A COMPANION TO HELLENIS

BLACKWELL COMPANIONS TO THE ANCIENT WORLD

This series provides sophisticated and authoritative overviews of periods of ancient history, genres of classical literature, and the most important themes in ancient culture. Each volume comprises approximately twenty-five and forty concise essays written by individual scholars within their area of specialization. The essays are written in a clear, provocative, and lively manner, designed for an international audience of scholars, students, and general readers.

Ancient History

Published

A Companion to the Roman Army
Edited by Paul Erdkamp

A Companion to the Roman Republic
Edited by Nathan Rosenstein and Robert Morstein-Marx

A Companion to the Roman Empire
Edited by David S. Potter

A Companion to the Classical Greek World
Edited by Konrad H. Kinzl

A Companion to the Ancient Near East
Edited by Daniel C. Snell

A Companion to the Hellenistic World
Edited by Andrew Erskine

A Companion to Late Antiquity
Edited by Philip Rousseau

A Companion to Ancient History
Edited by Andrew Erskine

A Companion to Archaic Greece
Edited by Kurt A. Raaflaub and Hans van Wees

A Companion to Julius Caesar
Edited by Miriam Griffin

A Companion to Byzantium
Edited by LIZ James

A Companion to Ancient Egypt
Edited by Alan B. Lloyd

A Companion to Ancient Macedonia
Edited by Joseph Roisman and Ian Worthington

A Companion to the Punic Wars
Edited by Dexter Hoyos

A Companion to Augustine
Edited by Mark Vessey

A Companion to Marcus Aurelius
Edited by Marcel van Ackeren

A Companion to Ancient Greek Government
Edited by Hans Beck

A Companion to the Neronian Age
Edited by Emma Buckley and Martin T. Dinter

Literature and Culture

Published

A Companion to Classical Receptions
Edited by Lorna Hardwick and Christopher Stray

A Companion to Greek and Roman Historiography
Edited by John Marincola

A Companion to Catullus
Edited by Marilyn B. Skinner

A Companion to Roman Religion
Edited by Jörg Rüpke

A Companion to Greek Religion
Edited by Daniel Ogden

A Companion to the Classical Tradition
Edited by Craig W. Kallendorf

A Companion to Roman Rhetoric
Edited by William Dominik and Jon Hall

A Companion to Greek Rhetoric
Edited by Ian Worthington

A Companion to Ancient Epic
Edited by John Miles Foley

A Companion to Greek Tragedy
Edited by Justina Gregory

A Companion to Latin Literature
Edited by Stephen Harrison

A Companion to Greek and Roman Political Thought
Edited by Ryan K. Balot

A Companion to Ovid
Edited by Peter E. Knox

A Companion to the Ancient Greek Language
Edited by Egbert Bakker

A Companion to Hellenistic Literature
Edited by Martine Cuypers and James J. Clauss

A Companion to Vergil's *Aeneid* and its Tradition
Edited by Joseph Farrell and Michael C. J. Putnam

A Companion to Horace
Edited by Gregson Davis

A Companion to Families in the Greek and Roman Worlds
Edited by Beryl Rawson

A Companion to Greek Mythology
Edited by Ken Dowden and Niall Livingstone

A Companion to the Latin Language
Edited by James Clackson

A Companion to Tacitus
Edited by Victoria Emma Pagán

A Companion to Women in the Ancient World
Edited by Sharon L. James and Sheila Dillon

A Companion to Sophocles
Edited by Kirk Ormand

A Companion to the Archaeology of the Ancient Near East
Edited by Daniel Potts

A Companion to Roman Love Elegy
Edited by Barbara K. Gold

A Companion to Greek Art
Edited by Tyler Jo Smith and Dimitris Plantzos

A Companion to Persius and Juvenal
Edited by Susanna Braund and Josiah Osgood

A Companion to the Archaeology of the Roman Republic
Edited by Jane DeRose Evans

A Companion to Terence
Edited by Antony Augoustakis and Ariana Traill

A Companion to Roman Architecture
Edited by Roger B. Ulrich and Caroline K. Quenemoen

A Companion to Sport and Spectacle in Greek and Roman Antiquity
Edited by Paul Christesen and Donald G. Kyle

A Companion to the Ancient Novel
Edited by Edmund P. Cueva and Shannon N. Byrne

A COMPANION TO HELLENISTIC LITERATURE

Edited by

James J. Clauss
and Martine Cuypers

WILEY Blackwell

This paperback edition first published 2014

Edition history: Blackwell Publishing Ltd (hardback, 2010)

Registered Office
John Wiley & Sons Ltd, The Atrium, Southern Gate, Chichester, West Sussex, PO19 8SQ, UK

Editorial Offices
350 Main Street, Malden, MA 02148-5020, USA
9600 Garsington Road, Oxford, OX4 2DQ, UK
The Atrium, Southern Gate, Chichester, West Sussex, PO19 8SQ, UK

For details of our global editorial offices, for customer services, and for information about how to apply for permission to reuse the copyright material in this book please see our website at www.wiley.com/wiley-blackwell.

Library of Congress Cataloging-in-Publication Data

A companion to Hellenistic literature / edited by James J. Clauss and Martine Cuypers.
p. cm. – (Blackwell companions to the ancient world)
Includes bibliographical references and index.
ISBN 978-1-4051-3679-2 (hardcover : alk. paper) ISBN 978-1-118-78290-3 (pbk. : alk. paper)
1. Greek literature, Hellenistic–History and criticism.
I. Clauss, James Joseph. II. Cuypers, Martine.
PA3081.C63 2010
880.09–dc22

2009025321

A catalogue record for this book is available from the British Library.

Cover image: Jean-Claude Golvin, Alexandria, showing the Canopic street, watercolour. Courtesy of Editions Errance
Cover design by Workhaus

Set in 10/12.5pt Galliard by SPi Publisher Services, Pondicherry, India

1 2014

Contents

Maps

Notes on Contributors

Benjamin Acosta-Hughes is Professor of Greek and Latin at the Ohio State University. His principal interests are Hellenistic poetry and Archaic lyric. He is the author of *Polyeideia: The Iambi of Callimachus and the Archaic Iambic Tradition* (2002), and of *Arion's Lyre: Archaic Lyric into Hellenistic Poetry* (2010). With Susan Stephens he is currently co-authoring a book on Callimachus.

Annemarie Ambühl has taught at the University of Basel and the University of Groningen. Her publications include *Kinder und junge Helden: Innovative Aspekte des Umgangs mit der literarischen Tradition bei Kallimachos* (2005) and articles on Hellenistic epigram. She is currently working as a post-doctoral researcher at Groningen on the reception of Attic tragedy and Hellenistic poetry in Lucan's *Bellum civile.*

Jon S. Bruss has taught at Bethany Lutheran College, St. Olaf College, the University of the South, and the University of Kansas. He is the author of *Hidden Presences: Monuments, Gravesites, and Corpses in Greek Funerary Epigram* (2005) as well as various articles on epigram and Hellenistic poetry, and he is the co-editor of *Brill's Companion to Hellenistic Epigram: Down to Philip* (2007).

Anthony W. Bulloch is Professor of Classics at the University of California, Berkeley. He is the author of *Callimachus: The Fifth Hymn* (1985), the section on Hellenistic poetry in *The Cambridge History of Classical Literature*, vol. 1 (1985), and co-editor of *Images and Ideologies: Self-definition in the Hellenistic World* (1993). He is also joint editor of the ongoing University of California Press series *Hellenistic Culture and Society.*

James J. Clauss is Professor of Classics at the University of Washington, Seattle. He is the author of *The Best of the Argonauts: The Redefinition of the Epic Hero in Book 1 of Apollonius' Argonautica* (1993), the co-editor of *Medea: Essays on Medea in Myth, Literature, Philosophy, and Art* (1997), and the co-translator of *Rome and Environs: An Archaeological Guide* by Filippo Coarelli (2007).

Martine Cuypers is Lecturer in Greek at Trinity College Dublin. She is preparing a commentary on Apollonius' *Argonautica* and the co-editor of *Beginning from Apollo: Studies in Apollonius and the Argonautic Tradition* (2005). She also maintains the online *Hellenistic Bibliography*.

Jacco Dieleman is Assistant Professor of Egyptology at the University of California, Los Angeles. He is the author of *Priests, Tongues, and Rites: The London-Leiden Magical Manuscripts and Translation in Egyptian Ritual* (2005), and co-editor of the UCLA *Encyclopedia of Egyptology*.

Andrew Erskine is Professor of Ancient History at the University of Edinburgh. A specialist in Hellenistic history, he is the author of *Troy between Greece and Rome: Local Tradition and Imperial Power* (2001) and *The Hellenistic Stoa: Political Thought and Action* (1990). He is also the editor of *A Companion to the Hellenistic World* (2003) and *A Companion to Ancient History* (2009).

Elena Esposito is Lecturer at the University of Florence, Istituto papirologico "G. Vitelli," and Tutor in Greek Literature at the University of Bologna. Her main interests are Hellenistic poetry and Greek lexicography. She has published *Il Fragmentum Grenfellianum (P.Dryton 50)* (2005) and many articles on Herodas and the mime. Her current project is a commented edition of Greek lexica preserved on papyri for the series *Commentaria et Lexica Graeca in Papyris Reperta*.

Marco Fantuzzi teaches Greek literature at Columbia University, New York, and at the University of Macerata. He has published widely on Hellenistic poetry and Athenian tragedy, and is the author of *Bionis Smyrnaei Adonidis epitaphium* (1985), *Ricerche su Apollonio Rodio: diacronie della dizione epica* (1988), and, with Richard Hunter, *Tradition and Innovation in Hellenistic Poetry* (2004). He is close to completing a commented edition of the *Rhesus* ascribed to Euripides. His next book project is a commentary on Dionysius of Halicarnassus' *De compositione verborum*.

Alain M. Gowing is Professor of Classics at the University of Washington, Seattle. His chief interests lie in the area of Roman historiography and literature, especially of the Imperial period. His publications include *The Triumviral Narratives of Appian and Cassius Dio* (1992), and *Empire and Memory: The Representation of the Roman Republic in Imperial Culture* (2005). He is currently working on a book tentatively titled "*Genius urbis*: The City of Rome in Latin Historiography."

Erich S. Gruen is Gladys Rehard Wood Professor of History and Classics Emeritus at the University of California, Berkeley. His contributions in Hellenistic and Jewish studies include *The Hellenistic World and the Coming of Rome* (1984), *Heritage and Hellenism* (1998), *Diaspora: Jews amidst Greeks and Romans* (2002), *Cultural Borrowings and Ethnic Appropriations in Antiquity* (ed. 2005), and survey articles in the Blackwell *Companion to the Hellenistic World* (2003), the *Cambridge Companion to the Hellenistic World* (2006), and the *Oxford Handbook of Biblical Studies* (2006). He is currently completing a book tentatively titled "Confronting the 'Other': Greek, Roman, and Jewish Impressions of the Alien."

Kathryn J. Gutzwiller is Professor of Classics at the University of Cincinnati. She has published widely in Hellenistic literature, the interaction of art and text, and literary criticism. Recent books are *Poetic Garlands: Hellenistic Epigrams in Context* (1998), *A Guide to Hellenistic Literature* (2007), and an edited volume entitled *The New Posidippus: A Hellenistic*

Poetry Book (2005). Her current projects include the collaborative publication of new Menander mosaics from Antioch and a commentary with critical edition for the epigrams of Meleager.

Annette Harder is Professor of Ancient Greek Language and Literature at the University of Groningen. She has written on Greek tragedy and published a number of mythographic papyri, but her main field of interest is Hellenistic poetry, on which she has published extensively. She is the organizer of the Groningen Workshops on Hellenistic Poetry, held biennially since 1992, and co-editor of their proceedings in the series *Hellenistica Groningana*. She has also published a Dutch translation of a selection of Callimachus' poetry (2000), and is in the process of finishing a commented edition of Callimachus' *Aetia*.

Silke Knippschild is Lecturer in Ancient History at the University of Bristol. Her main research interests lie in the field of intercultural relations and cross-cultural influences between the ancient Near East, Greece, and Rome. She is the author of *"Drum bietet zum Bunde die Hände": Rechtssymbolische Akte in zwischenstaatlichen Beziehungen im orientalischen und griechisch-römischen Altertum* (2002) and co-editor of *Ceremoniales, Ritos y Representación del Poder* (2004) and *Imagines: Antigüedad en las Artes Escénicas y Visuales* (2008). She is currently working on a monograph entitled "Spoils and Iconoclasm," dealing with the destruction and theft of political and religious identifiers in the first millennium BCE.

Adolf Köhnken is Emeritus Professor of Classics (Greek) at the Westfälische Wilhelms-Universität Münster. He is the author of *Apollonios Rhodios und Theokrit* (1965), *Die Funktion des Mythos bei Pindar* (1971), and *Darstellungsziele und Erzählstrategien in antiken Texten* (2006). He has published widely on Archaic and Hellenistic poetry, the Argonautic tradition, narratology, historiography, drama, ancient literary criticism, and the history of Classical scholarship, and is co-editor of the journal *Hermes* and the series *Texte und Kommentare*.

Susan Lape is Associate Professor of Classics at the University of Southern California. She has published *Reproducing Athens: Menander's Comedy, Democratic Culture, and the Hellenistic City* (2004) and various articles on Menander and Roman comedy. Her book *Before Race: Citizen Identity in Democratic Athens* is scheduled to appear with Cambridge University Press in 2010.

Enrico Magnelli is Lecturer in Greek Literature at the University of Florence. He has published widely on Greek poetry from the Hellenistic to Byzantine periods, Attic comedy, and meter, including *Alexandri Aetoli testimonia et fragmenta* (1999) and *Studi su Euforione* (2002). He is currently preparing a monograph on the use of Homer in Greek comedy and satyr-play, a critical edition of Greek epigrams on poets of the Imperial period and late antiquity (with Gianfranco Agosti), and a commented edition of the fragments of Euphorion.

Ian S. Moyer is Assistant Professor of History at the University of Michigan, Ann Arbor. He has published articles on Herodotus and Egypt, ancient cross-cultural interactions, and Graeco-Egyptian magic. He is currently completing a book entitled *Egypt and the Limits of Hellenism*, in which he explores the history and historiography of cultural and intellectual encounters between Greeks and Egyptians.

Jackie Murray is Assistant Professor of Classics at Skidmore College. Her principal interests are Hellenistic, Archaic, and Latin poetry, and she has published articles on Apollonius Rhodius, Callimachus, Ovid, Homer, and epigram. She is presently co-editing *The Cambridge Companion to Apollonius Rhodius' Argonautica* and revising her dissertation *Polyphonic Argo* (2005) into a monograph.

Mark Payne is Associate Professor of Classics at the University of Chicago. He is the author of *Theocritus and the Invention of Fiction* (2007) and articles on Greek poetry and poetics from the Archaic to the Hellenistic periods. He is currently working on a book about the representation of animals in poetry.

J. D. Reed is Professor of Classics at Brown University. His interests lie mainly in Hellenistic and Latin poetry, especially in questions of cultural identity. He is the author of *Bion of Smyrna: The Fragments and the Adonis* (1997), and *Virgil's Gaze: Nation and Poetry in the Aeneid* (2008). He has also published on the ancient cult and myth of Adonis and their reception in modern literature.

Ruth Scodel is D. R. Shackleton Bailey Collegiate Professor of Greek and Latin at the University of Michigan, Ann Arbor. Her publications include *Credible Impossibilities: Strategies of Verisimilitude in Homer and Greek Tragedy* (1999), *Listening to Homer* (2002), *Whither Quo Vadis* (2008, with Anja Bettenworth), and *Epic Facework: Self-presentation and Social Interaction in Homer* (2008).

Alexander Sens is Joseph Durkin SJ Professor of Classics at Georgetown University. He is the author of a commentary on Theocritus' *Hymn to the Dioscuri* (1997) as well as (with S. Douglas Olson) editions of Archestratus of Gela (2000) and Matro of Pitane (2000). He recently completed an edition of Asclepiades of Samos for Oxford University Press, and is currently at work on a commentary on select Hellenistic epigrams. His interest in Lycophron continues to grow, and he hopes to pursue further work on that poet's *Alexandra* in the future.

Susan Stephens is Professor of Classics at Stanford University. Her work includes contributions to the *Oxyrhynchus Papyri* and *Yale Papyri in the Beinecke Library*, vol. 2 (1985); with Jack Winkler she co-authored *Ancient Greek Novels: The Fragments* (1995). The political and social context of Hellenistic poetry has been the focus of her recent research, articulated in *Seeing Double: Intercultural Poetics in Ptolemaic Alexandria* (2003) as well as numerous articles on individual poets. She is currently working on "geo-poetics," or how poets created a collective identity for the newly established city of Alexandria.

Rolf Strootman is Lecturer in History at Utrecht University. His main interest lies in the history, ideology, and organization of imperial states in the ancient Middle East and Central Asia, particularly the Seleucid Empire. He completed his dissertation "The Hellenistic Royal Court" in 2007, and has contributed to the *Encyclopaedia Iranica* and published articles on aspects of monarchy and empire in the Hellenistic period.

Katharina Volk is Associate Professor of Classics at Columbia University. She is the author of *The Poetics of Latin Didactic: Lucretius, Vergil, Ovid, Manilius* (2002) and *Manilius and his Intellectual Background* (2009), as well as many other publications on Greek and Latin poetry and its relation to philosophy, science, and the history of ideas.

Stephen A. White is Professor of Classics and Philosophy at the University of Texas at Austin. He is the author of

Sovereign Virtue: Aristotle on the Relation between Prosperity and Happiness (1992) and articles on many areas of ancient philosophy and literature, including Callimachus, Stoicism, and Hellenistic ethics; co-editor with W. W. Fortenbaugh of two volumes on the Hellenistic Lyceum, *Lyco of Troas and Hieronymus of Rhodes* (2004) and *Aristo of Ceos* (2006); and area editor for philosophy and science for the *Oxford Encyclopedia of Ancient Greece and Rome.* He is currently preparing a translation of Diogenes Laertius.

Tim Whitmarsh is Tutorial Fellow in Greek and E. P. Warren Praelector at Corpus Christi College, Oxford. His books include *Greek Literature and the Roman Empire: The Politics of Imitation* (2001), *Ancient Greek Literature* (2004), and *The Second Sophistic* (2005). He edited *The Cambridge Companion to the Greek and Roman Novel* (2008), and co-edited *Ordering Knowledge in the Roman Empire* (2007). He is currently finishing a book on narrative and identity in the Greek novel, and running a research project on Greek and Near Eastern fiction.

Jessica Wissmann lectures at the Ruhr-Universität Bochum. Her publications include *Motivation und Schmähung: Feigheit in der Ilias und in der griechischen Tragödie* (1997) and articles on Imperial Greek literature. She is working on a monograph on Homer in ancient education.

Preface

This *Companion* is intended to serve as an introduction to the Greek literature of the Hellenistic period (323–31 BCE) for slightly advanced students of Classics. Its organization largely follows genre, and therefore quite a few authors are discussed in more than one chapter (Callimachus and Theocritus were especially lucky). Poetry takes up more space than prose, as the state of the evidence commands, but a variety of prose texts are also discussed in the Contexts and Neighbors sections. The latter section is perhaps the most unusual feature of this volume. It explores the cultural dialogue between the Greeks and their Egyptian, Jewish, Western Asian, and Roman literary interlocutors.

Although we underscored particularly apposite connections among the chapters through cross-references and offered an overview of the contributions in the Introduction, we chose not to synthesize, generalize, or construct a grand narrative. Collectively authored companions are by nature polyphonic, and this one is perhaps even more so than others. Our contributors represent three scholarly generations and a wide range of academic traditions, experiences, and fields, and their topics invite or rather require very different approaches. It is our hope that the volume we have produced reflects the variety of scholarship on the Hellenistic world as well as the state of the field and current trends in research. Certainly included among these trends is an emphasis on the contexts of literature production and cultural continuity.

Greek and Latin are cited more frequently than in most other volumes in this series because we felt the absence of the original text and a total ban on "philological" discussion would have impoverished discussions of Hellenistic literature, especially given the fact that this was the era when philology was born. All Greek and Latin are translated and, where discussions turn technical, we have tried to organize them so that their general drift should also be clear to readers who have no access to the original text. Among omissions, inevitable even in a volume of this size, we want to single out reception. Because so many Latin authors directly engage with Hellenistic literature, we felt this topic could not be satisfactorily discussed even in a number of wide-ranging chapters.

We are very grateful to our contributors for the time and energy they have invested in this project and for putting up with our editorial demands and interventions. Many went beyond the call of duty in commenting on the contributions of others and tailoring their own chapters to them. All have been remarkably patient, given the fact that this project has taken longer than planned. The volume has also benefited from the suggestions of the three anonymous reviewers for the press, and from the input of the final year Greek classes of 07/08 and 08/09 at Trinity College Dublin, who test-drove many of its chapters. At Wiley-Blackwell, Al Bertrand and Ben Thatcher were there at the beginning, Galen Smith, Haze Humbert, Janey Fisher, and Rebecca du Plessis at the end; all showed admirable fortitude during the long time in between.

Seattle and Dublin
James J. Clauss and Martine Cuypers

Acknowledgments

The editors and publishers gratefully acknowledge the permission granted to reproduce the copyright material in this book.

Maps 2.1 and 4.1 on pp. 18 and 50 reprinted by permission of John Wiley and Sons, Inc. from pp. xiii and 18 of Kathryn Gutzwiller, *A Guide to Hellenistic Literature*, Malden, Oxford, and Carlton: Blackwell Publishing Ltd. © 2007.

Material on p. 117 reprinted by permission from page 145 of *First Things: A Journal of Religion, Culture, and Public Life*, Issue 145, © August 2004.

Every effort has been made to trace copyright holders and to obtain their permission for the use of copyright material. The publisher apologizes for any errors or omissions in the above list and would be grateful if notified of any corrections that should be incorporated in future reprints or editions of this book.

Abbreviations

Ancient Authors

A.R.	Apollonius of Rhodes (unspecified references are to *Arg.*)
Arg.	*Argonautica*
CA	see Reference Works
Ach. Tat.	Achilles Tatius
Ael.	Aelian
VH	*Varia Historia* (*Historical Miscellany*)
Aesch.	Aeschylus
Eum.	*Eumenides*
Alex. Aet.	Alexander Aetolus
Anac.	Anacreon
Antim.	Antimachus
Antipat. Sid.	Antipater of Sidon
Antipat. Thess.	Antipater of Thessalonica
AP	*Anthologia Palatina* (*Palatine Anthology*)
APl.	*Anthologia Planudea* (*Anthology of Planudes*)
App.	Appian
Mith.	*Mithridatica* (*Mithridatic Wars*)
Syr.	*Syriaca* (*Syrian Wars*)
Ar.	Aristophanes
Av.	*Aves* (*Birds*)
Eccl.	*Ecclesiazusae* (*Assemblywomen*)
Thesm.	*Thesmophoriazusae* (*Women at the Thesmophoria*)
Arat.	Aratus
Phaen.	*Phaenomena*
Archestr.	Archestratus
Archil.	Archilochus

arg.	*argumentum* (introductory summary of a literary work)
Arist.	Aristotle
(Ps.) *Ath. Pol.*	*Athenaiōn Politeia* (*Constitution of the Athenians*)
Poet.	*Poetics*
Rhet.	*Rhetoric*
Arr.	Arrian
An.	*Anabasis*
Asclep.	Asclepiades
Ath.	Athenaeus
b.	born
Bacch.	Bacchylides
c.	*circa*
Call.	Callimachus
Aet.	*Aetia*
Dieg.	*Diegeseis* (ancient summaries)
ep.	*Epigrams*
h.	*Hymns*
Hec.	*Hecale*
ia.	*Iambs*
Pf. and *SH*	see Reference Works
Char.	Chariton
Cic.	M. Tullius Cicero
Ac.	*Academica*
Arch.	*Pro Archia* (*Defense of Archias*)
Att.	*Letters to Atticus*
Brut.	*Brutus*
de Orat.	*de Oratore* (*On the Orator*)
Div.	*de Divinatione* (*On Divination*)
Fin.	*de Finibus bonorum et malorum* (*On the Ends of Good and Evil*)
Leg.	*de Legibus* (*On the Laws*)
ND	*de Natura Deorum* (*On the Nature of the Gods*)
Sen.	*de Senectute* (*On Old Age*)
Tusc.	*Tusculanae Disputationes* (*Tusculan Disputations*)
Clem. Al.	Clement of Alexandria
Strom.	*Stromata* (*Miscellanies*)
Curt.	Q. Curtius Rufus
d.	died
D.H.	Dionysius of Halicarnassus (unspecified references are to *AR*)
AR	*Antiquitates Romanae* (*Roman Antiquities*)
Comp.	*de Compositione Verborum* (*On the Arrangement of Words*)
Isoc.	*de Isocrate* (*On Isocrates*)
Lys.	*de Lysia* (*On Lysias*)
Orat. Vett.	*de Oratoribus Veteribus* (*On the Ancient Orators*)
Pomp.	*Epistula ad Pompeium* (*Letter to Pompeius*)

D.L.	Diogenes Laertius
D.S.	Diodorus Siculus
Dem.	Demosthenes
Phil.	*Philippica* (*Orations against Philip*)
Demetr.	Demetrius
Eloc.	*de Elocutione* (*On Style*)
Diod.	Diodorus (epigrammatist)
Dio Chrys.	Dio Chrysostom
Or.	*Orations*
Dion. Scyt.	Dionysius Scytobrachion
Dion. Thr.	Dionysius Thrax
Diosc.	Dioscorides (epigrammatist)
Enn.	Ennius
Ann.	*Annales*
Sk.	see Reference Works
Euph.	Euphorion
Eur.	Euripides
El.	*Electra*
Hec.	*Hecuba*
Med.	*Medea*
Or.	*Orestes*
Phoen.	*Phoenissae* (*Phoenician Women*)
(ps.) *Rh.*	*Rhesus*
Eus.	Eusebius
PE	*Praeparatio Evangelica*
F or fr.	fragment
fl.	*floruit* (flourished; i.e., active around a certain date)
Gal.	Galen
h.Ap.	*Homeric Hymn to Apollo*
Hdt.	Herodotus
Heraclit.	Heraclitus
All.	*Allegoriae* (*Homeric Allegories, Homeric Problems*)
Hermes.	Hermesianax
Hermog.	Hermogenes
Id.	*Peri ideōn* (*On Types of Style*)
Herod.	Herodas
Mimi.	*Mimiambs*
Hes.	Hesiod
Th.	*Theogony*
WD	*Works and Days*
Hor.	Horace
Ars	*Ars Poetica* (*The Art of Poetry*)
Carm.	*Carmina* (*Odes*)
Ep.	*Epistulae* (*Letters*)
Sat.	*Satires*
Hsch.	Hesychius

Il.	*Iliad*
Is.	Isocrates
Jos.	Josephus
AJ	*Antiquitates Judaicae* (*Jewish Antiquities*)
Ap.	*contra Apionem* (*Against Apion*)
Leon. Tar.	Leonidas of Tarentum
LetArist	*Letter of Aristeas*
"Longin."	Pseudo-Longinus
Subl.	*de Sublimitate* (*On the Sublime*)
Luc.	Lucian
Hist. Conscr.	*Quomodo Historia Conscribenda sit* (*How to Write History*)
DDS	*De Dea Syria* (*On the Syrian Goddess*)
Lucr.	Lucretius
Lyc.	Lycophron
Lys.	Lysias
Macc.	*Maccabees*
Manetho	Manetho
Dyn.	*Dynasty*
Men.	Menander
Asp.	*Aspis* (*Shield*)
Sam.	*Samia* (*Samian Girl*)
Mimn.	Mimnermus
Nic.	Nicander
Al.	*Alexipharmaca*
Cyn.	*Cynegetica*
Georg.	*Georgica*
Heter.	*Heteroioumena*
Oit.	*Oitaica*
Sik.	*Sikelia*
Th.	*Theriaca*
Theb.	*Thebaica*
obv.	obverse
Od.	*Odyssey*
Ov.	Ovid
Ars	*Ars Amatoria* (*The Art of Love*)
Am.	*Amores*
Met.	*Metamorphoses*
Rem. Am.	*Remedia Amoris* (*Love's Remedies*)
Tr.	*Tristia*
Parth.	Parthenius
Erot. Path.	*Erōtika Pathēmata* (*Love Stories*)
Paus.	Pausanias
Philostr.	Philostratus
VS	*Vitae Sophistarum* (*Lives of the Sophists*)
Phld.	Philodemus
Mus.	*On Music*

Po.	*On Poems*
Rh.	*On Rhetoric*
Pi.	Pindar
I.	*Isthmian Odes*
N.	*Nemean Odes*
O.	*Olympian Odes*
P.	*Pythian Odes*
Pl.	Plato
Crat.	*Cratylus*
Phdr.	*Phaedrus*
Prot.	*Protagoras*
Rep.	*Republic*
Sym.	*Symposium*
Plb.	Polybius
Plin. *NH*	Pliny the Elder, *Natural History*
Plin. *Ep.*	Pliny the Younger, *Epistulae* (*Letters*)
Plu.	Plutarch
Alex.	*Life of Alexander*
Ant.	*Life of Antony*
Cato Ma.	*Life of Cato the Elder*
Cic.	*Life of Cicero*
Cleom.	*Life of Cleomenes*
Conv.	*Convivium Septem Sapientium* (*Banquet of the Seven Sages*)
Crass.	*Life of Crassus*
De Is. et Os.	*De Iside et Osiride* (*On Isis and Osiris*)
Dem.	*Life of Demosthenes*
Demetr.	*Life of Demetrius*
Mor.	*Moralia* (*Ethical Treatises*)
Pyrrh.	*Life of Pyrrhus*
Sol.	*Life of Solon*
Posidip.	Posidippus
pr.	prologue, foreword
proleg.	*prolegomena* (introductory matter)
Procl.	Proclus
in Ti.	*in Timaeum* (*On Plato's Timaeus*)
Prop.	Propertius
Ps.	Pseudo- (falsely attributed to)
Quint.	Quintilian
Inst.	*Institutio Oratoria*
Rh.	*Rhesus*, a tragedy falsely attributed to Euripides
Rhet. Her.	*Rhetorica ad Herennium* (anonymous handbook)
schol.	*scholion* (commentary note in a manuscript)
sed. inc.	*sede incerta* (fragment of unknown location)
Semon.	Semonides
Sen.	Seneca the Younger

Ep.	*Epistulae* (*Letters*)
Sext. Emp.	Sextus Empiricus
Math.	*Against the Mathematicians*
PH	*Pyrrhōneioi Hypotypōseis* (*Outlines of Pyrrhonism*)
Sib.	*Oraculae Sibyllinae* (*Sibylline Oracles*)
Soph.	Sophocles
Stob.	Stobaeus
Str.	Strabo
Suet.	Suetonius
de Gram. et Rhet.	*de Grammaticis et Rhetoribus* (*On Teachers of Grammar and Rhetoric*)
T or test.	*testimonium* (evidence for an author's life or work)
Theoc.	Theocritus (unspecified references are to the *Idylls*)
ep.	*epigrams*
Id.	*Idylls*
Theod. Prisc.	Theodorus Priscianus
Eup.	*Euporiston* (*Household Remedies*)
Theophr.	Theophrastus
Char.	*Characters*
Thgn.	Theognis
Thuc.	Thucydides
Val. Max.	Valerius Maximus
Var.	M. Terentius Varro
LL	*On the Latin Language*
Men.	*Menippean Satires*
Verg.	Vergil
Aen.	*Aeneid*
Ecl.	*Eclogues*
Vitr.	Vitruvius
Xen.	Xenophon
Mem.	*Memorabilia* (*Memories of Socrates*)

Reference Works

AB	Austin, C. and Bastianini, G. *Posidippi Pellaei quae supersunt omnia*. Milan 2002.
ABC	Grayson, A. K. *Assyrian and Babylonian Chronicles*. Locust Valley 1975.
ANRW	Temporini, H. and Haase, W. (eds.). *Aufstieg und Niedergang der römischen Welt*. Berlin 1972–98.
BCHP	Finkel, I. and Van der Spek, R. J. *Babylonian Chronicles of the Hellenistic Period*. Prepublished at www.livius.org/babylonia.html.

Bl.	Blänsdorf, J. *Fragmenta poetarum latinorum epicorum et lyricorum praeter Ennium et Lucilium*. Stuttgart and Leipzig 1995.
BM	*British Museum Catalogue*. London.
BNJ	Worthington, I. *Brill's New Jacoby: The Fragments of the Greek Historians*. At www.brillsnewjacoby.com.
CA	Powell, I. U. *Collectanea Alexandrina*. Oxford 1925.
CAF	Kock, T. *Comicorum Atticorum fragmenta*. 3 vols. Leipzig 1880–8.
CEG	Hansen, P. A. *Carmina Epigraphica Graeca*. 2 vols. Berlin 1983, 1989.
CG	*Catalogue général du Musée de Caire*. Cairo.
CGFP	Austin, C. *Comicorum Graecorum Fragmenta in Papyris reperta*. Berlin 1973.
CID	*Corpus Inscriptionum Delphicarum*. Paris 1977–.
CIL	*Corpus Inscriptionum Latinarum*. Berlin 1853–.
Cr	Cribiore, R. *Writing, Teachers, and Students in Graeco-Roman Egypt*. Atlanta 1996.
Cu.	Cunningham, I. C. *Herodae Mimiambi, cum Appendice Fragmentorum Mimorum Papyraceorum*. Leipzig 1987.
DK	Diels, H. and Kranz, W. *Die Fragmente der Vorsokratiker*. 6th edition. Berlin 1952.
EGF	Davies, M. *Epicorum Graecorum Fragmenta*. Göttingen 1988.
EK	Edelstein, L. and Kidd, I. G. *Posidonius I: The Fragments*. Cambridge 1972.
FGE	Page, D. L. *Further Greek Epigrams*. Cambridge 1981.
FGrH	Jacoby, F. *Die Fragmente der griechischen Historiker*. Berlin 1922–56, Leiden 1994–. See also *BNJ*.
FHSG	Fortenbaugh, W. W., Huby, P., Sharples, R., and Gutas, D. *Theophrastus of Eresus: Sources for his Life, Writings, Thought, and Influence*. 2 vols. Leiden 1992.
GLP	Page, D. L. *Select Papyri: Literary Papyri*. Cambridge, MA 1941.
GP	Gow, A. S. F. and Page, D. L. *Hellenistic Epigrams*. 2 vols. Cambridge 1965.
GPh	Gow, A. S. F. and Page, D. L. *The Garland of Philip*. 2 vols. Cambridge 1968.
GS	Gow, A. S. F. and Scholfield, A. F. *Nicander, The Poems and Poetical Fragments*. Cambridge 1953.
GSHE	Irby-Massie, G. I. and Keyser, P. T. *Greek Science of the Hellenistic Era: A Sourcebook*. London.
ID	*Inscriptions de Délos*. Paris 1926–37.
IEG	West, M. L. *Iambi et Elegi Graeci ante Alexandrum cantati*. 2nd edition. Oxford 1992.
IG	*Inscriptiones Graecae*. Berlin 1873–.

IKyme	Engelmann, H. *Die Inschriften von Kyme.* Bonn 1976.
IMEG	Bernand, É. *Inscriptions métriques de l'Égypte gréco-romaine.* Paris 1969.
KA	Kassel, R. and Austin, C. *Poetae Comici Graeci.* Berlin 1983–.
Loeb	*Loeb Classical Library.* Cambridge, MA.
Lom.	Lomiento, L. *Cercidas, testimonia et fragmenta.* Rome 1993.
LP	Lobel, E. and Page, D. L. *Poetarum Lesbiorum fragmenta.* 2nd edition. Oxford 1963.
LSCG	Sokolowski, F. *Lois sacrées des cités grecques.* Paris 1962.
MP^3	Mertens, P. and Pack, R. A. *Catalogue des papyrus littéraires grecs et latins.* 3rd edition. Prepublished at http://promethee.philo.ulg.ac.be/cedopal/index.htm.
MW	Merkelbach, R. and West, M. L. *Fragmenta Hesiodea.* Oxford 1969.
OCT	*Oxford Classical Texts.* Oxford.
OLD	*Oxford Latin Dictionary.* Oxford 1982.
PCG	see KA
PEG	Bernabé, A. *Poetae Epici Graeci.* Part 1. Stuttgart and Leipzig 1996.
Pf.	Pfeiffer, R. *Callimachus.* 2 vols. Oxford 1949, 1953.
PMG	Page, D. L. *Poetae Melici Graeci.* Oxford 1962.
PMGF	Davies, M. *Poetarum Melicorum Graecorum fragmenta.* Oxford 1991.
Powell	see *CA*
RE	Pauly, A. von, Wissowa, G. and Kroll, W. *Realencyclopädie der classischen Altertumswissenschaft.* Stuttgart 1893–1980.
ROL	Warmington, E. H. *Remains of Old Latin.* 4 vols. Cambridge, MA 1932.
SEG	*Supplementum Epigraphicum Graecum.* Amsterdam 1923–.
SH	Lloyd-Jones, H. and Parsons, P. *Supplementum Hellenisticum.* Berlin 1983.
SIG^3	Dittenberger, W. *Sylloge Inscriptionum Graecarum.* 3rd edition. Leipzig 1915–24.
Sk.	Skutsch, O. *The Annals of Quintus Ennius.* Oxford 1985.
SLG	Page, D. L. *Supplementum Lyricis Graecis.* Oxford 1974.
SSH	Lloyd-Jones, H. *Supplementum Supplementi Hellenistici.* Berlin 2005.
SVF	Arnim, H. von *Stoicorum Veterum Fragmenta.* Berlin.
TrGF	Snell, B., Radt, S. L. and Kannicht R. *Tragicorum Graecorum Fragmenta.* Göttingen 1971–2004.

Papyri

P.Col.Zen.	Papyri from the Zenon archive in the collection of Columbia University, New York
P.Egerton	Papyri of the Egerton collection in the British Museum, London
P.Heid.	Papyri in the collection of the University of Heidelberg
P.Herc.	Papyri found in Herculaneum, Italy
P.Hibeh	Papyri found in el-Hibeh, Egypt
P.Köln	Papyri in the collection of the University of Cologne
P.Lond.Lit.	Greek literary papyri in the collection of the British Museum, London
P.Mich.	Papyri in the collection of the University of Michigan, Ann Arbor
P.Mil.Vogl.	Papyri in the collection of the Università degli Studi, Milan, initially edited by A. Vogliano
P.Oxy.	Papyri found in Oxyrrhynchus, Egypt, kept in the Bodleian Library, Oxford
P.Par.	Papyri in the collection of the Musée du Louvre, Paris

CHAPTER ONE

Introduction

James J. Clauss and Martine Cuypers

Under Alexander and his successors, new Greek civic centers arose throughout the Eastern Mediterranean and Western Asia, and the political structure of the *oikoumenē*, the "inhabited world," changed drastically, as the competition between *poleis* and regional leagues became subordinated to a competition between imperial states ruled by Greco-Macedonian kings. Once a balance of power had been reached, these rulers turned toward the project of transforming their courts and capitals into fully Hellenized centers, replicating the traditional Greek city for those living in diaspora and showcasing their power and refinement to the world, eager to prove their right to represent and manage Hellenic culture. Local elites followed suit, for very similar reasons.

In their eagerness to establish Greekness abroad, the Hellenistic rulers and cities could be said to have created a sort of virtual reality whereby all could have the experience of living, if not in Greece, at least in an idea of Greece. Alexander led the way toward the creation of this Virtual Greece when he paid his respects at Troy on his way to do battle with the Persians. He self-consciously assumed the role of a new Achilles, heralding a return to an age of heroes (Erskine). In its modern use, virtual reality involves interaction with a computer-simulated environment. The Hellenistic Virtual Greece was a political game played by way of creative postures and literary illusions. In the film *The Matrix*, the world was in fact a post-holocaust wasteland but people experienced reality through a computer program (the Matrix) that created what human minds, based on past experience, were conditioned to perceive as normal lives. Hellenistic Greekness is likewise a construct, mindset, or concept, based on a past presented as common and cultural traditions perceived as shared. Yet the Hellenistic world crucially differs from the world of *The Matrix* in that Hellenized minds were not disconnected from the Real. Although reality was sometimes literally a desert, it was metaphorically far from that. The citizens of Virtual Greece were in the end still denizens of Egypt, Asia Minor, or Mesopotamia, regions with their own history, literature, and culture, their own economic and social infrastructures, their own religions and ideologies of kingship. Although the impact of these realities on Hellenistic literature and culture is not always obvious, it should not be ignored (Stephens).

In their patronage of the arts and sciences, Hellenistic kings were following in the tradition of tyrants such as Polycrates and Pisistratus. Their courts supported generations of intellectuals who studied and rescripted traditional literature and knowledge in a competitive environment that fostered innovation (Strootman). Their achievements provided entertainment for the new elites at customary venues, such as festivals and the symposium, only this time situated in multicultural enclaves far from Hellas. Here all "friends of the king" jockeyed for attention and influence, whether they were poets or soldiers, diplomats or astronomers, philosophers or administrators. Regardless of pursuits, all were courtiers first. Alexandria even went so far as to vie with Athens as an intellectual center, creating the massive Library and think-tank Museum in imitation of Aristotle's Lyceum, and asserting its cultural affinity with Athens by giving prominence to tragic performances and applying the name Eleusis to the quarter that housed its principal cult site of Demeter. The famous anecdote about a Ptolemy relinquishing the huge deposit paid for original copies of the plays of Aeschylus, Sophocles, and Euripides likewise hints at the transference of cultural prestige from Athens to Alexandria (Stephens).

The importance attached to literature by the highest strata of society, local no less than royal, is reflected in education (Wissmann). In support of Virtual Greece, gymnasia sprouted throughout the Hellenic *oikoumenē*. They played a critical role in the education of the young, promulgating traditional concepts considered central to Greek culture, not in the last place through poems such as the Homeric epics. A substantial number of school texts from locations throughout Egypt provide a sense of the average curriculum. More can be gleaned from the many references to education in Hellenistic literature, which sketch a picture of the schooling not just of ordinary children but also of mythological figures such as Heracles, the ultimate icon of Greekness. These testify to a general interest in the practice of education, which in this period became increasingly formalized and professionalized, assuming the general shape it was to retain until well into the Byzantine period.

The literary work that stands out as quintessentially Hellenistic and that dominated the literary discussion in its day and beyond was Callimachus' *Aetia*, which, as fate would have it, survives only in random citations, translations, and papyrus scraps (Harder). Featured in this (paradoxically) playful and scholarly elegiac poem of four books is a non-continuous and impressionistic history of Hellas from Minos to Berenice through "origins" (*aitia*), making of Ptolemaic Alexandria the culmination of Greek advancement, the obvious model for Ovid's future *Metamorphoses*. The apparent seamlessness of the transition from Greek to Macedonian cultural hegemony represents perhaps the greatest illusion of its time.

The primacy of the *Aetia* is also to some extent an illusion, one which is actively and openly propagated by its poet. Modern critics sometimes create the impression that Callimachus' poetry created a kind of Copernican revolution, establishing a new poetics which caused a radical paradigm shift and obliterated "old-fashioned" types of poetry. It is perhaps more accurate to say that Callimachus identified and appropriated the poetic spirit of his time. It is not at all obvious, for example, with whom or what he is actually polemicizing at the start of the *Aetia* and elsewhere, and many of the tropes and features which are generally considered emblematic of "Callimachean" poetics are already prefigured in Archaic and Classical poetry, including, indeed, its self-consciousness and polemical stance (Acosta-Hughes). In Hellenistic poetics, tradition and innovation are paradoxically intertwined. The themes, forms, and principles of the poetic past are scrutinized, appropriated, and developed further, and then further, until they become something that is at the same time daringly novel and surprisingly familiar.

Nowhere does the figure of Callimachus loom as large as in elegy, where, due to the Roman poets' embracement of the *Aetia* as a prime model, other incarnations of the genre were virtually eclipsed (Murray). It is telling that Quintilian in the first century CE recommends only Callimachus and Philitas as reading for the aspiring orator and not, for example, the fourth-century BCE innovator Antimachus or any of the earlier elegists, such as Mimnermus or Simonides. If, however, one looks backward not from Roman poetry but from Callimachus, one might argue that the *Aetia* successfully revised the history of elegy and established itself as the new *aition* of a protean genre. Elegy took many forms from Archaic times onward, and it underwent many crucial developments in the late fifth through fourth centuries BCE due to changes to the way poetry was produced and consumed. The demarcation between long elegiac poems and hexameter poetry became even vaguer than before, and short elegiac poetry and epigram melted together in the genre of literary epigram, composed for the book roll and symposium, which included much of the thematic ground of earlier elegy.

The writing of epigrams in fact became a major literary fashion of the Hellenistic age (Bruss). Many of these pose as genuine inscriptions, playing with the conventions and teasing out the possibilities of poems such as commonly found on tombstones and dedicated objects. Epigrams imagine, for example, conversations between the deceased and passersby and suitable epitaphs for famous people. They present ordinary and bizarre dedications never made, some mimicking the shape of the item dedicated. Others, such as sympotic, erotic, or scoptic epigrams, forego the inscriptional fiction entirely. Drawing their inspiration primarily from the sympotic poetry of the past, elegy and iambos, they present imaginary symposia, fantasy love affairs, and staged feuds. Labels and classifications, however, do not do justice to the versatility of this genre, which offers an exceptionally large scope for experimentation and seems infinitely capacious of ideas, motifs, and forms from other types of literature. These brief, polymorphic poems generally demand an intensive interpretational effort from the reader, and many remain ultimately elusive.

While the inscribed epigrams of earlier days rather straightforwardly reflect the interests and ideology of those wealthy enough to commission such poems and the dedications and monuments on which they were inscribed, Hellenistic literary epigram, whether produced at court or in other elite circles, displays throughout a keen interest in ordinary people and everyday life, a "realism" that is also manifested in other literary genres and in the art of the period. However genuine or voyeuristic this interest in artisans, herdsmen, and prostitutes may also be, their *mimēseis* in any case functioned as a virtual alternative reality, a looking-glass image of the concerns of the court and public life. A song from the musical *Camelot* captures this elite fascination as well as any scholarly discussion:

GUENEVERE
What do the simple folk do
To help them escape when they're blue?
The shepherd who is ailing, the milkmaid who is glum,
The cobbler who is wailing from nailing his thumb.
When they're beset and besieged
The folk not noblessly obliged,
However do they manage to shed their weary lot?
Oh, what do simple folk do we do not?

ARTHUR
I have been informed by those who know them well
They find relief in quite a clever way.
When they're sorely pressed, they whistle for a spell
And whistling seems to brighten up their day.
And that's what simple folk do,
So they say.

Although composed in a more traditional genre and on a much larger scale than epigram, Apollonius' epic *Argonautica* was no less in tune with contemporary tastes (Köhnken). In fact, it has many points of contact with Callimachus' *Aetia*, belying the ancient biographical tradition that promulgated the story of a bitter argument between the two poets. Like the *Aetia*, the *Argonautica* contains numerous "origins" and is related by a prominent narrator who relies on the Muses but also talks like a historian. And like the *Aetia*, it is highly episodic but by no means disjointed, its episodes being connected through numerous thematic links, shared intertexts (from Homer to Pindar, Herodotus, and Euripides), cross-references, foreshadowing, and bridging devices. Quintessentially Hellenistic is also the epic's main hero, Jason. Apollonius has so reduced Jason's stature that modern scholars question his heroic status, particularly as he appears to have been fully upstaged in the course of the poem by a seemingly all-powerful Medea. Jason's diminished abilities resonate, however, with contemporary interest in realism. In reality, an average young man like Jason cannot handle fire-breathing bulls or single-handedly kill scores of earthborn warriors. This could only happen through the intervention of some superhuman force. Apparently, Hellenistic audiences found such a figure more engaging than a godlike hero, predetermined for success.

Unfortunately, apart from the *Argonautica* no other long narrative hexameter poems survive from the Hellenistic era. We have titles and fragments of other epics, but not enough to determine if Apollonius' approach to the genre was an exception or the rule. What do survive are short narrative poems on mythological topics which scholars have come to call *epyllia*, "little epics" (Ambühl). Such poems typically treat select episodes of familiar stories from novel angles, leaving out key parts of the story to be supplemented by the readers. A number of the surviving texts focus on the ultimate Greek hero, Heracles, in unconventional ways, presenting him in love, childhood, disguise, or *absentia*. Remarkably often in Hellenistic poetry the interest in the human side of the great mythological figures takes the form of a prequel. Theocritus' Heracles (*Idyll* 24), Callimachus' Theseus (*Hecale*), and Apollonius' Jason and Medea (*Argonautica*) are represented in the process of becoming the figures celebrated in earlier literature. In this way Hellenistic literature turns literary chronology on its head.

Hellenistic hymnal and encomiastic poems raise many thorny questions, first and foremost regarding their context and function. While earlier praise poems, from the *Homeric Hymns* to Simonides' encomia, were first and foremost scripts to be performed at some sort of public occasion, many of their Hellenistic incarnations are more redolent of the library than the festival (Bulloch). The borders between hymn, encomium, and epyllion are often blurred, as gods, heroes, and kings are matched up in poems that praise but also, as in mythological epic, show their subjects' human side. In evidence throughout the extant corpus is a novel mixture of traditional religious-political thought and contemporary ideologies, from Egyptian concepts of kingship, as in Callimachus and Theocritus, to Stoic theology, as in Cleanthes.

Several of Callimachus' hymns create the illusion of a festival, including, as it were, their performance context within the text. Something similar happens in contemporary paeans, songs for Apollo and Asclepius composed by otherwise unknown poets (Fantuzzi). All are preserved in inscriptions which elaborately contextualize the paeans' lyrics, providing a key to, for example, the original performance context, the propagandistic subtext, the authority of poet, patron, and poem, and in some cases even the music. These texts with their tendency toward self-conscious innovation, intertextuality, and self-justification suggest that even far from the courts poets were touched by contemporary poetic trends. They also show that a tradition of sung poetry still flourished in the sanctuaries of the Greek homeland at a time when avant-garde poets used dactylic meters even for themes that were originally melic, creating a sort of virtual music.

No poetic genre reflects Hellenistic writers' interest in learning more clearly than didactic. It therefore seems appropriate that the key representative of this genre, Aratus' *Phaenomena*, should vie with Callimachus' *Aetia* for the title of the period's most influential poem (Volk). The *Phaenomena* refashions contemporary research on astronomy and meteorology along the lines of the *Works and Days*, and to such an extent that Callimachus observed about the *Phaenomena* that "the song and manner are Hesiod's." As in the case of the *Aetia*, modern scholarship has found it difficult to see past the poem's Roman reception, which fogs up Aratus' relationship to his predecessors and sources, and his intentions in this poem. Although the *Phaenomena* has been widely used as a textbook, its explicit didactic goal of teaching farmers and sailors is clearly a conceit. Nor is the *Phaenomena* merely an attempt to show that a good poet can make pleasing poetry out of any material. Rather, it is didactic in a broad sense, providing lessons about the nature of the universe, the divine, and the human condition – be they Stoic or more generally philosophical – focusing on the importance of "signs" and their interpretation.

Much the same applies to the *Theriaca* and *Alexipharmaca*, the didactic diptych of Nicander, who at least a generation later achieved a comparable result in reconstructing Hesiod's *Works and Days*, this time with poisonous creatures and antidotes as the unlikely subjects (Magnelli). Here too, common laborers are the explicit beneficiaries, but the ideal audience would consist of those who not only knew Hesiod but also Aratus, Callimachus, Theocritus, and Apollonius well enough to appreciate Nicander's allusions, verbal plays, and metrical finesse. More so than in the *Phaenomena*, verbal virtuosity takes center stage, in keeping, it seems, with the underlying didactic agenda. Nicander's display of poetic *technē* mirrors his emphasis on the technicalities as opposed to the practicalities of toxicology in these poems, which both open without a reference to the gods but with a triumphant "easily," a catch word that matches Aratus' "signs" and may suggest that, in Nicander's worldview, human control comes not through recognizing signs but through *technē*.

Theocritus' bucolic poetry takes the creation of fictional realities even further than other Hellenistic genres. Its humble herdsmen spend their time singing and in love in pleasurable surroundings without pressing needs, inhabiting a fiction that belongs to no world, mythological or real, outside the individual poems in which they appear (Payne). While these poems have a dramatic setting, they are largely plotless: the action revolves around the performance of songs, in which the herdsmen poets, all highly conscious of their predecessors, identify themselves with figures such as Daphnis or Polyphemus, creating microcosms within the poem that are somehow related to, yet separate from, the world of the dramatic frame. There can be little doubt that Theocritus himself appears as a fictional character in *Idyll* 7 under the guise of Simichidas, which raises the question of whether the poet is also represented in the other poems. While Callimachus and Herodas receive their inspiration in dreams, Theocritus inserts himself as a sort of avatar into an illusory world in order to actualize an aspect of the self that cannot be attained otherwise: he achieves the status of a Hesiodic poet through the re-enactment of a poetic investiture overseen by a mysterious goatherd. Ironically, only by becoming another can the poet, like his characters, realize the self to which he aspires.

Later writers of bucolic poetry followed Theocritus' precedent and freely inserted themselves into fictional worlds of their own invention. Some also inserted other historical figures, from historical predecessors, such as the poet Bion in the *Epitaph for Bion*, to contemporaries, such as Augustus in Vergil's *Eclogues*. Vergil's move proved a crucial one, as it gave rise to a tradition of bucolic poetry that creates a full-fledged counter-image of historical reality to offer a social critique. By Vergil's time, however, Theocritus' experimental poems about herdsmen had spawned a literary genre with its own conventions and a coherent fictional world, recognizable, for example, in Moschus and Bion. At an early point in the process of genre-formation stand three poems preserved among the works of Theocritus: *Idyll* 6, ascribed to Theocritus himself, and *Idylls* 8 and 9, generally considered post-Theocritean (Reed). All three seem to be synthesizing Theocritus' (earlier) bucolic poetry. Treating its innovations as conventions with which to work, they codify a specific type of herdsmen's exchange and pastoral world, and stereotype its intertextual tropes in such a way that they become stepping-stones to a new poetics.

The Archaic iambic poet Hipponax was resurrected during the Hellenistic era, even literally in Callimachus' first *Iamb*. As was the case for other authors whose works were appropriated as models at this time, iambographers updated Hipponactean verse in tune with the intellectual trends and literary tastes of the day (Scodel). Most importantly, Hellenistic iambos and its sister parody are no longer vitriolic and cruel but relatively mild and amusing. The people lampooned are largely straw men, and personal invective and gross obscenity have been replaced by general moral advice. Where the Archaic iambographer presented himself as a drinker, brawler, and seducer, the main models of his Hellenistic incarnation are philosophers such as Socrates, Diogenes, and Pyrrho, socially marginal "wise men" who mock common behavior and teach virtue and detachment – but most of all, happiness. As far as Hellenistic iambos is still hostile and contemptuous, it is to conventional beliefs, to wealth and power, in short, to any sort of pretension, including literary. Beyond this overall "philosophical" atmosphere the extant satiric-parodic texts vary widely. Boundaries between genres, styles, and illocutionary modes are porous, and so are those between schools of philosophy. Phoenix's choliambs dispense lighthearted moral advice, perhaps with a Cynic flavor. Callimachus' learned and complex *Iambi* are only loosely attached to the spirit and form of Archaic iambos, containing poems in different meters and on non-satiric topics; in some Plato is an important model. Cercidas introduced meliambic verse, a meter related to the dactylo-epitrite, to sing a Cynic tune in a Doric literary dialect. Macho's *Chreiai* are vulgar anecdotes with punch lines in prosaic diction and regular iambic trimeters. The hexameters of Timon of Phlius satirize the philosophical schools from a Skeptical perspective; those of Crates of Thebes sell Cynicism through poetic parody (White). A mixed bag indeed.

Herodas' *Mimiambs* offer another take on the iambic genre, blending iambos and mime, with Hipponax himself showing up for Herodas' consecration as iambic poet, a Hesiodic theme explored by so many Hellenistic and, later, Roman poets (Esposito). Herodas' depiction of the lives of ordinary people, such as cobblers, housewives, and school masters, is also typical of the period. The *Mimiambs*' unpretentious subject matter and seemingly realistic dialogue led some earlier critics to evaluate them as popular poetry or even, with a Marxist twist, as an indictment of the elitist literature of the court. Yet the simplicity of these poems is deceptive. Just like Theocritus' hexameter "urban mimes" (*Idylls* 2, 14, and 15), they address an audience equipped to appreciate complex allusions and philological games, and they likewise seem to support a Ptolemaic cultural agenda. They are, in fact, far removed from the anonymous "popular" mimes which were performed by traveling troops throughout Hellenistic Egypt. These, as fragmentary scripts and related documents testify, drew their effect from various combinations of scripted dialogue, improvisation, music, song, and dance. Although the *Mimiambs* too may have been performed in some manner and context, Herodas clearly had attentive readers in mind as well.

The passage of time was not kind to Hellenistic drama, but Menander's comedies were so ubiquitous in Greco-Roman Egypt that many chunks and scraps survived in the dry sands, to resurface only in recent years. We have one virtually complete play (*Dyskolos*) as well as large parts of a handful of others from which to get a good sense of what was happening on the comic stage. To this we can add the surviving Roman adaptations by Plautus and Terence, although their evidence should be handled with care. Throughout the Hellenic *oikoumenē*, rulers and civic elites embraced drama to advertise their allegiance to Greek culture in general and Athenian culture in particular – for despite the rise of an international theatre industry and professional theatrical guilds, drama retained its special connection with Athens and drama produced in Athens enjoyed a broad appeal. What makes this remarkable in the case of Menander is that his comedies, complex five-act marriage plots, are centered around problems which are highly specific to life in the Athenian *polis* with its exclusive citizenship laws

(Lape). Why, one might ask, would a Syracusan living in Alexandria want to see the travails of a young Athenian in love? One reason is surely that citizenship was an issue of intense interest to the mixed populations of the Hellenistic kingdoms, and that Menander's plays, although they are ultimately faithful to the tenets of Athenian civic identity – legitimacy, nativity, and freedom – also kick against them by constantly exploring the relationship between character and birth. But we may be dealing with a more generic issue as well. Asking why Menander's comedy appealed to a non-Athenian audience is like asking why modern audiences across the world like westerns, police dramas, and martial arts flicks. What these genres have in common is that they offer audiences who are not Athenian citizens, cowboys, police officers, or kung fu masters a fictional world with clearly defined parameters and conventions as a counter-image of their own reality. In this respect, the worlds of Menander and bucolic have something in common.

Hellenistic tragedy is almost entirely covered in darkness. We know that mythological dramas continued to be produced, and that there were historical tragedies as well as satyr-plays, but little more (Sens). What might the plays written by members of the so-called Pleiad, the most important dramatists of the time, have looked like? Would we encounter the mixing and blending of genres, Homeric glosses, and intrusion of contemporary issues observed elsewhere? To judge from the names of tragedians we know, which include the scholarly poets Alexander Aetolus, Lycophron, Philicus, and Sositheus, and from the evidence for actual texts, it would appear that like so many genres, tragedy came to Alexandria through the rabbit hole. In Sositheus' *Daphnis or Lityerses*, Daphnis, searching the world for the nymph he loved, found her as a slave at the court of the Phrygian king Lityerses, who required strangers to engage in a contest of reaping and killed them when he won; the play ended with Heracles decapitating Lityerses and returning the nymph to her lover. The main hero is a bucolic icon, the outcome that of a Euripidean tragedy, while the overall plot recalls satyr-play, epic, and the later novel. Whatever this play was, it was just as remarkable as the two best preserved Hellenistic "tragedies," Ezekiel's *Exagoge*, which dramatizes the story of Exodus (Gruen), and Lycophron's *Alexandra* (Sens). Lycophron's curious piece consists entirely of what represented only one scene of a typical tragedy, the messenger speech. In almost 1,500 lines, a messenger reports to King Priam an oracular utterance by Alexandra (i.e., Cassandra, the sister of Alexander/Paris), the prophet whom no one believed, couched in mystifying neologisms and recherché kennings. Cassandra's words provide an account of the Trojan cycle, but in such a way that the original audience would have required the equivalent of a PhD to understand their meaning. For the *doctus lector* able to decrypt it, the *Alexandra* explores the interrelationship between epic and tragedy, the historical conflict between East and West culminating in the rise of Rome, and last but not least the very hermeneutic effort required to access Hellenistic poetry's manifold levels of signification, "winding and traversing, pondering with wise mind, the obscure path of riddles" (lines 9–11). Such pondering presupposes reading, and it is indeed hard to imagine any audience deciphering the entire *Alexandra* in performance.

Whereas for poetry we possess a substantial number of key texts by key authors in their original form, the situation is radically different for prose. The three centuries after the death of Alexander are unquestionably important in intellectual history, showing crucial developments in fields such as philosophy, literary criticism, oratory, mathematics, astronomy, and medicine. Yet our evidence for these developments is almost entirely indirect. With some notable exceptions (such as the *Histories* of Polybius and technical works) we are able to access the prose literature of the period only through its reception, through discussions, summaries, and the occasional quotation in the works of later authors, writing in Latin as often as in Greek. Such testimonies and fragments allow us to say something – and sometimes even a lot – about the content of texts, but they rarely tell us much about the text as a text. For this reason Hellenistic prose tends to fill relatively few pages in literary histories.

Rhetoric and its most immediate application, oratory, are cases in point. Formal speeches doubtless played an important role in law, politics, and display within and among courts and cities. Yet not a single speech, whether forensic, epideictic, or diplomatic, survives: nearly all our information about Hellenistic speech-writing comes from authors such as Cicero and Dionysius of Halicarnassus, who were active at the very end of our period and favored the orators of the fourth century over Hellenistic styles (Cuypers). For theoretical thinking about language use and text composition – usually covered under rhetoric and literary criticism – we rely on largely the same set of authors, but with one crucial addition. Thanks to modern imaging techniques and new editions, we are increasingly able to interpret the carbonized papyrus texts of early first century BCE works by Philodemus of Gadara, found at Herculaneum. In addition to providing insight in Hellenistic theoretical discussions we previously knew little about, they show that many strands of criticism which were once thought to be peculiar to later writers in fact perpetuate centuries-old discussions (Gutzwiller). Philodemus treats fundamental questions regarding the function of literature, the nature of the poetic, the relationship between poetry's subject matter, language, style, and thought, and how to judge a literary work; he also discusses the so-called euphonist critics, who prioritized the sound of poetry over all other aspects, and allegorical approaches, which emphasized poetry's hidden lessons.

As an author of works on phenomenology, theology, ethics, rhetoric, music, poetry, and the history of philosophy, Philodemus also illustrates the breadth of the territory covered by *philosophia* after Aristotle and the interconnectedness of the fields within it (White). Of the three basic spheres of Hellenistic philosophy, physics dealt with the natural world as a whole, encompassing not only cosmology, theology, and metaphysics, but also, for example, biology, geology, and meteorology. Ethics covered all aspects of human conduct and therefore studied not only character and values but also the organization of cities and empires and the responsibilities of leaders and intellectuals. Logic went beyond formal logic and epistemology to include grammar, rhetoric, and literary criticism. Many who bore the label philosopher ranged even wider: Philodemus wrote poetry and was a historian (of philosophy at least); others were, for example, mathematicians. Although there are differences between first-century Rome and third-century Alexandria, there can be little doubt that in Callimachus' time philosophy, rhetoric, and literary criticism were as strongly interconnected, as established within Hellenic *paideia*, and as relevant to poetry production as they were in Philodemus' time. On the impact of these interrelated spheres on Hellenistic poetry much work remains to be done.

As for philosophical literature in the narrower sense, all that survives intact of the colossal production of Hellenistic Peripatetics, Stoics, Epicureans, Skeptics, and Academics are three letters by Epicurus and collected excerpts from his writings; short poems (notably Cleanthes' *Hymn to Zeus*); some pseudepigrapha preserved under the names of Plato, Aristotle, and others; and a few documents such as wills (White). For everything else we rely on the testimony of authors such as Cicero, Lucretius, and Sextus Empiricus. In the many forms philosophical literature took, a feature that stands out is the prominence of the persona and voice of the philosopher himself, engaged in communication in genres such as dialogues, biographies, anecdotes, and letters; this phenomenon may be usefully compared to trends in contemporary poetry and historiography. As in the case of oratory, the close of the era saw a renewed interest in the originary texts of the discipline. Unlike Hellenistic oratory, however, Hellenistic philosophy was not obliterated by this development but remained the basis for interaction with the works of Classical authors such as Plato and Aristotle for a long time to come.

It is a tenet that philosophers increasingly led what we would call an academic life, devoted to study and reflection. Yet they could and did wield influence. As intellectual icons of their community they could be paraded, for example, on diplomatic missions (Erskine), and they instructed the future political and intellectual elite. Just as Aristotle had taught Alexander, his successor Demetrius of Phalerum, after governing Athens for Cassander, became a tutor to the Ptolemies, whose Museum, as we saw, was modeled upon the Lyceum. At Alexandria and elsewhere, philosophers participated in the intellectual competition and complex politics of the court just like all other courtiers, be they poets or generals.

Ironically, the area of Hellenistic prose where most texts are extant also happens to be the one least accessible to most students of Greek literature. Scientific writing, even if it could be classified under philosophy, was somewhat separate back then as it is now. It addressed an audience of specialists through concise verbal explanation with visual illustration, using formal conventions which are surprisingly similar across disciplines (Cuypers). Substantially preserved (occasionally in Arabic translation) are works on mathematics, optics, astronomy, and mechanics by over a dozen authors, including key figures such as Euclid and Archimedes. As in the case of poets and philosophers, the biographical tradition often insists that these men were primarily motivated by intellectual challenges per se and regarded real-world applications with disdain; but although there are indeed important similarities in spirit between science and contemporary poetry, it is a fact that the mechanical treatises of Biton and Philo describe war machines and artillery – also the area where Archimedes proved his worth to Hiero of Syracuse – and that Apollonius of Citium, the author of the only extant medical treatise of the era, criticizes his predecessors precisely for their lack of hands-on experience. Scientists too had patrons and were expected to make themselves useful.

In historiography the only text to survive (though not completely) is Polybius' *Histories*, which forms an island in the sea of fragments that leads from the fourth century BCE to Dionysius of Halicarnassus in the late first (Gowing). Features of some pre-Polybian histories can be gleaned from Polybius' criticism of them, even if, as in the case of Callimachus' *Aetia* prologue, we should perhaps be slightly wary of Polybius' insistence that the "dramatic" and "universal" histories of his predecessors were much inferior to his own Thucydidean "pragmatic" history. Not only do veridical polemics come with the territory, many of Polybius' predecessors also worked in a different tradition, which privileged romantic storytelling, exoticism, and wonder. This tradition can be traced from Herodotus through fourth-century authors such as Theopompus and Ctesias to various ill-demarcated literary categories of the Hellenistic period, including paradoxography, utopia, biography, and local history, in which history and myth, fact and fiction, Greek and non-Greek were closely interwoven (Whitmarsh). There were, for example, countless local historians who wrote about the peoples, places, and events associated with their own towns and regions in stories and histories, putting them on the cultural map of the Hellenic *oikoumenē*. Local lore and wonders likewise occupy a prominent place in poems such as Callimachus' *Aetia* and Apollonius' *Argonautica*, both of which also include their share of eros. The exploits of Alexander the Great, first recorded by "serious" historians whose works we can now only glimpse through Diodorus, Plutarch, and Arrian, also gave rise to many tales of wonder, as preserved in the *Alexander Romance*. Although there is no straight road from Hellenistic literature to the erotic-exotic novels of Imperial times, it is clear that in this period a crucial development occurred. Various Hellenistic innovations in what we would call prose fiction are the products of genuine cross-cultural hybridity, fusing Greek, Egyptian, and Western Asian elements into something recognizably new.

This cross-cultural dialogue goes far beyond prose fiction. Although Greek became the *lingua franca* in all lands under Greco-Macedonian rule, this did not imply that indigenous elites were simply "assimilated" or that the Hellenic elite was ignorant of local cultural traditions. Literature continued to be written in Egyptian, Akkadian, and Aramaic. Some genres remained exactly as they were, others underwent more or less substantial developments, but few disappeared completely. When indigenous elites adopted the Greek language and Greek literary forms, it was often not so much to demonstrate their Greekness but for self-presentation to a broad audience. Jewish writers penned dramas, epics, *ktisis* tales, histories, letters, and dialogues, and through these insinuated themselves brilliantly into Greek cultural history and reached out to an increasingly Greek-speaking Jewish population in diaspora (Gruen). A similar ploy can be seen in the *Alexander Romance*, in its origin a product of Ptolemaic Egypt, where Nectanebo, the last pharaoh of Egypt, goes to the court of Philip II and impregnates Olympias with Alexander, persuading her that she would be sleeping with Amun. Accordingly, Alexander and his successors could be seen as the natural successors of indigenous rulers (Dieleman and Moyer). The strategy is also employed in the *Babyloniaca*, written by Bel-re'-ushu (Berossus). In this historical work, the Seleucids were portrayed as the final stage in the succession of empires stretching back to Nabopolassar and his son Nebuchadnezzar (Knippschild). Much like the *Aegyptiaca* of the Egyptian priest Manetho, Berossus' work was not a straightforward imitation of Greek historiography but to some extent adhered to indigenous conventions of form; and with respect to their message both works cut both ways, flattering not only the rulers but also the ruled, whose cultural pride was clearly very much intact.

While Greeks had dealt with the peoples of Western Asia and Egypt for centuries, Rome was a new power which established itself on the Mediterranean stage in a relatively short time in the third century and proceeded to swallow up the Hellenistic kingdoms at a swift pace. Apart from being unfamiliar to the Greeks and being the ruler instead of ruled, the Romans also did not have a long and distinguished literary history, even if they had a strong and distinct cultural tradition. For all these reasons the interaction between Greeks and Romans was fundamentally different.

Greek historiography provides us with a fascinating view of how the Greek attitude toward the Romans shifted over time (Gowing). For Polybius, writing in the second century, the Romans were still the Other who had recently gained an empire, for which reason it was necessary to explain to Greeks who they were and how they had become so successful. In the later writings of Polyhistor, Posidonius, and Dionysius of Halicarnassus, we see the perspective gradually change as Roman hegemony becomes more and more a fact of life and a new symbiosis develops between the Roman elite and the Greek intellectuals streaming into Rome: not an uneasy pact between conqueror and conquered, but a relationship of mutual interest and respect. In time, Dionysius would go so far as to see the Romans as honorary Greeks, which is not so startling a thought when one considers the extent to which Roman writers, thinkers, and artists absorbed Hellenic culture.

This should not, however, be taken to imply that Roman literature simply took over Greek concepts, forms, and styles; rather, it assimilated them, individuating itself from Hellenistic literature with great success. This process of assimilation and individuation culminated in the first century but began as early as the third. In their adaptation of Greek poetic genres, Roman authors managed to maintain their own voice from the start. Enough survives of the earliest Roman epics by Livius Andronicus, Naevius, and Ennius to demonstrate a keen awareness of Hellenistic sensitivities (Clauss). With respect to their learnedness, playfulness, and self-consciousness these poems might have been at home in Alexandria; yet in their content and ethics they are unmistakably Roman. The contemporary comedies of Plautus, which are both firmly connected to and significantly different from Hellenistic comedy, allow a similar analysis.

Historians almost universally let the Hellenistic period end in 31/30 BCE, the years of the Battle of Actium, the fall of Alexandria, and the death of Cleopatra, after which Augustus ruled, effectively with sole power, over much of the area once dominated by Alexander and his successors. It was also shortly after Actium that Dionysius of Halicarnassus arrived in Rome, an event that provides an appropriate book-end to a chapter in literary history whose beginning was marked by the deaths of Aristotle and Demosthenes. The city in which Dionysius arrived must have looked to him very much like a Hellenistic metropolis. It was filled with Greek sculptures and paintings, peripteral temples in foreign marble instead of the local stone, public buildings and porticos faced with Corinthian columns and ornate entablatures. Intellectuals from all over the *oikoumenē* flocked to the Seven Hills to give displays of their erudition. In the decades that followed Actium, Rome came to resemble a Hellenistic city even more, and Alexandria in particular, as intellectual life blossomed and construction boomed. Among other allusions to Alexander's great city, Augustus built a magnificent mausoleum in imitation of the great Macedonian general's tomb, in front of which stood two obelisks. He also commissioned a monumental Horologium whose gnomon was another obelisk, and to his home he added a temple to Apollo and libraries, an obvious nod to the Alexandrian Library and Museum. It seems fitting, therefore, that Medieval and Renaissance Europe would become acquainted with Hellenistic literature primarily through Rome. While the Roman poets, rhetors, philosophers, and historians of the early Empire went their own way, they indirectly preserved much of the Hellenistic literary tradition of which they were the immediate heirs. Due to the vagaries of history, many of their works survived while the Hellenistic texts did not. Our direct knowledge of these texts has begun to grow significantly only since the nineteenth century, thanks to finds such as the Herculaneum scrolls, the Archimedes palimpsest, and most of all, of course, the numerous literary papyri that have emerged from the sands of Egypt, with the "New Posidippus" as the most spectacular recent example. It is to be hoped that such finds will continue to increase our understanding of Hellenistic literature in the future.

FURTHER READING

Hellenistic literature often fares poorly in histories of Greek literature, most of which explicitly or implicitly offer a rise-and-fall narrative that privileges the Classical period and sees the Hellenistic period as a time of decline. The almost complete loss of much of the period's prose literature makes it even easier to give it short shrift. Kassel 1987 is an informative survey of the demarcation and evaluation of the Hellenistic period in literary histories from Vossius to modern times, which foregrounds the rehabilitation of Hellenistic poetry, if not of Hellenistic literature at large, at the end of the nineteenth century, the time of the first major papyrus finds. Kassel rightly singles out the contribution of the vehemently anti-Classicistic Wilamowitz, directly through publications (see notably 1912, 1924) and indirectly through his students. Tellingly, the Hellenistic section of Schmid and Stählin's revision of Christ's *Geschichte der griechischen Literatur* grew to 506 pages in the fifth edition of 1911, then to 662 in the sixth edition of 1920. This work, which remains the most comprehensive survey of Hellenistic literature to date, posits a cultural break at 146 BCE between "the creative period of Hellenistic literature" and "the period of the transition to Classicism," which it lets end around 100 CE – an analysis challenged by various chapters in this *Companion*.

An accessible book-length introduction to Hellenistic literature is Gutzwiller 2007a, which inevitably focuses on poetry but includes substantial discussions of prose that survives in its original form (Polybius, technical treatises). Almost half of the volume is devoted to analytic discussions of topics such as historical context, learning, book culture, aesthetics, and the critical impulse in literature and art. Recent bite-sized introductions are Hunter 2003b and Krevans and Sens 2006, both largely restricted to poetry. Substantial discussions of Hellenistic literature in broader literary histories include Lesky 1971 (German) and 1966: 642–806 (English); Dihle 1991 (German) and 1994: 231–311 (English); Saïd 1997: 277–402 (French; a radically abbreviated English version in Saïd and Trédé 1999: 93–118). Schmitt and Vogt 2005 includes substantial entries on all major Hellenistic authors and genres.

Recent surveys of Hellenistic poetry in particular include Bulloch 1985, Hutchinson 1988, Fantuzzi and Hunter 2004, and Manakidou and Spanoudakis 2008 (in Greek). Influential older surveys are Couat 1882 (English version 1931), Susemihl 1891–2, Legrand 1924, Wilamowitz 1924, and Körte 1925 (English version 1929; revised as Körte and Händel 1960). Fowler 1990 anthologizes Hellenistic poetry in English translation; Hopkinson 1988, in the original Greek.

PART ONE

Contexts

CHAPTER TWO

From Alexander to Augustus

Andrew Erskine

For a Greek at the time of Alexander's accession in 336 BCE the Persian Empire was part of the very structure of the world, a superpower whose territory stretched from Asia Minor to Bactria, or in modern terms from Turkey to Afghanistan. Under the Achaemenid dynasty it had dominated the East for almost two centuries and had long stirred the imagination of Greek observers. Yet, within a few years it would have ceased to exist, defeated by a young Macedonian king who would himself take the place of the Great King. Alexander's empire, however, would not have the longevity of its predecessor. When he died in Babylon in 323, he left no viable heir to hold these diverse territories together; instead his death inaugurated several decades of war between members of the Macedonian elite, who shaped kingdoms for themselves out of parts of Alexander's empire.

This chapter is concerned to offer some sense of the historical context in which Hellenistic literature was produced. The fundamental shift from the Classical period is the appearance of powerful Greco-Macedonian kings with vast territories and enormous wealth. These kings resonate throughout the chapter. After briefly examining the emergence of the Hellenistic kingdoms, I move on to explore three key themes which have particular relevance to our understanding of literature in this transformed world: first, the relationship between royal power and literary culture (discussed in more detail by Stephens and Strootman in this volume), then the place of the *polis* in this world after Alexander, and finally the impact of Rome.

After Alexander

Alexander's death left a vast empire without an obvious ruler. The kingship was initially shared between his infant son, Alexander IV, and his allegedly mentally disabled half-brother, Philip Arrhidaeus, neither of whom were in a position to rule. Nor was there

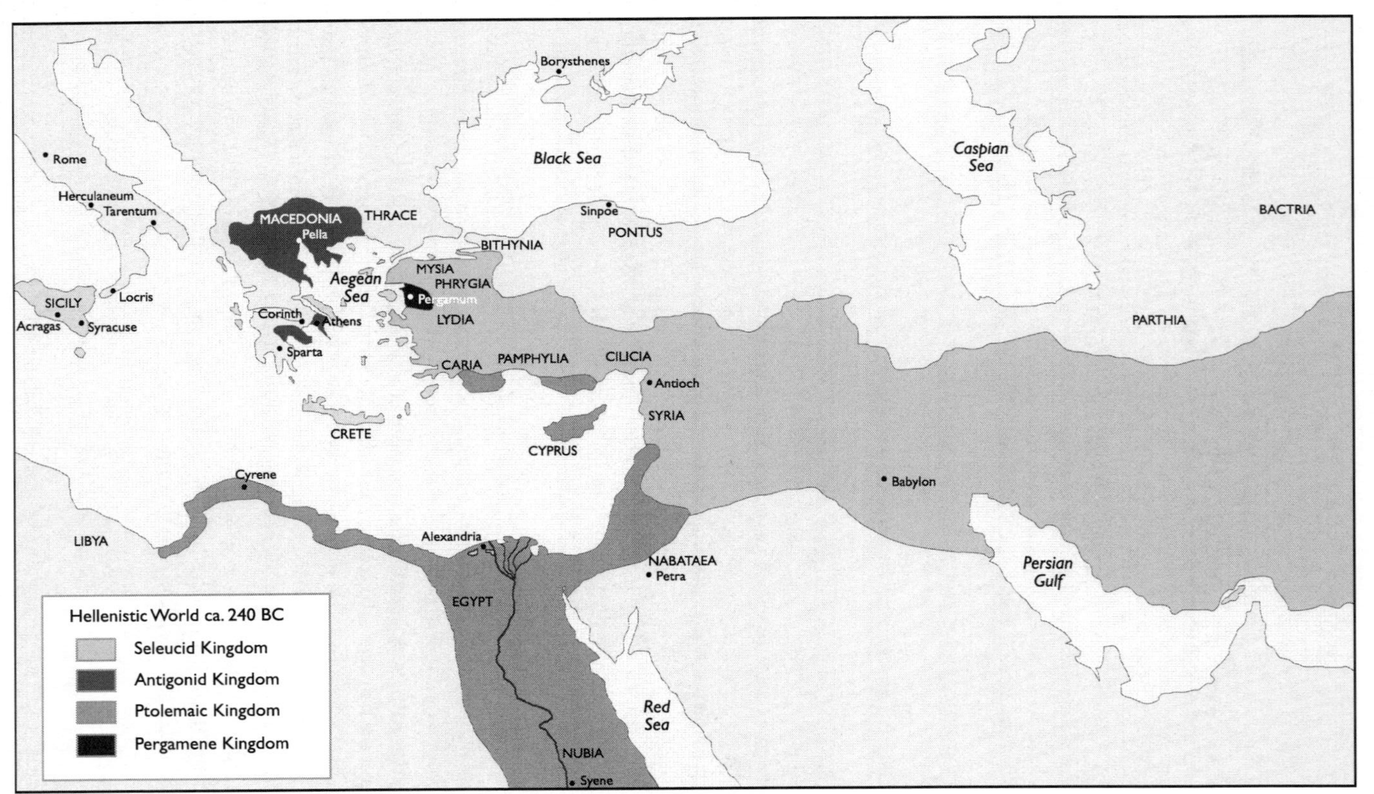

Map 2.1. *The Hellenistic Kingdoms (c. 240 BCE).*

anyone who ruled undisputed on their behalf. Instead Alexander's generals seem to have tried to carry on as before, administering the empire, allocating governorships, minting Alexander's coins and putting down the revolt in Greece. They were in all likelihood also planning their individual strategies for the future, but whatever plans they may have had, they affected support for the empire and the two kings. Even so, in the turbulent years that followed Alexander's death the casualty rate was high. Antipater, Craterus, and Perdiccas must number amongst the political and military heavyweights at the end of Alexander's reign but none made effective use of the new situation and all were dead within four years of Alexander's own death, the result of old age, battle, and mutiny respectively. Eumenes, who had been victorious over Craterus, went on to achieve significant success despite being Greek rather than Macedonian, until he himself succumbed to Antigonus Monopthalmus. Polyperchon, entrusted with Alexander IV and Philip Arrhidaeus by Antipater, failed to follow up this advantage and was soon bettered by Antipater's son Cassander. Kingship did not save Philip Arrhidaeus and his wife Eurydice, who met their end at the hands of Philip's stepmother Olympias. She in turn was executed by Cassander.

Few would have predicted that within fifteen years of Alexander's death the leading figures in this Macedonian Empire would have been Antigonus, Cassander, Ptolemy, Lysimachus, and Seleucus. Even Alexander IV was no more, secretly executed by Cassander before he came of age and thus called into question Cassander's position as ruler of Macedon. Ptolemy had laid claim to the governorship of Egypt when the satrapies were distributed after Alexander's death and had defended it against any assault, such as the invasion in which Perdiccas lost his life; similarly Lysimachus had taken over Thrace. While not foregoing expansionist adventures, both men concentrated on strengthening their positions in their acquired possessions. Seleucus had a more difficult time establishing himself as governor of Babylon; toppled by Antigonus, he was only reinstated with the assistance of Ptolemy. The dominant figure in the latter part of the fourth century, however, was Antigonus, whose ambition, it is believed, was to reunite the empire under his sole rule. Constantly at war and controlling Asia Minor and at times central Asia too, he prompted his rivals to unite against him on several occasions, decisively so at the Battle of Ipsus in Phrygia in 301, where he died on the battlefield and his son Demetrius Poliorcetes fled.

Significantly, even after the murder of Alexander IV none of these warlords hurried to claim the title of king. Indeed so strong was the need to maintain some form of belief in the existence of a unified Macedonian Empire that Alexander IV's regnal years continued to be used for dating purposes in both Babylon and Egypt until 306/5, several years after his death. In 306 Antigonus, perhaps predictably, was the first to claim the royal title for himself, but his rivals soon followed suit. This marked the end of any pretense that Alexander's empire still existed, and opened the way for the development of separate kingdoms and their accompanying royal ideologies. Becoming a king, however, did not entail founding a dynasty. That required taking suitable care of the succession, something both Cassander and Lysimachus failed to do. On Cassander's death in 297, his sons fought it out in a civil war in which their mother, Philip II's daughter Thessalonice, was a victim. Neither son gained the kingdom, which was seized and soon lost by Demetrius. Lysimachus, on the other hand, made the mistake of executing his eldest son so it was already a weakened kingdom that he left behind him when he was killed in battle against Seleucus at Corupedium in 281.

Such instability in the northern regions of Macedon and Thrace created the conditions for one of the events fundamental in shaping the worldview of the third-century Greek. Early in the 270s groups of Celts, usually called Galatians by the Greeks, broke through Macedon and so exposed the vulnerability of the Greek world. They succeeded in reaching as far south as the great sanctuary of Apollo at Delphi, an opportunity for divine intervention and a heroic defense by the Aetolians. Some, going through Thrace across into Asia Minor, eventually settled in the area that would come to be known as Galatia, and became a constant irritant for neighboring Greeks. For the Greeks of the time this was their equivalent of the Persian invasion, complete with its own Battle of Thermopylae (279). When Antigonus Gonatas, son of Demetrius and grandson of Antigonus Monopthalmus, defeated some 15,000 Celts at Lysimacheia on the Thracian side of the Hellespont in 277, he was hailed as Savior (*Soter*) for a victory that helped to establish him as king of Macedon (Mitchell 2003). Finally, the Antigonids had won a kingdom that they would keep, at least until the arrival of the Romans.

Of these kingdoms, therefore, three key dynasties survived to be significant forces throughout the third century. The Ptolemies were based in Egypt, although at various times their power extended to Cyprus and into the Aegean Sea; the Seleucids established themselves in Syria and Babylonia and thus took over the heart of the old Persian Empire; and the Antigonids came to rule Macedon itself and to exert considerable influence over mainland Greece. Powerful Greco-Macedonian families thus ruled the East, but this was no mere change in political superstructure. Macedonian rule brought new Greek foundations and a Greek immigrant population to go with them. Most prominent amongst these new cities was Alexandria in Egypt, but there were many others, such as Antioch on the Orontes in Syria or Seleuceia on the Tigris not far from Babylon. There were even Greek cities as far east as Bactria, as the excavations at Ai-Khanoum demonstrate (Holt 1999). The relationship between the new and the old populations is one of the major questions of Hellenistic scholarship. Kings with large multi-ethnic populations took care to appeal beyond the Greek and Macedonian core to other ethnic groups; thus, for example, Antiochus I takes on the guise of a native king at Babylon, while in Egypt portraits of the Ptolemies could depict the king either within a Greek tradition or in the manner of an Egyptian pharaoh (Kuhrt and Sherwin-White 1991; Walker and Higgs 2001: 40–5). Where scholarship previously considered Alexandria to be emphatically Greek, archaeology is now showing that visually the city was far more complex than this, and that the Ptolemies themselves appear to have promoted Egyptian and Egyptian-influenced architecture and sculpture within the city as well as Greek (Ashton 2004; McKenzie 2003; Stephens in this volume).

These kings were to hold sway over the Eastern Mediterranean and beyond for more than a hundred years, the only challenges to their rule coming from each other. In the West, however, Rome's victories over Carthage in the first two Punic Wars (264–241 and 218–201) revealed a new and dynamic military power. Within ten years, at the beginning of the second century, two major Hellenistic dynasties, the Antigonids and the Seleucids, were defeated by Roman legions, making Greeks aware of the emergence of a new world order. By the middle of the century the Antigonid dynasty was no more. The Seleucids remained a significant power in Asia for much of the second century, but with the loss of Babylonia to the Parthians their dynasty was considerably weakened, and in 64 BCE it was finally laid to rest by Pompey. Caught up in the Roman civil wars, the last of the original successor kingdoms ended with the suicide of Cleopatra in 30 BCE, the year frequently designated by scholars as the end not only of the Ptolemaic dynasty but also of the Hellenistic Age.

The Dagger and the *Iliad*

Within a year of Alexander's accession a rumor reached Thebes that the new Macedonian king had died in battle. The Theban response was to revolt; only when Alexander and his army were a few hours from the city did the Thebans learn the unfortunate truth. After their revolt was crushed, the city was razed to the ground and the population sold into slavery, an example to any who might consider resisting Alexander's authority in the future. There was, however, a striking exception to the general destruction. The house of the poet Pindar was to be left intact and his descendants were to be exempted from the fate of their fellow citizens (Arr. *An.* 1.7–9; Plu. *Alex.* 12). This combination of violence and literary sensibility was to be a continuing feature of the Hellenistic world. Alexander was a man who slept, so it was said, with two objects under his pillow, a dagger and a copy of Homer's *Iliad*, the latter considered by him to be a manual of the art of war. Indeed, when he had to choose his most precious possession to place in a valuable casket seized from Darius, it was the *Iliad* that he selected (Plu. *Alex.* 8, 26).

By 334 Alexander had asserted his control over Macedon and the Greek mainland. Any rivals for the Macedonian throne were dead, Thebes was a ruin, and Alexander was ready for the crossing to Asia. The manner of the crossing is telling. On the European side of the Hellespont Alexander paid his respects at the sanctuary of the hero Protesilaus, the first man ashore in the campaign against Troy. In doing this he recalled the heroic age while also contrasting his own religious observance with the earlier Persian desecration of the shrine (Hdt. 7.33, 9.116–20). Landing in the Troad at the so-called harbor of the Achaeans, Alexander is said to have been the first to leap from the ships before going on to lay claim to the territory with the throw of a spear (D.S. 17.17; Arr. *An.* 1.11.5; Stewart 1993: 78). Imitation here blurs the boundaries between history and myth, literature and life.

This evocation of the *Iliad* and the age of heroes is further reinforced by a visit to Troy. Many stories circulated about this visit: he paid homage to the tomb of Achilles while his close friend Hephaestion did likewise at the tomb of Patroclus; he viewed relics from the Trojan War in the temple of Athena and exchanged his own armor for some of the weapons on display there, including a shield which was later carried before him into battle; and he sacrificed to Priam at the altar of Zeus Herceius, where his ancestor Neoptolemus had killed the Trojan king. Throughout his career Alexander created an image of himself as an epic hero, a new Achilles. He is said to have been nicknamed "Achilles" as a child by his tutor, to have lamented that there was no Homer to celebrate his deeds, to have mourned Hephaestion as Achilles mourned Patroclus. Such stories may be the result of later elaboration but they are based on an image that Alexander himself was projecting during his lifetime. For Alexander, a powerful leader with a large army of followers, operating outside the structure of the *polis*, the analogy with the Homeric hero was especially appealing and appropriate. The influence of this idea is seen in the way that Hellenistic kings are later depicted in the heroic manner, beardless and sometimes nude. Alexander was not only leading a campaign against the Persians, he was also leading a return to the age of heroes (Plu. *Alex.* 15, Arr. *An.* 1.11–12; Erskine 2001: 227–30).

Alexander's journey across Asia to the river Indus can be portrayed as a drunken orgy of killing and destruction, yet quality reading material was a necessary accompaniment. Even in the furthest reaches of Asia Alexander did not forget his Greek literature, and he is reported to have dispatched an instruction to Harpalus to send him some books. He received, writes Plutarch, the histories of Philistus, tragedies by Aeschylus, Sophocles, and Euripides, and poetry by Telestes and Philoxenus (*Alex.* 8; Brown 1967). Such a request highlights the barbarian, non-Greek setting he now found himself in and serves to repudiate those who wished to insinuate that the Macedonians were not proper Greeks (Dem. *Phil.* 3.31–2; Badian 1982).

It is indicative of the political and social changes brought about by Alexander that in the third century BCE the largest collection of Greek books in the ancient world was to be found not in mainland Greece, housed in a famed city of culture such as Athens, but in Egypt (Stephens and Gruen in this volume). Nor was this the collection of some intellectual or philosopher but rather of a military commander who had accompanied Alexander on his campaign and participated in the bloody warfare along the Indus. Ptolemy, son of Lagus, who converted his governorship of Egypt into a kingship and himself into Ptolemy Soter, took note of Alexander's lesson on the need for Greek literature in barbarian lands and used his newly acquired power to lay the foundations for the Library and Museum of Alexandria. Ptolemy's literary aspirations were such that not only did he collect books, he also wrote his own, namely an account of Alexander's campaigns, since lost but a major source for Arrian's history of Alexander.

The Museum and the Library were complementary institutions, the former a community of scholars, the latter a collection of books. They can be viewed from two perspectives, both as part of the history of literature, scholarship, and science, and also within the context of the goals and ideology of the Ptolemaic monarchy and court. The first perspective would emphasize the names of those who worked there (Euclid, Callimachus, Eratosthenes), the range of disciplines (literature, medicine, mathematics, astronomy), and especially the innovative literary activity, whether that be the writing of poetry or the editing of classic texts such as those of Homer and the Athenian dramatists. The two institutions were, however, the creation of the Ptolemaic kings and operated in a monarchic framework, the physical manifestation of which was their location within the palace complex. The patronage of writers and intellectuals was not new among rulers, not even among Macedonians; Archelaus, the fifth-century Macedonian king, had played host to Euripides and Philip II had employed Aristotle as tutor to Alexander. But this Ptolemaic venture was on an unprecedented scale, so much so that it was in effect something quite different: this was institutional patronage that continued from generation to generation.

The Ptolemies no doubt did seek the kudos that comes from patronage just as their predecessors had, but they were also driven by their own particular situation. They and their Greek and Macedonian subjects were far from their homeland; in Egypt they were effectively on the periphery of the Greek world. By gathering together and taking control of Greek literature and scholarship in this way the Ptolemies assert that they are part of that Greek world, both to themselves and to others. Indeed they are staking an ambitious claim to be its cultural center, one that mirrors and reinforces their claim to political leadership in the Greek world. In this capacity they presented a gymnasium and library to the city of Athens, a gift from the new cultural capital of Greece to the old (Paus. 1.17.2; Habicht 1992). Later the upstart Attalids would signal their arrival as major players in Hellenistic international relations by imitating the Ptolemies. They set up a rival library and they too acted as benefactors to Athens, sponsoring the construction of the Stoas of Attalus and Eumenes (Erskine 1995; Nagy 1998).

Not all kings went so far as to institutionalize patronage in this way but Greek intellectuals and literary men were a feature of courts throughout the Hellenistic world, their presence a statement of common Greek culture (Strootman in this volume). The court of mid-third-century Macedon under the lengthy rule of Antigonus Gonatas is well represented in our somewhat scattered and anecdotal evidence. Power, wealth and importantly stability brought many leading figures here. There were at various times philosophers such as Menedemus of Eretria, the Stoic Persaeus, and the Cynic-inspired Bion of Borysthenes, and poets such as Aratus, whose *Phaenomena* was said to have been written at Antigonus' request, and the now obscure Antagoras of Rhodes (*Vita Arati* 15; for philosophers, Erskine 1990). Antagoras, the author of an epic *Thebaid*, is the subject of a revealing anecdote recorded by Athenaeus (8.340f). When Antigonus finds Antagoras cooking conger eels, he asks him whether Homer would have ever written the *Iliad* celebrating Agamemnon if he had spent all his time cooking conger eels. Antagoras replies that Agamemnon would never have done those famous deeds if he had spent his time nosing around to see who was cooking eels in his camp. A similar informality is evident in another story, this time from the court of Antiochus III, the Seleucid warrior king, face battle-scarred and teeth missing. Antiochus and his court are taking turns to dance in arms; the historian Hegesianax of Alexandria Troas asks permission to substitute a reading of his poetry for dancing and is rewarded for his poetic eulogy of the king with the status of king's friend or *philos* (Ath. 4.155b; Ma 1999: 226). Here in both the Antigonid and Seleucid courts we can observe the recurring Hellenistic interplay between war and literature, the dagger and the *Iliad*, on the one hand the violence that brought about and maintained the kingdoms of the eastern Mediterranean, on the other hand the common Greek culture that bound them together.

The Place of the *Polis*

Kings and their courts tend to be highlighted as distinctive features of the Hellenistic world, while the *polis*, the city-state, is downplayed. Indeed it has often been claimed that the *polis* died with Demosthenes in 322 or even earlier with Philip's victory at

Chaeronea in 338. Increasingly, however, scholarship has been showing that this view will not stand up to examination; it reflects the common prioritizing and idealization of the Classical period in contrast to the "debased" Hellenistic period that followed. Advocates of the death of the *polis* have argued that with the rise of the kings, the *polis* was no longer the independent entity it had once been. Yet, was it ever? It is primarily the focus on Athens that leads anyone to suppose that independence should be treated as a defining characteristic of the *polis.* Many cities may have found their freedom constrained by the new monarchies, but many too had suffered similar restrictions in earlier centuries when faced with the power of Athens or Sparta. What is less evident in the Hellenistic period is the presence of hegemonic *poleis* of this latter sort. Instead *poleis* are often found organized in federations, the most prominent of which were the Achaean and Aetolian Leagues in Greece.

If we direct our attention towards the thousands of published inscriptions from the cities of the Hellenistic world, a different picture emerges. What we see here is the tremendous vitality of civic life in this period. Assemblies and councils are passing decrees, honoring the city's benefactors (*euergetai*), organizing festivals, producing regulations for local education and the gymnasium, receiving and responding to letters from kings, arranging embassies to kings and to other cities near and far. Much of this is as before. Even local wars continue, often over land and boundaries. What is new, at least in its pervasiveness, is the emergence of the king and the powerful citizen benefactor as significant influences on civic life, their status reflected in honorary decrees. The king, transformed into the object of cult, could even become part of the religious structure of the city.

Far from the death of the *polis* one might even see its reinvigoration as kings, following the example of Alexander, set about founding new cities and in this way simultaneously affirmed their power and their Greek identity. Seleucus I was reputed to have been especially fond of founding cities (App. *Syr.* 57, trans. White 1899):

> He built cities throughout the entire length of his dominions and named sixteen of them Antioch after his father, five Laodicea after his mother, nine after himself, and four after his wives, that is, three Apamea and one Stratonicea. Of these the two most renowned at the present time are the two Seleuceias, one on the sea and the other on the river Tigris, Laodicea in Phoenicia, Antioch under Mount Lebanon, and Apamea in Syria. To the others he gave names from Greece or Macedonia, or from his own exploits, or in honor of Alexander; whence it comes to pass that in Syria and among the barbarous regions of upper Asia many of the towns bear Greek and Macedonian names, such as Berrhoea, Edessa, Perinthus, Maronea, Callipolis, Achaea, Pella, Oropus, Amphipolis, Arethusa, Astacus, Tegea, Chalcis, Larissa, Heraea, and Apollonia; in Parthia also Sotera, Calliope, Charis, Hecatompylos, Achaea; in India Alexandropolis; among the Scythians an Alexandreschata. From the victories of Seleucus come the names of Nicephorium in Mesopotamia and of Nicopolis in Armenia very near Cappadocia.

There is, no doubt, some exaggeration here, but even if Seleucus founded only a quarter of these it is clear that he attached considerable importance to the *polis.* Furthermore, the names themselves are revealing about the post-Alexander world. Where Alexander monotonously founded cities bearing his own name, Seleucus is thinking dynastically. It is not the name of Seleucus alone that is being stamped across his empire but those of his relatives as well, both male and female; thus the dynasty and the land they control become one. The other theme that emerges from the nomenclature of the cities is nostalgia for the homeland, as Greece and Macedon are built anew in the East. This phenomenon recalls the Ptolemies' desire to lay claim to their Greek heritage through their library.

Polis status became something to aspire to and the king was the person who could make it happen. There is a fascinating letter from the Attalid king Eumenes II to a community in Phrygia, dating from the first half of second century, in which he grants the inhabitants' request that their community become a *polis*. The letter was subsequently inscribed as public confirmation of their new status. We see too what might be required for such an elevation. They had requested, writes Eumenes, that "a *polis* constitution be granted to [them], and [their] own laws, and a gymnasium, and as many things as consistent with those" (Jonnes and Ricl 1997; Bagnall and Derow 2004: no. 43). The Phrygian community in this text is not only becoming a *polis*, it is also becoming visibly Greek. The almost contemporary case of Jerusalem, however, shows that taking on the trappings of Greekness might not come without tension in the community; in the Jewish accounts of the controversial high-priesthood of Jason it is the gymnasium which symbolizes the Greek way of life (*1 Macc.* 1.10–15, *2 Macc.* 4.9–19).

Greekness may always have been a fairly flexible notion, as the fluctuating perception of the ethnic identity of the Macedonians demonstrates, but from the fourth century onwards there seems an increasing willingness for peoples who would most naturally be seen as non-Greek to represent themselves in Greek terms and even to claim Greek identity. The Lycians, for instance, were a non-Greek people from Asia Minor with their own language, funeral practices, and religious customs, but more and more they borrowed from their Greek neighbors until in the Hellenistic period Lycian public inscriptions are in Greek (Bryce 1986: 42–54, 214–15). In the late third century the Lycian city of Xanthus is visited by an embassy from Cytinium on the Greek mainland seeking funds for the reconstruction of their city-walls. The ambassadors in a learned speech full of complex genealogical arguments show how the Xanthians and the Cytinians are kin, with a shared ancestry that can be traced back to heroic times. The speech clearly excited the interest of the Xanthians, who proudly inscribed a summary of it, proof that they were part of the community of Greeks (Bousquet 1988; Erskine 2005: 126–7). Further east in Asia Minor, something similar was happening: cities in Pamphylia and Cilicia, such as Aspendos, Soloi, and Mallos, were turning themselves into Greeks with an Argive past (Scheer 2003: 226–31). Greekness could be further affirmed by participation in one of the Panhellenic festivals that flourished in the Hellenistic period, not only the old festivals at Olympia, Delphi, Isthmia, or Nemea but newly created ones, such as the festival of Artemis Leucophryene, established at Magnesia-on-the-Meander in the late third century, or that of Athena Nicephorus at Pergamum, which achieved Panhellenic status in 182 under Eumenes II (Rigsby 1996: 179–85, 363–6).

Within this broad community of Greeks, cities also had a very strong sense of civic identity; on the one hand they looked to what they shared with other Greeks, on the other they emphasized and prided themselves on their distinctiveness. This is apparent from the number of local histories that are known to have been written, although their parochial nature did little for their chances of survival. This pride in the community and its past comes out clearly in the opening of a verse inscription from Halicarnassus, which takes the form of a question addressed to Aphrodite: "What is it that brings honor to Halicarnassus?" Aphrodite then answers, first with an account of the gods and heroes that had had some part in the early history of the area, then with the city's poets and historians, among whom Herodotus is prominent. The section on gods and heroes is especially interesting; it illustrates how each city, while sharing in the common Greek mythology, had its own distinctive version. The names and characters are familiar, but their activities and contexts are not: Zeus is born in Halicarnassus, Hermaphroditus is the inventor of lawful marriage, Bellerophon and Endymion are somehow involved in the foundation of the city. All these stories are unique to this inscription and to Halicarnassus (Isager 1998; Lloyd-Jones 1999).

This inscription may honor the city itself but far more common are decrees that honor rich citizens who have acted as civic *euergetai*, "benefactors," for instance by going on an embassy or assisting in a grain shortage. This culture of elite benefaction has become known as euergetism. Especially important among this group of citizens are those who act as intermediaries between the city and the king and who may be numbered among the *philoi*, "friends," of the king, as Hegesianax of Alexandria Troas was a *philos* of Antiochus III. This proximity to the power of the king confers great prestige on the individual within his home community. An early example is an Athenian inscription of 283/2, which honors the comic poet Philippides, a *philos* of Lysimachus. Philippides' interventions with the king on behalf of Athens are traced over a period of circa fifteen years. He requests successfully that Lysimachus release those Athenians who had fought on the Antigonid side at Ipsus, he obtains gifts of grain from the king and support for the Panathenaic festival, and he wins assurances of help after the city has won its freedom from Demetrius Poliorcetes in 287. Philippides' services to the city are not limited to soliciting these favors from the king in which the king himself is the chief benefactor. Philippides is clearly a very rich man and repeatedly used his wealth on behalf of the city. In addition to paying the cost of the burial of the Athenian dead at Ipsus and providing money for the repatriation of survivors, he spent a considerable amount on contests and sacrifices in Athens. Noticeably absent from the inscription is any explicit reference to his successful career as a dramatist, although it is alluded to by the decision to crown him during the Great Dionysia and to place a bronze statue of him in the theatre (*SIG*^{3} 374; Bagnall and Derow 2004: no. 13; Plu. *Dem*. 12). It is the great power of the Hellenistic monarchs, operating outside civic structures, that gives rise to men like Philippides and Hegesianax, men whose lives and influence cross between the city and the court, the one reinforcing the other.

The Impact of Rome

Where Greeks of the fourth century had grown up with the Persian Empire as a fact of political life, their late third-century descendants grew up with the Hellenistic kings. For the Achaean historian Polybius what needed explaining was the rise of Rome and the collapse of the political world his contemporaries had known, a world which until Rome appeared must have looked unlikely to change. This was the subject of his history, clearly stated at the beginning (1.1.4–5):

> For the very unexpectedness of the events about which I have chosen to write is enough to challenge and provoke everyone, old and young, to read my history. For who is so petty or apathetic that they would not wish to know how and by what sort of government in less than 53 years almost the whole inhabited world was subjugated and brought under the sole rule of the Romans, the like of which has never happened before.

Polybius' 53 years begin with the 140th Olympiad (220–216), during which he believes the history of Italy and Libya merged with that of Greece and Asia; the period concludes with the end of the Macedonian Kingdom following Rome's defeat of Perseus at the Battle of Pydna in 168, after which point all must obey Roman orders (Plb. 1.3, 3.4). The transformation was that much more unexpected because in 220 all three main dynasties could be seen as recently revitalized by the accession of young kings, at least two of whom were impressively dynamic: Philip V, who at the beginning of his reign was felt to promise so much for Greece, and Antiochus III, who would spend the next 30 years systematically reclaiming the vast empire of his ancestor Seleucus I. But two decisive battles, Cynoscephalae in 197 and Magnesia in 189, put an end to the ambitions of each of these two kings in turn and left them paying war indemnities to Rome.

Polybius' claim that by 168 the whole world was subject to Rome might seem questionable; Rome did not, for example, maintain occupying forces in Greece after the dissolution of the Macedonian monarchy. For Polybius, however, it was not garrisons or taxes that defined power, but the capacity to enforce obedience (Derow 1979). This was a capacity that Rome had, as was dramatically illustrated in the same year by its response to Antiochus IV's invasion of Egypt. A single and abrupt instruction from the Roman legate, C. Popillius Laenas, was sufficient to force Antiochus to abandon his invasion and withdraw; famously he drew a circle round Antiochus and told the king he could not leave it until he had given him a decision (Plb. 29.27).

The Attalids of Pergamum, longstanding Roman allies in the East, had been early beneficiaries of these radical changes. A third-century break-away from the Seleucid Kingdom, they took advantage of the weakening of their Antigonid and Seleucid neighbors to establish themselves as a major power in Asia Minor. They publicized themselves as saviors of the Greeks against the troublesome Celts of central Asia Minor. Their palace complex on the acropolis of Pergamum became an advertisement for Attalid political and cultural aspirations. Here they embarked upon an elaborate building program, the construction of the Great Altar with its lavish and distinctive sculptural decoration, and the establishment of a library. Again the complex character of Hellenistic kingship is evident as Attalids look not only to a Greek heritage but also to an Anatolian one, laying claim to the leadership in the Greek world but also rooting themselves in Asia (Kuttner 2005). The end of the Macedonian Kingdom in 168 brought the Attalids to even greater prominence in the East but also strained their relationship with Rome. When the last of the dynasty, Attalus III, died prematurely in 133, he left his kingdom to Rome in his will. It is a reflection of the changing nature of Roman involvement in the East that rather than installing a new ruler the Romans took control themselves and the kingdom became the Roman province of Asia. Whether this development took place fairly quickly or at a leisurely pace is a matter of debate among scholars, whose differences here reflect broader differences on the character of Roman imperialism.

The second century saw a gradual transformation of the East as Roman control deepened. Initially Rome had announced itself as the liberator of Greece with a celebrated proclamation at the Isthmian Games near Corinth in 196, but by the end of the century Macedon and Asia had Roman governors and were paying tax to Rome. An ill-considered assertion of independence by the Achaean League in the 140s led to the destruction of Corinth by the Roman consul L. Mummius, the choice of city starkly symbolic of the end of Greek freedom. Yet Roman control could still be shaken, as Mithridates was to show in the following century, when he seized first Asia Minor then mainland Greece in a campaign that revealed the fragility of Roman rule and also the hostility felt towards Rome by some Greeks. The notorious massacres of Romans and Italians that took place in Asia Minor at this time could only have happened with the participation of Greeks there (App. *Mith.* 22–3). Sulla's destructive siege of Athens in 86 during the First Mithridatic War marked a striking contrast to Ptolemaic and Attalid patronage of the city (Hoff 1997).

Rome's increasing influence in the East is matched by a corresponding increase in the presence of intellectuals and literary figures in Rome. Initially they tended to come to Rome as ambassadors. Hegesianax of Alexandria Troas, the historian and friend of Antiochus III, was in Rome in the 190s to negotiate an alliance on behalf of the Seleucid king; Crates of Mallos, the Cilician city which used Argive ancestry to affirm its Greek identity, visited Rome on behalf of Attalus II, reputedly breaking his leg and thus being forced to remain in the city and give lectures; and in 155 there was the famous Athenian embassy, led by the heads of the three philosophical schools, although it was the disturbing skepticism of the Academic Carneades that most engaged the Romans rather than the embassy itself (Suet. *de Gram. et Rhet.* 2; Plu. *Cato Ma.* 22; Pliny *NH* 7.112–13). Not all came to Rome so willingly. Polybius himself was among 1,000 hostages from the Achaean League and spent more than 15 years there until allowed to leave in 150 BCE. While in Rome he became a friend of the Scipio family, a relationship that might echo those between prominent Greek citizens and the kings, but now it is one between a Greek and a single powerful family. Even in the mid-second century Polybius is commenting on the large number of learned men coming to Rome (31.24), something that was to become even more common in the next century. Greeks such as these are frequently found associated with a leading Roman, whether in Rome or elsewhere. Thus the philosopher Panaetius of Rhodes is associated with Scipio Aemilianus, the poet Archias from Antioch with L. Licinius Lucullus, and the Mytilenian politician and historian Theophanes with Pompey (Erskine 1990: 211–14; Gold 1987: 71–107).

This movement towards Rome can be explained by a number of factors. There is the condition of the Hellenistic kingdoms, deceased or in decline; thus of the two great sponsors of Greek culture, the Attalids bequeath themselves to Rome in 133 and the Ptolemaic tradition of cultural sponsorship never recovers from Ptolemy VIII

Euergetes II's expulsion of Alexandria's leading intellectuals and scholars in the later 140s. One can also point to the widespread disruption caused by the Mithridatic Wars, not least the sack of Athens; again some came voluntarily looking for patronage while others such as the poet Parthenius and the scholar Tyrannio came as prisoners. Above all, however, there is the simple pull of Roman power (Rawson 1985: 14–18).

The Hellenistic period began with a single monarch whose kingdom encompassed the eastern Mediterranean and beyond as far as Afghanistan, but Alexander's empire was soon fragmented into smaller kingdoms. When these met defeat at the hands of a city-state from the West, the focus of power moved from the eastern part of the Mediterranean to its center. Sole rule, however, was not to be so easily put to one side. The period ends with the re-establishment of a single ruler, as Augustus emerges victorious from Rome's civil wars in 31 BCE. Senatorial government is replaced by an emperor, and the Hellenic world has to adapt yet again.

FURTHER READING

Shipley 2000 offers the best recent single-author introduction to the Hellenistic world and can be supplemented by the essays in Erskine 2003 and Bugh 2006. In addition there are Walbank 1992 (a succinct survey), Green 1990 (readable and distinctive), Will 1979–82 (political history), Préaux 1978 (a more thematic approach), and the chapters in vol. 7.1 of the *Cambridge Ancient History* (2nd edition, 1984). All students of the Hellenistic world should also consult Rostovtzeff's 1941 classic. Translated source material, including inscriptions and papyri, is conveniently collected in Austin 2006, Bagnall and Derow 2004, Burstein 1985, and Sherk 1984.

The early wars of the successors are treated by Bosworth 2002, while the dominating figure, Antigonus, is the subject of biographies by Billows 1990 and Wehrli 1968. On Lysimachus, see Lund 1992 with Delev 2000; on Seleucus, Mehl 1986 and Grainger 1990, with Austin 2003 and Sherwin-White and Kuhrt 1993 on the Seleucid dynasty; Ptolemy I is best approached through the studies of the Ptolemies by Hölbl 2001 and Huss 2001; for the various rulers of Macedon, Hammond and Walbank 1988 and Errington 1990. On the Attalids Hansen 1971 is now rather dated but still the fullest account; it should be supplemented by Koester 1998, Gruen 2000, Kosmetatou 2003 and Kuttner 2005. On the nature of Hellenistic kingship, Austin 1986, Koenen 1993, Ma 2003; for the complexity of court life, Ogden 1999 and Herman 1997.

On the character of the Hellenistic *polis*, see Shipley and Hansen 2006, Billows 2003, Ma 1999, Gruen 1993, Gauthier 1993; Giovannini 1993 is an excellent study of the relationships between cities. The essential study of the practice of civic euergetism is Gauthier 1985. Much of the material for ruler cult is collected in Habicht 1970, which should be read together with later studies by Chaniotis 2003 and Price 1984. On warfare, both between kings and as it affected cities, Chaniotis 2004.

For Roman conquest of the Greek world, see in particular Gruen 1984 and Derow 1989, 2003. Holleaux 1921 has been fundamental to the way the debate over the Roman conquest of the East has developed (for his thesis in English, volumes 7 and 8 of the first edition of the *Cambridge Ancient History*, 1928) and is now revived by Eckstein 2008 in terms of international systems realism. For the cultural interaction between Greece and Rome, see Ferrary 1988, Gruen 1990 and 1992, with Erskine 2001 on the Trojan myth in Rome.

CHAPTER THREE

Literature and the Kings

Rolf Strootman

Although literature also thrived in the *poleis* (Hunter 2003b: 477–9), the most successful writers were drawn to the major centers of power. Most of the key Hellenistic texts that survive today were written at the royal courts, under the patronage of kings, queens, and powerful courtiers. Discussions of this backdrop (including the present one) tend to focus on poetry, but it is important to emphasize that poets stayed at court in the company of philosophers, historians, geographers, astronomers, botanists, technicians, physicians, sculptors, and painters. As royal patronage of art and science is most successful in times of economic and political stability (De Bruijn, Idema, and Van Oostrom 1986), it is unsurprising that art and science flourished notably at the Alexandrian court under the first three Ptolemies and to a lesser degree at the Seleucid and Antigonid courts of the same age. Third-century Alexandria did not become the unrivaled center of art and learning because of the Ptolemies' greater wealth, as is commonly thought. With an annual revenue of 15,000–20,000 talents of silver from taxes alone (Aperghis 2004: 251), the Seleucids in their heyday presumably were richer. Rather, it was the stability of Alexandria as an imperial center that gave the Ptolemies a crucial advantage over their main rivals, the Seleucids, whose court was peripatetic and traveled between several capitals throughout their vast empire.

This chapter focuses on the position and function of literature at the royal courts of the Hellenistic kingdoms, starting with a brief outline of the court culture, in which Achaemenid, Macedonian, and Greek traditions came together and developed into a new phenomenon which, transmitted to Western Europe via the Roman Empire, left its imprint on the courts of the Renaissance and the Ancien Régime. We will then look at the position of men of letters within the court society and look at the reasons why they aspired to become courtiers, and, conversely, why kings attracted them to their courts. It is my contention that their position did not fundamentally differ from that of the "regular" courtiers, who commanded the king's armies and fleets, administered the empire's revenues or served as diplomats. I will also argue that

Hellenistic court patronage in general was characterized by an atmosphere of experiment and innovation. Originality was a requirement of the court, which may have been an ivory tower of sorts but not one which produced "art for art's sake."

The Hellenistic Royal Court

The court culture of the three great Hellenistic dynasties – Seleucids, Ptolemies, and Antigonids – was strikingly similar, due to intermarriage, diplomatic contact, competition, and a shared Macedonian background. The royal court was essentially the *oikos*, "household," of the royal family, and is often referred to as such in the sources. Another common designation is *aulē*, "court," derived from the fact that the architectural center of the Hellenistic palace was an open courtyard surrounded by *andrōnes*, banqueting rooms (Nielsen 1994). However, in ancient historiography and documentary evidence the royal court is usually defined as the people surrounding the king, with terms like "retinue" (*therapeia*), "the people of the court" (*hoi peri tēn aulēn*), and notably "the friends of the king" (*hoi philoi tou basileōs*); in fact, *philos*, "friend," may be regarded as the technical term for courtier in the Hellenistic age.

The *philoi* constituted a status group that shared in the power and prestige of the king. They were neither servants nor officials, but free men who were bound to the king by *philia*, a form of ritualized friendship between individuals with traits of fictive kinship. They were drawn to the courts by *xenia* (or *philoxenia*), a ritualized friendship between families usually translated as "guest-friendship." From Archaic times onward, *xenia* networks constituted supranational, "horizontal" elite structures, linking together families of approximately equal social status but of separate social units, i.e., of different *poleis* (Herman 1987). Gift exchange, a fundamental aspect of *philia* and *xenia*, was central to social relations at court. The Hellenistic courts were imbued with competition for favor, power, and status, and were frequently torn apart by faction strife and dynastic infighting.

The friends of the king were for the most part Greeks and Macedonians (Habicht 1958), although Hellenized non-Greeks also sometimes turn up in the role of "favorites" (Strootman 2007: 172–8) or as lesser officials (Sherwin-White and Kuhrt 1993: 121–5). They came from a wide range of cities, often from beyond the empires' borders, making the court a kind of "cosmopolis" (Herman 1997: 208). Through family ties and their own *xenia* networks, *philoi* maintained bonds with their cities of origin, where they promoted the interests of the monarchy; conversely, they promoted the interests of their families, friends, and cities at court. The *philoi* served the king as military commanders, diplomats, administrators, and so on. They were rewarded for their services with favors, privileges, estates and other material gifts, and status. From Macedonian and Achaemenid antecedents an increasingly elaborate system of court titles developed, first at the Seleucid and soon after also at the Ptolemaic court. This court titulature included honorific titles such as Relative of the King or Most Honored Friend, and more functional titles like Major-Domo, Chamberlain, and Master of the Hunt. They reflected the hierarchy among the courtiers, particularly the degree to which a courtier had access to the king. Men who had served together with the reigning king as Royal Pages (*basilikoi paides*, sons of aristocrats) received the title of Foster-Brother (*suntrophos*) of the King, and were addressed by the king as "brother." In the early Hellenistic Age kings presumably were able to control the social composition of their courts to a large extent; from the second half of the third century, however, it became increasingly more difficult for kings to remove courtiers from important positions and replace them by others (Strootman forthcoming b). It is generally assumed that in the second century the court system, notably in the Ptolemaic Kingdom, became more rigid, with a hereditary court aristocracy at the top and professional administrators at the lower levels of the hierarchy.

Court Culture and the Arts

Royal patronage of the arts was a Macedonian tradition predating the Hellenistic Age. Already at the end of the fifth century, the philhellene Macedonian king Archelaus had been the host of the tragedians Euripides and Agathon, and the painter Zeuxis. Philip II and Alexander had also earned themselves a reputation as magnanimous patrons. Cultural patronage by rulers is in fact an almost universal phenomenon. Historians of early modern Europe have long recognized that during the Renaissance and Ancien Régime royal patronage guided the emergence of modern science and art (Lytle and Orgel 1981; Kent, Simons, and Eade 1987; Moran 1991b; Biagioli 1993; Griffin 1996). For Renaissance rulers, this type of patronage "seemed . . . to have a moral and political dimension and to be part of statecraft" (Stroup 1991: 211); or in other words, "the practice of art patronage and art collection were obviously regarded as activities related, but not secondary, to the exercise of power, [and] were considered operational expenses" (Gardini 1986: 93). Galileo Galilei, as one historian put it, "fixed one eye on the moons of Jupiter and the other on his patron" (Moran 1991a: 196). In the study of Hellenistic culture, however, the romantic modern notion that art and science are incompatible with politics is still widespread, and it has been common to characterize Hellenistic poetry as *l'art pour l'art*, "art for art's sake" (e.g., Schwinge 1986; Bulloch 1989; Green 1990; Kerkhecker 1997). This view is now losing ground, and Hellenistic literature is more often related to the social and cultural context in which it was produced and received, in particular the royal court (Weber 1993; Stephens 1998, 2000, 2003). But what exactly *is* the relevance of this context?

Some Hellenistic literary works obviously made a direct contribution to royal propaganda. Explicitly laudatory texts include panegyric, paeans, epinician odes, epic, and epigrams celebrating special events or successes of the dynasty. Philosophers elaborated the genre of the *Fürstenspiegel*. Court historians recorded military campaigns. Most surviving court literature, however, at first sight does not seem explicitly concerned with kingship. How do genres such as mime, bucolic poetry, mythography, geography, or ethnography pertain to the court? Some scholars have tried to evade this problem by stating that Hellenistic literature, although written *at* court, was not written *for* the court (Zanker 1983; Cameron 1995a; Kerkhecker 1997).

Others have focused on the political dimensions of explicitly encomiastic poetry (Griffiths 1979; Mineur 1984; Gutzwiller 1992; Hunter 2003a) or tried to find "hidden" ideological messages, particularly references to pharaonic ideology (Merkelbach 1981; Gelzer 1982; Koenen 1983; Bing 1988; Stephens 2002, 2003; Noegel 2004). There is, however, more to say about the way Hellenistic literature relates to the royal court.

First, literature was functional within the social milieu of the court. Poetry, as well as philosophy and science, entertained courtiers and guests during symposia (Weber 1993: 165–70; Cameron 1995a: 71–103), and provided them with subjects for debate and thus opportunities to compete. Learned allusion and suggestion prompted the audience to "decode" the text (Zanker 2004), as E. A. Barber unwittingly acknowledged when he despairingly exclaimed that Lycophron's *Alexandra* is "one vast riddle" and that even Callimachus "does not spare his audience," for example when in his elegiac *Victory of Sosibius*, "he refers to the victor on the strength of his Isthmian and Nemean successes as "twice-crowned by both children, the brother of Learchus and the infant who was suckled with Myrine's milk." A hard nut to crack without a mythological dictionary!" (Barber 1928: 271; Call. fr. 384.24–6 Pf.). The virtuosity and inventiveness of Hellenistic poetry, its preference for rare words and obscure versions of myths, its fascination for faraway lands and the remote past – it all marks out Hellenistic poetry as typical court poetry, written for the sake of a privileged, self-confident, and highly educated upper class. It is not surprising that such genres as riddle poetry, didactic poetry, and bucolic fiction matured at the courts, where courtiers competed in learning and wit, or made fun of people of lesser standing, as in Theocritus' *Idyll* 15, which humorously portrays the rabble that is allowed into the Alexandrian palace gardens for the royal Adonis festival. It was customary for courtiers to discuss philosophical and literary topics during symposia (Ath. 6.211d) as if they had as much time on their hands as the herdsmen of pastoral poetry – like Bion's Cleodamus, who asks: "Of spring, Myrson, and winter and autumn and summer, which do you prefer?... Come, tell me..., as we have plenty of time for a chat" (fr. 2.1–8 Reed 1997).

As amusement and subject for debate, literature served a similar purpose to the devices that Hellenistic engineers (*mēchanikoi*) developed for their royal patrons, such as Ctesibius' pneumatic organ or Hero's robot in the shape of Heracles, which could automatically shoot an arrow at a hissing serpent. Peter Green has called these inventions, "a collection of elaborate mechanical toys [and] curiosities [of] complete irrelevance" (1990: 478–9). But the technological principles demonstrated through these toys could also be applied in agriculture, mining, or construction (Schürmann 1991; White 1993), and could be employed to awe the crowd during public celebrations. Court poetry likewise could be double-edged. It could, for instance, be written for religious festivities connected with kingship. The poet Hermocles, an Antigonid courtier, composed paeans in praise of Antigonus Monophthalmus before writing the notorious ithyphallic hymn that the Athenians sang for Demetrius Poliorcetes when he entered their city in 291 or 290 BCE (Duris *FGrH* 76 F 13 = Ath. 6.253b–f).

Men of letters, especially scholars and philosophers, were assigned the task of educating the children of the king together with the Royal Pages. The intellectual education of princes and pages was a principal responsibility of the head of the Museum at Alexandria (Str. 17.1.8; *P.Oxy.* 1241); it was arguably the principal reason why the Museum was founded in the first place and why the other dynasties, too, maintained libraries in their capitals (Strootman 2007: 186; Plu. *Ant.* 28 and 58; *Suda* s.v. "Euphorion"; Malalas 235.18–236.1). The pages at the court of Ptolemy Soter were educated by Strato of Lampsacus and others, and at the court of Ptolemy Philadelphus by Philitas of Cos, Apollonius of Rhodes, and Aristarchus of Samothrace (Delia 1996: 41–51). Antigonus II Gonatas brought the Stoic philosopher Persaeus to his court for the same reason (D.L. 7.6–9; cf. Plu. *Mor.* 1043c); the philosopher and tragedian Euphantes of Olynthus was tutor and subsequently *philos* of Antigonus III Doson, to whom he dedicated a treatise *On Kingship* (D.L. 2.110). Furthermore, prominent representatives of major philosophical schools – Aristotle, Zeno, Cleanthes, and many others – wrote treatises on the art of kingship for the benefit of the king's children.

Another reason why rulers acted as patrons was the fact that patronage as such added to their prestige. By accommodating poets and scholars at his court, a king met several of the requirements for being an ideal ruler. He proved that he was hospitable, benevolent, and generous. The accumulation of art and knowledge in the house of the king added to his charisma. Famous writers and scholars were living status symbols, and by patronizing such men a ruler demonstrated wisdom, learnedness, and good taste. Better still was to write oneself. Throughout history, rulers have been actively involved in science and literature. Princes such as Charles d'Orléans, Süleyman the Magnificent, or Lorenzo de' Medici were not only great patrons of the arts, but poets of distinction themselves. In Renaissance Italy, the connection between rulership and the arts had a theoretical basis in the ideal of the "learned prince" (Eamon 1991: 32). The Hellenistic period likewise cherished this ideal. Alexander the Great (a pupil of Aristotle) was called "a philosopher in arms" by a contemporary (Onesicritus *FGrH* 134 F 17a = Str. 15.1.64). Ptolemy Soter was celebrated as a historian and wrote a tragedy *Adonis* (*TGrF* 1.119). Antiochus VIII wrote didactic poetry (Pliny *NH* 20.264). Ptolemy II Philadelphus, Ptolemy III Euergetes, and Philip V were epigrammatists of some renown.

Competition with rival courts constitutes a further reason. Just as kings would send athletes and horses to Panhellenic Games, so too they competed with one another in poetry, scholarship, and science. Plutarch says that "kings hunt for men by attracting them with gifts and money, and then catching them" (*Cleom.* 13.5). Indeed, various anecdotes emphasize the efforts kings made to attract famous intellectuals to their courts, even using force if necessary (D.L. 2.115 and *passim*). Thus, Aristophanes of Byzantium was reputedly locked up in Alexandria when it came out that he planned to join the Attalid court (Vitr. 7 *pr.* 5–7). The intellectual and artistic competition between courts – a phenomenon that is common to court culture throughout the ages (Kruedener 1973: 21–2) – induced kings to look for poets and philosophers whose work would amaze the world.

This competition to a large extent accounts for the innovative and experimental nature of Alexandrian literature and scholarship. Poets and scholars who worked for kings did not barter away their integrity and intellectual freedom. Kings were not particularly keen on docile propaganda-makers. On the contrary, the court offered opportunities to freely do and say things that public morality in the Classical *polis* prohibited. The early Ptolemaic court in particular was a safe haven for intellectuals with unorthodox, even subversive views. The philosopher Theodorus of Cyrene, called the Blasphemer, was allegedly banished from Athens because he denied the existence of the gods; but a later notorious "atheist," Euhemerus of Messene, found a warm welcome first at the court of Cassander and later in Alexandria (D.L. 2.102–3; Ath. 12.611b; Cic. *Tusc.* 1.102). Under the protection of Ptolemy Philadelphus, the astronomer Aristarchus of Samos formulated the unorthodox theory that the sun was the center of the universe, even though his ideas were widely criticized on moral grounds (D.L. 7.174). The Ptolemies likewise ignored public morality when they enabled the physicians Herophilus and Erasistratus to perform systematic dissections on human cadavers, which allowed them to chart the human vascular and nervous systems, causing a revolution in medical science. The work of other courtiers was less controversial but equally revolutionary. Protected and encouraged by kings, Eratosthenes calculated the circumference of the earth, Hero built a steam engine, Euclid and Archimedes innovated mathematics. Originality was a requirement of the court, in literature no less than in any other field.

Literature could also be more directly employed for competition. The perennial war between rival dynasties regularly continues in poetry, particularly epigram, a genre practiced by kings, courtiers, and "professional" poets alike. A straightforward example is the votive inscription which Leonidas of Tarentum wrote for the Celtic shields dedicated by Pyrrhus of Epirus after he had defeated Antigonus Gonatas (*AP* 6.130 = 95 GP; cf. Plu. *Pyrrh.* 26.5 and Paus. 1.13.2):

τοὺς θυρεοὺς ὁ Μολοσσὸς Ἰτωνίδι δῶρον Ἀθάναι
  Πύρρος ἀπὸ θρασέων ἐκρέμασεν Γαλατᾶν,
πάντα τὸν Ἀντιγόνου καθελὼν στρατόν· οὐ μέγα θαῦμα·
  αἰχμηταὶ καὶ νῦν καὶ πάρος Αἰακίδαι.

These shields, now dedicated to Athena Itonis,
  Pyrrhus the Molossian took from the fearless Celts
after defeating the entire army of Antigonus: no great wonder:
  the Aeacids are valiant spear-fighters, now as in the past.

An indirect attack is contained in the notorious epigram of Timon of Phlius, in which he ridicules the Alexandrian Museum (*SH* 786 = Ath. 1.22d = fr. 12 Di Marco 1989):

πολλοὶ μὲν βόσκονται ἐν Αἰγύπτωι πολυφύλωι
βιβλιακοὶ χαρακῖται ἀπείριτα δηριόωντες
Μουσέων ἐν ταλάρωι.

In the thronging land of Egypt there are many who are feeding, many scribblers on papyrus, ever ceaselessly contending, in the birdcage of the Muses.

Since Timon was an Antigonid courtier, this is surely not mere squabbling between scholars, it has a clear political dimension. The same may be true for the end of Callimachus' *Hymn to Apollo*, where the poet writes that "the Assyrian river (i.e., the

Euphrates) has a broad stream but carries down much filth and refuse on its waters" (*h.* 2.108–9), which apart from its metapoetic significance, I would suggest, constitutes a quip against the Seleucids.

Collecting art and knowledge at royal courts demonstrated political control (Eamon 1991: 39; Griffin 1996: 39–44). Just as an epigram to Lorenzo de' Medici proclaimed that "because you know everything, you are all-powerful" (Eamon 1991: 32), so, too, did the efforts of Hellenistic kings to control art and science mirror their efforts to control territory, wealth, and manpower. The accumulation of knowledge and objects at the imperial center showed how far-reaching and all-embracing royal power was. Exotic animals and plants were gathered in the palace gardens of Alexandria and exhibited to the public during the Ptolemaia festival. Geographers and ethnographers described faraway lands and peoples. One may also think of Berossus' *Babyloniaca*, a history of Mesopotamia commissioned by Antiochus I, Manetho's *Aegyptiaca*, written at the request of Ptolemy I or II, and Josephus' statement that Ptolemy II ordered a translation of the Torah principally to create "a work glorious to himself" (*AJ* 12.49; on these works see Knippschild, Dieleman and Moyer, Gruen in this volume). Collecting books, and translating them into Greek, was a means of accumulating and controlling knowledge. According to Josephus, it was Ptolemy I's ambition "to gather together all the books that existed in the entire inhabited world" (*AJ* 12.20), and tradition has preserved colorful accounts of the Ptolemies' efforts to lay their hands on them (Stephens in this volume).

A last explanation is the wish of kings to present themselves as philhellenes to acquire the goodwill of the Greek, or Hellenized, elites of the cities. This was important because their own ethnicity was ambiguous. The Ptolemaic, Seleucid and Antigonid kings were ethnic Macedonians and needed to emphasize their Macedonian identity vis-à-vis the Macedonian soldiers who constituted the backbone of their armies and the small Macedonian aristocratic class constituting the core of their courts. The rulers of the smaller Hellenistic states in Asia Minor and the Seleucid vassal kingdoms in the Middle East, most of whom were patrons of Greek culture too, were not even semi-Greek Macedonians, but (mainly) Iranians. Whatever their background, Hellenistic kings had to maintain good relations with various indigenous civic and priestly elites, whether these consisted of Iranians, Babylonians, Jews, Egyptians, or Greeks. But they singled out the Greeks because their power rested to a large extent on the support of, and tribute paid by, cities. The city was the place where the agrarian surplus of its hinterland was collected, and part of it turned into cash. Keeping good relations with the many cities in the realm was therefore a principal concern of royal administrations. Most cities in the Seleucid west, the Ptolemaic Mediterranean and, of course, Antigonid Greece, were either Greek cities or cities whose ruling families had adopted aspects of Hellenic culture precisely because of their connections with the monarchy. The court, too, was for the greatest part composed of Greeks from the *poleis*.

Notwithstanding the cultural heterogeneity of the empires and the cosmopolitan character of some of their capital cities – Antioch on the Orontes, Seleucia on the Tigris, Ptolemaic Alexandria – the culture of the court was predominantly Hellenic. Non-Greeks were not entirely absent from the courts, but they seldom held important positions. Due to intermarriage with Iranian dynasties and a system of delegating power to vassal kings, the Seleucid court probably on the whole included more non-Greeks than the Ptolemaic, but they were rarely among the king's principal advisors and commanders. When in both empires non-Greeks do turn up in the upper echelons of the court, they are mostly "favorites" of the king, a position they could obtain precisely because they were outsiders (Strootman 2007: 172–8).

Non-Greek artists, writers, and scholars were likewise almost completely absent from court circles as *philoi*. Those who were present – Berossus, Manetho – wrote in Greek for a Greek-speaking audience. In other words, kings protected not culture in general, but *Greek* culture in particular, and for this reason they promoted the study of the Greek past. Hellenistic scholars and poets (often scholar-poets) studied "classic" Greek literature (such as the poetry of Homer), and were obsessed with the Greek mythological legacy. Hellenistic literature differed from Classical literature in its tendency to iron out regional differences among the Greeks, redefining Greek culture in the light of a more cosmopolitan worldview in which non-Greek culture and knowledge, after being Hellenized, could be integrated. It was this "non-ethnic" Hellenism that provided the umbrella culture of empire.

Thus, the Hellenism of the court was instrumental in creating an imperial elite culture, intensifying a process of Hellenization that was also at work independently in the *poleis*. In world history, court culture has often served to tie together local elites, creating coherence in culturally and ethnically heterogeneous empires, and binding these elites to the political centre by "the power of memory, of imagination, and of language" (Burke 1992: 57; cf. Strootman 2007: 215).

Kings and Poets

Cultural patronage was an organic part of court society. Men of letters were considered genuine courtiers, "friends of the king" (*philoi tou basileōs*). Some even reached the upper echelons of the court and were given political, diplomatic or military responsibilities (Erskine in this volume). Onesicritus of Astypalaea, a pupil of Diogenes and the author of an account of Alexander's campaigns, served Alexander as a navigator in India, and in 325/4 was lieutenant to Alexander's admiral Nearchus. The historian Hieronymus of Cardia served as military commander for the Antigonids. Antigonus Gonatas put the Stoic philosopher Persaeus in charge of the Acrocorinth citadel.

If poets, artists, and intellectuals were not servants, what was the nature of their relationship with the king? The contemporary evidence that is most illuminating in this respect is Theocritus' *Idyll* 16. This poem is principally an encomium of the Sicilian ruler Hiero II. It is also a request for a gift and an attempt of the poet to be accepted by Hiero as his *philos*. Because Theocritus came from Syracuse (*ep.* 27 Gow) it is usually assumed that the poem was written at the beginning of his career, and that he moved to Alexandria because Hiero was not interested in his services (Gow 1952b: xvii; Green 1990: 240), but this is far from certain (Bulloch in this volume). In the poem, Theocritus evokes the styles of Bacchylides, Pindar, and Simonides (Hunter

1996: 82–90, 97–109). All three had enjoyed the patronage of Hiero's namesake and predecessor, the fifth-century Syracusan tyrant Hiero I, a ruler who was particularly renowned for his protection of the arts (Gold 1987: 21–30). Theocritus now urges the second Hiero to support poetry too, in particular his own (16.22–9, trans. Verity 2002):

> τί δὲ κέρδος ὁ μυρίος ἔνδοθι χρυσὸς
> κείμενος; οὐχ ἅδε πλούτου φρονέουσιν ὄνασις,
> ἀλλὰ τὸ μὲν ψυχᾶι, τὸ δέ πού τινι δοῦναι ἀοιδῶν·
> πολλοὺς εὖ ἔρξαι πηῶν, πολλοὺς δὲ καὶ ἄλλων
> ἀνθρώπων, αἰεὶ δὲ θεοῖς ἐπιβώμια ῥέζειν,
> μηδὲ ξεινοδόκον κακὸν ἔμμεναι ἀλλὰ τραπέζηι
> μειλίξαντ' ἀποπέμψαι ἐπὴν ἐθέλωντι νέεσθαι,
> Μοισάων δὲ μάλιστα τίειν ἱεροὺς ὑποφήτας.

> What is the point of hoarding masses of gold?
> Wealth, says the man of sense, should be used to indulge
> yourself – and after that, perhaps, to give a poet a little;
> to do a good turn to one's relations, and to others, as far
> as you can; to offer regular gifts on the gods' altars;
> to be a generous and kindly host, not sending your guest from
> your table until he's ready to go; but above all, to honor the Muses'
> priestly interpreters.

With these words Theocritus appeals to the Hellenistic ruler's self-image as a generous host who entertains many *philoi* in his house. Theocritus wants to be invited too, and he embeds his request in the moral complex of *xenia* ("guest-friendship") with its ideals of generosity, gift exchange, and reciprocity, a central Greek virtue and of particular importance in royal courts. The reciprocal nature of *xenia* is stressed throughout the poem, notably in its play with the double meaning of *charites*, "graces," as favors and as goddesses. The latter represent poetry, making it clear that Theocritus offers his writings to Hiero as gifts, for which he expects gifts in return.

Apart from the prestige to be gained from hospitality and generosity, Theocritus mentions another reason why Hiero should extend his *xenia* to him. The argument is as simple as it is, by modern standards, presumptuous: reward me, and you will buy yourself immortality. After all, "who would ever have known the long-haired sons of Priam" (48–9), or Achilles (74), or wandering Odysseus (51–4), had not Homer put their deeds into words? Now, thanks to the poet, not only the heroes are remembered, but even Odysseus' swineherd, Eumaeus (54–5). Hiero, the Achilles of our age, also needs a poet to immortalize his heroic exploits (listed in 76–100), and spread his glory "across the Scythian Sea" (99), that is, to the end of the earth (16.30–3, trans. Verity 2002):

> ὄφρα καὶ εἰν Ἀίδαο κεκρυμμένος ἐσθλὸς ἀκούσηις
> μηδ' ἀκλεὴς μύρηαι ἐπὶ ψυχροῦ Ἀχέροντος,
> ὡσεί τις μακέλαι τετυλωμένος ἔνδοθι χεῖρας
> ἀχὴν ἐκ πατέρων πενίην ἀκτήμονα κλαίων.

so that men may speak well of you
even when you're hidden deep in Hades. Do this, and you won't
be forced to grieve without honor on Acheron's chill banks,
like a poor man, his hands callused by the spade's toil,
who complains about his inheritance of helpless poverty.

Alluding to the exclamation of Achilles' spirit that he would rather be a farmhand on earth than a king in the underworld (*Od.* 11.489–91), Theocritus here pushes the point that all a man has left after death is *kleos* ("reputation") and that great deeds become null and void unless they are celebrated in poetry (Griffiths 1979: 14). Only praise sung by a *great* poet will for all posterity reach such a large and widespread audience that the poem's protagonist will be truly immortalized. Conversely, the ambitious poet is also in need of *great* subject matter to attain fame. The prestige of the poet will, in a sense, be added to the prestige of the patron.

What more concrete benefits did poets expect to gain from patronage? Of course one must first think of material rewards. Ptolemy Soter allegedly gave Strato of Lampsacus the astronomical sum of eighty talents for tutoring his son (D.L. 5.58). Unlike long-term labor for hire, which was considered tantamount to servitude, gift exchange was honorable, operating in a sphere of *philia* that was free of subordination (Konstan 1997: 82). Even so it was also a mechanism to confer and confirm social status. This means that the value of rewards went beyond the material. Antiochus the Great rewarded the polymath Hegesianax with money *and* a court title for reciting his work (Ath. 4.155b). The Epicurean philosopher Diogenes received status gifts, including the purple costume of a *philos*, from Alexander Balas (Ath. 6.211d). The Ptolemaic title of Head of the Museum (*epistatēs tou Mouseiou*) was a genuine court title, like Chamberlain or Master of the Hunt. Consequently, we may infer that the production of literature or scholarship was instrumental in obtaining access to the presence of the king, or more precisely, to be admitted to royal symposia. This in turn was a means to acquire status, favors, and privileges, not only for oneself but also for one's family, friends or hometown.

The court was a place where the lines separating the hierarchical layers of society could be crossed. But to gain access to the king – or the queen, a prince, or an important courtier – one had to attract attention by distinguishing oneself, and so win favor and build a personal network of influential *philoi.* This in-house competition, too, which challenged men to prove their worth and demonstrate their skills, is reflected in the mannerism and erudition of Hellenistic literature, with its in-crowd allusions and partiality for obscure myths and rare words. One reason why the work of court poets was so subtle and intellectual was that they had to distinguish themselves before an audience of courtiers – an audience that was perceptive and critical, and expected to be confirmed in its self-image as an educated leisure class. The entire set-up was predicated on competition – hence the envy that according to some sources spoiled the atmosphere at the Alexandrian Museum (Timon *SH* 786; Call. fr. 191 Pf.). The rivalry could take the form of open contest, when for instance poets and courtiers competed by writing epigrams on a given subject during symposia (Cameron 1995a: 83).

Another benefit of patronage was that the court provided, on a regular basis, an ideal audience – an audience that was educated, influential, and rich. Mainly at symposia, when the king entertained guests and courtiers, poems and treatises were read, inventions were demonstrated, and new ideas proposed. Besides *philoi*, foreign guests and ambassadors would frequently be present. Not all court poetry of course was aimed exclusively at court circles. Some of it was written for a broader audience, for example epigrams inscribed at sanctuaries, or hymns sung during festivities. We can be sure, however, that most poetry was in the first instance written for an elite circle of educated royal friends and other aristocrats. Competition for honor and prestige was a major drive in the life of a Greek poet, and to be associated with such an elite milieu increased one's status more than success among lower levels of society. The members of the upper level of the court each had their own network of *xenoi* and maintained relations with their families' cities of origin. Thus the court was the nucleus of an international elite infrastructure through which texts, ideas, and reputations could circulate throughout the Hellenistic world. For an ambitious poet, the court was the gateway to international success.

The Poetics of Power

While most of the surviving texts are not explicitly concerned with kingship, enough panegyric survives to prove that this was a cardinal aspect of Hellenistic poetry and to allow us to identify some motifs that recur throughout Hellenistic poetry as ideologically charged. One of these is the image of the ruler's empire encompassing the entire inhabited world (*oikoumenē*). On an ideological level, the Ptolemies, Seleucids, and Antigonids cultivated claims to universal dominion, regardless of the actual political state of affairs (Strootman forthcoming a). Although in diplomatic contacts Hellenistic kings negotiated as equals, in propaganda rivals were routinely presented as rebellious princelets. The Hellenistic image of world-empire was in part an elaboration of Near Eastern royal ideology (Liverani 1990), and would in turn influence images of empire in Roman panegyric (Asche 1983; Rees 2002: 88–9; also Weinstock 1971: 371–84; MacCormack 1981: 17–61).

In court poetry we often find the themes of the victory of Order over Chaos, and the spread of (Greek) civilization to the ends of the earth. A recurring topic in Callimachus' *Aetia* is the expansion and progress of civilization, often featuring the "royal god" Heracles in his role as savior and culture hero (Harder 2003b and in this volume). In Apollonius' *Argonautica*, Greeks travel to the edge of the world, leaving a trail of sacred objects and rituals wherever they go (Hunter 1993a: 152–69; Stephens 2003: 171–237). Another crucial element of Hellenistic royal ideology, obvious from royal ceremonial and iconography, which recurs in court poetry, is the association of the king with the sun and the conception of his rule as a Golden Age. Here the sun god Apollo, vanquisher of barbarians, and conquering Dionysus, the bringer of good fortune, figure most prominently. Last but not least, there is the equation of the earthly rule of the king with the cosmic rule of Zeus.

The association of king and Zeus is made explicit in Theocritus' seventeenth *Idyll*, an encomium of Ptolemy II Philadelphus (also discussed by Bulloch in this volume). In the opening lines Theocritus says (17.1–4):

ἐκ Διὸς ἀρχώμεσθα καὶ ἐς Δία λήγετε Μοῖσαι,
ἀθανάτων τὸν ἄριστον, ἐπὴν† ἀείδωμεν ἀοιδαῖς·
ἀνδρῶν δ' αὖ Πτολεμαῖος ἐνὶ πρώτοισι λεγέσθω
καὶ πύματος καὶ μέσσος· ὁ γὰρ προφερέστατος ἀνδρῶν.

From Zeus let us begin, and at Zeus make your end, O Muses,
the best of the immortals, whenever we celebrate in song.
But among men Ptolemy should be named first
and last, and also in the middle, for he is the greatest of men.

Zeus is King of Heaven, Ptolemy King of the World. Theocritus later refines this notion. When Ptolemy was born the heavens opened and a great eagle descended, "a bird of omen, a sign from Zeus." Three times the eagle cries above the cradle, thus making it known that Ptolemy is Zeus' chosen one (71–6). At that point Theocritus has already described how the king's father, Ptolemy I Soter, acquired a place among the Olympian gods: in the house of Zeus three thrones have been set up; on one of these sits Ptolemy, while beside him sit the deified Alexander and his ancestor Heracles (16–25). The presence of Heracles is significant. As a mortal who became an Olympian god (according to most sources, in reward for the help he gave to the gods in their struggle against the forces of chaos, i.e., the Giants), Heracles provided a model for Hellenistic royal apotheoses (Strootman 2005; Huttner 1997).

Ptolemy Soter, Theocritus continues, has bequeathed to his son a limitless empire and inexhaustible wealth (75–94), making the Ptolemaic household the symbolic center of the world: "All the sea and all the land and the rushing rivers are subject to Ptolemy.... He is wealthier than all other kings together, such riches arrive each day at his sumptuous *oikos* from all directions" (91–2, 95–7). Where Philadelphus rules, there is harmony: "His people can work their fields in peace, for no enemy crosses the teeming Nile by land to raise the battle cry in towns that are not his, no enemy jumps ashore from his swift ship to seize with weapons the cattle of Egypt. Too great a man is settled in those broad fields, golden-haired Ptolemy, skilled with the spear" (97–103). The image of the king as a "spear-fighter" was pivotal to the ideology of all Hellenistic kingdoms. The king was presented as a Homeric hero, whose personal bravery as a *promachos* ("fore-fighter") in battle brought his kingdom victory (Gehrke 1982; Strootman 2007: 31–53). In lines 5 to 8, Theocritus declares that he will celebrate the "noble deeds" (*kala erga*) of Ptolemy as Homer honored the deeds of Trojans and Achaeans. And in lines 53 to 56 Ptolemy is even directly equated with Achilles, who once was, as Ptolemy is now, the best of men.

In his *Hymn to Zeus*, Callimachus too compares the rule of Philadelphus with the rule of Zeus. There are other kings, of course, but Callimachus presents Philadelphus as the only *real* king on earth because he is Zeus' chosen one (*h.* 1.79–90). In the *Hymn to Delos* Callimachus in turn equates his patron directly with Apollo. When the pregnant Leto is approaching the island of Cos to give birth to Apollo and Artemis, suddenly Apollo's voice sounds from her womb, urging his mother not to give birth on that island because it is destined to become the birthplace of "another god," a Macedonian of "the sublime lineage of the Saviors." Under his rule, Apollo prophesies, "will be the two lands and the countries that lie on the sea, as far as the ends of the earth, where the swift horses always carry Helius" (*h.* 4.162–70).

Ptolemy's power is thus presented as limitless: his empire stretches from sunrise to sunset. Although the reference to "the two lands" presumably is a reference to Egypt (Hunter 2003a: 168), it would be rash to understand the solar imagery in this hymn, as in other Alexandrian poetry, as simply a continuation of pharaonic ideology. The image of the sun as a symbol of universal monarchy is a generic one. We see it also in connection with ancient Mesopotamian and Persian monarchy (L'Orange 1953). But it was in the Hellenistic kingdoms that the solar iconography of kingship reached its zenith (Bergmann 1998; Strootman forthcoming a). Already in the ithyphallic hymn for Demetrius Poliorcetes (291/290 BCE, quoted in Ath. 6.253b–f = Duris *FGrH* 76 F 13 = *CA* pp. 173–4) we read (9–12):

σεμνόν, ὅθι φαίνεθ', οἱ φίλοι πάντες κύκλωι,
ἐν μέσοισι δ' αὐτός,
ὅμοιος ὥσπερ οἱ φίλοι μὲν ἀστέρες,
ἥλιος δ' ἐκεῖνος.

An august picture is revealed: all the friends around him, and he in the middle of them. Just as the friends are like the stars, his semblance is like the sun.

At the same time that this hymn was sung, the Athenians commissioned a fresco depicting Demetrius enthroned on the *oikoumenē*, the "inhabited world" (Ath. 12.535f). The sun surrounded by stars also turns ups as a heraldic emblem on early Antigonid and Seleucid shields (Liampi 1998). The Hellenistic equation of monarchy to the sun, with its radiant crowns and other solar imagery, was transmitted to the Roman and Sassanid empires, and eventually provided a model for the image of Christ in late antiquity.

A related image is the expectation of a new Golden Age. In the introduction to his astronomical poem *Phaenomena*, Aratus evokes an image of the universe as an all-embracing, harmonious unity under the universal rule of Zeus, who appears as "an absolutist god-king" (Hose 1997: 62), in control of everything (*Phaen.* 1–4, quoted by Volk in this volume). These first lines are complemented by an extensive celebration of the Golden Age and the rule of Justice (*Phaen.* 98–136). Aratus, who worked at the court of Antigonus Gonatas, does not mention his patron by name, but his image of the universe under Zeus' reign perfectly mirrors the universalistic pretensions in Hellenistic royal ideology. In the *Hymn to Zeus*, Callimachus places the birth of Zeus not on Crete, but gives preference to an Arcadian birth myth. According to this myth, Arcadia, once a dry and inhospitable country, becomes instantly fertile when Zeus is born, and changes into a land of bliss (*h.* 1.18–35). In the *Hymn to Delos*, Callimachus contrasts the disorderly world before Apollo with the peace and harmony after the god's birth (Bing 1988: 30–5), and links the god's birth to the birth of Ptolemy Philadelphus. In Theocritus' encomium of Philadelphus, too, images of fertility and peace abound (17.75–80, trans. Verity 2002):

πολὺς δέ οἱ ὄλβος ὀπαδεῖ,
πολλᾶς δὲ κρατέει γαίας, πολλᾶς δὲ θαλάσσας.
μυρίαι ἄπειροί τε καὶ ἔθνεα μυρία φωτῶν
λήιον ἀλδήσκουσιν ὀφελλόμεναι Διὸς ὄμβρωι,

ἀλλ' οὔτις τόσα φύει ὅσα χθαμαλὰ Αἴγυπτος,
Νεῖλος ἀναβλύζων διερὰν ὅτε βώλακα θρύπτει (...).

Great wealth goes hand in hand
with such a man, and his rule spreads far abroad over land and sea.
There are numberless lans peopled by numberless nations
who harvest their crops through the generosity of Zeus' rain,
but none is as fertile as low-lying Egypt when the overflowing Nile
saturates and crumbles its soil.

Theocritus' *Idyll* 16 even more explicitly emphasizes the causal connection between kingship and prosperity, peace, and harmony. The poet first describes a confused, violent world in which greed prevails over honor, war over peace, and the barbaric Carthaginians have the better of the civilized Greeks. The coming of Hiero, Theocritus prophesies, will change everything. In fact, the Carthaginians already tremble from fear as the warrior Hiero girds himself for battle. Only a handful of barbarians will be left alive to return to Africa and spread the fame of Hiero "with tidings of the deaths of loved ones to mothers and wives" (86–7). When this work has been done, Theocritus prays, harmony will be restored to Sicily (16.88–97, trans. Verity):

ἄστεα δὲ προτέροισι πάλιν ναίοιτο πολίταις,
δυσμενέων ὅσα χεῖρες ἐλωβήσαντο κατ' ἄκρας·
ἀγροὺς δ' ἐργάζοιντο τεθαλότας· αἱ δ' ἀνάριθμοι
μήλων χιλιάδες βοτάναι διαπιανθεῖσαι
ἂμ πεδίον βληχῷντο, βόες δ' ἀγεληδὸν ἐς αὖλιν
ἐρχόμεναι σκνιφαῖον ἐπισπεύδοιεν ὁδίταν·
νειοὶ δ' ἐκπονέοιντο ποτὶ σπόρον, ἁνίκα τέττιξ
ποιμένας ἐνδίους πεφυλαγμένος ὑψόθι δένδρων
ἀχεῖ ἐν ἀκρεμόνεσσιν· ἀράχνια δ' εἰς ὅπλ' ἀράχναι
λεπτὰ διαστήσαιντο, βοᾶς δ' ἔτι μηδ' ὄνομ' εἴη.

May the cities which enemy hands have cruelly razed
be once again peopled by their former inhabitants.
May rich harvests repay their toil, and may sheep in their
countless thousands fatten in pastures, bleating across
the plain; and may herds of cattle as they wander back
to their folds quicken the evening traveler's steps.
May fallow land be ploughed again, ready for seed-time,
at the season when the cicada, keeping watch over the shepherds
in the noonday sun, sings loudly high up in the tree branches.
May their armor be covered with spiders' fine-spun webs, and
even the name of the battle-cry be forgotten.

This image is comparable with the idyllic pastoral world of bucolic poetry. However, to bring peace, first war must be waged. To secure order, chaos has to be defeated. A central theme in royal ideology was the presentation of the king as a savior from barbarians, just as the Olympian gods once brought peace and order by defeating Titans and Giants (Strootman 2005). In *Idyll* 16 the Carthaginians are staged as the barbarian foes (Hans 1985), but the archetypal enemies of the Hellenistic order were the Celts. In 279 BCE Celts had invaded Greece, to be defeated only when they had come as far as Delphi. The saving of Delphi was attributed to the intervention of Apollo himself. Soon after kings took over the role as the protectors of civilization from the gods. In the summer of 276 BCE, Antigonus Gonatas defeated a Celtic army near Lysimacheia – a feat commemorated in a lost poem by Aratus (Tarn 1913: 175–6) – and used this victory to legitimize his usurpation of the Macedonian throne in the same year. Celtic tribes invaded Asia Minor as well. Both Antiochus I and Attalus I styled themselves *sōtēres*, "saviors," after defeating the invaders in battle, and were subsequently awarded divine honors by the Greeks of Asia Minor. The triumphs were abundantly celebrated in epic poetry (Barbantani 2001), in victory monuments, and on coins. The divine salvation of Delphi figures in the *Hymn to Delos* (*h.* 4.171–90), where Callimachus manages to give Ptolemy Philadelphus a share of the honor, even though he had no part in the action, by linking Apollo's *sōtēria* with Philadelphus' suppression of a mutiny of his own Celtic mercenaries in Egypt during the First Syrian War (274–271 BCE). By directly equating Philadelphus' triumph in Egypt with Apollo's victory in Greece over these "later-born Titans" (*h.* 4.174), Callimachus presents Philadelphus as a savior god who has delivered the civilized world from barbaric chaos. In a similar vein, the *Hymn to Apollo* claims (*h.* 2.26–7):

ὃς μάχεται μακάρεσσιν, ἐμῶι βασιλῆϊ μάχοιτο·
ὅστις ἐμῶι βασιλῆϊ, καὶ Ἀπόλλωνι μάχοιτο.

Whoever fights against the blessed gods, fights with my king;
whoever fights against my king, fights with Apollo.

Being the earthly champions of the gods was not an exclusive privilege of the Ptolemies. The Antigonid king Philip V used a famous poem on Zeus by his courtier Samus to claim the same. In 218 Philip had demolished Thermus, the holy place of the Aetolians, in retaliation for some sacrilegious act of the Aetolian League. When the army departed, a line from Samus' poem was left behind as a graffito on a ruined wall (Plb. 5.8.5–6): "Seest thou how far the divine bolt hath sped?" This single line has far-reaching implications. Its comparison of Philip's military action with a bolt of lightning associates Philip with Zeus, presents his power as irresistible and boundless, reaching even the remotest of places, and portrays Philip as a just ruler who punishes wrongdoers on behalf of the supreme god, restoring order and peace.

The Ivory Tower

Unlike the literature of the Classical *polis*, the literature of the Hellenistic courts was not "national." It leveled the differences between the various Greek "tribes" and reinvented Hellenicity in the light of a new cosmopolitan worldview. In the worldview propagated by the Hellenistic empires a shared culture united all, from the Macedonian imperial upper class to the Hellenized non-Greeks in the cities. At the same time the literature of the court was elitist, being aimed in the first instance at a court audience. Although produced in an atmosphere of competition, it was instrumental in the creation of group cohesion and identity among the royal *philoi*, who had disparate origins. Moreover, by their appreciation of complex and erudite literature, courtiers distanced themselves from other social groups. This is typical of court culture: "the court, shielded from the outside world, projects an image of itself as mysterious and inaccessible; its power is enhanced by the double aim of seeming both very learned and very glorious" (Bertelli 1986: 17). Hellenistic court poetry was not "art for art's sake," but it was produced in, and for the sake of, an ivory tower: the ivory tower of the court.

In the second instance, court poetry spread to an audience of regional and civic elites, Greeks as well as non-Greeks. Hellenism became a means of defining who did and who did not participate in the imperial order of the Hellenistic kings. Indigenous upper-class families developed a multiple identity (e.g., Greek-Egyptian, Greek-Babylonian, Greek-Jewish) when their political prevalence depended on allegiance to the empire and the favor of the king. The adoption of Greek culture bound them to the monarchy and distanced them from those who did not share in the power. Thus Hellenism became the "high culture" of empire, creating, at the highest level of society, a sense of commonwealth in states that were characterized by their political, ethnical, and cultural heterogeneity. It was a non-national, "cosmopolitan" form of Greekness in which indigenous ideas and forms could be amalgamated, not unlike Ottoman culture in the empire of the sultans. Royal patronage of the arts made it manifest that the court was the heart of this unifying culture.

FURTHER READING

Seminal works on the royal court are Elias 1969 and Kruedener 1973, although many of their theories concerning the function of the court have now been adjusted or even wholly rejected: see Duindam 1995. The courts of the Renaissance and Ancien Régime are discussed in Dickens 1977, Bertelli, Cardini, and Garbero Zorzi 1986, Asch and Birke 1991, Adamson 1999, and Duindam 2003. Specifically on patronage of the arts and sciences at early modern courts see Trevor-Roper 1976, Lytle and Orgel 1981, and Moran 1991b. Biagioli 1993 is a revealing case study on Galileo. The essays in Spawforth 2007 discuss various ancient courts, including Alexander's.

Although studies of individual aspects of the Hellenistic royal courts abound, so far only Herman 1997 and Weber 1997 offer a broader perspective. On court titulature and prosopographical aspects see Berve 1926 and Heckel 1992 (the Argead court under Alexander); Peremans, Van't Dack, and Mooren 1968, Mooren 1975 and 1977, Herman 1981 (Ptolemies); and Savalli-Lestrade 1998 (Seleucids and Attalids). For Hellenistic palace architecture see Nielsen 1994, Brands and Hoepfner 1996; on the ideology of Hellenistic kingship Walbank 1984, Ma 2003, and Chaniotis 2003. A general overview of patronage of literature in the ancient world is Gold 1987. Literary patronage at the courts of the Argeads and early Antigonids is discussed in Weber 1992 and 1995. Weber 1993 and Meissner 1992 are extensive studies of poets and historians respectively at the Hellenistic courts.

CHAPTER FOUR

Ptolemaic Alexandria

Susan Stephens

In 333 BCE Alexandria did not exist. Fifty years later, at the accession of Ptolemy II Philadelphus, it was well on the way to becoming the first city of the Mediterranean, a status it enjoyed for two centuries until displaced by Rome. The story goes that following the dictates of an oracle or a prophetic dream Alexander himself laid out the city that was to become the capital of the Ptolemies, the rulers of Egypt for the next 300 years. The new city sat on a slender neck of land that ran above Lake Mareotis, on the site of an older Egyptian village or border fort called Rhacotis (McKenzie 2007: 36–9). The island of Pharos lay before the harbor and about 15 miles to the east was the westernmost (Canopic) branch of the Nile and the promontory of Cape Zephyrium. The city was connected to the Canopic branch by a channel that allowed efficient transport of grain from Upper Egypt as well as of luxury goods brought from the Red Sea overland to Coptos and then shipped down river. How large the city was, who lived there, even when the Ptolemies first took up official residence (320/19 or 312/11 BCE) are all matters of debate. The first surviving description of the city's layout is that of Strabo, who visited in the 20s BCE, and is therefore to be used with caution in assessing the early city; archaeological excavations are hindered by the overlying modern city; underwater work in the harbor area is very recent and the finds not well understood; and the inevitable baggage, both ancient and modern, continues to cloud the picture (McKenzie 2007). The physical and psychological space that was early Ptolemaic Alexandria must have shaped the literature produced there. At the same time the glimpses we get from third-century and later authors undoubtedly condition modern impressions of the city. In what follows I will use modern historical and archaeological analyses to contextualize what writers such as Callimachus and Theocritus, assorted epigrammatists, historians, and pseudo-historians say. Ancient writers are eclectic: sometimes their observations converge with what we learn from other sources; more often what they tell us belongs to the mythology of Alexander or derives from the ideological positioning of the Ptolemies as they negotiate a space for themselves between Macedon, Greece, and Egypt.

The People

In the absence of accurate population data for Alexandria, Walter Scheidel has compared two pre-modern cities, London and Tokyo, to provide "probabilistic predictions" for size and growth patterns of the new foundation. On the basis of these data he observes that Alexandria should have seen a very steep growth curve during its initial fifty years, reaching a total population of around 150,000 by 270 BCE. It may then have grown to a population of about 300,000 by 200 BCE (Scheidel 2004: 12–15), though even these figures may be too high. Recent estimates for the size of the land occupied by the early city are in the range of 200 to 250 hectares, a size capable of supporting a population of 60,000 to 80,000 (Grimm 1996). These numbers bring the early Ptolemaic city closer in size to an Athens than a Rome, though with different social and political hierarchies. For the period when most of the surviving Alexandrian poetry was produced (c.285–c.240 BCE), the population of Greek elite males must have been a relatively discrete group, and principally attached to the royal house. The larger population would have consisted of mercenary soldiers and the trades- and craftsmen that the court and court-centered elite groups required to support their lifestyle. Egyptians would have already been resident in Rhacotis and the surrounding villages, and would have been needed in some numbers for manual labor; they will have constituted at least half and more likely a higher percentage of the urban population. Sustained population growth, however, would have depended on a constant stream of immigrants from other locations in the Mediterranean and Egypt proper, and, in the second century BCE, Jews (Scheidel 2004: 27; Fraser 1972: 1.73).

Katja Mueller's recent study of foreign ethnic designations found on papyri and inscriptions within Hellenistic Egypt provides a rough snapshot of migration in the first three centuries. Regional and city ethnic designations for the whole period in decreasing order of frequency include: Cyrenaica (201) and Cyrene (173), Thrace (199), Judaea (102), Attica (63) and Athens (58), Crete (80), Thessaly (58), Caria (53), Ionia (37), Miletus (21), Syracuse (19), Corinth (18) (Mueller 2005: 87–92). The preponderance of immigrants from Cyrene or the Cyrenaica in Egypt makes it likely that Alexandria (although no evidence survives for the city) saw a similarly high number of Cyrenean immigrants. If so Callimachus would have been a member of one of, if not the largest Greek-speaking ethnic group in the city. Posidippus, from Pella, would also have found a substantial immigrant community, and Theocritus was unlikely to have been an isolated Syracusan. From third-century literature we can infer that under the early Ptolemies there was as yet no pervasive sense of Alexandrian identity. Callimachus in the *Aetia* provides the instructive vignette of Pollis, a recent immigrant from Athens, who is hosting a private symposium (fr. 178 Pf.). The guests include Theogenes, a visitor from the island of Icus, and Callimachus from Cyrene, who critiques Thessalian drinking practices. Neither Callimachus nor Pollis regard themselves as "Alexandrian," and if permanent immigrants (rather than visitors), they remain closely tied to their places of origin. The women in Theocritus' *Idyll* 15 describe themselves as immigrants, and they take pride in the fact that they are Syracusans (90). The singer within the poem is described simply as "the Argive woman's daughter" (97). By the Roman period "Alexandrian" was a desirable status distinct from the Greeks (or more likely Greco-Egyptians) living in the rest of Egypt, but this cannot be assumed for or retrojected onto the reigns of the earliest Ptolemies. In fact, the ethnicities most often mentioned in the early poets – Cyrenean, Athenian, Thessalian, Syracusan – would seem to be a reliable reflection of the earliest migration patterns to the new city and this raises the possibility that when poets refer to places outside of Egypt (like Cyrene, Syracuse, or Athens) they are appealing to recent immigrants from those locations.

We do not know whether the Ptolemies provided financial incentives for immigration, but their immense wealth, and Alexandria as a magnet for those seeking wealth is a recurring theme in early poetry. Herodas' much-quoted statement from his first *Mimiamb* describes the city as a place for those in search of economic advancement (1.26–31):

τὰ γὰρ πάντα,
ὅcc' ἔcτι κου καὶ γίνετ', ἔcτ' ἐν Αἰγύπτωι·
πλοῦτος, παλαίςτρη, δύναμις, εὐδίη, δόξα,
θέαι, φιλόcοφοι, χρυcίον, νεηνίcκοι,
θεῶν ἀδελφῶν τέμενος, ὁ βαcιλεὺc χρηcτός,
Μουcῆιον, οἶνος, ἀγαθὰ πάντ' ὅc' ἂν χρήιζηι,

All that exists and is produced anywhere can be found in Egypt: wealth, wrestling grounds, power, leisure, reputation, spectacles, philosophers, money, young men, the precinct of the *Theoi Adelphoi*, a king who is good, the Museum, wine, every fine thing that one can desire.

Posidippus echoes this sentiment in a newly discovered roll of his epigrams. Throughout the first section of the collection there is movement from the eastern periphery of Alexander's empire towards the land of the Ptolemies (mentioned in the final poems of the section) as luxury goods and individuals are inexorably drawn to Egypt (1–20 AB; Stephens 2004: 63–86; Bing 2005: 119–40). The most obvious group attracted to Egypt would have been soldiers. The frequent wars between Alexander's successors meant that the new reign had a constant need for troops and that loyalties went to the general with the best pay package. The early literature provides us with a picture of military service under the first Ptolemies as a character in Theocritus' *Idyll* 14 gives his friend the following advice: "Ptolemy [sc. II] is the best paymaster for a free born man . . . so if you are bold enough to stand against a bold man's charge, then go quickly to Egypt" (59, 66–8). Troops of soldiers figure prominently in the celebration of the Ptolemaia (Callixenus in Ath. 5.201d), and we see the intersection of the civilian and military and the clash of cultures in the city also in Theocritus, where the women on an outing to enjoy the Adonia complain about the king's horsemen (15.46–8). Macedonian soldiers would have constituted the palace guard and thus may have been the most visible military force in early Alexandria, even if they were not otherwise significant in the composition of the army (Fraser 1972: 1.52–4). The Ptolemies were successful in retaining soldiers by making provisions of land on which they might settle. To this end a region west of Memphis (the Fayum) was opened up under Ptolemy II. The new land generated income, provided a stable Greek-speaking population, and de facto a military class as sons of soldiers in turn served in the army (Bagnall and Rathbone

2004: 127–54). This policy will have guaranteed a certain loyalty to the reign and may well stand behind the poetic enthusiasm for Ptolemaic wealth or Ptolemy as paymaster.

Any consideration of the demographic gives us a substantial Egyptian population, and that should be factored into the picture. Their presence within the city is felt in Theocritus' *Idyll* 15 when the Syracusan ladies praise Ptolemy for reducing the thievery of Egyptians (47–50). We can infer that they were numerous and mingled freely with, if not welcomed by, the Greek populace. Callimachus' fragment from the opening of the victory poem for Berenice II (*SH* 254) presents a slightly different picture: he alludes to the Egyptian ceremony of mourning for the death of the Apis bull, an event that took place early in Philadelphus' reign and again towards its end (Thompson 1988: 190–209). We also know that under the first two Ptolemies some Egyptians were closely associated with the new monarchy: Manetho, a high priest from Sebennytos, wrote a history of Egypt and a tract on Egyptian religion that took into account Greek philosophical speculation on the elements (Dieleman and Moyer in this volume). A number of hieroglyphic inscriptions testify to Egyptians holding what appear to be high military and administrative offices under the first Ptolemies, one even bearing the title of Overseer of the King's Harem (Lloyd 2002: 117, 136). Since the Ptolemies needed a bilingual bureaucracy to administer the new state, reliance on Egyptians is not surprising, and recent studies continue to expand the role of natives in central areas like the army and the regional administration (Clarysse 1985; Thompson 1994; Lloyd 2002: 119–22).

Alexander in Alexandria

Egyptian Alexandria was only one of the numerous cities founded in the wake of Alexander's conquests, though it is the one that subsequently was most closely associated with him. Myth-making about Alexander began in his own lifetime, and increased at his death as the successors enhanced their own status via association with the now divinized king. Ptolemy I Soter was assiduous in his efforts to reinforce Alexander's status as a god and promote himself as his legitimate successor. He wrote a history of Alexander's campaigns (now lost), and recent scholars credit him with the original version of the *Liber de morte*, an account of Alexander's death that now stands at the end of the *Alexander Romance* (Bosworth 2000: 206–41). This fictive pastiche, the oldest parts of which seem to have originated in Ptolemaic Alexandria, indicate Alexander's centrality to Ptolemaic ideology (Fraser 1996: 211–12; Dieleman and Moyer, Whitmarsh in this volume). The text links Alexander first with Egypt as its rightful king and then with Alexandria as its founder. Here we are told that Egypt's last pharaoh, Nectanebo II, fleeing the Persians, escaped to Macedon disguised as a magician. He ingratiated himself with Olympias, seduced her by pretending to be the Egyptian god, Amun, and decked out as the god (with a ram's head) fathered Alexander. Alexander as both Macedonian and Egyptian serves as a model for the dual aspects of Ptolemaic rule and for the city itself (Stephens 2003: 64–73). In the *Alexander Romance*, he asks the Egyptians to give to him the tribute they formerly paid to the Persians "not so that I may add it to my treasury, but so that

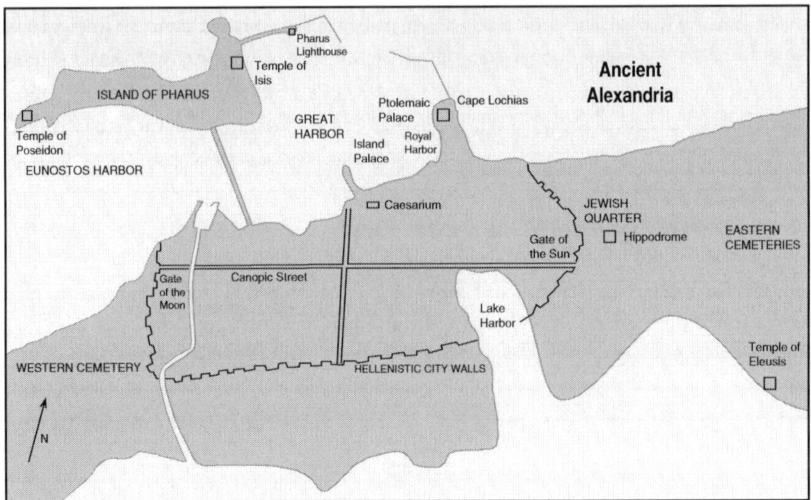

Map 4.1. *Ancient Alexandria.*

I may spend it on your city of Alexandria, which lies before Egypt, and is the capital of the whole world" (1.34.9, Recension B).

A clever move in this high stakes game was Ptolemy I Soter's appropriation of Alexander's body. According to Diodorus he intercepted the funeral cortege carrying the embalmed body from Babylon to what was to be its final resting place in the shrine of Zeus Amun in Libya. Details are murky, but the likeliest scenario is that the body was first taken to Memphis, the old capital of Egypt, after which either Soter or Philadelphus entombed it in a central place in the new city (D.S. 28.3–5; Curt. 10.5.4, 10.20; *Liber de morte* 129). The fourth Ptolemy is credited with building the mausoleum that held Alexander and the Ptolemies themselves. As part of the process of legitimating their own dynasty, the Ptolemies established the cult of the divinized Alexander and associated members of their own family with him in the cult (Erskine 2002). The Ptolemies also capitalized on a crucial story in Alexander's life: his trek to the shrine at Siwah in the Libyan desert, where the local priests apparently proclaimed him the son of the god, Amun (Plu. *Alex.* 27.5–9; Curt. 4.7.9). The Ptolemies issued coinage featuring either Alexander in conjunction with themselves or members of the royal family in the accoutrements of Alexander, for example, depicted with Amun's ram's horn above the ear. Statues of Ptolemy and Alexander together are mentioned in Callixenus' description of the procession for the Ptolemaia around 276 BCE (Ath. 5.201d), and Theocritus links Alexander and Soter, now dead, on Olympus (17.16–19):

τῆνον καὶ μακάρεσςι πατὴρ ὁμότιμον ἔθηκεν
ἀθανάτοις, καί οἱ χρύσεος θρόνος ἐν Διὸς οἴκωι
δέδμηται· παρὰ δ' αὐτὸν Ἀλέξανδρος φίλα εἰδώς
ἑδριάει, Πέρσαισι βαρὺς θεὸς αἰολομίτρας.

[Ptolemy] the father [sc. Zeus] made equal in honor with the blessed immortals, and he established a golden throne for him in the house of Zeus. By his side in friendship sits Alexander, bane of the Persians, god of the glittering diadem.

Alexander and his mythical ancestors – notably Dionysus, Perseus, and Heracles – became the de facto ancestors of the Ptolemies, and they along with ancestors of the Macedonian royal house – Argaeus, Coeneus, and Temenus, who were said to be descended from Heracles – are commemorated in the names of Alexandrian civic units or "demes" (Fraser 1972: 1.44–8; Satyrus, *On the demes of Alexandria* = *P.Oxy.* 27.2465 fr. 1 col. 2).

Buildings and Monuments

Recent archaeological work in Alexandria makes it clear that while the Ptolemaic buildings were mainly in the Greek style, Egyptian decorative elements such as sphinxes, obelisks, and columns, imported from elsewhere in Egypt, were used as ornamentation (McKenzie 2007: 33–4, 121–45). We have at least one example found within Alexandria of Ptolemy II and Arsinoe II represented in the pharaonic mode, just as they were in numerous other locations throughout Egypt (Stanwick 2002: 100 A10). In the *Alexander Romance*, Alexander is particularly attentive to the religious life of Egyptians. He worships the Apis bull and establishes a temple to Isis after moving the local Egyptians into the newly founded city (1.31.4). A papyrus letter from 257 BCE confirms that at least one Isis festival was celebrated within the city (*P.Col.Zen.* 59154). A Greco-Egyptian religious liaison was created when the Ptolemies introduced the divinity Sarapis, who blended elements of Egyptian Osiris and Greek Dionysus. The so-called Great Serapeum, erected by Ptolemy III upon an earlier foundation, was the most important religious structure in the new city. Dedicatory plaques inscribed in Egyptian hieroglyphs and Greek found in the foundations of the building testify to the dual ethnicity of the new god (McKenzie 2007: 53–6).

In the *Alexander Romance* Alexander gives orders for the foundation known as Parmenion's Serapeum. After he received an oracle about his death and the prediction that Alexandria would be his permanent resting place (this was blatant propaganda for the Ptolemies, since after his death they gained possession of his corpse), Alexander ordered Parmenion to build a shrine to Sarapis that seems not to have been the precursor to the Great Serapeum but an early separate temple (Fraser 1972: 1.270–1; *P.Col.Zen.* 59355). According to the scholiast on Callimachus' first *Iamb* (*Dieg.* VI 2.3 Pf.), this is the temple to which Hipponax, returning from the dead, summons the "critics" in order to chastise them for their quarrelsomeness: "[come] here to the shrine that stands in front of the city wall, when the old man who fashioned Pangaean Zeus of old [sc. Euhemerus] chatters scratching out his impious books" (9–11). Euhemerus, a somewhat older contemporary of Callimachus who wrote in the court of Cassander, had acquired the reputation for impiety because he invented gods or rather presented divinities like Zeus as once human and having achieved divine status though their services to mankind (Whitmarsh in this volume). Callimachus' association of Euhemerus with a temple of Sarapis may be a pointed allusion to the newly created status of Sarapis as well as to Ptolemies' habit of turning their family members into gods.

One of Alexandria's earliest monuments was the lighthouse built on the Pharos, the island that stood before the harbor. According to Posidippus (115 AB, trans. Austin):

Ἑλλήνων σωτῆρα, Φάρου σκοπόν, ὦ ἄνα Πρωτεῦ,
  Σώστρατος ἔστησεν Δεξιφάνους Κνίδιος·
οὐ γὰρ ἐν Αἰγύπτωι σκοπαὶ οὔρεος οἷ' ἐπὶ νήσων,
  ἀλλὰ χαμαὶ χηλὴ ναύλοχος ἐκτέταται.
τοῦ χάριν εὐθεῖάν τε καὶ ὄρθιον αἰθέρα τέμνειν
  πύργος ὅδ' ἀπλάτων φαίνετ' ἀπὸ σταδίων
ἤματι, παννύχιος δὲ θοῶς ἐν κύματι ναύτης
  ὄψεται ἐκ κορυφῆς πῦρ μέγα καιόμενον,
καί κεν ἐπ' αὐτὸ δράμοι Ταύρου Κέρας, οὐδ' ἂν ἁμάρτοι
  Σωτῆρος, Πρωτεῦ, Ζηνὸς ὁ τῆιδε πλέων.

As a savior of the Greeks, this watchman of Pharos, O lord Proteus,
  was set up by Sostratus, the son of Dexiphanes, from Cnidus,
for in Egypt there are no look-out posts on a mountain, as in the islands,
  but low lies the breakwater where ships take harbor.
Therefore this tower, in a straight and upright line,
  appears to cleave the sky from countless furlongs away
during the day, but throughout the night quickly a sailor on the waves
  will see a great fire blazing from its summit.
And he may even run to the Bull's horn and not miss
  Zeus the Savior, O Proteus, whoever sails this way.

A statue of Zeus Soter probably stood on the top of the monument, and he may have been the principal dedicatee. Five centuries later Lucian claims that the original inscription was to the Savior Gods – from the context he surely means the Dioscuri –, but covered over in plaster on which the name of the current king was written (*Hist. Conscr.* 62). Given the importance of the Dioscuri in protecting sailors, their inclusion in the dedication would be appropriate, and they are elsewhere well represented in Ptolemaic Egypt. There was a temple to them in Naucratis, an early temple to the Dioscuri in the city (noted in Satyrus), and the two are individually commemorated with Alexandrian deme names (Fraser 1972: 1.207; Satyrus, *P.Oxy.* 27.2465 fr. 11.5). Divinities associated with the lighthouse may have included the first royal couple, Ptolemy I Soter and Berenice I, who after their deaths were added to the Alexander cult with the title of *Theoi Soteres*, "Savior Gods."

The other monument frequently commemorated in early poetry was the temple of Aphrodite Zephyritis, located on a promontory facing the Mediterranean some fifteen miles east of the city. The subject of several epigrams and mentioned tangentially in Callimachus' *Lock of Berenice*, the temple was unique because its divinity at a very early date was associated with the deified Arsinoe II, the sister-wife of Ptolemy II (Posidippus 39, 116, 119 AB; Call. *ep.* 5 Pf. = 14 GP and *Aet.* fr. 110 Pf.; Hedylus 4 GP). This was not a case of the Egyptian practice of co-templing, in which there were two associated divinities and two cult statues. The dead queen was completely identified with or assimilated to Aphrodite. Again we are indebted to Posidippus for the temple's dedicatory epigram (119 AB, trans. Austin):

τοῦτο καὶ ἐν πόντωι καὶ ἐπὶ χθονὶ τῆς Φιλαδέλφου
  Κύπριδος ἱλάσκεσθ' ἱερὸν Ἀρσινόης,
ἣν ἀνακοιρανέουσαν ἐπὶ Ζεφυρίτιδος ἀκτῆς
  πρῶτος ὁ ναύαρχος θήκατο Καλλικράτης·
ἡ δὲ καὶ εὐπλοίην δώσει καὶ χείματι μέσσωι
  τὸ πλατὺ λισσομένοις ἐκλιπανεῖ πέλαγος.

Both on land and sea make offering to this shrine
  of Aphrodite-Arsinoe-Philadelphus.
She it was, ruling over the Zephyrian promontory
  whom Callicrates, the admiral, was the first to consecrate,
and she will grant safe sailing and in the midst of the storm
  will make smooth the wide sea for those who entreat her.

Louis Robert has argued that Callicrates of Samos, who was the head of Ptolemy's naval forces, dedicated this temple as a promotional policy for the Ptolemaic fleet (Robert 1966). The temple is one of many monuments dedicated to Arsinoe II found throughout the lands under Ptolemaic influence. Towns and whole regions, like the Arsinoite nome of Upper Egypt, were named for her; and her cult quickly gained acceptance in Egypt proper, where she was co-templed with Egyptian divinities.

The temple of Arsinoe-Aphrodite Zephyritis was located near the Canopic mouth of the Nile. An underwater excavation nearby has produced a colossal statue of the Nile god, Hapi, represented with pendulous breasts that must have been standing during the early Ptolemaic period. The fusion of mortal (Arsinoe II) with immortal (Aphrodite) in the Cape Zephyrium temple and the Egyptian Hapi are typical of the divinities found in the new city and its environs. They differ from the traditional Olympic pantheon, who are not represented in the city's early buildings (the exception is Demeter, on whom see below). There was no temple to Zeus or Apollo or Hera or Athena, although temples to Olympian Zeus and to Athena were to be found in the older Greek city of Naucratis, some fifty miles up the Canopic branch of the Nile. Instead of shrines for Olympians we find Serapea, Isis temples, or monuments like the Arsinoeion, which was apparently mentioned by Callimachus in his poem on the deification of Arsinoe (fr. 228 Pf.). This was a mortuary temple built for Arsinoe II by Ptolemy II. If the description in Pliny is even close to correct the building was an extravagant tour de force that featured a magnetic roof under which a statue of the dead queen was suspended in air (*NH* 34.148). Pliny tells us that the mortuary temple had an Egyptian element: an obelisk carved in the reign of Nectanebo I or II (McKenzie 2007: 51) apparently stood in front of the edifice (*NH* 36.67). These monuments, if only in a small way, provide us with a glimpse of the visual dynamics of early Alexandria and its surroundings, whose "Greek" identity was constructed alongside of a self-consciously appropriated native tradition.

The initial building phase of the city under Soter and Philadephus included an imperial palace that seems to have been complete by the time of Theocritus' *Idyll* 15. It is here that Arsinoe II stages the tableau that he describes as part of a festival for Adonis (the Adonia). The palace buildings, which included the Museum and the tomb of Alexander, extended along the waterfront from the promontory of Antirrhodos to Cape Lochias (McKenzie 2007: 173–5). A number of large houses datable to the early Ptolemaic period have been found here, many with their elaborate mosaic flooring nearly intact (McKenzie 2007: 66–9). In some houses dining rooms with their placement of couches are still discernable, remnants of the elegant dinner parties that contemporary poets might have graced. Callimachus gives us a glimpse of one such party in the *Aetia* (fr. 178.2–8 Pf.):

> Ἰκαρίου καὶ παιδὸς ἄγων ἐπέτειον ἁγιστύν,
>   Ἀτθίσιν οἰκτίστη, cὸν φάος, Ἠριγόνη,
> ἐc δαίτην ἐκάλεccεν ὁμηθέας, ἐν δέ νυ τοῖcι
>   ξεῖνον ὃc Αἰγύπτωι καινὸc ἀνεcτρέφετο
> μεμβλωκὼc ἴδιόν τι κατὰ χρέοc· ἦν δὲ γενέθλην
>   Ἴκιοc, ὧι ξυνὴν εἶχον ἐγὼ κλιcίην

> Celebrating the annual ceremony of Icarius' child, your day, Erigone, lady most lamented by Attic women, [Pollis] invited friends to a banquet, and among them a guest who had just arrived in Egypt, having come on some private affair. He was an Ician by birth, and I shared a couch with him.

Pollis, the Athenian immigrant, celebrates his own version of an Athenian festival, and his guests include Callimachus, a Cyrenean, and a visitor from the island of Icus. Here Callimachus and Theocritus, who in *Idyll* 14 describes a symposium at some unknown country location (outside of Egypt), show us the importance of these private events in forging and maintaining Greek social bonds.

Museum and Library

Traditionally the Museum and the Library have been assigned to the reign of Ptolemy II, although the evidence is late and problematic. According to Strabo the Museum was part of the palace complex (13.608, 17.793–4). Herodas is the earliest to mention the Museum, as we saw above (1.26–31), but the earliest explicit information about the Library comes from a fictional letter of one Aristeas urging Ptolemy II to underwrite a translation into Greek of the holy books of Jewish law. This intriguing text, also discussed by Gruen in this volume, opens with Demetrius of Phalerum urging Ptolemy II to build the library (*LetArist* 9–11):

> Placed in charge of the king's library, Demetrius of Phalerum received large sums to gather together, if possible, all the books in the world. Making purchases and copies he accomplished as best he could the wishes of the king. Now in my presence he was asked: "How many tens of thousands of books are there?" He responded: "More than twenty (sc. 200,000), O King, and in a short time I will collect the remainder, up to fifty (sc. 500,000)."

If Demetrius of Phalerum was instrumental in the Library's establishment, it must have been a project of the first Ptolemy, since he fell out of favor at Philadelphus' accession as sole ruler (D.L. 5.78). Demetrius is attractive as the facilitator because of his connection with Aristotle, whose philosophical school, the Lyceum, with its shrine of the Muses (Museum) and Library has often been seen as the model for the Ptolemies (Fraser 1972: 1.312–19). However, Ptolemy I, who began his rule in Memphis and depended on the Egyptian elite to consolidate power, would have had an Egyptian model at hand as well. Many Egyptian temples featured Houses of Life and Houses of Books in which priests and scholars collected, copied, and commented on religious works, medicine, geography, chronological and historical narratives, and even fiction. When Greeks are credited with studying in Egypt (for example, Thales, Pythagoras, Eudoxus, and Plato) or consulting priests for information (Hecataeus of Miletus, Herodotus) these are the institutions that might have accommodated them. The House of Life also served as a scribal school and played a role in educating elites (Strouhal 1989: 235–42). An Egyptian model for the Library becomes more cogent if, as many scholars have argued, the library within the Great Serapeum that is attested in the Roman period began its life under the early Ptolemies (Fraser 1972: 1.323–4; McKenzie 2007: 55).

Aristeas asserts that the total number of manuscripts housed in the Library was 200,000 to 500,000 rolls, and other writers report even higher numbers. Rudolf Blum questioned these numbers, as has Roger Bagnall (Blum 1991: 107; Bagnall 2002). Even if we take into account that the book roll was considerably shorter than the codex (which only came into use during the second to fourth centuries CE), and that the bulk of the Library might have consisted of copies, Aristeas' estimates are far greater than holdings of any pre-twentieth-century library in the West, at a period when the total number of books available for collection would have been significantly larger (Bagnall 2002: 356 and n.36). Bagnall also points out that Callimachus' *Pinakes* (catalogue notes) could not possibly have held enough information to catalogue holdings of hundreds of thousands of rolls. Every work of Greek that we know to have been written before the end of the third century BCE would occupy no more than about 250 to 350 rolls. Even if we assume that what survives represents no more than a hundredth of all that was written, the increase (25,000–35,000 rolls) is still far below traditional estimates unless the bulk of the collection consisted of duplicates (Bagnall 2002: 353–6). Even within these lower numbers, it is important to recognize that the reading and collating would have been a task for professional readers (*anagnōstai*) and scribes (*grammateis*). Callimachus and the associated librarians and scholars surely functioned as overseers and the final authority for decision-making. They would have been the final arbiters of a reading or assignment to genre or authentication of authorship, but they were not cataloguers in the modern sense.

The real significance of the library is that the Ptolemies were engaged in the competitive collecting of Greek literature and its commodification as a symbol of political power. They began a process that, because of its scale and their apparent desire to possess as much of Greek literature as possible, turned what earlier had been a small-scale civic or religious or private act (as in the case of philosophers' libraries) into a major political statement. What the Ptolemies did in Egypt, the Attalids did in Pergamum. Anecdotes that surround collecting, for example, that of a Ptolemy depositing 15 talents to "borrow" Athens' official copies of the tragedies of Aeschylus, Sophocles, and Euripides, then foregoing the talents for the original rolls, are not about building a library (Galen 17A.606–7 Kühn; Fraser 1972: 1.305–35;

Erskine 1995). It would have been easier, cheaper, and more conventional to have had the tragedies copied in Athens. The point of the anecdote is to enhance the status accruing to the possessors (now the Ptolemies) of the most distinguished literary production of the Athenian state, and to mark via the physical transport of the Athenian books to Egypt the passing of power from old Athens to this new city.

Festivals

The new city initially lacked cults and festivals, the time-honored means of forging a cultural identity. The challenge for the Ptolemies was to establish the city as a Greek space, especially since the Greek population was so diverse, yet also to accommodate the large number of non-Greeks and the even larger number of ethnic Egyptians.

The public performance of tragedy was one means of accomplishing the first goal, since the repertory with its familiar myths would have reinforced a collective "Greekness." Traditional tragedy and comedy were staged in Alexandria as well as mime or farce, rhapsodic competitions, and musical events. The theatre of Dionysus is not mentioned before Polybius (15.30.4, referring to events of 204 BCE), but "artists of Dionysus" (*technitai Dionusou*) are participants in the Ptolemaia around 276 BCE (Ath. 5.198b–c). They are led by Philicus, who has on plausible grounds been identified as a member of the Pleiad, a group of Hellenistic tragedians associated in the sources with the reign of Philadelphus (Rice 1983: 55–6; Fraser 1972: 2.859 n.407). How many tragedians actively produced for the Alexandrian stage is not known, but the number of early Hellenistic papyri of tragedy with musical notation discovered in Upper Egypt suggests an active performance culture (Pöhlman and West 2001: 12–55). The fourth Ptolemy (Philopator) is even credited with writing a tragedy on Adonis in the manner of Euripides (schol. Ar. *Thesm.* 1059).

City dwellers could and did attend the theater, and festival occasions in Alexandria, like those found elsewhere in the Hellenistic world, featured a growing number of musical, athletic, and other events. Theocritus, for example, alludes to Alexandrian poetic competitions, although the specific event cannot be identified (17.112–16):

> οὐδὲ Διωνύϲου τιϲ ἀνὴρ ἱεροὺϲ κατ᾽ ἀγῶναϲ
> ἵκετ᾽ ἐπιϲτάμενοϲ λιγυρὰν ἀναμέλψαι ἀοιδάν,
> ὧι οὐ δωτίναν ἀντάξιον ὤπαϲε τέχναϲ.
> Μουϲάων δ᾽ ὑποφῆται ἀείδοντι Πτολεμαῖον
> ἀντ᾽ εὐεργεϲίηϲ.

> A man never comes to the sacred contests of Dionysus without receiving from Ptolemy the gift his art deserves, if he knows how to sing a clear-voiced song. And those interpreters of the Muses sing of Ptolemy for his benefactions.

The richness of their public spectacles seem to have characterized the reign of the early Ptolemies. Court-sponsored festivals included the Basileia, which apparently combined an older Macedonian festival of Zeus Basileus and royal birthday celebrations. Callimachus' *Hymn to Zeus* and Theocritus' *Heracliscus* (*Id.* 24) may have been written to celebrate the Basileia at the time of Ptolemy II's assumption of the co-regency in 285/4 (Clauss 1986; Cameron 1995: 58; Stephens 2003: 77–9, 125–7). Other festivals for which we have evidence include the Soteria (probably in honor of Ptolemy I Soter), the Arsinoeia (in honor of Arsinoe II), the Adonia (a festival of Adonis, delineated in Theocritus' *Idyll* 15), and more than one festival in honor of Demeter (Perpillou-Thomas 1993: 151–75). There were also the Egyptian events mentioned above, Isis festivals and the ritual mourning that took place at the death of the Apis bull, and very possibly notionally Greek festivals included elements to appeal to the Egyptian population.

The Ptolemaia, for which Callixenus provides a detailed (and the only) account (Ath. 197c–203b), gives us considerable insight into the ideological underpinnings of Ptolemaic rule. The festival was first celebrated around 276 BCE by Ptolemy II in honor of his father. It began with a procession that wound through the city stadium (this has been identified as the Lageion, near the Great Serapeum). It was timed for the appearance of the Morning Star, whose wagon opened the procession, followed by the divinized parents of the royal couple, and all the gods, and finally the Evening Star. Figures of temporality, Eniautos ("yearly") and Penteteris ("every five years"), carried the *persea* crown and palm, pharaonic signs of reign and long life (Stephens 2002: 249). Next in order of appearance came the priest of Dionysus and the artists of Dionysus. The tableaus presented on wagons included events from Dionysus' life: Semele, his mother; Nysa, the city of his nurture; the "return of Dionysus from India," which assimilates him to Alexander; his pursuit by Hera; and finally a phallus pole. The procession included statues of Alexander, the king's throne with a crown, and a variety of subjects, animals, and objects that signaled the wealth and breadth of the empire, including (if true) an extraordinary number of infantry (57,000) and cavalry (23,000).

Both Callimachus and Posidippus celebrate the athletic contests that were part of the Ptolemaia, in contexts that reinforce the status of the events as "isolympic" (*SIG*[3] 390). One of the new epigrams attributed to Posidippus, from the section labeled *Hippika*, reads (76 AB, trans. adapted from Austin):

> ἐκτέτα[τ]αι π[ρ]οτ[ρ]έχων ἀκρώνυχος, ὡc Ἐτεάρχωι
> [οὗ]τοc κ[λεινὸc Ἄ]ραψ ἵπποc ἀεθλοφορεῖ·
> [ν]ικήc[α]c Πτολεμαῖα καὶ Ἴcθμια καὶ Νεμέαι δὶc
> [τ]οὺc Δελφοὺc πα[ριδ]εῖν οὐκ ἐθέλει cτεφάνουc·
>
> This famous Arab horse is stretched out, galloping on the edge of its hooves, and thus it carries off the prize for Etearchus. Victorious at the Ptolemaia and the Isthmia, and at Nemea twice, it refuses to overlook the Delphic crowns.

Callimachus, in celebrating Sosibius' victory at Nemea in a now fragmentary elegiac epinician, contextualizes the win by mentioning Sosibius' earlier victories at the Athenian Panathenaia and in the Ptolemaia (fr. 384.40–2 Pf.). He celebrates the uniqueness of the victor by stressing the fact that Sosibius was born in Egypt. The Nile proclaims: "a beautiful reward my nursling has brought me, for until now no one had brought a . . . trophy to the city from these sepulchral festivals" (i.e., the Nemean Games), and all of North Africa is imagined as turning out to celebrate (29–31).

Demeter was introduced in Alexandria probably in the reign of Soter. At least one reason for her introduction was her close connection to the Egyptian goddess, Isis, whose cult already in the fourth century had been exported from Egypt into the northern Mediterranean. Demeter's principal cult site seems to have been in an eastern suburb of the city called Eleusis, after the district of Attica where the famous Eleusinian mysteries were celebrated. Hereditary priests of Demeter were credited with bringing her cult to Alexandria, though some modern scholars reject the stories (Fraser 1972: 1.199–202; Hopkinson 1984a: 32–9). It is, however, worth considering the naming of Eleusis in conjunction with the procession of Dionysiac artists and the phallus pole in the Ptolemaia – are these events in some measure deliberately staged to compete with Athens? Eleusis appears in a recently discovered poem of Posidippus in a way that leaves ambiguous until the final line whether Eleusis is in Attica or in Egypt (20 AB, trans. adapted from Austin; Lehnus 2002):

ὡς πάλαι ὑψηλὴν Ἑλίκην ἐνὶ κύματι παίςας
  πᾶςαν ἅμα κρημνοῖς ἤγαγες εἰς ἄμαθον,
ὥς κ' [ἐ]π' Ἐλευςῖνα πρηςτὴρ ἑκατόγγυος ἤρθης
  εἰ μὴ Δημήτηρ ςὴν ἐκύνηςε χέρα·
νῦν δέ, Γεραίςτι' ἄναξ, νήςων μέτα τὴν Πτολεμαίου
  γαῖαν ἀκινήτην ἴςχε καὶ αἰγιαλούς.

As long ago you struck lofty Helike with a single wave and reduced it, cliffs and all, to sand dunes, so you would have come against Eleusis as a gigantic hurricane, had Demeter not kissed your hand. Now, Lord of Geraestus (sc. Poseidon), along with the islands, keep Ptolemy's land and shores unshaken.

And the scholiast on Callimachus' *Hymn to Demeter* claims the cult was introduced in imitation of Athens (Pfeiffer 1953: 77):

Ptolemy Philadelphus in imitation established some customs of the Athenians in Alexandria, among which was the procession of the basket; for in Athens customarily the basket was carried on a designated day on a vehicle in honor of Demeter.

"The basket carried in honor of Demeter" refers to the Eleusinian Mysteries, and it is Callimachus' only hymn that hints of an Alexandrian connection, though we saw above that the first *Iamb* is set in a local temple, and he does mention other local monuments in his poetry. Because there was also a Thesmophorion in the city, at least by the time of Ptolemy IV, Callimachus' hymn, whether or not it was written for a specific occasion, will have had a local resonance (Plb. 15.29.8).

Theocritus' poem on the Adonia (*Idyll* 15) rounds out our picture: here we see Greek housewives in Alexandria, immigrants from Syracuse or the Peloponnese, approaching the royal palace to view an elaborate tableau of Aphrodite mourning Adonis. The Adonia, like the Mysteries, was celebrated in Athens, but well suited for transportation to a city located in Egypt. The underlying story of Aphrodite mourning her lover – who is promoted as "bridegroom" in Theocritus – has the contours of the Egyptian myth of Isis mourning her dead husband Osiris (Reed 2000). Equally the event reinforces the wealth of the Ptolemies by implicitly associating it with nature's abundance in the tableau of the dead Adonis. Like Sarapis, Adonis had dimensions that both Greek and Egyptian might appreciate, though in Theocritus the Egyptian population is kept at a distance and referred to as an underclass (47–50). It is interesting that the Adonia and the mourning for the Apis bull are the only two Alexandrian religious events that Hellenistic poets mention explicitly, and neither is for a traditional Olympian deity.

The Mythological Landscape

Apart from the connection with Alexander, the new city lacked heroes. From the earliest period therefore, we see poets forging links between the new city and earlier Greek myths in which Egypt was prominent. The most important were stories that associated the region with Homer or with Homeric poetry. One version of the founding of Alexandria, for example, relates that when Alexander had, with the advice of his architects settled on a site, the following dream came to him (Plu. *Alex.* 26.5–7):

> A man with very white hair and venerable in aspect seemed to stand by him and speak the following lines: "Now there is an island in the much buffeting sea, in front of Egypt. Men call it Pharos" (*Od.* 4.354–6). Immediately Alexander arose and went to Pharos, which was still an island . . . , not yet attached to the mainland by a causeway. When he saw the natural advantages of the site . . . , he said that Homer was not only marvelous in all other respects, but also the wisest of architects, and he had his city plan drawn to suit the location.

Alexander's dream of Homer provides a different version of the founding of Alexandria than the instructions he received from Amun when he visited the Siwah oasis. But alternative versions of the foundation should not be thought of as mutually exclusive so much as mutually reinforcing – each serves a particular purpose in locating the new city within existing Greek and/or Egyptian culture at the same time that it delineates the city's uniqueness. Alexandrians cannot boast of autochthony but they can lay claim to a land with ancient Greek connections. In addition to the story of Alexander's dream of Homer, prior Homeric myth allows the new city to be inscribed into the oldest and most venerable of Greek stories, that of the Trojan War. Useful for this purpose are figures such as Helen and Menelaus and Proteus, who are connected with Egypt as early as the *Odyssey* (el-Abbadi 2004).

The Egyptian town of Canopus, lying to the east of Alexandria, was according to Stephen of Byzantium named for the helmsman of Menelaus, who died there. Apollonius wrote a choliambic poem on the subject, from which only two scant fragments have survived. A scholium to Nicander tells us that in Apollonius' poem Canopus fell asleep on the shore, was bitten by a poisonous snake, and died (Powell 1925: 4–5; Krevans 2000: 76–8). Somewhat later, pseudo-Eratosthenes lists Canopus among those turned into stars (*Catasterisms* fr. 37), and according to Conon, a court astronomer under Ptolemy II, Proteus' daughter Theonoe was in love with him, and when he died of snakebite, Menelaus and Helen buried him locally (*FGrH* 26 F 1 VIII). Although their origin is now impossible to determine, these stories featuring Canopus provide clear examples of how one seemingly obscure Greek myth might come to assume regional prominence.

Helen and Menelaus are also important figures in the mythology of Alexandria. In the *Odyssey,* Menelaus tells Telemachus how he was blown off course on his return from Troy (now in possession of his erring spouse) and stranded in Egypt, but the version attributed to Stesichorus, recounted in Herodotus' *Histories* (2.112–20), and the basis of Euripides' tragedy *Helen*, seems to have been preferred by local poets. In the passage from Callimachus quoted below, "Helen's island" can only allude to her sojourn in Egypt, and to the version of her story in which she remains the faithful wife. In this version Egypt can claim to be the land that preserved her virtue. In *Idyll* 18, Theocritus gives us an epithalamium for Helen and Menelaus, and Callimachus associates her with Arsinoe II in his now fragmentary poem on Arsinoe's deification (fr. 383 Pf.). Both poets emphasize Helen's quasi-divine status, and like Alexander she comes to function as a local hero.

Proteus is a central actor in the story of Menelaus and Helen in Egypt. In the *Odyssey* Proteus is "the old man in the sea" and a seer, tending his seals on the Pharos (4.351–570), but in Euripides' *Helen* he becomes an Egyptian king, noted for his wisdom, who guards Helen until Menelaus can claim her. The most explicit (in a manner of speaking) Hellenistic version is found in Lycophron's *Alexandra*. Here Proteus rescues Helen from Paris, her abductor, and we learn that Proteus had married a nymph in Thrace, Pallene, but overcome by the lawlessness of the place returned to Egypt via an underground river (111–29; Sens in this volume). Thus for Lycophron's Proteus too, Egypt is a space of moral integrity.

Callimachus depends on these mythologies in the opening of his elegy for Berenice's chariot victory at the Nemean games to create the link between Greece and Egypt (*SH* 254.1–6):

Ζηνί τε καὶ Νεμέηι τι χαρίϲιον ἕδνον ὀφείλω,
 νύμφα, κα[ϲιγνή]των ἱερὸν αἷμα θεῶν,
ἡμ[ε]τερο.[......]. εων ἐπινίκιον ἵππω[ν.
 ἀρμοῖ γὰρ ⌊Δαναοῦ γ⌋ῆϲ ἀπὸ βουγενέοϲ
εἰϲ Ἑλένη[ϲ νηϲῖδ]α καὶ εἰϲ Παλληνέα μά[ντιν,
 ποιμένα [φωκάων], χρύϲεον ἦλθεν ἔποϲ.

To Zeus and Nemea I owe a debt of gratitude, bride, holy blood of the Sibling Gods, in the form of a victory song for your . . . horses, because recently a gilded tale has come from the land of cow-born Danaus to Helen's island and to the Pallenean prophet, shepherd of seals.

Via "Helen's island" (Pharos) and the "Pallenean prophet" (Proteus) Callimachus provides a Greek pedigree for the Egyptian space, while Greece is redefined as "the land of cow-born Danaus," that is, in terms of Egypt. Danaus, like Alexander in the *Alexander Romance,* is Greco-Egyptian. His ancestor was Io, the Argive girl who was turned into a cow by her lover, Zeus, to keep Hera from detecting the affair. Hera then drove her in her cow form to wander the earth until she arrived in Egypt where she bore Zeus' son, Epaphus ("Touching"). In the *Prometheus Bound* (846–55)

Prometheus informs Io about the end of her wandering and her destiny as mother of nations:

> There is a city, Canopus, at the end of the earth, by the very mouth and outpouring of the Nile. There Zeus will make you sound, touching you with a touch that does not cause fear... You will give birth to dark-skinned Epaphus, whose name recalls his begetting by Zeus. He will reap the fruit of all the land the broad-flowing Nile inundates, and in five generations his descendants, fifty female children, will return to Argos, against their will, fleeing a marriage with their cousins.

Epaphus' descendants in the fourth generation were the brothers Danaus and Aegyptus, eponymous ancestors to the Greeks (Danaans) and Egyptians respectively. Alexandria and its landscape by means of reciprocal Greek and Egyptian tales (Pharos, Canopus) is linked to a distant Greek past, and endowed with heroes who, if not the founders, are long established in the place and complement the myths of Alexander. It is important to note that both sets of myths – those related to Alexander and those derived from earlier Greek literature – emphasize that the city is both Greek and Egyptian. Mythologically speaking, the two cultures are no longer defined as polar opposites, as they are in Herodotus. They are now related by blood.

FURTHER READING

Although written almost forty years ago, Fraser's *Ptolemaic Alexandria* (1972) remains the most helpful source on the subject. More recent studies have challenged many of his assertions, but the encyclopedic quality of the notes alone make it indispensable, and virtually all subsequent work is dependent on him. Two more recent essay collections worth consulting are *Alexandria and Alexandrianism* 1996 and Harris and Ruffini 2004. Scheidel in the latter sets out desiderata for a better historical understanding of the city. The Library has generated a considerable literature: Bagnall 2002: 348 has a useful bibliography. McKenzie 2007 provides the most up-to-date archaeological reconstruction of the ancient city with a full bibliography. Our understanding of the Egyptian presence under the early Ptolemies continues to grow; see Lloyd 2002 and Baines 2004. For the relationship of Alexandrian poetry to the Ptolemies see Weber 1993, Stephens 2003, Strootman in this volume, and specifically on Posidippus of Pella, Stephens 2004 and Bing 2005, Fantuzzi 2005, and Thompson 2005.

CHAPTER FIVE

Education

Jessica Wissmann

There are two ways in which literature and education converge. Literature, especially poetry, was an important part of education and schooling. The numerous school texts from Hellenized Egypt that survive thanks to the arid climate contain a substantial amount of poetry and some prose. Those from the Hellenistic period are especially important in that they constitute the earliest extensive evidence concerning the use of literature in education. Literature and education also converge in the many references to education found in Hellenistic literature, especially poetry, which reflect an increased interest in everyday life in general and the practice of education in particular.

Poetry was used in ancient schools to teach reading and writing, but also because knowledge of poetry was a staple of education. In the first half of this chapter I will examine what texts were selected and how they were used. Cribiore (1996, 2001a) and Morgan (1998a) have discussed literate education in the Greco-Roman world extensively. Here, the focus will be on school texts from the third to first centuries BCE. In this period, education became more formalized and institutionalized than before; and even though, by and large, schools in the Roman Empire well into the Byzantine period followed the patterns laid out in the Hellenistic era, there are some differences between Hellenistic and schools of subsequent centuries in their dealings with literature. A short discussion of the afterlife of Hellenistic poetry in classrooms of the Roman and Byzantine periods will conclude the examination of school texts.

The second half of the chapter will deal with what we can learn about education in the Hellenistic period from the literature of that time. Although many theoretical treatises and practical manuals were written about the topic, unfortunately none have survived, and there is little one can say about them based on only a few titles, even fewer fragments, and their use by later writers. We do, however, have surprisingly many Hellenistic poems (as well as some prose texts) that touch upon education. This topic has not yet been studied systematically, perhaps because education was seen as an everyday activity like all the others depicted in poetry of that time. It is, however, of special importance because education is immediately relevant to the production and reception of literature. The poets' interest in education mirrors an increased practical concern with the subject, and their works in many ways complement the evidence of the school texts.

Literature Used in Education: School Texts

Stories have always been part of education. Mothers and nurses tell stories to little children (Pl. *Rep.* 377c); in school, the poetic praise of "good men of old" was supposed to set an example for students to emulate (Pl. *Prot.* 325c–326a). It is this latter use of stories that the school texts from Hellenistic Egypt can illuminate, providing – like other evidence from Egypt concerning education – "a window on the vast panorama of educational practices around the Mediterranean" (Cribiore 2001a: 1–2). More than 400 school texts from Greco-Roman Egypt have been collected by Cribiore (1996) based on criteria such as writing material, handwriting, signs facilitating the reading of continuous writing, and content. In addition to these texts, there are numerous papyri, ostraca, and writing tablets that do not show the typical signs of school exercises, yet may have been used in school, for example, for studying an author at a more advanced level. As certainty is impossible, our picture of what was read in ancient classrooms is by no means complete.

Still, it is worthwhile to examine which authors pupils in Hellenistic Egypt encountered. Dramatic texts are represented in 13 of the 33 extant school exercises from the third to first centuries BCE that contain literary texts, yielding 28 fragments. Of these, nine fragments, found in five exercises, are from comedies, mostly *adespota*; of the tragedians, Euripides is represented with 17 passages in 10 exercises, Aeschylus with two fragments; Sophocles is absent. Euripides outdoes Homer, who is represented with nine passages in eight exercises. This is surprising: within the corpus of ancient school texts as a whole Homer easily surpasses any other author (Cribiore 1997, 2001a: 195–7; Morgan 1998a: 104–9). The distribution of the Homeric passages also holds a little surprise: five are from the *Iliad*, four (in three school texts) are from the *Odyssey.* Even though such a mere handful of texts does not warrant any definite conclusions, this ratio is quite different from that in the school texts of the Roman and Byzantine periods, where passages from the *Iliad* outnumber those from the *Odyssey* by a significant degree. The four passages from the *Odyssey* were taken from books 5, 11, 18, and 21; the books of the *Iliad* represented are 1, 5, 6, 10, and 18, a wider range of books than in school texts from subsequent centuries. Because so few Hellenistic school texts have survived, we cannot be certain, but these facts may well indicate a greater diversity of reading in the Hellenistic period, preceding a stricter canonization. There are also other indicators of more varied reading than in subsequent times. Hellenistic school texts contain passages from Archaic poets: Hesiod, Hipponax, Sappho, and Theognis; Hesiod alone appears in later school texts, and even he only once. They also contain Hellenistic, i.e. "contemporary" poets, such as Antimachus, Menander, Leonidas, Philemon, and (probably) Posidippus. School teachers of later centuries seem to have no interest in Hellenistic authors (with the exception of Menander), let alone writers of their own time.

The diversity of the attested readings makes it difficult to detect the criteria behind the selection of certain genres, authors, and passages. But an attempt to find such criteria is by no means hopeless, because the type of exercise can help determine its purpose and thus the criteria for the choice of texts. Two of the Hellenistic school texts that contain literature (Cribiore 1996 [henceforward Cr]: no. 129, 130) are writing exercises, intended solely for improving the student's handwriting (Cribiore 1996: 43–5). It is probably not a coincidence that both contain the opening line of a play by Euripides (*Bacchae* 1 and *Phoenissae* 3, the original beginning). It is easy to imagine a school teacher giving his student a line to copy that he himself easily remembered (for the *Bacchae* as a popular school text, see Cribiore 2001b).

Soon thereafter the student would be confronted with the first coherent pieces of poetry (Cribiore 1996: 46–7). Of the extant "short passages" (as Cribiore calls them), three were copied by a younger student (Cr 177, 178, 180). One of these reproduces *Iliad* 6.147–9, part of the simile where Glaucus compares the short life-cycle of humans to that of leaves. This image, frequently reworked in later poetry (e.g., Simonides *IEG* 19), was clearly selected for the lesson it contained (Cribiore 1994). The other two texts are epigrams, a genre not frequently found among the ancient school texts overall. One illustrates Spartan virtue in the form of an anecdote about a lame Spartan soldier who stands his ground (Cr 178, with 179 = *SH* 971). The competition of numerous cities to be Homer's birthplace is the topic of the other (Cr 177 = *SH* 973), which "solves" the issue by proclaiming the *Odyssey* Homer's "fatherland." Based on such admittedly lacunose evidence, one might say that the "minimal cultural package" (Cribiore 2001a: 178) already included two major icons of Greekness: Homer and Sparta (Wissmann 2002: 218–22). Sparta was, of course, not so much the political entity but the *idea* of Sparta, with an educational system that fostered typical Spartan virtues. The veneration of Homer, and his use in education, goes back at least to the Classical era; obviously a poem about Homer as *the* Greek poet instilled a long-lasting reverence for the poet in the young pupil's mind, especially if such texts were also memorized, as was likely the case.

Copying and memorizing went on for years in a student's life, the passages becoming longer over time. Although the exercises which Cribiore classifies as "long passages" cannot easily be assigned to a particular level (1996: 47–9), it is clear that these texts were not primarily used to improve the student's reading and writing skills but were studied for their content under the guidance of a grammarian. It is here that a search for selection criteria can yield the best results. Because not all texts of this type can be examined within the confines of this chapter, I will focus on three illustrative collections of texts: two sets of ostraca or papyri, each written by the same individual, and a teacher's textbook. I will be referring to these collections as "anthologies," understood in the broadest possible sense. Even though not all texts of these sets can be subsumed under a single category, each set shows a clear tendency towards certain types of texts: moralizing content, interest in literature and culture, and language seem to have been the prevalent criteria for the selections made.

Anthology (1): Moralizing

Gnōmai, or maxims, were regarded as an especially suitable tool for conveying moral lessons about life: they are short statements of a generality that makes it difficult to question their truthfulness and authority. It is hardly surprising, then, that they were extensively collected and used in school (see Morgan 1998a: 120–51, on the importance of such collections and the range of topics covered). The first set, a series of ostraca (Cr 234–6) in the hand of either a teacher or an advanced student, is a good example of this tendency: they abound with *gnōmai*, but also contain shorter passages from poetry that were probably also supposed to contribute to the moral development of the students. On the ostracon Cr 234, which contains 11 extracts, the first five are probably from comic poets (*PCG* 1 F 248 [(Ps.) Epicharmus, two passages] and 8 F*1029–31); the subjects illustrated are good sense, the dangers of pleasure, the true value of a man, learning, justice. More gnomic statements follow: "the strong arm does not withstand battle any better than the weak" (Eur. *El.* 388–9); "not even Zeus can please everyone, neither when he lets it rain nor when he withholds it" (Thgn. 25–6). But then the sequence of *gnōmai* is interrupted by the beginning of a speech from the *Odyssey* – Antinous scolding the beggar Irus, 18.79–80, lines which may have been taken as paraenetic. And after Hesiod's gnomic insight that "it is easy to seize baseness in quantity" (*WD* 287), another quotation from Euripides again does not fit the category of maxims but certainly embodies a moral (Hecuba scolds orators for playing along with the mob, *Hec.* 254–6). The last two passages are again decidedly gnomic (the authors are not known): the student learned that "stupidity is not a good excuse" and, as part of a prose-story about a man and pigs, that everything is relative.

The other two ostraca in the series show the same mixture of gnomic and non-gnomic passages, with the *gnōmai* setting the heavily moralizing tone. One ostracon contains a few lines from Theognis (434–8) in an order that follows Plato's *Meno* (95e), and a short comic fragment addressed to someone who was only concerned about his own safety and abandoned others (*PCG* 8 F 1049). The third ostracon contains a tragic maxim about excellence to be displayed also in death by a man who has stumbled (Eur. *Aegeus TrGF* 5 F 11), a maxim of Socrates about not living in order to eat but eating in order to live (turned into a *chreia*), and finally a list, culled from a comedy, of character-flaws such as rashness, heedlessness, thoughtlessness, "and countless other such traits" (*PCG* 8 F*1050). The editor of these two ostraca, arguing from, among other things, the fact that one reproduces Plato's order of the lines from Theognis, which does not quite make sense outside its Platonic context, surmised that a student had been given the assignment to read through various writings and collect sayings and quotations about virtues and vices (Viereck 1925: 257). Whether it was a student who gathered these lines or a teacher who handed them to a student for copying, it was the teacher who set the criteria for the selection of texts. The extracts show a deeply moralistic slant, covering many areas of life. Not many of them would have been applicable to the life of a young student yet; but the character-flaws on the list are typically attributed to youths. All in all, the selection of texts on these ostraca represents the purest form of a "utilitarian" reading of poetry not for its own merits but for the lessons to be taken from it.

Anthology (2): Literature and Culture

The second set of texts (Cr 244–6) has much less of a moralizing character and is more "literary" in nature. The passages were copied by a certain Apollonius, about whom we know more than we do about most students in ancient Egypt (Thompson 1988: 212–65). His brother was confined to the Serapeum in Memphis, where young Apollonius temporarily joined him. It is not quite clear whether the texts Apollonius copied were part of a school exercise (he may have attended school in the Serapeum; Thompson 1988: 245) or copies he made independently (Cribiore 2001a: 188–9); but even if he just copied them for his own use, they certainly reflect a practice typical of the ancient school: making excerpts. To some degree, they may also reflect a literary taste shaped in school. Of the four passages Apollonius copied on Cr 244 and 246, two are narrative speeches, from Euripides' *Medea* (5–12) and *Telephus* (*TrGF* 5 F 696 = *GLP* 17). As parts of prologues, both passages provide the necessary background information to the plot in a nutshell, supplying a conveniently epitomized version of the relevant myth. The same is true of the third tragic excerpt, from Aeschylus' *Carians*: Europa narrates the story of her abduction by Zeus and the birth of his sons (*TrGF* 3 F**99). Also from a prologue, a comic one this time, is a fragment in which a young man describes how he was "reborn" after joining a philosopher's school in Athens (*PCG* 8 F 1001; attributed to Menander by Koerte 1.145b = *GLP* 53). So was Apollonius or whoever selected these passages specifically excerpting dramatic prologues? And if so, why?

Another text on Cr 244 may help here: Apollonius also copied a comic passage (falsely attributed to Euripides) that had been written by a different hand on the other side of the same papyrus (*PCG* 8 F 1000). In this passage, which clearly does not come from a prologue, a young woman complains to her father about his plans to separate her from her present husband and marry her off to another man. Only with difficulty could Apollonius have copied the passage from the other side of the same papyrus. More likely, he learned it by heart and then wrote it down from memory (Thompson 1988: 259–60), a common procedure in the memorization of poetry within a school context (Cribiore 2001a: 213). It would appear, then, that Apollonius was memorizing dramatic passages. Longer narrative *rhēseis* were more suitable for memorization than dialogue, and as prologues usually take this form, they were an obvious choice. As the collection of texts in Cr 244 has a header – probably "Lessons of Aristo, the philosopher" – Apollonius possibly followed the instructions of a teacher.

This does not, however, exclude more personal selection criteria (either of the teacher or of Apollonius himself). The dramatic excerpts display an atmosphere of turmoil, illustrate the difficulties of living in a foreign country, or have a religious dimension that has affinity with life in the Serapeum (Thompson 1988: 260–1). The co-existence of Egyptian and Greek culture was probably very keenly felt by Apollonius, who shared his life in the temple with Egyptian detainees, in a bilingual and bicultural environment (Thompson 1988: 261–5). Apollonius' daily contact with Egyptians and their culture, probably combined with a personal interest in dreams (his brother, Ptolemaeus, apparently wrote down some dreams he had; Thompson 1988: 259) may have been the reason why Apollonius became interested in, and made a copy of, "Nectanebo's Dream," a tale about the last native pharaoh (Cr 245; Dieleman and Moyer in this volume).

Apollonius' interest in Egyptian culture does not correspond to the overall picture one gets from the school texts (Cribiore 2001a: 179–80). Even in the case of those few that contain Egyptian material, the primary interest appears not to have been in the different culture, but, as in the anthology discussed in the previous section, in moral lessons in the form of gnomic sayings and injunctions. One school text, an ostracon, contains a Greek version of the Egyptian "Commandments of Amenotes" (Cr 239, perhaps a teacher's model; for the text see Totti 1985: no. 46). These commandments are combined with other maxims, among them three that also form part of a collection of maxims that Stobaeus attributes to Sosiades, who apparently collected them from the inscriptions at Delphi (Stob. 3.1.173). They were so popular that they were also collected by philosophers and copied on stones found as far away as Afghanistan (Oikonomides 1980: 179–81). They were an obvious choice for use in school, as is indicated also by the fact that some of the same maxims recur in another school text, written in a beginner's hand (Cr 238). Their very brief injunctions – "follow the god," "save time," "respect your parents" – would have been especially suitable for teaching young pupils, offering short phrases for letter practice and moral guidance in one.

This is about as far as the interest in Egyptian culture went. In fact, even "Nectanebo's Dream" was clearly adapted for a Greek audience (Koenen 1985: 172), and Greek interest in the tale may have had a lot to do with one of the Greeks' own cultural heroes: Nectanebo plays a major role in the first 15 chapters of the *Alexander Romance*, where he is said to have been Alexander's real father (Stoneman 1991: 16–7; Whitmarsh, Dieleman and Moyer in this volume). Alexander himself figures prominently in another school papyrus (Cr 380, probably written by a teacher), the second half of which offers a list of famous men, the Seven Wonders, largest islands, highest mountains, rivers and springs – the sort of facts an educated Greek ought to know. The text about Alexander himself is a dialogue with the Gymnosophists, the "naked philosophers" of India. Versions of this conversation recur in the *Alexander Romance* (3.5–6, where the Gymnosophists act as one body) and Plutarch's *Life of Alexander* (64). It is a competition of cleverness: Alexander asks subtle questions, such as whether the dead or the living are more numerous, and the Gymnosophists offer their answers. Considering the lack of practical relevance of the questions and answers, one may wonder why this specific text was used in school. The question-and-answer format was popular in school, as is clear from the so-called *Erōtēmata* in later papyri, which contain entries such as "Who was the father of Hector?" (Cr 405–6; Cribiore 2001a: 208–9). In the dialogue with the Gymnosophists, however, the questions and answers are not anonymous but asked by Alexander and answered by the ring-leaders behind a rebellion against him. The Gymnosophists' answers are judged to be poor and unhelpful, proving their intellectual inferiority to the king, who comes out as an icon of Greekness. Texts about Alexander seem to have remained a staple of the curriculum well into the Roman era (Cr 347–50).

Heracles is the other Greek hero whose importance is reflected in the school texts. One advanced student in the second century BCE copied or composed a narrative of Heracles' labors (Cr 344). The text is a paraphrase, perhaps of a drama or an epic poem; on a purely technical level it shows that paraphrasing, a frequent exercise in the rhetorical training of later times, was already practiced in the Hellenistic era (similarly

Cr 345, a combination of lines from the *Iliad* and summaries of events in books 18 and 19). Heracles as a subject was an obvious choice, for the Ptolemies traced their descent back to him (Fraser 1972: 1.202–3; Koenen 1993: 44–6; Huttner 1997: 124–45). Dionysus was another putative ancestor (Fraser 1972: 1.201–7), and he too appears in the school texts: a papyrus from the second or first century BCE contains the first 23 lines of the first *Homeric Hymn to Dionysus* (Cr 251).

Anthology (3): Language

One of the most informative extant school texts is a teacher's textbook from the third century BCE (Cr 379, in the *editio princeps* erroneously thought to be a student's book). Even in its damaged state (the upper part of the papyrus roll has broken off and a considerable amount of text is lost), this book clearly reflects a curriculum of education, predominantly literate. It starts out with very basic exercises (a syllabary, a list of Macedonian months, a series of numbers, a list of monosyllables, one of names of divinities, another of polysyllabic nouns), then moves on to literary texts, and concludes with some mathematical exercises.

The literary texts show an astonishing variety. The first two are moralizing speeches from Euripides on the dangers of ambition and arrogance (*Phoen.* 529–34; *Ino TrGF* 5 F 420). Like the preceding exercises, they have been facilitated for beginning readers by dividing the words into syllables. One of the main obstacles in learning to read was that texts were written in *scriptio continua*, i.e. without any spaces between words. Beginners were therefore trained to identify syllables and words with the help of lectional signs (Cribiore 2001a: 174–5). It cannot be ruled out that the two passages also served as models for copying in a writing exercise, and their moralizing content was also appropriate to an educational context; but their principal use appears to have been that of a primer for reading. Apparently writing, in the strict sense of copying, and reading were taught independently (Cribiore 2001a: 176–8).

The next passage, under the heading "Epic Poetry," consists of a few lines from *Odyssey* 5. As the lectional signs are no longer used, the reading of a text is taken to a more advanced level. The choice of this passage is surprising: it is the beginning of Calypso's complaint that Hermes and the other gods begrudge her relationship with Odysseus (116–24). It cannot possibly have been regarded as very edifying; perhaps its interest lay in the story of Orion, coveted by Dawn as Calypso covets Odysseus. However, the excerpt probably continued beyond this exemplum at the missing top of the next column of the papyrus, and the rationale for its inclusion remains ultimately unclear.

The selection criterion for the remaining texts seems more obvious: the distinctive feature of these texts, two epigrams and three passages from comic poets, is that they abound in difficult words. This makes perfect sense if the book was a primer for reading – there was a tendency in antiquity to give exercises of greater difficulty than was actually necessary. Syllabaries, for example, contain almost unpronounceable and sometimes nonsensical words, so-called *chalinoi*, the most notorious being *knaxkhbi* (Cribiore 2001a: 166). So in school the student encountered words he would hardly use in everyday life. Not all the texts in the teacher's handbook show the same density of unusual words. Of the two epigrams (*SH* 978–9 = *FGE* anon. 151a/b = *GLP* 105a/b), the first (perhaps by Posidippus: *113 AB) is over-fraught with the technical vocabulary of architecture; the remnants of the second, however, are a simple dedication of a building to Homer (further discussed below). Perhaps the teacher copied the two poems from a collection of epigrams on buildings: the first of the pair drew his interest on account of its vocabulary, the second, which might have followed in the collection, was included because it praised the cultural icon Homer and reflected the Ptolemies' interest in education.

An interest in unusual words possibly also is behind the choice of the three comic fragments, all monologues of cooks (*PCG* 8 F 1072; 1073 = *GLP* 59; Strato *Phoenissae* 1 *PCG* 7 = *GLP* 57). Cooks who used elaborate culinary vocabulary and boasted about their art in great detail were stock-characters in Middle and New Comedy (Nesselrath 1990: 298–309). Of the first passage only a few lines survive, which contain some technical terms for the preparation of food. The second passage is almost like a catalogue of culinary jargon and types of food and spices. In the third passage, preserved also in Athenaeus (9.382c), the cook is so educated that he uses Homeric words in inquiring about the details of the meal to be prepared. His employer is at a complete loss and complains that one would need the "books of Philitas," who wrote a glossary of obscure words, to understand what the man is talking about. Clearly, "difficult words," especially Homeric glosses, are what this passage is all about. The memorization of Homeric vocabulary had already been part of teaching Homer for a long time (in Aristophanes' *Banqueters*, for example, a father quizzes his son on it, *PCG* 3.2 F 233), and the great number of Homeric glossaries among the school texts from the Roman era testifies to its continued importance. This probably explains why the teacher used the comic passage replete with Homeric words in class.

Striking about the textbook as a whole is the large proportion of texts outside the "mainstream" which it contains. In general, Hellenistic school texts include a wider range of authors than school texts of subsequent centuries. It has been mentioned already that Hipponax, Sappho, and Theognis appear only in school texts from the Hellenistic era (Cr 234–5, 237, 247). Hesiod is included in one Hellenistic and only one later school text (Cr 234 and 386). Finally, two of the three school texts with Aeschylus are Hellenistic (Cr 244, 250), and the later example (Cr 277) is uncertain, reflecting perhaps a line from Euripides' *Hypsipyle* (*TrGF* 5.2 F 757, verse 891) rather than Aeschylus' *Persians* (483). The presence of these authors in Hellenistic school texts may reflect the academic interest Alexandrian scholars took in the poets of old (Cribiore 2001a: 202). But antiquarian interest cannot have been the sole principle governing the selection of texts, for Hellenistic school texts also contain more Hellenistic poetry than later school texts.

The Reception of Hellenistic Poetry in School Texts

The textbook just discussed (Cr 379) is extraordinary in that at least three and possibly even five of its eight reading passages are Hellenistic. It is perhaps no coincidence that two of these texts are epigrams. In addition to these, there are the three epigrams mentioned above used as writing exercises (Cr 177, 178/9). Another school text (Cr 243 = *SH* 976) contains only the beginnings of a number of epigrams, two of them by Leonidas (25, 46 GP = *AP* 9.322, 6.13). Apparently epigrams were considered particularly suitable for use in school: they were short and easy to memorize, usually not too difficult to understand (the epigram *SH* 978 on Cr 379 with its technical vocabulary is an exception), frequently about everyday life, and oftentimes funny and entertaining. Strangely, they disappear almost entirely from school papyri after the Hellenistic period. One possible reason is that as the fifth and fourth centuries were increasingly regarded as the "glory days" of Greek culture, the school canon narrowed. Genres and authors without "classical" status, regardless of their pedagogical expedience, disappeared from the curriculum (Wissmann 2002: 228–9).

Much of what makes epigrams suitable for educational purposes also holds for comic passages, especially those taken from New Comedy. It is difficult to identify such passages – many of which are *adespota* – as Hellenistic or sometimes even as comic. Still, some observations can be made. About half of the comic fragments used in school are found in texts from the Hellenistic period; the other half, in texts from the Roman period. In mere numbers, there is no indication that the interest in comic poets decreased. But what has changed in the Roman period is the mode of reading. If one looks more carefully at the reception of the most popular Hellenistic comic poet, Menander, in the Roman school texts, it turns out that he was mainly used as a quarry for moralizing statements (Cribiore 2001a: 199–201). One always has to take into account the possibility that texts were used in school that do not show the typical characteristics of school texts, especially at a higher level of education (Cribiore 2001a: 138), and so entire plays of Menander may very well have been studied. The fact that the prologue of the *Misoumenos* appears in one school text of the Roman era suggests this possibility (Cr 290 = *CGFP* 147). Nonetheless, whereas Hellenistic school texts include passages of various lengths from a range of comic authors, the vast majority of comic extracts in later school texts are maxims taken from Menander's plays or attributed to him, the so-called *Monostichoi*. This kind of "instructional reading" also included misogynist statements, as on the two ostraca Cr 267–8 (*PCG* 8 F 1047–8).

In the case of three pieces of Hellenistic literature their use in school at first sight seems puzzling. Yet it is possible to identify selection criteria similar to those established above, for example an interest in "difficult" words. A glossary, written on an ostracon by a teacher or advanced student in the third century BCE, quotes a passage from Antimachus' *Lyde* for its use of the noun *souson* (Cr 237 = fr. 68 Matthews 1996), as it happens mistakenly (the word which Antimachus actually wrote, and knew from *Od.* 21.390, must have been *ouson*). Several passages from Callimachus' *Hecale* appear on a writing tablet from the fourth to fifth century CE (Cr 303 = *SH* 288 = frs. 69, 70, 73, 74.14–28 Hollis 2009). These fragments describe the great moment when Theseus has finally subdued the bull and also include the tale of the crow that is part of the Cecrops myth and the story about Apollo's raven. The copying of these lines is probably to be explained from a strong "historical" interest in the heroes of the Athenian past, observable also throughout ancient rhetorical instruction (Cribiore 2001a: 231–8). A similar interest in history may explain why a student in the first century CE transcribed an elegy, possibly of Posidippus (118 AB = Cr 381 = *SH* 705 = *GLP* 114). The perspective of an old man taken in this poem is not exactly tailored to the interests of young students, but perhaps this was seen as less important than the fact that both (Egyptian) Thebes and Pella in Macedonia are mentioned. Even more importantly, if this poem was indeed a *sphragis* or "poetic seal" (Lloyd-Jones 1963), its prominent position within a collection may have been the reason for using it in school.

Education as Reflected in Hellenistic Poetry

The Hellenistic period not only provides substantial evidence of actual school texts; education also became a pervasive topic in literature. Philosophers (Plato, Aristotle, not to mention the sophists) had long theorized about education, and they continued to do so. We know of numerous works by Hellenistic philosophers about education, for example from the lists of works in the *Lives* of Diogenes Laertius, but only small fragments survive. The Stoics had a special interest in the subject (Inwood and Donini 1999: 705–14), as, in his own way, had Epicurus, who seems to have rejected the standard approach to education (the *enkyklios paideia*; Asmis 2001). In Hellenistic poetry, however, very many aspects of education are represented, providing almost enough material to sketch instruction from early childhood to higher education. Often, especially in the case of Herodas, the descriptions are exaggerated and humorous. Consequently, this material is to be used with caution, that is, not as "hard evidence." The discussion of references to education in poetry and in Theophrastus' *Characters* in the next few pages is not intended as a substitute for a comprehensive account of education in the Hellenistic period, but rather to show how important a position education had in Hellenistic poetry and culture.

Educators

If we are to believe the epigrammatists, "children are trouble; but a childless life is a crippled one" (Posidippus *133 AB = 22 GP = *AP* 9.359; cf. Metrodorus *AP* 9.360 = *FGE* 1). If a child died young, both the toil and the pleasure vanished with the deceased (Antipat. Sid. 54 GP = *AP* 7.467). Not just the parents, the nurse too played a major, and lasting, role in a child's life: Callimachus has a grateful Mikkos not only look after his old Phrygian nurse her entire life but also set up a tombstone for her after her death (*ep.* 50 Pf. = 49 GP = *AP* 7.458; cf. Theoc. *ep.* 20 Gow 1952b = 11 GP = *AP* 7.663). A *paidagōgos* frequently accompanies the young man, sometimes even into battle, as in Menander's *Aspis* (14). The central control, however, remained with the parents, who also had expectations of their children – different ones for boys and girls. To his young daughter, a dying father gives the useful advice to stick to the spindle and emulate her mother's virtue so that she might be of value to her future husband (Antipat. Thess. *AP* 9.96). A mother would expect support from her son in old age, as Metrotime does from her son Kottalos in Herodas' *Schoolmaster*, although there is little hope this young good-for-nothing will ever fulfill her expectations (*Mimi.* 3.29; on education as an "investment," see Cribiore 2001a: 107–8).

Unable to cope with Kottalos, Metrotime seeks the help of the teacher. The young lad's father is apparently too old to hold him in check (32), so that the neighbors have started complaining about his acts of vandalism (47–8). At the mother's request, the teacher must now wield the whip of authority. Corporal punishment was not unusual (Cribiore 2001a: 65–73), and Herodas' teacher does not hesitate to administer it. The instruments typically used for this – a stick and a shoe – are among the tools of his trade that a retired teacher dedicates to Hermes in an epigram by Phanias (2 GP = *AP* 6.294). According to the Cynic philosopher Teles, a young individual is continuously vexed by his educators, namely his *paidagōgos*, his teachers of physical and musical education, of grammar and painting, of mathematics, of geometry, and of horseback riding; and when he is older, he is beaten and controlled by his instructors in physical education and fighting with weapons, even by the official who is in charge of the gymnasium (Teles fr. 5, pp. 49–50 Hense).

Teachers were not necessarily regarded with respect. Elementary teachers in particular had a low social standing. In literature they are regularly pitied for their profession, and it was an insult to call someone a "teacher of letters" (*grammatodidaskalos*; Cribiore 2001a: 59–65). Aratus laments the fate of the poet Diotimus, who has to teach the children of the Gargarians "the alpha and beta" (2 GP = *AP* 11.437). In *Iamb* 5, Callimachus mocks a school teacher, likewise teaching "alpha beta" (3), pointing out that his pederastic inclinations may get him into trouble some day. Parents, on the other hand, would express their lack of respect most effectively by not paying the teacher: in Herodas, Kottalos' mother complains about the fee (3.9–10); Theophrastus tells us that a greedy man typically would deduct a percentage from the teacher's fees if his sons missed classes due to illness, and not even send his children to school in months with many holidays (*Char.* 30.14). Lampriskos, the teacher in Herodas' mime, at first appears to be a figure of authority, for, after all, the exasperated mother turns to him for help in disciplining her son; but in the end, she is convinced that he has been too lenient with Kottalos, so much so that her old and largely incapacitated husband could deal with their son more successfully than the teacher (3.94–7).

Learning the Basics

Bad behavior is only one of Kottalos' problems; to the despair of his mother, he also neglects his studies. He habitually ditches classes and hardly ever uses the tablet his mother once a month laboriously coats with wax; instead, he plays dice all the time (3.8–22). As a result, he does not even know the most elementary things: like some nitwits in Callimachus' *Iamb* 1 (88), who had "learned not even the alpha," Kottalos "cannot even recognize an alpha syllable" (3.22–3). Kottalos is very far behind indeed. Syllabaries were among the very first reading-exercises students encountered

(Cribiore 2001a: 172–5), and in an epigram Asclepiades characterizes Eros as an infant by having him mispronounce written love-charms sitting beside his mother (23 GP = *AP* 12.162).

Kottalos' attempts at spelling names reflect another common teaching practice: lists of names figure in many of our school texts. When asked to spell the name "Maron" – a name that typically occurs in lists of names used in school (Rusten 1985) – Kottalos fails miserably, spelling "Simon" instead, the name of a throw of the dice.

An advanced level of writing skills occurs in an epigram of Asclepiades, the inscription for a comic mask which a boy has dedicated to the Muses as thanks for "winning the boys' contest" in calligraphy ("because he wrote beautiful letters"), carrying off a prize of 80 knucklebones, popular toys (27 GP = *AP* 6.308). A related epigram by Callimachus is spoken by a tragic mask of Dionysus that has been dedicated to the Muses by Simos, son of Mikkos, with a request for "easy learning" (48 Pf. = 26 GP = *AP* 6.310; quoted by Bruss in this volume). The mask's mouth "yawns twice as wide as the Dionysus of Samos." This playful allusion to the cult of Dionysus *Kechēnōs* ("with the open mouth") shows how tedious the study of poetry in classrooms often was: the mask has to listen to the boys incessantly reciting "my lock is holy," a line spoken by Dionysus in "his" tragedy, Euripides' *Bacchae* (494), which, as has been mentioned above, was a popular school text.

The dedication to the Muses also indicates how difficult memorizing poetry was felt to be; Herodas' Kottalos would certainly agree. His mother complains bitterly that when she or her husband ask him to recite a (dramatic) speech (*rhēsis*), as one would expect from a young man, all that trickles out are disjointed words – a feat even his grandmother could perform ("and she does not even know letters") or indeed "any passing Phrygian" (3.30–6). Kottalos is a hard, if probably not uncommon, case of a youngster's indolence. It is more astonishing to read of a grown-up, who has undergone the cumbersome process of memorizing poetry, refusing to display his *paideia*, as Theophrastus' "Antisocial Man," who "won't sing or recite a speech or dance" (*Char.* 15.10). Quite the opposite is another of Theophrastus' characters, the "Late Learner." He performs enthusiastically what is normally expected of a youngster, even if, at the age of sixty, he is no longer able to recall the passages he has so laboriously memorized when he tries to recite them at a drinking party (*Char.* 27.1–2).

Grammar and Higher Education

Although probably not as formalized as in later centuries, grammar was part of secondary education (when longer passages of poetry were read) already in the Hellenistic period (Cribiore 2001a: 210–15). But apparently not all agreed with this practice. According to Timon (*SH* 835), grammar is "no concern at all for someone who is being taught the Phoenician signs of Cadmus," i.e., writing and reading. Perhaps, as Sextus Empiricus, to whom we owe this quotation, understood it

(*Math.* 1.53), Timon considered the art of grammar totally useless. Alternatively, it could be a warning not to start with grammar too early.

Only a few disciplines of higher learning appear in Hellenistic poetry. We hear of professions such as a physiognomist or teacher of dancing (Theoc. *ep.* 11 Gow = 10 GP = *AP* 7.661; *FGE* anon. 171); perhaps poetic references to various disciplines reflect the higher learning practiced at the Alexandrian Museum (Weber 1993: 322). In addition to these, philosophers or philosophical schools are mentioned, typically to be ridiculed on grounds of their ostentatious appearance (e.g., *FGE* anon. 155).

More importantly, Hellenistic poetry reflects the intellectual climate of its time. What made Egypt an interesting place were, among other things, *palaistrai*, philosophers, and the Museum (Herod. 1.28–32; quoted in full by Stephens in this volume). Theocritus praises Ptolemy Philadelphus as a benefactor of poets (*Id.* 17.112–20) and as "friend of the Muses" (*philomousos*, *Id.* 14.61). Perhaps this is an allusion to the Museum, the most famous expression of the Ptolemies' interest in intellectual culture (Strootman and Stephens in this volume). Homer was given special attention, as the epigram in *SH* 979 attests; it is unclear, though, whether the Homereion that this epigram dedicates was a place of worship or included an institution of learning (as the remnants of a word beginning with *did-* in the text may indicate). The poem praises Ptolemy (probably Philopator) enthusiastically as "the best leader in both war and culture." Homeric scholarship, for which Alexandria was made famous by scholars such as Zenodotus and Aristarchus (Pfeiffer 1968: 87–279), is not only echoed by, for instance, a poem about a statue of the poet and scholar Philitas, set up at the order of the king in order to honor this "perfectionist" (Posidippus 63 AB). It even inspired a harsh and satirical tone. In an invective against the school of Aristarchus, Herodicus (*FGE* 1), perhaps a follower of the school of Crates at Pergamum, ridicules the Aristarcheans for focusing on linguistic matters. More explicit is an epigram ascribed to Crates (whether the scholar or another person by that name is unclear): using terminology and names that, understood at face value, are associated with Homeric scholarship, he in fact attacks the sexual practices of the librarian and poet Euphorion (Crates 1 GP = *AP* 11. 281).

The Gymnasium

It was not only the great centers of scholarship that stood for Greek culture and education. By the Hellenistic period, gymnasia, which had always been locations for the physical training of young male citizens, were a key feature of cities, old or newly (re)founded, throughout the Hellenic *oikoumenē* (Hesberg 1995: 14; Gauthier 1995). It is indicative of the increased status of gymnasia that it became a matter of great prestige to be a gymnasiarch or a benefactor to a gymnasium (Ameling 2004; Schuler 2004). The gymnasium served as a location for competitive athletics and cultural entertainment, but also as the central place for the intellectual and physical education of the ephebes (Delorme 1960; Scholz 2004a). Needless to say, such a public space provided much material for literary productions, oftentimes with a penchant for eccentric behavior. Theophrastus' portrait of the "Late Learner" – ludicrously competing with the *paidagōgos* of his sons in disciplines such as throwing the javelin and archery – also illustrates the typical elements of the ephebes' physical training in the gymnasium (*Char.* 27.3–4, 6, 13–14). These included athletic disciplines such as running and wrestling as well as military training, although this aspect apparently became less and less important (Burckhardt 2004). Success in athletic competitions not only brought about respectable insignia, such as a statue awarded to a victor in the boys' wrestling competition ("Simonides" *FGE* 30). It also paid off in terms of a man's sex-appeal, at least according to Herodas' Gyllis, who tries to persuade Metriche to begin an extra-marital affair with such a man (*Mimi.* 1.51–3). Even though athletics were practiced under the supervision of a *paidotribēs*, parents had some influence on the extent of the physical training: Theophrastus' "Absent-minded Man" forces his children to practice wrestling and running to utter exhaustion (*Char.* 14.10). For grown-ups, the gymnasium was a place to hang out and watch the ephebes exercising; an enthusiast might even have his own training arena (*Char.* 5.7, 9–10). Sometimes the motivation was to pass the time by talking endlessly to the instructors in the arena and to the teachers in schools, thus keeping the young from exercising or learning (*Char.* 7.4). The gymnasium was also the place for the sort of pederastic desires expressed in the Pseudo-Theocritean *Idyll* 23; how real a concern this was becomes clear, for example, from a Gymnasiarchal Law from Verroia in Macedonia that bans homosexuals from disrobing in the gymnasium (*SEG* 27.261 = Miller 2004: no. 185).

Closely connected with the ephebes' age of transition from boyhood to adulthood was Hermes, to whom a boy would dedicate the toys he no longer played with (Leon. Tar. 45 GP = *AP* 6.309). The god had his place in the gymnasium (see, e.g., the inventory of the gymnasium in Delos, *ID* 1417AI.118–54 = Miller 2004: no. 180), where he was worshipped either in a shrine or simply as a statue that, as in an epigram by Nicias, was crowned with flowers by the boys (7 GP = *AP* 16.188; cf. Xenocritus of Rhodes *FGE* 2). The worship of Hermes was often combined with that of Heracles, who represented physical training (Aneziri and Damaskos 2004: 248–51) but was also closely associated with moral and intellectual education.

Famous Students and Teachers

The education of famous individuals became a matter of great interest in the Hellenistic period. The historian Duris, for example, identified the flute teacher of Alcibiades. He also reported that Eumenes of Cardia received a traditional education and impressed King Philip with his skills in wrestling, and that the artist Lysippus of Sicyon, originally a coppersmith, did not learn his craft from a master but was self-taught (*FGrH* 76 F 29, 23, 53, 32). In the footsteps of Xenophon's *Cyropaedia*, entire treatises, now lost, were written on the education of kings: Onesicritus and Marsyas of Pella, for example, wrote on the education of Alexander, Lysimachus on that of Attalus I. But the notion of education was also used to ridicule famous individuals. Timon of Phlius makes fun of Plato by accusing him of plagiarism, alleging that the philosopher purchased a book (on Pythagorean doctrine), "for the desire of learning seized him," and from it "he was taught" to write the *Timaeus*

(*SH* 828). Even worse, Timon lampoons Epicurus' opposition to traditional education by pointing out that even though he was the son of a schoolmaster, he was the most uneducated individual (*SH* 825).

The interest in the education of prominent individuals was not restricted to humans: even Zeus was "educated" at some point (Dion. Scyt. *FGrH* 32 F 8). The most famous student, however, was Heracles, the hero who became a god and as such presented an exemplary model for Hellenistic kings (Huttner 1997). The two sides of this hero, violent brute and civilizing force, are mirrored in accounts of his youth and his education (Ambühl 2005: 54–8 and in this volume). Already Prodicus' Choice of Heracles, in which the hero is faced with the decision whether to take the path of laborious Virtue or that of pleasurable Vice, is an expression of these two sides of his nature (Xen. *Mem.* 2.1.26–34). An actual clash of these two sides is represented in fifth-century vase-paintings which show Heracles in the act of killing his music teacher, Linus (Beck 1975: pls. 4–6; Arnott 1996b: 404–6). The civilizing side is also unable to prevail, albeit with less violence involved, in Alexis' comedy *Linus*. Here, Linus asks his pupil to choose a book from his library to read. Heracles' character is revealed when he chooses, to the dismay of his teacher, not Orpheus, Hesiod, Choerilus, Homer, Epicharmus, or a tragedy, but a cookbook (*PCG* 2 F 140). Linus' sarcastic remark that Heracles is a "real philosopher" and Heracles' absolute concentration on his stomach underline the contrast between civilization and nature: the attempt to educate and thus civilize Heracles is thwarted by the young hero's gluttony.

As a child of exceptional strength, Heracles does not seem predestined to be a representative of refined intellectual education. Theocritus' *Idyll* 24, however, portrays both his family and the young hero himself as ordinary human beings (Ambühl in this volume). The poem includes a long catalogue of Heracles' teachers and their subjects, which creates the suggestion that the young man is to a large extent like any other ephebe training in a gymnasium, going through the typical exercises in archery, wrestling, boxing, pancration, and the use of weapons as well as some less typical ones, such as chariot-driving and commanding an army (103–33). Other subjects are lyre-playing and letters, the latter taught by Linus, as in Alexis. The results of this education are unclear, if only because the poem breaks off shortly after. What is clear is that Theocritus uses education in order to emphasize the "domestic" side of Heracles. Even more intriguing is the anachronism of a mythological hero learning letters. In this, Theocritus' depiction resembles that of Alexis, who gives the anachronism yet another twist in that Heracles himself would appear as a character in some of the poetry Linus recommends to him. On a somewhat less humorous note, in *Idyll* 13, Theocritus gives a more domesticated version of Heracles in portraying him not just as a "tame" educatee but also an educator himself: Heracles teaches his beloved, Hylas, "as a father teaches his son, everything he needs to learn to become as noble and renowned as himself" (8–9). This Heracles, an educator *par excellence*, corresponds to the Heracles worshiped in gymnasia all over the Hellenistic world. Another mention of his educating Hylas, in Apollonius' *Argonautica*, apparently makes fun of this notion. Apollonius' Hylas is sent out to fetch water in preparation for dinner, and we learn that "these were the habits in which Heracles had trained him" when he was a little boy (1.1211). This appears to be a very "domestic" education, but it is important that it is within the context of food: what Hylas has been taught is how to cater to his educator's appetite. Also, the word Apollonius uses for "training," *pherbō*, usually means "feed" or "nourish": in the otherwise civilized dinner scene the gluttonous side of Heracles shines through.

* * *

It is highly unlikely that anyone actually believed that a mythological character such as Heracles had a formal education that resembled the contemporary one in so many respects. Yet giving heroes and gods an education was more than just one part of humanizing them by giving them a "biography"; it also shows how important a part education played in an individual's life in the Hellenistic period. If education had not been widely spread, it would not have contributed to making a hero more human.

In spite of its oftentimes humorous slant, the representation of education in Hellenistic poetry fills a significant gap left by the evidence of the school texts: that of the atmosphere in the classroom. School exercises suggest that much of what was done in class was rather repetitive and tedious; but nothing could illustrate better to what degree of boredom even such highly emotive texts as Euripides' *Bacchae* were reduced than Callimachus' yawning mask of Dionysus. Herodas' *Schoolmaster* gives a good impression of the violence that teachers might exert, of the parents' helplessness, of a young boy's recalcitrance. But even so, there are many things we will never fully know, above all, how teachers talked about the texts they used in class.

FURTHER READING

Pfeiffer 1968 still provides the most extensive collection and discussion of sources on the intellectual culture in the Hellenistic period. Regarding Hellenistic gymnasia, Nilsson 1955 is still illuminating and Delorme 1960 presents an impressive range of literary, epigraphical, and archaeological sources. The articles in Kah and Scholz 2004 address the topic from a variety of angles. Schaaf 1992: 62–83 focuses on the gymnasium foundations in Athens and Miletus and the motivations behind them.

On ancient education in general, Cribiore 1996, 2001a, Morgan 1998a, and the papers in Too 2001 replace Marrou 1982 (1948), presenting an up-to-date picture and systematic analysis of the evidence and thought-provoking ideas about the operation and role of education in ancient society.

Rhetorical training has deliberately been excluded from this chapter. On this topic see Cuypers in this volume.

PART TWO

Poetry

CHAPTER SIX

The Prefigured Muse: Rethinking a Few Assumptions on Hellenistic Poetics

Benjamin Acosta-Hughes

καὶ τὰ μὲ̣ν ἂ[ν] Μ̣οίcαι cεcοφι̣[c]μ̣έναι
εὖ Ἑλικωνί̣δε̣[c] ἐμβαίεν †λόγω[ι·
θνατὸ̣c δ' ο̣ὔ̣ κ[ε]ν̣ ἀνὴρ
διερ.[......]. † τὰ ἕκαcτα εἴποι.

On these themes the learned Heliconian Muses might embark (in story?), but no mortal man could tell each detail (clearly?).

The theme in these lines seems a variation of a traditional statement of a poet's *aporia* faced with the magnitude of his subject (compare *Il.* 2.489 "not even if I had ten tongues and ten mouths were mine"), and the imagery of Heliconian Muses contrasted with mortal man appears conventional. Yet Muses termed cεcοφιcμέναι, "learned" or "skilled," cannot but startle a modern reader. The standard parallel given by the commentaries on these lines, that of Theognis 19–20, Κύρνε, cοφιζομένῳ μὲν ἐμοὶ cφρηγὶc ἐπικείcθω / τοῖcδ' ἔπεcιν ("Cyrnus, may these words be the proven token of my skill"), does not assuage the reader's disquiet, for the skill or learnedness here is the poet's, not of his divine source of inspiration. Nor does the Hesiodic parallel at *Works and Days* 648–62, where it is again the poet himself who is "not cεcοφιcμένοc of sailing and ships" (649), elucidate the seeming paradox of our educated Muses. As to song, it is the Muses who taught Hesiod "to sing an unimaginable hymn" (Μοῦcαι γάρ μ' ἐδίδαξαν ἀθέcφατον ὕμνον ἀείδειν, 662). *They* trained *him*. The lines cited above have a very different characterization. That the Muses here have their learning at second degree, a learning not inherent but acquired, might be understandably assumed at first glance to be a typically "Hellenistic" gesture, as in Hellenistic poetry the relationship between Muses and poet comes to be more varied, and is sometimes even inverted (Paduano Faedo 1970; Fantuzzi and Hunter 2004, esp. 1, 6–7, 52–4, 58–9). But these lines are not taken from a poem of the Hellenistic period.

Rather they are part of an encomium of Polycrates that is widely attributed to the sixth-century poet Ibycus of Rhegium (*PMGF* S151 = *P.Oxy.* 1790 fr. 1; text after Hutchinson 2001: 41). Ibycus, though from the western Greek world, sang at the court of Polycrates of Samos and, after Polycrates' death, under the patronage of the Pisistratid tyrants, at Athens. The court of Polycrates attracted poets from different parts of the Greek world. Set geographically across from the kingdom of Lydia, subsequently a western satrapy of the Persian empire, Samos came face to face with another people and its ancient culture. The parallels with Ptolemaic Alexandria are many, and indeed this may help explain Ibycus' later popularity with Hellenistic poets. Nonetheless, Ibycus' encomium, for all of its apparent novelty and experimentation, is a late sixth century poem. It might be added that scholars of Ibycus generally do not like this poem any more than those of Theocritus like his encomium of Ptolemy Philadelphus (*Id.* 17). And for many of the same reasons.

These lines are in fact emblematic of a larger problem in approaching the poetry of the Hellenistic period. The term "Hellenistic" has its origins in the study of history (it was coined by Droysen, 1833–43), and as a historical term it has a clear definition: it defines the period from the death of Alexander the Great to the death of Cleopatra VII (323–30 BCE). As a discursive term for literature, "Hellenistic" is much more problematic. For example, if one defines "Hellenistic literature" as the literature of the Hellenic diaspora instantiated by Alexander's conquests, a valid argument can be made that Hellenistic literature only ended, at least in the Mediterranean, with the violent nationalism of the twentieth century, when the Greek populations largely vanished from Asia Minor and Egypt. And that still leaves in question the present-day Greek populations of the Americas, Africa, and Australia, who live, as did many of their post-Alexander forebears, among other peoples and cultures, with the Athenian Acropolis and the temples at Delphi (though now in ruins) as their imagined *heterotopia*, the marker of their Hellenicity (Leontis 1995: 43). A valid argument can be made, too, that the early twentieth century poet Constantine Cavafy was the ultimate "Hellenistic" poet (Scodel 2003); in his allusivity, his engagement with a distant and largely mythical past, his oblique perception of figures, his emphasis on the refined and intricate, Cavafy epitomizes many of the qualities Classicists associate with "Hellenistic poetry."

If "Hellenistic" is to be defined through characteristics rather than date, there is also no clear beginning. Ibycus' encomium of Polycrates is but one of many compositional movements in Archaic and Classical literature that not only prefigures a poetics often termed "Hellenistic," but might indeed be cited as an example of this poetics. The 48 surviving lines – the papyrus begins with an antistrophe – effect a catalogue of heroes of the Trojan War whose excellence the singer will *not* tell, thus at once evoking the Muse invocation opening the Catalogue of Ships in *Iliad* 2 and clarifying our singer's act of variation. The rhetorical form is a *praeteritio*, reminiscent of Sappho's priamel fr. 16 LP; like that poem, Ibycus' composition prefers the erotic to the military, and segues to the celebration of beauty (that of Polycrates).

Ibycus launches into his *praeteritio* with the words "now mine is not to hymn the desirous deceiver of his host, Paris, nor Cassandra of the slim ankles" (ν]ῦν δέ μοι οὔτε ξειναπάτ[α]ν Π[άρι]ν / [..] ἐπιθύμιον οὔτε τανί[σφ]υρ[ον / ὑμ]νῆν Κασσάνδραν, 10–12). The adversative νῦν δέ μοι both juxtaposes singer and Muses and heroic and contemporary time and further sets this poem against the Homeric ones. Contrast of a heroic past and the present, as here, is a hallmark of Alexandrian poetry, and the avoidance of the Trojan War and its associated themes is a central feature of Hellenistic poetics (Sistakou 2008). There are many features of these lines that might lead a modern reader to assume this is a Hellenistic work. And this reader would be wrong.

In a recent monograph on the narrative voice in Hellenistic poetry, Andrew Morrison has made a strong case for a reading of Greek poetry that prefers the integral continuity of its poetics over a historical period division with an implicit teleological prejudice (Morrison 2007). This chapter, while far more modest in scope, is related in its focus. In the following pages I consider a small selection of moments in Archaic and Classical poetry that not merely prefigure some of the most cited compositional gestures of Hellenistic poetics but are essentially the same gestures, and suggest the need for a nuanced re-evaluation of the literary critical term "Hellenistic poetics." For convenience this study is composed of three sections. The first two survey passages in several lyric, elegiac, and epic poets (Anacreon, Simonides, Timotheus, and Choerilus) that concern poetic program and artistic innovation; the third looks at the portrayal of Aeschylus and Euripides as rivals in art in the *agon* of Aristophanes' *Frogs*.

Two Programmatic Passages

οὐ φιλέω, ὃς κρητῆρι παρὰ πλέωι οἰνοποτάζων
νείκεα καὶ πόλεμον δακρυόεντα λέγει,
ἀλλ' ὅςτις Μουςέων τε καὶ ἀγλαὰ δῶρ' Ἀφροδίτης
ςυμμίςγων ἐρατῆς μνήςκεται εὐφροςύνης.

I don't like the man who when drinking wine by a full mixing-bowl talks of strife and tearful war. Rather I like the one who, mingling the splendid gifts of the Muses and Aphrodite, makes mention of lovely festivity.

ἄγε δηῦτε μηκέτ' οὕτω
πατάγωι τε κἀλαλητῶι
Σκυθικὴν πόςιν παρ' οἴνωι
μελετῶμεν, ἀλλὰ καλοῖς
ὑποπίνοντες ἐν ὕμνοις.

Come again, let us no longer so practice drinking in the Scythian manner, with clatter and shouting, but drink moderately with beautiful songs of praise.

These two fragments of poems attributed to Anacreon, one in elegiac couplets (*IEG* 2), the other in anacreontics (*PMG* 356b), both outline a "poetics" of the symposium in a series of contrasts: other/ours, war/love, gross/discrete, hateful/joyful. The singer of the first passage associates himself (through the gesture οὐ φιλέω … ἀλλά) with the singer of the Muses and Aphrodite, the singer of the second with a preference for the orderly over the noisy and foreign ("drinking in the Scythian manner"). That the elegiac fragment is so little cited, even in studies of elegy, may well be due to the unfortunate fact that standard selections of lyric poetry omit poetry in non-lyric meters by the poets they showcase.

Comparison with two lines from Callimachus, now generally thought to have come at the beginning of *Aetia* 2 (D'Alessio 2007: 555 n.14; Zetzel 1981), reveals a similar use of symposiastic decorum (fr. 178.11–12 Pf.):

καὶ γὰρ ὁ Θρηΐκίην μὲν ἀπέcτυγε χανδὸν ἄμυcτιν
  ζωροποτεῖν, ὀλίγωι δ' ἥδετο κιccυβίωι.

For he too despised drinking unmixed wine without pause, mouth open, in the Thracian manner and rather took pleasure in the small drinking-bowl.

The Callimachean elegiac lines parallel several Anacreontic images. Thracians substitute for Scythians as disorderly foreigners. The fragment of Callimachus has been much studied for its programmatic significance, especially as echoed in Roman elegy, but the Anacreon parallels suggest that a nuanced reconsideration, and an important one, is in order. Is not already Anacreon defining a type of elegy, here that of the symposium, as the appropriate setting for certain themes and an inappropriate one for others? The disinclination for military themes at the symposium in fact has a long tradition in elegy (e.g., Xenophanes fr. 1.13–24 Gentili and Prato 2002; Thgn. 757–64). So, is not Callimachus here, as elsewhere in the *Aetia*, underlining his adherence to an earlier elegiac poetics?

A new fragment of the fifth-century poet Simonides of Ceos offers a similar paradigm for Hellenistic poetics. This is fr. 11 (*IEG*) of the so-called "Plataea elegy," a poem for those who fell against the Persians at Plataea that appears to have been much imitated by later poets (Hunter 1996: 97–109; Barchiesi 2001b). The structure of the poem is commonly agreed to be at least tripartite (Rutherford 2001b: 38; Obbink 2001: 65–6, 69–73). It begins with a hymnic proem celebrating Achilles and the East–West conflict of the heroic past, but then transitions to Simonides' own time and contemporary subject matter (text after Sider 2001: 18):

ἁγέμαχοι Δαναοί[
οἷcιν ἐπ' ἀθά]ν̣ατον κέχυται κλέος ἀν̣[δρὸc] ἕκητι
  ὃc παρ' ἰοπ]λοκάμων δέξατο Πιερίδ[ων
—⏖ —]θείην καὶ ἐπώνυμον ὁπ̣[λοτέρ]οιcιν
  —⏖ ἡμ]ι̣θέων ὠκυμόρον γενεή̣[ν.
ἀλλὰ cὺ μὲ]ν νῦν χαῖρε, θεᾶc ἐρικυ[δέοc υἱέ
  κούρηc εἰν]αλίου Νηρέοc· αὐτὰρ ἐγώ̣ [
κικλήcκω] c' ἐπίκουρον ἐμοί, π[. . . . . .]ε Μοῦcα,
  εἴ πέρ γ' ἀν]θρώπων̣ εὐχομένω[ν μέλεαι·
ἔντυνο]ν̣ καὶ τόνδ[ε μελ]ί̣φρονα κ[όcμον ἀο]ιδῆc
  ἡμετ]έ̣ρηc, ἵνα τιc̣ [μνή]c̣ε̣τ̣α̣ι̣ ὑ̣[

... the Greek generals [upon whom imm]ortal fame was poured because of that man [who] received from the [violet]-tressed Pierian Muses [all truth] and made famous for later men the short lived race of demi-gods. [But you] farewell, famed son of the divine [daughter] of Nereus of the sea. But I [call upon] you as my ally... Muse, [if you have a care for] men's prayers [make] this delightful adornment of [my] song so that someone [will remember] ...

The lines develop an equation of present poet (Simonides) with past poet (Homer), present East–West conflict (the war against the Persians) with past East–West conflict (the Trojan War), and so confer on the present subjects of song the fame (κλέοϲ, 15) of the earlier heroes. This evaluation of present conflict and present fighters in terms of the heroic past is key to understanding the cultural significance of Simonides' poem, and later imitations of it, especially by Theocritus in his encomium of Ptolemy Philadelphus (*Id.* 17; Hunter 2003a: 185–6, 195–9). An important effect of this transition is the portrayal of the warriors of Plataea not just in heroic terms but specifically in Homeric ones. By, for example, importing the figures of Menelaus and, probably, the Tyndarids into his poetic narrative of the Battle of Plataea (31), Simonides maintains the figure of Homer before his audience as one of both his own poetic identity in a tradition of singers of battle, and at the same time of disassociation, for these are his warriors and his "epic" battle. His is at once a poem of emulation and one of artistic self-definition. And, yes, this is a compositional gesture we often term "Hellenistic."

Artistic Novelty and its Problems

A later fifth-century poem on the Persian Wars, Timotheus' *Persians*, makes a different compositional gesture that became a Hellenistic theme, the defense against critical reception of artistic novelty. Timotheus is representative, along with, for example, Philoxenus and Cinesias, of an artistic movement that flourished toward the end of the fifth century, known as the New Music (the term is something of a misnomer), one that found distinct disfavor with Plato (Csapo 2004: 236 for citations, 207–8 on the term). Timotheus' *Persians* is a "citharodic nome," a poem sung to the lyre in "lyric" meters. It is astrophic (typical also of Hellenistic lyric poetry: Fantuzzi in this volume), polymetric, and marked by an often strikingly innovative vocabulary (particularly in compounds and metaphors). Timotheus' own commentary on his poetry's reception at Sparta is very revealing (text after Hordern 2002a):

ἀλλ' ὦ χρυϲεοκίθαριν ἀέ-
ξων Μοῦϲαν νεοτευχῆ,
ἐμοῖϲ ἔλθ' ἐπίκουροϲ ὕ-
μνοιϲ ἰήϊε Παιάν·
ὁ γάρ μ' εὐγενέταϲ μακραί-
ων Σπάρταϲ μέγαϲ ἁγεμὼν
βρύων ἄνθεϲιν ἥβαϲ
δονεῖ λαὸϲ ἐπιφλέγων
ἐλᾶι τ' αἴθοπι μώμωι,
ὅτι παλαιοτέραν νέοιϲ
ὕμνοιϲ Μοῦϲαν ἀτιμῶ·
ἐγὼ δ' οὔτε νέον τιν' οὔ-
τε γεραὸν οὔτ' ἰϲήβαν
εἴργω τῶνδ' ἑκὰϲ ὕμνων·
τοὺϲ δὲ μουϲοπαλαιολύ-

μας, τούτους δ' ἀπερύκω,
λωβητῆρας ἀοιδῶν,
κηρύκων λιγυμακροφώ-
νων τείνοντας ἰυγάς.

But you who boost the new-fashioned Muse of the golden lyre, come as ally to my hymns, iēie Paian. The well-born and long-lived Spartan great leader, the people teeming with the flowers of youth, harass me with fire and chase me with burning blame, alleging that I, with my new hymns, dishonor the more traditional Muse. But I keep nothing new, nor old, nor contemporary at a distance from these hymns. Rather the ancient-Muse-soilers, these I keep off, destroyers of singers, straining cries of far-heard-shrill-voiced heralds.

The poem is from a late fifth century poet but the terms are very like those we associate with Callimachus: tradition versus novelty, dishonoring the Muse, Pindaric μῶμος ("criticism") in an aesthetically critical setting, physical violence (real or metaphorical) directed against the innovative singer. The singer's stance, like that of Callimachus in his thirteenth *Iamb* (fr. 203 Pf.), is at once defensive and offensively programmatic: he seeks to ally himself with the best of an earlier tradition while distancing himself from those who have corrupted the Muse. The detractors of these poets of the late fifth century, Plato among them, fault this innovative music for its πολυειδεία and ποικιλία, its constant shifts in mode and mood and "baroque" elaboration – some of the very features that come to mind in essaying a simple classroom definition of the term "Hellenistic."

A passage from the proem of another late fifth century poem on the Persian Wars, Choerilus of Samos' epic *Persica* (*SH* 317 = *PEG* fr. 2), frames the poet's engagement with his poetic predecessors as one of artistic belatedness:

ἆ μάκαρ, ὅςτις ἔην κεῖνον χρόνον ἴδρις ἀοιδῆς,
Μουσάων θεράπων, ὅτ' ἀκήρατος ἦν ἔτι λειμών·
νῦν δ' ὅτε πάντα δέδασται, ἔχουσι δὲ πείρατα τέχναι,
ὕστατοι ὥστε δρόμου καταλειπόμεθ', οὐδέ πηι ἔστι
πάντηι παπταίνοντα νεοζυγὲς ἅρμα πελάσσαι.

Blessed was he who was skilled in song in that time, a servant of the Muses, when the field was yet undefiled. Now when everything has been allotted, and the arts have limits, we are left behind in the race, and for someone looking there is nowhere to drive a newly yoked chariot.

Choerilus' lines not only lament the lack of novel directions in which the contemporary poet might go, they do so in a series of images taken from earlier poets and poetry, a gesture also to be performed by much Hellenistic poetry. The overtones of Archilochus, Pindar, and Homer discernible in Choerilus' proem themselves illustrate the singer's *aporia* – he phrases his lack of novel direction in others' voices. It is not surprising that Callimachus in turn, when he eschews composition on the Persian Wars (*Aetia* fr. 1.15–16 Pf.), does so in a setting that markedly recalls Choerilus' mosaic of earlier poets (Acosta-Hughes and Stephens 2002). Yet if "Hellenistic" poetry defines itself in terms of earlier poetry that makes the same compositional gesture, the lines of demarcation between them become blurred. Choerilus already finds himself overwhelmed by the poetic past, and at the same time his poetry is an amalgam of intertexts. A traditional definition of "Hellenistic poetics" might single out precisely these two characteristics as symptomatic of the artistic period; but temporally we are not even close.

Antitechnai – Rivals in Art

Hitherto I have discussed brief passages of poems that prefigure, whether in language, imagery, or tone, concepts we tend to regard as "Hellenistic." There is, however, an extant work that encompasses many of the signal elements of "Hellenistic poetics" at some length – this is Aristophanes' *Frogs*. First performed at the Lenaia of 405, *Frogs* is, among other things, Aristophanes' comic treatment of Athens' poetic past. The play's very conceit, Dionysus' journey to Hades in search of Euripides, marks the play as retrospective; it is a reaction to, or perhaps better result of, earlier poetry. The long *agon* or "formal contest" in the second part of the drama between Aeschylus and Euripides, an artistic duel between two ἀντιτέχναι or "opponents in art" (*Frogs* 816), pitches a newer, lighter, cleverer poetics against an older, heavier, more bombastic one, as each is contending for the underworld "chair of tragedy" (769) on grounds of artistic excellence, which in the value system explored by the play is intrinsically connected to moral excellence and educational value (esp. 1007–13).

The echoes of this confrontation in later poetry are many, and I touch only on a few here that are entwined in the opening of Callimachus' *Aetia*. In the weighing of verses, Aeschylean "heavy" topics, such as "death," outweigh Euripidean "airy" ones, such as "persuasion" (1364–1410). *Aetia* fr. 1.9–10 picks up the general concept of weighing and measuring poetry, but with an artful reversal of Aristophanes' outcome: in Callimachus it is apparently the lighter poem that prevails, paradoxically "outweighing" (καθέλκει at fr. 1.9 recalls καθέλξει at *Frogs* 1398) the longer and therefore "heavier" one (Acosta-Hughes and Stephens 2002; Harder in this volume). The chorus at *Frogs* 814 gives Aeschylus Zeus' Homeric epithet "thunderer" (ἐπιβρεμέτας); at *Aetia* fr. 1.20 Callimachus declares: "to thunder is not for me, but for Zeus" (βροντᾶν οὐκ ἐμόν, ἀλλὰ Διός). And if we remember that the conceit of the *agon* in the *Frogs* is to judge which of the two poets is τὴν τέχνην σοφώτερος (780), Callimachus' injunction to judge σοφία by τέχνῃ (fr. 1.17–18) becomes the more intriguing.

In the introduction to his edition of the *Frogs*, Dover details the rapport of literary criticism and popular culture in the late fifth century (1993: 24–37). The play's discourse, as Dover convincingly shows, is not above the heads of Aristophanes' audience, nor, we should note, is that of the opening of Callimachus' *Aetia* above the heads of his readers. These are metaphors accessible to anyone. The "advice" of the *Aetia*'s prologue consists largely of the reworking of fairly well tried literary tropes, although in terms of intertextuality it is a complex work (Asper 1997; Acosta-Hughes and Stephens 2002). This not to deny the originality of Callimachus' composition, nor to re-awaken the tired claim that Hellenistic poetry is a derivative form of art, but rather to call attention to its place in a continuum of artistic production. The critical discourse on poetic style and content not only existed already at the time of the performance of *Frogs* in 404, it was familiar enough to a general audience to be viable material for comedy.

Among the thematic charges laid against Euripides in the *Frogs* (and also elsewhere in Aristophanes, notably in the *Thesmophoriazusae* and *Acharnians*), is his treatment of heroic characters. In particular Euripides is criticized for representing male heroes in "unheroic" situations (for example, Telephus and Menelaus as exiles in rags) and female heroines overcome by illicit passion (Phaedra, Stheneboea). Euripides' "unheroic" heroes are indeed an innovative creative feature, and they in many ways prefigure the downscaling that is one of the signal features of Hellenistic poetry, heroes likewise tend to appear in less than heroic settings: in Callimachus' *Aetia*, Heracles visits the poor farmer Molorcus (Harder in this volume); in Theocritus' *Idyll* 24, he appears as a baby in homely surroundings; and in the post-Theocritean *Idyll* 25, he joins his host Augeas for a cattle inspection (Ambühl 2004; Ambühl and Harder in this volume). Another signal Hellenistic feature is the creation of heroes whose heroism is more psychologically complicated, such as Apollonius' Jason and the Heracles of Theocritus' *Idyll* 13. Heroines overwhelmed by erotic impulse are another recurring feature of Hellenistic poetry (the narratives preserved in Parthenius' *Love Stories* are indicative here: Lightfoot 1999), and indeed the in-depth reading of psychological trauma was at one time seen as the period's contribution to Greek erotic poetry. Yet the Phaedra of Euripides' *Hippolytus* is a telling example of earlier detailed treatment of passion outside of lyric. Among the lost plays of Euripides that might have been even more revealing here is the original *Hippolytus* (*TrGF* 5 F 34), where the scene that allegedly drew the opprobrium of contemporary viewers, the face-to-face confrontation of Phaedra and Hippolytus, would be of great interest as a comparandum, notably for the confrontation between Medea and Jason in Apollonius' *Argonautica*.

Two other, related charges laid against Euripides in the *Frogs* deserve brief consideration here. These are a preoccupation with the domestic and with humble characters (948–1003). Dionysus' list of mislaid household items at 980–90 is of course ridiculous, but Aristophanes' basic point is again accurate. An interest in domestic detail is also a feature of much extant Hellenistic poetry. Callimachus' *Hecale* is the outstanding example, and some of the similes in Apollonius' *Argonautica* (e.g., 3.291–95, 755–70), while these have Homeric models, are at the same time remarkable for their homely subject matter. Euripides in the *Frogs* prides himself on the wide social range of his speaking characters: "then from the first works I wouldn't leave anyone idle, but the wife in my play would speak, and the slave no less, the master, the young girl and the old woman too" (948–50). This play on Euripides' "democratic" (952) composition is again parodic, but it does take into account the large speaking presence of characters like the farmer of the *Electra* and Phaedra's nurse in the *Hippolytus*. Figures like Callimachus' Molorcus, Theocritus' Simaetha, and the cast of Herodas' *Mimiambs* owe something to the larger role given to humbler characters in Euripidean tragedy as well as comedy. Both domestic detail and humble character return as topics in Aeschylus' extended parody of Euripidean choral song and monody further on in *Frogs*, in a passage that is startlingly like a miscellany of different Hellenistic authors (1298–1363).

Monody itself is a late development on the tragic stage, preserved for us in Euripides and in Aristophanes' parodies of his style (Battezzato 1995). Tragic monodies and long soliloquies are a clear antecedent of the solo "arias" of later elegiac and hexameter poetry, as varied as Acontius' in Callimachus' *Aetia* (preserved largely in later imitations and in Aristaenetus' prose rendition: Rosenmeyer 1996), Simaetha's in Theocritus' *Idyll* 2, and Ariadne's in Catullus 64; the *Fragmentum Grenfellianum* is another obvious example (Esposito 2005: 62–5 and in this volume). In particular, monody allows for expanded psychological characterization. Medea's soliloquy of tormented indecision at *Argonautica* 3.771–801, for example, owes a great deal to the conventions of tragic monologue in general and to Medea's speeches in Euripides' *Medea* in particular, especially to her soliloquy of tormented indecision at 1022–55 (Fusillo 2001); the focus in both passages on parents, children, and fear of humiliation is very telling.

As Euripides and Aeschylus prepare to engage, the chorus frames their artistic duel as one of operatic grandeur or cεμνότηc against intellectual cleverness or λεπτότηc (814–17):

ἦ που δεινὸν ἐπιβρεμέταc χόλον ἔνδοθεν ἕξει,
ἡνίκ' ἂν ὀξύλαλόν περ ἴδηι θήγοντοc ὀδόντα
  ἀντιτέχνου· τότε δὴ μανίαc ὑπὸ δεινῆc
    ὄμματα cτροβήcεται.

And, I think, thundering mightily, he (Aeschylus) will have a fearsome rage in his heart, when he sees his rival in art whetting his sharp-talking tooth. Then will he roll his eyes in fearsome frenzy.

Thundering characters, rolling eyes, and inspired frenzy convey epic grandeur, but in the eyes of Euripides they lack subtlety and sophistication, are empty bombast; sharp-talking teeth suggest mental acumen and verbal skill, but also, in Aeschylus' diagnosis, wordiness and sophistry, speech without substance. Thus the chorus captures the essence of both antagonists' styles and artistic programs in terms that speak as succinctly and effectively as the images of Callimachus' *Aetia* prologue.

The term ἀντιτέχνηc in this passage suggests a way of looking at poetry both as a τέχνη and as competitive. Opposition in any agonistic setting is quintessentially Greek, and the idea of rivalry between two artists has a longer history, both in earlier and later Greek poetry (Duchemin 1968; Collins 2004). Such pairs of rivals include Homer and Hesiod (in the tradition of the *Contest of Homer and Hesiod*), Pindar and Simonides (where too the antagonism has a distinctly ethical dimension), Plato and Isocrates (in a different discursive realm), and, of course, Callimachus and Apollonius. Scholarship on Hellenistic poetry has often framed the perceived "quarrel" of Callimachus and Apollonius in terms of the cultural setting of the Alexandrian Museum. Here the oft-cited text is a fragment of Timon of Philius (*SH* 786 = Ath. 1.22d = fr. 12 Di Marco 1989):

πολλοὶ μὲν βόcκονται ἐν Αἰγύπτωι πολυφύλωι
βιβλιακοὶ χαρακῖται ἀπείρατα δηριόωντεc
Μουcέων ἐν ταλάρωι.

In Egypt of many peoples many papyrus nestlings, quarreling incessantly, are fed in the Muses' basket.

It is likely enough that the Museum was the center of intense literary polemic (Lelli 2004; Strootman in this volume). Yet we should perhaps also view the references of the biographical tradition to rivalry between Apollonius and Callimachus, two artists who are in so many ways remarkably alike and whose work contains unmistakable cross-references, as part of a Greek cultural tradition that sets "masters of truth" in opposition to one another (what Detienne has called the "whole current of dichotomic thought . . . a way of thinking in terms of alternatives," 1996: 126). There is, further, a distinct parallelism observable in the pairs of rivals: one figure is framed as "traditional" (Aeschylus, Pindar, Apollonius), the other as "innovative" (Euripides, Simonides, Callimachus – though it is interesting that Apollonius, the one representative of the "older" art form, is given in his biographical tradition as the "pupil," μαθητής, of Callimachus). At issue in all three cases are questions of language, genre, the purpose of poetry, and ultimately ethics.

We need to distinguish here between the cultural tradition that establishes this antithesis between poets and the poets themselves. Just as the contest in the *Frogs* need not reflect what Aeschylus and Euripides in fact thought of one another, so too we should perhaps not make too much of the comment preserved in a scholion to the concluding lines on Envy and Apollo of Callimachus' *Hymn to Apollo*: "he reproaches with these words those who make fun of him for not being able to compose a large poem, hence he was forced to compose the *Hecale*" (schol. *h.* 2.106).

The epigram ascribed to Apollonius at *AP* 11.275 is another case in point:

Καλλίμαχος τὸ κάθαρμα, τὸ παίγνιον, ὁ ξύλινος νοῦς,
αἴτιος, ὁ γράψας Αἴτια Καλλιμάχου.

Callimachus the rubbish, the toy, the wooden head, is the cause, the one who wrote *Callimachus' Causes.*

Do these lines reflect the opinions of the poet Apollonius, or are we dealing with a constructed poetic rivalry? There is no way to be sure.

Popular reception of Greek cultural figures often seeks, in an almost carnivalesque fashion, to downplay their socio-cultural importance. Low birth, unseemly deaths, accusations of rape, theft, and other crimes pervade their biographical traditions. Aeschylus' repeated quips in the *Frogs* about Euripides' alleged less-than-noble parentage ("son of the vegetable goddess," 840; cf. 947) and less-than-happy marriage (1045–8) are part and parcel of artistic slugfests. Both Callimachus in his fourth *Iamb* (and Ovid in *Amores* 3.1) may be playing on this tradition (in fact, Callimachus' reference in the opening lines of the fourth *Iamb* to a popular fable may be a tongue in cheek reference to just such popular reception of art). But this need not mean that such battles actually occurred. Reception is not necessarily reality, and this is especially true of laughing at high art.

***

To a certain extent Hellenistic poetry's interstitial position in Classical Studies is responsible for the way the traditional perception of "Hellenistic poetics" has evolved. Latinists who look to Hellenistic poets for models for Roman authors do not necessarily read extensively in earlier Greek literature; conversely scholars of Archaic and Classical Greek do not necessarily read post-fifth-century poetry, and hence do not draw the connections that the later evolution of Greek poetry provides. The discourse in which scholarly discussion of Hellenistic poetry is framed is also at fault here; the qualities of "belatedness" and "cultural anxiety" are a given rather than even points of discussion. Even the vocabulary in which this discourse is conducted is not unproblematic: the "re" of "refashioning," "recalling," "reconsidering" already suggests something at a second remove.

There are however signs of change. A relatively recent development in the scholarship on Hellenistic poetry is one that not so much emphasizes its relationship to the Greek poetic past, though this remains integral to this literature, as highlights its place as origin of the literary present, of *our* literary present, to see in Hellenistic poetry, as indeed in other aspects of the post-Alexander Mediterranean world, the origin of modernity. This scholarship foregrounds more the inventive than the reactive in Hellenistic poetics, and, together with recent work on Hellenistic as post-Platonic poetry and on Hellenistic literary criticism, may well further change the way we discuss Hellenistic poetry – less as an art burdened by a Golden Age past but rather one that enhances the principles it inherits from earlier artists and develops further, and then further.

FURTHER READING

Recent work on Hellenistic poetry and its use of poetic models includes Cusset 1999, Asper 1997, Fantuzzi and Hunter 2004, Morrison 2007, and Acosta-Hughes 2009. Cameron 1995a, though not uncontentious, is a signal re-evaluation not only of Callimachus himself but also of the history of scholarly evaluation of him. Green 1993 in his chapters on Callimachus and Apollonius takes a more traditional approach to their "quarrel." Among recent studies that highlight the "modern" character of Hellenistic poetry, including its use of the poetic past, are Selden 1998, Payne 2007, and Radke 2007. Csapo 2004 provides a very helpful discussion of the significance of the New Music in later fifth-century Athens; see also Prauscello 2009 on the New Music and Callimachus. On Plato's role in re-figuring the discourse on poetry and its value for later poets see Weineck 1992, for Plato and Callimachus, Acosta-Hughes and Stephens 2007, and on Hellenistic literary criticism Gutzwiller in this volume.

CHAPTER SEVEN

Callimachus' *Aetia*

Annette Harder

The elegiac *Aetia* was Callimachus' main work, probably written in several stages in the course of his career as a poet at Alexandria in the first half of the third century BCE. Thanks to a considerable number of papyrus finds we are now able to form a reasonable picture of this typically Hellenistic poem, which has inspired so many subsequent poets.

In its overall structure the *Aetia* was a catalogue poem, which contained a collection of aetiological stories. It explained, for instance, the origins of unusual rituals, such as that for Heracles at Lindos, where the priests scolded the hero during sacrifices, or of surprising statues, like that of Artemis at Leucas, which carried a mortar on its head. Other stories, such as the love story of Acontius and Cydippe, which explained the origin of a ruling family at Ceos, were not related to ritual, but were aetiological in a broad sense. Many contained secondary *aitia* as well, like the story of the Argonauts at Anaphe, where, apart from the origin of a ritual for Apollo Aegletes, we also find a number of foundation stories.

The *Aetia* consisted of four books and fell into two clearly distinguished parts. In Books 1 and 2 the stories were told within the framework of a dialogue with the Muses, who answered the questions of "Callimachus" in a dream that carried him as a young man to Mount Helicon. In Books 3 and 4 the stories were juxtaposed without this kind of framework and there is no evidence that Callimachus created any kind of transition from one story to the next. The work opened with a prologue (fr. 1 Pfeiffer) in which "Callimachus" defends himself against the criticisms of the so-called Telchines, who reproach him for not writing a continuous work in many thousands of lines about kings and heroes. "Callimachus" then claims to follow Apollo's instructions to cultivate a "slender Muse" and go along "untrodden paths" when writing poetry (1.23–8). The views on poetic style expressed in the prologue are underlined by a large number of allusions to other authors and seem to have been put into practice in the rest of the *Aetia*.

The appearance of the work as we know it may reflect the stages in which Callimachus wrote it. The view which is almost generally accepted nowadays is that of Parsons, proposed upon the discovery of the papyri of the *Victory of Berenice* in 1976. Parsons suggested that Callimachus wrote *Aetia* 1–2 as a young man, and that he continued writing aetiological poems which later in life he collected in *Aetia* 3–4, framed by two poems for Berenice II, the *Victory of Berenice* at the beginning of Book 3 and the *Lock of Berenice* at the end of Book 4, resulting in "a bipartite *Aetia*, to which a new prologue (fr. 1) and a new epilogue (fr. 112) gave external unity" (Parsons 1977: 50). With this proposal he refined an earlier idea of Pfeiffer (1953: xxxvi–vii), who had suggested that the *Aetia* was an early work, written before 270 BCE, and that the old Callimachus had made a second edition of it, framing it with a prologue (fr. 1) and epilogue (fr. 112) and including the *Lock of Berenice* (fr. 110) some time after the beginning of 246, when Ptolemy III Euergetes married Berenice II. The references to old age in the prologue seem to support the reconstruction of Pfeiffer and Parsons, even though one cannot be sure how much of the emphasis on old age is poetic fiction. Recently their ideas have been challenged by Cameron (1995a), who argues that *Aetia* 1–2, including the prologue and epilogue, were written around 270 BCE, and that *Aetia* 3–4 were added in 245/240. His arguments, however, are far from cogent (Harder 2002b: 600–3).

The *Aetia* was an influential poem. It was admired and imitated by many later Greek and Latin poets, commented on by such scholars as Theon and Epaphroditus, and circulated widely, to judge from the number of surviving papyri, the latest of which dates from the seventh century CE and contains many learned marginal comments. Somewhere in the thirteenth century the work seems to have been lost, to be gradually rediscovered only in the twentieth century thanks to papyrus finds. To mention some highlights, the story of *Acontius and Cydippe* was first published in 1910, the prologue in 1927, the *Diegeseis*, which gave us summaries of most of Books 3 and 4, in 1934, and the *Victory of Berenice* in 1976. In addition to these, there were many smaller finds, which all helped to form a clearer picture of what the *Aetia* had been like.

The reactions to the papyrus finds were not immediately favorable, and among scholars in the first half of the twentieth century one can often hear some disappointment about newly rediscovered parts of the *Aetia*. Scholars judged that the story of Acontius and Cydippe, although it was very learned, did not show a great deal of "art" and emotion, and therefore was of limited literary quality. In a similar vein, they found the *Lock of Berenice* stiff and artificial. Although in the course of the first half of the twentieth century there was a growing interest in Hellenistic poetry, for a long time it seemed unlikely that the *Aetia* would ever attract many admirers who would work on it and advance its interpretation.

Still, the situation gradually improved. In the development of interest in and appreciation of the *Aetia*, Pfeiffer's edition of 1949 must be regarded as a milestone. Here for the first time all the fragments were assembled and placed in the order which to a large extent is still accepted today, and Pfeiffer's notes helped to form a better idea of the work's character and incited further study. In the second half of the twentieth century Classical scholarship increasingly moved away from "romantic" aesthetics and came to appreciate Hellenistic poetry on its own terms. There was a growing interest in and understanding of the workings and importance of intertextuality and of the new social context in which poetry was produced and received. These new approaches have also affected and fostered research on the *Aetia*. Especially during the last three or four decades, there has been a general reappraisal of Callimachus' work and an increasing awareness of the particular qualities of his poetry. The playful and experimental character of the *Aetia* and the intertextual subtleties of its literary technique, as well as its function as Alexandrian court poetry, are objects of ongoing research.

Callimachus and his Audience

Although from the literary point of view Callimachus' work has received a great deal of attention and scholars have made much progress with its interpretation, we still find rather extreme views on the place of Callimachus' work, and particularly that of the *Aetia*, within the context in which it was produced and received, i.e., the Ptolemaic court of the third century BCE (a subject further discussed in this volume by Strootman and Stephens). On the one hand, until recently scholars generally held the view that Hellenistic poetry should be regarded as "art for art's sake" (*l'art pour l'art*). Thus, for example, Schwinge (1986) has forcefully argued that one should read Callimachus' poetry as guided by purely aesthetic criteria and unrelated to contemporary society, and explains the particular character of Hellenistic poetry in general from the loss of the social function which poetry had in Archaic and Classical Greece and from the new context of philological research in which the poets operated at Alexandria and other Hellenistic courts. On the other hand, Cameron (1995a) has claimed that there was no "ivory tower" at all. According to him, we should reckon with a lively tradition of public performances of Hellenistic poetry, because the Ptolemies organized many festivals at which poetry was performed and traveling artists gave all sorts of recitals throughout the Hellenized world. In this picture, Hellenistic poetry is much more part of public life, and Callimachus appears as one within a generation of poets who traveled widely and whose poetry was not confined to a select audience.

The view of Callimachus' poetry as art for art's sake seems hard to maintain, if only because it does not explain why Callimachus wrote so many poems celebrating the Ptolemies, such as the *Victory of Berenice*, the *Lock of Berenice*, and the hymns to Zeus, Apollo, and Delos (*h.* 1, 2, 4). Cameron is thus surely right in challenging this view. Yet his own conclusions are not entirely convincing either. Instead of proving that all Hellenistic literature was produced for a broad audience, his evidence rather suggests that there were different kinds of literature then as there are today, and that texts written to be performed for larger audiences co-existed with more sophisticated texts intended for more exclusive audiences and/or individual readers. A first key argument for this view is that evidence for performances for larger audiences is not available for major Hellenistic poets such as Callimachus, Theocritus, or Apollonius Rhodius – as Cameron himself also admits, but without investigating possible explanations for this fact, like the rather obvious explanation that some works were too difficult for a general audience. Secondly, poets' efforts to create intertextual and structural subtleties in works like the *Aetia* would be hard to account for if their works were meant only or primarily for performance: full appreciation of such texts depends on their being read to or by a select audience of peers, and this suggests that their reception context was primarily the Alexandrian Museum, and secondarily a select audience of highly educated readers beyond the Ptolemaic court.

The diametrically opposed approaches of Schwinge and Cameron have been useful in focusing the discussion and provoking new thoughts about the context of Callimachus' work, and particularly the *Aetia*. In recent research we see attempts to refine and reconcile their views, with scholars arguing that Callimachus' poetry is much more engaged with contemporary issues than Schwinge allows, but yet not likely to have been part of public culture in the way Cameron thinks. Such evaluations tend to be based on a fuller examination of the evidence – for it is revealing that in Schwinge's book we find discussions of the prologue and the two poems for Berenice, but none at all of the other fragments of the *Aetia*, while Cameron pays very little attention to the highly allusive character of the prologue, on which much of his argument depends. A good example is the article by Asper (2001), who, focusing on the *Aetia*'s aetiological contents and its use of intertextuality, argues that the work served to establish a sense of common identity among the Greeks in Egypt, and in this respect fits in with the cultural politics of the Ptolemies, exemplified notably by the foundation of the Museum and the Library (Stephens and Strootman in this volume; for a political interpretation of Callimachus' use of aetiology, see also Selden 1998).

In this chapter I shall give some further examples of the insights generated by the new approach described above, focusing on the *Aetia*'s content, intertextuality, genre, and structure – aspects which are closely related and therefore will partly overlap in the discussion – concentrating on the text of the preserved fragments, as this is where we can learn most about the work. By analyzing these aspects we may gain a better picture of the *Aetia* as a typically Hellenistic work of art and get a sense of the purpose it may have served within the cultural politics of Ptolemaic Alexandria.

Content and Structure

Although much of the *Aetia* is lost, we have enough evidence to allow us to analyze the content of the *poem* as a whole. Surprisingly, such explorations have only been undertaken in a systematic manner in recent years. As we have seen, Asper (2001) has drawn attention to the fact that the antiquarian and aetiological stories of the *Aetia* "unite" the Egyptian Greeks, hailing from different areas in Greece proper and its colonies to the East and West, and that in this way the poem helps to create a sense of shared identity through a shared past, fitting in with Ptolemaic cultural politics. These observations are supported by an attractive suggestion of Fantuzzi and Hunter (2004: 54), who propose that we regard the *Aetia* as a continuation of Hesiod's *Theogony*, since it begins where the *Theogony* ends, with the myths of Minos, Heracles, and the Argonauts. In this reading, the *Aetia* continues the genesis of the Greek pantheon on the human level and shows the history of the Greek world as a continuum incorporating both gods and mortals. Starting from the earliest stages of human history, the poem moves through various phases of Greek history in all parts of the Greek world (Harder 2003b).

The period before the Trojan War is represented by the very characters mentioned at the end of the *Theogony.* We find evidence of Minos' imperial rule over the Cyclades in the first story of *Aetia* 1, which deals with the cult of the Graces at Paros (frs. 3–7). This story is followed by an episode from the expedition of the Argonauts (frs. 7–21) and stories about Heracles (frs. 22–5). Apart from this opening cluster, stories from the earliest period of human history also recur elsewhere in the *Aetia.* Heracles is the main character in the *Victory of Berenice* at the start of *Aetia* 3 (*SH* 254–68C), while Minos' son Androgeos appears in fr. 103 and the Argonauts are found again in fr. 108, both towards the end of the *Aetia.* Thus we see an emphasis on this early period at the beginning of the *Aetia*, where it belongs chronologically if we regard the *Aetia* as a kind of sequel to the *Theogony.* However, we find the same characters in structurally significant positions later in the *Aetia*, at the start and towards the end of the "added" second half of the work, shortly before we read about events in contemporary Alexandria in the *Lock of Berenice* (fr. 110). The effect seems to be that of a deliberate "disturbance" of chronology.

The Trojan War is largely absent from the *Aetia.* We find only a few stories about the return journeys of the Greek heroes and related events, such as Ajax's death at the Gyrades (fr. 35), Peleus' miserable death at the small island of Icus (fr. 178), and the defeat of the so-called Hero of Temesa, one of Odysseus' companions, whose ghost terrorized Temesa and was put to rest by Euthymus of Locri in the fifth century BCE (frs. 98–9).

Historical events from the Archaic period have left their traces in several parts of the *Aetia.* Events in Asia Minor reflecting the early period of colonization of the area in the tenth and ninth centuries BCE are prominent in *Aetia* 3–4. These stories include the love story of Phrygius and Pieria, which leads to peace between the towns of Miletus and Myus (frs. 80–3) and the treacherous murder of Pasicles of Ephesus (fr. 102). Seventh-century conflicts in the Aegean, also known from the poetry of Archilochus, are represented by the story of the Thracian Oesydres and the wars of the people of Paros with the Thasians and their Thracian allies (fr. 104). Another group of stories focuses on the western world, particularly the settlement of Sicily in late eighth century during the second wave of Greek colonization. These include a catalogue of Sicilian foundation stories and an explanation of the founder cult of Zancle (fr. 43), a story about Phalaris, the evil tyrant of Acragas who roasted strangers in a bronze bull (frs. 44–7), and a story about a war between Lipara and the Tyrrhenians that led to human sacrifice (fr. 93).

Finally, we also find references to later events, though somewhat more rarely. Some of the western stories bring us to the early Classical period, like those about the Panhellenic victors Euthycles and Euthymus of Locri (frs. 84–5 and 98–9) and about the tomb of Simonides, destroyed and built into the walls of Acragas, where he died in the early 460s BCE (fr. 64). Callimachus touches on the beginnings of Rome in the story of Gaius, a young Roman wounded during a siege of the city (frs. 106–7). And at the end of the *Aetia* we even reach third-century Alexandria where, after Berenice II sacrifices a lock of hair, a new constellation is discovered and a ritual established (fr. 110).

Of course all of this looks much neater than it would have appeared in a linear reading of the *Aetia*: one needs to reshuffle the episodes to make this chronological line visible. It appears as if Callimachus has deliberately made his "aetiological world-history" as discontinuous as possible (as one would also expect after reading the poem's prologue), but within an overarching framework that is chronological, starting with Minos, at the point where Hesiod stopped, and ending with Berenice in his own time. If Callimachus indeed shaped the *Aetia* in two stages, he seems to have provided a new perspective to his own work by including the catasterism of the lock of Berenice at the end of the new second half of the poem and so taking the poem to the present as "past of the future."

Within this general framework of an unobtrusive but purposeful chronology, the selection of stories also invites observations. On the one hand, one may detect topical elements. Callimachus' attention for islands like Sicily and Ceos fits in with their contemporary political importance for the Ptolemies, who had important contacts with Sicily and a fleet base on Ceos. The attention given to Argos and Heracles recalls the Ptolemaic claim of Argive descent through Heracles as well as the notion that Argos was refounded from Egypt by Danaus and his daughters, descendants of Epaphus, the son of Io, daughter of the Argive Inachus (Stephens in this volume). Thus the poem implicitly credits the Ptolemies with an intricate mixture of Greek and Egyptian origins and legitimates the presence of Greeks in Egypt. It also contains notions of progress and increasing civilization (Clauss 2000), exemplified by Heracles' killing of monsters and punishment of villains, and of cultural and political expansion, as shown by the stories about Minos, the Argonauts, and the Greek colonization of the Archaic period. Some *aitia* in fact present the idea of progress in a nutshell, like the one about the increasing sophistication of statues, which in the distant past were simple pieces of wood and gradually developed into works of art (fr. 100), and that of the various temples of Apollo at Delphi (fr. 118).

On the level of poetics, the absence of the Trojan War make perfect sense from the poet's expressed intention to move along untrodden paths (fr. 1.25–8), as there is no overlap in content between the *Aetia* and the Homeric poems. The absence of Trojan subjects is, however, counterbalanced by the prominence of allusions to the *Iliad* and *Odyssey*, which illustrates the complexity of Callimachus' engagement with the literary tradition: even this explicitly un-Homeric elegiac poem owes a great debt to, and constantly pays homage to, Homer. This is obvious, for instance, in the story of Peleus' death on Icus, set within the narrative framework of a symposium where "Callimachus" hears the story from Theogenes, a fellow guest from Icus (fr. 178). The framework recalls Odysseus' stories to the Phaeacians, and the narrator, Theogenes, is related to Odysseus by means of a number of allusions. Thus the reader is invited to view the un-Homeric story against a Homeric background and to appreciate the subtlety of Callimachus' innovative and experimental poetry.

The *Aetia*, we may conclude, is not a random collection of stories driven only by antiquarian interest and aesthetic criteria. A careful consideration of the stories' contents indicates that there is more at stake: they seem to have been selected and developed to create a sense of Greek identity and a notion of progress from the beginning of human civilization to third-century Alexandria. The fact that the arrangement of the stories looks rather random compared to Ovid's similar project in the *Metamorphoses*, where the chronological line is evident, may partly be due to the state of the transmission but it is also in line with Callimachus' explicit refusal, in the prologue, to write "one continuous song" (ἓν ἄειϲμα διηνεκέϲ, fr. 1.3). It is the reader's responsibility to identify the larger issues and worldview which emerge from the collection. These issues cannot have been immediately clear to a large listening audience, particularly because a performance could not easily encompass the whole of the *Aetia*. Clearly the views of Schwinge and Cameron are both hard to reconcile with the *Aetia*'s contents.

At first sight the stories in the *Aetia* seem to have been woven together more or less at random. In the prologue Callimachus himself admits to having written "not one continuous song" (fr. 1.3) and the remains of the *Aetia* (together with the scholia and *diegeseis*) seem to confirm the idea of discontinuity. As we have seen, there is no clear chronological order. Nor is there any obvious thematic organization: there are a few groups of related *aitia*, like those about scurrilous rituals, statues with strange features, scapegoats, and love, but one searches in vain for broader themes. Even so it is clear that certain programmatic and topical considerations underlie the structure of the poem (Harder 1993; Fantuzzi and Hunter 2004: 44–9). After the introduction of the dialogue with the Muses (fr. 2), the first *aition* is devoted to the Graces, as we have seen (frs. 3–7), the second to Apollo, the god of poetry (frs. 7–21), and the third and fourth are devoted to Heracles, ancestor of the Ptolemies (frs. 22–3 and 24–5). The second half of the poem is framed by poems about Berenice, with the *Victory of Berenice* opening *Aetia* 3 and the *Lock of Berenice* closing *Aetia* 4. Moreover, the *Victory of Berenice* focuses on Heracles, so that in this respect the start of *Aetia* 3–4 echoes that of *Aetia* 1–2.

A dialogue with Apollonius may also account for some aspects of the poem's structure. The Argonautic stories in the *Aetia* appear at the beginning of Book 1 (frs. 7–21 about Anaphe) and towards the end of Book 4 (fr. 108 about the anchor at Cyzicus), the opposite of their order in the *Argonautica*, where the former appears just before the end of Book 4 (1689–1730) and the latter in Book 1 (955–60). In other words, just as the *Aetia* starts where the *Theogony* ends, it also starts where the *Argonautica* ends, but while the poem moves forward in time from the end of the *Theogony*, it moves backwards in the story of the Argonauts, ending with one of their early adventures. Moreover, *Aetia* 3 contains two love stories, the story of Acontius and Cydippe (frs. 67–75) and the story of Phrygius and Pieria (frs. 80–3), and one may speculate whether this placement does not reflect the contents of the third book of Apollonius' *Argonautica*, with its focus on the love of Medea. It is also possible to read the end of the *Aetia*, the *Lock of Berenice* (fr. 110) with its emphasis on the love between king and queen (a prominent motif in Ptolemaic ideology throughout), as a counterpoint to the less-than-perfect relationship of Jason and Medea at the end of the *Argonautica*.

Within the individual stories that make up the *Aetia* the presentation can appear similarly random, but here too there is surely always a rationale to be identified by the attentive and well-informed reader. Callimachus' version of the Argonauts' adventures at Anaphe (frs. 7–21) presents a good example of his mode of operation at this level, and it also illustrates his engagement with Apollonius' *Argonautica* in detail. In this story the Argonauts are suddenly struck with utter darkness. After a prayer by Jason, Apollo sheds light, enabling the Argonauts to discover and land on the small island of Anaphe, where they honor Apollo as Aegletes ("the Radiant One"). The celebrations end in jesting between the Argonauts and Medea's Phaeacian servants, which explains the peculiar nature of the ritual for Apollo Aegletes that is still performed on Anaphe "today." As we saw, this is one of the last stories in the *Argonautica* but one of the first in the *Aetia*. This inversion is flagged with an allusion to the *Argonautica* at the start of the story, where Calliope instructs "Callimachus" as follows (fr. 7.23–6):

Αἰγλήτην Ἀνάφην τε, Λακωνίδι γείτονα Θήρηι,
  π]ρῶ̣τ̣[ον ἐνὶ μ]νήμηι κάτθεο καὶ Μινύας,
ἄρχμενος ὡς ἥρωες ἀπ' Αἰήταο Κυταίου
  αὖτις ἐς ἀρχαίην ἔπλεον Αἱμονίην.

First commit to memory Aegletes and Anaphe, the neighbor of Laconian Thera, and the Minyans (i.e., the Argonauts), beginning with how the heroes sailed back from Cytaean Aeetes to old Haemonia.

The words with which the Muse encourages the poet to start at the Argonauts' return journey recall not only the end of Apollonius' Anaphe story (4.1730 Αἰγλήτην Ἀνάφης τιμήορον, "Aegletes, the tutelary god of Anaphe") but also the very beginning of the *Argonautica*, and with it the "orthodox" starting point of the story (1.1–4):

ἀρχόμενος σέο, Φοῖβε, παλαιγενέων κλέα φωτῶν
μνήσομαι, οἳ Πόντοιο κατὰ στόμα καὶ διὰ πέτρας
Κυανέας βασιλῆος ἐφημοσύνῃ Πελίαο
χρύσειον μετὰ κῶας ἐύζυγον ἤλασαν Ἀργώ.

Beginning with you, Phoebus, I shall tell of the fame of the ancient men who drove the well-banked Argo through the entrance of the Pontus and the Cyanean rocks, following the command of king Pelias, in search of the Golden Fleece.

In the Anaphe story Callimachus incorporates events from various parts of the *Argonautica*, so that it looks as if the whole of the *Argonautica* has been squeezed into a single episode of the *Aetia*. The fragments contain references to the Argonauts' departure from Greece (A.R. 1.358–62 and 402–4), prayers of Jason that recall prayers at different stages in the *Argonautica* (1.411–24, 4.588–94, 4.1701–5), the anger of Aeetes when the Argonauts have left with the Fleece (4.210–40), the activities of the helmsman Tiphys (who died on the outward journey in the *Argonautica*, 2.851–63, but not in the *Aetia*), the various colonies founded by the pursuing Colchians (4.507–21), the Argonauts' stay with the Phaeacians (4.982–1169), and of course the events at Anaphe (4.1694–1730). Callimachus appears to have dealt with all this within the compass of 150 elegiac lines, against the close to 6,000 hexameters of Apollonius. Even from the little that survives it is clear that verbal similarities were frequent. Typical is Jason's prayer in fr. 18.5–11:

ἀλλ' ὅγ' ἀνι]άζων ὃν κέαρ Αἰcονίδηc
coὶ χέρας ἠέρ]ταζεν, Ἰήιε, πολλὰ δ' ἀπείλει
ἐc Πυθὼ πέ]μψειν, πολλὰ δ' ἐc Ὀρτυγίην,
εἴ κεν ἀμιχ]θαλόεccαν ἀπ' ἠέρα νηὸc ἐλάccηιc·
]. ὅτι cήν, Φοῖβε, κατ' αἰcιμίην
πείcματ'] ἔλυcαν ἐκ[λ]ηρώcαντό τ' ἐρετμά
]πικρὸν ἔκοψαν ὕδωρ.

But the son of Aeson, grieved in his heart, raised his hands to you, Ieius, and promised to send many (gifts) to Pytho and many to Ortygia, if you would drive the dark mist from the ship ..., because according to your oracle, Phoebus, they had loosened the ropes and allotted the oars... and beaten the bitter water.

These lines recall the Argonauts' allotment of the benches in *Arg.* 1.395–400 and Jason's following prayer at their departure (ἄλλα δὲ Πυθοῖ, / ἄλλα δ' ἐc Ὀρτυγίην ἀπερείcια δῶρα κομίccω, "but I shall brings endless gifts to Pytho and others to Ortygia," 1.418–19) as well as his prayer at Anaphe, towards the end of their travels, where it is given in indirect discourse as in the *Aetia* (πολλὰ δὲ Πυθοῖ ὑπέcχετο, πολλὰ δ' Ἀμύκλαιc, / πολλὰ δ' ἐc Ὀρτυγίην ἀπερείcια δῶρα κομίccειν, "he promised to bring many gifts to Pytho, many to Amyclae, many to Ortygia," 4.1704–5). In addition, Callimachus' prolepsis in fr. 12.6 regarding the future movements of the Colchian settlers (καὶ τὰ μὲν ὣc ἤμελλε μετὰ χρόνον ἐκτελέεcθαι, "and these things were thus to be fulfilled in later times") is verbally identical to Apollonius' prolepsis about the death of the Boreads in *Arg.* 1.1309, whereas the same notion is also conveyed in different words in the context of the Colchian settlements in *Arg.* 4.1216 (ἀλλὰ τὰ μὲν cτείχοντοc ἅδην αἰῶνοc ἐτύχθη, "but these things were fulfilled when a great deal of time had passed") – yet another allusion which evokes the first and last book of the *Argonautica* in conjunction.

Clearly the way in which Callimachus has shaped his Anaphe episode invites comparison with Apollonius, since there is a clear connection between these two texts. One may ask what this means. I have suggested in this section that Callimachus reacts to Apollonius and shows how one could treat a large-scale epic theme in one brief episode in an elegiac poem and, as it were, squeeze the whole of the *Argonautica* into a single episode of the *Aetia*. Others (e.g., Köhnken 2001) suggest the opposite order, which would imply that Callimachus' concise elegiac version was stretched out in a full-scale epic by Apollonius. Simultaneous interaction, with the poets composing their works at the same time and showcasing their different approaches, would be yet another option. Certainty is impossible to reach, but on the whole I think that it is most plausible that at least when Callimachus gave the *Aetia* the final form in which we know it, the complete *Argonautica* was available to him.

Intertextuality and Genre

Although scholars have long recognized that allusion is an important part of Callimachus' literary technique, they tended to regard it largely as a display of erudition, and only gradually embraced the idea that allusion has a crucial function in creating poetic and topical meaning (see, e.g., Reinsch-Werner 1976 on Callimachus and Hesiod; Fuhrer 1992 on Callimachus and Pindar; Harder 2002a). It is now more or less generally accepted that allusion creates a subtext to be read along with the main text, which comments on it and adds another level of meaning. Scholars have also become increasingly aware that allusion is rhetorically important, because it invites an active participation of readers and engages their goodwill and interest (Schmitz 1999; Harder 2002a). Another, more general function of allusion is, as we have seen, that it relates texts to the literary tradition of which they form part and thus makes readers aware of their cultural legacy and identity (Asper 2001). A few examples may illustrate these points, as they show how allusions help to embed the *Aetia* in the literary tradition as well as in its social context, and how Callimachus takes part in the cultural and political discourse of his age.

(1) We are told in the prologue that "the bountiful Demeter outweighs by far the tall (oak?)" (καθέλκει /....] πολὺ τὴν μακρὴν ὄμπνια Θεςμοφόρο[ς, fr. 1.9–10). "Demeter" here most probably refers to the title of a work by Philitas, which is to be compared favorably with another, longer poem (by Philitas or another poet; see Murray in this volume). Also present, however, are allusions to two other texts, which add further interpretive dimensions.

In the first place the lines recall the poetry weighing contest in Aristophanes' *Frogs*, where Aeschylus with "heavy" and martial lines trumps Euripides, who keeps throwing "light" and airy lines into the scales (see also Acosta-Hughes in this volume), and especially Dionysus' encouragement of Euripides in lines 1397–8: "now try to find some other item, in the heavyweight category, which will make the scales go down (καθέλξει) for you, a mighty and big one." Here the same verb as in fr. 1.9, καθέλκω, has as its subject the heavier item, which wins because it makes the scale go down, whereas in Callimachus its subject is the lighter item, which, although it goes *up*, wins by "outweighing" the heavier item in a metaphorical sense: the modern, lighter Euripides, who was the loser in *Frogs*, is here associated with the modern, lighter poetry that now *wins*. Thus the statement invites the reader to consider the issue of weight in the light of the literary tradition and of changing literary taste and values.

In the second place we are reminded of *Il.* 8.68–74 and 22.208–12. In these two passages the notion of weight appears in a context where Zeus is weighing the fates of mortals and the fates of those who are destined to die go *down*, i.e., those who go down are the losers as in Callimachus. Thus the reader is invited to interpret the passage of the *Aetia* against the background of epic as well and to pick up the notion that going down implies the death of heroes as well as the failure of the wrong kind of poetry.

(2) Somewhat further on in the series of metapoetic images of Callimachus' prologue, we find the statement: "let the crane who enjoys the blood of the Pygmies, fly away over a long distance to the Thracians" (μακρ]ὸν ἐπὶ Θρήϊκας ἀπ' Αἰγύπτοιο [πέτοιτο / αἵματ]ι Πυγμαίων ἡδομένη [γ]έρα[νος, fr. 1.13–14). These words allude to *Iliad* 3.2–7:

> The Trojans went with noise and shouts, like birds, as the sound of the cranes is in the sky, who, when they flee from winter and immeasurable rain, fly noisily over the streams of Oceanus, bringing the fate of death to the Pygmy men, and in the air they carry evil strife.

Again the allusion is more than a show of erudition. The movement away from Egypt in Callimachus is opposed to that in the *Iliad*, where the cranes are moving towards the Pygmies, and this change of direction has been thought to suggest that all long, i.e., wrong, poems should leave Egypt. The sound of cranes was considered particularly unpleasant, and this characteristic is also invoked by the allusion, because sound is the simile's *tertium comparationis*. Thus the image combines long distance and unpleasant sound, i.e., the wrong length and the wrong style of poetry, which continues the ideas of lines 9–12, where brief was sweet. Both notions are further developed in the images that follow – see, for example, the emphasis on length in the reference to the "Persian land-measure" (18) and on sound in those to the cicada and ass (29–36).

(3) An allusion with topical implications occurs at the start of the story of Heracles and Thiodamas (fr. 24). In the tale which immediately precedes (frs. 22–3), Heracles brutally slaughtered and ate the ox of a Lindian farmer, a rather surprising portrayal of the hero from which the poets' patrons claimed to descend. Subsequently Callimachus seems to create the impression that this has been a false start, because in the next story Heracles is, as it were, rehabilitated: he saves his starving son Hyllus by confiscating an ox from the rude farmer Thiodamas, and civilizes Thiodamas' people, the unruly Dryopians. When in fr. 24.1–3 the starving Hyllus pulls out the hair from Heracles' chest, the narrator comments: "and for you, lord, laughter was mixed with pain" (τὶν δ', ὦνα, γέλωϲ ἀνεμίϲγετο λύπηι, 3). This surprisingly recalls Andromache's emotions when, in *Iliad* 6, she receives Astyanax from her husband Hector after he has expressed the hope that his son may become "much better than his father" (479): "and she took him to her fragrant breast, crying and laughing at the same time" (ἡ δ' ἄρα μιν κηώδεϊ δέξατο κόλπωι / δακρυόεν γελάϲαϲα, 483–4). By associating Hyllus with Astyanax, who died while still a child and was not able to continue the Trojan dynasty, Callimachus suggests what is at stake in this story: by saving Hyllus, Heracles is saving the Ptolemaic dynasty.

Generically the *Aetia* is a complex and highly experimental poem (Fuhrer 1992; Harder 1998). In the first place, its overall framework recalls the didactic poetry of Hesiod. As was argued above, there are good reasons for regarding the *Aetia* as a continuation of the *Theogony* because it starts where Hesiod stops. The dream which opened and framed *Aetia* 1–2 (fr. 2) and the epilogue which capped the poem as a whole (fr. 112) both also evoke the *Theogony*, referring as they do to Hesiod's opening description of Chaos and his meeting with the Muses while tending his flocks on Mount Helicon. The *Aetia* also shares with the *Theogony* its movement from chaos to order and the notions of gradual progress and increasing civilization, and one might say that its climax in the Alexandrian present in the *Lock of Berenice* (fr. 110) mirrors the establishment of the power of Zeus at the end of the *Theogony*, suggesting a close association between the rulers of Egypt and the Ruler of Gods and Men as guarantors of order and stability, an idea also prominent in Callimachus' *Hymn to Zeus*.

The influence of *Works and Days* is harder to fathom from what survives of the *Aetia*, but that this Hesiodic poem was also of structural importance is suggested by the almost verbal quotation of one of its central lessons at the start of *Aetia* 1: fr. 2.5, "for whoever devises an evil thing against another devises an evil thing against his own heart" (τεύχων ὡϲ ἑτέρωι τιϲ ἑῶι κακὸν ἥπατι τεύχει) restates *WD* 265, "who devises evil things against another devises evil things against himself" (οἷ αὐτῶι κακὰ τεύχει ἀνὴρ ἄλλωι κακὰ τεύχων). Several stories in the *Aetia* illustrate this truth, for instance that of Phalaris, who fails to heed it when he starts roasting strangers in a bronze bull, but successfully teaches it to the bull's inventor, whom he throws in first of all (frs. 44–7). The flip side of the coin is, of course, that whoever does good will experience good. This is illustrated for instance in the *Victory of Berenice*, where Molorcus gives a friendly reception to Heracles and is rewarded with a mule and perhaps also a ritual.

In contrast with Hesiod, Callimachus composed the *Aetia* in elegiac distichs rather than hexameters. Reasons for his choice of meter may be that, on the one hand, it seems to allow more room for extensive, and sometimes playful, personal interventions of the narrator and on the other hand, particularly in contrast with the limited number of applications of hexameter poetry before the Hellenistic period, more freedom to choose a variety of subjects ranging from epic adventures (like those of the Argonauts, frs. 7–21) to grim and sordid stories (like the death of the adulterous Leimonis and her lover at Athens, frs. 94–5) to romance (as in the love story of Acontius and Cydippe, frs. 67–75). The moralizing character of the *Aetia* also recalls early elegiac wisdom poetry such as that of Solon and Theognis. Callimachus' choice of "elegiac didactic," as it were, enables him to pick up the moral issues of Hesiod, but apply them to more divergent aspects of human life.

On lower compositional levels numerous other genres are evoked. We find extended passages and even whole sections in the shape of a hymn (fr. 7), epic catalogue (fr. 43), funeral epigram (fr. 64), dedicatory epigram (fr. 110) or Pindaric epinician (the *Victory of Berenice*). Within these passages Callimachus exploits generic conventions to create extra layers of meaning. Two examples may help to illustrate this and to show how it affects the interpretation of the *Aetia* in its literary and social context.

Programmatic issues are prominent in fr. 7.13–14, where the story of the Graces (Charites) on Paros is given a hymnal closure when Callimachus prays to them to give his poem lasting fame:

> ἔλλατε νῦν, ἐλέγοιcι δ' ἐνιψήcαcθε λιπώcαc
> χεῖραc ἐμοῖc, ἵνα μοι πουλὺ μένωcιν ἔτοc.
>
> Be gracious now and wipe your shining hands on my elegies, in order that they may live for many years.

Although the story of the Graces is the first *aition* of the *Aetia*, i.e., the first part of the poem's "body," this hymnal ending gives it the status of a hymnal proem like the hymn to the Muses which begins Hesiod's *Theogony* and like the *Homeric Hymns*, which were intended as introductions to a performance of epic. Thus Callimachus alludes to epic practice and to the *Theogony*, but he diverges by asking the favor, not of the Muses, but of the Graces, who are not so much associated with Hesiod as with Pindar, who refers to them frequently. Even so we should not forget that the story of the Graces is told by the Muse Clio within the framework of a dialogue between "Callimachus" and the Muses, which results in a double claim: the *Aetia* will be authoritative because its information comes from the Muses, and graceful because it is backed by the Graces.

Programmatic issues may also be observed in Callimachus' genre-play in the *Victory of Berenice.* This poem has the form of a Pindaric epinician (Fuhrer 1992), but it is by no means a slavish imitation. The mere fact that it is elegiac rather than lyric already implies a different mood and register, and Callimachus' choice of the myth is un-Pindaric as well. The poem's central story of Heracles' stay at the cottage of Molorcus on his way to Nemea features a rural setting, a poor farmer, trouble with mice, and the construction of mousetraps. Molorcus' struggle against the mice that have infested his home in fact replaces the heroic story of Heracles killing the Nemean lion (which was probably left out altogether, as we may infer from fr. 57; see also Ambühl in this volume). Moreover, the *Victory of Berenice* celebrates Berenice not in a traditional choral performance, as was the case with the Pindaric epinicians, but by its conspicuous position at the beginning of Book 3 of the *Aetia*, framing *Aetia* 3–4 together with the *Lock of Berenice.* In this, and more generally in the virtuosity of the text, which only a – very perceptive – reader would have been able to fully appreciate, Callimachus "epinician" is clearly the product of a more literate society.

The *Victory* must be read against the background not only of epinician, but also of epic. Homer is evoked, for example, in *SH* 257.15–20, where even the scanty remains allow us to see that Molorcus' reception of Heracles is modeled after Eumaeus' reception of Odysseus in *Odyssey* 14. In *SH* 259 an epic style time-indication and a simile likewise give the story an epic flavor and draw the reader's attention to Callimachus' manipulation of the epic conventions. The former, "when the evening star was about to loosen the yoke from the oxen" (ἀcτὴρ δ' εὖτ'] ἄρ' ἔμελλε βοῶν ἄπο μέccαβα [λύcειν / αὔλιοc], 5–6), indicates the onset of evening in an image taken from the *Iliad*, where the farmer's well-deserved rest from labor is typically contrasted with the exertions of the heroes, who throw themselves into battle at that very moment (e.g., 11.86–91, 16.779–80). We see the same thing occur in Callimachus, but ironically on a domestic level: the approach of evening signals the mice's invasion into Molorcus' cottage and the beginning of his "epic" battle against them. Callimachus achieves a similar effect with the simile (*SH* 259.9–11):

ὁ δ' ὅτ' ἔκλυεν ἠχ[ήν,
ὡc ὁπότ' ὀκν]ηρῆc ἴαχ' ἐπ' οὖc ἐλάφου
cκ]ύμνοc, [μέ]λλ[ε] μὲν ὅccον ἀκουέμεν, ἦκα δ' ἔλ[εξεν· . . .

And when he heard the noise (at the door), as when a lion cub roars at the ear of a frightened deer, he paused briefly to listen and then spoke softly: . . .

On seeing Molorcus compared to a deer, an animal which in Homer always is the frightened victim of stronger beasts, the reader may expect him to give up in despair; instead, however, he stands his ground against the mice and puts up a fight. The allusion underlines the character of Callimachus' narrative, opposed as well as indebted to epic, and illustrates how the intertextual and generic subtext which Callimachus creates in the *Aetia* is crucial to the poem's interpretation and enhances its "messages" at various levels.

* * *

Recent scholarship on the *Aetia* has done a great deal for the appreciation and understanding of this intriguing and influential Hellenistic poem. It continues to move away from an interpretation of the poem as art for art's sake and at the same time keeps illustrating the level of sophistication it expects of its audience. The *Aetia* deals with obscure facts and stories and presents them in a learned and apparently random way, so that at first sight it gives the impression of an antiquarian at play. Yet on closer inspection the poet proves to be thoroughly engaged in the literary and political discourse of his time as well as the entire Greek literary and cultural tradition, and behind the chaos of his poem there proves to be an intricate order. In its discontinuity and protean versatility, the *Aetia* perhaps demands more than any other Hellenistic poem of its readers in terms of the preparation, commitment, and ingenuity required to decode its complex messages and formulate answers to such questions as why these specific stories have been selected, why they have been arranged and framed in this manner, and why they are told in this specific form, voice, and language. At the time when it was composed, the *Aetia* must have been not only boldly innovative but also deviously challenging, and it is not surprising that it soon became an emblem of third-century Alexandrian poetry and a major source of inspiration for other poets, Greek and Roman.

FURTHER READING

Recent introductions to the *Aetia* include Hutchinson 2003, Fantuzzi and Hunter 2004: 44–88, and Asper 2004: 23–31. On the important prologue (fr. 1) one may also consult Acosta-Hughes and Stephens 2002, and on the *Victory of Berenice* Parsons 1977. The standard edition of the Greek text is still Pfeiffer 1949, with additions in Lloyd-Jones and Parsons 1983 (*SH*) and Lloyd-Jones 2005 (*SSH*).

Recently the *poem* has been explored in partial commentaries such as Massimilla 1996 (*Aetia* 1–2), Fabian 1992 (*Aetia* 2), Marinone 1997 (fr. 110), Torraca 1973 (fr. 1), and Hopkinson 1988 (frs. 1 and 67–75 Pf.). For the whole of the *Aetia* useful tools are the text, Italian translation and brief but very helpful commentary of D'Alessio 2007; the English translation by Nisetich 2001, which offers very helpful transitional passages between the fragments; and the text with German translation and brief notes by Asper 2004. My own commented edition of the whole of the *Aetia* will appear in 2010.

CHAPTER EIGHT

Hellenistic Elegy: Out from Under the Shadow of Callimachus

Jackie Murray

Tunc et elegiam uacabit in manus sumere, cuius princeps habetur Callimachus, secundas confessione plurimorum Philetas occupauit.

Quint. *Inst.* 10.1.58.6–7

Then he will also be free to take up elegy, of which Callimachus is held to be the prince, and Philitas occupies second place in the opinion of most.

Precious little Greek elegy survives and most of what does survive predates the Hellenistic period. Unsurprisingly, scholars trying to determine the distinctiveness of Hellenistic elegy have for a long time approached Hellenistic elegy largely through its reception in Roman poetry. Here we not only have a larger body of evidence with which to work, but Roman elegists also explicitly present themselves as continuators of a specific Hellenistic stream of the genre, often identifying their own poetics as "Philitan-Callimachean" or simply "Callimachean" (Prop. 2.34.31–2, 3.1.1–4, 3.52; Ov. *Ars* 3.329, *Rem. Am.* 759–60). Yet this well-trodden route is strewn with pitfalls, and there is a growing consensus among scholars that, since Roman poets had their own culturally and ideologically specific poetic agenda, we should be very cautious in using Roman poetry as a guide to Hellenistic poetry (Ziegler 1966; Cameron 1995a; Hinds 1998; Hunter 2006a; Ambühl and Acosta-Hughes in this volume). The problem of periodicity presents another potential obstacle to understanding "Hellenistic elegy." As Benjamin Acosta-Hughes demonstrates in his chapter in this volume, many of the gestures that we have long identified as hallmarks of "Hellenistic" poetics are in fact already present in the works of poets from earlier historical periods, raising the question of whether it is at all valid to apply modern historiographical boundaries to literature. Yet, there does seem to be something quite different about this literature, as is also suggested by the fact that so many Roman poets exploit for their own poetic and political ends a contrast between the earlier Greek poets and those who flourished in the historical Hellenistic period (Hunter

2006a: 42–80). But the questions of precisely what this difference is and how its demarcations can be recognized need more attention. Only through a careful study of "Hellenistic" poetics both in relation to more general notions of Greek poetics and in relation to Roman poetics can this distinctiveness be accurately described. In the small compass of this chapter, I will entirely forego the backward glance from Roman poetry and instead broach this issue, the distinctiveness of Hellenistic elegy, by looking forward from earlier manifestations of the genre. In particular, I will consider the tangible influence of changes to poetic production in the late fifth and fourth centuries BCE on the development and demarcation not only of elegy but also the adjacent genres of epigram and epic, in the third century and beyond.

Toward a Definition of Hellenistic Elegy

Elegy is one of oldest Greek poetic genres. It is at least as ancient as hexameter poetry and inscriptional epigram, and is closely related to both in meter and language (Friedländer and Hoffleit 1948: 65–70; West 1982: 35–46; Gentili 1968: 39–81; Aloni 1981: 80–103; Bowie 1986: 13–14; Powell 1991: 142–80). Yet from its earliest manifestations onward elegy is far more difficult to define as a genre. This is not so much a consequence of the paucity of the specimens that have come down to us as of their abundant variety. This variety is so puzzling that scholars have yet to reach a satisfactory description of early Greek elegy that says more than simply "a poem composed in elegiac couplets" (Gerber 1997: 91; M. L. West 1974: 2–21). Philosophical, military, sympotic, and personal erotic themes are well attested in the poems that survive, but there is also sufficient evidence to confirm later reports about the existence of elegies resembling long hexameter poems on mythical and "historical" themes, for example, in the fragments of Mimnermus' *Smyrneis*, Tyrtaeus' *Politeia* or *Eunomia*, Panyassis' *Ionika* (Bowie 1986: 27–34), and last but not least Simonides' so-called Plataea Elegy (first published in West 1992, frs. 10–18; cf. Boedeker and Sider 2001). Elements in this last poem additionally point to the existence of early hymns composed in elegiac couplets (Rutherford 2001b: 38). In fact, no theme seems to have been out of bounds for the elegist. It has been suggested that early elegy did not extend to the "scurrilous or obscene" (Bowie 1986: 14; cf. Gerber 1997: 91), but the absence of examples of such elegies may be simply an accident of preservation.

There is a tendency among modern scholars of early elegy to privilege the poetic forms of the Archaic period as stable and fixed prototypes devoid of any self-consciousness, and to regard any subsequent variation as an illegitimate degeneration. Ironically, this also applies to the subject matter which in modern literature, through Roman poetry, has become inextricably linked with the label "elegy": mourning. Some have argued that funerary or threnodic elegies (dirges) are no "real" forms of the genre but an artificial development of the fifth century inspired by sophistic and philosophical debates about the origins of the genre (Bowie 1986: 21–7; Gerber 1997: 91; differently Page 1936: 206–30; Aloni 2001). According to this view, Archilochus *IEG* 13 (seventh century BCE), which has references to grieving the dead (κήδεα μὲν cτονόεντα, 1) and the elegiac threnody in Euripides' tragedy *Andromache* (420s BCE) are to be dismissed as evidence for a subgenre of threnodic elegy, the former because of its sympotic performance context and the latter as a self-conscious product of contemporary musical theory that postulated a derivation of the term *elegos* from ἒ ἒ λέγειν, "say *e e*" (Bowie 1986: 22–3; cf. Pfeiffer 1968: 53–62). Yet we have so few examples of elegy from the Archaic period that we are not in a position to say categorically that there were no threnodic elegies composed before the fifth century BCE. Moreover, it is possible to read the Archilochus fragment as exploiting a tension between threnodic and sympotic elegy. Certainly, the poem's exhortation to "bear it and quit womanly lament" (τλῆτε, γυναικεῖον πένθος ἀπωcάμενοι, 10) differentiates what men should sing in symposia from what women sing at funerals, and something like the elegiac lament in Euripides' *Andromache* may well lie behind the opposition. Finally, the fragments of Simonides' Plataea Elegy, composed shortly after the 479 BCE battle that it commemorates, provide an early example of mourning in elegiac couplets (Allan 2000: 55–7; Aloni 2001: 90–1; Yatromanolakis 2001: 211–12, 219–20; differently Mace 2001). So, there is no good reason to doubt that at least some elegiac poems from the Archaic period did conform in their content to the later common understanding of elegy, even if they may not have been explicitly labeled as "threnodic elegy" (Aloni 2001: 105). This example strongly cautions against treating the limited number of extant examples as if they represented clearly defined and fixed prototypes of the genre. In fact this notion of the genre being fixed in the early period is blatantly inaccurate since the early elegists can be shown to be self-consciously negotiating the boundaries of the genre in their poetry in gestures that we have come to associate only with Hellenistic poets (see Acosta-Hughes in this volume).

Elegy Versus Epigram

The variety of early elegy means that it cannot be distinguished sharply from other genres on the basis of theme or subject matter. Occasion and mode of performance do not set it apart either. Longer elegies on subjects that were of interest to the community were performed publicly, but so were epics on similar themes. Similarly, as Bowie observes (1986) shorter elegies were performed in symposia, but by the fifth century symposiasts were in the habit of performing (singing and reciting) various kinds of poetry and even prose as part of the festivities. Even meter, ostensibly the genre's only distinctive characteristic, is not entirely unproblematic, since hymns and epigrams were also composed in elegiac couplets.

Elegy and epigram are completely separable only in the Archaic and early Classical periods when, as Kathryn Gutzwiller (1998) observes, they occupied different spheres of experience. The communicative context that defined the aesthetics of Archaic and Classical poetry, including elegy, was performance; the writing down of poems had only a mnemonic function (Immerwahr 1964: 17–48; Herington 1985: 45–7, 201–6). Poetry existed on the lips of the performer, not independently as words on a tablet or book roll. This put epigram in a different category: the physicality of the text and the surface upon which it was inscribed were integral aspects of epigram's aesthetic value. Location was also important, since most epigrams were anonymously composed and read by random passersby. Indeed, early epigram's meaning often depended more upon the monument that bore it and its context than upon the words per se (Raubitschek 1968: 3; Häusle 1979: 88–105). Moreover, prior to the Persian Wars epigrams rarely exceeded two couplets; thereafter, epigrams between two and four couplets seem to be standard (West 1974: 2). By the same token, the exigencies of performance seem to dictate that Archaic and Classical elegies be no shorter than five couplets (Faraone 2005a, 2008: 71–92). Two exceptions are worth noting: a five-couplet inscription of the mid-sixth century found on a *polyandrion* in Ambracia (Bousquet 1992; D'Alessio 1995) and a five-couplet Megarian inscription attributed to Simonides (*FGE* 16 = *IG* VI.53). In both cases, we seem to have a threnodic elegy that was performed and then transcribed onto to a monument to commemorate the dead (Faraone 2005b, 2008: 31–42, 134–5). Although these poems in their final form do blur the distinction between elegy and epigram, the manner of this blurring is hardly self-conscious; it is simply the result of inscribing the elegy (compare Fantuzzi in this volume on inscribed paeans). So, despite similarities in meter, language, function, and even content, elegy and epigram in the Archaic and Classical period were notionally different animals (Gutzwiller 1998: 2).

That situation changes radically in the third century. In Hellenistic manifestations of elegy and epigram the borders between these genres have become permeable. These borders only remained solid so long as written versions of elegies remained mere mnemonic devices for performance and these texts never acquired an aesthetic status equivalent to the performance, and epigrams remained inscribed on their monuments and were never performed or recorded in book rolls. This distinction began to break down as early as the end of fifth century with the development of symposia where the recitation of speeches (*rhēseis*), notably from drama, became prevalent alongside singing elegies and other types of sympotic song (Murray 1990; Cameron 1995a: 72–3; Bowie, 1994, 2007: 95–6; Wissmann in this volume). In this same period written texts began to be used more widely and certain compositions took on the aesthetic status of literature as opposed to functional documents (Thomas 1989: 45–94; Gutzwiller 1998: 47). A consequence of these changes was generic seepage between elegy and epigram. By the mid-fourth century, inscriptional and mock inscriptional epigrams were being recited at symposia (Pl. *Phdr.* 264d; Gutzwiller 1998: 116), and by the early Hellenistic period collections of "elegiac poems" consisting of elegies *and* epigrams began to circulate for use in symposia; the examples that survive are the *Theognidea* and the collection of Simonides' epigrams (West 1974: 57; Page 1981: 123; Molyneux 1992: 13–15; Sider 2007). With the creation of the *Theognidea*, the textual "transcript" was transformed from an aide-mémoire into a "script" for recitation, which expanded the performance possibilities of the elegies it contained beyond those dreamt of by their composers. Elegies could now be performed both from memory and by someone reading directly from the text (Immerwahr 1964: 17–48; Herington 1985: 45–7, 201–6). The activities of copying and collecting had an even more interesting effect on the relationship between elegy and epigrams. The epigrams of Simonides were composed to be meaningful in conjunction with the monument on which they were inscribed. However, once these inscribed epigrams were replicated in a collection, they existed in a medium that allowed them to be performed.

In other words, the advent of the book roll transformed elegy and epigram into a new kind of homogeneous elegiac book poetry (Gutzwiller 1998: 3–8). By the third century, poets were writing elegies and epigrams to be appreciated ultimately as book poetry, regardless of whether they were *also* performed or inscribed (Gutzwiller 1998: 115–82). Thematically, elegy and epigram also merged as poets started composing erotic epigrams suitable for a sympotic performance context (real or imagined). Thus in the book rolls shorter elegies became "virtually indistinguishable" from longer epigrams (Gutzwiller 1998: 5, cf. 115–20). Whereas in Archaic and Classical poetry we can securely separate shorter elegies from longer epigrams by looking at the poems' implied medium of communication, performance versus inscription, in the case of Hellenistic poems in elegiac couplets we seem to be forced to rely on generic labels applied by scribes, grammarians, and scholiasts (Gutzwiller 1998: 47–53). What is interesting is that the ancient scholars and poets applied the generic label *epigrammata* to many of these third-century collections of elegiac poems. Thus a new type of "epigram" emerged in the third century: the sympotic epigram (Gutzwiller 1998: 115–82; Bowie 2007; Bruss in this volume). In other words, third-century epigrams covered the same thematic ground as Archaic and Classical elegy. The implication seems to be that epigram became the favored genre and that shorter elegy became assimilated to it. Effectively, shorter elegies came to be considered epigrams.

Elegy Versus Epic

The scholarly consensus follows Ewen Bowie's important study which argues that in the Archaic and Classical periods shorter elegies were performed at symposia, whereas longer narrative elegies – some reaching hundreds or thousands of lines – were composed for public performance (Bowie 1986; cf. Dougherty 1994). These longer poems seem to have functioned as a less prestigious alternative to hexameter poetry on civic occasions (Aloni 2001: 90). The scant evidence we have suggests there may have been a basic thematic difference between the two forms: narrative in hexameters appears to have been restricted to mythological events set no later than the Heroic Age, whereas narrative in elegiac couplets could extend into the Iron Age and even into the recent past. Mimnermus' elegiac *Smyrneis* celebrated the war between Smyrna and Gyges and the Lydians, Tyrtaeus' *Politeia* (or *Eunomia*), Spartan prowess in the Messenian Wars. Semonides composed an elegiac *Archaeology of the Samians*, Panyassis a *History of Ionia* (*Ionika*), Simonides elegies on the Battle of Artemisium (*IEG* 1–4) as well as the Battle of Plataea. The meter of Ion of Chios' *Foundation of Chios* is uncertain, but this poem too was most likely in elegiacs (Bowie 1986; Aloni 2001). Mimnermus, according to Pausanias (9.29.4 = Mimn. *IEG* 13), referred to two sets of Muses in his proem to the *Smyrneis*: the more ancient Muses, daughters of Ouranos, and the more recent Muses, daughters of Zeus. There are various ways to interpret this distinction, but one obvious way is to see the reference as demarcating the different time periods covered by the narrative: events set in the Heroic Age are governed by the older Muses and events set in the Iron Age, by the younger Muses (Bowie 1986: 29). Similarly, as Eva Stehle (2001) argues convincingly, Simonides in his Plataea Elegy constructs a poetic voice for himself as a bard of the Iron Age in opposition to Homer, the bard of the Heroic Age, by beginning his Plataea Elegy with a hymn to Achilles. She argues that by staging the Muses not as the source of his song, as they are in Homeric epic, but as his "allies" (*epikouroi*) Simonides opposes his poetic enterprise – the glorification of the heroes of Plataea – to that of Homer – the glorification of the heroes of the Trojan War.

The thematic distinction between hexameter and elegiac public poetry seems to have crystallized when the Persian Wars created a strong demand for public performances celebrating its themes and heroes. We can discern a tendency among poets and historians alike to claim for more recent events equal, if not greater status, than events of the mythical past (e.g., Hdt. 1.1, Thuc. 1.1–21). The popularity of the Persian Wars as a theme in public poetry of the Classical period is clear. Aeschylus not only staged his *Persians*, he is also said to have rivaled Simonides with an elegiac poem on the Battle of Marathon (*Vita Aeschyli* 2.28–30 = *TGrF* 3.33–4). Simonides in addition to elegies on Artemisium and Plataea composed a lyric poem on the Battle of Salamis (*PMG* 536). Timotheus composed a lyric *Persika* and Phrynichus a tragic *Phoenissae*. Yet despite its popularity as a theme, the Persian Wars did not become established as a subject of hexameter epic until the end of the fifth century, when Choerilus of Samos composed his *Persika* (*SH* 316–23, *PEG* 1–25b; 425–395 BCE? see MacFarlane 2009). There is some evidence suggesting that Empedocles may have composed a hexameter *Persika* earlier (Sider 1982; Kingsley 1996), but what distinguishes Choerilus' achievement is its recognition and influence: Choerilus was granted the extraordinary privilege of re-performing his work alongside the Homeric poems at the Panathenaic Festival in Athens (*SH* 315 = *PEG* test. 1). Moreover, in what survives of his proem, Choerilus implies by his complaint that there is no place for his poetic chariot in the race of the Muses that he is striking out in a new poetic direction (*SH* 317, quoted by Acosta-Hughes in this volume). In fact, Choerilus seems to be making the claim that he is refashioning the genre (MacFarlane 2009). Obviously, composing a poem on the Persian Wars was not in itself innovative; but composing an epic on this theme was. Choerilus' "invention" of historical epic probably had important ramifications for the long public elegy. Since epic always enjoyed the status of top genre, by breaking down the thematic boundary between these two adjacent genres Choerilus effectively paved the way for the retroactive elevation of long elegies on historical themes, notably the Persian Wars, to the status of epic. Indeed, this would have been facilitated by the fact that the term *epos* could refer to elegiacs as well as hexameter poetry. In other words, it is highly likely that by the fourth century "epic" as a generic concept became less of an indicator of meter and more of an indicator of theme (Boedeker 1995: 226–9, 2001).

The Classical elegies celebrating the Persian Wars were read in Ptolemaic Egypt and probably in most of the Greek-speaking world (Barbantani 2002/3: 32). Their influence on the development of "historical" or "encomiastic" poetry in the Hellenistic period seems to have been substantial. For example, there are allusions to Simonides' Plataea Elegy in Theocritus' encomia for Hiero II and Ptolemy II Philadelphus (*Id.* 16 and 17; Hunter 1996: 9–109; Fantuzzi 2001; Bulloch in this volume). Indeed, the only obvious examples of historical elegy from the Hellenistic period, *SH* 958 and 969 (which may be sections from the same poem), are consistent with the language and style of the remains of earlier historical elegies (Barbantani 2001). The importance of the Persian Wars as a theme to the genre as a whole is evident in *SH* 958, where in an exchange between a messenger and a king, the Galatians are compared with the Persians (*SH* 958.7–16, text after Barbantani 2001):

χὼ μὲν] ἐπεὶ μάλα πάντα δι' οὔατος ἔκλ[υε μῦθον
  ὠργίcθη, βρι]αρὸν δ' αὐτίκ' ἄνεcχε λόγ[ον.
"ἀνέρε]c ὑβριcταί τε καὶ ἄφρονεc, ἀλλὰ μ̣[άλ' ὦκα
  [τίcουcι]ν ταύτηc μιcθὸν ἀταcθαλίηc,
γνώcον]ται δὲ μαθόντεc, ἐπεὶ καὶ ἀρεί[οναc ἄλλουc
  τούτων] εἰc κρατερὴν δουλοcύνην ἔθεμ[εν.
οὖδ' ἔμπ]ηc Μήδοιcι βαθυκτεάνοιcιν ὁμ[οίωc
  οἶδε βιώ]cαcθαι θοῦροc ἀνὴρ Γαλάτηc.
οὐ γὰρ πο]ρφυρέοιcιν ἐν εἵμαcιν οὐδὲ μύροιc[ιν]
  κοιμᾶται] μαλακὸν χρῶτα λιπαινόμενο[c
ἀλλὰ χα]μευνάδιόc τε καὶ αἰθρι[ά]α<ι> ἐνι[αυτόν."

When the whole report came to his ears, he flared up with rage and immediately raised a threatening speech: "These arrogant and foolish men! Well, they will soon pay the price for this outrage and learn the hard way, because we have put into harsh slavery men better than them. And yet the bold Galatian man does not at all live like the Medes, deep in wealth. For he does not fall asleep in crimson garments after anointing his soft skin with sweet perfume, no, he lies down on the ground and in the open all year round."

There is some debate among scholars about which events are being alluded to in this passage and whether the "Medes deep in wealth" refers to the forces of Xerxes, Darius III, or even the Seleucids (Barbantani 2001: 188–223, 2002/3: 36–45). It seems reasonable to rule out Xerxes, since by the Hellenistic period the Persian Wars theme would have been focused more squarely on Alexander's conquest of the Persian Empire and less on the Athenian and Spartan forces thwarting the invasion of Greece, which by now must have paled by comparison. But in any case, the reference to the Persians evokes the Classical elegiac and hexameter poems celebrating military victories over the Barbarian. Thus, it can be read as an attempt to bolster the value of this elegy by placing it in the older tradition of "epic" *Persika*, which by the third century would have notionally included (without metrical distinction) elegiac poems such as those composed by Simonides and Aeschylus, and hexameter poems like those composed by Choerilus and possibly Empedocles.

The dawning book culture not only caused short elegy to be swallowed up by "epigram," it also contributed to the most important innovation in long elegy. Around 400 BCE, Antimachus of Colophon, a younger contemporary of Choerilus, composed the *Lyde*, which seems to have been the most remarkable elegiac poem prior to Callimachus' *Aetia*. The *Lyde* had its roots in public catalogue poetry, the most important Archaic representative of which was the Hesiodic *Catalogue of Women* (Hunter 2005b). As far as the scanty fragments (in Matthews 1996) allow us to discern, the *Lyde* was a catalogue of mythological stories in at least two books, organized around the common themes of misfortune and grief. What made the poem different was its personal narrative frame: Antimachus presented the mythological stories in the context of consoling himself after the death of the woman he loved, Lyde. The *Lyde*'s personal frame would have made it unsuitable for a festival or public performance, whereas its length probably precluded presentation of the poem in its entirety at a symposium. Clearly Antimachus reckoned with readers as well as listeners.

In terms of content, the *Lyde* is often mistakenly described as featuring the sad love affairs of heroes (Del Corno 1962: 77–8). In fact, the pseudo-Plutarchan *Consolation to Apollonius*, one of our primary sources for the poem's general theme, describes it as follows (*Mor.* 106b–c = Antim. test. 12 Matthews 1996):

> ἀποθανούϲηϲ γὰρ τῆϲ γυναικὸϲ αὐτῶι Λύδηϲ, πρὸϲ ἣν φιλοϲτόργωϲ εἶχε, παραμύθιον τῆϲ λύπηϲ αὐτῶι ἐποίηϲε τὴν ἐλεγείαν τὴν καλουμένην Λύδην, ἐξαριθμηϲάμενοϲ τὰϲ ἡρωικὰϲ ϲυμφοράϲ, τοῖϲ ἀλλοτρίοιϲ κακοῖϲ ἐλάττω τὴν ἑαυτοῦ ποιῶν λύπην.
>
> After his wife Lyde died, toward whom he was very affectionate, [Antimachus] composed the elegy called the *Lyde* to soothe his pain by cataloguing the misfortunes of heroes, to lessen his own pain with the troubles of other people.

It would be wrong to follow Hecker in changing the text to read "erotic misfortunes" (ἐρωτικὰϲ ϲυμφοράϲ). "Misfortunes of heroes" (ἡρωικὰϲ ϲυμφοράϲ) is consistent with the Homeric description of the theme of Phemius' epic song to the suitors in *Odyssey* 1 and Demodocus' epic song to Odysseus and the Phaeacians in *Odyssey* 8 (1.326–7 "he sang the disastrous return [νόϲτον λυγρόν] of the Greeks," 350 "the miserable doom [κακὸν οἶτον] of the Greeks"; 8.498, 578 "the doom [οἶτον] of the Greeks"). Antimachus apparently used heroic, i.e., epic stories, to assuage his grief at the loss of his beloved – more probably his mistress than his "wife," as the moralizing *Consolation to Apollonius* claims (Matthews 1996: 27). There is indeed hardly any evidence from the fragments of the *Lyde* to suggest that the myths narrated were especially erotic in nature (Matthews 1996: 32). Ovid in *Tristia* 1.6.1, which invokes the *Lyde* as a model, uses very much the same strategy (Cairns 1979: 219–20). The fragments also suggest that the language or style of the *Lyde* was not significantly different from Antimachus' great epic poem, the *Thebaid*. In fact, it seems that it is exactly the "epicness" of the elegiac *Lyde* which Callimachus criticized with the notorious words Λύδη καὶ παχὺ γράμμα καὶ οὐ τόρον, "the *Lyde*, a fat piece of writing and not sharp" (fr. 398 Pf. = Antim. test. 15 with Matthews 1996: 27–39; Cameron 1992: 309).

The *Lyde* seems to have shown the way for poets in the fourth and third centuries to compose similar thematically arranged subjective catalogue elegies of considerable length on themes suitable for the symposium and/or private reading but not for public performance (Hunter 2005a: 259–64). From the frequent coupling of Antimachus and his *Lyde* with Philitas and his "Bittis," it seems reasonable to assume that Philitas also composed a substantial catalogue poem dedicated to his girlfriend which may or may not have been named after her (Cameron 1995a: 381; Spanoudakis 2002). *Loves* or *Beautiful Boys* of Phanocles was a substantial catalogue poem on pederastic love affairs (*CA* pp. 106–9; Hopkinson 1988: 177–81). The *Leontion* of Hermesianax of Colophon comprised a three-book-long catalogue of love affairs which included poet lovers in the third book (*CA* pp. 96–106). Alexander Aetolus, a contemporary of Aratus (Fraser 1972: 1.555; Magnelli 1999), composed an *Apollo* which was a catalogue of famous clients of Apollo's oracle at Didyma (*CA* pp. 122–3). It is also possible that his other elegy, the *Muses*, may have been a catalogue of poets and/or their corresponding literary genres (Cameron 1995a: 382; *CA* pp. 124–6). The strangest example is the so-called Tattoo Elegy (*SH* and *SSH* 970), an elegiac catalogue of cautionary mythological scenes that the speaker threatens to tattoo upon the body of his enemy (probably his erotic rival). The extant lines describe a fight between Heracles and the Centaur Eurytion, the punishment of Tantalus, and the Calydonian boar hunt (Huys 1991; Slings 1993; Lloyd-Jones 1994; Rawles 2006; Bernsdorff 2008). Outside of Callimachus' oeuvre, the longest specimen of Hellenistic elegy to survive is Hermesianax's *Leontion* (*CA* pp. 96–106), originally three books in length, of which 98 lines are quoted in Athenaeus' *Learned Banqueters* (Ath. 13.597b = *CA* 7; Asquith 2005; Hunter 2005a; Caspers 2006). This passage is a catalogue of poets both mythical and historical in which Hermesianax assigns to each poet a beloved whose name seems to be drawn from his poetry. For example, in addition to Antimachus and Lyde and Philitas and Bittis, he includes Hesiod and Ehoie (alluding to the *Catalogue of Women*), Mimnermus and Nanno (alluding to the title of Mimnermus' collected erotic poems) and Homer and Penelope (alluding to the *Odyssey*). His own poem apparently inserted itself into this series of poetic love affairs: it was named after his own mistress Leontion.

All of these elegiac catalogues are often treated as successors to the Hesiodic *Catalogue of Women*, but they should also be considered direct descendants of the *Lyde*, with which they all seem to share a subjective narrative frame (Asquith 2005: 279–86). And as Krevans (1993) and Cameron (1995a: 382) both point out, even Callimachus' *Aetia*, though it draws heavily on Hesiod's hexametric *Theogony* (Fantuzzi and Hunter 2004: 51–60), nevertheless owes much to Antimachus' elegy. The *Aetia*'s catalogue of stories, however, seem to embrace all the generic diversity of Archaic poetry in elegiacs (Harder 1998), including epigram (e.g., in the story of the inscribed apple in Acontius and Cydippe, frs. 67–75 Pf.), sympotic elegy (e.g., the banquet of Pollis, fr. 178 Pf.), and encomiastic elegy (e.g., in the *Victory of Berenice*, *SH* 254–68). So, in a sense, Callimachus' *Aetia* is a subjective catalogue of different types of elegy.

Callimachus' Big Lady

There is very little we can say for certain about the nature of Hellenistic elegy on the basis of the fragments that survive. Yet, as we have seen, it is possible to show without recourse to Latin elegy that Greek elegiac poetry of the third century BCE was significantly different from its Archaic and Classical predecessors. What has emerged is an interesting picture. In the case of shorter sympotic or private elegy, the evolution of the literary epigram resulted in a merger of the two forms. It seems fair to say that once the literary epigram became popular, shorter elegy was assimilated to it and effectively disappeared. A similar process of assimilation is likely to have taken place between long public elegy and hexameter epic. After it became acceptable to treat "historical" themes in hexameter poetry, the border between the two forms collapsed. Accordingly, a long poem on heroes and kings would have been considered epic, regardless of whether it was composed in hexameters or elegiac couplets. Thus by the third century, elegy had lost most of its variety. Following Antimachus' *Lyde*, the main form of elegy became the long subjective catalogue poem, culminating in Callimachus' long catalogue of "origins," the four-book *Aetia*.

There is, nevertheless, no escaping recourse to the prologue of the *Aetia* in any exploration of Hellenistic elegy. Callimachus began his poem as follows (fr. 1.1–12 Pf.; on the supplements see Luppe 1997; Müller 1998; Acosta-Hughes and Stephens 2002):

πολλάκ]ι μοι Τελχῖνες ἐπιτρύζουςιν ἀ˻οιδῆ,
νῆιδε˻ς οἳ Μούςης οὐκ ἐγένοντο φίλοι,
εἵνεκε˻ν οὐχ ἓν ἄειςμα διηνεκὲς ἢ βαςιλ[η
......]ας ἐν πολλαῖς ἤνυςα χιλιάςιν
ἢ.....].ους ἥρωας, ἔπος δ' ἐπὶ τυτθὸν ἑλ[ίςςω
παῖς ἅτ˻ε, τῶν δ' ἐτέων ἡ δεκὰ˻ς˼ οὐκ ὀλίγη.
......].[.]και Τε[λ]χῖςιν ἐγὼ τόδε· "φῦλον α[
.......] τήκ[ειν] ἧπαρ ἐπιςτάμενον,
Κώιος οὐ] γὰρ ἔην [ὀλ]ιγόςτιχος· ἀλλὰ καθέλ˻κει
δρῦν] πο˻λὺ τὴν μακρὴν ὄμπνια Θεςμοφόρο[ς·
τοῖν δὲ] δυοῖν Μίμνερμος ὅτι γλυκύς, α[ἱ γ' ἁπαλαὶ μὲν
νήνιες,] ἡ μεγάλη δ' οὐκ ἐδίδαξε γυνή.

Often the Telchines grumble at my song –
fools who are not friends of the Muse! –
because I haven't written a single, continuous song
in thousands of verses on kings
[or ...] heroes, but I [tell my stories] little by little
just like a child, though the decades of my years are not few.
... to the Telchines I reply this: "You race [of ...],
knowing only how to devour the liver,
[the Coan poet to be sure was not] a man of few verses,
but his bountiful Thesmophoros drags down by far his tall [oak],
[and] of [the] two it is Mimnermus' [delicate girls] that teach
how sweet he is, not his big lady.

For the longest while, scholars have understood this passage as implying that Callimachus was taking a stand against epic poetry. Recently, Cameron (1995a: 307–38) cast doubt on this reading by arguing that the object of Callimachus' scorn was not epic, but long catalogue elegy in general and Antimachus' *Lyde* in particular. As I have argued, after Choerilus the distinction between epic and elegy disappeared in respect to long public poems. So, when Callimachus rejects long poems about heroes and kings, it is likely that he means both elegiac and hexameter "epic." In fact, I would submit that Callimachus is engaged here in a typically elegiac strategy, already deployed by the Archaic elegists, namely establishing the thematic boundaries of elegy vis-à-vis other types of elegy as well as adjacent genres (compare, for example, Xenophanes fr. 1.13–24 Gentili and Prato 2002, Thgn. 757–64; see Acosta-Hughes in this volume). In lines 9 to 12, Callimachus allusively points out to his critics that the long poems of Philitas of Cos and Mimnermus are aesthetically inferior to their shorter works. In the case of Philitas, "Thesmophoros" points to his influential elegy, *Demeter*. This analogy alludes to Demeter's introduction of agriculture which caused grain ("Thesmophoros") to replace acorns ("tall oak") as the main source of human sustenance (Müller 1998). Callimachus thus asserts the superiority of this comparatively short poem to a longer Philitan poem. Since oak trees symbolized Homeric epic, I suggest that the other poem was in hexameters, most likely Philitas' *Hermes*, since it reworked Homer's account of Odysseus' visit with Aeolus, the king of the winds. Mimnermus'"big lady" seems to refer to his long historical elegy, *Smyrneis*; this poem Callimachus compares unfavorably to the collection of Mimnermus' short sympotic elegies that circulated under the title *Nanno* ("delicate girls"; West 1974: 72–6; Bowie 1986: 13–35; Allen 1993: 20; Asquith 2005: 281–2; Hunter 2005a: 260–1). Thus the prologue to the *Aetia* seems to equate the long poems of Philitas and Mimnermus, whether composed in hexameters or elegiacs, thematically, formally, and/or aesthetically and stylistically with long poems about kings or heroes (3–5), i. e., "epic." As a result, the long subjective catalogue elegy which it introduces, the *Aetia*, is set up as the new measure for long elegy, supplanting any pre-existing standard, notably the *Lyde*. Any elegy that does not fit the *Aetia*'s definition of the genre is rated inferior. The success of the *Aetia* in revising the history of elegy and establishing itself as the *aition* of Hellenistic elegy is evident in Quintilian's canon of Greek elegists, quoted at the beginning of this chapter. For, despite the fact that it was Antimachus who started the trend of subjective catalogue elegy, Quintilian only prescribes Callimachus and Philitas to the aspiring orator.

FURTHER READING

The most recent discussion of the complex relationship between Hellenistic and Latin elegy is Hunter 2006a. Cameron 1995a is a controversial but important treatment of Callimachus' role in shaping taste in Hellenistic elegy. Gutzwiller 1998 has much that is relevant to the distinction between epigram and elegy. The papers in Boedeker and Sider 2001 on Simonides' Plataea Elegy contextualize the proliferation of historical elegy in the Hellenistic period. MacFarlane 2002, 2006, and 2009 are similarly important for Choerilus' innovation in epic. The extant fragments of Hellenistic historical elegy are discussed by Barbantani 2001 and 2002/3. On the influence of Antimachus, see Matthews 1996 and Krevans 1993; on that of the Hesiodic *Catalogue of Women*, Hunter 2005a and Asquith 2005.

Fragmentarily preserved Hellenistic elegies are collected in Powell 1925 (*CA*) and Lloyd-Jones and Parsons 1983 (*SH*), with additions in Lloyd-Jones 2005 (*SSH*). For individual authors see also: Antimachus: Matthews 1996 and Cameron 1995a: 303–38; Philitas: Spanoudakis 2002; Eratosthenes: Rosokoki 1995; Alexander Aetolus: Magnelli 1999; Euphorion: Van Groningen 1977 and Magnelli 2002; Hermesianax: Hunter 2005a, Asquith 2005, and Caspers 2006; Phanocles: Hopkinson 1988: 45–6, 177–81; Parthenius: Lightfoot 1999; the Tattoo Elegy: Huys 1991, Rawles 2006, and Bernsdorff 2008.

CHAPTER NINE

Epigram

Jon S. Bruss

At Arlington

Two dates carved in stone above his grave
tell us he was seventeen, not how
this soldier died, nor whether he was brave
or terrified, or both. No matter now:
the only life he had to give, he gave.

This short poem by Wiley Clements (2004: 145) uses the five-beat meter standard for poetic epitaphs in English. Yet it is not an epitaph but a reflection on an epitaph: a wanderer through Arlington National Cemetery interprets the inscription on one of the thousands of gravestones that, in neat, criss-crossing lines populate the undulating hills. This much we can gather if we combine the information the poem supplies with our knowledge of the location specified by its title. The curtness of the soldier's epitaph – no more than two dates and, presumably, a name – makes the poet speculate about the implications of the information the stone provides (this soldier was seventeen years old when he died) and about what it does not and even cannot tell him ("not how this soldier died, nor whether he was brave or terrified, or both"). The curtness of Clements' poem in turn begs us to inquire further. Who is the young man who lies under the stone, and where was he from? He must be an American, or he would not be buried at Arlington. His young age suggests that he died in battle, so to which war did he give his life? The age supplies a clue: it must have been an early war, when seventeen-year-olds could enlist. While we formulate such hypotheses, we are, as sophisticated readers, aware that it is the poet who has made us experience the soldier's grave in this way. Our experience of the tombstone comes from words on a page. We have no way of telling whether the stone is even real, nor can we, in the end, be completely confident about the "reading" which we have put on it and on the poet's reflection about it (Does it matter that this poem was published during the war in Iraq? What do we know about the author? What about the journal in which it was published?). The best among Hellenistic epigrams present many of the same challenges and rewards. They too invite the reader to read closely the little that is there so that they may be able to supplement what the poem does not say but the reader must realize in order to truly appreciate the poet's creation (*Ergänzungsspiel*: Bing 1995). What is more they similarly often resist a final interpretation.

Two Byzantine collections, the *Palatine Anthology* and *Planudean Anthology* (abbreviated *AP* and *APl.*), preserve for us many thousands of lines of short poetry composed in elegiac distichs, testifying to the continuing popularity of the genre of literary epigram until late antiquity. In addition, a substantial number of epigrams has survived in other ways, such as quotations in Athenaeus' *Learned Banqueters*. From this body of material Gow and Page (1965) identified roughly a thousand poems as deriving ultimately from Meleager's *Garland* (*Stephanos*), the earliest attested anthology of epigrams (c.100 BCE; Cameron 1993), running to 4,700 lines and composed by over 60 poets, some represented with a large number of poems (e.g., Leonidas of Tarentum with 103, Meleager himself with 132). To give this figure some sense of scale, it is the equivalent of roughly three tragedies or a third of the *Iliad*. Thousands of further lines can be ascribed to another early anthology, composed around 40 CE by Philip of Thessalonica, whose *Garland* included epigrammatists who wrote between Meleager and his own time (Gow and Page 1968).

Since Gow and Page published their editions of the *Garlands* of Meleager and Philip, the process of collection and arrangement of epigrams in "poetry books" and anthologies has received a fair amount of scholarly attention (Cameron 1993; Gutzwiller 1998; Sider 2007; Krevans 2007; Argentieri 2007). This debate has been fueled recently by the appearance of the "New Posidippus," a papyrus from the third century BCE (*P.Mil.Vogl.* VIII 309) preserving the (in some cases scanty) remains of 112 epigrams. Of these epigrams 110 are new to us, but two are attested elsewhere under the name of Posidippus (15, 65 AB = 20, 18 GP), which has led many scholars to conclude that all 112 poems are from the hand of that poet. Whether that is so or not, the papyrus underscores how much of the epigram production of the Hellenistic period is lost. It also provides us with an insight into the organization of an epigram collection that predates the *Garland* of Meleager by more than a century, confirming, for example, the arrangement of epigrams by subgenre and preserving the title of eight such entries.

Whatever the status of this specific collection, it is likely enough that anthologies of epigram existed well before Meleager. I have argued elsewhere that the 22 epigrams which constitute the preserved oeuvre of Alcaeus of Messene (fl. 200 BCE) may have appeared within a multi-poet collection drawn together by Alcaeus himself (Bruss 2002/3). What has come down to us from Alcaeus includes an uncharacteristically large percentage of political-satiric epigrams, a type meagerly represented in Meleager's *Garland*, and then under other headings. As in the case of the "New Posidippus," which contains various types of epigram meagerly or not at all represented in the *Garland*, one wonders what we have lost because it did not fit Meleager's selection criteria.

"Inscribed" Epigrams

Many types of literary epigram from the Hellenistic period pose as epigrams inscribed in stone, such as those commonly found on tombstones and dedicated objects (Day 2007; A. Petrovic 2007; Bettenworth 2007). In what follows I will attempt to give an impression of how such poems play with the conventions, and explore the possibilities of, their inscribed "ancestors." As my starting point I will use a literary funerary epigram by the poet Dioscorides in which many of the influences and currents in Hellenistic epigram come together. As for most Hellenistic epigrammatists, Dioscorides' dates are uncertain, but he was in any case active after the death of the comic poet Macho (in the second half of the third century BCE), for whose Alexandrian tomb he composed an epitaph (24 GP = *AP* 7.708). The following epitaph, too, is for a writer of sorts: the name of Philaenis, apparently a famous courtesan, is attached to what seems to have been a notorious manual on courtship and sex, fragmentarily preserved for us in *P.Oxy.* 2891, from which we can gather that it opened with sections on making passes, flattery, and kissing (what followed is easy to guess). But the attribution, Philaenis insists, is incorrect and her notoriety undeserved (26 GP = *AP* 7.450):

τῆϲ Σαμίηϲ τὸ μνῆμα Φιλαινίδοϲ. ἀλλὰ προϲειπεῖν
  τλῆθί με, καὶ ϲτήληϲ πληϲίον, ὦνερ, ἴθι.
οὐκ εἴμ᾽ ἡ τὰ γυναιξὶν ἀναγράψαϲα προϲάντη
  ἔργα καὶ Αἰϲχύνην οὐ νομίϲαϲα θεόν,
ἀλλὰ φιλαιδήμων, ναὶ ἐμὸν τάφον. εἰ δέ τιϲ ἡμέαϲ
  αἰϲχύνων λαμυρὴν ἔπλαϲεν ἱϲτορίην,
τοῦ μὲν ἀναπτύξαι χρόνοϲ οὔνομα, τἀμὰ δὲ λυγρήν
  ὀϲτέα τερφθείη κληδόν᾽ ἀπωϲαμένηϲ.

The tomb of Samian Philaenis. Talk to me,
  if you dare, and come up close to the pillar, sir.
I'm not the one who wrote up for women these
  repugnant tricks and who didn't think Modesty was a god.
No, I was a lover of modesty – on my grave, I was! And if anyone
  has written a scurrilous treatise, putting me to shame,
may time spew out his name; and may my bones
  rejoice when I've shaken off my sorry reputation.

The inscriptional derivation of this poem is obvious. Its opening combines two distinct modes of self-presentation familiar from Greek funerary epigram: that by the monument ("[this is] the tomb of Samian Philaenis") and that by the deceased ("talk to me"). The first mode is attested from a very early date in Greek funerary inscriptions and is the main mode in Archaic one-line inscriptions. On a sixth-century Attic grave column, for example, we find the hexameter "[Thi]s is the tomb of [name missing], a good and [prude]nt man" (. . . τόδ]ε ϲῆμ᾽ ἀγαθοῦ [καὶ ϲώφρον]οϲ ἀνδρόϲ, *CEG* 36.ii; the spelling has been normalized, as in the following examples). But the same conflation of forms as in Dioscorides' epigram already appears in the inscription on the "Phrasicleia *korē*," a funerary statue of an unmarried girl which is contemporary with the grave column of the "good and prudent man" and may been sculpted by the same artist (*CEG* 24.i; Svenbro 1993):

> cῆμα Φραcικλείαc. κούρη κεκλήcομαι αἰεί,
> ἀντὶ γάμου παρὰ θεῶν τοῦτο λαχοῦc' ὄνομα.

> The *sēma* of Phrasicleia. I shall be called a girl forever,
> having received from the gods this name as my share instead of a marriage.

The first half of the first line identifies the monument as a grave marker for Phrasicleia. Then, as in Dioscorides' poem, the voice breaks, becoming first-person: the dead girl, represented by the statue, now presents herself, relating her circumstances in death – unmarried – which itself serves as an aetiology for her monumental presentation as a *korē*. Phrasicleia's *korē* is one of only a handful of Archaic funerary monuments with epigrams for females, almost all of which are for unmarried girls. If the surviving evidence is in any way representative, this puts the epitaph of Philaenis, whose highest goal in life was certainly not marriage and who supposedly lived her life to the full, in an ironic light.

Dioscorides' poem also plays on another trope common to funerary epigram: seeking to attract the passerby's attention. Witness, for example, this c.510 BCE epigram inscribed on the base of a funerary *stele* (*CEG* 51):

> οἴκτιρον προcορῶ[ν] παιδὸc τόδε cῆμα θανόντοc,
> Σμικύθ[ου], ὅc τε φίλων ὤλεcεν ἔλπ' (*sic*) ἀγαθήν.

> Mourn as you take in this *sēma* of a dead child,
> Smicythus, whose death has destroyed the great expectations of his loved ones.

The address envisions an individual reader and demands grief as a response (οἴκτιρον), a move which, as Day 1989 has convincingly shown, seeks to "reactivate" the mourning ritual. Smicythus' death at a young age has bereft his loved ones, likely his parents, of what in the Greek world was a fervent hope, support in their old age. The reader is asked to place himself in the position of the decedent's parents as an incentive to mourn. In Dioscorides 26 GP, the address to the passerby is comprised entirely of Philaenis' speech. But instead of invoking a "you," or a generic "wayfarer" (ὁδίτηc, παροδίτηc) or "stranger" (ξεῖνοc), Philaenis, in keeping with the very trade from which she tries to disassociate herself, specifically beckons a *man* (ὦνερ, 2). Her opening words, "talk to me, if you dare, and come up close to the pillar, sir," figure the addressee as morally superior, a decent man less than eager to be involved in conversation by a woman like Philaenis, whether she be dead or alive.

In literary funerary epigram (collected largely in Book 7 of the *Palatine Anthology*), such games with the addressee – a passerby who now travels through a scroll rather than by road – are nearly ubiquitous. For example, in an epigram by Asclepiades (third century BCE), the "owner" of a cenotaph provides the passerby with the following instruction: "tell my father Melesagoras, whenever you arrive in Chios, how an evil Eurus destroyed me and my ship and my business and that the name of Euippus is the only thing left" (31 GP = *AP* 7.500). The poem exploits the tension between the fixedness of Euippus' tomb and the mobility of the wayfarer, who is not merely expected to stop, read, and mourn (expectations so standard that they need not be expressed), but also to memorize or write down the epigram's message, carry it with him, and report it to Euippus' father in Chios. In another Asclepiadean epigram, similarly for the victim of a shipwreck (30 GP = *AP* 7.284), the address to the passerby is humorously inverted into an address to the sea, whom the drowned man urges to "stay eight cubits away" and not destroy his grave on the seashore. Such addresses are a mimetic device that assists in the realization of the fiction it perpetrates; within the confines of a collection of poems, such inversions also maintain a reader's attention by arresting it.

Hellenistic literary epigram also plays with the inscriptional genre of the dedicatory epigram. Greek temples were full of objects dedicated by worshippers who came to petition or thank the gods for success or salvation, and many of them bore metrical inscriptions such as the following epigram from Rhamnus in Attica, accompanying a marble statue of a youth (*CEG* 320, c.420 BCE):

Λυσικλείδηc ἀνέθηκεν Ἐπανδρίδου υἱὸc ἀπαρχὴν
τόνδε θεᾶι τῆιδε, ἣ τόδ' ἔχει τέμενοc.

Lysicleides, son of Epandrides, dedicated this as a first-fruits offering
to this goddess who holds this sacred precinct.

The physical context of this epigram obviates the need to specify a number of basic details. The reader who encounters this text *in situ* can see that the dedicated object ("this") is a statue of a youth, and knows he is in the sanctuary of Themis ("this goddess who holds this sacred precinct," with overuse of the near-field deictic ὅδε). Specified are only the dedicator's name – Lysicleides son of Epandrides – and the reason for the dedication – a first-fruits offering.

Most literary dedicatory epigrams appear in Book 6 of the *Palatine Anthology*, a grouping that seems to derive ultimately from Meleager's *Garland*. Six dedicatory epigrams also make up a section in the "New Posidippus" under the heading *Anathēmatika* (36–41 AB). Some of these epigrams may once have been inscribed on actual objects, others are likely to be entirely fictional; all have in common that they can be appreciated in isolation, in a context where the object(s) and locations to which they refer must be imagined on the basis of the information the epigram provides. Contrast Lysicleides' dedication with the following poem by Perses, one of the earliest Hellenistic epigrammatists, active at the end of fourth century BCE (1 GP = *AP* 6.112):

τρεῖc ἄφατοι κεράεccιν ὑπ' αἰθούcαιc τοι, Ἄπολλον,
ἄγκεινται κεφαλαὶ Μαιναλίων ἐλάφων,
ἃc ἕλον ἐξ ἵππων †γυγερῶι χέρε† Δαΐλοχόc τε
καὶ Προμένηc, ἀγαθοῦ τέκνα Λεοντιάδου.

Three heads with antlers that leave one speechless
are dedicated in your porch, Apollo, from Maenalian stags,
which Dailochus † . . . † took on horse,
and Promenes, sons of noble Leontiadas.

Promenes and Dailochus, sons of a notable Theban family, appropriately dedicate trophies of their (bow-?) hunt to the far-shooting god, Apollo. The fact that the family is known gives the poem an air of realism; but deictics are absent. All the reader is to "see" is provided by the text – up to a point: the poem has no real "here," except wherever one might imagine the sanctuary where the stags' heads are dedicated to stand. It also remains unclear why these Theban aristocrats should have gone all the way to Arcadia to hunt stags on a mountain associated with Apollo's stag-hunting sister Artemis (e.g., Call. *h.* 3.89, 224). Such breaches in realism may also be observed in other epigrams by Perses that seem to refer to actual people and events (e.g., 4 GP = *AP* 7.501). They suggest that this poem, too, is not a real dedication but about the sort of dedication people like the sons of Leontiadas might make after doing the sort of thing one imagines such people do.

A distinct subgenre of literary dedicatory epigram is formed by poems about professionals dedicating objects associated with their trade (Rossi 2001: 131–4). Such dedications have a basis in reality – Greek temples must have been full of appropriate objects dedicated to ask or thank for professional success – but as in the case of epitaphs Hellenistic poets exploited the potentials of the basic setup and conventions in imaginative and often humorous ways, producing epigrams one would be very surprised to find inscribed on an actual object. This applies, for example, to a pair of dedicatory epigrams incorporated not in Book 6 but in Book 5 of the *Palatine Anthology*, which contains "erotic" epigrams (*erōtika*) – illustrative of the problems of categorization faced by ancient anthologists and modern scholars alike. These epigrams, one by Asclepiades (6 GP = *AP* 5.203), the other possibly by Posidippus (127 AB = *AP* 5.202) rather than Asclepiades (35 GP), commemorate the dedication of spurs, whips, and reins by two rather extraordinary jockeys; and in the latter we encounter a familiar name (127 AB for text and translation):

πορφυρέην μάcτιγα καὶ ἡνία cιγαλόεντα
  Πλάγγων εὐίππων θῆκεν ἐπὶ προθύρων,
νικήcαcα κέλητι Φιλαινίδα τὴν πολύχαρμον
  ἑcπερινῶν πώλων ἄρτι φρυαccομένων.
Κύπρι φίλη, cὺ δὲ τῇιδε πόροιc νημερτέα νίκηc
  δόξαν, ἀείμνηcτον τήνδε τιθεῖcα χάριν.

Her purple whip and glittering reins
  Plango dedicated on the portico of fine horses,
having defeated as a jockey Philaenis, the hardened campaigner,
  when evening colts had just begun to neigh.
Dear Cypris, grant her the true glory of her victory,
  by having this favor remembered forever.

Plango, doubtless a practitioner of the world's oldest profession, can boast of "riding" skills to beat those of epigram's most famous prostitute, Philaenis. The poem borrows tropes from several genres of epigram. The recall of Philaenis' defeat at her hand and the speaker's plea for "the true glory of her victory" explicitly link the poem to victory epigram (Köhnken 2007). The placement of the tools used to accomplish her victory at Cypris' temple, along with the very language of dedication, borrows from dedicatory epigram. And the "event" in which Plango defeated Philaenis evokes the world of erotic epigram. The ingenuity of the poem lies in its conflation of these tropes within what was probably a common metaphor (worked out in great graphic detail in Asclepiades 6 GP, which Posidippus may have intended to cap) in a surprising direction: if prostitutes "riding" customers are like jockeys, they can be imagined as competing in races with other prostitutes and, after winning such a race, dedicating the sort of objects jockeys dedicate and praying for the eternal fame that equestrian victories bring (if they are commemorated in poetry).

In addition to the large corpus of dedicatory epigrams in elegiacs, there also survive some Hellenistic dedicatory poems of a somewhat different nature, the so-called figure poems (*technopaignia*), included in Book 15 of the *Palatine Anthology*. The genre is associated especially with the early third-century poet Simias of Rhodes, for whom three such poems are attested. Other figure poems, equally replete with riddles and glosses, are ascribed (not in all cases convincingly) to Dosiadas, Besantinus, and Theocritus. It is still a matter of debate where these poems first debuted: on papyrus (Bing 1988: 15 and 1990: 281–2) or as inscriptions on actual objects (Cameron 1995a: 33–7)? What is clear is that in these poems the poet manipulates the length of the lines so that the shape of the poem mimics the dedicated object, real or imaginary, to which it refers. For example, the first line of Simias' *Wings* (*AP* 15.24) runs to 23 syllables, but each of the next lines becomes shorter by one choriambic foot (—⏑⏑—) until in line 6 only the three-syllable clausula is left (⏑–⏓). This pattern is reversed in the second half of the poem, where the lines increase from one foot in line 7 to six in line 12, forming the second wing of "swift-flying" (9) Eros. We might imagine the poem inscribed on the wings of a statue of Eros, but the practicalities of its arrangement pose problems. The same applies to Simias' *Egg* (*AP* 15.27). As this poem has come down to us in the *Palatine Anthology*, its lines ascend in length from the first to the tenth, and descend in length from the eleventh to the twentieth, but they must be read in the order first, last, second, second-last, third, third-last, etc. (in line with the poem's own riddling "reading instruction"). Wilamowitz (1906: 245), followed by Gow (1952b: 179) and Cameron (1995a: 35), suggested that the only way the poem makes sense is as an inscription on the top half of a bronze or stone egg, such that what are now lines 1 and 20, which must be read sequentially, wrapped around the top of the egg (inscribed on opposite sides), lines 2 and 19 below that, and so on to lines 10 and 11, which would have been circumscribed around the egg's girth. A mirror image of *Egg* (but in the meter of *Wings*) is Simias' *Axe* (*AP* 15.22), a dedication by Epeus of the axe he used to build the Wooden Horse, which has been nonsensically arranged in the *Anthology* to form a two-headed axe. Printed in the proper order, the lines of the poem form an up-ended triangle in which every third line becomes one choriamb shorter, in such a way that one can imagine it being inscribed on opposite sides of a (single-headed) axe. The question of whether *Axe* was originally inscribed is ultimately unanswerable. What can be said is that, just like Hellenistic "inscriptional" epigrams in elegiacs, these poems do not *require* any other context than the papyrus scroll to work.

Epigram and Symposium

The world of the symposium provides another originary locus for epigram (Bowie 2007). In fact, Richard Reitzenstein (1893) suggested that the very conduit through which inscribed epigram became literary was the Classical-era symposium, which in his eyes formed an ideal habitat for the (competitive) exchange of short, witty poems and which was in any case the context for much of the elegiac poetry of the Archaic period. The theory was for a long time roundly rejected, but has been recently revived by Alan Cameron (1995a), who posited a lively Hellenistic culture of poetry composition and performance for and at symposia – and incurred many of the same criticisms that Reitzenstein did from scholars who emphasize the bookishness of Hellenistic epigram. The truth in this issue (which is bound up with a broader discussion about orality and literacy in Greek culture) probably lies somewhere in between the two poles; though closer to which remains to be seen. What we may safely assume, however, is that the symposium also in Hellenistic times remained a key locus for social interaction between adult males, featuring drinking, musical entertainment, games, sexual excitement, and the exchange of speeches and poetry (Murray 1990; Strootman in this volume). Illustrative of the continuing importance of poetic exchange at Hellenistic symposia is the grisly story, told by Plutarch (*Alex.* 51.1–6) and Arrian (4.8.7–9), of how a poetic barb at a royal symposium led Alexander the Great to drive a spear through his general Cleitus. Alexander's reaction to Cleitus' attempt to send a message through what is in itself normal sympotic behavior – citing poetry – implies he assumed the other symposiasts would also grasp that the aim of Cleitus' first thrust, "alas, what an evil regime in Hellas" was to evoke the next lines from Euripides' *Andromache*, about a tyrannical general who alone claims credit for the work of a whole army.

Hellenistic epigram, if not a product of the symposium in the first place then at least a product of a world in which the symposium mattered, often addresses sympotic themes. For example, Dioscorides' epitaph of Philaenis, discussed above (26 GP), through its very protagonist evokes this setting, the courtesan's natural playground; it also takes the moralizing that is typical of Archaic sympotic poetry in elegiacs in a rather cheeky direction. From the sympotic setting, real or imagined, whole subgenera of Hellenistic epigram arise. So-called sympotic epigrams directly evoke the symposium by explicit reference to drinking. Erotic epigram is also closely connected with it, directly as well as indirectly through the influence of Archaic erotic lyric arising from the sympotic setting (Giangrande 1968; on erotic epigram in general, see Garrison 1978; Gutzwiller 2007b).

No other epigrammatist's extant oeuvre is as steeped in the world of the symposium as that of Hedylus of Samos. All 12 poems attributed to him (two perhaps falsely) have sympotic themes, and it is probably not coincidental that in Meleager's introduction to the *Garland* (1 GP = *AP* 4.1) he is mentioned in one breath with Asclepiades, his elder compatriot (and source of inspiration?), and with Posidippus (45–6), both also prominent contributors to Meleager's selection of sympotic-erotic verse. Two poems in particular by Hedylus, both quoted by Athenaeus (11.473a), preserve a lively understanding of the symposium as a source for subject material for epigram – if not also as a performance setting and locus of epigrammatic invention (5 and 6 GP):

πίνωμεν, καὶ γάρ τι νέον, καὶ γάρ τι παρ᾽ οἶνον
  εὕροιμ᾽ ἂν λεπτὸν καί τι μελιχρὸν ἔπος.
ἀλλὰ κάδοις Χίου με κατάβρεχε καὶ λέγε, παῖζε
  Ἡδύλε· μισῶ ζῆν ἐς κενὸν οὐ μεθύων.

Let's drink, and maybe, maybe in my cups
  I'll be able to find something new and slick, some sweet epigram.
Come, drown me in jars of Chian wine and say: "Play,
  Hedylus." I hate living in vain – not being drunk, that is.

ἐξ ἠοῦς εἰς νύκτα καὶ ἐκ νυκτὸς πάλι Σωκλῆς
  εἰς ἠοῦν πίνει τετραχόοισι κάδοις,
εἶτ᾽ ἐξαίφνης που τυχὸν οἴχεται· ἀλλὰ παρ᾽ οἶνον
  Σικελίδεω παίζει πουλὺ μελιχρότερον,
ἐστι δὲ †δὴ πολὺ† στιβαρώτερος· ὡς δ᾽ ἐπιλάμπει
  ἡ χάρις ὥστε, φίλος, καὶ γράφε καὶ μέθυε.

From dawn to dusk and again from dusk to dawn
  Socles has been drinking from gallon-sized jugs.
And then – snap – he's off on a whim. Still, even drunk
  he tosses off a funny one much sweeter than Sicelides (i.e., Asclepiades);
but, you know, that's his constitution. So brilliant
  is his charm, that, friend, well ... write – and drink up, too!

Here, drinking orders are given in epigrammatic form. In 5 GP, drinking inspires the creation of epigram, and Socles in 6 GP can toss off epigrams in a state of utter inebriation. Latent in the comparison of Socles with Asclepiades is not only Socles' supposedly superior poetry, but perhaps also his ability, unlike Asclepiades, to compose a good epigram off the cuff. At the end of the poem, although Socles has departed the symposium, Hedylus instructs his addressee to bask in the residual charm left behind. A lesser poet than Socles (one more like Asclepiades?), the addressee is to set to epigram-writing with stylus and wax tablet in hand while seeking Socles-like inspiration in his wine. Here, epigrams are created and communicated during a symposium through both writing and oral expression, and the dynamics of this process are preserved in poems which have come to us only because they made their way onto papyrus. The extent to which these poems mirror reality is, as was indicated above, a matter of long-standing debate among scholars, and remains in need of further exploration.

While these poems of Hedylus zero in on drinking and intellectual exchange in the symposium, notable others by slightly older contemporaries such as Asclepiades, Posidippus, and Callimachus move sympotic epigram in the direction of eros. In the *Palatine Anthology*, erotic epigram is subdivided into heteroerotic and homoerotic verse: Book 5 contains most of the heteroerotic poems, Book 12, the homoerotic. Book 12 seems to be in origin the collection *The Boy-Muse* (*Mousa paidikē*) of the second century CE poet Strato of Sardis, into which a Byzantine editor, led by moral concerns, later shuffled off the homoerotic poems from a unified book of erotic epigrams within Meleager's *Garland*. Yet some homoerotic epigrams remain in Book 5, many epigrams that are not obviously homoerotic appear in Book 12, and on the whole the classification has been executed with a remarkable lack of care (Gow and Page 1965: 1.XIX). For example, in two poems by Meleager (66–7 GP) the editor evidently took the female name Phanion (which appears also in a Meleagrian epigram in the funerary section, *AP* 7.207 = 65 GP) as an inflected form of the male name Phanio(s), and so they landed in Book 12 (53 and 82). Another poet who has suffered much under the hands of the editor is Asclepiades (Gow and Page 1965: 2.117–18). Of his 26 erotic-sympotic epigrams, 16 appear in Book 5 and 10 in Book 12. However, two epigrams in Book 5 are homoerotic, and two in Book 12, heteroerotic (12, 14; 19–20 GP); two epigrams in Book 5 and four in Book 12, concerned with eros but not gender-specific (1, 11; 15–18 GP); and two in Book 5 (25–6 GP; Bettenworth 2002), concerned with symposium preparation but not directly erotic (beyond the invitation of a prostitute in 26.6). The arrangement of these epigrams in the *Anthology* (and Gow and Page 1965) to some extent obscures the thematic relationships between these poems; many *topoi* recur throughout the set.

One of Asclepiades' non-gender-specific epigrams gives us an internal monologue of the poet, his audible thought (Walsh 1990). At a symposium, Asclepiades drowns his sadness in wine, and attempts, apparently, to console his unfulfilled love (16 GP = *AP* 12.50):

Πîν, 'Ασκληπιάδη· τί τὰ δάκρυα ταῦτα; τί πάσχεις;
  οὐ σὲ μόνον χαλεπὴ Κύπρις ἐληΐσατο,
οὐδ' ἐπὶ σοὶ μούνωι κατεθήξατο τόξα καὶ ἰούς
  πικρὸς Ἔρως· τί ζῶν ἐν σποδίηι τίθεσαι;
πίνωμεν Βάκχου ζωρὸν πῶμα· δάκτυλος ἀώς·
  ἦ πάλι κοιμιστὰν λύχνον ἰδεῖν μένομεν;
†πίνομεν, οὐ γὰρ ἔρως μετά τοι χρόνον οὐκέτι πουλύν,
  σχέτλιε, τὴν μακρὰν νύκτ' ἀναπαυσόμεθα.

Drink up, Asclepiades. Why these tears? Why are you suffering?
  It's not you alone that harsh Cypris has taken as her booty,
nor is it at you alone that sharp Eros has shot his bows
  and arrows. Why do you bestrew yourself with ashes when you're still alive?
Let's drink up Bacchus' neat drink; dawn is but a finger away;
  Do we expect to see the bed-time lamp again?
†We drink, for there will not *be* eros. After not much more time,
  poor chap, we shall be at rest for one long night.

Asclepiades' consolatory gestures are typical, paralleled in many other love poems within and outside epigram: he is not the only one to have been seized by love; the love wound inflicted by Cupid's arrows has not robbed him of his life; dawn will come and go, and there will be a next day – and importantly, a next evening. But the drunken, love-sick poet's words catch up to him: the consolation of the prospect of another evening is evoked by the lamp that topically stands guard over lovers' trysts (6). In the oeuvre of Asclepiades, that lamp is nothing if not a symbol of futile hope. It appears, for example, in 9 and 10 GP (*AP* 5.7 and 150), where instead of silently watching Asclepiades tossing on the sheets with a girl, it mocks the gullibility that has kept him waiting for her – not to arrive. And Asclepiades' lack of control over his own feelings and vocabulary – he tellingly calls the lamp "bed-time lamp" – trips another, disconsolate thought that drives him back to drinking. The bed-time lamp evokes night-time rest, and with that the long night of death, when eros ceases forever. A similar incarnation of the *carpe diem* motif appears in one of Asclepiades' explicitly heteroerotic poems (2 GP = *AP* 5.85), where a girl is urged not to be stingy with her virginity because "it is among the living that the entertainments of Cypris lie" (3).

In another Asclepiadean sympotic-erotic epigram, wine appears not as a source of comfort but as a betrayer of a fellow symposiast's love (18 GP = *AP* 12.135):

οἶνος ἔρωτος ἔλεγχος· ἐρᾶν ἀρνεύμενον ἡμῖν
ἤτασαν αἱ πολλαὶ Νικαγόρην προπόσεις·
καὶ γὰρ ἐδάκρυσεν καὶ ἐνύστασε καί τι κατηφές
ἔβλεπε, χὠ σφιγχθεὶς οὐκ ἔμενε στέφανος.

Wine is love's reproof. That he's in love, though he denies it, was demonstrated to us
by the state Nicagoras' many first-round drinks put him in.
Indeed, he even shed a tear and drooped his head and looked
somewhat downcast – and his garland didn't even stay fixed.

The speaker, we might imagine, observes to a fellow symposiast the state their friend Nicagoras is in; like the self-consolatory Asclepiades, Nicagoras has overdone it on the neat wine – the first few rounds at a symposium were libations of neat wine to the gods, above all Dionysus. Perhaps drawing on his experience in 16 GP ("let's drink Bacchus' neat beverage," 16.5), the speaker recognizes in Nicagoras' heavy drinking, bodily carriage, and lack of concern for decorum the funk of love.

A slightly less depressed sympotic vignette is given by an explicitly homoerotic epigram by Callimachus, whose thematic connection with Asclepiades 16 GP is clear. If the block *AP* 12.49–51 has been taken from the *Garland*, this connection was noted also by Meleager (Callimachus 5 GP = *AP* 12.51):

ἔγχει καὶ πάλιν εἰπὲ "Διοκλέος"· οὐδ' Ἀχελῷιος
κείνου τῶν ἱερῶν αἰσθάνεται κυάθων.
καλὸς ὁ παῖς, Ἀχελῷιε, λίην καλός, εἰ δέ τις οὐχί
φησίν, ἐπισταίμην μοῦνος ἐγὼ τὰ καλά.

Pour and say it again: "Diocles!" Not even Achelous
gets to touch that wine's holy ladles.
The boy is pretty, Achelous, pretty in the extreme, and if anyone
denies it, then I might just be the sole arbiter of beauty.

Like the neat drinkers in Asclepiades, in his exuberance over the beauty of the boy Callimachus' speaker hyperbolically denies his wine all water, even from the sacred river Achelous, as he toasts to Diocles. At that, the insularity of love is not absent from this epigram. The speaker's asseverations of Diocles' beauty are figured as having gotten no traction. The appeal is made now to the river-god Achelous; and if Achelous does not agree either, it changes nothing. It just means that the speaker alone knows true beauty. In another epigram, Callimachus also follows in the implicit steps of the Asclepiadean progression from 16 to 18 GP, offering a "me too" stance that conjures up Asclepiades' evaluation of Nicagoras' behavior (Callimachus 13 GP = *AP* 12.134; since Asclepiades 18 GP = *AP* 12.135, Meleager may again have noted the connection):

ἕλκος ἔχων ὁ ξεῖνος ἐλάνθανεν· ὡς ἀνιηρόν
  πνεῦμα διὰ cτηθέων – εἶδες; – ἀνηγάγετο,
τὸ τρίτον ἡνίκ᾽ ἔπινε, τὰ δὲ ῥόδα φυλλοβολεῦντα
  τὠνδρὸς ἀπὸ cτεφάνων πάντ᾽ ἐγένοντο χαμαί.
ὤπτηται μέγα δή τι. μὰ δαίμονας, οὐκ ἀπὸ ῥυcμοῦ
  εἰκάζω, φωρὸς δ᾽ ἴχνια φὼρ ἔμαθον.

The stranger was trying to keep his wound a secret. How painfully
  – did you see it? – he drew his breath through his chest
when he took his third drink and the roses, losing their petals,
  all fell to the ground from the man's garlands.
Wow, he's really cooked! By god, my guess isn't out of
  tune – as a thief, I've learned the tracks of a thief.

This speaker too can be imagined as leaning over and speaking to a fellow symposiast, describing and diagnosing the stranger's symptoms on the basis of his own experience of eros, explicitly mentioned in the final line of the epigram, but also inferable from the Diocles poem. The pathos is drawn with a heavier hand than in Asclepiades: Nicagoras' garland was askew, the flowers of Callimachus' stranger's have fallen to the floor. Callimachus also emphasizes his powers of observation – he notes the heavy, pained breath of the stranger, a not-so obvious clue ("did you see?") – and makes his credentials as an interpreter explicit in the final line. The thief recognizing the tracks of a thief underscores the surreptitiousness of both observed and observer and returns to the poem's first assertion that the stranger was trying to keep his love-sickness hidden. The distant surreptitiousness of the lover in hunt in fact pervades Callimachus' homoerotic epigrams. One features the figure of the hunting lover (1 GP = *AP* 12.102), another, a vagabond soul "boring holes in house walls" (4 GP = *AP* 12.73), yet another, a dialogue in which a would-be lover is told to flee lest he be caught (10 GP = *AP* 12.149). These themes climax in a poem in which the pursued expresses alarm at the closing distance between himself and Menexenus, his sly pursuer (9 GP = *AP* 12.139; text after Bruss 2002):

ἔcτι τι, ναὶ τὸν Πᾶνα, κεκρυμμένον, ἔcτι τι ταύτηι,
  ναὶ μὰ Διώνυcον, πῦρ ὑπὸ τῆι cποδιῆι.
οὐ θαρcέω· μὴ δή με περίπλεκε· πολλάκι λήθει
  τοῖχον ὑποτρώγων ἡcύχιος ποταμός.
τῶι καὶ νῦν δείδοικα, Μενέξενε, μή με παρειcδύc
  οὗτος – ὃc εἶ γ᾽ ἀρνῆι c᾽ – εἰc τὸν ἔρωτα βάληι.

There's something, by Pan, yes; there's something hidden there,
  by Dionysus – fire under the ashes!
I'm not up to it; don't embrace me; often a quiet river,
  unbeknownst, will undercut a wall.
And so even now I fear, Menexenus, that by penetrating me
  that one (so I'll say, for you deny who you are!) might cast me into love.

Hiddenness pervades the poem: fire under ashes, a quiet river, surreptitious penetration (that evokes the borer of Callimachus 4 GP), and denial of intentions. This is compounded by an ambiguity – do the metaphors speak of what the speaker is becoming aware of in himself or in Menexenus, or is it both? The cool distance of a diagnostician is observable here, too. Yet, up against a strange or extraneous power (the name *Menexenos* evokes the *xe[i]nos*, "stranger," of 13 GP) applied with an indefensible surreptitiousness, the coolness of the unattached observer is warmed by his realization that he has succumbed to the very danger he sees.

Influences and Uses

Epigram, like almost all Hellenistic poetry, seems infinitely capacious of ideas, motifs, and forms from other types of literature and intellectual discourse. Funerary epigram, for example, not rarely reflects philosophical ideas about body and soul (Clayman 2007). This phenomenon already has precedents in inscribed epigram, such as a fourth-century epitaph (*CEG* 535, before c.350?) which states that "the mighty moist aether holds Eurymachus' soul (*psychē*) and intellectual capacities (*dianoiai*); this tomb, his body (*sōma*)." The conceptualization – location of the soul in the aether, moisture, separate mention of *dianoia(i)* – suggests influence of the myth of Plato's *Phaedrus.* Epitaphs of philosophers, a thriving subgenre of literary epigram, naturally reflect these philosophers' doctrines. Thus an epitaph of Plato (attributed to Speusippus) explains that "This body of Plato's earth holds in her bosom; but his divine soul has taken its places in the array of the blessed" (*AP* 14.31.2), in accordance with the Myth of Er of *Republic* 10. Many poems on philosophers lob bombs at their subject, such as an epigram in the "New Posidippus" for the cenotaph of Lysicles, a contemporary head of the Academy who was lost at sea (89 AB, the first of the *Nauagika* or "shipwreck poems" that extend to 94 AB; Bruss 2005: 113–16). The poem seems neither very philosophical nor very amusing until one reads it through the tradition of Platonic-Academic epitaphs and its many variations on the theme "his body lies here, but his soul is elsewhere." What then if there is no body?

Other notable influences on epigram are iambic invective and comedy. Dioscorides' epigram on Philaenis (26 GP = *AP* 7.450) seems to have been directly inspired by a poem of a certain Aeschrion (c.300 BCE?) that is generically an epigram but is composed in choliambs, "limping iambs." This meter, primarily associated with the Archaic invective poet Hipponax, enjoyed a revival in the Hellenistic period, with Callimachus and Herodas as prominent practitioners (Scodel and Esposito in this volume). Aeschrion's poem, like that of Dioscorides, poses as the inscription on Philaenis' tomb, which is here imagined as standing on a headland, visible to passing ships (1 GP = *AP* 7.345):

ἐγὼ Φιλαινίϲ, ἡ 'πίβωτοϲ ἀνθρώποιϲ,
ἐνταῦθα γήραι τῶι μακρῶι κεκοίμημαι.
μή μ', ὦ μάταιε ναῦτα, τὴν ἄκραν κάμπτων
χλεύην τε ποιεῦ καὶ γέλωτα καὶ λάϲθην,

οὐ γάρ, μὰ τὸν Ζῆν', οὐ μὰ τοὺϲ κάτω κούρουϲ,
οὐκ ἦν ἐϲ ἄνδραϲ μάχλοϲ οὐδὲ δημώδηϲ.
Πολυκράτηϲ δὲ τὴν γονὴν Ἀθηναῖοϲ,
λόγων τι παιπάλημα καὶ κακὴ γλῶϲϲα,
ἔγραψεν οἷ' ἔγραψ'· ἐγὼ γὰρ οὐκ οἶδα.

I Philaenis, slandered by men,
have been laid to rest here by long old age.
Do not, flippant sailor, when rounding this headland,
make jest or joke or insult.
For, by Zeus, no – no, by the Kouroi below! –
I was not lewd toward men, nor a prostitute.
Rather, Polycrates, an Athenian by birth,
himself the very subtlety of verbiage and an evil tongue,
he wrote whatever it was he wrote. See, I don't know!

Ironically, such self-defenses quickly turn against the speaker(s) to become self-pillorying, which is, of course, exactly the intention. In a sense, the permanence of the ill repute of Philaenis is guaranteed by these very epitaphs. Her self-defense in Aeschrion's poem is self-incriminating first and foremost because it contains a number of words which recall the sort of sexual puns familiar from Old Comedy. On a "flat" reading, κεκοίμημαι in line 2 is the equivalent of epitaph's ubiquitous κεῖμαι, "I lie," meaning "I have been laid to rest." But in the mouth of this speaker it also begs to be taken as "I have been laid" (Ar. *Eccl.* 723–4). And the adjective ἐπίβωτοϲ in the first line, which has a basic sense of "shouted at," can be interpreted as referring to notoriety ("cried out against"), or fame ("acclaimed"), or sex appeal ("called to"), depending on one's predisposition. Read in this light, some elements in what follows also invite a sexual interpretation. Sailing is a common metaphor for sexual intercourse (Henderson 1991: 163–6), which explains why Philaenis has been made to address a sailor rather than a generic passerby, and suggests that τὴν ἄκραν κάμπτων (3) means more than just "rounding this headland." Perhaps we are to think of the use of κάμπτω as "bending someone over" to be penetrated from behind (Pherecrates fr. 145.15 KA; Henderson 1991: 175, 179–80), a position ("the lioness") which literature and vase painting associate with prostitutes. Alternatively, the expression may refer to sexual climax. Likewise, the reference to Polycrates as a "bad tongue" (8) may suggest not only speaking ill but also (badly performed?) sexual acts (Henderson 1991: 183–6) that would befit someone who is μάχλοϲ and δημώδηϲ (7), adjectives which conveniently do not distinguish between masculine and feminine endings (and printing a period at the end of 7 is an interpretive decision). In addition, the poem's last line seems to contain two ambiguities of a slightly different nature. The elided ἔγραψ' is *prima facie* a third-person form (ἔγραψε, "he wrote") but it can also be taken as a first person (ἔγραψα, "I wrote"), producing an admission of guilt; and what follows can be read as "see, I don't know [how to write]" (rather than "know [such things]"), producing a lie – because, within the fiction set up by this poem, she in any case composed the epigram we are reading, written on her gravestone. These *double entendres* are bound to elicit the very chuckle Philaenis fears (3–4). A translation which more fully exploits them might run as follows:

I Philaenis, called to by men –
here in my long old age, I've been laid.
Silly sailor boy, when you wriggle round my headland (if you know what I mean),
don't jest or joke or insult.
For, by Zeus, no – no, by the boys below! –
I was not lewd toward men or loose –
but Polycrates, an Athenian by birth, was!
A subtle chap with words who gave bad tongue –
He wrote whatever I – or he – wrote. See? I don't know!

In Dioscorides' Philaenis epigram, as we saw, Philaenis' opening move already constitutes proof of guilt: she disavows her lewdness while beckoning the passerby like a hooker (26.1–2 GP). Equally incriminating, if in a different way, is the sequence οὐκ εἴμ' ἡ ... Αἰσχύνην οὐ νομίσασα θεόν, / ἀλλὰ φιλαιδήμων (3–4), translated above as "I'm not the one who ... didn't think Modesty (*Aischunē*) was a god. No, I was a lover of modesty (*philaidēmōn*)." This is surely what Philaenis wants us to understand, but it seems as if she herself realizes that by making *Aischunē* rather than the more usual *Aidōs* into a goddess she might be creating the wrong impression: *aischunē* can be used positively as "sense of shame, modesty," like *aidōs*, but is more frequently used negatively as "shame." Therefore Philaenis could also be saying that she was devoted to doing shameful things – a Freudian slip? In her attempt to disambiguate this move with *philaidēmōn*, "lover of *aidōs*," she unfortunately undercuts her credibility even more. This word is attested only here and has surely been coined for the occasion. It plays with the speaker's own name (*Philainis*, *philaidēmōn*) but also hides another, less harmless pun. Although *aidēmōn* is a current adjective, it is not the obvious form to use in a compound adjective derived from *aidōs*. The word which Philaenis should have formed is *phil-aidoios*, and this indeed seems to be what she is in the process of forming until she realizes that she is hanging herself yet again: because *ta aidoia* is a well-established euphemism for private parts ("the shameful things"), the words *phil-aidoios*, coming from the mouth of Philaenis, would almost inevitably be interpreted as "lover of dicks." To make matters worse, the word which Philaenis forms to *avoid* saying *philaidoios*, *philaidēmōn*, itself introduces a verbal echo of the qualification *dēmōdēs*, "public," i.e., "a prostitute," in Dioscorides' model, Aeschrion 1.6 GP. When Philaenis then also, by saying *aischunōn*, "putting to shame" (6), unstrategically restages the concept of *aischunē* in the very sense she is trying to dispel, she has gotten completely tangled up in her web of "shame" words and her credibility is irrevocably lost.

Dioscorides' Philaenis poem varies that of Aeschrion, addressing the same theme in a somewhat different manner, and for optimal effect should be read against it. In another epigram, Dioscorides applied the same trope to a situation taken from Archaic invective, Aeschrion's source of inspiration: in the epitaph 17 GP (*AP* 7.351) the daughters of Lycambes defend their reputation after having been so maligned by the iambic poet Archilochus that they were driven to suicide (on Archilochus' row with Lycambes, see Gerber 1997: 50–1). That poem in turn spawned a companion piece on the exact same theme, perhaps composed by Meleager (132 GP = *AP* 7.352).

In Hellenistic literary epigram we in fact often see motifs or themes being developed from multiple perspectives in a series of poems ("the art of variation": Tarán 1979; Ludwig 1968), a practice that flows almost naturally from inscribed epigram. Funerary epigram, for example, had already for centuries generated, within its formal and generic strictures, variations on circumstances of death, the sadness of the bereft, consolation, and the address to the passerby (the organization in Peek 1955 provides a helpful guide). From here it is a small step to the conscious "capping" of other poets' work that is prominent in, for example, the erotic poetry of Callimachus and Asclepiades. We also see poets creating their own mini-cycles by writing a number of poems on the same or similar themes. Dioscorides' Philaenis epigram is part of a putative series of (funerary) epigrams on authors that can be culled from Book 7 of the *Anthology* (where their arrangement largely reflects the anthologist's rather than what seems to have been the poet's agenda: 18–26 GP = *AP* 7.407, 31, 410–11, 37, 707–8, 485, 450).

Such epigrams on authors are a subgenre in themselves. They may sing the praise of the Archaic and Classical masters, such as Dioscorides' poems on Sappho, and Sophocles (18, 22 GP) and the numerous epitaphs for Homer, but also contemporaries, such as Dioscorides' epitaph for Macho (24 GP) and Callimachus' famous praise of Aratus (56 GP = 27 Pf. = *AP* 9.507; Volk in this volume). Such poems (collected in Gabathuler 1937) have long been considered "book-tag epigrams," epigrams for an edition of an author's work(s), to be written as a sort of blurb either before the author's text or on the tag by which scrolls on shelves were identified. It is indeed not hard to see how Dioscorides' epigram on Philaenis might have accompanied an edition of the erotic manual ascribed to her, and it is interesting that *epigramma* initially seems to have referred to identifying tags on papyrus scrolls – it is not found as a technical term for the range of poetry we now call "epigram" until the second century CE (Puelma 1996). While some details of Gabathuler's view are now regarded as outdated, it remains the case that epigrams modeled on the "book-tag" pattern served both to introduce and conclude collections of, at least, epigrams. Such poems are now for the most part collected in Book 4 of the *Anthology* (Van Sickle 1981; Gutzwiller 1998: 279–80; Meyer 2007: 189).

Aesthetic Interests

Perhaps the most striking discordance between Hellenistic literary epigram and its inscribed forebears is the widely divergent aesthetic that drives it. Archaic and Classical epigram essentially commented on key moments in the life of the elite, reflecting the interests and ideology of a part of the population wealthy enough to commission poems and the monuments to inscribe them on. As taken over by Hellenistic poets, the genre, although not always self-deflating, was deeply influenced by the contemporary aesthetic interest in everyday life and the lower strata of society that is also apparent in other types of literature and art (Ambühl in this volume). Typically Hellenistic is also literary epigram's often unconventional, if not hostile, engagement with the heroes of the past, whether mythological such as Heracles, historical such as Leonidas, or literary such as Homer. In Callimachus' epigrams that deal with earlier poetry, the genuine praise of the poem on Aratus' *Phaenomena* alternates with tongue-in-cheek humor in poems such as the following, where the great tragedian Euripides is made to reside in the Hellenistic world and so cut down to size (26 GP = 48 Pf. = *AP* 6.310; see also Wissmann in this volume):

εὐμαθίην ἠιτεῖτο διδοὺϲ ἐμὲ Σῖμοϲ ὁ Μίκκου
  ταῖϲ Μούϲαιϲ, αἱ δὲ Γλαῦκοϲ ὅκωϲ ἔδοϲαν
ἀντ' ὀλίγου μέγα δῶρον. ἐγὼ δ' ἀνὰ τῆιδε κεχηνὼϲ
  κεῖμαι τοῦ Σαμίου διπλόον, ὁ τραγικὸϲ
παιδαρίων Διόνυϲυϲ ἐπήκοοϲ· οἱ δὲ λέγουϲιν
  "ἱερὸϲ ὁ πλόκαμοϲ," τοὐμὸν ὄνειαρ ἐμοί.

Simus the son of Miccus, when he gave me to the Muses, asked
  for good progress in his studies, and they, like Glaucus, gave it –
a large gift for a small one. Now, up here I sit, with a yawning gape
  twice as wide as the Samian Dionysus', I the "tragic"
Dionysus who has to listen in on the boys. They keep on saying
  "Holy is the lock!" and all they're doing is telling me my own dream.

Instead of, say, poetic inspiration, Simus ("Snub") the son of Miccus ("Tiny") has asked for something down to earth: good progress in school, grammar school. The god Dionysus, represented by the mask Simus has dedicated, is unimpressed not only with the nature of the request but also with the gift and with Simus' aptitude for learning ("a large gift for a small one"). Dionysus is also unimpressed with *what* Simus is learning: hanging on the classroom wall, he is forced to listen to the boys' lispings as they recite but a snippet of one of antiquity's greatest tragedies, in honor of the god himself, the *Bacchae* (line 494). His gaping mouth is not that of the Dionysus *Kechēnōs* ("with open mouth") worshipped at Samos but that of boredom: they tell him nothing new ("my own dream"), an *ad nauseam* repetition of *his* line in *his* tragedy.

The dedicator in Callimachus' poem is illustrative of Hellenistic epigram's inclusion of humble, even low-life, figures as its subject matter (on the general aesthetic, see Fowler 1989: 66–78). Leonidas of Tarentum, one of the first-generation Hellenistic epigrammatists, seems to have specialized in this, a tack that Gutzwiller (1998: 88–114), among others, credits to the palpably Cynic nature of Leonidas' poetic persona, which elevates the humility of his subjects by the brilliance of his language, as in his poem on the carpenter Theris (7 GP = *AP* 6.204). Upon his retirement the craftsman Theris dedicates to his patron goddess Athena the tools of his trade: "an uncurved ruler, a straight saw with bent handle, his axe and bright plane, and rotating borer" (Gutzwiller 1998: 92). The poem's juxtaposition of curved and uncurved items, of the meanness of Theris' trade and the brilliant coinage "skillful-handed" (δαιδαλόχειρ), is a reflection of Leonidas' ensconcing of the retirement of a humble tradesman within verse traditionally associated with the lives of the elite. Leonidas enhances this effect by the sophisticated precision in his description of the tools of Theris' mundane trade. Many of the Archaic and Classical dedicatory epigrams are for statues or statuettes of the god, or for relatively generic items, such as tripods. In these, the god takes center-stage and the personality of the dedicator fades into the background; here, conversely, the personality of the human actor comes to the fore: what Theris dedicates to the god represents himself, the pride he takes in his humble trade. The tone is touching.

The genre also descends to less respectable levels of society, as we have seen in the pair of Philaenis epigrams. A mini-series in the *Anthology*, within a longer Meleagrian sequence, consists of epigrams by Callimachus, Leonidas of Tarentum, Dioscorides, and Aristo on drunks (*AP* 7.454–7). Like the Philaenis epigrams, they owe a large debt to iambos and comedy, which Leonidas' poem advertises most openly: it is composed in iambic trimeters (68 GP). This funerary epigram for Maronis, "the wine-lover, the wine-jar-sponge," describes her grave as being decorated with an Attic kylix (wine goblet). The tone of these racing iambics is condescendingly humorous. The inflated language of the first line, where Maronis is "Maronis the . . . ," draws from the laudatory "grammar" of funerary epigram and epinician poetry only to present to the reader a picture of a drunk. The tomb's peculiar decoration, a kylix, is as representative of Maronis' lifetime occupation as are Theris' ruler, saw, axe, plane, and borer. The punch in the poem for Maronis consists of an inversion of a typical funerary topos wherein the deceased or the survivors mourn for their separation from their loved ones; Maronis groans for a kylix. She remains in death what she was in life: a "wine-lover," a drunk.

* * *

It is this complex interplay of interests and influences that gives life to Hellenistic literary epigram. Our central example, Dioscorides' Philaenis epigram (26 GP), is remarkable for its complexity but by no means exceptional. It is in form a funerary epigram and plays with the language and conventions of inscribed epitaphs. It is one of a pair, capping a poem by Aeschrion on the same theme, and forms part of a wider set of epigrammatic self-defenses by slandered women. It can also be serialized on the basis of numerous other criteria: as an epigram on an author, an erotic epigram (and as such a sympotic epigram?), an epigram on a low-life character, an epigram on a prostitute, a satiric epigram, or a curse epigram. It draws for its language and themes not only on various epigrammatic subgenres but also on iambos and comedy. In its brevity and polymorphism, the poem demands an intensive interpretational effort from the reader, and yet it ultimately remains elusive, impervious to finalizing interpretations. In all these respects it is typical of the genre.

FURTHER READING

Collections of inscriptional epigram include Peek 1955 (funerary epigrams from the eighth century BCE into the Byzantine era), Hansen 1983 and 1989 (*CEG*; funerary, dedicatory, and miscellaneous epigrams from the eighth century BCE through the fourth), and Merkelbach and Stauber 1998–2004 (funerary, dedicatory, and miscellaneous epigrams from the Greek East into the Byzantine period). Gow and Page 1965 (GP) includes all epigrams known at that date for poets who wrote before or concurrent with Meleager, who compiled his *Garland* around

100 BCE; Gow and Page 1968 goes down to c.40 CE, the date of the *Garland* of Philip. Page 1981 and 1975 contain early epigrams not included in these two editions, such as many of the so-called Simonidea. Paton's five Loeb volumes, 1916–19, contain the text of the entire *Palatine Anthology* with English translation. Sens forthcoming will provide a useful introduction to Hellenistic epigram for students. Recent single-author editions include Galán Vioque 2001 (Dioscorides), Guichard 2004 (Asclepiades), and Austin and Bastianini 2002 (Posidippus); various others are underway, e.g., of Meleager (Gutzwiller), Asclepiades (Sens), and Alcaeus of Messene (Bruss). Bing and Bruss 2007 is a comprehensive collection of contemporary approaches to Hellenistic epigram and contains a full bibliography.

CHAPTER TEN

Apollonius' *Argonautica*

Adolf Köhnken

The *Argonautica* of Apollonius of Rhodes, an epic poem in four books (of 1362, 1285, 1407, and 1781 hexameters respectively), is addressed to Apollo and sets out to tell the memorable voyage of the Argonauts of old to the Black Sea to fetch the Golden Fleece (1.1–4). Although the poem everywhere recalls the language, style, and subject matter of the *Iliad* and *Odyssey*, it is nevertheless quite un-Homeric, but rather characteristically Hellenistic in its startling presentation of events and characters, human and divine, and markedly "Callimachean" in its allusive narrative technique and striking preference for pointed aetiological topics. Yet in contrast to contemporary Alexandrian poetry such as Callimachus' *Aetia* and *Hymns*, and Theocritus' *Idylls*, the *Argonautica* does not mention contemporaneous events or Ptolemaic kings or queens and always remains within the mythical timeframe of the story of the Argonauts. Apollonius' poem, which not long ago was often brushed aside for no compelling reason as a traditional epic running against the unconventional spirit of contemporary Hellenistic poetry, has only recently come into its own right and been shown to be a complex, innovative, and fascinating work of art. In what follows I shall single out significant aspects that highlight these qualities.

Aetiology

The *Argonautica* may be termed an aetiological poem in the Callimachean manner as far as the account of the Argo's voyage to and from Colchis in Books 1, 2, and 4 is concerned. These three books contain 77 of the 80 *aitia* in the epic (Valverde Sánchez 1989: 309–11), a characteristic element that is sometimes underrated (e.g., by Hutchinson 1988: 93–5, who counts only "about forty" *aitia*, and Hunter 1993a: 105; contrast DeForest 1994: 8). There is, however, a difference in narrative perspective between Callimachus' *Aetia* and Apollonius' *Argonautica*. In Callimachus, as a rule, strange cults and customs of the present are explained by looking back to a distant mythical past; in Apollonius the Argonauts' journey initiates future cults and customs still existing. Callimachus' aetiological stories begin by asking "how is it that . . ." (e.g., *Aet.* frs. 7.19–21, 43.84–7 Pf.), those of Apollonius finish by stating "thus it came about that . . ." (e.g., 1.1019–20, 4.1770–2; Gummert 1992: 91; Köhnken 2003: 207). Book 3 on the other hand, Apollonius' intricate account of Medea's falling in love and Jason's ἄεθλος, the centerpiece of the narrative, has very few *aitia* (Valverde Sanchez 1989 lists three) and is thus clearly set apart from the voyage books (DeForest 1994: 100).

Apollonius' *aitia* generally highlight the significance of places and events connected with the route of the Argo, such as the Altar of Apollo Actius Ecbasius (1.402–4), the Place of Argo's Embarkation (591), the Temple of Jasonian Athena (958–60), Jason's Way (988), Anchor's Rock (1019–20), Jason's Spring (1145–9), the river Acheron later named Soonautes (2.746–8), a place called Lyre because Orpheus dedicated his lyre there to Apollo Savior of Ships (927–9), Ram's Bed and the Altar of Zeus Phyxius, where Phrixus dedicated the golden ram (4.115–21), the Harbor of Argo (658, 1620), and the Cave of Medea (1153–5). Of particular interest, however, are those *aitia* which are not only fascinating in themselves but which are also clearly positioned in the narrative to serve a structural function, thus underscoring the poem's overall sense of balance and cohesiveness. Spectacular examples are the epiphany of Apollo Heoios, containing three *aitia* (the Island of Apollo Heoios, the origin of the invocation *hiē hiē paiēon*, and the foundation of the Temple of Concord, 2.674–719), and the epiphany of Apollo Aegletes, containing two (the Temenos of Apollo Aegletes and the name of the island Anaphe, 4.1706–30). Both epiphanies are modeled on the same sequence in Callimachus' *Aetia* and by their evident intratextual relationship within the *Argonautica* create a striking correspondence between Books 2 and 4 (Köhnken 2001, 2003; Harder 1993: 107–9; for the *aitia* in Book 2 also Fusillo 1985: 116–58; Paskiewicz 1988).

The Gods

Gods are very much in evidence in the *Argonautica*, but their activity is quite un-Homeric and peculiar (Klein 1931). There is no council of gods as in the *Iliad* and *Odyssey*, and although Zeus' wife, Hera, "is as much part of the narrative as any Argonaut," Zeus himself "is not with her ever, nor once represented in the narrative" (Feeney 1991: 65). Although there are Olympic scenes in the *Argonautica*, the Homeric assemblies of the gods, presided over by Zeus, are replaced by a meeting of individual goddesses in private chambers (Hera, Athena, and Aphrodite, 3.7–166), with the narrator explicitly emphasizing that they meet "apart from Zeus himself and the rest of the immortal gods" (3.8–10; cf. also the summoning of Thetis to Olympus for a private interview with Hera in 4.780–841). Zeus is in evidence only as guarantor of fate and divine order. Thus Glaucus refers to the labors of Heracles as decreed by "the plans of Zeus" (1.1315–50) and Hera, through the voice of the ship Argo, transmits to the Argonauts Zeus' "wrath" (*cholos*) about the treacherous murder of

Apsyrtus (4.576–92). On the other hand there is a noticeable emphasis on divine interference in human affairs throughout, first and foremost that of Apollo, Hera, and Athena. Apollo, who inaugurated the Argonautic expedition by his oracle to Pelias (1.5–17), acts as a savior god for the Argonauts and their expedition in the voyage books 1, 2, and 4, although he remains a somewhat aloof and distant divinity (the fact that he is missing from Book 3 underlines the peculiar status of that book). Athena in Books 1–2 and Hera in Books 3–4, on the other hand, watch over the wellbeing of Jason and his fellow Argonauts much more closely and intimately. In addition, there are also striking lesser divinities of some importance, like Glaucus in Book 1 and mischievous Eros and sinister Hecate in Book 3 – Eros exemplifying the interest of Alexandrian poets in the portrayal of extraordinary and prodigious divine children (compare, for example, Heracles in Theoc. 24.26–59 and Artemis in Call. *h.* 3.4–43; see also Ambühl and Wissmann in this volume), and Hecate the dark and uncanny aspects of the poem's plot. Finally, Thetis, the Libyan Heroines, the Hesperides, and Triton/Eurypylus all play a role in Book 4 (see below).

Structure and Main Characters

The *Argonautica* was often, and sometimes still is, classified as an "episodic" epic consisting of a string of loosely connected scenes (Herter 1955: 336–400, for example, divides the poem into 32 separate units, without regard for the author's book divisions). More recently, this view has been considerably modified and scholars have paid much more attention to cross references between the events narrated, to the position of the scenes Apollonius chose to elaborate and their overall significance within the narrative, and also to the impact upon his poem of genres other than epic and predecessors other than Homer, above all Pindar's fourth *Pythian Ode* and Euripides' *Medea*, but also Herodotus (Zanker 1987: 195–209; 1998: 229–31; Clauss 1993: 5–10; Cuypers 2004a).

Analysis of the structure of the *Argonautica* shows that Apollonius has given his poem a novel kind of cohesion by a network of cross references; for example:

(1) He has established meaningful links between events in the outward and return journeys. Most conspicuous are the spectacular accounts of the Argonauts' passage through the Cyanean Rocks or (Sym)Plegades in 2.537–603 (prepared by Phineus' directives in 2.317–45 and already highlighted in the proem, 1.2–3) and their journey past the Planctae in 4.930–67 (prepared by the meeting of Hera and Thetis in 4.753–841 and Thetis' instructions to Peleus in 4.856–64). These scenes, evidently designed as structural analogues, are both framed and marked off by the intervention of a helper goddess, that of Athena pushing the Argo through the Cyanean Rocks (2.537–48 and 598–603) and the even more amusing one of Thetis and the Nereids playing ball with the Argo high above the Planctae (4.930–8 and 966–7; cf. the simile in 4.948–55).

(2) He has introduced structural devices bridging the divisions between Books 1 and 2, 2 and 3, and 3 and 4 (see below).

(3) He has made sudden deaths of prominent members of the crew correspond. As Hunter observes (1993a: 44), "no Argonaut is killed in battle. The expedition does

lose eight members – four by death (Idmon, Tiphys, Mopsus and Canthus), two by something more than death (Hylas, Boutes) and two who 'miss the boat' (Heracles and Polyphemus). The four deaths occur in two groups of two." The passages describing the deaths of the seers Idmon (2.815–50) and Mopsus (4.1502–36) begin with nearly identical statements, and in both cases the narrator notes that both Argonauts, though seers, did not foresee their own fate; both deaths are, moreover, accompanied by the deaths of other Argonauts, those of Tiphys and Canthus (Manakidou 1995: 192, 196–7).

(4) He has given a prominent role to prophecies foreshadowing future developments within or beyond the timeframe of the poem. Here belong the intriguing guidelines and veiled advice of the old blind seer Phineus (2.309–530), which prepare the Argonauts for dangers and encounters in the rest of the outward journey and after their arrival in Colchis (including hints at the importance of Eros). Of this advice the Argonauts are reminded more than once afterwards. Noteworthy are also the corresponding epiphanies and prophecies of the marine deities Glaucus and Triton at the end of Books 1 (1310–28) and 4 (1551–1619, cf. 1732–54) respectively, both referring to *aitia* of future cities in Mysia and Libya (founded by *Polyphemus* in Book 1 and *Euphemus* in Book 4) and both explicitly confirmed by authorial comments (1.1345–57 and 4.1755–64).

The *Argonautica* confronts the reader with three proems, instead of merely one at the outset like the *Iliad* and *Odyssey.* The two additional ones, introducing Books 3 and 4, underscore the poem's macro-structure by highlighting the importance of Book 3 (the Argonauts' confrontation with king Aeetes in Colchis, Medea's love for Jason, and Jason's "contest" for the Golden Fleece) and Book 4 (the winning of the Fleece and the return journey) as against Books 1 and 2 (the outward journey). They have also been formally linked with each other and with the proem of Book 1: 3.2 ἐϲ Ἰωλκὸν ἀνήγαγε κῶαϲ Ἰήϲων looks back to 1.4 χρύϲειον μετὰ κῶαϲ ... ἤλαϲαν Ἀργώ. In addition, there is a structural correspondence between the appeal to Erato at 3.1 and that to "the Muse" at 4.1–2, both followed by γάρ-clauses justifying the appeals. Moreover, each of the three proems contains an element of surprise. The first one, contrary to the reader's expectation, does not embrace the poem as a whole but exclusively refers to adventures of the Argonauts on their outward voyage (1.1–4 and 20–2); in other words, it is, in contrast to the proems introducing the Homeric poems, only concerned with the narrative up to the end of Book 2 (*pace* Hunter 1993a: 119 and others). The special proem to Book 3, on the other hand, does not restrict itself to the main issue of this book (Medea's love for Jason) but already looks forward to Jason's successful return journey to Iolcus with the Golden Fleece (3.2–3); i.e., it goes beyond Book 3 to include subject matter of Book 4. This, however, raises the question of why we get a new proem at the beginning of Book 4. The answer is that this third proem marks a radical change of focus, from the adventures of the Argonauts on their way from Iolcus to Colchis (proem 1: Books 1 and 2) and Jason's contest for the Fleece won by Medea's help (proem 2: Book 3) to Medea's own struggle (4.1–5):

αὐτὴ νῦν κάματόν γε θεὰ καὶ δήνεα κούρηϲ
Κόλχιδοϲ ἔννεπε Μοῦϲα, Διὸϲ τέκοϲ· ἦ γὰρ ἔμοιγε

ἀμφαςίηι νόος ἔνδον ἑλίςςεται, ὁρμαίνοντι
ἤέ μιν ἄτης πῆμα δυςίμερον ἦ τό γ' ἐνίςπω
φύζαν ἀεικελίην ἧι κάλλιπεν ἔθνεα Κόλχων.

Tell me now yourself, goddess, of the struggle and concerns of the Colchian maiden, Muse, daughter of Zeus. For indeed my mind within me turns around in speechlessness as I wonder whether I should call it the pain of ill-guided passion or rather shameful desertion which made her abandon the tribes of the Colchians.

The first line of Book 4 (Medea's κάματος) refers back to and contrasts with the last line of Book 3 (Jason's ἄεθλος). Jason and the Argonauts, of whom there is no word in the proem of Book 4, have left center stage and Medea takes their place. This new development is underlined by a sophisticated ring-composition bridging the book division. Book 3 narrates the story of Jason's contest engaging King Aeetes' fire-breathing bulls and the earthborn men (1223–1401), followed by a reference to the chagrin of Aeetes and his men at the unexpected outcome (1402–6), and it closes with an ambivalent sentence about the day and Jason's contest having come to an end (3.1407). Book 4 in turn starts off with the announcement of Medea's imminent struggle (1–5), then returns to the outrage of the furious and revengeful Aeetes and his men (nocturnal council, 6–10), and proceeds with the actual account of Medea's struggle, her securing the Golden Fleece for Jason, and her flight from Colchis with the Argonauts (11–240). The narrative clearly follows a pattern: the events of the final part of Book 3 and the first part of Book 4 are presented in the order a–b–c: c–b–a (Köhnken 2000: 59–62).

This device may be compared to a similar but simpler one linking Books 2 and 3. Here the book division is bridged by a repeated reference to the Argonauts hiding in the marshes of the Phasis river after their arrival in Colchis, first at 2.1283 and again at 3.6–7. In the latter place the reference is refocalized, as Hera and Athena are said to be the only ones who notice the Argonauts in their hiding place (perspective of the onlooker). They thereupon launch into action, setting the events of Book 3 into motion. The repetition is designed to introduce divine interference as a new factor and give the narrative a different turn.

A more complex linking device is found at the division between Books 1 and 2. At the end of Book 1, Heracles and Polyphemus are inadvertently left behind in Mysia while searching for Hylas, who has been kidnapped by a nymph. At the beginning of Book 2, Apollonius narrates the boxing match of Amycus and Polydeuces. These two elements of the Argonautic saga seem to have little in common, except that they are both also found in Theocritus (*Idylls* 13 and 22) and are therefore primary evidence in a still ongoing priority debate. But Apollonius has managed to establish a close connection between them by means of the unexpected comment of an anonymous Argonaut at the end of the episode in Book 2 (144–54):

καὶ δή τις ἔπος μετὰ τοῖςιν ἔειπε·
"φράζεςθ' ὅττι κεν ἧιςιν ἀναλκείηιςιν ἔρεξαν,
εἴ πως Ἡρακλῆα θεὸς καὶ δεῦρο κόμιςςεν.
ἤτοι μὲν γὰρ ἐγὼ κείνου παρεόντος ἔολπα
οὐδ' ἂν πυγμαχίηι κρινθήμεναι· ἀλλ' ὅτε θεςμοὺς
ἤλυθεν ἐξερέων, αὐτοῖς ἄφαρ οἷς ἀγόρευε

θεcμοῖcιν ῥοπάλωι μιν ἀγηνορίης λελαθέcθαι.
ναὶ μὲν ἀκήδεcτον γαίηι ἔνι τόνδε λιπόντες
πόντον ἐπέπλωμεν· μάλα δ' ἡμέων αὐτὸc ἕκαcτοc
εἴcεται οὐλομένην ἄτην ἀπάνευθεν ἐόντοc."
ὣc ἄρ' ἔφη· τὰ δὲ πάντα Διὸc βουλῆιcι τέτυκτο.

And then someone among them said: "Imagine what they would have done in their cowardice if by chance a god had brought Heracles also to this place. For if he had been present, I for one believe the issue would not even have been decided by a boxing match, but when he (Amycus) would have come to proclaim his laws, he would at once have been made to forget his laws as well as his arrogance by means of the club. Indeed, thoughtlessly we left this man (Heracles) behind on land and set out on the sea again. Certainly each one of us will personally experience deadly ruin because he is far away." Thus he spoke, but all of this had come to pass by the plans of Zeus.

This gloomy, Homeric-style anonymous comment or "*tis*-speech," highlighting the feelings of the Argonauts, is surprising and hard to understand if taken by itself, because it does not really seem justified by the course of events, intervening as it does between the utter defeat of Amycus and his Bebrycians, and the Argonauts' celebration of their victory and the outstanding achievement of their champion Polydeuces (2.155–63). Why introduce a reminiscence of Heracles' superior power at this place where it seems least called for, and so soon after Heracles has been lost for good?

A clue is supplied by the narrator's comment closing the *tis*-speech, "but all of this had come to pass by the plans of Zeus" (154). This refers to the inadvertent abandonment of Heracles in Mysia, explicitly recalled by the anonymous Argonaut (151). The narrator's closing tag specifically harks back to two interrelated phrases in the final part of the Heracles–Hylas–Polyphemus narration at the end of Book 1, namely the first words of the prophecy of the sea god Glaucus to the Argonauts, "why do you wish to bring mighty Heracles to Colchis, against the will of Zeus?" (παρὲκ μεγάλοιο Διὸc ... βουλήν, 1315), and the beginning of the corresponding final résumé by the narrator, which confirms that Heracles and Polyphemus had to pursue an agenda of their own "by the will of Zeus" (Διὸc βουλῆιcιν, 1345). The Homeric-epic expression Διὸc βουλῆιcιν is found only in these two passages in the *Argonautica*, 1.1345 (varying 1315) and 2.154, both referring above all to the destiny of Heracles. The *tis*-speech at 2.154 – "what would Heracles have done to Amycus if he had still been with us?" – is the first in a line of reminders of Heracles, who in spite of his absence remains present in the background of the narrative and is brought back to the minds of the Argonauts and the readers at significant points throughout the *Argonautica* – for example, in King Lycus' story of an earlier visit of Heracles (2.762–95), Amphidamas' reference to a helpful Heraclean invention (2.1046–68), the narrator's comment that only Heracles would have been able to withstand Aeetes' spear (3.1231–4), and the Argonauts' ordeal in the Libyan desert, where they are saved by a spring created by Heracles (4.1396–1405, 1432–84). Obviously, the first of these reminders, at the beginning of Book 2, is designed to link the first event without Heracles (the encounter with Amycus) to the last one in which he was actually present (the disappearance of Hylas). Thus the *tis*-speech complaining about the loss of Heracles and worrying about the consequences, added at the end of a successful exploit of the Argonauts in which Heracles played no part, is a bridging device pointedly relating the beginning of Book 2 to the finale of Book 1. At the same time this structural arrangement provides a chronological clue: by making Heracles a common element of his Hylas and Amycus episodes Apollonius connects the two stories which are treated separately and independently from each other in the Hylas and Amycus poems of Theocritus, *Idylls* 13 and 22, of which the latter has nothing to do with Heracles, suggesting strongly that Apollonius' epic postdates the Theocritean poems (*pace*, among others, Hunter 2004a: 87 and 90).

Finally, it is interesting to note (with Mooney 1912 on 2.146) that Valerius Flaccus in his *Argonautica* transfers the Argonauts' longing for Heracles to a position immediately *before* the conflict with Amycus (*redit Alcidae iam sera cupido*, 4.247). Apparently, Valerius thought it more plausible that the Argonauts should wish Heracles back before rather than after Polydeuces' dangerous fight against Amycus. On the level of the action, this is certainly reasonable, but it confirms in retrospect that Apollonius' arrangement primarily serves a structural purpose. By reintroducing Heracles at this unexpected place, he concludes the encounter with Amycus at the beginning of Book 2 with a reminder, for the Argonauts and the reader, of the outcome of the preceding Hylas story at the end of Book 1.

Taking our clues from the bridging and linking devices discussed, and from the three proems and their intratextual relationship, we can form a clear idea of the sophisticated design of Apollonius' *Argonautica* and of the interplay of traditional and striking new features concerning the structure of the plot and the presentation of leading characters. The proem of Book 4 in particular directs the reader's attention to the ambiguous and dangerous position and suffering of Aeetes' daughter Medea, who gives up her parents and her country to join Jason and the Argonauts (foreshadowed by 3.1132–6). The expectation raised here, that Medea will from now on be the focus of attention, is explicitly confirmed by the often-discussed address of the narrator to Eros at 4.445–51 (e.g., Fränkel 1968: 493–6; Hunter 1993a: 166), preparing the reader for the hideous murder of Medea's brother Apsyrtus, and by the overall course of events in Book 4, from Medea's elimination of the dragon guarding the Golden Fleece at the beginning, via her manipulation of the wavering and treacherous Jason, her unscrupulous scheming to get rid of her brother, and her winning the sympathy and support of Arete, and through her of Alcinous, against the extradition demands of the pursuing Colchians, up to her defeat of the nearly invincible giant Talos at the end. The striking emphasis Apollonius gives to Medea's role represents a major shift from the inherited layout of the Argonaut story. This is found, above all, in one of Apollonius' most important models, Pindar's fourth *Pythian Ode* (214–50, cf. 9–58), where Medea's contribution, though important, nowhere impinges on Jason's standing as leader of the expedition.

The emphasis on Medea in Books 3 and 4, like that on Heracles in Book 1 and, indirectly, in Books 2 through 4, should be seen together with Apollonius' striking redefinition of the role of Jason. Contrary to the mainstream of the tradition from Homer through Theocritus, Apollonius' *Argonautica* is no longer about *Jason*, *his* men and *his* ship, but about the Argonauts as a group (contrast, e.g., *Od.* 12.69–72; Hes. *Th.* 992–1002; Mimn. fr. 11 *IEG*; Pi. *P.* 4.188–9; Theoc. 22.31 with 13.16–18). This refocusing already emerges clearly from the phrasing and structure of the three proems. According to the first, addressed to Apollo and the Muses (1.1–4 and 18–22),

Apollonius will remind his readers of the famous exploits of the *Argonauts* (παλαιγενέων κλέα φωτῶν, 1), sailing for the Golden Fleece by order of King Pelias, and this focus returns in the poem's coda (4.1773–81, esp. 1773 ἵλατ' ἀριϲτῆεϲ, μακάρων γένοϲ, modeled on Medea's address to the Argonauts in Pi. *P.* 4.13, παῖδεϲ ὑπερθύμων τε φωτῶν καὶ θεῶν). Already in the poem's opening Jason is reduced to an instrument of destiny, feared by Pelias (1.5–17). In the second proem, addressed to Erato, the Muse of *eros* or "love" (3.1–5), Jason's recovery of the Fleece is attributed to Medea's love, and Eros is emphatically identified as the crucial force behind the events to come. Finally, from the third proem, addressed in Homeric style to "the Muse" in general (4.1–5), Jason is dropped altogether in favor of Medea: *her* ordeal is now the issue that is on the narrator's mind (Hunter 1993a: 12; differently Clauss 1997: 149–77; Zanker 1998: 229–30).

The clues provided by the proems are borne out by the narrative. In Book 1, Jason, instead of being the principal hero of the Argonauts, plays second fiddle to mighty Heracles and only becomes the Argonauts' leader because Heracles does not accept their unanimous nomination and forcefully authorizes Jason's leadership instead (1.341–50). At a later stage in the book, though, Heracles' words and deeds clearly indicate that Jason is not up to his job (see 861–78, where Heracles scolds the Argonauts in general, and Jason in particular, for forgetting their mission while making love to the Lemnians). In Book 2, the Argonauts more than once deplore the loss of their natural leader Heracles and realize, or are reminded of, how slim their chances have now become to fulfill their mission (see especially 144–54, discussed above, and 772–5). In Book 3, Jason's success in the contest imposed by King Aeetes is wholly due to Medea's magic and instructions (3.1246–62, cf. 1026–62, 1168–9, 1305, and 1363–4, as well as 1232–4, where the narrator notes that only Heracles would have been up to Aeetes in straight combat). In Book 4, Jason is, on the one hand, presented as passive and dependent on Medea (see, e.g., the narrator's comment at 149 and the simile at 4.165–73, discussed below), or waiting for the initiative of fellow Argonauts (Argos, Peleus, Castor and Polydeuces, Orpheus, Euphemus, or even the absent Heracles; characteristic is Jason's stance at 4.1331–44), or relying on divine help (Hera, Thetis, the Libyan heroines, the Hesperides, and Triton). On the other hand, he can be unreliable and deceitful, especially towards Medea, as is already apparent from his misleading and dishonestly selective presentation of the Ariadne story in Book 3 by which he succeeds in winning her over. The reader knows the truth Medea cannot know (3.975–1007, cf. Medea's reaction in 1008–21; Bulloch 2006: 44–8, 67–8). In Book 4, he all but sacrifices her to Apsyrtus and the pursuing Colchians in exchange for keeping the Golden Fleece (339–49). Medea counters with a bitter and scathing reproach (355–90), eliciting from Jason a timid and unconvincing answer (393–410), in a dialogue that foreshadows Euripides' *Medea* (Dyck 1989: 456–7, 459–62; Hunter 1987: 129–39; 1989: 18–19). From now on Medea no longer believes in Jason's love or unconditional support and loyalty. Telling are 4.1011–12 and 1030–53, where she is again forced to appeal for help, but this time implores each of Jason's fellow Argonauts in turn, passing by Jason himself.

Jason's assets in the *Argonautica* are his overwhelming beauty and a persuasive charm by which he easily succeeds in winning support, above all that of women. A key passage is the description of the radiant divine cloak, a present of Athena, which he puts on to impress the Lemnian queen Hypsipyle at 1.721–68 (the Apollonian equivalent of the Homeric description of the divine shield of Achilles, magisterially analyzed by Bulloch 2006). Equally revealing is the star simile which follows (1.774–81), illustrating the beauty and impact on the Lemnians of – as Goethe put it – "Jason, attractive to women" ("Jason Frauen angenehm," *Klassische Walpurgisnacht* 7374).

However, Jason also has a hidden dark and destructive side, as Apollonius makes clear, for example, in what is perhaps the most splendid of his many intriguing similes, inserted at the crucial moment when Medea is waiting for her first rendezvous with Jason (3.956–63):

> αὐτὰρ ὅ γ' οὐ μετὰ δηρὸν ἐελδομένηι ἐφαάνθη,
> ὑψόϲ' ἀναθρώιϲκων ἅ τε Σείριοϲ Ὠκεανοῖο,
> ὃϲ δ' ἤτοι καλὸϲ μὲν ἀρίζηλόϲ τ' ἐϲιδέϲθαι
> ἀντέλλει, μήλοιϲι δ' ἐν ἄϲπετον ἧκεν ὀιζύν·
> ὣϲ ἄρα τῆι καλὸϲ μὲν ἐπήλυθεν εἰϲοράαϲθαι
> Αἰϲονίδηϲ, κάματον δὲ δυϲίμερον ὦρϲε φαανθείϲ.
> ἐκ δ' ἄρα οἱ κραδίη ϲτηθέων πέϲεν, ὄμματα δ' αὔτωϲ
> ἤχλυϲαν, θερμὸν δὲ παρηίδαϲ εἷλεν ἔρευθοϲ.

> But not long afterwards he appeared before her who was eagerly waiting for him, like Sirius leaping up high from Ocean; and Sirius rises indeed beautiful and clear to look at, but to flocks he brings immense suffering: just like that the son of Aeson came up to her, beautiful to behold; but by his appearance he called forth the suffering of ill-guided passion. Her heart dropped from her breast, her eyes became misty for no clear reason and a hot flush covered her cheeks.

Scholars have drawn attention to the sinister connotations of this simile, which foreshadows 4.1–4 *κάματον*... κούρηϲ Κολχίδοϲ... ἄτηϲ πῆμα *δυϲίμερον*, i.e. the next stage of Medea's story (Hunter 1989 on 3.956–61; for the destructive power of Sirius see also the *aition* of the Etesian winds at 2.516–24). The simile reworks *Iliad* 22.25–36, where Achilles in his shining armor, looking for Hector, recalls in the eyes of Priam, the first among the Trojans to become aware of his approach, the brilliant but ill-boding dog-star. Apollonius has introduced a number of subtle and significant changes:

(1) In the *Iliad*, Sirius is set firm in the center of the sky, shining brighter than a multitude of other stars, just as Achilles is shining among the Greek warriors in the plain as he races along; in the *Argonautica*, Sirius is rising: Jason appears before Medea's eyes leaping up as Sirius (leaps up) from the Ocean (956–7); he comes into her view like a beautiful apparition (958 and 960–1). Apollonius stresses the act of appearing, beautiful to watch, Homer the menacing brilliance.
(2) In the *Iliad*, Achilles' "brilliance" is due to his shining armor (22.32); in the *Argonautica*, Jason's "brilliant beauty" is that of his person (beautiful Sirius – beautiful Jason).
(3) In the *Iliad*, Priam *dreads* Achilles' imminent clash with his son Hector, whom he expects to be killed; in the *Argonautica*, Medea *looks forward* to Jason's appearance: the narrator prepares the stage for her infatuation (956, 960–1).

(4) In the *Iliad,* the simile illustrates a specific event, foreboding Hector's death at the hands of Achilles (22.30 λαμπρότατος μὲν ... κακὸν δέ τε cῆμα, of the dog-star; 32 ὥc τοῦ χαλκὸc ἔλαμπε, of Achilles); in the *Argonautica*, its significance comprises the whole of Medea's relationship with Jason, of which it marks the beginning. Jason's beauty is ravishing to look at but devastating in its effect (960–1 in conjunction with 4.1–5).

In the *Argonautica*, similes are often used to disclose truths that are not immediately apparent or hidden beneath a misleading surface. Another revealing simile concerning Jason occurs at the end of Apollonius' account of Medea's and Jason's recovery of the Golden Fleece from the dragon guarding it: "*like a young girl* trying to catch the gleam of the full moon in her dress – her heart delighted at the radiance – *Jason* full of joy lifted the great Fleece with his arms, and its golden blush was reflected in his beautiful cheeks" (4.167–73). This striking simile with its strange contrast of protasis (167 παρθένοc, "young girl") and apodosis (170 "Jason") contains the essence of the whole scene (4.109–82), which shows Medea consistently in charge – a fact Jason himself partially admits (193) – and Jason following her "panic-stricken" (4.149; Reitz 1996: 110–15; missed by Effe 2001: 152).

Jason's role in this scene is even less consistent with that of a dominant leader in charge of a mission than the part he plays in the Libyan desert, later in Book 4, where helpful Libyan heroines find him utterly despondent and incapable of thinking without the assistance of his fellow Argonauts. There, too, the reader is confronted with a curious "non-simile" (Hunter 1993a: 33, 133; but see also Reitz 1996: 136–41), in which the decidedly unheroic apodosis runs against the expectations raised by the protasis, which, in good Homeric style, compares Jason to a lion (4.1337–43), achieving "a destruction of the epic hero with the means of an epic poet" (Reitz 1996: 136–7, cf. 140–1).

Other Members of the Crew

Of the 55 Argonauts mentioned in the Catalogue (1.23–232, including the introduction of Jason), Jason and Heracles receive the largest amount of space in Apollonius' narrative, but among the remaining 53 there are a number of others who receive special attention, such as the pairs of brothers Polydeuces and Castor, Lynceus and Idas, Zetes and Calais, and Peleus and Telamon, or the seers Idmon and Mopsus and the pilots Tiphys and Ancaeus. Most important among the "others," however, are Orpheus, "said to be the son of Calliope," the Muse of epic poetry (1.23–34), and Euphemus, son of Poseidon (1.179–84).

Orpheus heads the catalogue, immediately after the invocation of the Muses in the last line of the proem (1.22), and his prominence is also underlined by the number of lines he receives – 12, more than any other single Argonaut in the catalogue. Both Orpheus and Euphemus are also part of Pindar's small catalogue of leading Argonauts (*P.* 4.171–83), and their characterization and relevance in Pindar have apparently influenced their role in the *Argonautica*. In both cases, however, Apollonius has made significant modifications.

In Pindar, Orpheus joins the Argonauts "at the instigation of Apollo" and is acclaimed, in the center of the catalogue, as "the phorminx-playing father of songs, highly praised Orpheus" (ἐξ Ἀπόλλωνος δὲ φορμιγκτὰς ἀοιδᾶν πατὴρ ἔμολεν εὐαίνητος Ὀρφεύς, *P.* 4.176–7). In the context of an epinician ode praising the accomplishments of the Argonauts and their descendants, Orpheus is evidently to be seen as the mythical ancestor of the encomiastic poet, and he may be regarded as a figure of identification for Pindar himself. In the *Argonautica*, this function is certainly also alluded to (as is suggested, for example, by the mention of Calliope as his mother and his closeness to the Muses of the proem), but Apollonius has given his Orpheus a much wider significance by introducing him as a key helper of Jason, putting his magic art at Jason's disposal to overcome the obstacles facing him (Ὀρφέα μὲν δὴ τοῖον ἑῶν ἐπαρωγὸν ἀέθλων Αἰσονίδης … δέξατο, 1.32–4). The first *aition* of the poem illustrates Orpheus' effectiveness and importance: the oak trees which he once moved down from Pieria to the Thracian coast by means of his enchanting music are still standing there in rows bearing witness to the power of his art (26–31). Thus there is a shift of focus: Orpheus' art in the *Argonautica* is less concerned with the author or with posterity or the lasting fame of the expedition than with its successful completion.

Orpheus' activity is restricted to the voyage, Books 1, 2 and 4.241–1785; he has no part in Book 3 and the beginning of Book 4, where Medea takes over as Jason's most conspicuous helper. Orpheus' functions are clearly defined. With his enchanting songs, he secures or restores harmony among the Argonauts, which is often strained, for example, ending a quarrel among Jason, Idas, and Idmon (1.460–515) and inaugurating a temple of Concord after leading communal celebrations in honor of Apollo Heoios (2.683–719). More than once he suggests cultic measures for the safety of the Argonauts on their journey: he leads the Argonauts into the mysteries of Samothrace (1.915–21), supervises the building of an altar and sacrifice for Apollo Neossoos at the Tomb of Sthenelus (2.927–9), and dedicates a tripod to the divinities of Libya (4.1547–55). His phorminx-playing rescues the Argonauts from danger, for instance by defeating the Sirens (4.902–11) and placating the Hesperides (4.1409–23). He creates a harmonious atmosphere in difficult circumstances, such as the hastily improvised wedding of Jason and Medea (4.1155–60 and 1192–98).

All of these interventions serve a single purpose. They help to overcome internal and external problems which threaten the security and concord of the entire crew due to Jason's lack of authority. Orpheus never acts on Jason's orders or in his stead as has been suggested (e.g., by Busch 1993: 322) but always spontaneously and independently for the sake of the crew as a whole. Thus he supports Jason's mission and contributes to the success of the Argonauts' expedition in his own peculiar way. The interventions of Orpheus are always successful and his advice is immediately followed, but he never enters into the discussions and conflicts of his fellow Argonauts. His roles are those of an arbitrator and mediator between men and gods. On the whole he is designed as an integrating figure, whose voice and lyre have an enchanting and soothing effect on the heterogeneous crew.

Euphemus, on the other hand, may be called the most Pindaric among Apollonius' Argonauts. In Pindar's fourth Pythian Ode, he is of paramount importance because he is the Argonaut to whom Arcesilaus IV of Cyrene, Pindar's addressee, traces the origins of his family and the foundation of his city (Jackson 1987: 23–30). In the *Argonautica*, Euphemus is a main character in two key sequences of the narrative, the passage through the Cyanean Rocks (2.531–606) and the adventures in the Libyan desert (4.1381–624). His role in the second event corresponds to the part he plays in Pindar's ode. In Apollonius as in Pindar, Euphemus receives as a gift of hospitality from the local divinity Triton/Eurypylus, a son of Poseidon like himself, a clod of Libyan soil which foreshadows the colonization of the country by his descendants (4.1552–3, cf. 1734; Pi. *P.* 4.37, 42–3). Euphemus' encounter with Eurypylus as told in the *Argonautica* closely resembles that of Pindar and even contains a number of verbal reminiscences. In both cases the Libyan clod is linked to the island of Thera, from which Euphemus' descendants will colonize Libya. Apollonius' narrative, however, takes a peculiar turn thanks to a few striking changes vis-à-vis Pindar's account and an innovative characterizing feature of Euphemus:

First, Apollonius has replaced Pindar's accidental loss of the Libyan clod near the island of Thera (*P.* 4.38–56, cf. 254–62) by an explicit instruction in a dream which Euphemus remembers when the Argonauts leave a small island to which they have given the name "Anaphe" (4.1732–46):

> Euphemus remembered a dream which he had had in the night passed on Anaphe. For it had seemed to him that the divine clod which he held in his hand close to his breast became wet from white drops of milk, and the clod, though being small, turned into a woman looking like a young girl. He made love to her overcome by an incontrollable desire, and he lamented as if he had bedded his daughter whom he had himself nourished with his own milk. But she cheered him up with gentle words: "Of Triton's race I am, dear friend, the nurse of your children, not your daughter, for Triton and Libya are my parents. Come now, put me down beside the maiden daughters of Nereus to inhabit the sea near Anaphe. Later on I shall go towards the rays of the sun, where I shall be ready for your descendants." This Euphemus remembered in his heart.

Euphemus' dream is reported by the narrator as a fact remembered at the very moment when the Argonauts leave Anaphe, the island near which the Libyan clod (represented by the woman in the dream) wants to be dropped into the sea. And throwing it into the sea is what Euphemus does (1755–7), having been told by Jason, himself informed by prophecies of Apollo, that the gods will turn the clod into an island which the youngest of Euphemus' grandchildren will eventually settle (1749–54). This island, the emergence of which is the finishing stroke of Apollonius' colorful Libyan canvas, is "Kalliste, the sacred nurse of Euphemus' children" (1758). It is "to the island Kalliste" (1763) that in later times Theras, Euphemus' descendant, brought Spartan settlers, and "in honor of him it changed its name to Thera" (4.1761–4). The elaborate aetiological sequence closes with a break-off statement: "but these events occurred long after Euphemus" (ἀλλὰ τὰ μὲν μετόπιν γένετ' Εὐφήμοιο, 1764) – "words that echo Callimachus" with which "the narrator leaves the reader to finish the story" (DeForest 1994: 141–2; Call. *Aet.* fr. 12.6 Pf.).

It has often been claimed that the "foundation myth of Cyrene" in the *Argonautica* has to be understood in the context of contemporary Ptolemaic politics and that

Apollonius here "evokes an explicitly 'political' frame of reference for his epic" (Hunter 1993a: 153). One should note, however, that Apollonius, unlike Pindar, curiously stops short of actually narrating or even referring to the colonization of Libya. His story pointedly ends with Kalliste, the island designed for the descendants of Euphemus to settle, through the chiastic repetition of 4.1757–8 νῆcoc ... Καλλίcτη in 1763 Καλλίcτην ἐπὶ νῆcoν, and the repeated verbal linking of Kalliste with Euphemus in the opening and closing lines (1758 Καλλίcτη ... Εὐφήμοιο and 1762–3 Καλλίcτην ... Εὐφήμοιο). Evidently, Apollonius is not so much interested in the colonization of Libya itself (contrast Pi. *P.* 4.256–61, 19–25 and Hdt. 4.145–57) as in its starting point, the clod which turns into the island Kalliste. What is the reason for this exclusive and surprising emphasis on Kalliste, and what is the connection between Kalliste and Anaphe, which does not appear in Pindar's ode?

At this point, a closer look at the non-Pindaric credentials of Apollonius' Euphemus, which have not received much attention in Apollonian scholarship, may be helpful. In the catalogue, Euphemus is introduced as the "most swift-footed" of the Argonauts (ποδωκηέcτατοc ἄλλων, 1.180), a qualification explained as follows (182–4):

> κεῖνοc ἀνὴρ καὶ πόντου ἐπὶ γλαυκοῖο θέεcκεν
> οἴδματοc, οὐδὲ θοοὺc βάπτεν πόδαc, ἀλλ' ὅcoν ἄκροιc
> ἴχνεcι τεγγόμενοc διερῇ πεφόρητο κελεύθῳ.
>
> That man used to run even over the waves of the grey sea and did not moisten his swift feet; but dipping in only the tips of his toes he passed along on his wet path.

Euphemus' exceptional swiftness explains his remarkable importance in the most crucial event of the outward journey, the passage through the Cyanean Rocks in Book 2 (531–606), as well as his participation in the attempt to catch up with Heracles and make him rejoin the Argonauts in the Libyan events of Book 4 (1461–71, 1482–4). Traditionally, however, the title of honor "swiftest of men" belongs to another Argonaut, Iphiclus (Hes. fr. 62 MW; Call. *Aet.* fr. 75.46–7 Pf.), who is also listed in Apollonius' catalogue but deprived of his swiftness (1.45–8). Apparently, Apollonius has transferred this characteristic from Iphiclus to Euphemus to give additional significance to this central figure of the Libyan foundation legend. For this transfer he again seems to have been inspired by Pindar, who makes his Medea prophesy to the Argonauts on the island of Thera, i.e. Kalliste, that the Libyan descendants of Euphemus "will exchange dolphins for swift mares and instead of oars handle the reins of wind-swift chariots" (*P.* 4.17–18). Thus the "swiftness" attributed by Pindar to the descendants of Euphemus is given to Euphemus himself by Apollonius. Seen against the backdrop of Pindar's Thera/Kalliste in Medea's prophecy, this change highlights the significance of the island of Kalliste in the *Argonautica*.

The purpose of this focus on Kalliste at the end of Apollonius' narrative finally becomes clear when one considers the function of the *aition* of the name Anaphe, taken over from Callimachus' *Aetia* (frs. 7–21 Pf.). Near this "Island of Appearance," made visible by Apollo (Aegletes) when the Argonauts are lost in darkness, Euphemus is to throw into the sea the Libyan clod which turns into the island of Kalliste, the idea apparently being that the etymologically ambivalent "Anaphe" will also make "Kalliste" visible. Within the framework of the Callimachean *Aetia* with which Apollonius' *Argonautica* draws to a close (the story of Euphemus and the Libyan clod is preceded by the Apollo Aigletes *aition* and followed by the Hydrophoria *aition*, the last *aition* of the narrative), the striking prominence of *Kalliste*, origin of Cyrene in Libya, evoking the name of *Kalli*machos of Cyrene, seems to be designed as a tribute by the poet of the *Argonautica* to the poet of the *Aetia* (Köhnken 2001: 78–9; 2003: 207–11; 2005).

* * *

This chapter has focused on four peculiar features that exemplify the unorthodox quality of the *Argonautica* as compared to the tradition Apollonius inherited: (1) the intriguing patterns and interplay of Apollonius' three proems and the means used to tie together the four books of the epic; (2) a novel selection and presentation of divine helpers, on the one hand Apollo, "the far-darter," who intervenes, effectively, from a distance, on the other female gods, especially Hera and Athena, who provide hands-on and intimate support; (3) striking modifications of epic devices such as similes and ecphrases; (4) a strong interest in aetiological matters. Characteristic attractions of Apollonius' narrative art are its sophisticated play with intertexts with which the reader is supposed to be familiar, purposefully selected, adapted, and rearranged, as well as its pointed pregnancy and multi-layeredness, which challenges the narratees to take hints and read between the lines. Apollonius is a master in subtle and indirect storytelling.

FURTHER READING

Vian's edition, 1974–96 (followed in this chapter), with introduction and concise notes as well as a French translation by Delage, is exemplary; Fränkel 1961 (edition only) contains too many arbitrary changes and transpositions. Commentaries: on Book 1, Ardizzoni 1967, Clauss 1993, Vasilaros 2004; on Book 2, Matteo 2007, Cuypers 1997 (1–310); on Book 3, Gillies 1928, Ardizzoni 1958, Vian 1961, Hunter 1989, Campbell 1994 (1–471); on Book 4, Livrea 1973. In addition, Fränkel 1968 is worth consulting, and Mooney 1912, on all four books, is still sometimes useful. Wendel 1935 provides access to the important scholia on the poem.

Recent English translations are Hunter 1993b, Green 1997, and Race 2008. Helpful for orientation are Hutchinson 1988: 85–142, Nelis 2005, Hunter 1993a, and the essays in Papanghelis and Rengakos 2008 (2001), Harder, Regtuit, and Wakker 2000.

On the characterization of Jason, see Carspecken 1952, Lawall 1966, Beye 1969, 1982, Vian 1978, Hunter 1988, 1993a: 8–45, Clauss 1993, Köhnken 2000; on Medea, Hunter 1987, Dyck 1989, Clauss 1997 (the proems as "programmatic introductions"), Bulloch 2006 (a brilliant analysis of the Ariadne paradigm). Discussions of narrative structure, techniques, and "voice" include Hurst 1967, Fusillo 1985, Hunter 1993a: 101–51, 2001, Byre 2002, Cuypers 2004a. On the *Argonautica* and Homer, see for example Fantuzzi 1988, Clauss 1993, Knight 1995, Fantuzzi and Hunter 2004: 246–82. Erbse 1953 is a seminal article on Apollonius as a scholarly poet; see further Rengakos 1993, 2001. For the *Argonautica* as an aetiological poem, its relationship with Callimachus' *Aetia*, and relative chronology, see Valverde Sánchez 1989, DeForest 1994, Cameron 1995a, Köhnken 2001, 2003, 2005, Harder in this volume; and on the *Argonautica* and contemporary culture, Hunter 1993a: 152–69, Stephens 2003. On Apollonius' similes, see Carspecken 1952, Reitz 1996, Effe 2001; on his gods, Klein 1931, Feeney 1991, Hunter 1993a: 75–100; and on his descriptions, Zanker 1987, 2004, and Williams 1991. For Apollonius' influence on Vergil, see especially Nelis 2001.

CHAPTER ELEVEN

Narrative Hexameter Poetry

Annemarie Ambühl

What is a typically Hellenistic epic? Is it a miniature epic ("epyllion") in the style of Callimachus' *Hecale* or a multi-book epic in the manner of Rhianus? In modern scholarship, this issue has provoked a long-standing and sometimes ideologically charged debate. Konrat Ziegler has notoriously postulated hundreds of thousands of lines of lost Hellenistic historical and mythological epic, whereas Alan Cameron has questioned the very existence of full-scale epics celebrating Hellenistic kings, and instead argued for a tradition of short hexameter encomia performed at festivals (Ziegler 1966: 15–23; Cameron 1995a: 263–302; on historical/encomiastic elegies such as *SH* 958, see Barbantani 2002/3). The scarcity of the evidence has favored hypothesizing. Notably, the modern critical debate has led to the construction of an analogous Alexandrian debate about epic as a genre. As signal witnesses of this debate, scholars have regularly adduced the Prologue to the *Aetia*, where Callimachus seems to reject long, continuous epics on kings and heroes in favor of shorter, lighter compositions (fr. 1 Pf.; Acosta-Hughes and Harder in this volume), as well as ancient testimonies for a quarrel between Callimachus and Apollonius, the main contemporary epicist, which was construed as a clash between modern and old-fashioned poetics (for an overview see Benedetto 1993: 27–91). Because there is now wide agreement that Apollonius' *Argonautica* is essentially a "Callimachean epic" (Köhnken in this volume), the phantom of a quarrel has been more or less laid to rest, but Callimachus' alleged ban on (long) epic poems still haunts modern discussions. Only recently, the polemical stance of the Prologue has been identified as mainly a literary strategy of its author, testifying to the lasting success of Callimachus' self-fashioning as an innovative poet rather than to an actually existing ancient controversy (Cameron 1995a: 358, 452–3; Schmitz 1999; Acosta-Hughes and Stephens 2002). Even if one does not subscribe to Cameron's thesis that the Prologue is not about epic at all, but about different styles of elegy, it seems advisable to leave Callimachean polemic aside and instead look at the texts from an unbiased perspective.

Moreover, the difference between epic and "epyllion" has been defined primarily as a matter of length. But length is relative, as can be gauged from the fact that even within the modern category of epyllion the scope varies widely, from an *eidyllion* of fewer than a hundred lines such as Theocritus 13 up to a full-blown miniature epic such as Callimachus' *Hecale*, which employs complex structural devices and may have run to well over a thousand lines (Hollis 2009: 337–40). Ultimately, the preoccupation with length as the sole criterion for judging the value of poetry once again derives from Callimachus, who set up this absurdly extreme position in order to make fun of his – real or fictitious – critics (fr. 1.17–18 Pf.). Therefore it seems preferable to frame the discussion not only in quantitative but also in qualitative terms regarding style and treatment. But does a Hellenistic "epyllion" then necessarily have to be innovative and preferably anti-heroic, and heroic epics conventional and boring? (Lloyd-Jones 1990: 236–7; Bing 1988: 50–6). How can we judge, if no full-scale epics have survived apart from Apollonius' *Argonautica*, which in its unconventional character may or may not have been representative of the contemporary epic production? Perhaps we should reckon with a diversity of markets and audiences for different kinds of epic poems rather than with a sterile opposition between Callimachean and un-Callimachean poetry.

The Evidence

Regrettably, with the exception of Apollonius' *Argonautica* no specimen of extensive narrative hexameter poetry from the Hellenistic period has survived intact. There exist titles and fragments of historical-encomiastic epics (with the reservations of Cameron 1995a regarding their scope mentioned above) and of regional-ethnographic epics such as the *Messeniaca*, *Achaica*, *Eliaca*, and *Thessalica* by Rhianus (*CA* 1–65 and *SH* 715–16) or the *Ktiseis* (foundation poems) by Apollonius (*CA* 4–12); the latter may however have been quite short compositions. A third group is made up by mythological epics such as those on Heracles, discussed below. Collections of metamorphoses like Nicander's *Heteroioumena* (frs. 43, 50, 59, 62 GS and *SH* ?562; cf. Boeus' *Ornithogonia*, Parthenius' *Metamorphoses* [*SH* 636–7 = 24 Lightfoot 1999], and ultimately Ovid's *Metamorphoses*) might be linked more appropriately with didactic poetry. In most cases, the length and contents of these poems can no longer be determined. Moreover, there are no strict boundaries between the subgenres, since foundation poems, for instance, regularly include mythological as well as historical material. An important precursor of this kind of epic apparently was Antimachus' *Thebaid*, in which he revived the Archaic mythological epics about Thebes by updating them with the help of his philological research. Later critics regularly commented upon the poet's verbosity, a criticism which perhaps reflects in distorted form characteristics of his narrative: Antimachus may have padded his narrative with devices such as ecphrasis rather than driving the plot on (Matthews 1996: 20–6 and 64–76, on fr. 2).

With respect to the relatively short narrative hexameter poems on mythological subjects conventionally designated as epyllia (a label that will be explored below), the situation looks more promising. In this category we might include Theocritus 13 (*Hylas*), 24 (*Heracliscus*), and 25 (*Heracles the Lion-Slayer*, probably not by Theocritus himself), as well as Moschus' *Europa*, the *Megara* (Ps.-Moschus 4) and the fragmentary *Epithalamius of Achilles and Deidamia* ascribed to Bion. Significant fragments exist from Callimachus' *Hecale*, allowing a basic reconstruction of its outline (Hollis 2009). Considerably fewer fragments are left of Philitas' *Hermes* and Eratosthenes' *Hermes*. Despite their shared title, they had very different subject matters. Eratosthenes' poem was an Alexandrian reworking of the *Homeric Hymn to Hermes*, treating the childhood adventures of the wily god and his invention of the lyre, and culminating in a description of cosmic harmony by the god himself, a topic which reflects the author's astronomical interests (*CA* 1–16, *SH* 397–8, 922; Geus 2002: 110–28). In contrast, Philitas' *Hermes* apparently did not have a divine protagonist at all, but dealt with Odysseus' stay on the island of Aeolus, enriching this episode from *Odyssey* 10 with the pathetic story of the illegitimate love between the hero and Aeolus' daughter Polymele, the girl's abandonment, and her subsequent incestuous marriage to one of her brothers (*CA* 5 – 9 = 1 – 5 Spanoudakis 2002; reconstructions in Latacz 1999 and Spanoudakis 2002: 95–141; speculations in Geus 2000).

Alexander Aetolus, Euphorion, and Parthenius also composed short mythological poems in hexameters on such subjects as the metamorphosis of Glaucus (Alexander's *Halieus*, *CA* 1 = 1 Magnelli 1999) or the unhappy love story of Byblis and her brother Caunus (Parthenius *SH* 646 = 33 Lightfoot 1999; cf. Nicaenetus' *Lyrcus*, *CA* 1). Euphorion had a reputation for especially obscure mythological poems which made him fashionable with the Roman neoteric poets (Lightfoot 1999: 57–64). He seems to have written epyllion-style compositions as well as catalogue poems on curses and mythological punishments (*Chiliades*, *Curses or the Cup-stealer*, *Thrax*; on the genre see Watson 1991), all of them in hexameters (*CA* 1–139, 142–77; 3–195 Van Groningen 1977; *SH* 413–54).

Finally, there are several anonymous fragments classified as epyllia in Powell's *Collectanea Alexandrina* (*Epica adespota* 1–4, 8, and 9 col. viii, ix). Some of them share traits with poems by Callimachus and Theocritus. The meeting of the son of Iphis with the old Pheidon on Diomedes' estate in fr. 2 recalls the bucolic setting of Heracles' meeting with the old ploughman on Augeas' estate in Ps.-Theocritus 25, and the speech of an impoverished old woman in fr. 4 recalls Hecale's recollections of her former wealth in Callimachus (fr. 41, Hollis 2009: 29–30, 179–80). Among the anonymous hexameter fragments in the *Supplementum Hellenisticum*, there are remains of Hellenistic poems on Hero and Leander (901A, 951), but as the editors remark (on 951): "omnia incerta" – a cautionary label that might be applied to much of the other material as well. Indeed, these collections contain many more hexameter fragments consisting of only a few words or lines which frustratingly defy further analysis. In cases where a single hexameter has been transmitted, it cannot even be decided whether it derives from an epic or an elegiac work.

Definitions and Questions

In line with general directions in Hellenistic scholarship, the study of Hellenistic epic has recently profited from new approaches that combine close reading with methods deriving from genre theory, narratology, and studies in intertextuality, and take into consideration the social, political, and cultural contexts in which these texts were produced. Nevertheless, taxonomically oriented debates about modern critical terms and concepts, and their application to ancient literary texts, have tended to become an end in themselves, as is exemplified by the case of the so-called epyllion. Apart from the well-known fact that the term originates in nineteenth-century criticism and is therefore strictly speaking anachronistic (Allen 1940; Most 1982), modern reconstructions of the "genre" of Hellenistic and Roman miniature epic run two risks.

The first trap is a teleologically oriented perspective, which applies a biological model to the development of the genre from its "birth" to its "maturity" and subsequent "death," thus projecting a linear evolution onto the categorized works (Toohey 1992: 100–20). It may be true that the development of a genre can be reconstructed through the history of its reception, in the sense that individual poems mark their affiliation with a certain genre through continuity with, as well as modification of, their predecessors (as is the case, for example, with bucolic: Nauta 1990; Thomas 1996; Reed in this volume). Yet in the case of "epyllion," in view of the lack of a genuine ancient equivalent for the term, it is doubtful whether the texts we categorize as such were perceived of as belonging to an identifiable subgenre of epic at all.

Second, genre definitions easily become normative instead of descriptive. The search for the "perfect epyllion" that matches all the criteria predetermines the selection of examples and excludes texts that do not conform sufficiently to the pattern. Expectations thus shape interpretation in a circular manner: if an epyllion by definition has to be ironical or anti-heroic, it is likely to produce readings that in turn confirm the definition (Effe 1978). This phenomenon can be observed in most modern studies of the Hellenistic epyllion, whose selection of material is firmly linked to the agendas of their respective authors. Thus Marjorie Crump (1931) identifies a "digression," rather loosely defined as a second story contained within the first, as an essential feature of the epyllion, and she accordingly defines long, direct speeches such as the crow's story of Erichthonius in Callimachus' *Hecale* or ecphrases such as Moschus' description of the pictures of Io on the basket of Europa as digressions. Kathryn Gutzwiller (1981) analyzes epyllia by Theocritus, Callimachus, Moschus, and Bion in order to demonstrate the subversion of epic norms and values that in her view characterizes these poems. The most recent monograph on the subject by Carol Merriam (2001) focuses on female characters as a central feature of the epyllion and accordingly highlights the heroines Alcmena in Theocritus 24, Moschus' Europa, Thetis and Ariadne in Catullus 64, and other women in Latin epyllia.

This is not to say that the term epyllion should be abandoned altogether, for it has proven its merits as a term for grouping together poems with similar characteristics. But at least any definition for the "genre" should be as open as possible, allowing for a variety of forms and taking into account the differences between individual texts as well as their similarities. Such a definition could start from the shared characteristics that distinguish these works from other epic subgenres such as hymns, encomia, and didactic and bucolic poetry. They are predominantly narrative as opposed to mimetic texts, although they may include a sizeable percentage of direct speech (the *Megara* being the most striking example). Their subject matter is mainly mythological as opposed to factual/scientific, fictional/pastoral or cultic/religious. As will be discussed below, the definition should perhaps even include thematically related compositions in elegiacs. Many of the texts covered by this definition can of course also be discussed under other generic headings, according to different criteria regarding form, content, function, and possible performance context (for example, the mythological narrative Theocritus 24 seems to have been concluded with a hymnic ending), while texts which are generally discussed under other categories may also include mythological narrative (for example, Callimachus' *Hymn to Demeter* with its inset tale of Erysichthon or Theocritus' hymn to the Dioscuri, *Id.* 22).

The selection and combination of different generic traditions has thus to be taken into account when we analyze the formal and thematic variety of Hellenistic "epyllion." Probably the main reason for this variety is the fact that from the fourth century onwards dactylic hexameters and elegiacs increasingly replaced lyric meters, with the result that contents formerly belonging to other (sub)genres were adapted to hexametric and elegiac poetry (Fantuzzi and Hunter 2004: 17–37; Fantuzzi in this volume). Given the prominence of elegiac verse in the oeuvres of third-century poets, an especially intriguing issue is the relationship between short mythological poems in hexameters and in elegiac distichs. For instance, besides their hexameter poems mentioned above, Philitas composed a *Demeter* (*CA* 1–4, *SH* 673–5; 5a–21 Spanoudakis 2002) and Eratosthenes an *Erigone* (*CA* 22–7; Rosokoki 1995) in elegiacs. Alexander Aetolus and later Parthenius, too, seem to have written narrative poems in both meters (Magnelli 1999: 12–26; Lightfoot 1999: 17–49), and in his preface to the *Erotika Pathemata*, the latter recommends his love stories to Gallus for "rendering into hexameters and elegiacs" (εἰς ἔπη καὶ ἐλεγείας ἀνάγειν).

Is this simply a matter of variation and personal taste, or are there significant narratological and stylistic differences between epic and elegiac compositions? Alan Cameron compares Callimachus' parallel stories about Theseus' meeting with Hecale in the hexametric *Hecale* and Heracles' meeting with Molorcus in the elegiac *Victory of Berenice* in the *Aetia* on the lines of scholarship on Ovid (Heinze 1919; Hinds 1987), identifying the two narratives as a model epic and a model elegy respectively (Cameron 1995a: 437–53). According to him, one of the main differences is the greater prominence of the narrator in elegiac verse: "personal elegy as against impersonal epic" (1995a: 439; similar conclusions in Harder 2004: 63–72; Morrison 2007: 190–2). But can such statements based on statistical data concerning the frequency of authorial intrusions into the narrative really be trusted given the fragmentary nature of the corpus? Moreover, the narrator in the hexametric *Argonautica* is, in his own way, no less prominent than the narrator in the *Aetia* (Cuypers 2004a, 2005). The differences in treatment of the two related myths in the hexametric *Hecale* and the elegiac *Victory of Berenice* cannot be explained simply as deriving from generic differences between epic and elegy. Additional generic debts, such as to tragedy, comedy, and satyr-play, and specific intertextual and metapoetic issues must also be taken into account (Ambühl 2004; see also Harder 2002a: 217–23 on the elegiac and epic treatments of the Anaphe episode in the *Aetia* and in Apollonius' *Argonautica* respectively). In short, the issue of the similarities and differences between hexametric and elegiac "epyllia" needs further investigation.

Finally, what does their reception in Roman poetry tell us about Hellenistic epic and "epyllion"? Can Ennius' *Annals*, for all its Hellenistic features, really be claimed as the only existing example of a Hellenistic historical epic (Ziegler 1966: 23–37, 53–77)? If Philitas, Callimachus, Euphorion, and Parthenius are remembered by Roman poets as prime exponents of elegy (e.g., Prop. 3.1.1, Verg. *Ecl.* 10.50; cf. Quint. *Inst.* 10.1.58), does this reflect the original balance between hexameter and elegiac works in their oeuvres? Or is this rather a case of name-dropping in a "do-it-yourself literary tradition" manner (Hinds 1998: 123), in the sense that Roman poets are fond of making up Greek predecessors for a certain genre or style? The complete lack of evidence that Euphorion wrote any elegies at all (Jacoby 1905: 69; van Groningen 1977: 251–3) would seem to plead for the latter. In general, the fact that so many Hellenistic works have been lost has often been used as a license to project certain features of Roman "epyllia" back onto the Greek texts. Yet it has become increasingly clear that behind the opposition between epic and elegy in Roman poetry there lies a specific Roman cultural and political agenda that should not be superimposed onto Alexandria (Cameron 1995a: 454–83; Hunter 2006a). It may therefore be advisable to study the surviving Greek poems first on their own terms, taking into account their specific literary and cultural context, before comparing them to their Roman successors.

The Metamorphoses of Heracles

In what follows, I will focus on a selection of texts that have been preserved (almost) intact in order to examine their relationship to epic as well as to other generic traditions, their adaptation of myth, and their narrative techniques: Theocritus 13 (*Hylas*) and 24 (*Heracliscus*), Ps.-Theocritus 25 (*Heracles the Lion-Slayer*), and Ps.-Moschus' *Megara*. All four feature the quintessential hero Heracles, who offers an excellent test case to study these crucial aspects of Hellenistic hexameter poetry. The poems put Heracles into different environments that range from the heroic to the domestic, the bucolic, and the erotic. They present him at different times in his life – from his childhood to his death and apotheosis – and have him interact with a variety of persons: boys, women, and old men, relatives and strangers, characters known from the literary tradition and otherwise unknown figures. The texts employ various narrative techniques, combining authorial narrative with direct speech, exhibiting inset stories, prophecies, and dreams, and evoking different genres such as epic, lyric, tragedy, and hymn. Like the metamorphosing mythological figures the Hellenistic writers were so fond of, Heracles adapts his shape to various textual environments and points of view.

In Hellenistic times, epics about Heracles continued to be written, among them Rhianus' *Heracleia* (*CA* 2–10, *SH* 715), Diotimus' *Heracleia* (*SH* 393) and *Heracles' Labors* (*SH* 394), and Phaedimus' *Heracleia* (*SH* 669). Although not much of them remains, they will probably have described his deeds in chronological order in the manner of the Archaic and Classical Heracles-epics by Pisander and Panyassis (on the latter see Matthews 1974). For the type of poem that focuses on a single episode there exist precedents as well: for example, the *Sack of Oichalia* by Creophylus (the subject of an epigram by Callimachus, 6 Pf.), the pseudo-Hesiodic *Shield* with its extensive ecphrasis of Heracles' shield, or the anonymous *Meropis*, whose datings range from the Archaic to the Hellenistic Age (*SH* and *SSH* 903A).

An especially popular topic in Hellenistic poetry seems to have been Heracles' fight against the Nemean lion. The fight may either be narrated directly or indirectly, forming the background for another story, or evoked by way of allusion. In Ps.-Theocritus 25, a full account is put into Heracles' own mouth. In contrast, in Callimachus' *Victory of Berenice* (*SH* 254–68C), the introductory elegy of the third book of the *Aetia* whose mythic centerpiece shares some traits with hexametric epyllia, a direct narrative seems to have been avoided by means of a double narrative ellipsis, as first the narrator and then Heracles himself explicitly refuse to tell the full story (*SH* 264 with Ambühl 2004: 42; for a contrastive metapoetic reading of the two texts, see Seiler 1997: 29–110). Nevertheless, Callimachus apparently did include certain aspects of the fight, probably in the form of an *aition* of the lion-skin (*SH* 267–8C), and certainly indirectly by mirroring Heracles' struggle against the lion in miniature with Molorcus' fight against a plague of mice (*SH* 259). In the *Hecale*, too, Heracles' lion-skin may have played a role as part of the story of Theseus' childhood. When Heracles visits Pittheus at Troezen, the boy Theseus bravely attacks what he mistakes for a living lion, a childish feat that nevertheless points to his future prowess (frs. 13 and 101 Hollis 2009: cf. Hollis 1994; Ambühl 2005: 54–5). Unfortunately, not enough survives of an anonymous Hellenistic Heracles-poem (*CA epica adespota* 8) to tell in which manner the fight was treated there.

The killing of the Nemean lion is the first of Heracles' 12 canonical labors, accomplished when he was still a young man at the beginning of his heroic career. This choice of subject can be linked with the Hellenistic interest in aetiology, as it provides the *aition* of Heracles' emblem, the lion-skin (Gutzwiller 1981: 38). On the whole the shift of focus from the adult hero Heracles to his childhood and youth implies not so much an ironical "destruction of tradition" (Effe 1978) or a penchant for realism (Zanker 1987), but is rather to be identified as an aetiological strategy which seeks to trace the character of the hero back to its origins and thus to re-invent literary tradition (Hunter 1998; Ambühl 2005). In the four poems to be considered next, references to the fight as well as to other elements of the Heracles myth are employed in various narrative contexts to form creative re-writings of his story.

Theocritus 13 and 24: The Hero in Love and the Hero to Be

At the beginning of Theocritus 13 (*Hylas*), the narrator identifies Heracles as the "bronze-hearted son of Amphitryon, the one who withstood the savage lion," only to add that he too succumbed to Eros and fell in love with a beautiful boy (ἀλλὰ καὶ

Ἀμφιτρύωνος ὁ χαλκεοκάρδιος υἱός, / ὃς τὸν λῖν ὑπέμεινε τὸν ἄγριον, ἤρατο παιδός, 5–6). As has often been pointed out, Heracles' erotic passion for Hylas stands in an uneasy relationship with his heroic character, here symbolized by his feat of killing the Nemean lion (Effe 1978: 60–4; Gutzwiller 1981: 19–29; Van Erp Taalman Kip 1994; Hunter 1999: 261–89). This tension is reflected by competing models within the text. Heracles himself understands his role as that of a father who teaches his son how to become a "real man" (καί νιν πάντ' ἐδίδασκε, πατὴρ ὡσεὶ φίλον υἱόν, 8; ἀλαθινὸν ἄνδρ', 15). In his view, he himself, the ἀγαθὸς and ἀοίδιμος hero (9), is the ideal role model for Hylas. As in *Iliad* 6.358, where Helen prophesies that she and Paris will become a theme of song for future generations, and in Callimachus' *Hymn to Athena* (*h.* 5.121), where Athena promises Teiresias eternal fame, the adjective ἀοίδιμος here has a self-referential quality, for it refers to Heracles' fame in poetry, presumably in heroic epic. Ironically, thanks to Theocritus' poem (and Apollonius' *Argonautica*), Hylas will indeed become ἀοίδιμος and, like Heracles, immortal (72), but not because of his heroic deeds, as Heracles intended. The term thus also points to the ambiguous status of Theocritus' "epyllion," between heroic epic and love poetry.

Sure enough, the handsome Hylas soon becomes the prey of nymphs, who also fall in love with him (46–9). Heracles' dubious ideal of an heroic education, which has already been undermined by the chick simile where he is associated with a fussing mother-hen (12–13), is now replaced by the similarly ambiguous image of "mothers" who comfort the crying boy on their knees with gentle words (ἀγανοῖσι παρεψύχοντ' ἐπέεσσιν, 53–4). Heracles' reaction is in character. He rushes to the rescue with bow and club (55–7), and three times shouts "Hylas" "as loud as his deep throat could bellow" (τρὶς μὲν Ὕλαν ἄυσεν, ὅσον βαθὺς ἤρυγε λαιμός, 58), while Hylas each time replies faintly from under the water (ἀραιὰ … φωνά, 59–60). The cry is Heracles' only utterance in the poem, and it has an almost animal quality. Indeed the lion imagery from the beginning now returns, as Heracles' frenzied reaction to the loss of his beloved is described by means of an epic simile: "a ravening lion hears a fawn cry upon the mountains and hastens from his lair in search of the ready prey" (νεβροῦ φθεγξαμένας τις ἐν οὔρεσιν ὠμοφάγος λὶς / ἐξ εὐνᾶς ἔσπευσεν ἑτοιμοτάταν ἐπὶ δαῖτα, 62–3). Heracles the lion-slayer is now associated with a lion himself. The animal simile that in a straightforward epic context would underline Heracles' heroism, here rather points to his loss of rational control and to the problematic fusion of his heroic identity with erotic passion. Hylas, the beloved boy he wants to protect, by way of the simile becomes his helpless prey. Ultimately Heracles fails both as an epic hero and as a lover: on the level of the simile as the lion who cannot reach his ready prey, and on the level of the narrative as the passionate lover who cannot keep his beloved safe. In Theocritus 13, Heracles' epic-heroic past as a lion-slayer is thus evoked in incompatible circumstances, and his present erotic endeavor is bound to result in failure, as he wanders aimlessly through the wilderness (64–7, 70–1).

The opposite strategy is employed in Theocritus 24 (*Heracliscus*), for here Heracles is a ten-month-old baby whose first heroic feat, the strangling of the snakes sent by Hera, prefigures his future character as a hero and god. Although in prophesying the amazing career of the extraordinary boy Tiresias does not specify the beasts to be subdued by Heracles later in life (81–3), the strangling of the snakes exhibits narrative patterns associated in other texts with some of his canonical labors, such as the strangling of the Nemean lion with his bare hands (26–33, 55; cf. Ps.-Theoc. 25.262–71) or the fear of onlookers as they are presented with the catch (54–9; cf. Eurystheus' fear at seeing the dead Nemean lion in Apollodorus 2.5.1 or Cerberus in Euphorion *CA* 51 = 57 Van Groningen 1977). Towards the end of the poem, there is also a more direct hint at the Nemean lion, when Heracles uses as a bed "a lion-skin that pleases him much" (εὐνὰ δ' ἦς τῶι παιδὶ τετυγμένα ἀγχόθι πατρὸς / δέρμα λεόντειον μάλα οἱ κεχαρισμένον αὐτῶι, 135–6).

Through such allusive references, Heracles' future is already present in the text, unknown to the boy himself and his family but recognizable to the reader familiar with the mythological and literary tradition. At the same time, some of his well-known features have been transformed into something new. This metamorphosis becomes tangible in the passage describing the boy's education (103–40). In pointed reversal of the comic Heracles, this Heracles is no unmusical brute and glutton. On the contrary, he receives an education worthy of a Hellenistic prince (Gow 1952b: 2.432), including grammar (105–6) and music (109–10). Moreover, his traditional gluttony is restrained by a diet. For dinner he receives roast meat and a big loaf of bread, "enough to satisfy a hard-digging gardener" (ἀσφαλέως κε φυτοσκάφον ἄνδρα κορέσσαι, 138), which alludes to his notorious appetite, but in compensation he is allowed only a frugal cold lunch (αὐτὰρ ἐπ' ἄματι τυννὸν ἄνευ πυρὸς αἴνυτο δόρπον, 139). In a metapoetic reading, this refinement of Heracles' character points to a similar refinement of the literary tradition in Theocritus' poem.

The domestic atmosphere within which the story is set does not necessarily detract from Heracles' heroism. Much has been written about the "bourgeois" character of Amphitryon's household and the prominent role of Alcmena, who with her resoluteness inevitably drives her slower husband into the background – after all, Tiresias prophesies that *her* name will be sung by many Greek women (75–8; Effe 1978: 53–9; Gutzwiller 1981: 10–18; Zanker 1987: 88–9, 176–9; Merriam 2001: 25–49). Certainly there are touches of irony – including intertextual irony directed, for instance, at epic arming scenes or specific intertexts such as Pindar's *Nemean* 1 – but this is not all that is going on in the poem. There is a more serious level of intertextuality that points to the divine character of the baby Heracles, for instance allusions to the omens foreshadowing Odysseus' victory over the suitors in the *Odyssey* (Fantuzzi and Hunter 2004: 208). Other models include the *Homeric Hymns* as well as their adaptation in Callimachus' *Hymns*, where divine children such as Hermes and Apollo reveal their divinity through their precocious deeds. The hymnic features of the Heracles narrative in Theocritus 24 are underlined by the original hymnic ending, of which some traces survive on a papyrus (141–72), and the poem has convincingly been placed in the context of the Ptolemaic court and interpreted as an encomium of the young Ptolemy II Philadelphus, perhaps performed at the occasion of his birthday and accession as co-ruler in 285/4 BCE (Koenen 1977: 79–86; Stephens 2003: 123–46; Fantuzzi and Hunter 2004: 201–4).

The variety of generic markers and intertexts which the poem employs to highlight the complex literary character of its new Heracles manifests itself especially in the numerous direct speeches interspersed through the narrative (Fantuzzi and Hunter

2004: 201–10, 255–66): Alcmena's lullaby (6–10) reworks Danae's lyric lullaby in Simonides (*PMG* 543), a song sung by another mother to another son of Zeus in the face of danger (and of course Perseus is Heracles' ancestor, as Theocritus reminds his readers by having Tiresias address Alcmena as Περcήιον αἷμα in 73). Tiresias' prophecy in 73–100 calls tragedy to mind, and the sequence of exclamations by master and servant in 48–50, which is not interrupted by the narrator, imitates the manner of comedy or mime. In contrast, Heracles never speaks himself in the poem. This feature corresponds to his characterization as a (laconic?) hero in the making.

Ps.-Theocritus 25: The Anonymous Hero

In this poem, transmitted among Theocritus' *Idylls*, Heracles' identity is initially unclear. The text starts *in medias res*, revealing information about its hero as it proceeds. First an old ploughman explains to an inquiring stranger (ξεῖνε, 3, 22) the extent of Augeas' estate (1–33), and asks him about the purpose of his visit, remarking that he does not look like an ordinary fellow but like a son of immortals (34–41). Then the narrator calls the stranger "the valiant son of Zeus" (Διὸc ἄλκιμοc υἱόc, 42). At this point the reader can surmise that the visitor is Heracles, if he had not drawn this conclusion already at the mention of Augeas (7). In contrast, the old man does not dare to ask the stranger who he is, although he wonders about the lion-skin and the club (62–7). Immediately afterwards the narrator for the first time explicitly identifies him as "Heracles, son of Amphitryon" (Ἀμφιτρυωνιάδηι Ἡρακλέι, 71). Thus there exists a striking contrast between the readers, to whom the narrator gradually reveals the stranger's identity, and the old ploughman who, being neither informed by his interlocutor nor able to read his tell-tale attributes, remains completely in the dark. It is surely significant in this respect that the closing action of the poem's opening section, when Heracles is assaulted by dogs (68–84), evokes Odysseus' arrival at the hut of Eumaeus (*Od.* 14.29–47). The readers are invited to compare and contrast the behavior of the two visitors, neither of whom reveals his identity to his host: Odysseus because he deliberately hides it, Heracles seemingly only because his host is too afraid to ask (but see below).

It is not until the third section of the poem (153–281) that Heracles' identity comes close to being revealed also to the internal audience. Here our stranger, identified anew by the narrator as "mighty Heracles" (βίη Ἡρακληείη, 154) and "the son of Zeus All-high" (Διὸc γόνον ὑψίcτοιο, 159), is addressed by the son of Augeas, Phyleus, who tells him that he is wondering about a *mythos* he has heard long ago. The reader is made to expect a recognition scene but, as it turns out, Phyleus has only heard about "a certain man from Argos" (167) who killed the Nemean lion. Moreover, his information is second-hand, as he stresses repeatedly (162–88, trans. Sargent 1982):

> "ξεῖνε, πάλαι τινὰ πάγχυ cέθεν πέρι μῦθον ἀκούcαc,
> εἰ περὶ cεῦ, cφετέρηιcιν ἐνὶ φρεcὶ βάλλομαι ἄρτι.
> ἤλυθε γὰρ cτείχων τιc ἀπ' Ἄργεοc – ἦν νέοc ἀκμήν –
> ἐνθάδ' Ἀχαιὸc ἀνὴρ Ἑλίκηc ἐξ ἀγχιάλοιο,

ὅς δή τοι μυθεῖτο καὶ ἐν πλεόνεσσιν Ἐπειῶν
οὕνεκεν Ἀργείων τις ἔθεν παρέοντος ὄλεσσε
θηρίον, αἰνολέοντα, κακὸν τέρας ἀγροιώταις,
κοίλην αὖλιν ἔχοντα Διὸς Νεμέοιο παρ' ἄλσος.
"οὐκ οἶδ' ἀτρεκέως ἢ Ἄργεος ἐξ ἱεροῖο
αὐτόθεν ἢ Τίρυνθα νέμων πόλιν ἠὲ Μυκήνην"·
ὥς κεῖνος ἀγόρευε· γένος δέ μιν εἶναι ἔφασκεν,
εἰ ἐτεόν περ ἐγὼ μιμνήσκομαι, ἐκ Περσῆος.
ἔλπομαι οὐχ ἕτερον τόδε τλημέναι Αἰγιαλήων
ἠὲ σέ, δέρμα δὲ θηρὸς ἀριφραδέως ἀγορεύει
χειρῶν καρτερὸν ἔργον, ὅ τοι περὶ πλευρὰ καλύπτει.
εἴπ' ἄγε νῦν μοι πρῶτον, ἵνα γνώω κατὰ θυμόν,
ἥρως, εἴτ' ἐτύμως μαντεύομαι εἴτε καὶ οὐκί,
εἰ σύγ' ἐκεῖνος ὃν ἧμιν ἀκουόντεσσιν ἔειπεν
οὑξ Ἑλίκηθεν Ἀχαιός, ἐγὼ δέ σε φράζομαι ὀρθῶς.
εἰπὲ δ' ὅπως ὀλοὸν τόδε θηρίον αὐτὸς ἔπεφνες,
ὅππως τ' εὔυδρον Νεμέης εἰσήλυθε χῶρον·
οὐ μὲν γάρ κε τοσόνδε κατ' Ἀπίδα κνώδαλον εὕροις
ἱμείρων ἰδέειν, ἐπεὶ οὐ μάλα τηλίκα βόσκει,
ἀλλ' ἄρκτους τε σύας τε λύκων τ' ὀλοφώιον ἔθνος.
τῶι καὶ θαυμάζεσκον ἀκούοντες τότε μῦθον,
οἵ δέ νυ καὶ ψεύδεσθαι ὁδοιπόρον ἀνέρ' ἔφαντο
γλώσσης μαψιδίοιο χαριζόμενον παρεοῦσιν."

"Stranger, long ago I heard a tale about you – if it was about you – and just now it comes back to my mind. For a man arrived from Argos – I was then still a boy – an Achaian from Helike that lies by the sea, and he told a story – and to many other Epeians too – about how in his presence some Argive had killed a wild beast, a terrible lion, a curse to the countryfolk, who had a hollow lair by the grove of Nemean Zeus. "I don't rightly know whether he was from holy Argos itself or lived in the city of Tiryns or in Mycenae" – so the man said. But he told us he was descended – if indeed I still remember correctly – from Perseus. I am convinced that no other Achaian but you could have performed such a deed, and the skin of the beast slung over your ribs clearly proclaims a great labor. Now, hero, come tell me first, that I may know in my heart whether I have divined truly or not, and if you are indeed that one of whom, as we listened, the Achaian from Helike spoke, and I have gauged you aright. Tell me how you killed that dreadful beast single-handed, and how it got to the well-watered countryside of Nemea. For in all Apia you would not find such a monster, not if you longed to, for it does not support a beast of that kind, but only bears and boars and the fierce tribe of wolves. Those who heard the tale at the time were astonished, and some even claimed that the wayfaring stranger was lying, endeavoring with idle chatter to entertain those around him."

Within Phyleus' speech, there are several levels of narration. First, he mentions his own doubts about the identification of his interlocutor with the Argive lion-slayer he has heard about from a man from Argos (162–5). He goes on to summarize the latter's tale in indirect speech (166–9, 172–3) and even quotes two lines in direct speech (170–1). Somewhat paradoxically, he cites the exact words of this alleged eyewitness (167; but according to Heracles himself there was no one around: 218–20), not in order to prove their truthfulness, but on the contrary to cast doubt on the reliability of the information, for the witness himself was not sure about the provenance of the anonymous hero (in fact a reflection of the mythological variants concerning Heracles' hometown). Moreover, Phyleus even doubts his own memory (173), which is underlined by his situation of the whole incident, surprisingly, in a distant past (πάλαι πάγχυ, 162) when he was still a young man (164; Gow 1952b: 2.459–60). Finally, he reveals that the whole *mythos* told by the stranger was suspected by the audience to be a lie (186–8). In contrast, the lion-skin "clearly proclaims" (ἀριφραδέως ἀγορεύει, 175) the heroic deed of its bearer.

The stress on the process of information-gathering and truth-finding and on the questionability of stories from hearsay prepares for Heracles' own account of his deed (193–281), for he should of course be the most reliable witness himself. But although he complies willingly with Phyleus' request, remarkably not even here does he reveal his name, thus leaving open the questions that could not be answered by the man from Argos. Instead, he acknowledges the limits of his own knowledge (like the other Argives he cannot tell for sure where the lion came from, 197–200), while at the same time establishing his credentials as a narrator of his own story, which he will tell in detail (195–6).

Through the emphasis on the topics of identity, falsehood, and truth, the attention of the external as well as the internal audience is directed to the chances and dangers of transmission. This ultimately constitutes a reflection on the origins of literary tradition and the workings of fiction. Therefore the question emerges whether or not Heracles is really such a reliable narrator as he presents himself and Phyleus expects him to be. As has been noted, Heracles' long account of the killing of the lion constitutes a major narrative ellipsis (in fact the poem's title *Heracles the Lion-Slayer* was only added by the editor Callierges in 1516), for the apparent main theme of the poem – Heracles' cleaning of Augeas' stables – is never narrated nor even mentioned explicitly (Gutzwiller 1981: 30–8; Zanker 1996; Hunter 1998). Heracles himself explains the aim of his visit in very vague terms to the old man (43–50), and in his conversations with Augeas and Phyleus he does not bring up the topic either. In his account of his struggle with the Nemean lion, he mentions in passing that this was the first labor imposed upon him by Eurystheus (204–5), but he does not specify the others which were to follow.

How does this striking omission relate to the anonymity of the poem's hero? The poem has attractively been interpreted by Richard Hunter as reconstructing a world "before *kleos*," where neither Heracles himself nor the other characters are conscious of his future fame in the literary tradition (Hunter 1998; Fantuzzi and Hunter 2004: 210–15). Indeed, within the poem Heracles is not yet famous as Heracles, but figures merely as the anonymous killer of the Nemean lion; for although his story has spread (162), his name is known only to the external narrator, not to the characters. But does Heracles himself really "not yet know, or at least understand, his own identity" (Hunter 1998: 122–3), or does he dissimulate his identity on purpose, using his incognito as a camouflage? After all, his actual task of cleaning Augeas' stables does not constitute a truly heroic enterprise. In the end, the old man may not be far off the mark when he fears to offend the stranger by asking him an inopportune question about his identity (64–7).

Heracles' lion-skin, which in this text does not function as an unmistakable token of his identity, nevertheless plays a crucial part in the second section of the poem

(85–152). While visiting the herds together with Augeas and his son Phyleus, Heracles is attacked by the bull Phaethon as soon as the beast catches sight of his lion-skin (142–4). Heracles then subdues him by pure strength, anticipating his fight against the Cretan bull, which in the traditional order of the labors follows after the present undertaking. The two major themes of the poem that unfold around the untold tale of the cleaning of the stables, the narrator's account of Heracles' struggle with the bull Phaethon and Heracles' own "epic" account of his fight against the Nemean lion, thus reflect his famous heroic deeds in an oblique way, compensating for the unheroic setting. In this way, they are not digressions but essential components of the poem that help to define the character of Heracles as he is seen by others and as he wants to see himself.

Ps.-Moschus, *Megara*: The Absent Hero

In the last poem to be considered here, the *Megara* (Ps.-Moschus 4), Heracles does not even appear in person. Nevertheless, he is the central figure on whom the story hinges. In a way similar to Ps.-Theocritus 25, the plot is therefore based on a kind of ellipsis. The text consists of an exchange of speeches between two women with no authorial narrative apart from a short transition (56–61). First, Heracles' wife Megara speaks (1–55), then his mother Alcmena (62–125). Again the reader has to reconstruct the situation from their words without guidance from the narrator, as Megara is not named at all, Alcmena not until the middle of the poem (60), and Heracles, the subject of their conversation, only toward the end (95). Megara acts on behalf of the reader by asking Alcmena a series of questions that gradually lead to the main topic of the poem, Heracles' madness, his murder of his own children, and his subsequent labors in the service of Eurystheus (1–16). Megara then gives an eyewitness account of the murder of her children and laments her lonely fate far from her family (17–55). She is comforted by Alcmena, who reassures her that she loves her daughter-in-law as her own daughter, but fears for her son because of an ominous dream (62–125). Despite Heracles' terrible deed, both women long for his return (41–5, 88–90). They do not blame him but the gods (8–16, 125), and they lament his unworthy servitude (a topic also reflected in Alcmena's dream, 94–8) "as of a lion under a fawn" (λέων ὡϲεί θ' ὑπὸ νεβροῦ, 4–5), an indirect reference to his heroic status as a lion-slayer comparable to the simile in Theocritus 13. Heracles is thus characterized indirectly through the perception and words of the two women most affected by his fate. In this poem Alcmena's worst fears, as dispelled by Tiresias in Theocritus 24 (64–85), have come true.

The mainly dramatic form of the poem sets it at the margins of narrative poetry and points to its intertextual affiliation with the genre of tragedy, an aspect not yet fully taken into account in previous interpretations (Breitenstein 1966; Vaughn 1976). One might identify specific verbal echoes and point out the differences from Euripides' *Heracles* with regard to the underlying mythological facts, but I think that it is more profitable to look more generally for narrative patterns derived from tragedy (as is briefly suggested by Fantuzzi and Hunter 2004: 195). The intimate dialogue between two women in distress may be seen as constituting an extract from a tragedy, comparable perhaps to Cassandra's dramatic monologue in Lycophron's *Alexandra*. However, in contrast to a tragic exchange of *rhēseis*, it does not lead to any progress on the level of action. Nor does the section exactly correspond to the prologue of a tragedy such as the exchange between Deianeira (Heracles' *other* wife) and the nurse in Sophocles' *Trachiniae* or the dialogue between Amphitryon and Megara in Euripides' *Heracles*, for it does not function as an exposition of a play to follow, and the reader is left to puzzle things out to a far greater extent than in those dialogic prologues. As in the *Trachiniae* (1–982) and in the *Heracles* (1–522), the dramatic "action" mainly consists in waiting for Heracles, but in contrast to these tragedies he never actually appears on stage. The recollections and premonitions of the two women result in a narrative standstill encompassing the whole of Heracles' life from his birth (83–7) to his death, which is anticipated in Alcmena's dream of a fire threatening her son (91–125). This dream is indeed characteristic of a tragic prologue – compare Hecuba's dream announcing the death of her last two children in Euripides' *Hecuba* – but its fulfillment will take place outside the timeframe of the poem.

The poem thus reworks elements from tragedy by placing them in a new setting. Most of all, the extended lamentation of the two women corresponds to a tragic *thrēnos*. This is reflected in a self-conscious way in Alcmena's speech (63–7, text in 67 following the manuscript tradition; cf. Marcovich 1980):

πῶϲ ἄμμ' ἐθέλειϲ ὀροθυνέμεν ἄμφω
κήδε' ἄλαϲτα λέγουϲα τά τ' οὐ νῦν πρῶτα κέκλαυται;
ἦ οὐχ ἅλιϲ, οἷϲ ἐχόμεϲθα τὸ δεύτατον, αἰὲν ἐπ' ἦμαρ
γινομένοιϲ; μάλα μέν γε φιλοθρηνήϲ κέ τιϲ εἴη
ὅϲτιϲ ἀριθμήϲειεν ἐφ' ἡμετέροιϲ ἀχέεϲϲι.

Why do you want to upset us both with talk of those unforgettable sorrows, which have not been bewailed now for the first time? Are not those sorrows enough which have last befallen us, as they keep coming upon us day by day? Very fond of wailing indeed would be he who wanted to add up all our griefs!"

By having Alcmena stress the repetitious nature of her laments, the poet comments upon the place of his poem in the literary tradition. He tells of sufferings that have indeed been lamented before (64), especially in tragedy. Thus he himself assumes the role of the hypothetical person who is "fond of wailing" (φιλοθρηνήϲ, 66).

* * *

The four texts studied above have all been categorized as epyllia. While the sample may be too small to allow a general conclusion about all related poems, it seems clear that a definition of this category in narratological terms that leaves room for a considerable variety within relatively wide generic parameters suits the evidence best. We should therefore perhaps supplement the formal definition provided at the start of this chapter with a more detailed description of some narrative characteristics. Poems conventionally designated as epyllia cover a comparatively small section from a mythological continuum through extensive narration, either focusing on select episodes or on specific points of view, such as those of Heracles' wife and mother. The narrative techniques may range from predominantly authorial narrative to an almost exclusively dramatic mode containing large portions of direct speech. Interestingly, some of the texts are built around a narrative ellipsis, which does not just follow from their small format but reflects a deliberate poetic choice. At the same time, the wider context of the myth is incorporated by various narrative techniques, such as prolepses or analepses, or by allusively appealing to the readers' knowledge of earlier texts. In this way, the poets work the literary history of the Heracles myth into the fabric of their texts, not only by evoking previous treatments but also by self-conscious reflection on the metamorphoses of the hero through different genres and texts and ultimately on the character of literary tradition itself.

FURTHER READING

Fragmentarily preserved Hellenistic hexameter poems are collected in Powell 1925 (*CA*) and Lloyd-Jones and Parsons 1983 (*SH*), with additions in Lloyd-Jones 2005 (*SSH*). Gow 1952a and Beckby 1975 provide the Greek text (the latter with German translation) of all poems ascribed to Theocritus, Moschus, and Bion. For individual authors the following editions and commentaries may be consulted: Antimachus: Matthews 1996; Philitas: Spanoudakis 2002; Callimachus, *Hecale*: Hollis 2009; Theocritus: Gow 1952b, Hunter 1999: 261–89 (*Id.* 13); Moschus, *Europa*: Bühler 1960, Campbell 1991; Ps.-Moschus, *Megara*: Vaughn 1976; Ps.-Bion, *Epithalamius of Achilles and Deidamia*: Reed 1997; Nicander: Gow and Scholfield 1953; Alexander Aetolus: Magnelli 1999; Euphorion: Van Groningen 1977, Magnelli 2002; Parthenius: Lightfoot 1999. Recent essays on some of the poets discussed in this chapter can be found in Harder, Regtuit, and Wakker 2006.

On the "genre" of the epyllion see Crump 1931, Gutzwiller 1981, and Merriam 2001; on the Latin epyllion, Perutelli 1979 and Bartels 2004 (a narratological analysis). Critical discussions of the term and its application may also be found in Allen 1940, Hollis 2009: 23–6, Cameron 1995a: 447–52, and Fantuzzi and Hunter 2004: 191–6. Important recent treatments of Hellenistic hexameter poetry include Cameron 1995a (challenging the *communis opinio* since Ziegler 1966) and Fantuzzi and Hunter 2004: 191–282.

On Heracles in the Greek literary tradition (and beyond) see Galinsky 1972, Effe 1980, and Ambühl 2005: 58–97 (on Callimachus' *Victory of Berenice*); on his importance in Hellenistic royal ideology, see Huttner 1997.

CHAPTER TWELVE

Hymns and Encomia

Anthony W. Bulloch

At some point between the sixth and the fourteenth centuries CE, someone whose identity is not known to us, and who lived we know not where in the Greek-speaking world, was motivated to put together a collection of hymns. Into one book he assembled the hymns ascribed to Homer and Orpheus, and those of Callimachus and Proclus. What his purpose was and who may have been the putative readership, we do not know. What is clear, though, is that we owe the survival of the text of Callimachus' hymns into the modern world to this one compiler. Without his efforts – and the interest and efforts in later centuries of other readers and appreciators of pagan Greek culture, who made, or commissioned, copies of that original collection – our knowledge of Callimachus' hymns would be limited to a small number of quotations and a few scraps of papyrus, and we would know even less about them than we know about three other major works of this author, the *Aetia*, the *Hecale*, or the *Iambi*. This would have been especially regrettable because the hymns are witnesses to, and expressions of, many facets of the world of Alexandria in the first half of the third century BCE – the realms not just of poetry, art and the artist, but also of society, the intelligentsia, fashion, politics and power, and the intersection of all of these.

Callimachus' Hymns

What did Callimachus write his hymns for? Who were his audience? And indeed, what will the term "hymn" (*hymnos*) have meant to them and to the poet? That Callimachus and his contemporaries will have called these poems "hymns" seems certain. First, we possess extensive remains of a comprehensive set of narrative summaries, or synopses, to many of Callimachus' major poetic works, dating from the first century BCE or CE and referred to as the *Diegeseis*. The *Diegeseis* seem to have been based on a "collected edition" of Callimachus' poetry, and although they date from a time two or three hundred years after the poet's death, there are several indications that the text and collection on which this work was based was made by Callimachus himself, probably late in his career after Ptolemy III Euergetes had ascended to the throne in Alexandria. Included in the *Diegeseis* are the hymns, classified as a set of poems distinct from other works such as the *Aetia*, the *Iambi*, and the *Hecale*. Second, earlier writers closer to the age of Callimachus refer to poems written in celebration of gods as "hymns," and, although later Greek theorists delighted in hair-splitting and defined multiple sub-categories within the overall genre of *hymnos* (e.g., Menander Rhetor, in his *Division of Epideictic Speeches*, distinguishes between eight types of hymn: invocatory, valedictory, on gods' nature, "mythic," genealogical, fictional, precatory, and deprecatory: Furley 1993; Furley and Bremer 2001: 1.295), the term seems to have been used for most poems whose objective was celebration of a divinity. So the Athenian in Plato's *Laws* 700b, describing the good old days in contrast to the decadent status quo of his own modern society, remarks that music used to be divided into distinct basic categories, such as hymns for prayers to the gods, contrasted with dirges (*thrēnoi*), paeans and dithyrambs. Or, again, the nurse in Euripides' *Medea*, lamenting that no music has been invented that can cure mankind's sorrows, observes "(men of old) invented the hymn for festivals, banquets and feasts to bring pleasurable sound to our lives" (192–4). *Hymnoi*, then, are poetic celebrations of divinities, written to be performed, or presented in some manner, presumably, at some sort of public occasion. And that is indeed how the earliest poets who wrote hymns described their activity. Hesiod recounts how he once traveled to Euboea to compete in the festival for Amphidamas there and won a prize, a tripod, with his *hymnos* (*WD* 654–7). As Martin West points out (1978: 321), the *hymnos* could as well have been the *Theogony*, or something like it. Similarly, the singer of the *Homeric Hymn to Apollo* describes his work as a hymn in that poem's famous "autobiographical" passage (146–78), and he describes the activity of the celebrants of Apollo as "hymn-singing" (*hymnein*). There is a famous story, preserved in the *Contest of Homer and Hesiod* (315–21), that Homer went to the sacred island of Delos and there delivered his *Hymn to Apollo* standing at the sacred altar made of horn, for which the Ionians rewarded him with citizenship and the people of Delos had the poem inscribed on tablets which they dedicated in the temple of Artemis.

Conventional wisdom amongst critics and readers of the Hellenistic poets is that the Hellenistic era was the age of books – that this was the time when true literacy came into its own, and that the poet was now an artist whose creations were no longer composed out of social demand and for performance at specific community occasions, as they had been in the Archaic and Classical periods. Book culture, not song culture; private, not public; reading, not listening. There is clearly an amount of truth in this, but we should be careful not to go too far. When we piece together the evidence we have for the typical role and context of hymns and similar works in the pre-Hellenistic period, the picture is quite rich: the poet was the artist who composed the words and music, and often the choreography, for choruses of young men and/or women, typically 30 to 50 in number, to perform, under the direction of a chorus-master and accompanied by the lyre or flute, on significant festival and ritual occasions, in procession, or at or around the altar, or perhaps at the door of the temple.

Although the Hellenistic hymnal poems which have survived would seem to be less obviously a product of this kind of context (especially the "mimetic," or mime-like, hymns of Callimachus), we should not assume that they were mere words on a page, divorced from the reality of cultic ritual, and we should certainly not assume that they were, because of their "bookishness" and self-consciousness, any less religious in either sentiment or perception. Recent scholarship has begun a healthy readjustment of the "art for art's sake" view of Hellenistic poetry and shown that when we take proper account of their production and reception context, the works of Callimachus, Theocritus, and others prove to be as deeply rooted in the religious and other public concerns of their communities as any works by, say, Pindar and Bacchylides before them (Cameron 1995a; see further Stephens, Strootman, Harder in this volume). It would even be difficult, for example, to prove that Callimachus' first hymn, the *Hymn to Zeus*, was *not* sung by a large chorus of 50 young men dressed in white at the ritual banquet on the eve of the great Basileia festival in Alexandria, in front of a very large crowd which included Ptolemy Soter and/or Philadelphus himself. The essential thing for modern readers to realize is that Callimachus' hymns are indeed authentic *hymnal* texts, regardless of their complexity and their refusal to fit into a tidy mold (Fantuzzi and Hunter 2004: 364).

Callimachus' set of hymns comprises six poems, all written in dactylic meter (five in continuous hexameters, one in elegiac couplets). The gods they celebrate are, in order, Zeus, Apollo, Artemis, again Apollo (now focusing on Delos, his birthplace), Athena, and Demeter. Since the order in which they have come down to us most probably goes back to Callimachus' own publication of his collected works (Depew 2004: 117), it is reasonable to consider if there is any significance to their arrangement. First, the whole set begins with a spirited hymn to Zeus. Poems praising the Father of Men and Gods were entirely normal, and although it is notable that the *Homeric Hymns*, which Callimachus certainly knew and draws on, contain no full-scale work addressed to this god, his choice of a hymn to Zeus to open his collection has other precedents. For example, as Pindar observes at the beginning of one of his epinician poems associated with Nemea, one of Zeus' main Panhellenic sites, "the Homeric bards generally begin their rhapsodies with a prelude to Zeus" (*N.* 2.1–3), and so indeed does Hesiod, one of Callimachus' main sources of inspirations in the first hymn (*WD* 1–10). The opening lines of Callimachus' poem – "who better to sing of at his libations than Zeus himself, forever great, forever lord" (Ζηνὸς ἔοι τί κεν ἄλλο παρὰ σπονδῇσιν ἀείδειν/λώϊον ἢ θεὸν αὐτόν, ἀεὶ μέγαν, αἰὲν ἄνακτα, 1–2) – constitute both an expression of standard social ritual and a programmatic statement. They mark the beginning of an evening of celebration, since a toast to Zeus was traditional when a symposium turned from the meal to its aftermath of wine and song. But while these first lines provide a nice preamble into the hymn itself, at the same time they also present a whole collection with the highest and most kingly of all gods at its head. A commanding opening. And an opening that closely resembles that which the Alexandrian editors (possibly Callimachus himself) had given to the collected works of Pindar, when they placed *Olympian* 1 at the head of his epinicians.

There are clearly many connections between the hymns – aesthetic, programmatic, thematic, political, and structural. How one evaluates these connections, and the set of six as a collection, eventually depends on what one sees as significant. For example, at the simplest organisational level, the gods of the first two hymns are male while the gods of the last two are female, with the twins Artemis and (Delian) Apollo in the middle. Another way of framing what many readers sense – that there does seem to be a logic to the poems' arrangement – without insisting that they must have profound programmatic unity as conceived from the start for their position in a "poetry book," is to view them as a group of five hymns introduced by a sort of rhapsodic preface, the *Hymn to Zeus*. Of these five, the first and last, to Apollo (*h.* 2) and Demeter (*h.* 6), focus on young males, Apollo and Erysichthon, the former redolent with vitality and effectiveness, the latter equally vigorous but directing his energy toward an enterprise which is impious and perverse; the *Hymn to Apollo* celebrates youthfulness as an ideal, the *Hymn to Demeter* cautions against its misapplication. Bracketed inside this pair is another pair, to Artemis (*h.* 3) and Athena (*h.* 5), the two virgin Olympian deities, each accompanied by their band of nymphs. And at the center is the longest of the hymns, the *Hymn to Delos* (*h.* 4), birthplace of Apollo; and this is also the hymn which contains the most explicit reference to contemporary politics and the most blatant acknowledgement of Ptolemy as a ruler with essentially a divine mission (*h.* 4.160–95, a topic prepared for by the *Hymn to Zeus*): from Leto's womb, Apollo himself authoritatively ensures that his mother cedes place to the impending birth of "another god" (θεὸϲ ἄλλοϲ, 165), King Ptolemy Philadelphus, by not giving birth to her twins on Cos.

Another approach to the hymns should be addressed at this point. From time to time modern critics, observing that Callimachus and other poets of the third century BCE could be outspokenly contentious about what constituted "real" art, and truly "creative" poetry, are tempted to extend occasional vituperative snide remarks into a full-time obsession, and think that almost every poem must have been "programmatic" and conceived with an artistically political purpose in view. There is hardly a single Hellenistic poem which has not, at some time or other in the last hundred years, been read as an allegory, as a poem whose "real" topic is poetry itself. Indeed Callimachus is at times explicitly programmatic – for example, he replaces the traditional concluding prayer at the close of his *Hymn to Apollo* with an explicit description of the god's hostility to turgid writing as he kicks out Phthonos (Envy), just as earlier the hymn mentioned Pytho, the dragon that Apollo expelled when he took over Delphi. Nonetheless, those who see allegory and metapoetic subtexts everywhere in the hymns are mostly unconvincing. It is usually critics who want art to be self-regarding: artists, however self-centered they may sometimes be as individuals, mostly have more important things to obsess about than solipsistic self-predication.

Some of the most innovative work that has been done recently on third-century Alexandrian poetry has come from scholars who are well acquainted with Egyptian customs and beliefs. They have demonstrated that once we alert ourselves to some of the basic features of life in the land of the Nile, whether geography, social organization, economy, politics, culture, or religion, much that hitherto has appeared puzzling or dissonant in authors such as Callimachus, Theocritus or Apollonius Rhodius becomes explicable (Selden 1998; Stephens 2002, 2003, and in this volume). Our understanding of Callimachus' hymns has progressed considerably, and not just in the matter of some of the more abstruse details. If we regard the hymns within their Greco-Egyptian context – a process which has been very aptly described as "seeing double" (Stephens 2003) – our understanding of them shifts fundamentally: we can now see them as not merely reworkings of a rich Greek legacy but highly original and experimental creations of a complex bicultural experience.

Comparison of Callimachus' *Hymn to Zeus* with another Hellenistic hymnal text is illuminating. Callimachus' contemporary Aratus began his astronomical poem, the *Phaenomena*, with a hymn to Zeus as a sort of immanent patriarch, source of orderliness in the natural world (1–18; Volk and White in this volume). To a modern reader Aratus' poeticizing of astronomy and his laborious achievement of setting science to verse seems esoteric, and in comparison Callimachus' hymn can seem more conventional and regular, even a bit stiff. But in actuality it is Aratus' poem that is the more uniform of the two, and his introductory hymn to Zeus helps us identify what is so distinctive about Callimachus' poem. Where Aratus describes Zeus as a cosmic force in terms that are familiar and historically rather ordinary (however "Stoic" they may also be), for Callimachus what comes immediately to the fore is the possibility of dramatically wayward origins of the god, and his associations with the awesome, venerable and strange regions of Arcadia and Crete, even if the hymn turns ultimately to discoursing on the nature of political power both on Olympus and in the world of Ptolemaic Egypt. While the association of Zeus with Arcadia was of long and respectable standing, it was not poetically mainstream, and Callimachus' extended untraditional exploration of Zeus must have caught the attention of his Alexandrian audience, and especially of his Macedonian-Greek ruler with aspirations to Pharaonic divine authority. It would have been so easy for Callimachus to call up images of a more orthodox supreme deity, in the manner of Aratus, and to allow his patron to identify unthinkingly with the Olympian autocrat who defeated Titans and Giants (the image that Eumenes II would draw on for his political statement a hundred or so years later when he built the great "Altar of Zeus" in Pergamum). Instead, Ptolemy, and his subjects at the Alexandrian court who will have been Callimachus' audience, are openly asked to reflect on the mortal ruler and his political power as being validated by Zeus only after ruminating on the difficulties of childbirth, the aridity of the Arcadian landscape, the wonders of being nurtured by a goat, and the trickiness of obtaining, and holding onto, supreme power. And it deepens our understanding of the *Hymn to Zeus* once we realize that many of these motifs were resonant with long-standing Egyptian ways of thinking about royal power and its origins (Stephens 2003: 77–114).

To some extent the poem's attitude and even politico-religious philosophy can be viewed as Hesiodic – Callimachus was always interested in the quirky poet from Ascra, and there is plenty of Hesiod in the *Hymn to Zeus*. But his engagement with Hesiod is by no means straightforward, and as so often, it is the fifth-century lyric poet Pindar, another maverick who was something of a soulmate for Callimachus, who helps us to see how various themes configure. In *Pythian* 1, written to celebrate a victory at Delphi, the sanctuary of Apollo, by Hiero I, king of Syracuse, Pindar shapes his epinician into a declaration of the power of Apollo-inspired song combined with a hymn celebrating Zeus as a dynast, wielding both military might and civic strength; by extension the glory and power of the mortal Hiero are also magnified. In similar fashion Callimachus' poem narrating the birth of Zeus, and events associated with it, emerges as a statement about power and the nature of the virtuous ruler, with an emphasis on dispensation of justice (*h.* 1.81–3, cf. *P.* 1.86) and the divine origin of the authority of kings (*h.* 1.77–8 "it is by Zeus that kings are kings," ἐκ δὲ Διὸϲ βαϲιλῆεϲ; *P.* 1.41–2 "it is by the gods that all human virtues are contrived," ἐκ θεῶν γὰρ μαχαναὶ πᾶϲαι βροτέαιϲ ἀρεταῖϲ). And like Pindar Callimachus insists on veracity as a cardinal principle (*h.* 1.65, *P.* 1.86). Something which would merit more investigation is the manner in which this formal hymn in praise of the divine becomes an epinician of the ruler through deployment of contemporary and historical political theory. The comments in the hymn about rulership, power, policy and effective implementation (*h.* 1.85–90) are similar to the description of the character of fifth-century Athenians ascribed by Thucydides (1.70) to the Corinthians, and similar ideas are implicit even as early as Homer, for example in the "Diomedeia" (*Il.* 5) or Nestor's reflections on kingship (*Il.* 9.96–102), and they were certainly a feature of Hellenistic treatises on the topic.

It is becoming increasingly apparent, in fact, that Callimachus' hymns, like much of his other poetry, were resonant with their contemporary political context, even if many of the more subtle details are now lost to us. The *Hymn to Apollo* is explicit about linking Apollo and Ptolemy (*h.* 2.26–7), and the *Hymn to Delos* both has Apollo himself foretelling the rise to power of Ptolemy and his achievements against the Celts who invaded Greece (*h.* 4.165–90), and is full of political ideology and symbolism. Indeed, specific local events may well have prompted Callimachus to write some of the hymns. It has been suggested quite convincingly that the *Hymn to Zeus* was composed on the occasion of the Basileia festival in the reign of Ptolemy Philadelphus (Clauss 1986; Stephens 2003: 77–9; Cuypers 2004b), that the *Hymn to Apollo* was occasioned by the festival which is afforded a major section in the hymn (2.65–96), the Carneia, in Callimachus' home town, Cyrene, and that even the *Hymn to Demeter* has a political dimension, since a comment in the scholia suggests that the poem is to be linked to the introduction in Alexandria of the Athenian Thesmophoria festival (Hopkinson 1984a: 32–43). Some have even suggested that as poems portraying male and female power, all of the hymns have symbolic political significance and concern imperial identity, with Zeus and Apollo as "divine prototypes" of the kings and Artemis, Athena, and Demeter of the queens of Egypt (although one-on-one identification of regal and divine seems mostly too broad and vague to be helpful in interpreting these texts).

The hymns of Callimachus have traditionally been divided into two groups by modern critics: the mimetic (in the sense of mime-like) and the non-mimetic. Three of the hymns (to Zeus, Artemis, and Delian Apollo) are addressed directly to the divinities themselves and are in the familiar, one could say traditional, form of the *Homeric Hymns*: they focus on topics like the god's origin and familiar accomplishments, and would be in place on any kind of occasion where the god was being celebrated. Three (to Apollo, Athena, and Demeter) are addressed to celebrants, in the voice of a festival official or group leader of some kind who is calling out instructions as they all wait for the god to arrive at their celebration and for the next stage of the ritual to begin. Thus the *Hymn to Athena* begins with a call from, probably, a priestess to other women to assemble in readiness for the ceremony that is about to begin. The opening lines of the poem provide enough information for the reader (or listener, in the case of an oral presentation) to envision the scene right from the start (1–4):

ὅσσαι λωτροχόοι τᾶς Παλλάδος ἔξιτε πᾶσαι,
ἔξιτε· τᾶν ἵππων ἄρτι φρυασσομενᾶν
τᾶν ἱερᾶν ἐσάκουσα, καὶ ἁ θεὸς εὔτυκος ἕρπεν·
σοῦσθέ νυν, ὦ ξανθαὶ σοῦσθε Πελασγιάδες.

All you bath-pourers of Pallas (Athena), come on out everyone!
Come out! The sacred horses were just whinnying –
I heard them. The goddess is ready to go.
Hurry, now! Hurry, fair daughters of Pelasgus.

We are in Argos, waiting for Athena (that is, her statue) to emerge on a horse-drawn wagon. The atmosphere is one of eager anticipation, and the appearance of Athena, coming out from the sanctuary on the way down to the river, where she will be ritually bathed, is experienced as being almost like an epiphany of the goddess herself. Callimachus skillfully sets a scene and draws us, his audience, in to participate, effortlessly and unselfconsciously since we identify so naturally with the celebrants being addressed. After a while the hymn, that is the priestess whose voice we are listening to, turns from addressing the celebrants admonitorily to narrating a story about a figure and an event set in the mythic past: it is the story of Tiresias, who once encountered the goddess in person and found himself transformed from an ordinary young male into an extraordinary blind prophet. Like so many Greek *mythoi* this is a paradeigmatic narrative reflecting on the nature of god and man, power and mortal vulnerability, sexuality and knowledge, innocence and transformation.

The other mimetic hymns are equally enticing. The *Hymn to Demeter*, which needs very little background knowledge to be appreciated by a modern audience, consists primarily in a striking cautionary tale. As in the *Hymn to Athena*, the directly mimetic part of the poem, the second-person address of the priestess instructing and encouraging her fellow celebrants, forms a frame, within which Callimachus' audience, identifying with the priestess' audience, is told the satisfying tale of a rebellious youth, Erysichthon, who tried crassly to ignore the orderly world of civilized values that Demeter stands for, and was duly punished by being condemned to a world in which everything is inside out. His father had introduced worship of the goddess of grain to his community; the son deals with his need for food by perversely violating Demeter, chopping down the trees in her grove as timber to build a grand banqueting hall. The result is not just failure, or suspension of Demeter's beneficence: her bounty becomes an actual weapon, as Erysichthon is driven into a state of perpetual hunger which can never be satisfied, until he ends up begging at the crossroads, having eaten everything his family has. It is typical of Callimachus' sharp, allusive style, for which "indirection" is a central mode, that (again, like Pindar before him), when he reaches the narrative climax, he elides out the real ending of Erysichthon. Everyone in his audience will have known well what Callimachus only hints at, in characteristic mock-coyness: that the heretic continued eating to the end, reduced, finally and inevitably, to autophagy.

The tone and manner of these texts are typically Hellenistic and, especially, typically Callimachean: familiar but indirect, formal yet shifting and unpredictable, grand but quick. But both types of hymn, the non-mimetic and the mimetic, are grounded in a long tradition of celebratory writing. The former are easy to place, in direct line from the *Homeric Hymns*, and even though we have few other examples of dactylic hymns written in the period between the Archaic (when we surmise the earliest *Homeric Hymns* must have been composed) and the Hellenistic era, we know that hymns in dactylic meter were normal throughout. The mimetic hymns owe a debt to a type of choral poetry that is attested as early as the seventh century BCE, when the Spartan poet Alcman wrote partheneia or "maiden songs," poems which, just like Callimachus' mimetic hymns, adopt the voice of a chorus member addressing the other chorus members. But whereas Alcman's poems are melic, i.e., composed in lyric verse form, as was common for poems written for performance by a chorus in honor of a god (Fantuzzi in this volume), Callimachus' mimetic hymns are written in dactylic meter, continuous hexameters (*Hymn to Apollo* and *Hymn to Demeter*) or elegiacs (*Hymn to Athena*). One might describe this as a good example of "mixing the genres," and see the use of a non-melic verse form which is more formally "narrative" as another indication that these hymns are purely literary in nature and not cultic, but Callimachus was not just a chef adjusting the flavors of different cuisines in a fashionable salon. The verse form which Callimachus chose for his mimetic hymns, the dactylic, was, after all, the form appropriate for celebratory narratives, declaratory works proclaiming the god's main attributes and virtues, such as the *Homeric Hymns*. In other words, it is misleading to regard these hymns as Hellenistic versions of earlier melic works such as Alcman's partheneia or Pindar's paeans. Rather, they are hymns with an added vividness achieved by casting them in the voice of a celebrant explicitly addressing other celebrants (a mode which is to some extent prefigured in the *Homeric Hymn to Apollo*: Nünlist 2004: 40–2; Harder 2004: 63–7).

At one time modern scholars seriously considered the possibility that Callimachus' mimetic hymns were written for specific festivals, indeed were the result of commissions from patrons who hired the poet to compose for their religious rituals. The *Hymn to Athena*, for example, which concerns the cult of the goddess in the Peloponnesian city of Argos, was thought to have been written by request from the city itself. This approach is not really tenable: Callimachus' mimetic hymns are so specific about such momentary details as the neighing of the horses that are pulling the festival chariot in the *Hymn to Athena*, that they cannot possibly have been written for an actual ceremony, when the author could only hope that the real-life horses would behave themselves and do what his text described on cue. What such "realistic" details show is that Callimachus' mimetic hymns, regardless of the function they may have fulfilled at real-life occasions, in Egypt or elsewhere, were at one level fictive, written to re-create the very occasion they describe. What marks them as distinctively Hellenistic is not so much their "allusiveness," or their supposedly cerebral qualities, but the close attention that they pay to artful illusion, the vivid creation of a sense of immediacy and reality. This concern with illusion is a very Hellenistic trait which goes well beyond the hymns of Callimachus. In fact it is of the essence of much third-century BCE Alexandrian poetry that it explores reality through the creation of illusions, imaginary situations played out in the moment, snapshots in time.

Theocritus

Although Theocritus is thought of today almost entirely as a writer, indeed as the creator, of pastoral poetry, this is an accidental identity which has been created for him by later history. Already by the time of the Roman poet Vergil it was the bucolic poems of Theocritus that were considered typically Theocritean, and it is those poems that lead off the first part of the "collected works" of Theocritus that have come down to us in the medieval manuscripts. But unlike the poems of Callimachus, Theocritus' poems were not assembled into any kind of definitive collection until several hundred years after the poet's own lifetime. The pastoral mimes stand where they do only because later critics and editors put them there, and it seems unlikely that Theocritus thought of himself as primarily a writer of bucolic. The pastoral mimes in fact comprise the lesser part of his extant corpus, which includes also urban mime, love poetry, short works cast in the language and verse-form of traditional Homeric epic on mythic themes ("epyllia": Ambühl in this volume), and, most important for the purposes of this chapter, a hymn and two encomia (although "political praise poems" might be a better term). The common thread that runs through the corpus is that, regardless of genre, Theocritus' poems are generally situational studies, set in an illusory moment. Sometimes they are mimetic, scripts that play out short scenes, and sometimes they are more detached third-person narratives; but it is almost always the occasion, or the illusion of an occasion, that his poems present and explore.

About Theocritus' life – who he was, where he lived, when and in what circumstances he wrote those poems that have survived – we know almost nothing. We know much less, even, than most modern scholars would have us believe. What is apparent, though, is that his immediate social circumstances, for example the world of the royal court at Alexandria, where he appears to have enjoyed patronage, form part of the backdrop to his poetry, to be alluded to and woven into the fictional world of his poetic characters. Thus the rustic Italian goatherd in *Idyll* 4 is thoroughly familiar with the songs of a popular Alexandrian singer who was reputed to be a favorite, and maybe mistress, of Ptolemy; and the urban mimes, *Idylls* 14 and 15, almost turn into encomia of the Egyptian royal couple and their role as patrons. It is no surprise, therefore, that Theocritus' "epic"-style poems include two that are concerned with patronage and patrons (whether actual or potential), one being quasi-encomiastic and the other encomiastic in form: *Idyll* 16, referring to Hiero II of Syracuse, and *Idyll* 17, addressed directly to Ptolemy Philadelphus.

Idyll 16 (also discussed by Strootman in this volume) is often viewed as an appeal by Theocritus to the tyrant of Syracuse for patronage, an appeal that was made in the early years of Hiero's long reign and was unsuccessful, with the result that Theocritus moved to Egypt and transferred his affiliation to the more receptive Ptolemy Philadelphus. Our evidence for the dating of the poem is slim, though, and based mostly on a combination of *ex silentio* and circular arguments; furthermore, although we have good grounds for regarding Theocritus as a native of Syracuse, we have no external evidence at all that he had any relations with Hiero or Hiero's court. Indeed, if *Idyll* 16 is an appeal for patronage dressed up as a poem in praise of the ruler, it reads as a rather clumsy effort. The poem begins solidly enough, with an unexceptional formal prologue (16.1–4):

> αἰεὶ τοῦτο Διὸc κούραιc μέλει, αἰὲν ἀοιδοῖc,
> ὑμνεῖν ἀθανάτουc, ὑμνεῖν ἀγαθῶν κλέα ἀνδρῶν.
> Μοῖcαι μὲν θεαὶ ἐντί, θεοὺc θεαὶ ἀείδοντι·
> ἄμμεc δὲ βροτοὶ οἵδε, βροτοὺc βροτοὶ ἀείδωμεν.

> It is ever the job of Zeus' daughters, ever that of the singer,
> to hymn the immortals, to hymn the glorious deeds of great men.
> The Muses are gods, so of gods as gods they sing:
> we here are mortals, so of mortals as mortals we should sing.

The poet then goes straight into a long complaint – elegantly written, but a complaint, nonetheless – about the miserliness of the wealthy and their lack of appreciation for poets and poetry (16.5–21), followed by a reminder that death levels all, and only the patron who is wise enough to hire a poet leaves any record for others to remember him by (16.22–67). As examples he cites first the famous fifth-century rulers of Thessaly (who were patrons of the poet Simonides), then the rulers of Troy, and finally the famous wanderer Odysseus, adding an outspoken rejection of material wealth in favor of other men's respect and friendship. All this seems quite implausible as an appeal for patronage, even if at lines 68–9 Theocritus states "I seek a man who will take delight in my presence with the Muses" (δίζημαι δ' ὅτινι θνατῶν κεχαριcμένοc ἔλθω/cὺν Μοίcαιc), and despite his anticipation of great deeds worthy of a poet's song as the Syracusans defeat their enemies and establish peace, with the help of Hiero. Most of this poem seems more like a trope, a loose set of reflections on an established theme in an imagined realm which allows more freedom of thought than would a begging letter delivered at Hiero's court. We should not forget that complaints by artists about their impoverished circumstances were common in Greek poetry of all periods (Hunter 1996: 92–109), and tell us nothing about their real lives. It seems just as likely that *Idyll* 16 is not a direct appeal to Hiero at all. Indeed, it is even worth considering that the actual context of the poem's composition (as against its purported Syracusan context) may have been the court at Alexandria. The pointed complaining and sermonizing will then have been nicely droll, not clumsy, safely projected onto a world outside Ptolemy's court and not unlike the expressions of poverty by the rustic characters in Theocritus' illusionistic pastoral poems.

Idyll 17 is more straightforward, addressed directly and clearly to a patron, and manages to be both a hymn and an encomium (Hunter 2003a: 8–24; Strootman in this volume). This is enabled by a significant development of the Hellenistic Age, the ruler cult, as well as the fact that in Egypt the Ptolemies continued the Egyptian practice of regarding the ruler as a son of god. Theocritus is careful at the beginning of his poem to keep Zeus and Ptolemy separate, but he also uses language that is ambiguous enough for the two rulers to merge in perception, and by line 16 the poem has Ptolemy Soter established by Zeus himself on a throne in Zeus' palace, sitting alongside Alexander the Great and their common ancestor Heracles (17.16–27). And although Theocritus uses vocabulary that maintains throughout the distinction between mortal and immortal, the tone of the poem is that of a hymn to a god, familiar from the *Homeric Hymns* as well as Theocritus' contemporary Callimachus. In addition two of the poem's main components, accounts of the birth of Ptolemy and then of the nature and extent of his power and efficacy as a ruler, are typical of hymns to gods, which routinely recount the divinity's origins and major accomplishments. It is notable also that the poem begins with a standard hymnal prefatory declaration (17.1–2):

> ἐκ Διὸc ἀρχώμεcθα καὶ ἐc Δία λήγετε Μοῖcαι,
> ἀθανάτων τὸν ἄριcτον, ἐπὴν† ἀείδωμεν ἀοιδαῖc.
>
> From Zeus let us begin, and at Zeus make your end, O Muses,
> the best of the immortals, whenever we celebrate in song.

Yet it ends with the standard final invocation made not to Zeus but to Ptolemy, albeit only as a demi-god (17.135–7):

> χαῖρε, ἄναξ Πτολεμαῖε· cέθεν δ' ἐγὼ ἶcα καὶ ἄλλων
> μνάcομαι ἡμιθέων, δοκέω δ' ἔποc οὐκ ἀπόβλητον
> φθέγξομαι ἐccομένοιc· ἀρετήν γε μὲν ἐκ Διὸc αἰτεῦ.
>
> Farewell, lord Ptolemy. You equal to other
> demi-gods shall I remember. And I think the song I pronounce
> posterity will not reject. As to virtue, ask it from Zeus.

In a neat maneuver Theocritus manages to have Ptolemy receive the concluding prayer, even while Zeus retains the final focus (Hunter 2003a: 195–6).

The modern reader may find the encomium to Ptolemy difficult to engage with. Our own post-Romantic notions of artistic freedom of expression limit our ability to appreciate art in the open service of patronage with objectivity. It is true that the encomium, both prose and verse, was a long-established genre in ancient Greece and will have been regarded by Theocritus' audience as normal and ordinary, and that praise of a patron was a standard component of the system of patronage upon which artists and art depended for their subsistence. But despite that, and even though *Idyll* 17 may stop short of being blatantly sycophantic and is of great interest to scholars, it is a fact that it has aged less well than, say, Pindar, all of whose victory poems were written in the service of a paying patron but lyrically transcend their historical context. The poem also has nothing to match the penultimate section of *Idyll* 16, whose description of the impact of peace on the countryside, once war is put away, for a moment transcends that poem's immediate concerns (16.82–100).

Idyll 22, addressed to the Dioscuri, is the only one of Theocritus' extant poems that is a straightforward hymn in praise of divinity. This is a work which has puzzled modern readers, to say the least, and many regard it as a disjointed failure (Sens 1997: 13–23). The problem lies in its very nature as a hymn: to all outward appearances this is a poem which declares itself, tonally and rhetorically, as a traditional celebratory text, laudatory of the twin brothers Castor and Polydeuces. And yet, while the first narrative section, on Polydeuces and his boxing victory over Amycus, seems morally straightforward (Amycus, after all, is a bully of Cyclopean proportions), the second narrative section deals with Castor's defeat and slaughter of his cousin Lynceus. To a modern reader the latter episode seems morally much more dubious, since Lynceus was only defending himself against aggression initiated by the Dioscuri, who were abducting his and his brother's brides. How can this be a "hymn"? Many critics have followed Wilamowitz in declaring the text to be badly damaged, diagnosing a lacuna after line 170 in the Castor–Lynceus section, which will have contained some sort of justification by Castor of the treatment meted out to his opponent. Yet recently discovered fragments of a second-century CE papyrus text of Theocritus (*P.Köln* 212) seem to afford no room for a lacuna. Some scholars have attempted to "save the phenomena" by seeing the narrative of Castor's brutal victory as a kind of literary game by Theocritus, who will have been pointing up the difference between himself and Homer – the modernist wryly eschews the archaic – but this too seems an awkward solution (Griffiths 1976; Sens 1992, 1997: 190–1). More likely, we should acknowledge that what appears to a modern readership as unjustified brutalism will have been viewed as a normal consequence when a mortal ignores the overwhelming superiority of divinity: power is its own justification. This was a basic assumption about reality in the Greek worldview, both at the divine and heroic level: the raw might of Zeus and the physical superiority of his hero children, such as Heracles and other semi-divine heroes like them, are often demonstrated in the world of Greek myth, and without any apparent felt need that the defeat of opponents or rivals be justified morally. And that will surely also have been a self-evident feature of the monarchic circles upon whose patronage the Hellenistic writers depended.

But for all its possible socio-political undercurrents and possible hints at contemporary figures and events, *Idyll* 22 is still a work whose primary engagement is with the literary tradition. First, the poem opens quite explicitly as a hymn in the traditional Homeric mold. Castor and Polydeuces are the subject of *Homeric Hymn* 33, a work which is generally considered to be at least as old as the sixth century BCE. *Idyll* 22 has even been described as "a version in the Alexandrian style" of the Homeric poem (Gow 1952b: 2.382). Once we proceed beyond the Archaic-Homeric form of the opening, though, the hymn's Alexandrian character emerges very clearly, and in several intertwined ways. Within the oeuvre of Theocritus, *Idyll* 22 connects closely to *Idyll* 13, a narrative non-hymnal poem which uses the theme of loss to reflect on the nature of love and the impact of the unpredictable on even heroic emotional attachment. In *Idyll* 13 Heracles' lover Hylas steps into a lush, seductive landscape (a *locus amoenus*) only to find himself drawn into it forever when he is pulled to the bottom of a pool by nymphs; in *Idyll* 22 what begins as a hymn turns, in its first part after the introduction, into an extended narrative in which Castor and Polydeuces step into an equally lovely *locus amoenus* to find themselves confronted with a threat of their own. Then, in terms of their larger narrative, both of these poems deal with incidents experienced by members of Jason's Argonautic expedition, as the Argo was making its way out to Colchis. Then, in another layer of meaning, both also have an important intertextual relationship outside themselves, with a work by another Alexandrian writer, the *Argonautica* by Apollonius of Rhodes. Theocritus' two poems are patently linked not just thematically but textually with Apollonius' epic poem; and even though the nature of the relationship between the two authors and their poems is debated, along with different possible chronologies and intentions (Sens 1997: 24–36; Hunter 1999: 264–5; Köhnken 1965, 2001, and in this volume), that they are so linked is indisputable. *Idyll* 22 is hymnal, then, in form, and epic in diction and mode, but its role and stance as an incidental narrative piece, emphasizing mood and the episodic, and inviting comparison with other contemporary writing, are more significant than its genre. We could say, in fact, that *Idyll* 22 is at heart not so much a hymn as another situational study – another glimpse into the slightly disassociated and disconcerting world of rural Greece, whose landscape is populated by strange and intrusive Cyclops figures (*Idyll* 11) or mysterious goatherds that materialize at the noonday hour out in the hills (*Idyll* 7). Castor, Polydeuces, Amycus, Lynceus, Polyphemus, Hylas' water-nymphs – all are characters whose solitariness and power to disrupt are more highly charged than any specific literary "genre" to which they may temporarily belong.

Other Hymns

A number of hymns have been preserved from other poets of this period. Quoted in Diogenes Laertius (4.5.26) are seven hexameters on Eros by the poet Antagoras of Rhodes, who was active at the court of Antigonus Gonatas in Macedon. Antagoras' hymn (*CA* 1) opens with a conventional trope, a deliberation about how the god should best be celebrated, and Diogenes reports that the Platonic philosopher Crantor seemingly agreed with Antagoras that Eros was a god of split personality. These lines are similar in rhetorical structure to line 5 of Callimachus' *Hymn to Zeus*, and most scholars assume that Callimachus was explicitly alluding to his contemporary here (Cuypers 2004b: 96–102).

Another writer from whom hymnal poetry has survived is the prominent Stoic philosopher Cleanthes, who was an almost exact contemporary of Callimachus. The anthologist Stobaeus (1.1.12) has preserved 39 hexameter lines by Cleanthes extolling Zeus in the traditional verse-form and familiar language of epic, but promoting him as the Stoic first principle, the prime mover and origin of the universe (see also White in this volume). Although we know nothing about the context or occasion for these lines, they do seem to have been quite literary and not performative in intent: their main purpose seems to have been to promote Stoic philosophical ideas. Cleanthes did use verse (hexameters and iambic trimeters) quite extensively to express Stoic philosophy, probably with a view to making it more accessible to a general audience, and his lines on Zeus seem similarly doctrinal in mode. Another hymn, or, at least, hymnal address, to Zeus with a similarly philosophical view of the world to promote was the hymn to Zeus with which Aratus opens his *Phaenomena* (mentioned above).

Other hymns survive from the Hellenistic period not because they were written by well-known authors and preserved as works of literature, but because they were recorded epigraphically on stone in the sanctuaries with which they were associated (*CA* pp. 132–73; Käppel 1992: 375–94; Fantuzzi in this volume). Several of these are anonymous, but in some cases the inscription attests the name of the author. Thus from the great healing sanctuary at Epidaurus we have six late-fourth-century BCE inscriptions containing 84 lines by a local poet Isyllus, who wrote in trochaic tetrameters, dactylic hexameters, elegiacs, and ionics. These are partly declaratory texts, aimed at establishing and enhancing the authority of Asclepius as an Epidaurian, but they include a paean to Asclepius and Apollo which, with its opening address to celebrants and concluding prayer to deity for increase and good health, resembles the frame of the mimetic hymns of Callimachus and serves to remind us of the latter's verisimilitude. Another paean, from the sanctuary of Asclepius in Athens, preserved in an inscription from the Roman era but thought by some scholars to date, as a text, from the third century BCE, is attributed to Macedonicus (41 Käppel; *CA* pp. 139–40). Written in dactylic lines of varying length, it addresses Apollo and Asclepius jointly, and, just like Isyllus' paean and the mimetic hymns of Callimachus, begins and finishes with instructions to celebrants and with prayers for divine benefaction.

An inscription found in 1904 near Palaikastro on Crete preserves a hymn in trochaic meter to Zeus sung by the Curetes, the legendary warrior-guardians of the king of the gods while he was a baby (*CA* pp. 160–2). In contrast to the hymns of Callimachus, Aratus, Cleanthes, or even the paeans to Apollo and Asclepius just mentioned, this text is simple and repetitive and does little more than implore the divinity to come and join the ritual dance, which was clearly performed as part of a regular, perhaps annual, celebration of the birth and rise to power of Zeus, along with the special association of the local region with him; there is no attempt at narrative of any kind, and the hymn serves as a reminder how straightforward the everyday cultic prayers which form the context for Callimachus and other writers of highly "literary" hymns will most likely have been. The inscription which preserves the *Hymn of the Curetes* dates from the second century CE, but, like the Asclepius paean from Athens, the hymn itself was almost certainly a traditional text dating from many centuries earlier.

Other hymns, or celebratory texts, include paeans to Apollo preserved in inscriptions at Delphi, one anonymous, another by an Athenian called Limenius (45–6 Käppel; *CA* pp. 141–59). Both of these are accompanied, most unusually, by musical notation. Also from Delphi are two fourth-century paeans, one to Apollo and another to the hearth goddess Hestia, by Aristonous of Corinth, preserved on the Athenian Treasury (*CA* pp. 162–5; 42 Käppel), as well as a long paean to Dionysus (who was equally at home in Delphi as his half-brother Apollo) by one Philodamus (*CA* pp. 165–71; 39 Käppel). From elsewhere in Greece, Eritrea, comes a fourth-century anonymous hymn (headed "Hymn") to the Idaean Dactyls (*CA* pp. 171–3).

From the forecourt of a temple precinct of Isis at Medinet Madi in the Fayum in Egypt come four Greek hymns, inscribed on two piers, probably in the first quarter of the first century BCE (Vanderlip 1972; Dieleman and Moyer in this volume). Two are in hexameters, two in elegiac couplets, and although the author, who calls himself Isidorus, seems not to have been a native Greek speaker, he was clearly familiar with Homer and Hesiod and the *Homeric Hymns*. These hymns are usually referred to as aretalogies, since they describe the powers of Isis-Hermouthis as they affect every aspect of mankind's life, from climate and natural phenomena of all kinds (including the inundation of the Nile) and the crops, to health, prosperity and general wellbeing. Like the hymns of Callimachus and Theocritus some two hundred years earlier, Isidorus' are much concerned with the role of the monarch, his power, and his relation to the divine, and these aretalogies come across as a fascinating mixture of traditional Greek concepts and sentiments and quite otherworldly Egyptian beliefs. They were clearly intended to form a bridge between the two cultures.

These epigraphic texts were recorded because of their importance as cult songs, and in order to assure their preservation, along with continuity and regularity in ritual. One of the things about them that is striking is that they were written in a variety of lyric meters, and they remind us that in using almost exclusively dactylic meter for their songs of praise, the literary authors were distancing themselves from the mainstream of traditional religious practice.

FURTHER READING

Furley and Bremer 2001 offer a collection of Greek hymns from Archaic to Hellenistic times. On Hellenistic praise poetry in particular, see Hunter and Fuhrer 2002, Stephens 2003, Fantuzzi and Hunter 2004: 350–403.

The standard edition of Callimachus' *Hymns* is Pfeiffer 1953; English translations in Lombardo and Rayor 1988, Nisetich 2001. Recent studies on the hymns as a corpus include Depew 2000, 2004, Harder 2003a, 2004, Vamvouri 2004, and Morrison 2007; see also Haslam 1993, Henrichs 1993a. For specific poems see, on *Zeus*: McLennan 1977, Tandy 1979, Clauss 1986, Hopkinson 1988, Winder 1997, Cuypers 2004b; on *Apollo*, Williams 1978, Bing 1993; on *Artemis*: Bornmann 1968, Bing and Uhrmeister 1994, Plantinga 2004, I. Petrovic 2007; on *Delos*: Mineur 1984, Ukleja 2005; on *Pallas*: Bulloch 1985, Hopkinson 1988, Hunter 1992, Morrison 2005, 2007: 160–70; on *Demeter*, Hopkinson 1984a, Müller 1987, Murray 2004.

On Theocritus' encomia, *Idylls* 16 and 17, see notably Hunter 1996: 77–109 and 2003a; further Griffiths 1979: 9–50, 71–82, Fantuzzi 2000, Goldhill 1991, Gutzwiller 1983, Gow 1952b; on the hymnal *Idyll* 22, see Sens 1997, Hunter 1996: 46–76, Köhnken 1965, Gow 1952b.

Thom 2005 and Hopkinson 1988 provide commented editions of Cleanthes' *Hymn to Zeus*; see also White in this volume. Further reading on Aratus is provided by Volk in this volume. For the text of the cultic hymns and paeans mentioned in the last section of this chapter, see Powell 1925: 132–73 and Käppel 1992: 375–94; see further Pöhlmann and West 2001, and Fantuzzi in this volume. For texts of the Isidorus aretalogies, see Vanderlip 1972; further references are provided by Dieleman and Moyer in this volume.

CHAPTER THIRTEEN

Sung Poetry: The Case of Inscribed Paeans

Marco Fantuzzi

In answer to his father's exhortation to follow the traditional custom of the symposium and sing some lyric poetry (*melē*) of Simonides, Aristophanes' Pheidippides protests that he would rather perform a tragic speech (*rhēsis*) by Euripides because singing a song to the lyre at a symposium is terribly passé (*Clouds* 1353–71). A movement away from song is also observable in Athenian drama. In the fourth century BCE the most prominent lyric sections of tragedy and comedy, the choral odes, became repertory pieces, more or less remote from the dramatic action and only occasionally composed by the dramatists themselves. The trend was never reversed. In the next century, Theocritus and Callimachus often adopted the two recitative meters *par excellence*, the dactylic hexameter and the elegiac couplet, for types of poetry that would formerly have commanded lyric meters. As for these meters themselves, the increasing separation between music and meter, which Plato laments especially in connection to the dithyramb (*Laws* 2.669d–e), may explain why we find Hellenistic poets using lyric meters, which the Archaic poets had employed in responsive strophic structures, in stichic or epodic poems, or composing free-flowing songs comparable to the monodies of the later plays of Euripides and the *Fragmentum Grenfellianum*. And although Hellenistic stichic poetry occasionally mimics the strophic structure of sung poetry (notably in Theocritus; lastly Prauscello 2006: 185–213), no actual strophic lyric survives from any of the major Hellenistic poets. In this light it comes as no surprise that there is almost no evidence for singing competitions in Hellenistic Egypt, and although such competitions are recorded elsewhere (for example in mainland Greece and Delos), it is clear that reciting dactylic poetry was the dominant form of poetic performance throughout the Hellenistic world (Hardie 1983: 206).

The Hellenistic poems that still employ lyric meters fall into a number of groups. Callimachus' four short *Melē* (frs. 226–9 Pf.), Theocritus' short *Idylls* 28–31, and a small number of epigrams by Callimachus, Theocritus, Asclepiades, and others (listed in Fantuzzi and Hunter 2004: 39 n.155) take up, if not in meter at least in language and imagery, the tradition of short lyric poetry such as that composed by Sappho, Alcaeus, and Anacreon. We also find stichic re-use of lyric meters in a small number of "popular," mainly mime-like texts (*CA* pp. 180–96) of a kind similar to the *Fragmentum Grenfellianum* (Esposito in this volume). Other poems are the work of experimental virtuosos who are little more than names to us – indeed they are mentioned by later writers only for their metrical "inventions." Philicus, one of the members of the Alexandrian Pleiad, who composed a *Hymn to Demeter* in choriambic hexameters in the first half of the third century, explicitly offered his abstruse invention as a "gift to the grammarians" (*SH* 677); and Boiscus of Cyzicus, who dedicated his invention of the catalectic iambic octameter to Apollo, presented himself as the proud "author of a new poem" (*SH* 233). Lyric-iambic meters feature in the so-called *technopaignia* or "figure poems" ascribed to Theocritus, Simias of Rhodes, Dosiadas, and Besantinus, which are perhaps the most playful and virtuosic kind of poetry produced by the Hellenistic Age. They are replete with arcane glosses and riddles, and the succession of verses of different length gives the poem itself the shape of a particular object. The length of the lines is dictated by pictographic necessity, without any regard for the traditional strophic organization of lyric *cola*: here metrics has really become "the art of measuring," a manipulation of length. Lyric meters were also adopted for social satire. The *poète maudit* Sotades produced lyric verses of a new kind that subsequently took their name from him, sotadeans. In this meter he wrote hard-hitting attacks on the political powerhouse of the Ptolemies, and he likewise expressed a subversive spirit towards the highest power of literary tradition by re-writing the *Iliad* in sotadeans. Another satirical moralist, Cercidas from Megalopolis, invented iambic-lyric meters (*meliamboi*) based on the *kat' enoplion* epitrites of the lyric-choral tradition (Scodel in this volume).

A small number of lyric texts of the Hellenistic Age continued to be composed in strophes. Most of them are paeans or religious hymns preserved on stone (metrical analyses in Parker 2001: 32–5). Through indirect literary transmission we have testimonia or fragments of a few other paeans and encomiastic hymns, celebrating kings or military leaders, but in most cases too little to ascertain their precise structure. Honorands of such compositions were Antigonus Monophthalmus and Demetrius Poliorcetes (*SH* 492; for the latter is also *CA* pp. 173–4, in strophes of iambic trimeters and ithyphallics), Craterus (*SH* 40), Seleucus (*CA* p. 140), and Titus Quinctius Flamininus (*CA* p. 143). The context of all these texts is not Alexandrian or even Egyptian (apart from the *Erythraean Paean*, a copy of whose text was also found in Ptolemais, an exception which confirms the rule): they rather appear to be linked to a conservative tradition of religious singing, which still flourished in the sanctuaries of the Greek homeland, and to the practice of the epinician paean, which was as old as Homer (*Il.* 22.391–4; Rutherford 2001a: §5d). The cultic paeans that survive epigraphically are all either anonymous or by authors who are otherwise unknown, and none of them, as far as we know, was ever recorded in any other medium than stone. Set against Callimachus' and Theocritus' preference for recitative meters and stichic composition, these poems would seem perfect examples of the activity of "minor" or "popular" poets, writing for hire or for agonistic festivals

(Cameron 1995a: 47–53) in a tradition that was more or less uninfluenced by "Callimachean" tastes. This impression, we will see, is only in part correct.

Isyllus

Not long after the Macedonian king Philip (perhaps Philip II, 338 BCE, but more probably either Philip III, 317/16 BCE, or Philip V, 218 BCE) "had led his army against Sparta with the intention of dismantling the power of the kings" (lines 63–4), the Epidaurian Isyllus, son of Socrates, dedicated "to Apollo Maleatas and Asclepius" (2) a long inscription of 84 lines in the sanctuary of Asclepius at Epidaurus, which includes a short paean to both gods but notably to Asclepius (40.37–61 Käppel 1992; *CA* pp. 132–6). Isyllus may have composed the entire text himself or had parts of it composed by a hired versifier; in any case, hardly any parallel can be found for the complex form and the artistic engagement and ambitions of this inscription, which, together with the paean itself, includes a full narrative of the events leading to its composition, instructions for its performance, and several expositions of Isyllus' political views. It is structured in seven sections, some in prose, others in various meters, each with its own topic and goal.

The first two lines, in prose, introduce the dedicator, Isyllus, and dedicatees, Apollo and Asclepius. Surprisingly, there is no object here for ἀνέθηκε, "dedicated," a technical term which usually introduces the offering, for example a statue, a trophy, or professional tools, which the dedicatory inscription (supposedly) accompanies and "explains." Here the verb remains self-referential and points not simply to the paean, which might be expected to be the dedicated "object," but to the whole inscription, a point which the final line of the text restates more clearly (ταῦτά τοι … ἀνέθηκεν Ἴϲυλλοϲ, 79).

The section that follows this heading starts with an undisguised political declaration, which is at first sight surprising in a religious inscription. Lines 3–9 state, in trochaic tetrameters, that the demos is stronger if it empowers aristocrats to be "directed" (ὀρθοῦται) by their "manly virtue" (ἀνδραγαθία, 4); but in case one of the nobles is affected by "baseness" (πονηρία, 5), the demos must restrain him for the sake of stability: "this is the opinion I had in the past; I expressed it then and express it now. I vowed to inscribe this opinion if the law which I presented ratified it for us. This has indeed happened, and not without the gods' will" (7–9).

In Section 3, composed in dactylic hexameters (10–26), it becomes clear that Isyllus' sacred law ratified his political ideas because it involved or presupposed a specific role for the nobles in the celebration of Phoebus and Asclepius. Cleverly stressing his personal vow, which he presents as almost atemporal and thus less arbitrarily partisan, Isyllus legitimates the inclusion in the inscription of his political advice to the Epidaurians with the fact that the existence of a noble leading class is a necessary requisite for the procession in honor of Asclepius that he proposes. At 14–26 Isyllus prescribes that the demos of Epidaurus choose among themselves "those who are the best" (οἵ τ' ἀριϲτεύωϲι, 14), publicly proclaim their names, charge them to march in a procession "in honor of Phoebus and of his son Asclepius" bearing wreaths of laurel for Apollo and olive branches for Asclepius (17–21), and pray that "good health for children" (τέκνοιϲ ὑγίεια), "physical and ethical excellence" (καλοκαγαθία), "peace" (εἰράνα), "good order" (εὐνομία), and "irreproachable wealth" (πλοῦτοϲ ἀμεμφήϲ) may last forever at Epidaurus (21–4). If the Epidaurians respect this law in years to come, they may hope that Zeus will keep them from harm (25–6). Isyllus' faith in the Epidaurian aristocracy perhaps also intrudes upon his religious language in the following paean. The name of the daughter of Malos quoted at 45, Kleophema, recalls two key aristocratic values, κλέοϲ and φήμη, and later Asclepius is called ὦ μέγ' ἄριϲτε θεῶν (83) with an epithet, ἄριϲτοϲ, that is very rare for gods but a crucial term in aristocratic ideology (Sineux 1999: 165; Vamvouri 2004: 171).

The lines that express Isyllus' political credo (3–9) also show what is in my opinion a key goal in his self-presentation: they invite readers of the inscription to identify him as a sort of new Solon, an intertextual connection which so far does not seem to have received any scholarly attention. Isyllus' idea that the demos has to accept to be directed by a morally superior oligarchic class, but also has to monitor the nobles constantly to ensure that they do not become "base" (πονηρίαϲ, 5) and their wealth is "irreproachable" (ἀμεμφῆ, 23) find precise parallels in Solon's appreciation of only wealth that is "rightful" (δίκαιοϲ), his criticism of the excesses (ὕβριϲ) of the wealthy, and his appeal to the demos to obey the leading class but also control it and restrain its tendency toward excess. These thoughts are expressed, for example, in fr. 13.7–32 (*IEG*), on righteous wealth and Zeus' punishment of unlawful people, and in fr. 4, which warns the rich to avoid excess for the sake of political stability (εὐνομία), claiming that "through the dispensation of Zeus" (κατὰ Διὸϲ αἶϲαν) the city of Athens would never perish, but that the foolishness of the "leaders of the demos" (δήμου ἡγεμόνεϲ) might lead to its destruction (1–8). Similar points emerge in fr. 4c.1–3, 6.1–4, and 11.3–4.

Solon's preference for an enlightened "pre-democratic" rule over the demos by the traditional leading class and Isyllus' encouragement of an enlightened oligarchy might be deemed a casual and partial coincidence. For example, Isyllus' oligarchic ideas also to some extent match Tyrtaeus' defense of the Spartan political system (fr. 4; although the idea that the demos has to check the aristocracy seems to have no parallel in Tyrtaeus). What is strikingly Solonian, however, is the way in which Isyllus frames his political credo and accomplishments in order to fashion himself as a successful authority figure. Isyllus' claim that the opinion he expresses at this moment is an opinion he has also defended and communicated in the past (τάνδε τὰν γνώμαν τόκ' ἦχον καὶ ἔλεγον καὶ νῦν λέγω, 7), and his statement at the end of the introduction that what he undertook and vowed to do "has indeed happened, and not without the gods' will" (ἔγεντο δ', οὐκ ἄνευ θεῶν, 9), voice the same feelings Solon expresses about his own political project, most probably after accomplishing it, in order to defend himself against criticism: "for what I said I would, I have accomplished with the gods' will" (ἃ μὲν γὰρ εἶπα, ϲὺν θεοῖϲιν ἤνυϲα, fr. 34.6). Moreover, while the poetry in which Solon explicates his moral and political ideas is composed in elegiac distichs, the fragments of his "apology" for his reforms, in which he emphasizes that his opinions are as they were before, significantly use the more conversational iambic trimeter (36–7) and trochaic tetrameter (32–4; Noussia forthcoming). It will hardly be coincidental that it is precisely the trochaic tetrameter, a meter seldom found in Hellenistic poetry outside Menander, which carries the political program in lines 3–9 of Isyllus' inscription. Apart from this specific connection, Isyllus may have also more broadly followed the paradigm of Solon in adopting different meters for the different contents and tones of the sections of his inscription, just as Solon varied between elegiacs, iambics, and tetrameters. And on a more speculative note, one may wonder if there is not also a connection between Isyllus' choice to present his sacred law (lines 10–26) in dactylic hexameters and the story that Solon started composing his laws in hexameters but in the end abandoned this form for prose, found by Plutarch in his sources for the *Life of Solon* (3.5) together with the purported opening lines (Solon fr. 31). The lines and the story are surely spurious, but it is a fact that, with the exception of sacred laws decreed by oracles, we have no other evidence for inscribed regulations such as that of Isyllus composed in metrical form until the early Empire, i.e., well after Isyllus' time (Sokolowski 1962; A. and I. Petrovic 2006). It is at least possible, therefore, that Isyllus' choice for the hexameter was directly inspired by the Solonian tradition.

It should come as no surprise that Isyllus, a supporter of an enlightened aristocracy, adopted Solon as a validating figure. Already in fourth-century Greece "even critics of popular rule could put up with democracy, if only it was ancestral" (Hansen 1989: 75), and the Athenian lawgiver had attained an almost mythical status. Although there is a tendency in the orators to position Solon as the father of the radical democracy of the fifth century, Aristotle interpreted Solon's original constitution as an indirect and representative democracy, where the role of the demos mainly consisted in electing the magistrates. Similarly, Isocrates suggests a return to Solon's constitution as a remedy against the problems of radical democracy, and the oligarchic Council of the Four Hundred, established in Athens in 411 BCE, also seems to have used Solon's constitution as its model (Hansen 1989: 88–9, 93–7; Ruschenbusch 1958: 407).

The two sections that follow Isyllus' *nomos* on the ritual for Apollo and Asclepius (Sections 4 and 5, lines 27–31 and 32–6) provide authoritative justifications for both the ritual and the paean that follows. Section 4 starts with an elegiac distich commemorating how a certain Malos founded the cult of Apollo Maleatas by building an altar and sacrificing to the god (the dedicatory character of the lines probably explains the choice of meter). The three dactylic hexameters that follow state the vitality and Panhellenic importance of these sacrifices: even in Asclepius' sanctuary at Trikkala nobody can enter the inner sanctum without first sacrificing to Apollo Maleatas. Section 5, composed in prose, is parallel in structure and immediately juxtaposed to Section 4, suggesting an analogy between Malos' and Isyllus' contributions to the cult: it was Malos who built the first altar; it was Isyllus who composed a paean, consulted the Delphic oracle, and was told to inscribe it "for the present and future time" (36).

The text of the paean proper, in ionics, follows (37–56, Section 6). The introduction indicates who are to sing it: all the demos (ἀείcατε λαοί, / ζαθέαc ἐνναέτα[ι] τᾶcδ' Ἐπιδαύρου, 37–8), and not only, for example, the aristocrats leading the procession or the city's *kouroi* (as in the *Erythraean Paean*, discussed below). The body of the song is almost completely devoted to legitimizing the joint cult of Apollo

Maleatas and Asclepius at Epidaurus through an elaborate Epidaurian genealogy. According to this genealogy, which is authoritatively presented as a "revelation" that "came to the ears of our ancestors" (ὧδε γὰρ φάτις ἐνέπους' ἦλυ/θ' ἐς ἀκοὰς προγόνων ἁμετέρων, 39–40), Zeus married his daughter, the Muse Erato, to Malos; then Phlegyas, who came from and lived at Epidaurus (43), married the daughter of Erato and Malos, Kleophema; from them was born Aigla, also called Koronis, who was raped by Apollo "in the house of Malos," i.e., at Epidaurus; with the help of the Moirai and Lachesis, Aigla gave birth to a child whom Apollo called "Asclepius" after the name of its mother. Most of these details are unique. The marriage between Malos and Erato, the figure of Kleophema, and Aigla as the name of Asclepius' mother are not found elsewhere. In all other sources Phlegyas comes from Thessaly, not Epidaurus, and Asclepius' mother is simply called Koronis. The etymological connection of the god's name to the otherwise unattested Aigla, as linguistically far-fetched as it may seem, effectively caps a genealogy devised to appropriate Asclepius as an Epidaurian god (cf. τὰν ϲὰν Ἐπίδαυρον ματρόπολιν, 59), which is licensed by its presentation in a paean – and not just any paean but one which Apollo himself, through the Delphic oracle, told the Epidaurians to inscribe and preserve for all time.

The beginning and end of the paean's final section are marked by the cry *ie Paian ie Paian* (58, 61), the formula which makes a paean a paean (Ford 2006: 287–8) but which elsewhere in this song appears only in the very first line (ἰὲ Παιᾶνα, 37). It seems significant that the first cry comes immediately after Asclepius has been qualified as "healer of illnesses, giver of health" (νόϲων παύ/[ϲ]τορα, δωτῆρ' ὑγιείαϲ, 56–7) and the second caps the wish "may you bestow upon us manifest health in mind and body" (ἐναργῆ δ' ὑγίειαν ἐπιπέμποιϲ φρεϲὶ καὶ ϲώ/μαϲιν ἁμοῖϲ, 60–1). Paian (also called Paiēōn) was perhaps in origin an independent healing god, but in literature and cult this name typically appears as an epithet or allonym of Apollo as a healing or apotropaic god. Isyllus' song is certainly not the first to address Asclepius with the words *ie Paian*: the earliest version of the *Erythraean Paean to Asclepius* dates from 380–360 BCE and already Sophocles may have composed paeans to this god (*PMG* 737b). Yet it seems that Isyllus, by directly linking the cry *ie Paian* to Asclepius' healing powers, justifies its own existence as a paean to Asclepius by way of a subtle aetiology, the implicit argument being that *ie Paian* addresses Apollo as a healing god, and therefore it can be transferred to his son Asclepius, who is also a healing god. That this connection is not self-evident is shown by the "miniature paean" within Callimachus' *Hymn to Apollo* (97–104) and Orpheus' song to Apollo in Apollonius' *Argonautica* (2.705–13), which provide a competing *aition* of [*h*]*ie Paian* focusing on the first element ([*h*]*ie*), which they explain from the Delphians' exhortations to Apollo to shoot (*hie*) his arrows at the dragon Pytho (cf. also Ephorus *FGrH* 70 F 31).

The final section of Isyllus' inscription, in dactylic hexameters (57–79), celebrates Asclepius' power by describing one of his achievements. These lines are in form an aretalogy (καὶ τόδε ϲῆϲ ἀρετῆϲ, 62), reminiscent in style and form of the *Homeric Hymns*. Yet they are also a personal testimony of the greatness of the god, because the event which Isyllus records does not derive from the realm of myth but from his own experience. When "Philip" (on whose identification see above) led an army against Sparta in order to abolish the power of the kings, Asclepius came to the Spartans' aid from Epidaurus. At that moment "the boy" Isyllus (67 ὁ παῖς, 72 μοι, 77 ἐμέ) returned from the Bosporus with an illness and prayed to Asclepius. The healer then appeared to him in golden armor and said (73–82):

"θάρσει· καιρῶι γάρ cοι ἀφίξομαι – ἀλλὰ μέν' αὐτεῖ –
τοῖc Λακεδαιμονίοιc χαλεπὰc ἀπὸ κῆραc ἐρύξαc,
οὕνεκα τοὺc Φοίβου χρηcμοὺc cώζοντι δικαίωc
οὓc μαντευcάμενοc παρέταξε πόλῃ Λυκοῦργοc."
ὣc ὃ μὲν ὤιχετο ἐπὶ Σπάρτην· ἐμὲ δ' ὦρcε νόημα
ἀγγεῖλαι Λακεδαιμονίοιc ἐλθόντα τὸ θεῖον
πάντα μάλ' ἑξείαc· οἳ δ' αὐδήcαντοc ἄκουcαν
cώτειραν φῆμαν, Ἀcκλαπιέ, καί cφε cάωcαc.
οἳ δὴ ἐκάρυξαν πάνταc ξενίαιc cε δέκεcθαι
cωτῆρα εὐρυχόρου Λακεδαίμονοc ἀγκαλέοντεc.

"Do not worry, I will come to you in due course – just wait here! – but first I must save the Spartans from dire destruction. For they justly observe the decrees of Phoebus which Lycurgus imposed upon the city after consulting the oracle." After speaking these words he was off to Sparta, and my mind urged me go and report the epiphany to the Spartans, all of it, word for word. They listened to the prophecy of salvation I spoke, Asclepius, and saving them you did; upon which they sent word that all should receive you hospitably, addressing you as savior of Sparta with the broad dancing-places.

When immediately after these lines Isyllus closes his text with the formula "Isyllus dedicated this" (ταῦτά τοι ... ἀνέθηκεν Ἴcυλλοc, 79), these words, like the opening formula "Isyllus dedicated" (Ἴcυλλοc ... ἀνέθηκε, 1), clearly do not point just to the central sections of the inscription, the sacred law and the paean: all sections – Isyllus' political advice, his ritual prescriptions, the text of the paean, and the account of his encounter with Asclepius and embassy to the Spartans – form part of an encompassing persuasive strategy to build up Isyllus' political authority through divine validation. Isyllus is the new Solon whose political views are confirmed by a sacred law approved not just by the people of Epidaurus but by Apollo himself. His service to Apollo and Asclepius is comparable to that of Malos, founder of the joint cult of Apollo Maleatas and Asclepius and ancestor of the latter. Isyllus is on familiar terms with and dear to both gods: Apollo, who in an oracle told him his paean was to be preserved for all time, as well as Asclepius, who appeared to him when he was a child and whose message of salvation he conveyed to the Spartans, to the benefit of the Spartans, Asclepius, and himself. Isyllus' strategy resembles that of Zaleukos of Locri, whose code of laws, if we are to believe to Plutarch, "found favor with the Locrians not least because he asserted that Athena had constantly appeared to him and had in each case guided and instructed him in his legislation" (Plu. *Mor.* 542e–543a; cf. Arist. fr. 548 Rose 1886). Indeed, Asclepius' speech to the boy Isyllus in the final lines brings us back to the project of the older Isyllus enshrined in this inscription. The reason, so Asclepius declares, why he supports the Spartans against the Macedonians is that the Spartans had respected Apollo's oracle by adopting the laws of Lycurgus. The Epidaurians, then, would be fools to disregard the law of Isyllus, the protégé of Apollo and Asclepius, who as an eyewitness of Asclepius' epiphany, a beneficiary of his healing power, and carrier of his message of salvation, constituted living evidence of the god's power and benevolence.

Long and detailed inscriptions recording religious laws are not uncommon in the Classical and Hellenistic periods. The Milesian *nomos* of the Molpoi, which was re-inscribed at the end of the third century BCE but dates from 450/449 and probably resumes even older ritual prescriptions, runs to 45 lines (Herda 2006); the prescriptions about ritual purity preserved in a third century BCE inscription from Cos (*LSCG* 154) fill more than 90, and the 92 BCE rules of the mysteries from Andanie (*LSCG* 64) no fewer than 193 lines. The constituent parts of Isyllus' inscription are also partly unsurprising. Cults were often supported through oracles, which could be proudly evoked in inscriptions recording their foundation or revival. A case in point is the long text set up by a certain Mnesiepes for the cult of the poet Archilochus in Paros, which records no fewer than three oracles of Apollo to Mnesiepes and one to Archilochus' father Telesicles (Archil. test. 3 Gerber 1999 = *SEG* 15.517). Even so, there do not seem to be any parallels for a religious song being cast in an explanatory and legitimizing framework as elaborate as that of Isyllus' inscription, where the paean constitutes less than a third of the entire text.

In order to appreciate the boldness of Isyllus' framing of his religious law and song and the peculiarity of his paean, it helps to compare his text to an inscription from Erythrae in Asia Minor which has already been mentioned several times above. Datable to 380–360 BCE, this inscription is at least half a century older than Isyllus. Recorded in 40 lines of prose on the recto of the stone is a sacred law detailing rituals and sacrifices to be performed for Asclepius and Apollo, including the instruction to sing a paean (παιωνίζειν), first to Apollo and then to Asclepius, after a successful incubation in the temple or the fulfillment of a prayer. The verso contains the scanty remains of a paean to Apollo and a much better preserved paean to Asclepius (36 and 37 Käppel). The *Erythraean Paean to Asclepius* became the standard paean to Asclepius and may have been initially composed with this goal in mind. The person who devised the inscription not only chose to completely separate the paean from the sacred law that regulates its performance (inscribed in prose on the opposite side of the stone, as was the most common epigraphic practice, rather than integrated with the paean in a prosimetric text as in Isyllus' inscription) but he also composed, commissioned, or selected an entirely generic song.

The *Erythraean Paean*, structured in strophes with a mesymnion and ephymnion *ie Paian*, faithfully reproduces the most marked formal features of the traditional paean to Apollo ("automatization of the form" in the terminology of Käppel 1992: 189–206), while limiting the song's content to a bare genealogy of the god, a list of his children, and an appeal to Asclepius to "be gracious to my city of the broad dancing-places" (ἵλαοc δ' ἐπινίcεο/τὰν ἐμὰν πόλιν εὐρύχορον, 19–20) and allow "us" (ἡμᾶc, 20) to enjoy a healthy life. This reduction is only partly explainable from the fact that while there was a stock of paeanic stories for Apollo from which a poet could draw, such a tradition did not really exist for his son Asclepius. In comparison with what remains of the earlier literary paeans of authors such as Pindar and Bacchylides, we find among the paeans inscribed during the Hellenistic era a noticeable fluctuation in authorial individuality and narrative ambition. This applies first and foremost to the *Erythraean Paean*, whose narrative section consists in – or rather is substituted by – a meager list of Asclepius' children, which seems to place it in a class of less ornate cult poetry, without the literary aspirations of texts such as the paeans of Pindar or Isyllus

(Schröder 1999: 62–96). Yet, as was recently argued by LeVen (2008: 262–7), even this at first sight unambitious paean shows a certain degree of self-consciousness and subtly justifies its status as a paean not to Apollo but to Asclepius. The sacred law on the recto of the stone, listing the rituals to be performed by the worshippers praying for *Asclepius'* help, ends with a paean to *Apollo*, which runs on from the bottom of the recto to the top of the verso. The paean to Asclepius on the verso opens immediately after the end of the paean to Apollo, with the following words: "Sing of Paian, famous for his skill ... who fathered a great joy for mortals..., iē Paian, Asclepius, most famous god, ie Paian" (Παιᾶνα κλυτόμητιν ἀείcατε / ... ὃc μέγα χάρμα βρότοιcιν ἐγείνατο ... / ἰὴ Παιάν, Ἀcκληπιὸν / δαίμονα κλεινότατον, ἰὲ Παιάν, 1–9): the song seems to open as if it is going to be another paean to Apollo, but in reality "transfers" the appellation Paian to Asclepius. Significantly, Asclepius' epithet κλεινότατοc, "most famous," in line 9 is a standard epithet for Apollo; here it picks up Apollo's epithet κλυτόμητιc, "famous for his skill," in line 1, a word which allegedly qualified not Apollo but Asclepius in Sophocles' prototypical paean to this god (*PMG* 737; but cf. Rutherford 2001a: 461–2).

As indicated, this "generic" or "essential" paean became a classic, which was still sung more than five centuries after its first attestation. Copies of it, more or less unchanged, were recorded at Ptolemais in Egypt (97 CE), Athens (first or second century CE), and Dion in Macedon (late second century CE). The absence of details restricting this paean to a specific location or context meant that it could be used in every circumstance and place. It could also be easily adapted as desired, as has happened in the version from Ptolemais, which includes an additional fourth strophe with the wish for regular floods of the Nile. In the same vein, a paean composed by a certain Macedonicus (41 Käppel), found near the Athenian Asclepieum and datable to the first century BCE, closely follows the structure of the time-honored Erythraean model but adds some final verses asking for Asclepius' protection specifically for Athens. It may not be just a matter of chance that the *Erythraean Paean* remains the only instance among the epigraphically attested paeans from the fourth to the first centuries BCE whose author remains unknown to us. That is to say, it is quite possible that the author of this song or his patrons purposely chose not to record his identity exactly because anonymity was essential to its desired dissemination as a standard text. However this may be, read against the *Erythraean Paean*, Isyllus' provision of a uniformly "literary" and authoritative form for every aspect of the political and religious context of his message appears bold and original indeed.

Philodamus

As it turns out, Isyllus' inscription is not a completely isolated phenomenon. Some other paeans of the Hellenistic Age, though not as elaborately and artistically framed and presented as that of Isyllus, likewise have a religious-political dimension and show similar rhetorical strategies. Close in time to the earliest possible date for Isyllus is a Delphic inscription which contains a long paean to Dionysus going under the name of Philodamus of Skarpheia (39 Käppel). The paean itself, which is fragmentarily preserved, is followed by a prose subscription which not only specifies who wrote the paean – Philodamus and his brothers Epigenes and Mantidas – but also authorizes the preceding song. It states that, under the eponymous magistrate Etymondas (probably 340/339 BCE), the Delphians granted Philodamus, his brothers, and their descendants a number of privileges (including proxeny, preferential consultation of the oracle, first-rank seats at ceremonies, and exemption from fees) to honor them for the preceding paean to Dionysus, which the three brothers composed "according to the oracular command of the god" (κατὰ τὰ]ν μαντείαν τοῦ Θεοῦ ἐπαγγεἰλατ[ο]). This official endorsement is particularly significant because the paean, like Isyllus' paean to Asclepius, takes an innovative approach to its subject, pushing an identification of Dionysus and Apollo which goes far beyond what we find in earlier sources.

Forms of association between (Delphic) Apollo and Dionysus may already have been promoted by the Pisistratids (Ieranò 1992) and are not foreign to fifth-century Athenian tragedy (Aesch. *Eum.* 24–6; Rutherford 2001a: 133). Delphic evidence includes, for example, a fifth-century inscription of the Labydae detailing sacrifices for Dionysus to be performed at Delphi in mid-summer (*CID* 1.9.43–5), and the much later testimony of Plutarch, who reports that it was customary to celebrate Dionysus at Delphi with dithyrambs in winter, when Apollo was supposed to be among the Hyperboreans (*Mor.* 388e–f; cf. Bacch. 16.5–12). Our paean, however, pushes a far more radical idea. It opens with an invitation to Dionysus to come to the Delphic Theoxenia, the spring feast that celebrated Apollo's return from the Hyperboreans (3–4). This in itself already seems odd. One would expect Delphic Dionysus to be celebrated with a dithyramb, while a paean, especially one for this occasion, would naturally be addressed to Apollo; in antiquity these two genres were often seen as opposed (Philochorus *FGrH* 328 F 172; Plu. *Mor.* 389a–b; Rutherford 2001a: §7g and §12). Philodamus' paean self-consciously draws attention to its crossing of genres and syncretistic agenda right from its first line, where Dionysus is addressed as Διθύραμβε, and it continues to blur the distinction between Apollo and Dionysus, and between paean and dithyramb throughout. For instance, the epithet καλλίπαις usually qualifies Apollo's mother, Leto; here, and here alone, it is the mother of Dionysus who is "with beautiful child" (7). Many other moves of this type, some more, others less obvious, can be identified.

The text of the paean consists of twelve strophes, each including a mesymnion (5, 18, etc.) and ephymnion (11–13, 24–6, etc.) As we saw, strophes with such refrains were perceived as a key formal feature of the traditional paean. Yet the phrasing of this mesymnion is by no means traditional. Its formula εὐοῖ ὦ ἰὸ Βάκχ' ὦ ἰὲ Παιάν prefixes a Dionysiac address εὐοῖ ὦ ἰὸ Βάκχ' to the traditional Apollinian invocation ὦ ἰὲ Παιάν, achieving an equation of Dionysus to Paean and hence to Apollo – an equation which automatically extends to the invocation of Paean in the song's more traditional ephymnion, "ie Paian, come as savior, be benevolent and protect this city so that it may continue to prosper" (ἰὲ Παιάν, ἴθι σωτήρ, etc.).

The first five strophes describe a series of locations where Dionysus brought his blessings, landmarks of his cult. After seeing the light in Thebes (strophe 1) and establishing his rites there, Dionysus is presented as first visiting Delphi (strophe 2), where "revealing his starry frame [he] stood among his Delphic maidens in the folds of Parnassus" (21–3). He then went to Eleusis, where he came to be invoked in the

Mysteries as "Iakchos" (strophe 3), and after the unreadable strophe 4 we find him in Olympus and Pieria (58–61):

> Μοῦcαι [δ'] αὐτίκα παρθένοι
> κ[ιccῶι] cτε[ψ]άμενοι κύκλωι cε πᾶcαι
> μ[έλψαν] ἀθάνα[τον] ἐc ἀεὶ
> Παιᾶν' εὐκλέα τ' ὀ[πὶ κλέο]υ-
> cαι, [κα]τᾶρξε δ' Ἀπόλλων.

> And immediately the maiden Muses, having crowned themselves with ivy, in a circle all hymned you as forever immortal and famous Paian, and Apollo led their chorus.

Because strophes 6–8 are almost completely unreadable we cannot say for certain whether Olympus was the last stop on Dionysus' journey. However, the content of strophe 5 and the preserved letters πυθοχρη[cτ?] in strophe 6 strongly suggest that in that strophe the narration came full circle and Dionysus returned to Delphi, the location where he had established his own chorus at the very start of his journey. This is also where Philodamus and his brothers, in the present, honor him under the title of "Paean," as is licensed by the "owner" of this appellation, Apollo, through the song of the Pierian Muses in strophe 5, and paralleled by Dionysus' acquisition of the sobriquet "Iakchos" at Eleusis in strophe 3.

Regardless of whether Philodamus' song is really the first paean ever composed for Dionysus, it certainly aetiologizes its own existence. In strophe 9 the main point of its mythological tale – legitimizing the singing of paeans to Dionysus – is sanctioned once again by Apollo, this time explicitly. Here the god is said to have ordered the Amphictyons (the Delphic confederation), surely by means of an oracle (compare the oracle given to Isyllus), first of all to "present this hymn for his brother (Dionysus) to the family of the gods" (110–12) on the occasion of the Theoxenia; secondly, to restore the old temple built by the Alcmeonids, which had been destroyed by a landslide in 373; and finally, to set up a statue of Dionysus in a holy grotto and honor the god with a sacrifice and a choral competition.

The reference to the new temple of Apollo, built between 370 and 320 BCE, might be said to provide the key to Philodamus' song, since its decorations parallel the syncretistic program of the paean on significant points. Whereas the east pediment of the new temple displayed the usual Apollo *kitharōdos*, accompanied by Artemis, Leto, and the Muses, the decorations of the west pediment showed Helios, Thyades (maenads), and a Dionysus who holds a *kithara* and lacks any trace of that ecstatic mobility which is typical of this god and which the presence of the Thyades would lead one to expect. Furthermore, this Dionysus is not clad in any of his usual garments, but "wears the heavy, high-belted, full-length chiton and cloak of Apollo *kitharōdos*" (Stewart 1982: 209). If we are here indeed dealing with a Dionysus Musagetes ("leader of the Muses"), as seems likely, mirroring the Apollo Musagetes of the east pediment, then the song of Philodamus and his brothers can plausibly be read as an *aition* for this arrangement: the syncretistic paean supports the syncretistic decorations and vice versa. Apollo's approval, in the song, of Dionysian paeans as well as his instructions regarding the new temple, involving the accommodation of a cult of Dionysus within the precinct, provides an explanation for the iconographical syncretism of the temple decorations. The decorations meanwhile, there for all to see and made to last, lend a tangible and lasting authority to the divinely sanctioned song.

The ideological project supported by Philodamus' song may also have had a political dimension, because the push toward a closer association of Apollo and Dionysus at Delphi probably came from one specific direction: from Athens. On a very general level our paean, as a poem celebrating a god that provides an *aition* for the building of a temple to Apollo, invites comparison with the indirect pro-Athenian propaganda constituted by the "aetiological" references in the *Homeric Hymn to Apollo* (56, 76, 80, 253–60, 285–93) to the temple of Apollo erected by Pisistratus at Delos (Burkert 1979; Aloni 1989: 47–61). It is a fact that Athenian artists, Praxias and Androsthenes, were in charge of the iconographic planning of Apollo's new temple at Delphi, and there is evidence to suggest that Praxias was also involved in the decoration of the temple of Dionysus at Thasos; this temple featured a Dionysus *kitharōdos* dressed in the garb of Apollo Musagetes and surrounded by personifications of tragedy, comedy, and dithyramb, i.e., in the role of patron of the performative arts which he held most prominently and iconically in Athens. It is not implausible that at Delphi, too, the promotion of Dionysus in a role which hitherto had been reserved for Apollo was essentially an Athenian project (Vamvouri 2004: 200–7).

Athenaeus, Limenius, Aristonous

Other Hellenistic paeans whose religious discourse is interwoven with politics are two texts which were inscribed on the Athenian Treasury at Delphi, one by an Athenaeus (45 Käppel; on the name, see Bélis 1988), the other by Limenius (46 Käppel). The latter advertised itself as "the paean and prosodion to the god which the Athenian Limenius, son of Thoinos, composed and performed to the lyre." The prosodion or "processional song" is not physically marked off from the paean but unquestionably starts in the middle of line 33. Both parts (so the introduction implies) were to be sung to the lyre (D'Alessio 1997: 30) and interlinear musical annotation is provided throughout to facilitate future performance. Next to Limenius' song stood an inscription in prose (*Feuilles de Delphi* 3.2.47.22) which functioned somewhat like the framing elements of Isyllus' integrated text: it includes Limenius in a list of *technitai Dionysou* ("artists of Dionysus") who in 128/127 BCE participated in the Pythais, a ritual procession from Athens to Delphi organized by the Athenians. This context suits the prosodion as well as the lines of the paean that present the *technitai* singing the paean (19–21):

Παιήονα κικλήισκ[ομεν ἅπας
λ]αὸς αὐ[το]χθόνων ἠδὲ Βάκχου μέγας θυρσοπλὴ[ξ
ἑσμὸς ἱ]ερὸς τεχνιτῶν ἔνοικος πόλει Κεκροπίαι.

Paian we celebrate, we the entire nation of autochthonous people and the great sacred thyrsus-banging throng of artists of Bacchus living in the city of Cecrops.

These lines stand between a description of Apollo's stay in Attica during his voyage from his birthplace Delos (13–19) and the narration of the rest of his voyage to Delphi (21–33), and thus also at the level of the inscription function as a *trait d'union* between Athens and Delphi. The Athenian stop-over is otherwise only mentioned at *Eumenides* 9–11, where the scholiast comments that Aeschylus included it to "flatter" Athens. The text of the paean also advertises Apollo's connection with Athens in other places. At 6–7, Leto holds a branch of olive, symbol of Athena and Athens, against the pains of childbirth (contrast *h.Ap.* 117–18 and Call. *h.* 4.210, where Leto holds a palm branch). At 15–17, the Athenians, and not the Delphians, seemingly invent the address παιὰν ἰὲ παιάν to, as they welcome the god's arrival in Attica with *kithara*-songs that present an *aition* for the *technitai*'s performances in the Pythais. And last but not least, the Athenians are presented as an autochthonous Greek race of peaceful farmers (19–20, 13–14), the very opposite of the wandering Gauls, the warlike barbarians (31–2) whom Apollo turned away from Delphi (in 278/277 BCE).

The objectives of Athenaeus' paean seem to have been less ambitious. This text too includes musical annotation and it resembles Limenius' paean in structure. Both paeans start with a long invocation to the Muses, inviting them to come, and praise Apollo (Limenius 1–5, Athenaeus 1–8), while the last part of Athenaeus' paean that survives (19–27; the stone is in a bad condition), just like the final section of Limenius' paean (23–33) associates Apollo's killing of the dragon Pytho (the foundation myth of Delphi) with the god's defeat of the Gauls. The middle sections differ. Athenaeus does not seem to have dealt with the journey of Apollo from Delos to Delphi and his stop-over at Athens but to have included instead a lengthy self-description of the *technitai*, who present the Athenians as worshipping and themselves as playing the *kithara* for Apollo at Delphi (9–18). The *technitai*'s song for Apollo (16) parallels the songs sung for him by the Muses in the opening section (4), and the architecture of the passage as a whole recalls *Homeric Hymn to Apollo* 146–76, where we find a description of a blissful gathering of Ionians at the festival of Apollo at Delos next to a description of the chorus of Delian maidens and an authorial self-reference (Lonsdale 1993: 68–70).

As we saw, the longer remains of Limenius' inscription include at the end some lines which its preface calls a prosodion. In these lines, the singer asks Apollo to assist and protect Athens and support the military power of Rome (33–40). The setup of the song as a whole (a paean closing with a prosodion) and the content of the prosodion (a prayer for the wellbeing of the patron city) have a parallel in Pindar's *Paean* 6 (Snell and Maehler 1964 = D6 Rutherford 2001a), a text composed for a Delphic Theoxenia that has survived on papyrus. Here the lacunose final section (123–83) is marked off by an *asteriskos* and identified as a prosodion in a scholion to line 124. It is certainly concerned with Aegina and its local hero, Aeacus, and very likely contained a prayer to the gods involved in the Theoxenia for Aegina's wellbeing (so D'Alessio and Ferrari 1988; D'Alessio 1997: 49–59).

The precise relationship between the poems of Limenius and Athenaeus cannot be established with certainty. Were both performed on the same occasion or does Athenaeus' paean belong to another Pythais, for example the previous one of 138 BCE? The inscription honoring the *technitai* participating in the Pythais of 128 includes, together with Limenius, an "Athenaeus son of Athenaeus," whom it is tempting to identify with the author of the preserved paean. The main objection to this identification is that Athenaeus' paean is very similar in wording, topoi, and music to Limenius' paean: it would be odd if two so similar songs had been performed at the same festival by the same *technitai*. A text for the Pythais of 97 BCE throws some light at least on the similarity of the compositions in referring to the song performed by the *technitai* on that occasion as πάτριος παιάν, "the traditional paian." The paeans of Athenaeus and Limenius indeed look like variations on an established pattern (Furley and Bremer 2001: 130–1). Yet their variance in the middle section (Athenaeus 9–18, Limenius 6–22) is substantial and significant. Limenius' paean emphasizes the connection between Athens and Apollo in the past, focusing on the celebration of Apollo's coming to Athens with the first paean. With this it provides an *aition* for the Athenian *technitai*'s singing of paeans to Apollo in Delphi, the focus of Athenaeus' paean, which emphasizes the connection between Athens and Apollo in the present. Regardless of whether the two paeans were performed on the same occasion, it seems plausible that they were inscribed on the Treasury together because they complement each other as propaganda for the city and *technitai* of Athens. What is more, it cannot be ruled out that the particle δέ in the preface to Limenius' paean (Παιὰν δὲ καὶ π[ροσό]διον, κτλ.) points to a placement close to Athenaeus' (earlier) text, inviting a complementary reading of the two inscriptions.

A third paean to Apollo, composed by Aristonous of Corinth, was found close to the Athenian Treasury (42 Käppel). Although its inscription, which dates to the fourth or third century BCE, cannot be linked to the Treasury with certainty, the discourse of this paean too seems to have an Athenian dimension. The prose preface resembles that of the paean of Philodamus and his brothers, stating that the Delphians endorsed Aristonous' paean by awarding him many privileges (proxeny for him and his offspring, preferential consultation of the oracle, etc.). The paean itself emphasizes Apollo's gratitude for favors he receives, using myth as a paradigm for present worship. In its treatment of Apollo's coming to Delphi, a standard theme we already saw in Limenius, it focuses on the help provided to the god by Athena, who advised him to go to Delphi and persuaded Gaia and Themis to let him take over their oracle (19–24), and on the honors with which he thanked her for her assistance, to wit a share in his Delphic cult as "Athena Pronaia" (25–32). After outlining Apollo's gratitude to Athena, Aristonous adds that in fact many immortals – Poseidon, the Corycian Nymphs, Dionysus, Artemis – bestowed gifts on Apollo, enhancing the prestige of his cult (33–40). The logical connection is not made explicit, but it is clearly implied that these gods give gifts because Apollo is a grateful god who knows how to reciprocate. This idea is applied to the present in the next and final strophe (41–8), where the author presents himself and other singers of this song also as givers of gifts, which he hopes will be reciprocated: "May you find favor with our songs, o ie Paian, and always give us wealth obtained with decency and grace me with your protection" (χαρεὶς ὕμνοις ἡμετέροις, / ὄλβον ἐξ ὁσίων διδοὺς / ἀεὶ καὶ σώιζων ἐφέποις / ἡμᾶς, ὦ ἰὲ Παιάν, 44–8).

This commerce of favors between singer and god in a hymnic context (*do ut des*) recalls the *Homeric Hymns*, but by selecting the cult of Athena Pronaia as his key example of Apollo's generosity, Aristonous has focused the topos in a very specific way. It is commonly assumed that this emphasis reflects a pro-Athenian agenda, not in the last place because both the prominence of Athena Pronaia and Aristonous' list of other gods associated with Delphic Apollo recall the prayer of the priestess of Delphic Apollo which opens Aeschylus' *Eumenides* (1–33, cf. esp. 21–9). But if this is true it is strange that Athens is never mentioned in the paean. It is possible that Aristonous, a Corinthian, was simply inspired by the construction at Delphi of a new porch to Athena Pronaia (Vamvouri 2004: 212–16).

Tentative Conclusions

For the Archaic and Classical periods we have no archaeological or testimonial evidence for paeans inscribed on stone. Paeans such as those composed by Pindar and Bacchylides were transmitted through performance, oral transmission, and probably a manuscript tradition of some sort; there is no reason to believe they were ever inscribed. Yet their commissioners were surely no less concerned with durability than their fourth-century and Hellenistic counterparts. A plausible reason why these texts were inscribed seems to me that their authors or patrons were less prepared than their predecessors to rely on re-performance as a sole or primary means of preservation. This might also explain the elaborate contextualization of the songs, which provides a key to a propagandistic subtext which might not have been so obvious in later re-performances. The texts of Isyllus, Philodamus, Athenaeus, Limenius, and Aristonous all show more or less complex strategies of self-legitimation and contextualization. All in one way or another establish their own authority. Some of them thematize and justify hymning a god other than Apollo, the original addressee of paeans. Some reserve much space for promoting the author or patron. Some include, either within the paean or in an accompanying text, the rules of the ceremony in which they were or are supposed to be performed. This last element may perhaps be compared to Callimachus' presentation, in his hymns to Apollo, Athena, and Demeter, of the celebration of a god at a festival through a "master of ceremony" (*h.* 2, 5, 6), or to his re-use of sacred *nomoi* especially in the hymn to Apollo (on which see I. Petrovic forthcoming). But it may also draw on the tendency in Pindar's victory odes "to represent the poet as creating the song as the audience hears it" and mimic "the performance as experience" in the text of the song (Carey 1995: 100 and 101; see also Slater 1969; Pfeijffer 1999).

The odd one out among the songs discussed in this chapter is the *Erythraean Paean*, the oldest of the epigraphic paeans. Although it too subtly justifies the singing of paeans to Asclepius, it is by far the least contextualized and most generic paean of the series, easily separable from (and in later versions indeed separated from) the religious law that accompanies its earliest incarnation. I have suggested above that the conformity to generic rules and sheer simplicity of this paean may be a stratagem rather than a sign of literary poverty, as has often been assumed. It would be wrong to conclude on the basis of this text that after the fifth century religious poetry became less concerned with its function and occasion of performance, or more broadly its social setting. While the conditions for the composition and performance of religious poetry changed in the fourth and third centuries – as did the position of authors, patrons, and sanctuaries – context remains a vital concern in these poems and crucial to the interpretation of their underlying messages. In this respect they are not far removed from the topicality of the paeans of Pindar and Bacchylides or from the self-propaganda which Pisistratus or Polycrates managed to include in the *Homeric Hymn to Apollo*.

Perhaps more typically Hellenistic in these paeans is their tendency toward self-conscious innovation, intertextuality, self-justification, and self-reflection. This is not to say that we should imagine their poets as local Callimachuses, eager to construct a new poetics and redefine the genre (Kolde 2002/3: 163). What we can see at work in these poems is a general awareness of contemporary poetic trends and techniques in conjunction with a pronounced concern with contextualization. Their "reality effects" differ somewhat from those pursued in "high" poetry in hexameters and elegiacs which represents the experience of taking part in a religious festival, such as Theocritus' *Adoniazusae* (*Id.* 15) and Callimachus' hymns to Apollo, Athena, and Demeter, poems whose "realism" is at least in part fictional (Bulloch in this volume). Yet the concern with realism per se is shared, and these poems likewise brim with encomiastic elements and politically charged discourse. We should therefore perhaps not rule out the possibility that, in its concern with politics and contextualization, the fictionalized festival poetry of authors such as Callimachus and Theocritus reflects religious poetry such as the paeans discussed in this chapter, that is to say, poetry composed for actual religious festivals.

FURTHER READING

The most comprehensive edition of the paeans and other religious lyric poems from the Hellenistic Age is still Powell 1925. All the paeans have been re-edited in Käppel 1992, with testimonia for the genre and extensive bibliography, and most of them also appear in Furley and Bremer 2001, with English translations and commentary.

Good surveys of the genre, from the Archaic to the Hellenistic Age, are provided by Käppel 1992 and Rutherford 2001a. Käppel's analyses of the *Erythraean Paean* and Philodamus' paean should be read with the qualifications of Schröder 1999. See also Vollgraff 1924–27, Reiner 1975, and Stewart 1982. For the political implications of the paeans of Limenius, Athenaeus, Philodamus, and Aristonous, see especially Vamvouri 2004 (on Limenius, already Vamvouri 1998); on Limenius and Athenaeus, see further Bélis 1988. For Isyllus' inscription, Kolde 2003 is fundamental; see also Kolde 2002/3, Sineux 1999, Stehle 1997: 132–7, Wilamowitz 1886. For a survey of Greek sacred laws, see Lupu 2005: 3–112.

CHAPTER FOURTEEN

Aratus

Katharina Volk

Students are often surprised to learn that Aratus of Soloi was one of the most popular writers of antiquity. His *Phaenomena* was hailed by contemporaries, quickly became a school text, gave rise to an extensive commentary tradition, and continued to be widely studied into the Middle Ages. It also engaged the imagination of Roman writers like no other Greek work, inspiring an unparalleled number of Latin translations and imitations. To modern tastes this success is hard to understand. How is it possible that readers from Callimachus to Cicero and beyond were so fascinated by a poem on constellations and weather signs, a subject matter that, as Quintilian observed, "is without liveliness, variety, emotions, characters, or a single speech" (*Inst.* 10.1.55; not entirely correct: the character Dike delivers a short speech in 123–6)? The fact that we are so well informed about the *Phaenomena*'s reception makes it harder for us to look at the poem without prejudice; how can we abstract from what we know about the reactions of, say, Hipparchus or Ovid? As far as his modern readers are concerned, Aratus is a poet undone by his own success.

If we try to understand not what became of Aratus but where he was coming from, we also run into problems. The ancient biographical evidence (surveyed by Martin 1998: xi–xlviii) does not allow us to construct a coherent picture of the intellectual and political context of Aratus' work. It is reasonably well established that the poet spent time in Athens consorting with early Stoics such as Zeno and Persaeus, and that he accepted an invitation to the court of Antigonus Gonatas in the early 270s. Yet we are unable to trace the influence of specific individuals or circumstances on Aratus' poetry. As for the literary affiliations of the *Phaenomena*, the work's apparent originality may to some extent be a mirage: it is possible that Aratus was the first to write a scientific didactic poem based on prose sources, but we know next to nothing of the didactic poetry of the fourth century, and what appears as innovation may well have been part of an ongoing trend. Finally, the identity of Aratus' sources themselves remains controversial: Jean Martin has recently challenged the *communis opinio* (in place since Hipparchus) that the astronomical part of the poem is based on Eudoxus' *Phaenomena* and *Enoptron*, maintaining that the "Eudoxan" quotes in Hipparchus' commentary come from a work that postdates Aratus (1998: lxxxvi–cxxv). Regarding the section on weather signs, numerous theories have addressed its source and its relationship to the pseudo-Theophrastan *On Weather Signs*; David Sider now suggests that, like the first part of the poem, it is based on Eudoxus, who may have treated both astronomy and meteorology in the same work (Sider and Brunschön 2007: 16–18 and 42).

Reading Aratus through his reception runs the risk of introducing anachronisms, while viewing him in his historical and cultural context is made difficult by the dearth of evidence. In this chapter I will therefore concentrate largely on the poem itself and through a discussion of a (necessarily limited) number of its features attempt to arrive at a general understanding of what the *Phaenomena* "is about," before concluding with a brief look at the work's later fortune.

As has often been pointed out, there are fundamentally three ways of interpreting the poem's character and purpose. An obvious first approach is to view it as a manual intended to teach astronomy and forecasting the weather. Within the text, the poet explicitly instructs an anonymous student in these arts, which – as he points out repeatedly – are especially useful to those engaged in agriculture and navigation. While it is fairly obvious that this is a conceit and that Aratus was not writing for actual farmers and sailors (compare Magnelli in this volume on Nicander), it is perfectly possible to use his poem, especially the first part, as a genuine source of information, and generations of Greek and Roman schoolchildren actually learned their constellations from the *Phaenomena*. Still, the poem was clearly not intended as a textbook, and while the history of its use as such is interesting (Why was a poem used for teaching a scientific subject?), it must not distract us from trying to understand the text itself.

If the *Phaenomena* is not serious about teaching astronomy, is it instead simply a bravura piece of verbal art? This second interpretation, which casts Aratus as an aesthete first and foremost interested in creating a charming and original poem, is characteristic of the school of thought that considers Hellenistic poetry primarily sophisticated play and art for art's sake. Whether this is viewed as positive or negative depends largely on the taste of the individual critic: Kroll (1925: 1847–50) delivers a famous and amusing piece of Aratus-bashing, while Fakas (2001) puts a more positive spin on the poet's perceived aestheticism.

Most scholars agree, however, that rather than being straightforwardly didactic or playfully formalist, the *Phaenomena* is expressive of larger themes that have to do with the nature of the universe and the place of man in this world (Erren 1967; Effe 1977a: 40–56; Fantuzzi and Hunter 2004: 224–45; Hunter 2008a: 1.153–88). Individual readings of this third type differ considerably, but some kind of "philosophical" interpretation (in the widest sense) appears to be the most common approach to the poem today. The following observations fall in the same category.

The Song and Manner of Hesiod

One of the earliest critical responses to the *Phaenomena*, and by far the most famous, is an epigram by Callimachus (27 Pf. = 56 GP), whose first two-and-a-half lines run as follows:

> Ἡσιόδου τό τ' ἄεισμα καὶ ὁ τρόπος· οὐ τὸν ἀοιδὸν
> ἔσχατον ἀλλ' ὀκνέω μὴ τὸ μελιχρότατον
> τῶν ἐπέων ὁ Σολεὺς ἀπεμάξατο.

> The song and the manner are Hesiod's. The man from Soloi has not copied the singer to his full extent but has without a doubt wiped off the honey-sweetest of his verse.

The poet's typically opaque language and complex syntax have given rise to heated scholarly discussions that are closely bound up with beliefs about Hellenistic aesthetic ideas and "Callimachean" poetics. Many critics have understood the phrase τὸν ἀοιδὸν ἔσχατον (or, with Scaliger's emendation, τὸν ἀοιδῶν ἔσχατον) as "the ultimate poet" and interpreted it as referring to Homer (Reitzenstein 1931: 42–6; Reinsch-Werner 1976: 9–12). On this reading, the epigram is evidence for the supposed preference of Hellenistic poets (especially Callimachus) for Hesiod over Homer as a poetic model, on the grounds that no one could rival Homer anyway. Aratus would thus be commended for his prudent choice of imitating the sweetest poet while leaving alone the best. This interpretation is suspect on linguistic grounds alone, however, and it is far preferable to understand τὸν ἀοιδὸν ἔσχατον as "the poet to the very end," i.e., to his full extent (Kaibel 1894: 120–3; Gow and Page 1965 *ad loc.*; Cameron 1995a: 374–9): Aratus did not follow Hesiod in everything, but "skimmed off" (ἀπεμάξατο) only particularly attractive features of his poetry. As we shall see, this makes excellent sense as a description of Aratus' eclectic practice of imitation and in no way implies that he – or, for that matter, Callimachus or any other Hellenistic poet or critic – considered Hesiod an *a priori* more eligible model, whether as opposed to Homer (who plays no role in the epigram) or anybody else.

But what makes the *Phaenomena* a Hesiodic poem? Callimachus' designation need mean little more than that it is a didactic poem, a genre believed to have originated with Hesiod. However, more detailed examination shows that Aratus consciously endeavored to create his own version specifically of the *Works and Days*, at points adhering closely to his Archaic model, at others deviating from it (Fakas 2001). On a purely stylistic level, his metrical practice is remarkably similar to Hesiod's (Porter 1946), even though his choice of vocabulary is very much indebted to Homer: Aratus rejoices in employing rare Homeric words in new and surprising contexts (Ludwig 1963: 442–5; Kidd 1997: 24–5) and he even attempts to mimic the Homeric *Kunstsprache* by inventing archaic-sounding morphological variants (Kroll 1925: 1849–50; Kidd 1997: 25–6). As we can still tell from the biographical sources, ancient critics were therefore undecided whether Aratus might not be an emulator of Homer rather than Hesiod (*Vitae* 2 and 4 in Martin 1974, pp. 12.7–18 and 21.7–8; Reitzenstein 1931: 43–4).

In terms of content, however, the parallels to the *Works and Days* are clear. Both poems fall into two parts – *Works* followed by *Days* vis-à-vis *Phaenomena* followed by *Diosemeiai* – while also employing a kind of agglutinative method of composition, by which new topics are "tacked on" without readily apparent motivation (Fakas 2001: 66–84). Both Hesiod and Aratus address themselves, at least nominally, to farmers and sailors, offering instructions to help them do their jobs more successfully. At the same time, it is clear that the ultimate topic of their works is the human condition in general: both the Archaic poet and his Hellenistic follower endeavor to explain why life is the way it is and how human beings ought to deal with it. Both ascribe a central role to Zeus as the power that has brought about and is in charge of the current state of affairs.

Apart from these large-scale similarities, the nitty-gritty concerns of the *Works and Days* and the *Phaenomena* are mostly different: Hesiod chides his brother, offers advice to the kings, and gives instructions on farming, while Aratus describes in detail the constellations and the various methods of foretelling the weather to an anonymous addressee. Hesiod's use of equinoxes and solstices and the rising and setting of constellations to mark the seasons would appear to be an interesting parallel to Aratus' topics, but this particular practice is for the most part only implied in the *Phaenomena*. There are but two passages in Aratus where the poet engages closely with comparable sections of Hesiod. These are the proem with its hymn to Zeus (1–18), which harks back to the beginning of the *Works and Days* (1–10), and the myth of Dike (96–136), an amalgam of Hesiod's account of the races of men (*WD* 109–201) and his description of the "maiden Dike" as a guardian of justice (*WD* 220–62). Both passages are central to the worldview of the *Phaenomena* and have been much discussed (on the proem, see Erren 1967: 9–31; Fakas 2001: 5–66; on Dike, Schiesaro 1996; Fakas 2001: 149–75; Bellandi, Berti, and Ciappi 2001). They cannot be treated in detail here, but the general difference in outlook between Hesiod and Aratus will become clear in what follows.

A World Full of Signs

Aratus famously begins his poem "from Zeus, whom men never leave unmentioned" and who is said to fill the roads, squares, sea, and harbors (1–4). He, whose progeny we are (5), "kindly gives propitious signs to humans" (ὁ δ' ἤπιος ἀνθρώποιϲι / δεξιὰ ϲημαίνει, 5–6), with the intention of rousing them to work; in particular, he has fixed the stars as signs (ϲήματα, 10) in the sky, so that they might signal (ϲημαίνοιεν, 12) the appropriate times for agricultural activities (10–13). Because of all this Zeus is worthy of worship, and the poet calls upon him (14–16) before turning to the Muses and asking them for assistance with his song about the stars (16–18).

In addition to announcing the poem's topic, this proem neatly states the *Phaenomena*'s conception of the world as a cosmos full of benevolent signs from an omnipresent god who has the welfare of human beings at heart. The contrast to Hesiod could not be more pronounced: Zeus as described in the proem to the *Works and Days* (3–7) is all-powerful, but his ability to raise and oppress human beings at will is threatening rather than reassuring, and in hiding the livelihood of men (42, 47, 50), he acts in a manner diametrically opposed to that of Aratus' Zeus, who by means of his propitious signs "reminds people of their livelihood" (μιμνήϲκων βιότοιο, 7; Hunter 2008a: 1.157–8).

Scholars have often characterized the worldview of the proem, and of the *Phaenomena* as a whole, as fundamentally Stoic (Erren 1967; Gee 2000: 70–91; White in this volume; differently Fakas 2001; Lewis 1992: 105–8; Bulloch in this volume). After all, the Stoics identified Zeus with the fiery *logos* or *pneuma* that is present throughout the cosmos, shaping and directing everything according to divine *pronoia*. This belief is in evidence in Cleanthes' *Hymn to Zeus*, which is contemporary to the *Phaenomena* and shows a number of similarities to its proem (James 1972; Bulloch and White in this volume). As we have seen, the biographical tradition, too, associates Aratus with members of the Stoic school, and later readers of the *Phaenomena* clearly interpreted the poem as a Stoic text (Lewis 1992: 105–8).

However, while there are certainly similarities to and affinities with Stoic ideas, the philosophy of the poem can hardly be described as orthodox Stoicism (and note at any rate that, as Hunter 2008a: 1.158–9 points out, Stoic dogma was probably still being developed at the time Aratus was writing). Unlike Cleanthes, Aratus does not use typical Stoic vocabulary (Lewis 1992: 107, with n.41), and his cosmology shows crucial differences from the Stoic view. Stoic natural philosophy is characterized by pantheism: the god ("Zeus") is everywhere in the sense that he physically permeates the universe, which is entirely material and forms an unbroken continuum. Despite scholars' repeated claims to the contrary (James 1972: 36; Kidd 1997: 10; Gee 2000: 72–3), this view is absent from the *Phaenomena*. When Aratus observes that all roads, squares, and harbors as well as the sea are "full of Zeus" (μεϲταὶ/ἡ Διόϲ, 2–3), he is referring not to a physical presence but to the god's interaction with human beings (Erren 1967: 18–19; Martin 1998 *ad loc.*). The places enumerated are not features of the natural world as much as areas of human activity. This is true even for the sea, which was no doubt chosen qua locus of navigation and forms a pair with the harbors: the sea leads to the harbors as the roads lead to the squares. Any human activity, Aratus stipulates, depends on the support of Zeus: "at all times we are all in need of Zeus" (πάντη δὲ Διὸϲ κεχρήμεθα πάντεϲ, 4); and this unending support consists in the propitious signs given by the god (10–13). This is a far cry from Stoic physics: instead of physical continuity, we have a continuity of communication.

The idea of the sign is central to the *Phaenomena*, as is apparent from the fact that forms of the noun ϲῆμα (*sēma*, pl. *sēmata*) "sign" appear 47 times in the course of the poem, those of the verb (ἐπι)ϲημαίνω "to signal" 11 times. The near-obsessive repetition of these and similar keywords – another frequent one is (ἐπι)τεκμαίρομαι "to conjecture on the base of a sign" (15 times) – drives home the message that Aratus is not interested in natural phenomena (e.g., the constellations) as such, but only in as much as they are part of the cosmic system of signs that has its origin in the benevolence of Zeus. In Aratus' universe, we are constantly confronted with signs that speak to us and, if we but know how to listen, signal important information.

But what exactly is the signified of Aratus' signs? It very much depends – and it is not always entirely clear. In the proem, Zeus is said to have fixed the stars in the sky to signpost agricultural activities, which would point to the use of the risings and settings of individual constellations as seasonal markers, a time-honored practice that we see reflected in Hesiod's *Works and Days* and in the Greek and Roman farmer's almanac-type astrometeorological calendars known as *parapēgmata* (on this tradition, see Lehoux 2007). However, when describing the constellations, Aratus makes only occasional mention of this use of the stars or indeed of their seasonal risings and settings (149–55, 158–9, 264–7, 285–310, 329–37); only later, and then very much in passing, does he refer to the possibility of marking the seasons by means of the stars, taking the morning rising of Arcturus as his example (741–51).

In the course of his description of the constellations (which has often been compared to an ecphrasis of a work of art and which the poet may very well have composed with an actual star globe in hand), Aratus often uses the word *sēma* to refer to a star or star group in its capacity, not as a sign for something outside the sky (the beginning of the plowing season, say), but as a pointer to something within the sky, for example, another constellation (which in turn, of course, has the potential to be a sign for something else). Consider, for example, the following description of the head of Taurus (168–71):

τὰ δέ οἱ μάλ' ἐοικότα cήματα κεῖται,
τοίη οἱ κεφαλὴ διακέκριται· οὐδέ τις ἄλλωι
cήματι τεκμήραιτο κάρη βοός, οἷά μιν αὐτοὶ
ἀcτέρες ἀμφοτέρωθεν ἑλιccόμενοι τυπόωcι.

The way the head is marked out, there are very clear signs for that. And one need not conjecture the head of the Bull by any other sign, given how the revolving stars themselves model it on both sides.

Usually, Aratus enables the reader to find a constellation by explaining its spatial relationship to another one, which acts as its sign, as in the following (246–7):

Ἀνδρομέδηc δέ τοι ὦμοc ἀριcτερὸc Ἰχθύοc ἔcτω
cῆμα βορειοτέρου· μάλα γάρ νύ οἱ ἐγγύθεν ἐcτίν.

Let the left shoulder of Andromeda be your sign for the more northerly Fish, for it is very close to it.

With the Bull, such an external sign is not needed, as the stars that make up the constellation are sufficiently clear as signs on their own, defining the outline of the head in such a way that it is obvious to any observer. However, in both cases we are dealing with signs of signs: while the constellations themselves are, it is implied, signs of (for instance) seasonal change, human beings are also in need of, as it were, secondary signs in order to be able to identify the more important signs in the first place.

The idea of the secondary sign returns in the section on simultaneous risings and settings (559–732). Aratus explains that one can tell time at night by observing the risings of the signs of the zodiac (of which six rise in the course of every night). Since, however, the zodiacal constellations may well be obscured at the moment they come over the horizon, the poet recommends watching out also for stars that rise (or set) at exactly the same time: these, he says, will be useful signs (565), for they point at the signs of the zodiac, which in turn signal the time of night.

After a short transitional passage about the phases of the moon and the seasons of the year, Aratus in line 758 turns to the topic of weather signs. In this discussion, unlike in the preceding astronomical section, every sign is immediately correlated with its significance: a slender and clear moon on the third day forecasts good weather (783–4), cackling chickens predict rain (960–2), etc. Part of the poet's treatment is even arranged, not by sign, but by signified, that is, by type of weather (909–1043: signs for wind, rain, fair weather, and storm). Generally speaking, then, in the course of the *Phaenomena* Aratus' signs become more and more concrete, just as they become more lowly and commonplace. We start with the constellations, whose status as signs is repeatedly asserted but rarely explained, while the poet dwells instead on what I have called secondary signs. We then move to the observation of everyday environments, objects, and especially animals, whose signification, if we believe Aratus, is entirely straightforward. It has been argued that this movement from the theoretical ("there are signs everywhere") to the practical ("here are a few dozen specific signs") has a protreptic function: Aratus introduces the student into his world full of signs and gradually accustoms him to observing and making use of these signs himself (Erren 1967: 227–64). Fittingly, the poem ends with an exhortation to watch out for signs at all times (1142–54). If we do so, we will "never make a conjecture in vain" (οὐδέποτε cχεδίωc κεν ... τεκμήραιο, 1154); we will always be able to count on the unceasing communication from Zeus.

The *Phaenomena* is all about signs: not about imparting a body of knowledge about specific signs, but about the idea of signification itself. Aratus may give us a fairly complete description of the constellations and an at least rather extensive catalogue of weather signs (which he himself once interrupts with the rhetorical question, "Why should I tell you all the signs there are for humans?" 1036–7). However (and despite its later reception), the purpose of the poem is not to provide a full course in astronomy or meteorology. As Richard Hunter puts it, "'didactic poetry' does not have to be comprehensive to be 'didactic'" (2008a: 1.174); by selectively treating only part of a specific scientific field, Aratus makes the larger point that nature is an infinite divine sign system.

But what, we may ask, are the theoretical underpinnings of Aratus' semiotics? This question is by no means anachronistic. Greek thinkers, especially in the Hellenistic period, were deeply concerned with the nature of signification and with the relationship between the sign and its signified, or, as they typically thought of it, that which can be inferred from it (Manetti 1993; Allen 2001; Barnouw 2002). A crucial question was whether sign and signified necessarily had to be in a causal relationship or whether a sign was simply that which repeated observation had shown to accompany or precede a given phenomenon. The topic is discussed in Cicero's dialogue *On Divination*, where the author's interlocutor, his brother Quintus, sticks to the empirical position while he himself upholds the necessity of causal explanation (Hankinson 1988a; Lehoux 2006). In the course of his exposition, Quintus quotes a number of passages from his brother's own translation of the weather signs section of the *Astronomica*, arguing that these signs are valid even though it is quite unclear how, if at all, they physically relate to the outcomes they predict (*Div.* 1.13–16). In Cicero's view, Aratus' signs are at the very heart of the debate.

But what about the *Phaenomena* itself? On the whole, Aratus gives little indication how the signs he describes relate to the phenomena they signify. As we have seen, he does not even always indicate exactly *what* they signify, and in the grand scheme of his poem, the fact that there *is* ubiquitous signification is more important than what each of the single innumerable signs actually has to tell us. However, once we look more closely, we find that signification is in fact presented in a wide variety of ways. Most signs are simply signs, but some of them actually appear to be caused by the very (meteorological) phenomena they predict. Thus, for example, when the sun's center is very bright, but its rays are dispersed to the south and north (829–30), this may be because it "is passing through either rain or wind" (831). The bad weather causes the sun to look the way it does, which is why in turn its appearance can serve as a sign of bad weather (cf. also 787, 798, 834–5, 874–6, 1006–7). Conversely, a sign may be the cause of its signified: the Kids and Capella, for example, are said to "put into motion" (κινῆcαι, 682) storms (cf. also 816–17, 838–9, 887–8, 1084–5). On a few occasions, a sign appears to work by analogy. Thus, both hens (961–2) and ravens (966–7) are said to imitate the sound of approaching rain with their cries, while the fruit-bearing patterns of mastich and squill mirror those of the harvest (1044–63) and the arrival of the crane coincides with the arrival of winter (1075–81).

At some fundamental level, of course, all signs can be traced back to the agency of Zeus, and Aratus comes back periodically to the god's role as the ultimate giver of signs (264–7, 741–3, 769–72, 963–6). But other figures are credited with giving signs as well, including Dionysus (71–3), personified Night (408–12, 418–19), and the gods in general (732), and on a number of occasions the signs themselves are said to communicate with humans, for example, the moon, which "teaches" (734, 793) and "speaks to" (739, 773) its observers (cf. 775–6, 1048, 1071). Most strikingly, at least some of the animate signs are readers of signs in their own right: the calves, whose behavior serves as a weather sign for humans, themselves "conjecture" (τεκμαίρονται, 1121) the arrival of a storm, as does the dog, which behaves as it does because it "expects" (δοκεύων, 1136) a particular kind of weather.

In a properly Stoic universe, all these phenomena could be explained with reference to the world's physical continuity, in which everything is connected to everything else by the principle of *sympatheia* and everything happens according to an unbroken chain of cause and effect. Aratus' universe is compatible with the Stoic universe, but it is not described in Stoic terms. Rather than offering a coherent theory of the link between sign and signified, or between sign and signifying agent, the poet concentrates instead on the fact of signification itself. His attitude may be expressed in the line that concludes the discussion of weather signs (1141), where mice are described as desiring rest at the approach of rain, ὅτ' ὄμβρου cήματα φαίνει. The reading φαίνει is not unanimously transmitted (though preferable to the variant φαίνοι), and it is unclear how the verb is to be construed. But as there is no other possible subject, it is probably best to take cήματα as a nominative and posit an unparalleled impersonal use of the verb (Kidd 1997 and Martin 1998 *ad loc.*): cήματα φαίνει thus simply means "signs show." This, in a nutshell, is the message of the *Phaenomena*.

Signs and the Poet

It is Aratus' avowed purpose to "speak of the stars" (17) and to tell his students at least some of the overwhelmingly many signs that exist for the benefit of human beings (1036–7). Just as the world is a continuum of signification, the *Phaenomena*, too, is full of signs that are made apparent (φαινόμενα) by the poet. The text is thus a microcosm of the universe it describes (Gee 2000: 70–91; Hunter 2008a: 1.160–6), and scholars have pointed in particular to one passage where Aratus appears to comment self-consciously on the process of identifying and interpreting signs that his work endeavors to teach. This is the famous acrostic in lines 783–7, first identified by Jean-Marie Jacques in 1960 (see also Levitan 1979; Haslam 1992):

> **Λ**επτὴ μὲν καθαρή τε περὶ τρίτον ἦμαρ ἐοῦϲα
> **Ε**ὔδιόϲ κ' εἴη, λεπτὴ δὲ καὶ εὖ μάλ' ἐρευθὴϲ
> **Π**νευματίη, παχίων δὲ καὶ ἀμβλείῃϲι κεραίαιϲ
> **Τ**έτρατον ἐκ τριτάτοιο φόωϲ ἀμενηνὸν ἔχουϲα
> **Η** νότωι ἄμβλυνται ἢ ὕδατοϲ ἐγγὺϲ ἐόντοϲ.

> When the moon is slender and clear around the third day, it should be a sign of fair weather; if it is slender and very red, of wind; but if, thicker and with blunted horns, moving from the third to the fourth day, it shows feeble light, then it is blurred by a south wind or because rain is near.

The word λεπτή (*leptē*) "slender, thin, subtle" is there for us to detect just as we will be able to detect – once instructed by Aratus – the various signs in the natural world. That we are to take the acrostic as a comment on the nature of signs and sign reading is made additionally likely by a shortly preceding passage, in which Aratus avows that "men do not yet know everything from Zeus, but many things are still hidden" (768–70). Even these, however, the god may reveal "if he wishes" (770–1), as he generally "benefits the human race openly" (771) and "shows signs everywhere" (772). To the observant reader, λεπτή is such a hidden sign that is suddenly revealed. Of a similar "meta-semiotic" nature is the much-remarked-on pun in the poem's second line, where the word ἄρρητον ("unmentioned") cleverly alludes to the poet's own name (Levitan 1979: 68 n.18; Kidd 1981: 355; Hopkinson 1988: 139; Bing 1990). As has been shown, at least some of Aratus' more sophisticated early readers apparently caught on to both the pun and the acrostic (Bing 1990; Cameron 1995a: 321–8).

Modern scholars have been fascinated by the fact that the word formed by Aratus' acrostic (which also shows up twice in the text of the five lines: 783, 784) should, of all things, be λεπτή. While the poet is apparently alluding to an (accidental) acrostic in *Iliad* 24.1–5, which spells out the similar word λευκή ("white"), it is certainly suggestive that he is using an adjective long associated with the poetic program of Callimachus. What is more, Callimachus himself in epigram 27 hails the *Phaenomena* as λεπταὶ / ῥήϲιεϲ, "subtle discourses" (3–4). Critics have been happy to jump to the conclusion that Aratus was an adherent of the Callimachean aesthetic ideal of λεπτότης ("slenderness, subtlety"); that he cleverly signaled his allegiance not only in the *Phaenomena* as a whole, but in his cunning acrostic, which was exactly the sort of thing to be picked up by the sophisticated readers able to appreciate the kind of poetry Callimachus and Aratus were trying to promote; and that Callimachus in turn recognized Aratus as a soul mate and advertised his achievement in epigram 27 (Jacques 1960: 53–9; Reinsch-Werner 1976: 12–4; Bing 1990: 281–2).

This scenario is the current *communis opinio*. However, there are serious problems with it (Cameron 1995a: 321–8). Leaving aside the vexed question of what Callimachus' poetic ideal actually was, and whether the *Phaenomena* would have conformed to it, we should note that there is nothing in the acrostic and its context to suggest that λεπτή has a metapoetic significance (Asper 1997: 182). Holders of the majority view would respond that the adjective would easily have been recognizable as a Callimachean buzzword – as indeed it is to students of Classics today. There is no reason to believe that this is true, though. While Callimachus certainly likes to use metaphors of size when talking about poetry (Asper 1997: 135–207), the word λεπτός is hardly ever found in the extant Callimachean corpus: besides the λεπταὶ ῥήσιες of epigram 27, there is only the famous Μοῦσα λεπταλέη ("slender Muse") of the *Aetia* prologue (fr. 1.24 Pf.), which employs a derivative of the adjective. As for the κατὰ λεπτὸν ῥήσιες ("discourses in the slender style") of Mimnermus putatively mentioned earlier in that same prologue (11–12), not only is ῥήσιες a conjecture by Augusto Rostagni (whose unlikelihood Cameron 1995a: 321–2 demonstrates), but as has recently been shown, κατὰ λεπτόν is not in fact a possible reading of the London scholia (on which we rely for this part of the text). The early editors appear to have been misled exactly by their desire to find an additional form of λεπτός in Callimachus (Bastianini 1996b; Luppe 1997).

Unless λεπτός made a frequent appearance in those parts of Callimachus' oeuvre lost to us but known to Aratus, it seems unlikely that the author of the *Phaenomena* would have been able to identify the adjective as a keyword of his contemporary's poetics and use it accordingly in his own work (that Callimachus and Aratus were contemporaries is assured, but the relative chronology of their works is unclear, and there is no reason to believe that they knew each other personally: Negri 2000). On the contrary, it appears that λεπτός was associated by Hellenistic poets not so much with Callimachus as indeed with Aratus himself, whom Leonidas of Tarentum praises for expounding the stars λεπτῆι φροντίδι "with a subtle mind" (101 GP = *AP* 9.25), and a King Ptolemy calls λεπτολόγος "of subtle speech" (*SH* 712.4). It is possible that these authors, as well as Callimachus in epigram 27, are simply responding to the λεπτή-acrostic. I would argue, however, that λεπτότης is indeed a central concept of the *Phaenomena*'s poetics, though in a sense that has very little to do with the presumed aesthetics of Callimachus.

Forms of the word λεπτός appear nine times in the *Phaenomena*, a not inconsiderable number. Two occur in the passage that forms the acrostic and refer to the crescent moon (783, 784), one concerns light spider webs (1033), and another describes the faint glow inside a burning piece of charcoal (1042). In all other cases, Aratus uses λεπτός to indicate stars or constellations of little brilliance: parts of Ophiuchus (80), the Kids (166), Libra (607), and the Asses (894, 906). Throughout the *Phaenomena*, the poet takes great care to distinguish between greater and smaller, brighter and less visible stars, and λεπτόϲ is but one of his expressions to designate constellations that are less easy to make out. Others include ἐλαφρόϲ "light" (81, 337, 519), νωθήϲ "dull" (228), ἀνάϲτεροϲ "starless" (228, 349), ἀφαυρόϲ "weak" (256, 277, 569), ἀφεγγήϲ "lightless" (264), ἠερόειϲ and ἠέριοϲ "murky" (276, 317, 349, 385), κυάνεοϲ "dark" (329, 398, 702), γλαυκόϲ "gray" (369), χαροπόϲ "dull" (394, 594), and ἀναλδήϲ "feeble" (394). Differentiation by stellar magnitude is, of course, a scientific procedure, but it seems that Aratus is not aiming solely at astronomical exactitude. It would appear that he has a special fondness for signs that are λεπτόϲ – small, subtle, and difficult to read – as we can infer already from his famous juxtaposition of the two Bears (Hübner 2005: 142–9). While the Greeks navigate by Helice, the Great Bear, the Phoenicians rely on the Little Bear, Cynosura (37–9). Helice is very bright and easy to make out (40–1), but Cynosura – though "slight" (ὀλίγη, 42) – is the much better sign (42–4). In this, his very first description of two constellations, Aratus is signaling to his readers that when it comes to signs, smaller (or more λεπτόϲ) is often better.

The poet's fascination with hard-to-perceive stars continues throughout the astronomical section of the *Phaenomena*. He calls special attention to an unnamed star cluster underneath Lepus that has little brilliance (ὀλίγηι … αἴγληι, 367) and no name (νώνυμοι, 370). As these stars do not appear in a recognizable shape (370–3), they were ignored by the name-giver of the constellations (373–85). However, they are not ignored by Aratus, who by his negative *aition* (the story of the first astronomer does *not* explain anything about the non-constellation) draws disproportionally great attention to them. Another cluster difficult to make out (ἐπιϲκέψαϲθαι ἀφαυραί, 256) are the Pleiades, which are so faint that only six of their supposed seven stars are actually visible (258–61). Nevertheless, the poet stresses, the Pleiades are extremely important, for their risings and settings signal (ϲημαίνειν, 267) the changing seasons (264–7).

An extreme example of Aratus' wish to find signs where (next to) none are perceptible is his description of the constellation Argo (342–52). As is apparent from the name, Argo's stars were believed to outline a ship – but only its rear half. Aratus describes this phenomenon as follows (349–50):

> καὶ τὰ μὲν ἠερίη καὶ ἀνάϲτεροϲ ἄχρι παρ' αὐτὸν
> ἱϲτὸν ἀπὸ πρώρηϲ φέρεται, τὰ δὲ πᾶϲα φαεινή.
>
> On the one side, from the prow all the way to the mast, it is carried along dim and starless; on the other side, it is entirely bright.

This is a paradoxical way of talking about the constellation: after all, Argo *does not have* a prow. It is as if the poet is able to make out signs where no one else can see them and to conjecture the existence of the second half of the ship, which to his discerning eye is there, even if on the surface of appearances, there are no stars to indicate its outline.

Anybody can identify the Great Bear or, presumably, the bright stern of Argo. Aratus' poem teaches us to distinguish more subtle signs – and the subtler, the better. One of the poet's terms for the subtle nature of a sign is λεπτόϲ, and I suggest that this is why he chose this word for his acrostic, which is itself a subtle sign and encapsulates the poetics of the *Phaenomena*, a poem in which a poet with a subtle mind (λεπτῆι φροντίδι, Leonidas of Tarentum) expounds subtle signs and thus creates a subtle discourse (λεπταὶ ῥήϲιεϲ, Callimachus; cf. λεπτολόγοϲ, King Ptolemy). In his ambition to "speak of the stars" (ἀϲτέραϲ εἰπεῖν, 17) "Aratus" (Ἄρητοϲ) endeavors not to leave anything "unspoken" (ἄρρητον, 2, 180; ἄφραϲτοι, 608), but to reveal, by means of his poetry, even the most hidden of signs.

In a recent book (2009), Reviel Netz points to the predilection of both Hellenistic mathematicians and Hellenistic poets for what he calls the minute and the asymptotic: they delight in exploring ever smaller details or fractions, while at the same time attempting to approach infinity. Both tendencies are present in Aratus, who rejoices in identifying the small, faint, and hidden sign and who is aware of the infinite multitude of signs (not to mention signs of signs), many of which have not yet been revealed. In this context, we may consider an argument put forward by William Levitan in 1979. Levitan descries two further acrostics in the *Phaenomena*, πᾶϲα in 803–6 and ϲεμειη in 808–12 (see now also Haslam 1992 and Cusset 1995, as well as Fakas 1999 for a possible telestich in 234–6). He fully acknowledges that the second of these is either incomplete or misspelled, as we would expect ϲημεῖα "signs," which would indeed be of great programmatic significance. Levitan goes on to argue, however, that the imperfection may have been introduced on purpose to drive home a central message of the poem, namely that the reading of signs is a dynamic, never-ending process: "The signs may be hard to discern or their interpretation obscure, but if the design appears unfinished, it is Aratus' trust that it is complete nonetheless" (1979: 64). Levitan himself compares the "missing" star of the Pleiades (1979: 68 n.20); we may point additionally to the "invisible" prow of Argo. As Aratus exhorts us again and again (Bing 1993: 109), we must continue to pay attention, look out, discern, and interpret: in this world, there will always be more signs.

From Aratus to *Aratea*

Aratus took the astronomical and meteorological information he found in his prose sources and shaped it into his own version of the "song and manner of Hesiod," a "subtle discourse" on the human condition, which he saw as characterized by the continuous exposure to signs and the necessity of deciphering them. Aratus' readers took the *Phaenomena* – and made it into whatever they pleased. The poem's enormous cultural significance in antiquity comes from the fact that it was not so much read and studied in its own right as used over the centuries as a fertile source of inspiration and material by many different people with many different agendas. This, as mentioned above, accounts for some of the difficulties that modern readers face in approaching the *Phaenomena*. It also makes for a fascinating narrative of intellectual history (Lewis 1992).

As we have seen, Hellenistic poets such as Callimachus appreciated the *Phaenomena* as a work of poetry, and the same appreciation must have persisted into the Roman world (despite the disparaging remarks of Quintilian quoted above). Otherwise, Latin poets such as Cicero, Varro of Atax, Ovid, Germanicus, and Avienius (on the correct form of the latter's name, see Cameron 1995b) would not have undertaken to translate all or part of the *Phaenomena*, and Vergil, Manilius, and again Ovid (in the *Fasti*) would not have adapted individual passages or aspects of it. To some extent, all these efforts are part of the larger phenomenon of the Roman *imitatio* and *aemulatio* of Greek poetic models, and one imitates only what one admires.

At the same time, Aratus would never have attained his high status were it not for the fact that at least from the second century BCE onward, the first part of his poem was used as a school text of astronomy (Weinhold 1912; Marrou 1956: 184–5; Lewis 1992: 113–18) and that in the imagination of the Greeks and Romans, he was thus inextricably linked with his subject matter, the stars. In the words of the neoteric poet Cinna, the *Phaenomena* is the source "by which we know the heavenly fires" (*quis ignes nouimus aerios*, fr. 11.2 Bl.), and according to Ovid, "Aratus will always be with the sun and the moon" (*cum sole et luna semper Aratus erit*, *Am.* 1.15.16), that is, his poems will be read as long as there are heavenly bodies – and they will always be associated with each other. Aratus' status as an "astronomer" (he is depicted as such in manuscript illuminations and other works of art: Maass 1898: 172–4; Marrou 1956: 408; Lewis 1992: 108) was certainly taken seriously by Hipparchus, the famous second-century BCE astronomer, who wrote a commentary on the *Phaenomena* in which he showed in detail where the poet (and already Eudoxus) had been scientifically mistaken. The fact that this is the only work of Hipparchus to have come down to us attests to the important role of Aratus in the cultural imagination of antiquity.

For the Hellenistic Greeks and even more for the Romans, the stars (which for Aratus had been just one set of signs observable in our surroundings) were a culturally increasingly significant phenomenon that took on a variety of meanings and engendered a number of different discourses, and as the *Phaenomena* was *the* repository of knowledge about the stars, the poem came to be associated with these discourses as well. One of these was myth: while Aratus himself had used stories of catasterism sparingly, his constellations became closely associated with aetiological myths, many of which were collected in the so-called *Catasterisms* of Ps.-Eratosthenes and made their way into the Latin adaptations of the *Phaenomena*. Another was Stoicism: Cicero, for example, used quotations from his own translation of Aratus in the *De natura deorum* to support the Stoic "argument from design" (Gee 2001: 527–36), and Manilius in his *Astronomica* refigured the Aratean cosmos in terms of Stoic physics. As Manilius' work shows, astrology was another worldview to become bound up with the reception of the *Phaenomena*; this is apparent also in the translation of Germanicus, who seems to have replaced Aratus' weather signs with a section on planetary astrometeorology (frs. 2–6 Le Boeuffle 1975; Montanari Caldini 1973).

As this all-too-brief survey shows, the reception of Aratus quickly turned into a cultural phenomenon in its own right, one only tangentially related to the original concerns of the *Phaenomena*. But if the poet perhaps had not expected his work to become a science text for schoolboys or a source book for mythographers, the fact that it did in a way proves Aratus' own point. Humans are always in the process of reading and interpreting signs, and the *Phaenomena* was one of the most widely read and interpreted sign systems of the ancient world, capable of continually producing new meaning.

FURTHER READING

Aratus can be studied in two excellent recent editions with translation and commentary, Kidd 1997 (English) and Martin 1998 (French). The ancient commentaries have been edited by Maass 1898, the scholia by Martin 1974. For the commentary of Hipparchus, see Manitius 1894; for the fragments of Eudoxus, Lasserre 1966; and for the pseudo-Theophrastan *On Weather Signs*, Sider and Brunschön 2007.

The best general introduction to the *Phaenomena* remains Erren 1967 (idiosyncratic but inspiring), to be supplemented by Effe 1977a (the classic "philosophical" reading), Fakas 2001 (on the poet's reworking of Hesiod), and especially the outstanding discussion of Hunter 2008a: 1.153–88 (also Fantuzzi and Hunter 2004: 224–45). For the poetic style and structure of the *Phaenomena*, see Ludwig 1963 and Hutchinson 1988: 214–36; Pendergraft 1990 raises important issues about the nature of Aratus' constellations. On the whole, Aratus remains remarkably understudied; especially welcome would be interdisciplinary work that examines the links between his poem and contemporary science and philosophy.

Generally on the reception of the *Phaenomena* in antiquity, see Lewis 1992. The Latin *Aratea* are most easily approached through the Budé editions of Soubiran 1972 (Cicero) and 1981 (Avienius) and Le Boeuffle 1975 (Germanicus; see also Gain 1976). A recent monograph on Germanicus is Possanza 2004. For a comparative study of the Dike episode in Germanicus and Avienius (with a nod to Cicero), see Bellandi, Berti, and Ciappi 2001. A general investigation of Aratus' reception as a cultural phenomenon remains a desideratum.

My thanks go to Daryn Lehoux, Reviel Netz, and David Sider for kindly making unpublished material available to me.

CHAPTER FIFTEEN

Nicander

Enrico Magnelli

Readers who chance upon Nicander's poetic oeuvre of nearly 1,600 lines, devoted almost entirely to snakes, spiders, and poisons and marked by an arcane style and recondite vocabulary, typically do not fall in love with their discovery. Professional classicists also sometimes run from Nicander as if from a venomous creature. Even A. S. F. Gow, who in the mid-twentieth century made a key contribution to Nicandrian studies, had mixed feelings about the texts he was editing, seeing in them "the combination of a repulsive style with considerable metrical accomplishment" (Gow and Scholfield 1953: 8; for other unfavorable judgments by modern scholars, see Jacques 2002: LXVI–VII). And yet in Nicander, as in other Hellenistic poetry, content, style, and meter are intimately interconnected aspects of the same literary program. Nicander's diction more particularly reflects how linguistic trends noticeable in early Hellenistic poetry developed during the mid-Hellenistic period, just as his poetics offers an invaluable insight into the evolution of Greek didactic poetry after Aratus. Both features of his work merit close consideration. But first we need to confront the issue of Nicander's chronology.

How Many Nicanders?

Ancient sources ascribe many works to a Colophonian poet named Nicander, and a "Nicander of Colophon" indeed explicitly claims to be the author of two extant hexameter poems, the 958-line *Theriaca*, "On Venomous Animals," and the 630-line *Alexipharmaca*, "On Antidotes" (*Th.* 958, *Al.* 9–11). The evidence for Nicander's life is scanty and inconsistent. The *Life of Nicander* quotes from an unknown work a line in which he advertised himself as "the son of the memorable Damaeus" (fr. 110 GS). The same source preserves the five opening lines from a *Hymn to Attalus* (fr. 104 GS) that links the poet with the Pergamene court – although it is unclear whether the addressee was Attalus I (Cazzaniga 1972; Cameron 1995a: 200–2) or Attalus III (Pasquali 1913; Touwaide 1991: 100–1; Jacques 2006: 24–6, 2007b: 104–5; Spatafora 2007: 11 and, more cautiously, Massimilla 2000: 135–6). The ancient biographical tradition makes Nicander live either in the age of Ptolemy II Philadelphus (283–246 BCE; test. C i–ii GS), or under Ptolemy V (204–181; test. C iv–v GS), or under Attalus III (138–133; test. A–B GS). Apart from the biographical sketches preserved in our manuscripts, in which it is very hard to sort truth from fiction, we also have a decree from Delphi that confers proxeny on "Nicander, son of Anaxagoras, of Colophon, the epic poet" (*SIG*³ 452 = test. D GS). Once dated around the mid-third century, this inscription now appears in the light of recent research to have been produced shortly before 210 BCE. Consequently, one Nicander of Colophon, son of Anaxagoras, was writing poetry during the reign of Attalus I (241–197; Massimilla 2000: 132–5); but the name Anaxagoras is hard to reconcile with the Damaeus of fr. 110. Although scholars have tried to console the biographical sources, arguing that Damaeus was Nicander's father by adoption (for the relevant data, see Massimilla 2000: 130 n.14), we may well be dealing with *two* poets named Nicander. If so, the *Theriaca* and *Alexipharmaca* may have been written either by Nicander, the son of Anaxagoras, at the end of the third century BCE, or by a younger poet, son of Damaeus, possibly in the second half of the second century BCE. Attalus III had a strong interest in poisons and antidotes (Hansen 1971: 144–5), and his reign (138–133) would offer an appropriate context for the two iological poems (Touwaide 1991: 100–1; Massimilla 2000: 135–6; Jacques 2006: 27–8). Furthermore, interesting arguments have recently been advanced for seeing in *Alexipharmaca* 15 an allusion to the destruction of Heracleia Pontica by Prusias II shortly before 154 BCE (Hautcourt 2001). However this may be, it seems unlikely that the *Theriaca* and *Alexipharmaca* were written by a poet who was active under Ptolemy II (*pace* Cameron 1995a: 194–207): the two poems not only show a remarkable allegiance to Callimachean poetics but also numerous points of contact with actual lines by Callimachus, Apollonius, Theocritus, and Euphorion. Regardless how one analyzes individual instances (echo, imitation, allusion?) there can be little doubt that Nicander is not engaged in a dialogue with contemporaries but looking back at predecessors. The *Theriaca* and *Alexipharmaca* are not the work of a first-generation literary pioneer (Magnelli 2006a).

Regarding the other works attributed to "Nicander" in antiquity, some 150 lines remain of the *Georgica* (frs. 68–91 GS). Their style and diction are almost identical to those of the two extant poems (Pasquali 1913: 95–7 = 1986: 373–6). Works of which much less survives – the *Oitaica*, *Thebaica*, *Sikelia*, *Heteroioumena*, and possibly a *Cynegetica* (the existence of such a poem remains doubtful: Cazzaniga 1976: 320–4; Martínez 2000) – also have various features in common with the *Theriaca* and *Alexipharmaca*, for example:

lists of zoological names: *Oit.* fr. 18, *Heter.* fr. 59;

typical Nicandrian vocabulary: *Theb.* fr. 19 ὑπὲρ Παμβωνίδας ὄχθας ~ *Th.* 214 ὑπὸ Σκείρωνος ὄρη Παμβώνιά τ' αἴπη; *Sik.* fr. 22 ὄμβρωι τε κρυμῶι τε, δέμας τότε δάμνατο μάλκηι ~ *Th.* 381–2 ὅτ' ἐν παλάμηισιν ἀεργοί / μάλκαι ἐπιπροθέωσιν ὑπὸ κρυμοῖο δαμέντων, 724 μάλκη ἐνισκήπτουσα, *Al.* 540–1 ὑπὸ μάλκης / δάμνανται;

Callimachean phrases: *Heter.* fr. 62.3–4 μορφὴν / γρήϊον ~ Call. *Hec.* (?) fr. 173 (Hollis 2009) γρήϊον εἶδος ἔχουσα; *Cyn.* (?) fr. 98 ἑσμὸν ἄγει ~ Call. *Aet.* fr. 12.3 Pf. ἑσμὸν ἄγων;

Callimachean topics: *Sik.* fr. 21 ~ Call. *Aet.* fr. 43.69–71 Pf.; *Heter.* fr. 50 ~ Call. *Aet.* fr. 67–75 Pf.

Some of these features were pointed out long ago by Giorgio Pasquali in his magnificent and still fundamental study on "the two Nicanders" (1913). Pasquali assigned the *Theriaca*, *Alexipharmaca* and most of the fragmentary works to a poet living under Attalus III, leaving to an elder Nicander the *Europia*, *Aitolika*, and possibly *Ophiaka*. Yet his distinction between this small group of fragments and the rest seems unwarranted. The mere nine surviving lines of the *Ophiaka* (fr. 31–2 GS) do not allow a meaningful stylistic comparison (and at any rate fr. 32 is hardly more unsophisticated than, say, *Theriaca* 8–18); we do not even know whether the *Aitolika* (test. A GS) was in poetry or prose (Cazzaniga 1973 and Grilli 1973, with references to earlier discussions); and Pasquali's evaluation of *Europia* fr. 26 ("the giant Athos hurling peaks from the promontory is much grander an image than those of the *Theriaca* and *Alexipharmaca*," 1913: 108 = 1986: 384) seems arbitrary, all the more since this passage imitates both Callimachus' *Hymn to Delos* (*h.* 4.133–6) and Apollonius' description of the bronze giant Talos throwing rocks at the Argonauts (*Arg.* 4.1638–40). All in all, there are no serious objections against assigning any of the fragments to the author of the *Theriaca* and *Alexipharmaca* (Cameron 1995a: 204–5). If indeed there were two Nicanders, one of them remains an elusive figure.

In the Footsteps of the Alexandrians

The author of the *Theriaca* and *Alexipharmaca* appears to have been particularly fond of third-century Alexandrian poetry. He not only borrows a good number of words and phrases from Apollonius, Theocritus, and especially Callimachus, but in fact often exploits their texts in quite sophisticated ways (Magnelli 2006a). A good example is *Alexipharmaca* 232–4:

ἤ ἔτι καὶ κλήροισιν ἐπήβολα τοῖά περ ὧραι
εἰαριναὶ φορέουσιν ἐνεψιήματα κούραις,
ἄλλοτε δὲ στρούθεια…

or even those belonging to the fields, the kind of girls' playthings the spring seasons bear;
or again pear-quinces…

Here Nicander is reworking lines 80–3 of Callimachus' *Hymn to Apollo* (Jacques 1955: 19):

ἰὴ ἰὴ Καρνεῖε πολύλλιτε, σεῖο δὲ βωμοὶ
ἄνθεα μὲν φορέουσιν ἐν εἴαρι τόσσα περ Ὧραι
ποικίλ' ἀγινεῦσι ζεφύρου πνείοντος ἐέρσην,
χείματι δὲ κρόκον ἡδύν.

Hiē hiē Karneios, much-supplicated god. Your altars bear the manifold flowers gathered by the Seasons in spring, when Zephyrus breathes dew, and in winter they bear sweet saffron.

The subject is similar, but Nicander's choice of words is far more complex and clearly inspired by Homeric scholarship (Magnelli 2006a: 191). Thus Callimachus' simple ἄνθεα, "flowers," become both the redundant κλήροιϲιν ἐπήβολα, "(fruits) belonging to the fields" and ἐνεψιήματα κούραιϲ, "girls' playthings." As it happens, ἐπήβολοϲ was a Homeric *hapax legomenon* of disputed meaning, and the otherwise unattested ἐνεψίημα may well reflect Callimachus' and Apollonius' interest in Homeric ἐψιάομαι (Rengakos 1994a: 92). Nicander is apparently trying to be more Alexandrian than the great Alexandrian. The same applies to *Theriaca* 266–8,

αὐτὰρ ὅγε ϲκαιὸϲ μεϲάτωι ἐπαλίνδεται ὁλκῶι
οἶμον ὁδοιπλανέων ϲκολιὴν τετρηχότι νώτωι,
τράμπιδοϲ ὁλκαίηϲ ἀκάτωι ἴϲοϲ.

[the snake called cerastes] slithers on clumsily with movements of his middle, wandering on a skewed path with his scaly back, like the dinghy of a merchant vessel.

Nicander's dense text engages no fewer than three different lines from the fourth book of Apollonius' *Argonautica*: 1463 ἴχνια γὰρ νυχίοιϲιν ἐπηλίνδητ' ἀνέμοιϲιν (both ἐπαλίνδομαι and ἐπαλινδέομαι appear to be *hapax legomena*), 838 δολιχήν τε καὶ ἄϲπετον οἶμον ὁδεύειν (which Nicander imitates changing ὁδεύω into the rare ὁδοιπλανέω), and 1541 ὡϲ δὲ δράκων ϲκολιὴν εἱλιγμένοϲ ἕρχεται οἶμον. In the last passage a ship is slithering like a snake; Nicander wittily reverses the simile, making the cerastes move like a ship (Magnelli 2006a: 194–5; cf. Livrea 1973: 429; Jacques 2002: 22; Cusset 2006a: 82–4).

Another predecessor is targeted in *Alexipharmaca* 433 μήκωνοϲ κεβληγόνου ... δάκρυ, "the tears of the poppy, whose seeds are in a head," including an adjective which appears elsewhere only in Euphorion: κεβληγόνου Ἀτρυτώνηϲ, "of Athena (Atrytone) born from the head" (*CA* 108). Nicander amusingly transfers the epithet from the goddess to the humble flower (changing its meaning in the process: Magnelli 2006a: 192) in a way that calls to mind a passage of the parodist Matro (on whom see Scodel in this volume) where the Homeric Tityus, "the son of glorious earth" (*Od.* 11.576–7) is turned into a cucumber (*SH* 537 = fr. 4 Olson and Sens 1999).

Nicander's relationship with the poets of the early Hellenistic age is never servile or without point. It often takes the form of ironic reworkings, erudite allusions, *oppositio in imitando*, and so on. In other words, he applies to his Alexandrian predecessors the same literary approaches they had successfully applied to their Archaic and Classical models, notably Homer. That these poets had become the new classics is unsurprising; they were already regarded as such by Euphorion, who flourished just a few decades after Callimachus and Theocritus. Yet there is a crucial difference. Euphorion's engagement with Callimachus and his contemporaries is reverential: his imitations of their poetry show none of the irony and subversiveness of his imitations of Homer (Magnelli 2002: 54–6). In the second century, it seems, poets felt free to play with Callimachus as well. Nicander, in any case, appears to treat the Alexandrians with a lighter touch.

Nicander challenges even the most patient reader. His language is full of rare words, new coinages, and morphological peculiarities, and his style is the opposite of clear and concise. It is not by chance that he is often compared to Lycophron. Nonetheless his poetics are tangibly different: whereas Lycophron intentionally fills his verses with forbidding riddles, Nicander does not primarily aim at obscurity. Strange as his diction may seem, if you are familiar with poetic language and are not shocked at such irregularities as καναχός instead of καναχής or θέρω in the place of θεραπεύω, you might remain uncertain about the exact meaning of an adjective here or there, but on the whole you will understand what Nicander says (whether you will like the way he says it, is a different matter). His vocabulary abounds more in morphological innovations than in inscrutable dialectal glosses (Jacques 2002: XCIV–CIII). Something similar applies to Nicander's mythical digressions and references, which for the most part deal with well-known stories and characters. One does not have to be a scholar to make sense of, for example, "the Nemean plant, evergreen celery" (*Th.* 649): every ancient reader could be expected to know that a victory at the Nemean games was rewarded with a crown of celery, and explanations of the origin (*aition*) of this custom were provided by Callimachus (*SH* 265.5–9) and Euphorion (*CA* 84). In the case of myths that are not well known, Nicander invariably provides sufficient detail for comprehension, as in his digressions on Canobus (*Th.* 309–19; Jacques 2002: 115–16), Alcibius (*Th.* 541–9, 666–75), and the nymphs of Samos (*Al.* 148–52).

The most-discussed passage in Nicander is certainly his aetiological digression on why mankind does not live forever, inserted in a description of the snake called dipsas, whose name is etymologized from "thirst" (Brelich 1958; Davies 1987: 71; Hopkinson 1988: 143–6; Toohey 1996: 64–7; Reeve 1996/7; Jacques 2002: 28–9, 120–1). These elegant lines, which contain the poet's signature in an acrostic (Lobel 1928; Jacques 2002: LXXX with n.179), provide a particularly clear impression of Nicander's style (*Th.* 343–56):

ὠγύγιος δ' ἄρα μῦθος ἐν αἰζηοῖϲι φορεῖται,
ὡϲ, ὁπότ' οὐρανὸν ἔϲχε Κρόνου πρεϲβίϲτατον αἷμα,
Νειμάμενοϲ καϲίεϲϲιν ἑκὰϲ περικυδέαϲ ἀρχὰϲ
Ιδμοϲύνηι, νεότητα γέραϲ πόρεν ἡμερίοιϲι
Κυδαίνων· δὴ γάρ ῥα πυρὸϲ ληίϲτορ' ἔνιπτον.
Αφρονεϲ· οὐ μὲν τῆϲ γε κακοφραδίηιϲ ἀπόνηντο.
Νωθεῖϲ γὰρ κάμνοντεϲ ἀμορβεύοντο λεπάργωι
Δῶρα· πολύϲκαρθμοϲ δὲ κεκαυμένοϲ αὐχένα δίψηι
Ρώετο· γωλειοῖϲι δ' ἰδὼν ὁλκήρεα θῆρα
Οὐλοὸν ἐλλιτάνευε κακῆι ἐπαλαλκέμεν ἄτηι
Σαίνων. αὐτὰρ ὁ βρῖθοϲ, ὃ δή ῥ' ἀνεδέξατο νώτοιϲ,
ἤιτεεν ἄφρονα δῶρον, ὁ δ' οὐκ ἀπανήνατο χρειώ.
ἐξότε γηραλέον μὲν ἀεὶ φλόον ἑρπετὰ βάλλει
ὁλκήρη, θνητοὺϲ δὲ κακὸν περὶ γῆραϲ ὀπάζει.

There is an ancient tale going around among men how, when the first-born blood of Kronos acquired heaven, in his wisdom he allotted to each of his brothers their illustrious realms, and to mortals he gave the gift of youth to honor them for telling on the fire-thief [Prometheus]. The fools! Through their bad judgment they got nothing out of it. For being lazy, they grew tired and entrusted the gift to an ass to carry; and the skittish animal, its throat burning with thirst, ran off. Seeing in its hole the deadly, crawling beast, it weedled and begged for help in its sore plight. The snake then asked the silly animal for the very gift it had taken on its back, and the ass did not refuse the snake's request. Since then crawling reptiles always slough their old skin, but mortals are subject to grievous old age.

This narrative passage is largely free of the technical vocabulary that characterizes the zoological and pharmacological descriptions, but it is by no means straightforward. A fair number of relevant conceits are expressed with uncommon poetic words and kennings: ὠγύγιος for ἀρχαῖος, κάσιες for ἀδελφοί, αἰζηοί and ἠμερίοι for ἄνθρωποι and/or θνητοί, λέπαργος for ὄνος (Jacques 2002: 28), θὴρ ὁλκήρης for διψάς, Κρόνου πρεσβίστατον αἷμα for Ζεύς, πυρὸς ληίστωρ for Προμηθεύς. Yet none of these expressions is particularly opaque. As Jean-Marie Jacques has repeatedly stressed, Nicander's aim appears not to be to puzzle the reader, but rather to impress him with the involved refinement of his diction (Jacques 2002: CI; 2004: 117–18; 2006: 39–40).

Nicander's metrical practice sheds further light on his overall artistic intentions. It is well known that his smooth and elegant hexameters perfectly conform to the standards set by the most refined Alexandrian poets, and recent research has stressed his allegiance to Callimachean practice in particular (Brioso Sánchez 1974; Jacques 2002: CXXIII–IX; Oikonomakos 2002b: 135–52; Magnelli 2002: 70–81 and 2006a: 198–201). Sometimes he goes even further. In Hellenistic hexameter poetry in general, we may observe a tendency to place monosyllabic nouns at the end of the line (West 1982: 156), but Nicander pushes this to the point where he only once uses a monosyllabic noun in another position (Maas in Kroll 1936: 261). His linguistic and stylistic habits seem to follow a similar rationale: he follows in the footsteps of his illustrious forebears but takes their practices one step further. If third-century Alexandrian poetry was a successful blend of erudition, superb technical skill, and "thinness" (λεπτότης), i.e., subtle simplicity, in later poetry the first two seem to overshadow the third: for some poets to be refined apparently meant to fill their lines to the rim with glosses and new coinages. It is this tendency among the later generations of Hellenistic writers that appears to elicit an "anti-Callimachean" reaction from a number of Macedonian epigrammatists in the first century BCE, exemplified by Antipater of Thessalonica's famous harangue against the "tribe of thorn-gathering poets" (*AP* 11.20 = *GPh* 185–90). In fact, Callimachus might not have approved of Nicander's style. Nonetheless I sense it was precisely his devotion to Callimachus which shaped that style.

In the light of all this evidence, it is quite surprising to find Nicander defining himself at the end of the *Theriaca* as "Homeric" (Ὁμηρείοιο … Νικάνδροιο, 957). It is well possible that this passage echoes the end of the "Delian" section of the *Homeric Hymn to Apollo* (165–78; De Martino 1982; doubts: Fakas 2001: 54 n.157), but this echo in itself hardly explains "Homeric Nicander." One possibility is that Nicander alludes to the alleged Colophonian origin of Homer, and/or that he belonged to a guild of poets associated with Colophon's Homereion (Pasquali 1913:

89 = 1986: 368). Others think that the epithet is "not inappropriate to a self-satisfied poet writing hexameters with an archaic vocabulary" (Gow and Scholfield 1953: 189) or that it stages Homer as Nicander's model of style (Jacques 2002: LXXI, 2007b: 102). Others yet suggest that it is due to his use of epic glosses and his knowledge and reworking of the Homeric text (so, approximately, Vian 1991: 5 = 2005: 469; Spatafora 2007: 202). No explanation is fully satisfactory. Whatever the meaning of Homeric here, it cannot but evoke the image of a poet whose most evident feature is his allegiance to Homer. This does not suit Nicander: his debts to Homeric language are relevant (Jacques 2002: CVII-IX), but those to the Alexandrian poets are even greater, and as such he cannot be labeled as a traditionalist. I am therefore inclined to think that the epithet was intended to sound paradoxical and that Nicander, who elsewhere displays a detached, ironic attitude towards his own poetry (as we will see), deliberately chose it in order to challenge the reader. Whatever the solution may be, at least one ancient reader took *Theriaca* 957 at face value. The anonymous epigram *AP* 9.213 (*FGE* 1246–9) runs as follows:

καὶ Κολοφὼν ἀρίδηλος ἐνὶ πτολίεσσι τέτυκται
 δοιοὺς θρεψαμένη παῖδας ἀριστονόους,
πρωτότοκον μὲν Ὅμηρον, ἀτὰρ Νίκανδρον ἔπειτα,
 ἀμφοτέρους Μούσαις οὐρανίῃσι φίλους.

Colophon too is famous among cities, having bred two sons excellent in wisdom: Homer it bore first, then Nicander, both dear to the heavenly Muses.

Other first-rank poets were born in Colophon, such as Mimnermus, Xenophanes, Antimachus, Hermesianax, and Phoenix. The author of this epigram selected Nicander alone as Homer's counterpart. Possibly he was very fond of toxicological poetry, but it is perhaps more likely that he took the idea from Nicander himself. So, in the company of Homer and thanks to the good will of an unknown versifier, the author of the *Theriaca* finally meets those Muses he had carefully avoided to mention in his own proem.

A Theriological Diptych

The *Theriaca* and *Alexipharmaca* are clearly conceived as a diptych. Both begin with an appeal to the dedicatee and a statement of the poet's skill and aims:

ῥεῖά κέ τοι μορφάς τε σίνη τ' ὀλοφώια θηρῶν
ἀπροϊδῆ τύψαντα λύσιν θ' ἑτεραλκέα κήδευς,
φίλ' Ἑρμησιάναξ, πολέων κυδίστατε παῶν,
ἔμπεδα φωνήσαιμι.

Th. 1–4

Easily, dear Hermesianax, most honored of my many kinsmen, will I expound the shapes of deadly creatures, the wounds they inflict unforeseen, and the remedy that counters the harm, all in due order.

εἰ καὶ μὴ σύγκληρα κατ' Ἀσίδα τείχεα δῆμοι
τύρσεσιν ἐστήσαντο τέων ἀνεδέγμεθα βλάστας,
Πρωταγόρη, δολιχὸς δὲ διάπροθι χῶρος ἐέργει,
ῥεῖά κέ τοι ποσίεσσιν ἀλέξια φαρμακοέσσαις
αὐδήσαιμ' ἅ τε φῶτας ἐνιχριμφθέντα δαμάζει.
Al. 1–5

Even though the peoples from whom you and I, Protagoras, have derived our births did not set up the walls of their strongholds side by side in Asia, and we are separated by a long stretch of space, yet I can easily tell you the remedies for poisonous liquids which strike men and bring them down.

Both also have a very similar two-line closure:

καί κεν Ὁμηρείοιο καὶ εἰσέτι Νικάνδροιο
μνῆστιν ἔχοις, τὸν ἔθρεψε Κλάρου νιφόεσσα πολίχνη.
Th. 957–8

And you will also in the future remember Homeric Nicander, whom the snowy town of Clarus nurtured.

καί κ' ἔνθ' ὑμνοπόλοιο καὶ εἰσέτι Νικάνδροιο
μνῆστιν ἔχοις, θεσμὸν δὲ Διὸς ξενίοιο φυλάσσοις.
Al. 629–30

And now you will also in the future remember Nicander the singer, and heed the command of Zeus, Protector of Friendships.

Both poems show the same organization and narrative techniques (Effe 1974b, 1977a: 56–65), and structural and stylistic differences between them (Crugnola 1961: 151–2; Schneider 1962: 36) are few and insignificant. Their cumulative length of almost 1,600 lines would fill a single papyrus roll (compare the 1,781 hexameters of the fourth book of Apollonius' *Argonautica* or the 1,474 trimeters of Lycophron's *Alexandra*), and it is likely that Nicander wrote them with such an arrangement in mind.

But there is more. At the start of the *Theriaca*, the poet quotes Hesiod as an authority for the origin of spiders and reptiles: these creatures were born from the blood of the Titans, "if indeed the man from Ascra spoke the truth, Hesiod, on the steps of secluded Melissēeis by the waters of Permessus" (*Th.* 10–12). He then relates the origin of the scorpion, created by Artemis as a weapon against the rapist Orion (13–20), and this, as Effe (1974a) has convincingly demonstrated, alludes to Aratus' *Phaenomena* (636–46). Whatever Nicander may have had in mind when referring to Hesiod (perhaps a *Titanomachy* once intruded into the Hesiodic corpus, as was proposed by Cazzaniga 1975; other possibilities are scrutinized by Jacques 2002: 77–8), it is clear that he is situating his own work within the tradition of didactic poetry by staging his two most important antecedents: Hesiod and Aratus. No other programmatic passage appears either at the end of *Theriaca*, whose brief coda (quoted above) comes almost unexpected, immediately following the detailed recipe for a panacea, or at the beginning of *Alexipharmaca*, where the address to Protagoras (also quoted above) immediately proceeds to the entry for aconite. But the section on myrtle in *Alexipharmaca* 616–28, just before the final two-line cφραγίc, reveals something interesting:

> καὶ τὰ μὲν οὖν Νίκανδρος ἑῆι ἐγκάτθετο βίβλωι
> μοχθήεντα μύκητα παρ' ἀνέρι φαρμακόοντα.
> πρὸc δ' ἔτι τοῖc Δίκτυννα τεῆc ἐχθήρατο κλῶναc
> Ἥρη τ' Ἰμβραcίη μούνη cτέφοc οὐχ ὑπέδεκτο,
> κάλλεοc, οὕνεκα Κύπριν, ὅτ' εἰc ἔριν ἠέρθηcαν
> ἀθάναται, κόcμηcεν ἐν Ἰδαίοιcιν ὄρεccι·
> τῆc cύ γ' ἀπ' εὐύδροιο νάπηc, εὐαλθὲc ὄνειαρ,
> καρπὸν πορφυρόεντα cυναλδέα χειμερίηιcιν
> ἠελίου θαλφθέντα βολαῖc δοίδυκι λεήναc,
> χυλὸν ὑπὲρ λεπτῆc ὀθόνηc ἢ cχοινίδι κύρτηι
> ἐκθλίψαc πορέειν κυάθου κοτυληδόνα πλήρη
> ἢ πλεῖον, πλεῖον γὰρ ὀνήιον – οὐ γὰρ ἀνιγρὸν
> πῶμα βροτοῖc – τόδε γάρ τε καὶ ἄρκιον αἴ κε πίηιcθα.

> Such medicines as a man may use against harmful fungi Nicander has already presented in his book. In addition to these, there is the plant (i.e., the myrtle) whose branches Dictynna hates and which Imbrasian Hera alone does not accept for a garland, because when the immortal goddesses were up against each other in a beauty contest, it adorned Cypris on mount Ida. From this pluck in a well-watered valley as a healing remedy the scarlet berries that ripen in the warmth of the winter sun's rays, crush them with a pestle, strain the juice over fine linen or with a rush sieve and administer a full cyathus-sized cup of it, or more – in fact, more is fine, because this potion is not harmful to men; but drinking a cup of it should already be enough.

Fungi, already discussed in 521–36, seem out of place here: this, and the absence of the whole passage in Eutecnius' paraphrase, has led most scholars to delete it (Schneider 1856: 156–8; Klauser 1898: 55 n.3; Gow and Scholfield 1953: 200; Jacques 1955: 34–5; Effe 1974b: 65 n.21; Oikonomakos 2002b: 245–6; Spatafora 2007: 292; Jacques 2007a: 249). I have argued elsewhere that these lines are perfectly Nicandrian in language, style and meter (Magnelli 2006b), featuring some prominent Callimachean echoes: line 616 reworks *Aetia* fr. 75.54–5 Pf. ἀρχαίου Ξενομήδεοc, ὅc ποτε πᾶcαν / νῆcον ἐνὶ μνήμηι κάτθετο μυθολόγωι and 66 γέρων ἐνεθήκατο δέλτ[οιc, both dealing with "books" rather than "songs"; and 621 varies *Hymn to Zeus* 51 Ἰδαίοιc ἐν ὄρεccι. Therefore, rather than rejecting the entire passage as an interpolation, we should perhaps assume that "fungi" (μύκητα) at 617 is corrupted or some two half lines have been omitted after it (for details see Magnelli 2006b). It is also worth noting that the two myths alluded to at 618–21 are markedly Callimachean. For Dictynna and the myrtle, the only extant literary source that predates Nicander is Callimachus' *Hymn to Artemis* (200–3); and while the Samian cult of Hera and her link with the river Imbrasus are well known, for a proper treatment of the story alluded to here one must turn to two episodes from the fourth book of Callimachus' *Aetia* (fr. 100–1 Pf. and possibly 599 Pf. = 127 Massimilla). As we already saw, allusive brevity with respect to stories told by Callimachus is very typical of our poet. On the whole it is tempting to think that Nicander, who had opened the *Theriaca* staging Hesiod and Aratus as his models in the genre of didactic poetry, now ends the *Alexipharmaca* under the sign of Callimachus as his foremost model of style and refinement, in a ring composition that underscores the symmetry and complementarity of the two iological poems.

Pushing the Didactic Envelope

The openings of Nicander's poems are also significant in other ways. The very first word of the *Theriaca* is ῥεῖα, "easily," which also appears at line 4 of the *Alexipharmaca*. As Fakas (2001: 63 n.190) acutely pointed out, this is something of a revolution within the tradition of didactic poetry. Hesiod's *Works and Days* starts with the typical Muse-invocation; Aratus opens his Stoicizing astronomical *Phaenomena* by praising the cosmic power of his god (ἐκ Διὸc ἀρχώμεcθα, "let us begin with Zeus"), while the Muses are entrusted with a secondary role at the end of the proem (16–18; Volk and White in this volume). Nicander goes much further, foregoing the mention of any divine being (Brioso Sánchez 1994: 268) and opening instead with a triumphant "easily," which asserts his self-confident attitude: to write his poem he needs nothing but his own genius and erudition. In this "secularization" of didactic poetry we are surely dealing with a fair degree of self-irony. For what sort of reader would seriously believe that composing refined hexameters on so unfriendly a matter and in so abstruse a style might be an easy task?

Such irony and self-consciousness is widespread in Hellenistic poetry and may also be observed elsewhere in the *Theriaca* and *Alexipharmaca* – Toohey rightly argued that both poems feature "a strong strain of playfulness" (1996: 66; cf. 70–2). As we saw, when Nicander mentions the myth of the Titans in the proem of the *Theriaca*, he adds "if indeed Hesiod spoke the truth" (10–12). Such disclaimers are a literary commonplace (Stinton 1976) and sometimes the disbelief that they express is more apparent than real. Yet they are not what one would expect in the prologue to a didactic poem, and especially not with reference to the very founder of that poetic genre. Hesiod seems not to be much of an authority for the detached Nicander.

Nicander treats other stories in the same way: εἰ ἔτυμον, "if the tale is true," prefaces the death of Canobus (*Th.* 309); ἐρέει φάτιc, "the tale states," introduces a digression on Demeter and Ascalabus (*Th.* 484); and λόγοc γε μέν, "the story goes," frames Odysseus' death by the sting-ray (*Th.* 835). On the other hand, he employs no such phrase when he narrates the amusingly indecent *aition* of the appearance of the lily (*Al.* 405–9, cf. also *Georg.* fr. 74.29–30 GS):

> αἴνυcο δ' αὐτὴν
> ἶριδα λειριόεν τε κάρη τό τ' ἀπέcτυγεν Ἀφρώ,
> οὕνεκ' ἐριδμαίνεcκε χρόηc ὕπερ, ἐν δέ νυ θρίοιc
> ἀργαλέην μεcάτοιcιν ὀνειδείην ἐπέλαccε
> δεινὴν βρωμήεντοc ἐναλδήναcα κορύνην.

Take also the very iris and the head of the lily, which Aphrodite abhors, since it was her rival for color; and so she put something terribly shameful in the middle of its petals, making grow there the shocking shaft of an ass.

The ridiculous story is recounted as an unquestionable fact. Is the reader to assume that in Nicander's world the gods are more likely to quarrel with humble plants and to take vengeance on them than to wage a cosmic war against the Titans?

Nicander's self-confident attitude transfers from metapoetic passages to the context itself. As Clauss (2006) has aptly shown, the two poems are framed by the idea that knowledge makes life easier: "easily" will the poet expound his matter (ῥεῖα, *Th.* 1) and "easily" (ῥηϊδίως, *Th.* 22) will his addressee dispel all deadly creatures with what Nicander has taught him (cf. also *Th.* 117 "you may readily save yourself by our precepts," αἶψά κεν ἡμετέρηισιν ἐρωήσειας ἐφετμαῖς). If our author indeed had in mind the Hesiodic lines on Zeus who "*easily* makes strong and *easily* oppresses the strong, *easily* diminishes the conspicuous one and magnifies the inconspicuous, and *easily* makes the crooked straight and withers the proud" (ῥέα ... ῥέα ... ῥεῖα ... ῥεῖα, Hes. *WD* 5–7: Clauss 2006: 162–9), this seems to suggest that "Nicander's knowledge of poisonous creatures and how to deal with them gives him a status comparable to that of a god," thus wittily opposing the triumphant, Zeus-like poet to the harmful brutes originating from the Titans (Clauss 2006: 164; on the "rhetoric of ease" see also Hunter 2004b: 223–7). Therefore I would hesitate to subscribe to Toohey's interpretation of Nicander's stance as "doleful pessimism" (1996: 72). Dreadful as the beasts may be, the poet appears to say, you can easily deal with them if you just read my poem.

But who will benefit from Nicander's precepts? Aratus often speaks to his addressee explicitly, who nonetheless remains anonymous and faceless throughout (Toohey 1996: 55). Instead, the names of Nicander's addressees are declared at the very start of each poem, but this does not make them any less elusive or the reason why they are addressed any more obvious – contrast the named addressee of the *Works and Days*, Hesiod's brother Perses, who has taken more than his share of the inheritance and is therefore in obvious need of a lesson in justice (δίκη). About Protagoras, the addressee of the *Alexipharmaca*, we learn nothing except that he is Nicander's guest-friend (ξένος, 630) and hails from Cyzicus (1–11); why he might require instruction on antidotes remains unclear. The address to Hermesianax, "most honored" of Nicander's "many kinsmen," at the start of the *Theriaca* is framed in the following way (4–7; on these lines, see Brioso Sánchez 1994: 268; Fakas 2001: 101; Jacques 2002: LXXXIV):

> σὲ δ' ἄν πολύεργος ἀροτρεὺς
> βουκαῖός τ' ἀλέγοι καὶ ὀροιτύπος, εὖτε καθ' ὕλην
> ἢ καὶ ἀροτρεύοντι βάληι ἔπι λοιγὸν ὀδόντα,
> τοῖα περιφρασθέντος ἀλεξητήρια νούσων.

> And the hard-working plowman, the cowherd, or the woodcutter, whenever he is in the forest or plowing and one of these creatures sinks its deadly teeth in, shall respect you for being steeped in such means for averting illness.

Paying attention to humble workers is common in Hellenistic poetry, but here it is not clear whether "they shall respect you" means "they will wish that they too had read my poetry" (thus Hunter 2004b: 227) or "they will be grateful to you for healing them." In the latter case, Hermesianax should be a doctor (thus Jacques

2002: LXIX–LXX); yet there is nothing to support this elsewhere in the poem. In some passages, Nicander seems to be talking to a young country gentleman who occasionally has to spend the night in the fields (*Th.* 25, 55–6, 78–9); other passages, however, presuppose a farmer or the like (*Th.* 58 ἔργον ἀνύccαc, "when your work is done," and 113–4 μεθ' ἀλώια ἔργα / ζωcάμενοc θρίναξι, "when you gird yourself after work at the threshing-floor"), in fact more like the plowmen, herdsmen, and woodcutters who according to the proem will respect Hermesianax for having taken to heart Nicander's teachings. This inconsistency is hardly an oversight on the part of the poet. Nicander is simply uninterested in pinning down his addressee, which makes his didactic fiction looser than those of Hesiod and Aratus (on which see Semanoff 2006). The poet depicts himself as a dispenser of knowledge, but seems less concerned about constructing a realistic and coherent frame for the reception and his addressees' use of the information he provides. From this point of view, "the poet's solicitous professions of concern for his 'patients' should fool no one" (Hopkinson 1988: 143).

Nicander's lack of commitment to the "rules" of didactic does not necessarily lead to the conclusion that his subject held no intrinsic interest for him and that his primary goal was to show that a skillful poet can make good poetry out of virtually anything, as was once widely held. Schneider, for example (1856: 181–201), saw Nicander as nothing but a metaphrast, the versifier of a prose model which he identified with the now lost iological treatises of the third-century BCE scholar Apollodorus of Alexandria. More recent research has shown that Apollodorus was just one of many iological writers available to our poet (Touwaide 1991: 71–5; Jacques 2002: XLIX–LII), and that Nicander's knowledge of medical, zoological, and botanical literature is much more profound than earlier scholars imagined (Jacques 1979, 2002: LII–LX, 2004: 111–3, 2006: 28–31; Oikonomakos 1999; De Stefani 2006b: 57–65). Nicander, we can safely assume, was genuinely interested in snakes and plants, poisons and antidotes; the problem is rather that he is not interested in them in the way modern biologists and toxicologists are, and that his agenda differs from that of other didactic poets. Nicander's main interest in the *Theriaka* and *Alexipharmaca* is in description, in carefully listing the ingredients of his recipes, ailments, and animals, in which he sometimes shows a bent for the paradoxical (e.g., the reproduction of vipers, *Th.* 128–34) and the macabre (e.g., the crying head just cut from the body at *Al.* 215–16; Toohey 1996: 66–7; Spatafora 2005: 257–62). He does not provide details about the dosage of ingredients in antidotes nor seriously pretend in any other way to offer practical precepts to his addressees and readers. Nicander's approach to toxicology is not practical but theoretical, a fact he does not bother to hide – it is worth recalling the terse evaluation of Gow and Scholfield: "whereas the uninstructed reader may learn a good deal of astronomy from Aratus, the victim of snake-bite or poison who turned to Nicander for first-aid would be in sorry plight" (1953: 18). In other words, in Nicander the theoretical description one associates with ancient science and medicine predominates over the practical instruction one might expect in didactic poetry. In this respect as in others, his poetry is perfectly at home in the cultural climate of the Hellenistic Age, when the gap between cutting-edge science and the educational curriculum of the upper class was growing exponentially and waiting to be filled. Nicander was not a professional scientist, nor did he aim at producing a handbook that could help save human lives. Guido Gozzano's unfinished *Epistole entomologiche* ("Entomological Letters," c.1909–11) offers a modern parallel for his poems. Gozzano combined a profound interest in, and admirable command of the style and form of eighteenth-century didactic poetry with a passion for butterflies and moths. Surely, a love of "Callimachean" aesthetics and a passion for poisons and snakes would not have been seen as incompatible by Hellenistic Greeks – and least of all by scholar-poets such as Callimachus.

FURTHER READING

The standard editions of the *Theriaca* and *Alexipharmaca* are Jacques 2002 and 2007a, including the Greek text with French translation, extensive introductions, and detailed exegetical notes (for an assessment, see Spanoudakis 2005 and De Stefani 2006a). At present Schneider 1856, the first modern edition, still offers the only complete collection of all Nicandrian fragments (poetry and prose, 19–135, 203–7; additions in *SH* 562–563A; see also *FGrH* 271); Schneider's introduction and apparatus are also still worth consulting. Gow and Scholfield 1953 offers the two extant poems, poetic fragments, and testimonia with English translation and brief but helpful notes. Other editions include Oikonomakos 2002a–b (*Alexipharmaca* with important *prolegomena*); Crugnola 1971 and Geymonat 1974 (scholia on *Theriaca* and *Alexipharmaca*); and Gualandri 1968, Geymonat 1976, Papathomopoulos 1976 (Eutecnius' late-antique paraphrases).

Kroll's 1936 survey on Nicander is still useful. Pivotal studies of the structure of *Theriaca* and *Alexipharmaca* and their place in the tradition of didactic poetry are Effe 1974a–b and 1977a. For the interaction between pharmacological knowledge and literary aims in Nicander's poetry, see Jacques 1979, 2006, and Touwaide 1991; on Nicander's ideology in the *Theriaca*, Clauss 2006. Schneider 1962, Toohey 1996: 62–77, Spatafora 2005, and Cusset 2006a: 75–103 offer important insights on Nicander's style and poetic technique; on Nicander's language, see further Klauser 1898, Gow 1951, Crugnola 1961, and Bartalucci 1963. Studies devoted to Nicander's reception in Latin poetry include Hollis 1998 on Lucretius; Cazzaniga 1960 and Harrison 2004 on Vergil; and Vollgraff 1919, Herter 1941, Montanari 1974, and Griffin 1991 on Ovid.

CHAPTER SIXTEEN

The Bucolic Fiction of Theocritus

Mark Payne

The bucolic poems of Theocritus are generally understood to be those that feature a herdsman of one kind or another and they take their name from this central character, the *boukolos*: *Idylls* 1, 3–7, and 10–11. Some scholars have considered this an unwarranted restriction of the term to poems that are easily assimilated to the later pastoral tradition. They would include a larger selection of poems under the heading "bucolic," and point to the critical engagement with the earlier literary tradition that is missed when the *Idylls* are considered from the perspective of their future imitators. However, insofar as these poems limit themselves to the portrayal of herdsmen in a circumscribed rural setting, where their only activity is the production of song, they are recognizably the origin of the Western pastoral tradition that has as its primary model Vergil's *Eclogues* (*Bucolica* as he himself called them) and are rightly considered a new kind of literary fiction (Gutzwiller 1991: 3–19 and 2006; Alpers 1996: 145–7; Reed in this volume).

The fictionality of the bucolic world Theocritus created can hardly be exaggerated: the herdsmen come and go as they please, without masters to answer to or flocks with pressing needs. They spend their time singing and in love, and their surroundings are a pleasure zone of trees, streams, springs, and breezes. Nothing obliges them to act and the poems they inhabit are largely plotless as a result; the performance of song takes the place of action as such. The herdsmen are manifestly fictional, yet the nature of their fictionality is elusive: some look like ordinary mortals with invented names, or no name at all, others have a history in earlier literature. Moreover, characters with the same name look very different from one poem to the next, to the point where it is virtually impossible to reconcile the differences (Kossaifi 2002: 355–6). While the bucolic *Idylls* make use of elements from earlier Greek poetry, the fictional world that results from their recombination is unprecedented and the poems are immediately recognizable in these terms as a new genre. To understand their novelty better, it will be helpful to briefly review the various understandings of literary representation that were current at the time of their appearance.

Fictionality in Greek Literary Theory and Hellenistic Poetry

It is widely agreed that the concept of fictionality is first articulated in Aristotle's *Poetics*. While the distinction between truth and deceptive semblance has a long history in the poetic and sophistic tradition, Aristotle, for the first time, formulates an understanding of poetic narrative that endeavors to free it from judgments of truth or falsehood (Ford 2002: 231; Halliwell 2002: 166–8). In the terms of contemporary philosophy, poetic narrative is "verification-transcendent" insofar as it does not make direct truth claims about the world but offers a representative image of human life. Plot and direct speech by characters are the two aspects of fiction-making that Aristotle values most, for the first reveals what particular types of people do when placed in particular kinds of situations, while the second ensures that the story advances with the minimum of intervention on the part of the poet (*Poet.* 9, 24).

Aristotle's understanding of fiction's value leaves little room for the otherworldly. Fictional worlds peopled by beings who are not recognizably moral agents like ourselves, or worlds where the rules of possibility and causality bear little resemblance to those that obtain in our own, can have little value as models for understanding the behavior of real people. Such worlds are incapable of being an object of analysis for philosophically informed discussion, and literary criticism that abides by this Aristotelian understanding of mimesis will struggle with the fantastic. So, for example, a famous scholion on the *Iliad* tries to explain (and explain away) such elements as Zeus and Hera's lovemaking, or the monsters of the *Odyssey*, as the poet's intrusive fantasies, rather than integral parts of the poems' fictional worlds (Gutzwiller in this volume). New Comedy provides the scholiast's normative literary model; in Menander, human types such as misogynists, tricksters, and loudmouths act within a fictional world that has minimal deviation from the real world, so that his plays are easily understood as modeling real-life behaviors (Meijering 1987: 68–9; Lape in this volume). In the famous words of Aristophanes of Byzantium, "O Menander and Life, which of you imitated the other?"

In the Hellenistic period, the other genre that might seem to offer cognitive possibilities similar to those of New Comedy is the urban mime. In these poems, as represented by the *Mimiambs* of Herodas, and *Idylls* 2, 14, and 15 of Theocritus, a small cast of characters engages in conversation in an intimate domestic setting. The conversation is worldly, ranging over such topics as the possibilities for mercenary service in Ptolemaic Alexandria, and the purchase of sex toys in this same metropolis. The characters are housewives, soldiers, shopkeepers, and domestic slaves, but the brief scope of the poems (fewer than 200 lines) gives little opportunity for character to unfold in action; they are genre scenes rich in circumstantial detail rather than a representative image of human life.

An interest in the lives of humble people is also apparent in the mythological narrative poetry of the Hellenistic period. In Callimachus' *Hecale*, Theseus stays with a poor old woman before fighting the Bull of Marathon; in the *Aetia*, Heracles has to hear about the invention of the mousetrap from the pauper Molorcus before proceeding against more formidable foes; in Theocritus' *Idyll* 24, Hera's fearsome serpents find their way into a hero's home, where a shield has been repurposed as a crib. The effect is less to ironize or demystify these stories, and more a kind of re-enchantment of myth that comes from placing the fantastic in a setting that is immediately familiar. What would it really be like to have Heracles under your own roof, these poems ask us to imagine; what would it be like to see an infant strangle snakes? The emphasis is less upon the story itself, as a myth to be remembered, than on the act of imagination necessary to envision its story world.

If the main attraction in Hellenistic mythological narrative is not the story but the storytelling, poems in which mythical narratives have an encomiastic function might seem to present the writer with a problem: how to compare a king with a hero if myth itself lacks charismatic authority? Pindar could assimilate his athletic victors to their heroic counterparts in all seriousness, but how was a Hellenistic poet to make comparisons with beings that had lost their ontological prestige? The answer, it seems, was allegory. If the plot had a clear enough ideological content (the defeat of monsters by an Olympian god, or the emergence of order from chaos) its allegorical quality would be readily apparent, and the audience would understand it was really hearing about Ptolemy, not Heracles. When the relationship between history and myth is an intellectually apprehended analogy, rather than full ontological re-enactment, a certain amount of hilarity in the fictional construct is easily tolerated. So, in Callimachus' *Hymn to Delos*, for example, the unborn Apollo explains from his mother's womb that he is unwilling to be born on the island of Cos because Ptolemy Philadelphus is going to be born there in the future, and goes on to praise the successful campaigns against the Gauls the king has recently concluded (162–88). As the poet jests with the myth, its real function, to present Apollo as an analogue of his patron, becomes apparent. In this propagandistic use of the story world of myth, its gods and heroes do not instantiate human universals, as in the Aristotelian account of tragedy (a democratic fiction). Rather, the poet treats historical particulars (kings and tyrants) as if they were instantiations of mythical archetypes (Henrichs 1999: 223–6; Stephens 2003: 251).

More work needs to be done in this area, as it is not easy to see how poems such as Callimachus' *Hymn to Demeter* (especially the grotesque punishment of Erysichthon), or Theocritus' *Idyll* 26 (on the dismemberment of Pentheus), which share many of the lurid and fantastic features of the overtly encomiastic poems, would fit within the ambit of court poetry. What is clear, however, is that Hellenistic poems that include mythical narrative usually have formal features that draw attention to the way in which myth is deployed within them. To give the best-known example, Callimachus' hymns alternate between poems that feature a speaker fixed in a fictional time and space (the "mimetic" *h.* 2, 5, and 6) and poems that are spoken by an uncharacterized and seemingly colorless narrator (*h.* 1, 3, and 4). In the former, the speaker makes use of apparently omniscient sources to recount the sacred narrative that is the centerpiece of the poem; in the latter, the speaker tends to interfere with the story he is telling (Harder 1992: 384–94). In both cases, the mode of presentation invites attention to the relationship between teller and tale in mythical narrative, even as particularly fabulous episodes from it are selected for retelling.

A similar caution is apparent in the didactic poetry of the Hellenistic period. Here we can see a radical restriction of the sphere within which a poet can hope to make legitimate truth claims in his own voice. While Hesiod may claim knowledge about the birth of the gods, or Pindar offer prescriptive maxims for moral behavior, the Hellenistic poet offers a poetry of fact, presented with the elegance proper to scientific knowledge, but manifestly non-fictional. The points of departure for Aratus' poetry on the movements of the stars, or Nicander's on the bites of venomous animals, are prose treatises by scientific authorities (Eudoxus, Apollodorus), with which their poems could easily have been compared. While the poems may narrativize their scientific material (Nicander in particular proceeding by imagined vignettes of reptile and insect attack), neither poet offers special knowledge derived from his vocation as poet. What makes a text poetic is the way it presents its material rather than the material itself (Hunter 2008a; Gutzwiller in this volume).

To better appreciate the generic innovations of Hellenistic poetry, we must analyze them with due regard for the kinds of world-making they enable – how formal experiments are related to fictionality and the mimetic function. The formal structures of narrative genres are most productively considered in close relationship with the fictional worlds they transmit, and fictional presence – how a story world is brought close or kept at a distance by the way in which it is presented – should have a central place in their study, as it does in the narrative theory of Plato and Aristotle (Hardie 2002: 6). Likewise, manifest differences in content with regard to Archaic and Classical predecessors should not automatically be regarded as signs of an author's antagonistic relationship to the literary tradition, but may be more usefully thought of as additions to the fictional repertoire available to the poet (Fantuzzi and Hunter 2004: 133–41).

The Fictionality of the Bucolic Poems

Aristotle's conception of genre proposes a sustained correlation between objects and modes of representation. Tragedy is the representation of people better than ourselves in the dramatic mode, comedy of people worse than ourselves, and so on (*Poet.* 2–5). Aristotle does not address the interlopers who occasionally make their presence felt – Thersites in the *Iliad*, or the slaves and messengers of tragedy – but it would probably be correct to suppose that these characters would have had a focusing function for him insofar as they draw our attention to the kind of people the genre is really about.

The most common mode of presentation in the bucolic poems is dramatic; while Theocritus experiments with a variety of framing devices, a dramatic scene is at the heart of each, and this scene in turn contains some form of song. These songs range from the merest scrap of a refrain in *Idyll* 4 to the dramatic re-enactment of "The Sorrows of Daphnis" in *Idyll* 1, the competitive song contest of *Idyll* 5, the song exchanges of *Idylls* 7 and 10, and the solo love songs for an absent beloved in *Idylls* 3 and 11. However, while the poems have the generic consistency that comes from the combination of a particular kind of character with a particular mode of representation, this character is hard to place on the scale of human types – better, worse, or just like ourselves – that Aristotle envisages.

The poems in which the herdsmen appear are short, and virtually plotless, like the urban mines, but they themselves are not rural counterparts of the slaves in those poems. The herdsmen take part in musical competitions with Pan and the Muses, they pretend to be Daphnis and Polyphemus in their songs, they elaborate on the pleasure they have taken in contemplating works of art, and offer their thoughts on Hellenistic literary theory. Not only does their speech belie what their occupation suggests, the reality effects drawn from the world of rural labor that is the backdrop to the songs only enhance the manifest fictionality of their characterization as herdsmen.

Nor do they belong to myth. The nameless goatherd of *Idyll* 1 cannot, by his very anonymity, be located in the mythical record. Anonymity is a marker of fiction where it is found in earlier literature (Finkelberg 1998: 130), and the centrality of an unnamed character in this poem seems to be programmatic: while fictional beings elsewhere people the interstices of mythical narratives – the shield of Achilles in the *Iliad*, whose invented cities are filled with anonymous inhabitants, or the messengers and minor characters of tragedy – here one occupies center stage, identified by his occupation alone. On the other hand, the herdsmen are highly conscious of their predecessors – in *Idyll* 1, Thyrsis impersonates Daphnis, who is on speaking terms with the Olympian gods; in *Idyll* 6, Daphnis and Damoetas impersonate Polyphemus and a nameless companion; in *Idyll* 7, Lycidas imagines the lives of Daphnis and Comatas; in *Idyll* 5, Comatas compares himself with Daphnis and Melantheus, the evil goatherd of the *Odyssey. Idyll* 11 further problematizes the question of what ontological category to assign the herdsmen to, for in this poem Polyphemus is re-imagined as a lovesick shepherd like those of the other bucolic poems.

An imagined version of the bucolic world they themselves inhabit is thus a constant obsession of the herdsmen, and forms the substance of their songs. Yet this bucolic past is not anchored to any particular time; it is an image generated by longing and mirrored inconsistently from one poem to the next. Lycidas, who is the superlative singing herdsmen in *Idyll* 7, longs for the world of Daphnis and Comatas, yet Daphnis, when we see him in person in *Idyll* 6, is imagining the world of Polyphemus. So too Comatas, the embodiment of bucolic consolation in Lycidas' song, is salacious and aggressive when he appears in person in *Idyll* 5. The irreducibility of the bucolic world's origins enhances its ontological mystique; what is sourced from myth and actuality has undergone a thorough fictionalization in its transduction to its new home, and the bucolic characters belong to no world that we can identify outside the poems in which they appear.

Discovering the Fiction

Ancient commentators regarded *Idyll* 1 as the most delightful and best constructed of Theocritus' poems, which for these reasons was rightly placed at the beginning of the collection as its "gleaming front" (*Id.* 1 arg. b at Wendel 1914: 23). It is a dialogue between Thyrsis, a shepherd and singer, and an unnamed goatherd who is also a syrinx player. An introductory conversation between the two (1–14) sets the scene of their encounter, and is followed by a long speech by the goatherd (15–63) in which he describes a decorated bowl or *kissubion* (27–60) that he promises to give to Thyrsis if the latter will sing "The Sorrows of Daphnis" for him. Thyrsis responds by performing the song (64–145), and the goatherd greets his performance with enthusiastic admiration when it is over (146–52).

The opening speeches carefully identify human and natural music; as a pine tree by springs sings its whispering song, so the goatherd sweetly pipes (1–3); likewise, the goatherd replies, Thyrsis' song falls more sweetly than water from a nearby rock (7–8). Beginning with this elaborate and highly patterned praise, the herdsmen extend their gaze to a landscape of trees and gentle hills as they seek out a spot in which to attend to one another's music. As they gesture to their customary haunts, they invite us to picture their delightful surroundings for ourselves.

Thyrsis is reluctant to sing at first, and the goatherd has to draw him out with a reward. He offers him a *kissubion*, or wooden bowl, decorated with an ivy pattern and scenes with figures. Not having the bowl before him, he elaborates on its adornment; in one scene (32–8), men with beautiful hair "contend with words" beside a woman, though they do not touch her mind: as she "looks at one man smiling and then turns her mind to the other," they, "long since hollow-eyed with love, labor in vain." In the next (39–44), an old man strains with all his might to cast a net, so that "you would say that he is fishing with all the strength of his limbs." In the final scene (45–54), a young boy is guarding a vineyard, poorly. He is intent on weaving a cricket cage from some plants, with the result that scheming foxes are wrecking the vines and about to devour his lunch.

In all three cases the ecphrasis of the recollected object contrasts the fixity of the visual image with the interpretive additions the goatherd introduces to explain what he sees, as he finds psychology and a back story in the first scene, identifies physiologically with the fisherman in the second, and imagines the mental states of boy and fox in the third. The interpretive movement on the goatherd's part recapitulates the energies we bring to bear on the poem's opening dialogue as we connect the details the poem supplies in order to imagine a fictional world with extension and temporality. Now, in 23 verses, we enter and leave three fictional microcosms in succession, with new settings, new characters, and new stories to imagine each time. The ecphrasis offers the reader a concentrated experience of fictional involvement and a paradigm of the way in which this involvement can further fictionalize fictional facts by providing them with all kinds of imagined motivations and contexts. For the goatherd's account of the bowl leaves us in no doubt that what we are listening to is in part invention. The ecphrasis is a fictional character's imaginative engagement with a work of visual fiction (Miles 1977: 147; Payne 2007: 38–40).

The goatherd's description appears to work the same magic on Thyrsis as it does on the reader, for he agrees to perform "The Sorrows of Daphnis" as requested. His song is an elaborate, histrionic performance. It includes impersonation, of Daphnis himself, and of the visitors who visit his deathbed, dramatic pauses as the dying herdsmen refuses to answer his interlocutors, and a final theatrical outburst as he reproaches Aphrodite for her cruelty in bringing about his death. Thyrsis incorporates his audience into the performance with references within the song itself to the sexual proclivities of goatherds and to the syrinx that the goatherd shares with Daphnis. The fiction of live performance in which the singer can respond directly to the living presence of his audience confronts his listener with an imaginary world that maps itself actively onto his own time and space (Pretagostini 1992: 71).

Thyrsis cannibalizes a variety of literary genres for effect (epic, hymn, tragedy, comedy, funeral epigram). At the textual level, the poem deconstructs its own illusion of primitive oral song even as it produces it. Likewise, the story of Daphnis is impossible to reconstruct from the song, even in outline (Ogilvie 1962: 110). Yet, at the level of the poem's fiction, the goatherd sees none of this. He responds to it as song, wishing that the "lovely mouth" of Thyrsis might be filled with honey since he sings "better than a cicada" (146–8). The poem exploits the cognitive dissonance between his experience of the song and our own – to understand his delight, we have to imagine the material pleasure of Thyrsis' voice, the very thing we cannot get from the text, nor from any performance of it. The poem's hexameters elide the difference between speech and song so that the source of delight within the poem's fictional world cannot be produced by staging it (Wilamowitz 1906: 137). The poem playfully dramatizes its own distance from orality and its impossibly melodious shepherd is the invention of a poet who knows he can depend on the imagination of readers to bring his world to life. The non-performativity of the text is another marker of its fictionality. While face-to-face storytelling (as the poem portrays it) responds directly to its audience's desires, the text must seduce its readers with an imaginary experience they cannot have outside it.

In other bucolic *Idylls*, narrative framing plays with the reader's desire for the poetic fiction, particularly insofar as this fiction is made present by the direct speech of the herdsmen. The distinction between narration by the poet and the invented speech of his characters is the basis of Plato's analysis of literary effect in the *Republic* (Book 3, 395c–d, 401b–c; Book 10, 605c–606b), and remains central to the understanding of genre in the *Poetics*, where the dramatic mode is virtually equated with fictionality (24). Experimentation with the modes of literary representation remains vital in Hellenistic poetic practice and in ancient commentary on the resulting works (McLennan 1977: 147; Fantuzzi 1988: 65–81). The prolegomena to the Theocritus scholia, for example, discuss the formal variety of the bucolic poems in these terms (proleg. D and E at Wendel 1914: 4–5), and *Idyll* 11 is an experiment with storytelling modes that can be approached rewardingly from this perspective.

Idyll 11 begins with a suggestion addressed to a named addressee (1–3): "There is no other medicine for love, Nicias, either rubbed or sprinkled, than the Pierides." As an example of the successful application of the Muses to the wounds of love, the poet proposes Polyphemus, who "fared better" (ῥάιστα διᾶγε, 7; cf. 81) with this treatment. It has been suggested that the opening is a fictionalized version of the exchange of maxims between friends in the performative contexts of Archaic lyric, iambic and sympotic poetry (Fantuzzi and Hunter 2004: 170–1). In keeping with these models, the poet sets out the salient points of his example: wounded by a dart from Aphrodite, the adolescent Cyclops let his flocks wander while he sat on the sea shore singing of his love for the sea nymph Galatea.

At this point, however, the poem takes a very surprising turn, as the poet drops the narrative mode and lets the Cyclops speak (or rather sing) for himself (19–21): "O white Galatea, why do you spurn one who loves you, you who are whiter than cream cheese to look upon, softer than a lamb, friskier than a calf, sleeker than an unripe grape." As the poem morphs into dramatic fiction before our very eyes, the difference between exemplum narration and fictional presence could hardly be more apparent. Instead of a discursive object held at arm's length for the sake of a point, Polyphemus is suddenly present in his own words in all his irrepressible alterity. As a fictional creation, Theocritus' Polyphemus is manifestly different from those of Homer and the comic tradition. As he tells it, his ugliness is now all on the outside; no longer the cannibalistic negation of civilization as he is in Homer, nor an embodiment of its laughable excesses as he is in Euripides, the Cyclops is now a "monster" merely by virtue of his snub nose and hairy brow. His heart is pure, his love as sincere as that of any singing herdsman, his mind as full of visions. He cannot even, it seems, distinguish memory from dream, and his waking life is devoted to recapturing the images his sleeping mind produces unsummoned (22–33).

While the Cyclops is aware of his own unattractiveness, he also knows that he is well endowed with pastoral riches, and contemplation of them seems to do him good as he reviews them in his imagination: his cattle, the fine milk and cheese they produce, his musical skills, the abundance of baby animals he can offer as playthings, his shady cave, and its cool water from the snows of Mount Etna (34–48). He passes all these before his mind as he sits upon the shore, and, in doing so, he turns the pastoral world he has temporarily abandoned into an imaginary object, a secondary desire that can take the nymph's place. By being pictured in this way, as an imaginary presence rather than a real one, his world is able to exert the same attraction over him as the absent body of Galatea. "Come forth," he says, one last time, "and having come forth forget, as I do now, sitting here, to go home" (63–4). But no sooner is the claim that he has forgotten his home out of his mouth (as if he had not spent most of his song describing it), than he comes to his senses and pledges to return to it. "O Cyclops, Cyclops, where has your mind wandered" (72), he concludes, acknowledging his imaginary journey as he turns back towards his lambs and his cheese.

Polyphemus achieves his return to reality by picturing in song an imagined double of the bucolic world he himself inhabits as an alternative to erotic fantasy. In this he resembles Theocritus' other herdsmen. Lycidas, in *Idyll* 7, imagines an idealized pastoral scene he might have shared with Comatas (86–9), Thyrsis, in *Idyll* 1, imagines himself as Daphnis (100–36). Less happily, the goatherd in *Idyll* 3 invokes a series of mythical doubles for his own experience (40–51), but cannot quite identify with them successfully. The pastoral world he imagines remains rooted in myth, and will not allow him to re-imagine his own world in its image. Polyphemus, however, can stand outside himself for a while, and see himself as another; he desists from re-inflicting his erotic wound by imagining himself as someone worthy of love by virtue of the world that he inhabits. The effects are evidently therapeutic, but the process is nothing like progress towards self-knowledge (Holtsmark 1966: 253–9; Cozzoli 1994: 95–110). Rather, his song fulfills the healing function that is claimed for it in the poem's opening by replacing the imaginary object that has occupied the Cyclops' mind with another that can substitute for it.

There is, however, a second, and perhaps more important way in which his song instantiates (rather than simply demonstrates) this claim. For Polyphemus has not just himself as audience, but Nicias too. Many of the bucolic poems feature listening to bucolic song as their centerpiece. In particular, Thyrsis' performance of "The Sorrows of Daphnis" in *Idyll* 1, and the song that Lycidas imagines being performed for him in *Idyll* 7, demonstrate the pleasures of imaginative absorption for the listener. Just as the goatherd of *Idyll* 1 professes extreme pleasure in the performance he hears (146–8), so Lycidas imagines the power of pastoral song to distract him from his love for the boy Ageanax, and concludes by wishing that he might have been able to hear the voice of Comatas himself (7.71–89). It is in hearing, rather than performing, pastoral song that its healing power resides for him (Walsh 1985: 13).

By allowing Nicias, then, in *Idyll* 11, to overhear the song of a famous pastoral musician – Polyphemus "can pipe like no other Cyclops" (38–9), just as Lycidas is "the best of pipers among the herdsmen and reapers" (7.27–9) – the poem restages the listening scenes that occur between fictional characters in other poems across the boundary that separates fictional character from real world reader. Listening to Polyphemus, we forget about the universe of discourse that surrounds him for the duration of his song. We are absorbed by the Cyclops' performance until we are suddenly jarred out of it by the unexpected return of the poet's voice at the end of the poem: "So Polyphemus tended his desire with song, and did better than if he had paid money" (80–1).

Making the reader aware of his absorption in the poem's fictional world resembles the ecphrastic technique of *Idyll* 1, where in quick succession we enter and leave a series of miniature scenes on the surface of the goatherd's decorated bowl. In *Idyll* 11, the transition from one narrative level to another is combined with a change in mode, as the poet's voice suddenly replaces that of his character, and the self-consciousness this induces is the most telling proof of the poem's gnomic proposition, that song is an effective treatment for desire. For as long as the Cyclops' song lasts, the reader forgets about his own preoccupations. The example does not just work by demonstration, inviting Nicias to inspect Polyphemus' state of mind at the beginning and end of his performance, and so judge the therapeutic effect of the song upon its singer. It works as imaginative experience, drawing the reader in, and thereby demonstrating its power over us. The poem enacts the powerful form of mental distraction exercised by fictional speech, a willing forgetfulness of the self in imaginary experience that is all the more palpable because we return to reality so abruptly at the end of it.

Mimetic Desire and Metafiction

Rather than lamenting a fall from performance culture to literacy, *Idyll* 1 and *Idyll* 11 exploit the conditions of textuality to present their fictional worlds in ways that foreground the acts of imagination involved in conceiving them. The centrality of the imagination to their literary project is further evidenced by the role it plays within the poems. For a key element in the subjectivity of the bucolic characters is their ability to imagine, project, and identify with singers who inhabit bucolic worlds that are doubles of their own. Insofar, then, as being a bucolic character means having a self that is consciously shaped by imitation of a self-elected literary model, it is proper to speak of the herdsmen as acting under the influence of what René Girard has called "mimetic desire" (1978: 3).

So the performance by which Thyrsis proves his exemplary status as bucolic singer in *Idyll* 1 is a re-enactment of the herdsman Daphnis. So the goatherd of *Idyll* 3 introduces mythical paradigms that lead not so much to the persuasion of his addressee Amaryllis, but to a partial identification with his legendary predecessors. So Comatas in *Idyll* 5 contrasts his positive and negative models, Daphnis and Melantheus. So Lycidas, the exemplary herdsman singer in *Idyll* 7, wishes he could have heard the voice of the famous Comatas. To have heard bucolic song is to have been inspired with a desire to emulate its leading characters, and dramatic impersonation is one way in which this desire expresses itself. By imagining themselves as others, the herdsmen try out roles from the bucolic repertory, and so stage their own imaginative involvement with the bucolic world of which they are a part.

This aspect of bucolic song is staged at length in *Idyll* 6 (on which see also Reed in this volume). The poem begins, like *Idyll* 11, with an address to a friend. However, in this case, there is no indication of what point the ensuing dramatic scene is meant to illustrate; Aratus, the addressee, is simply told that "Damoetas and Daphnis the cowherd once drove their herd together into one place," and that in the exchange of songs that followed, "Daphnis began first, because he first proposed a contest" (1–5). More surprisingly still, when Daphnis begins, he appears to be talking to someone other than Damoetas: "Galatea throws apples at your flock, Polyphemus, and calls you a wretched lover and a goatherd. And you do not look at her, you wretch, but sit sweetly playing your pipe" (6–9). The dramatic situation is hard to construe, to put it mildly: why is Daphnis pretending to talk to Polyphemus, and why is Theocritus telling Aratus about it?

If this were not puzzling enough, the way Daphnis presents the Cyclops to Damoetas quite explicitly contradicts what we know about him from *Idyll* 11. Now it is Galatea who is in love with him, and who has left the sea to solicit his affections, while Polyphemus is either indifferent to her charms, or master of his own desire to such a degree that he is able to feign indifference to her. So, too, when Damoetas adopts the role of Cyclops in his response, the eye that was the source of his ugliness in *Idyll* 11 is now the instrument of his power over the nymph, and, like his gleaming teeth, an object of beauty when he views himself reflected in the ocean (35–8). Not content with fictionalizing the Polyphemus of the tradition in *Idyll* 11, Theocritus brackets the ontological claims of his own fiction by allowing his bucolic impersonators to reinvent him in this poem.

The lability of the Cyclops matches that of his impersonator Daphnis. For Daphnis is more palpable, more present, when he is projected by Thyrsis' impersonation of him in *Idyll* 1 than he is when he appears in his own person in *Idyll* 6. The bucolic characters do not have a self that can be discovered by inspection, either by themselves or by the reader. Their subjectivity is rather a site for fictional projection and identification – it is by pretending to be others that they are most truly who they are. At the end of the poem the herdsmen exchange instruments and play on, their calves dancing around them. Even the definition of character by musical accomplishment that distinguishes the syrinx-playing goatherd from the singer Thyrsis in *Idyll* 1 is abandoned: "One gives the other a syrinx, the other gives a lovely flute. Damoetas plays the flute, and Daphnis the cowherd plays the syrinx" (43–4). Now there is nothing to choose between them, and the idea of contest is abandoned: "Neither won, they were both undefeated" (46). The lability of the bucolic character is fully manifest.

The theme of bucolic imitation is dramatized most strikingly in the poem that has been by far the most discussed by modern scholars, *Idyll* 7, the "Thalysia," or "Harvest Festival." In this poem, a speaker named Simichidas recalls how he traveled from the city of Cos to a harvest festival at the country estate of some friends (1–9). On the way, he met a goatherd named Lycidas (10–20), and the two of them exchanged songs before going their separate ways. Lycidas sings of his love for a boy, but soon turns from erotic to bucolic themes. He imagines the songs that will be sung for him at a rustic symposium he is to host, and recalls famous bucolic singers of long ago (52–89). Simichidas' song remains within the present, but is full of bucolic touches as it cautions his friend Aratus against unrequited love (96–127). Lycidas gives Simichidas a staff as a token of his esteem, and the two parties go their separate ways (128–34). In the last part of the poem, Simichidas gives an account of his surroundings at the festival that is both rapturous in tone and exceptionally rich in descriptive detail. He concludes by comparing the wine he drank there with wine drunk by Heracles and Polyphemus, and wishes that he might be allowed to experience the festival again in the future (135–57).

What sets the poem apart is its precise, real-world location, and the form of its narration; while the other bucolic *Idylls* are enacted in a dramatic present (sometimes framed by a discursive present in which the poet addresses a friend), *Idyll* 7 is a retrospective first-person account of past experience that ends with an unprecedented wish for the future (Puelma 1960: 144; Meillier 1993: 104). The poem reads like autobiography and it was understood as such by its ancient commentators, who identified Simichidas with Theocritus (*Id.* 7 arg. at Wendel 1914: 76–7). Lycidas, on the other hand, is clearly a bucolic character – he looks like one and sings like one, although the contrast between small-scale composition and emulation of Homer that precedes his song touches on some topical issues in Hellenistic poetics (45–7). Further complicating the picture is the fact that his sudden appearance has elements of Homeric epiphany scenes (Williams 1971: 137–45), and that his gift of a staff to Simichidas closely resembles Hesiod's meeting with the Muses in the *Theogony* (Puelma 1960: 155–6).

How, then, to put these elements together, and so make sense of the poem as a whole? Like most interpreters, I think Lycidas is the key to understanding the poem. Lycidas looks like a goatherd, and smells like one too (16), but his familiarity with contemporary poetics belies the suggestion that he is a figure drawn from the countryside from which he emerges so mysteriously. He invites Simichidas to "begin the bucolic song" (36) in words that recall the refrain song of Thyrsis in *Idyll* 1. He sings of desire, and of the freedom from desire that emerges in the contemplation of bucolic predecessors, singing in landscapes of their own (Walsh 1985: 13). His song nests a series of increasingly smaller stories within it, and the singers within his song point back to Lycidas himself, the master singer enclosed in the narrative of *Idyll* 7.

Lycidas, then, would seem to be the instantiation within the world of the poem of the singing herdsmen who exemplify the bucolic fiction as a whole (Kühn 1958:

64–74; Meillier 1993: 115). What Simichidas appears to learn from him is the ability to understand his own bucolic experience as a desire for identification with such models. At the end of the poem he gives a point-by-point account of the beauty of his surroundings at the festival and concludes with an imaginative question (148–57):

> Νύμφαι Κασταλίδες Παρνάσιον αἶπος ἔχοισαι,
> ἆρά γέ παι τοιόνδε Φόλω κατὰ λάϊνον ἄντρον
> κρατῆρ' Ἡρακλῆϊ γέρων ἐστάσατο Χίρων;
> ἆρά γέ παι τῆνον τὸν ποιμένα τὸν ποτ' Ἀνάπωι,
> τὸν κρατερὸν Πολύφαμον, ὃς ὤρεσι νᾶας ἔβαλλε,
> τοῖον νέκταρ ἔπεισε κατ' αὔλια ποσσὶ χορεῦσαι,
> οἷον δὴ τόκα πῶμα διεκρανάσατε, Νύμφαι,
> βωμῶι πὰρ Δάματρος ἁλωΐδος;

> Castalian nymphs, who inhabit the slopes of Parnassus, did old Chiron set a cup such as this before Heracles in the stony cave of Pholus? Did nectar such as this persuade that shepherd by the Anapus, the mighty Polyphemus, who hit ships with mountains, to dance about the sheepfolds with his feet, such a drink as you then mixed beside the altar of Demeter of the Threshing Floor, Nymphs?

The contrast with the witty ironic song he sang earlier for Lycidas (the best in his repertoire, he boasted) is clear. From the studied introduction of bucolic motifs in that piece, he has progressed here to an understanding of what bucolic song can be in the hands of a master such as Lycidas: the ability to imagine bucolic paradigms so seductive that one's identity as a bucolic singer merges with them. He has not yet achieved the mastery of a Thyrsis or a Lycidas in this respect, for these characters are able to instantiate for others the very archetypes they imagine for themselves. Simichidas is more like the goatherd of *Idyll* 3; he is still trying out the relationship between paradigm and personal experience, and he does so without a great deal of confidence (Fantuzzi 1995: 28). He has, however, glimpsed what it would be like to be bucolic in the way that they are.

Lycidas calls Simichidas "fashioned for the sake of truth" (ἐπ' ἀλαθείαι πεπλασμένον, 44), and, when we read a poem by Theocritus that is a poet's autobiography, and the defining moment in this autobiography is this poet's encounter with a bucolic singer, it is difficult to avoid the idea that the autobiography is that of Theocritus himself, the inventor of bucolic fiction. Why, then, does the poem thwart this identification even as it suggests it? Story time and moment of narration never converge in *Idyll* 7, and its narrator does not tell us how the younger version of himself whose meeting with Lycidas is recorded in the poem became the person who writes of that meeting (Starobinski 1980: 78–9). More obviously, the name of this narrator is Simichidas, not Theocritus, and this might seem to preclude the identification of character with author in the first place (Lejeune 1989: 4–5). If *Idyll* 7 is autobiography, why the detour through fiction?

The answer lies, I think, in the kind of autobiography that the poem is, namely, an inspiration narrative. As Callimachus in the *Aetia* prologue, and Herodas in *Mimiamb* 8, defer to dreams the encounter with the inspiring being that results in their distinctive poetic creation – the encounter that for Hesiod and Archilochus happens in the waking world (*Theogony* 22–34; Clay 2004: 14–16) – so *Idyll* 7 points to the mystery of inspiration by recounting this event as fiction. Significantly, the transforming encounter is not with a god but with a goatherd. While Lycidas is invested with divine characteristics, he is, most obviously, a figure from Theocritus' own bucolic poetry. By employing the heteronym Simichidas, Theocritus allows a version of himself to encounter his invention Lycidas in a fictional narrative in which he is transformed by his own creation. By creating a poem in which the fictionalized author emulates his own fictional character, Theocritus offers us a form of autobiography that remains faithful to the message of the bucolic *Idylls*, that we free ourselves to change by identifying with the products of the literary imagination.

The Poet in the Poem

The presence of the author in a fictional world of his own invention, encountering there what is recognizably one of his own fictional creations, is an innovation in literary world-building that will be vitally significant to the future of bucolic poetry. For if Simichidas is Theocritus, and Simichidas can meet Lycidas, the poet can be discovered in his poems in all kinds of guises and disguises.

Traces of the interpretive questions this possibility raises can be found in the scholia to the *Idylls* where commentators dispute whether the goatherd of *Idyll* 3 is rightly identified as the poet (*Id.* 3 arg. 3.1a at Wendel 1914: 116–17; Gutzwiller 1991: 180–1). Theocritus' poetic successors respond to the possibility creatively. The *Epitaph for Bion* presents a scene in which the historical poet Bion was known to, associated with, and continues to be lamented by, his own bucolic characters (58–63): "Galatea too weeps for your song, whom you used to delight as she sat beside you on the shore … Now she sits upon the lonely sands, and tends your flocks till this hour." The poem does not merely call a historical poet a herdsman for the first time (Van Sickle 1976: 27; Alpers 1996: 153). More ambitiously, it posits a bucolic world in which beings from different ontological domains can mingle freely.

It is, however, Vergil's *Eclogues* that utilize the possibility in a way that will prove decisive for the future of bucolic poetry. Vergil's Roman contemporaries occupy the same fictional world as his bucolic characters, and the poet moves in and out of alignment with the fictional singers that represent him (Patterson 1987: 19–59; Martindale 1997a: 116–19; Hunter 2006a: 125–30). The visible presence of the author and other historical figures within the poems makes the bucolic world legible as a counter-image of their own historical reality, and the Renaissance revivalists of bucolic fiction will cherish its ability to offer a utopian critique of their age (Iser 1989: 75).

FURTHER READING

The most convenient place to read the bucolic poems in Greek is in the edition with commentary by Hunter, 1999; see also Gow 1952b and Dover 1971. The essays collected in Fantuzzi and Papanghelis 2006 offer a broad range of perspectives upon the development of pastoral in antiquity. The ideas in this chapter are developed at greater length in Payne 2007. The best introductions to fictional-worlds theory and its emergence from the possible worlds theory of Anglo-American philosophy are Pavel 1986 and Doležel 1998; Ronen 1994 is a clear account of the ways in which the two theories differ. Edmunds 2001 contains a rewarding discussion of the relationship between fictional worlds and genre in Latin poetry. Iser 1993 brings a unique theoretical acumen to bear on the thematization of fictionality in Renaissance pastoral. Among twentieth-century pastoralists, the Portuguese poet Fernando Pessoa most repays comparison with the bucolic experiments of Theocritus and Vergil; I discuss his version of the encounter between the bucolic poet and the bucolic master he invents for himself in Payne 2007: 141–4. Pessoa 1998 and 2001 are representative selections of his poetry and prose. McHale 1987 is a fascinating study of world-building in the postmodern novel.

CHAPTER SEVENTEEN

Idyll 6 and the Development of Bucolic after Theocritus

J. D. Reed

The transition from the work of Theocritus to the poetic line it inspired – mime-like poems involving herdsman-singers and other country people, labeled "pastoral" or "bucolic" – is one of the most tantalizing questions in ancient, and indeed in all Western, literature. It has proved difficult to resist essentialist solutions, particularly those that purport to recover a core plan of the author's own, perpetuated by his followers – even once we have abandoned the ancient "mimetic" conception of bucolic that conflates its poets and their compositions with its characters, herdsmen-singers, and their own performances. Origins seem always to be privileged in the question of this poetic category: who invented it? Theocritus, according to the consensus; but the question remains: what did he invent? Surely not the "pastoral" as modern critics know it. The moment of change, and its dynamics, then become our object: is it to be found in early modern pastoral? Vergil's Roman imitators? Vergil's own *Eclogues*? One of the Greek followers of Theocritus? It is perhaps preferable to refocus and ask, instead, about the picture yielded by any provisionally adopted point of origin; that is, about how any given text in this poetic line reads (or makes us read) others – especially, from the historical standpoint, the texts that precede it.

Our focus here is on an early stage in the tradition. Of the three names preserved in the ancient canon of bucolic poets – Theocritus of Syracuse, Moschus of Syracuse, and Bion of Smyrna (*Suda* θ 166, schol. *AP* 9.440) – the first lived under Ptolemy Philadelphus in the early to mid-third century, and the last two must have lived roughly in the latter half of the second century BCE. The historical facts at our disposal offer poor means to reconstruct the development of bucolic poetry from Theocritus down to Moschus and Bion, let alone to the anonymous authors whose poems, mistakenly ascribed to one or another of the canonical three, are transmitted in the bucolic manuscripts with theirs. This chapter will examine the transition from Theocritus that is attested in the anonymous *Idylls* 8 and 9 in the Theocritean corpus, poems that have been seen as representing the earliest examples of post-Theocritean bucolic. Rossi, for example, calls 8 our first example of "sentimental" pastoral poetry

(1971b: 5; cf. Effe 1977b: 9–10). What we seem to observe in them is a building on, a rereading of, the precedent set by Theocritus' poetry (e.g., Effe 1977b: 25–6; Nauta 1990: 125). We shall pay especial attention to their connections to *Idyll* 6, which in many ways they closely resemble, and which critics have often seen as a transitional step from the bucolic of Theocritus to that of his followers, especially as concerns the crystallization of bucolic conventions and the development of an idealized pastoral world.

At 45 lines, *Idyll* 6 is the shortest of the mime-like hexameter poems that modern scholarship ascribes to Theocritus (*Idylls* 1–7, 10, 14–15; *Idyll* 9 is shorter). After a few introductory lines of narrative addressed to one Aratus, the poem proceeds to a singing contest between two herdsmen, Daphnis and Damoetas, who act out a version of the legendary love of the Cyclops Polyphemus for the sea nymph Galatea. The contest concluded, they happily exchange musical instruments. The prologue, mime-like dialogue, herdsmen characters, singing contest, romantic undertones, and Cyclops myth all seem typical of Theocritean bucolic. The dialect is that of epic poetry with a Doric admixture, as in his other mime-like poems; the meter, as usual, is the hexameter. A recent critic says, "*Idyll* 6 ... seems to me to encapsulate the bucolic world in a more concise way than any of the other pastoral idylls ... We not only meet the mythical Daphnis, but we witness again the quintessential bucolic motifs: the herdsmen and their herds, the meeting at noontime, the springs, the songs and piping ... In addition to all of these, the amoebean contest, the only bucolic element missing in *Idyll* 1, is highly prominent in 6 ... *Idyll* 6 is the application of bucolic principles: it is, perhaps, the pastoral poem *par excellence*" (Lushkov 2003: 1–2). Yet we should not let hindsight and the conventions of later pastoral lead us to *expect* a constellation of features here that is really rather remarkable, and that points to a new consolidation of motifs out of Theocritus' typically Alexandrian experiments.

Idylls 8 and 9, although transmitted under the name of Theocritus, are now generally agreed to be the work of one or two others, variously on linguistic, dialectal, metrical, and stylistic grounds, as well as for perceived anomalies in portrayal and characterization (Valckenaer 1779; cf. Brinker 1884; Kattein 1901; Arland 1937: 9–11; Gow 1952b; Bernsdorff 2006: 168–70 nn.9, 11). Their narrative form and use of earlier literature suggest that if 8 and 9 imitate Theocritus, they took 6 as their foremost model (Arland 1937: 20–2 on 8). All three poems are titled *Boukoliastai*, "Herdsmen-Singers," a term doubtless adopted with its use at *Idyll* 5.68 especially in mind; although the titles may not go back to the original authors, they mark all three poems as being about Theocritean herdsman-singers. Like 6, 8 and 9 each frame a singing-contest between two herdsmen with a few lines of introduction and conclusion. The introductory passages of 6 and 8 are remarkably similar in both ideas and wording (Kattein 1901: 42–3). Daphnis is one of the two named speakers in each of the three, and he is a winsome, childlike Daphnis far removed from the legendary Sicilian herdsman who defies the gods in *Idyll* 1.

Idylls 8 and 9 also recall 6 in their style. The latter poem's proportion of Doric to epic dialect is relatively light and its meter at the high end of the scale of Alexandrian refinement (Di Benedetto 1956; Fabiano 1971). Its syntax and diction are relatively plain and lucid, with very few recherché words; it is notable for its intensive use of the epithet καλός (6.11, 14, 16, 33, 36 twice, 43; cf. 19). *Idylls* 8 and 9 are comparable linguistically. Di Benedetto (1956: 58–9) finds that the metrics of 8 and 9 depart from Theocritean norms, including those of 6 – but the relatively small number of lines in these poems may prohibit firm conclusions on these grounds. The style of these three poems may mark the beginning of a trend: late bucolic will employ a more superficially Doric language and mostly eschews the erudite vocabulary and linguistic constructions of the early Alexandrians. The stylistic lucidity of 8 and 9 is abetted by a paucity of thematic particulars, especially in contrast to the pastorals of Theocritus, and here too they coincide with 6. All three poems share an idealized, schematic rural setting in Sicily, which is specified at 8.56 and 9.15 and may be presumptive – because of Daphnis – in *Idyll* 6. The herdsmen in 6 meet "at some spring, at noon on a summer's day" (6.3–4; Ott 1969: 70–1); those of 8 only "in the high mountains" (8.2); 9 gives no background details outside its characters' songs. Contrast the richly detailed setting, replete with offstage characters and intrigues, that emerges from the herdsmen's conversation in the first few dozen lines of *Idylls* 4 and 5.

More particular background elements in 6 are limited to the narrator's named addressee at line 2 and the superstition at lines 39–40, taught to the Cyclops (according to his impersonator Damoetas) by the old woman Cottytaris. The (very literary) proverbial color and the gaming metaphor at lines 17–19 represent the only approach to the usual bantering, almost racy colloquial effect of the language of Theocritus' herdsmen. *Idylls* 8 and 9 share this lack of texture (Arland 1937: 11–28; Merkelbach 1956; Rossi 1971b: 6; Bernsdorff 2006: 183–4; already stressed by Brinker 1884 and Kattein 1901). A few realistic details appear in 8: the strict parents in lines 15–16, the painful finger in 23–4. At 9.10–11 the accidental death of sheep results in soft sheepskins, one detail of a *locus amoenus* within Daphnis' song. Like 6, *Idylls* 8 and 9 leave in the furthest background any social or sociopolitical significance attached to their characters and their worlds, unlike the rurally set *Idylls* 1, 3, 4, 5, 7, and 10 (Stephens 2006).

In *Idyll* 6, then, we seem to have an important site of the codification of Theocritus' innovations, their hardening into genre, and it is followed by 8 and 9. Theocritus' body of work shows a variety of forms, among which the poems with pastoral themes are not easily segregated from the others; recent criticism has moved toward an unpacking of the category "bucolic" (or "pastoral") and a disaggregation, particularly in the work of Theocritus, of the themes, motifs, and modes of representation that from the standpoint of the later tradition seem naturally to accompany literary herdsmen (Van Sickle 1976; Effe 1977b; Halperin 1983; Nauta 1990; Thomas 1996; Reed 2006; Stephens 2006). Late bucolic, comprising the mostly fragmentary work of Moschus and Bion and many of the pseudonymous bucolic poems, will show a proliferation of themes and narrative forms (Arland 1937; Trovati 2001; Reed 2006; Bernsdorff 2006). But it was Theocritus' casting of pastoral themes in dramatic form that seems to have been most influential in the long term. If the genre instigated by Theocritus is considered historically, and pastoral dialogue is not considered its original essence, then it becomes a matter of interest to clarify the route by which pastoral dialogue – particularly in an idealized representation – became its signal form in the post-Theocritean tradition down to Vergil and beyond.

Reasons of space forbid close readings of all the relevant passages and parallels between our three poems and others, and a full appreciation of the formal and thematic complexities not only of *Idyll* 6 but of the two later poems; instead I will refer frequently to more detailed discussions. Our investigation falls under four general rubrics, mainly to organize the observations of critics of the last century and especially the last two decades: the song competition, the formal narratological structure of the poems, the character of Daphnis, and the theme of the Cyclops and Galatea (which, although specific only to 6, can introduce thematic questions relevant to 8 and 9). Our approach will thus be formalist, but also historicist. Without prejudicing the issue by invoking the authors' intentions, I would like to explore the effect of Theocritus' poems as seen against earlier literature, and those of his followers as seen against his.

Competition

The exchange of songs in *Idyll* 6 is described as a contest (ἔρισδεν, 5). The only other pastoral music competition in Theocritus is in *Idyll* 5; the musical exchanges in 7 and 10 also have affinities to competition (and note the ethos of bantering and verbal exchange that we see in 4 and elsewhere). *Idyll* 6 shows a development of 5's form (Serrao 1977: 189–94). Yet in 6 there is none of the zero-sum competitiveness that lends vigor and earthy humor to the contest in 5: at the end of 6 Damoetas kisses Daphnis and they exchange pipes (Hutchinson 1988: 184–5). Even the amity between the singers of *Idylls* 7 and 10 is more complicated, more edgy. Ott emphasizes the insistent assimilation of the two "competitors" (1969: 68–9). No discussion of where to meet and what to sing is part of *Idyll* 6 as it is of 5 (Bernsdorff 1994: 41); the characters seem spontaneously to enact the Cyclops story. Whereas in 5 each response both caps the previous utterance and, setting a challenge, conditions the next, in 6 each speaker has a single speech, that of Damoetas echoing that of Daphnis point by point (Ott 1969: 76; Serrao 1977: 194; Köhnken 1996: 175). There is no judge, no winner or loser: neither has won, yet both have won, proclaims the last line. Thus this is not really a contest; the poetic economy is represented as something else (Bernsdorff 1994: 43–4). *Idyll* 9 takes this development of Theocritean bucolic competition even further. In 9 both competitors win; that is, both receive gifts from the unnamed judge, the narrator. In both idylls the "contest" emerges as an assumed convention, a function of the pastoral setting. One might schematically read both 6 and 9 as adopting the amicable relations that obtain between herdsmen in *Idylls* 1 and (to some degree) 7, and between the reapers who sing in 10, and putting them into a bucolic contest similar to the one that 5 depicts.

Thus *Idyll* 6, apparently followed by 9, in a sense creatively misreads the realia of bucolic exchange, particularly as they are represented in the other idylls, reducing them to givens while playing up new elements – an impression often expressed of *Idyll* 8 too. That poem (in which, as in *Idyll* 5, the songs cap each other, corresponding closely point by point until the lengthy final sets) is often thought to have been modeled on 5, particularly as by an author ignorant of or uninterested in pastoral reality: 8 adapts its herdsmen from Theocritus, not from life (Merkelbach 1956; Rossi 1971b; cf. Kattein 1901: 23–4, and 54 on 8.33–60). We need not mistake

Theocritus' own characters for unmediated imitations of real herdsmen to find in his follower's depiction a secondary remove from the referent. Van Sickle (1976: 25), describing the post-Theocritean tradition in terms of "bucolic mannerism," whose best-known characteristic is "its tendency to simplify Theocritean multiplicity into generic commonplace," finds that 8 reduces Theocritean poetic contests "to a highly stylized convention." In 8 Daphnis wins (motivating the etiological function of the poem: see below), to the chagrin of his competitor, Menalcas, but even here the rivals are extremely nice, calling blessings down on each other (for their herding, not for their singing). As in 6 and 9, we are far from the scrappy one-upmanship of other bucolic competitions. Each singer already has an identical pipe: the winner will get what he already owns. Merkelbach notes that in 8.82–3 Daphnis wins because his voice is sweet – not because Menalcas' song runs out or proves unequal to his, as *Idyll* 5 posits the criterion of competitive song. There is no *eris*, in other words, as 5 knows it. The competitions of all three of our poems represent creative reinterpretations of those in other Theocritean poems.

Narrative Frame

In all three poems under discussion a narrative frame enfolds the herdsmen's dialogue (Kattein 1901: 25, 41). This form represents a creative development of what Theocritus was doing with his literary tradition. Apart from *Idyll* 6, his pastoral mime-like poems are straight dramas: monologues or dialogues without an external narrating voice (1, 3, 4, 5), like his non-pastoral mime-like poems (2, 10, 14, 15). *Idyll* 7, although pastoral in theme, is not like a mime in form, but is rather a narrative, autobiographical monologue with an undefined addressee. The frames in 6, 8, and 9 recall the authorial addresses to Nicias in two of Theocritus' mythological poems, *Idylls* 11 and 13 – the former, which like 6 is on the Cyclops and Galatea, has notable thematic affinities to the pastoral mimes by virtue of its topic. Our three poems again combine motifs that in Theocritus originally had different uses.

The narrative modes of our three poems are complex. In 6 and 8 the frame is narrative at both beginning and end, and intermittently between the sections of dialogue, which (especially in 8) almost become part of the narrative, not dramatic dialogue at all (6.1–5, 20, 42–6; 8.1–10, 28–32, 61–2, 71, 81–93). The storytelling element is strong: note 6.2 ποκα, a traditional opening like "once upon a time," and 8.2 ὡς φαντί, "as they tell." In 8 the introductory narrative includes direct speech; that is, the dialogue begins as speech embedded in narrative before turning into dramatic dialogue – which at the end slips back into narrative again. The narrators of these two poems, anonymous and characterless, do not figure in the action. The structure of 9 is even more complicated. The poem is either a drama, with a fellow-herdsman at the scene directing the "contest" at beginning, middle, and end (where he himself delivers a song), or a narrative, with a narrator issuing injunctions to his characters in an extreme form of the "author's metalepsis." Insofar as the latter reading is valid, the structure parallels those of 6 and 8: narrative frames the poem at beginning and end, and between blocks of dramatic speech (9.1–6, 14, 28–36). But the narrator presents himself as a participant: "thus Daphnis sang to me" (9.14), "which I sang when I was with those herdsmen" (29). Thus Bernsdorff suggests that "the first-person narrator of *Idyll* 9 ... seems to combine the two main characters of *Idyll* 7" (2006: 174–5); and as in 7, the judge is also a singer (we might say that, in a sense, 9 distracts the two main characters of 7 into three). *Idyll* 9 lets itself be read as a memoir of pastoral song, like 7, though without the elaboration of a fictional persona that the narrator of 7 has. Van Sickle, who also compares 9 to 7 (1976: 26; cf. Arland 1937: 24), characterizes the poem as "a pastiche of conventions and Theocritean tags" that gives us a sharp sense of what the author felt those conventions were – and how he innovated on them.

The narrator's address to Aratus in *Idyll* 6 represents another re-interpretation of Theocritus' various forms, another recombination. *Idylls* 11 and 13 spell out the lesson their contents hold for Nicias. What lesson does *Idyll* 6 hold for Aratus? No doubt something about love, if anything, and particularly about the Cyclops' strategy of withdrawal from Galatea (Gow 1952b: 2.120; Hunter 1999: 243–4). Recent critics have speculated on the intimations of love between the two speakers in *Idyll* 6 and its covert bearing on the songs they sing (Gutzwiller 1991: 130; Stanzel 1995: 178–80; Bowie 1996: 91–5; Payne 2007: 98–100). But the address to Aratus is quite perfunctory, the characters' relationship is drawn with the sketchiest of brushstrokes, and any conclusions we draw in this regard must come from outside the text and be based on speculation (Walker 1980: 61). In fact, *Idyll* 6 reduces the frame and its significance as much as it reduces the pastoral dialogue: conjoined, both are subjected to new uses, and are now barely interpretable on their own. The poem is more generous to attempts at reading its alleged lesson intertextually. Critics have found a moral for Aratus in parallels between the legend of Daphnis and that of Polyphemus, with implications for the way *Idyll* 6 (re)interprets the Daphnis story of *Idyll* 1 as well as the Polyphemus story of *Idyll* 11 (Gutzwiller 1991: 131–2; Bernsdorff 1994: 45–8; Hunter 1999: 247–8; Lushkov 2003: 11–12). A key passage here is 6.7, where the rebukes "backward in love" (Hunter's translation of δυcέρωc) and "goatherd," which Daphnis' song attributes to Galatea, repeat Priapus' words to Daphnis at 1.85–6 (they are also used of Polyphemus in Posidippus 19.7–8 AB). Moreover, the addressee's name, Aratus, picks up the narrator Simichidas' addressee Aratus, unhappily in love, in *Idyll* 7 (esp. Stanzel 1995: 179–80). What is significant in this intertext is that in 7 Aratus is *fictional* (whether or not he is based on one of Theocritus' real-life friends). That is to say, as read against 7, 6 takes Aratus out of poetry and puts him in the world that frames poetry – or reduces the frame to an implicit fiction, analogous to the ambiguities of the narrative element of 9 and its relationship to *Idyll* 7.

The frames of *Idylls* 11 and 13, by proffering to Nicias authorial interpretations of the stories they enclose, invite the suspicion of semantic complexity and even duplicity. Here is a seam, a joint, where dissonance in perspective may irrupt into the text. To put it one way, the frames of 11 and 13 make Theocritus and Nicias characters in the poems; poet and addressee are expressly subjected to the interpreting eye of the reader, and an additional viewpoint is introduced, sometimes coinciding with, sometimes going against those in the narrative section. In 6, on the other hand, the apostrophic frame serves only to set the scene, not to interpret the myth. Rather than keep us aloof from the enclosed narrative and give us a wider perspective on the story, the frame pulls us deeper into the fiction and reinforces its illusions (compare

Ott 1969: 67–84). In 8, where there is no addressee, only narrative stage-setting, we are even further removed from 11 and 13.

In a later critical tradition, dialogue became a distinguishing feature of the bucolic (or pastoral) genre that traced itself to Theocritus; but as Halperin, whose analysis of this genre is foundational, warns us: "The originality of Theocritus takes on a different meaning when it is viewed from the vantage point of the previous artistic tradition instead of with the steady gaze of historical hindsight" (1983: 118). Analyzed without regard to the later pastoral tradition that they gave rise to, Theocritus' dramatic poems (1–6, 10, 14–15), with their flavorful dialogue or monologue in "real time" between heavily characterized common people, appear as innovative hexameter versions of lighter, popular dramatic performance, in particular literary mime (Wendel 1914: 270.5, 305.7; Halperin 1983: 206–9; Fantuzzi and Hunter 2004: 133–4; Hordern 2004: 27–8; Reed 2006: 212–13). This typically early Hellenistic "mixture" or "hybridization of genres" (Kroll 1924: 203–4) yields, again typically, a potentially piquant or even humorous incongruity, with humble or quotidian subject matter foregrounded in an elevated form. Herodas' *Mimiambs*, which set the matter and dramatic form of mime in iambic meters, offer a close parallel. Theocritus' original touch may have been the inclusion of pastoral themes in this mixture, although Herodas too has a mimiamb about shepherds (8; Effe 1977b: 15 rightly emphasizes the affinities between Theocritus' mime-like poems, both pastoral and non-pastoral). Seen from this historical angle, the dialogue in *Idyll* 6, framed and interrupted (between the two songs) by a narrator's commentary that violates the dramatic illusion, does something with the literary tradition that goes beyond the other dramatic idylls. We might (with due caution) imagine the following transitional scenario: 6 mixes into the mime-like pastoral exchange the apostrophic frame from 11 (along with its basic subject matter Polyphemus and Galatea), then 8 and 9 treat that combination as standard.

Moreover, the exchange between Daphnis and Damoetas in *Idyll* 6 does not exploit the veristic character of mime or create a vivid or satirical sketch of personalities. The two young herdsmen themselves remain decorative mouthpieces for their performance, with none of the quirks that make memorable (for example) the vivaciously uncouth herdsmen of 4 and 5, the platitudinous reapers of 10, or the catty festival-goers of 15. *Idyll* 6 does not perform the way the other pastoral dialogues and monologues do: the rustic background does not set off incongruous urban or high-culture motifs (as perhaps most noticeably in 1, 3, and 7). In much of Theocritus, an idealized rusticity runs along underneath the construction of the countryside as "other," partly supporting it, partly undermining it. It is as if this idealization were expanded in 6 to exclude the otherness of rustic life. Ironic distance is reduced (Effe 1977b: 14–21, with special emphasis on the loss of this ironic distance as a feature of the post-Theocritean tradition): the reduced scope of the dialogue diminishes the characterizations of the herdsmen, and the frame offers the reader no firm standpoint from which to view them. It is in the songs of the poem's two characters that we get the lively details: the sea nymph throwing apples, the Cyclops' dog running along the beach and barking at her, the sly strategy of Polyphemus. *Idyll* 6 downplays the features that set its speakers apart from its readers, and plays up their charm and the appeal of their leisurely life of song. *Idylls* 8 and 9 do likewise.

Idyll 9 is in some ways most interesting of the three for this kind of innovation on Theocritean precedent. Very short, only 36 lines long, it is dominated by its frame. The narrator closes it with his own song, prefaced by a prayer: "bucolic Muses (βουκολικαὶ Μοῖϲαι), be of good grace, and reveal the song that I once sang when I was with those herdsmen (i.e., Daphnis and Menalcas)" (28–9). Now, in Theocritus the word "bucolic," βουκολικόϲ, and its cognates only need to refer literally to things (especially musical) having to do with herdsmen (not exclusively "cowherds": Dover 1971: lv), and their referents belong to the world the poem describes, not to that of the poet (Nauta 1990: 126–9). So in *Idyll* 1 Thyrsis, as a shepherd, naturally calls upon the "bucolic Muses" (1.20, etc.). In *Idylls* 5 and 7 the verb βουκολιάϲδειν refers to herdsmen's song quite remote from the form and character of the idylls themselves (5.44, 60; 7.36, 49). In 9 too "bucolic Muses" literally means "Muses that preside over the songs of herdsmen." And yet the identity of the imprecator there with the narrator of the poem, with all the complications discussed above, suggests more. The figure of the herdsman ends up appropriating the narrative frame. If the frames of *Idyll* 6 and 8 disrupt the dramatic illusion only to endorse the fiction into which the reader enters, the frame of 9 ambiguously draws the narrating author into the world of the dialogue. We are drawing close to the identification of the bucolic poet with his subjects that is the central trope of the anonymous *Epitaph for Bion*, and to the genre-marking, metapoetic use of βουκολικαὶ Μοῖϲαι by the first-century BCE philologist Artemidorus (Van Sickle 1976: 26).

Daphnis

Daphnis is a character in all three of our poems; in 6 he is joined by one Damoetas, and in 8 and 9 by Menalcas. Neither of the latter two appears elsewhere in Greek bucolic. The name Damoetas may derive from Archaic lyric (Bowie 1996: 93–4). Menalcas is already a character in literature about herdsmen before Theocritus (Clearchus in Ath. 14.619c–d); that he is connected with Daphnis – as musical competitor or lover – in Theocritus' contemporaries Sositheus (*TrGF* 1 F 1a–3) and Hermesianax (*CA* 2) suggests that *Idylls* 8 and 9 are drawing on several early Hellenistic sources. Those two poems give Daphnis a companion almost equal to him in legendary and literary power.

For Daphnis is the legendary hero of the song Thyrsis sings in *Idyll* 1. His treatment in our three poems offers another example of how they build on a motif established in Theocritus. The story of the legendary Sicilian cowherd and his doomed love was first introduced to literature by the fourth-century dithyrambist Stesichorus (Ael. *VH* 10.18; West 1970: 206) and is found in various types of Hellenistic literature (apart from Sositheus and Hermes, cf. Alex. Aet. *CA* 15, Timaeus *FGrH* 566 F 83). The first audience of *Idyll* 1, insofar as they were able to analyze the poem against its literary background, would have felt that they were reading a pastoral mime that included an aria from dithyramb, with the whole thing put into Doricized hexameters – the poem is of course more complicated than that, but that is its basic schema as viewed historically. Theocritus performs similar generic transformations in the hymn to Adonis included in *Idyll* 15 and the ritual epithalamium that constitutes 18, to take two non-pastoral examples, though the adaptation is more piquant among the lowly characters of *Idyll* 1. There Daphnis is not a character in the mime, but a legendary figure referred to with reverence and under a cloud of antique mystery by herdsmen-singers who look back to him as a sort of predecessor. He also appears within herdsmen's songs in 5.20 and 80–1. In 7.73 he is even further distanced: a character in a song within a song within the narrative. This is why his role in 8, which alludes to the story known from 1 and elsewhere and in fact etiologizes his preeminence as a herdsman-singer (92–3; cf. 85–6), should come as such a surprise. He is re-imagined as a herdsman like Thyrsis (Arland 1937: 11–12).

Idylls 6 and 9 invite the same surprise, although neither elaborates on the identity of its Daphnis as 8 does. In 6 he is "Daphnis the herdsman" (1 Δάφνιc ὁ βουκόλος; 44 Δάφνιc ὁ βούτας, cf. 7.73). The poem leaves barely open the possibility that despite these determiners, Daphnis here is an ordinary herdsman named for his legendary predecessor, as in *Idyll* 5 the herdsman-singer Comatas is nowhere said to be identical with the legendary goatherd Comatas, of whom Lycidas sings in 7.78–89 (so Fantuzzi 1998, with the further argument that the poet of 8 conflated Theocritus' two different Daphnises, the legendary one and the ordinary one). Yet Comatas lacks the legendary status that Daphnis has (he is unknown outside of Theocritus, though schol. 7.78–9 attributes his story to one Lycus of Rhegium: Wendel 1914: 99–100). For the character Comatas himself, Daphnis is a legendary figure, for it is Comatas who sings of Daphnis at 5.80–1. Discussing *Idyll* 6, Hunter concludes, "although the goatherd Comatas of Idyll 5 is most naturally understood to be a latter-day namesake of the legendary goatherd of *Idyll* 7, it is reasonable to understand Δάφνιc ὁ βουκόλος here as *the* legendary Daphnis of *Idyll* 1, as the poet of *Idyll* 8 seems to have done" (1999: 245). All three of our poems project the Theocritean pastoral world back onto its legendary past. All three are about Daphnis' boyhood – "prequels" to the story Thyrsis sings of, winning a playful illusion of priority to *Idyll* 1 and other treatments of the myth? – imagining it in terms taken from Theocritus' herdsman-mimes (and re-imagining that mime form in legendary terms). In all three, Daphnis has become a stepping-stone to a new synthesis, his pre-Theocritean associations unresonating and his character melded into a persona typical of Theocritus' pastoral idylls.

Cyclops

The most conspicuous innovation of *Idyll* 6 is its variation on the story of the Cyclops and Galatea as we know it from *Idyll* 11 and from the fragments of Theocritus' model. This theme is not directly present in 8 and 9, but they show comparable thematic innovations. Theocritus' addressee in *Idyll* 11, Nicias, like the first readers of *Idyll* 1, had the novel experience of reading a dithyrambic aria set in hexameters: this story, like that of Daphnis, became literary in lyric performances of the century before Theocritus, first in Philoxenus (*PMG* 822), then in works by Stesichorus and Oeniades (Didymus on Dem. *Phil.* 11, col. 12.59–62). As with Daphnis, contemporaries of Theocritus treat the same myth in various literary forms (Hermes. *CA* 1; Call. *ep.* 46 Pf. = *AP* 12.150; cf. Posidip. 19.7–8 AB). In the extant treatments, including *Idyll* 11, the Cyclops' song provides the remedy (φάρμακον) for his (fierce, unrequited) passion for Galatea. *Idyll* 6 drops this theme (late bucolic returns to it: Reed 2006: 225–33). In 6.9 his sweet piping (ἁδέα cυρίcδων) is without its classic significance. Polyphemus has not sublimated or cured his desire; he has adopted a new strategy, that of pretending to ignore Galatea (6.32–3; Stanzel 1995: 186–90; Hutchinson 1988: 183–7). He has taken advantage of the lesson that it is the absent one who provokes desire, the one who withdraws, the one who seems unable to love (cf. *Idyll* 10.8). *Idyll* 9, in the reading of Bernsdorff (2006: 199), further purges this Cyclops-related theme of erotic meaning: the narrator's concluding song, in thanking the Muses for providing a remedy against Circe's potions, implicitly disregards the whole idea of a cure for one who is already in love.

As Polyphemus in 11.76 reassured himself that he would find another, more beautiful Galatea, so Damoetas as Polyphemus in 6.26 says that he has "another woman" with whom to make Galatea jealous. The revision is notable. Scholars have long regarded 6 as a kind of sequel to 11, not unreasonably: our poem takes off from and pointedly revises the very words of the other one (Ott 1969: 72–84; Köhnken 1996: 171, 180–1). The general impression is that 6 builds on the story in 11, reads its Polyphemus as not exactly cured of his love, but able to control it and try a new tactic. In this regard 6 is taking advantage of an ambiguity in the way 11 conceives of the φάρμακον of song (Spofford 1969: 34–5; Köhnken 1996: 181–2). The conclusion to his song in 11 is the premise here and the pivot of the revision in 6. An allusion at 6.17 by Daphnis, speaking in the guise of an anonymous questioner (derived from dithyramb?), to Galatea's former unwillingness ("she flees one who loves her and pursues one who does not") takes the form of an answer to Polyphemus' consolatory words to himself in 11.75: "milk the cow that's nearby" (that is, "love the one you're with"); "why are you chasing one who flees you?" Lover and beloved have switched places.

It is as if 6, in putting the theme of 11 into a herdsmen's dialogue, assumed that the Galatea myth has already been absorbed into bucolic poetry – that is to say, bracketed together with Theocritus' other poems. *Idyll* 11 makes no such assumption; its emphasis on the rustic details of the Cyclops' life can be explained as an Alexandrian foregrounding of the quotidian matter of the *Odyssey* (following, for example, Euripides' *Cyclops*) rather than as a consequence of genre. So *Idyll* 6 again seems to take for granted a combination of motifs that in the earlier idylls is dynamic and tension-filled, and to build on it creatively. This is also true of the poem's engagement with Homer. At 6.22–4 Damoetas in the persona of the Cyclops swears an oath "by my one sweet [eye], wherewith I pray that I may see to the end – but that seer Telemus who spoke evil, may he bring evil back home to keep for his children." The allusion is to *Odyssey* 9.509, where the Cyclops realizes the truth of the prophecy of the seer Telemus, that he would lose his sight at the hands of Odysseus. The passage has the effect of a proleptic allusion: the poet gains a kind of ironic priority to Homer by treating a famous story from the *Odyssey* as in the future. At 11.50–3 the Cyclops says to Galatea, "but if I myself appear too shaggy, yet I have logs of oak and an imperishable fire under the ash; and I would submit to being burned by you, both my soul and my eye, than which nothing is sweeter to me." Gow (1952b) emphasizes the metaphorical sense of burning: the fires of love seem almost real to the Cyclops, who unwittingly tropes his own future blinding as the price of Galatea's love. His cherished fire, here an enticement for the sea nymph, will become the means of his destruction, when Odysseus heats the sharpened olive beam "under the ash" in the Cyclops' cave (*Od.* 9.375–6). And further on, at 11.60–2, he promises to learn to swim, to join Galatea in the sea, if some stranger arriving in a ship should teach him how. Τις ξένος, "some stranger": but of course the most famous stranger to sail to the land of the Cyclops will be, not τις, but Οὔτις, "Nobody."

These allusions achieve more than prolepsis; they engage the text of the *Odyssey* and win from it new meaning for the young Polyphemus' lament. The word ξένος introduces a remarkably broad program of confrontation. Odysseus in his wanderings is the stranger *par excellence*, and the cave of the Cyclops is a theatre for his status as ξένος and its discontents: what it means to be a guest far from home, measuring oneself against different models of behavior and hospitality, and so on. By introducing this notion, however obliquely and unwittingly, Theocritus' Polyphemus appropriates a whole thematic network of the *Odyssey* and re-orients it, putting himself at its center. And the frame matters here too: Theocritus approaches Polyphemus not as "other" (as so paradigmatically in Homer), but empathetically (11.7 ὁ παρ' ἁμῖν, "my fellow countryman" Polyphemus), and therefore slips ineluctably into a play of identities, egos and alter egos, that enrich the personae of this poem.

By contrast, "the Cyclops of *Idyll* 6 responds almost as though *Odyssey* 9 did not exist" (Hunter 1999: 247). The "allusive art" in the reference to Telemus at 6.23 is minimal. It enters through a mention of his eye (which is tied to the poem's insistent thematic of vision), and then is dropped, unlike the deeply involved allusions to the *Odyssey* that recur in 11 and color Polyphemus' whole outlook as we perceive it. The story of the Cyclops and Galatea often seems to attract ironic distance, a knowing viewpoint on the naive monster – perhaps a persisting reflex of the frame in *Idyll* 11. One can trace this even in the four-line fragment of Bion's treatment of the story (fr. 16 Reed 1997) and in Vergil's transmutation of Polyphemus into Corydon in *Eclogue* 2. This distance is less evident in *Idyll* 6. How can the role-playing by Damoetas acquire complexity if Damoetas himself is so minimally differentiated from the Cyclops – and from ourselves? A chance to accommodate multiple, competing viewpoints within a single persona has been eschewed, along with the effects of such a play of identities on levels both of narratology and literary history. A play of identities operates elsewhere in 6; the intertext with the *Odyssey* is not the living, dynamic creator of meaning in the poem that it is in 11. *Idyll* 6 blocks the analysis of the story against earlier literature that 11 invites, setting it instead against a new background. Theocritus' generic experimentation again provides the basis for a new, fully coherent restructuring of his poetry's formal and thematic elements.

In *Idyll* 8 as well, the intertextual dynamics of Theocritus' mime-like poems are turned to conventions that support quite different effects. The first section of dialogue is in elegiac couplets (28 lines in the manuscripts, but a quatrain has evidently been lost after line 52). This is a remarkable innovation, since it was the uniformly hexametric cadence of Theocritus' mime-like poems that transumed dramatic works like mime and dithyramb into a different sphere, setting up a contrast between different sets of expectations. In order to set the first part of the singing contest into elegiacs, one has to be already familiar with hexameters in this type of poem – even a little numb to their effect.

What does the new meter bring to the poem? Hubbard recalls that the elegist Hermesianax wrote on Daphnis and Menalcas (*CA* 2–3): against that background, 8 will have been combining two early Hellenistic poets (1998: 35; Trovati 2001: 52 n.70). More generally, the elegiac exchanges invoke the traditions of Archaic elegy and contemporary epigram, particularly erotic; Arland (1937: 20) notes the thematic difference between the elegiac and hexametric sections of the contest. Menalcas' words at 8.53–6, for instance, transfigure a typically elegiac rejection of conventional standards of riches and power into particularly pastoral values: not the realm of Pelops, nor the wealth of Croesus, nor swiftness beyond that of the winds, but music and love in the countryside are this elegist's desires. The quatrain transplants Archaic symposiastic elegy (Gow 1952b) into a conventionalized pastoral landscape, a Theocritean synthesis of motifs that can now be taken for granted. But the elegiacs in 8 recall elegy specifically through its Alexandrian successor, epigram (Brinker 1884: 28; Kattein 1901: 55–7; Merkelbach 1956: 122–4), which was a medium for symposiastic recitation and relaxed competition under the early Ptolemies (Cameron 1995a: 71–103). The tradition of variation in epigram, the effect of capping the epigram of another, can sometimes still be felt in the *Greek Anthology.* In 8 this effect melds with the capping native to the herdsman's song that Theocritus had more studiously evoked. In the mouths of Menalcas and Daphnis, this high-culture technique has a piquant effect, very much in the manner of the Homericizing rustics and city-dwellers of Theocritus. One might say that the Theocritean contrast between verse-form and subject matter has been taken a step further, perhaps to preserve the contrastive effect despite the semantic languor of the hexameters – although in 8 the rustic features of the persons and their surroundings are so muted that there is little opportunity for any contrast along those lines. As in 6, the play of contrasts in 8 operates elsewhere.

Idyll 6 and the Bucolic Tradition

For every basic difference between *Idyll* 6 and Theocritus' other pastorals, there is a basic similarity between it and *Idylls* 8 and 9. *Idyll* 6 uses earlier literature differently from Theocritus' other poems: their play with mime, with dithyramb, with Homer, and so on becomes in 6 the foundation for a different emphasis, especially the innovative treatment of the myth of Polyphemus and Galatea, which reworks *Idyll* 11 more than it does the myth per se. The intertextual dynamics of 6 are operating at a stage beyond the other Theocritean poems: again and again, 6 stereotypes their intertextual tropes and uses them as stepping-stones to a new poetics. We see this poetics in 8 and 9 as well.

Idyll 6 is vividly intertextual with several of Theocritus' poems, particularly 1, 3, 5, and 11. Theocritus' success with such poems as those might have inspired him, at a later stage of his career, to combine and crystallize their motifs into the conventions that other poets, like those of 8 and 9, then took up. An alternative explanation also suggests itself. If *Idylls* 6, 8, and 9 all equally treat the innovations of Theocritus' similar poems as conventions with which to work and thus represent a secondary stage in the history of bucolic, and are closely similar in form, content, and intertextual program (especially as seen against the other pastoral poems), then it may be wondered whether *Idyll* 6, rather than being the Theocritean model for a new phase of bucolic poetry, is part of that phase itself, composed by a later poet as were 8 and 9. To my knowledge the Theocritean authorship of 6 has never been doubted. But that possibility would not affect the present thesis: that we are looking, in all three poems, at the crystallization of Theocritus' artistic experiments and at how texts make us read other texts. The new emphasis falls on, and the new tensions arise from, the narrative frame and the way it distances us readers – or does not distance us – from the characters.

The particular poetic form that these three poems establish has no exact continuation in Greek literature that we can observe, but some of its elements do re-appear or even become standard in the later bucolic tradition. The anonymous *Idyll* 21, whose dramatic dialogue between fishermen is introduced by a narrator's moralizing apostrophe, approaches the synthesis of narrative forms we have been observing. In late bucolic – the extant remains of Moschus, Bion, and certain anonymous poets found in the bucolic manuscripts (datable roughly between the mid-second and mid-first centuries BCE: Reed 2006: 209–10) – pastoral themes, including song and dialogue between herdsmen, remain common; but here generic hybridization and the assimilation of new themes, combined with the metrical and dialectal features of Theocritus' mime-like poems and pointing back to them, constitute a new, different assumption of Theocritus' work as a norm, and a new building on it. Moschus' *Runaway Love*, for example, is a sustained epigrammatic exercise on the nature of Eros, and Bion's *Adonis* is a mythological vignette partly in the tradition of Callimachus' mimetic hymns. The anonymous *Epithalamius of Achilles and Deidameia* (Ps.-Bion 2) starkly incorporates an amorous mythological narrative as a herdsman's performance within dialogue. Still typical of these poems is the diminished distance between reader and rustic character; it is reflected also in such bucolic-inspired works in other genres as Longus' novel *Daphnis and Chloe*. The narratological play with boundaries between author, narrator, and character will be renewed by the anonymous *Epitaph for Bion* and in Latin by Vergil's *Eclogues*. These richly aware texts look back both to the type of herdsmen's exchange codified in 6, 8, and 9 and directly to their Theocritean models, and press to a new limit that poetry's ambiguities of voice and potentially permeable boundaries between narratological spheres.

FURTHER READING

Studies of post-Theocritean bucolic per se are few. Arland 1937 can still reward the reader; for recent surveys see Bernsdorff 2006 and Reed 2006, whose references will lead back to other recent and not-so-recent scholarship. New texts and commentaries on later bucolic are fortunately increasing in number: for Bion see Fantuzzi 1985 and Reed 1997; for Ps.-Theocritus 20, 21, and 27 see Kirstein 2007 and Belloni 2004. The most complete commentaries on *Idylls* 8 and 9 remain those in Gow 1952b; for *Idyll* 6 see also Hunter 1999. For the historical study of the development of the genre from the work of Theocritus particularly useful are Van Sickle 1976, Effe 1977b, Halperin 1983, and Nauta 1990.

CHAPTER EIGHTEEN

Iambos and Parody

Ruth Scodel

Poetry in "low" genres, defined by hostility to social or literary pretension, flourished in the Hellenistic period. Phoenix of Colophon and Callimachus take Hipponax as a model in reviving the Archaic iambos. Homeric parody had already become an independent genre in the late fourth century; the Hellenistic period produced mock-epics in which tiny animals act as if they were great heroes. There was also satiric philosophical poetry: the hexameters of Crates of Thebes argue for Cynicism through poetic parody, while Timon of Phlius composed hexameter satire of the philosophical schools from a skeptical perspective, with Xenophanes as a character and probably model. Macho, primarily a comic poet, composed the *Chreiai* ("Useful Sayings"), vulgar anecdotes with punch lines. Cercidas wrote both choliambs and meliambs, lyric iambos. Timon and Sotades wrote "cinaedic" poetry – abusive and obscene. The new and newly adapted forms may be learned, allusive, and complex in the Alexandrian style, like Callimachus' *Iambi*, or straightforward and pedestrian, like the *Chreiai*, but they share an attitude of distance from wealth, power, and the literary forms associated with them. Most are relatively mild. Parody is now amusing, not cruel; iambos is no longer vitriolic.

Popular philosophy is an important influence on this poetry. Some poets may have been Cynics. Scholars have seen Cynicism in Phoenix (Gerhard 1909) and it is important for Cercidas, though scholars disagree about whether it should be the center of interpretation (Williams 2002; Livrea 1986; López Cruces 1995). Plato is clearly important for Callimachus (White 1994). However, the poets are more broadly steeped in the Socratic tradition, with its stress on a search for inner happiness that depends on self-control, virtue, and wisdom, and its contempt for wealth and power (Long 1996a). The Cynic habit of making fun of conventional beliefs became deeply embedded in literary practice.

Philosophy helps explain the mildness of Hellenistic iambos and parody, because its mocking, moralizing discourse was a filter through which Hellenistic readers re-invented the personal attacks of Archaic iambos. The figures of Socrates and of the Cynic philosopher, with his voluntary poverty and witty raillery, influenced how the iambographer pictured himself and his models. The Archaic iambographer presents himself as a drinker, brawler, and seducer. His poems often represent themselves as revenge on people who have injured him, and his counter-attacks do not pull their punches. However, when the Hellenistic poet-reader assimilates this character to the philosopher or "wise man," a socially marginal figure who criticizes common behavior, he can imitate the iambographer while replacing personal hatred with general moral advice. Dio Chrysostom says that Antisthenes compared Diogenes to a wasp (*Or.* 8.3), while Hellenistic authors often refer to Archaic iambographers as wasps, following Callimachus (fr. 380, with Pfeiffer 1949: 306; Gerhard 1909: 175).

Boundaries between philosophy and poetry, and between different schools of philosophy, could be porous. Crates of Thebes, an important early Cynic, composed extensively in verse: surviving fragments include elements of comedy, parody, direct address, self-satire, and moralizing. The iambics of his *Ephemeris* ("Account") are typical (*SH* 362):

> τίθει μαγείρωι μνᾶς δέκ', ἰατρῶι δραχμήν,
> κόλακι τάλαντα πέντε, cυμβούλωι καπνόν,
> πόρνηι τάλαντον, φιλοcόφωι τριώβολον.
>
> Pay ten minas to a cook, a drachma to a doctor, five talents to a flatterer, smoke to an advisor, a talent to a whore, a half-drachma to a philosopher.

The cook is well paid, the doctor poorly; the flatterer gets a fortune, the advisor nothing. The philosopher's pittance stands against the whore's fat fee. This complaint about false values, although it originates in Plato's *Gorgias* (464d–465) does not belong to any particular philosophical school; it invites the reader to think about why a philosopher is to a whore (rather than to a rhetorician, his more obvious opposite) as a doctor is to a cook; and by suggesting that the philosopher might like to do better, it undercuts itself.

The Iambic Revival (1): Phoenix

In the early third century BCE, both Callimachus and his older contemporary Phoenix of Colophon claimed to revive the manner of the sixth-century iambographer Hipponax. Both use Hipponax's characteristic meter, the choliamb or "limping iamb" (also employed by Herodas), along with his Ionic dialect and some of his unusual vocabulary. Callimachus announces the relationship by having Hipponax return from the dead to speak most of the first *Iamb* (fr. 191 Pf.). Yet something peculiar happens on the way from Archaic Ephesus: Hipponax is afflicted with niceness, and abandons vehement self-assertion. The surviving fragments of Hipponax use his name at least five times. Although Callimachus' Hipponax speaks of himself in the third person, Callimachus does not name himself, and neither do other Hellenistic iambographers. Hipponax is a vivid, dominant personality; Phoenix and Callimachus employ masks or characterize themselves blandly. Hipponax viciously attacks the same characters repeatedly, characters who seem real whether they actually were so or not (Hellenistic readers believed they were); Callimachus rebukes straw men.

The philosophical turn is partly responsible for this change, since the poets evidently think iambos should be (somewhat) edifying. But there are other reasons, too. Hipponax's abuse belongs to particular situations; even though some Hellenistic iambos is clearly occasional, it is aimed at a reading public and must transcend its immediate occasion. The major authors prefer to avoid the extravagant obscenity of the Archaic style, as a matter of taste. And in a world where poets often depended on autocrats as patrons, iambic freedom was not what it was in the Classical *polis*. It was neither safe nor profitable to attack anyone really worth attacking. Indeed, iambic freedom expresses itself negatively: because iambos is not expected to address grand themes, it does not need to praise kings and princes, at least not overtly.

Fierce invective is not entirely missing from Hellenistic poetry. Sotades' famous line on the marriage of Ptolemy II to his sister (*CA* 1) meets Hipponactean standards of license: "you are driving your stick into an unholy hole" (εἰϲ οὐχ ὁϲίην τρυμαλιὴν τὸ κέντρον ὠθεῖϲ). If the iambs of Alcaeus of Messene had survived, Hellenistic iambos would probably look harsher, to judge from his epigrams against Philip V (2–5 GP). Hipponactean obscenity and violence, though, are separated from Hipponax as stylistic model. Indeed, Callimachus' first *Iamb* announces its kinder, gentler Hipponax, who comes "bearing an iamb that does not sing the fight with Boupalus" (φέρων ἴαμβον οὐ μάχην ἀείδοντα / τὴν Βουπάλειον, 1.3–4).

The speaker of Phoenix's "Crow-song" (*CA* 2 = Ath. 8.359e) is a ritual beggar. Carrying a model crow (sacred to Apollo), he goes from house to house, singing blessings and requests (1–3):

> ἐϲθλοί, κορώνηι χεῖρα πρόϲδοτε κριθέων,
> τῆι παιδὶ τἀπόλλωνοϲ, ἢ λέκοϲ πυρῶν
> ἢ ἄρτον ἢ ἥμαιθον ἢ ὅτι τιϲ χρήιζει.
>
> Good people, reach out a handful of barley-grains to the crow, the daughter of Apollo, or a dish of wheat, or bread, or a penny, or what anyone wants to give.

Meter, language, and the poor-man's persona evoke Hipponax. Nothing, however, could be less Hipponactean than this poem's impregnable good will. Hipponax is aggressive, boastful, or whiny, but never affable. The Rhodian swallow-song, another ritual begging-song from Athenaeus (8.360b = *PMG* 848), warns the householder that if he does not give, the singers will carry off his door, his lintel, or his wife (12–16). Phoenix's performer, however, makes no threats, showers flattery and blessings on the entire family, and emphasizes how easily satisfied he is, concluding, "So ends my song. Give something, and it will be enough." Similarly, the Hipponax of Callimachus' first *Iamb* comes from Hades to lecture the disputatious intellectuals of Alexandria on humility and intellectual generosity, telling the story of the cup of Bathycles: inscribed as a prize for the wisest of men, it was given by each of the Seven Sages to the next until it had made the rounds of them all.

What, then, is Phoenix's poem doing? Scholars have interpreted it as a request for patronage, comparing it with Theocritus' *Idyll* 16 (Wills 1970; Furley 1994). Yet

Theocritus' poem emphatically mentions a particular individual, Hiero. It does not call on the ordinary reader to be a patron, but to sympathize with the poet's difficulties. Phoenix's poem is addressed to the householder before whose door he stands – that is, metapoetically, the reader – and its requests are so modest that anyone could afford them. It celebrates the happy and generous bourgeois family. The poem thus seems less a request for patronage than a *captatio benevolentiae* aimed at all readers, a self-presentation of the poet as Apollo's very humble servant. The gap between the stylistic reminiscences of Hipponax and the naive and harmless speaker, and between the expertise of meter and dialect with the folkloric content, is precisely the point, and typically Hellenistic (De Stefani 2002).

The other surviving choliambs of Phoenix direct hostility only at general targets. They deserve some attention beyond the ongoing problem of priority between Phoenix and Callimachus (Pfeiffer 1949 on fr. 191.1; Hutchinson 1988: 49; Cameron 1995a: 173; Kerkhecker 1999: 29–30). Athenaeus cites a choliambic poem on "Ninus," a variant of Sardanapalus, a legendary king of Nineveh who devoted himself completely to pleasure (*CA* 1). The army of Alexander had seen a tomb with a statue making an apparently disdainful gesture, and a (cuneiform) inscription whose (probably invented) translation, claiming that only the pleasures enjoyed in life remained postmortem property, became a topic of variation in Hellenistic poetry. There were hexameters by Choerilus (*SH* 335) and ripostes by Crates of Thebes (*SH* 355) and Chrysippus (*SH* 338). Phoenix makes no explicit reference to his being a king, although the statement "he was not a judge; he did not study census-taking and counting" (οὐ δικαcπόλοc κεῖνοc· / οὐ λεωλογεῖν ἐμάνθαν', οὐκ ἀμιθρῆcαι, 7–8) implies the political responsibilities that he ignored:

ἀνὴρ Νίνοc τιc ἐγένετ', ὡc ἐγὼ 'κούω,
Ἀccύριοc, ὅcτιc εἶχε χρυcίου πόντον,
τάλαντα πολλῶι πλεῦνα Καcπίηc ψάμμου.

There was a man, Ninus, as I hear, Assyrian, who had a sea of gold, more talents by far than the sand of the Caspian.

Ninus is just like you and me, except that he had more money. He "was best at eating, drinking, and lovemaking" (ἦν ἄριcτοc ἐcθίειν τε καὶ πίνειν / κήρᾶν, 9–10) and cared for nothing else – although his epitaph includes song among his pleasures, too (18).

Athenaeus also cites *CA* 3 (10.421d):

Νίνου κάδοι μάχαιρα καὶ κύλιξ αἰχμή,
κύμβη δὲ τόξα, δήϊοι δὲ κρητῆρεc,
ἵπποι δ' ἄκρητοc, κἀλαλὴ "μύρον χεῖτε."

Ninus' sword is jars, his spear-point a cup, his bow a bowl, enemies mixing-bowls, horses unmixed wine, his battle-cry "pour myrrh."

The speaker does not seem to disapprove of Ninus, and in a symposiastic context, these substitutions are appropriate. Similarly, while the speaker of fr. 1 does not endorse Ninus' hedonism, he is not overtly hostile to it.

A choliamb addressed to an unidentifiable Posidippus is preserved in *P.Heid.* 310, subscribed "Iamb of Phoenix" (*CA* 6). It is a complaint about rich men (unnamed) who have no idea how to use their money (7–12):

τῶι πλούτωι δὲ πρὸς τί δεῖ χρῆ[cθ]αι,
τοῦτ' αὐτὸ πάντων πρῶτον οὐκ ἐπίcτανται·
ἀλλ' οἰκ[ία]c μὲν ἐκ λίθου cμαραγδίτου,
εἴ πω[c] ἀνυcτόν ἐcτι τοῦτ' αὐτοῖc πρήccειν,
[. .]τ̣[. .] ἐχούcαc καὶ cτοὰc τετραcτύλουc
[πολλῶ]ν ταλάντων ἀξίαc κατακτῶνται·

But what money is supposed to be used for, this, first of all, they don't know. But they get houses made of emerald stone, if it is manageable for them to do this, with ... and porticoes with four pillars, worth many talents.

What is the best use for wealth, then? Line 13 seems to mention "the necessary soul" (τ]ὴν ἀναγκαίην̣ ψ̣υ̣χήν), while a little below "made self-controlled by helpful words ... knows what is helpful and advantageous" seems to have the soul as subject (λ]όγοιc χρηcτοῖcι cωφρονιcθεῖcα / [......] τὰ χρηcτὰ καὶ τὰ cυμφέροντ' εἰδῆι, 16–17). How would one use money to provide *logoi* that would give *sophrosyne* to the soul? Perhaps by hiring a philosopher, or moralizing poet, to assist. This poem looks less like a genuine satire of the rich than a comment on their failure to support poets and philosophers, and perhaps the reader should turn this complaint against the speaker, recognizing his resentment. The last line, "for they also think about stones" (...]ν γὰρ καὶ λίθων φροντίζουcιν, 23), is peculiarly tantalizing, since one of the possible addressees, Posidippus the epigrammatist, composed an impressive number of epigrams about precious stones. The poem would thus end with a wry allusion to what a poor poet has to do to make a living: to flatter the rich and powerful by praising their luxury possessions (Petrain 2005: 340–3).

The Iambic Revival (2): Callimachus

The *Iambi* of Callimachus are partially preserved in *P.Oxy.* 1011 (frs. 191–208a Pfeiffer 1949); the reconstruction of those in poor condition and thus of the book depends on the Milan *Diegesis.* The first five follow in the tradition of Hipponax at least insofar as they are moralizing and critical. In the first, Hipponax criticizes the learned men of Alexandria, and tells them the story of the cup of Bathycles. The story was surely familiar to Callimachus' audience, and its simplicity stands in sharp contrast with the poem's allusive style. The poem compounds its ironies. The author is among the presumed objects of its satire; it critiques an excessively critical attitude; its internal audience is very learned but has evidently not taken the moral of a well-known tale.

In the second *Iamb*, an unnamed speaker tells the fable of how animals could once talk, but Zeus, angered by their complaints, gave their voices (unjustly!) to people, as if people didn't talk too much already. A series of specific but obscure people are associated with unpleasant animal sounds. The whole story turns out to be a quotation from Aesop. By inserting invective into the aetiology, the poem creates a certain confusion: what animals lose (articulate speech) is not exactly what people get (articulate voices that sound like the noises the animals still make). Furthermore, if the fable, as the *Diegesis* claims, had Zeus act in part because the fox complained that he ruled unjustly, Aesop ignores his own moral, since he calls Zeus unjust.

In the third poem the speaker appears to be the poet, complaining that the times favor money over merit, as demonstrated by the bad treatment he has received from a boy named Euthydemus. He thought he had found the Good, but now wishes he had served Cybele or mourned Adonis instead of following Apollo and the Muses. Yet complaints that money alone matters "now," in contrast to some past pederastic utopia, are themselves old (Pi. *I.* 2.1–12, Anac. *PMG* 384). The speaker may be less pathetic than ridiculous.

The fourth poem starts with a rebuke to the son of Charitades (Simon, according to the *Diegesis*), who is "not one of us," and it continues with the fable of the laurel and the olive. Each delivers a long speech in praise of itself. When a bramble urges them not to quarrel, the laurel angrily responds that the bramble has no standing to intervene (4.98–103):

> "οὐκ ὦ τάλαιναι παυcόμεcθα, μὴ χ̣α̣ρ̣τ̣αὶ
> γενώμεθ' ἐχθροῖc, μηδ' ἐροῦμεν ἀλλήλας
> ἄνολβ' ἀναιδέωc, ἀλλὰ ταῦτά γ' .β̣..μ̣.;"
> τὴν δ' ἆρ' ὑποδρὰξ οἷα ταῦροc ἡ δάφνη
> ἔβλεψε καὶ τάδ' εἶπεν· "ὦ κακὴ λώβη
> ὡc δὴ μί' ἡμέων καὶ cύ;"

> "Shouldn't we stop, losers, lest we become a joy to our enemies, and not shamelessly talk trash to each other, but these things ..." But then the laurel, giving her an angry look, like a bull, said: "You lousy disgrace, so you're one of us?"

Most interpreters interpret the allegory as a literary quarrel. The olive seems to be the "winner" and the representative of Callimachean poetics. If that is so, this poem inverts the first. The bramble is an easy symbol for Hipponax, practitioner of a "low" genre (Alcaeus of Messene 13 GP puts one on his tomb), and again the symbol of aggression and vulgarity preaches solidarity and good manners to his social/generic betters – who openly reject him. "Callimachus" would seem to play three roles – he rebukes the intruder in the frame, he is represented by the olive, and the bramble stands for the iambic voice he has assumed.

In *Iamb* 5, which combines choliambs with iambic dimeters, the speaker rebukes a schoolmaster for sexually molesting his pupils. The theme is worthy of the old iambos, but the object is apparently unnamed, and the tone superficially friendly: it begins "friend – for advice is a holy thing – listen to these heart-felt words" (ὦ ξεῖνε – cυμβουλὴ γ[ὰ]ρ̣ ἕν τι τῶν ἱρῶν – / ἄκουε τἀπὸ καρδ̣[ίηc). If the speaker is the same as that of *Iamb* 3, he is hardly in a position to advise.

At this point the book abandons its already diluted attachment to the spirit of Archaic iambos. The following six poems are in varying meters and elements of non-Ionic dialect appear in them. These poems involve ecphrasis or aetiology or both. When they are read together, their author is recognizably the Callimachus of the

Aetia and *Hymns*, but each by itself has an individual tone and voice, and each is independent of any grand project. *Iamb* 6 describes Phidias' Zeus at Olympia with measurements of virtuosic precision. The seventh is an aetiological story of the statue of Hermes Perpheraios at Ainos. The wooden statue, attributed to Epeus, builder of the Wooden Horse, tells his own story of shipwreck and eventual safety. The eighth celebrates a victory of Polycles of Aegina in a local race commemorating the Argonauts' search for water on Aegina. In the ninth, a lover of Philetades asks a statue of Hermes whether his erection is owing to desire for Philetades; the statue answers that his erection has a secret religious meaning (κατὰ μυστικὸν λόγον), but the inquirer's passion is destined to end badly or indicates bad intentions (ἐπὶ κακῶι). The tenth explains why at Aspendos in Pamphylia they sacrifice pigs to Aphrodite, and praises Artemis at Eretria, who accepts all animals. The eleventh concerns the proverb ἁρπαγὰ τὰ Κοννίδα, "Konnidas' property is up for grabs."

Several display an ironic attitude akin to that of the earlier poems. Hermes corrects the obsessive lover. The simple statue of Perpheraios is indestructible. A pig-friendly Aphrodite is more sensible than other Aphrodites. Both Konnidas and the people who plunder his estate are contemptible. The race at Aegina commemorates the need even of epic heroes for water, the most basic human requirement. Six seems to make fun of the speaker's fascination with the size and value of Phidias' work. Still, these poems apparently lack even the genial moralizing of those in choliambs. As individual poems, they are clever, occasional trifles. Within the collection, they further redefine the genre and the implied author, whose interests and personality become a theme in themselves. This iambographer is unmistakably a scholar-poet, fascinated by odd stories and aetiologies: he mentally wanders around the Greek world, exclaiming "This is interesting!" These poems further mitigate the "iambic" qualities of those that preceded them. The implied author knows that the world is full of a number of things, not all of them nice, but not all nasty, either, many worth thinking about and remembering.

Iamb 12 returns to moralizing themes, honoring the infant daughter of a friend of the poet by telling how the gods competed with gifts for the infant Hebe. Apollo demonstrates that his gift of song is the best because it is neither perishable nor morally dubious (as gold is). If Apollo's song points to this very book, song includes the book's attitude of amused fascination with odd aetiologies and human folly. The thirteenth returns to choliambs and defends the author's poetic practices against critics who complain that he has not visited Ephesus (Hipponax's home), improperly mixes dialects, and writes in too many genres – not, however, that he satirizes too harshly or too weakly. The answer insists that the gods have not established generic boundaries for each poet (31–3), and after a lacuna it adduces the examples of the carpenter and of Ion of Chios in defense of *polyeidcia*, "multiformity." Finally, it presents the horrors of a literary world consumed by envy, where poets insult each other and the Muses fly past in fear for their own reputation (58–9). Finally the speaker proudly turns his critic's words against him (63–6):

ἀείδω
οὔτ' Ἔφεσον ἐλθὼν οὔτ' Ἴωσι συμμείξας,
Ἔφεσον, ὅθεν περ οἱ τὰ μέτρα μέλλοντες
τὰ χωλὰ τίκτειν μὴ ἀμαθῶς ἐναύονται.

I sing without having gone to Ephesus or hung around with Ionians – Ephesus, where those planning to give birth to the lame meters learnedly light their fires.

Like the first, the poem is invective against invective, but the critics' objections themselves mark how harmless this iambos is. They complain exclusively in literary terms; nothing in the content has hurt anyone.

What is the point of iambos when it becomes so pacific and its topics so wide? The moralizing of the new iambos demands an ironic attitude to social norms, to literary traditions, and to the self, but this irony itself limits invective force, since to be really nasty a speaker must take himself seriously. Its fun lies in deflating both self and others. In *Iamb* 10, the claim that there is more than one Aphrodite evokes the Platonic distinction between the heavenly and the common Aphrodite (*Sym.* 180c–185c2), but the issue at hand is sacrificing pigs. In what other genre could a tree not only talk but have the angry look of an epic hero (4.101–2, quoted above), or one's annoying colleagues be compared to flies around a goatherd, wasps pouring from the ground, or Delphians at a sacrifice (1.26–7)? The first two similes have epic antecedents, but the echo is absurd. This fun, though, makes one significant implicit claim. The opponents in *Iamb* 13 call the iambographer crazy (19–21):

οἱ φίλοι ϲε δήϲ[ουϲι
κ[ἢ]ν νοῦν ἔχωϲιν, ἐγχέουϲι τὴν [κρᾶϲιν,
ὡ̣ϲ̣ ὑ̣γ̣ιείηϲ οὐδὲ τῷ̣νυχ̣ι ψαύε̣ι̣ϲ.

Your friends will tie you up, and if they are wise, they will pour your mixture [i.e., either a medicine or much-watered wine], since you aren't in contact with Health even with a fingernail.

Behind the various personae of the poems, however, the implied author is very sane. He is no Cynic trampler of norms, but he is detached from even his own participation in the follies of life. So the genre is defined largely by what it seems to exclude: besides royal flattery, passionate love (though not of course sex), really serious thinking, pathos.

A further problem complicates the generic status of the *Iambi*. The thirteen poems in iambic meters are followed in the *Diegesis*, without any notation (though it marks the end of the *Aetia* and the start of the *Hecale*), by another four poems (frs. 226–9 Pf.). It also looks as if at least one ancient copy had these poems on a single roll with the *Iambi*. Yet the ring-composition of 1 and 13 delimits the thirteen poems, and there are no certain quotations of the *Iambi* that are not from the thirteen (recently favoring a book of seventeen, D'Alessio 2007: 43–7; Cameron 1995a: 163–73; of thirteen, Kerkhecker 1999: 271–82). And while the first of these four, in phalaecians, warned young men to avoid the fate of the Lemnians – a possibly iambic topic, in a possibly iambic meter – the next concerns an all-night festival, and its opening implies the presence of a most uniambic chorus (ἔνεϲτ' Ἀπόλλων τῶι χορῶι, "Apollo is there in the chorus"). The next is on the apotheosis of Arsinoe, the last on Branchus, a shepherd loved by Apollo and founder of his sanctuary at Didyma near Miletus. It is hard to imagine that any reader would have read these through iambic conventions (one, at least, is clearly court poetry). Yet if all these poems stood in one book, the variety of the author's concerns would be even more salient, the invective element even weaker.

Iambos in Song: Cercidas

Only one choliamb of Cercidas survives: "there was once a pair of girls with beautiful asses in Syracuse" (ἦν καλλιπύγων ζεῦγος ἐν Συρακούcαιc, *CA* 14), which sounds like the beginning of an aetiology on the temple allegedly founded by sisters who argued who had a more beautiful butt. However, we have rich fragments of the genre he invented, meliamb. There is now general agreement that poet is the Megalopolitan statesman and legislator of the latter half of the third century. This identification, though, creates other complications. *P.Oxy.* 1082 (second century CE) is subscribed "Meliambs of Cercidas the Dog," and the ancient tradition identifies the poet Cercidas as a Cynic, though a Cynic as public servant is hard to imagine. I will discuss only the first two fragments, on wealth and sexual desire, which are extensive enough to give a sense of how the arguments develop.

The *Meliambs* are literary Doric in dialect, vigorous in language, and metrically a relative of dactylo-epitrite, "in the fourth and third centuries the normal meter for what may be called educated bourgeois lyric" (West 1982: 139). They thereby claim a peculiar territory that is both elevated and direct, a potentially high poetic voice whose moral energy demands an expanded register. All are reflections on moral topics (for example, fr. 3 Livrea 1986 [= 3 Lomiento 1993] is on old age, fr. 6 [= 6] on pederasty). Explosions of stylistic energy serve arguments and exhortations that are simultaneously straightforward and unpredictable, conveying more powerfully than Phoenix or Callimachus the sense of hearing thoughts as they develop. Cercidas quotes earlier authors by name and without circumlocutions (καὶ τοῦθ' Ὅμηρος εἶπεν ἐν Ἰλιάδι, "Homer said this also in the *Iliad*," fr. 1.19–20 = 1.58 Lom.), consonant with his combination of loftiness and plain speaking.

In fr. 1, whose theme of wealth in the wrong hands is reminiscent of Phoenix's poem to Posidippus, a string of comic compounds can barely express the speaker's indignation (1.5–11 = 1.44–50 Lom.):

> κα[ὶ] τί τὸ κωλύον ἦc, αἴ τίc φέρο[ι]το;
> ῥεῖα γάρ ἐcτι θεῶι πᾶν ἐκτελέc<c>αι
> χρῆμ', ἐπὶ νοῦν ὅ̣κ' ἵηι, ἢ τὸν ῥυποκιβδοτόκωνα
> καὶ̣ τε̣θ̣νακ̣οχαλκίδαν ἢ τ̣<ὸ>ν παλινεκχυμενίταν,
> τὸν κτεάνων ὄλεθρον, τοῦτον κενῶcαι
> τᾶc cυοπλουτοcύναc, δόμεν δ' ἐπιταδεοτρώκται
> κοινοκρατηροcκύφωι τὰν ὀλλυμέναν δαπάνυλλαν;
>
> And what was in the way, if someone were to carry it off? For isn't it easy for a god to accomplish anything to which his mind turns, the usurer-of-counterfeit-filth and dead-penny-grasper, or the re-outpourer, the destruction of possessions, to empty him of his pig-wealth, and give his damned bit of expense to the appropriate-muncher, the cup-from-the-shared-mixing-bowl guy?

He continues with rhetorical questions about the gods. Justice has gone blind, Phaethon (i.e., Helios) can't see straight, Themis has gone dim; and "how can there still be gods, when they have neither hearing nor sight?" (πῶc ἔτι δαίμονεc οὖν τοὶ μήτ' ἀκουὰν / μήτ' ὀπὰν πεπαμένοι; 15–16 = 54–5 Lom.). Zeus is the climax (16–19 = 55–7 Lom.):

καὶ μὰν τὸ τάλαντον ὁ cεμνὸc
ἀcτεροπαγερέταc μέccον τὸν Ὄλυμπον [. . . . .]
ὀρθὸν [τιταίνει],
[κ]αὶ νένευκεν οὐδαμῆι.

And indeed the revered fixer of the stars, who sits at the center of Olympus, extends the scale straight, and does not incline it anywhere.

Homeric epic offers a normative model for the god, which the speaker is not following. Zeus is a paternal uncle to some, a father to others. But he then decides to leave these matters to the "astronomy-fussers" (μετεωροκόποιc), while we concern ourselves with Paean, Nemesis, and Μετάδωc, "Share" – "for she is a god" (θεὸc γὰρ αὕτα). The poem ends with a warning to honor Nemesis, for if a storm-wind comes and blows against one's prosperity, "we will have to vomit these things out from the bottom" (ταῦτ' ἕ[ccεθ' ἁμὶν] / νειόθεν ἐξεμέcαι, 37–8 = 75 Lom.).

Livrea argues that the poem must refer to a specific crisis and program, probably the dire situation in Megalopolis after the Battle of Sellasia in 222/221, while López Cruces relates it more precisely to the issues described in Polybius 5.93 (Livrea 1986: 2–3; López Cruces 1995: 123–30). The citizens were divided over whether they should reduce the city's area and over a proposal that the rich contribute one-third of their property for new citizens, while the law-code produced by Prytanis, a Peripatetic, caused intense strife. Yet the poem is oddly unspecific. The abusive epithets attack two categories of rich people, the cheap/usurious and the wasteful. To be sure, the speaker clearly thinks he could use Xenon's money for better purposes, and the reference to Share describes what the rich should do. However, this is not a poem about the plight of the poor. The proposed recipient of wealth is "ourselves," and is a man of moderation (ἐπιταδεοτρώκταc). That he fills his cup from a shared *krater* (κοινοκρατηροcκύφοc) presumably means that he belongs to a society that shares meals, but it suggests full participation in community life rather than extreme poverty. The poem does not mention specific problems caused by the selfishness of the rich. While the poem may have addressed the crisis at Megalopolis, it is applicable to other situations; this generality is typical of Hellenistic iambos.

The poem's values are conventional: the target of the attack gained money wrongfully and/or uses it badly. More striking is the vehemence with which it rejects the traditional gods, especially Zeus, because they do not do what the speaker's understanding of the poetic tradition says they should. Most of the extant fragment is about the gods. Zeus is not only "father of gods and men" but "the one who planted and begot us all" (a more philosophical than mythological description of the god), making his failure to intervene even worse. Yet Cercidas still warns of the Nemesis typically associated with Zeus.

Fragment 2 Livrea looks more Cynical. The poem opens by reminding the addressee, Damonomus, how "somebody" (τιc) said that there are two ways Eros can blow upon us (nautical imagery dominates). He can be gentle and blow from the right, but he can also blow from the left and cause storms and a rough voyage; Euripides (now named) was right. But suddenly the argument shifts. We can control what happens (11–14 = 2.19–22 Lomiento, who transposes οὐκοῦν δύ' ὄντων and κάρρον ἐστίν):

> οὐκοῦν δύ' ὄντων
> κάρρον ἐςτὶν ἐκλέγειν τὸν οὔριον ἇμιν ἀήταν,
> καὶ μετὰ Σωφροςύνας οἴακι Πειθοῦς
> χρώμενον εὐθυπλοεῖν.
>
> So of the two it is better to select the breeze favorable for us, and to sail straight, using Persuasion's tiller in the company of Moderation.

After some poorly preserved lines (Icarus is mentioned), Cercidas warns of the dangers of the wrong kind of sexual entanglement and recommends, instead, prostitutes (30 – 2 = 26 – 30 Lom.):

> κ̣αὶ προκοθηλυμαν[ὲς] φέρει τ̣αναβλαψιτέλειαν
> καὶ μ̣ε̣ταμελλοδύναν· ἁ δ' ἐξ ἀγορᾶς Ἀφροδ̣ίτα
> καὶ τὸ μη[δε]νὸς μέλειν, ὁπ[α]νίκα λῇις, ὅκα χρήιζηις,
> οὐ φόβος, οὐ ταραχά· τα̣[ύ]ταν ὀβολῶ κατακλίνας
> Τ[υν]δαρέοιο δόκει γαμβ̣ρ̣ὸς τ[ό]κ' ἦμεν
>
> And deer-woman-madness [i.e., stag-like craziness for a female] brings extended-end-damage and grief-of repentance. But the "Aphrodite from the marketplace," the "worry about nothing," "each time you want, whenever you need," "no fear, no disturbance": bedding her for an obol think then you are the son-in-law of Tyndareus.

Exotic compounds describe the wrong kind of sex, while everyday clichés summarize the advantages of readily available sex. To conclude, he quotes yet another proverb (31 – 2 = fr. 7 Lom.):

> τὸ τᾶς ῥ̣⌊ικνᾶς⌋ [ἐν
> γᾶι ⌊χελώνας μναμόν⌋ευ'· οἶκο̣ς γ̣ὰ̣ρ ἄριςτος ἀλαθέως,
> καὶ φίλο⌊ς⌋. [πά]ρ̣ε̣ςτ' ἀεί.
>
> Remember the saying of the wrinkled tortoise in the ground: "Home is truly best, it's always there and dear."

This is probably praise of masturbation; Euripides' distinction between kinds of love has taken a surprising direction. Yet the benefit of using prostitutes is a commonplace of popular philosophy, most familiar from Horace (*Sat.* 1.2.119), and the poem remains within the traditional language of moderation.

We do not need to attribute everything in these poems to a fully coherent set of beliefs. The *Meliambs* are fully iambic in imitating a spontaneous voice. The tendency to rant in fr. 1 characterizes the speaker as much as Xenon, and it is funny as a performance. The fun of fr. 2 lies in the very practical form that traditional wisdom takes. If Cercidas sounds more excited than Phoenix or Callimachus, his basic interest in general ethical questions places him just as far as they are from Archaic iambos.

Macho

The fragments of Macho's *Chreiai* (all preserved by Athenaeus) are not stylistically impressive. Filler is frequent, diction prosaic, and reading the fragments through is stultifying. The poem, composed sometime around the middle of the third century BCE, consists of a string of anecdotes without formal connection with each other – names are repeated from anecdote to anecdote, and Stratonicus is called "the citharode" in 141 and 149 (there is an occasional δέ, but it does not mark real connection). Readers would presumably hunt for bits they could use socially. Each anecdote has as its point a (presumably) clever remark; the characters are hetaerae, musicians, and parasites. Some stories include famous people, some not. A few take place in the fifth century, many in the fourth, and some concern Macho's contemporaries. Although anonymous figures – a bad lyre-player, an unsuccessful boxer – figure in many, there is always a named character. Many are obscene. Most have some Athenian connection, in the setting or characters. The milieu is familiar from comedy and epigram (Lape, Bruss in this volume), but the effect is quite different, since these characters are the center, not the periphery, of this iambo-comic world.

The preoccupations are sex, food, poetry/music, and money, while the implicit attitude is a worldly wise hedonism. Several jokes are at the expense of bad musicians – who should be providing enjoyment but offer its opposite instead. Some concern rates of exchange: one Morichos approaches the hetaera Phryne, who demands a mina. He complains that she was with a foreigner two days before for two gold pieces. She answers (454–5 Gow 1965):

περίμενε τοίνυν καὶ cύ, φηc', ἕωc ἂν οὗ
βινητιάcω καὶ τοcοῦτον λήψομαι.

You, too, wait until I want a fuck, and I'll take that much.

One of the few jokes at a hetaera's expense begins when Lamia rejects a variety of perfumes Demetrius offers her; finally he puts a cheap scent on his fingers and fondles his genitals. When she calls that the worst of all, he comments that it is "from a royal acorn" (ἀπὸ βαλάνου ... βαcιλικῆc, 187). Kings may make jokes or provide the occasion for them, but they are not their targets ("Ptolemy" appears in 1–5, 25–45, 439–49). Only one story has an obvious moral: Stratonicus jokes after a king's wife farts and tries to hide it by noisily crushing almond shells; the king has him drowned (156–62). The anecdotes do not respect the powerful, but they do not challenge power, either.

One story about the death of the poet Philoxenus is strongly reminiscent of Phoenix's Ninus. Philoxenus bought a huge octopus, overate, and became sick. A doctor warned him to settle his affairs. Philoxenus speaks of his poems as if they were children who have done well and are provided for, and ends (81–6):

ἀλλ' ἐπεὶ
ὁ Τιμοθέου Χάρων cχολάζειν οὐκ ἐᾶι,
οὐκ τῆc Νιόβηc, χωρεῖν δὲ πορθμὸν ἀναβοᾶι,

καλεῖ δὲ μοῖρα νύχιος ἧς κλύειν χρεών,
ἵν' ἔχων ἀποτρέχω πάντα τἀμαυτοῦ κάτω
τοῦ πουλύποδός μοι τὸ κατάλοιπον ἀπόδοτε.

But since the Charon of Timotheus allows no waste of time, the one from the Niobe, and he yells that the ferry is leaving, and the "fate of night is calling" which you have to listen to – so that I can go off below with everything I own, give me the rest of the octopus.

Dying, he parodies a poetic rival, and then echoes Ninus' assertion that all he really owns is what he consumed and enjoyed. Deathbeds and famous last words were common in moralizing literature (Cercidas describes the death of Diogenes by holding his breath, apparently with sincere admiration, fr. 54 Livrea = 60 Lom.). Philoxenus' heroic hedonism evokes this usually uplifting genre.

More generally, popular philosophy made heavy use of anecdotes. The Socratic tradition in both Plato and Xenophon already relied on exemplary but entertaining tales of Socrates, and stories about Diogenes constitute the basis of Cynicism. It may be significant that Athenaeus preserves no anecdotes about philosophers, although there were many philosopher-hetaera stories, and philosophers were standard comic characters; perhaps Macho actually respected them. Yet most of the stories, while dirty, are good-natured, and most of the targets were dead. Macho has no more bite than Callimachus. His implicit morality urges adaptation to circumstances, sensibly controlled hedonism, and self-knowledge that is not philosophical but social and economic: wise moderation is knowing what you want, what the traffic will bear, and what you can get away with.

Parody

Epic parody was already a tool of Greek humor in the Archaic period. In the late fifth century, parody came to have its own formal competitions. Its first celebrated poet is Hegemon, who presents himself as poor, old, and apparently among those who "badly perform bad epic" (κακῶς κακὰ ῥαψωιδοῦςιν, fr. 1 Brandt 1888). This implies that good epic and good performances are possible, even if the speaker has not encountered any.

We know almost nothing about the four books of parodies by Euboeus of Paros in the fourth century. Thanks to Athenaeus, though, we have considerable fragments of Archestratus of Gela. He discusses where to find the best food in the Mediterranean, combining snippets of Homeric phraseology with a clear didactic voice: his knowledge is the result of extensive travel (fr. 2.1–3 Olson and Sens 2000); he will treat the topic systematically (*ibid.*); he frequently addresses two internal addressees; he admits that judgments may differ (14.4); and he respects the gods (there may be divine vengeance on someone who does not buy Ambracian boar if he can, no matter how expensive it is, 15.1–4). The poem is at once funny and informative. Satire is directed only at how seriously the speaker takes gourmandizing, not at those who have a reasonable interest in food.

At the end of the fourth century, Matro of Pitane narrates an immense banquet given by the politician Xenocles in Athens (two characters, Stratocles and the parasite Chaerephon, also appear in Macho). The narrator, who does not usually eat like this, is willing to fight for an especially desirable item, but so are others; there is a mock-heroic struggle both to grab the best goodies and to surpass natural capacity. Xenocles and Stratocles were well-known supporters of the restored democracy and Demetrius Poliorcetes; Olson and Sens (1999: 29–33) make a strong case that there is a political subtext in the poem, warning of the hidden greed of apparent democrats. Still, the political satire is not especially salient.

In these texts, epic reminiscences work against the mundane subject matter, but epic itself is not mocked. However, parody can satirize primarily epic itself. *SSH* 1190 (*P.Mich.* 6946) is a fragmentary epic about a war between mice and a weasel. A fable is the likely basis; "mouse and weasel" is the typical childish fable at Aristophanes *Wasps* 1181–4, and there is an Aesopian fable about a mouse–weasel war (Perry 1967: no. 165; Hausrath and Hunger 1957–70: no. 174). The surviving fragments include a messenger's report; Hermes' approach to a rack for drying figs; a decision-monologue; a gathering, and an assembly-speech by a wise, elderly mouse. The language points strenuously to Homer, including Homeric whole-line speech introductions. When a mouse named Trixos dies in the front line, the narrator comments on the pathos of his death outside his ancestral field, and his widow grieves. This probably parodies the familiar story of Protesilaus and Laodamia (Schibli 1983: 2–3). The target of the burlesque is conventional epic action. The *Suda* mentions battles of spiders, starlings, and cranes (3.526.6, 527.8 Adler).

The "Battle of Frogs and Mice" (*Batrachomyomachia*) overtly satirizes not just the conventions of epic, but heroic attitudes. Scholars now generally agree on a Hellenistic date for the poem, which uses some Homeric expressions, often recombining them, but makes no effort to be consistently Homeric (Kirk 1966: 161–3). The narrative is based on the fable found in one of the Lives of Aesop (Perry 1967: no. 133; Hausrath and Hunger 1957–70: no. 302) in which a frog's attempt to bring a mouse-friend to his house kills both of them. In the poem, a mouse named Psicharpax ("crumb-grabber") is drinking by a pond when he is accosted by the frog-king Polyphemus ("noisy" or "famous," named for the Cyclops of the *Odyssey*), who suggests that they could become friends, if the mouse's genealogy is as impressive as his warlike appearance. Psicharpax does not think friendship possible, defining the difference in their environments by their different diets – he eats human leftovers, while frogs eat vegetables (evidently, he knows nothing about frogs). Polyphemus criticizes his boasting about food, but offers to give him a ride around his territory.

Psicharpax soon regrets accepting, finding himself terrified; when a snake appears, Polyphemus dives underwater, and Psicharpax drowns, cursing Polyphemus. In the mouse-assembly, Psicharpax's father calls for war. Polyphemus lies outright to the frogs (147–9):

οὐδὲ κατεῖδον
ὀλλύμενον· πάντωϲ δ' ἐπνίγη παίζων παρὰ λίμνην,
νήξειϲ τὰϲ βατράχων μιμούμενοϲ.

And I didn't see him perish. He must have drowned playing by the pond, imitating frogs' swimming.

The frogs do not ask how he knows if he wasn't there, since it is plausible to them that a mouse would imitate them; they too arm for battle. So it is not just that tiny animals think they are great warriors; Psicharpax is gullible and cowardly; Polyphemus vain, thoughtless, and deceitful. Both sides are stupidly bellicose. When it appears that the mice will overwhelm the frogs, Zeus sends a thunderbolt, but even that is inadequate, and he sends an army of crabs, before whom the mice flee. The joke is on both epic mannerisms and the epic view of human life. The *Batrachomyomachia* alludes to Callimachus and Moschus as if to suggest that Hellenistic poetry's new "realism" about the mythological past did not go far enough (examples in Wölke 1978).

So one type of mock epic treats food as worthy of heroic energy; the other attributes heroic posturing to mice, those greedy little parasites. In both, we sense how the attitudes of the high genre are out of touch with a hedonistic world. Yet the reader is presumably at a certain distance from both epic pretension and excessive hedonism. Moderation implicitly wins again, and as often in Hellenistic satire, the reader is invited to share amusement instead of indignation.

Iambic and parodic poetry seem to be composed by and for tolerant people. They are not about to convert to the philosophical life but enjoy being mocked, exhorted, and entertained. It is an extraordinarily difficult task to make the voice of moderation lively, and this is the achievement of the low Hellenistic genres. Parody combines the period's delight in the tiny and trivial with its devotion to Homer. The success of Hellenistic iambos required a misreading of the Archaic genre so that it could be adapted to the new conditions of Hellenistic literary production: refined taste, reading rather than performance, patronage. The outcome is something quite new.

The clever reader will probably have recognized that while the Hellenistic iambographer filters his Archaic predecessors through the figure of the philosopher, this essay filters Hellenistic iambos through its own future: historically, the greatest success of Hellenistic iambos may have been its creation of a literary space for Horace. While Horace does not share Callimachus' delight in the antiquarian wonders to be found in an excellent library, and no Hellenistic iambographer seems to share Horace's unappealing interest in witches, the gently satiric, loosely philosophical poetry created in the Hellenistic world became a long-enduring tradition.

FURTHER READING

Phoenix needs a new edition: still standard is Powell 1925 (*CA*); translation (into rhyming couplets) in the Loeb, Knox 1929. There is a good translation and discussion in Furley 1994. For Cercidas, the standard edition of *P.Oxy.* 1082 (commentary and translation into Italian) is Livrea 1986; a new edition is in preparation by Livrea and F. Williams. Livrea heavily stresses Cercidas' Cynicism. Lomiento 1993 edits, translates, and comments on the testimonia and fragments quoted in ancient authors as well as the papyrus; López Cruces 1995 is a study of the biographical tradition and fragments that argues against overemphasizing Cynicism in Cercidas. For Callimachus' *Iambi*, the most recent edition is D'Alessio 2007 (with Italian translation); English translation, Nisetich 2001. There are two recent complementary monographs: Kerkhecker 1999 almost replaces a commentary; Acosta-Hughes 2002 is thematic. Cameron 1995a: 167–73, argues for Callimachus' priority to Phoenix and for a book of 17

Iambi. For Macho, Gow 1965 is an exemplary text and commentary. A new Loeb translation of Athenaeus (sole source for the fragments of Macho) by S. Douglas Olson is in progress (2007–). Studies of Macho are mostly devoted to the many problems of text and interpretation; the only general recent study is Kurke 2002, which argues, interestingly but not convincingly, that the poem is a protest against Macedonian domination in Athens. On Archestratus, see Olson and Sens 2000; on Matro, Olson and Sens 1999. Wölke 1978 is the most important work on the "Battle of Frogs and Mice." Most 1993 suggests that the mice represent the *Iliad*, the frogs the *Odyssey*.

CHAPTER NINETEEN[*]

Herodas and the Mime

Elena Esposito

Like so many other genres, the mime, which is generally assumed to have begun its life as a literary genre with Sophron of Syracuse in the fifth century BCE, came to flourish once again during the Hellenistic Age (Mastromarco 1991: 171–2). This rebirth can be explained at least partly from the principles that inspire Hellenistic poetry as a whole, more specifically a widespread taste for attenuated poetry and realistic representation. Mimes, short compositions that focused on character portrayal and features of everyday life, offered poets the opportunity to observe aspects of the lower middle class, but filtered through the lens of a carefully defined and refined, "aristocratic" art form. Mime-like features occur in two hymns of Callimachus (5 and 6) and many of Theocritus' *Idylls* (the "bucolic mimes" 1, 3, 4, 5, 10, and "urban mimes" 2, 14, 15), and it is likely that both were inspired by Sophron and other writers in this tradition (although direct connections between Sophron and Theocritus or Herodas are hard to establish, see Hordern 2004: 26–9). Even a number of epigrams take the form of little sketches, including realistic conversations with questions, exclamations, and responses, that in all respects show the characteristics of genuine mime (for example, Asclep. 25–6 GP = *AP* 5.181, 185; Posidip. 124 AB = 10 GP = *AP* 5.183; Call. 31 GP = *AP* 7.524; Phalaecus 3 GP = *AP* 13.5; see also Bruss in this volume). Yet only Herodas, by calling his poems "mimiambs," explicitly links his work with mime as a genre and as such he can be considered the most representative exponent of literary mime of the Hellenistic era.

[*] Translated by James J. Clauss and Martine Cuypers.

The Rediscovery of an Author

Except a few citations preserved at second hand, nothing remained of Herodas until 1891, the year of publication of a papyrus that contained eight largely complete mimiambs and fragments of a ninth (*P.Lond.Lit.* 96 = *P.Egerton* 1; cf. MP^3 485). This rediscovery has granted us access to Herodas' work and the ability to date it, even with some hesitation, to the reign of Ptolemy II Philadelphus on the basis of internal features. Nonetheless his city of origin and the location where he engaged in his literary projects remain to some extent uncertain and controversial (an issue discussed below), and the same applies to the exact form of his name. Herodas, the Doric form, is generally preferred by English-speaking and Italian scholars; Herondas, the Boeotian form, by French and German scholars; and the Ionic-Attic form Herodes was used by A. D. Knox in most of his work on the poet.

Although Herodas' poetry now seems to have found a more favorable critical response, it was at first negatively received and deemed of very little value on the basis of what were mostly anachronistic aesthetic and moral norms. Typical reactions are the reductive judgment of the first editor, F. G. Kenyon ("it cannot be said to be of high literary merit," 1891: 1), and the condemnatory pronouncements recorded in *La Civilità Cattolica*, a magazine published by the Jesuits in Italy, according to which "Herodas sadly reflects the corruption of his times" and turns out to be a "true artist" only where "he avoids wallowing in the mud" (no. 43, 1892: 281). Soon, however, the poet was embraced as a realist *ante litteram*: his poetry was characterized, for the most part, as naive, steeped in bourgeois and popular culture, an interpretation which reflects the ideals of realism and naturalism cultivated at the time, and which continued to rule until the 1920s. During that decade, a number of excellent scholarly works appeared which radically re-appraised Herodean poetry, notably the editions and commentaries of Groeneboom (1922), Headlam and Knox (1922), and the critical studies of the eighth mimiamb by Herzog (1924) and Knox (1925). All of these contributions fostered, in a different though decisive manner, the image of Herodas as a *doctus poeta* that had been anticipated by Blass (1892: 230) and Wilamowitz (1896: 221; 1924: 1.211–12). Forty years later several Soviet scholars attempted to revive the realistic/naturalistic Herodas of early scholarship, arguing that the mimiambs were composed as a sort of social indictment that appealed to the masses and opposed the elitist literature of Alexandria, the ideological mouthpiece of the ruling class (Smotrytsch 1962, 1966; Luria 1963); but they were clearly fighting a rearguard action. Herodas did not write for the uneducated, nor did he preach social reform. His interest in realistic representations of the daily life of ordinary people is purely literary in nature.

A number of telling features associate Herodas' poems with the *docta poesis* of the time. Among the most obvious are the mimiambs' meticulous detailing in form and concept, facilitated by *brevitas*, and their renovation of traditional genres through a painstaking recovery of archaic genres or other literary features that were no longer current (Fantuzzi 1993; Rossi 2000) and thus at risk of disappearing, such as the long-forgotten choliambic meter. What we observe in the mimiambs is a combination of genres, notably, of course, the *mimos* and *iambos* (Kroll's *Kreuzung der Gattungen*,

1924: 202–24; Fantuzzi and Hunter 2004: 17–26). Characteristically Hellenistic are also Herodas' appeal to a literary authority of the past – Hipponax – in order to justify a poetic project (Fantuzzi and Hunter 2004: 3–5) as well as his "realism" and exploitation of marginal themes and humble or even déclassé characters which had been excluded from "high" literature. The mimiambs also refer to literary polemics and link poetry and philology; they are highly intertextual and show a notable dependence on Homer; and as such they appeal to a select audience. Among these various issues, the ones which seem to be most in need of further attention, and on which I will therefore focus in this chapter, are, on the one hand, the relationship between the mimiambs and epic and their reflection of (Homeric) philology, on the other, Herodas' place within the "literary scene" of the early third century BCE and his connections with the Ptolemies.

Herodas, *Doctus Poeta* (1): *Mimiamb* 8

Richest in their poetic self-consciousness and in the "Alexandrian" features mentioned above are Herodas' first and eighth mimiambs (together perhaps with the fourth: see below). These poems reveal that Herodas' rapport with the Homeric epics is anything but mechanical or superficial. Their intertextuality far transcends the borrowing of individual terms, motifs, and stylistic features, and suggests that Herodas followed Hipponax, the founding father of the choliamb, in employing for programmatic purposes entire Homeric scenes or theme clusters, reworked to support the poet's specific goals (Degani 1995: 135; Esposito 2001a).

In the programmatic eighth mime, a farmer who is later revealed to be the poet dreams he is dragging a goat. The goat is sacrificed and his hide prepared for the game of *askōliasmos*, which involved staying upright on top of an inflated and greased skin bag. The protagonist participates in the competition and, as far as we can tell from the damaged text, triumphs over the other contestants, but his victory is compromised by the appearance of an angry old man who threatens him with a stick and claims a share of the prize. As a variation of a scene of poetic consecration (topical since Hesiod, *Th.* 22–35), the author, interpreting his nocturnal vision, foresees for himself on the one hand literary polemics, but on the other, future glory as the successor of the famous Hipponax.

The character of the poem, an elegant literary *lusus* sustained by a lively comedic/ parodic mood, becomes apparent immediately from the initial verses. It opens with a domestic scene in which our farmer scolds his servants (8.1–15, text after Di Gregorio 2004):

ἄcτηθι, δούλη Ψύλλα· μέχρι τέο κείcηι
ῥέγχουcα; τὴν δὲ χοῖρον αὐονὴ δρύπτει·
ἢ προcμένειc cὺ μέχριc εὖ ἥλιοc θάλψηι
τὸ]ν̣ κ̣ῦcον ἐcδύc; κῶc δ', ἄτρυτε, κοὐ κάμνειc
τὰ πλ]ευρὰ κνώccουc'; αἱ δὲ νύκτεc ἐννέωροι.
ἄcτη]θ̣ι, φημί, καὶ ἅψον, εἰ θέλειc, λύχνον,
κα]ὶ̣ [τ]ὴν ἄναυλον χοῖρον ἐc νομὴν πέμψ[ο]ν̣.

τ̣ό̣ν̣θρυζε καὶ κνῶ, μέχρις εὖ παραστά[ς σοι
τὸ] βρέγμα τῶι σκίπωνι μαλθακὸν θῶμα[ι.
δει]λὴ Μεγαλλί, κα̣[ὶ] σ̣ὺ Λάτμιον κνώσσεις;
οὐ] τὰ ἔριά σε τρύχ[ο]υ̣σιν· ἀλλὰ μὴν στέμμ[α
ἐπ' ἱρὰ διζόμεσ̣[θ] α· βαιὸ̤ς οὐχ ἧμιν
ἐν τῆι οἰκίηι ἔτι μα[λ]λὸς εἰρίων. δειλή,
ἄστηθι. σύ τε μοι τ̣[οὖ]ν̣α̣ρ, εἰ θέλεις, Ἀννᾶ,
ἄκουσον· οὐ γὰρ νη̣[πία]ς̣ φρένας βόσκεις.

Get up, Psylla, you slave. How long are you going to lie snoring? The sow is rent by drought. Perhaps you're waiting until the sun warms your bum, crawls into it? You indefatigable thing, don't you wear out your sides with all this sleeping? These nights last for ages. Get up, I say, and light the lamp – please! – and send that unmelodious(?) sow to the pasture. Sure, mutter and scratch yourself – until I get over to you and bash your head in with my cane. Megallis, you wretch, also in a Latmian sleep? Can't be the work that's making you tired. Should we ever seek a wreath for a sacrifice, there isn't the tiniest shred of wool left in the house. You wretch, get up! And you, want to know what I dreamed, Annas? Listen then, because you don't feed a silly mind.

Although the first debt is obviously to comedy, where masters frequently scold their lazy slaves, this opening also evokes Homeric scenes where a character who is resting or idle is called to action (*Il.* 3.250, 10.159, 16.126, 18.170; *Od.* 6.255, 15.46, 23.5; imitated at Theoc. 24.35–6). The phrase μέχρι τέο κείσηι specifically recalls the "war poet" Callinus rebuking young soldiers in *IEG* 1.1–2 (μέχρις τέο κατάκεισθε . . . / ὦ νέοι;) and uses Homericizing language redolent of epic verse (μέχρι τέο, cf. *Il.* 24.128–9 τέκνον ἐμόν, τέο μέχρις . . . / σὴν ἔδεαι κραδίην;); but the decidedly non-heroic ῥέγχουσα, "snoring," added in enjambement undermines the epic tone and produces a comic effect. Similarly, the second verse contains both the rare word for "drought," αὐονή (earlier attested only in Archil. *IEG* 230, Semon. *IEG* 7.20 and Aesch. *Eum.* 333, 345) and the high-sounding δρύπτω that belongs to the tradition of female laments long associated with epic and tragedy. The overall result is clear: much of the comic effect of Herodas' poem derives from a clash between low and high, banal and lofty, prosaic and poetic, straightforward and sophisticated.

The rest of the passage confirms this impression. The solemn adjective ἄτρυτος in line 4 (cf. Pi. *P.* 4.178, Aesch. *Eum.* 403) is here ironically attributed to a slave who is "indefatigable" in sleeping. The name Ψύλλα in line 1 can be taken both as an ethnic name like Greek masters often used for their slaves – the Psylli being a (rather obscure) African tribe – and as a significant name, "Flea," suggestive of the parasitical character of the servant or perhaps, antiphrastically and with a studied reversal of the conventions of serious poetry, the agile rapidity of the movements of the insect that are the opposite of the sluggish slave. Of solid epic pedigree is κνώσσους' in line 5, a verb which occurs only once in Homer, in the same form, when the industrious Penelope is having a dream (*Od.* 4.809), just like the master of Herodas' profoundly unindustrious slave. At the end of the same line, ἐννέωροι is another Homeric rarity, which would appear to take up and expand on the idea of deep sleep expressed by the verb κνώσσω immediately preceding. The literal sense of ἐννέωρος seems to be "of nine years," which in our context produces the sort of hyperbole that is also common in Hipponax (Degani 1984: 33). Psylla's long nights of sleep are mirrored by the

"Latmian sleep" of Megallis in line 10, a learned allusion to the eternal slumber of Endymion, associated with Mount Latmus in Caria; and the second half of 5 also echoes, in structure, rhythm, and sense, the Homeric clause αἵδε δὲ νύκτες ἀθέςφατοι, "these nights are interminable," spoken by the swineherd Eumaeus in *Odyssey* 15.392. If the nights are endless for the "illustrious swineherd" (δῖος ὑφορβός) Eumaeus, they are nine years long for his counterpart in Hellenistic mime, which has the effect of dramatically reducing the level of discourse. In short, we are dealing with an odd but far from random mix of Homeric intertexts, which produces a comic effect.

Up to this point, the mime comes across as "subversive" in its playful re-use of the diction and metaphors of high poetry. After line 17 the text preserved on the papyrus is badly damaged, but enough survives to suggest that here too Herodas' relationship with high poetry, and notably epic, remains complex and profound. In line 37, the making of the skin bag for the game seems to have been explicitly associated with "Aeolus' gift to Odysseus" (Ὀδ]υςςέως . . . Αἰόλ[ου] δῶρον), evoking the episode of the *Odyssey* in which Aeolus offers Odysseus the bag of winds (compare 10.19 δῶκε δέ μ' ἐκδείρας ἀςκὸν βοὸς ἐννεώροιο, with the rare adjective Herodas employed in line 5). The allusion may be programmatic and may evoke Hipponax, if indeed this episode was included among the parodied Odyssean themes on the pottery of the sanctuary of the Cabiri in Thebes, and this pottery drew its inspiration from Hipponax's *Odyssey* (fr. 74–8 Degani 1991; cf. Miralles and Pòrtulas 1988: 15–21; Miralles 1992: 110). At the very least, the jealousy of Odysseus' comrades about the bag of winds prefigures that of the protagonist's competitors in the game with the inflated goatskin bag, i.e., Herodas' literary rivals (69–72).

In the better-preserved lines 40–7 our dreamer describes the actual contest. The participants' efforts of maintaining balance with one foot on the greased goatskin are compared to Dionysian dance (ὥςπερ τελεῦμεν ἐν χοροῖς Διωνύςου, 40), but their falls are described in images and terms straight from Homer. Like warriors on the Iliadic battlefield, they tumble on their faces and backs in the dust, resembling divers, drawing a reaction from the bystanders (in this case, laughter).

When we pick up the dream again in 58 (lines 48–57 are almost completely lost), an old man is making threats and generic evocation of epic has made way for a sustained allusion to a specific Homeric episode that pulls together the various associations provided earlier in the poem, solving, as it were, the riddle posed by the author (58–60):

τὰ δεινὰ πνεῦςαι λὰξ πατε[
ἔρρ' ἐκ προςώπου μή ςε καίπ̣ερ ὢν πρέςβυς
οὔληι κατ' ἰθὺ τῆι βατηρίηι κό[ψω.

to blow terribly trampl(ing?) with the heel get out of my sight, lest I, even though I am old, strike you fully with the force of my stick.

The angry old man recalls without a doubt Hipponax (Esposito 2001a: 147–50), but he evokes at the same time the "old beggar" Odysseus, who at the start of his clash with Irus over the "begging rights" of the Ithacan palace warns his opponent: "Do not provoke me excessively with your hands, lest you anger me, and lest, even though I am an old man, I shall smear your chest and lips with blood" (*Od.* 18.20–2, esp.

21 μή cε γέρων περ ἐών). The fact that traces of the same Odyssean episode appear throughout the poem (Esposito 2001a: 148, n.42) reminds us of the mode of operation of Hipponax, who was clearly fascinated by the comic potential of certain Homeric episodes and turned them into programmatic models. Odysseus' clashes with Thersites, Euryalus, and Irus were particularly suited for re-employment in Hipponax's poetry of blame (ψόγοc), and in the creation of some of the roles acted out in his own person, he was inspired by none other than Odysseus himself. The iambic poet found in Odysseus the "eternal underdog" (Rosen 1990: 11) whose modest demeanor hid an awesome physical force and extraordinary intellectual subtlety. The fact that Herodas stages Hipponax with the mask used by the iambic poet himself, that of Odysseus, supports the identification of the angry old man with the iambographer from Ephesus and signals Herodas' intention to follow Hipponax closely. The peculiar poetic initiation featured in the eighth mimiamb, which represents the poet's model as furious with his disciple and successor and which, for this reason, has generated not a little embarrassment for modern critics (Esposito 2001a: 149 n.44), can be justified with the fact that Herodas "in the name of not violating his preferred model . . . could not but dress him in the clothes that suited him best" (Degani 1984: 53). On the other hand, the clash between the old and young poets reveals symbolically the dynamic of imitation and emulation, the relationship of conflict that the epigone, in search for his own identity and originality, feels with the past, in sum, the necessary contrast that gives birth to and sanctifies a new literary genre, within which – in this particular case – the mime and "sweetened" iamb intermingle (as for Callimachus: Hughes 1996: 206–10). Conte expresses the concept well: "every work in every part is the result of a conflict between originality and convention, between the demand of the new and traditional structures, imposing forms of the collective memory" (1985: 69; cf. Bing 1988: 50–90).

Herodas, *Doctus Poeta* (2): *Mimiamb* 1

A further example of the relationship that Herodas entertained with epic, and of his affiliation with the *docta poesis* of the Hellenistic courts, is found in the first mimiamb. Its protagonist is the elderly procuress Gyllis, the former nurse of Metriche (Di Gregorio 1995: 686), whom she visits to convince her to accept the amorous proposals of a suitor. It has now been ten months since Metriche's previous lover went off to Egypt and, Gyllis stipulates, it is unlikely that he will return. The sensible Metriche, a faithful lover, rebukes the old woman and tells her to direct such proposals elsewhere.

The opening verses of the poem reveal several traits that are clearly Homeric. Lines 8–12, in which Metriche expresses her surprise at the visit of her old nurse, and 13–14, which contain Gyllis' reply, recall the scene in *Odyssey* 4 where Penelope welcomes Athena posing as her sister, Iphthime (795–837, esp. 810–14). Both contexts share the surprise aroused by the unexpectedness of the visit, the reason given as distance, and the visitor's intention to console loneliness and grief, caused by the prolonged absence of a loved one (in Herodas expressed esp. in lines 21–3 and 37–8).

Among the reasons that Gyllis offers to excuse her long-term absence, she states: ἐγὼ δὲ δραίνω μυῖ' ὅϲον, "I have the strength of a fly" (15). The verb δραίνω is a Homeric *hapax*, used solely at *Iliad* 10.96, by Agamemnon with reference to Nestor. We are invited, it seems, to compare the physical condition of Gyllis to that of the old Homeric hero who, though old, "did not yield to grim old age" (*Il.* 10.79). The verb, which in Homer alludes to the noble action of a hero, here designates the debilitating weakness of an elderly crone. Gyllis may indeed present herself as weak as a fly, but this weakness is clearly exaggerated and the emphasis she puts on it is part of her persuasive strategy. So even if Gyllis seems dissimilar to Nestor, in the end the old woman proves to be an interesting match: her power, like that of Nestor, consists in her ability to persuade as a speaker, to negotiate. In fact throughout the *Iliad* it is emphasized that Nestor no longer has his former strength, that physically his best days are behind him, but that he compensates with his mental and social abilities and his experience. These are also Gyllis' strengths. Here again we encounter an intertextual comparison that elicits a smile and a lowering of the narrative register to such an extent that we devolve from the heroic to the petty bourgeois. The exploits of a warrior give way to the amatory machinations of a procuress. Besides activating the Homeric context, Herodas also implicitly expresses a scholarly opinion about the meaning of δραίνω (which he uses once more at 2.95) which goes beyond and against the ad hoc explanations of the ancient "glossographers" but fits in very well with the Homeric usage of ὀλιγοδρανέων (e.g., *Il.* 15.246) and other Hellenistic poets' usage of ἀδρανίη/έω (e.g., Arat. 471, A.R. 2.200), "weakness, to be weak" (on Herodas as a Homeric critic, see Esposito 2001a: 151–5; further Bonanno 1990, 1995, 2004; Rengakos 1992, 1993, 1994a–b, 2001; Rossi 1995; Tosi 1997).

The reason of Gyllis' fly-like strength, so she claims, is that "old age drags [her] down and the shadow of death stands by [her]" (τὸ γὰρ γῆραϲ / ἡμέαϲ καθέλκει χἠ ϲκιὴ παρέϲτηκεν, 15–16). The image of death approaching someone (rather than the other way around) is common in Homer, but its verbal expression points to one Iliadic subtext in particular, namely the gloomy words spoken by Patroclus to Hector at 16.852–3, and once more by Thetis to her son, Hector's killer, at 24.131–2: ἀλλά τοι ἤδη / ἄγχι παρέϲτηκεν θάνατοϲ, "but death already stands close by you" – featuring the only Homeric instance of the perfect of παρίϲτημι. The context of 24.131–2 allusively spells out Gyllis' message to Metriche, because Thetis' opening gambit, immediately preceding the quoted words, runs: "My child, until when will you eat your heart out in sorrow and lamentation, remembering neither food nor bed? It is a good thing to lie with a woman in love – for you will not live long!" (128–31). The message that is implied, and that is hammered home by Gyllis as the poem proceeds (15–16, 19–20, 36–46, 63, 90) is simple and clear. Life is short, before she knows it Metriche will, like Gyllis and Achilles, be on the brink of death, and rather than crying over spilled milk she should enjoy certain pleasures of life while she still can – by letting Gyllis bring a new man into her life and fill her empty bed.

Additionally, as in the case of Herodas' use of δραίνω, the allusion to *Il.* 24.128–32 can be read against the background of Homeric scholarship. As emerges from the Homeric scholia, *Il.* 24.130–2 were criticized and even athetized by some ancient scholars as "inappropriate" (ἀπρεπέϲ, ἀνοίκειοι) and "inopportune" (ἀϲυμφορώτατον, ἄκαιρον) words for a goddess addressing a hero or a mother speaking to her son. Regardless of whether we should read the allusion as a learned poet's defense of the transmitted lines, using his poetry as an "alternate vehicle" to philology (Rossi 1995: 19), if the discussion about the propriety of Thetis' words in these Homeric lines goes back to Herodas' time, this would give an extra dimension to their echo in the mouth of Gyllis.

In the lines that follow, the intertextual dialogue with Homer remains intense. For example, Gyllis' reference to Metriche's "widowhood" and empty bed (21–2) parallels in sense and alliterative structure *Od.* 16.33–5, where Telemachus asks Eumaeus whether his mother Penelope still endures her loneliness "or some other man has now married her and the bedroom of Odysseus lies abandoned, covered in cobwebs." In line 38 the expression τέφρη κάψει ("ashes will devour") recalls in sound *Il.* 23.251 κάππεσε τέφρη ("ashes fell"). And in 52 the image of the first beard as "bloom" (τοὺϲ ἴουλον ἀνθεῦνταϲ) somewhat worryingly associates Metriche's suitor, the boxer Gryllus, with the Homeric description of the giants Otus and Ephialtes, killed by Apollo for their *hybris* (*Od.* 11.319–20 ἰούλουϲ / ἀνθῆϲαι; the metaphor is common, but recurs in these precise terms only here and at Call. *Hec.* fr. 45.1 Hollis 2009). In short, by the time readers reach the final section of the text, containing Metriche's reaction to Gyllis' "indecent" proposal, they are well prepared to recognize the key Homeric model underlying the poem (67–77, text after Di Gregorio 1997):

Γυλλί, τὰ λευκὰ τῶν τριχῶν ἀπα[μ]βλύνει
τὸν νοῦν· μὰ τὴν γὰρ Μάνδριοϲ κ̣α̣[τ]άπλωϲιν
καὶ τὴν φίλην Δήμητρα, ταῦτ' ἐγὼ [ἐ]ξ ἄλληϲ
γυναικὸϲ οὐκ ἂν ἡδέωϲ ἐπ̣ήκουϲ̣α,
χωλὴν δ' ἀείδειν χώλ' ἂν ἐξεπαίδευϲα
καὶ τῆϲ θύρηϲ τὸν οὐδὸν ἐχθρὸν ἡγεῖϲθαι.
ϲὺ δ' αὖτιϲ ἔϲ με μηδὲ ἕν, φίλ̣η, τοῖον
φέρουϲα χώρει μῦθον· ὃν δ̣ὲ γρήιαιϲ̣<ι>
πρέπει γυναιξὶ ταῖϲ νέαι̣ϲ̣ ἀ̣πάγγελλε·
τὴν Πυθέω δὲ Μετρίχην ἔα θάλπ̣ειν
τὸν δίφρον· οὐ γὰρ ἐγγελᾶι τ̣ι̣ϲ εἰϲ Μ̣άνδριν.

Gyllis, the whiteness of your hair dulls your mind. By Mandris' return and Demeter dear to me, I would not have endured hearing this from another woman, but would have taught her to sing her lame song with a limp and to consider the threshold of my door enemy territory. Don't come to me, my dear, bringing any such story in the future. Tell what is suited to old hags the young women. As for Metriche, the daughter of Pytheēs, let her keep her seat warm. No one will laugh at Mandris.

The educated reader will not miss in Metriche's tirade the echo of the verses in which Penelope scolds the old nurse, Eurycleia, at *Odyssey* 23.11–24:

Dear Nurse, the gods have made you insane who are able to make foolish even one that is very smart and even provide the dullard with good sense; they have struck you, you who were once right-minded . . . But come now: go down and return to the hall. If one of the other women who serve me had come to announce such things and awakened me from sleep, I would have sent her back to the hall in sorry shape. Your old age, however, will protect you.

It is tempting to see Gyllis as a foil evolving almost naturally from the faithful Eurycleia in the context of Hellenistic mime. Where Eurycleia hastens to Penelope and urges her to welcome her spouse after a journey of 10 years, Herodas' procuress pushes Metriche, whose partner Mandris has been absent only 10 months, toward a lover who, far from being princely and domineering like the Homeric suitors, is inexperienced in matters of love, not in control of his emotions, and dependent on an intermediary to help him attain the woman of his dreams. Through the same process of "imborghesimento," of lowering the social register turning the heroic and ideal into the bourgeois and (highly mannered) "real," the wise Penelope has become Metriche, the *bona meretrix* or "noble courtesan" awaiting her Mandris-Odysseus who set out by sea not for a perilous Troy out of necessity but for the enticing Egypt to seek his fortune (26–35; Di Gregorio 1995; Esposito 2005: 54–5). Moreover, to assert himself as a poet of mimes in "limping iambs" (χωλίαμβοι) and insert himself rightfully in the iambic tradition, Herodas uses as a mouthpiece Penelope/Metriche, who threatens Eurycleia/Gyllis with an exemplary punishment: "I would have taught her to sing her lame song with a limp" (71–2). Similarly, to construct the comic character of Gyllis, target of the iambic "blame" (ψόγοc) of this poem, he enlists the archetype of the caring and wise nurse, which he transforms and enriches with features derived from other genres that had developed her as a character (Di Gregorio 1997: 47–8).

From a metapoetic perspective, another detail of the poem is also telling. In line 76, Metriche refers to herself as "the daughter of Pytheēs." According to our ancient biographical sources, Pytheēs was the name of the father of Hipponax. Consequently, behind Metriche there lies none other than the old master of the "lame song" himself, whom Herodas, his aspiring successor, revives in a mime-like environment. The name Pytheēs provides a hidden *sphragis* or "authorial seal" that secures the metapoetic significance of the preceding reference to "lame song" (71) just as firmly as mention of the actual name "Hipponax" dictates the interpretation of τ]ὰ κύλλ' ἀείδειν, "sing the crippled ones" at the end of the explicitly programmatic eighth mimiamb (78–9). And it will be no coincidence that in both mimiambs Herodas uses an episode from the *Odyssey* – Odysseus' encounter with Irus in the eighth and Penelope's conversation with Eurycleia in the first – as a vehicle to express his debt to Hipponax who likewise, as we saw, "brought down" the *Odyssey* to the register of iambic poetry.

Herodas' inversion, subversion, and degrading of epic and other high poetry substantially follows two routes. First, he juxtaposes and contaminates subject matter and styles that are heterogeneous, his Hipponactic distortion (Degani 1982: 23 and 1984: 187–205) and general avoidance of slavish imitation of the Homeric epics reflecting the sort of polemical approach toward traditional poetry that we also find in Callimachus and other Hellenistic poets. Secondly, Herodas pillages the Homeric epics for anti-heroic material, intrinsically comic and suitable for being included, expanded, and revitalized within the newly created genre of the mimiamb. Notably, he uses non-heroic characters – such as the swineherd Eumaeus, the beggar Irus, the nurse Eurycleia – and the private sphere of the epics to assign literary status and a new "Hellenistic" identity to characters and themes marginalized in the heroic tradition. In general, the continuous incursion of the mimiambs into the domain of epic, their allusions, citations, arcane echoes, parodic verve, all elements that require a high level of critical awareness and technical skill, confirm Herodas' place as poet and scholar in the tradition of Hipponax, one of the most refined poets of the Archaic era (Degani 1984: 163–225), and in the intellectual tradition of the third century BCE.

Herodas and the Ptolemies

Among the many questions regarding Herodas that are unanswered, there remains the place where he practiced his trade. That said, it is a fact that the mimiambs contain a series of references, often encomiastic, to the Ptolemies and to Cos, which pinpoint Herodas' location more precisely as at least within the Ptolemaic sphere of influence, and which seem to bind the poet to this dynasty. Most prominent among these are lines 26–35 of the first mimiamb (also discussed by Stephens in this volume), which praise Egypt and its "good king" (ὁ βαcιλεὺc χρηcτόc), a ruler whom most scholars identify as Philadelphus. Mimiamb 2 surely, 4 almost certainly, and perhaps also mimiambs 1 and 3, are set on the island of Cos, which held a central position in Ptolemaic politics (Fraser 1972: 1.307; Sherwin-White 1978). Cos is named directly at 2.95 and 4.2, it is famous for its temple of Asclepius, featured at 2.97 and in the fourth mimiamb (Solimano 1976; Di Gregorio 1997: 244–9), and some want to see in the reference to Phoebe giving birth to Leto on Cos at 2.98 an allusion to the sojourn of Berenice I on the island, where in 308 BCE she gave birth to Ptolemy Philadelphus (Nairn 1904: 28). Potentially significant is also the setting of the *askōliasmos* contest in the eighth mimiamb at a festival of Dionysus, a god whom Ptolemy Philadelphus claimed as an ancestor and with whom he was associated in ideology and cult (Hazzard 2000: 8–9, 107–8, 110, 154; Di Gregorio 2004: 358–9).

The recently published papyrus with epigrams of Posidippus (*P.Mil.Vogl.* VIII 309; Bastianini and Gallazzi 2001; Austin and Bastianini 2002) adds further ammunition to the case. A comparison between Posidippus' *Andriantopoiika* or "epigrams about statues" (62–70 AB) and the fourth mimiamb seems to confirm the link between Herodas and the Ptolemies. In the fourth mimiamb, two women go to the temple of Asclepius to perform a sacrifice and, while waiting to learn the outcome of their offering, they admire the works of art in the sanctuary and, by talking about them to each other, describe them to us. In lines 20–40 and 56–78 they praise various sculptures, a painting, and finally some other paintings by Apelles.

These lines are at the center of a lively critical debate over the question of whether or not Herodas expressed his personal artistic opinions through the statements of the two commoners. In my opinion, this is altogether likely (Esposito 2004: 198–200). The description and evaluation of a work of art, the process of evoking, and in a sense reproducing in writing, the work itself, echoes to a certain extent the author's tastes, aesthetics, and literary creed. As such, it offers a privileged space for poetic reflection and experimentation, and for this reason it does not surprise that in the Hellenistic period poets start to show a particular interest in descriptions (ecphrases) of works of art (Männlein-Robert 2007). In some cases, however, their artistic project has a broader ideological significance.

Through his *Andriantopoiika*, Posidippus constructs a sort of short history in verse of bronze statuary (Gutzwiller 2002), honoring in particular the oeuvre of Lysippus, the famous fourth-century sculptor from Sicyon, as the pinnacle in the development of naturalism in Greek art. Lysippus opens and closes the *Andriantopoiika* and features once more in the central part of the collection, forming its backbone and heart (62, 65, 70 AB). In his praise of Lysippus' realism, technical virtuosity, and ability to express character and psychology, as well as that of his precursors and followers, Posidippus seems to invite his readers to admire the same qualities in his epigrams. But apart from this metapoetic goal, according to Gutzwiller, the sculptural tastes of the poet of Pella also belie a political agenda (2003; cf. Kosmetatou 2004). By celebrating Lysippus, the sculptor whom Alexander the Great chose to shape the official iconography of his monarchy, Posidippus indirectly flatters the Ptolemies, suggesting that they are the true successors of Alexander also in having inherited his aesthetic tastes, i.e., by promoting the artistic values of Lysippus – and poets such as Posidippus.

Herodas' fourth mimiamb may be interpreted along the same lines. Through his characters' conversation, the poet shows himself to be in tune with the contemporary aesthetic that privileged subject matter closer to everyday life, and creating the illusion of reality, over representing traditional topics in an elevated and idealized fashion, inviting a comparison between the described works of art and his own poetry. And as in the case of Posidippus' praise of Lysippus, Herodas' celebration of Apelles may not only express an artistic preference but also possesses a political dimension: Apelles was the official painter of Alexander as well as the early Ptolemaic court. Since the fourth mimiamb already has a Ptolemaic subtext through its setting – the Temple of Asclepius on Ptolemaic Cos – it is attractive to conclude that, through its celebration of Apelles, this poem also promotes the Ptolemies as the true heirs of the culture – and political power – of Alexander and Macedon (on this poem, see further Männlein-Robert 2006 and 2007: 261–83; Zanker 2006).

Herodas' Audience and Reception

In modern scholarship, Herodas' audience is typically defined as "elite," the sort of audience implied for Hellenistic poetry in general and exemplified notably by the Ptolemaic court of Alexandria, an environment in which, as Rossi puts it, "literature is 'consumed' by the same ones who produce it" (1971a: 80). Indeed it is true that only a highly cultivated audience would be able to appreciate the constant allusions to the literary tradition and sophisticated humor of the mimiambs fully. Yet nothing prevents their being enjoyed by a public less educated and less capable of recognizing all nuances: even on the level of pure sitcom, they are very entertaining.

The question of *how* the mimiambs were enjoyed remains unresolved. Were they written to be acted out, to be recited by one person, or merely intended for private reading? In the absence of external evidence that might allow us to answer this question, we must have recourse to arguments from the poems themselves; and these ultimately "depend upon subjective assessments of what is and is not possible in performance" (Hunter 1993c: 39). Mastromarco has argued that, for example, the absence of stage directions pleads for performance because a viewing audience does not need them (1984: 21–3). Yet this same fact has also been employed in support of the opposite conclusion, with the argument that ancient dramatic texts such as tragedies and comedies typically abound in explicit references to entrances and exits of characters and scenographic details such as locations and props (Parsons 1981; Puchner 1993: 12–14, 30–4). Comparison with various scenes of Menander and with the mime-like *Idylls* of Theocritus, which appear "much less concerned than Herodas with the (real or fictional) dramatisation and scenic quality of the poems" (Fantuzzi and Hunter 2004: 33), would also seem to suggest that "the mode of the *mimiamboi* is that of genuinely 'performed' texts" (Hunter 1993c: 42). Nevertheless from a similar comparison of Herodas and Theocritus, Stanzel (1998) inclined toward the view that both the mimes and the *Idylls* were read, arguing that the narrative element prevails in both. It has even been proposed that Herodas, although intending the mimiambs for a reading public, actually composed them *as if* they were supposed to be performed (Fantuzzi 1979: 723). This explanation has its attractions, but leaves some puzzling passages unexplained, such as certain demonstratives that point to items not identified in the text (e.g., αἵδε, "these here," to designate the Muses at 3.57).

Regardless of whether or not the mimiambs were composed originally for performance, in a bookish age as the third century BCE there must have been a written circulation of some sort. Just as the mimiambs may have been appreciated by diverse audiences, so too they may have been "consumed" in several ways: from private reading, above all by the more learned, to the recitation by a single performer who modulated his voice to suit the various characters portrayed, to an actual staging by actors at a symposium, at court, or at the homes of the well-to-do and cultured.

As we have seen, Herodas predicted fame for himself as the successor of Hipponax. From a modern perspective this prediction can be said to have come true: thanks to the papyrus finds, Herodas has become for us the main representative of the literary mime. How his poems were received by his contemporaries we can only guess, but it is probably safe to infer success from the fact that in Imperial times they were still in circulation and enjoyed the status of classics.

P.Lond.Lit. 96, the papyrus that restored the mimiambs to us, dates to the first or second century CE. It includes a series of corrections which suggest a second exemplar has been collated. *P.Oxy.* 22.2326 is later by almost a century. It restores the right margin of lines 67–75 of the eighth mime, and is interesting because within the course of a few verses it presents two variants with respect to *P.Lond.Lit.* 96, indicating perhaps the degree of variation that may result from wide circulation.

What is more, the mimiambs were familiar to the intellectual circles of Rome in the first century CE. In a letter addressed to Arrius Antoninus (4.3), Pliny the Younger praises his friend's epigrams and mimes by comparing them to those of Callimachus and Herodas, whom he clearly considers the most illustrious exponents of the two literary genres. We can deduce from this compliment that Herodas was a household name to Pliny's friends and the quality and status of his work a matter of agreement, even if we cannot tell if and how much they actually read him. At least Arrius Antoninus and Vergilius Romanus (mentioned by Pliny in *Ep.* 6.21 as the author of mimiambs) probably used him as their model. Beyond Pliny's circle, Cn. Matius (first century BCE) might also have been a follower of the Alexandrian poet (Kroll 1930), and we cannot exclude the possibility that the poems of Herodas also inspired Catullus, Vergil, Ovid, Seneca, Persius (Tartari Chersoni 2003), and Petronius (Di Gregorio 1997: 49; 63–4).

When our author fell silent is difficult to determine. He is cited once in Athenaeus' *Learned Banqueters* (c.200 CE) and seven times in Stobaeus' *Anthology* (early fifth century CE). These citations, which constitute nearly all that was available to modern readers of Herodas until 1891, suggest that the mimiambs may have followed a trajectory similar to Menander's comedies: appreciated for their sententious and proverbial content by those in search of γνῶμαι, but read less and less and eventually lost until they re-emerged from the Egyptian sands. Herodas was still known in the ninth century, as the one reference to him in Photius' *Library* shows (115a; Esposito 2000: 226). Some time thereafter, during the Byzantine era, when hard choices were made regarding what works were to survive, the poet and his works seems to have been forgotten (Arnott 1971: 121).

Herodas' rediscovery at the end of the nineteenth century and the crop of editions, translations, commentaries, and studies which the publication of *P.Lond.Lit.* 96 generated also soon led to creative responses. The first literary figure to take notice of the new author was Konstantinos Kavafis (1863–1933) who composed a poem entitled *The Mimiambs of Herodas*, written as early as 1892 but published only after his death. In this composition, Kavafis comments on the rediscovery and evaluates some of the mimiambs, demonstrating a keen understanding and appreciation of his Hellenistic predecessor's artistic refinement (Kutzko 2003). The mimes of the erudite French intellectual Marcel Schwob (1867–1905), dated to 1894 and published in 1903 as part of the collection *La lampe de Psyché*, state their debt to Herodas in the prologue: "The poet Herodas . . . sent my way a subtle shade from the netherworld that he had once loved here . . . I immediately felt the desire to write mimes." The Italian author Giovanni Pascoli (1855–1912) seems to have been influenced by a number of Herodean expressions in *La civetta*, one of the *Poemi conviviali*, published in 1904 (Puccioni 1950). Somewhat later, another Italian poet, Umberto Saba (1883–1957), wrote a lyric poem, first published in 1914, with the title *Còttalo*, from the name of the young boy featured in the third mimiamb (Condello and Esposito 2003). A final reminiscence of Herodas' work occurs in the tragedy *Lunga notte di Medea* (1949) of the Italian author Corrado Alvaro (1895–1956; Zumbo 2004: 138). From then on, Herodas' poems continued to generate numerous specialized studies, but, to my knowledge, no more artistic recreations. The only exception seems to be a dramatic rendition of *The Cobbler* in Italy, at Paestum, in 1932, which was favorably received by the public – something which cannot be said of a first attempt to stage the mimiambs in 1902 (Pace 1932; Di Gregorio 1997: 105).

"Popular" Mimes

If the mimiambs of Herodas, together with the mime-like *Idylls* of Theocritus, represent the most refined version of the mime in the Hellenistic Age, a series of papyrus texts and documents (such as hiring contracts, lists of professionals, performance information: Maxwell 1992; Tedeschi 2011) bear witness to the dissemination in

Greco-Roman Egypt of what is customarily called "popular" mime. These texts, all of which have come down to us anonymously, are less sophisticated than the mimiambs or the *Idylls* from a stylistic and structural point of view, suggesting that they served an audience less exacting than the one targeted by the two *docti poetae*. In any event, literary and "popular" mimes should not be viewed as separate spheres but as interdependent and engaged in an intense and dynamic exchange, an example of which is provided by the similarities between the fifth mimiamb and the *Moicheutria* (see below).

The preserved fragments of "popular" mime date from different periods (some are Hellenistic, most belong to the first centuries CE) and appear heterogeneous both in style and in formal arrangement. Some are in lyric meters, such as the *Fragmentum Grenfellianum* (*Mim. Pap.* fr. 1 Cunningham 1987 = Esposito 2005) which has been tentatively ascribed to forms of entertainment such as the μαγωιδία, ἱλαρωιδία, or λυσιωιδία mentioned by Athenaeus (14.620d–621d). Others are prosimetric, such as the mime *Charition* (fr. 6 Cu.) or entirely in prose, such as the *Moicheutria* (fr. 7 Cu.), at least in the parts that have come down to us.

The themes vary just as widely. Some texts derive their subject matter from myth, for example, the mime preserved by *P.Köln* 6.245, which stages the exploits of Odysseus when he secretly entered Troy dressed as a beggar (Parca 1991; Gianotti 2005), an episode handled previously also in tragedy (Soph. frs. 367–9 and Ion frs. 43a–49a *TrGF*). Other pieces likewise take up motifs and themes from well-known literary works. The *Charition*, for example, portrays a young woman, a priestess of Selene, taken prisoner by Indians but liberated by her brother and his Greek associates, who get her Indian captors drunk. The author clearly looked to texts such as the *Iphigenia in Tauris*, *Helen*, and *Cyclops* of Euripides (Crusius 1904: 357, Santelia 1991: 12–37; Andreassi 2001a: 31–5). Many mime fragments recall everyday life, like Herodas' mimiambs, or popular motifs typical of comedy. In one a man laments the loss of his fighting cock, which has apparently run off with a hen (fr. 4 Cu.); the *Moicheutria* or "Adulteress" focuses on the erotic adventures of a married woman and her attempt to poison her husband (fr. 7 Cu.); the *Fragmentum Grenfellianum* reworks the motifs of the "lament of the abandoned woman" and of the *paraklausithyron*; in yet another fragment a young girl seems to have been violated during the night of a festival, a motif familiar from New Comedy (fr. 13 Cu.); and in *P.Oxy.* 53.3700 (fr. 3a Cunningham 2002) it is not certain whether the names Heracles and Omphale represent a mythological allusion (Cunningham suggests that a man, at the door of a woman's house, compares himself to Heracles visiting Omphale) or refer to the characters of the mime.

The common feature of these compositions is that, regardless of any circulation in writing they may also have enjoyed, they all appear to have been originally conceived for performance. Their scripted lines represented only one of many elements that contributed to the success of the piece: music, mime, dance, and improvisation also played a significant role. In the *Fragmentum Grenfellianum*, for example, the conspicuous presence of dochmiacs indicates that the passage was meant to be sung, even if the person who transcribed it, the cavalry officer Dryton, probably intended it for private reading (Esposito 2005: 41–50). The *Charition* contains instructions for instrumental accompaniment (with drums and cymbals), and in fact the papyrus which preserves this text on the recto and the *Moicheutria* on the verso seems to be the work of someone in the mime business – an actor? manager? scriptwriter? What we have of the *Moicheutria* are mainly the non-continuous words of the principal character, i.e., the part of the actor representing the "adulteress," and regarding what happened between her speeches we can only guess. At the very end of the text we get what seem to be the lines of two male characters in the mime's final scene. The recto, meanwhile, provides an almost full text of the *Charition*, but a different version of one of its scenes is written on the verso after the *Moicheutria*.

In general, a variety of elements – dance, musical accompaniment, dialogue, and song – are in evidence and performance will have varied considerably from text to text and occasion to occasion. We can imagine stagings that were sparse or essential, perhaps above all in the case of solo performances, where the gestures of the actor would have constituted the entire dramatic action. Other texts would require a fully articulated *mise-en-scène* by a troop of actors, such as the *Charition*, whose plot presumes not only the presence of different actors on stage at the same time but even the availability of a "chorus" of Indian men and women (Andreassi 2001a: 22).

FURTHER READING

On the rediscovery of the Herodas papyrus, see Bastianini 1996a and Martin 2002. Esposito 2000 reviews the principal editions of Herodas, the most recent of which is Zanker 2009 (with English translation and commentary); see also Di Gregorio 1997, 2004 (with extensive Italian commentary), Cunningham 1971 (with English commentary), 1987 (revised 2004; edition only), 2002 (with English translation), and Headlam and Knox 1922. Among older works on Herodas, Will 1973 is still useful as an accessible introduction in English. Classic works on the language of Herodas are Bo 1962 and Schmidt 1968; see further Redondo Moyano 1995 and Tzamali 2000.

Mastromarco 1984 remains the main study of the poet's audience, even if his conclusions regarding the editorial presentation of the text and the use of *paragraphoi* are open to argument (see Fantuzzi 1979 and Parsons 1981); recent contributions to the discussion include Bettenworth 2006, Kutzko 2006, and Fernández 2006.

On the literary mime, see in particular Mastromarco 1991 and Fryer 1993. Cunningham 2002 and Hordern 2004 offer a text and English translation of Sophron (the latter with commentary). Simon 1991: 19–82 and Ypsilanti 2006 discuss the relationship between Herodas and Theocritus; Degani 1984: 50–6 and 1995: 117–21, Esposito 2001a, and Palumbo Stracca 2006 that between Herodas and Hipponax; and Hunter 1995 similarities between Herodas and Plautus and their models, i.e., "popular" mime and farce.

Swiderek 1954 still offers many good points on the relationship between literary mime and "popular" mime, a topic also discussed by Fountoulakis 2002 and Fantuzzi and Hunter 2004: 33–4; on the connection between "popular" mime and "high" literature in general see Andreassi 1997, 2001b, and 2002. The fragments of the "popular" mime are collected in Cunningham 2002, with additions in Parca 1991 and Elliott 2003. Recent studies dedicated to these texts include Santelia 1991, Gianotti 1996, Andreassi 2001a, and Esposito 2001b, 2005. On productions of mimes and actors, see Leppin 1992, Maxwell 1992, Roueché 1993, Fountoulakis 2000, and Tedeschi 2002.

CHAPTER TWENTY

Menander's Comedy

Susan Lape

New Comedy is the name conventionally given to the brand of comic drama that flourished in Athens and throughout the Greek world during the beginning of the Hellenistic Age, roughly from the death of Alexander the Great in 323 to the death of Philemon, one of the genre's leading figures, in 260 BCE. New Comedy differs from its forebears, Old and Middle Comedy, in its content, form, and conditions of production. Old Comedy, as known from the plays of Aristophanes, deals in a highly topical way with political and intellectual issues specific to Athens' democratic culture. Its heroes or protagonists are mostly ordinary citizens and sometimes women who are given fantastic scope to carry out their grand ideas, whether it means journeying to the heavens or implementing a transnational sex strike. By contrast, poets of Middle Comedy seem to retreat from direct engagement with contemporary politics, turning instead to the mythic tradition to cull their characters and adapt their plots, at least as far as we can discern from the fragments quoted by late authors and other evidence. By the time we get to New Comedy, comedy has returned, at least notionally, to the realities of life in the Athenian *polis*. But rather than treating the world of politics, war, or pressing social issues, New Comedy portrays the struggles of young citizens in love in a realistic, if heavily stylized, five-act marriage plot. This is striking both because it is unprecedented in the Athenian dramatic tradition and because it occurs during a time in which comedy was garnering an increasingly cosmopolitan appeal.

Although Athens had long been exporting its drama, particularly its tragedy, the conquests and foundations of Alexander the Great and his successors in the late fourth and early third centuries created an increased interest in drama throughout the Mediterranean world. This demand arose from a variety of sources and interests. On one level, the Hellenistic rulers' support for comedy (and drama generally) enabled them to assert their own cultural legitimacy while simultaneously spreading Hellenic culture in their territories. But the demand for drama was hardly a top-down phenomenon. Depending on the community, comedy allowed local elites to advertise their Greekness, Athenian-ness, and/or to protest prevailing power structures and large-scale changes in the international landscape (Lape 2004a). In response to the heightened international demand for drama, theatrical guilds, known as "artists of Dionysus," were created by the early third century BCE (Ghiron-Bistagne 1976; Lightfoot 2002). The establishment of these guilds completed a process of professionalizing theater workers that had begun earlier in the fourth century and that enabled non-Athenians to work as actors and in other theater jobs. Similarly, although there are a few attested non-Athenian poets who competed in fifth-century tragic competitions in Athens, it became much more common during the fourth century for non-Athenian poets to compete in both tragic and comic competitions. The impact of these changes on New Comedy is readily detected: many of its poets are either non-Athenians or naturalized Athenians.

Thus, although Athens retained its status as the theatrical capital of the Hellenic world, drama itself was increasingly produced and performed by a Panhellenic cast of characters for audiences throughout the Greek-speaking *oikoumenē*. So far, the only New Comic poet whose works have been certainly identified on Egyptian papyri is Menander – a native Athenian. We have one complete play, the *Dyskolos*, one near complete play, the *Samia*, substantial portions of five more, and fragments from many others. Although Menander's comedies do not represent New Comedy in its entire breadth, they do form an important subtype of the genre (Henrichs 1993b). Moreover, since Menander is the poet whose works crop up most frequently on papyri after Homer and Euripides, we know that his comedy was extremely popular in Ptolemaic and Roman Egypt, and we can infer from archaeological finds that his plays were famous in cities throughout the Hellenistic world (Arnott 1979: xxi; Bernabò Brea 1981; Webster 1995).

Comedy's Athenocentric Conventions

The evident appeal of Menander to Athenian and non-Athenian audiences alike raises a number of questions, since many of his comedies articulate a narrowly Athenocentric perspective. Athenian citizens not only take center stage in such plays, but Athens' highly specific laws and norms pertaining to citizenship and family membership also underpin their generic conventions and plot structure (Fredershausen 1912; Lape 2004a; Ogden 1996; Préaux 1960). The Athenian *polis* strictly limited marriage to native Athenians, forbidding its male citizens to marry freeborn women from other cities – no matter how exceptional they were in birth, character, or wealth (Humphreys 1974; Patterson 1998; Wolff 1944). It also controlled the borders of the conjugal family by excluding bastards from both civic and family membership (Lape 2002/3). In essence, it established the conjugal family as the Athenian or democratic family form.

These laws and norms are the unstated assumptions that lend coherence to the standard twists and tropes of Menander's romantic plots. First and foremost, Athenian men always marry legitimate freeborn Athenian women. But this often happens in a backhanded way, with Athenian citizen protagonists falling in love with women who seem not to have the status to support marriage, because they appear to be foreign or otherwise not respectable. As the plot develops, however, these women are discovered to be female citizens after all. By affirming the norms of Athenian marriage as if by accident, Menander's plays offer an ideologically potent endorsement of the norms of Athenian marriage and citizenship (Konstan 1995).

If the first rule of Menander's comedy is that Athenian citizens always marry Athenian women, the second rule is that they always procreate according to the state's norms of family and *polis* membership. Although comedy's young Athenian protagonists have sexual affairs outside marriage, they never accidentally father bastards. This conceit is most clear in plays that employ a rape plot (Lape 2001; Omitowoju 2002; Pierce 1997; Rosivach 1998; Sommerstein 1998). In plays of this type, an Athenian citizen rapes a woman usually in a festival context in which Athenian and non-Athenian women are present. In every case, the rape proves fertile. Yet, it never happens that the citizen fathers a genuine bastard: the woman he impregnates is invariably discovered to have the status to support a legitimate marriage and thus to make the child legitimate.

We can imagine that such representations would have been especially comforting in Hellenistic Athens in times when Macedonian backed oligarchies instituted a wealth requirement for citizenship, superseding the longstanding democratic correlation of citizenship and legitimate native birth (Habicht 1997; Lape 2004a; Wiles 1984). But why would such comedies have been so popular outside Athens, in cities whose citizens appear in them as second class, if they appear at all? Why would plays that consistently endorse Athenian biases against bastardy and interpolis marriage have been popular in Greek cities that lacked or relaxed such exclusionary practices or in new foundations in Egypt and Asia, where Hellenic men of various provenance freely married and procreated with Hellenic women of various provenance as well as women from the native population (Modrzejewski 2005; Pomeroy 1984; Vatin 1970)? Finally, Menander's comedies not only depict a highly Athenocentric vision of law and the family; that vision is also decidedly masculinist. Although the marriage plot pattern portrays what might be called be mating strategies, these strategies often elide the female side of the equation entirely. In extreme cases, the "romantic" plot focuses exclusively on the negotiations between men to establish the marriage of an unnamed and unseen female character. Assuming that women were sometimes among the audience members at performances of Hellenistic comedy, we might consider how they identified with plots that not only ignore their perspective but also champion a view of marriage that was fast becoming archaic (Modrzejewski 2005: 349).

Comedy, of course, offered ways for audience members to engage with its plots that transcended local practices, ideologies, and even gender. It was possible to identify with comic characters on the basis of their character traits, common humanity, and/or their situation in the plot. As Kathleen McCarthy (2000) has shown, Roman citizens could identify with the clever slaves who are so prominent in Roman versions of New Comedy because they lived in common conditions of status mobility and anxiety. The question of how non-Athenian audiences identified with Menander's comedies is an issue simply because many of the comedies highlight Athenian exclusivity so strongly, underscoring that only Athenian citizens get the prizes of love, marriage, and reproduction. Since this emphasis would have inevitably hindered at least some forms of identification, in this chapter I focus on comic themes and plot motifs that for non-Athenian audiences might have compensated for the plays' overall Athenian parochialism.

I examine three instances in which comedy undermines the salience of so-called "given identities" that were at the heart of Athenian civic ideology. Given identities encompass what anthropologists call primordial ties and connections, basic group identities consisting of "the ready-made set of endowments and identifications that every individual shares with others from the moment of birth by the chance of the family into which he is born at that given time and place" (Isaacs 1975: 38–9). Given identities – unchosen identities that we are born into – include social identities such as nationality, ethnicity, race, kinship, and legitimacy (the kinship of the conjugal family). To describe these identities as given is not to claim that they have a special ontological status (Stevens 1999: 104). Rather, the point is that to the bearers of these identities they seem to be natural, to follow from birth, and hence to be in place before one enters into any particular political or cultural environment. But this is precisely what endows given identities with the appearance of being given – namely the fact that they seem natural and inevitable despite the fact that they are ultimately political creations.

The Athenian *polis* made particularly effective use of given identities: legitimacy (being born from married parents), nativity (being born from two Athenian parents), and free birth (being born from free parents) worked together to create connections and attachments between citizens, and to differentiate citizens from non-citizens (Lape 2002/3, 2003). Although Menander's comedy is ultimately faithful to the laws and conventions that produced and supported these key identities, the comedies were also able to step outside them, to question not only their naturalness but also their relevance as a basis on which to assign moral worth and/or social goods. As we will see, Moschion in Menander's *Samia* and a character from an unknown play explicitly argue against using various Athenian birth norms as determinants of character. Both speakers effectively articulate an outsider's perspective by insisting that those lacking a culturally and politically sanctioned given identity might nevertheless have moral worth. Questions of identity are also at the heart of Menander's *Aspis*. While this play too intimates that at least some outsiders might deserve the privileges of belonging, it also critiques Athenian given identities from a different perspective by showing that some insiders are conspicuously undeserving.

Bastards and Belonging

Most Greek cities defined children born outside the marriage context as bastards (Ogden 1996: 224). The Athenians in particular attached severe disabilities to bastardy, completely excluding bastards from familial, civic, and religious participation. Although Menander's comedy strongly supports these exclusions by effectively imposing a generic ban on bastardy, there are nevertheless near misses, cases in which an Athenian citizen seems to have fathered a bastard. The plot of Menander's *Samia* hinges on two such incidents. Prior to the play's opening, Moschion raped and impregnated Plangon, the daughter of his next-door neighbor. The baby is born in the course of the play and is – temporarily – a bastard. Before the baby's status is normalized by the belated marriage of its parents, the play uses it to explore the social significance of bastardy and, less explicitly, to dramatize the performativity of kinship. By depicting legitimacy and bastardy as statuses dependent on the actions of the baby's parents, it queries the status of bastardy as a given identity.

In the crucial scene, Moschion tries to convince Demeas, his adoptive father, to raise his own bastard child (temporarily) by pretending that the child belongs to Demeas and Chrysis, his mistress who was once a *hetaira* (Arnott 2000b). When Demeas determines to throw Chrysis out of his house for raising a bastard child against his wishes, Moschion intercedes. Demeas is incredulous, objecting that to raise a bastard would be wrong (136). At this juncture, Moschion asks (*Sam.* 137–8):

> τίϲ δ' ἐϲτὶν ἡμῶν γνήϲιοϲ, πρὸϲ τῶν θεῶν,
> ἢ τίϲ νόθοϲ, γενόμενοϲ ἄνθρωποϲ;
>
> Who of us is legitimate, by the gods, or a bastard, being born a human being?

With this query, Moschion intimates that legitimacy and bastardy are not "natural" statuses, but rather artificial designations added by society – an interpretation reinforced by the status of Moschion's child. When Demeas assumes that his son is joking, Moschion adds (*Sam.* 139–42):

> μὰ τὸν Διόνυϲον, <ἀλλ'> ἐϲπούδακα·
> οὐθὲν γένοϲ γένουϲ γὰρ οἶμαι διαφέρειν,
> ἀλλ' εἰ δικαίωϲ ἐξετάϲαι τιϲ, γνήϲιοϲ
> ὁ χρηϲτόϲ ἐϲτιν, ὁ δὲ πονηρὸϲ καὶ νόθοϲ.
>
> No, by Dionysus, I'm serious. I don't think there's any distinction with regard to birth (*genos*), but if you scrutinize rightly, the moral man is legitimate and the wicked man a bastard.

Although the next few lines of dialogue are too fragmentary to interpret, it is clear that Moschion convinced his father to allow Chrysis and their supposed bastard child to remain in the house. But how significant is Moschion's argument? Although Gomme and Sandbach (1973: 559) find it more striking than any parallels that can be found, Ogden (1996: 204) sees a basic continuity between Moschion's moralizing rhetoric and the sentiments expressed by tragic characters in Sophocles and Euripides. Unfortunately, the pre-Menandrean parallels adduced by Ogden (Eur. fr. 141, 168 and Soph. fr. 84 *TrGF*) are bare fragments, virtual one-liners devoid of the context needed to tease out their ideological meaning. We do, however, find critiques of bastardy in Sophocles' *Ajax* and Euripides' *Andromache* that illuminate the status of Moschion's claims in the *Samia*. When taunted as a bastard and slavish by Agamemnon, Teucer in the *Ajax* defends his innate nobility and aristocratic birth (1299–1302, 1304). His behavior in the play bears out his positive self-image. Similarly, in the *Andromache*, the aged Peleus warns Menelaus that his grandson will one day take vengeance against him, even if he is three times a bastard (636). Although Teucer and Peleus contest the idea that bastards are necessarily inferior to legitimate sons, they do so in a way that retains the notion that the birth (nobility) determines identity and character. By contrast, Moschion redefines bastardy and legitimacy in moral terms (*chrēstos* and *ponēros*), employing language that does not anchor identity in the circumstances of one's birth but rather in character, which in New Comedy arises from one's behavior. In so doing, he pushes against the idea that moral worth is a matter of natural endowment limited to a privileged subset of human beings.

It is worth pointing out that Moschion's ability to assail the state's conjugal kinship regime may be linked to his own status as an adopted rather than a natural son (Keuls 1973; Blume 1974: 140; Lape 2004a). Although adoption served a crucial function in Athens, allowing men to secure an heir for their estates when they had no legitimate sons of their own, there remained a bias against adopted children. In Attic inheritance cases, juries often privilege the claims of blood relatives over those of adopted children (and of nearer blood relatives over more distant relatives who had been adopted; e.g., Is. 3.61). Sally Humphreys has argued that these cases reflect an "opposition in Athenian minds between natural affections and legal rules" (1983: 8). The assumption seems to be that adopted kinsmen are incapable of mustering the same affection and loyalty as blood or "natural" kin. In the *Samia*, however, both Moschion and Demeas implicitly contest this notion. While Moschion himself emphasizes his filial loyalty, Demeas insists that Moschion is a good son, even though he happens to be adopted (343–7). Demeas' defense is all the more pointed, of course, because he makes it after coming to believe, mistakenly, that Moschion has fathered a child with his own mistress.

Although Demeas may have ultimately decided to keep Chrysis and their bastard child because it is what he really wanted to do anyway, the very fact that Moschion could employ such an explicit argument against the state's official kinship designations remains highly unusual. The apparent efficacy of this critique may suggest that it taps into a pre-existing cultural awareness or suspicion that bastards were stigmatized unfairly and/or arbitrarily. We have already seen that tragedy contests the view that bastards are necessarily inferior to legitimate sons. Although such representations were probably not intended to promote bastard rights, the tragic critique may have nevertheless shaped the way contemporary Athenians thought about and perceived bastards, paving the way for the revisionist definition we find in the *Samia*.

Accordingly, an awareness, no matter how dim, that there is something odd and even unfair about the bias against bastards may underlie Demeas' decision to rear a bastard child. What lends his decision special point, however, is that the child qualifies as a bastard on two counts: it is extramarital and, because Chrysis, the presumed mother, is a Samian, the product of a mixed (interpolis) union (Mossé 1992: 274). By restricting citizenship and hence marriage to native Athenians, the Periclean citizenship law of 451/450 effectively expanded the definition of bastardy to include children of unions between Athenians and non-Athenians (Ogden 1996). For this reason, Moschion's argument that no one is a bastard by birth undermines the norms of both familial and *polis* membership. Demeas' willingness to accept a child of Samian extraction into his household pushes against these same nativity rules. It does not matter whether or not he was planning to pass off the child as a citizen; the Attic lawsuits well attest that a citizen could be accused of *xenia* (citizenship fraud perpetrated through marriage fraud) for having a courtesan and her child in his household (Ps.-Dem. 59; Lape 2004a). At the same time, a citizen who lived with a courtesan placed the status of any children he had from a prior legitimate Athenian marriage in jeopardy. It is precisely the awareness of the judicial peril in which his living arrangements placed him – and Moschion – that accounts for Demeas' excessive concern to conceal the goings-on in his household from outsiders and enemies.

Although Moschion's critique of bastardy challenges the given identities (legitimacy and pure Athenian-ness) usually privileged in comedy, thus opening the door for various forms of outsider identification, its force might seem to be offset by the broader circumstances in which he offers his revisionist definition. After all, the child on whose behalf he makes his pleas is his own, and hence not a true bastard in the Athenian sense of the term. Yet, these circumstances actually add weight to Moschion's argument. In Athenian culture, kinship status was supposed to be significant: it not only identified a person as belonging a particular family and the larger family of citizens, it also described that person in terms of certain qualities and characteristics. At any rate, this is how speakers in the Attic lawsuits justify and defend the kinship norms of Athenian citizenship. By having Moschion and Plangon marry only after their child is born, the *Samia* depicts one and the same child transitioning from bastardy to legitimacy in response to the behavior of its parents. In so doing, the play undermines the moral salience of legitimacy by showing that it has nothing to do with the character or behavior of its bearer.

From Birth to Character

A fragment from another Menandrian play, of unknown title, contains a stronger critique of assigning social and political significance to identities ascribed at birth. A speaker begs his mother (it is actually unclear whether it is a male or female character) not to evaluate people (his or her friend, prospective spouse?) on the basis of *genos*, "birth" or "family" and *eugeneia*, "good birth" (F 835 KA = *CAF* 612):

> ἀπολεῖ με τὸ γένοc. μὴ λέγ', εἰ φιλεῖc ἐμέ,
> μῆτερ, ἐφ' ἑκάcτωι τὸ γένοc. οἷc ἂν τῆι φύcει
> ἀγαθὸν ὑπάρχει μηδὲν οἰκεῖον προcόν,
> ἐκεῖcε καταφεύγουcιν, εἰc τὰ μνήματα
> καὶ τὸ γένοc, ἀριθμοῦcίν τε τοὺc πάππουc ὅcοι.
> οὐδένα δ' ἔχοιc ἰδεῖν ἂν οὐδ' εἰπεῖν ὅτωι
> οὐκ εἰcὶ πάπποι· πῶc γὰρ ἐγένοντ' ἄν ποτε;
> εἰ μὴ λέγειν δ' ἔχουcι τούτουc διά τινα
> τόπου μεταβολὴν ἢ φίλων ἐρημίαν,
> τί τῶν λεγόντων εἰcὶ δυcγενέcτεροι;
> ὃc ἂν εὖ γεγονὼc ἦι τῆι φύcει πρὸc τἀγαθά,
> κἂν Αἰθίοψ ἦι, μῆτερ, ἐcτὶν εὐγενήc.
> Σκύθηc τιc; "ὄλεθροc." ὁ δ' Ἀνάχαρcιc οὐ Σκύθηc;

This "birth" is killing me. If you love me, mother, don't keep bringing up birth all the time. For only those who have nothing good in them, nothing their own, take refuge in these things – tombs and *genos* and counting up all their grandfathers. But everybody has grandfathers, how else could they have been born? If they can't name them, because

> they've moved or have no friends, how are they less well born (*dusgenesteroi*) than those who can? The person of good birth (*eugenēs*) is the one well endowed with a good nature, mother, even if he's Ethiopian. Someone is Scythian? "A wretch." But wasn't Anacharsis Scythian?

Although the term *genos* can be translated as family in this passage, we should bear in mind that it refers specifically to a descent group – a collection of individuals perceived to be related by birth and blood (Jones 1996; Kamtekar 2002). In some contexts, *eugeneia* refers specifically aristocratic birth – which was loosely defined in Greek culture as belonging to a family with a supposed divine or heroic family founder (Arist. *Rhet.* 1360b 34–5; Thomas 1989). Although the Athenian democracy came into being largely by suppressing the political significance of good birth in this sense, it never undermined the cultural and symbolic value of having such birth. Throughout the democracy, citizens belonging to traditional aristocratic families leveraged their lineage for gain of all sorts, including acquittals in the democratic courts (Ober 1989). At the same time, however, the democracy itself appropriated the concept of *eugeneia* to characterize the birth of its own citizens (Loraux 1986: 186–7; Ober 1989: 259–61; Thomas 1989). Accordingly, in democratic civic discourse *eugeneia* was employed to figure the birth nobility of all Athenian citizens, a nobility issuing from having two native Athenian parents (Loraux 1993; Ober 1989; Thomas 1989).

The speaker is likely attacking the latter conception, and by extension, the nativity norms of Athenian citizenship. For the claim that only those without good natures take refuge in mentioning tombs and grandfathers recalls the terms in which Athenian citizenship was established and contested. At the scrutiny for Athenian magistracies, candidates had to verify their citizen standing by identifying their mothers and fathers, and their maternal and paternal grandfathers (Ps.-Arist. *Ath. Pol.* 55.3; Rhodes 1981: 617–19). Likewise, in lawsuits, identifying mothers and grandparents was crucial to establishing and defending citizenship (Dem. 57), as was having a family tomb (*mnēmata*) and being able to show its location (Is. 6.51; Dem. 57.28, 40). In one case, a litigant claims that furnishing a name is hardly sufficient to prove a woman's citizen status: "We must know where she is buried and in what sort of tomb" (Is. 6.65). Accordingly, the speaker's devaluation of grandfathers and tombs as markers of identity appears to replace the nativity norms of Athenian citizenship with a more universal notion of kinship.

After the speaker has made the point that a person's ancestors and birth should not be used as a basis for assigning moral or social worth, he/she extends the logic to another given identity: ethnicity. By citing Anacharsis, a famous Scythian wise man, the speaker refutes the notion that non-Greek (i.e., "barbarian") peoples are by definition inferior or worthless ("a wretch"). In this way, the critique of *genos* is made to cover descent groups of varying size: the individual family, the citizen family, and nations and ethnic groups.

The speaker's logic recalls an argument offered by Socrates in Plato's *Theaetetus* to weaken the aristocratic ideology of noble birth. According to Socrates, it is silly to think that having one noble ancestor makes a person special because, in the fullness of time, every person has had many ancestors, slave and free, Greek and barbarian (174e). This passage is similar in that it discredits *eugeneia* by placing beliefs about the significance of a particular person's ancestry/kinship in a more universal context, i.e., the human condition. Our comic speaker, however, does not seek to jettison the concept of *eugeneia* altogether but rather to revise it: nobility should be based on character rather than birth. While character may be envisioned to follow from *physis*, "nature," *physis* on this model is not the result of having a distinguished pedigree. It need not even refer to innate disposition but rather to nature as it has been shaped by nurture, designating "the way in which a person grows" based on environmental influences (Dover 1974: 84). Accordingly, the argument is very much in the spirit of what we saw in the *Samia*. Whereas Moschion critiqued bastardy as an arbitrary status and redefined it in moral terms, the speaker in this fragment attacks and revises the birth nobility specifically associated with democratic citizenship (bilateral Athenian nativity). In both cases the critique of Athenian norms creates a conceptual space for outsiders – non-Athenians – to identify with what might otherwise appear to be ruthlessly Athenocentric comedy.

The claim that character rather than birth is what really matters in making one's associations seems to have been fairly common in New Comedy, and also works to challenge the norms of Athenian exclusivity from within; that is, Athenian citizens argue that one ought to judge other citizens on the basis of character rather than birth. For instance, a speaker in a fragment from an unknown play attributed to Menander specifically assails marriage strategies based on traditional considerations of birth and wealth as follows (F 804.1–12 KA = *CAF* 581.1–12):

> καὶ τοῦτον ἡμᾶϲ τὸν τρόπον γαμεῖν ἔδει
> ἅπανταϲ, ὦ Ζεῦ cῶτερ, ὡϲ ὠνήμεθα·
> οὐκ ἐξετάζειν μὲν τὰ μηθὲν χρήϲιμα,
> τίϲ ἦν ὁ πάπποϲ ἧϲ γαμεῖ, τήθη δὲ τίϲ,
> τὸν δὲ τρόπον αὐτῆϲ τῆϲ γαμουμένηϲ, μεθ' ἧϲ
> βιώϲεται μήτ' †ἐξετάϲαι μήτ' ἰδεῖν·
> οὐδ' ἐπὶ τράπεζαν μὲν φέρειν τὴν προῖχ', ἵνα
> εἰ τἀργύριον καλόν ἐϲτι δοκιμαϲτὴϲ ἴδῃ,
> ὃ πέντε μῆναϲ ἔνδον οὐ γενήϲεται,
> τῆϲ διὰ βίου δ' ἔνδον καθεδουμένηϲ ἀεὶ
> μὴ δοκιμάϲαϲθαι μηδέν, ἀλλ' εἰκῇ λαβεῖν
> ἀγνώμον', ὀργίλην, χαλεπήν, ἐὰν τύχῃ,
> λάλον.
>
> We should all – God, how we should! – go about marrying as we go about shopping, not asking useless questions like "Who was the girl's grandfather? Her grandmother?" while never asking about or investigating the character (*tropos*) of the woman you're going to spend your life with. It's senseless to bring the dowry to the bank (so that the manager can assure you it's not counterfeit), when it's not going to stay in the house for five months, but not to scrutinize the woman who's going to settle down in your house for the rest of her life, but rather to take a wife at random, one who's silly perhaps, quick-tempered, difficult, a chatterbox.

The speaker (a father as we know from later in the fragment) argues that what matters in choosing a wife is neither her ancestry nor her dowry, but rather her character. While his argument seems to work within the conventional Athenian norms, it contests the salience normally attributed to them. And although his critique of marriage practices is animated by some conventional negative female stereotypes, his advice is nevertheless based on the recognition that they can be avoided. Like Moschion in the *Samia*, the speaker of the fragment discussed above, and many other comic characters, he makes the point that people should not be evaluated or esteemed on the basis of given identities but rather on the basis of who they really are, a principle that, in at least some cases, extends to women as well as men.

The Play of Character

In the examples discussed so far (save the last one), we have seen characters defending people who seem to be outsiders, bastards and/or foreigners against bias and exclusion; although it is likely that in all of these instances the person in question turned out to be a free citizen, the basic point is still made: one does not have to be a legitimate Athenian citizen to be a good person (*chrēstos*), a person of moral virtue, and/or deserving of life and the goods of society. In this way, comedy suggests that there is no deep significance to being born a citizen; to put it another way, it shows that the overlapping norms of family and civic membership pick out who the legitimate citizens are, but do not identify who they really are, i.e., the kind of people they are. A stronger way of making the same point, however, would be to demonstrate that legitimate citizens are neither good nor morally upright simply because they have what counts as the right birth. This is precisely what we find in Menander's *Aspis.* The play depicts a bearer of Athens' privileged given identity, legitimate Athenian kinship (which, of course, also means citizenship), not only behaving badly but also exploiting kinship duties and obligations for his own financial gain. Although no character in the play openly disparages kinship, the play dramatizes the failure of a key given identity to shape or positively influence the character of its bearer. In other words, the *Aspis* allows us to see that character rather than kinship is the source of behavior (the actions that disclose character), even when those behaviors are mandated as kinship obligations.

The *Aspis* belongs to the subcategory of New Comic marriage plots involving an *epiklēros* or heiress. A brotherless woman in Athens became an *epiklēros* when her father died without adopting an heir (Karnezis 1977; Rubinstein 1993; Schaps 1979: 25–41; Sealey 1990: 29–30). The woman temporarily inherited her father's estate. If she was wealthy, her father's closest male relative had the option of marrying her or allowing another close relative to do so; significantly, a man could claim an heiress even if he or the heiress were already married to other people. The situation was slightly different when the heiress was poor, belonging to the thetic, i.e., lowest wealth class. In this case, her father's closest male relative had a more precise legal obligation: he either had to marry the girl himself or provide a dowry for her (Harrison 1968: 135–6; MacDowell 1978: 96). He could not, as in the case of the wealthy heiress, pass her off to the next closest relative. While marrying a wealthy heiress was regarded as a boon, there was a significant catch. The *epiklēros* was to produce an heir for her father first – rather than her husband (Wolff 1944: 50). Upon coming of age, this child was normally adopted into his maternal grandfather's household. In practice, this meant that the heiress and her husband only had control of the wealth temporarily, until their son came of age. This system worked to preserve the number of households in the state and to prevent the accumulation of wealth in a small number of families (Gernet 1921).

This legal situation forms the backdrop of Menander's *Aspis*. In the play, Smikrines attempts to manipulate the rule requiring the *epiklēros* to marry her father's next of kin, like other New Comic characters, in order to leverage a questionable marriage (Scafuro 1997: 293–4). Prior to the play's opening, Kleostratos had served as a mercenary on a campaign to win booty to provide a dowry for his sister. Although he succeeded in this, his loyal slave Daos mistakenly reports that Kleostratos was killed in battle. His presumed death transforms his sister into an *epiklēros* (MacDowell 1982: 48). Kleostratos had left her in the care of their uncle, Chairestratos. Kleostratos' sister and Chairestratos' daughter grew up together, like sisters (128). Chairestratos treated his niece so much like a daughter that he also arranged a marriage for her with his stepson, Chaireas, and provided a hefty dowry. The marriage was to take place on the very day the news of Kleostratos' presumed death arrived. But when Smikrines, Chairestratos' older brother, sees Kleostratos' loot (600 gold coins, foreign slaves, pack animals, and young girls), he determines to marry his niece himself, thereby gaining control of the wealth.

The other characters, including Fortune, the divine prologue speaker, are outraged at Smikrines' conduct. They view him as greedy and as decidedly too old for the girl (114, 258–9, 267). Although we do not know exactly how old Smikrines is, the characters call him a *gerōn*, an old man over 40, while the girl is described as a *pais*, a young girl probably between 14 and 18 years of age (Golden 1990: 122). The Athenians were well aware that male fertility decreased with age. This is why speakers in the Attic lawsuits express the view that a man could become so old that he ought not to marry at all (Isager 1980/1). Although procreation was the stated purpose behind Athenian marriage, in the case of marriage with an *epiklēros* there was extra and explicit legal pressure to procreate. Solon reportedly passed a law requiring that men who married *epiklēroi* have intercourse with them three times a month (Plu. *Sol.* 20.2–3). Presumably the purpose of the law was to ensure that the *epiklēros* produced an heir and to prevent men from marrying *epiklēroi* simply for their money. By harping on Smikrines' advanced age, the characters may be intimating that he will be unable to perform his legally prescribed procreative duties (310–11).

Although the other characters see Smikrines as too old for the marriage he desires, Smikrines himself insists that his age gives him the right and indeed the obligation to marry the heiress. For Smikrines and his brother Chairestratos have exactly the same degree of affinity to the heiress, and in such situations the Athenians seem to have decided the case on the basis of seniority (MacDowell 1982: 47; Karabelias 1970: 375–8). This play, however, is the main evidence for the practice. Scholars accept that Smikrines is technically correct to claim that the law gave him the first option of marrying the girl. But there is a complication here. MacDowell argues that, since Smikrines has the law on his side, the play depicts a conflict between love and law in order to critique the unfairness of inheritance practices that compel unwanted marriages (MacDowell 1982: 51). In a subsequent study, however, Brown challenged this interpretation, arguing that Smikrines misrepresents the compulsory force of the law, and that the play's aim is therefore not to condemn the epiklerate itself but solely Smikrines' greed (Brown 1983; cf. Scafuro 1997). Although Brown is certainly right to point out that Smikrines is a highly biased legal interpreter, it is worth mentioning that Athenian law gave him ample scope to interpret the law generously, that is, in his own interest. In the Athenian context, there were no legal professionals who would test Smikrines' claim against the wording of the law in question. Rather, the meaning of laws (particularly those pertaining to inheritance) was determined by whether or not a litigant could convince a jury that the law should be applied as he argued in the particular case in question (Todd 1993; Yunis 2005). Since there were no legal constraints on what a litigant could say in court, Smikrines would be free to misrepresent the compulsory force of the law if it suited his interest to do so.

Kleostratos' presumed death makes his sister undeniably wealthy. Accordingly, Smikrines was under no strict legal obligation to marry her, as Brown points out. Yet, in overstating the law's compulsory force, Smikrines is doing no more than what actual Athenian litigants did; that is, they sometimes justified their behavior in, say, killing someone by claiming that the law not just allowed them but in fact obliged them to perform an execution (Lys. 1.25, 26, 29; Harris 1990). Such arguments were not an aberration or abuse of Athenian law but rather an expected use of the system. Athenian laws have been described as "open textured," referring (in one sense) to the fact that they name rather than define the offenses they regulate (Osborne 1985; Carey 2004). This gave litigants an exceptionally wide scope to argue that a given action fell within the law's purview. Moreover, the people who ultimately decided whether a legal argument or interpretation was valid were in most cases ordinary citizen jurors rather than professionals. In such a system, justice and equity depended on the character, actions, words, and interpretations of the citizens themselves rather than on an abstract legal apparatus (Dem. 21.224–5).

Smikrines is not at all sure that the law obliges him to marry his niece. When he tells Daos that he intends to marry the girl, as his friends have advised him to do, he explains: "that's pretty much what the law says, I think" (186–7). As his use of the adverb *pōs* signals, Smikrines is not entirely certain what the law means, but like an actual litigant, he does not hesitate to argue that the law is on his side. When an Athenian died without leaving a direct heir, no one had an indisputable legal right to the estate (Gomme and Sandbach 1973: 78). In order to marry his niece, Smikrines would first have to convince a jury that he was actually her closest male relative (Karabelias 1970: 381). Although this might seem straightforward, in practice it was often complicated because the law allowed multiple disputants to make the same claim (Todd 1993: 228–9). Athenian jurors seem to have enjoyed considerable discretion in determining who should get an *epiklēros.* When Philocleon in Aristophanes' *Wasps* boasts that jurors award *epiklēroi* to whomever they wish (583–6), this is surely a comic exaggeration, but it is clear from other evidence that Athenian juries did not feel compelled to base their decisions solely on the biological facts of kinship (Cohen 1995: 163; Christ 1998). They could and did decide closeness on the basis of who seemed to be the better kinsman. Accordingly, if Chairestratos had disputed Smikrines' claim in court, a jury might well have favored him for the very fact that he was already playing the part of a good kinsman, serving as his niece's guardian, whereas Smikrines had formerly avoided responsibility.

The circumstances of the play, however, pre-empt this possibility: since Chairestratos was already married and had decided to allow his stepson to marry his niece, he would not have been expected to come forward as a rival claimant for the heiress. In other words, Smikrines probably could have convinced a jury that he was the heiress' closest male relative, and this gives him the power to compel the marriage.

Since all of the characters come to believe that Smikrines will be able to use the law to leverage an iniquitous marriage, the play does launch an implicit critique, a critique not of the law per se but rather of the criterion that the law privileged: it calls into question the legal preference granted to Smikrines on the basis of bare biological kinship. By privileging biological kinship, Athenian inheritance laws risk rewarding someone like Smikrines who regards kinship as something to be exploited or ignored depending on financial incentive. Throughout the play we are repeatedly reminded that Smikrines fails to recognize or accept social kinship, the obligations, affective ties, and scripts associated with biological kinship but not determined by it (Schneider 1984: 165–6; Faubion 2001a: 12; Stevens 1999; Lape 2004b). For example, Fortune, the divine prologue speaker, introduces Smikrines like this (*Asp.* 114–20):

> ὁ γέρων δ' ὁ πάντ' ἀνακρίνων ἀρτίως
> γένει μὲν αὐτῶι θεῖός ἐςτι πρὸς πατρός,
> πονηρίαι δὲ πάντας ἀνθρώπους ὅλως
> ὑπερπέπαικεν· οὗτος οὔτε συγγενῆ
> οὔτε φίλον οἶδεν οὐδὲ τῶν ἐν τῶι βίωι
> αἰςχρῶν πεφρόντικ' οὐδέν, ἀλλὰ βούλεται
> ἔχειν ἅπαντα.

> This old man, the one who's just been asking about everything, he's his paternal uncle by birth, but in baseness he exceeds all men. He knows neither kinship nor friendship, and he doesn't worry about shame, but wants to have everything.

Fortune identifies Smikrines twice: first by kinship and then by character. To leave us in no doubt about the relative significance of Smikrines' two identities, the goddess adds that Smikrines does not actually recognize kinship as important. In so doing, she implicitly acknowledges that given identities such as kinship do not actually guarantee character; they do not ensure that kinsmen like Smikrines will uphold the social scripts of kinship. This is further emphasized when Fortune compares him with his brother, Chairestratos (*Asp.* 122–8):

> οὗ δ' εἰςελήλυθ' ὁ θεράπων ἐν γειτόνων
> ἀδελφὸς οἰκεῖ τοῦδε τοῦ φιλαργύρου
> νεώτερος, ταὐτὸν προςήκων κατὰ γένος
> τῶι μειρακίωι, χρηςτὸς δὲ τῶι τρόπωι πάνυ
> καὶ πλούσιος, γυναῖκ' ἔχων καὶ παρθένου
> μιᾶς πατὴρ ὤν· ὧι κατέλιπεν ἐκπλέων
> ὁ μειρακίςκος τὴν ἀδελφήν·

> Where the slave's gone in next door, lives the younger brother of this money lover. He has exactly the same degree of affinity to the young man, but he has a very good character as well as wealth, and he has a wife and he's the father of one daughter; when the young man sailed away he left his sister with him.

Although Smikrines and Chairestratos stand in exactly the same kin relationship to Kleostratos and his sister, they behave in diametrically opposed ways. We might be tempted to conclude that the difference between the brothers is that Chairestratos, in contrast to Smikrines, is a good kinsman. While this is true, it is not the salient point. That is, Chairestratos does not behave as he does merely because of kinship. Certainly, Chairestratos seeks to make an appropriate marriage for the heiress because he is her uncle and recognizes the responsibilities of kinship. But he acts this way because he is *chrēstos*, his character is upright, rather than because he happens to be a kinsman. Just as in the case of Smikrines, character is prior to kinship as a source of motivation and action.

Although virtue may not be its own reward in Menander's reality, bad character (or a lack of moral virtue) is perhaps its own punishment; for character not only motivates action, but also shapes and constrains the way one sees reality and one's choices. Smikrines' key flaw – wanting to have everything – renders him vulnerable to mistakes of perception and judgment (326–7). Accordingly, although kinship and age give Smikrines legal leverage, the real advantage in the play belongs to those who understand character. Just as kinship identities come with certain scripts, so too ethical identity carries a degree of predictability. Smikrines' money-loving greed is apparent to everyone. Chairestratos even tries to strike a deal with him by appealing to it (263–9), but Smikrines refuses it because he knows that an Athenian jury might well take it away from him in the future if the heiress should have a child. Fortunately, Daos, the Phrygian slave, has a firmer grasp of Smikrines' likely behavior. Acting as folk psychologist and amateur playwright, he scripts and directs a play within the play to foil Smikrines' nefarious marriage plot in which he calculatingly exploits precisely the old man's desire to have it all.

As it happens, the fake tragedy that Daos convinces Chaireas and Chairestratos to stage mirrors the larger dramatic frame (329; Blänsdorf 1982: 37–41; Gutzwiller 2000: 132; Vogt-Spira 1992: 84–5; Scafuro 1997: 348). They are to pretend that Chairestratos has become depressed and died, succumbing to his well-known melancholic side (306–7, 338–9). Chairestratos' supposed death will make his daughter an heiress too, and a far wealthier one than Kleostratos' sister. Daos predicts that Smikrines will immediately lay claim to her, leaving Chaireas free to marry Kleostratos' sister. When Chairestratos subsequently appears alive and well, it will presumably be too late and too embarrassing for Smikrines to claim Kleostratos' sister. Although the play's continuous text breaks off after the scene between Smikrines and the fake doctor summoned to play up Chairestratos' illness and eventual death, we know that Daos got it right and that the play ended happily, with the return of Kleostratos and with the right marriage between Chaireas and his sister.

In the examples discussed in the previous sections, Athenian civic kinship norms were critiqued by speakers arguing that outsiders ought to be judged not on the basis of birth but rather in terms of character. The *Aspis* stages the other side of the coin, showing an insider – a legitimate Athenian citizen – who exploits his kinship for self-interested and disreputable motives. In so doing, the play creates a space for theater-goers to identify with the romantic plot irrespective of their national affiliation or social status. In fact, the *Aspis* seems especially concerned with creating such a broader perspective. For the character who saves the day is Daos, the foreign slave.

When he learns that Smikrines will use the law to get his hands on the heiress, Daos immediately intuits a plan to outwit him, which he subsequently explains to the slow but eager citizens. The *Aspis* thus casts a foreign slave as the hero (or at least most clever character and crucial enabler) and as a figure for the playwright within the play. At the same time it portrays an Athenian citizen, oblivious to the constraints and duties of kinship, as the villain. With this setup, it underscores the folly of judging people on the basis of given identities – in this case, ethnic and social identities (Sherk 1970) – and suggests that given identities may not actually determine or even shape the motivations of their bearers, implying their inadequacy as a basis for apportioning political goods and privileges.

Yet, although the play includes a variety of perspectives, its inclusivity is not without limits. That there is no perspective for the greedy and apparently unredeemed Smikrines is not surprising. But in addition, the notional heroine, the *epiklēros* herself, remains silent and unnamed throughout. While this made her a good, that is, respectable Athenian girl, it also risked alienating audiences outside Athens where women enjoyed slightly better conditions (Schaps 1977). There is, however, no evidence that Menander's Hellenistic audiences outside Athens were bothered by the elision of the heroine's perspective from the *Aspis*, or from any other Athenocentric comedy. It is striking, however, that when Menander's plays are adapted for the Roman stage, we suddenly find marriage plots in which the heroine's view and desire matter (e.g., Plautus' *Cistellaria*). But whether and how such representations created and molded female identification is another story.

FURTHER READING

For the text of Menander's plays and fragments, see Sandbach 1990 (Greek text only) and Arnott 1979, 1996a, 2000a (with English translation), for the fragments of Menander and other New Comic poets also Kassel and Austin 1983– (the volume containing Menander's substantially preserved works is not yet published). The basic commentary on all plays and fragments is Gomme and Sandbach 1973; the numerous commentaries on individual plays published since then are listed by Katsouris 1995, who provides a complete bibliography on Menander up to that year. Useful general introductions are Webster 1974, 1970 and Hunter 1985.

For Menander's comedy in the Hellenistic world, see Lape 2004a. In addition to investigating the politics of comic romance in the Athenian historical context, this work also discusses Menander's *Perikeiromenē* and *Misoumenos*, plays that articulate and promote the perspective of the Greek cities over and against the Hellenistic kingdoms. Several recent studies investigate aspects of gender in Menander's comedy; see, in particular, Konstan 1995 (for gender and ideology), Rosivach 1998 (for the comic rape plot and male maturation), and Traill 2008 (for perceptions of women). Goldberg 1980, Traill 2008, Wiles 1991, and Zagagi 1994 investigate different aspects of the poetics of Menander's comedies. Scafuro 1997 analyzes the disputing behavior of comic characters in New Comedy, connecting it to pre-trial judicial practice in Athenian culture. Omitowoju 2002 reviews the social and legal questions raised by Menander's rape plays and considers the more general issue of female consent to sexual relations in Athenian law. For the poetics of Menander's comedy, see Gutzwiller 2000 and Wiles 1991.

CHAPTER TWENTY-ONE

Hellenistic Tragedy and Lycophron's *Alexandra*

Alexander Sens

Among the texts carried by Alexander on his campaigns, according to Plutarch, were the works of the Attic tragedians Aeschylus, Sophocles, and Euripides (*Alex.* 8.3). This transportation of Attic tragedy deep into Asia is a striking index of a change already well under way at the time Alexander set off against Persia: inscriptional and material evidence reveals that by the mid-fourth century, comedy and tragedy, forms originating in a specific Athenian performance context, had far transcended the boundaries of Attica (Sifakis 1967; Vinagre 2001). The "classic" plays of the fifth century, and especially Euripidean tragedy, were widely re-performed (and sometimes augmented with additional material) by guilds of artisans ("artists of Dionysus"; Pickard-Cambridge 1968: 279–321; Lightfoot 2002), including actors, musicians, and choral instructors as well as poets, while new plays were composed for dramatic festivals throughout the Greek-speaking world. But apart from the uncertain case of the *Rhesus* preserved among the works of Euripides, only scraps of fourth-century tragedy have survived. In the third century, the Ptolemies (like other Hellenistic dynasts) seem to have patronized the public performance of drama, for example by exempting the guild of dramatic artists known as "craftsmen of Dionysus and of the Savior Gods" from the salt-tax (Fraser 1972: 1.618–19).

As an epigram of Dioscorides on the playwright Sositheus (33 GP = *AP* 7.707) implies, the works of the third-century tragedians known corporately as the "Pleiad" were probably performed occasionally at public festivals, though it is clear that these men had higher literary pretensions than run-of-the-mill "artists of Dionysus." The exact composition of the Pleiad (a name that implies a group of seven men) varies in the ancient sources (Fraser 1972: 1.619), and it is dangerous to generalize or to assume uniformity of style and substance within the group. But the fact that it included the scholar-poet Philicus (author *inter alia* of a metrically innovative *Hymn to Demeter*), Alexander Aetolus (who produced learned compositions in several meters and forms), and Lycophron of Chalcis (the *grammatikos* charged with work on comedy at the Library), gives a sense of its general literary concerns and aspirations.

Of the tragedies that can be dated with some confidence to the Hellenistic period, only a few fragments survive. The best-preserved fragment of what may be a tragedy is a passage, probably drawn from the prologue, of Sositheus' *Daphnis or Lityerses* (*TrGF* 99 F 2). Something of the plot of that play can be gleaned from a passage of Servius Auctus (on Verg. *Ecl.* 8.68), who reports that when a nymph Daphnis loved was abducted, he searched the world for her, and eventually found her as a slave at the court of the Phrygian king Lityerses, who required strangers to engage in a contest of reaping and killed them when he won; Heracles, pitying Daphnis, decapitated Lityerses and returned the nymph to her lover. The play also seems to have contained a singing contest judged by Pan, in which Daphnis defeated Menalcas (F 1 = schol. Theoc. 8 arg. b at Wendel 1914: 203–4); whether that contest was acted on stage or simply described is unclear. The work, which has often been considered a satyr-play, shows the influence of comedy and satyr-play in its diction and in the focus on Midas' folly and Lityerses' gluttony (F 2; Xanthakis-Karamanos 1997). On the other hand, there is no evidence that Silenus or his children appeared in the play, and that fact, together with the metrical strictness of the fragment, which contrasts with the fragments of Lycophron's satyr-play *Menedemus* (in which Silenus and the satyrs do appear) in its avoidance of resolution and observance of Porson's Law, has been taken to suggest that it is a tragedy, though substantial uncertainty remains (tragedy: Webster 1964: 129; Xanthakis-Karamanos 1994; contra, Cipolla 2003: 404–6; Cozzoli 2003: 283–4). Whatever the case, the rigidity of metrical practice is reminiscent of early tragedy, but the sentimental tragicomic plot seems indebted to Euripides (Xanthakis-Karamanos 1997). Given the apparent popularity of his works in the late Classical and early Hellenistic periods, it is perhaps significant that the best-preserved Hellenistic "tragedy," Ezekiel's *Exagoge*, is also essentially Euripidean in style (*TrGF* 128; Jacobson 1983: 50–67; Holladay 1989: 344–405; Gruen in this volume).

Beyond this, the fragments of Hellenistic tragedy offer little to go on (for discussion, Fantuzzi and Hunter 2004: 432–7). A fragment of a play recounting the story of Gyges and Candaules (*TrGF* 664) is perhaps more likely a Hellenistic dramatization of the tale told in Herodotus than that historian's source, but its date remains debated. Few surely Hellenistic titles survive; the only author for whom our sources provide a substantial list is Lycophron of Chalcis. Most of his tragedies seem to have treated mythological themes, some relatively obscure, but the list transmitted by the *Suda* includes a *Cassandreis*, which likely dealt with the recent history of the Macedonian city of Cassandreia in Chalcidice or with its fictional mythic past, and a *Marathonioi*, which, like the *Themistocles* of Philicus and the homonymous tragedy by Moschion, likely dealt with an episode from the Hellenic past. Indeed, the treatment of specifically Athenian history in the *Marathonioi* and the two Themistocles plays may perhaps be read as evoking the Athenian origin of the form, as well as, more generally, the theme of contact and conflict between Greeks and non-Greeks. How prominent a role historical topics, already found in fifth-century tragedies such as Aeschylus' *Persians* and Phrynichus' *Sack of Miletus*, played in Hellenistic tragedy generally is hard to know.

As for satyr-play, already in the fourth century, Python had turned the form into a vehicle of personal abuse in his *Agen*, in which he lampooned Alexander's companion Harpalus; Timocles, too, poked fun at Hyperides in his *Icarian Satyrs* (F 15–19 KA;

TrGF 86 F 2), although that play is more likely a comedy. In the third century, too, Lycophron composed a satyr-play in which he poked fun at a living individual, the Eretrian philosopher Menedemus, whose diet is treated with humorous irony (Xanthakis-Karamanos 1996). To the extent that this personal abuse can be thought to represent a broader trend, post-Classical satyr-play seems to have taken over one of the original features of comedy, which in the Hellenistic period apparently no longer engaged in extensive *ad hominem* attacks on contemporaries (Fantuzzi and Hunter 2004: 437). Python's play was performed at the Dionysia celebrated by Alexander at the river Hydaspes (Ath. 13.595d). It cannot be said for certain whether Lycophron's *Menedemus* was intended for performance and under what circumstances, but the play included a speech by Silenus to his sons the satyrs, who will have served as the chorus. Indeed, the evidence, including titles like *Cassandreis*, *Pheraioi*, and *Marathonioi*, suggests that the chorus continued to play a meaningful role in tragedy and satyr-play well into the Hellenistic period (Sifakis 1967: 116–20; Vinagre 2001).

Lycophron's *Alexandra*

If little is known about Hellenistic tragedy, much more can be said about a work that, while not a tragic drama in the strict sense, depends on and plays with the conventions of the form: the *Alexandra* ascribed by ancient sources to the scholar and playwright Lycophron of Chalcis. Some modern scholars have questioned the attribution, for reasons discussed below. Although nothing excludes the possibility that sections of the poem were read aloud to an exclusive, private audience (Cameron 1995a: 81), the work as a whole must have been intended for elite, learned readers rather than broad public performance (West 2000: 155); there is no reason to think that its effect depended on recitation (*pace* Fountoulakis 1998). The poem consists of 1474 iambic trimeters and takes the form of a first-person monologue in which a messenger reports to Priam (never directly named) the prophecies of Cassandra, whom the speaker calls Alexandra. The narrative is framed by the messenger's words, but the bulk of the poem consists of Cassandra's prophecy, reported as direct, first-person speech. The poem's most striking feature, noted since antiquity, is its riddling obscurity: both the prophecy itself and the messenger's speech that frames it use elaborate, high-style language, with numerous compound adjectives and obscure words, many of which occur nowhere else or are first attested here. Moreover, identification of the individual humans, gods, and places treated in the poem often requires tremendous erudition, since they are usually not named directly but introduced metaphorically and periphrastically. In addition, Cassandra's prophecy draws on a wide array of mythical material, much of it recondite, and that fact combined with the linguistic difficulty makes the poem demanding reading (though undoubtedly it would be less demanding had we more of the texts on which Lycophron drew, as the discovery of the Cologne Alcaeus [*SLG* 262] and the fragments of Sophocles' *Locrian Ajax* [*TrGF* F 10] show). As a result, the *Alexandra* has often been dismissed as merely a curiosity of Hellenistic erudition.

In fact, however, closer consideration shows the *Alexandra* to be a rich and complex work that engages with the literary traditions on which it depends in sophisticated and interesting ways. Most obviously, the poem occupies a "liminal" position between tragedy and epic (Fusillo 1984). First, the poem locates itself in an imaginary dialogue between the messenger and Priam (ἅ μ' ἱcτορεῖc, 1), but is itself a monologue. In a basic sense, Lycophron has isolated and expanded a constituent feature of tragedy, while playing with its conventions. Whereas tragic messenger speeches commonly report unpleasant or unviewable events that have already taken place off stage, in the *Alexandra* the messenger reports a direct speech (for which the closest antecedent in tragedy is the report of the public meeting at Eur. *Or.* 866–952) – but one that looks to the future rather than the past, though it moves with serpentine fluidity from anticipated events to their background in the present and in the distant past (Cusset 2006c). More importantly, whereas in tragedy messenger speeches are delivered to an addressee who appears on stage, here the internal audience is only implicitly present, and the Trojan king, addressed as "master" in the third verse (cf. 1467), merely serves as an internal doublet of the external reader (who in 9–11 is thus invited, like the Trojan king, to "wind and traverse, pondering with wise mind, the obscure path of riddles"), and thus perhaps of Lycophron's royal patron (Kosmetatou 2000: 35–9).

In its apocalyptic character, Cassandra's prophecy has something in common with Egyptian and Near Eastern prophetic literature such as the so-called "Oracle of the Potter" (West 2000: 160–3; Fantuzzi and Hunter 2004: 440; Dieleman and Moyer in this volume), but one need not look far beyond Greek sources for the primary literary background of the *Alexandra*. The predictions, which find parallels in the use of prophecy as a narrative device elsewhere in Hellenistic poetry (e.g., in the *Apollo* of Alexander Aetolus, on which see Magnelli 1999: 15–17; cf. Call. *Hec.* fr. 74.10–20 Hollis 2009; A.R. 2.311–407; West 2000: 160), develop and expand on Cassandra's speech in the second half of Aeschylus' *Agamemnon*, a connection reinforced both by specific allusions and by the generally Aeschylean style and meter. Indeed, the proliferation of animal imagery, one of the most striking features of the *Alexandra*, may productively be taken as a development of Cassandra's speech in the *Agamemnon*, where, like her counterpart in Lycophron, she refers to humans as animals (e.g., 1258–60; Saïd 1997: 344; Cusset 2001), though such imagery is a common feature of prophecy in general. The apocalyptic prophecies of the fates of Agamemnon and Odysseus find a parallel elsewhere in tragedy in Cassandra's predictions about the suffering of these heroes in Euripides' *Trojan Women* (353–405, 424–61). These models have been widely noted; what has been less widely observed is that the prologue in particular evokes the prophecies of Prometheus, whose comprehension of the sweep of universal history mirrors Cassandra's own, in the *Prometheus Bound* (for the possibility of connections between the *Alexandra* and the *Prometheus Unchained* as well, cf. West 1984: 150). Although the authorship of that play is now widely questioned, it was ascribed to Aeschylus already in the Hellenistic period, and Lycophron's engagement with it may thus be read as part of a broader strategy to affiliate his poem with Aeschylean tragedy. Indeed, the connection is established by a specific allusion. In the opening lines of the *Alexandra*, the speaker promises to tell his master all he asks of him: "I will tell you accurately everything you inquire of me from the very beginning" (λέξω τὰ πάντα νητρεκῶc ἅ μ' ἱcτορεῖc / ἀρχῆc ἀπ' ἄκραc). On the whole, the first verse resembles – and may be read as a variation of – the openings of Homeric speeches in which the speaker promises to speak the entire truth (e.g., *Od.* 24.123 coì δ' ἐγὼ εὖ μάλα πάντα καὶ ἀτρεκέωc καταλέξω, "I will tell you all things very well and truly"; cf. *Il.* 10.413, 427; *Od.* 24.303), but the speaker's opening words also engage with *Prometheus Bound* 609–11, where Prometheus promises to avoid riddles in telling Io what she wishes to know:

> λέξω τορῶc coι πᾶν ὅπερ χρῄιζειc μαθεῖν
> οὐκ ἐμπλέκων αἰνίγματ', ἀλλ' ἁπλῶι λόγωι
> ὥcπερ δίκαιον πρὸc φίλουc οἴγειν cτόμα.
>
> I will tell you clearly everything you want to learn, not weaving riddles, but with a simple story, as it is just to open one's mouth to friends.

The verbal similarity is reinforced by what is most easily explained as deliberate thematic variation. Like the opening of the *Alexandra*, Prometheus' words are the prelude to an extended and detailed account of future suffering. But whereas Lycophron's messenger immediately emphasizes the confusing and obscure character of Cassandra's prophecy (3–12; cf. 1462–6), Prometheus insists that he will speak clearly. That in the *Alexandra* it is the messenger rather than the princess herself who initially lays claim to the authority of truth is an important feature of the poem and is discussed in greater detail below.

Other allusions to specific extant tragedies can be found throughout the poem (Cusset 2003); were more Athenian drama extant, we could surely identify others. The thematic and generic connection to tragedy, however, is only a piece of a more complex puzzle. Cassandra's prophecy focuses on the Trojan War and its aftermath, and especially the sufferings experienced by Trojans and Greeks as a result of the rape (or seduction) of Helen by Paris, and the assault on Cassandra herself by Locrian Ajax. Her speech thus covers topics treated in the major Homeric poems and the epic cycle – Cassandra's prophecies on the occasion of Paris' abduction of Helen were already a feature of the *Cypria* – though it also draws on a wide range of now lost texts from genres other than epic and tragedy. Cassandra's prophecy rewrites the *Iliad* briefly and the *Odyssey* more extensively; and in general the contents of the lengthy monologue are strongly evocative of epic, despite the difference in narrative voice between Cassandra's emotional, first-person account and that of the remote (or at least ostensibly remote) third-person epic narrator (Fusillo 1984). In that sense, the poem plays on the interrelation between epic and tragedy in general, and between epic and tragic messenger speeches in particular.

But at a basic level the narrative complexity and temporal fluidity of the *Alexandra*, with its numerous digressions and seamless movement between future events and their antecedents, resembles the narrative style of Herodotus' *Histories.* A good example of such "Herodotean" digressiveness is Cassandra's treatment of the settlement of Cyprus by Greeks returning from Troy. That narrative opens with the summary statement that "five shall come to the Horned Wasp Island and Satrachus and the land of Hylates [i.e., Cyprus] and dwell beside Morpho the Lady of Zerynthus [i.e., Aphrodite]" (447–9). Each of the first three, Teucer, Agapenor, and Acamas, is then treated in a detailed narrative, while the fourth and fifth, Cepheus and Praxandrus, are treated more briefly (584–91). The story of Acamas, the third (and thus the central) figure discussed, expands to include an extended account (itself containing other digressions) of the battle between the Dioscuri and their cousins, Idas and Lynceus, which Cassandra frames as a gift to the Trojans from Zeus.

Indeed, the complex Herodotean structure of the narrative is mirrored by its broader theme. It is worth noting that the poem as a whole is couched as a response to the "inquiry" posed by the king (ἱcτορεῖc, 1); although the verb used by the messenger to describe this act is common in tragedy, for the reader who knows the entire composition it may also evoke the "research" (ἱcτορίη) fundamental to Herodotus' own project and essential to the work of learned scholar-poets such as Lycophron. More important, in the final section of the prophecy it becomes clear that the immediate focus of Cassandra's concern, the Trojan War and its aftermath, forms part of a larger, ongoing conflict between East and West (1283–1450). Like Herodotus' Persian *logioi*, Cassandra views the conflict as beginning with the Phoenician abduction of Io and the Cretan counter-abduction of Europa and continuing through a series of misdeeds and reprisals, including Paris' involvement with Helen and its aftermath, so that the subject of her account is shown to be part of a broader historical dialectic. The series of reprisals Cassandra describes reaches a climax with the Persian campaigns against Greece, the subject of Herodotus' own research, so that the final section of the *Alexandra* may be understood as both a rewriting and a continuation of the *Histories*. In this sense, the end of Cassandra's prophecy answers the teleological problem, "when (and how) will it end?" left open by Herodotus. According to Cassandra, the campaigns of Alexander, whose ancestry is explicitly connected to both Aeacus (grandfather of Achilles) and Dardanus (great-grandfather of Priam), and thus to both sides of the coming Trojan conflict, will end the hostility between Europe and Asia. This unification was a crucial feature of Alexander's own self-representation and must have resonated powerfully with his Macedonian successors (Hurst 1996). Unfortunately, problems of date and uncertainties about the text make larger conclusions about the ideology of the poem difficult.

The Problem of Authorship and Date

The *Suda* (λ 827) treats the *Alexandra* as the work of the grammarian and tragic playwright Lycophron of Chalcis, who was charged with work on comedy in the Library. If this is correct, the poem belongs to the early third century. Two passages, however, raise problems for that dating. First, since antiquity (schol. Lyc. 1226, p. 226 Leone 2002) critics have wondered whether the glorification of Roman power that opens the extended account of Aeneas' foundation of Rome would have been possible in a poem written under the early Ptolemies, or even before the Roman victory at Cynoscephalae in 197 BCE (1226–31):

γένουc δὲ πάππων τῶν ἐμῶν αὖθιc κλέοc
μέγιcτον αὐξήcουcιν ἄμναμοί ποτε
αἰχμαῖc τὸ πρωτόλειον ἄραντεc cτέφοc,

γῆς καὶ θαλάςςης cκῆπτρα καὶ μοναρχίαν
λαβόντες, οὐδ' ἄμνηςτον, ἀθλία πόλις,
κῦδος μαρανθὲν ἐγκατακρύψεις ζόφωι.

Someday my descendants will again exalt to the highest the glory of the race of my ancestors, when they have won with the spear the foremost garland, obtaining the scepter and monarchy of earth and sea. Nor, wretched city, will you hide your withered glory in the darkness of oblivion.

Second, what seems at first glance to be the culmination of Cassandra's prophecy, the campaigns of Alexander, whose ancestry makes him a fitting agent of the end of strife between Europe and Asia, is followed immediately by a puzzling reference to a mysterious "kinsman" (1446–50):

ὧι δὴ μεθ' ἕκτην γένναν αὐθαίμων ἐμός,
εἷς τις παλαιςτής, ςυμβαλὼν ἀλκὴν δορὸς
πόντου τε καὶ γῆς κεἰς διαλλαγὰς μολών,
πρέςβιςτος ἐν φίλοιςιν ὑμνηθήςεται,
ςκύλων ἀπαρχὰς τὰς δορικτήτους λαβών.

With him after the sixth generation my kinsman, a unique wrestler, having joined battle on land and sea and come to terms, will be sung of as best among friends, taking the spear-won first-fruits of the spoils.

Although this passage has been read as referring to the Persians, the verbal and thematic similarities between it and 1226–31 support the now generally accepted view that Cassandra is referring to a specific Roman or to the Romans generally here as well (West 1984: 134). But the proper method of calculating the six "generations" specified by Cassandra, the identities of the "kinsman," the "wolf general of Galadra" mentioned in 1444, and the antecedent to the relative pronoun ὧι in 1446 continue to be disputed (synopsis in West 1984; Fusillo, Hurst and Paduano 1991: 17–27; Fernández-Galiano 1991).

The problems of chronology and authorship raised by these passages have been the principal focus of scholarship on the *Alexandra*, and are closely connected to questions of ideology. If one discounts the possibility that Lycophron was prescient, discussion of the issue takes three basic approaches. First, some scholars argue that references to Roman power are not in fact inappropriate to an early third-century context, especially given the diplomatic contact between Rome and the Ptolemies (Momigliano 1942, 1945; Hurst 1976). Others argue that the bulk of the work belongs to that period, but that the problematic passages (and perhaps others) are later intrusions (West 1983, 1984). Finally, some would move the date of the *Alexandra* to the second century, assigning it to different author, perhaps of the same name (recently, Gigante Lanzara 1998, 2000; Kosmetatou 2000; Musti 2001; Stirpe 2002). None of these approaches has yet won the day, and a detailed examination of the questions falls outside the scope of this essay. It must nonetheless be said that, despite recent arguments for a second-century date, there is much in the style and interests of the poem to recommend the view that the poem, or at least most of it, is a product of early Hellenistic Alexandria (cf. West 1984: 129–30).

The strongest argument for the view that the lines 1226–80 are interpolated is the fact that 1281–2, "so many difficult woes will they who are about to destroy my country suffer," seem out of place after the long account of the successes of Aeneas and his descendants in the West (a story which, however, it is hard to imagine Cassandra passing over entirely), but would fit nicely after 1225. In addition to their obscurity, 1446–50 come as an anticlimax to the account of Alexander's campaigns, which are treated only briefly. Indeed, the name Alexandra (30), comparable to Paris' doublet Alexander and perhaps containing a reference via false etymology (Ἀ-λέξ-ανδρα) to Cassandra's difficulties in communicating believably with her audience (cf. 1 λέξω; Lambin 2003: 134; Cusset 2006c), may be read as anticipating the natural culmination of her prophecy, in which she anticipates the reconciliation of Asia and Europe by Alexander. Thus the end of her predictions as they are transmitted seems an odd appendage (West 1983, 1984).

One piece of support for the view that the *Alexandra* was produced in the early Hellenistic period is that the last dateable event mentioned is the murder of Alexander's son Heracles by Polypherchon in 309 BCE (801–4; Paus. 7.9.2). If the poem were from well after the first few generations following Alexander, the absence of any reference to intervening Hellenistic history would be striking. The view that the entire poem belongs to the second century has nonetheless recently received some favor: Musti (2001; followed by Stirpe 2002) has argued that it should be associated with the last Antigonid kings of Macedon, Philip V and his son Perseus, while Kosmetatou (2000) suggests that it was composed in the Attalid court at Pergamum. That the *Alexandra* would resonate in interesting ways if it were written in a second-century Antigonid or Attalid context is beyond question. It is important to recognize, however, that despite the fact that the *Alexandra* does not directly refer to the Ptolemies or evidence detailed knowledge of Egyptian geography, several passages might easily have had particular significance for a Ptolemaic audience, especially in the early third century. Given the range of the poem's subject matter, it is perilous to isolate any story or feature to privilege a particular political context. Still, it is arguable that individual Alexandrian interests, for instance, might help account for the attention paid to the settlement of Cyprus, an important Ptolemaic territory, by Greeks returning home (446–591), whatever one makes of the argument that the passage could not have been written before the latter part of the third century (Fraser 1979).

More striking is the emphasis Cassandra places on Proteus' role as arbiter and upholder of divine justice (128–9; see also Stephens in this volume). According to the prophetess, Proteus, whose residence in the Nile delta is explicitly noted ("the coastland furrowed by the effluence of Triton," 118–19), deprives Paris of Helen, whisking her off to Egypt and leaving a phantom in her stead (113–14). Cassandra stresses that the stern Proteus (whose hostility to Paris' act is recounted extensively in Herodotus, 2.115) returned to his Egyptian homeland from Pallene, in Macedonian Chalcidice, and in this sense his connection to both Macedon and Egypt may be seen to mirror, however imperfectly, that of the Ptolemaic line itself. The connection cannot be pushed too far (it is hard to imagine that a Ptolemy would have relished any implication of a resemblance between the unjust children of Proteus, whom he left Pallene to escape, and his own progeny), but it is nonetheless striking that, other than Zeus, Proteus is the poem's most important agent of divine justice. The prominence of this figure, called the "Pallenean prophet," in the programmatically and ideologically fraught opening of the *Victory of Berenice* at the beginning of Callimachus' *Aetia* 3 is a telling parallel for the potential significance of Proteus and his connections to Pallene in a Ptolemaic context (*SH* 254.5; Stephens in this volume). In this regard, the prominence of North Greek and Macedonian geography in key passages in the poem (408–10, where the Greek North, including Macedon, is used as a synecdoche for all of Hellas; 1342 and 1404–8 focus on Asian encroachment on Macedonian landmarks in the long struggle between East and West) is interesting, if ambiguous: such references may have been particularly meaningful to an original audience in Macedon, but the early Ptolemies also took pains to emphasize their Macedonian roots, and emphasis on Macedonian geography would probably have resonated powerfully for them as well (cf. Posidip. 88.4 AB; Bearzot 1992; Sens 2004: 74–5).

Cassandra and Poetic Authority

When Callimachus declares that he sings of "nothing without a witness" (ἀμάρτυρον οὐδὲν ἀείδω, fr. 612 Pf.; cf. *h.* 5.56, fr. 75.54–77), he seems to be laying claim (perhaps ironically) to the authority afforded by the literary and scholarly tradition on which he relies. To judge from a famous programmatic passage of Theocritus, truthfulness and accuracy were important metaphors for a broader set of literary qualities that third-century Alexandrian poets admired (Theoc. 7.44; Posidip. 63 AB; Sens 2005: 209–12). Moreover, Hellenistic poets were often concerned to link their poetic enterprise with authoritative literary ancestors, real or imagined, and to establish the legitimacy both of their own projects in general and of their own versions of particular myths in particular. In that connection, Cassandra, guaranteed the power of accurate prophecy but denied believability, is *ipso facto* a powerful if problematic emblem of poetic authority, since her words carry the weight of divine sanction. In a sense, her embedded speech, drawing as it does on a wide gamut of models, may be read as a "prophecy" of Lycophron's own literary heritage – a tradition that in the poem is at once the poet's past and his narrator's future. As in other Hellenistic poetry, we see the poet writing himself into the literary tradition: like, e.g., Apollonius in the *Argonautica* or Theocritus in *Idyll* 11, Lycophron represents his own narrative as a precursor to the very texts that he draws on. It is useful in this regard to consider Cassandra's role as (embedded) narrator in the context of the competitive intellectual environment in which the work was likely composed (Strootman in this volume). By making her the voice for his own reworking of a series of texts, Lycophron implicitly claims authority for his rendition of Greek literary history, while simultaneously acknowledging the problematic character of that authority: however much the accuracy of *his* version of individual myths (like the reliability of Cassandra's prophecies) might be subject to disagreement, they are the "correct" versions.

The poem's interrogation of "poetic truth" is a complicated one, however. From a Hellenic perspective, Cassandra's speech is manifestly biased, and her characterization as anti-Greek, anti-war, and anti-sex is an important feature of the work. Her prophecies, moreover, are reported by the messenger, who himself emphasizes their accuracy in the opening and closing frame (1 νητρεκῶϲ, 1471 ἐτητύμωϲ). The assertion of veracity is a conventional feature of messenger speeches, but in the context of the *Alexandra* the assertion is rendered problematic by the length, difficulty, and complexity of the speech the speaker claims to report. Lycophron's use of the frame thus not only establishes a dramatic context for Cassandra's prophecy but raises the question of whether they are accurately reported: Cassandra may be infallible, but given the nature of her words, how can the messenger be, except to the extent that his voice is identical to that of the omniscient poet? (For messenger speeches generally, cf. Barrett 2002, esp. 56–101; Lowe 2004 on the multiple narrators and audiences of the *Alexandra*.)

Indeed, in several passages the poem explicitly calls attention to the problem of narrative authority. The issue is most overtly framed by Cassandra's treatment of the *Odyssey*, and in particular by her comments about Odysseus' role as a storyteller. Cassandra's account of the death of Idomeneus near Colophon describes the hero as "the very brother of Aethon in fictitious writings" (ἐν πλαϲταῖϲ γραφαῖϲ, 432), a reference to Odysseus' lying claim to be Aethon, brother of Idomeneus, at *Od.* 19.181–4. Similarly, Cassandra characterizes Odysseus' account of his wanderings as a μυθοπλάϲτην ... γόον, "fictitious lament" (764). In both cases, the words may be understood as a bitter comment on Odysseus' veracity and (in the latter case) on the fact that as narrator, he controls how he is represented in *Odyssey* 9–12. But there is also a pointed irony to Cassandra's snide description of Odysseus' narrative at the climax of an account that, with variations and material drawn from other sources, covers the same ground as the hero's own (648–765). That fact may suggest that the phrase ought to be read at another level as well, as a broader observation (by Lycophron *qua* author rather than by his narrator Cassandra) about the fundamentally fictitious nature of poetry, and especially epic poetry, generally (Fantuzzi and Hunter 2004: 441), and implicitly about its power to shape the reception and reputation of the heroes whose deeds it recounts (cf. Pi. *N.* 7.22–3 "I expect that through sweet-voiced Homer the story of Odysseus was enhanced beyond his suffering, since there is something impressive [ϲεμνόν] in lies [ψεύδεϲι] and a winged device").

Elsewhere, Cassandra's words raise the problem of poetic authority in other ways. At 512–16, for instance, her expressed hope that the Dioscuri never join the Greek expedition against Troy resonates significantly against readers' familiarity with their fate as represented elsewhere. In this passage, the Trojan princess couches what is functionally a claim about the future as a wish:

> οὓϲ μήποτ', ὦ Ζεῦ ϲῶτερ, ἐϲ πάτραν ἐμὴν
> ϲτείλαιϲ ἀρωγοὺϲ τῆι διϲαρπάγωι κρεκί.
> μηδὲ πτερωτὰϲ ὁπλίϲαντεϲ ὁλκάδαϲ
> πρύμνηϲ ἀπ' ἄκραϲ γυμνὸν αἰψηρὸν πόδα
> εἰϲ Βεβρύκων ῥίψειαν ἐκβατηρίαν.

> May you never send them, Savior Zeus, to my fatherland as defenders of the twice-snatched *krex*, nor arming winged ships may they throw from the end of the stern their swift, naked foot onto the landing place of the Bebrycians.

The engagement with the literary and mythological tradition is complex. On the one hand, Cassandra's hope that the Dioscuri will not set foot in Troy is "realized" in a famous passage of the *Iliad*, where Helen, surveying the Greek forces arrayed on the battlefield, wonders why her brothers have stayed away, only to have the narrator observe that they are already dead and buried in Sparta (*Il.* 3.236–44). Indeed, the focus on Helen (whose identification with the now unidentifiable bird called the *krex* depends on the belief that that creature was inauspicious for marriage; cf. Call. fr. 428 Pf.; Euph. *CA* 4) invites the reader to think of the "aftermath" of Cassandra's prayer as it plays out in Homer, and in this sense Cassandra's prayer may be understood not only as a precursor but perhaps even as the reason for the absence of Helen's brothers from the war at Troy.

At the same time, the phraseology of the last line (516) involves an irony that depends on the reader's knowledge of a different story involving the Dioscuri. As the scholia recognize, the designation of the Trojans as Bebrycians derives from the identification of Troy as the area once occupied by the people of that name. The equation of Trojans with Bebrycians recurs at 1305 and 1474, but the word's first occurrence here is highly significant: while it is true that the Dioscuri never set foot in Troy to aid Helen, Polydeuces' triumphant boxing match with the inhospitable king of the Bebrycians, Amycus, was a prominent feature of the Argonautic saga, and was treated at length by other Hellenistic poets (A.R. 2.1–154; Theoc. 22.27–134; cf. Euph. *CA* 77; Gengler 2003). Indeed, Theocritus in *Idyll* 22 explicitly recounts the Argonauts' disembarkation onto Bebrycian territory (30–3):

> ἔνθα μιᾶς πολλοὶ κατὰ κλίμακος ἀμφοτέρων ἓξ
> τοίχων ἄνδρες ἔβαινον Ἰησονίης ἀπὸ νηός·
> ἐκβάντες δ' ἐπὶ θῖνα βαθὺν καὶ ὑπήνεμον ἀκτὴν
> εὐνάς τ' ἐστόρνυντο πυρεῖά τε χερσὶν ἐνώμων.
>
> There many men descended a single ladder from both sides of Jason's ship. And debarking on the broad strand and windless shore, they spread beds and brandished firesticks in their hands.

Cassandra's wish that the twins never set foot on the "landing place of the Bebrycians" thus recalls an episode from the Argonautic saga not explicitly treated by Lycophron (for the Argonauts in the poem, cf. Schmakeit-Bean 2006) and complicates any simple reading of the success of her wish for the future. On the one hand, Cassandra, armed with prophetic power, correctly anticipates the absence of Castor and Polydeuces from Troy. But her prayer, if taken at face value, evokes a story in which the Dioscuri did land in the territory of the Bebrycians, and thus subtly raises the issue, once again, of the troubling multi-valence of Cassandra's words – and of literary narrative in general.

The Style and Poetics of the *Alexandra*

We have already observed that the thematic affiliation between the *Alexandra* and Aeschylean tragedy is signaled in the opening verse, which evokes Prometheus' prophecies in the *Prometheus Bound*, and is continued in Cassandra's prophecies, which by their nature recall her namesake's words in the *Agamemnon*. That evocation of Aeschylean tragedy also operates on the stylistic plane. At a metrical level, Lycophron's trimeters (like those in the fragments of Hellenistic tragedy) resemble the earliest extant tragedies in their avoidance of resolution (Del Ponte 1981). More important, the diction, with its numerous rare words and elaborate compound adjectives, and the complexity and obscurity of the poem's many circumlocutions create an impression of stylistic grandeur and weight that evoke Aeschylean drama (Schade 1999: 22–3; Cusset 2003a).

Lycophron's Aeschylean (or proto-Aeschylean: Fantuzzi and Hunter 2004: 439) weightiness may profitably be read against the backdrop of what we can know about the values expressed by other early Hellenistic poets. The most widely discussed passage in this regard is the reply to Callimachus' critics at the opening of the *Aetia*, where the poet opposes his own "fine" style with the weighty one of his adversaries. Whatever the chronological relationship between the poems, there is little reason to see in one a *direct* response to the other. The opposition set up in the *Aetia* prologue may nonetheless serve as an interesting touchstone for evaluating Lycophron's literary project. As scholars have recognized, the critical language of the *Aetia* prologue finds a precursor in the debate between Aeschylus and Euripides in Aristophanes' *Frogs* (Acosta-Hughes and Harder in this volume). There, the stylistic qualities attributed to Euripides – including clarity, subtlety, and cleverness or wisdom – conform closely to what Callimachus later claims for his own poetry. The bombast and weight ascribed to Aeschylus, on the other hand, is picked up in the treatment of Callimachus' enemies, whose work is represented as excessively large – i.e., excessively grand and insufficiently refined. Indeed, the extant Hellenistic epigrams on Aeschylus emphasize (in a laudatory way) the figurative "size" of his poetry (Diosc. 21.3 GP = *AP* 7.411.3 ἐξύψωcεν, "brought to a height"; Antip. Thess. *GPh* 141–2 = *AP* 7.39.1–2 ὀφρύοεccαν ἀοιδὴν / πυργώcαc, "have made a tower of haughty song"; Diod. *GPh* 2167 = *AP* 7.40.1–2 τὸν μέγαν, "the great"). Thus at a basic level an attempt to emulate Aeschylus' grand style might seem to contradict the values praised in the *Aetia* prologue, despite the resemblance between the two poems in (among other things) their interest in aetiology, their fondness for rare or disputed diction, and their love of obscure mythology. Read in this light, the *Alexandra*'s engagement with Aeschylus may be seen as, in part, a project to write in a manner at once "Aeschylean" and "refined" – stylistic qualities which, to judge from Callimachus, might arguably be understood as opposed.

But if the style of the *Alexandra*, insofar as it may be called Aeschylean, is superficially at odds with the qualities recommended in the *Aetia* prologue, the poem remains broadly speaking "Alexandrian" in other respects. It is worth noting in this regard that the messenger's opening frame may be read as a self-referential statement of poetic program (Durbec 2006). Thus the messenger draws on the image of the path of song, used by other poets of their own work (e.g., Pi. *O.* 9.47; Call. fr. 1.25–8 Pf.), to call attention to the learning required of his audience (9–12), but in so doing varies convention by applying the metaphor to the experience of the listener (and thus the reader), who must make his way through the complicated byways of her prophecy, rather than to the project of the poet. Indeed, in calling attention to the "literary" quality of the prophecy, the messenger furthers the gap between the poet and his embedded narrator Cassandra: to the extent that Cassandra is represented as a poet, she is distanced from Lycophron by the mediation of the messenger's report.

Other than its obvious lexical difficulty, the most notable feature of Lycophron's style is its use of riddling periphrases: mortals and gods are rarely referred to directly by their proper names, but are instead identified by circumlocutions or identified with animals, especially wolves and lions (Cusset 2001, 2003: 142); gods are typically identified by local cult names, often strung together in asyndeton; large geographical areas are generally identified by synecdoche through reference to specific local features or other periphrases; and other kennings abound (e.g., 22–4, of Paris' ships at sea: "the wooly-footed, fair-faced, stork-colored Phalacraean maidens struck maiden-killing Thetis with their blades"). Moreover, these circumlocutions, which occur without stylistic distinction in both the messenger's frame and Cassandra's reported prophecies, are labile, so that an individual first identified as one beast may be treated as another shortly thereafter. Although the difficulties thus created have often been emphasized, sufficient information is usually included to allow the learned reader (or at least the ideal reader with access to more texts than now survive) to puzzle them out. In some cases, the very instability of the metaphor is itself helpful: Helen, for example, is referred to within a single verse (87) as both "dove" and "Pephnian hound," the latter a nod to her characterization as a "bitch" already in Homer and a clue to her identity.

Lycophron's riddling style, often denigrated as a mark of Hellenistic self-indulgence, requires patience and learning on the part of the reader, but it is important to emphasize that the circumlocutions used by Cassandra are sometimes meaningfully appropriate to their context. A single example may suffice to illustrate the point: when the prophetess reports that Proteus will intervene to deprive Paris of Helen (i.e., by stealing her away and leaving a phantom in her place), she calls him the "gloomy husband of the Phlegraean spouse Torone" (ὁ ... cυλλέκτροιο Φλεγραίας πόcιc / cτυγνὸc Τορώνηc, 115–16), emphasizing his status as a husband and his role as a protector of the marriage bonds that Helen and Paris violate. A further example, the use of the cult title Melanthus to refer to Poseidon, will be discussed below; systematic consideration of the literary function of Lycophron's periphrases would doubtless yield interesting results. Moreover, in cases where we have access to Lycophron's models his kennings often have a specific allusive point, and this fact suggests that many similar points are now lost to us. Thus, for example, the point of treating Odysseus' men as "mullets" at 664–5 (οἳ πάντα θρανύξαντες εὔτορνα cκάφη / cχοίνωι κακὴν τρήcουcι κεcτρέων ἄγρην, "who smashing all the well-lathed hulls will pierce their evil catch of mullets with reeds") would be obscure were the passage not recognizable as a reworking of Odysseus' account of the Laestrygonian attack on his crew at *Od.* 10.1223–4 κόναβοc ... / ἀνδρῶν τ' ὀλλυμένων νηῶν θ' ἅμα ἀγνυμενάων· / ἰχθῦc δ' ὣc πείροντεc ἀτερπέα δαῖτα φέροντο, "the sound ... of men dying and ships being broken up at the same time; and piercing them like fish they carried off their unpleasant feast"), with the Homeric simile turned concrete and specific (Fusillo, Hurst, and Paduano 1991: 233, noting Lycophron's broader tendency to make concrete what is metaphorical in his model; Gigante Lanzara 1997: 47–8), and the phrase κακὴν ... ἄγρην picking up and varying Homer's ἀτερπέα δαῖτα.

Indeed, the *Alexandra* shows an engagement with the text of Homer similar to that found in other early Hellenistic poetry. Lycophron's diction, for example, seems to exhibit a familiarity with scholarly debates about the constitution and interpretation of early epic texts, as may be suggested by a number of cases where words are used in senses debated in the Homeric scholia (Rengakos 1994b). A different sort of erudite engagement with prior literature may be seen in 1375, where the poet applies a rare adjective meaning "mute" (μυνδός) to the word used since early epic to refer (both as adjective and as substantive) to "fish" (ἔλλοψ) – a word said by some ancient sources to derived from ἰλλεcθαι "be barred" and ὄψ "voice" (Olson and Sens 2000: 61 on Archestr. fr. 12.1), so that the adjective may be understood as a gloss on the supposed etymology of the noun (for the muteness of fish, cf. Aesch. *TrGF* F 307). Indeed, the *Alexandra* is replete with typically Hellenistic evocation and variation of Homeric language, as in 661, where ἐπιδόρπιον in the context of Odysseus' encounter with the Cyclops varies Homer's use of ποτιδόρπιον at *Od.* 9.234 (cf. Theoc. 13.36), or 679, where the use of μῶλυc as an adjective suggests that Lycophron is engaging in an interpretation of μῶλυ, famously used as the name of a plant at *Od.* 10.305 (Hurst 1999: 121).

Cassandra's "*Odyssey*" and Lycophron's Literary Technique

The loss of so many of the texts with which Lycophron engages has hindered the study of the *Alexandra* as a work of literature, and has made it difficult to evaluate the poem's intertextuality in a systematic way. There are, however, a few passages about the literary background of which we are better informed, and in them one can catch a glimpse of the extent to which what at first glance might seem erudition for its own sake can prove meaningful. The most extended such passage is Cassandra's account of Odysseus' return from Troy, an account that engages intensively with the *Odyssey* itself but also draws on and exploits a number of other texts, including tragedy and local history, especially in its identification of the places visited by the hero with sites in Italy (Gigante Lanzara 1997; Hurst 1999; Schade 1999). What follows is merely a selective treatment of areas of interest to illustrate possible avenues of approach for future scholarship.

Cassandra's account of Odysseus' wanderings (648–765) is a masterpiece of hostile rhetoric, which subtly diminishes Odysseus' accomplishments as he describes them in *Odyssey* 9–12 and, even when acknowledging his suffering, puts it in the most humiliating light possible. Thus whereas Odysseus in the *Odyssey* claims that in order to avoid Charybdis he hung from a fig tree "like a bat" with no way to support himself with his feet or climb on the branch (*Od.* 12.432–4), Cassandra eliminates the difficulty of the labor and grandness of the accomplishment by representing him as a gull sitting on (προcκαθήμενοc) the branch of the fig (Gigante Lanzara 1997: 54). So, too, Odysseus' seven-years-long suffering on Calypso's island, where, Homer emphasizes, he lived in constant grief, having grown tired of the goddess and sleeping with her unwillingly (*Od.* 5.151–5), is reduced in Cassandra's narrative to a brief and pleasurable tryst (744 βαιὸν … τερφθείc, "having taken brief pleasure," a phrase that the scholiast struggles to explain). Whereas Homer emphasizes the craftsmanship with which Odysseus constructs his raft (*Od*. 5.249–51), Cassandra dismisses it as "a thrown-together vessel" (αὐτοκάβδαλον σκάφος, 745; Gigante Lanzara 1997: 54–5). Similarly, in her account of the hero's experience in disguise on Ithaca (where Cassandra acknowledges the extent of the hero's suffering), she notes that he endured having pottery thrown at him, an embarrassing detail not found in Homer but imported from Aeschylus (as the scholiast to 778 notes; cf. *TrGF* F *180), where the vessel in question is a chamber pot.

Indeed, a closer consideration of Cassandra's account of Odysseus' experiences in Ithaca (766–88) may help illustrate the richness of Lycophron's engagement with earlier literature. As we have seen, the long account of Odysseus' adventures at sea that precedes this section culminates with ironic self-reflexivity in Cassandra's description of the story told to the Phaeacians as a "fictitious lament" (μυθοπλάστην ... γόον, 764). In the succeeding verses, Cassandra opens her account of Odysseus' continued sufferings upon his safe return to Ithaca by expressing the hope that Poseidon will not lose interest in punishing her nemesis for wounding Polyphemus (765 ἀρὰς τετικὼς τοῦ τυφλωθέντος δάκους, "having paid for the curses of the blinded monster"), to continue (766–7; for the text and translation, cf. West 1983: 117):

> οὔπω μάλ', οὔπω. μὴ τοσόσδ' ὕπνος λάβοι
> λήθηι Μέλανθον ἐγκλιθένθ' Ἱππηγέτην.
>
> Not yet, not yet! Let not such sleep take Melanthos, Lord of Horses, yielding to forgetfulness.

And in fact, on his return the hero will see his house "overturned by lewd wife-stealers" (769–71) and his vixen wife acting coquettishly and spending his wealth on banquets, a tendentious and nasty interpretation of Penelope's behavior that reflects Cassandra's burning hostility to Odysseus and his family (771–3; Hutchinson 1988: 262–3; Gigante Lanzara 1995: 92–4; Hurst 1999: 123). Odysseus himself, Cassandra reports, will be forced as a parasite to endure great suffering, including threats and physical abuse at the hands of his own servants (774–8):

> αὐτὸς δὲ πλείω τῶν ἐπὶ σκαιαῖς πόνους
> ἰδὼν μολοβρός, τλήσεται μὲν οἰκετῶν
> στυγνὰς ἀπειλὰς εὐλόφωι νώτωι φέρειν
> δέννοις κολασθείς, τλήσεται δὲ καὶ χερῶν
> πληγαῖς ὑπείκειν καὶ βολαῖσιν ὀστράκων.
>
> He himself, a parasite, seeing more labors than at the Scaian gates, will endure bearing the hateful threats of his domestics on his back, punished by jeering, and will suffer to yield to blows from their hands and to the throwing of pottery.

At least two points are worth making about the engagement with Homer in this passage. First, the word μολοβρός, "beggar," is a Homeric rarity, applied, as the scholiast notes, derogatorily to Odysseus by his goatherd Melanthius at *Od*. 17.219 and by the beggar Irus at *Od*. 18.26. By having Cassandra use the word of Odysseus in her account of his treatment at the hands of his own servants, Lycophron enacts the very abuse she describes. Second, Cassandra's description of Odysseus' experiences on

Ithaca lends special significance to her use of the cult name Melanthus in the exclamation of 766–7. According to the scholiast, that title was an Athenian name for Poseidon. At the same time, however, the name evokes, for readers who have reached the description of Odysseus' treatment at the hands of his domestics several lines later, the names of the archetypal abusive servants of the *Odyssey*, Melanthius and Melantho, who together serve as the named representatives of the community of bad domestics. Far from being merely a display of obscure erudition, therefore, the use of the name Melanthus to refer to Poseidon links Cassandra's wish that the god's wrath continue to its realization in the treatment afforded the hero by his disloyal servants.

The next stage of Cassandra's account of Odysseus' return home is equally interesting in its engagement with the Homeric text. Immediately after describing the hero's mistreatment on Ithaca, Cassandra turns to an episode mentioned earlier in the *Odyssey*: a spying mission to Troy, in preparation for which Odysseus had his comrade Thoas whip him, leaving scars that, Cassandra says, will still remain (779–80). In the *Odyssey* Helen says that Odysseus "tamed himself with unseemly blows" (4.244), but a beating by Thoas seems to have been mentioned in the *Little Iliad* (*PEG* 7 [*EGF* 8] = schol. Lyc. 780; for other versions of Odysseus' infiltration of Troy, cf. Soph. *TrGF* F 367–*9a; Eur. *Hec.* 239–50; *Rh.* 503–7; Arist. *Poet.* 1459b6; Euph. *CA* 69). Lycophron has thus taken advantage of the reference to Odysseus' suffering and mistreatment at the hands of his domestics in Ithaca to introduce a different, thematically related story from an earlier phase of the Trojan cycle. At the same time, Cassandra's insistence that, at the time of his arrival home, Odysseus will still bear the scars of Thoas' mistreatment recalls an episode from the end of the *Odyssey* that Lycophron omits from his own narrative: the story of how Odysseus got the scar which is recognized by his old nurse Eurycleia (*Od.* 19.392–475). Just as in the *Odyssey* Eurycleia's recognition of her master's scar triggers a narrative "flashback" that explains how he got it, so too, in the *Alexandra*, the presence of scars on Odysseus' body at the time of his arrival on Ithaca is explained by a narrative flashback – albeit to a different story drawn from a different source: Lycophron's Cassandra, hostile as ever to the Greek hero, omits the aristocratic hunting mishap of the *Odyssey*, substituting in its stead another instance of Odysseus' deceptiveness.

FURTHER READING

The most accessible translation of the *Alexandra* into English remains that of Mair in the Loeb series (1921). Readers seeking commentary on the entire poem in English must still resort to Mooney 1921; there is a short selection of Greek text from the poem (348–72), with commentary, in Hopkinson 1988. The Teubner edition of Mascialino (1964) can be consulted, but warrants updating. The poem has fared better in languages other than English, especially Italian: Gigante Lanzara 2000 and Fusillo, Hurst and Paduano 1991; and French: Lambin 2005 and Hurst and Kolde 2008. The essays of Stephanie West (1983, 1984, 2000, 2003a) remain fundamental for framing the question of date and authorship, as well as for raising larger literary questions. Fusillo 1984 treats the problems of genre in interesting ways, and

Hunter's brief but suggestive discussion of the poem in Fantuzzi and Hunter 2004: 437–43 raises important areas for future work. Lowe 2004 is a crucial study of the multiple narrative levels on which the poem operates. The abundant ancient scholia (and ancient and Byzantine paraphrases) are now best accessed through Leone 2002. Scheer 1908 remains important for the extensive twelfth-century commentary by Tzetzes.

PART THREE

Prose

CHAPTER TWENTY-TWO

Historiography, Rhetoric, and Science: Rethinking a Few Assumptions on Hellenistic Prose

Martine Cuypers

While this chapter owes its chimerical shape to practical considerations, including limitations of space and overlap with other *Companions* (Marincola 2007, Worthington 2007), I would like to make a virtue out of necessity by using it to discuss some wider issues as a background to the chapters that follow, all but the last dealing primarily with prose texts. As was noted in Chapter 1, Hellenistic prose typically fills little space in surveys of Greek literature. For example, in Easterling and Knox 1985, Hellenistic science, literary criticism, and rhetoric are absent, and Hellenistic historiography fills only five pages, devoted largely to Polybius. Only philosophy fares better with 20 pages. Hellenistic poetry, in contrast, receives 81 pages. The choices made reflect the surviving evidence only to some extent: scientific texts are by far the best-preserved Hellenistic prose genre, the evidence for Hellenistic historiography beyond Polybius is sizeable, and the output of the Hellenistic philosophers is no better preserved than that of historians, rhetors, and literary critics. Clearly, then, we are also dealing with assumptions about the purpose of a literary history and, more importantly, about the significance of the Hellenistic period for the history of ancient literature at large. Bluntly put, many surveys of Hellenistic literature create the impression that poetry, philosophy, and Polybius made a difference, and that other genres and texts did not. In essence this reproduces the Classicistic stance of Greek and Roman authors of the late Hellenistic period and Empire on whom much of our knowledge about Hellenistic literature depends.

Literary history is no exception to the truth that history is written by the victors; and the victors' truth in due course tends to become the reality that dominates diachronic overviews. Yet in the past decades, in line with general trends in the field of history, there has been a growing inclination among literary scholars to take ancient evaluations of Hellenistic literature and culture as merely a perspective, a product of the cultural and political dynamics of their time and perhaps also of a more general tendency in Greco-Roman literature to claim originality by rejecting the immediate past and turning a more remote past into an idealized source of inspiration. This curious discourse of tradition and innovation is shared between the early Empire and the Hellenistic period (at least), and a polemic stance is part and parcel of it. Ancient authors' verdicts about their predecessors should not always be taken at face value (Acosta-Hughes, Murray, and Clauss in this volume): no matter how loudly they may deny it, the status quo which these predecessors produced still forms their own point of departure. Just as Hellenistic philosophy formed the basis of Imperial authors' interaction with the oeuvre of Plato (White in this volume), developments of the Hellenistic period in other spheres, too, could not simply be undone. It is from such considerations that many chapters in this volume and in other recent surveys (e.g., Worthington 2007) look beyond ancient evaluations and emphasize continuity and shared ground among forms of literary expression and types of intellectual activity across the cultures of the Mediterranean world from the Classical period through the Hellenistic period to the Empire. One of the gains of this approach is a rehabilitation of Hellenistic intellectual pursuits other than poetry and philosophy as subjects of interest not only to historians but also to students of literature – a development which fits into a more general blurring of boundaries between literary and historical approaches in Classical scholarship and beyond.

In the following three sections, I will discuss Hellenistic historiography, rhetoric, and science (or technical prose) in order and without any pretension to comprehensiveness. For the last two topics extensive further reading suggestions are provided at the end of the chapter. Historiography is discussed in more detail in the chapters of Erskine, Gowing, Whitmarsh, Gruen, Knippschild, and Dieleman and Moyer. My emphasis for this genre, in line with what was said above, will be on the problems which indirect transmission poses for the evaluation of individual texts and for tracing developments. Rhetoric and oratory, also touched upon in the chapters of Wissmann and Gutzwiller, raise similar issues. For science, where many works are in fact extant, the question is rather how these texts, which were food for specialists then as they are now, relate to the "mainstream" of Hellenistic literature.

The Trouble with Fragments: Historiography

Most brief treatments of Hellenistic historiography have recourse to Polybius' *Histories* as a haven in the sea of murky evidence that stretches from Xenophon in the fourth century BCE to Dionysius of Halicarnassus and Diodorus Siculus in the first. There are many reasons for doing so. First of all, Polybius' work is much better preserved than any other history from this period. Secondly, it provides a contemporary account of the political sea-change caused by the military exploits of Rome. Thirdly, it does so in a manner that is sufficiently in line with Thucydidean and modern concepts of history to earn its author respect as a "serious" historian. And last but not least, Polybius while defending his own ideas about writing history extensively reflects on the achievements of his predecessors, so that he is now a key witness for the lost historiography of the fourth through second centuries. While all of this makes sense, it is to be feared that the primacy of Polybius in literary surveys has left generations of Classicists with a skewed picture of Hellenistic historiography, and has steered them away from material that is no less significant and interesting, if considerably harder to access and navigate.

To start with navigability, it should be said that Polybius' *Histories* do not present particularly fair sailing either. Of its original 40 books only the first five survive intact. Books 6 to 18 we know largely from the so-called "Excerpta Antiqua," a Byzantine epitome of Books 1 to 18, and for the remaining 22 books we rely primarily on a collection of excerpts made for the Emperor Constantine VII Porphyrogenitus (912–50 CE). These sources can be supplemented from citations by other authors, ranging from a few to none for some books (nothing at all survives of Books 17 and 40) to very many for the geographical Book 34. Arranging and interpreting this evidence is fraught with difficulties (Walbank 1979: 1–62).

This, then, is the best a scholar of Hellenistic historiography may hope for. On the opposite side of the evidence spectrum are historians who are little more than a name, such as a certain "Demetrius who wrote about his fatherland," named in Stephanus of Byzantium's sixth-century CE encyclopedia of geographical names (*Ethnica*) for no other purpose than to illustrate the ethnic "of Odessus" (*FGrH* 808). Demetrius' local history *On Odessus* is as easily imaginable in the Empire as in the third century BCE, and such dating problems are persistent throughout the evidence even where more information is available. This in itself says something about the continuities in Greek historiography and spells trouble for attempts to construct a developmental history of the genre.

Somewhere between Polybius and Demetrius fall historians such as Nymphis, a third-century author from Heraclea on the Black Sea, whose best-known work, like that of Demetrius, dealt with his fatherland, and who, like Polybius, played a political role of some significance within his community. In Felix Jacoby's *Fragmente der griechischen Historiker* (*FGrH*), our principal guide to most of the hundreds of known Hellenistic historiographers, the evidence for Nymphis consists of six testimonies (T), remarks in other authors which tell us something about the author and his oeuvre, and 19 fragments (F), citations of various sorts (e.g., paraphrases, summaries, or verbatim quotations) which tell us something about the content of his work. Their nature and contents are fairly representative of the evidence for many Hellenistic local historians (*FGrH* 432):

T 1 The entry "Nymphis" in the *Suda*, an encyclopedia of the tenth century CE, which says that Nymphis wrote a work about Heraclea in 13 books, ending with Ptolemy III Euergetes; and a work on Alexander, the Successors, and their successors in 24 books.

T 2 Ps.-Chion 13.3, of uncertain date, a passage in a fictional letter written in the name of Chion, one of the Heraclean notables who murdered the tyrant Clearchus in 353 BCE. To add verisimilitude, the author has used the names of well-known Heracleans, including Nymphis who lived a full century later.

T 3, 4	Photius, *Library* 224.226a and 228b, two passages from this ninth-century patriarch's summary of Books 9–16 of the Heraclean history of Nymphis' compatriot Memnon (first or second century CE). The first says that after the death of Lysimachus (281 BCE) "Nymphis, advised the remaining exiles, being also one of them himself, to return to Heraclea." The second mentions "Nymphis the historian" as the leader of a Heraclean embassy to the Galatians.
T 5	= F 3, a scholion on Apollonius, *Argonautica* 2.729–35, which ends with the words "(this) says Nymphis in Book 1 of *On Heraclea*, from whom Apollonius seems to have taken it" (in fact borrowing in the opposite direction, Nymphis using Apollonius, cannot be entirely excluded).
T 6	A citation of the third-century CE Neoplatonic philosopher Porphyry by Stobaeus, *Anthology* 1.49.52 (fifth century CE), which mentions a work by Philo of Heraclea entitled *Reply to Nymphis Concerning His Wonders.*
F 1, 2	The entries "Phrixus" and "Hypius" in Stephanus' *Ethnica*, which cite Nymphis as an authority for the topographical names "Phrixus' Harbor" and "Hypia Mountains."
F 3, 4, 5a, 8, 11, 12, 13, 14, 15, 16	Scholia on Apollonius of Rhodes, *Argonautica* 2.729–35a, 752, 780–3b, 4.247–53, 2.168b, 649–50, 672–3, 786–7a, 815, and 854, citing Nymphis for mythical events and facts on the south coast of the Black Sea relating to the locations and stories mentioned in Apollonius' epic.
F 5b, 9, 10, 18	Athenaeus, *Learned Banqueters* 14.619f–20a, on a ritual of the Pontic Mariandynians and its origin, including a long quotation of Nymphis' actual words; 12.536a–b, an anecdote about the corrupt Spartan general Pausanias, also with a quotation; 12.549a–d, an anecdote about the mortally obese Heraclean tyrant Dionysius, with a long quotation; and 13.596e, on Sappho's love for Phaon, curiously referring to "Nymphis' *Periplus of Asia*" – surely Nymphodorus is meant.
F 6	*Lexicon Rhetoricum Cantabrigiense* 353.2, a note in the margin of a Cambridge manuscript of Harpocration's *Lexicon of the Ten Attic Orators*, citing Nymphis for an explanation of the Persian term *orosangēs*.
F 7	Plutarch, *Virtues of Women* 9.248d, citing Nymphis for the origin of the custom of using metronymics rather than patronymics in Lydian Xanthos, where women once persuaded Bellerophon to lift a curse he had imposed for non-payment for a service.
F 17	Aelian, *On the Nature of Animals* 17.3, on giant snakes in the land of the Troglodytes, mentioned "in Book 9 of Nymphis' work on Ptolemy."
F 19	The Byzantine lexica *Etymologicum Magnum* and *Etymologicum Genuinum* under "Gargaros," a city in the Troad named after a son of Zeus of that name, "as Nymphias (*sic*) the philosopher (*sic*) explains."

I have included this lengthy assemblage of *disiecta membra* primarily to illustrate the complexity of the evidence and the number of interpretive moves required to make sense of it. Engagement with Nymphis implies dealing not only with a very broad array of source texts – many non-mainstream and quite a few untranslated – but also with the works on which some of these sources comment, and with other authors and works cited in the same context. To make informed judgments, one needs a basic familiarity with all of these texts: their nature, content, and aims; their intended audience and production context; their state of transmission; the author's interests, citation habits, and overall accuracy. Many general caveats apply (Marincola 2007: 2). Ancient authors often cited from memory, which is far from infallible: they may get various bits wrong – from the precise words to the context or title of the cited work – while still providing significant information on other points. Furthermore, it is often hard to tell to what extent an author is following the cited historian – for example, whether he is quoting verbatim or paraphrasing, where the citation ends and his own words start, and whether he has perhaps misrepresented his source text through misunderstanding, or has purposely tailored it to suit his own argument. One must also take into account the distortion caused by selection. This is most obvious in summaries of entire works, such as those of Photius, but also applies to incidental citations. For example, because most of our evidence for Nymphis comes from *Learned Banqueters* and the scholia on Apollonius, it looks as if Nymphis dealt primarily in anecdotes and myths; but this was precisely what the Apollonian commentators and Athenaeus were looking for and may not be representative of the work they mined. And in the case of evaluative discussions we must also reckon with polemical bias: an author keen on showing the superiority of his own knowledge, understanding, or approach may not be doing justice to the work he discusses.

Despite all these problems, surprisingly much can often still be elicited from little scraps. In the case of Nymphis, where we are lucky enough to have book numbers in most citations, we can reconstruct the overall layout of *On Heraclea* with a reasonable degree of plausibility (*FGrH* vol. 3b.259–61). Book 1, the source of most citations in the scholia to Apollonius, appears to have dealt with mythical events in northwestern Asia Minor before the foundation of Heraclea (an "archaeology" comparable to those in Herodotus and Thucydides). Books 2 to 9 covered the period from the city's foundation to the start of the tyranny and the Heracleans' dealings with Achaemenid Persia (660/50–365/4 BCE). Books 10 and 11 dealt with the tyranny of Clearchus and perhaps also that of his successor, Timotheus (364/3–353/2 or –338/7), and the final Books 12 and 13 treated the later history of the tyranny, its fall, and events down to at least the succession of Ptolemy III Euergetes (247/6). Although Books 2 to 13 covered "historical" events, it is clear from the citations that aetiological, ethnographical, and geographical excursus were not restricted to Book 1 but occurred throughout the entire narrative, as they do in Herodotus. Therefore, and because of Nymphis' inevitable interest in Persian matters, it is perhaps no coincidence that there is a significant change of theme after nine books, precisely the length of Herodotus' *Histories*. The relatively limited space reserved for recent history may be explained by the fact that Nymphis dealt with this period at much greater length in his work on Alexander and the Successors. And apart from such structural observations, the evidence also allows some analysis of Nymphis narrative style in digressive passages, thanks to the three lengthy verbatim quotations in Athenaeus (F 5b, 9, and 10).

The example of Nymphis stands for hundreds of Hellenistic historians whose work is lost and can now only be gleaned from testimonies and citations. The practical explanations for their disappearance vary per author and genre. In the case of the local historians, their regional focus certainly did not help their chances of survival; to a wider audience such works held a limited appeal. In the case of Nymphis in particular one may also cite the tyranny of compilations. When Memnon continued the history of Heraclea to the late Hellenistic period or early Empire, his work in due course supplanted that of Nymphis (which he used to compile his own version) as the first port of call for all things Heraclean and as a handy continuous account of the entire Hellenistic period (albeit one written from a local vantage point). In very much the same way Nymphis had obliterated his own predecessor, Promathidas (*FGrH* 430), and the accounts of Arrian, Diodorus, and Plutarch supplanted the early histories of Alexander.

But an ideological explanation also looms in the background, which one might call "the tyranny of Thucydides," exemplified notably by Dionysius of Halicarnassus. Dionysius' developmental scheme of Greek historiography (which may go back to Theophrastus) identifies as the genre's originators "local" historians who in plain language recorded the traditions of the past of their own towns, including not only the evidence of monuments and records but also marvelous stories ("myths"). Herodotus in turn did not write about one time or place, but included all important events of the Greek and non-Greek world in a single narrative. Thucydides then rejected both the marvelous stories of the early writers and Herodotus' broad scope and wrote about a single war, basing his account solely on his own inquiry and autopsy (*On Thucydides* 5; Marincola 2007: 4–5). In Dionysius' view, then, local history is primitive, Herodotus a pivotal figure, and Thucydides the *telos* of the genre (at least in content if not in style).

A teleological model of historiography that culminates in Thucydides underlies the thinking of virtually all ancient theorists, including Polybius, Plutarch (*On the Malice of Herodotus*), and Lucian (*How to Write History*). It persists also in modern evaluations of the genre, even if their taxonomies of the evidence differ. For example, Jacoby's collection (*FGrH*) arranges Greek historiography into five subgenres in the order in which he believed they developed (Jacoby 1909; Marincola 2007: 5–7; Schepens 1997). First, Jacoby thought, mythography appeared, which sought to organize the many different stories about the mythical past. The second subgenre, ethnography, focused on the distinctive features, customs, and marvels of lands and peoples and was a hybrid form, containing both narratives of events and descriptions. Chronography, the third, took as its point of departure the events within a certain time period, organizing them by year. The fourth and best subgenre, contemporary history (*Zeitgeschichte*), Jacoby saw emerging in Books 7 to 9 of Herodotus (whom he, like Dionysius, constructed as a pivotal figure) and coming to maturity in the work of Thucydides. The key features of this type were an emphasis on the author's own time and a Panhellenic perspective. The fifth subgenre, local history (horography), limited itself to a local perspective, treating not only "historical" events but also mythographical and ethnographical material. Unlike Dionysius, Jacoby saw this as a late development inspired largely by Herodotus (a view which has its attractions). He agreed with Dionysius, however, in evaluating it as an inferior genre, and more generally in seeing Thucydides' work as the pinnacle of Greek historiography and all that followed as a step back.

Most scholars now seem to agree that such models do injustice to the sheer variety of Greek historical writing throughout antiquity and that they ignore that historiography as a genre is far from clearly demarcated. For the Hellenistic period in particular, they disqualify a very substantial slice of the evidence (texts such as the *Letter of Aristeas*, Euhemerus' *Holy Account*, and the *Periplus* ascribed to Scymnus are also, in their own way, historical writing) and so rather hinder our understanding of the period's literary culture. We should keep in mind that Nymphis and his colleagues were no less familiar with Thucydides' work than we are; if they wrote something different, this is surely not a matter of incompetence but one of choice. It is more fruitful to look beyond the bias of our sources and modern historiographical norms and "read" these authors as working in a different tradition. While the remains of most Hellenistic historians are not generous in providing hard historical data, they do furnish important evidence for social and political ideology and identity building (Erskine in this volume), building blocks for the development of prose fiction (Whitmarsh in this volume), and a context for the interests of contemporary poets (Harder and Köhnken in this volume). For all these reasons this material deserves more attention, and it is to be hoped that the current re-edition of Jacoby's collection with English translations and commentaries (Worthington 2006–) will make an important part of it more accessible.

The Trouble with Silence: Rhetoric and Oratory

The fate of Hellenistic rhetoric and its practical application, oratory, resembles that of historiography. Here too the Classicism of the late Hellenistic period and Empire hangs as a shadow over what preceded, and here too modern scholars have often taken the judgment of later authors for granted. This is perhaps more excusable than for historiography because the evidence is both more limited and more biased. Not a single Greek rhetorical treatise or oration written between c.300 and the late first century BCE survives (with the possible exception of Demetrius' *On Style*), and while historical texts are often cited and summarized in a fairly neutral way for the facts and narratives they contain, our information about Hellenistic rhetoric almost entirely comes from later treatises and handbooks on the topic (which are evaluative by nature) and much depends on a relatively small number of authors (notably Cicero, Dionysius of Halicarnassus, and Quintilian). These sources allow us to say a fair bit about the theoretical interests and tenets of Hellenistic rhetors but only little about the practical application of their teachings; what they do provide us with are negative evaluations of Hellenistic styles of speaking as opposed to the oratory of Classical Athens. Their grand narrative of the history of rhetoric eventually underlies modern assessments such as the following (Kühnert 1993: 666, my translation):

> Practical rhetoric reached its highpoint in the fourth century BCE, especially in Demosthenes. When after the Battle of Chaeronea (338) Greece had become politically insignificant and for this reason free speech had lost its most important application, the play of political forces, practical rhetoric swiftly declined and the art of rhetoric more and more retreated into the schools. Rhetoric's scholastic nature determined its further development in the Hellenistic period, characteristic of which are the central position of rhetoric in education, the primacy of stylistic issues in rhetorical theory and practice, a spread of rhetoric to literature at large, and last but not least, a detailed expansion of rhetorical theory through far-reaching systematization and ever more complicated classification and differentiation.

Although today few scholars of ancient rhetoric would compose this passage as it stands, it provides a convenient starting point for an attempt to move beyond the bias of our literary sources and construct a picture of the innumerable Hellenistic theoreticians and practitioners of eloquence whom they reduce to near-silence.

First of all, contrary to Kühnert, "Greek political eloquence did not die at Chaeronea" (Pernot 2005: 73) because "the Greek city did not die at Chaeronea" (Robert 1969: 42). In the new political world wrought by Alexander and his successors, the *polis* continued to be the primary focus of social life for most people (Erskine in this volume). Independence had always been the privilege of a relatively small number of hegemonic *poleis*, and for the majority of Greek cities the new status quo changed relatively little. If anything, the *polis* became more important because the number of Hellenic cities grew, thanks to new foundations and foreign cities' adoption of the institutions of the *polis*. In all Hellenistic *poleis*, old and new, factions vied for power, individuals brought their disputes to court, and councils and assemblies deliberated about internal and foreign affairs. Countless men defended themselves against charges, proposed decrees, praised the benefactors of their city, and spoke to its interests in other cities, leagues, and royal courts. Their immense production does not survive and is barely visible in our literary sources, but it is omnipresent in the epigraphic record. Each of the innumerable Hellenistic decrees preserved on stone is a testimony to speeches delivered, and the text of the inscription often gives a fair impression of the content of such speeches (examples in Erskine 2007). Occasionally we even have an actual address, as in the case of epistles sent by rulers to cities, which were read aloud in public as well as recorded on stone. These observe many of the conventions of public address and give us some first-hand evidence for Hellenistic styles of oratory (Pernot 2000: 103–14 = 2005: 73–82).

The epigraphic evidence and common sense, then, defy the claim that "practical rhetoric swiftly declined" at the end of the fourth century. This implies that it is dangerous to approach Hellenistic rhetoric as a "scholastic" discipline in the modern sense of the word, i.e., as a subject that is primarily of theoretical interest and of limited practical use. If in the Hellenistic period rhetoric came to occupy a crucial position in higher education, this is not merely as a symbol of Greekness, to inculcate Greek cultural values, but first and foremost as a system to equip elite youths from different places and backgrounds with the power of the word, spoken and written, which was key to a successful completion of many of the tasks that were expected of them in later life. Rhetoric in the Hellenistic period became the single most important educational tool to promote good citizenship, achieving a status already promoted by

Isocrates and later theorized notably by Cicero and Quintilian. A rhetorical education became "virtually a minimum requirement for full elite status" (Vanderspoel 2007: 129), and it is for this reason that philosophers of all persuasions theorized about it in one way or another, handling the competition between rhetoric and philosophy in different and often confusing ways – from embracing rhetoric as part of philosophical knowledge (*epistēmē*) to degrading it to a "routine" (*tribē*; Quint. *Inst.* 2.15, 17; Philodemus' *Rhetoric*: Gutzwiller in this volume).

Yet theorizing by rhetors and theorizing by philosophers cannot really be separated, and rhetoric never *retreated* into the schools, be they schools of philosophy or schools of rhetoric; practical education, and not contemplation, remained the context of its development. It is in this context that the Hellenistic drive towards systematization, classification, and differentiation must be understood (Connolly 2007: 147–8). Critics who observe that the practicing orator does not need such detailed taxonomies are missing the point. Ancient rhetors were well aware of the importance of experience and talent. They knew that oratory in action tends to blur the lines drawn by theory, and that their classifications and differentiations were open to argument. While they may have found pleasure in intricate description (as did contemporary poets, historians, geographers, and mathematicians), system building was not a goal in itself. Formal analysis played an important role in the system of literary education, which was in place already at the beginning of the Hellenistic period and, though continually tweaked and refined, remained in essence the same during the Empire.

Its first serious stage, after students had learned their letters, was grammatical training, well documented in the school texts of Greco-Roman Egypt (Wissmann in this volume) and a handbook ascribed to Dionysius Thrax (170–90 BCE), to whom at least the work's introduction goes back. According to Dionysius, the purpose of grammatical training was to make pupils familiar with poets and, to a lesser extent, prose authors of the canon. It consisted of six parts: reading aloud and learning poetic meters; identification of tropes; explanation of the meaning of rare words and historical references; etymology; declining nouns and conjugating verbs; and finally, "judgment," comprising textual criticism, questions of authenticity, and esthetic evaluation. Standard elements of rhetorical training, typically starting at age 12 to 14, would have been the different types of speeches, techniques of argument and organization, and aspects of style (sentence structure, word choice, prose rhythm), the nature, effect, and appropriateness a great variety of tropes or figures of speech and thought (*schēmata*, including personification, irony, anaphora, antithesis, aposiopesis, preteritio, climax, and simile). These were ingrained through the study of various types and styles of prose writing and through written exercises on set themes, ranging from preliminary exercises (*progymnasmata*) for specific modes (such as narrative, ecphrasis, comparison, fable, and speaking in character) to declamations (*meletai*) on imaginary themes drawn from mythology, history, and daily life (such as "advise Agamemnon whether or not to sacrifice his daughter Iphigenia"). Analysis of language, style, structure, and arguments, formalized in a theoretical framework that combined elements of literary criticism, grammar, logic, dialectic, and psychology, formed a crucial intermediary step in the learning process, helping students appreciate the qualities of the examples and providing them with guidelines for their own attempts at text composition.

A practical factor which must also be taken into account is that most rhetors were paid directly by their students, so that their income depended on how many (and which) students they managed to attract. This in turn depended not only on their location (major cities attracting the best teachers and students) and reputation as an active speaker (i.e., their perceived ability to teach by example), but also on the efficiency of their teaching system. Since the set examples and exercises did not leave much room for innovation, the realm where a rhetor could prove himself better than the competition was the "system" on which he based his teaching. In a sense, therefore, there were as many rhetorics as there were rhetors, which goes a long way to explaining why so little of Hellenistic rhetorical writing survives: most texts had the status of handbooks; they were "operator's manuals" (Vanderspoel 2007: 130) of a type well attested in Latin during the Empire (Kennedy 2003). Like modern textbooks, they were swiftly superseded as educational practice adapted to developments in rhetorical theory, a "finite, logical system capable of meshing with the virtually infinite disorder of the world" which continually evolved to "compensate for contingencies with a superabundance of possibilities for classification" and to "impose systematic order on speech that always threatens to escape its proper bounds" (Connolly 2007: 152, 148).

The educational context is also important for a proper assessment of what Kühnert calls "the spread of rhetoric to literature at large," with a metaphor (*das Ausgreifen*) that suggests uncontainable infection, unruly horses, and trespassing. In light of educational practice, there can be no doubt that nearly all Hellenistic authors had rhetorical training; yet it is difficult to trace the influence of this training in the works we possess. Where in the Second Sophistic we see the world of rhetorical exercises enter literature with spoofs such as Lucian's *Encomium of the Fly*, few such tell-tale signs of educational practice appear in Hellenistic literature. When it comes to less obvious influence, the most rewarding objects of study would seem to be texts such as Polybius' *Histories* and Apollonius' *Argonautica*. Yet using the set speeches and representation of public speaking in these works as evidence for Hellenistic rhetoric is tricky. It is true that both works emphasize the power of the spoken word and that features of their set speeches can be mapped onto the instructions of later rhetorical handbooks. Such observations, however, equally apply to numerous pre-Hellenistic texts, from Thucydides' *Histories* to the Homeric epics. Rhetors in fact loved to trace the origin of their profession back to the *Iliad*, pointing to Phoenix's claim that he taught Achilles everything to make him a "speaker of words" (9.440–4), but surely they did not seriously believe that Homer derived his eloquence and that of his characters from a rhetorical handbook. Rather they assumed that the ancient poets intuitively or through experience knew the very parameters of effective speech making which they themselves elaborately spelled out for their inexperienced and, on average, considerably less talented students. In the end, then, the reason why rhetorical training is hard to trace in what survives of Hellenistic literature is not that rhetoric was an abstract system without practical use for literary composition, but that good literature tends not to reveal how the author learned his métier.

Finally, let us look at Kühnert's "primacy of stylistic issues in rhetorical theory and practice." This observation, it seems, is to a significant extent inspired by the prominence of the discussion about Attic and Asiatic style in the late first century BCE. Leaving this discussion aside for the moment, we may observe that what is perhaps the most crucial Hellenistic contribution to rhetorical theory does not concern style but content and organization. Hermagoras of Temnos (active c.150 BCE) developed a classification of "types of issues" (Greek *staseis*, Latin *statūs*) which had a decisive influence on theorizing about invention (*heuresis*), one of the key aspects of speech making – together with arrangement (*oikonomia*), diction (*lexis*), memory (*mnēmē*), and delivery (*hypokrisis*). It was further developed by authors such as Cicero (*On Invention*), Quintilian, and Hermogenes (*On Issues*), who give us a good impression of Hermagoras' ideas. The purpose of his so-called *stasis* theory was to define the key point on which a case turned, i.e., what a speech had to establish. This defined the nature and structure of its argument. Discussions of Hermagoras' system tend to focus on its usefulness for forensic oratory ("Did X kill Y? If so, was it murder or homicide? Were there mitigating circumstances? Should it be tried in this court?"). Yet by including not only issues concerning particular situations (*hypotheseis*: "should Socrates marry?") but also general issues (*theseis*: "should a man marry?"), Hermagoras also made an important contribution to bringing moral and philosophical subjects within the scope of rhetorical education. On style he had relatively little to say (Cic. *Brut.* 263, 271).

Another Hellenistic development was refinement of the basic Aristotelian division of oratory into forensic (*genos dikanikon*), deliberative (*symbouleutikon*), and epideictic (*epideiktikon*). The epideictic *logos* in particular was subdivided into a large number of subgenres, including the *logos epitaphios* (funeral speech), *basilikos* (speech to a king), *panēgyrikos* (festival speech), *epithalamios* (wedding speech), *genethliakos* (birthday speech), and *presbeutikos* (ambassador's speech), each with its own do's and don'ts. Theophrastus provided at least some of the drive for such refinements. Building on Aristotle's groundwork, he wrote about 20 works on a wide range of rhetorical topics (all lost). They included separate treatments of forensic, deliberative, and epideictic oratory and treatises on examples, maxims, non-technical proofs, praise, slander, statement of the case, narration, and humor (D.L. 5.42–50; fragments in FHSG 2.508–59). Theophrastus may also have been the first to systematically discuss delivery (the use of voice and gestures), in a work which also covered the performance of music, acting, and poetic recitation. If later authors primarily cite Theophrastus' treatise *On Style* and its distinction of four stylistic "virtues" (*hellenismos*, correctness; *saphēneia*, clarity; *to prepon*, appropriateness; *kataskeuē*, ornamentation) and three types of style (*ischnos*, plain; *megaloprepēs*, grand; and *mesos*, mixed), this primarily reflects the focus of their own interest and an overall agreement with Theophrastus' advice always to seek the mean between extremes and to use a style appropriate to the subject.

The Stoics made a significant contribution to the philosophical acceptability of rhetoric by defining it as a part of logic. Their technical contributions came largely from the study of language and the overlapping spheres of grammatical theory and literary criticism. They may have been responsible for the distinction between figures of thought and figures of speech, and for the concept of tropes (*tropoi*), single words used in "novel" ways (including metaphor, metonymy, and hyperbole).

Exclusively devoted to style but not focusing exclusively on oratory is the treatise *On Style* which the manuscript tradition attributes to Demetrius of Phalerum (Chiron 1993; Innes 1995). Its date has been heavily debated, with some scholars placing it as early as the third century BCE and others as late as the second century CE. An early-first-century BCE date is perhaps most plausible – somewhere between the rediscovery of Aristotle's *Rhetoric* and the rise of Atticism, which the treatise does not discuss, and well after the "critics" of the third and second centuries BCE of whom it includes concepts (Gutzwiller in this volume). The author describes four styles – plain, grand, elegant, and forceful – in terms of appropriate diction, composition, and subject matter, copiously illustrating his statements with examples drawn from poetry and prose. In light of the evidence from Philodemus, the distinction of four styles (instead of Theophrastus' three) no longer seems as remarkable as it once did, which serves as a warning that we should also not make too much of the treatise's "idiosyncratic" inclusion of a substantial discussion of letter-writing. Since the letter was a popular literary form (White in this volume), manuals of letter-writing probably existed. Given the state of our evidence, it means little that the earliest surviving example of such a manual dates from late antiquity.

In short, Hellenistic rhetoric was concerned with describing in increasing detail *all* the facets of planning, writing, memorizing, and delivering a speech. Style was one of these facets and an important one, but it surely did not eclipse everything else. That it nevertheless appears all-important has, it seems, much to do with how a polemic originating in the first century BCE has colored the perception of Hellenistic rhetoric from Imperial to modern times. I am deliberately using "polemic" rather than other terms that often appear in scholarly discussions about the opposition between "Atticism" and "Asianism." Take for example the following assessment (Vanderspoel 2007: 133):

> What had begun as a dispute between the philosophers and the sophists about the utility and nature of rhetoric became a disagreement between different schools of rhetorical thought on the proper style for oratory. In some ways, the Asianists replaced the sophists in what was by and large the same debate, a battle now fought in technical terms rather than centering on issues of morality.

This approach is confusing for two reasons. First, it reduces the issue to style and technical matters whereas, as we shall see, the opposition between Atticism and Asianism is more complex and in fact very similar to that between the philosophers and sophists of the Classical period. Secondly, we are not really dealing with two debating schools of rhetoric, but with a one-sided move of the rhetorical proponents of Classicism, who call themselves Atticists and define their enemy by opposition (Wisse 1995). If Atticism stands for good, Asianism stands for bad. Asianism is not so much a school but a stigmatizing label like Callimachus' Telchines, which could be applied with a fair degree of liberty.

Significant is the case of Cicero, in whose *On Invention* of c.80 BCE and *On the Orator* of 55 BCE *Asianus* simply means "from Asia." The term "Atticism" first appears in a letter to Atticus of 54 BCE (4.19.1), and by 46 BCE Cicero is writing *Brutus* and *The Orator* in response to accusations of composing in the Asiatic manner. He defends himself by citing Attic antecedents in the speeches of Demosthenes and claiming for his own style the label "Rhodian" (*Brut.* 51, *Or.* 25; cf. Quint. *Inst.* 12.1.16–19), which he defines as a mean between the two extremes of Atticism and Asianism – the mean being good and extremes by definition bad, as we saw with Theophrastus. Attempts to describe Attic, Asiatic, or Rhodian style outside the context of individual authors' stylistic polemic run into trouble: there is no less variation in style between the canonical Attic orators (Lysias and Demosthenes could not be further apart) than there is between the orators whom our sources stigmatize as Asiatic. Ancient descriptions of Asiatic style typically comprise two very different modes: one that is ornate and impetuous and another that is terse and epigrammatic, full of Gorgianic figures (Cic. *Brut.* 325–6). The key similarity is that they are both extreme and therefore bad; otherwise they could not be more different. And no one ever sold himself as an Asiatic orator – in fact, Hegesias, an alleged third-century "inventor" of Asianism, apparently claimed Lysias as his model (Cic. *Or.* 226).

A passage in Strabo about this same Hegesias gives a good impression of the spirit in which the war against Asianism is conducted, and may lead us back to the question of the actual importance of style in this polemic (Str. 14.1.41):

> Well-known Magnesians are the rhetor Hegesias, who primarily invented the so-called Asiatic style, corrupting the existing Attic ethos; also Simus the melic poet, who in a similar way corrupted the ways of earlier melic poets by introducing free song ... and Cleomachus the boxer, who fell in love with a pervert (*kinaidos*) and with some slave-girl raised by this pervert, and started speaking and behaving like a pervert. The first to use pervert-speak in poetry was Sotades, and then Alexander Aetolus. But they did so in recited poetry, Lysis in sung poetry, and Simus even earlier than him. Another Magnesian is Anaxenor the lyre-singer, who was exalted by theatre audiences in general but especially by Antony, who granted him the right to collect tribute from four cities and supplied soldiers to give him a hand.

While the words about Hegesias refer to his corruption of the Attic style, all that follows tarnishes him further by association. The birthplace of the Asiatic style is also the home of *kinaidoi*, inventors of suspect song, effeminate boxers, slave prostitutes, and histrionic opera singers who are admired by despotic Roman politicians. Stylistic corruption, moral corruption, and political corruption go hand in hand. What is at stake here is more obvious in the opening of Dionysius of Halicarnassus' *On the Ancient Orators* (1, translation adapted from Usher 1974):

> We ought to acknowledge a great debt of gratitude to the age in which we live, my most accomplished Ammaeus, for an improvement in certain fields of serious study, and especially for the considerable revival in the practice of civil oratory (*politikos logos*). In the epoch preceding ours, the ancient wisdom-loving Rhetoric (*philosophos rhētorikē*) was so badly smeared and suffered such terrible abuse that she was obliterated. From the demise of Alexander of Macedon she started to expire and wither away bit by bit, in such a way that by our time she was almost completely dead. Another rhetoric sneaked in and took her place, one who was intolerably theatrical, without dignity, ill-educated, without even a hint of philosophy or any other aspect of liberal education. By deceiving the ignorant mob she not only managed to live in greater wealth, luxury, and splendor than the other rhetoric; in fact, she made herself indispensible for positions of honor and leadership in the cities, which ought to have been the prerogative of her wisdom-loving rival. She was vulgar and disgusting and in the end made Greece like a house abandoned by morality and the gods. Just as in such a house the free-born, prudent wife has no control over what is hers by right while a senseless harlot claims control of the entire estate and runs it into the ground, terrorizing the wife and treating her like dirt – just

> so in every city... the ancient, autochthonous Attic Muse sat deprived of the respect and privileges which were rightfully hers, while her antagonist, who had arrived only yesterday or the day before from some Asian pit, a Mysian or Carian or Phrygian pest, claimed the right to administer Greek cities, expelling her rival from public life. Ignorance thus expelled love of wisdom, and insanity expelled prudence.

Our own age, however, Dionysius continues, has corrected this wrong and swiftly restored the ancient Rhetoric to her former glory, thanks to the Romans (2–3):

> But this is perhaps not the only reason for praising the present age and our allies in the love of wisdom (*sumphilosophountas*), that they started to make what is good more honored than what is bad... Equally recommendable is how swiftly they have given us this change and how much the situation has improved. Apart from a few Asian cities which because of their ignorance are slow to learn what is good, the world has ceased to admire vulgar, frigid, and senseless oratory... Yes, I think the cause and origin of this great change has been Rome, the ruler of all, who has turned the eyes of the entire world upon her, and those who administer her public life according to what is virtuous and best, highly educated men, noble in their judgments.

Excavating the ideological depths of these paragraphs would command a chapter by itself (Hidber 1996). Like many passages in Dionysius' *Roman Antiquities*, they are the product of a complex symbiosis between the elite of Rome and the Greek intellectuals streaming into the city in the late first century BCE (Gowing in this volume). For Dionysius the Romans are not just honorary Greeks but the true heirs of Classical Athens. Athenian moral, political, educational, cultural, and literary values are equated with Roman values. The key to these values, in Dionysius' presentation, is the *philosophos rhētorikē*, the philosophical rhetoric advocated by Isocrates as a complete education in itself, which provides its students not only with the power of the word but also with the moral and political attitudes required to wield it justly. In time, in the first century CE, this position in the debate over the respective remits of the philosopher and the rhetor would give birth to "sophists" who occupied a niche somewhere between the two poles, and with them to the Second Sophistic. Meanwhile the role Isocrates had envisaged for rhetoric in education was firmly established; in this respect rhetoric never needed rescuing by the Atticists, the Romans, or anyone else. Practical oratory probably did not need quite as much rescuing either, but unfortunately we will never know for sure. When Dionysius wrote "I should be surprised if the craze for that silly sort of oratory survives another generation" (*Ancient Orators* 3), he accurately predicted that Atticism would obliterate Hellenistic oratory swiftly and completely. Already in Philostratus' *Lives of the Sophists* of the early third century CE, the history of rhetoric jumps straight from the fourth century BCE to the time of Nero.

The Trouble with Specialization: Science

This final section takes the form of that most annoying of rhetorical figures, the praeteritio, its length being in inverse proportion to the number of subjects and authors covered. As systematic learning flourished, the Hellenistic period produced innumerable texts in fields which Classical scholars tend to label as "science," loosely used to include all disciplines which endeavor "to understand or model some aspect of the natural world on the basis of investigation and reason" (Keyser and Irby-Massie 2008: 1). This definition covers, in alphabetical order, agriculture, alchemy, architecture, astrology, astronomy, biology, cosmology, geography, harmonics, mathematics, mechanics, human and veterinary medicine, meteorology, metrology, optics, pharmacology, physiognomy, and psychology.

Even a superficial survey of what we know about developments in these fields during the Hellenistic period would fill a book. My primary aim here is to draw attention to the fact that, differently from most areas of Hellenistic prose, quite a few scientific texts are actually extant in their original form or something resembling it. The survivors are unevenly spread over the disciplines and they are not always what we would have wanted to have, but the corpus is sizable. Of Euclid, active in Alexandria under Ptolemy I (ruled 323–283), we have the mathematical *Elements* and *Data*, the astronomical *Phaenomena*, and the *Optics*; his *On Divisions of Figures* partially survives in Arabic translation. Aristarchus of Samos (c.310–230 BCE), who famously advocated a heliocentric model of the universe, is meagerly represented with *On the Sizes and Distances of the Sun and the Moon*. The extant works of Archimedes (c.287–212 BCE) include *On the Equilibrium of Planes*, *On the Measurement of a Circle*, *On Spirals*, *On the Sphere and the Cylinder*, *On Conoids and Spheroids*, *On Floating Bodies*, *The Quadrature of the Parabola*, *(O)stomachion*, *The Cattle-Problem*, *The Sand-Reckoner*, and last but not least, *The Method of Mechanical Theorems*, surviving in a palimpsest which is currently being re-examined (Netz and Noel 2007). The *Conics* of Apollonius of Perga (c.262–190 BCE) exist in Greek and Arabic, and much of the treatise *On Burning Mirrors* by his contemporary Diocles is preserved in Eutocius' commentary on Archimedes' *On the Sphere and the Cylinder*.

In the field of engineering, Hero of Alexandria (c.10–70 CE) falls slightly beyond the cutoff point of this volume, but since science was largely unaffected by Classicism, little changed from the Hellenistic period to the early Empire. We have his *Pneumatics*, *Mechanics* (in Arabic), *On Measurement*, *On the Dioptra*, *Catoptrics*, *On Artillery Construction*, and the strange treatise *On Automaton Construction*, which deals with the construction of mechanical showpieces. Hero's predecessors include Philo of Byzantium (c.280–220 BCE), of whose *Compendium of Mechanics* the sections on poliorcetics and artillery construction survive in full, and the nebulous Biton, who addressed his extant work on war machines to Attalus I of Pergamum (ruled 241–197 BCE). The monumental *On Architecture* by Vitruvius (first century BCE) is in Latin but gives a good impression of Hellenistic achievements in this field. Medicine and biology are represented by Theophrastus' *Inquiry into Plants* and *Causes of Plants* and Apollonius of Citium's commentary on the Hippocratic treatise *On Joints*. For the debate between the various Hellenistic medical "sects" (Herophilus, Erasistratus, Asclepiades of Bithynia, the empiricists) we depend entirely on later authors such as Galen.

Most of the texts in this dry list do not appear on the radar of the average Classicist and belong primarily to historians of science. There are two obvious explanations for this state of affairs. The first is that many of these texts are hard to access without specialized knowledge, especially in fields that involve mathematics (including astronomy, geography, optics, mechanics, and harmonics). Secondly, these texts do not really look like literature to modern eyes. Just like modern science dissertations, they follow strict formal conventions, and at first sight they appear to contain little that commands the attention of literary scholars. It is perhaps mainly on this last point that there has been a change in atmosphere in recent decades, in tune with what I called a "general blurring of boundaries between literary and historical approaches" in the introduction to this chapter. In practical terms, there is a growing interest in scientific texts not merely as repositories of factual information but also as forms of discourse, and more generally in their position within the intellectual, cultural, and literary space of their time. For no matter how intractable the content of Aristarchus' *Sizes and Distances* may be for non-specialists, it is a fact that it was produced at the same time and in the same place as the poetry of Callimachus, Theocritus, and Apollonius, namely at the Ptolemaic court of Alexandria in the first half of the third century BCE.

If scientists and poets did not inhabit separate physical spheres, they also did not inhabit separate intellectual and literary spheres. This is perhaps most obvious from extreme examples such as Philodemus (Gutzwiller and Clauss and Cuypers in this volume), Eratosthenes, whose diverse production comprised poetry, philosophy, grammar, musical theory, history, chronography, mathematics, astronomy, and geography (Geus 2002), and Posidonius, who wrote on philosophy, historiography, military tactics, descriptive geography and ethnography, mathematical geography, physics, meteorology, and astronomy (Gowing in this volume). Modern demarcations between disciplines are clearly of limited value for assessing Hellenistic "intellectual profiles." Mythology and reasoned investigation of the natural world were also married by others than Eratosthenes. Aratus' *Phaenomena* and Nicander's *Theriaca* and *Alexipharmaca* have scientific subjects, and not only because these poets wanted to show off their skill by creating poetry out of unpromising material (Volk and Magnelli in this volume). Science is also omnipresent in the work of other poets. Posidippus wrote epigrams on precious stones (Sider 2005b), Callimachus alludes to theories about epilepsy (Lang 2009), and Apollonius' *Argonautica* is informed by, at the very least, astronomy, biology, cosmology, geography, mechanics, medicine, meteorology, and psychology. Hellenistic poets read around, and it is clear that they were not bound by the distinction between scholarship and science which defines the modern academic world – and which has perhaps restricted our understanding of the Hellenistic literary space more than we care to admit.

What then about the extant scientific treatises themselves? Much remains to be done here. As the Further Reading section below shows, editions are often quite old, and studies which discuss these texts as discourse are still relatively thin on the ground. This is a pity because they raise many interesting questions, notably regarding their authors' communication strategies. All scientific texts are didactic in one way or another, and most have an explicit addressee. Archimedes wrote his *Cattle Problem* and *Method of Mechanical Theorems* in the form of letters to his colleague Eratosthenes. Other works, including Biton's *On Artillery Construction*, are addressed to royal patrons. Beyond these explicit addressees there are also implicit addressees, because Archimedes and Biton counted on others than Eratosthenes and Attalus reading their work. The identity of explicit and implicit addressees is reflected in the voice, content, and aims of a treatise. These authors' attitude towards the work of predecessors and colleagues/competitors also merits consideration – for example, how they sell their own contribution to the topic at hand, and how they present material borrowed from others (synopses, paraphrases, and epitomes abound, and with them, questions of authorship). An issue specific to technical texts, finally, is the relationship between verbal explanation and visual illustration.

What can be done with a "literary" approach has been exemplarily illustrated for the mathematical texts by Reviel Netz (2009), who identified in them a playful aesthetic akin to that of Hellenistic poetry. Similar studies in other fields would be welcome, as the opening lines of two of the extant mechanical texts may illustrate:

> The study of automaton construction has been considered an acceptable pursuit by our predecessors because of the complexity (*to poikilon*) of the craftsmanship involved and because it produces a baffling (*ekplēkton*) spectacle. For, briefly put, automaton construction encompasses every part of mechanics in its step by step construction . . . Avoid old-fashioned scenarios so that your presentation will look modern. For it is possible . . . to vary and create different scenarios while using the same techniques.
>
> Hero, *On Automaton Construction* 1.1, 12

> Philo to Aristo, greetings. The volume I sent you before dealt with harbor construction. Now it is time to explain, in accordance with the program I laid out for you, the subject of artillery construction, which some call engine construction. If all who previously dealt with this field of mechanics had used the same method, all I needed to provide would be a description of the standard artillery designs. But since previous writers disagree not only about the proportions of interrelated parts but also about the prime guiding factor, namely the hole that is to receive the spring, it is fair to ignore old authors but explain those methods of later specialists which can achieve the required effect in practice. Now I know you are not unaware that for the mass of people this art has something inscrutable and unfathomable. Many people who have tried to build engines of the same size, using the same design, similar wood, and identical metal of the exact same weight, have produced some engines with long range and powerful impact but others that fall short. Asked why, they had no explanation. The remark of Polycleitus the sculptor applies here. He maintained that "perfection is achieved gradually in the course of many calculations." Likewise in this art, where constructions require many calculations, if you produce a small discrepancy in particular parts, you get a large error in the end.
>
> Philo, *On Artillery Construction*, preface

Both authors create an interesting conspiracy with their addressee – Aristo in the case of Philo, anonymous in Hero – but these conspiracies have a very different feel. Hero is evidently addressing a specialist in mechanics and does not beat around the bush. The enemy is detractors who might say that automaton-making is trite – Hero and his addressee know better: automata are a true test of skill – and spoiled audiences which need to be baffled with "new" shows which are technically speaking really the same shows, in order to earn applause and respect. Philo's addressee, on the other hand, has a general interest in engineering and is reasonably knowledgeable, but he is not a specialist. He needs to be made curious and seduced into reading this treatise. Artillery construction is a noble art (the Polycleitus quotation), it has something mysterious, and even seasoned specialists often cannot get it right (including the overpaid Alexandrian engineers whom Philo ridicules in the next paragraph). Philo, however, has the keys: the size of the hole for the spring, getting the dimensions spot on and, because theory goes only so far, not being afraid to get your hands dirty.

FURTHER READING

Historiography is discussed in more detail by Erskine, Gowing, Whitmarsh, Gruen, Knippschild, and Dieleman and Moyer in this volume who provide further guidance on individual authors and genres. On the problems associated with indirect transmission, see for example Marincola 2007: 1–9 and 1997, Erskine 2003: 4–14, Brunt 1980, and Schepens 1997. Most of the fragmentary evidence can be found in Jacoby 1923–58 (*FGrH*), currently re-edited with English translations and commentaries in Worthington 2006– (*BNJ*). Brief introductions include Marincola 2001: 105–49, Connor 1985: 458–71, and Saïd 1997: 384–402. Marincola 2007 includes many chapters relevant to the Hellenistic era, all of which provide further reading at the end; see notably those on the Alexander historians, local history, Western Greek historiography, the Greek historians of Persia, Western Asia, and Rome, Hellenistic Jewish historiography, and early Roman historiography; also the chapters on the relationship between history and myth, fiction, tragedy, antiquarianism, ethnography, and biography. For local history, see further Scheer 1993, 2003, and Clarke 2008; for biography, Bollansée 1999 and Erler and Schorn 2007; for early Roman historiography, Ruschenbusch 2004; and for the shadow Polybius has cast over his predecessors, Schepens and Bollansée 2005.

Greek rhetoric and oratory are surveyed in Worthington 2007 and Porter 1997. Helpful Hellenistic chapters in single-authored overviews include Kennedy 1963: 264–336 and 1994: 81–101, and Pernot 2000: 82–114 = 2005: 57–82. Martin 1974 and Lausberg 1973 = 1998 remain useful tools for the technical aspects.

On Hellenistic oratory, see Erskine 2007 (on the continued importance of the *polis* and civil rhetoric), Wooten 1973 (on ambassadors' speeches) and 1975 (on Asianism), Smith 1974 (on oratory in Alexandria), and Pernot 2000: 103–14 = 2005: 73–82 (on the epigraphic evidence). The speeches in Polybius' *Histories* are discussed by Wooten 1974, Walbank 1985a, Champion 1997, Oliver 2006, and Fox and Livingstone 2007; those in Apollonius' *Argonautica*, by Clare 2002: 261–85 and Mori 2007, 2008.

On rhetorical education, see Marrou 1982 (1948) and Morgan 1998, 2007. Cribiore 1996 and 2001a focus on Egypt; Kennedy 1969 and Morgan 1998a, on Quintilian. On the early stages of education, see Wissmann in this volume; on literary criticism, Gutzwiller in this volume and Laird 2006; on grammar and philosophy of language, Sluiter 1990, 1997, Ildefonse 1997, Lallot 1998, Frede and Inwood 2005. Hock and O'Neill 2002 and Kennedy 2003 are crucial for rhetorical school exercises; Russell 1983 and Berry and Heath 1997 discuss the technicalities of declamation (for which most of our evidence is of Imperial date) and *stasis* theory. On the latter topic, see also Dieter 1950 and Heath 1994, 1995; Matthes 1962 collects the fragments of Hermagoras of Temnos (discussion in Matthes 1958 and Kennedy 1963: 303–21). The evidence for Theophrastus' rhetorical work can be found in FHSG 2.508–59, with commentary in Fortenbaugh 2005; see also Fortenbaugh and Mirhady 1993.

On Greek rhetoric in Rome, see Connolly 2007, Wisse 1995, Clarke 1996, Dominik 1997, and Dominik and Hall 2007; further Kaster 1995 on early teachers of rhetoric at Rome; May 2003 on Cicero; De Jonge 2008 on Dionysius of Halicarnassus; Sussman 1978 and Bonner 1949 on Seneca the Elder and Roman declamation; generally on intellectual life in late-

Republican Rome, Rawson 1985; and on the birth of the Second Sophistic, Jones 1978 (focusing on Dio Chrysostom).

Short introductions to Hellenistic science and technical prose include Gutzwiller 2007: 154–67, Keyser and Irby-Massie 2006, and Fraser 1972: 1.376–434. Irby-Massie and Keyser 2002 provides selected passages from Hellenistic and Imperial treatises in English translation. Accessible book-length surveys of ancient science at large include Lloyd 1973, Rihll 1999, and Lindberg 2007. Collective volumes give a good impression of current interests: see Giannantoni and Vegetti 1985, Argoud and Guillaumin 1998, Rihll and Tuplin 2002, Santini 2002, Celentano 2003, Horster and Reitz 2003, Lang 2005, Keyser and Irby-Massie 2008.

The discourse strategies and literary context of ancient technical treatises are discussed by Meissner 1999, Formisano 2001, Asper 2007, and Netz 2009. On their social and political contexts, see Lloyd 1983, 1987, 1991, and 1996, Schürmann 1991, White 1993, Rihll and Tuplin 2002, and Cuomo 2007. Early modern science is a useful comparandum: see Moran 1991b, Biagioli 1993, and Long 2001.

Hellenistic mathematics is covered in Chapters 3–4 of Cuomo's 2001 survey; Heath 1921 is seminal but demands considerable mathematical competence. Translations include Thomas 1939–41 (a selection), Heath 1926 (Euclid's *Elements*), Netz 2004b (Archimedes' *On the Sphere and the Cylinder*), Heath 1912 (Archimedes' other works), Heath 1896, Fried 2002, and Rashed, Decorps-Foulquier, and Federspiel 2008– (Apollonius of Perga, *Conics*), Toomer 1976 (Diocles' *On Burning Mirrors*), and Burton 1945 (Euclid's *Optics*). See further Dijksterhuis 1987 and Jaeger 2008 on Archimedes, Netz, and Noel 2007 on the Archimedes palimpsest, and Netz 1999, 2004a, 2009 on the intellectual principles underlying Hellenistic mathematics.

For mathematical astronomy Neugebauer 1975 is indispensible but not easy reading. Evans 1998 and Heath 1932 are accessible introductions to this topic, the latter including translations of key Hellenistic texts. Other translations include: for Euclid's *Phaenomena*, Berggren and Thomas 1996; for Archimedes' *The Sand-Reckoner*, Heath 1912; for Aristarchus' *On the Sizes and Distances of the Sun and the Moon*, Heath 1913; Bodnár and Fortenbaugh 2002 and Zhmud 2006 discuss the evidence for Eudemus of Rhodes. Work on astrology includes Neugebauer and Hösen 1959, Barton 1994, Jones 1999, Swerdlow 2000, and Beck 2006. On meteorology and time-reckoning, see Taub 2003, Cusset 2003b, Feeney 2007, Lehoux 2007, Sider and Brunschön 2007, and Hannah 2008.

For Hellenistic geography Fraser 1972: 1.520–53 is a good starting point. Hübner 2000 includes chapters on Eudoxus, Eratosthenes, Hipparchus, and geographical poetry. Thomson 1948 and Tozer 1964 provide readable though somewhat outdated introductions in English; Jacob 1991, in French. For Eratosthenes' measurement of the earth, see Aujac 2001, Bowen and Todd 2004, and Nicastro 2008; see further on this polymath Geus 2002, Pàmias and Geus 2007, Cusset and Frangoulis 2008. Cartography is discussed in Dilke 1985 and Talbert and Unger 2008. On the relationship between geography and ethnography, paradoxography, and fiction, see Whitmarsh in this volume, Dihle 1961, Romm 1992, Schepens and Delcroix 1996, Clarke 1999, Geus 2003, Dench 2007, and Engels 2007. Kish 1978, a sourcebook for ancient geography at large, includes some Hellenistic material. Translations of individual authors include Dicks 1960 for the geographical fragments of Hipparchus; Roseman 1994 and Bianchetti 1998, for Pytheas of Massilia; and Burstein 1989, for Agatharchides.

Rihll 2009 is a short introduction to ancient technology at large. Book-length surveys include Landels 1978, White 1984, Schürmann 2005, Schneider 1992, 2007, and Oleson 2008. Extracts from various Hellenistic works in this field can be found in Humphry, Oleson, and Sherwood 1998. Drachmann 1963 translates Hero's *Mechanics*; Marsden 1969–71, the treatises *On Artillery Construction* by Biton, Hero, and Philo; Garlan 1974 and Lawrence 1979, Philo's *Poliorcetics*; see also the helpful illustrations in Campbell and Delf 2003a and 2003b. Hero's *On Automaton Construction* is translated by Murphy 1995; his *Pneumatics*, by Woodcroft 1971. Schmidt, Nix, Schöne, and Heiberg 1899–1914 in five thick volumes edits the Greek text of Hero's entire extant oeuvre with German translation. For Vitruvius' *On Architecture*, see Granger 1931–4 and Rowland and Howe 1999.

Brief discussions of Hellenistic medicine include Flemming 2003 and Fraser 1972: 1.338–76; Nutton 2004 surveys ancient medicine at large. For discussion of the various Hellenistic "sects," see also Hankinson 1995 and Lloyd 1995; von Staden 1996 imaginatively explores the connections between medicine, mechanics, and philosophy. Kollesch, Kudlien, and Nickel 1965 contains the text, illustrations, and a German translation of Apollonius of Citium's commentary to *On Joints*. Von Staden 1989 collects the evidence for Herophilus; Garofalo 1988, for Erasistratus; Deichgräber 1965, for the "empiricists"; Vallance 1990, for Asclepiades of Bithynia; various extracts also in Longrigg 1998.

French 1994 and Wöhrle 1999 survey ancient biology and natural history. For Theophrastus' work in these fields, see Fortenbaugh, Huby, and Long 1985 (introduction), Fortenbaugh and Gutas 1992 (translations of preserved treatises), and Fortenbaugh, Huby, Sharples, and Gutas 1992: 106–253 (fragments of lost works).

For Hellenistic scientific poetry, see in general the essays in Horster and Reitz 2005, Cusset 2006, and Harder, Regtuit, and Wakker 2009. On Aratus and Nicander, see Volk and Magnelli in this volume; on Eratosthenes, Geus 2002, Cusset and Frangoulis 2008, and Trachsel 2009; on Posidippus, Sider 2005b; on the *Periplus* attributed to Scymnus, Bianchetti 1990, Korenjak 2003, and Hunter 2006b: 123–40 = 2008: 503–22.

CHAPTER TWENTY-THREE

Literary Criticism

Kathryn J. Gutzwiller

The three centuries after the death of Alexander were a period of intense and lively debate about the nature and purpose of literature. The concepts about literature that originated with the sophists, Plato, and Aristotle were scrutinized, refined, and reworked into new formulations. In fact, most of the critical discussion of poetry and prose found in later Greek and Latin texts derives from ideas and typologies developed in the early Hellenistic period and extensively debated over the course of the next two centuries. Because of the loss of almost all key texts from this period, the modern tradition of literary criticism, as well as Classical scholarship, has remained largely ignorant of the historical importance and sophistication of this body of thought. It is now clear, however, that Hellenistic philosophers, literary theorists, textual scholars, and poets engaged seriously with such fundamental questions as the nature of the poetic, the function of literature, and how to judge a literary work.

In recent years it has become increasingly possible to piece together major critical trends of the Hellenistic period. Essential to the process have been new and better editions of the texts of Philodemus, especially his *On Poems* (Janko 2000 on Book 1 and 2011 on Books 3–4; Mangoni 1993 for Book 5) and *On Music* (Delattre 2007 on Book 4). The library of this Epicurean philosopher, who was friend and mentor to Vergil, was discovered in the eighteenth century, preserved in a lavish villa at Herculaneum on the Bay of Naples (Armstrong, Fish, Johnston, and Skinner 2004; Sider 2005a). Through new imaging techniques and brilliant editing, the works of Philodemus on poetry, rhetoric, and music, as well as other traditional philosophical subjects, have been, and will continue to be, restored for us (Delattre 2006). Interpretation of this material remains difficult, the province of specialists, because of the fragmentary nature of the charred papyri and the author's method of quoting earlier thinkers, usually out of context, in order to refute their theories. But even so, our knowledge of Hellenistic literary criticism is undergoing a renaissance in terms of new material and new understanding of old material. For instance, scholars generally agree that Demetrius' *On Style*, a treatise of perhaps the early first century BCE which deals with types of style in both prose and poetry, contains critical concepts important to the theories of the so-called "critics" of the third and second centuries, who are known almost exclusively through Philodemus. Likewise, it is now clear that the literary critical works of Dionysius of Halicarnassus, most importantly his *On Composition*, do not contain the idiosyncratic thoughts of an inventive thinker, as earlier scholars sometimes suggested, but rather explore in pragmatic detail literary critical topics basic to the Hellenistic period, such as the euphonious arrangement of words and phrases. Even *On the Sublime* by "Longinus" now seems to advance a strand of Hellenistic criticism, one that favored stylistic grandeur and promoted authorial inspiration. A still largely untapped benefit of this new knowledge of Hellenistic criticism is the opportunity it affords to understand how the literary artists of the age reflected, and contributed to, the theoretical debate going on around them in and through their own compositions.

What's in a Name?

At the dawn of the Hellenistic Age, scholars and theoreticians of literature were apparently called κριτικοί, "critics." Strabo (14.2.19) referred to Philitas of Cos as "both poet and critic" (ποιητὴϲ ἅμα καὶ κριτικόϲ), and according to Plutarch (*Mor.* 1095c–e), Epicurus in his *On Kingship* advised even cultivated kings to banish from their symposia conversation about "musical problems and the philological inquiries of critics" (προβλήμαϲι δὲ μουϲικοῖϲ καὶ κριτικῶν φιλολόγοιϲ ζητήμαϲιν). Plutarch further asserts that if the Ptolemy "who founded the Museum" (Ptolemy I) had encountered Epicurus' advice, he would have rejected it out of hand and that Epicurus was foolish to prefer the pleasure of the theater to that of hearing, over wine, Theophrastus, Aristoxenus, or Aristotle discoursing on music or Homer. It appears, then, that already at the beginning of the Hellenistic Age literary criticism was practiced by a wide range of educated persons and that royal courts were a hotbed for discussion and debate about such issues.

With the increasing specialization typical of the age, terminology developed to sort out different categories of persons working on literary questions. Zenodotus and the later textual scholars of Alexandria were called γραμματικοί. The term was in use by the time of Philicus of Corcyra, a priest of Dionysus during the reign of Ptolemy II Philadelphus, who addressed his *Hymn to Demeter* in choriambic hexameters to γραμματικοί, apparently as experts in metrics (*SH* 677). In the second century BCE, Diogenes of Babylon, a leader of the Middle Stoa, referred to a group of earlier writers on literature as κριτικοί (Phld. *Mus.* 136.26 Delattre). His contemporary Crates of Mallus, an important literary theorist working at Pergamum, distinguished the κριτικόϲ, one concerned with systematic knowledge of discourse, from the γραμματικόϲ, who was concerned only with explaining glosses, prosody, and the like. In sum, he said, the critic is like an architect and the grammarian comparable to his assistant (Sext. Emp. *Math.* 1.79 = F 94 Broggiato 2001). Or as a later source tells us (schol. Dion. Thr. pp. 169.30–170.5, 471.34–472.2 Hilgard 1901), the grammarian judges whether a poem is genuine or spurious but the critic judges whether it is good or bad. In making such a distinction, Crates was aligning himself with a theoretical approach to literature that descends from the Classical Age; he was claiming for it superiority over the more specialized studies of the Alexandrian grammarians, such as his settled opponent, Aristarchus of Samothrace. In this positive sense, Crates called himself a κριτικός, as heir to certain literary thinkers of the third century BCE, whom he seemed to have discussed in a lost work (or works) refuted by Philodemus in *On Poems* (Janko 2000: 125–7).

At the same time, within the Hellenistic philosophical schools there developed theories about literature that reflected technical views on knowledge, language, ethics, and the psychology of the soul. For those who were primarily philosophers, literary criticism was just another branch of philosophy. The Peripatetics continued the work of Aristotle and Theophrastus in defining, categorizing, and analyzing the formal aspects of literature. Peripatetic influence on literary critical thought in Alexandria is indicated by the presence of Demetrius of Phalerum and later Strato of Lampsacus at the court of the first two Ptolemies, and by Callimachus' treatise against the Peripatetic Praxiphanes (fr. 460 Pf.). The Stoics found poetry a method of expressing truths, and sometimes employed allegory to extract these truths. Cleanthes, who wrote philosophical poetry, believed that poetic diction was better at conveying the power of the gods than was prose, and among the titles of treatises by Chrysippus are *On Poems*, *On the Right Way to Read Poetry*, and *Against the Critics* (D.L. 7.200). The Cynics and Skeptics, who lived rather than argued their philosophies, preferred to demonstrate the uses of poetry by composing works, such as Menippus' satires and Timon of Phlius' *Silloi* (*SH* 775–840; Scodel in this volume), which satirized other philosophers through literary parody. Although Epicurus did not consider poetry and music serious enough occupations to warrant philosophical speculation, Philodemus' efforts in writing *On Poems*, *On Rhetoric*, and *On Music* reflect a later Epicurean tradition of dealing seriously with such topics, especially in opposition to Peripatetic and Stoic views on the subject.

Distinctions between the three categories of grammarians, literary critics, and philosophers were far from absolute. Almost all intellectuals of the Hellenistic Age had philosophical training and sympathies, and technical exegesis of Homeric language and passages was widely practiced (Wissmann in this volume). In addition, judgments about whether a poem was good or bad were surely made by most lovers of literature, whether or not they were committed theorists of the subject. To take one example, Crates of Mallus, who laid claim to the title κριτικός, also wrote on grammatical problems in Homer and proffered allegorical interpretations in the Stoic manner. The terms developed, then, not only to define the increasing specialization of the age but also to promote the superiority of one's chosen approach over that of opponents.

What is the Function of Literature?

Early Greek poets perceived no conflict between the cognitive benefits and the emotional pleasures provided by their verse. With the advent of critical thinking about poetry by those who were not necessarily its practitioners, this integrated duality of purpose began to be interrogated, its logical inconsistencies analyzed, and even the value of poetry questioned. Plato knew already of "a long-standing quarrel between philosophy and poetry" (*Rep.* 607b). In the Hellenistic Age the debate about the goal of literature, colored by the oppositional positions staked out by Plato and Aristotle, crystallized around the terms διδαςκαλία, "instruction," and ψυχαγωγία, "enthrallment." In this dichotomy, διδαςκαλία was associated with benefit (ὠφελία), and ψυχαγωγία with pleasure (ἡδονή).

The old argument about the purpose of poetry, now formulated as instruction versus enthrallment, or cognitive/ethical benefit versus aesthetic pleasure, was further complicated by the emergent importance of prose. The question posed in our heading "What is the function of literature?" could not be directly asked by Hellenistic critics because they lacked a term that united both artistic prose and poetry in a single category. Originally, the literary had been synonymous with the poetic. By the early Hellenistic Age, however, prose treatises had come to assume one of the functions earlier performed by poetry, namely, the transmission of knowledge; and poets often acquired, sometimes with acknowledgment, the material for their poetry from prose sources. In addition, by the third century sophisticated theories of prose styles had developed, as well as technical rules for achieving them, with parallels for poetic technique, for which our main extant source is Demetrius' *On Style*. So while the practice of the literary had expanded in scope, the conceptual framework for defining it had not.

A commonly held position throughout the Hellenistic period was the assignment of διδαςκαλία to prose and ψυχαγωγία to poetry. In this view, the function of prose was cognitive, to convey to the reader information ("truth," ἀλήθεια), often with the added benefit of instilling moral principles, and that of poetry was aesthetic, to produce a sensation of pleasure, such as often comes from an account of the unusual, distant, or impossible ("falsehood," ψεῦδος). The word ψυχαγωγία, often translated "entertainment," retained much of its etymological sense of "leading the soul," as in necromancy; it commonly refers to the quasi-magical, physically entrancing effect that language can have on its audience. This dual division in the function of literature was in formation as early as Theophrastus, who criticized poetic effects in serious speeches, such as overuse of antithesis and other types of word play (D.H. *Lys.* 14.1 = F 692 FHSG). We can also trace the idea through Andromenides, one of the earlier critics, who said that the skilled prose writer seeks truth but the poet commonly accepts ideas from others; for him the most beautiful style is the one that enchants the common reader, not the one that is admired for its learned correctness (Phld. *Po.* 1, 161.2–6, 13–15 Janko 2000). Andromenides' purpose, as it seems, was to defend the aesthetic pleasure of hearing beautiful language, and as we will see, a feature common to all the critics was their detailed theoretical analysis of the means by which poetic language produced ψυχαγωγία.

One of the clearest statements of the division of purpose between poetry and prose comes from Eratosthenes, an Alexandrian librarian, scientist, and scholar of the late third century BCE, who also composed poetry. He described himself as a φιλόλογος, a term designed to accommodate his wide-ranging knowledge in such diverse fields as astronomy, mathematics, and geography (Suet. *De gram. et rhet.* 10 Brugnoli 1963). Near the beginning of his important treatise on geography, Eratosthenes rejected traditional claims that Homer was a polymath, and so a source of knowledge, by asserting that "every poet aims at enthrallment, not instruction" (ποιητὴϲ πᾶϲ ϲτοχάζεται ψυχαγωγίαϲ, οὐ διδαϲκαλίαϲ, Str. 1.1.10; cf. 1.2.3). In the original context of the *Geographica*, the point was no doubt to distinguish the scientific truth of his own prose treatises, based on observation, reliable reports of others, and astronomical studies, from the embellished, sometimes mythical, descriptions of geography in Homer. He made the colorful remark that someone would as soon find the shoemaker who sewed up the bag of winds as the places where Odysseus wandered (Str. 1.2.15). It is reasonable to assume that Eratosthenes' lost *Erigone* (*CA* 22–8b, more fully in Rosokoki 1995), a short epic concerned with the origin of wine and Attic festivals, and his *Hermes* (*CA* 1–16, *SH* 397–8; discussion in Geus 2002: 110–28; Ambühl in this volume), a fragment of which (16) describes the five heavenly circles, converted the knowledge available from prose resources, or his own scientific/historical investigations, into imaginative poetry that had as its goal enjoyment, rather than learning. When Ps.-Longinus calls the *Erigone* an "altogether blameless little poem" (*Subl.* 33.5), in contrast to the divinely inspired but disordered outbursts of Archilochus, he suggests that Eratosthenes followed the Alexandrian emphasis on technical proficiency in poetry. It seems likely, then, that Eratosthenes accepted for his own poetic practice the view that poetry was a τέχνη, "art," requiring precision and skill and having as its goal ψυχαγωγία, rather than the διδαϲκαλία offered in prose treatises on technical and scientific subjects.

While the φιλόλογοϲ Eratosthenes allows a place for the ψυχαγωγία of poetry alongside the search for truth characterizing non-rhetorical prose, Polybius expresses anxiety about the encroachments of dramatic, or poetic, elements upon history. In a number of passages, Polybius makes clear that the goal of his *Histories* was to benefit the elite members of society through models of good and bad behavior provided by accurate accounts. He is highly critical of those historians who imported poetic elements into their narratives (Whitmarsh in this volume). These writers of "tragic history," such as Duris of Samos and Phylarchus, dwell, he claims, on the emotional aspects of events and aim to arouse pity in the reader (2.56.10–12):

> A prose author (i.e., historian; ϲυγγραφέα) should not provide his readers a thrill (ἐπιπλήττειν) by incorporating marvels (τερατευόμενον) into his history, nor should he seek to invent possible speeches and recount events only incidental to his subject, as writers of tragedy (τραγωιδιογράφοι) do, but rather report in full what was actually (κατ' ἀλήθειαν) said and done, even if it should be rather ordinary. For the goal (τέλοϲ) of history is not the same as that of tragedy, but the opposite. The tragedian should thrill and charm (ἐκπλῆξαι καὶ ψυχαγωγῆϲαι) his audience for the moment by presenting the most plausible (πιθανωτάτων) speeches, but the historian should instruct and persuade (διδάξαι καὶ πεῖϲαι) those eager to learn for all time by reporting true (ἀληθινῶν) deeds and words, since in the first case the plausible even if false (ψεῦδοϲ) compels its viewers through illusion (ἀπάτην), while in the other case truth compels by benefiting lovers of learning (φιλομαθούντων).

It is unfortunate that we do not know how the "tragic historians" justified their more dramatic and emotional style of writing. In all likelihood, their goal was not simply to provide the reader aesthetic pleasure, since Dionysius of Halicarnassus (*Comp.* 4) criticizes a group of Hellenistic historians, including Phylarchus, Duris, and Polybius (as well as Stoic writers like Chrysippus), for their inattention to beauty of style. The quarrel over "tragic history" probably centered on the historiographical question of how best to convey truth, and the role that imaginative accounts may have in that. Polybius here revises Aristotle's assertion that "poetry is more philosophical and more serious than history" because it relates the universal through possible events while history relates the particular through actual events (*Poet.* 1451b3–8). In Polybius' vehemence we hear a sympathetic echo of Plato's opposition to poetry and its qualities, which he believed harmful to an ideal society based on philosophical truth.

Despite the widespread acceptance of the division in purpose between poetry and prose in the Hellenistic Age, the problems raised by its absolute application underlay much of the theoretical debate of the era. Some thinkers, most prominently the Stoics, sought to defend poetry as a source of knowledge, through such interpretative approaches as allegory or etymology. The Stoics also defended music as having ethical and educative value, as pure sound apart from words, a position that reflects the new reality of lyric poetry composed and recited without musical accompaniment. This belief regarding music helps to explain Stoic sympathies toward the "critics," even though their euphonist position advocated aesthetic pleasure as the goal of poetry and, for some, of prose as well. As the Epicurean Philodemus makes clear in *On Rhetoric*, "sophistic rhetoric," which focused on linguistic τέχνη rather than content, was discussed by early Epicureans and had become a settled trend by the first century BCE; this display of rhetorical and poetic features developed as a mark of cultured prose in the imperial era.

The rivalry between διδασκαλία and ψυχαγωγία as dichotomous goals of literature came, then, to define the oppositional poles in theoretical discussions of both prose and poetry. At the same time, some thinkers advocated a more synthetic position, as is evident from Book 5 of Philodemus' *On Poems.* Among them was Philodemus himself, who argued that good poetry offered the reader a mixture of instruction and pleasure, a position famously enshrined in Horace's reference to the *utile* and the *dulce* (*Ars* 343). In looking now more closely at the concepts and trends that define Hellenistic literary criticism, we will see that differing beliefs about the function of literature underlie these various attempts to theorize the literary.

How to Divide Poetic Art?

The existence of a τέχνη or "art" that applied to poetry was a generally accepted premise of the Hellenistic period. Various approaches to poetic theory were differentiated on the basis of the definition given to this τέχνη ποιητική, "poetic art," and its position within differing divisions into species (εἴδη) relating to poetry. A separation of the τέχνη ποιητική from the ποιητής, "poet," is implied by Aristotle's two treatises, *Poetics* and the lost *On Poets*, and other early Academic and Peripatetic scholars, like Heraclides of Pontus and Praxiphanes of Mitylene, offered discussion of poetry in works whose titles suggest a continuing dual conception. Within the third century there developed a new tripartite division, in which the ποιητής was grouped with ποίηϲιϲ and ποίημα to form the three species of the τέχνη ποιητική. The terms ποίηϲιϲ and ποίημα are not translatable without context, and their variable meanings, such as "composition of poetry" versus "a poetic composition," "subject" versus "style," or "long poem" versus "short poetic unit," are discussed below. The tripartition was widely adopted by later grammarians and continued to influence literary discussions of the imperial period. In *On Poems* 1 Philodemus reports that Crates of Mallus accepted the three species, which he knew from Andromenides (132.23–7 Janko), and in Book 5 (13.33–16.28 Mangoni 1993) he attributes the same division to Neoptolemus of Parium, on whose precepts Horace modeled, at least in part, his *Ars Poetica* (Pomponius Porphyrio on *Ars* 1 Holder 1894). Since Andromenides is apparently one of the earliest euphonists and Neoptolemus is cited in the late third or early second century by Aristophanes of Byzantium (F 19 Mette 1980 = 194 Slater 1986), the dating of this new categorization to the third century is secure. Despite similarities to Academic discussions of rhetoric (Asmis 1992c), most scholars have pointed to the Peripatetic affinities evident in the thought of both Andromenides and Neoptolemus.

Neoptolemus was clearly a major theorist of the tripartite division. Although his views must be reconstructed through the filter of Philodemus' polemic, certain key ideas can be established. For Neoptolemus (15.1–3 Mangoni), ποίημα is synonymous with ϲύνθεϲιϲ τῆϲ λέξεωϲ, "arrangement of the language," which was separated from διανοήματα, the "ideas" expressed. The new division is justified by Neoptolemus' belief that ποίημα is "no less, or greater, a part" of the poetic art (13.33–14.3 Mangoni). In his view, the division called ποίηϲιϲ consists of only "subject matter" (ὑπόθεϲιϲ), which includes "thoughts, actions, and characterizations" (διανοί[αϲ ...] καὶ πράξειϲ καὶ [προϲω]ποποιίαϲ, 14.26–8, 15.3–6). He considers ποίημα "the first of the three divisions" (πρωτεύ[ει]ν τ[ῶν] εἰδῶ[ν], 15.27–8), and since the arrangement of the language could scarcely occur before selection of the subject matter, he likely means that verbal composition ranks above subject matter as the most essential element of poetry qua poetry. Neoptolemus' separation of ποίηϲιϲ from ποίημα reduces to two categories Aristotle's list of the four component parts shared by tragedy and epic – plot (μύθοϲ, based on action or πρᾶξιϲ), character (ἦθοϲ), thought (διάνοια), and language (λέξιϲ). As a result, λέξιϲ is now separated off from the other three, which fall together into one category, and style thus becomes, in a reversal of Aristotle's ordering, the category of primary importance.

Etymologically, ποίηϲιϲ should mean the process of composing poetry and ποίημα the object so created, the poetic composition itself. Conceptual difficulty ensued, however, when ποίηϲιϲ and ποίημα began to be treated as different aspects or kinds of texts, rather than action and product. For instance, the Stoic Posidonius of the first half of the first century BCE defines ποίημα as "metrical or rhythmical language that exceeds prose form with elaboration" and gives a line of Euripides as an example; ποίηϲιϲ he defines as "ποίημα with meaning, containing an imitation of divine and human affairs" (D.L. 7.60 = F 44 EK). For Posidonius, as it seems, the two terms are interrelated, the ποίημα being a verbal and metrical building block of the more complex ποίηϲιϲ. Similarly, in refuting Neoptolemus, Philodemus views ποίημα as potentially nothing more than a poetic passage, such as the first thirty lines of the *Iliad*, while the ποίηϲιϲ is the epic as a whole, that is, a "web" (ὕφη) or interweaving of the many ποιήματα or ἔργα, "units of poetic work" (14.12–17, 31–6 Mangoni).

For some Hellenistic thinkers, the ποίημα could be an independent composition with its own semantic coherence, defined by its brevity. Lucilius (338–47 Marx 1904) defines the *poema* as a *pars parva*, such as an epistle (presumably in verse), and the *poesis* as a complete and unified work like the *Iliad* or Ennius' *Annals*. Likewise, Varro (*Men*. fr. 398 Astbury 2002) gives an epigram of a single couplet as an example of the *lexis enrythmos* called *poema* and cites epic poems to illustrate the *perpetuum argumentum* that constitutes a *poesis*. Philodemus was also familiar with the concept of ποίημα as a short independent poem, since he specifies that "writers of epigrams and Sappho" are considered composers of ποίηcιc only in a general rather than specific sense (38.7–15 Mangoni); he means that ποίηcιc in the specific sense would refer to long poems such as epics and exclude such short ones.

The separation of ποίηcιc from ποίημα as distinct literary types on a quantitative basis – long versus short poetry – has significant implications if good verbal composition is associated with one type more than the other. Reflecting the changed nature of poetry in the Hellenistic Age, the tripartite division accommodated a broader range of what might be considered poetry, such as shorter stichic poems that do not involve narrative or action. It also provided terminology that could designate the shorter hexameter narratives, called epyllia in modern terminology, that were popular in the Hellenistic period. The privileging of verbal composition as the essential quality of poetry (its ἴδιον) provides justification for emphasizing the technical aspects of poetic production and fits well with aesthetic practice and programmatic statements found in third-century poetry.

Other information about Neoptolemus indicates that he was not only a literary theorist but also a scholar and a poet, in the manner typical of the third century. The titles of two poems survive, a *Dionysias* (F 1 Mette 1980) and *Trichthoniai*, from which we have one partial hexameter about Oceanus surrounding the earth (F 2). Like Philitas of Cos, he was a glossographer, and his treatise explaining rare words ran to at least three books (F 9). Also attributed to him are *On Witticisms* (F 8) and *On Epigrams* (F 7). In light of the identification of epigrams as ποιήματα by Varro and Philodemus, it is tempting to speculate that in the latter treatise Neoptolemus explored a theoretical basis for the new literariness granted the epigram form. He quoted there an epitaph for the sophist Thrasymachus (F 7 = Ath. 10.454f):

> τοὔνομα θῆτα ῥῶ ἄλφα cὰν ὖ μῦ ἄλφα χῖ οὖ cάν,
> πατρὶc Χαλκηδών, ἡ δὲ τέχνη cοφίη.

> His name is theta rho alpha sigma upsilon mu alpha chi omicron sigma,
> his country Chalcedon, his profession wisdom.

Athenaeus' report that the epitaph was engraved on the sophist's tomb in Chalcedon carries no weight, and πατρίc need only give his native land, not the reputed location of the grave. Athenaeus quotes it in a section on riddles, just before a passage by Castorion that refers to Hellenistic critical practice (discussed below). Neoptolemus' inclusion of the epitaph, possibly his own composition, in *On Epigrams* surely had to do with his theoretical concerns. Thrasymachus is now best known from Plato's *Republic* as a political theorist. In antiquity, however, he was famous for his Τέχνη ῥητορική (*Suda* θ 462; cf. Pl. *Phdr.* 266c, 269d, 271a; schol. Ar. *Av.* 880), and the

Suda reports that he introduced the concept of the period and colon. Thrasymachus was, then, deeply involved in the sophistical development of rhetorical and linguistic theory, and the epitaph, as an illustration of the building blocks of speech, demonstrates this expertise, or τέχνη, perhaps with allusion to his famous treatise. The hexameter consists of the first elements of language, that is, letters, spelled out as syllables. When pronounced together, they form the οὔνομα "Thrasymachus," which can be understood both as the deceased's "name" and in the grammatical sense of "word" or "noun," one of the parts of speech from which sentences are formed. With letters, syllables, and words illustrated in the first line, the pentameter gives two examples of cola, the building blocks of periods, of which the couplet as a whole could be viewed as an example. From the perspective of grammatical theory, the epitaph constitutes a period that illustrates the letters, syllables, words, and clauses from which it is composed, and ends by naming the linguistic or rhetorical art that is the goal of combining these elements (cf. Plato's similar analysis of grammatical art in *Crat.* 424e–5a). From the perspective of Neoptolemus' poetic theory, however, it offers a basic ποίημα – a single couplet forming an epigram. Philodemus reports, intriguingly, that Epicurus' close friend Metrodorus discussed Thrasymachus' τέχνη in the first book of his Περὶ ποιημάτων in which he argued against another writer on ποιήματα (*Rh.* 2, Cols. 49.27–51.1 Sudhaus 1892: 85–7 = 1895: 42.14–43.12). We might speculate, then, that Thrasymachus' linguistic theories somehow foreshadowed Neoptolemus' own analysis of the poetic art and that inclusion of the epitaph was an acknowledgment of that. Certainly, it illustrates the potential for even the briefest of ποιήματα, when composed with expert, technical knowledge, to provide not only complex information but also poetic pleasure.

Callimachus' programmatic statements fit remarkably well with the new emphasis on ποίημα, as the poetic division focused on the poet's technical skill. His rejection of ἓν ἄεισμα διηνεκές, "one continuous song," in many thousands of lines on kings and heroes (cf. *perpetuum argumentum*, Var. fr. 398 Astbury; *perpetuum carmen*, Ov. *Met.* 1.4; Hor. *Ars* 146–7) is associated, in the flow of the *Aetia* prologue, with his accusation that his critics, the Telchines, judge poetry not by "art" (τέχνηι) but by a measure of length called the Persian chain (fr. 1.3–5, 17–18 Pf.). The implication is that the essence of poetry lies in its verbal artistry, within the confines of manageable subject matter. Here issues of style are intertwined with length and content because the third-century debate about poetics involved the opposition between those who continued the Aristotelian emphasis on plot and character as developed in drama and epic and those who turned the focus to the stylistic component (λέξις), which could be more artfully demonstrated in small poems or free-standing parts of larger ones. Such an understanding of Callimachean poetics against the theoretical background of third-century criticism obviates modern scholarly debates about whether his quarrel with the Telchines was about length, genre, or style, and suggests that Callimachus' passion was to prize poetry away from the Aristotelian emphasis on subject matter and to center it on linguistic practice. Such a view is supported by his treatise criticizing the Peripatetic theorist Praxiphanes (fr. 460 Pf.) and by the presence of Praxiphanes' name in the list of Telchines provided by the Florentine scholiast to the *Aetia* prologue. According to this scholiast, the Telchines "found fault with [Callimachus] because of the thinness of his short poems" (τὸ κάτισ[χνον τῶν ποιη]μάτων, 8–9 Pf.). The new division of the poetic art may also illuminate another scholiast's remark that Callimachus was forced to write the *Hecale* by the critical accusation that he could not compose a μέγα ποίημα (schol. *h.* 2.106 = test. 1 Hollis). Since this poem was a short epic of perhaps about a thousand lines (Hollis 2009: 337–40), the term ποίημα, which eventually became the standard way to refer to a single book of Homer, is apparently used in a specific sense. The challenge to Callimachus was not to write a full-scale epic, which would be a ποίηcιc, but to demonstrate his skill at refined language in a ποίημα of sustained length.

It is more difficult to assess Neoptolemus' third category, that of ποιητήc. In vehemently accusing him of illogicality, Philodemus fails to clarify Neoptolemus' thoughts on this division of the poetic art. Horace relies on Neoptolemus, however, in an early section of the *Ars Poetica* (Brink 1963) where he discusses the poet's technical or natural capacity (*vis*) with reference to subject matter (*sumite materiam vestris, qui scribitis, aequam viribus*, "you writers should choose a subject equal to your powers," 38–9) and style (*cui lecta potenter erit res, nec facundia deseret*, "eloquence will not desert the writer who chooses a topic within his capacity," 40–1), divided into arrangement (*ordo*, 42–5) and word choice (*verba*, 46–72). In all likelihood, then, Neoptolemus' discussion of the ποιητήc in his tripartite division focused on the poet's "technical skill and compositional capacity," or τὴν τέχνην κ[αὶ τὴν] δ[ύν]αμιν, as Philodemus phrases it (14.5–7 Mangoni). It was through this skill and capacity that the elements of the other two divisions could be realized – the linguistic substance of the text (ποίημα) and the ideas expressed therein (ποίηcιc).

Perhaps in reaction to the complexity of the tripartite scheme, there developed a simpler, dual division of the poetic art, which excluded the poet. Just after his discussion of Neoptolemus in *On Poems* 5, Philodemus presents a certain "one of the Stoics," whose name has been read as Aristo (16.28–30 Mangoni). If this is the correct reading, he is likely Aristo of Chios, a student of Zeno, and an independent thinker; he rejected both logic and physics and concerned himself only with ethics (D.L. 7.160–4). This Aristo, as I will call him, made a dual categorization of the poetic art, dividing it into thought (διάνοια) and stylistic composition (cύνθεcιc). The order of Philodemus' discussion suggests that he considered Aristo's dual division a reaction to, or improvement upon, the tripartition theorized by Neoptolemus, although their relative chronology is unknown. While in many ways analogous to the separation of ποίηcιc from ποίημα, the διάνοια–cύνθεcιc division avoids the confusing use of the terminology to refer to longer versus shorter poems and eliminates the complication caused by the parallel category of ποιητήc. While the tripartition is often acknowledged in later sources, the simpler opposition of thought to style also becomes commonplace in the late Hellenistic and imperial eras.

The Euphonist Critics

The poetic theorists called κριτικοί are known to us primarily through Philodemus' *On Poems* and to a lesser extent through another Epicurean work preserved at Herculaneum, Demetrius of Laconia's *On Poems*, written about 100 BCE (Romeo

1988). Chrysippus' *Against the Critics* and Aristo's adaptation of the doctrine of euphony (21.10, 21.16–17, 23.26–33 Mangoni) indicate that some critics' views on the aesthetic quality of poetry were known before the middle of the third century. In the second century, Crates of Mallus revised the earlier work of the critics for his own poetic theories, and it may have been Crates' sympathetic treatment of them, from a quasi-Stoic perspective, that provoked the interest of loyal followers of the Garden. The critics focused their attention on the category of ποίημα, which was furthered subdivided into arrangement (cύνθεcιc) and diction (λέξιc). Philodemus claims, however, that what unites them, what "remains as if engraved on a *stele* for all the critics" (παρὰ πᾶcι μὲν ὡc ἐν cτήληι μένει τοῖc κριτικοῖc) is that "the supervening euphony is the unique characteristic" (τὸ τὴν μὲν ἐπιφαινομένην εὐφωνίαν ἴδιον εἶναι) of poetry, while "the ideas and phrases must be considered external and common" (τὰ δὲ νοήματα καὶ τὰc λέξειc ἐκτὸc εἶναι καὶ κοινὰ cυνάγεcθαι δεῖν; *P.Herc.* 1047 + 1081 + 1676, Col. 17.2–9 Sbordone, p. 253). For these euphonists, the desired effect of poetry was the pleasure of hearing beautiful sound, a physical sensation in the ears; it was thus a purely aesthetic, "irrational pleasure" (χάριν τὴν ἄλογον, 83.24–5 Janko), independent of thought. Other aspects of a poem were considered "common," shared with other speech acts, but the euphonic component was the peculiar poetic feature, the basis on which a poem was to be judged *qua* poem. While this separation of the sound of poetry from the meaning of its words may seem extreme to us, as it did to Philodemus, the development of the euphonist theory should be understood within the literary problematic of the third century. Since prose writers had largely usurped the traditional role of poets as purveyors of the truth, what was left to poetry was to delight its audience, through the pure beauty of sound. The poet was an expert in how to put together language, a wordsmith, and the job of the critic was to establish criteria by which to judge whether a poet had succeeded or failed to produce a pleasing composition.

Andromenides is probably the earliest identifiable euphonist (named in Phld. *Po.* 1, 131.2–3, 132.24–5 Janko; Demetrius of Laconia *On Poems* 1, 14.7–8 Romeo 1988; Hsch. ε 3231). He has clear Peripatetic affinities and shares with Aristotle an interest in high-style poetry – that concerned with gods and heroes – but he also knows and accepts the tripartite division of the poetic art. His particular concern was choice of diction (ἐκλογή). Much like Theophrastus in his *On Style* (D.H. *Comp.* 16 = F 688 FHSG), Andromenides believes that good poetry is dependent on the use of words that are naturally beautiful, or luminous (λαμπρόc; cf. Arist. *Poet.* 1460b4–5 where the term describes ornamental diction and Hermog. *Id.* 1.9 where luminosity is an aspect of thought that produces grandeur). The job of the poet is to move the soul by appealing to the sense of hearing through beautiful diction. At the same time, diction should be appropriate to its content, and luminous words are well suited to the stories of gods and heroes. Philodemus' quotations or paraphrases from Andromenides illustrate his views: "poets are suited to working out the language and vocabulary"; "for human beings there exists by nature attention to and instinctive kinship with the Muses, as revealed by the lulling to sleep of children by illiterate song"; and "beautiful effects of words exist for the hearing as do luminous (λαμπρά) letters, and from the quality and quantity of letters are produced the beautiful effects" (131.5–132.2 Janko). While the idea of a natural human affinity for poetry is easily recognizable as an Aristotelian heritage, Andromenides' emphasis is on the emotional, comforting effects of lovely sound, as the comparison to simple lullabies indicates.

Another passage attributed to Andromenides by Janko reveals his unusually metaphorical language, which tends to explain the aural effects of poetry through synaesthesia (181.4–19 Janko):

> The composer of fictional narrative (ψευδορήμονα) must choose (ἐκλέγειν) not only words exotic to the mouth (ξενός[τ]ομα) but also very beautiful ones, and the most beautiful are those having syllables densely woven (ἐcπαθημένα[c) with many letters, and the mouth must grasp onto euphonious ([εὐη]χῆ letters and hurl weighty (ὀγκώδεις) syllables made of very luminous sounds; and the most luminous is lambda, for it is the most beautiful and the peak of luminosity and gleaming.

Here Andromenides provides the reader the sensation of the "exotic to the mouth" with his unique compounds (ψευδορήμονα, ξενόcτομα), the heavy feel of densely woven consonant clusters with his word choices (ἐcπαθημέναc), and the quasi-visual effect of lambda's gleaming brilliance with his repetition of that letter (ἀ[λλ]ὰ λαμπρότ[α]τον εἶναι τὸ λάβδα, καὶ γὰρ κά[λλιcτον κ]αὶ τοῦ λαμπρο[τάτου] κορυφαῖον). Elsewhere the same critic makes explicit the visual quality of sound by claiming that "ears seem to hear heroic bodies" (τὰc ἀκοὰc δοκεῖν ἡρωϊκῶν cωμάτων ἀκούειν, 171.2–4 Janko) when the poet "marshals his language out of pure colors" (τ[ὴν] γῆρυν ἐξ εἰλικρινῶ[ν] χρωμάτων cυντάξηται, 170.24–171.1). Andromenides, as it seems, explains further that in the Homeric line "braids which were plaited with gold and silver" (πλοχμοί θ', οἳ χρυcῶι τε καὶ ἀργύρωι ἐcφήκωντο, *Il.* 17.52) the luminous exists not in the mention of gold and silver but in the dense sound of πλοχμοί "braids" and ἐcφήκωντο "plaited" (producing a spondaic line) (23.27–24.12; cf. 185.13–186.3 Janko). It is significant that πλοχμοί, a Homeric *hapax*, appears next in Apollonius of Rhodes (*Arg.* 2.677), where it refers to the "golden locks" of Apollo, who carries a "silver bow." It is just the type of word that delighted Philitas and other early Hellenistic glossographers. What becomes evident from these precepts preserved by Philodemus is that scholarly study of diction also functioned as a form of poetic criticism in the third century and so influenced poetic practice. Apollonius' motivation for alluding to this Homeric passage with πλοχμοί and the references to gold and silver was perhaps not just to display his learnedness but also to adorn his verse with sounds of epic splendor, to convey the "pure colors" of Apollo's dawn epiphany through the sound supervening on his diction.

Another euphonist critic discussed in *On Poems* is Heracleodorus, for whom, if we follow Janko's reconstruction, poetic excellence lay not in the choice of beautiful words, but in arrangement (cύνθεcιc). Heracleodorus (named in Col. 201.23 Janko; *P.Herc.* 1074 + 1081 + 1676, fr. n Sbordone, p. 221; Col. 3.28 Sbordone, p. 225; Col. 24.28 Mangoni) seems to have been opposed to the views of Peripatetic critics such as Andromenides since he rejects the idea of generic distinctions. The following fragments show this: "[There is] not one epic [style], one tragic, another iambic, and another comic or whatever some people say" (192.13–17 Janko); "it is not possible for generic kinds to be differentiated" (193.1–3). He thus disavows, it appears, the doctrine of styles, with appropriateness for certain genres, which existed as early as the fifth century in its simplest form of the grand style and the more bookish or technically polished plain style (O'Sullivan 1992). He rather advocates a mixture of generic forms and levels of diction, and even went so far as to consider the prose writings of Demosthenes, Xenophon, and Herodotus to be ποιήματα, "poetic texts" (197R.19–25 Janko). In Heracleodorus' view, the poet's task is not the construction of thought, common to other forms of communication, but the arrangement of rhythms and words to produce poetic pleasure through beautiful sound. This critic's means to prove that sound alone is the source of poetic effect is metathesis, the re-arrangement of words to show that the emotional appeal of poetry disappears when the word order is altered. As an example, he points out that the lovely Homeric line ἔϲπετε νῦν μοι, Μοῦϲαι Ὀλύμπια δώματ' ἔχουϲαι (*Il.* 16.112) is deprived of its beauty when rearranged as ἔϲπετε Μοῦϲαι Ὀλύμπια δώματα νῦν μοι ἔχουϲαι (38.28–39.5 Janko). Citing another Homeric line, τὼ μὲν ἀναρρήξαντε βοὸϲ μεγάλοιο βοείην (*Il.* 18.582), the same theorist credits it with a quality that Janko reconstructs as "sonority" (λιγυροτάτηι), destroyed when the words are re-ordered (40.7–14). Metathesis, which became a common critical tool in the early Hellenistic period, continued to be used well into the imperial era (Demetr. *Eloc.* 185; D.H. *Comp.* 4, 7; "Longin." *Subl.* 39.4; De Jonge 2005).

There are a number of correspondences between the views attributed to Heracleodorus and the innovative practices of third-century poets. The rejection of rules for genres is strikingly close to the position of Callimachus, who in *Iamb* 13 defends himself against criticism of his πολυείδεια, or composition in multiple genres and dialects (Janko 2000: 164). The fragments of this critic's views thus give us an ancient theoretical precedent for the "mixture of genres" that has long been an established element in modern analysis of Hellenistic poetry. In addition, his claim that content has nothing to do with the ἴδιον of poetry, provides a theoretical support for the phenomenon of reworking prose treatises of a scientific or technical nature into verse, as in the didactic poets Aratus and Nicander. I call attention as well to a text in which the critical tool of metathesis is incorporated into poetic practice. Castorion of Soli, a poet of the early Hellenistic period, composed a *Hymn to Pan*, of which we have the opening lines (*SH* 310):

ϲὲ τὸν βολαῖϲ νιφοκτύποιϲ δυϲχείμερον
ναίονθ' ἕδραν, θηρονόμε Πάν, χθόν' Ἀρκάδων,
κλήϲω γραφῆι τῆιδ' ἐν ϲοφῆι πάγκλειτ' ἔπη
ϲυνθείϲ, ἄναξ, δύϲγνωϲτα μὴ ϲοφῶι κλύειν,
μωϲοπόλε θήρ, κηρόχυτον ὃϲ μείλιγμ' ἱεῖϲ.

You who dwell in a wintry home struck by blasts of snow,
the land of the Arcadians, Pan the herder of wild beasts,
I will celebrate in this learned text where I have arranged
words renowned to all that are hard for the uneducated to understand,
Muse-tending beast, you who send forth a wax-molded melody.

Athenaeus (10.454f–455a) preserves the lines in his section on literary puzzles, just after the Thrasymachus epitaph, because each of its iambic trimeters consists of three segments of 11 letters that can be rearranged without changing the meaning.

By specifying that he has "arranged in this learned text words … hard for the uneducated person to understand," Castorion alerts the reader acquainted with contemporary poetic theory to the game he is playing with metathesis. Peter Bing (1985) has shown that any re-arrangement of the metrically equivalent segments produces a harsh collocation of sounds, such as a clash of sigma's or nu's. What now becomes clear is that Castorion is self-consciously poeticizing the practice of metathesis, which critics used to demonstrate an excellent arrangement producing beautiful sound. The poet expressly invites the reader to perform the test of excellence on his own poem and arranges his verses to facilitate that process. The result is proof of his poetic expertise, since the poem is to be judged stylistically good, while the invitation to judge also demonstrates the poet's learned knowledge of critical theory.

Pausimachus of Miletus, known only from Philodemus (Janko 2000: 165–6), continued the euphonist emphasis on good sound but modified the approach of Heracleodorus. Playing down the importance of arrangement, Pausimachus located the ἴδιον of poetic beauty purely in εὐηχία, "good sound" (*P.Herc.* 994 W.24–6 Sbordone, p. 15). Explaining that it is insufficient simply to analyze the successes and failures of poets, as through metathesis, Pausimachus criticizes earlier euphonists for not explaining systematically what they mean by good and bad sound (*P.Herc.* 994 frs. 14.25–11.11, as joined and quoted in Janko 2000: 165 n.4; cf. 80.6–20 Janko). In Janko's reconstruction, Pausimachus contributed a detailed study of sounds at the level of letters, syllables, and words, accompanied by critical analysis of exemplary passages. In the view of this critic, broad vowels such as alpha, eta, and omega are more beautiful than closed ones like iota, and he praises words that combine broad vowels with liquids, especially lambda. He argues that sound governs word choice and gives examples from Homer, such as κίονα μακρήν, "long column," which he claims Homer chose for its broad vowels to create aural pleasure. Another example is πλατεῖ Ἑλληcπόντωι, "wide Hellespont," used even though the strait is narrow (103.12–21 Janko) because syllables combining stops and lambda, as in πλατεῖ are especially lovely. He attaches great importance to onomatopoetic words, such as Homer's ὑλακτεῖν and μυκᾶcθαι (perhaps also τρίζειν and cίζειν, as Janko conjectures, 106.6–10), which "move the hearer" by reproducing through the physical sensation of "tickling" the ears (γαργαλιcθῆναι, itself onomatopoetic) the experience being described (49.5–10 Janko). The more unattractive sounds also have, then, a poetic role in physically conveying to the reader certain types of subject matter, as he advises the poet to "try to [produce] imitations of content" (49.26–8).

For Pausimachus, the poetic experience is entirely conditioned by sound, which moves us to sympathetic engagement even against reason. From birds, especially the nightingale, he draws an analogy to the good poet who is "naturally talented" and who succeeds because he has an affinity for producing sounds suggestive of his subject; he seems to have held that poets with less innate ability can learn to compose through τέχνη, as parrots imitate articulate speech without understanding (114.19–115.23 Janko; cf. 100.3–6). He concludes that excellent poets can compose in any genre because genres are conventional, but poets compose by nature when "they name their subject by finding sound that is noble, primary, and entirely fitting" (117.16–21). With Pausimachus, the euphonist tradition reached its most extreme point, through the denial of any poetic value in content and even the rejection of art as an essential component in the poet's skill. Like Heracleodorus, he was such a radical exponent of ψυχαγωγία that for him not even prose writers should aim at the truth rather than pleasing the many (49.1–5 Janko).

The question of poetic sound, which lies at the heart of euphonist theories of composition, is often the subtext in passages of Hellenistic poetry that seem to address issues of genre, style, and content. To return to the *Aetia* prologue, we may note that Callimachus' rejection of long compositions "on kings and heroes" places him in critical opposition to the early euphonist theory of diction, apparently Andromenides', which pertains to epic subject matter (ἥρωcι κα[ὶ] βαcιλε[ῦcι] πρεπωδέcτερον, "more appropriate for heroes and kings," 170.18–19 Janko). Callimachus' imagery for the poetry he rejects is the long flight of cranes from Egypt to Thrace or the far bow shot of the Massagetae against the Medes; in contrast, he offers the simple statement that "nightingales are sweeter" (fr. 1.13–16 Pf.). If the issue were merely the length of poetry, the nightingale image would be a non-sequitur. The point seems to be rather that, however we want to understand the cranes and the Massagetae, as examples of distance or epic subjects or allusions to specific poems, they do not as images exemplify the essential poetic quality of beautiful sound (for the harsh sound of cranes, see Lucr. 4.181–2 = 910–11); it is in this sense that nightingales are sweeter. While the loveliness of the nightingale's song is represented by Callimachus' melodious ἀ[ηδονίδεc] ... μελιχρ[ό]τεραι (still the best conjecture, fr. 1.16 Pf.), the onomatopoetic word for the harsh sound made by both cranes and the bow, κλαγγή, is absent from Callimachus' text, to be supplied by the reader's knowledge of Homer (e.g., *Il.* 1.49, on Apollo's bow, and *Il.* 3.3, 3.5, on cranes battling Pygmies). A few lines later, Callimachus tells us expressly that some poets produce unpleasant and harsh sounds, like the braying of the ass (ὀγκήcαιτο, fr. 1.31). The word for braying is here chosen to suggest the weightiness, or ὄγκοc, of the grand style (cf. ὀγκώδειc cυλ[λαβάc], "weighty syllables," 181.12–13 Janko). It is an appropriate word for its purpose because it features the ugly short "o" sound as well as a harsh consonant cluster combining a guttural with nasalization (as in the absent κλαγγή). Callimachus prefers a style of more studied polish, with a charming sweetness of sound. In a fragment of *On Poems*, a euphonist, perhaps Heracleodorus, attributes to Homer "sonority and musicality" (λιγυρότητα καὶ ἐμμέλειαν), qualities he associates with that poet's "winged words" (*P.Herc.* 1677, 6.21–2, 7.3–5 Romeo 1992: 196). It can scarcely be unrelated that Callimachus claims for his song the "sonorous sound" (λιγὺν ἦχον) of the cicada and describes himself as "the small one, the winged one" (fr. 1.29–30, 32 Pf.).

A principal theme of bucolic poetry, as it develops from Theocritus' *Idylls*, is the beauty of song, particularly in terms of its relationship to the sounds of nature. In the pseudo-Theocritean *Idyll* 8, which likely belongs to the late third century, the goatherd who judges (κρινεῖ, 25; κρίνειν, 29) the singing match between Daphnis and Menalcas declares Daphnis the winner on the following basis (82–3):

ἁδύ τι τὸ cτόμα τοι καὶ ἐφίμεροc, ὦ Δάφνι, φωνά·
κρέccον μελπομένω τευ ἀκουέμεν ἢ μέλι λείχειν.

Sweet is your mouth and lovely your voice, Daphnis;
hearing you sing is better than licking honey.

To decide the contest on the basis of the pleasing sweetness of Daphnis' song would unavoidably evoke, for Hellenistic intellectuals, the critical practices of the euphonists. In particular, the emphasis on the physical pleasure of hearing through the synaesthetic comparison to taste (emphasized by the aural similarity in μελπομένω … μέλι) recalls euphonist argumentation. For instance, Dionysius of Halicarnassus argues that not all words affect the ear in the same way but produce sweetness or bitterness, roughness or smoothness, "just as not all visible objects affect in the same way the perception of sight, or tasted objects the perception of taste or other stimuli other forms of perception" (*Comp.* 12). An even more elaborate example of synaesthesia occurs in the Theocritean passage that is the model for *Idyll* 8.82–3. The goatherd of *Idyll* 1 compliments Thyrsis on his song by wishing that his month be full of honey or sweet figs since he sings better than a cicada (146–8). He then gives him a carved wooden cup, saying "see how sweet it smells" (149). Here we have taste, sight, and smell as the aesthetic equivalent of lovely sound. Another important model for the poetic judging in *Idyll* 8 comes from the fifth *Idyll*, where Morson declares Comatas the winner over Lacon, but without expressly stating the basis for his judgment. In his last song, however, Comatas has just boasted of his own superiority by proclaiming that "a nightingale should not compete with magpies or hoopoes with swans" (5.136–7). Morson apparently accepts Comatas' judgment, based on an analogy of human singers to birds. The passage strongly suggests that Pausimachus' comparison of the nightingale, as the emblem of the poet naturally talented in producing beautiful sound, to the parrot, as an emblem of the less talented composer who must rely on mimicking others through art, develops euphonist discussions known already to Theocritus.

Another point of intersection between bucolic poetry and euphonist criticism involves onomatopoetic words. A theory of word origin in imitation of natural sounds is found in Plato's *Cratylus* (423b–c) and was further developed by the Stoics. Working from a derivation of onomatopoeia as a "coining of words," Demetrius (*Eloc.* 94) claims that many such words are "uttered in imitation of an emotion or action," and he gives as examples cίζε and λάπτοντες, both from Homer (*Od.* 9.394, *Il.* 16.161). Pausimachus advised poets to attempt imitations of their subject matter (49.26–8 Janko) and posited that the hearer was stimulated by imitative words "on account of their similarity to the experience of the [ears]" (106.13–14 Janko). The Theocritean corpus famously opens with an onomatopoetic imitation of the sound of the syrinx, a feat that Demetrius (*Eloc.* 185) claims also for Plato's reference to the herdsman's pipe (*Rep.* 399d). In *Idyll* 1.1–3 the sound pattern dominated by π, τ, and c replicates the aural similarity between the song of the whispering pine and the goatherd's piping, while the anaphora in ἁδύ, ἁδύ points to pleasure as the goal of their music, as it is of bucolic poetry in general. A bucolic scholiast points out that the key word ψιθύριcμα, "whispering," is onomatopoetic, chosen for "its particularity of sound as mimetic of voice" (1c). In defining it, through a false etymology from ψίω and θύρα, as "sounding out in the ears some thin sound (λεπτὸν ἦχον ἠχεῖν) like 'pssss' at doors" (1d), the scholiast gives precise evidence that the "thin" style of the Alexandrians was associated with the quality of their sound.

Many of the standard onomatopoetic words cited in ancient sources appear in Theocritus and his successors, often to provide a harsher-sounding counterweight to the prevailing sweetness of sound produced by long alpha and omega, and by the combination of liquids with voiceless stops. Theocritus, for example, juxtaposes two of these imitative words in *Idyll* 6.29 – cίξα δ' ὑλακτεῖν, "I hissed [to a dog] to bark" – to convey something of the Cyclops' harsh character (on the use of rough letters such as ξ, ζ, c, and even ρ, see Phld. *Po.* 2, *P.Herc.* 994, Col. 33.3–8 Sbordone, p. 103). Another passage filled with sonorous imitation of nature is Theocritus' description of the sounds produced by insects and birds during the Thalysia. In introducing the scene, Theocritus describes the lovely gurgling of the water flowing from the nymphs' cave with a half line taken from *Il.* 21.261: κατειβόμενον κελάρυζε (*Id.* 7.137). Significantly, a critic identified by Janko as Pausimachus discusses the sound of this very Homeric passage, an effect he attributes largely to the onomatopoetic κελαρύζει (107.26–108.21 Janko; cf. schol. Theoc. *Id.* 1.1d, Hsch. κ 2139–41). In adapting the Homeric phrase, Theocritus appears to be signaling, by allusion to a critical tradition followed by the euphonists, his own creative use of imitative sound in the lines to follow. Another example comes from Moschus' *Europa*, a poem that throughout displays evidence of attention to the type of sweet sound favored by the euphonist critics. When Europa is enchanted by the white bull that is Zeus in disguise, touches him all about, wipes the foam from his mouth, and kisses him, he "moos gently" (μειλίχιον μυκήcατο), like the "sweet sound of a Mygdonian flute" (αὐλοῦ Μυγδονίου γλυκὺν ἦχον, 97–8). Here Moschus enhances the sound-sense of the standard onomatopoetic word μυκᾶcθαι by further conveying the animal noise it imitates through the alliteration in μ supported by the gutturals γ, κ, χ and assonance in sonorous υ.

Another well-known passage from Theocritus alludes, I suggest, to the euphonist interest in cύνθεcιc as a vehicle for conveying beautiful sound. In the third and last scene on the goatherd's cup in the first *Idyll*, a boy who guards a vineyard sits on a rock wall weaving a grasshopper's cage as foxes plunder the fruit and plot to steal his lunch. In Theocritus' words (52–4):

> αὐτὰρ ὅγ' ἀνθερίκοιcι καλὰν πλέκει ἀκριδοθήραν
> cχοίνωι ἐφαρμόcδων· μέλεται δέ οἱ οὔτε τι πήραc
> οὔτε φυτῶν τοccῆνον ὅcον περὶ πλέγματι γαθεῖ.
>
> He plaits a lovely grasshopper's cage by fitting together rush
> with flowering asphodel, and he pays no notice to his wallet
> or to the plants since he takes such great joy in his plaiting.

The boy has often been interpreted as an emblem of the poet, and certainly weaving may stand for poetic composition, just as tuneful insects were associated with song. I believe there is here a more specific allusion to Hellenistic theories of poetic art. The words πλέκει and πλέγματι evoke the technical usage of words from the same root, such as πλοκή and cυμπλοκή, to refer to ordering of letters or words (as in Phld. *Po.* 1, 80.7 Janko; D.H. *Comp.* 2, 16). In addition, ἐφαρμόcδων recalls the use of ἁρμονία for melodious arrangement (Theophr. F 691 FHSG = D.H. *Isoc.* 3; cf. Phld. *Po.* 1, 117.19, 131.14–15 Janko; D.H. *Comp.* 2–3). The grasshopper, playing the same role here as do the nightingale and the cicada in the *Aetia* prologue, likewise points to euphonist theories. A parallel is offered in *Idyll* 7.39–41, where Simichidas professes that in poetic skill he is inferior to Philitas and Asclepiades as a frog is to grasshoppers (βάτραχος … ποτ' ἀκρίδας ὥς τις); a scholiast's comment that grasshoppers "pipe harmoniously" (συρίζουσιν ἐναρμόνιον, 41b) points to the insect's connection with musical harmony. For knowledgeable ancient readers, then, the harmonious plaiting of rush and asphodel would emblematize good poetic composition, as the grasshopper who will occupy the "lovely" cage would represent the sound that supervenes upon it. Vergil reworks this image at the end of the *Eclogues* to close his own textual plaiting: "this will be enough for your poet to have sung, goddesses, while he was sitting and plaiting a basket from slender marsh mallow" (10.70–1). Servius explains, using technical terms, that Vergil "means allegorically he has composed (*composuisse*) in the thin style."

Stoic Uses of Poetry and Allegorical Interpretation

Another dominant trend, contrasting sharply with that of the euphonists, emphasized the didactic utility of poetry. The Stoics provided much of the theoretical basis for this view, which found in poetry moral instruction and even accurate information about the nature of the universe. According to a Herculaneum papyrus (*P.Herc.* 403, fr. 4.12–18, quoted by Mangoni 1993: 251–2), the true Stoics held that a beautiful poem was one containing wise thought and a good poet was the maker of such poems. Uncovering the particular Hellenistic manifestations of Stoic critical practice is difficult, however, since the views of the major philosophers in the early Stoa are known only in fragmentary form. It is clear, however, that etymology and allegory played an important role in Stoic exegesis from the time of Zeno of Citium, the founder of Stoicism, even if the more sustained form of allegorical interpretation was a secondary development.

The early Stoics were more interested in literary topics than their contemporary Epicureans, were because they found interpretive ways of reading poetic texts in accordance with their own philosophical beliefs (Ramelli and Lucchetta 2004: 79–203). Among the known writings of Zeno are *On Styles*, *Homeric Problems* in five books, and *On the Reading of Poetry* (D.L. 7.4); he also wrote on Hesiod in an unrecorded work (Cic. *ND* 1.36 = *SVF* 1.167). The fragments of his literary criticism suggest that he brought a Stoic approach to scholarly problems, particularly the interpretation of epic passages. As a general principle, Zeno taught that Homer "composed some things in accordance with opinion (κατὰ δόξαν) and some things in accordance with truth (κατὰ ἀλήθειαν)," in order to show that the poet did not contradict himself in passages of seemingly oppositional content (Dio Chrys. *Or.* 53.4–5 = *SVF* 1.274). It appears that Zeno believed some parts of Homer to be directly accurate and others composed in accordance with the primitive understanding of the era (cf. Cic. *ND* 2.63 = *SVF* 1.166). Strabo reflects this view in an important passage (10.3.23):

> Every discourse about the gods investigates ancient opinions and myths (δόξας καὶ μύθους), since the ancients hid in riddles their physical understanding of affairs and

> always imposed myth on their discourses. It is not easy to solve all the riddles accurately, but ..., though some (myths) agree with each other and others are contradictory, one could successfully conjecture the truth (τἀληθές) from them.

The Stoic method of solving the riddles in earlier myth was allegory, which was already in use in a certain strand of Homer interpretation and in ritual practice, as shown by the Derveni Papyrus (Obbink 2003). Etymology was a favorite device for revealing that the divine figures of early poetry represented the physical nature of the universe as the Stoics understood it. Zeno interpreted Hesiod's *Theogony* in this way, since he argued, for instance, that χάος stands for water, one of the elements forming the universe, through a derivation from χέεσθαι (*SVF* 1.103). Cleanthes, who is credited with a treatise about Homer entitled *On the Poet* (D.L. 7.175), created even more extravagant etymologies. He rewrote as one word – ἀναδωδωναῖε – part of Homer's phrase Ζεῦ ἄνα, Δωδωναῖε, "lord Zeus, of Dodona" (*Il.* 16.233), and explained that his new compound referred to exhalation (ἀνάδοσις) of air (i.e., Zeus) from the earth (Plu. *Mor.* 31d–e = *SVF* 1.535). He also supported his interpretation of Atlas as "unwearying" divine providence by rewriting his Homeric epithet ὀλοόφρων, "destructive-minded," with a rough breathing, as if it were derived from ὅλος, "whole," and φρήν, "mind," to signify the divine thought pervading all (schol. *Od.* 1.52 = *SVF* 1.549). Similarly, in his *On the Nature of the Gods* Chrysippus accommodated the poetry of the earliest poets – Orpheus, Musaeus, Homer, and Hesiod – to Stoic belief in the pantheistic presence of the divine by interpreting the gods as synonymous with physical features of the universe (Cic. *ND* 1.39–41 = *SVF* 2.1077). Among the early Stoics, only Chrysippus is known to have made a sustained allegory, that of a painting on Samos. In his infamous reading, the depiction of Hera fellating Zeus represents the diffusion of seminal reason into matter (*SVF* 2.1071–4). Scholars have often focused on the question of whether the early Stoics believed that information about the physical universe was *knowingly* encoded in mythical stories by philosophers or poets living in a primitive age (Long 1992; Boys-Stones 2001: 28–43 and 2003a). What seems clear, however, is that the Stoics, at least the early ones, were working from a belief in a divine λόγος that pervades everything, including the mythical language of poetic texts and artistic depictions. The surviving etymologies and allegories rather monotonously identify gods with basic elements such as water, air, and fire or find yet another reference to the rational principle controlling all.

Some Stoic thinkers of the Hellenistic Age still found poetic expression useful for conveying their philosophical beliefs. From the perspective of Stoic criticism, these were likely considered "good" poets who composed "beautiful" poetry. Aratus' *Phaenomena* begins with a tribute to Zeus as pervasively present, revealing to mortals beneficial signs, including the constellations. In Cleanthes' *Hymn to Zeus*, the phrase διὰ πάντων (*CA* 1.12) not only expresses the god's pantheistic presence throughout the universe but also etymologizes his name. For Cleanthes, as reported by Philodemus in *On Music* (142.5–14 Delattre 2007 = *SVF* 1.486), philosophical prose had a sufficient capacity to explain divine and human matter, but since it was unadorned, it lacked a poetic style appropriate for conveying divine grandeur. In Cleanthes' view, meter, melody, and rhythm more effectively bring the hearer to contemplation of the divine in accordance with the truth (cf. Sen. *Ep.* 108.10 = *SVF* 1.487). This surprisingly strong belief in the utility of poetry for the philosopher is related to the Stoic belief in the power of music to move the soul toward virtue and to guide the intellect (vigorous opposed by Philodemus in *On Music*). It helps to explain Cleanthes' own verse production. Though Chrysippus apparently did not compose poetry, he filled out his hundreds of prose treatises with citations from lyric and dramatic poets as well as early epic. He copied out practically all of Euripides' *Medea* in his *On the Soul* (D.L. 7.180), where he argued for the heart as the seat of an undivided soul in which emotions and reason interact (Galen, *On the Doctrines of Hippocrates and Plato* 3.3.13–18 De Lacy 1978 = *SVF* 2.884–90; Gill 1983, 1996: 226–36; Dillon 1997). He offered as evidence for this Stoic concept Medea's process of decision making in her monologue (Eur. *Med.* 1021–80), not an allegorical reading. As suggested by Chrysippus' *Against the Critics*, the Stoics were interested in the usefulness of poetry in terms of its content, whether that was straightforwardly truthful or obscured by the conventions of the age in which it was composed. Poetic expression was of concern only to the extent that it could enhance the cognitive or ethical message (Nussbaum 1997).

More extended allegorical readings of Homer were conducted by Crates of Mallus in the second century. His Stoic credentials have been disputed, but Hesychius calls him a "Stoic philosopher" (κ 2342 = T 1 Broggiato 2001) and Panaetius is said to have been his student (Str. 14.5.16 = T 21). In the Stoic manner, he identified the gods with natural elements, such as Zeus with the sky (F 131 Broggiato) and Apollo with the sun (schol. A *Il.* 18.240 b = F 26). Borrowing from the third-century poet Moero, he interpreted the πέλειαι, "doves," that bring ambrosia to Zeus in *Od.* 12.59–65 as the constellation of the Pleiades (Ath. 11.490e = F 59). What underlay these interpretations of specific passages was Crates' belief in Homer's πολυμαθία, or wide understanding of natural principles discovered by scientists only much later (Str. 3.4.4 = F 75). He attributed to Homer the understanding that the universe was a sphere with the earth at its center, the view of most Hellenistic scientists; this cφαιροποιία, as it was called, refers to Homer's re-creation of the cosmic sphere in poetic form (Phld. *Po.*, *P.Herc.* 1074 + 1081 + 1676, Col. 2.23–5 Sbordone, pp. 223 = F 99 Broggiato; Geminus 16.21–8 = F 37). To establish this interpretation, Crates explained Homer's description of Agamemnon's shield (and probably Achilles' shield as well) as a μίμημα τοῦ κόcμου (schol. bT *Il.* 11.40 b = F 12). Related was his interpretation of the scene in which Hephaestus is thrown from heaven as an attempt by Zeus to measure the universe (*Il.* 1.590–3). Since the sun's crossing of the sky in one day was equal to the duration of Hephaestus' fall, it was proven that the universe is equally distant horizontally and vertically (Heraclit. *All.* 27.2–4 Russell and Konstan 2005 = F 3); this of course would prove its sphericity. In his reading of the passage, Crates also employed an etymology. He derived the problematic word βηλόc, normally understood as the "threshold" from which Hephaestus was tossed to earth, from ἧλοc, "nail head," to associate it with the nail-like appearance of the stars in the sky (F 21).

Our most complete record of a Hellenistic allegorical interpretation of Homer comes from a work entitled *On Nestor's Cup* by Asclepiades of Myrlea (Pagani 2004). This scholar of the first half of the first century BCE offered a thorough explanation of Homer's description of the famous gold cup (*Il.* 11.632–7), much of which is preserved in Athenaeus (11.489c–94b). Asclepiades explains that those of the ancients who ordained for humans the equipment of civilized life, through their belief in the spherical shape of the universe, developed "vivid mental images" (ἐναργεῖc φαντacίαι, 11.489c) from the sun and moon, from which they produced round tables, tripods, and circular loaves. In "imitation of the cosmos" (μίμημα τοῦ κόcμου, Ath. 11.489d), they also made cups. But Nestor's cup is special because it had upon it stars, which Homer compares to nail heads (ἥλοιc), and doves, by which Homer means the Pleiades who offer to humans signs of the agricultural seasons. Asclepiades' debt to Crates is thus clear. The passage continues with increasingly strained interpretations based on philological arguments, including the claim that the cup was adorned with not two or four doves as usually assumed, but six to match the number of visible stars in the Pleiades. It is indisputable, then, that by the first century BCE, one strand of poetic interpretation sought to find in Homer – through etymology, philological contrivance, and allegorical interpretation – evidence that the earliest Greek texts are true sources of knowledge, expressed in the forms available to the poets of that age.

We have been tracking the Hellenistic use of allegorical interpretation in establishing the didactic benefits of poetry. It is important to note, however, that the practice of what was called "allegory" was a widespread phenomenon that often served other literary goals. The term ἀλληγορία, in its general sense, designated a stylistic trope common to both poetry and prose (Innes 2003: 19–20). In *On Rhetoric* 4 (Col. 3.20–2 Sudhaus 1892: 164; Cols. 22.24–5, 23.18–25 Sudhaus 1892: 181) Philodemus describes allegory as a figure akin to metaphor and divides it into riddle (αἴνιγμα), proverb, and irony. What unites these three species of allegory is that more is meant than what is said (cf. Quint. *Inst.* 8.6.44, ἀλληγορία . . . *aliud uerbis, aliud sensu ostendit*). Demetrius finds the trope of allegory useful in his various styles – in the elegant style to produce wit (*Eloc.* 151) and in the forceful and grand styles to produce shock and fear (99–102, 243, 282–6). As a favorite example, he cites the threat of the Syracusan tyrant Dionysius to the Locrians that their cicadas would sing to them from the ground, which, as Demetrius says, is more fear-inspiring in its cryptic brevity than an explicit threat to denude their land of trees (99, 243). Demetrius points out that allegory was used in the mysteries, like "darkness and night," to provoke "shock and shuddering" (101). He recommends avoiding a succession of allegories so that the "language does not become a riddle (αἴνιγμα)" (102; cf. Cic. *de Orat.* 3.167). Quintilian (*Inst.* 8.6.44–7) defines the trope as sustained metaphor and gives a series of useful examples from Latin poetry: Horace's ship of state (*Carm.* 1.14; cf. Heraclit. *All.* 5.5–9 Russell and Konstan 2005, on Alcaeus), Lucretius' claim to wander upon the "untrodden places of the Pierides" (1.926–7 = 4.1–2), and Vergil's veiling of his own persona in the bucolic figure of Menalcas (e.g., *Ecl.* 10.20). Clearly, then, allegory in its simpler form was a type of imagery commonplace in Greek and Latin literature and was considered an effective adornment for enhancing literary speech. The interpretive practice that provoked controversy was finding sustained allegory in texts where it was far from obvious that any had been intended, in order to use the authority of literature to authenticate truth claims. Philodemus in *On Poems*, for instance, condemns those, like Crates in his *sphaeropoeia*, who understand that the signified content of the *Iliad* begins with the word μῆνις but still desire that the poet present other meanings; he even considers "clearly mad" those who try to show that the *Iliad* is about the physical nature of the universe or laws and customs by identifying heroes and gods with celestial bodies or organs of the body (*P.Herc.* 1074 + 1081 + 1676, Cols. 2.18–3.14 Sbordone, pp. 223, 225).

Allegorical imagery was used by many Hellenistic authors. Greek models for Quintilian's examples of Latin allegory include Callimachus' image of the "untrodden places" in the *Aetia* prologue (e.g., τὰ μὴ πατέουσιν ἅμαξαι τὰ στείβειν, "to go on the tracks not trampled by wagons," fr. 1.25–6 Pf.) and the identification of the bucolic poet with the cowherd, as in Bion fr. 10 Gow 1952a or the *Epitaph for Bion*. It is altogether likely, then, that Hellenistic poets thought of their programmatic imagery, in which they self-consciously reflected their own poetic choices, as, technically, allegory. The treatise *On Tropes* ascribed to Tryphon (first century BCE; West 1965) cites as an example of allegory (1.1 West = Spengel 1856: 3.245) a passage from *Iamb* 5 in which Callimachus bids a pederastic school teacher to contain his flame from blazing forth and to hold back his horses from a second running of the chariot race (23–9). In offering his addressee this erotic "riddle" to solve, Callimachus expressly names himself a prophetic Bacis, a Sibyl, an oracular laurel and oak (31–3). Other poetry of the era displayed a more sustained, "enigmatic" form. The *technopaignia* are of this sort. The reader must decode the riddling language to understand what object is described, and the visible shape on the page provides a clue to solving the riddle. All descend to us with scholia in which the cryptic language is translated into the true meaning. The most sustained example of allegorical composition in the Hellenistic period is Lycophron's *Alexandra* (Sens in this volume). The messenger who reports Cassandra's inspired prophecies to Priam characterizes them with language descriptive of the strongest forms of allegory: she "mimics the speech of the black Sphinx" (7), and the king must "pursue the ill-spoken paths of her riddles" where a "learned track guides that which is in darkness" (10–12). In the figure of Cassandra, Lycophron may be presenting an image of the god-inspired poet, flinging out a torrent of words and driven by *enthousiasmos*. The "mad" poet, such as Horace's Empedocles who thinks he will become a god (*Ars* 453–76), was often mocked in an age that preferred the learned art of the technically proficient composer. Ps.-Longinus, however, seems to reflect a contrary stand of critical thought in which authors could be so inspired by older poets of natural talent that they speak with like grandeur of style. His model for such inspiration is the Pythia's experience of issuing prophecies as a result of inhaling divine vapors (*Subl.* 13.2). In Lycophron, Cassandra ends her ranting prophecy by predicting that, although her words will be of no "benefit" (ὠφελεῖν, 1459) to her homeland because they will be disbelieved, in time everyone will learn of their accuracy. This is a basic claim made by those practicing the strong form of allegorical interpretation for early poetry – that mythical language conceals underlying truths understood by wise men only in the fullness of time. The *Alexandra* can thus be read, metapoetically, as an allegorical text that self-consciously challenges its reader to decode the ancient inspired predictions of mad Cassandra from the later perspective of known history.

Other Hellenistic authors seem to encourage allegorical readings of their texts. For instance, a scholiast explains the embroidered figures on Jason's cloak in Apollonius'

Argonautica (1.721–68) as referring to "cosmic order and the deeds of human beings"; in addition, Athena is said to have given him the cloak because "the cosmos came about through divine intelligence" (schol. 1.767). Such interpretations were perhaps influenced by allegorical readings of Homeric objects, such as Crates on Agamemnon's shield and Asclepiades on Nestor's cup. It is also possible that the Stoic idea of manufactured objects reflecting the wisdom of primitive men about the universe is related to Hellenistic interest in poetic ecphrases, like Jason's cloak, with evident symbolism. If so, Crates' concept of cφαιροποιία was perhaps not so unique, but had precedents in earlier Hellenistic critical thinking.

Yet other poets represented dramatically the process of interpreting the more sustained αἰνίγματα. Many of the ecphrastic epigrams preserved in the *Greek Anthology* dramatize the process of "reading" a work of art to unravel the figure depicted and its attributes. In a few, the art object was created as a figure of allegory. For instance, in an epigram by Posidippus (142 AB = 19 GP = *AP* 16.275), Lysippus' statue of Kairos speaks in dialogue with a viewer to explain his peculiar physical appearance and the sculptor's purpose in making him, namely, to offer διδαcκαλίη, "instruction." A series of epigrams that represent a passerby attempting to decipher the symbols placed on a grave monument (*AP* 7.421–9) seem to function differently, to interrogate the reliability of allegorical exegeses and so of its didactic utility. In one such epigram, by Alcaeus (16 GP = *AP* 7.429), a passerby thinks of various explanations for the two phi's (διccάκι φεῖ) engraved on a gravestone, before deciding that they must indicate the burial of a poor woman named Pheidis, meaning "phi twice," but also suggesting "Thrifty." In self-satisfaction, he proclaims himself an "Oedipus" who has solved "riddles of the Sphinx," praiseworthy for working out an αἴνιγμα that is "light to the wise and darkness to the unwise." What the reader does not know is whether the clever interpretation of the emblems, that they representing a linguistic game with letters and a name should be construed as correct (Gutzwiller 1998: 268–70). It is certainly possible to read the passerby's triumphal boasting as mimicking the misplaced confidence of an allegorical critic.

Synthetic Approaches

To summarize, this survey has shown that Hellenistic literary theory struggled at its core with a debate about whether ψυχαγωγία or διδαcκαλία was the proper goal of literature. This debate descends from dichotomous reactions provoked by Plato's challenge to the conventional view of poetry as a source of knowledge and a basis for moral education. One response was to refocus on technical expertise as the province of the poet, independent of the truth or falsehood of content, as in euphonist criticism, which judged poetry in terms of the material, aesthetic pleasure it gave. The other response, given a theoretical basis by the Stoics, continued to defend poetry as utilitarian and instructive, differentiated from prose treatises through its reliance on such tools as etymology and allegory. To the modern mind, this privileging of pleasure or instruction, form or content, seems overly simplistic, and throughout the Hellenistic period some literary theorizers attempted more synthetic analyses. The theorists discussed in Book 5 of Philodemus' *On Poems* may have been selected to represent this more moderate or synthetic approach which Philodemus himself championed, and it is fitting that we conclude with a survey of his final book.

First, let us review the current thinking about the contents of *On Poems*. In Books 1 and 2, Philodemus discusses primarily the euphonists, who are criticized for their focus on how poetic form affects the recipient. The less well preserved Books 3 and 4 take up questions of genre and engage with Aristotelian principles, including whether the concept of *mimēsis* is an adequate means of defining the poetic. It is not unreasonable to surmise that Philodemus discussed in the first two books those theorists who privileged form and then in the next two those focused on content, such as the earlier Peripatetics. Book 5 contains summaries with refutation of the major ideas advanced by several literary thinkers. The surviving portion of the book appears to be organized by philosophical schools: first the Academics, then Peripatetics, next Stoics, and finally the Epicurean reaction. Although it is unclear whether the theorists are presented in chronological order, there does appear to be a progression of thought, as if each thinker was responding to the one before. The central question addressed is the nature of poetic excellence (ἀρετή) with subsidiary questions about the intended effect of poetry (ὠφελία or ἡδονή) and the proper divisions of the poetic art, a topic that involves the relationship between subject and style. In short, Book 5 offers a brief history of what Philodemus may have considered the best or most important theories about the nature of poetry.

Because the name Heraclides twice appears (3.14–16 Mangoni) in the first section of *On Poems* 5 yielding any readable text (1.1–12.9), a number of scholars, starting with Jensen (1936, correcting his 1923 attribution to Neoptolemus; cf. Mangoni 1993: 36–44; Janko 2000: 137–8), have attributed all or part of that material to Heraclides of Pontus. This fourth-century follower of the Academy, who later attached himself to Aristotle, wrote numerous works on literary and musical topics, including *On Poetic Art and the Poets* and *On Genres* (D.L. 5.87–8). Philodemus' presentation of ideas that look back to Plato's criticisms of poetry supports the identification of Heraclides as one opponent, and we know that Philodemus discussed Heraclides in the lost Book 3 of his *On Music* (138.5–7 Delattre). In *On Music* 4 (49.1–20, 137.27–138.4 Delattre), he reports that Heraclides was interested in what melodies were appropriate for what types of (dramatic?) character and how musical practice shapes dispositions toward virtue. Here in *On Poems* 5, he discusses his opponent's position that a poet both pleases and benefits his audience (3.3–32 Mangoni), apparently with moral virtue as the goal. He objects that, according to Heraclides' argument, the most useful poetry would be the best (4.21–4) and that Heraclides excludes from excellence the most famous poets because their poetry lacks utility. He also points out that his opponent has laid upon the poet the burden of having accurate knowledge of various technical disciplines, such as geometry, geography, and navigation (5.11–6.1). The views here attributed to Heraclides suit well an attempt to accommodate Plato's complaints against traditional poetry and yet salvage a social role for verse by assigning an educative and moral value to certain types of music and poetry.

After a brief lacuna, Philodemus reports that the same theorist (as it seems) prescribes as a requisite for both the poet and his art a concise preconception of his subject and plausible, clear development of thought (6.12–19). Philodemus' following remarks indicate that this opponent made a division of poetic styles (7.25–8.34), like the four χαρακτῆρες of Demetrius or the three *genera loquendi* known from Roman sources. In addition to the preceding poetic qualities, the opponent mandated, for his first stylistic category of poems that are very solid and rather substantial (ϲτερεώτατα καὶ μείζω), the qualities of richness (πολυτελῶϲ) and weight (ἐμβριθῶϲ), not commonness (εὐτελῶϲ) and lightness (ἐλαφρῶϲ). These qualities are attainable because the poet draws raw material (ὕλη) from an abundant supply of personages (πρόϲωπα) and ethical traits (ἤθη) as well as unique stories (μύθοι) and plots (ὑποθέϲειϲ), chosen for their truth and novelty. The opponent's second or "intermediate" type of poem likewise required some richness (πολυτελεία) and had plot. The third type, which the opponent apparently did not commend, was common (εὐτελέϲ) and light (ἐλαφρόν), lacking unique narrative, plot, truth, and individuality. The preferences behind this categorization of literary styles are strikingly reminiscent of the views that Callimachus assigns to the Telchines, who championed lengthy poetry on epic themes and muttered against his "slender Muse" (Μοῦϲα λεπταλέη, fr. 1.24 Pf.). In turn, Callimachus defends his style by vaunting his role as the "small" cicada (οὐλαχύϲ, fr. 1.32). Philodemus worries that the poems favored by his opponent, if they lack forcefulness, would not differ from the swollen or bombastic (ὀγκώδεϲιν, 8.14), just as Callimachus rejects the bombastic braying of the ass (ὀγκήϲαιτο, fr. 1.31) and criticizes Antimachus' *Lyde* as a "fat and unclear" composition (παχὺ ... καὶ οὐ τορόν, fr. 398 Pf.). Behind the literary quarrels of Callimachus and his contemporaries seem to lie, then, the critical theories of philosophers such as Heraclides. Philodemus ends the section in agreement with his opponent, arguing that excellent poets, such as Homer and Sophocles, are more than just good composers because they also incorporate thought through their selection of subject matter (10.20–3). He thus signals his own belief in the importance of content for good poetry.

In the next section, on Peripatetic theorists (12.10–13.32 Mangoni), Philodemus accepts the contention that the best poet should excel more or less equally in subject matter, in character portrayal, and in style, but he criticizes the Peripatetics for not distinguishing the poet from mime writers or other prose authors who also excel in these categories (cf. Arist. *Poet.* 1447b2–4; Hordern 2002b on Demetrius of Laconia's treatment of Sophron's prose mimes). After mentioning Praxiphanes, against whom Callimachus wrote a prose treatise, and Demetrius of Byzantium, who held elegant (ἀϲτείωϲ) thought to be the first element of a good poem followed by appropriate word choice and then a beautiful execution of style, Philodemus turns to Neoptolemus' tripartite division of the poetic art, discussed above. At the end of the passage (16.4–28 Mangoni), Philodemus comments on Neoptolemus' claim that the perfect poet, identified with Homer, provides not only enthrallment (ψυχαγωγία) but also benefit and edifying instruction, the origin, it seems, of Horace's famous endorsement of the *utile* mingled with the *dulce* to both delight and advise the reader (*Ars* 343–4). Philodemus' complaint is that Neoptolemus does not make clear what sort of benefit derives from poetry, though Philodemus surmises it is philosophical wisdom or other forms of knowledge. Again, he seems to have chosen theorists who found some way of accommodating both form and content.

There follows the Stoic, likely Aristo of Chios (16.28–24.22 Mangoni), whose dual division of the poetic art was discussed above. Aristo provided a Stoic perspective on the question of how to judge poetry. Poetry was to be judged as (1) good, (2) neither good nor bad, or (3) bad, a division derived from the Stoic idea that all things are good, bad, or indifferent. In his synthetic approach, the interaction of the thought and the composition determines the overall value of the poem. A poem that falls into the category of good has both good content, which means that it contains fine thoughts and actions and aims at education (17.14–20), and good or artful composition, which includes the "euphonies of the critics" (21.16–17). Aristo's Stoic orientation is evident in his category of the absolutely good poem, which would, presumably, be the poem written by a sage, and Philodemus complains that no poet has ever written or will ever write such a poem (17.20–4). A poem may be classed as bad simply on the basis of faulty composition (21.1–5), and he condemned some poems of the ancients as absolutely bad, apparently on the basis of content, even though their composition was meritorious. It appears, then, that the category into which would fall actual poems commonly judged to be of superior quality would be the intermediate one, neither good nor bad.

Aristo was a great admirer of Antimachus, apparently for both his technical precision and his "educational" content (παιδευτικά, 17.24–31). In this, he followed Plato, who reportedly so admired Antimachus that he sent Heraclides of Pontus to Colophon to collect his poetry (Call. fr. 589 Pf. = Procl. *in Ti.* 21c). Aristo finds original or ingenious explanations for mythical material in Antimachus, whose use of narratives as "consolation" to soothe his grief for his beloved in the *Lyde* suggests that his educational value lay partly in ameliorating passion, thus countering the arousal of emotions to which Plato objected. Diogenes of Babylon's claim that one benefit of music was to soothe the pains of love (Phld. *Mus.* 4, 129.1–4 Delattre) may contribute to our understanding of why Antimachus was appreciated by certain Hellenistic poets, such as the erotic epigrammatists Asclepiades (32 GP = *AP* 9.63) and Posidippus (9.1–2 GP = *AP* 12.168.1–2; Gutzwiller 1998: 157–69 on his Stoic inclinations). In Aristo's analysis, Antimachus' poetry modeled the "therapy of desire" that was the general goal of Hellenistic philosophy. Aristo's emphasis on the importance of euphony with its musical qualities, indicating acquaintance with the critics, may not be far from Cleanthes' view that sound clarifies the grandeur of thought. It appears that Aristo managed to integrate an analysis of poetry in terms of content and form with Stoic views of how the rational mind cooperates with irrational perception to form judgments that lead toward virtue.

Next comes a summary refutation of the views of Crates (24.23–29.23 Mangoni), who is Philodemus' intermediary source for earlier poetic criticism, just as the Stoic Diogenes is his intermediary in *On Music*. While some of Crates' interpretations of Homer reflect Stoic allegorical readings, his views on judging poetry, that is, what he wrote as a κριτικός, blend the focus on style and euphony typical of the euphonist critics with Stoic views on language as a natural system. In opposition to certain philosophers (perhaps early Epicureans) who based literary judgment on conventions that vary from one group to another (25.2–30 Mangoni), Crates argues for a standard of judgment based on a rational method of composition involving art, that is, a λόγος that constitutes a single, universal principle of language use independent of genre, meter, or other poetic variables. This overarching principle involved euphony, which could be created in any poem through the proper combination of sounds. Crates' focus on letters, discussed more fully in lost parts of Book 2 (29.7–18 Mangoni), points to his grounding in the Stoic theory of natural language, which underlies his acceptance of, and interest in modifying, euphonist views.

A key doctrine for Crates is that, although pleasure comes from poems through hearing, "a poem is to be judged good not whenever it pleases the hearing but whenever it is realized in accordance with the *logos* of art" (ὅταν κατὰ τὸν τῆϲ τέχνηϲ λόγον ἐνεργηθῆι, 28.2–4 Mangoni). Unlike the earlier critics, Crates does not base poetic judgment on the irrational faculty of hearing, despite the fact that sense perception was the means through which the pleasure of poetry was received; for him, judgment should be directed to the artistic acts of the composer. Likewise, he objects to judging the contents of poetry, although contents remain essential to poetry qua poetry (in opposition, for instance, to music), because he understands content to be pre-existing thought, not that which the poet creates in his art. Crates wants to exclude from poetic judgment both the irrational element of hearing, since hearing might find pleasure in accidental euphony, and the cognitive assimilation of meaning, since the utility of the thought is not a specifically *poetic* effect, so that judgment is directed only to the poet's activation of artistic principles (28.19–29 Mangoni). In doing so, Crates is shifting from judgment based on the reader's response, whether that be to the pleasure of hearing or the usefulness of content, to judgment based on the poet's skills. It is not surprising, then, that he, "like Andromenides" (and like Neoptolemus), agrees with the tripartite division of the poetic art into ποίηϲιϲ, ποίημα, and ποιητήϲ (132.23–7 Janko), since this division allows judgment to be directed, through analysis of both style and content, to the creative artist. Despite Philodemus' attempt to link Crates with some extreme views of the critics, it is clear that his theory of poetic judgment was one of the most sophisticated and synthetic of the Hellenistic era. The great attention given in *On Poems* to the euphonists and Crates' sympathy for them indicates Philodemus' desire to respond, from an Epicurean perspective, to this critical theory with its (partially) Stoic underpinnings.

Philodemus' own views on poetry, to the extent that we can reconstruct them, are also synthetic. Throughout *On Poems*, as in *On Music*, he prefers to refute his predecessors rather than to argue his own theoretical positions. This approach is likely rooted in Epicurean practice, which developed from the master's relative indifference to music and poetry. Epicurus considered music to be simply sound that could give physical pleasure, lacking in intellectual content, and likewise he found no philosophical utility in poetry. For the Epicurean master, a theatrical performance was an enjoyable experience (Plu. *Mor.* 1095c), but literary criticism was a waste of time. Later Epicureans took poetic and musical theory more seriously, at least in part in order to refute the falsehoods that they found in other philosophers. Zeno of Sidon, an eminent scholar at Athens who taught Philodemus and whose lectures Cicero attended, was respected for his acute intelligence and clarity in interpretation (Cic. *Ac.* 1.46, *Fin.* 1.16, *Tusc.* 3.38). In the Epicurean manner, he made a list of thirteen *doxai* encapsulating the principal views of others about poetry. Philodemus reproduces these as the closing section of Book 5 (29.23–39.14 Mangoni), with refutations that also likely emanate, at least in part, from Zeno.

It is because of the nature of the Epicurean approach, then, that Philodemus' statements of his own opinions so often concern what he does not like. He does not believe that poetry has any natural utility in either diction or content (25.31–4 Mangoni). In this, he stands opposed to the Stoic attempt to enlist poetry in the service of teaching wisdom. He considers "clearly mad" those who think the *Iliad* means something other than what it says (*P.Herc.* 1074 + 1081 + 1676, Col. 2.25–6 Sbordone, p. 223). For Philodemus, the goal of poetry is pleasure, and this point of agreement with the euphonists is likely one reason that he takes them so seriously. He disagrees, however, with the fundamental euphonist belief that sound produces a physical sensation of pleasure without any cognitive component. Analogously to the "mad" Stoic allegorizers, the euphonists, he says, become downright Corybantic in their enthusiasm for the effects of sound on the hearer (*P.Herc.* 1074 + 1081 + 1676, fr. c, Col. 2.5–13 Sbordone, p. 201; cf. Col. 181.1–4 Janko). For Philodemus, thought is an essential component in poetic pleasure. Musical rhythm, he believes, may produce in the ears an irrational physical pleasure, but the sounds of language do not (26.29–27.2 Mangoni). As he says elsewhere in *On Poems*, "verbal arrangement is the particular quality of poets, not being essential and praiseworthy in itself, but rather because it presents thoughts by which [poets] lead the soul (ψυχαγωγοῦcιν), not taking them from anyone else but creating them from themselves" (*P.Herc.* 1074 + 1081 + 1676, Col. 17.19–27 Sbordone, p. 253). The latter part of this comment signals disagreement with one of the *doxai* listed by Zeno which encourages the poet "to imitate well the works of Homer and other poets similarly handed down" (33.24–8 Mangoni). This principle of writing well by imitating earlier authors took hold in the theoretical thought of the imperial period ("Longin." *Subl.* 13.2–14), and is evident already in the late Hellenistic period, for instance, in the imitation of Theocritus in bucolic poets or in the epigram variations by Antipater of Sidon and Meleager (Gutzwiller 1998: 227–322). Perhaps reacting to a contemporary trend, Philodemus sets in opposition the idea that poets should convey through verbal composition compelling and original thought.

Since for Philodemus there is no natural utility in diction or thought, the underlying goals for creating poetic excellence are two: to imitate in poetic diction language that benefits by teaching the useful and to participate in the thought that lies between the wise and the vulgar (26.1–7 Mangoni). The first part of this directive indicates that ultimately Philodemus approves of poetry that brings some instruction in addition to its strictly poetic qualities, and there may be a degree of support here for didactic poetry such as that of Lucretius. The second part of the directive looks toward the Epicurean idea of common "preconceptions" about good and bad poetry as a basis for judgment. For Philodemus as an Epicurean, poetry should not provide hidden meanings that offer wisdom only to the enlightened elite, nor does it simply provide physical pleasure from the beauty of well-arranged letters and words. Poetry is rather something accessible to all and subject to judgment that can be commonly held, without a specialized knowledge of conventions as a standard of excellence. In justifying pleasure as a response to poetry that both moves the soul and provides instruction, *On Poems* modifies to only some degree Epicurus' disinterested interest in poetry while it also provides a sophisticated defense to the views of other literary theorists.

FURTHER READING

A history of Hellenistic literary criticism remains to be written. Pfeiffer 1968 is mostly concerned with Hellenistic scholarship, and Kennedy 1989: 200–19 is now quite inadequate. More useful are Fantuzzi and Hunter 2004: 449–61, and Sider 1997: 24–39, 2004 on Philodemus' poetic theory in relationship to his epigrams.

Although much important scholarship on Philodemus, especially *On Poems*, has been completed in recent years, the situation remains somewhat chaotic, and difficult for the non-specialist. With the aid of new technologies, improved editions with translations and commentaries are being published through the Philodemus Translation Project, edited by D. Blank, R. Janko, and D. Obbink. To date there have appeared only *On Poems* 1, Janko 2000, which includes a history of the papyri and discussion of the theorists analyzed in Books 1 and 2, and *On Poems* 3–4, Janko 2011, on genre and Aristotle's theories of drama. Although not universally accepted (Asmis 2002), Janko's reconstruction of the text and identification of Philodemus' opponents is fundamental. Sbordone's 1976 edition of the papyri preserving *On Poems* 2 (and 3?) has been superseded in parts by publications listed in Janko 2000: 12–13. Jensen's 1923 edition of *On Poems* 5 has been replaced by Mangoni 1993, with English translation in Armstrong 1995. Greenberg 1955, with translations from Book 2, should be used with caution because many readings have been improved. The following editions of *On Poems* are in progress: Janko for Book 2 and D. Armstrong, J. Fish, and J. Porter for Book 5. Important for Philodemus' aesthetic thought is Delattre's 2007 edition of *On Music* 4. Sudhaus' 1892/6 and 1895 editions of *On Rhetoric* have been replaced for Books 1–2 by Longo Auricchio 1977; for translation of these books, see Chandler 2006, partially based on Blank's forthcoming edition.

There exists a growing body of scholarship, editions in some cases as well as articles or books, on individual Hellenistic theorists and on philosophical approaches to literature. On Eratosthenes' writings, see Geus 2002. Neoptolemus of Parium has been edited by Mette 1980; for the theories of Neoptolemus, see Brink 1963: 43–78; Asmis 1992c; Mangoni 1993: 53–61; and Porter 1995. On Andromenides, Heracleodorus, and Pausimachus, see Janko 2000: 143–89. For the *kritikoi* as materialists, see Porter 1995: 133–42; for sound and sense in Philodemus' discussion of the euphonists, Asmis 2004; and for the Classical background to euphonism, Porter 2004.

For Stoic use of allegory and etymology, see Whitman 1987: 31–47; Most 1989; Long 1992; Boys-Stones 2003a; Ramelli and Lucchetta 2004. For allegorical readings more generally, see Dawson 1992a; Struck 2004; Russell and Konstan 2005: xiii–xxvii. For Aristo, see Ioppolo 1980: 256–78; Asmis 1990; and Porter 1994. Crates of Mallus has been edited, with Italian translation and commentary, in Broggiato 2001; discussion of his poetics also in Mette 1936 (with the fragments); Asmis 1992a; Porter 1992: 85–114; and Janko 2000: 120–34.

On Epicurean poetics, see Asmis 1991, 1992b, and 1995. The fragments of Demetrius of Laconia are collected in Romeo 1988. The essays in Armstrong, Fish, Johnston, and Skinner 2004 demonstrate the importance of Philodeman studies for Latin poetry.

CHAPTER TWENTY-FOUR

Philosophy after Aristotle

Stephen A. White

Philosophy attained full maturity in the fourth century, and its institutionalization established an Athenocentric orientation that endured through most of the Hellenistic period. At Socrates' death in 399, philosophy had no permanent base, nor any substantial literature. Still largely an avocation pursued among likeminded friends, it was confined mainly to homes, gymnasia, and similar retreats. By 322, when Aristotle followed his pupil Alexander to the shades, it had come of age, both studied and taught as a distinct professional discipline with its own set of methods and aims. Thanks principally to a pair of centers for advanced study, Athens had become its capital. Plato's Academy, a private estate beside a suburban sanctuary from which it acquired its name, had grown into a thriving school under his successors; and Aristotle's Lyceum, associated with another suburban shrine, was already a friendly rival though barely a dozen years old. These two centers, the minds they attracted, the work they fostered, and the libraries they housed, mark the acme of ancient philosophy as we know it. That is in part a tribute to the genius of their founders. But it is also an accident of survival: the works from the following three centuries that eclipsed their influence for generations are almost entirely lost. For philosophy, far from faltering in the Hellenistic Age, exploded with intense creative energy, spawning an enormous literature, captivating cities and courts around the vast Hellenic realms, and acquiring a steadily larger role in the acculturation of Greeks and foreigners alike. By the end of our period, philosophy is fluent in other tongues, most notably Cicero's Latin. When Octavian entered Alexandria after Actium, at his side was one of the city's leading philosophers, the Stoic Arius, in whose honor, reportedly, he spared the new jewel in Rome's imperial crown (Plu. *Ant.* 80).

Orientation

The boundaries of philosophy have always been flexible and porous. The label, apparently a fifth-century coinage that initially had very broad scope, was hotly contested. Inquiring minds and intellectuals of various stripes laid claim to it from the start: learned scholars and polymaths, "sophists" and teachers, scientists and logicians, even Isocratean advisers and orators. But by the end of the fourth century, a formal demarcation of its terrain had gained a currency that would persist throughout antiquity. Like Gaul, Hellenistic philosophy had three parts: physics, ethics, and logic. Physics, the study of the natural world as a whole and in its manifold parts, encompassed cosmology, theology, and metaphysics as well as special sciences such as biology, geology, and meteorology. Ethics, the study of human conduct, character, and value, addressed both normative and psychological issues, both theoretical and applied, and for both individuals and groups, from households to cities and empires. Logic, the study of language, reasoning, and knowing, covered mainly formal logic (standardly called "dialectic") and epistemology but also grammar, rhetoric, and literary criticism. Many philosophers ranged even more widely, into history (political, cultural, literary), anthropology, biography, mathematics, and more, not to mention poetry and public affairs.

It was not only by subject matter that philosophy defined its boundaries. After all, its vast domain overlapped and intersected with many other disciplines. More to the point, it had distinctive methods and aims. The universalizing impulse apparent in its all-encompassing three fields reflects its central ambition: nothing less than a theory of everything, formulated in clearly defined and rigorously argued terms. Its regulative norms demand dispassionate inquiry governed by objective canons of evidence (observation, correlation, corroboration) and reasoning (semantic precision, formal validity, systematic explanation). Adherence to these norms could hardly ensure accuracy or understanding any more than it does today. But they were the newly articulated rules of a game that had truth and universality as its primary objectives.

The methods of conceptual analysis and logical argument that we can see evolving in Plato's dialogues reach maturity with Aristotle and his colleagues. At Aristotle's death, the discipline called "philosophy" addressed many of the same basic questions using many of the same basic methods as philosophers do today. Serious pursuit of these questions required substantial training and leisure, and it gained strength in numbers. The upshot was a "reflective" (*theōrētikos*) and "studious" (*scholastikos*) way of life, roughly what we now call an "academic" life after its most famous base: withdrawal from politics and the marketplace in order to maximize time for theoretical inquiry and discussion. The new institutions, and the explosion of philosophical study they fostered, soon made Athens the capital for philosophers everywhere, and the impact of their work rippled steadily outward until it won over the leading minds of Rome.

Disciplines develop at their own pace, and the standard chronological boundaries fit ancient philosophy only loosely. Aristotle's death marks an epoch for us mainly because it closes our book: very little philosophical writing survives from the next three centuries. But the appearance of closure is deceptive. The Academy, under Xenocrates and Polemo, continued to explore its founder's lines of thought well into the third century. Likewise Theophrastus and Strato pressed ahead with Aristotle's encyclopedic agenda in the Lyceum, which benefited from the political authority of a star pupil, Demetrius of Phalerum. Even Cynic iconoclasm soldiered on with Theban Crates and his natural law partner, Hipparchia. But others were already raising new questions and devising new theories that would shift the direction of philosophical discussion for the next two centuries.

The impetus for change came from many quarters, but chiefly four figures, all well versed in ongoing debates, each radically innovative in similar but starkly opposed ways. Epicurus (342/1–271/0), born to Athenian settlers on Samos, was in Attica for his ephebic service by 322, having already shown a bent for philosophy by challenging his teachers to explain the origin of "chaos" in Hesiod's *Theogony*. After building a following in Mytilene and Lampsacus, he returned to Athens around 306 and established a base for "co-philosophizing" (as he calls it) on a suburban estate – the famous "garden" (*kēpos*) – near the Academy. Zeno of Citium (c.334–262/1) left Cyprus for Athens around 315. Inspired by Socratic dialogues (reportedly Xenophon's), he first sought out the Cynic Crates, then studied under Theophrastus in the Lyceum, Polemo in the Academy, as well as Stilpo of Megara and the master dialectician Diodorus "Kronos," before venturing to expound his own ideas on the edge of the agora in the Stoa Poikile, from which his followers acquired their familiar name. Pyrrho of Elis (c.365–c.275), after accompanying his teacher, Anaxarchus of Abdera, in Alexander's entourage all the way to the Indus, returned home to live out his long life with a cluster of followers attracted by his cultivation of tranquil indifference to the world around him. Story has it they had to rescue him repeatedly from wild dogs, precipices, and onrushing wagons; more likely his novel brand of ascetic skepticism inspired comic caricature. The youngest of the four innovators was Arcesilaus of Pitane (316/5–241/0), an exact contemporary of Callimachus. Trained in mathematics by his compatriot Autolycus, he too studied with Theophrastus before joining Polemo in the Academy, which he soon transformed into a bastion of critical argument, chiefly targeting Zeno's theories. The skeptical stance of his "New Academy" (as it came to be called) remained a dynamic force down to Cicero, its leading Roman proponent.

Philosophy enjoyed great prestige at the opening of the third century, and occasional assaults notwithstanding, its public stature generally continued to increase. Young minds from all around the Mediterranean – even from Carthage and Rome – flocked to Athens to study with its leading lights. In return, new outposts of Hellenism like Alexandria and Pergamum competed with towns from mainland and periphery alike to attract philosophers, if only to visit, and the subvention of their schools became a popular form of benefaction, both local and royal (Scholz 2004b). Strabo, writing at the end of our period, repeatedly gives philosophers pride of place in the catalogues of local heroes he compiles for the sites on his itinerary. But the focal points of philosophical debate gradually shifted in the first century. When Sulla laid siege to Athens in 86, denuding the original groves of Academe in the process, many of its philosophers sought safety elsewhere: the Stoic Posidonius in Rhodes, prominent Epicureans in Campania, the Academic Philo in Rome, and his neo-Aristotelian rival Antiochus in Alexandria. The ensuing diaspora undercut Athenian dominance and promoted other centers for philosophical study. It also signals a threefold shift in focus that would shape the next three centuries: a return to the texts of Plato and Aristotle that launched a growing stream of constructive exegesis; a vigorous revival of Pyrrhonian skepticism; and renewed interest in Pythagorean traditions. Hellenistic philosophy endured well into the third century CE, as Epicureans, Stoics, and Pyrrhonists proliferated around the Mediterranean. But the first century BCE inaugurates a return to earlier work that became increasingly influential in the following centuries, culminating in the magisterial synthesis Plotinus developed in Rome in the mid-third century, now known as Neoplatonism.

Texts and Sources

By the end of Aristotle's life, philosophy had accumulated a substantial literature of its own. Joining the extant works of Plato and Aristotle, numerous enough on their own, are hundreds of titles by their colleagues (attested mainly in booklists recorded by Diogenes Laertius): Heraclides, Speusippus, and Xenocrates; Theophrastus, Eudemus, Clearchus, Dicaearchus, and others; not to mention Xenophon and many fellow "Socratics." But their production, massive as it was, was dwarfed by the harvest of philosophical writing generated during the next three centuries. As the number of teachers and students grew from the dozens to hundreds and then thousands, so the production of texts increased exponentially, as we can see from a handful of extant booklists. The most prolific were Epicurus ("about 300 cylinders"; a shortlist of his "best writings" runs to over 40 titles and over 80 rolls: D.L. 10.26–8) and the Stoic Chrysippus (over 700 works: D.L. 7.180; a truncated catalogue in 7.189–202 lists 161 titles comprising over 400 rolls). But records for some of their associates (16 works, one in 22 rolls, by two Epicureans: D.L. 10.24–5; 82 works, some in multiple rolls, by two Stoics: 7.174–8) indicate that the total volume of writing was colossal – and it almost entirely vanished long ago.

What survives in its original form is swiftly catalogued: a trio of summary letters by Epicurus to his followers; a handbook of excerpts from his writings (entitled *Kuriai Doxai* or "Key Doctrines"); a short hexameter *Hymn to Zeus* by the Stoic Cleanthes; scraps of occasional verse by a few others; various pseudepigrapha preserved under the names of Plato, Aristotle, and others; and a few documents, most notably wills. A thorough census would include two treatises on botany and several short studies by Theophrastus (372/0–288/6), all or most composed after Alexander's death; essentially extensions of Aristotle's projects, they illustrate continuity, not the new trends that are the focus here. Everything else, if not entirely lost, has suffered gravely from the depredations of time. Remnants of more works by Epicurus and over 20 by later followers, most notably Philodemus of Gadara (c.110–c.40), survive on Herculanean papyri, as do scraps of a logical work by the Stoic Chrysippus (280/76–208/4); and some excerpts from Teles illustrate the stylized sermonizing of third-century "Cynic diatribe" – essentially rhetorical rather than philosophical in method and form. The rest is scattered citations in later authors, occasionally exact quotations but mainly paraphrase, more or less distorted by abbreviation or expansion, friendly, hostile, or ostensibly neutral.

Four of our later sources loom largest, and the first two, both written in Latin, fall within our period: Lucretius' exuberant hexameter presentation of Epicurean physics; Cicero's stately dialogues and treatises, typically matching Roman proponents of Epicurean and Stoic theories against Academic critics; lengthy skeptical critiques by the Pyrrhonian Sextus Empiricus (later second century CE); and the tantalizing "lives" of philosophers by Diogenes Laertius (early third century CE), roughly a third on Hellenistic figures. Many other works of Imperial date play supporting roles, most notably Seneca's essays, letters, and treatises, all rich in summary and citation; Plutarch's dialogues and essays, which include sustained critiques of Stoic and Epicurean theories; a monumental display of Epicurean texts erected in Lycian Oenoanda by an ardent follower named Diogenes; and the voluminous commentaries on Aristotle's treatises by diverse hands, from the Aristotelian Alexander of Aphrodisias (fl. 200 CE) to Neoplatonists such as Simplicius (fl. 530 CE). Also deserving mention are the discourses of Epictetus recorded by Arrian, the *Meditations* of Marcus Aurelius, detailed critiques by Galen, introductory courses on Stoic ethics by Hierocles and Stoic cosmology by Cleomedes, the magpie compilations of Aelian and Athenaeus in Greek and Aulus Gellius in Latin, polemical works by Clement of Alexandria and Eusebius, and the chalcenteric anthologist Stobaeus.

Philosophers in Action: Dialogues, Lives, Anecdotes

Philosophical writing before Plato took mainly two forms: didactic verse, usually hexameter, as in Parmenides and Empedocles; or expository prose, typically magisterially terse, starting with Anaximander and continuing through the following century. The charismatic Socrates, however, inspired a number of companions to recreate his conversational exploits by adapting dramatic techniques from mime and the stage. The resulting hybrids, conversations in prose presented either directly as scripts or embedded in narratives, acquired a new name: initially "Socratic *logoi*" and eventually *dialogoi* or "dialogues" (from *dialegesthai*, "discuss" or "converse"). Plato had many rivals in composing textual memorials to Socrates in action, but most he soon eclipsed, and for us his corpus stands almost alone, joined only by Xenophon's efforts and meager fragments of a few others. Why Plato restricted himself to this novel form is a perennial controversy, encouraged by his own writings. But two points are paramount here. Dialogue can, and in Plato's corpus usually does, highlight two essential features of philosophical practice: the dynamic interplay of question and assent or dissent; and thereby an explicit articulation of premises and inferences (whence the label "dialectic" for logic).

The motives behind this hybrid varied among its varied authors: apologetics for a condemned hero, reaching wider audiences, deflecting authorial authority, and so on. But the form itself is inherently protreptic: an invitation to engage in the practice portrayed. On the surface, dialogues purport to depict or mimic actual discussion, and as verbal mimesis, the form is continuous with other narrative and dramatic modes. But it depicts a radically different kind of activity, and in ways that reflect its protreptic ambitions: the depiction of philosophical debate induces readers and listeners to engage in philosophy themselves. To some extent, other modes achieve something comparable: ecphrasis mimics the process of observant viewing, encomium and invective an attitude of admiration or reproach, soliloquy a focused intensity of thought or feeling. But in no other mode does the text induce readers to engage in the act itself – to see or denounce or deliberate – as readers of a philosophical dialogue must do in order to follow its course and grasp the train of thought. In short, the very act of reading such dialogues is itself an exercise in philosophical thinking.

A number of shorter dialogues in the Platonic corpus are plainly spurious, and some of them probably have Hellenistic origins. No others survive from our period, apart from Cicero's in Latin, and evidence for continuing composition is scarce and mainly circumstantial. Many of Plato's associates and their colleagues employed the form: certainly Heraclides, Aristotle, Clearchus, and Dicaearchus, probably Speusippus, Xenocrates, and Theophrastus. But apart from some diehard Socratics and minor Peripatetics, dialogues are securely attested for very few after the fourth century. One by the Peripatetic Praxiphanes imagined a conversation between Plato and Isocrates "on poets" (D.L. 3.8), which makes it a likely locus of ideas Callimachus associated with his Rhodian Telchines and addressed in a *Reply to Praxiphanes* (frs. 1 and 460 Pf.; Brink 1946). Stilpo of Megara (c.360–c.280) is credited with "nine frigid dialogues," one entitled *Aristotle* and another *Ptolemy* (D.L. 2.120). But he is the last we hear of who wrote dialogues exclusively – if indeed he did, for one of his "dialogues" was entitled *To His Daughter*, and the names forming the other eight titles could signify recipients of letters or criticism too.

Stilpo's case highlights the tenuous nature of our evidence. In the later authors on whom we must rely, the term *dialogos* does not refer uniquely to dialogues (witness Seneca's ten *Dialogi*); and titles are an unreliable index of form, not least because proper names are also standard in titles for encomiastic works. Cicero, in his dialogue doubly entitled *Cato* and *On Old Age* (*Sen.* 3), cites as one of his models a discourse by Tithonus from a work by Aristo of Ceos, head of the Lyceum after 225 (or Zeno's dissenting associate, Aristo of Chios: the text is uncertain; Stork 2006: 62–5). The context readily suggests a dialogue (*sermo* in Cicero), possibly entitled *Tithonus*, or (after Aristo's teacher) simply *Lyco*, a work noted for its blend of theory and myth. Evidence for others is even more tenuous. A few works entitled *Symposium*, *Erotic Discourses*, or the like are probable suspects; similarly a *Platonicus* and *Aristo* by Eratosthenes, a student of both Arcesilaus and Aristo of Chios. But dialogues by Epicureans are unlikely; we have no firm evidence for any by Academics; and even if some of Zeno's associates composed a few, later Stoics apparently did not, perhaps on principle (Sedley 1999).

The decline of philosophical dialogue is probably due in part to the continuing popularity of fourth-century works. Cicero's efforts, which highlight their debt to Plato's and Aristotle's, are part of the Classical revival that marks the end of Hellenistic philosophy. But broader trends are also involved. Once entrenched in cultural literacy, philosophy had less need to advertise its distinctive methods, and interest shifted to supplying its larger audience with portraits of philosophers in action. Platonic dialogue seeks to capture live argument on the page, and so did Aristotle's, in which he typically took the leading role himself, speaking at length and magisterially. But the volumes of *Recollections* and *Discourses* (*Diatribai*) attested for

Zeno and others apparently shifted the emphasis from rigorous argument to moral instruction, as in the series of vignettes that make up Xenophon's *Memories of Socrates*. Antigonus of Carystus evidently did much the same in the *Lives* of philosophers he composed for many of his elder contemporaries: Pyrrho, Zeno, Polemo, Arcesilaus, Lyco, Menedemus of Eretria, and others. Unlike Hermippus of Smyrna and previous Peripatetics, who wrote mainly on earlier figures and with more historical aims, Antigonus concentrated on character and conduct, reporting revealing encounters and intellectual habits along with major events and accomplishments. Philosophical conversion was apparently a special interest: a drunken Polemo (like Alcibiades in Plato's *Symposium*) stumbling into a lecture by Xenocrates, whose imposing dignity inspires the dissolute youth to turn to philosophy (D.L. 4.16); the Academic Crantor quoting Euripides' Perseus rescuing Andromeda and the young Arcesilaus reciting her reply (D.L. 4.29).

On a still smaller scale, collections of the episodes called *chreiai* or "anecdotes" exhibited insight and character even more succinctly. As found in Aelian, Athenaeus, and Diogenes Laertius above all, they have been reworked repeatedly, often sharply condensed or freely expanded. Although some must come from Hellenistic collections, many plainly derive from continuous compositions like dialogues, "lives," or even plays. Accounts of the frugal symposia that Menedemus of Eretria hosted stem from a satyr-play by Lycophron, excerpted already by Antigonus (Ath. 419e–20c; D.L. 2.139–40); Zeno figured in comedies by Philemon and Posidippus (D.L. 7.27–8); and the stage is the likely source of an amusing story about Lacydes, head of the Academy after Arcesilaus, being fleeced by his servants (D.L. 4.59; Eus. *PE* 14.7). Extant *chreiai* involving philosophers often have edifying themes: they chastize common foibles and failings, usually with wit, sometimes stinging. But some target their ideas, often at symposia amongst illustrious company: Ptolemy Philopator trying (and failing) to confute the Stoic Sphaerus by serving him wax pomegranates (D.L. 7.177); Diodorus Kronos, with a dislocated shoulder, hearing the doctor Herophilus recite back to him his argument that nothing can move (Sext. Emp. *PH* 2.245).

Much of this work reflected encomiastic impulses. As Socrates was lionized in dialogues, so was Plato in posthumous eulogies, and traces of tributes to several Hellenistic figures survive. Epicurus in particular gave commemoration a central role in his teaching, composing memorials to his closest associates, including his own family, that were read aloud at monthly and annual ceremonies to inspire emulation of their exemplary Epicurean conduct (Clay 1998: 62–74).

Philosophers at Work: Notebooks and Treatises

Most philosophical writing in our period was technical and professional, texts for teaching and study or ongoing research. The output of notebooks and treatises (*hypomnēmata* and *pragmateiai*) was industrial in scale, and booklists for the major figures record only a fraction of the total. Strato of Lampsacus (330s–270/68), tutor to Ptolemy Philadelphus on Cos before heading the Lyceum after Theophrastus, wrote some 45 works spanning all three fields of philosophy, almost all in the form of technical studies of technical topics: *On Void*, *On Time*, *On Definition*, and so on (D.L. 5.59–60). Here, and in a few other cases, a stichometric total enables us to estimate the scale: over 332,000 lines, which is roughly 12 times all of Thucydides (Sedley 1998: 103). Few others besides Epicurus and Chrysippus were so prolific, but their steadily increasing numbers produced mountains of texts. The vast majority of this work resembled Strato's in focus and format: mostly treatises *On X* (*Peri tinos*), often flagged by *Reply to X* (*Pros tina*) as contributions to specific debates (as in over half the titles in Chrysippus' catalogue), or comprehensive studies of an entire field, like *Physics* or *Ethical Theory*. Another common format, illustrated by the 38 books of *Problems* transmitted under Aristotle's name but compiled early in our period and expanded repeatedly, were collections of material for study and discussion: multiple volumes of *Arguments* (*logoi*), *Puzzles* (*aporēmata*), *Investigations* (*zētēmata*), and the like, often with a field or topic specified.

Philosophy, as an intellectual practice and discipline, is fundamentally an oral activity. Its lifeblood is discussion, the give and take of vigorous argument, claim and counter-claim, reasons and rejoinders, proof proffered and objections marshaled. For many, therefore, Socrates was its model practitioner, and the literary recreation of his *viva voce* inquiries the ideal textual format. But the impact of this oral context is evident in other formats as well. Both treatises and shorter studies typically grew out of collaborative inquiry, discussion, and instruction. Whether fodder for teaching or its fruit, they were typically framed by questions or problems to be resolved, and studded with alternative solutions, objections, and replies. Some of these texts circulated only among the writer's associates and students as informal "notebooks" (*hypomnēmata*). But many were reworked into more accessible form, sometimes by other hands. The will of Lyco of Troas, head of the Peripatos after Strato, distinguishes works "already read" (*ta anegnōsmena*) from his "uncirculated" works (*anekdota*), which require further attention from a colleague (D.L. 5.73). And although the brilliant Academic skeptic Carneades of Cyrene (214/13–129/8) wrote nothing himself, many of his disquisitions (ostensibly imitated by Cicero in the *Tusculan Disputations*: 1.7–8 and 3.54) were recorded by associates, who duly continued to dispute the master's point and purport (Cic. *Ac.* 2.78).

A typical "course" (*akroasis*, *scholē*, or *diatribē*) can be sampled in the remnants of Epicurus' magnum opus *On Nature*, which filled 37 books composed over the course of two decades. The whole, as reconstructed by David Sedley (1998: 94–144) on the basis of parallels between fragments (both papyrus remains and later reports) on the one hand and the extant letters and Lucretius on the other, had two distinct sequences, apparently reflecting stages of composition: an initial presentation in Books 1–13, then subsequent elaborations and revisions in the remainder. What survives smacks of the classroom: expansive and informal in diction, syntax, and style, with hiatus and hiccups in grammar; stretches of quasi-dialogue with critics or opponents, both real and imagined; and references to his colleague Metrodorus and others present. But the detail of these volumes and the tortuous progress of their arguments could deter even avid readers, as Epicurus acknowledges in his extant letters, all intended to make his teaching more digestible.

Summaries can be a boon to novice and expert alike, and epitomes of major works such as Plato's *Republic* and treatises on logic and physics are attested already for

Aristotle and his colleagues. But some works, thanks to their conceptual or linguistic obscurity, or simply their authoritative status, received the opposite treatment. Plato's *Timaeus*, which stimulated intense discussion well into the third century, elicited detailed exegesis from the Academic Crantor (d. 276/5), the first in the long and distinguished tradition of commentaries on Plato (Sedley 1997). Works by Epicurus and Zeno provoked similar efforts, as key texts and problematic passages were studied and debated by followers and critics alike (Sedley 1989; Erler 1993).

Philosophical Pulpits: Essays and Letters

The boundary between classroom and society, though ordinarily clear enough, often blurs in writing. Since technical treatises had little appeal outside the schools, many philosophers distilled some of their thinking and clothed it in more appealing form. Crantor's "golden booklet" *On Mourning* (Cic. *Ac.* 2.135) was a signal success. Addressed to a father in mourning, it was the fountainhead for a rich tradition of literary consolations, which drew on it repeatedly: the Stoic Panaetius (c.185–110/109) addressing Scipio's nephew, Aelius Tubero; Cicero's lost *Consolatio* on the death of his own daughter; another by Arius to Livia on the death of Drusus; the *Consolation to Apollonius* transmitted under Plutarch's name; and many more. Taking a specific event as an occasion for general reflections, these works targeted very broad audiences, including but never limited to fellow philosophers. Crantor, for example, leavened his case for sensitive fortitude with abundant exempla from history and poetry, including frequent quotations, and a parable of his own in which a personified Andreia, speaking before a Panhellenic assembly, wins the prize over Health, Pleasure, and Wealth. The result must have resembled the discourses on ethical topics by Seneca and Plutarch now widely labeled "essays." Nor was Crantor the originator of this format; short works on similar topics go back at least to Plato's associates: *On Friendship*, *On Wealth*, *On Fortune*, and so on.

The range of this protean format, though largely restricted to ethical themes, was extremely wide. Crantor's *libellus* probably fell near the middle in its union of philosophical content and rhetorical dress. Near the rhetorical end of the spectrum stood the moralizing "diatribes" of itinerant teachers and speakers such as Teles (mid-third century BCE). Marked by narrow thematic focus, earthy imagery, colloquial style, feigned dialogue, and a hectoring tone, his harangues against the laxity of conventional values and attitudes are long on oratorical flair but very short on philosophical argument or analysis. Incidentally, it is probably inaccurate, and definitely misleading, to label this style of discourse "Cynic diatribe." As previously noted in passing, the term *diatribē* spans very diverse forms and styles, from school discussions (like the *diatribai* of Epictetus) to epideictic lecturing; and neither Teles nor his putative models – which include Socrates and Socratics as well as avowed Cynics like Diogenes and Crates – were distinctly or exclusively Cynic, while Bion as well studied in the Academy and Lyceum (Trapp 2007). At the other end of the spectrum, and differing little from technical treatises, fall works like Cicero's *De officiis*, which he modeled closely on a work *On Duty* by Panaetius. Addressed to his son studying in

Athens (in part to indicate the target audience of serious students), its three books present a methodical introduction to a distinctly Stoic system of applied ethics.

Dedicatory prefaces, their occasional significance aside, signal a calmer tone suitable for studious reading, and typically also the kind of audience envisioned. In effect, they announce an open or public letter: Cicero writing to his son, or to Atticus, Brutus, or others, speaks beyond them to corresponding segments of Rome if not to Romans at large. The core idea of letters is then near to hand, and some exploited the affinity between philosophical and epistolary stances. Letters, as virtual conversations interrupted and delayed by distance, are implicitly dialogical (Demetr. *Eloc.* 223–35), and by mediating the intimacy of oral exchange with the reflective distance of textuality and lapse of time, they offer effective ways to promote serious reflection. Even more than dialogues, they can moderate the impersonality of abstract reasoning by establishing an intimate tone of sincere concern. Here again Plato led the way, if any of the 13 letters preserved under his name are genuine. The longest and richest seventh is illustrative by omission: its elaborate apology for *not* providing a more substantive discussion, though in part a reflex of peculiarly Platonic reservations about *ex cathedra* discourse, shows how natural a context letters provide for candid self-presentation, however illusory in fact.

Letters are attested for many Hellenistic philosophers. But rarely is there any reason to think they had much philosophical content. An exchange between Zeno and Antigonus Gonatas, authentic or not, affords a glimpse of philosophy's prestige: a fervent invitation and a polite refusal (D.L. 7.6–9). The first distinctly philosophical epistles evidently came from Epicurus. Necessity was one of his motives, since many of his followers lived abroad. Intense discussion with friends and associates in Athens was the furnace in which he forged his theories, working out new ideas and arguments, wrestling with problems and objections, testing rejoinders and solutions. But the resulting texts, exemplified by papyri of *On Nature*, were prolix and rambling, hard to follow, and sorely lacking in the clarity and simplicity that many of his followers required. Epicurus tackled the problem by adapting his ideas to epistolary form. The chief need, as the extant letters acknowledge, was brevity, which he achieved by producing concise epitomes: a synopsis of atomic physics in a letter *To Herodotus*, of meteorological theories in one *To Pythocles*, and of ethics in one *To Menoeceus* (all in D.L. 10). The opening of the second is instructive (D.L. 10.84–5):

> Epicurus to Pythocles, glad greetings. Cleon brought me a letter from you in which you continue to show a friendliness to us worthy of our concern for you. Clearly you are trying to commit to memory the reasonings that lead to a happy life, and you ask me to send you a concise outline of my reasoning about celestial phenomena, so you can readily remember it. For our other writings are hard to remember, even though, you say, you review them constantly. We were pleased to receive your request, and we retain high hopes. So now that we have finished writing everything else, we shall provide what you request, these reasonings which will be useful to many others, especially to those who are just getting their first taste of genuine physical theory, and those who are tied up with more demanding work than any of the standard subjects. So read these points carefully, store them in your memory, and study them diligently along with the rest of what we sent Herodotus in the short summary (*mikra epitomē*).

Epicurus relied heavily on letters both to extend the reach of his teaching and to lend it the requisite pastoral tone and authority. Fragments of many of his letters survive, addressed to over 20 different correspondents and preserving some of his most famous remarks. The three that survive intact show how well the form suits concise instruction. The shortest, addressed to an otherwise unknown Menoeceus, is a model of brevity that deploys a simple but supple style marked by flashes of elegance (D.L. 10.122–3):

> Ἐπίκουρος Μενοικεῖ χαίρειν. μήτε νέος τις ὢν μελλέτω φιλοσοφεῖν, μήτε γέρων ὑπάρχων κοπιάτω φιλοσοφῶν· οὔτε γὰρ ἄωρος οὐδείς ἐστιν οὔτε πάρωρος πρὸς τὸ κατὰ ψυχὴν ὑγιαῖνον. ὁ δὲ λέγων ἢ μήπω τοῦ φιλοσοφεῖν ὑπάρχειν ὥραν ἢ παρεληλυθέναι τὴν ὥραν ὅμοιός ἐστι τῶι λέγοντι πρὸς εὐδαιμονίαν ἢ μὴ παρεῖναι τὴν ὥραν ἢ μηκέτι εἶναι. ὥστε φιλοσοφητέον καὶ νέωι καὶ γέροντι, τῶι μὲν ὅπως γηράσκων νεάζηι τοῖς ἀγαθοῖς διὰ τὴν χάριν τῶν γεγονότων, τῶι δ' ὅπως νέος ἅμα καὶ παλαιὸς ᾖ διὰ τὴν ἀφοβίαν τῶν μελλόντων. μελετᾶν οὖν χρὴ τὰ ποιοῦντα τὴν εὐδαιμονίαν, εἴπερ παρούσης μὲν αὐτῆς πάντα ἔχομεν, ἀπούσης δὲ πάντα πράττομεν εἰς τὸ ταύτην ἔχειν. ἃ δέ σοι συνεχῶς παρήγγελλον, ταῦτα καὶ πρᾶττε καὶ μελέτα, στοιχεῖα τοῦ καλῶς ζῆν ταῦτ' εἶναι διαλαμβάνων.
>
> Epicurus to Menoeceus, glad greetings. No one who is young should delay studying philosophy, nor anyone who is old tire of it. For no one is either too young or too old to have a healthy soul. Anyone who says it is either too soon or too late for philosophy is like someone who says it is too soon or too late to be happy. Therefore, both young and old ought to study philosophy: the one so that as he ages, he may stay young in good things because he is thankful for what is past, and the other so that he may now be both young and old at once because he is fearless of what will come. So one must study what produces happiness, given that we have everything when it is present, and we do everything to get it when it is absent. Both perform and study the instructions I continually gave you, recognizing them to be the basic elements of living honorably.

A series of elaborately balanced antitheses creates a powerful exordium. Sharp polarities heighten the sense of urgency, universalizing singulars create a tone of personal intensity, and the central moral imperative is underscored by an insistent train of injunctions, sustained but varied in form (third-person imperatives, verbal adjectives, impersonal *chrē*). Two sudden and significant shifts in the final sentence mark the transition from exhortation to theory: from third-person generality to intimately direct address (I/thou singulars for shared concerns), and from philosophy in general to specifically Epicurean precepts.

The body of the letter proceeds to summarize the famous "fourfold cure" (*tetrapharmakos*; cf. *Kuriai Doxai* 1–4), a catechism of four basic principles designed to yield what the exordium loudly advertises: a healthy soul and thereby a happy life. The principles which Menoeceus is advised to "study," and which he is told everyone should ponder, whether young or old, are these. First, a radically revisionist conception of the gods: imperishable paradigms of happiness, but never the agents of either benefit or harm for anyone, living or dead. Second, death is "nothing to us": a total extinction of life and awareness that leaves us immune to the posthumous pain and sorrow imagined by the misguided multitude. In short, gods exist, and forever; but the dead do not, ever. The main external sources of anxiety thus banished, Epicurus turns to its internal sources, which he defuses by sketching the two linchpins of his decidedly austere brand of hedonism. First, a pleasant life is readily within our reach if we live naturally; in particular, the natural needs we must meet to be happy are few and readily satisfied, and the resulting state of pleasure is the happiness that is (as announced at the start) the fulfillment of all we naturally desire. Finally, the sole remaining threat to happiness, physical pain, is either "short if strong, or weak if long": even intense pain can be overcome by the joy of a healthy soul, happy in its memories of pleasure past, secure in its prospect of pleasure to come, hence fully content in its present state, whatever pains may assail the body.

Epicurus concludes by capping his fourfold cure with a pair of rebuttals: no one can ever be happy without virtue, or virtuous without happiness; and we always have sufficient control over our lives to attain the happiness envisioned, since no power either divine or natural – neither "Dame Destiny" nor atomic determinism – can defeat the power of "sober reasoning." A muscular peroration recaps the argument in a sprawling rhetorical question that delineates the devout Epicurean in a string of isocola (D.L. 10.133):

> For who do you think is superior to one who has pious beliefs about the gods, who is entirely fearless about death, who has rationally determined the goal of nature, who realizes that the limit of good things is easy to fulfill and maintain, whereas the limit of bad things is either brief or not intense?

His cure recapitulated, Epicurus closes with an exhortation (D.L. 10.135):

> So study these and the related points day and night both by yourself and with someone like yourself, and you will never feel anxiety either awake or asleep, and you will live like a god among men; for anyone living with immortal boons bears no resemblance to a mortal creature.

The farewell, though addressed to Menoeceus, extends the letter's reach by urging him to study it with likeminded companions. Their reward, promised to all who master the principles outlined therein, is a virtual immortality: the release from all anxiety called *ataraxia*.

Philosophers in Verse

Prominent poets repeatedly paid homage to leading philosophers. Witness epitaphs for Polemo by Antagoras of Rhodes (1 GP = D.L. 4.22), for Crantor by Theaetetus (2 GP = D.L. 4.25; cf. Call. *ep.* 7 Pf. = 57 GP = *AP* 9.565), for Zeno by Antipater of Sidon (35 GP = D.L. 7.29), and so on. Well schooled in poetry themselves, philosophers were often proficient in verse as well. Specimens of occasional verse survive in various sources. From Arcesilaus, who wrote no books, we have two polished memorials: one commemorating an Attalid chariot victory, the other the untimely death of a colleague's friend (*SH* 121–2 = D.L. 4.30–1). From the end of our period come 35 epigrams by Philodemus, and incipits of many more (Sider 1997). Most have erotic themes, but one, inviting his Roman patron Piso to a modest dinner honoring Epicurus (27 Sider), illustrates the vitality of the Epicurean community outside Naples, and its impact on the Roman elite, including Vergil and friends.

Another famous example of the interaction of poetry, politics, and philosophy is Aratus, who studied under Zeno in Athens before visiting the court of Antigonus Gonatas alongside various other poets and students of Zeno. The catalogue of stars that forms the bulk of his *Phaenomena* embellishes work by Eudoxus, an associate of Plato's; and the accompanying survey of weather signs draws on Peripatetic work. A glance at the poem (discussed more fully by Volk in this volume) will highlight some of its Stoic inflections. Apart from the central theme of intelligent design, these are rarely prominent. But an opening invocation to Zeus gives traditional poetic motifs distinctly Stoic coloring (1–14):

ἐκ Διὸϲ ἀρχώμεϲθα, τὸν οὐδέποτ' ἄνδρεϲ ἐῶμεν
ἄρρητον· μεϲταὶ δὲ Διὸϲ πᾶϲαι μὲν ἀγυιαί,
πᾶϲαι δ' ἀνθρώπων ἀγοραί, μεϲτὴ δὲ θάλαϲϲα
καὶ λιμένεϲ· πάντη δὲ Διὸϲ κεχρήμεθα πάντεϲ.
τοῦ γὰρ καὶ γένοϲ εἰμέν. ὁ δ' ἤπιοϲ ἀνθρώποιϲι
δεξιὰ ϲημαίνει, λαοὺϲ δ' ἐπὶ ἔργον ἐγείρει
μιμνήϲκων βιότοιο· λέγει δ' ὅτε βῶλοϲ ἀρίϲτη
βουϲί τε καὶ μακέληιϲι, λέγει δ' ὅτε δεξιαὶ ὧραι
καὶ φυτὰ γυρῶϲαι καὶ ϲπέρματα πάντα βαλέϲθαι.
αὐτὸϲ γὰρ τά γε ϲήματ' ἐν οὐρανῶι ἐϲτήριξεν
ἄϲτρα διακρίναϲ, ἐϲκέψατο δ' εἰϲ ἐνιαυτὸν
ἀϲτέραϲ οἵ κε μάλιϲτα τετυγμένα ϲημαίνοιεν
ἀνδράϲιν ὡράων, ὄφρ' ἔμπεδα πάντα φύωνται.
τῶι μιν ἀεὶ πρῶτόν τε καὶ ὕϲτατον ἱλάϲκονται.

From Zeus let us start, the one we men never leave
unspoken. Full with Zeus are all routes
and all gatherings of people, full are the sea
and harbors; in all ways do we all have need of Zeus.
For we are also part of his family; and kindly to people
he shows apt signs. The folk he rouses to work
by reminding them of their living: he tells when the soil is best
for oxen and hoes; he tells when the seasons are apt
both for trenching plants and for casting all kinds of seeds.
For he himself fastened the signs in heaven,
forming constellations, and he saw to the annual
stars whose risings and settings would give the best signs
of seasons to men, so that everything always may grow securely.
Therefore they always pay homage to him first and last.

Nothing here requires philosophical training to follow. But Stoic theory informs the choice of emphasis. The world is "full with Zeus" not simply in contrast with Hesiodic pessimism (where earth and sea are full of ills: *Th.* 101), but because his power pervades the cosmos as the dynamic rational "principle" (*archē*, echoed in opening *archōmestha*) on which everything wholly depends (2–4). The essential rational nature of this principle is emphatically marked as "unspoken" (*arrhētos*): another echo of Hesiod, and a pun on the poet's own name, but also an allusion to the silent and ineffable cosmic mind. This unspoken but implicit order is most evident in perceptible signs (6, 10, 12) that tell us (*legei*, 7 and 8) more than eyes alone can see: as a divinely governed rational system, the world is an open book, to be read by intelligent human interpreters; and the cornerstone of Stoic empiricism is human aptitude for learning these inferential signs, observable facts and features that not only point to other facts but reliably entail them.

Although the poem presents no sustained argument for Stoic doctrines, its elaborate account of celestial pageantry corroborates and exalts the operation of divine providence that is central to the Stoic outlook and theories. Cosmology is Aratus' theme, his "phenomena" the visibly manifest signs that adorn both the heights of heaven and the realms below. Logic is effectively absent, and ethics receives only passing attention, most notably in an allegorical rewriting of Hesiod's myth of ages (96–136; cf. *WD* 106–201). But Aratus' celebration of Stoic physics finds its complement in a miniature hymn by Cleanthes (c.330–c.230), which focuses on ethics and theodicy.

Chronology is elusive and best left to the side. Ancient tradition has Aratus composing his poem at the request of Antigonus in the mid-270s; Cleanthes, who succeeded Zeno as head of the school a decade later, was then in his 50s, with over 40 years still to live. His hymn (so labeled in lines 6, 37, and 39) can stand alone (as it does in Stobaeus, 1.1.12), serving solely to exalt Zeus, not to introduce another theme (Bulloch in this volume). But its portrait of Zeus, while heavily indebted to traditional diction, is intensely argumentative and thick with correctives to traditional beliefs. Even its epithets, while modeled on epic phrasing, re-assemble their components in telling ways: "much might" becomes "almighty" (*pankrates*, 1) for the Stoic deity, and "bright-lightning" now "lightning-leader" (*archikeraune*, 32), to suit the cosmic mind or "command-center" (*hēgemonikon*) that in Stoic determinism governs everything in the universe as fate and providence (1–8; Thom 2005):

κύδιϲτ' ἀθανάτων, πολυώνυμε παγκρατὲϲ αἰεί,
Ζεῦ φύϲεωϲ ἀρχηγέ, νόμου μετὰ πάντα κυβερνῶν,
χαῖρε· ϲὲ γὰρ καὶ πᾶϲι θέμιϲ θνητοῖϲι προϲαυδᾶν.
ἐκ ϲοῦ γὰρ γενόμεϲθα, θεοῦ μίμημα λαχόντεϲ
μοῦνοι, ὅϲα ζώει τε καὶ ἕρπει θνήτ' ἐπὶ γαῖαν·
τῶι ϲε καθυμνήϲω, καὶ ϲὸν κράτοϲ αἰὲν ἀείϲω.
ϲοὶ δὴ πᾶϲ ὅδε κόϲμοϲ ἑλιϲϲόμενοϲ περὶ γαῖαν
πείθεται ᾗ κεν ἄγηιϲ, καὶ ἑκὼν ὑπὸ ϲεῖο κρατεῖται·

Most renowned of immortals, multinamed, almighty always
Zeus, nature's arch-leader, steering all with law,
hail, for righteous it is for every mortal to address you;
for from you we have come into being, a semblance of god our lot,
we alone among mortal creatures that live and crawl on earth.
Therefore I shall hymn you and always sing your might:
You this world entire as it spins around the earth
obeys wherever you may lead, and to you it freely submits.

Cleanthes adopts a very different tone. Whereas Aratus addresses his mortal readers, he directs his verses to Zeus himself, addressed directly and repeatedly, almost throughout. Zeus enters Aratus only alongside the Muses in a transitional invocation (15–18). But Cleanthes fills his proem with vocatives from the start, continues with personal pronouns and second-singular verbs (eight times in 3–8 alone), closes with a thicket of both (32–9), and steers clear of Zeus only in the latter part of his central exposition, when deprecating the impious follies of humankind at large (22–31). In effect, the entire poem is a prayer: first honoring Zeus with a litany of praise; then delineating his all-encompassing justice in an extended meditation that supplants the customary narrative; and after requesting – on behalf of a collective "us" (3–6, 33–8) – continued rational self-control (with three imperatives in 33–4), finally rejoicing in his beneficent justice (32–9).

ἀλλὰ Ζεῦ πάνδωρε κελαινεφὲς ἀρχικέραυνε,
ἀνθρώπους ῥύοιο ἀπειροσύνης ἀπὸ λυγρῆς,
ἣν σύ, πάτερ, σκέδασον ψυχῆς ἄπο, δὸς δὲ κυρῆσαι
γνώμης, ᾗ πίσυνος σὺ δίκης μέτα πάντα κυβερνᾷς,
ὄφρ' ἂν τιμηθέντες ἀμειβώμεσθά σε τιμῆι,
ὑμνοῦντες τὰ σὰ ἔργα διηνεκές, ὡς ἐπέοικε
θνητὸν ἐόντ', ἐπεὶ οὔτε βροτοῖς γέρας ἄλλο τι μεῖζον
οὔτε θεοῖς ἢ κοινὸν ἀεὶ νόμον ἐν δίκηι ὑμνεῖν.

But Zeus all-giving, dark-clouding, lightning-leader,
fend off baleful ineptitude away from humans;
scatter it, you our father, away from our soul, and grant us gaining
judgment, which you deploy in steering all with justice,
so that honored thus we may return you honor
hymning these your works continually, as is seemly,
mortal that we be, since no prize is greater for mortals
or for gods than always hymning justly the law we all share.

Thematically, the hymn wears its Stoic vision on its sleeve. Zeus is figured as cosmic reason, alias universal law of nature, fate, and providence: so much aligns with Aratus. But here divine intelligence is fully personalized, principally in political terms: an "arch-leader" (2) and "highest king" (*hupatos basileus*, 14) to be obeyed, or disobeyed to our own chagrin alone; and echoing Heraclitus, to whose work Cleanthes devoted four books of exegesis (D.L. 7.174), a thunderbolt-wielding helmsman (2, 10, 32, 35). His Zeus is also a benevolent "all-giving father" (32–4), because he has endowed us with the patrimony of rationality (4; cf. Arat. *Phaen.* 4), which makes humans alone among mortal creatures (5) fellow citizens and administrators of the cosmopolis (37–9).

Stoic ecumenism is indebted to Zeno's early flirtation with Cynicism, which cast a long shadow via his *Republic*, memorably impugned as "written on the cynosure" or "dog's tail" (D.L. 7.4). The Cynic vision, by contrast, was defiantly antinomian and earthbound. Crates (368/5–288/5), in a celebration of austerity modeled closely on the imaginary Crete of Homer's Odysseus, extols his beggar's pouch (*pēra*) as his *polis*, free from the frenzied vainglory of fools but rich in humble fare to slake his meager needs (*SH* 351 = D.L. 6.85). Other remnants of his verse (some 65 lines, mainly hexameters but also elegiacs and iambics) elaborate his rugged asceticism, often in similarly parodic manner (Scodel in this volume). A blatant parody of Solon's elegy to the Muses prays for "a dung-beetle's wealth": "easy to carry, easy to get, valuable for virtue" (*SH* 359); and he converts a vaunt from the Dolonia (*Il.* 10) into a hymn to the virtues of Frugality (*SH* 361). But verse was only instrumental to his true vocation: the cultivation of virtue in himself and others. A volume of letters "resembling Plato in style" (D.L. 6.98) might have engaged in theoretical debates, though he ridiculed Stilpo and others for toiling over empty verbal disputes (*SH* 347–8).

Philosophers, despite their increased prestige but also because of it, remained popular targets of satire. None cast his net more widely than one of their own: Pyrrho's eloquent publicist, Timon of Phlius (c.325–c.230), whose *Silloi* or "lampoons" spared few, living or dead. A first book narrated the poet's own *katabasis*; two more interviewed Xenophanes of Colophon about all the "busybody professors" from the first down to his own day (D.L. 9.111–12). Some 65 fragments (preserving over 140 lines) display masterly command of parody's arsenal: Homeric and colloquial diction cheek to cheek, cumbersome compounds, stilted phrasing, multivalent puns, farcical animal imagery, all pompously inflated by heroic meter and dialect. Miniature caricatures pinpoint idiosyncrasies both philosophical and personal: "stonemason" Socrates is a "snotty Attic ironist" (*SH* 799); "the giant platitude" Plato "equal to the cicadas singing in Hecademus' trees" (804); "Phoenician" Zeno a "voracious old lady in delusion's shade" (812); and Epicurus "last in the sty (*hustatos*) of physicists and most dogged" (825). But as a proponent of skepticism, Timon had his favorites, and he seasoned his satire with cameos of praise. Pyrrho he duly exalts as "alone delusion-free and indomitable" (783). Likewise Xenophanes, deemed a forerunner, is "all but free of delusion, basher of deceitful Homer" (834). A handful of others are also portrayed as proto- or quasi-skeptics: "mighty Parmenides, high-minded hero of disbelief," "Melissus, superior to many illusions," "Democritus keenest of minds, ambidextrous debater" (818–20). The upshot is a noble heritage for Pyrrhonian skepticism that still echoes in later sources (including D.L. 9).

Philosophical Scholarship

Timon's best-known lines deride the "endless polemics" of Alexandria's "cloistered pedants" (*SH* 786; Strootman in this volume). Ironically, his work was indebted to the pioneering labors of the Lyceum, which was both model and, via Demetrius of Phalerum and Strato, prime mover for the Ptolemies' Museum. Peripatetic research on archaic and Classical poetry is widely recognized; its *disiecta membra* preserved in Athenaeus and elsewhere are still a rich harvest of scholarship. Less familiar is their work on earlier philosophers. Studies of individual figures survive only as titles. But the fruits of this research appear repeatedly in Aristotle, whose dialectical methods rely heavily on compiling, analyzing, and assessing the rival claims and arguments of his predecessors and contemporaries.

Philosophy continued to study its past as it advanced in age. Plato was read more or less continuously, and signs of renewed interest in other fourth-century figures – including rival Socratics – appear in the second century. Epicureans kept detailed records of their school's history, with special attention to the founder and his closest associates, and similar but less hagiographic accounts were produced for the other schools and their leading members. Some of this material survives in the *Register of Philosophers* by Philodemus, originally in ten books; substantial portions of the two on Academics and Stoics have been recovered from Herculaneum (Dorandi 1991, 1994). One of its main aims is to trace the "succession" (*diadochē*) of each school: the lineage of its leading members, via lists of their teachers, students, and associates along with notable traits and accomplishments. Booklists reflect similar interests, but also doctrinal issues, since determining authenticity can affect school orthodoxy; debates about Zeno's *Republic* are a case in point (Schofield 1991: 3–21). The *Register* and other lost works like it supplied the framework for Diogenes Laertius. But their philosophical content was very thin. For meatier fare he and others had to look elsewhere.

Complementing these historical accounts were summaries and catalogues of "doctrines" (*doxai*) or "tenets" (*areskonta*). A major impetus for this work was the dialectical nature of the discipline. Epicurus, like Aristotle, developed many of his positions through critical reflection on claims made by others, and the recitation and rebuttal of rival positions continued to play a large role in later Epicurean writing. Collections of opposing views, whether held by rival parties or a single figure, were a powerful critical tool, widely deployed in skeptical arguments. Systematic surveys and summaries also had pedagogical value. The volume and complexity of many major works were daunting, and few had either the mind or the stomach to take their Chrysippus straight. Digests afforded easier access, and ready resources for discussion and debate. This kind of "doxography" (a label introduced by Diels 1879) looms large in many of our post-Hellenistic sources, and therefore in modern scholarship. Although its origins go back to Hippias and his fellow sophists, it came into its own during the third century, and some of the best surviving examples come from the end of our period: detailed surveys of Stoic and Aristotelian ethics (Stob. 2.57–152), and careful summaries of key points in Stoic and Aristotelian physics (some 40 excerpts: Diels 1879: 447–72). The authorship of this material has recently been questioned (Göransson 1995: 182–226), but at least some of it probably comes from Octavian's Alexandrian friend, the Stoic Arius, and it is tempting to conjecture that he compiled his digests while serving the Augustan household. In any event, in its attention to Aristotle, this material typifies the renewed interest in the originary texts of the discipline that marks the close of our period. Its critical treatment of fourth-century ideas, now construed in the light of subsequent theories, also indicates the continuity of Hellenistic philosophy both with earlier debates and with what would follow. For it was largely this constructive interaction between Hellenistic and older work that ushered Greek philosophy into a new phase under imperial Rome.

FURTHER READING

Study of Hellenistic philosophy remains heavily dependent on outdated editions and collections of source material; the standard works for major figures, schools, and sources are conveniently listed in Algra, Barnes, Mansfeld, and Schofield 1999: 805–19. More recent work of note includes editions of Antigonus of Carystus (Dorandi 1999); Demetrius of Phalerum and several Peripatetics (Fortenbaugh and Schütrumpf 2000; Fortenbaugh and White 2004 and 2006; Sharples forthcoming); Hermippus (Bollansée 1999); and Philodemus (Janko 2000; Delattre 2007). New editions are in preparation for Diogenes Laertius (Dorandi) and multiple works by Philodemus (see Gutzwiller in this volume), and also for Hellenistic Stoics (Mansfeld et al.) and Peripatetics (Fortenbaugh et al.).

Translations: Inwood and Gerson 1997 contains the extant letters of Epicurus and substantial excerpts from later sources; Long and Sedley 1987 provides short excerpts organized by topic along with analytical essays. Cicero's philosophical works are excellent introductions to major debates and styles of argument; notable translations include Annas and Woolf 2001; Brittain 2006; Graver 2002; Walsh 1997 and 2000. Similarly Sextus Empiricus, in Annas and Barnes 1994; Bett 1997 and 2005; Blank 1998; and for Diogenes Laertius, Goulet-Cazé 1999 and White forthcoming.

Algra, Barnes, Mansfeld, and Schofield 1999 surveys the main philosophical issues and positions by field and school, with succinct accounts of the sources, the history of the main schools, the "Socratic legacy," and the period's end; chapters in Gill and Pellegrin 2006 survey related issues. Habicht 1988 paints a vivid picture of philosophers in Hellenistic Athens; likewise Long 1986 on Arcesilaus, Sedley 1977 on Diodorus Kronos and dialectic, Clay 1998: 3–102 on Epicurean practices, Schofield 1983 on Stoic styles of argument, and Warren 2007 on Diogenes Laertius. For Aratus, see Volk in this volume, and Long 1978 on Timon. Goulet 1989– is a goldmine of prosopography. Critical discussion of philosophical issues is well represented in Ierodiakonou 1999 and Inwood 2003 on Stoicism, Warren 2009 on Epicureanism, Bett 2010 on skepticism, and volumes from the triennial Symposium Hellenisticum, most recently Ioppolo and Sedley 2007.

CHAPTER TWENTY-FIVE

From Polybius to Dionysius: The Decline and Fall of Hellenistic Historiography

Alain M. Gowing

What constitutes a "Hellenistic" historian? Or rather, when does a Greek historian writing after Alexander the Great cease to be Hellenistic and become something else? Most will agree that once we reach the Augustan period, the term Hellenistic is no longer apt, and that therefore characters such as Dionysius of Halicarnassus, Diodorus Siculus, and Strabo deserve a different label. Precisely what label is most appropriate for them is itself unclear (Greco-Roman? Augustan? Late Republican? Imperial?), but "Hellenistic" is obviously wrong. As most surveys of Hellenistic historiography rightly observe (e.g., Marincola 2001: 105), the expansion of Rome and the emergence of its territory between the third and second centuries BCE inevitably influenced and forever altered the nature of Greco-Roman historiography. Such surveys tend to stop with Polybius, recognizing that post-Polybian historiography is indeed different, yet they seldom articulate *how* it is different.

My concern in this paper is not to forge new ground in already familiar territory; the historians as well as the general historiographical trends discussed here have been the subject of numerous studies, some quite recent and extensive (e.g., Oliver 2006; Marincola 2001, 2007). Rather, my aim is to bring Polybius and Dionysius into play with one another, first, by tracing briefly the evolution of Greek historiography, specifically that which touches on Roman history, from the unproblematically Hellenistic historian Polybius down to Dionysius of Halicarnassus and the Augustan period; and secondly, by illustrating this evolution in concrete terms via a comparison of the prefaces of Polybius and Dionysius.

Between Polybius and Dionysius: Polyhistor and Posidonius

Polybius (c.200–118 BCE) is well known to students of Greco-Roman historiography. This aristocratic native of Megalopolis in the Peloponnese came to Rome as a political hostage shortly after the Roman defeat of Perseus in 168 BCE (Erskine in this volume). Befriended by P. Cornelius Scipio Aemilianus and subsequently part of the "Scipionic Circle," he composed a celebrated 40-book *Histories*, an account of the rise of Rome and its hegemony over the Mediterranean from 246 to 146 BCE. The scholarship on Polybius is extensive, though his views of Rome have perhaps received the most thorough attention. Of recent studies, Champion has persuasively argued that Polybius, via what Champion terms "indirect historiography," expresses in subtle ways both criticism of and admiration for Romans, resulting in a "politics of cultural indeterminacy" (2004: 4, 27–8, and *passim*). Champion's argument, complex and nuanced, nicely elucidates the undeniable ambiguity of Polybius' account. Despite Polybius' familiarity with them, his Romans remain an alien people, a people who may possess admirable, even "Hellenic" traits, but are still "other." As we shall see, Dionysius' attitude towards the Romans is conditioned by very different circumstances and in consequence bears little resemblance to that of Polybius.

Less familiar are Polybius' immediate successors, either because their works simply do not survive or survive only in a few fragments, or because their impact on historiography appears to have been minimal. In terms of gauging the impact the Roman conquest had on the way history would now be written, however, these authors have something to tell us.

Of the characters of whom we have any knowledge, one of the most intriguing is Alexander "Polyhistor" (born c.105 BCE in Miletus). As was Polybius' fate, war brought Polyhistor to Rome, though as a slave (a *paedagogus*) rather than a hostage, sometime in the 80s during the conflict with Mithridates. Made a citizen under Sulla, he went on to become a prodigious writer, among whose works may have been an *Italika* as well as a work *On Rome*.

The one secure fragment belonging to the former forms part of an aetiologizing story about an Etruscan king named Anius (from whom the Anio river is said to have taken its name), and the rape of his daughter by one Cathetus. This results in the birth of Latinus, from whom it is claimed the (Roman?) nobility are descended (*FGrH* 273 F 20), evidently another in the myriad accounts of the origins of the Latin king known best to us from the *Aeneid*. The fragment thus attests an interest in the pre-history of Rome, an interest that will be pursued in greater depth by Dionysius of Halicarnassus, who shares Polyhistor's curiosity about Latinus (e.g., 1.43). Along the same lines, Polyhistor attempted to account for the name of the Tiber (F 110). Other fragments suggest a similar concern for imparting to Greek readers recondite information about the origins of Rome and early Italic history. In one (F 104), for instance, perhaps to be assigned to either the *Italika* or *On Rome*, he builds on information found in Cato's *Origins* about the Oromobii, a mountain people living in northern Italy, proposing a Greek etymology for the name. The fragment suggests that Polyhistor had read Cato, an indication that by the early part of the first century influence in historical writing is no longer a one-way street, a point which I see as characteristic of a historiography that is no longer purely "Hellenistic" and to which I shall return. In short, Polyhistor appears to have moved beyond the sort of historical narrative favored by Polybius, as well as beyond Polybius' aims, to a brand of history that resembles Cato's *Origins* (Rawson 1985: 26) and anticipates the project of his successor Dionysius.

Roughly contemporary with Polyhistor is the far better known Posidonius (c.135–51 BCE), a towering figure in the intellectual history of the late Roman Republic (Yarrow 2006: 87–8, 161–6, and *passim*; Gruen 1984: 351–5). He was an even more prolific and wide-ranging author than Polyhistor; his historical writings represent but a very small portion of his output. Nonetheless, the most substantial of this, the *History*, is the most comprehensive treatment of Roman history attempted by a Greek since Polybius and indeed appears to be a continuation of Polybius, the chronological range being roughly 146–86 BCE (Kidd 1988: 1.277–80). Insofar as we can tell from the surviving fragments, in terms of approach Posidonius' universalizing history seems to have had more in common with Polyhistor and even with Cato than with Polybius (in the edition of Posidonius by Edelstein and Kidd 1972 – hereafter EK – 13 pages comprise F 51–78, which are assigned with certainty to particular books of the *History*, with an additional 32 pages for F 252–84, whose provenance is uncertain). It is distinctly a work of empire, an account of a world in the middle (rather than at the beginning) of the process of political and administrative consolidation that prefigured what we know as Imperial Rome.

A glance at some of the topics covered in Posidonius' *History* underscores the commonality of interests with Polyhistor as well as with Cato: Roman customs (e.g., F 53 EK, on banquets), the habits of various races (e.g., the Gauls, F 67–9, 274–275; Germans, 73, 277b; Parthians, 282; Celtiberians, 271); curiosity about various things Posidonius has encountered in his travels (e.g., rabbits seen near Naples, F 52; vegetables in Dalmatia, 70; perfume, 71). He is appalled by drunkenness and debauchery (e.g., F 63, 72a, 77). The Posidonian world, in short, is a vast but for the most part known world, not unlike the imperial world so vividly described a century later by Pliny the Elder. It is a world conquered by Rome rather than in the process of being conquered (Gruen 1984: 351); and thus Posidonius' history reads less like a narrative of conquest (like Polybius') than one of preserving and safeguarding a largely secured empire.

Posidonius' acknowledgment and acceptance of this fact are perhaps most apparent in the substantial fragment treating Athenion, the philosopher-tyrant who held sway over Athens in 88 BCE at the height of the First Mithridatic War (F 253 EK). Athenion had attempted to rouse the Athenians against a firmly entrenched Roman domination (lines 30–2) and restore their traditional "democracy" (28–9). Posidonius' colorful account, distinctly unsympathetic to Athenion, concludes, with no hint of disapproval or reproach directed against the Romans, with a massacre by the Roman commander Oribius of Athenion's supporters, the "senseless Athenians" (τοῖϲ ἀνοήτοιϲ Ἀθηναίοιϲ, F 253.159), who were attacked while in a drunken stupor.

The fragments in fact contain virtually no negative press for the Romans (Gruen 1984: 354). Posidonius speaks with approval of Scipio's relationship with Panaetius

(F 254 EK), and evidently found a place in his narrative for more than one flattering reference to Claudius Marcellus, the Roman general who took Syracuse for the Romans in 212 BCE (F 257; cf. 258–61). He seems, Cato-like, to have admired the old Roman virtues of frugality, justice, and piety (F 266–7). Polybius, to be sure, also admires Romans, but in Posidonius we find no trace of the ambiguity or diffidence that marks Polybius' work. He writes instead as a man entirely comfortable with Rome and the Romans and with the world they now dominate, but not yet as a man overly influenced by or indeed even interested in Roman culture. Marincola aptly summarizes the difference between Posidonius and his predecessor: "[he] … had far more catholic and cultural interests than Polybius" (1997: 239). Roman culture, however, evidently held little interest for him, a point that, as we will see, differentiates him from Dionysius of Halicarnassus.

It is worth noting in this connection the one reference to Posidonius in Cicero's correspondence (*Att.* 2.1.2 = 21 Shackleton Bailey 1965 = F 82 EK; in his youth Cicero had heard Posidonius lecture, Plu. *Cic.* 4). Cicero had sent Posidonius a *hypomnēma* or "memoir" that he had composed in Greek on the subject of his consulship, with a request that he should produce his own version, a more elaborate one (*ornatius*). Posidonius declined. Cicero implies that he did so on the grounds that the original was so perfect, it had no need of improvement by Posidonius, but the alternative explanation may be more plausible, that Posidonius simply had no interest in either the subject or Cicero (Shackleton Bailey 1965 *ad loc.*). Posidonius' reaction is revealing: it suggests no hesitation at refusing a request from Rome's greatest orator, no desire whatsoever to attach his name to this particular moment in Roman history, and complete deference on the part of Cicero toward the famous Greek he had hoped would write him into history. Significantly, Cicero similarly alleges that the Greek poet Archias, whom he defended in 62 BCE in a celebrated speech (the same year he wrote to Posidonius), had in fact written, or begun to write, an account of his consulship (*Arch.* 28).

Greeks and Roman History in the *Pro Archia*

The *Pro Archia* illustrates well the impact made on the Roman cultural and political scene by the many Greek intellectuals who came to Italy and Rome in the late Republic, of whom Polyhistor and Posidonius are representative. In this speech Cicero identifies as one of the chief benefits of cultivating Greek poets such as Archias the positive promulgation of Rome to the farthest flung reaches of the Empire (*Arch.* 23). Although Archias is a poet, his themes are nonetheless often historical, and here as elsewhere, Cicero blurs the line between historiography proper and historicizing poetry; both constitute a legitimate means of celebrating and recording the past. Thus Theophanes of Mytilene, the chronicler attached to Pompey the Great, of whose deeds he had written (as perhaps had Posidonius: F 79 EK), is adduced as an example of a Greek intellectual whose writings have served Rome well (*Arch.* 24; on this important character see Yarrow 2006: 54–67). Archias himself had as a young man penned poems about the Cimbrian campaigns of

Marius (*Arch.* 19), a theme also treated by his coeval Posidonius (F 272 EK). Later, he composed an evidently celebrated account of Lucullus' campaigns during the First Mithridatic War, spreading thereby the renown of not only his patron but also of the Roman people (*Arch.* 20–1). Posidonius, too, had treated this war in depth. Indeed, it seems highly likely that given their respective situations, circle of acquaintances, and overlapping interests, the paths of Archias and Posidonius had crossed, despite the absence of any evidence for a relationship.

Significantly, Cicero does not cite Polybius as an example of what he is talking about in the *Pro Archia*. For despite Polybius' relationship with Scipio (and the laudatory nature of his treatment of the Roman general), Polybius did not write the sort of history Cicero refers to in the *Pro Archia* nor for the same purposes; his relationship with neither Scipio nor Rome was precisely analogous to that, say, of Theophanes. Rather, the phenomenon to which Cicero alludes, of Greek intellectuals celebrating the achievements of Romans (and of Romans who are often their patrons), is a relatively *recent* development, characteristic of the late Republic, when Roman hegemony over the Mediterranean is not only essentially complete but also largely accepted.

The remarks on historical writing in the *Pro Archia*, however oblique, mark an important stage in the transition from the Hellenistic historiography practiced by Polybius and his predecessors to the increasingly "Rome-influenced" historiography of Polyhistor, Posidonius, and their successors. Those successors include a couple of important writers not surveyed here – Nicolaus of Damascus, for instance, the author of a universal history that covered Roman history from its beginnings and perhaps most notably of a biography of Augustus (Yarrow 2006, esp. 156–61), or the crucially important Diodorus Siculus, who also wrote universal history (for a fine analysis of the ways in which Diodorus marks the end of the Hellenistic period, see Wirth 1993). But this is the essential point: between Polybius and the middle of the first century BCE dramatic political as well as cultural changes have taken place. With the subjugation of Greece as well as the Hellenized world substantially complete, a new symbiosis develops between the Roman elite and the Greek intellectuals streaming into Rome. The relationship is hardly hostile, an uneasy pact between conqueror and conquered, but rather a relationship of mutual respect, each group recognizing the benefits of a rapport with the other (Wiseman 1979: 154–6; Rawson 1985: 3–18). More Greeks are living in Rome; more Greeks are writing Roman history (in both poetry and prose). Does this make their projects no longer "Hellenistic"? The circumstances in which Polyhistor or Posidonius wrote history in the early part of the first century BCE clearly differ from those operative for Polybius in the second, but all still write what we term universal history, a history that takes a holistic (rather than strictly localized) approach; and all are obviously interested in the actions of *both* Greeks and Romans. Yet even despite the fragmentary nature of late Republican Greek historical writing, we find little that is critical of Romans or even simply ambiguous, quite different from what one finds in Polybius. And again, the changes to which I allude are not strictly political. They involve equally significant developments in Roman cultural life, and linked to those developments is the emergence of a historiography that is no longer "Hellenistic." The best example of these "new" historians is Dionysius of Halicarnassus.

The Prefaces of Polybius and Dionysius

The *Roman Antiquities* of Dionysius of Halicarnassus represent a striking departure from Hellenistic models, and especially from Polybius (Gabba 1991: 118). Moving to Rome in 30 BCE, shortly after Octavian defeated Antony at Actium, he set to work on a 20-book account of Rome encompassing its mythical origins down to the beginning of the First Punic War in 264 BCE, a project that took him some 22 years (1.7.2–4). Simply in terms of subject matter, this differs significantly from the contemporary and universalizing history of Polybius, whose theater of action included virtually the entire Hellenistic world. While a full-scale comparison of Polybius and Dionysius is beyond the scope of this chapter, some sense of the evolution in their attitude – both toward the Romans and toward their historiographical task – may be obtained by comparing their prefaces. In the process we glimpse as well what differentiates the Hellenistic historian Polybius from a Greek historian who has moved beyond Hellenistic models and who prefigures his Imperial successors.

Although the two prefaces are in many respects standard and predictable and have certain qualities in common (Walbank 1957: 39), they differ at crucial points. It should be stressed that an enormously eventful century and a half separate the two authors, Polybius writing just as Rome emerges as a powerful military and political presence in the Mediterranean, Dionysius at a time when Rome's hegemony is not only fully established but extends over an area that even Polybius could perhaps not have imagined. It is true that Polybius asserts that Rome holds the "whole world" under its sway (3.3.9), but as Gruen rightly observes, such a remark owes more to rhetoric than reality: "The future mistress of the Mediterranean was not yet foreseen" (1984: 325). By Dionysius' day, rhetoric had become reality.

One apparent similarity between the two prefaces nicely captures this point. Both historians share the belief that the achievements of former empires pale in comparison with the nearly total domination of Rome. In Polybius' words, Rome had conquered "nearly the whole world" (cχεδὸν ἅπαντα τὰ κατὰ τὴν οἰκουμένην, 1.1.5). He then rattles off previous empires: Persians, Spartans, and especially Macedonians. The last deserves special comment: the Macedonians failed to take Sicily, Sardinia, Northern Africa, and knew nothing of the peoples inhabiting Western Europe. The Romans were better; they have conquered "nearly the whole world" (cχεδὸν ... πᾶcαν... τὴν οἰκουμένην, 1.2.7) – that phrase again.

Dionysius constructs his own list with differences that are small but significant (1.3). He begins with the Assyrians, then moves on to the Persians (who incidentally failed to overcome the European tribes), and finally, to the Macedonians, whose dominion he describes in much the same way as Polybius. Missing from the list to this point are the Greeks, but Dionysius reserves special comment for them. Greeks, he flatly admits, simply cannot compare with either those empires just mentioned or with the Romans: the Athenians (not even mentioned by Polybius) ruled not long and not much; the Spartans were no better. In the end, however, albeit with a greater flourish, Dionysius comes to the same point as Polybius: in distinction to these other powers, Rome has conquered nearly the whole world (1.3.3):

ἡ δὲ Ῥωμαίων πόλις ἁπάσης μὲν ἄρχει γῆς ὅση μὴ ἀνέμβατός ἐστιν, ἀλλ' ὑπ' ἀνθρώπων κατοικεῖται, πάσης δὲ κρατεῖ θαλάσσης, οὐ μόνον τῆς ἐντὸς Ἡρακλείων στηλῶν, ἀλλὰ καὶ τῆς Ὠκεανίτιδος ὅση πλεῖσθαι μὴ ἀδύνατός ἐστι, πρώτη καὶ μόνη τῶν ἐκ τοῦ παντὸς αἰῶνος μνημονευομένων ἀνατολὰς καὶ δύσεις ὅρους ποιησαμένη τῆς δυναστείας.

The city of Rome rules every land which is not unreachable and is inhabited; and she rules every sea, not only that within the Pillars of Heracles, but also of the sea of Ocean, except that part which cannot be sailed. And Rome is the first and the only nation of all those ever recorded who has made the rising and setting of the sun the boundaries of its Empire.

But Dionysius is able to make a point Polybius cannot, that Rome has experienced successes where others have failed, notably, in the conquest of Asia, Northern Africa, and Gaul. In the mid-second century, of course, these conquests had not yet happened. Thus the "nearly" in Polybius' "nearly the whole world" must carry more weight than appears at first sight; his claim is more rhetorical than it is credible.

Equally important is the acknowledgment of not only space – extent of conquest – but time as well. Polybius is impressed by the *speed* with which Rome has acquired its domain – only 53 years, measuring from the beginning of the Social War waged by the Aetolian League and its allies against Philip V down to the end of the Third Macedonian War (220–167 BCE), the period of time he originally intended to covered in his *History* (1.1.5; Erskine in this volume). Dionysius, on the other hand, is impressed by the *longevity* of Roman rule (1.2.1; Gabba 1991: 193). This he measures from the founding of Rome down to his own day (by his reckoning, 751 to 7 BCE), a period of 745 years; and interestingly, he dates by both consular year and Olympiads (1.3.3–4).

A further distinction emerges in the envisaged function of their work. Polybius famously describes his specific genre as "pragmatic history" (ἡ πραγματικὴ ἱστορία, 1.2.8; cf. 1.1.4; Walbank 1972: 56–8, 66–96); its aim is to educate those bent on a political career (1.1.2). But a political career where? Certainly not in Rome . . . or not exclusively in Rome. Polybius notably distances himself from Romans; when he speaks of "we," he means Greeks, not Romans (e.g., 1.3.7), and while he may anticipate that the lessons of his history will apply to Greek and Roman alike (Champion 2004, esp. 96–8), he writes with a Greek audience uppermost in his mind.

Dionysius, too, consistently refers to the Romans in the third person; like Polybius, when he says "we," he means "we Greeks" (e.g., 1.32.3). Yet while he may *seem* to distance himself from Romans in the same way as Polybius, in fact he does precisely the opposite. His aim is not to educate would-be politicians; nor is it merely to impress his reader with a litany of Roman virtues. Rather, he wishes to demonstrate that Romans are in fact Greeks (1.5.1; on Dionysius' tendency to identify Romans as Greeks see Gabba 1991: 87–8; Schultze 1986: 128–9). In so doing, of course, he brings Romans within the orbit of "we Greeks," effectively erasing the difference between "us" and "them" – a distinction rigorously maintained by Polybius.

It is in this context that the term Dionysius uses to characterize his work should be understood: ἡ κοινὴ ἱστορία (1.2.1). This is not "universal history" (as Cary 1943 renders it), but rather "common" or "shared history." This represents an important move away from Polybius' ἡ τῶν καθόλου πραγμάτων σύνταξις (1.4.2) – a "synthesis of events in general" or true "universal history," whose function he elaborates at some length (1.4.6–11). Incidentally, Dionysius' conception also suggests a still deeper engagement with Rome and the Romans than that which one encounters in Polyhistor or Posidonius. He demonstrates the fundamental unity of the Mediterranean peoples, and does not, like Polybius, merely narrate a series of interrelated events happening over an extensive geographic area that throw into relief the achievement of one discrete group, i.e., the Romans. Dionysius' approach, I would suggest, is the product of the emerging and increasingly ecumenical Roman Empire (and will find further expression in the writers associated with the Second Sophistic); the other, a characteristic of the Hellenistic period and of at least one form of Hellenistic historiography.

Polybius, therefore, would not have considered Dionysius' task a particularly profitable one, because it focused too exclusively on one people (cf. Polybius' criticisms of such narrowly focused histories at 1.4.3, with Walbank 1957 *ad loc.*). He may further have disapproved of Dionysius' lack of nuance in treating the Romans. This may be precisely why Dionysius feels compelled to defend his choice of subject. Ironically, he alleges that no historian has yet adequately celebrated Rome's achievement (1.2.1), yet this was exactly what Polybius himself implies he means to do (1.3.7–8). Polybius alleges that Greeks are unaware of the prior history of Rome and Carthage, a situation he intends to remedy; Dionysius, too, adduces the ignorance of his Greek reader as a motivating factor, though in this instance ignorance of "Rome's ancient history" (ἡ παλαιὰ τῆς Ῥωμαίων πόλεως ἱστορία, 1.4.2). It is an ignorance caused, however, not by inattention but, more seriously, by the falsifying and slanderous histories of his predecessors. It is difficult to resist the notion that Dionysius directs his criticisms here, at least in part, specifically at Polybius, a writer of whom he is elsewhere quite critical (e.g., *Comp.* 4), including once in the preface itself, where he lumps him together with other historians accused of producing "a few things carelessly thrown together" (ὀλίγα καὶ οὐδὲ ἀκριβῶς ... διεσπουδασμένα, 1.6.1; Fromentin 1998: 221 n. 4). Indeed, shortly before this he puts it even more baldly: there exists no history of Rome in Greek written by anyone of any competence (D.H. 1.5.4):

> οἱ δὲ σύμπαντες οἱ τοσοῦτο περιθέντες αὐτῆι δυναστείας μέγεθος ἀγνοοῦνται πρὸς Ἑλλήνων, οὐ τυχόντες ἀξιολόγου συγγραφέως· οὐδεμία γὰρ ἀκριβὴς ἐξελήλυθε περὶ αὐτῶν Ἑλληνὶς ἱστορία μέχρι τῶν καθ' ἡμᾶς χρόνων, ὅτι μὴ κεφαλαιώδεις ἐπιτομαὶ πάνυ βραχεῖαι.
>
> All of them (i.e., the Romans), despite having established for their country such a sizable hegemony, are unknown to Greeks: they have not yet found a worthy historian. For no truthful history of them has been published in Greek up to our time, except for some brief, summarizing epitomes.

Dionysius and the End of Hellenistic Historiography

It is, therefore, Dionysius *himself* who repudiates his Hellenistic predecessors, carving out a new historiographical niche, one which has far more in common with Cato and Livy – and, as we have seen, intermediary Greek historians such as Polyhistor and Posidonius – than it does with Polybius. However, the factors that contributed to the passing of Hellenistic historiography, of which Polybius was the last real representative, have nothing to do with whether or not Greeks "liked" or "disliked" Romans, or even whether the subject matter is Roman history or not. Rather, the increasing sophistication and growth of Roman literary and artistic culture, in absorbing and assimilating Hellenic culture (a process well documented by, among other texts, Cicero's *Pro Archia*), became a force to be reckoned with. The distinctive features of that culture would not have emerged without the infusion and influence of Hellenism, but nonetheless Roman culture managed to individuate itself from Hellenistic culture with stunning success. Polybius stands at the very beginning of that process, Dionysius witnessed its culmination.

In this regard, it is an obvious fact – but a fact that warrants emphasis – that there as yet existed no Latin historiographical tradition for Polybius to consult. While it is possible that he may have employed other types of Latin sources – documents, for instance, or perhaps the poet Ennius – they leave no discernible trace in the narrative, leading most Polybian scholars to conclude that his familiarity with or use of Latin materials was minimal (e.g., Walbank 1972: 81). In distinct contrast to Dionysius, Polybius wrote at a time when Roman historical writing was in its infancy. The tradition to which Polybius therefore looked (and indeed, to which the earliest Roman historians looked as well) was Greek, embodied in Herodotus, Thucydides, and Xenophon, to mention only the most famous. Thus despite its subject, in terms of conception, approach, and execution, the *Histories* of Polybius is purely Greek and purely Hellenistic. The same may not be said of Dionysius of Halicarnassus.

One further indication of this shift, to return to the evidence of the *Pro Archia*, is the fact that Cicero is able to place side-by-side chroniclers of Roman history who write in Greek with those who write in Latin. Ennius is the earliest of these. But closer to his own day, Cicero mentions Accius, another poet, who wrote about Decimus Brutus; and Lucius Plotius, who wrote of Marius' exploits as well as of Lucullus' (*Arch.* 20–7). It was Cicero himself who would lament the poverty of the Latin historiographical tradition (*Leg.* 1.5, written probably in the mid-40s BCE), though in the *Pro Archia* he views such commemorative writing as already firmly engrained in Roman culture, and practiced by Greek and Latin writers alike. And by the Augustan period, and in the Roman world in which Dionysius lived and worked, Roman historiography had acquired a vigor that even Cicero would have admired.

Dionysius in fact knew Latin well and had read broadly in Latin historians in the course of his research (1.7.2–4; Gabba 1991, esp. 1–4; Schultze 1986, esp. 121–4). He was thus fully conversant with the Latin historiographical tradition that had come into being and developed only *after* Polybius; Cato, the annalists, and Livy, to mention only the better-known examples, were all available to him (for Dionysius' possible use of Livy, whom he never actually cites, see Gabba 1991: 95–6). It is not, however, simply a question of the *historiographical* tradition. Dionysius' Augustan Rome was "cultured" in ways Polybius could not have imagined, a place now possessed of a literary tradition that had grown, flourished, and by the Augustan period reached what many would consider its apogee. It is no accident that Dionysius is as well known as a literary critic as he is as an historian. This dimension to his intellectual profile, so distinct from that of Polybius, may not *define* him as "Augustan" but it certainly aligns him with Augustan culture – that is, with the vibrant literary culture that defines the period. Dionysius is not adjacent to Augustan (and thus Roman) culture: he was *part* of it.

As often, it is Dionysius himself who proves the most trenchant analyst of his situation. Writing of the resurgence of rhetoric from the steady decline it had experienced in the period after Alexander, he praises the cultural renaissance, the "revolution" (μεταβολή) made possible by the Roman conquest (*Orat. Vett.* 3; Galinsky 1996: 340–2):

> αἰτία δ' οἶμαι καὶ ἀρχὴ τῆς τοςαύτης μεταβολῆς ἐγένετο ἡ πάντων κρατοῦςα Ῥώμη πρὸς ἑαυτὴν ἀναγκάζουςα τὰς ὅλας πόλεις ἀποβλέπειν καὶ ταύτης δὲ αὐτῆς οἱ δυναςτεύοντες κατ' ἀρετὴν καὶ ἀπὸ τοῦ κρατίςτου τὰ κοινὰ διοικοῦντες, εὐπαίδευτοι πάνυ καὶ γενναῖοι τὰς κρίςεις γενόμενοι, ὑφ' ὧν κοςμούμενον τό τε φρόνιμον τῆς πόλεως μέρος ἔτι μᾶλλον ἐπιδέδωκεν καὶ τὸ ἀνόητον ἠνάγκαςται νοῦν ἔχειν. τοιγάρτοι πολλαὶ μὲν ἱςτορίαι ςπουδῆς ἄξιαι γράφονται τοῖς νῦν, πολλοὶ δὲ λόγοι πολιτικοὶ χαρίεντες ἐκφέρονται φιλόςοφοί τε ςυντάξεις οὐ μὰ Δία εὐκαταφρόνητοι ἄλλαι τε πολλαὶ καὶ καλαὶ πραγματεῖαι καὶ Ῥωμαίοις καὶ Ἕλληςιν εὖ μάλα διεςπουδαςμέναι προεληλύθαςί τε καὶ προελεύςονται κατὰ τὸ εἰκός.

> The cause and origin of this revolution, I think, has been the fact that Rome has conquered everyone, compelling every city to look to her. Her leaders, in power because of their virtue, govern their commonwealth in good faith; they are exceptionally well educated, and with respect to their decisions, noble minded. Under their leadership the sensible portion of their city's population, being well governed, has improved still further, while the ignorant portion has been forced to come to its senses. As a result, many admirable histories have been composed by current writers, many satisfying political treatises and not insignificant philosophical tracts are being published; many other fine works as well are being produced and doubtless will continue to be produced by Greeks and Romans alike.

It is true, to be sure, that Dionysius provides no clue that he had read, for example, Horace or Vergil. In this he anticipates what will be generally true of his successors, especially in the Second Sophistic, who similarly took little interest in Latin literature in general. That said, it seems entirely credible that in this passage Dionysius is thinking of writers such as Cicero, Livy, and Sallust as well as poets such as Lucretius, Horace, and Vergil. His acute awareness and acknowledgment of a cultural revolution – and a revolution in which he imagines himself and other Greeks as full and equal participants – underscore the end of Hellenistic culture, supplanted by a literary and artistic tradition that would fuse the best of both worlds, Roman as well as Greek.

FURTHER READING

A good, recent survey of Hellenistic historiography may be found in Marincola 2001, though as is true of many such surveys, his concludes with Polybius; see also Connor 1985: 458–71, 786–7 and Oliver 2006. Gruen 1984: 316–56, with characteristic insight, places the Hellenistic historians in a useful context. For a more continuous account of historiography that reaches beyond Polybius, Lesky 1966: 772–80 is still valuable; so too Tarn 1927: 227–35, which, while dated, takes an unusually holistic view of Hellenistic historiography. Tarn terminates his survey essentially with Diodorus and, significantly, omits all mention of Dionysius of Halicarnassus. See also the comprehensive survey of Hellenistic historiography in Christ, Schmid, and Stählin 1959: 204–45. Yarrow 2006, an important book, contains much that is useful about the intellectual climate in which several of the authors discussed or mentioned in this paper worked and about the authors themselves (especially Posidonius, Diodorus Siculus, and Nicolaus of Damascus). With regards to Polybius and Dionysius of Halicarnassus specifically, I recommend, for the former, Champion 2004 (apart from proposing an innovative and interesting approach to the historian, this book is quite thorough in its use of previous scholarship on Polybius), and for the latter, Gabba 1991 and Pelling 2007.

CHAPTER TWENTY-SIX

Prose Fiction

Tim Whitmarsh

Hellenistic prose fiction is not a self-evident category. The Greek novel, as conventionally understood, is almost certainly a product entirely of Roman times (Bowie 2002). Xenophon of Ephesus, Achilles Tatius, Longus, and Heliodorus undoubtedly wrote in the first four centuries of our era; there is some debate over Chariton, but most commentators locate him in the first century CE. The various fragments are harder to date; recent critics have, however, tended to locate them in the first century CE or later.

This absence has not deterred the quest for traces of proto-fiction in the Hellenistic period; indeed, it has, perhaps predictably, stimulated it. The formative work of modern scholarship on Greek prose fiction – still subtly influential – has been Erwin Rohde's *Der griechische Roman und seine Vorläufer*, first published in 1876. Rohde's interest lay primarily in the Imperial novel, a phenomenon he sought to explain by revealing its "forerunners" (*Vorläufer*) in the Hellenistic period: principally, erotic poetry and prose travel narrative. The novel, in his view, was the hybrid offspring of these two Hellenistic forms.

Rohde's work has inspired a number of attempts to locate the origins of the Imperial novel (Lavagnini 1921; Giangrande 1962; Anderson 1984), but in general this kind of evolutionary narrative has fallen out of favor (see esp. Perry 1967: 14–15). There are, however, two consequences of his argument that are still with us. The first is a general reluctance to consider Hellenistic prose narrative on its own terms. Despite recent studies of individual works (Lightfoot 1999; Brown 2002; Winiarczyk 2002), scholars of ancient fiction have generally been too fixated upon the paradigm of the Imperial novel to acknowledge the existence of any culture of Hellenistic "fiction." If, however, we cease to view Hellenistic prose culture teleologically, that is to say simply as a stepping stone *en route* to the novel, then we can begin to appreciate a much more vibrant, dynamic tradition of storytelling. As we shall see below, there are indeed elements of continuity between Hellenistic prose and the Imperial novel; but the latter also self-consciously marks the break from its Hellenistic predecessors (Whitmarsh 2005a).

The second fallacy I wish to identify is the belief that Greek culture was insulated from non-Greek influence. Rohde's project is driven by a veiled racism, seeking to defend the novel against the charge (as he sees it) of oriental influence. "What hidden sources," he asks programmatically, "produced in Greece this most un-Greek of forms?" (Rohde 1914: 3). The identification of *echt* Hellenistic precursors allows him to preserve the Greekness of this superficially "un-Greek" form. Of course, few nowadays would formulate their views like this. Nevertheless, scholars of Greek literature tend to emphasize Greek sources, and hence tacitly to exclude the possibility of cultural fusion.

This chapter is principally designed to contest both these assumptions. The first half argues against the retrojection of anachronistic concepts of "fiction," arguing that we ought to look instead for challenges to dominant modes of narrative authority (conveyed particularly through the genres of epic and history). The second claims that Hellenistic narrative was energized by frictions both within Greek culture and between Greek and other cultures.

Ancient Fiction?

The category of fiction is not only philosophically complex, but also culture-specific: each society, in each historical phase, has its own different way of conceptualizing narratives that are accepted as not literally true, but instead serve as vehicles for a different order of moral or cultural truth. Fiction is not a linguistic pathology, but primarily and most fundamentally a way of expressing a culture's view of the logic of the world and the cosmos in narrative form (Pavel 1986; Newsom 1988; Currie 1990); it is, hence, responsive to changing ideas around the nature of the cosmos and humanity's place within it.

Although eternally aware of the potentially fictive properties of all discourse, Greeks only rarely acknowledged fiction as a *concept*: although partial exceptions can be found in forms of rhetoric and New Comedy (discussed below), it is not until the emergence of the novel in the Imperial period that one particular literary form became definitively fictive (Morgan 1993: 176–93; Schirren 2005: 15–37). In the Archaic, Classical, and Hellenistic periods, on the other hand, literary "fictions" were rather communicated through established narrative forms, which hovered ambiguously between truth and falsehood.

From earliest times it was accepted that poetry could mislead as well as pronounce authoritatively. Hesiod's Muses know how to tell "lies like the truth," as well as the truth (*Th.* 27). A similar phrase is used of Homer's Odysseus (*Od.* 19.203), who also prefaces his narration to the Phaeacians with a reminder that he is "famous among all for my deceptions" (9.19–20). Lyric poetry, from Archilochus to Pindar, is also full of reflections upon the truth status of stories and myths (Pratt 1983; Bowie 1993).

The fifth century, however, saw a set of cultural developments that increased consciousness of fictitious narrative (Finkelberg 1998; Rösler 1980, with reservations). When drama emerged as a major form in the fifth century, it too became a prime site for exploring questions of truth and fiction. The Sicilian sophist Gorgias famously claimed that in tragedy "the deceiver is more just than the non-deceiver, and the deceived wiser than the undeceived" (82 F 23 DK). Drama also presents the earliest examples of what critics would later call "plasmatic" narrative: stories based on neither historical nor mythical but on invented characters and events (Sext. Emp. *Math.* 1.263–5; Roman writers called this *argumentum*: *Rhet. Her.* 1.13; Quint. *Inst.* 2.4.2; further, Barwick 1928). This kind of plot can be found in mime, and even occasionally in tragedy (cf., e.g., Arist. *Poet.* 1451b), but is most prominent in comedy. Old Comedy often blends real figures (e.g., Cratinus' Pericles or Aristophanes' Cleon) with fictional, and uses scenarios that are fantastical distortions of contemporary reality. Hellenistic New Comedy, by contrast, is set in a "realistic" (if idealized) version of the democratic city, but uses entirely invented characters.

Comedy is thus one pre-Imperial literary genre that consistently handles people and events that are – and are recognized by the audience as – entirely conjured from the author's imagination. Another example is rhetoric: the scenarios of invented declamatory exercises (*progymnasmata* such as Lucian's *Tyrannicide* and *Disowned*), acted out by a speaker adopting the persona of another (a prosecutor, defendant or famous figure from the past), involve impersonation and make-believe (Webb 2006, esp. 43–4). Both set-piece rhetoric and comic drama are, indeed, as has long been acknowledged, key intertextual reference points for the Imperial novel, invoked as literary precedents (Fusillo 1989: 43–55, 77–83; Whitmarsh 2005b: 86–9).

Whether such dramatic and rhetorical acting actually constitutes fiction, however, turns entirely upon how we choose to define the concept. For the purposes of this chapter, I concentrate instead upon narrative forms, where the fictionality consists not in a performer mimetically assuming the role of another, but in the discursive presentation of invented scenarios as though they were true. This distinction is, admittedly, not absolute – genres such as epic and history could of course be performed mimetically, through recitation – but it will allow us to focus more sharply upon the literary techniques used by authors who wrote principally to be read.

Epic and Fiction

Pre-Imperial fiction, understood in this way, emerges not as a free-standing category, but as an ontologically ambiguous subcategory of existing narrative forms. Of these, the most evident is traditional hexameter epic. The Homeric and Hesiodic poems became a particular target of scorn in the early Classical period, when the so-called Ionian revolution shifted the burden of cosmic explanation from mythical narrative to physiological speculation. Xenophanes (early fifth century) mocks epic "inventions" (*plasmata*) about Centaurs (21 F 1.22 DK) and naive anthropomorphisms (F 13–14), chiding Homer and Hesiod for their depictions of divine immorality (F 10–12). Heraclitus too castigates his epic predecessors vigorously (F 42, 56–7, 105, 106). This process of decentering the cultural authority of epic continued within the philosophical tradition, most notably in Plato's famous critiques (in *Ion*, and especially *Rep.* 2–3 and 10).

Much of the anxiety, as the above examples show, focused upon the role of the gods, who were held to behave in ways that were either unbecoming or incredible (Feeney 1991: 5–56). For some ancient writers, the Homeric gods themselves were fictions. In a dramatic (perhaps satiric) fragment of the late fifth century, Critias has Sisyphus claim that the gods were invented by "a shrewd and thoughtful man," in order to terrify other humans into social conformity (88 F 25.12–13 DK). Whether this claim was undermined in the later narrative, we do not know; but it is clearly designed to reflect or refract contemporary sophistic beliefs, mimicking the patterns of social-constructionist anthropological aetiology elsewhere attributed to Prodicus and Protagoras (*P.Herc.* 1428 fr. 19, with Henrichs 1975: 107–23; Pl. *Prot.* 320c–323a).

This form of theological debunking is most fully realized in a Hellenistic text, Euhemerus of Messene's *Holy Account* (c.300 BCE; cf. below), which survives principally in the summary of Diodorus Siculus (6.1.3–10; contextual survey in Winiarczyk 2002). The author claims to have visited the Panchaean islands (supposedly off the eastern coast of Arabia), where he saw a golden pillar inscribed with the deeds of Ouranos, Kronos, and Zeus, three Panchaean kings (D.S. 6.1.7–10). The Greek gods were, it transpires, originally mortals, who were accounted gods because of their great achievements. Although it is not stated explicitly (at least in Diodorus' summary), Euhemerus' narrative clearly constitutes an implicit critique of Homeric fictionalizing. Euhemerus was influential upon Dionysius "Scytobrachion" (second century BCE), who composed prose versions of the Argonautic and Trojan events shorn of mythological apparatus (*FGrH* 32; Rusten 1982 adds three other fragments). In both cases, as far as one can tell from the fragments and summaries that survive, there is a playful tension between claims to narrative realism and the outrageously bathetic treatment of canonical myth (as emphasized by Rusten 1982, e.g. 112 [on the Libyan stories]: "a work of fiction"). As so often with literary innovation in the ancient world, new concepts emerge out of dialogue with the traditional narrative authority embodied in epic.

Further challenge to the veridical authority of epic came from the development of forensic oratory, beginning in fifth-century Athens. Particularly critical was the role of "plausibility" (*to eikos*): invoking or impugning the credibility of a particular account was a way of buttressing or assailing a speaker's trustworthiness (Goldhill 2002: 49–50). Rhetoric opened up a new language for assessing narrative: do we *believe* Homer's version of affairs? Is he a credible witness? Questions of narrative plausibility thus become central to literary criticism (they are famously prominent in Aristotle's discussion of tragic plotting in the *Poetics*). These debates persisted into the Hellenistic period. In the early third century, the scholar-poet Callimachus protests that "the ancient poets were not entirely truthful" (*Hymn to Zeus* 60) in their account of the gods' drawing of lots for heaven, earth and the underworld "it is plausible (*eoike*) that one should draw lots for equal things," not on such asymmetrical terms (62–3; Hopkinson 1984b). Later, in the first century CE, Dio Chrysostom would argue that Troy was not captured, making heavy use of the criterion of *to eikos* in his argument (11.16, 20, 55, 59, 67, 69, 70, 92, 130, 137, 139). Were such rhetorical confabulations promoted in the intervening Hellenistic period? We can, appropriately enough, appeal only to plausibility.

Back in late fifth-century Athens, such issues also allowed sophists to begin experimenting with alternative Homeric "realities." Hippias claimed to have an authoritative version of Trojan events, based not upon Homer alone but upon a synthesis of multiple sources (86 F 6 DK). Gorgias, followed in the mid-fourth century by Isocrates, defended Helen on the count of willing elopement, and composed a defense speech for Palamedes. Homer's most notorious woman could thus be re-appraised, and a figure who does not appear in the *Iliad* could be wedged into the Trojan War narrative. Sophistry also fostered a relativistic approach to storytelling. Around the turn of the fourth century, Antisthenes composed versions of Ajax's and Odysseus' speeches for the arms of Achilles. Once forensic rhetoric had permitted the idea that a single event could be narrated from multiple perspectives, then the Muse-given authority of the epic narrator ceased to be wholly authoritative.

This development allowed for the possibility of versions of the Trojan narrative told from alternative angles. The best-known examples are Imperial in date: in addition to Dio's *Trojan Oration*, noted above, we also have Philostratus' *Heroicus*, which impugns Homer's version of events for its pro-Odyssean bias, and the diaries of Dares and Dictys, which purport to offer eyewitness accounts of the Trojan War. This phenomenon has its roots in the numerous Hellenistic prose texts attempting to establish the truth of the Trojan War, now largely lost to us: philological works such as those of Apollodorus and Demetrius of Scepsis, and synthetic accounts like those of Idomeneus of Lampsacus and Metrodorus of Chios. Other late-Classical and Hellenistic versions seem to have come even closer to the fictionalizing accounts of the Imperial period. The fourth-century Palaephatus composed a *Trōika*, which seems to have concentrated on the rationalizing of wonders, like his extant *On Incredible Things*. A particularly captivating figure is Hegesianax of Alexandria Troas, a polymath of the third to second century BCE who composed a prose *Trōika* pseudonymously ascribed to one Cephalon (or, less probably, Cephalion) of Gergitha. "Cephalon" was probably not presented as a contemporary of the Trojan action, as is sometimes claimed: his account of the foundation two generations afterwards of Rome by Aeneas' son Romus (*sic*) seems to rule that out (*FGrH* 45 F 9). Nevertheless, the narrator certainly did pose as a voice from the distant past, and convincingly enough to persuade Dionysius of Halicarnassus, writing not much more than a century later, that he was an "extremely ancient" authority (1.72 = *FGrH* 45 F 9; cf. 1.49 = F 7).

Hellenistic texts also demonstrate a different kind of relativization of narrative authority, based upon the conflict between local traditions. Callimachus' *Hymn to Zeus* begins by noting the clash between two versions, the Cretan and the Arcadian, in relation to Zeus' birthplace. The poet professes himself "in two minds," before deciding upon the Arcadian version on the grounds that "Cretans are always liars" (4–9). The rejection of the "lying" tradition does not by itself guarantee that the other is true; in fact, the more emphasis one places upon partiality in traditional narrative, the less likely it becomes that any of it is true. Indeed, this is a poem that seems haunted by awareness of the fictionality of poetic traditions. Later, the poet mocks the story of the divine drawing of lots (discussed above), and expostulates: "May my own lies be such as to persuade my listener!" (65). Whatever the *narrator* means here – perhaps just "*if I ever lie*, I hope it's more persuasive than this" – readers can hardly miss the hidden author's wink, which playfully risks collapsing the whole poem into the black hole of untruth.

History and Fiction

These cultural shifts in the nature of narratorial authority also had implications for the writing of history. Prose records emerged in the fifth century, out of the same adversarial climate that produced cosmologists, scientists, and philosophers: a claim to speak the truth was at the same time a rejection of the falsehoods spoken by predecessors (Lloyd 1987: 56–70). As early as Hecataeus of Miletus (early fifth century) we find an author's programmatic assertion that he will deliver "the truth," in explicit contrast to the "many ridiculous stories" told by the Greeks (*FGrH* 1 F 1a). Herodotus (1.1–5) and particularly Thucydides begin with rationalized, scaled-down accounts of the Trojan War (1.1–22), which programmatically announce each author's factual reliability. Thucydides' austere rejection of "the mythical element" (*to muthōdes*, 1.22.4) in favor of "accuracy" (*akribeia*: 1.22.2; 5.20.2, 26.5, 68.2; 6.54.1, 55.3) marks his predecessors as inherently untrustworthy. Indeed, many extant authors of Greek history (Xenophon, the Oxyrhynchus historian, Polybius, Dionysius, Arrian, Appian, and so forth) do seem generally to replicate his fondness for relatively unadorned, linear narration.

Yet there was also a different tradition, stemming from Herodotus, which privileged storytelling, exoticism, and wonder (*thauma*). *Thauma* is, indeed, a key term in the history of fictional thought. Wonders occupy a peculiarly indeterminate epistemological position, between the plausible and the impossible (Packman 1991). Moreover wonders standardly form part of a discourse of geographical otherness, located at the margins of Greek ken (Romm 1992). *Thaumata* within a narrative are culturally or physiologically exotic, or both: they thus serve as a challenge to "our" received ideas as to what is plausible and what not.

Collections of *thaumata* and paradoxes become a genre in their own right in the Hellenistic period: such authors as Palaephatus, Callimachus, Antigonus of Carystus, Archelaus, Aristocles, Isigonus of Nicaea, and Apollonius compiled catalogues of extraordinary plants, animals, and events. Wonders also enriched the narrative texture of the now-fragmentary fourth-century historians Theopompus, Ephorus, and Timaeus. Dionysius of Halicarnassus remarks of Theopompus that "he tells of the inaugurations of dynasties and goes through the foundations of cities, he reveals the lifestyles of kings and the peculiarities of their habits, and includes in his work any wondrous paradox produced by land or sea" (D.H. *Pomp.* 6 = *FGrH* 115 T 20a[4]). These writers – famously excoriated by the austere Polybius (12.4a) – seem to have raised Herodotus' digressiveness (Theopompus *FGrH* 115 T 29–31; Ephorus 70 T 23; Timaeus 848 T 19) and prurience (Theopompus 115 T 2; Ephorus 79 T 18b) to new heights. Rather than seeing this habit in Polybian terms, as a deficiency of seriousness, it is preferable to see it as the sign of a distinctive literary aesthetic celebrating narrative polymorphousness – an aesthetic that seems to have exerted continued influence in swathes of Hellenistic history now largely lost (composed by figures such as Eudoxus of Rhodes, Myrsilus of Lesbos, and Zeno of Rhodes), and the influence of which can be seen everywhere in the Imperial novel (particularly evident in Antonius Diogenes' *Implausible Things beyond Thule*), as well as in the *Alexander Romance* (discussed below).

Allied to this textural experimentation was a willingness to embrace diverse content, including erotic narrative. The third-century historian Phylarchus – famously attacked by Polybius on the grounds of untruth and of presenting his narrative more like a tragedy than a history (Plb. 2.56.10–11 = Phylarchus *FGrH* 81 T 3; cf. Walbank 1960) – certainly incorporated erotic and mythological narrative. One of Parthenius' *Love Stories* (see below), a distinctive version of the attempted rape of Daphne by Apollo, is said in the manchette to derive from "Diodorus of Elaea and the fifteenth book of Phylarchus" (*Erot. Path.* 15 = *FGrH* 81 F 32). Another (*Erot. Path.* 23), detailing the love of Cleonymus of Sparta (third century) for his unfaithful wife Chilonis, is attributed by Plutarch to "Phylarchus and Hieronymus" (Plu. *Pyrrh.* 27.8 = *FGrH* 81 F 48; 154 F 14).

The most "romantic" of historians, however, according to tradition, was Ctesias of Cnidus, who served as the doctor to the Persian king Artaxerxes II (c.436–358 BCE). Ctesias' principal compositions were the *Persian Affairs* and *Indian History*, the former of which survives in summaries by Diodorus Siculus and Eusebius, as well as in numerous fragments (*FGrH* 688; Lenfant 2004; on Ctesias' importance in the history of fiction see esp. Holzberg 1993). These works were known in antiquity for their scurrility and exaggeration. Plutarch in his *Artaxerxes*, while using the *Persian Affairs* as a source for his own narrative, refers to Ctesias' "farrago of extravagant and incredible tales" (1.4 = *FGrH* 688 T 11d), which "turns away from the truth towards the dramatic and mythical (*to muthōdes*)" (6.9 = T 11e). Lucian cites him as one of his literary precursors in the prologue to his fantastical *True Stories*: "he wrote things about India and its customs that he had neither seen nor heard from anyone truthful" (1.3 = T 11h).

The surviving testimonia on Ctesias are uniformly critical of his mendacity, but he was clearly widely read in antiquity, particularly for the romantic themes and his orientalizing perspective upon Persia and the Middle East. If more of Ctesias survived then our understanding of the Persian scenes in Chariton and Heliodorus would no doubt be richer. Nor is his significance confined to this. He is our earliest known source for the story of the union between the Syrian (historical) Semiramis and the (mythical) Assyrian king Ninus (*FGrH* 688 F 1), which captivated later writers including Cornelius Alexander "Polyhistor" (*FGrH* 273 F 81) and the author of the fragmentary proto-novelistic work that modern scholars call the *Ninus Romance*, probably of the first century CE (Stephens and Winkler 1995: 23–71; Knippschild in this volume). This story clearly took on a narrative life of its own: Semiramis could be a hyper-powerful queen with divine elements as in Ctesias, who makes her the daughter of the Syrian goddess Derceto (~ Atargatis), and implicitly associates her with Astarte/Ištar; in the novel, she is transformed into a blushing maiden (Billault 2004); elsewhere we read that she was a prostitute who tricked Ninus out of his kingdom (*FGrH* 690 F 7; 681 F 1; Plu. *Mor.* 753d–e).

Ctesias is likely also to have been the source of an erotic intrigue between the Mede Stryangaeus and the Sacian Zarinaea, alluded to in a later source (Demetr. *Eloc.* 213; cf. *P.Oxy.* 2230 = *FGrH* 688 F 8b). This shows a range of motifs that will later re-appear in the Imperial novel: threatened suicide, a love letter, the bewailing of fortune (Holzberg 1993: 81–2). Again, the influence upon the later novels is arguably direct. Stryngaeus' letter to Zarinaea contained the phrase "I saved you – and although you were saved by me, I have been destroyed by you" (Demetr. *Eloc.* 213). The phrasing seems to have been picked up by Chariton and Achilles (perhaps via Chariton) in their letters of aggrieved lovers (Char. 4.3.10; Ach. Tat. 5.18.3–4).

Quasi-historical works such as these raise difficult questions. They are not "plasmatic": they deal with figures and events that already exist within the broad span of traditional records of the past. Moreover, while Lucian may cite Ctesias as a liar, and Polybius may reprove Phylarchus for mixing lies and truth, there is nothing to suggest that such texts were "fictional" at the level of a contract between reader and narrator. Ancient readers, presumably, turned to historians for truths, even if there were discrepancies between different kinds of truth and the different narrative registers through which they were communicated. Even so, neither is this history in the Thucydidean sense, of "realist" chronological sequence and meticulous accuracy. Ctesias, Theopompus, Ephorus, and Phylarchus, in their different ways, seem rather to have privileged (what they understood as) the Herodotean tradition of thrilling, episodic narrative; they re-instated "the mythical element" (*to muthōdes*) so famously excoriated by Thucydides (1.22.4; cf. 1.21.1). It is in the margins of historiography that Hellenistic prose culture develops its most vigorous storytelling.

Local Histories

In order to approach Hellenistic fiction, then, we need – paradoxically – to set aside the concept of fiction, and turn instead to the gray areas between history, mythology and creative storytelling, for it is here that Hellenistic culture typically locates its most exuberant narrative. I want to turn now to the local history of cities. "Local history" is, of course, not a coherent genre, but a modern label covering everything from verifiable recent history to the fantastic mythography of origin narratives. Such works were widely composed throughout Greek literature: I count over 85 titles alluding to specific locales that are securely datable to the Hellenistic period alone. Here more than anywhere, however, we are hampered by the fragmentary nature of sources. In the overwhelming majority of cases we have only brief snippets preserved in later sources, and reflecting the interests (often purely lexicographical) of the later author.

Nevertheless, there are good reasons to focus upon local history as a locus for fictional thinking. Greek accounts of the past that survive intact from antiquity are as a rule the synthesizing overviews that were too culturally authoritative for Christian late antiquity and Byzantium to ignore. Below this visible tip, however, lies a huge iceberg of diversity. Many of these stories may have circulated orally, whether jealously preserved as part of local culture or intermingled with more exotic stories thanks to cross-cultural traffic between travelers, traders, prostitutes, and soldiers. Oral culture is of course lost to us now, but some of its vibrancy can be detected in written texts that do survive.

The political organization of Greek society was highly conducive to generating stories. Each community advanced its own claims to prominence through local myths, often in the form of ktistic (dealing with foundation) or colonial narratives. For the Classical period, the works of Pindar and Bacchylides dramatize this phenomenon in abundance. Epigraphy in particular testifies to the genuine, ongoing importance to individual cities of ktistic myth in the Hellenistic period. Far from being simply a parlor game for intellectuals as was once thought, local myth-history was a politically important medium, through which a city might advance its claim to pre-eminence. Poets might be commissioned to add the luster of version: Apollonius of Rhodes and Rhianus were active in this field (*CA* pp. 5–8, 12–18; Cameron 1995a: 47–53), as of course was Callimachus (whose *Aetia* contains numerous examples of the type). Narratives might be inscribed on stone: an excellent example is the inscription recently discovered in the harbor wall of Halicarnassus, connecting the city's foundation with the nymph Salmacis and Hermaphroditus, the "inventor of marriage" (Lloyd-Jones 1999; Erskine in this volume). Another medium for preserving and disseminating local history was religious cult. The guides ("exegetes") whose role was to explain the sacred history of epichoric cult sites are more familiar from Imperial texts such as Plutarch's *On Why the Pythia No Longer Prophesies in Verse*, Pausanias, and Longus (Jones 2001); but the practice is already attested in Strabo (17.1.29), and would almost certainly have existed in the Hellenistic period.

What do these stories have to do with fiction? The first point to make is that local myths are both endowed with an intrinsic cultural authority and conceded (at least by the elite sophisticates who tend to record them) a license to confabulate, free from the rationalist strictures of more urbane narrative. Local history is expected to be bizarre, exotic: it tolerates stories of immortal intervention, of metamorphosis, of improper passion. It is no doubt for this reason that Longus' *faux-naïf* novel *Daphnis and Chloe* (second to third century CE) is dressed in the garb of a local myth, as told to the narrator by the exegete of a Lesbian cult of the Nymphs.

There is also a recurrent linkage between erotic narrative and local history: sexual union seems often to betoken some kind of foundational event (Rohde 1914: 42–59). Consequently, a number of texts emerged that used this form as a cover for scurrility and titillation. The most notorious example is the *Milesian Events* of Aristides: "lascivious books," according to Plutarch (*Crass.* 32.4). Ovid refers to Aristides in the same breath as Eubius, "the author of an impure history," and "he who recently wrote a *Sybaritic Events*" (*Tr.* 2.413–16). The *Suda* also attests to such works. Philip of Amphipolis (of unknown date) composed *Coan Events*, *Thasian Events*, and *Rhodian Events*, the last of which are styled "totally disgraceful" (*Suda* φ 351; cf. Theod. Prisc. *Eup.* Rose 1894: 133.5–12).

Late-Hellenistic prose collections of local narratives (by Nicander, Parthenius, Conon, and others; Lightfoot 1999: 224–34) point to the fact that they were increasingly perceived to have intrinsic narrative interest, independent of their original (or supposedly original) function in local ideology. Such collections are often united by narrative theme: Parthenius gathers love stories (like the pseudo-Plutarchan assemblage, which is probably later in date), and other later examples include the collection of metamorphosis stories of Antoninus Liberalis. What this suggests is that local history came to be viewed as a quarry for arresting and alluring narrative, independent of any "original" political, cultural or religious value to their communities. Parthenius, indeed, dedicates his collection to his patron Cornelius Gallus for use in his (Latin) hexameters and elegiacs: this is a collection designed not for locals but for the Empire's ruling class.

Local history is not fictional in the same way that the Imperial novel is (Lightfoot 1999: 256–63). Its subject matter veers from obscure mythology to central mythology to recent history, with plenty of indeterminate areas between. Nor is it "plasmatic," like the novel and New Comedy: so far from being invented *ex nihilo*, these stories tend to advertise their source history (witness, e.g., Callimachus' footnoting of Xenomedes in his story of Acontius and Cydippe, *Aetia* fr. 75.54–5 Pf.). For these reasons, it is misleading to present local history as a genetic predecessor of the Imperial novel (e.g., Lavagnini 1921). To grasp the fictionality of local history, we need to resist, once again, conceptions of fiction that are shaped by the Imperial period.

Greek and Near Eastern Narratives

The forms of local history and mythology emerging into view during this period were not just Greek. We have already discussed above the multiple versions of the story of the Syrian Semiramis and the Assyrian Ninus, which (for Greeks at least) stemmed ultimately from Ctesias. As the doctor of Artaxerxes II, Ctesias is likely to have had access to Persian narratives, and may well have spoken the language. Similarly culturally bifocal was Xenophon, whose experiences with the mercenary army of 10,000 fighting to support Cyrus – in his rebellion against Ctesias' patron Artaxerxes – will have brought him into contact with different traditions. Xenophon's most "novelistic" work was the *Cyropaedia*, an idealized biography of the king who united the Persians and Medes. Interwoven with the central section is a subnarrative dealing with the constant, enduring love between Panthea and Abradatas, before the latter is tragically killed in battle (4.6.11–12, 5.1.2–18, 6.1.31–51, 6.3.35–6.4.11, 7.1.15, 7.1.24–32, 7.1.46–9, 7.3.2–16). Critics have rightly emphasized the influence of this episode upon the Imperial novel, particularly upon the Persian episodes of Chariton's *Callirhoe* (Perry 1967: 166–73; Heiserman 1977). We also have a report in Philostratus (third century CE) of a work called *Araspes in Love with Panthea* (Araspes being a suitor of the Xenophontic Panthea), which some attribute to Dionysius of Miletus but Philostratus gives to a certain Celer (*VS* 524). Whether this was a "novel" (as modern critics tend to assume) or (more likely, in my view) a rhetorical declamation, it shows the iconic significance of this episode in amatory literary history.

Indeed, erotic prose seems to have been associated with eastern storytelling from the very beginning. Herodotus' *Histories* begins with the intriguing assertion that Persian *logioi* – the term seems to mean something like "prose chroniclers" (Nagy 1987) – tell the story of the Trojan War as an escalation in tit-for-tat woman-stealing after the Phoenician abduction of Io (1.1–4). The Phoenicians' version, Herodotus proceeds to tell us, is different: Io left willingly, having fallen pregnant by the captain of a Phoenician ship (1.5). Whether Herodotus is accurately reporting Persian and Phoenician traditions is simply unknowable: it is possible, but it is equally possible that it represents an orientalist mirage. The central point for our purposes, however, is that he is presenting himself as someone with access to Persian and north-Semitic cultural traditions – and also, crucially, implying that these traditions are preserved in a form alien to the Greek generic taxonomy, viz. "realist" (i.e., non-mythological) erotic prose. Nevertheless, thanks to Herodotus they become part of the Greek cultural repertoire, and part of the history of fiction (see in general Tatum 1997).

The allure of glamorous, oriental eroticism remains evident through the Hellenistic period. The Ninus and Semiramis story was undoubtedly the most popular "orientalist" narrative, but we can identify others too. Particularly notable is the association between (particularly erotic) prose fiction and Semitic culture. One striking example is the complex of narratives around Stratonice, the wife of Alexander's successor Seleucus, and her stepson Antiochus (later to be Antiochus I). According to the story, he fell in love with her, and began wasting away; the doctor Erasistratus diagnosed the problem, and then Seleucus ceded to him not only Stratonice but also his kingdom (Val. Max. 5.7 ext; Plu. *Demetr.* 38; Luc. *DDS* 17–18; App. *Syr.* 308–27; further sources at Lightfoot 2004: 373–4). Despite the historical characters, the main theme of the story is clearly folkloric: an inversion of the motif of the lusty older woman and the virtuous younger man, familiar from the Greek Hippolytus myth as well as the Hebrew story of Potiphar's wife (Genesis 39). The Semitic overtones of the story are strongly underlined in Lucian's version, which segues into an aetiology of the cult of the Syrian goddess Atargatis at Hierapolis (*DDS* 19–27; Lightfoot 2003: 373–402, with copious reference to Semitic parallels). It looks very much as though the historical story has been blended with a Syrian myth in order to explain the distinctive nature of the Hierapolitan cult.

This interpenetration of Greek and Semitic erotic narrative can be paralleled elsewhere. A certain Laetus composed a *Phoenician Events*, including accounts of the abduction of Europa and Eiramus' (i.e., Hiram's) presentation to Solomon of his daughter (together with an amount of wood – presumably Lebanese cedar – for ship-building; *FGrH* 784 F 1b). The latter story was also told by Menander of Ephesus, who was held (no doubt on his own testimony) to have learned Phoenician to access his sources (*FGrH* 783 T 3a–c). According to the *Suda*, Xenophon of Cyprus (undatable, but probably Hellenistic, and perhaps Ovid's source for the *Metamorphoses*) composed a *Cypriot Events*, glossed as "a history of erotic plots" including the stories of Cinyra, Myrrha, and Adonis. All of these figures are Semitic in origin, and no doubt reflect Cyprus' partially Phoenician heritage. We can point also to the *Nachleben* of the Phoenician setting in the Imperial romance, in Lollianus' *Phoenician Events* and Achilles Tatius' *Leucippe and Clitophon*.

Another erotic story that may be Semitic in origin is the notorious love between the children of Miletus, either of Caunus for his sister Byblis or the reverse. The major Hellenistic versions were in now fragmentary works of the epic poets Apollonius of Rhodes (*CA* 5) and Nicaenetus (*CA* 1), as well as the prose mythographers Parthenius (11, incorporating his own hexameter version, fr. 33 Lightfoot 1999 = *SH* 648) and Conon (2 Brown 2002; sources discussed at Rohde 1914: 101–3; also Lightfoot 1999: 433–6). The Semitic case (Brown 2002: 59–60) is based partly upon the incest motif (which superficially resembles that of the Cypro-Phoenician Myrrha narrative), and partly upon the name Byblis, which looks like an eponym for the Phoenician city of Byblos. It is also possible that Caunus is an originally Semitic name, given that Caria was a Phoenician settlement (Armand d'Angour suggests to me that it may derive from the root *qwn*, "sing" or "chant"). Again, a Semitic erotic myth has apparently entered the Greek tradition; as it has done so, its aetiological aspects have been gradually pared away to emphasize the erotic narrative.

A different kind of Semitic narrative hove over the Greek horizon with the translation of the Septuagint (discussed by Gruen in this volume): a number of the so-called apocrypha have been claimed as "novels," including Esther, Susanna, Judith, and Daniel (the Greek version of which is longer than the Hebrew, having taken on a life of its own: Wills 1995, 2002). To what extent gentiles actually read them is more difficult to ascertain: beyond the much-debated reference to Genesis in the treatise *On the Sublime* (9.9) – which is itself nigh-impossible to date – there is little evidence for a "pagan" Greek readership of Jewish texts. Even at the stylistic level, they manifest a certain intractability, their paratactic style (which renders the *vav* ["and"] constructions distinctive to the Hebrew language) marking their difference from "native" Greek. But the non-existence of evidence for circulation is not evidence for its non-existence: who knows how widely these stories traveled? In any case, direct influence is only one form of cultural contingency; they do in fact share motifs with Greco-Roman story culture. In particular, the focus upon the preservation of female integrity in the face of predatory monarchs (present in Judith and Esther) is a theme that we find in both Latin (Lucretia) and Greek (Chariton, Xenophon, Achilles Tatius, Heliodorus) narrative.

Certainly, Jewish narrative seems to have been influenced by the Greek erotic tradition. Retellings of the erotic segments of the Torah by Josephus and Philo seem to inflect them with Greek narrative motifs (Braun 1934). The convergences between Greek and Jewish are closest in the extraordinary *Joseph and Aseneth* (also discussed by Gruen in this volume), which elaborates upon the biblical story of Joseph's marriage to a young Egyptian maiden (Genesis 41:45; cf. 26:20). This text may be Hellenistic (S. West 1974: 80–1, tentatively suggesting the first century BCE), although it is probably overlain with Christian ideas (Philonenko 1968: 99–109, arguing for a second-century CE date), the latest strata perhaps being late-antique (Kraemer 1998: 225–42). Whatever the truth of that matter, the history of this text is clearly interwoven with the rise of the erotic novel. This narrative plays repeatedly upon the substitution of erotic with righteous motifs. She is egregiously beautiful like a goddess (4.2); she is immediately stupefied by the sight of him (6.1), grieves when they are separated after their initial meeting (8.8), and weeps in her room that night (10.2; Philonenko 1968: 43–8; S. West 1974). Yet their relationship is built around not just erotic obsession but also pious reverence of the Jewish god. Although this text is aimed at Jews and probably represents a translation from the Hebrew (it displays the same paratactic style as the apocrypha), it is clearly designed for a readership also familiar with the Greek literary (and particularly erotic) repertoire.

Greece and Egypt

The existence of significant Hellenistic prose stories on pharaonic themes, Egypt's prominence in the later, Imperial novel, and the significance of Hellenistic Alexandria as a point of intersection between Greek and Egyptian traditions (Selden 1998; Stephens 2003), have together led some to believe that the novel first developed in

Egypt (Barns 1956). Scholars have even detected in the Imperial novel survivals of narrative motifs from the pharaonic period (Rutherford 1997, 2000). While any crude hypothesis of a single cultural origin for the novel is unconvincing (in the light of the evidence discussed above for local Greek and Semitic elements), it is clear that Egypt played an important role in the novelistic *imaginaire*.

Two major traditions are of critical importance. The first is that surrounding the king and conqueror Sesonchosis (or Sesostris, Sesoosis), a mythical amalgam of various historical pharaohs (Stephens and Winkler 1995: 246; Dieleman and Moyer in this volume), credited with numerous conquests in Asia and Europe. In addition to the various historical (or quasi-historical) accounts of this figure (Hdt. 2.102–11; Manetho *FGrH* 609 F 2, p. 30; D.S. 1.53), we also have three papyrus fragments that seem to derive from a "novelistic" version of the story, composed in unassuming Greek (Stephens and Winkler 1995: 252–66). Two are military (one names the king's adversaries as an "Arab" [Palestinian?] contingent, led by one Webelis); a third, however, is erotic, describing the handsome young king's relationship with a girl Meameris, the daughter of a vassal king. This episode does not appear in any of the "historical" versions of the narrative, and the themes of young love, wandering, infatuation, erotic suffering, and distraction at a banquet (Stephens and Winkler 1995: 262) invite obvious comparisons with the Imperial novel. Thematically, the narrative resembles the fragmentary, novelistic version of the *Ninus Romance* (discussed above): each deals with a great national leader from the distant past, focusing upon both military exploits and erotic vulnerability.

What we are to conclude from these similarities is less clear: is *Sesonchosis* a text (or, at any rate, part of a now-lost tradition) that exerted a powerful influence on later erotic fiction? Or does it represent a specifically local-Egyptian, populist variant upon the Imperial novel? A third alternative, no doubt the safest, is to rephrase the terms of the question. "The Greek novel" and "the Sesonchosis tradition" were not monolithic and wholly independent traditions, nor was any traffic between the two necessarily unidirectional. As in the case of the Phoenician and Jewish material discussed above, Greek narrative prose proves to be a flexible and capacious medium, able to incorporate numerous cultural perspectives.

This is nowhere truer than in relation to the most important Egyptian-centered text, the text we call the *Alexander Romance* (Hägg 1984: 125–40; Jouanno 2002: 57–125; Stoneman 2003; Dieleman and Moyer, Stephens in this volume). The work survives in numerous different recensions, some prose and some (Byzantine) in verse; in all, there are over 80 versions from antiquity and the middle ages, in 24 languages (including Pahlavi, Arabic, Armenian and Bulgarian). Different versions contain different episodes, sequences and cultural priorities: the *Alexander Romance* is a prism, through which cultural light is sharply refracted.

The earliest recension is referred to as A, and represents a text probably compiled between the second and fourth centuries CE. The raw materials for this earliest stratum of the complete text were, however, Hellenistic: a bedrock of (creatively) historical narrative, an epistolary novel (manifested in the various letters that dapple the text, most notably Alexander's letters to his mother Olympias, 2.23–41), and a work of Egyptian propaganda. The latter is the motivation behind the identification of Alexander as the son, and hence continuator, of the last pharaoh Nectanebo

(1.1–12). The Persian invasion can thus be re-interpreted as a minor blip in the otherwise unbroken tradition of wise, powerful, and autonomous Egyptian kingship. On seeing a statue of Nectanebo, Alexander is told that a prophecy was delivered to his father: "the exiled king will return to Egypt, not as an old man but as a youth, and will beat down our enemies, the Persians" (1.34.5). Alexander's pharaonic credentials, indeed, are more deeply rooted than this. He visits monumental obelisks set up by Sesonchosis (1.33.6, 3.17.17), is hailed as a new Sesonchosis (1.34.2), and even receives a dream visitation from the man himself, announcing that Alexander's feats have outdone his. These episodes function on two levels: Alexander is appropriated into Egyptian history, as the restorer of Egypt's self-determination; and the *Alexander Romance* presents itself as a rejuvenated version of the Sesonchosis tradition.

In the substance of the narrative, however, he represents a figure with whom all peoples can identify: a wise, brave, questing prince, seeking out the edges of the earth. As so often in Greek narrative of this period, he is also a lover: a section towards the end, perhaps originally a separate romance, details his (entirely fictitious) liaison with Candace, queen of Meroe (3.18–23). Here too, there is a hint that the author is weaving together different traditions: Candace lives in the former palace of Semiramis (3.17.42–18.1). What is striking is not so much the tweaking (although the Ctesian Semiramis did in fact visit Nubia), but the author's self-conscious concern to portray this section of his narrative as a metamorphosed version of the Ninus and Semiramis story. If the fidelity to tradition is dubious, the negotiation of the anxiety of cultural influence is artful. The *Alexander Romance* presents itself as the summation of that tradition, outdoing each of its predecessors, just as its subject outdid all others in conquest.

Imaginary Worlds

The primary locations for such narrative confections were, then, Egypt and the Syrian coast. Others exist (for instance, the Black Sea littoral in the fragmentary *Calligone*, of uncertain date), but I want to conclude by focusing briefly upon two narratives set in imaginary worlds, Iambulus' "utopia," which modern scholars like to call *The Islands of the Sun* (second to first century BCE; Winston 1976), and the *Holy Account* of Euhemerus of Messene (c.300 BCE; Rohde 1914: 210–60; Winiarczyk 2002; Holzberg 2003). Each is preserved primarily in a summary by Diodorus Siculus (2.55–60 and 6.1.3–10 respectively), which gives little flavor of the tone and style of the originals, and moreover appropriates the content to suit Diodorus' own agenda, viz. a universal history in which all the individual elements cohere. Euhemerus' and Iambulus' narratives are geographically similar: both involve sea journeys beginning in Arabia (via Ethiopia in Iambulus), and into the Indian Ocean. It is tempting, given our discussion above, to see this journey as a self-conscious attempt to outdo the Semitic and Egyptian narrative traditions (as well as Alexander's conquests), by progressing beyond their geographical limits.

Despite the difficulties in peering through the Diodoran fug, certain features are evident. Euhemerus, as we have seen earlier, was concerned primarily to provide human, historical identities for the Homeric/Hesiodic pantheon. His actual journey to Panchaea seems not to have been described in any detail; the process of geographical dislocation is primarily a device allowing him to offer a perspective that is radically alternative to traditional Greek thought (in this respect, he is a forerunner of authors like Swift, the Butler of *Erewhon* and *Erewhon Revisited*, Edwin Abbott, Jules Verne, and Pierre Boulle). Certainly, the ancient tradition sees Euhemerus more as an atheist philosopher than as a travel writer (Winiarczyk 2002: 12–13, 28–52).

Iambulus is more difficult. Some have detected a philosophical, even political, promotion of a communist society "according to nature." The islanders "do not marry, but hold their wives in common, rearing any children that are born as common to them all, and love them equally ... for this reason no rivalry arises among them and they live their lives free of faction, extolling likemindedness to the highest" (2.57.1). Iambulus (or Diodorus) describes a society that embodies the ideals of Greeks politics (no "faction," *stasis*, only "likemindedness," *homonoia*) by following the principals of common property laid out in Plato's *Republic* (449c–50a; on the influence of this text on later philosophical utopias, see Dawson 1992b). Yet the socio-political aspects of the island in fact receive far less attention than the bountiful nature of the island, and the extraordinary health, size and longevity of its inhabitants. Diodorus prefaces his summary by promising to recapitulate in brief the "paradoxes" (*ta paradoxa*, 2.55.1) found on the island, a strong signal that he, at any rate, conceived of Iambulus as a purveyor of marvels rather than a systematic political theorist. Lucian too in his *True Stories* refers to his "paradoxes," adding that "it is obvious to everyone that he fabricated a fiction" (*pseudos*, 1). Iambulus seems to have found room enough within a supposedly veridical genre, the geographical travel narrative, to create a "fictional" work.

As recent scholarship has noted, there is an intrinsic connection in the ancient world between travel and fiction: alternative geographies are home to alternative realities (Romm 1992, esp. 172–214). Names of Hellenistic authors such as Antiphanes of Berge – who claimed to have visited a climate so cold that words froze in the air (Plu. *Mor.* 79a) – and Pytheas of Massilia became bywords for literary confection. It is important, however, to re-emphasize that there was no firm generic dividing line between "factual" report and "fiction." The writers we have discussed in this section inhabited the same literary space as more sober geographical writers like Strabo – which is why Diodorus felt licensed to include such material in his own purportedly historical work.

***

I have argued in this chapter that Hellenistic prose fiction needs to be understood on its own terms, not simply as a forerunner to the Imperial novel. In particular, prose fiction does not occupy its own generic category; rather, it nests in the form of supposedly veridical literature, especially history and travel narrative. I have also argued that imaginative storytelling often emerges from the friction between Greek history and exotic cultural traditions, whether *bizarreries* of local Greek cult, non-Greek traditions, or (in some cases) completely invented locales. Hellenistic Greeks who experimented with these new forms of exciting, episodic and/or erotic narrative tended to locate them in Greek backwaters, or in a cultural "elsewhere" (typically, but not exclusively, Egypt and the Near East. This is no doubt in part a defense mechanism: scandalous stories are less offensive if they are about other peoples.

This, however, is not the whole story. Hellenistic Greek literature was not written by Greeks peeking at other peoples over the crenellations of their own cultural traditions, as is so often assumed. The prose innovations of the period are the products of genuine cross-cultural hybridity, fusing Greek, Egyptian, Semitic, and indeed other elements into literary forms that are recognizably different from their predecessors. The works discussed in this chapter do not simply rehash barbarian stereotypes from the Classical period. Rather, they are composed by people with an impressive range of cultural competence: figures like Ctesias, Laetus, Alexander Polyhistor, and the authors of *Joseph and Aseneth*, the *Alexander Romance*, and *Sesonchosis*.

This, then, is the primary reason why so much searching for the "origins" of the Imperial novel in the Hellenistic period is wrong-headed: fiction is inherently hybrid; it has no single point of origin. Storytelling in this period is born of the kind of cultural dialogue between traditions that we have been discussing; it makes no sense to attempt to pinpoint a literary prime mover in (for example) Greek travel narrative or Egyptian resistance literature, and then hypothesize about its impact in other cultural fields. The story of prose fiction in antiquity is not clean, clear, and linear: we should imagine a much more tangled network of influences, contraflowing simultaneously between multiple narrative forms.

FURTHER READING

For the fragments of novels and related material (some of which may be Hellenistic) see Stephens and Winkler 1995; this corpus has since been supplemented by Hägg and Utas 2003, offering new material in relation to *Metiochus and Parthenope*, and *P.Oxy.* 4760–2, 4811. The larger fragments are also translated, together with the extant novels (including the *Alexander Romance* but not *Joseph and Aseneth*) in Reardon 1989. For a Greek text of the *Alexander Romance* see Van Thiel 1974, and (for book 1) Stoneman 2007. Hägg 1984: 125–40, Jouanna 2002, and Stoneman 2003 offer helpful introductions; see also the general account of Stoneman 2008. *Joseph and Aseneth* is best consulted in Philonenko 1968; see Humphrey 2000 for a recent translation, and Kraemer 1998 for discussion and bibliography. For translations of the Jewish apocrypha see Wills 2002, with Wills 1995 for discussion and further references. Fragmentary Hellenistic prose narratives can be consulted (in Greek, with German commentary) in Felix Jacoby's multi-volume *Fragmente der griechischen Historiker* (*FGrH*), presently being re-edited (with English translation and commentary) as *Brill's New Jacoby* (*BNJ*) under the direction of Ian Worthington. For text, translation, and interpretation of Parthenius and Conon respectively see Lightfoot 1999 and Brown 2002. Rusten 1982 offers a rich discussion of Dionysius Scytobrachion, focusing on papyrus fragments; Winiarczyk 2002 is a good contextual account of Euhemerus, while Winston 1976 discusses Iambulus. "Utopias" in general are surveyed by Ferguson 1975 (a rather superficial account) and Dawson 1992b (focusing on the influence of Plato's philosophical "republic"); see also duBois 2006. Paradoxography is a neglected field: Ziegler 1949 is still authoritative; see also Hansen 1996.

Among modern theories of fiction, the most helpful are Pavel 1986, Newsom 1988 and Currie 1990. Ancient theories are discussed by Barwick 1928, focusing on the division in rhetoric between historical, mythical and "plasmatic" (invented) narratives; Rösler 1980, arguing (not fully convincingly) that the spread of literacy caused awareness of fiction;

Feeney 1991, on the conceptual trouble caused by the gods in post-Homeric culture; Gill 1993, on Platonic ideas of falsehood; Morgan 1993: 176–93 and 2007, focusing on the Greek novel; Feeney 1993, a general discussion; Finkelberg 1998, on philosophical developments in the Classical period; Schirren 2005: 15–37, linking ancient ideas with semiotic theory. For older theories on the emergence of "fiction" in the Hellenistic period, see Lavagnini 1921; Braun 1934; Giangrande 1962.

PART FOUR

Neighbors

CHAPTER TWENTY-SEVEN

Jewish Literature

Erich S. Gruen

Hellenistic Jews inhabited a world dominated by Greek culture. Whether they dwelled in Alexandria, Cyrene, Antioch, Corinth, or even Palestine, they encountered (indeed became) Greek-speakers, gained exposure to Greek social and political institutions, and, at least among the educated classes, acquired a deep familiarity with Greek literature. Greek was the language of diaspora Jews everywhere in the Mediterranean (and a good number in Palestine too). As late as the fourth and fifth centuries CE the Jews of Rome still composed their epitaphs in Greek, a remarkable testimony to the tenacity of Hellenism in the far-flung communities of the Hebrews.

The lure of Greek culture did not entail "assimilation," a loaded and deceptive term. Jews retained their traditions, their distinctive traits, and their history. They simply found ways to express them in Greek. The surviving examples of Jewish writing in that language (and we have just a fraction of the corpus) show a command of Hellenic literature but also a drive to convert it to Jewish ends.

Translation of the Hebrew Bible into Greek, begun possibly as early as the third century BCE, emblematizes this process. The tale of that event as recorded in the *Letter of Aristeas* may be a fantasy. But the translation is a fact. The creation of the Septuagint probably did not come about on the initiative of the librarian in Alexandria or at the command of a Hellenistic monarch. The need for a Greek Bible arose largely because diaspora Jews had lost the mastery of Hebrew but clung to the centerpiece of their tradition. The new version acquired the sanctity of the old, not a replacement but an exact replica (so, at least, it was portrayed). The expression of the Jews' deepest beliefs and fundamental lore in the language of the diaspora signals the embrace of Hellenism for the advance of Judaism.

This mode of thinking characterizes at its essence the encounter of the cultures. There was no "clash of civilizations." Jews did not face a dilemma in which every adoption of Greek learning required them to sacrifice part of their heritage. The conquests of Alexander the Great brought a host of Greeks into the lands of the Near East. The removal of the Persian regime, the reshuffling of the political order, and the large-scale creation, re-foundation, and expansion of settlements that followed Alexander's invasion sparked a wave of migrations ushering in an era of mobility and relocation. Jews took advantage of it. The Greek diaspora inspired a Jewish one in its wake. Jews joined communities old and new in various parts of the Mediterranean that were at least partially Hellenic in makeup. And they found more and more Greek or Greco-Phoenician communities in and around the lands of Syria and Palestine. Jews met Hellenism in one form or other almost anywhere they dwelled. A gymnasium stood even in Jerusalem itself, installed on the directive of none other than the High Priest – not to cater to the Greeks but to delight the Jews (*2 Macc.* 4.9–14).

In view of this, a good grasp of Greek literature causes no surprise. Jewish intellectuals were well versed in most forms of Hellenic writings and wrote in a wide range of Greek literary genres. Those conversant with the conventions include epic poets like Theodotus and Philo, tragedians like Ezekiel, historians like Demetrius and Eupolemus, philosophers like Aristobulus, composers of prose fiction like the authors of the *Letter of Aristeas*, *3 Maccabees*, and *Joseph and Aseneth*, and those who engaged in cosmology and mythography like Pseudo-Eupolemus and the author of the *Sibylline Oracles*. But, although they wrote in Greek and adapted Greek literary modes, they held undeviatingly to the goals of rewriting biblical narratives, recasting the traditions of their forefathers, and shaping the distinctive identity of Jews within the larger Hellenistic world. Jewish intellectuals may have utilized Greek genres but they saw no value in recounting the tale of Troy, the labors of Heracles, the Persian Wars, or the contest of Athens and Sparta. Their heroes were Abraham, Joseph, and Moses.

Greek Genres and Jewish Content

A few examples will suffice to illustrate the Jewish penchant for appropriating Hellenic conventions to refashion their own heritage. Tragic drama, for instance, has a notable representative. Little of it survives from Hellenistic Greeks (Sens in this volume), but we have an extensive portion of a play produced by a Jewish dramatist named (and the name is almost all that we know of him) Ezekiel (text in Jacobson 1983: 50–67; Holladay 1989: 344–405; *TrGF* 128). His play, the *Exagoge*, was one of many Jewish tragedies, but the only extant one. Ezekiel was steeped in the tradition of Athenian drama, strongly influenced by Euripides, but also enamored of themes and motifs to be found in Aeschylus (Jacobson 1983: 23–8). He held to the traditions of the Greek theater, writing monologues and dialogues in iambic trimeter verse, keeping the battle scenes and the gore off stage, even bringing on the trusty messenger to summarize events. But the subject matter remained rigorously biblical. Ezekiel retold the story of the Exodus, employing the tragic mode to convey a familiar tale in a new form. He followed closely the narrative and language of the Septuagint (there is nothing to suggest that he consulted the Hebrew version or even knew the language), but did not refrain from injecting elements that went beyond material in the Book of Exodus. In one notable scene, he invented a dream in which Moses saw a great throne at the cleft of heaven and a noble man handed him a scepter and diadem and left the throne to him. Moses' father-in-law then interpreted the dream as signifying that

Moses would exercise a vast new authority and would serve as a guide to mortals everywhere (Eus. *PE* 9.29.4–6). The passage corresponds to nothing in the Book of Exodus. Indeed no other tale anywhere ascribes a dream vision to Moses. But Greek tragedy supplied ample precedents. And the Moses figure in the *Exagoge* would resonate with Ezekiel's contemporaries. His role as executor of God's will on earth, with absolute authority, plainly evokes contemporary royal rule. Moses becomes precursor of the Hellenistic kings (Gruen 1998: 128–35; Collins 2000: 224–30). The Greek influence is powerful, but the biblical tale holds center stage. Ezekiel has effectively commandeered a pre-eminent Hellenic genre and deployed it as a source of esteem for his Jewish readership.

Another venerable Greek genre attracted Jewish writers: epic poetry. A certain Theodotus, of unknown provenance and only approximate date (prior to the first century BCE), composed hexameters in Homeric language and style that exhibit parallels also with Hellenistic epic and epyllia (text in Holladay 1989: 51–99). A familiarity with the contemporary literary scene is plain. Form, genre, and expression in the fragments suggest an education of the most exemplary Hellenic sort. Yet the topic of his surviving fragments, all lamentably brief, is a strictly Hebrew one, the tale of Dinah's rape by the Shechemites and the rather questionable retaliation by the sons of Jacob in Genesis 34 (Eus. *PE* 9.22.1–11; Holladay 1989: 106–27). Theodotus cleans up the biblical story somewhat, softening the duplicity of the Israelites and treating the Shechemites more as impious violators than as victims, but he keeps in general to the Genesis narrative. He injects a palpable Greek element or two into the presentation, such as identifying Shechem's founder with the son of Hermes, treating the city's origins as a *ktisis* tale, and having its fate determined by an oracular forecast. Yet Theodotus unabashedly employed epic poetry and Homeric style to recast a biblical narrative in the interest of exculpating the Hebrew patriarchs (Pummer 1982: 177–88; Gruen 1998: 120–5).

We have the name and a few fragments of one other Jew who composed in the epic genre. Philo (c.100 BCE) produced an apparently lengthy poem, *On Jerusalem*, of which we have a bare fraction. The title may imply that this work fits into the frame of Hellenistic epic that celebrated the foundations of cities, such as Rhianus' *Messeniaca*, Pseudo-Moschus' *Megara*, and the *Ktiseis* of Apollonius Rhodius (*CA* 4–12). The extant fragments, a mere 24 lines, exhibit tortured language, enveloped in studied obscurity, the vocabulary rich in *hapax legomena*, and a variety of arcane allusions as if to outdo the opacity of a Lycophron (text in Holladay 1989: 234–45). The style of Philo's poetry is thoroughly Hellenistic. Yet the subject matter is again firmly rooted in Jewish tradition. The surviving verses treat Abraham, Joseph, and the waters of Jerusalem. And the inflated language that hails Abraham as "abounding in lofty counsels" and Joseph as holder of the scepter on the "thrones of Egypt" carries significance. Like Theodotus, Philo employed the epic genre to expand upon Scripture. In his verses the Hebrew patriarchs take on a pronounced eminence designed to resonate with a sophisticated audience (Gruen 1998: 125–7; Collins 2000: 54–7).

Historiography claimed additional Jewish practitioners. The first of whom we are aware, Demetrius, dates to the later third century. The remains of his work too are scanty but revealing. They show a keen interest in solving chronological and other historical puzzles, an understanding of critical method, and an adherence to rational inquiry that may owe something to Alexandrian scholarship (text in Holladay 1983: 62–79; Bickerman 1975: 72–84; Sterling 1992: 153–67). But Demetrius trains his focus exclusively on issues arising out of the Bible. So, for example, in case anyone wondered how Jacob managed to father 12 children in just seven years, he offered a solution: there were four different mothers (Eus. *PE* 9.21.3–5). On the question of how the Israelites, who left Egypt unarmed, managed to secure weapons in the desert, he had an answer: they appropriated the arms of Egyptians who drowned in the sea (Eus. *PE* 9.29.16). This was not frivolous exegesis. For Jews exposed to Greek learning and historical investigation, the Bible presented some vexing inconsistencies, chronological disparities, and historical perplexities. Demetrius took the authority of the Scriptures for granted but wrote for a sophisticated readership. He adapted Hellenic scholarly methods to re-inforce confidence in the biblical tradition and to corroborate the record of his nation's past (Gruen 1998: 112–18).

A final example in a different genre confirms the point. The enigmatic but entertaining prose narrative *Joseph and Aseneth*, which survives intact (in more than one version), defies ready categorization. Its date too remains a matter of controversy, with some seeing it as a Christian text and putting it as late as the fourth century CE (Kraemer 1998: 225–85). But common consensus puts it in the late Hellenistic period (Johnson 2004: 108–9). The work has clear affinities (though equally clear differences) with what we generally classify as Greek romances, such as those of Chariton, Xenophon of Ephesus, and Longus. The relative dates of these works and *Joseph and Aseneth* cannot be determined, but the genre or a form thereof goes back at least to the fragmentary *Ninus Romance*, which belongs to the late Hellenistic period (Whitmarsh in this volume). There can, in any case, be little doubt that *Joseph and Aseneth* belongs to the category of protreptic prose fiction (like Xenophon's *Cyropaedia*), composed for entertainment but also communicating values, ideas, or offering guidance (S. West 1974: 70–81; Wills 1995: 170–84; Chesnutt 1995: 85–92; Johnson 2004: 108–20). Hellenic and Jewish influences may well be mutual rather than one-sided. But the work certainly emerged in a literary climate that also produced the Hellenic novel. *Joseph and Aseneth*, like the other works discussed above, draws the inspiration for its tale from the Pentateuch. In this case, however, the Book of Genesis serves as the merest launching pad (the union of the Hebrew patriarch Joseph with the Egyptian noblewoman Aseneth) for a narrative that goes far beyond the scriptural text. The narrative combines two loosely connected fantasies, the first a love story in which the initially antagonistic principals, of different faiths and ethnicity, are brought together in a happy marriage, the second an adventure tale that divides the households of both Joseph and the pharaoh, culminating in a mighty battle and a final reconciliation. The close links with Greek prose fiction do not obviate the fact that this text has its setting entirely in the world of the ancient Hebrews and embellishes upon a core to be found in the Torah.

Jewish authors, in short, showed a wide familiarity with the genres, forms, and styles of Greek literature. But concluding that such familiarity betokened assimilation or acculturation misplaces the emphasis and misunderstands the process. Jews consistently employed Hellenic texts and conventions to express their own traditions, to recast and re-invigorate their ancient legends, and to convey their values in modes shared by the intellectual world of the Hellenistic era.

The *Letter of Aristeas*

Hellenistic Jewish authors did not by any means confine themselves to wrapping biblical tales in contemporary packages. They could incorporate Greeks themselves into their imaginative writings. It will be of value to discuss a few important texts that represent Jewish relations with real Hellenic figures (as they conceived them) and their significance for the Jews' own self-perception.

The *Letter of Aristeas* holds a central place in any such investigation. It purports to describe the events that led to the translation of the Hebrew Bible into Greek, an episode of the highest consequence for Hellenistic Judaism. And the story that it tells has traditionally served as the prime document of a harmonious and mutually beneficial interchange between Greeks and Jews.

The work is not, in fact a letter. The author describes it as a *diegesis*, an unspecific and widely applicable term referring to prose narratives (*LetArist* 1, 8, 322). This could encompass any number of genres and fits snugly into none. The treatise as a whole is *sui generis*. But individual features have close affinities with a range of Hellenistic writings. The Jewish author clearly had a strong education in the literature of Hellas.

First, a brief summary (text in Hadas 1951: 92–227). The narrative consists of a communication from Aristeas, supposedly a prominent figure at the court of Ptolemy II Philadelphus, to his brother Philocrates. It records Aristeas' eyewitness account of the decision and process that produced a Greek rendition of the Hebrew Bible. The initial impetus came from Demetrius of Phalerum, chief librarian in Alexandria, who persuaded King Ptolemy to authorize the addition of the "laws of the Jews," evidently the Pentateuch, to the shelves of the great Library. This required translation, for the available Hebrew texts were carelessly and improperly drawn up. Ptolemy duly composed a letter to the High Priest in Jerusalem, to be delivered by Aristeas and another courtier, seeking translators. He paved the way with the magnanimous gesture (suggested to him by Aristeas) of releasing the Jewish slaves who had been brought to Egypt by his father Ptolemy I. The High Priest Eleazer happily complied with the request (handsome gifts from Ptolemy helped to facilitate matters) and selected 72 scholars, six from each of the 12 Jewish tribes, experts in both languages, to do the job. Aristeas then pauses for a digression, in which he not only describes in detail the ceremonial gifts that Ptolemy had sent for the Temple in Jerusalem but also supplies an extensive description of the city, the countryside, the Temple itself and its furnishings, and even the vestments of the High Priest. He proceeds to recount Eleazer's gracious responses to his questions regarding the religious beliefs and dietary prescriptions of the Jews, a lengthy speech that extols the virtues of his own people and outlines the symbolic character of some of their practices, leaving a powerfully positive impression.

The Jewish sages reached Alexandria, where they were warmly welcomed. Ptolemy himself paid homage to the sacred scrolls that they had conveyed from Jerusalem. Indeed he organized a seven-day banquet (serving kosher food), during which the king put a different question to each of the 72 guests. Most of his questions concerned the appropriate means of governing wisely, and he found reason to praise every one of the guests for his sagacity. Aristeas cites court records as testimony to these events. Demetrius of Phalerum then found spacious quarters for the translators on the island of Pharos where they went to work, periodically comparing drafts, agreed upon a common version, and completed their task in precisely 72 days. Demetrius assembled the Jews of Alexandria and read out to them the finished translation, which they received with great applause. The priests and leaders of the Jewish community pronounced it a definitive version, not a line of it to be altered. Ptolemy joined them in admiration, paid reverence to the new Bible, and lavished gifts upon the Jewish scholars.

Such is the tale. No one can doubt that it derives from the pen of a Jewish author, cloaked in the garb of a learned court official. It bears little relation to historical events. But the work did not aim for historical accuracy, nor to deceive readers with the pretense of a verifiable narrative. The author offers verisimilitude rather than history, employing known figures and plausible circumstances to present Jewish learning and Hellenic patronage as mutually beneficial (Honigman 2003: 65–91; Johnson 2004: 34–8; Rajak 2009: 28–63).

The *Letter of Aristeas* supplies a showcase for the familiarity of Jewish intellectuals with diverse features and forms of Greek literature common in the Hellenistic period. For example, the lengthy segment on Aristeas' visit to Jerusalem, with its detailed description of the features of the landscape, the setting of the citadel, the terrain of the city, the geography of its surroundings, the appointments of the Temple, and the garb of the priests, much of it remote from reality, evokes Hellenistic geographical treatises and utopian literature (*LetArist* 83–120). Eleazer's exegesis of peculiar Jewish customs in turn has parallels with Hellenistic ethnographic excursuses (*LetArist* 128–70). The *Letter of Aristeas* also frequently cites and quotes documents, whether royal decrees, memoranda, administrative reports, or letters, a regular practice in Greek historiography. The extended symposium, of course, is a thoroughly Hellenic institution, and most of the Jewish sages respond to the king's questions with answers drawn from Greek philosophy or political theory (*LetArist* 187–294). The High Priest, in recounting the significance of Jewish dietary prescriptions, explains them in good Greek manner as either having a rational basis or requiring allegorical interpretation (*LetArist* 128–71). He himself receives description, in fact, in terms befitting a Greek aristocrat (a man of *kalokagathia*, *LetArist* 3). The text includes learned references to Greek intellectuals like Menedemus, Hecataeus, Theopompus, and Theodectus. Perhaps most striking is the process of translation itself as the narrative presents it. The project arose when the librarian found Hebrew copies to be deficient and inadequate (*LetArist* 29–30). And the Jewish scholars, when they set about their task, in comfortable quarters supplied by Ptolemy, did so by comparing translations and arriving at an agreed upon text (*LetArist* 301–12, 317–21). The activity (if not the result) surely evokes the scholarship subsidized by the court and carried out in the Alexandrian Museum (Honigman 2003: 13–35).

The author, steeped in Greek learning, brought it to bear on his construct of Jewish and Hellenic collaboration in the making of the Septuagint; the overlap of religious sensibility is striking. He begins with a notice that the available copies of the Hebrew Bible had been carelessly transcribed and ends with a definitive Greek text subject to no further revision (*LetArist* 29–30, 311). That implies a sanction of the

Septuagint that supersedes the Hebrew original. And, in a famous statement, Aristeas declared to Ptolemy that the Jews revere God, overseer and creator of all, who is worshiped by all including ourselves, except that we give him a different name, Zeus (*LetArist* 16).

On the face of it, the *Letter of Aristeas* appears to be the ultimate document of cultural convergence (Hengel 1974: 1.264–5; Barclay 1996: 138–50; Collins 2000: 191–5). That impression, however, reflects only the surface. The author, like others already discussed, exploits his profound familiarity with Hellenic literary genres and the Alexandrian scholarly scene, to advertise the advantages of Jewish tradition. The superiority of the Jews is never in question. The god to whom all bear witness, even though the Greeks may call him Zeus, is the Jewish god. Eleazer the High Priest happily sends Jewish scholars to Alexandria to render the Bible into Greek, but he reminds Aristeas of the transcendence of Jewish monotheism, ridiculing those who worship idols of wood and stone fashioned by themselves. He also insists that Mosaic law insulated the Hebrews from outside influences, erecting firm barriers to prevent the infiltration of tainted institutions (*LetArist* 134–42). The seven-day symposium may be a fundamentally Hellenic setting, but the Jewish sages answer every query put by the king with swift and pithy answers, adding a reference to God in each response. They earn the admiration not only of Ptolemy and his courtiers but of all the Greek philosophers in attendance, who acknowledge their inferiority to the erudite guests (*LetArist* 200–1, 235–96). The learned librarian Demetrius of Phalerum declares the wisdom of the Pentateuch to be both holy and highly philosophical, citing other Greek intellectuals for confirmation (*LetArist* 312–16). The king's munificence and encouragement make the whole scenario possible, but his awe-struck reverence (bowing seven times before the scrolls of the Law, supplying extravagant gifts to the Temple, providing a kosher meal for the visitors, praising the answer of every Jewish scholar no matter how banal, and ordering an annual festival to commemorate the translation) borders on caricature (Gruen 1998: 218–20). It is the Lord of the Jews who guides Ptolemy's actions and keeps his kingdom secure. And the High Priest observes that the Jews offer sacrifices to God to ensure the peace and renown of the Ptolemaic kingdom – a neat reversal of the patron–client relationship (*LetArist* 45). In short, the *Letter of Aristeas*, that quintessential text of Jewish Hellenism, testifies most eloquently to the appropriation of Hellenistic literature to express the pre-eminence of Jewish values.

Aristobulus

Pride in priority emerges more blatantly from another Hellenistic Jewish author. Aristobulus, a second-century BCE Jew of philosophical education and inclinations, played with what became a favored Jewish fiction: that Hellenic ideas derive from Hebraic roots. A mere handful of fragments survive, and the identification of Aristobulus is disputed (text in Holladay 1995: 128–97). But his acquaintance with Greek philosophy and his emphasis on Jewish precedence are plain enough.

Aristobulus' work, it appears, was cast in the form of a dialogue between himself and Ptolemy VI Philometor in the mid-second century. That frame may be a literary conceit, but it reflects the author's effort to place himself in a context comparable to that of the *Letter of Aristeas*, imparting Jewish wisdom to a Ptolemaic king. Aristobulus takes a leaf from Greek philosophy by propounding the allegorical method for biblical exegesis (Hengel 1974: 1.163–9, 2.105–10; Barclay 1996: 150–8; Collins 2000: 186–90). Allegory allows understanding of phraseology such as God's "hands," "feet," or "visage," and accounts for his "descent" at Sinai (Eus. *PE* 8.9.38–10.17). He rebukes those who employ only literal interpretations, thus embracing the methods of Hellenic allegorists. Indeed he refers to Judaism as "our philosophical way of thinking" (*hairesis*; Eus. *PE* 13.12.8).

Aristobulus does not, however, subsume Jewish tradition under Greek learning. Rather, the reverse. In Aristobulus' imaginative construct, Moses provided stimulus for Hellenic philosophers and poets, inspiring the loftiest achievements of Greek intellectuals. Aristobulus asserts that Plato's ideas followed the path laid out by the legislation of Moses, indeed that Plato was assiduous in working through every particular contained in it (Eus. *PE* 13.12.1). Nor did he stop there. Aristobulus cites a still earlier case, none other than the great sixth-century philosopher Pythagoras, who also found much in the Hebrew teachings that he could adapt for his own doctrines (Eus. *PE* 13.12.1). Knowledgeable readers might, of course, wonder how Greek sages would have had access to the Hebrew Scriptures generations or centuries before the composition of the Septuagint. Aristobulus had a prepared answer. He reassured potential skeptics by maintaining that translations of the Israelite law code were available long before the Septuagint came into being (Eus. *PE* 13.12.1). Aristobulus obviously had no qualms about fabricating one fiction to save another.

That accomplished, Aristobulus proceeded with additional flights of fancy. He included Socrates with Pythagoras and Plato among those whose reference to a divine voice in regard to the creation of the cosmos derives from the words of Moses. And he goes well beyond. Aristobulus offers an embracing doctrine that sweeps all of Greek philosophy within the Jewish orbit. He asserts universal agreement among philosophers that only pious opinions must be held about God. And, since that view is embedded in Mosaic law, it follows that Jewish conceptualizing supplied the wellspring for Hellenic philosophizing (Eus. *PE* 13.12.3–4, 13.12.8).

If Jewish inspiration could be claimed for Greek philosophy, why not for poetry? Aristobulus and others had no hesitation in extending the Jewish reach into that realm. The legendary Orpheus, fountainhead of Greek poetry, speaks of all things being in the hand of God, a sign, for Aristobulus, that his thinking paralleled the teachings of the Scriptures (Eus. *PE* 13.12.4). Aristobulus – or someone – even went to the trouble of composing or adapting a full-scale poem, ascribed to Orpheus and directed to his son Musaeus, that espoused a moving monotheism (Eus. *PE* 3.12.5; Holladay 1995: 165–71 and 1996). This composition, whether or not from the pen of Aristobulus, certainly represents a significant aspect of Hellenistic-Jewish thinking. By assigning to the ancestor of pagan poets a lofty monotheistic vision of the deity, the author has associated the inspiration for Greek literature with the doctrines of Judaism.

Nor did Aristobulus confine himself to distant or mythical poets. He quoted the near contemporary Hellenistic poet Aratus of Soli, finding suitable material in the opening lines of his great astronomical poem, the *Phaenomena* (discussed by Volk and White in this volume). But he made a notable emendation, substituting "God" for

"Zeus," and explained it as discerning Aratus' real meaning in his description of the divinity as permeating all on land and sea and guiding the fortunes of everyone (Eus. *PE* 13.12.6–7). The parallel with Aristeas' equation of Zeus with Yahweh is plain. Aristobulus succeeded in transforming Aratus' pantheistic paean to Zeus into a hymn for the Jewish deity.

Aristobulus' ingenuity stretched further still. He seized upon references to the number seven as evidence that the institution of the Sabbath had seeped into Hellenic consciousness. Aristobulus summoned up the verses of Greece's premier epic poets, Homer and Hesiod, to affirm that they endorsed the biblical sanctification of the holy day. This required some fancy footwork. Aristobulus (or perhaps his Jewish source) exercised special liberties in twisting the texts to his will. Hesiod's reference to a sacred seventh day of the month (*WD* 770) becomes the seventh day of the week, and Homer's "it was the fourth day and all his work was finished" (*Od.* 5.262) is transformed through emendation to "the seventh day." Other lines quoted by Aristobulus to support his claim are not attested in the extant texts of Homer and Hesiod and may simply have been invented (Eus. *PE* 13.12.12–15; Holladay 1995: 230–7). The subtle – or not so subtle – reworking had Homer and Hesiod acknowledge the consecration of the Sabbath. Aristobulus was also not above assigning fabricated lines to the mythical poet Linus, who came down in the tradition as son of Apollo, as music teacher of Heracles, or as both. He has Linus assert that all was made complete on the seventh morning, a perfect number also reflected in the seven heavenly bodies (planets) set shining in their orbits (Eus. *PE* 13.12.16). From the vantage point of Aristobulus, it was all for a good cause: to demonstrate the dependence of Greece's most ancient bards upon the teachings of the Torah. Observance of the Sabbath, in this conception, is no mere idiosyncrasy of an alien and self-segregated sect but a universal principle cherished in Hellenic song. Aristobulus thus harnessed some of the most celebrated Greek thinkers and artists, legendary or real, to the ancient traditions of the Jews (Gruen 1998: 246–51).

The Third Sibyl

Jewish ingenuity in adapting Hellenic forms has perhaps its most arresting expression in the *Sibylline Oracles.* Commandeering the voice of the divinely inspired Sibyl had a powerful and lasting impact. Her prophecies held a prominent place in Greek and Roman culture. A shadowy female figure assigned to distant antiquity and located in a variety of sites, she specialized in dire and doleful predictions for individuals and nations. Collections of the Sibylline oracles, duly edited, expanded, or invented, had wide circulation in the Greco-Roman world – long before Jewish writers exploited them for their own purposes. Those collections have largely been lost, surviving only in fragments or ancient reconstructions. The extant *Sibylline Oracles*, drawing upon but refashioning those models, derive from Jewish and Christian compilers, who had their own agenda to promote (Parke 1988: 1–50; Potter 1994: 171–93; Buitenwerf 2003: 92–123; Lightfoot 2007: 3–23). Fourteen books of oracles, gathered or reframed over a period of centuries, now constitute the corpus. Most date to the period of the Roman

Empire, some perhaps even to late antiquity. But the earliest portion, incorporated in the Third Sibyl, is a Hellenistic Jewish product from the era of the Maccabees (Barclay 1996: 216–28; Gruen 1998: 268–85; Collins 2000: 83–97; Buitenwerf 2003: 124–34). Echoes of Greek literature resonate in the text. The verses are delivered in Homeric hexameters, and the prophetess's fierce pronouncements of dreadful events to come have a noteworthy counterpart in Hellenistic writings: the darkly obscure poem *Alexandra* of Lycophron. This is not imitation or duplication. Alexandra (Cassandra) speaks in iambic trimeters rather than epic hexameters. But the parallel between the raving Trojan princess and the fiery Sibyl suggests that their respective authors shared a literary environment or tradition. Adoption of this pagan persona strikingly demonstrates how comfortable Jewish intellectuals were with Hellenic modes of presentation.

The Jewish thrust and goals, however, emerge unmistakably in the text. Tension and conflict dominate the Sibyl's prophecies. She twice gives a roll call of kingdoms that will rise and fall (*3 Sib.* 156–90). And forecasts of destruction recur repeatedly. Jews will be the ultimate beneficiaries of the carnage. They will endure much suffering at the hands of the wicked. Their devotion to righteousness and virtue, their rejection of idolatry and sorcery, and their adherence to the law guarantee that they will gain glory in the end when the terrible might of divine justice descends (*3 Sib.* 218–94, 573–600, 702–31).

Eschatology permeates this text. Ultimate glory for the Jews is a repeated refrain of the Third Sibyl. The apocalyptic vision, setting good against evil and proclaiming future desolation for all peoples while sparing the Jews, would seem to make it an unimpeachable document for alienation of the chosen people from the rest of humanity. But that inference may be hasty. The Jewish author's choice of medium is significant. By donning the garb of the Sibyl, he has taken on a persona with resonance in the Greco-Roman world. The thunderous pronouncements of the Lord, conventionally delivered through biblical prophets, here issue forth from the mouth of the pagan Sibyl in epic hexameters. And the author is widely learned, well beyond the traditions of the tribe. The Sibyl, in this text, can peer into the mysteries of Near Eastern, biblical, and Greco-Roman lore alike. She recounts the tale of the Tower of Babel, then connects it directly with the era of Kronos and Titan, proceeding to give a version of Hesiod's *Theogony* on the myths associated with the birth of Zeus and the struggles of Olympians and Titans (*3 Sib.* 97–155). One might note in particular a striking blend: the sons of Noah (Shem, Ham, and Japheth) become Kronos, Titan, and Iapetos, sons of Gaia and Ouranos (*3 Sib.* 110–15). The Sibyl knows the poems of Homer, whom she calls the blind bard from Chios, but, like Plato, regards him as purveyor of lies (*3 Sib.* 419–32). She forecasts both the fall of Troy and the Exodus from Egypt. The author sets her in the hoary mists of time that encompass a range of peoples and cultures. The Sibyl appears as a relative of Noah. She came from Babylon, then was dispatched to Greece where, in her mantic trance, she could deliver fiery prophecies that conveyed the message of God in divine riddles to all men. Her origins, she claimed, were assigned by different people to different places, including Erythrae, seat of the most renowned Sibyl, and her pronouncements reckoned as mad falsehoods, but she was the authentic prophetess of the great God (*3 Sib.* 809–29). She thus claims the most ancient lineage, embodying Hebrew traditions, Near Eastern legends, and Hellenic myths, all integral parts of the persona.

The glories of the eschaton, moreover, need not be confined to Jews alone. Evildoers, of course, will get their just deserts. But the hand of the Lord reaches out to the Greeks. The Sibyl exhorts the inhabitants of the Hellenic world to repent, urging them to acknowledge the true God, and offering hope of salvation. Oracular verses expose the folly of trust in mortal leaders and resort to idolatry. The appeal to repentance gains further vividness with prescriptions for sacrifices, prayers, and righteous behavior to earn divine favor (*3 Sib.* 545–72, 624–34, 732–61). The Third Sibyl includes Greeks among wayward peoples whose failure to see the truth has led them into arrogance, impiety, and immorality, thus provoking divine retaliation (*3 Sib.* 196–210, 295–365, 594–600). But the prophetess eagerly invites them to enter the fold of the true believers. The message is not one of cultural solidarity. Jewish traditions take clear precedence. Greeks who show themselves worthy are invited to partake of the values of the Jews. The oracular voice promises a happy fate for the Jewish faithful, and shows a willingness to extend that fate to the Greeks – provided that they embrace the ideals of the Chosen People (Gruen 1998: 287; Collins 2000: 160–1).

Here as elsewhere Jews successfully adapted the Hellenic medium. Employment of Greek forms, language, and themes in the service of advancing Jewish ideas inspired the intellectual circles of Hellenistic Judaism. The composers of the Third Sibylline Oracle had that goal in common with Ezekiel the tragedian, the historian Demetrius, and the imaginative Aristobulus, appropriator of Hellenic philosophy. They inhabited the same mental world that produced the fabricated verses and refashioned sentiments of Greek poets and thinkers in order to bring them into line with the teachings of the Torah. Jews reckoned themselves not only as an integral part of that world, but as its cultural forerunners.

The Significance

The fragmentary character of Jewish-Hellenistic writing makes assessment of its literary quality a frustrating endeavor. But its ideological thrust comes through with clarity. The bits and pieces do add up. Two other instances merit mention as reinforcing the conclusions already articulated. The historian Eupolemus, of whose oeuvre only a tiny portion survives, wrote in Palestine in the mid-second century BCE and composed a work entitled *On the Kings in Judaea* (text in Holladay 1983: 112–35), which included a revealing segment on Moses. Eupolemus has him hand down the knowledge of the alphabet first to the Jews, from whom the Phoenicians acquired it, and they in turn passed it on to the Greeks (Eus. *PE* 9.26.1). The fragment (we have only a couple of lines) is often interpreted as a shot fired in a polemical exchange conducted by intellectuals over which nation invented the alphabet (Wacholder 1974: 77–83; Hengel 1974: 1.92, 129; Sterling 1992: 218–19). That analysis misses the main point. Eupolemus does not actually credit Moses with inventing the alphabet. He simply "handed down the knowledge." At the very least, this suggests that the debate over priority was not uppermost in Eupolemus' mind. The historian aimed to rank Moses as first among the sages and to give the Jews a principal role in the transmission of literacy and literature in the ancient Mediterranean. Jewish intellectuals could take satisfaction from imagining that Moses' delivery of the Tablets constituted a milestone in the history of letters. And, equally important, Eupolemus' fancy made the Greeks indirect beneficiaries of the Hebrews (Gruen 1998: 153–4).

A comparable orientation emerges from the preserved lines of the imaginative writer Artapanus, a Hellenized Egyptian Jew of the second or first century BCE (text in Holladay 1983: 204–25). His creative rewriting of biblical stories includes an elaborate account of Moses' exploits that goes well beyond the scriptural foundation. Apart from crediting Moses with a host of Egyptian institutions and technologies, he adds a Greek connection. The name, Moses, Artapanus claims, induced Greeks to identify him with Musaeus, the legendary poet and prophet from Attica, son or pupil of Orpheus, who stands at the dawn of Hellenic song and wisdom. Artapanus, however, gives a slight but significant twist to the legend. He has Musaeus as mentor of Orpheus rather than the other way around. Moses therefore becomes the father of Greek poetry and prophecy (Eus. *PE* 9.27.3–4; Doran 1987: 258–63; Barclay 1996: 127–32; Gruen 1998: 155–60; Collins 2000: 37–46; Johnson 2004: 95–108). Artapanus neither rejects nor disparages those traditions. He simply goes them one better and counts them as part of a Hebrew heritage.

What is the significance of all this? Jewish literature in the Hellenistic Age did not constitute a mere game of one-upmanship. Intellectuals in Palestine and the diaspora could be inventive, witty, and playful. But they were doing more than showing off their learning or toying with the genres and conventions of Greek literature. These enterprises have a deeper purpose. The works discussed here – and they are typical – show a Jewish penchant for co-opting Hellenic forms to convey the priority of Jewish traditions, the precedents they set, and their continued relevance in a Greek intellectual world. The process, however, does not amount to borrowing or imitation or even influence. For Jews who grew up in literate communities and belonged to cultivated circles, Greek language and literature were also their language and literature. Most Jews in the diaspora had lost touch with Hebrew but not with their heritage. Epic poetry, tragedy, history, philosophy, prose fiction, and mythic recreations were the natural means to transmit that heritage. And, although several writers took pleasure in pointing to the Bible or to biblical figures as precursors and models for Greek achievements, the association itself, however artificial, carries the real significance. It is a mistake to see this as rivalry or competition. The Jews did not distance themselves from Hellenism; they were part and parcel of it. The recasting of scriptural narrative in epic or tragic form, the application of historical methods to straighten out biblical chronology, and the framing of sacred tales as romances exemplify the fundamental interconnectedness. The Jewish drive to embrace the literary legacy of Hellas exhibits itself again and again: in claiming biblical authority for Platonic teaching and Hesiodic cosmology, in having Jewish sages spout Greek political theory, and in transforming the Erythraean Sibyl into a prophetess who welcomes Greeks into the Jewish fold.

To what audiences were texts such as these directed? Many regard them as constituting "apologetics," i.e., an effort by Jewish intellectuals to explain the ways of the Jews to Greeks, to exhibit assimilation to the other's culture, and to address a

Hellenic readership that might otherwise be disapproving or hostile. The idea that Jews hoped to win over Gentiles as proselytes has largely (and wisely) been abandoned, as have interpretations that see Jewish writings as responding to anti-Semitism. These compositions could hardly have made converts of or softened the antagonism of the biased. But some see them still as a form of apologetics, an attempt at least in part to educate Greek readers about the virtues of Judaism and to reassure them of the compatibility of Jewish values and beliefs with Hellenism (Sterling 1992; Collins 2000: 14–16, 271–2). On that thesis Gentiles would constitute an important audience. The works considered in this chapter render the idea implausible.

Jewish writers, to be sure, underscored the connections, overlappings, and close affinities of Judaism with Hellenic culture. But they could hardly have expected many Greeks to find these claims congenial. The large corpus of Greek writings prior to the Christian era, whether highbrow literature or mundane transactions on papyri, shows barely a sign of acquaintance with Jewish texts (Tcherikover 1956: 169–93). Greek reading habits did not extend to that realm. And Jewish authors are unlikely to have harbored illusions about changing those habits.

Greek readers who happened to stumble upon Jewish compositions would not have found them especially welcome or agreeable. How many Greeks would have taken pleasure in the *Letter of Aristeas*, which had erudite Jews outshine Greek thinkers, the High Priest lecture Greeks on the absurdity of idolatry, and the Ptolemaic king ceremoniously bow down seven times to sacred Hebrew scrolls? How many would have regarded seriously Aristobulus' claims that eminent philosophers from Pythagoras to Plato and poetic giants from Homer to Euripides drew on biblical insights? How many would have enjoyed the pronouncements of a Sibyl who condescendingly encouraged pagans to embrace Judaism in order to obtain salvation? And how many would have found acceptable the idea that Greek literacy owed a crucial debt to the tablets of Moses?

The principal audience for such fantasies was surely the Jews themselves. They could take pride in the appropriation of Hellenic modes and figures to suggest Jewish priority and advantage and to advance Jewish values clothed in the conventions of the Hellenistic world. The texts emerged not in a spirit of antagonism or defensive reaction but as an authentic expression by writers fully at home in that world.

FURTHER READING

The classic work on this subject, unfortunately available only in Hebrew, is Gutman 1958, 1963. Although some of his suggestions are speculative, Gutman remains the most comprehensive study. A translation would be eminently desirable. The broad and influential work of Hengel 1974 is essential background reading, a seminal analysis that has done much to dissolve the long-standing divide between "Palestinian" and "diaspora" literature. The writing, however, is densely packed and demanding. Barclay 1996 offers a more readable survey, generally balanced and judicious in its assessments of the literature, although Barclay's categories of "assimilation," "cultural convergence," and "cultural antagonism" are somewhat strained and artificial. A fine overview, with succinct discussions of each of the writers and excellent bibliography, can be found in Schürer 1986. Many of the interpretations offered in this chapter are more fully developed in Gruen 1998. The second edition of Collins 2000 was prompted in part by the publications of Barclay and Gruen with which Collins often takes issue.

The most convenient access to many of the texts discussed in the chapter comes through Holladay 1983, 1989, 1995, 1996. His excellent editions provide texts, translations, notes, and extensive commentaries on numerous Jewish authors whose works survive only in fragments preserved by Church Fathers, primarily Eusebius and Clement of Alexandria. The very valuable collection by Charlesworth 1983, 1985 includes most of the writers in Holladay's volumes and many more, but supplies only translations with brief notes and introductions. For the *Letter of Aristeas*, the edition by Hadas 1951, with text, translation, and notes, remains quite serviceable. An original study by Honigman 2003 links that work closely to the scholarship of Hellenistic Alexandria and questions the very concept of Jewish literature as distinct from Hellenistic literature. Rajak 2009 offers an incisive interpretation of the work in its cultural context. For Aristobulus, in addition to the surveys and general treatments noted above, one should consult the more thorough investigation of Walter 1964 which set him in the Greek philosophical tradition and in the intellectual context of his time. The Third Sibyl as the earliest manifestation of the usurpation of that pagan symbol by Jewish writers has received much recent attention. Gruen 1998 and Collins 2000 offer quite different interpretations of its meaning. Buitenwerf 2003 has now supplied a new translation with extensive commentary and discussion – although not many are likely to adopt his notion of a literary unity and a composition between 80 and 31 BCE. For examination of other authors mentioned only briefly here, one can recommend the controversial but erudite study of Kraemer 1998 on *Joseph and Aseneth*, Jacobson's excellent 1983 dissection of Ezekiel, Bickerman 1975 on Demetrius, and Wacholder 1974 on Eupolemus. The issue of the relationship between Jewish fiction and the Greek romances is treated sensitively and intelligently by Wills 1995 and Johnson 2004; see also Whitmarsh in this volume.

CHAPTER TWENTY-EIGHT

Egyptian Literature

Jacco Dieleman and Ian S. Moyer

What happens when the Other writes back? This is a question far more open to investigation in the novel political and cultural conditions following the campaigns of Alexander than in the Classical period when Greek images of exotic barbarians first emerged. Within the frame of Ptolemaic Egypt, however, the most prominent current debate over the possibilities of communication between Greek literature and the surrounding Egyptian civilization is conducted on the relatively circumscribed terrain of Alexandrian poetry. Our joint contribution aims to shift the debate beyond these horizons to include the Egyptian *chora*, and to consider the traditions and innovations of indigenous literature in the mixed Greek-Egyptian milieus of Ptolemaic Egypt. We outline the framework of this approach by first considering the linguistic situation in Egypt, the social contexts of production and reception, as well as the problems created by the conditions of transmission and preservation. The conspectus of Ptolemaic Egyptian literature that follows is not exhaustive; it focuses on surviving examples in the major genres of Demotic and Greco-Egyptian literature of the Ptolemaic period. In the case of Demotic literature, these genres have antecedents in the long prior history of Egyptian literature and are considered as developments in this tradition. Several inherited Egyptian forms are also found in Greco-Egyptian literature, but in discussing examples of the latter, the focus naturally shifts to considering the positions these texts could occupy between traditions. The organization of this survey reflects the contention that this material, though divisible into other linguistic or generic categories, is best studied together in order to elucidate a spectrum of interrelated literary practices and their social contexts.

Imagining Egypt in Hellenistic Literature and Classical Scholarship

Over the last three decades, a number of scholars have argued that Alexandrian poetry contains references to the indigenous culture of Ptolemaic Egypt (Koenen 1977, 1983, 1993; Merkelbach 1981; Gelzer 1982; Mineur 1984; Bing 1988; Selden 1998; Stephens 2003). Especially prominent in this project has been the exploration of a dual poetics, capable of sustaining both Greek and Egyptian readings in the pluralistic cultural milieu of Ptolemaic Alexandria through allusions that connect the myths and ideologies of pharaonic kingship with parallel Greek ideas and narratives. Not everyone is convinced, and those who object often cast doubt on the suppositions of the enterprise (Zanker 1989; Goldhill 2005; for a more balanced overview, Hunter 2003a: 46–53). Such critics ask basic questions: Were Greek authors sufficiently aware of, or even interested in, Egyptian culture to make such allusions? Was a Greek readership capable of understanding the dual references? These are important questions to ask, but they often imply a fundamental social and cultural separation between Greeks and Egyptians, and construct a closed, purely Greek economy of literary production and consumption. Although many questions regarding the degrees and modes of cultural interaction in Ptolemaic Egypt are not yet settled, most historians have retreated from the extreme isolationist view that was commonly held in the 1970s and 1980s (e.g., Préaux 1978; Samuel 1983), and some, notably W. Clarysse and D. Thompson, have used the wealth of documentary evidence to assemble, incrementally, a history of overlapping and interconnected Greek and Egyptian social worlds, whose entanglements, though more pronounced in the second and first centuries, are nevertheless apparent already in early Ptolemaic Egypt (e.g., Clarysse 1985; Thompson 1988; Clarysse and Thompson 2006: 2.323–7; for a brief overview, La'da 2003). Broad lines of communication between the immigrants and the indigenes, sometimes members of the same families, cannot therefore be excluded (for case studies, see Derchain 2000 and Lloyd 2002). These facts can be joined to the evidence of Greek-Egyptian communication in the more restricted world of the early Ptolemaic court as represented by figures such as Hecataeus of Abdera, Manetho of Sebennytos, Soter's appointment of Nectanebo (a member of the last Egyptian royal house) as general, as well as the intermarriage of the families of Soter and Nectanebo (Clère 1951; Lloyd 2002: 119; Huss 1994). Particular double readings of Alexandrian poetry may or may not be successful, but arguments over their validity cannot presume that isolation deprived Greeks of competence in making connections between Greek and Egyptian ideas.

This leaves the question of what kinds of Egyptian references Greeks could plausibly comprehend, and how they learned about and interpreted Egyptian culture. In approaching this issue it is important to understand the references to Egyptian civilization in Greek poetry not simply as a product of the Greek reception and representation of Egyptian culture for Greek consumption. Contemporary Egyptians were undoubtedly involved as well. Greek knowledge of Egypt in all periods was the result of complex transactional processes of communication and exchange, in which Greeks and Egyptians each received and responded to the other's representations with their own motivations and strategies. Alexandrian poetry, to be sure, was produced primarily for a Greek audience, but debates over a Greek–Egyptian intercultural poetics must be sensitive to the broader contemporary context of cultural interchange.

Though pioneering and innovative, scholars proposing Egyptian readings of Alexandrian poetry at times make connections to Middle Kingdom or New Kingdom Egyptian literature that are historically improbable. Contemporary Egyptian literature provides a sounder basis for evaluating intercultural allusions, and works of Greco-Egyptian literature likewise provide the closest points of cultural and intellectual contact. In this chapter we present a survey of the genres and forms of these two related literary traditions. We foreground what they share with the age-old indigenous literary tradition, paying particular attention to issues of innovation and interplay with foreign literature. Our initial discussion of the social and cultural contexts of their production and reception aims to bring into focus the conditions and conduits that allowed a knowledge of Egyptian traditions to reach Alexandrian literature and its audience. It is our contention that the wealth and diversity of indigenous literature provide an opportunity to refine the broader picture of literary, intellectual, and cultural contacts in the Ptolemaic Period.

The Language Situation in Ptolemaic Egypt

In Ptolemaic Egypt indigenous literature was composed in Egyptian and Greek. Literature in Egyptian was marked by diglossia, i.e., certain texts were composed in Late Classical Egyptian ("Égyptien de tradition") and others in Demotic. Late Classical Egyptian represented by that time an extremely archaic form of the Egyptian language, which nonetheless retained its high status as the official written language of state and cult. Texts in Late Classical Egyptian were either executed in hieroglyphs on stone, such as royal decrees, temple texts, and (tomb) autobiographies, or in hieratic or cursive hieroglyphs on papyrus, such as ritual handbooks, priestly manuals, and funerary literature. The grammar and idiom of Late Classical Egyptian was basically the same as that of Middle Egyptian, an earlier language phase that had been in active use during the Middle Kingdom until the mid-eighteenth dynasty (c.2000–1350 BCE). As a consequence, texts in Late Classical Egyptian were composed and understood only by members of the Egyptian priesthood – and only by those who had received an in-depth scribal training.

Demotic had been adopted in the seventh century BCE as the language and script for administration, accounting, and law as well as business and private communication. The Demotic script was a cursive form of writing that had developed out of a Lower Egyptian variety of the hieratic script. It was usually written with a brush and ink on papyrus or ostraca, but Demotic inscriptions incised in stone also occur. By the Ptolemaic period it was the standard language for written communication between members of the indigenous population as opposed to Greek that was used for affairs related to the state and communication with the authorities. Demotic was now no longer used only for letters, accounting, and contracts, but also for composing texts of a literary and priestly nature for which previously (Late) Classical Egyptian had been the sole proper language.

Greek served as the *lingua franca* in Egypt after the conquest by Alexander the Great in 332 BCE, when it replaced Aramaic, the administrative language of Persian Egypt. It was the vernacular of the ruling elite and of the many immigrants and veterans who had come in the wake of the establishment of Macedonian rule. The majority of Greeks lived in the *metropoleis* and the Fayum region, where large-scale irrigation projects had secured large tracts of arable land from the desert fringes. Detailed studies of onomastics and family archives in Greek and Demotic have demonstrated that Greeks did not live in isolation from the indigenous population in the *chora*. Egyptians working for or with the Greek authorities, either on a local, regional or national level, were proficient in Greek and in regular contact with the culture of the immigrant population. These intercultural relationships are often difficult to trace in the sources due to the common practice of name-switching among these Egyptians. In their family and indigenous environment they carried an Egyptian name, whereas they adopted a Greek name when acting in a Greek milieu (Peremans 1970; Clarysse 1985, 1991). Authors such as Manetho demonstrate that some Egyptians even in the early Ptolemaic period were proficient in Greek to the level that they could use it as a language for literary expression.

Sources: Production, Transmission, and Preservation

Material for the study of Ptolemaic Egyptian literature is plentiful. However, as most of it is derived from archaeological sites, the texts are often fragmentary and the character of the corpus is subject to the hazards of preservation and recovery. Major discoveries of literary papyri were made in the Fayum settlements of Tebtunis and Soknopaiou Nesos, where a wide variety of cursive hieroglyphic, hieratic, Demotic, and Greek texts of what supposedly was once the temple library were found within the remains of a temple precinct (Ryholt 2005; Quack 2005: 11–12). The Demotic literary manuscripts date to the first and second centuries CE, but many are undoubtedly copies of texts that were already around in the Ptolemaic period. Another major group of literary texts was found in a papyrus dump in the temple precinct of the Sacred Animal Necropolis at North Saqqara (Smith and Tait 1983: IX–XI). These very fragmentary manuscripts range in date from the fifth to early third centuries BCE and attest to the existence of a mature tradition of Demotic narrative literature already at the beginning of the Ptolemaic period. Three late Ptolemaic manuscripts (two instruction texts and one narrative) were found in tombs in the region of Akhmim, where they were evidently deposited as prestigious burial goods. One of these, the "Instructions of Onchsheshonqy," was found rolled up together with a funerary manuscript inscribed for a certain "Hor, son of Petemin" (Smith 1994). The Ptolemaic period manuscript of Setne I was purportedly found in a tomb of Christian date. Many manuscripts are without known provenance and can only tentatively be assigned to a region and period with the help of palaeography and dialectology.

Despite the relative abundance of literary material in Demotic and Greek, it is not yet possible to write a linear history of Demotic and Greco-Egyptian literature due to the scattered nature of the source material, both chronologically and geographically, and to the fact that most texts are only attested in one copy. In those rare cases that multiple copies of one text are preserved, variants in phraseology and plot lines demonstrate that copyists felt free to make changes to the text. An Egyptian literary text was thus not fixed at any one time and then transmitted as the unique product of an individual author. Textual transmission could extend over a long period, as evidenced by the "Petese Stories." The oldest fragment comes from the Sacred Animal Necropolis at Saqqara, while the other three manuscripts belong to the Tebtunis temple library, attesting to a history of textual transmission and adaptation of at least 400 to 500 years.

Despite the limitations of our evidence, a few preliminary comments can be made about the contexts of production, transmission, and reception. Most Demotic literary manuscripts date to the late Ptolemaic or Roman period, but this should not necessarily lead to the conclusion that Demotic literature only bloomed late. The formative period of Demotic literature was probably the Saite period (664–525 BCE), even though only a single narrative in hieratic has been preserved for this period (Posener 1985). Of Persian date is a fragmentary Aramaic manuscript containing a narrative about the Egyptian magician "Hor, son of Pewenesh," who also occurs as a main character in a Demotic narrative preserved in a Roman-period manuscript (Porten 2004). Most likely the Aramaic text is a translation from the Egyptian, so that a version of the Demotic narrative must have circulated as early as the Persian period. These early texts confirm what is suggested by the abundance and variety of the narratives from the Sacred Animal Necropolis at Saqqara: already in the early Ptolemaic period Demotic literature had a rich and mature narrative tradition. The paucity of preserved literary texts for the period between the New Kingdom and the Ptolemaic period (1070–305 BCE) is no evidence for a dwindling literary output or a creative impasse, but the result of mere chance. Recent research has also demonstrated that several literary texts of pharaonic date kept being copied well into the Late Period, much longer than was previously assumed (Jasnow 1999; Verhoeven 1999). Demotic literature thus did not emerge in a wasteland, but continued a lively tradition of composing and transmitting literary texts.

The earliest manuscript preserving an Egyptian literary text written in Greek, here called Greco-Egyptian literature, dates to the second quarter of the second century BCE and comes from the *katokhē* archive from the Serapeum in Saqqara. It is a copy of the beginning of a narrative, merely the frame story, today known as "Nectanebo's Dream" (Gauger 2002), which has an almost word-for-word parallel in a very small fragment with Demotic writing from the Tebtunis temple library. Three Demotic scribal exercises, also from the Tebtunis temple library, preserve the opening of what probably was a sequel to the story (Ryholt 2002a). The works of the Egyptian priest Manetho and the Isis and Sarapis aretalogies, discussed below, also testify to the production of Egyptian literature in Greek in the early to middle Ptolemaic period. A recurring motif in these works is the presentation of the text as a translation of an Egyptian original. In a fair number of cases such claims may be true and should not be dismissed as a mere fiction to imbue the text with authority. Some texts are indeed attested in both a Demotic and Greek version. Whether or not the motif of translation was sometimes fictive, correspondences in genre, phraseology, and subject matter between Demotic and Greco-Egyptian texts demonstrate that they do not belong to separate traditions but were produced in a similar cultural environment, if perhaps for a different target audience.

The discovery of Demotic literary manuscripts in temple libraries, a dump within a temple precinct, and funerary contexts suggests that the production and reception of Demotic literature must be situated within an indigenous priestly milieu (Tait 1992). This agrees well with the subject matter and social setting of most of the narratives. The *katokhē* archive from the Memphite Serapeum, however, is of a different nature. Beyond the usual letters, petitions, and accounts, and the Greek version of "Nectanebo's Dream," it holds three short instruction texts in Demotic, excerpts from Greek drama (Euripides, Aeschylus, Menander, and another comic poet), epigrams of Posidippus, and Greek philosophical and astronomical works (Thompson 1988: 252–63). This bilingual archive belonged to Ptolemaeus, son of Glaucias, a man of Macedonian descent who lived as a recluse of very modest means in the Serapeum. Though Ptolemaeus, his brother Apollonius and his Egyptian friend Hermais were strictly speaking not priests, they lived within the temple precinct and probably acquired Egyptian literary texts through contacts with priests. This setting demonstrates that the audiences of Greek, Demotic, and Greco-Egyptian literature were not as distinct as earlier views have sometimes suggested. A similar conclusion is suggested by the numbers and distribution of manuscripts from the Fayum preserving Egyptian and Greek literature (Van Minnen 1998).

The Major Genres: Traditions and Transformations

Egyptian literature of the Ptolemaic period continued an age-old indigenous tradition of literary production. It should therefore not be studied in isolation from the earlier, formative periods of Egyptian literature. The most challenging issue for scholars of later Egyptian literature is the interplay between continuity and innovation with respect to motifs, themes, and narrative structures in light of the dramatic changes in the political, cultural, and demographic landscape that occurred in the Persian and Ptolemaic periods. These aspects can best be studied in the literary texts composed in Demotic and Greek. Texts written in Late Classical Egyptian were of a highly standardized nature and of limited distribution, either because they were executed in stone and thus immovable (e.g., temple texts and autobiographies) or because they contained specialized knowledge forbidden to all but priests (e.g., ritual handbooks, funerary literature and priestly manuals; Baines 2004). Demotic and Greco-Egyptian literature had a wider distribution and were the products of a lively scribal culture in which new texts were composed and earlier texts collected, copied, translated, and modified.

The pharaonic roots of Egyptian literature of the Ptolemaic period can best be observed in the main textual categories, which basically carry on the literary genres of earlier periods: autobiography, narrative, instruction, dialogue, lamentation or prophetic discourse, and satirical songs.

Autobiographies, which start to appear as early as 2500 BCE, constitute the earliest, simplest, and most significant genre of Egyptian literature, out of which instruction and narrative developed. In the Ptolemaic period autobiographies were composed in Late Classical Egyptian, but occasionally also in Demotic. They were written on a *stele* or statue, and commissioned only by high-ranking priests and officials for themselves or family members as part of their burial equipment or a votive gift to a deity. In addition to the usual list of priestly or official titles and succinct descriptions of career achievements the texts stress a person's rectitude, resolve and piety, usually in stock phrases, some of considerable antiquity, that continue a long tradition of moralistic self-presentation (Otto 1954; Derchain 2000; Jansen-Winkeln 2001). Rather than documenting particular biographical or historical events, most texts portray timeless model characters who are unaffected by historical circumstances (Zivie-Coche 2004: 291–3).

Narratives, judging from the number of preserved copies, represented the most popular and productive genre of literature in Ptolemaic Egypt. Compared to stories of the Middle and New Kingdom they also generally appear to have been of greater length. As a rule, the plot is set in a past when Egypt was still an independent state under an indigenous ruler. The opening line identifies the historical setting with a phrase such as "It happened one day in the reign of pharaoh N." The reigns to which the stories are dated range from the beginning to the end of pharaonic history (Quack 2005: 24–65). The frequent occurrence of anachronisms and fantastical elements demonstrates that the authors were led by a cultural memory of the past rather than historical facts.

The stories are told by an anonymous, external narrator who describes in relatively plain language the characters and events and seldom gives a comment or addresses the reader. Not infrequently an episode is narrated through a character's embedded speech, thus producing a story within a story, sometimes of considerable length. The plot develops around a main character, frequently a historic figure, who is a man of extraordinary abilities, either as a ritual specialist or as a warrior, and usually serving at, or in contact with, the royal court. The king plays most often a secondary, if not passive role, even if the events are critical to the survival of Egypt as an independent state and harmonious society. In most cases the royal court serves as the arena of dispute and display, where the story finds its beginning and happy ending. The world outside is a place of danger and conflict, where the main characters are tested, have to correct past mistakes, or fight against enemies of all sorts. Foreign regions from Nubia to Arabia, Mesopotamia, and India serve as places of action, but the texts are little concerned with describing these locations beyond mentioning names, and most characters seem to remain unaffected by their travel experiences (Vittmann 2006).

A characteristic of Demotic narrative literature is the existence of story cycles. Three cycles have been identified on the basis of the central characters and subject matter. One evolves around Setne Khamwase, whose interest in ancient texts and magic motivates the plots. He is modeled after the historic Khaemwaset, fourth son of Ramesses II (c.1279–1213 BCE), high priest of Ptah in Memphis, and renowned antiquarian. Knowledge of magic also plays a central role in the stories of the Atum priesthood at Heliopolis, of which the Petese story sequence is best preserved. This Petese may be identical with the sage Petese who was remembered for his arcane knowledge in the technical hermetica (Ryholt 1999: 81–2; Quack 2002; Ryholt 2006: 1–19). Of a different nature are the stories of the Inaros–Petubastis complex, which deal with the adventures and heroic deeds of Inaros and, after his death, of members of his extended family (Quack 2005: 44–61). Instead of magicians performing cunning feats, these tales portray warriors who prove their valor, loyalty, and honor in battle. Their historical background is the early seventh century BCE, when the local rulers Petubastis II of Tanis and Inaros of Athribis fought against the invading Assyrians.

Narratives were undoubtedly composed, read, and copied for multiple reasons. To assume that they were only appreciated for their entertainment value and literary merit is probably mistaken, since as much as 25 percent of the texts in the Tebtunis temple library are narratives. Given their historical subject matter, it is very well possible that priests perceived and collected the narratives as testimonies – or even historical records – of the heroes and glorious past of pharaonic Egypt (Ryholt 2005: 147, 154–7). This would also explain why Manetho's narrative accounts of Egyptian kings are strikingly similar in tone, structure, and subject matter. In fact, the Pherōs story, known from Herodotus (2.111), Diodorus Siculus (1.59), and Pliny the Elder (*NH* 36.74), is attested as a short story in the Petese story sequence (Ryholt 2006: 31–58).

In addition, the narratives propagate a set of traditional norms and values, which the main characters either embody or learn to recognize as just by bitter experience. As such the narratives also had a didactic function and served as vehicles for promoting and reinforcing a cultural and social identity for an indigenous elite that strove to maintain traditional values and social structures and sought for role models in the pharaonic past. In the stories about magic, the ideal is to be a "good scribe and wise man" (*sẖ nfr rmṯ rḫ*), a priest who is pious, conscientious, and strictly adheres to the cultic prescriptions and taboos (Dieleman 2005: 214–18, 237–8). In the Inaros–Petubastis texts the warrior (*rmṯ ḳnḳn*) sets the standard by his courage, loyalty, decisiveness, physical prowess, and knowledge of fighting (*sbꜥ mšs*). These are two rather different types, but both are capable through their respective skills, ingenuity, and determination, to overcome Egypt's enemies and restore order when the state comes under threat.

The story sequence of Petese son of Petetum, of which four fragmentary manuscripts have been preserved, is less concerned with male identity than with the virtues and vices of women (Ryholt 1999, 2006). Thirty-five stories of "praise of women" alternate with 35 stories of "scorn of women" embedded in a frame story about the Heliopolitan priest Petese. Petese learned that he had only 40 days left to live and ordered two baboons modeled out of wax to collect for him 70 stories of good and bad women as a literary testament to his memory. Female virtue is defined in terms of chastity, frugality, and restraint, whereas wicked women are adulterous, selfish, and prodigal. The stories are burlesque and racy and surely invited a good laugh within a male audience, but their didactic nature should not be underestimated, as is borne out by the fact that their view of female nature is in exact agreement with the discourse on women of the instruction texts (Dieleman 1998).

Narratives could also serve as a means to rewrite recent history, as the plot of the already-mentioned story "Nectanebo's Dream" suggests. The frame tells how king

Nectanebo II, Egypt's last native king (359–342 BCE), once saw in a dream the god Onuris complaining to Isis that the inscriptions in the sanctuary of his temple in Sebennytos were left unfinished. When he woke up Nectanebo immediately ordered the sculptor Petesis to complete the work, but Petesis failed due to his weakness for wine and women. At this point the Greek version breaks off, but references to Petesis' misery, a prophecy, and invading foreigners in the preserved portion of the sequel suggest that Petesis' indolence resulted in disaster (Ryholt 2002a: 232–7). In light of Nectanebo's role in the *Alexander Romance* and the below-mentioned prophetic texts, the story has often been read as a conscious effort on the part of the Egyptian priesthood to represent Alexander's invasion of Egypt as divine retribution for Nectanebo's failure to satisfy the gods (see also *Alexander Romance* 1.3.1–2 in Kroll 1926; translation Stoneman 1991: 36–7).

Animal fables, attested in very small numbers, constitute a distinct narrative genre. Several are embedded as moralizing tales in the "Myth of the Sun's Eye" (discussed below) and one is preserved as a scribal exercise; a canonical compilation of animal fables such as the Aesopica is not known for Egypt. These short, satirical narratives feature animals acting and speaking as humans with the aim of exposing and mocking human flaws such as arrogance, pride, and slyness. The earliest traces of the genre can be found in drawings of animals engaged in human activities dating to the Ramesside period (c.1290–1070 BCE; Brunner-Traut 1968). Parallels with foreign traditions are undeniable in certain fables, but it remains impossible to determine whether Egypt was the recipient or donor of the motifs. "The Fable of the Swallow and the Sea," preserved as a scribal exercise on a jar, reveals similarities in its basic plot structure with an animal fable in the Indian *Panchatantra* collection (1.12), which may be as old as the second century BCE; similarities have also been noted with a Jewish Aggadeh story and an episode in Plutarch's *Banquet of the Seven Sages* (*Conv.* 6, 150f–151e; Collombert 2002: 68–73). Embedded in the "Myth of the Sun's Eye" is "The Fable of the Lion and the Mouse," which is also known from the Aesop collection.

Instruction texts represented an important genre since the emergence of Egyptian literature in the Middle Kingdom. In the classic format, a father teaches his son the rules of proper conduct and how to be a competent, dependable, and responsible member of one's household and society at large. Unlike the instruction texts of the Middle and New Kingdom, Demotic teachings are not made up of stanzas which develop a thought over a few lines, but of self-contained aphorisms or maxims written on a single line each, and they display only a very loose sense of coherence and unity. This noteworthy shift was once explained with reference to the Hellenistic gnomological tradition, but the "Brooklyn Instruction Text" now suggests that the format was already under development in the Saite period (664–525 BCE) and thus probably came about without foreign influence (Lichtheim 1983; Jasnow 1992; Lazaridis 2007: 241–3). The relatively low number of instruction texts in the Tebtunis Temple Library may indicate that they were less popular than narratives (Quack 2005: 96). Nonetheless, both the so-called "Demotic Wisdom Book" and the "Instructions of Onchsheshonqy" are preserved in several (some very fragmentary) versions, which show considerable variation in the phrasing and sequence of the proverbs. The "Instructions of Onchsheshonqy" has a narrative introduction (also preserved as an independent composition) relating how Onchsheshonqy ended up in prison for not having divulged a plot against pharaoh's life sometime in the Saite period. As a prisoner, he had no other option for educating his son than by writing his teaching on the shards of the jars of mixed wine brought to him daily. The plot is strikingly reminiscent of the Aramaic "Tale of Ahiqar," whose earliest attestation is in a fifth-century BCE manuscript from the Jewish quarter at Elephantine (Porten and Yardeni 1993: 22–53; Knippschild in this volume). An Egyptian translation of the Ahiqar story is indeed attested in a number of Roman period papyrus fragments, so that influence from the Aramaic literary tradition cannot be excluded.

Dialogues are also attested as a literary genre since the Middle Kingdom. The format consists of two people discussing a topic of a moral nature, which setting allows for a difference of opinion, objections being raised, and further elaborations. Instead of giving straightforward instructions and prohibitions, this type of literature is rather concerned with documenting the process of acquiring knowledge and insight. The preserved versions of the "Myth of the Sun's Eye" and the "Book of Thoth," two elaborate dialogues in Demotic, contain editorial glosses indicating variant readings found in the earlier versions that were used for making the extant recensions. This method of glossing was an old scribal technique, but reserved for religious texts and priestly manuals only. Thus, rather than entertainment literature, these two dialogues were considered priestly knowledge, and they possibly circulated in temple scriptoria only.

The "Myth of the Sun's Eye," preserved in at least eight Demotic versions and a Greek translation, is a dialogue between a "small dog ape" and a "Nubian cat" which represent respectively the deities Thoth, god of knowledge and wisdom, and Tefnut, the daughter and eye of the sun god (Quack 2005: 128–39). The underlying plot is the "Myth of the Distant Goddess," well known from contemporary hieroglyphic temple texts and earlier sources, which relates how Tefnut was angry with her father Re, went to Nubia, and had to be entreated to come back to Egypt. In the present dialogue, the dog ape tactfully assuages the Nubian cat and persuades her to return and accept Egypt as her true homestead by telling animal fables and explaining proverbs to make her understand that each being has been assigned a particular role and position in nature and that god's plan and fate cannot be denied. Directions for the use of the voice included in the text may indicate that it was meant to be read aloud in front of an audience.

The "Book of Thoth" is a conversation, basically in question and answer format, between a mentor, called "He-of-Heseret" or "He-who-praises-knowledge," who is possibly identical with Thoth, and a student called "He-who-loves-knowledge" or "He-who-wishes-to-learn" (Jasnow and Zauzich 2005; Quack 2007). The composition is preserved in at least one hieratic and about 30 Demotic manuscripts, all of which date to the Roman period, except for one manuscript of possibly late Ptolemaic date. The mentor guides the aspiring initiate into the mysteries of the House of Life and the scribal profession. The House of Life was the temple's cultic library where ritual handbooks were composed, copied, and stored, and where rituals for Osiris and the preservation of life were performed. The text's tutorial format and the reference to Thoth as "The-thrice-great" (B02, 9/7) suggest that the "Book of Thoth" constitutes an early representative of the Greco-Egyptian traditions around Hermes

Trismegistus, which became widely popular in the Roman period and later. However, on the level of the subject matter, parallels between the "Book of Thoth" and the later Hermetica are less evident.

In Egyptian **lamentations** or **prophecies**, an inspired speaker delivers a dramatic monologue in front of an audience, usually the royal court, which listens without intervening to the speaker's descriptions of cosmic and social upheaval. The typical lamentations of the Middle Kingdom can be read as literary reflections on the validity and limits of society's ideal norms and values as propagated in official discourse (Parkinson 2002: 193–234). "The Words of Neferti," an *ex eventu* prophecy foretelling a return to order and stability under king Amenemhat I (c.1991–1962 BCE), mobilized this generic form to generate legitimacy and loyalty for the first rulers of the twelfth dynasty, who presented themselves as saviors bringing order out of chaos. In the Ptolemaic period the so-called "Oracle of the Lamb," "Potter's Oracle," and "Demotic Oracle" continued this tradition of prophetic chaos descriptions, with the difference that the return to indigenous rule and order was now projected into a distant or even undefined future (all relevant sources in Blasius and Schipper 2002). Nature and society will be in disarray, the cult will not be properly performed or abandoned altogether, and a foreign king will invade Egypt, taking over power and deporting the statues of the gods. Some scholars have termed these texts apocalyptic, even though they foretell a return to the old order rather than the advent of a radically new age (Blasius and Schipper 2002: 298–302).

The "Oracle of the Lamb," preserved in one Demotic manuscript from Soknopaiou Nesos (but known already to Manetho in the early Ptolemaic period), is allegedly an oracle spoken by a lamb in the days of King Bocchoris (722–715 BCE). The foreign king is identified as "the Mede" (I/22 and II/21), possibly a reference to Antiochus IV, who invaded Egypt in 170/69–168 BCE (Thissen 2002: 123–4). After 900 years, an indigenous savior king, "he of 55 (years)" (II/5) will overthrow the foreigners, ransack Nineveh, take control over Syria, and bring back the cult statues. The conflation of the Assyrian, Persian, and Seleucid empires demonstrates that the text, as it is preserved, is not concerned with one particular moment in time, but rather with the idea and trauma of foreign invasion and occupation.

The "Potter's Oracle," partly preserved in five Greek recensions of Ptolemaic and Roman date, is presented as the plea of an indignant potter to king Amenhotep III (c.1390–1353 BCE) predicting the destruction of Egypt just as he was mistreated, unjustly, himself. The text mentions the oracle of the lamb and "he of 55 (years)" as a savior king, but the foreigners are called here "Typhonians" and "girdle-wearers" whose king founded Alexandria. Due to their lawlessness and impiety the Typhonians will eventually destroy themselves, and the Agathos Daimon will leave Alexandria and return to Memphis as the primeval snake Kmephis, together with the statues of the gods. In the midst of this chaos, a hateful king from Syria will invade Egypt, but one day "he of 55 years, sent by the sun god" (P_3 IV.64) will regain control and establish law and order.

The "Demotic Oracle" (misleadingly named the "Demotic Chronicle" in the past) represents a prophetic text of a slightly different nature (Felber 2002). Preserved in an early Ptolemaic manuscript, it gives interpretations of oracular utterances and is primarily concerned with assessing in retrospect the piety and virtue of the indigenous rulers of the twenty-eighth to thirtieth dynasties (404–343 BCE) in relation to "the law," a new Late Egyptian concept reminiscent of Deuteronomistic kingship ideology rather than pharaonic *ma'at* theology (Johnson 1983; Assmann 2003: 378–81, 384). The text foretells how a native ruler from Herakleopolis will start an uprising and rule after the Greeks, but due to the text's enigmatic language much remains unclear.

In the past scholars have read the three texts as anti-Hellenic propaganda, possibly even written to legitimize and stir support for indigenous uprisings against Ptolemaic rule. However, purely "nationalistic" explanations of the major rebellions have come under question, and other social and economic tensions have been identified as factors in these unrests, which had Egyptians and Greeks on both sides (McGing 1997, 2006; Veïsse 2004). Recent scholarship, moreover, has played down the sharp divide between native Egyptians and Greeks by stressing the multicultural and bilingual character of society in the *chora* (Johnson 1992; Blasius and Schipper 2002: 294–8). The texts might just as well reflect tensions between *chora* and Alexandria, periphery and center, tradition and innovation.

Satirical songs stand out for their metrical form and bawdy character. To date only the "Harpist's Song" and the "Songs for the Bastet Festival" are known, but the genre may have been more popular and widespread than previously thought. These Demotic compositions celebrate sexuality, gluttony, and drunkenness. Due to their fragmentary state of preservation, their origin and performance setting remain controversial. The singular "Harper's Song," whose preserved five columns are a mockery of a harper named Hor-Oudja, has been regarded as an Egyptian adaptation of the Greek genre of the invective (Thissen 1992: 13–15). However, the newly discovered "Songs for the Bastet Festival" make it more plausible to associate the genre with the drinking festivals described by Herodotus (2.60) and known from other Egyptian sources (Depauw and Smith 2004; Hoffmann and Quack 2007: 305–11).

A Borderland of Greek and Egyptian Literature

The genres just surveyed lay out the boundaries of Demotic Egyptian literature, a literature that was produced and read by Egyptians of priestly background and education and that generally presumed and re-articulated the norms and values of this elite milieu. Several of the texts, however, have also attracted the attention of scholars pursuing the question of interplay between Egyptian and Greek literature. Narrative has been particularly prominent in this debate. The heroic deeds and one-on-one battles in the Inaros–Petubastis complex, it has been argued, were composed under the influence of Greek epic literature (Volten 1956 with ensuing discussions in Hoffmann 1996; Vittmann 1998; Thissen 1999), while the Egyptian narrative tradition, particularly in the period of Demotic literature, has been cited as a major factor in the development of the Greek novel. The fundamental early argument in favor of the latter (Barns 1956) pointed to the late emergence of prose fiction in the history of Greek literature, broad parallels in themes between the novels and Egyptian narratives, the prominence of Egypt in the Greek novels, and the existence of Greek translations from Demotic such as "Nectanebo's Dream" and the "Myth of the Sun's Eye." This was in part a refutation of the extremely Hellenocentric theories of Rohde (1876), but the debate over Egyptian influences in the novel continues. Classicists have tended to emphasize the Greekness of the Greek novel, and some have recently downplayed the impact of Egyptian narrative literature on the formation of the genre as a whole (e.g., Stephens and Winkler 1995: 11–18). Others accept that Greek–Egyptian interactions played a productive role (see the balanced assessment of Whitmarsh in this volume), and some studies have traced the origins of particular motifs such as magician-priests and stories of *boukoloi*-bandits to Egyptian literature (Rutherford 1997, 2000).

Whatever the outcome for the history of the Greek novel, this ongoing discussion emphasizes the place of narrative fiction as a borderland between Greek and Egyptian literary traditions. This fact in itself merits consideration for whatever light it can shed on the strategies of mutual interpretation or even misinterpretation at the interface between Greek and Egyptian literatures. Narrative, which has been described as "transcultural" and (unlike, e.g., lyric poetry) "translatable without fundamental damage" (Barthes 1977: 79, 121), appears to have been a privileged vehicle for this interaction; it more easily crossed the barriers of language or generic expectations that separated Greek and Egyptian literary communities. As outlined above, however, there were also clearly some individuals, predominantly among the indigenous elite, who could participate in both communities, and they were undoubtedly the ones producing translations of Egyptian narratives or composing new ones in Greek. In such texts, it is possible to detect continuities with Egyptian narrative literature, but also efforts to translate these traditions for a Greek audience while exploring the literary possibilities and complexities of a dual Greco-Egyptian readership.

The evidence for the transmission of narratives goes back at least to Herodotus, many of whose stories about Egyptian kings undoubtedly derived from indigenous sources (Lloyd 1988: 24–7, 38–44; Moyer 2002). This was long suspected, and is now given added support by the discovery of a Demotic version of the Pherōs story (mentioned above; Ryholt 2006: 31–58) and the legend of Sesostris in two Roman-period Demotic manuscripts (Widmer 2002: 387–93). The latter king, variously transliterated as Sesostris, Sesoösis, or Sesonchosis, conflates two great Middle Kingdom military pharaohs (Senwosret I and III) and possibly also the Libyan dynast Sheshonq I (Malaise 1966; Widmer 2002: 392). This composite legendary figure is also attested in other Greek sources (e.g., Manetho *Dyn.* 12.3 = *FGrH* 609 F 2, F 3a–b; A.R. 4.272–81; D.S. 1.53–9; Str. 15.1.6, 16.4.4), including papyrus fragments of a text known as the *Sesonchosis Romance* (Stephens and Winkler 1995: 246–66). Stories of a pharaoh of the glorious Egyptian past served to rival more recent conquerors, whether Persian (Hdt. 2.110.2–3) or Macedonian (D.S. 1.55.2–3). The *Sesonchosis Romance* treats a military campaign against Arabia (cf. D.S. 1.53.5), but also adds a love story between Sesonchosis and a certain Meameris. The names in these fragments, along with certain phrases paralleled in documentary papyri, suggest that this was an Egyptian composition or translation (Stephens and Winkler 1995: 248–9), perhaps related to the Demotic text which mentions, among other military ventures, Sesostris' campaign against Arabia (Widmer 2002: 390).

In the *Alexander Romance*, the Macedonian conqueror is assimilated to his Egyptian predecessor as the "new Sesostris, ruler of the world" (1.34.2 Kroll 1926; cf. 3.34.4), and in several versions Alexander finds the traces of Sesostris' earlier conquests as he pursues his own (e.g., 3.17.17). The Egyptian orientation of this comparison is also evident in other segments of the complex *Alexander Romance* tradition, the earliest elements of which have been identified as originating in early Ptolemaic Egypt (Stoneman 1994: 122–3; Fraser 1996: 211–14; Whitmarsh in this volume). The most notable evidence for this is the tale of Nectanebo's magical deception of Olympias (1.1–12), closely modeled upon the Egyptian myth of royal succession, which results in Alexander's over-determined paternal descent from both the last native pharaoh of Egypt and the god Amun. Since the Nectanebo episode begins with the pharaoh performing divinatory rites and realizing that the gods are against him, the story can be connected to "Nectanebo's Dream" (Ryholt 2002a). Whether a translation from Egyptian (Jasnow 1997) or a new composition loosely connected to the other Greek and Demotic Nectanebo stories, this episode provides an excellent example of the duality of Greco-Egyptian fiction, since its twists and turns can be read against both the ideological background of Egyptian kingship and Greek traditions of the divine ancestry of heroes (Stephens 2003: 64–72; see also Selden 1994). Like other Egyptian narratives, the Nectanebo episode is more than just salacious entertainment, since it also explains recent history as a continuation of Egyptian traditions and paradigms of kingship; Alexander's "illegitimate" birth makes him a legitimate pharaoh.

The normative and didactic dimensions of Egyptian narratives and their elaboration of religious, political, and social discourses were also exploited by Manetho in composing his *Aegyptiaca*, an Egyptian history in Greek now preserved only in epitomes and fragments (*FGrH* 609). Manetho, a priest from Sebennytos, served as an indigenous interpreter of Egyptian religion, history, and culture at the Alexandrian court under Soter and Philadelphus and probably into the early years of Euergetes (280s–240s BCE). Aside from the *Aegyptiaca*, his intercultural activities may have included a role in the development of the Alexandrian version of Sarapis and the composition of several works on Egyptian religion as well as *Criticisms of Herodotus* (*FGrH* 609 T 9, F 13–15, 16a, 17). The latter work, however, may be identical with the *Aegyptiaca*, in which he clearly engages with Greek traditions on the Egyptian past. The fact that he knew Herodotus and composed his history as a series of narratives has led many Classicists to view Manetho's work as dependent on Greek historiographical traditions (Murray 1972: 209; Fraser 1972: 1.506–9; Dillery 1999). This view inadequately addresses the overall structure of the work, which, as many Egyptologists have observed, takes the form of a traditional Egyptian king list elaborated by the insertion of stories derived from Egyptian narrative literature and other observations on various kings (Redford 1986: 225–6; Lloyd 1975–8: 1. 110–11). Manetho's history is thus not an imitation of Greek historiography, but rather a response to it in the form of an innovative combination of traditional Egyptian genres translated and re-interpreted for a Greek-reading audience (cf. Knippschild in this volume on Berossus and Mesopotamian king lists). Through a structure that looks like a series of *lemmata* and comments, Manetho elaborates an implicit pattern of ideal kingship based on a series of good and bad kings, and their fates. In this, his work is comparable to the "Demotic Oracle," discussed above, which consist of a series of oracular statements and interpretations retrospectively evaluating the reigns of late Egyptian kings (Johnson 1983; Felber 2002).

Manetho's history, fragmentary though its remains are, provides relatively straightforward evidence of knowledge passing between the Egyptian temple scriptoria and Greek intellectuals, but there are also tantalizing glimpses of such circulation in the papyri. Peter van Minnen's overview of literature preserved in Fayum villages (1998) reveals a large quantity of technical literature, especially medical, mathematical, and astrological texts, in both Greek and Demotic. The astrological texts from Tebtunis and Soknopaiou Nesos are especially noteworthy, since they provide a social and cultural milieu for one of the distinctive Greco-Egyptian contributions to Hellenistic literature: the astrological treatises penned under the names of Nechepso and Petosiris. The earliest datable references place their origins in second century BCE Ptolemaic Egypt, but they continued to have considerable authoritative weight in Roman-period astrological works (Fraser 1972: 1.436–7; fragments in Riess 1892). The literary conventions of the Nechepso–Petosiris tradition were used to integrate a heterogeneous array of ideas and practices into an Egyptian scheme for authorizing knowledge. Nechepso, the historical Necho II of the Saite twenty-sixth dynasty, is often referred to simply as "the king," while Petosiris seems to have played the role of a priest. Several fragments suggest that communications between the two provided the literary frame for the divine astrological wisdom transmitted under their names, recalling the Demotic literary convention mentioned above in which prophecies and narratives are recounted to the king at court. This has been given further support by the recent discovery of fragments of the Nechepso–Petosiris literature in Demotic (Ryholt 2008).

To the evidence of the Fayum survey and the Nechepso–Petosiris tradition must also be added a pair of Ptolemaic astronomical-calendrical texts that explicitly evoke the communication between Greeks and Egyptians. The *Art of Eudoxus* (*P.Par.* 1; Blass 1887; Neugebauer 1975: 2.686–9) is a pseudepigraphical work of the early second century BCE which draws on the astronomical ideas of the fourth-century scientist, some of which he allegedly developed while studying with Egyptian priests at Heliopolis (D.L. 8.8.87, 90; Str. 17.1.29, 30; Plu. *De Is. et Os.* 10; Lasserre 1966: T 7, 12–13, 17; Griffiths 1965). The manuscript, preserved in the bilingual Serapeum archive of Ptolemaeus mentioned above, seems to allude to these Egyptian connections with illustrations of a scarab, mummified ibis, and baboon (Neugebauer 1975: 3.1435, pl. VII; Thompson 1988: 252–4). A calendar for the Saite nome, dated 301–240 BCE, parallels phrases from the *Art of Eudoxus*, though in its short epistolary prologue the author refers to a wise man from Sais as his source (*P.Hibeh* 27.ii.19–22). These and other Ptolemaic Egyptian technical texts merit further investigation, not least for their possible connections to the Hermetic literature discussed above.

Tradition and Innovation in an Intercultural Poetics

Narrative literature and technical treatises reveal both continuities and transformations of traditional Egyptian forms. Authors of Greco-Egyptian literature could also adopt more strikingly innovative approaches (from an Egyptian perspective) when they used the language and formal conventions of Greek poetry. The range of possibilities is evident in the Greek hymns honoring Egyptian gods, particularly a group of closely related Isis hymns long studied as part of Hellenistic aretalogical literature. At the core of this group is the so-called Kyme aretalogy (*IKyme* 41; *IG* XII Suppl. 14, pp. 98–9), which consists of a long series of first-person self-predications by the goddess ("I am Isis, mistress of all the land; I was instructed by Hermes and I discovered writing with Hermes … I established laws for men"). This text is also preserved in three other partial versions: inscriptions from Thessaloniki (*IG* X(2).1.254) and Ios (*IG* XII Suppl. 14, p. 98), and a passage from Diodorus Siculus' account of Egypt (1.27.3–4). There are two other related inscriptions from Andros and Maroneia which treat many of the same themes, though in different forms (see below). The Kyme inscription explicitly claims Egyptian origins by stating that the Greek text was copied from a *stele* standing near the temple of Ptah in Memphis, a tradition partly confirmed by the testimony of Diodorus, who adds that the original was composed in hieroglyphs (1.22.2, 27.3–4). The Egyptian character of the text, its Memphite origins, and the question whether it was first composed in Greek or Egyptian have been much debated (Grandjean 1975: 12–15; Fowden 1986: 46–8; Versnel 1998: 41–4; Dousa 2002: 149–51; Quack 2003: 319–24). The initial case for Egyptian origins met with stiff resistance by those who saw the aretalogies as a thoroughly Hellenized representation of Isis, but their objections have been overcome by an accumulation of parallels in Egyptian hymns and other liturgical and mythical texts belonging to the formal religious literature of the temples (e.g., Harder 1944; Žabkar 1988; Quack 2003). In arguing for Greek or Egyptian identity, however, both sides have at times pursued an untenable cultural essentialism. Recent work has developed a more complex picture of continuity and transformation by analyzing traditional characteristics of Isis as they appear in both the Greek hymns and in contemporary Demotic literature (e.g., Dousa 2002, building especially on Ray 1976: 155–8, 174).

The formal qualities of these texts add to the complexities. The stichic declarations of the Kyme aretalogy owe little to Greek hymns, and bear a closer resemblance to the serial construction and *parallelismus membrorum* of poetic texts in Classical Egyptian (Quack 2003: 332–5). The aretalogies from Andros and Maroneia, however, use Greek literary forms to present much the same content (*IG* XII(5).739 = Totti 1985: no. 2; Grandjean 1975). This is particularly clear in the Andros inscription, which casts the simple self-predications of the Kyme aretalogy in hexameters filled with poetic vocabulary. This variation cannot be taken as evidence for a gradual process of Hellenization resulting from the articulation of Egyptian traditions in Greek (contra Fowden 1986: 45–8), since the inscriptions from Andros and Maroneia, dated to the first century BCE and the late second/early first century BCE respectively, are in fact among the earliest texts in this cluster of aretalogies. The Kyme, Thessaloniki, and Ios inscriptions, on the other hand, range in date from the first to third centuries CE. The original – if there ever was a single original – has not been recovered in Egypt or elsewhere, so it is impossible to be certain of its form or language. It would, therefore, be more prudent to consider the variations in poetic form as a spectrum of co-existent options drawing upon Greek and Egyptian literary forms. The content, the range of forms, and the dates of the earliest versions point to a genesis for this tradition in the mixed cultural milieu of Ptolemaic Egypt in the second century BCE or earlier.

The production of Greco-Egyptian poetry in an Egyptian context can be explored more directly through the Greek hymns of Isidorus found inscribed at the temple of

Renenutet in the Fayum village of Narmouthis (modern Medinet Madi). The most recent editor dated the inscriptions to the 80s BCE (Vanderlip 1972; cf. Bollók 1974), though composition in the third century BCE has also been proposed. The texts themselves furnish what little is known about the author. The name Isidorus is ostensibly Greek, but it is not uncommon for a theophoric name like this to translate an Egyptian equivalent, in this case perhaps Petese. In one of the hymns, he explicitly presents himself as translating Egyptian traditions for Greeks (4.18–19, 38–9), though he makes no overt claim to have read Egyptian texts himself. Isidorus' ethnic or socio-linguistic identity is not entirely clear, but these few facts, together with the content and form of the hymns, evoke a moment of literary communication between the Greek immigrant and indigenous Egyptian communities in the Fayum.

Isidorus' four hymns are arranged in two pairs on separate piers of the entry to the outermost forecourt, and each pair consists of one hymn in hexameters and one in elegiac couplets. The hymns on the west pier (1–2) honor Isis while identifying her with Renenutet (known in Greek as Thermouthis or Hermouthis), an Egyptian agricultural divinity prominent in the Fayum; those on the east (3–4) form a diptych on kingship. Their origin in the Egyptian *chora* does not prevent these texts from using a common Hellenistic language of praise and drawing on the same Greek poetic traditions as the poetry of the Alexandrian court (Fantuzzi and Hunter 2004: 350–3, 360–3). The texts combine these Greek models with material explicitly derived from Egyptian literature. This is especially apparent in the third and fourth hymns. The third, in praising Isis-Hermouthis as a patron of kingship, presents in hexameters and Homeric language an ideal ruler, likely an early Ptolemy, who is favored by the goddess: a king who controls Europe and Asia, bringing peace, prosperity, and victory in war. Though in line with Egyptian traditions, these are broad themes of Hellenistic kingship. Juxtaposed to hymn 3, however, is a much more direct appeal to pharaonic kingship. Hymn 4, the elegiac counterpart of hymn 3, honors Porammanres, i.e., the twelfth dynasty pharaoh Amenemhat III (c.1818–1770 BCE), who built the original Renenutet temple at Narmouthis, and was active in the extension of irrigation and settlement in the Fayum (like Ptolemy Philadelphus). The allusions in this hymn to tales of the ancient king's strange deeds and magical powers (4.11–20, 35–6), along with calques on Egyptian phrases (4.23, 31) support Isidorus' claim to have obtained the material of this hymn from Egyptian sources. These neighboring inscriptions thus embody not only the duality of Ptolemaic kingship, but also the double literary position that a Ptolemaic author from the Egyptian countryside could occupy.

A small collection of less intensively studied texts from the Egyptian *chora* provides further evidence for Greco-Egyptian poetry. Three *stelai* from Hassaia, the necropolis of Apollinopolis Magna near Edfu, preserve funerary epigrams, all composed by a certain Herodes, and all related to one small family (*IMEG* 5, 6, 35). The texts, which date to the late second century BCE, are composed in elegiac couplets, exhibit numerous Homeric usages, and dwell on themes familiar to Greek funerary epigrams. The individuals mentioned all have Greek names, and the men were officers in the Ptolemaic army, so the texts could have passed without much notice as the products of Greek immigrant society in Egypt. A few clues, however, allow us to identify these individuals with members of a priestly family with Egyptian names honored in hieroglyphic funerary *stelai* (Cairo *CG* 22018, 22021, 22050). The examination of these two sets of *stelai* reveals remarkable parallels between the titles, honors, and familial relations mentioned in the Greek epigrams and those in the hieroglyphic funerary texts, proving that we are dealing with two entirely different forms of literary self-representation, Greek and Egyptian, used by a single family from the *chora* (Yoyotte 1969). Read together, these texts also reveal the extent to which the outward appearances of Greek names and Greek poetry can mask the Egyptian milieu in which, and for which, Greco-Egyptian literature was produced. "Apollonius" is also "Pashu"; "Aphrodisia" is "Hathor-iity." Their home, "the steep, sacred city of Phoebus" (*IMEG* 5.10) is Edfu, the city of Horus. The "sacred seat of Persephone" in which they were laid to rest was in "the peaks of mountainous Bakhthis," a Greek rendering of Behdet, the ancient Egyptian name of Edfu (*IMEG* 35.1–6). This is not a Greek poetry of dislocation or diaspora, but one that has roots in the Egyptian landscape.

***

These inscriptions, then, like the papyrus texts discussed earlier in this chapter, provoke reflection on the boundaries that scholars set when they understand the language, generic categories, and formal conventions of Hellenistic literature in Ptolemaic Egypt as a set of expectations negotiated between writers and a particular readership. Such texts reveal that a Hellenistic literature in the language and idiom of Greek traditions was at times produced and read in a mixed Greco-Egyptian milieu, at least from the second quarter of the second century, when there was in any case more overlap and interconnection between the social worlds of Greeks and Egyptians. While these particular texts shed light only indirectly on the production and reception context of third-century Alexandrian poetry, they are part of a broader history of literary communication stretching back to the first Ptolemies. The outlines of this history are evident in the texts discussed above, whether Egyptian–Greek translations, or new compositions in Greek that have adapted inherited Egyptian genres or narrative patterns to a new social and linguistic situation. These Greco-Egyptian texts, together with the extensive (albeit fragmentary) evidence of Demotic literature, form a body of Ptolemaic Egyptian literature created primarily, but perhaps not exclusively, by the indigenous priestly classes. Egyptian writers produced and maintained a flourishing contemporary literature that continued and transformed long-standing traditions rooted in the earlier history of pharaonic Egypt. The further exploration of these texts, on which much work remains to be done, promises to provide a fuller picture of the cultural horizons of the indigenous elite in the Ptolemaic period and the knowledge, literary practices, and ideas they contributed to the Hellenistic literary and intellectual encounter between Greeks and Egyptians.

FURTHER READING

The best introduction to Egyptian literature in Demotic and Greek is provided by Quack 2005, a comprehensive and insightful survey of the genres and texts, in combination with Hoffmann and Quack 2007, an anthology of German translations of the major texts. Both contain an extensive bibliography with references to the editions of texts mentioned in this chapter. More concise introductions, though outdated in certain respects, are Tait 1994, 1996 and Thissen 2004. English translations of selected Demotic texts can be found in Lichtheim 1980 and Ritner's contributions to Simpson 2003. Convenient handbooks for the study of Demotic texts are Depauw 1997 and Hoffmann 2000. Translations of the relevant Greek texts are more scattered. The *Alexander Romance* and the fragments of *Sesonchosis* can be found in Reardon 1989; the latter is also included in Stephens and Winkler 1995. Recent German translations of the "Potter's Oracle" and "Nectanebo's Dream" along with discussion and bibliography can be found in Blasius and Schipper 2002. English translations of Manetho: Waddell 1940 (Greek text and translation); Verbrugge and Wickersham 1996. Bernand 1969 provides a collection of the Greek metrical inscriptions from Egypt with French translations. For English translations of Isidorus' hymns, see Vanderlip 1972. Several of the Greek papyri and inscriptions are included in the convenient collection of Totti 1985. For the socio-cultural context of indigenous literature, see Tait 1992, who addresses the question of who produced and read Demotic literature; Van Minnen 1998, who provides a useful survey of literary texts (both Greek and Demotic) found in Fayum settlements; and Ryholt 2005, a preliminary assessment of the holdings of the Tebtunis temple library. Issues of continuity and innovation in Demotic literature are discussed in Vittmann 1998. Arguments for or against Greek influence in Demotic literature are summarized in Hoffmann 1996, Thissen 1999, and Smith 2000. The most extensive recent treatments of Egyptian influence in Greek literature are Selden 1998 and Stephens 2003.

CHAPTER TWENTY-NINE

Literature in Western Asia

Silke Knippschild

After Alexander's conquest of Asia and the end of the Persian Empire, new sovereigns controlled Iran, Mesopotamia, and the Levant. The Seleucid dynasty, originating with Seleucus I who had been given Babylon as his share of Alexander's dominion, controlled large parts of Western Asia. However, the Seleucid kings never managed to establish lasting control over their possessions and during their reign various sections of their territories achieved autonomy under different rulers. One effect of this political instability manifested itself in the sphere of culture. Whereas tightly controlled successor states such as Ptolemaic Egypt exhibited a certain uniformity, the lands of Western Asia retained highly individual cultural characteristics. In other words, they remained culturally independent and diverse, much as they had been under Persian rule. One area in which this diversity is visible is literature, which thrived under the new sovereigns just as it had under each of the preceding dynasties.

In Greek and Roman literature we encounter two ways of representing Western Asia. On the one hand, authors present an idealized picture of the East and of its key city, Babylon, a place associated with riches, culture, and grandeur. But we also encounter an image of decline, decadence, and the downfall of culture, in particular again regarding Babylon (Boiy 2004: 77–8). The city is portrayed as a wasteland, mostly devoid of people, its buildings in ruins, the land within the famed city walls used for farming. Alongside these ancient *topoi* stands the portrayal of a Western Asia Hellenized in the wake of Alexander's conquest of the Persian Empire, which was created by twentieth-century scholarship. These images must be challenged.

As far as the material evidence is concerned, archaeology refutes the picture presented by ancient authors, both that of fabulous grandeur and that of decline and fall (Boiy 2004: 55–97). The surviving texts likewise prove the image of the waning of Western Asian literature and culture to be false. Literary traditions were cultivated and existing works copied down to the end of the use of cuneiform script in the first century CE (Geller 1997), and cuneiform texts were read until the second or third century CE (Geller 1995: 44; differently Westenholz 2007). Extant documents are written in the Sumerian and Akkadian languages, generally using the cuneiform script, although every now and then Greek characters appear. A group of Sumerian and Akkadian texts written in Greek script, apparently discovered in Babylon and now in the keeping of the British Museum, comprises administrative documents, practice texts from scribal schools, literary texts, incantations, and dedications. The reverse of these clay tablets is generally written in cuneiform, while the obverse contains a transliteration of the same text into the Greek alphabet. Although not many texts of this type survive (edited in Geller 1997), it appears that the practice started in the second century BCE, became popular in the first century BCE, and continued until the second century CE (Geller 1997: 83–4). The texts from scribal schools demonstrate familiarity with the enunciation of both Akkadian and Sumerian. The Greek may have been used as guide for pronouncing the cuneiform scripts. Geller suggests that the transliterations, which resemble Origen's transliterations of Hebrew with Greek letters of the third century CE, may be linked to the adoption of leather as writing material in the second half of the second century BCE, as attested by, e.g., astronomical diaries, which coincides with the rising popularity of the school texts (Geller 1997: 47–8, 68). Alphabetical scripts work well for writing on leather and Greek letters were highly suitable for representing Akkadian vowels and consonants. The adoption of this new system of writing for traditional literature shows that this literature was very much alive and is indicative of the flexibility of the people writing and reproducing it.

In addition to traditional forms of literature such as astronomical diaries or king lists, the intercultural contact with the Greek world produced new types of writing, such as the history of Western Asia in Greek by the Babylonian Berossus. In turn, Greeks such as Ctesias of Cnidus and Apollodorus of Artemita, living in Mesopotamia and Iran, also created reference works about their surroundings, their time, and the history of these areas, enabling their fellow countrymen to gain access to knowledge of these faraway regions in a familiar literary format. Some of the racier stories presented by authors such as Ctesias also influenced the budding literary genre of the Greek novel (Kuhrt 1995; Whitmarsh in this volume).

Nevertheless, this picture of continuity does not apply to all types of literature in the area. Specific genres vanish, such as medical texts, which become rare and eventually disappear completely in the early Hellenistic period (Oelsner 1986: 202 and 264). On the whole we have little indigenous narrative literature dating to Hellenistic times. It is unclear whether this is due to the chances of transmission or to other causes. Further, few Greek texts from Western Asia have survived, which may be due to the material used for writing: leather or papyrus perished, while the clay tablets used for cuneiform script (or Sumerian and Akkadian written in the Greek alphabet) were more likely to survive. Aramaic and Phoenician texts, too, were written in alphabetic scripts on perishable materials and are now mostly lost. A notable exception is Papyrus Amherst 63, an Aramaic text written in demotic script (Steiner 1995), which preserves a variety of literary forms, including a variation on a biblical Psalm and the so-called "Tale of Two Brothers," a story to which we will turn shortly.

Lists and Literature

The major and most varied part of Western Asian literature consisted of lists. The division between documentary and literary is particularly problematic for Western Asia once one goes beyond the realm of easily classifiable texts like administrative records. While lists may not appear to be works of literature to us at first glance, it is important to keep in mind that this distinction was probably not apparent to the inhabitants of ancient Western Asia. Within these lists, we encounter a wide variety of literary genres.

King lists were abundant in Hellenistic times. These texts list the names of kings in chronological order, often adding further information such as the number of their regnal years, the date of their accession to the throne, their death, and other pertinent details. A Babylonian example of the genre opens its record with Alexander and continues down to the Parthian period (Oelsner 1986: 202). When there was no acting king or the king was far away, the person exercising power would be named instead, such as the Macedonian generals Seleucus or Antigonus Monophthalmus when they governed Babylonia (Del Monte 1997: 208–9). A typical entry in the Babylonian king list on Seleucus I Nicator reads (*BM* 35603 obv. 6–8, trans. Van der Spek; cf. Glassner 2004: 134–5):

> Year 7, which is year 1: Sel(eucus was) king. He reigned for twenty-five years.
> Year 31, Ulûlu: Sel(eucus), the king, was killed in the land of the Haneans.

While this text is highly informative for the historian, for example as evidence for the chronology of the Seleucid era, it is sparse in narrative.

The related and more edifying genre of chronicles also catalogues important events under the headings of the regnal years of the ruling king. The most prominent Hellenistic example of this genre is the "Diadochi Chronicle" (*BCHP* 3 = Grayson 1975: no. 10), which starts its report in the third year of Philip Arrhidaeus and continues on to the ninth year of "Alexander the son" (321/20–308/7 BCE). It contains entries such as the following (23–5, trans. Van der Spek):

> That same month the king did battle with the satrap of Egypt, and the land ...
> The troops of the king were slaughtered. Month 8, day 10 ... the satrap of Akkad entered Babylon.

Astronomical diaries were another ancient Mesopotamian literary genre that flourished from Neo-Babylonian to Arsacid times (652/1–75 BCE). The latest known cuneiform document (75 BCE) belongs to this category (Geller 1995: 44), and astronomical diaries in fact make up the bulk of our extant texts (Hunger and Sachs 1988–96). They report the risings and settings of stars, eclipses, and other astrological phenomena in conjunction with the wind direction. They also list events which the observer considered to be omens, and occasionally we find endearing remarks such as "I did not watch" or "there were clouds in the sky" (Lendering 2008). Astronomy and astrology were not considered to be separate areas of investigation in antiquity; accordingly, these texts also functioned as horoscopes. Related are mathematical-astronomical lists predicting astral phenomena such as solstices and equinoxes. Other mathematical tablets list multiplication tables or square numbers. With these texts, it is important to keep in mind that labels such as astronomical, astrological, and mathematical are again no more than modern attempts at pigeonholing our evidence.

Another genre which continued in the Hellenistic period were prophecies. These were invariably recorded after the fact, a time-honored tradition not restricted to Western Asia (Grayson 1975: 24–37; Dieleman and Moyer in this volume). These texts list kings and differentiate their reigns by years and character: good or bad. One such prophecy from Babylon, today kept in the British Museum, represents a somewhat dubious source on Alexander the Great. In this so-called "Dynastic Prophecy," written at the earliest during the first regnal period after Alexander's death, Alexander's reign is unsurprisingly characterized as bad (Sherwin-White 1987: 11). Further, the reversal of Darius' defeat by a successor to Alexander is announced, after which the people will flourish (Sherwin-White and Kuhrt 1993: 8–9). Key to the people's future wellbeing, it appears, is a tax exemption, always an indicator of good kingship.

These forms of Western Asian literature represent the voice of the indigenous population. However, the new sovereigns employed traditional forms of writing as well. An outstanding example is the cylinder of Antiochus I Soter (280–262/1 BCE) from the temple of Nabu in Borsippa, the city's patron deity and god of writing. The text conforms largely to the standard formula of Babylonian foundation texts, although Antiochus included "the Macedonian" into the list of his royal titles, just as the Achaemenids incorporated their ethnic identity into the titulary. He calls himself caretaker of Esagila (the main sanctuary of Marduk, the highest god of the Babylonian pantheon and father of Nabu) and of Ezida, the sanctuary of Nabu in Borsippa where the text was buried. He goes on to describe how he restored those sanctuaries, forming bricks with his own hands as Babylonian kings were supposed to do, and relaid the foundations of Ezida. He prays for assorted blessings for himself and his family and promises tribute from his successes to the god for further construction in the sanctuaries. All this is standard behavior for a Babylonian king and just as standard writing, perfectly in keeping with the genre. Antiochus is presenting himself as a good Babylonian king, who takes great care to fulfill the religious obligations of his office. One feature, however, surprises: the text mentions Antiochus' wife Stratonice. Royal women do not normally appear in Western Asian royal texts. Exceptions are few and far between, one being the Assyrian queen Sammuramat, who lies behind the legendary Semiramis (Dalley 2005). Apparently, royal consorts appear in Western Asian literature when they played a key role in the dynastic succession, especially in times when the dynasty was perceived to be in peril (Kuhrt and Sherwin-White 1991: 84–5). This certainly applies to Stratonice, daughter of Demetrius Poliorcetes, who was married off to Antiochus' father Seleucus as part of a political transaction and passed on by Seleucus to his son, successor and co-regent. This deal resulted in the emergence of romantic legends about Antiochus' mad love for his father's young wife and the father's cure for his son's lovesickness (Whitmarsh in this volume). In other words, the appearance of Stratonice is, albeit unusual, consistent with Western Asian precedents. Her naming on an official document such as the foundation cylinder further suggests that the close bond of the royal couple was widely advertised, which is a typical feature of royal propaganda in the Hellenistic period: Mesopotamian and Hellenistic royal ideology concur on this point as on many others (Strootman in this volume). The truth behind the propaganda is, of course, a different matter. Nevertheless, it may have facilitated the formation of legends around Stratonice and Antiochus.

High Kings in High Halls

The question of whether or not a given text may count as literature is less pressing for religious texts, including incantations, laments, hymns, and cult songs (Linssen 2003), and for wisdom texts such as the tantalizingly obscure fable of the little *duqduqqu* bird (tentatively identified as a wren) preserved in a copy dated December 22, 242 BCE (Walker 1972: no. 93). Such texts enjoyed a wide dissemination in the Hellenistic period as before. Even more popular, however, are stories about the kings of old. The most prominent of these is the epic of Gilgamesh, which goes back to the twenty-first century BCE and continued to be copied at least down to the end of the Hellenistic period, as a colophon on a surviving version testifies (Oelsner 1986: 206). It tells the tale of Gilgamesh, the ruler of Uruk, his heroic feats, his friendship with the wild Enkidu, his sorrow at the death of this friend, and his unsuccessful quest for immortality. Its main characters appear as evil giants in Jewish mythology and even made it into Islamic incantations against evil demons (George 2003: 60–1). Aelian and the Nestorian Christian Theodorus bar Konia preserve the memory of Gilgamesh as a great king (George 2003: 61). The transmission through Aramaic, Phoenician, and Greek shows the enduring popularity of characters of the Gilgamesh story. Although the epic itself was apparently forgotten with the loss of the ability to read cuneiform, its legacy may be found in popular literary motifs such as the story of the wanderer, the water of life, and the land of the blessed (George 2003: 70; Geller 1995: 44).

The "Tale of Two Brothers," preserved on Papyrus Amherst 63, is another instance of narrative literature, albeit on a much smaller scale (Steiner and Nims 1985). The Aramaic text, written in the Egyptian demotic script, recounts the story of Sarbanapal and his brother Sarmuge, recasting the historical struggle between Ashurbanipal and his brother Shamash-shumukin. When their father Esarhaddon installed them as independent rulers of Ashur and Babylon in his succession treaty (Parpola and Watanabe 1988: 28–58), their relationship turned sour. The ensuing war ended with Ashurbanipal conquering Babylon and Shamash-shumukin either dying in the flames of his palace or killing himself in an intentionally kindled fire. The version of Papyrus Amherst 63 is remarkable both for its version of the death of the Babylonian king and for its representation of the background. The brothers' strife is portrayed as a rebellion on the part of Sarmuge who here holds the throne of Babylon by the grace of his brother rather than his father. The Assyrian king makes a valiant attempt at settling the dispute by diplomacy, sending his sister as an envoy, but her mediation fails due to the wickedness of the Babylonian king. The sister warns

Sarmuge that he is putting himself in deadly peril, and Sarbanapal reluctantly sends an army to conquer Babylon. Sarmuge ushers his family and his doctors into a specially built wooden contraption to burn them and himself to death, then changes his mind, surrenders, sets off to his kindly brother in Nineveh, and dies on the road of unspecified causes. This is an interesting example of storytelling based on history written by the victor: the victorious survivor is portrayed as a kindly ruler who is forced to bring his unthankful sibling to Nineveh after having made every attempt to reason with him. In this, it reflects the attitude of righteous outrage displayed by the historical Ashurbanipal (e.g., Borger 1996: 229). The ungrateful rebel then dies in a manner that leaves his brother blameless. This version of the "Tale of Two Brothers" is possibly a source for the legend of Sardanapalus we encounter in Ctesias (Steiner 1995: 203), who is also a source of stories about another historical Assyrian ruler, Queen Semiramis.

Two of the best examples of the continued popularity and transmission of Mesopotamian narrative literature through the Hellenistic period are the "Poor Man of Nippur" and the "Tale of Ahiqar." These folktales, which predate the Hellenistic period, both survived to make their way even into follow up collections of the *Arabian Nights.* The "Poor Man of Nippur" is the story of a trickster by the name of Gimil-Ninurta, who is disgraced by the mayor of his hometown. Robbed of his only possession, a goat, he obtains help from the king and pays back the ill treatment threefold: in a variety of disguises he swindles the mayor out of a sizable sum of money and beats him up three times. Our Akkadian source for this story, dating to 701 BCE (Gurney 1957: 147), constitutes the oldest extant example of a folktale which also appears in the sixth-century CE Sanskrit *Panchatantra*, in Medieval Europe, and finally in the "Tale of the First Larrikin" in the *Arabian Nights* published by R. F. Burton (Gurney 1972; Marzolph, Van Leeuwen, and Wassouf 2004). While the Gilgamesh epic may have influenced broad literary *topoi*, the "Poor Man of Nippur" shows specific similarities to later stories of a trickster repaying an ill treatment. As the literary tradition that produced the version of the *Arabian Nights* originates at least in part in the Mesopotamian story, its transmission through the Hellenistic period is presupposed.

The evidence for transmission and popularity during the Hellenistic period is more direct in the case of the "Tale of Ahiqar." Its main character is a high official – scribe, counselor, and keeper of the royal seal – at the court of the Assyrian king Sennacherib (704–681 BCE). After Sennacherib's death, Ahiqar continues his duties under the king's son and successor, Esarhaddon. He is in the king's good graces, is well thought of by all for his wisdom and fairness, and lives comfortably and contently, except for the fact that he has no children. Therefore, he adopts his sister's son Nadin and brings him up as his own. When old age rests heavily upon Ahiqar and he finally decides to retire, he asks for his office to be transferred to his son whom he trained for it, a wish the king grants gladly. Nadin proves unappreciative and falsely denounces his adoptive father, claiming that Ahiqar was plotting against the king. The angry Esarhaddon sends his executioner to kill Ahiqar. However, Ahiqar turns out to have once saved the executioner's life when Sennacherib decreed his death on a similar whim, and he now pleads for the favor to be returned. The executioner kills a slave of Ahiqar in his stead, ensuring that there is a body to be found if the king should send someone to look for proof. Then he hides his former benefactor in his own house, just as Ahiqar had done for him. Later, when the king misses his former counselor sorely, the executioner produces him, Ahiqar is reinstated, and his son severely punished for his evil deed. In one version, Ahiqar takes the mischievous Nadin prisoner and regales him with his wisdom until Nadin combusts and dies (Meyer 1912: 105–11). This story formed the narrative frame for a collection of sayings and fables, which constituted the main body of the text. Of these only a few disjointed fragments survive.

Although the names of the characters are proper Assyrian ones, we have no way of knowing how old the story of wise Ahiqar actually is. It was probably conceived soon after the lifetime of the protagonists (George 2003: 59), but the oldest extant version is a papyrus from Elephantine which contains the narrative frame in Aramaic as used in the Persian Empire, dating linguistically to approximately the sixth century BCE. The framed sayings already appear in Old Aramaic texts, dating back to the eighth or early seventh century, and may, based on linguistic evidence, stem from southern Syria or Lebanon, a detail that fits well with the provenance of the population of Elephantine (Kottsieper 1991: 321; Dieleman and Moyer in this volume).

In the Hellenistic period the story was widely known. There is a Babylonian parallel dating to 165 BCE, naming prediluvian kings and their wise men (Kottsieper 1991: 322). According to this text, the *ummanu* ("teacher") of Esarhaddon was Aba'enlil-dari, whose Aramaic name is given as "Achuqar." Theophrastus is said to have written an entire work about "Akicharos" (D.L. 5.50), and although we have no information about the content, the mere title suggests that Hellenistic Greeks were familiar with the character. Ahiqar also appears in the Book of Tobit (1.21–2, 2.10, 11.17, 14.10), generally believed to have been composed in the second century BCE. Here, Tobit from Naphtali is sent to Nineveh into exile. He lives during the rules of Sennacherib and Esarhaddon. Ahiqar appears as cupbearer, keeper of the royal seal, and vizier of Esarhaddon, and as a relation of Tobit's. A brief version of Ahiqar's life story appears as part of a warning speech Tobit delivers to his son, and in fact the entire work is to a certain extent modeled on the "Tale of Ahiqar."

Ahiqar remained a household name well beyond the Hellenistic period. Strabo names Ahiqar in a list of seers (16.762). According to Clement of Alexandria, Democritus appropriated teachings from a translation of the stele of Ahiqar (*Strom.* 1.15.69). The sage also features in the *Life of Aesop*. On the so-called Monnus mosaic from Trier of the third century CE, each of the Muses appears along with a character prominent in her specialty. Polyhymnia is accompanied by a seated man holding a book roll whose name was possibly "Acicar" (Parlasca 1959: 41–3 and fig. 43.1; differently Daniel 1996, cf. West 2003b).

Apparently, the "Tale of Ahiqar" continued to be told in Arab countries. In the late eighteenth century Dom Denis Chavis, a Christian monk, translated a number of Arabic tales into French, this story among them. The tales were linguistically polished by Jacques Cazotte (1719–1792) and published between 1788 and 1790 as books 38–41 of *Les Mille et Une Nuits.* The popularity of *1001 Nights* as published by Antoine Galland between 1704 and 1717 apparently inspired the imitation. The collection went on to be translated into English and was published in England as *Arabian Tales* (1792 and 1794). Here, a somewhat insipid Scheherazade entertains Schariar and her sister Dinarzade with stories. In this collection we find the "Story of

Sinkarib and His Two Viziers", named Hicar and Nadan (Chavis and Cazotte 1794: 197–222). It contains the main elements of the "Tale of Ahiqar," but omits the wisdom texts with the exception of one example: before Nadan takes over the office of vizier, his uncle offers advice on governing clothed in a metaphor about the flowering and fruit-bearing of the almond and mulberry trees. It adds to the original story the enterprising character of Hicar's first wife, Zesagnie, and an episode situated in Egypt in which Hicar and Zesagnie manipulate and outwit the pharaoh on behalf of the king of Assyria. The *Arabian Tales* version also curiously glosses over Nadan's death: the ungrateful nephew is cast into a dungeon, where he rids "the world of his crimes by becoming his own executioner" (Chavis and Cazotte 1794: 221). The "Tale of Ahiqar" stands out as an example of continuity in Western Asian literature. Widely popular and translated into most ancient languages, it survived in the Arabic tradition and was translated and again published in Early Modern Europe.

The stories of the Assyrian kings in this section stand in a tradition of their own: just as the rulers of Akkad symbolized the proverbial Great Rulers of the world in ancient Western Asia, the Assyrian kings and Queen Semiramis, who incidentally also presented themselves as successors of the rulers of Akkad, took their place in folktales after the fall of their empire. In a way they occupy a similar position to that of the popular figure of Harun ar Rashid in the *Arabian Nights*, the fifth Abassid caliph of Baghdad (786–809 CE), whose name translates as Harun the Just and who established diplomatic relations as far afield as India and Western Europe.

Western Asians Writing in Greek

We have seen how Antiochus I inscribed and buried a foundation cylinder in Nabu's sanctuary in Borsippa in good Mesopotamian tradition, reaching back to the second millennium BCE. Likewise some Mesopotamians took up the Greek language and addressed a Greek-speaking audience through Greek forms of writing.

Berossus, whose Greek name probably stands for the Babylonian Bel-re'ushu ("Bel/Marduk is his shepherd") was a native of Babylon and a contemporary of Alexander the Great (*FGrH* 680; Verbrugge and Wickersham 1996). Because he apparently had access to archaic records, it is generally assumed that he was a high official in Esagila, the Babylonian temple of Marduk (Kuhrt 1987: 48). He composed a history of Babylonia for Antiochus I Soter, probably called *Babyloniaka* (although alternative titles also appear). Unfortunately, only fragments of the work are extant, and these are often several steps removed from Berossus' orginal, such as excerpts by the eighth-century monk Syncellus from the *Chaldaika* of Eusebius, who himself probably epitomized a digest of the *Babyloniaka* by Alexander Polyhistor. It is worth pointing out that our most substantial sources for the work of Berossus are Jewish and Christian works, whose apologetic agenda informed the selection of passages (Kuhrt 1987: 35). Some astrological and astronomical works were also attributed to Berossus in antiquity in order to give them an aura of reliability, but this attribution lacks confidence (Kuhrt 1987: 36–44).

Berossus dedicated the first book of the *Babyloniaka* to geography, cosmogony, and anthropology, describing the beginning of civilization in Babylonia. In the second book he dealt with the kings before the Flood, the Flood itself, and postdiluvian dynasties and their wise men down to Nabu-nashir (747–734 BCE). The third contained the history of the Assyrian Empire and the Assyro-Babylonian conflict from Tiglath-pileser III (744–727 BCE) to the downfall of the last Assyrian king Sin-shar-ishkun (623?–612 BCE). Focal points in further books were the glorious reigns of the Babylonian kings Nabopolassar (625–605 BCE) and Nebuchadnezzar II (604–562 BCE), the Persian rule, and the conquest of Alexander. The last king to feature was Antiochus I Soter (281–261 BCE). Berossus appears to have used a late version of the "Dynastic Chronicle" for his list of kings and their wise men.

Of special interest is the story of the sage Oannes who brought civilization to mankind. Berossus is an important source for this figure, who was not attested in cuneiform literature until the beginning of the twentieth century, when his name was discovered in texts from Uruk and elsewhere (Van Dijk 1963: 217). In his *Ecloga Chronographica* (51) Georgius Syncellus reports (trans. Verbrugge and Wickersham 1996: 44):

> In the very first year there appeared from the Red Sea (i.e., the Persian Gulf) in an area bordering on Babylonia a frightening monster, named Oannes, as Apollodorus also says in his history. It had the whole body of a fish, but underneath and attached to the head of the fish there was another head, human, and joined to the tail of the fish, feet, like those of a man, and it had a human voice. Its form has been preserved in sculpture to this day. Berossus says that this monster spent its days with men, never eating anything, but teaching men the skills necessary for writing and for doing mathematics and for all sorts of knowledge: how to build cities, found temples, and make laws. It taught men how to determine borders and divide land, also how to plant seeds and then to harvest their fruits and vegetables. In short, it taught men all those things conducive to a settled and civilized life. Since that time nothing further has been discovered. At the end of the day, this monster Oannes went back to the sea and spent the night.

Berossus named six further fish-men who continued Oannes' work. These seven sages, the *apkallu*, are well known in Western Asian literature. Their fish bodies refer explicitly to the god Enki/Ea, god of wisdom and of the underground fresh water. Oannes' role as giver of culture is particularly associated with Enki as well. As giver of culture, Berossus also credits him with bestowing on mankind an account of creation that can be identified with the Western Asian creation epic *Enuma Elish*. In cuneiform texts, we now possess seven references to Oannes (Uan, "Light of An"). He is called all-knowing, is connected with temple building, and especially with the creation of literary works. Closest to Berossus' texts is the above-mentioned catalogue of *apkallu* ("sages") and *ummânu* ("teachers") from Hellenistic Uruk which names Oannes as first in a line of seven sages who taught in the time of King Ajjalu. This ruler may be identified with Alulim, the first king of Eridu according to the Sumerian king list and the first person to hold this office after kingship descended from heaven – that is, Berossus' Aloros (Streck 2005).

Berossus apparently explicitly criticized "the Greek historians" (Jos. *Ap.* 1.142) for what he considered to be errors and misconceptions. His primary target was certainly

Ctesias, even if, as far as we can tell, Ctesias was never identified by name. One example is Berossus' account of the end of the Assyrian Empire, preserved in the fragments of Abydenus (*FGrH* 685), who employed an epitome of Berossus' work as source for his *Chaldaean History.* Ctesias had the Assyrian Empire end with King Ashurbanipal, while it in fact continued to exist for nearly two decades after Ashurbanipal's death. According to Berossus, the last king of Assyria was Sarakos, a Hellenization of Sin-shar-ishkun, under whose reign the last capital, Nineveh, was indeed conquered (*FGrH* IIIC: 404). Another correction concerned the foundation of Babylon, which Ctesias attributed to Semiramis, the wife of the mythical founder of the Assyrian Empire, Ninus. Berossus corrects this notion along with Semiramis' association with the creation of the Hanging Gardens of Babylon, one of the seven wonders of the ancient world (Verbrugge and Wickersham 1996: 59 = Jos. *Ap.* 1.142). These corrections may spring from a genuine desire to set matters straight, but discrediting preceding authors also suits the competitive nature of Greek historiography, equally manifest in Ctesias' attitude toward Herodotus.

The assumption of Greek modes of discourse and a Greek frame of reference is a striking feature of Berossus' *Babyloniaka*. He described the world in Greek terms, reflecting Greek philosophy and using a Greek conception of the succession of empires (Kuhrt 1987: 54). One explanation why Berossus adopted this Greek voice is that he intended to provide the ruling Seleucids with a native dynastic legitimation similar to the one Hecataeus of Abdera and Manetho bestowed upon the Ptolemies (Dieleman and Moyer in this volume). He imported the Seleucids into the framework of local tradition, which he described in terms comprehensible to Greeks, and made their reign the final stage in the succession of empires. By describing in great detail the deeds of Nabopolassar and his son Nebuchadnezzar, founders of the Neo-Babylonian Empire, to whom he attributed control over Koile-Syria, Phoenicia and – historically incorrectly – Egypt, Berossus may have intended to refute the propaganda of the Seleucids' main competitors, the Ptolemies. In addition, he boosted their image by offering a local historical precedent for the successes of Seleucus I and Antigonus I (Kuhrt 1987: 56) and an ideological framework for accepting the new rulers as legitimate sovereigns (in itself an often practiced strategy in Babylonia). By showing that the Seleucids had come to rule subjects with a long and impressive history and had assumed the legacy of great kings, Berossus' work cut both ways: it not only flattered the Seleucids but also presented a source of pride for Babylonians who were able to read Greek, a competency which we may assume at least for the local elite who needed to co-operate with the Macedonians in order to gain and retain power.

In the end, the *Babyloniaka* proved to be a case of failed influence. By writing in Greek and using Greek ethnographical traditions as his model, Berossus clearly aimed at least in part at a Greek readership. However, he remained deeply rooted in the traditions of Western Asian literature, which, as we have seen, consisted to a considerable extent of lists. More often than not the sources Berossus used would have had this form, and it appears that he did not really flesh them out and offer the engaging narratives we find in authors such as Herodotus and Ctesias. This is probably a matter of choice rather than ability; he may have chosen to retain the literary style of lists in order to give his information greater authority. However this may be, Berossus' work did not catch on with a readership attuned to literature that paid more attention to marvelous details and entertainment. Ctesias' work continued to dominate the market. Furthermore, western interest in Mesopotamia seems to have faded when it fell under Parthian rule at the end of the second century BCE and thus ceased to be part of the Mediterranean world. The most avid readers Berossus' work encountered were scholars who used it to promote their own religious beliefs and vilify those of ancient Mesopotamia: Jewish historians used the *Babyloniaka* to corroborate the traditions of the Torah, Christian authors to show all pagans the error of their ways.

Greeks Writing about Western Asia

Working along the same lines as Berossus, some Greek authors also attempted to bring Mesopotamia closer to a Greek audience. In the *oikoumenē* created by Alexander, ambassadors and military commanders produced works on their surroundings, following in the footsteps of earlier Greek ethnographers, especially Herodotus. The historian Megasthenes (c.350–290 BCE) undertook several diplomatic missions to India for King Seleucus I between 302 and 291 BCE. His geographical and ethnographical work *Indika* consisted of three or four volumes, now extant only in fragmentary form (*FGrH* 715). It appears to have been based on autopsy, indigenous informers *in situ*, hearsay and quite possibly his Greek predecessors. Megasthenes' work was used as a source by Diodorus Siculus, Strabo, Pliny the Elder, and last but not least Arrian, who appears to have based his *Indika* on it. Another author writing about the East, Patrocles, was the Seleucid commander of Babylon from 312 BCE. Sent on a nautical expedition by Seleucus I and Antiochus in 285 and 282 BCE, he explored the Amu Darya (Oxus) and laid down his findings in a geographical work, also surviving only in fragments (*FGrH* 712).

Remarkably, in this changed world Greek views of the world changed very little. Although the margins had been pushed back further by authors such as Megasthenes, strange beings still populated the periphery of the *oikoumenē*, and the East remained alien. The reason for this appears to have been the work of Ctesias, by far the most influential author writing on Western Asia. Although he wrote before the conquests of Alexander, his work must be discussed here because of its enduring impact on the Greek perception of Asia: Ctesias created the reference works which no later author could choose to ignore.

Between 405 and 398 BCE, Ctesias of Cnidus lived as doctor of Artaxerxes II (404–358 BCE) at the Persian court in Susa (*FGrH* 688; König 1972; Lenfant 2004, 2007). His works included a *Periodos* (description of the world), the *Indika*, and the *Persika*, all designed for a Greek audience. The *Persika* comprised 23 books and dealt briefly with Assyrian and Median history (largely ignoring Babylon) before entering into the history and affairs of Persia proper. While the majority of Ctesias' work is now lost, substantial fragments are preserved in Diodorus Siculus, Nicolaus of Damascus, and Photius.

The *Persika* began with the reign of Ninus, a mythical king whose name is probably derived from the Assyrian capital Nineveh. He was married to Semiramis, who founded Babylon after her husband's death. Semiramis is probably based on the Assyrian queen Sammuramat, married to Shamshi-Adad V (824–811 BCE) and mother of Adad-Nirari III (811–783 BCE; Dalley 2005: 12–14). Ctesias, however, portrays her with details derived from the iconography of Ishtar, goddess of love and war: Semiramis is the daughter of a goddess, she is of exceptional beauty, courage, and intelligence, she builds palaces and devises cunning engineering works, creates wonders of the ancient world such as the Hanging Gardens and the walls of Babylon, leads armies, fights battles, travels to the furthest reaches of the earth, takes her most handsome soldiers as lovers, and disposes of them after the act. While the historical Sammuramat indeed played a prominent political role and accompanied her son on campaigns, she was obviously nothing like Ctesias' gaudy creation. His fictional queen more resembles, and indeed in many ways inspired, the character of Candace, Alexander's love interest in the *Alexander Romance* (Whitmarsh in this volume). Ctesias' account of Persian affairs ends with the eighth regnal year of Artaxerxes II (398/7 BCE), presumably the end of his stay in Persia. In good Western Asian tradition Ctesias offered a list of rulers for the period covered, now lost. Apart from that, his work was thoroughly Greek. It was also colored by the author's personal interests. Greco-Persian relations did not concern Ctesias at all. Medical matters, on the other hand, featured prominently.

Even through the haze of indirect transmission we can easily see that Ctesias' text was attractively written and offered colorful accounts of the lives of exotic kings and queens. Equally clear is that he was generally far off the mark in terms of accuracy. To give but one example, his description of the fall of Nineveh continues to puzzle. The scenarios that have been suggested to explain the mismatching pieces of his narrative are illustrative of the problems posed by his work.

In Ctesias' account of the fall of Assyria, Nineveh is situated on the Euphrates instead of the Tigris and Khosr. Its conquerors plunder the treasury, remove earth and tamper with the river so it washes away the remains of the destroyed city. Since Western Asian literature often portrays Nineveh and Babylon as mirror cities, this description may reflect the sack of Babylon by the Assyrian King Sennacherib in 689 BCE, where these events actually took place (Van de Mieroop 2004). In the record of his achievements, Sennacherib paralleled the fall of Babylon with the building of Nineveh. Accordingly, a Babylonian might draw on the sack of Babylon to create an account of the destruction of Nineveh by Babylonian and Median forces. If this is the case, Ctesias can hardly be blamed for getting it all wrong; he simply followed a Babylonian source (Van de Mieroop 2004: 4).

Alternatively, Ctesias may have conflated the fall of Nineveh with events that happened when King Ashurbanipal conquered Babylon after his brother Shamash-shumukin, the ruler of that city, rebelled against him (MacGinnis 1988: 37–42). As we saw, Ctesias refers to Ashurbanipal (Sardanapalus, reigned 668–631 BCE) as last king of Assyria, which is historically false: Assyria fell 19 years after his death. While we remain in the dark as to the circumstances of the deaths of the last kings of Assyria, Ctesias' account fits in nicely with the end of Shamash-shumukin, who reputedly burned to death. The two-year period Ctesias claims the siege of Nineveh lasted does not fit in with the cuneiform sources (who say it lasted two and a half months), but works nicely for Ashurbanipal's siege of Babylon in 650–648 BCE. As in the alternative explanation, the general conflation of Babylon and Nineveh accounts for Ctesias' mistake in locating the Assyrian capital on the Euphrates; and all further confusions may derive from no other source than the "Tale of Two Brothers" (Steiner 1995: 203).

Interestingly, Herodotus, whom Ctesias sought to emulate and, accordingly, criticized liberally, had gotten the location of the Assyrian capital right. In his eagerness to trump Herodotus, Ctesias frequently used sources of questionable reliability and came up with rather dubious results. Perhaps he prioritized entertainment value over veracity. At the very least, Ctesias' work appears to move away from the approach to *historiē* we encounter in Herodotus. Equally, as far as we can tell from the extant fragments, it does not seem to have contained an overarching concept of history or worldview. The general impression it makes is that of a collection of stories focusing on exotic and sensational events and people, aiming at amazement and one-upmanship rather than veracity and unity of thought. Nevertheless, the *Persika* ended up being the standard source of information on Western Asian in Greece, consulted, for example, by Plato, Aristotle, Theopompus, Ephorus, and Diodorus Siculus. In addition, authors such as Dino of Colophon and an otherwise unknown Athenaeus (late fourth century BCE) embellished Ctesias' story of Ninus and Semiramis, providing the story line for the *Ninus Romance*, one of the earliest known Greek novels (Kuhrt 1995: 61; Stephens and Winkler 1995: 23–71). Apparently, Greeks liked stories about racy, power hungry "oriental" women of questionable morals. As a rich source of such material, Ctesias' *Persika* made a significant contribution to the development of prose fiction that would lead to the Imperial novel (Whitmarsh in this volume).

Greeks and Greek Under Parthian Rule

While politically Mesopotamia ceased to be a part of the Greek world after the Parthian conquest of the late second century BCE, Greek literature continued to be appreciated and produced under Parthian rule. Plutarch informs us that Greek compositions were performed during the celebration of a royal marriage between the houses of Orodes II of Parthia and Artavasdes II of Armenia (*Crass.* 33). He emphasizes that the Parthian king knew the Greek language and Greek literature, while the Armenian even composed Greek tragedies, as well as historical and other prose texts, some of which were available to his day. When a messenger bearing the head of the decapitated Roman general Crassus reached the Parthian court, a staging of Euripides' *Bacchae* was allegedly in progress. The actor playing Agaue included the head into his performance of *Bacchae* 1170–9 and was put into his place by one of the wedding guests. The point here is not whether or not an actor actually improvised on Euripides at a historical event, but that Greeks such as Plutarch expected educated Parthians, Armenians, and presumably their subjects to be familiar with Greek literature. Greek poems produced in Hellenistic Parthia corroborate the impression that Hellenic culture was very much alive (Tarn 1938: 39). Furthermore, geographical works and descriptions of routes in Parthia were produced and transmitted in Greek, such as Isidorus of Charax's short

Parthian Stations, which may be drawing on a survey undertaken under King Mithridates II after Parthia had acquired Merv (before 115 BCE).

The most important representative, however, of Greek literature under Parthian rule is the historiographer Apollodorus, a Greek living in Artemita, a Greco-Parthian city situated at a vital crossroads east of the Tigris. His *Parthika*, in at least four books and most likely written around 100 BCE, recorded the rise of the Parthian Empire, along with information on geography and botany. A large section appears to have been dedicated to the successful Greek kings of Bactria, Demetrius (180–165 BCE) and Menander (155–130 BCE), whose conquests included India and outstripped even Alexander's military achievements. Menander is of particular interest, as he inspired later literary works, especially the semi-fictional character of the wise king Milinda. The work *The Questions of King Milinda*, written in India around or soon after the beginning of the Christian era, describes with didactic purpose the discussions of Milinda with the wise monk Nâgasena in the form of a historical novel (Rhys Davids 1975). Although little of Apollodorus' work is extant (*FGrH* 779), he was an important source for Pompeius Trogus and Strabo. Strabo probably drew largely on Apollodorus for his descriptions of Mesopotamia, Iran, and parts of Central Asia as well as in his accounts of the Scythians, Sakae, and Massagetae (Alonso Nuñez 1989: 2). He states that under Parthian rule, more information about these far-off lands and tribes had become known than was previously available (in, for example, Herodotus, Ctesias, or the Alexander historians) because authors like Apollodorus had seen them with their own eyes (Str. 11.6.3–4).

The scarcity of the evidence should lead us to speculate about Apollodorus' work only with the greatest caution. In his research he probably used both oral sources and written Parthian records (Nikonov 1998). He appears to have been enthusiastic about the Parthians. The emphasis in the fragments on the exploits of the Greek kings of Bactria, who outdid Alexander, may indicate that Apollodorus presented the Arsacids, the Parthian kings who conquered the Bactrians' realm, as the culmination of military prowess. If this is true, the *Parthika* may have been designed to do for the Parthian kings what Berossus' *Babyloniaka* did for the Seleucids: Apollodorus, the voice of Greco-Parthian nationalism, legitimated the Arsacids' rule by including them into the succession of dynasties (Alonso Nuñez 1989: 4).

***

In the Hellenistic period literature and culture flourished in Western Asia. Traditional literary forms such as lists continued to be produced by the native population and were adapted by the new rulers. While there is little evidence for the creation of new narrative literature, which may in part be due to the fragmentary nature of our sources, existing epics, wisdom texts, and folktales were retold, rewritten, and transmitted. Greeks living in Western Asia created historiographical, ethnographical, and geographical works about their surroundings, inspiring in turn the Babylonian priest Berossus to write a reference work on Babylonia in Greek. Much as during the Persian Empire, political instability and changes in power led to a diverse and independent culture of writing. Continuity in all genres, writing systems, and languages remains the most important characteristic of Western Asian literature at least to the beginning of the Christian era.

FURTHER READING

For lists as literature in Western Asia see Kuhrt and Sherwin-White 1987. Chronicles and king lists are easily accessible in transcription and translation with a commentary on the website www.livius.org, which contains a prepublication of I. Finkel and R. J. van der Spek, *Babylonian Chronicles of the Hellenistic Period* (indexed at www.livius.org/babylonia.html). Astronomical diaries are published in transcription and translation by Hunger and Sachs 1988–96. Maul 1991 discusses Greco-Babyloniaca and provides a list of Greek, Sumerian, and Akkadian transcriptions. Del Monte 1997 provides a succinct compilation of Hellenistic Mesopotamian texts in Italian.

The fragmentary Greek literature of Western Asia is available, with German commentary, in Felix Jacoby's multi-volume *Fragmente der griechischen Historiker* (*FGrH*) and partly, with English translation and commentary, in *Brill's New Jacoby*, edited by Ian Worthington (at present only available online). Verbrugge and Wickersham 1996 present a translation of Berossus with a helpful introduction. Lenfant 2004 provides a new edition of Ctesias with French translation and notes; König 1972 is still highly useful as a reference work on this author.

The ongoing online project Melammu (www.aakkl.helsinki.fi/melammu) has a useful database on the intellectual heritage of Assyria and Babylonia in East and West and provides easy access to information on many of the topics discussed in this chapter, with ancient sources in translation and bibliographies.

On the influence of the Western Asian literary tradition on Greek literature and culture see Kuhrt 1995, who emphasizes the literary quality of works such as that of Berossus. Geller 1995 and Gruen, Whitmarsh, and Dieleman and Moyer in this volume provide an outlook on Mesopotamian influences in areas not discussed in this chapter.

CHAPTER THIRTY

From the Head of Zeus: The Beginnings of Roman Literature

James J. Clauss

The topic of the reception of Greek literature in Rome, in particular poetry from the Hellenistic period, has been admirably covered over the past 50-plus years following the publication of Pfeiffer's epic two-volume work on Callimachus (1949–53), which, together with many other fundamental works on writers of the period, has made Hellenistic poetry more readily available to scholars of Roman literature. In a relatively short amount of time, so much of Roman poetry has come into greater focus. Not only can texts be interpreted on firmer ground now that we can securely identify specific Hellenistic models, but we also have a better understanding of how Hellenistic writers negotiated contemporary and earlier literature, which, as it turns out, furnished a significant model for Roman writers from the very beginning of their engagement with Greek literature. In what follows, I hope to take advantage of our greater appreciation of Hellenistic literary practices and push the interpretive envelope for the earliest Roman literature, with the understanding that the envelope may split here and there.

Once Rome, similar to other Mediterranean and Near Eastern lands, began to adopt the Hellenic mode of composition, their own meager native approaches to literary self-representation ultimately gave way. Such dependency is perhaps less surprising for the Romans than for the peoples of Egypt, Palestine, and Western Asia, who had been engaged in formal literary compositions for many centuries before the Greeks (Gruen, Knippschild, Dieleman and Moyer in this volume). Moreover, Rome, similar to Alexandria (Stephens in this volume), was from the beginning a multicultural city, the amalgamation of Latin, Italian, Etruscan, and even Greek cultures, as is evident from the city's physical remains and its distinctive blend of political and religious practices (Veyne 1979). In fact, there never existed an *ur*-Roman per se. Romans only came into being after the diverse inhabitants of the Seven Hills decided to pool their cultural resources and traditions and create an impressive melting-pot society. Rome's original strength lay not so much in its military might, impressive as it was, but in its wisdom of welcoming and incorporating the talents of others. Their loss of this original wisdom would in time lead to the kind of bunker mentality that builds walls instead of relationships, a phenomenon that sadly repeats from time to time.

Many excellent studies have already addressed the extensive influence of Hellenistic literature on the Romans (see Further Reading). In these few pages I will not attempt to examine the full array of authors and genres in the long history of Roman literature that could be discussed. Such a piece would of necessity be very superficial. Rather, I will attempt to highlight essential aspects of the Roman reception of Hellenistic modes of thought from its very beginning, which I hope will also function as a sort of conclusion to the present volume. In particular, I will focus on the epics of Livius Andronicus, Gnaeus Naevius, and Quintus Ennius, and argue that what we think of as "Hellenistic" writing migrated to, and established itself in, Rome definitively already in the mid-third century BCE, even during the Golden Age of Alexandrian literature.

Before I turn to the individual authors, however, I would like to illustrate a central feature of the Romans' earliest Hellenized literary productions by looking at an Italian movie of the early 1960s: *La Leggenda di Enea* (1962), directed by Giorgio Rivalta and released in America as *The Avenger*. The film is a cinematic rendition of the second half of the *Aeneid*. A glimpse at the cast shows that most of the actors and actresses are Italian. The star of the film, however, is American body-builder Steve Reeves, whose successful role as Heracles in *Le Fatiche di Ercole* (1958) and *Ercole e la regina di Lidia* (1959) earned him more work in Italy thereafter in other sword and sandal movies that, like *La Leggenda di Enea*, made it to America in dubbed versions. Like the *Aeneid* on which it is based, *La Leggenda di Enea* is a sequel, in this case to *La Guerra di Troia* (1961), a fanciful version of the *Iliad* in which, among other irregularities, Reeves' Aeneas competes at the funeral games of Patroclus. What struck me about the former film as I watched the American version is that, liberties aside, it replicated the *Aeneid* in a significant way: the majority of the characters were not speaking their original language. Although by Vergil's time Naevius and Ennius had already told the story of Aeneas' travels to, and his establishment of a Trojan presence in, Italy in Latin, nonetheless the Roman audience must have been well aware that their Anatolian ancestors entered literature, through the *Iliad*, as speakers of Greek. In Latin, then, at least in the early poems, they would have been experienced as dubbed. As for the *Aeneid*, not only was Vergil's Aeneas speaking Latin, but he stood out in the poem in another critical aspect: the heroic code he came to personify evolved in the course of the epic from Greek to Roman. He spoke and came to act like a Roman in an otherwise Greek genre. A comparable cultural disconnect can be observed in the 1962 film. Its hero differs from the rest of the cast not only in his physique (Reeves was a former Mr. Universe) but also by virtue of his body language, facial expressions, and original voice that stand out as patently American in an otherwise predominantly Italian milieu. Though approximate, I find this parallel helpful in reconstructing how the early Roman audiences might have encountered the translation and adaptation of Greek literature into Latin: the characters of the new literature were, figuratively speaking, dubbed in Latin and altered to fit the Roman ethos; the dynamic tension in the resulting product could not have been missed.

Livius Andronicus

As mentioned above, from the very beginning Roman culture, including religion, was composite in general and inclusive of Greek influence in particular. So, it should not come as a surprise that the history of Roman literature composed by professional writers began, in 240 BCE, with the introduction of Greek tragedies and comedies in translation at the ancient *Ludi Romani* (Cic. *Brut.* 72–3, *Sen.* 50, *Tusc.* 1.3). Nor should we be surprised that the first translator and adaptor was a Greek, Livius Andronicus from Tarentum, who also translated the *Odyssey* into Latin saturnians and composed a hymn to Juno Regina, presumably in a lyric meter (Livy 27.37.7; Festus 492.22). Significantly, the context for the introduction of these particular literary innovations was war: the successful completion of the First Punic War in the case of the first Greek drama and, for the hymn, a moment of crisis during the Second Punic War (207 BCE). The searing reality of war may account for the fact that roughly half of Livius' known tragedies involve events during or surrounding the Trojan War (*Achilles*, *Aegisthus*, *Ajax Mastigophorus*, *Equos Troianus*, *Hermiona*). War and its mediation through the Trojan cycle may also have motivated Rome's first national epic, about which more below.

Stephen Hinds' reading of the first line of Livius' *Odusia* (1998: 58–63) has shown decisively that the first epic in Latin foregrounded its scholarly pretensions. According to Hinds, the Tarentine's later negative reception was based on "renegotiations of the same cultural move" on the part of later writers staking out their position in Roman literary history (1997: 63). A glance at the opening of the poem reveals the hand of a *dicti studiosus*, to use Ennius' phrase (*Ann.* 209 Sk.): *Virum mihi, Camena, insece versutum* (1 Bl.) features an Italian water divinity whose name suggests *carmen*, an elegant Roman substitute for the Greek Muse; the rare and archaic *insece* replicates the similarly uncommon, similarly accented, and, and as it happens, etymologically related ἔννεπε (according to Sheets 1981: 68, an Umbrian gloss as well); and *versutum* not only translates πολύτροπον ("of many turns") but also incorporates the meaning "translate," *versio* being the technical term for "translation," and as such enacts a reference to the status of the work.

The other fragments, few though they are, reveal more evidence of linguistic and mythological playfulness. For instance, *in Pylum deveniens aut ibi<dem> ommentans* (9 Bl.) cleverly picks up the directional suffix -δε in the line ἠὲ Πύλονδ' ἐλθὼν ἢ αὐτοῦ τῶιδ' ἐνὶ δήμωι (*Od.* 2.317), with *aut ibi<dem> o-*, if correct, echoing αὐτοῦ τῶιδ' ἐνὶ δήμωι; *vestis pulla porpurea ampla* (27 Bl.) echoes the alliteration in χλαῖναν πορφυρέην οὔλην ἔχε δῖοc 'Oδυccεύc, / διπλῆν (*Od.* 19.225); *quando dies adveniet, quem profata Morta est* (23 Bl.) calls to mind such lines as ὁππότε κεν δὴ / μοῖρ' ὀλοὴ καθέληιcι τανηλεγέοc θανάτοιο (*Od.* 3.237–8; cf. 2.99–100), suggesting that Livius contracted the phrase μοῖρα θανάτοιο into a name for one of the fates, Morta, that also evoked the word for death (Livingston 2004: 7–11); the translation of ἦλθ' ἐριούνηc / Ἑρμείαc, ἦλθεν δὲ ἄναξ ἑκάεργοc 'Aπόλλων (*Od.* 8.322–3), *Mercurius cumque eo filius Latonas* (19 Bl.), includes what looks like a clever substitution of the god's matronymic, Λητοίδηc, which might look to the *Homeric Hymn to Hermes*, a text of great interest to Hellenistic writers, where this title is featured; his interest in matronymics recurs in the line *nam diva Monetas filia docuit* (21 Bl.), with *Moneta* an elegant allusion to Mnemosyne (Livingston 2004: 23–30). The attention to linguistic detail and nuance is sophisticated. "Livius Andronicus is a Hellenistic *poeta doctus*, whose poetic practice bears the stamp of literary reflection" (Albrecht 1997: 1.116).

What about the choice of the saturnian? Forced "by Roman conditions" (Williams 1982: 59)? I suspect not. Obviously Livius read and understood hexametric verse and composed poetry in iambic and lyric meters. He should have been able to manage a decent hexameter, had he wanted. Rather than imagining this choice as based on the author's lack of literary sophistication – which the fragments belie – or on the intended audience's expectations – why were Romans any more open to dactyls in the next century? – we might more productively think of the decision to choose the language of "fauns and *vates*," to use Ennius' deprecatory phrase (*Ann.* 207 Sk.), as strategic and influenced by Hellenistic practice. Alexandrian poets at this very time were exploring the application of archaic meters to new purposes with remarkable results (e.g., the resurrection of Hipponax's choliambic verse by Callimachus and Herodas; see Scodel and Esposito in this volume). What is more, Livius' articulation of the Homeric narrative in an old and established meter allowed the heroic narrative to feel both archaic, like the model text, and more familiar at the same time; the rhythm surely evoked a Roman sense of heroic identity, as could be heard in the funeral inscriptions of the Scipiones (*CIL* 1^2 6–9) or the poetic *elogium* of A. Atilius Calatinus that stood along the Appian Way (Cic. *Sen.* 61, cf. *Tusc.* 1.13); these were themselves already a gesture towards the elegiac Greek epigram (Van Sickle 1987). In this too, Livius can be said to have been a man of his time.

Of equal interest is Livius' choice of epic to translate. Gruen (1990: 84–5) provides a compelling answer: the orientation of the western Greek in Rome. In addition to the fact that Odysseus was an Adriatic prince, that his sons by Circe were believed to be founders of Italian cities, and that in some accounts Odysseus was a companion of Aeneas, the *Odyssey* also brought its hero to the Roman sphere of interest (Sicily, the Aeolian islands, the Tyrrhenian coast); one might compare fascination with stories that celebrate the presence in Rome itself of other Greek heroes, such as Evander and Heracles. Yet, I sense that the choice of the *Odyssey* involves more than what is, after all, a specious link between early Greeks and Romans (though speciousness should not be undervalued in the contentious longing for early membership in the pantheon of Greek heroes). The *Odyssey* is also a poem about a hero's return from war, an event that, including the war itself, took 20 years to complete. Although we do not know the date of publication of Livius' *Odusia* (on which, see Gruen 1990: 80–2), during a significant part of his lifetime the Romans were involved in a war that lasted 23 years, the First Punic War (264–241 BCE), at whose conclusion Livius staged the first Greek play in Latin for the *Ludi Romani*. It is difficult not to imagine that the *Odusia* responded to the most significant event of the period and reflected the anxieties of so many Romans at the time: a 20-year-plus war and the need to negotiate an eventual return home. Odysseus' successful homecoming from the Trojan War after undergoing a kind of rebirth, re-establishing his identity, and validating the right to be among his people once again would have been a meaningful narrative for Livius' audience. If the *Odusia* was composed after 241, I have to imagine that Livius was drawn to this

Homeric epic because he felt that it spoke to the audience's need for closure. The selection of an archaic theme that he explored in an archaic verse, infused with literary and mythological pyrotechnics and intended to reflect a critical issue of the day, however we ultimately explain that issue, looks and feels Alexandrian. Livius was a *vates* indeed, but more in an Augustan sense than Ennian.

Gnaeus Naevius

During and after the Second World War, Hollywood released over 600 films celebrating American victories and losses in both the European and Asian theaters. The desire for cinematic representations of America in armed conflict with Japan and Germany was intense. Director John Ford, a navy officer and combat photographer, made a documentary film during the course of the war, *The Battle of Midway* (1942). One film, *To Hell and Back* (1955), directed by Jesse Hibbs, was based on the autobiography of, and even starred, Audie Murphy, who won the Congressional Medal of Honor, among numerous other awards, for remarkable acts of courage during battle in Europe. Artistic representation of war by soldiers was nothing new. One such ancient military artist was Gnaeus Naevius who both fought in the First Punic War and later created the first national epic in Latin celebrating Rome's victory in this long and devastating conflict. We learn from Varro, by way of Gellius (17.21.45), that the poet mentioned his service in the war in his *Bellum Poenicum*, composed like Livius' *Odusia* in saturnians (perhaps a subtle nod to the association of that poem with the same event; similar to Livius, Naevius' tragedies also focused on the Trojan War: Albrecht 1997: 1.125). Ironically perhaps, the preface to Ovid's *Ars Amatoria* suggests a possible rationale for including such a statement (1.25–30). There, the Augustan poet, humorously contrasting his poetic authority with that of Hesiod and Callimachus, insists that he was not inspired by any god in the writing of this work but by personal experience; he could give instruction on the art of love because he could say, in the modern parlance: "been there, done that!" Might Naevius, then, have vouched for his personal participation in the war as part of a programmatic statement, explicitly or implicitly ascertaining the accuracy of his account? At any rate, the combination of personal experience and association with the Muses (Naevius referred to them in what may well be the opening line of the poem, *novem Iovis concordes filiae sorores*, 1 Bl.) finds parallel in the opening of Callimachus' *Aetia* where he recounts his dream of a conversation with the Muses. What is more, the fragments of the *Bellum Poenicum,* meager though they too are, also hint at an artist of Hellenistic sensibilities.

Naevius begins his historical epic with the founding of Rome by the grandsons of Aeneas, whose departure from Troy and journey to Italy appears to have been described, possibly as a flashback, with considerable detail. The fragments, in this section of the poem as elsewhere, reveal an interest in the origins of words that marks Naevius too as *dicti studiosus.* Varro informs us that Naevius derived *Palatium* from *Balatium* because of the presence of "bleating" (*balatus*) sheep on that hill (*LL* 5.43) and *Aventinum* from the *aves*, "birds," that assembled there (*LL* 5.53). The following lines appear to suggest an etymology for *auspicium*, which comes from the combination of *avem* and *specio* (25 Bl.):

> Postquam *avem aspexit* in templo Anchisa,
> sacra in mensa Penatium ordine ponuntur;
> immolabat auream victimam pulchram.
>
> After Anchises saw a bird within the duly apportioned precinct of the sky,
> offerings are placed appropriately on the table of the Household Gods;
> he began to sacrifice a splendid golden victim.

If correct, Naevius might be associating the taking of auspices with Trojan religious practice (compare the *figura etymologica* in the lines *virum praetor advenit, auspicat auspicium / prosperum* [39 Bl.] which, together with the previous passage, suggests more than passing interest in the rite). If the line *silvicolae homines bellique inertes* (10 Bl.) refers to the aboriginal people of Italy, Naevius might be anticipating the future rulers of Alba Longa who bore the name Silvius. When someone, most likely Venus, addresses Jupiter as *patrem suum supremum optumum* (15 Bl.), the poet plays with the cult title *Jupiter Optimus Maximus.* References to Roman rites, such as the traditional declaration of war (*scopas atque verbenas sagmina sumpserunt*, 35 Bl.), and topographical features, such as the *Pons Sublicius* (mentioned in the poem according to Festus 414.15), in addition to the other items listed above, suggest that Naevius imbued his account of early Roman history with cultural details the likes of which one would find in *ktisis*-poetry such as that written by Apollonius, in which the foundation of cities is traced back to legendary heroes (*CA* 4–12; for the likelihood that Naevius knew Apollonius, see Mariotti 1986: 16), or in chronicle poetry such as the *Messeniaca* of Rhianus or the *Mopsopia* of Euphorion.

Naevius' choice to incorporate the Trojan migration within his historical epic not only connected the origin of Rome, possibly even the Punic War, with the most important event in Greek literary history; it also afforded him the opportunity to engage in the sort of intertextual narrative we typically associate with later writers in Rome. For example, while the departure from Troy includes elements that probably come from the cyclic *Iliou Persis* in which Aeneas and his entourage are described as leaving Troy (e.g., 5 Bl.), Naevius' description of the storm that beset the Trojans on their way to Italy (which Servius on *Aen.* 1.198 tells us Vergil adapted in the first book of the *Aeneid*) was likely influenced by the passage from the *Odyssey* in which Odysseus is assailed by a storm sent by Poseidon (*Od.* 5.282–493). In fact, at some point in this part of the story, Anchises addresses Neptune, a detail that encourages us to think of this Odyssean passage (9 Bl.):

> Senex fretus pietatei deum adlocutus
> summi deum regis fratrem Neptunum
> regnatorem marum.
>
> The old man, trusting in his piety, addressed the god
> Neptune, brother of the almighty king of the gods,
> ruler of the seas.

This kind of interweaving of models can be observed again and again in Hellenistic authors such as Callimachus and Apollonius. We are fortunate in having evidence of it elsewhere in Naevius' poetry, as we learn from Terence (*Andria* 15–21) that he "contaminated" discrete dramatic narratives in his plays as well.

Still other possible connections with the Trojan War and the Homeric poems can be found among the fragments. The sheer length of the Punic War must have conjured up a parallel with the Trojan conflict; at one point, in fact, Naevius talks about a 17-year siege (*septimum decimum annum ilico sedent*, 44 Bl.). Moreover, we encounter a number of Homericizing phrases and conceits. The question put to Aeneas by someone during his journey to Italy or after reaching his destination (20 Bl.),

> Blande et docte percontat, Aenea quo pacto
> Troiam urbem liquerit.
>
> Agreeably, yet to the point, he asks how Aeneas
> left the city of Troy.

recalls such scenes as when Aeolus asks Odysseus about his travels (*Od.* 10.14–15):

> μῆνα δὲ πάντα φίλει με καὶ ἐξερέεινεν ἕκαϲτα,
> Ἴλιον Ἀργείων τε νέαϲ καὶ νόϲτον Ἀχαιῶν·
>
> For a whole month he hosted me and asked all sorts of questions
> about Troy, the ships of the Argives, and the return of the Achaeans.

The line that follows, "and I told him everything down to the last detail," gives us a good idea of what may have followed in the Naevian text. In the lines

> *manus*que susum ad caelum *sustulit* suas rex
> Amulius, *divis*<que> gratulabatur.
>
> And King Amulius raised his hands up toward the sky
> and thanked the gods.

(26 Bl., with Merula's widely accepted *manusque* for *isque*) Amulius' action echoes the many examples of phrases using χεῖραϲ plus a form of ἀνέχω and accompanied by the name of a god or gods in the dative that are found in both Homeric poems. In the line *sanctus Iove prognatus Pythius Apollo*, "holy child of Jupiter, Pythian Apollo" (24 Bl.), *Pythius Apollo* seems to toy with the Homeric clausula Φοῖβοϲ Ἀπόλλων, and the line as a whole with Homeric whole-verse formulas such as διογενὲϲ Λαερτιάδη πολυμήχαν' Ὀδυϲϲεῦ. *Topper capesset flammam Volcani*, "quickly it will lay hold of Vulcan's flame" (60 Bl.), recalls a phrase such as αὐτὰρ ἐπεὶ δή ϲε φλὸξ ἤνυϲεν Ἡφαίϲτοιο (*Od.* 24.71). We are even fortunate in having a brief ecphrasis (8 Bl.):

> Inerant signa expressa, quomodo Titani
> bicorpores Gigantes magnique Atlantes
> Runcus ac Porporeus filii Terras.
>
> Images were represented on it, such as the Titans,
> double-bodied Giants, huge Atlases,
> Runcus and Porporeus, sons of the Earth.

Whatever this described (a shield, perhaps, on the model of that of Achilles), the presence of such pre-Olympian monsters may have signified in some fashion the victory over the forces of chaos by a new Jovian regime: Rome? In sum, rather than translating and adapting Homer, as Livius did, Naevius was the first to use the Homeric poems as literary models for a Roman epic, and employed these texts to color and comment on their narratives in precisely the same way as Hellenistic poets and as his epic successors in Rome would do after him.

Quintus Ennius

Ennius (239–169 BCE), then, was not the first Hellenistic poet in Rome. He did, however, bring Hellenistic literary sensitivities to a new level, and stunningly so. In fact, the fragments and occasional details preserved by later writers suggest that he may have consciously fashioned his life and work along the lines of a Callimachus, if not Callimachus *ipse*. He claimed to be the descendant of the Oscan king and eponym of the Messapians, Messapus (524 Sk.), as Callimachus claimed to come from the family of the Cyrenian founder Battus (Barchiesi 1995). The assertion that he was poor at age 70 (Cic. *Sen.* 5.14) recalls Callimachus' claim of poverty in *Iamb* 3. His dream at the opening of the *Annales* clearly imitates the dream with which the *Aetia* proper opens (fr. 2 Pf.). Like Callimachus in the *Aetia*, Ennius speaks of his old age in the context of poetic composition (fr. 1.30–6 Pf.; 401, 522, *sed. inc.* LXX Sk.). Both poets added to their *magna opera*, Callimachus Books 3–4 of the *Aetia* and Ennius Books 16–18 of the *Annales*. In the preserved four-book format, the *Aetia* ends where Callimachus began, with the Muses; it seems possible that the first ending of the *Annales* in Book 15 concluded with the founding of the temple of Hercules of the Muses (Skutsch 1985: 6), a Roman Museum on the model of the Alexandrian institution (Gratwick 1982: 63), and thus passages celebrating the Muses similarly framed his great epic (the first line of which was *Musae quae pedibus magnum pulsatis Olympum*, 1 Sk.).

Even Ennius' impressive and varied literary output calls to mind, if not the Cyrenian, at least a learned scholar-poet of the Alexandrian mold. Space and the complexity of the questions prompted by the remains of Ennius' minor works do not allow any sort of treatment, but what we know of them provides the fascinating picture of a versatile, ambitious, and combative writer whose elegiac epitaph (*ROL* 1.402–3),

> Nemo me lacrimis decoret nec funera fletu
> faxit. Cur? Volito vivus per ora virum.
>
> Let no one adorn me with tears nor celebrate my funeral
> with lamentation. Why? I live through the winged words of men.

apart from imitating the frequent question-and-answer format found among the funeral epigrams in the *Greek Anthology*, also appears to cap the saturnian epitaph of Naevius, whose *Bellum Poenicum* was the main competition for the *Annales* (*ROL* 2.154–5; *Epitaphium Naevii* Bl.):

Immortales mortales si foret fas flere,
flerent divae Camenae Naevium poetam.
Itaque postquam est Orchi traditus thesauro
obliti sunt Romae loquier lingua latina.

If it were right for immortals to lament mortals,
the divine Camenae would lament the poet Naevius.
And so, after he was handed over to the chamber of Death
they forgot to speak Latin in Rome.

Not only has Ennius updated the meter, as it were, but his glory is such that he will not be consigned to the land of the dead!

In addition to the dramatic pieces, more tragic than comic, Ennius composed epigrams; *Sota*, an adaptation of a poem by the third-century poet Sotades; *Gastronomia*, a Latin rendition, in loose hexameters, of the mock-didactic food poem *Hedyphagetica* by the fourth-century poet Archestratus of Gela; the *Epicharmus* and *Praecepta* (or *Protrepticum*) in iambo-trochaic verse; and four books of *Saturae*, in various meters, that include fables, send-ups of stereotypical figures, proverbs, various comic scenes, and autobiographical stories, whose metrical and thematic *varietas* recalls the *Iambs* of Callimachus (Waszink 1972: 121–30). The *Euhemerus* or *Sacra Historia* stands as our earliest example of artistic prose in Latin. Moreover, his exploration of a variety of genres also calls to mind Callimachus' defense of his own *polyeideia* in *Iamb* 13. We even learn from Cicero (*Div.* 2.111) that in one of his works Ennius included the acrostic Q. ENNIUS FECIT, reminiscent of Nicander's famous signature acrostic at *Theriaca* 345–54 (quoted by Magnelli in this volume), and one fragment of the *Annales* may contain an acronym of the name MARS (156 Sk.; Hendry 1994). Not missing from Ennius' poetic resume are the sorts of encomia that recall Callimachus, Theocritus, and others: the *Scipio*, in which he stated that Homer alone could praise Africanus' deeds (*Suda* ε 1348), and the *Ambracia* that celebrated the Aetolian expedition of Ennius' patron M. Fulvius Nobilior, which was also featured in Book 15 of the *Annales*. The picture we get of a poet on intimate terms with the great leaders of Rome (e.g., Cic. *de Orat.* 2.276; Badian 1972), evokes the amicable relationships that the Ptolemies had with their literary protégés and anticipates the rapport that Vergil and Horace, among others, will have with Augustus (see also Erskine, Gowing in this volume).

Regarding the *Annales*, the fragments reveal a poem that includes programmatic self-consciousness, sophisticated word play, intertextuality, and association with Callimachean poetics, inter alia. What follows is a select survey of some of the features of the *Annales* that illustrate these points.

In the opening lines of the *Annales*, Ennius hijacked the dream motif featured in the first scene of the *Aetia* (fr. 2 Pf.). Callimachus dreamed that he conversed with the Muses on Mount Helicon, a trope that validates the authority of his material, itself a clever adaptation of Hesiod's encounter with the Muses in the *Theogony* (22–35). In his rendition of the Callimachean dream, Ennius, employing Pythagorean views of the soul, claims that Homer, a more appropriate model than Hesiod given the topic, appeared to him and informed him that, after becoming a peacock, his soul migrated to that of the Roman poet (1–11 Sk.). Ennius' dream thus trumps that of his Hellenistic model: validation for the content and presentation of the *Annales* lie in the poet himself as Homer *redivivus*. At the opening of the third triad of the *Annales* (Book 7), Ennius, according to Cicero, explained why he did not treat the First Punic War (206–7 Sk.):

> Scripsere alii rem
> vorsibus quos olim Faunei vatesque canebant.
>
> Others have written an account
> in verses which once the fauns and soothsayers used to sing.

He went on to state (208–10 Sk.):

> cum] neque Musarum scopulos ...
> ... nec dicti studiosus [quisquam erat] ante hunc
> nos ausi reserare.
>
> Nor [did anyone ascend the] cliffs of the Muses
> nor [was there any] philologist before him.
> We dared to lay open [the fountains?].

Ennius' decision not to treat the First Punic War is an early, if not the earliest, example of the *recusatio* motif in Latin. A Hellenistic parallel can be found in Apollonius' statement at the beginning of the *Argonautica* that he would not describe the building of the Argo because earlier poets had already done so (1.18–22), although in Ennius' case he disparages the unnamed *alii*. Closely linked with this statement is the claim that he was the first to ascend the mountain of the Muses as *dicti studiosus*, which scholars have long recognized as a translation of the Alexandrian term for scholar-poet, φιλόλογoς. As seen above, Livius and Naevius were in fact also practicing φιλόλογοι. In this prologue, introducing the First and Second Punic Wars, Naevius provided Ennius with precisely what he needed if he were going to be a Callimachus in Rome: someone to evoke as a seemingly inferior rival – a faun and a soothsayer – in order to distinguish his own work as innovative, just as Callimachus availed himself of the Telchines or, to cite a more recent example, when Michael Stipe of the 1990s pop group REM claimed that the Beatles produced "elevator music." That he borrowed much from Naevius' work, as Cicero observed (*Brut.* 19.76), was immaterial to the agonistic stance that his priority afforded. One final example. The prologue of the next triad (Books 10–12) contains the lines (322–3 Sk.):

> Insece Musa manu Romanorum induperator
> quod quisque in bello gessit cum rege Philippo.
>
> Tell, O Muse, what each commander of the Romans
> accomplished by force of arms in the war with King Philip.

It was suggested long ago that Ennius appears to "correct" Livius' *Camena insece*, substituting the Greek *Musa* for the archaic Italian water divinity but employing the same calque on ἔννεπε (Waszink 1979: 95). The correction might even go deeper. The object of ἔννεπε/*insece* in the Greek and Latin *Odyssey*'s was a single man, Odysseus; the object of *insece* in the *Annales* are the achievements of a number of

Roman generals. Roman greatness, one might deduce, lies not in individual but corporate *res gestae*. These three examples, despite their fragmentary state, reveal a poet self-consciously positioning his work within Greek and Roman literary history and in a manner that accords with Hellenistic practice.

Many of the fragments verify Ennius' claim to be *dicti studiosus*. Like his epic predecessors, Ennius gives his narrative a Homeric cast but to an even greater degree. For instance, *dia dearum* (22 Sk.) replicates the clausula δῖα θεάων and *endo suam do* (587 Sk.) echoes ἡμέτερον δῶ; the formula πατὴρ ἀνδρῶν τε θεῶν τε is imitated and varied in good Hellenistic style (see more examples of *variatio* below): *patrem divomque hominumque* (592 Sk.), *divom pater atque hominum rex* (203 Sk.), and *divomque hominumque pater, rex* (591 Sk.). Ennius translated whole formulaic lines, giving Roman battles the feel of an Iliadic conflict: *concidit et sonitum simul insuper arma dederunt* (411 Sk.) renders the line δούπησεν δὲ πεσών, ἀράβησε δὲ τεύχε' ἐπ' αὐτῶι (e.g., *Il.* 4.504). He even attempted to reproduce the sound of the Greek archaic genitive singular in *Mettoeo<que> Fufetioeo* (120 Sk.) and occasionally employed tmesis, elegantly as in *Hannibal audaci cum pectore de me hortatur* (371 Sk.), and playfully as in the unassigned fragment *saxo cere comminuit brum* (*ROL* 1.450–1, a reflection of Hellenistic practice: Zetzel 1974). There are the occasional puns, such as *alter nare cupit, alter pugnare paratust* (238 Sk.), *navibus explebant sese terrasque replebant* (518 Sk.), and *unus surum Surus ferre, tamen defendere possent* (540 Sk.), and glosses on Greek words such as *et densis aquila pennis obnixa volabat / vento quem perhibent Graium genus aera lingua* (139–40 Sk.) and *nec quisquam sophiam, sapientia quae perhibetur, / in somnis vidit priusquam sam discere coepit* (211–12 Sk.). Ennius introduced non-Latin words to add color, as in *summus ibi capitur meddix, occitur alter* (289 Sk.) and *Illyrii restant sicis sybinisque fodentes* (526 Sk.). He may also have picked up and toyed with Naevius' etymological play on *auspicium*, seen above (87–91 Sk.):

Simul aureus exoritur sol
cedunt de caelo ter quattuor corpora sancta
avium, praepetibus sese pulcrisque locis dant.
Con*spicit* inde sibi data Romulus esse propritim
auspicio regni stabilita scamna solumque.

As soon as the golden sun arises
twelve holy birds swoop down from the sky,
they betake themselves to propitious and pleasing places.
From this Romulus observes that a flight of birds established
a kingdom's throne and territory as his own.

Thanks to Macrobius, we know that Ennius recast a number of specific passages from the *Iliad*, applying them to new contexts in the *Annales*. The felling of trees for Patroclus' pyre (*Il.* 23.114–26) was borrowed to describe the funeral preparations after the Battle of Heraclea for the cremation of 11,000 men (175–9 Sk.); another comment on the corporate nature of Roman heroism? Ennius applied the episode of Ajax being pressed by the Trojans at *Il.* 16.102–11 to the struggle of a tribune (391–8 Sk.), which appears to have been a part of a larger Homeric *contaminatio* involving *Il.* 12.127–36 (see Skutsch *ad loc.*, and for a similar blending of Homeric passages, *ad* 432). He also adapted the celebrated horse simile assigned to Paris and Hector (*Il.* 6.506–11 and 15.263–8), likely a compliment to a conspicuous soldier. We learn from Cicero (*Sen.* 6.16) that Ennius included a speech by Appius Claudius in which he argued vehemently against making peace with Pyrrhus (199–200 Sk.). The line Cicero quotes recalls *Il.* 24.201–2, where Hecuba rebukes Priam for even thinking about going to the Achaeans to ransom the body of Hector; the assignation of words uttered by an unheroic female character to the aged Roman statesman is striking but also typical of Hellenistic gender reversals in the rewriting of Homeric passages.

Ennius, the purported re-incarnation of Homer, repeats himself, as it were, when he expresses inadequacy with regard to the magnitude of his topic (469–70 Sk. and *Il.* 2.487–9):

> Non si lingua loqui saperet quibus, ora decem sint
> in me, tum ferro cor sit pectusque revinctum . . .
>
> Not if I had ten mouths with which my tongue could speak,
> and if my heart and chest were bound with iron . . .
>
> πληθὺν δ' οὐκ ἂν ἐγὼ μυθήcομαι οὐδ' ὀνομήνω
> οὐδ' εἴ μοι δέκα μὲν γλῶccαι, δέκα δὲ cτόματ' εἶεν,
> φωνὴ δ' ἄρρηκτος, χάλκεον δέ μοι ἦτορ ἐνείη.
>
> I could not mention or name the multitude
> not even if I had ten tongues and ten mouths,
> and an unbreakable voice, and a heart of bronze within.

These and the previous passages indicate that the *Annales* possessed the kind of studied Homericizing narrative we find among the Hellenistic poets. The difference, of course, resides in the fact that all of the literary and linguistic niceties color our reading of Roman history, and not Greek mythology. Livius dubbed Homeric characters in Latin; Ennius, like Naevius, has historical Romans acting and talking like Homeric heroes, a fact that is further distanced by the self-consciousness of the language whereby the poet effectively shares the stage with his subjects.

Another feature of the poem that reflects Hellenistic tastes involves the inclusion of ethnographical and historiographical topics. Apart from the foundation of Rome featured in the first book, we find traces of the founding of Ostia (128–9 Sk.) and Carthage (472, *pace* Skutch *ad loc.*), with mention of the Carthaginian practice of child sacrifice (214 Sk.), all recalling Hellenistic *ktisis* poetry. Focus on decisive changes of fortune may reflect the kind of Hellenistic tragic history criticized by Polybius (2.56.10–12, quoted by Gutzwiller in this volume; 312–13 and 385–6 Sk.):

> Mortalem summum Fortuna repente
> reddidit †summo regno †ut famul †optimus esset.
>
> Fortune suddenly removed the highest mortal
> from the height of power to become a (a very fine?) slave.
>
> Infit, "O cives, quae me fortuna foro sic
> contudit indigno, bello confecit acerbo!"
>
> He begins to speak, "Citizens, what fortune so crushed me
> in a cruel forum, destroyed me in a bitter war!"

A particularly striking example of a dramatic reversal is the ambiguous oracle supposedly received by the great Roman nemesis Pyrrhus (167 Sk.):

> Aio te Aeacida Romanos vincere posse.
>
> I say, offspring of Aeacus, that you can defeat the Romans (or: the Romans can defeat you).

As Cicero who quotes the line noticed (*Div.* 2.116), Ennius replicated the famous prophecy given to Croesus (Arist. *Rhet.* 1407a; D.S. 9.31; cf. Hdt. 1.54):

> Κροῖϲοϲ Ἅλυν διαβὰϲ μεγαλὴν ἀρχὴν καταλύϲει.
> Croesus, crossing the Halys, will destroy a great power (i.e., his or that of Cyrus).

Though paralleled in epic poetry, piteous scenes in which the vanquished beg for mercy (*cogebant hostes lacrumantes ut misererent*, 162 Sk.) or women watch from city walls (*matronae moeros complent spectare faventes*, 418 Sk.) may also recall historians such as Phylarchus and his fourth-century BCE predecessor Duris who teased out the emotional reactions to historical events, like modern-day tabloids.

In the composition of literary epics, writers such as Apollonius evoked Homeric formulas but then varied their individual instances, eschewing wholesale repetition. We can observe Ennius aiming after a comparable effect for example in descriptions of galloping horses:

explorant Numidae, totam quatit ungula terram.	242 Sk.
consequitur. Summo sonitu quatit ungula terram.	262 Sk.
it eques et plausu cava concutit ungula terram.	431 Sk.

the night sky:

qui caelum versat stellis fulgentibus aptum.	27 Sk.
caelum prospexit stellis fulgentibus aptum.	145 Sk.
hinc nox processit stellis ardentibus aptum.	348 Sk.

and sailing (cf. also 294–6 Sk. and *ROL* 1.404–5.3):

poste recumbite vestraque pellite tonsis.	218 Sk.
pone petunt, exim referunt ad pectora tonsas.	219 Sk.

This tendency toward *variatio* is surely a conscious choice influenced by the practices of Hellenistic writers.

Ennius thus reveals himself in many ways as an artist of Hellenistic tastes. As we have seen, in this he built upon the work of Livius and Naevius, distancing himself from his predecessors by presenting himself as more "philological" than they were. Before concluding, I would like to explore two lines which suggest that he may also have been engaged in the kind of pointed inversion of Callimachean aesthetics that has been observed in later writers of the Neoteric and Augustan periods.

In his commentary on the *Georgics* (1988), Richard Thomas observes that on several occasions Vergil employed wording that conflicted with orthodox Callimachean imagery. For instance, in the prologue to *Georgics* 4 the poet states (3–7):

> Admiranda tibi levium spectacula rerum
> magnanimosque duces totiusque ordine gentis
> mores et studia et populos et proelia dicam.
> In tenui labor; at tenuis non gloria, si quem
> numina laeva sinunt auditque vocatus Apollo.

> In proper order I will recall for you the amazing spectacle of subtle things, both great-hearted leaders and the character and passions of an entire nation, and peoples and battles. Much work on a little topic: but no little glory, if propitious powers allow and Apollo listens when invoked.

As Thomas notes (*ad* 4.6), the stylistic approach taken is Callimachean (*tenuis* = λεπτόϲ), but the theme of war and the glory it will bring are non-Callimachean (see further Thomas 1985). Even the earlier and seemingly more conformist *Eclogue* 6 shows signs of inversion (Clauss 2004). At the opening of the *Metamorphoses*, Ovid's request that the Muses participate in his fine-spun "continuous poem" (*perpetuum* ... *carmen*, 1.4), strikes a similar dissonance (compare and contrast Callimachus' rejection of the "continuous" poem at *Aetia* fr. 1.4 Pf.), as do Latona's statements in the episode of the Lycian Farmers that the use of water is common to all and that nature does not make "fine waters" (*tenues undas*, *Met.* 6.351) the private property of anyone; even more strikingly, the mother of Lycian Apollo here claims to come to a common drinking-spot (*publica munera*), all of which runs counter to Callimachus' aversion to such places and the water found there (see especially *ep.* 28 Pf.). Similarly, at *Ars Poetica* 131–5 Horace states that one can write excellent poetry using "public material" (*publica materies*, 131; on this and the Ovidian passages see Clauss 1989). While one might imagine that pressure from the Augustan regime forced poets to abandon their Callimachean avoidance of epic themes, the same sort of contradictory phrases and imagery can be found in the previous generation, for example in Catullus 68b: the poem begins *non possum reticere* (41) and an audience of thousands is envisaged (45–6), a lofty spider is asked to weave a "non-tenuous" web (*nec tenuem texens sublimis aranea telam*, 49), a river that flows in the midst of many people brings relief (59–60), an enclosed area is made open where the poet's girlfriend places a soft foot on a well-worn threshold (67–72; Clauss 1995). In other words, poets of the first century BCE, even as early as the Neoteric Catullus, were fully comfortable with the idea of evoking and then subverting Callimachean programmatic imagery.

To return to the *Annales*, while it contains many features that are familiar from Hellenistic verse, in length and tone it resembles the "Persian chain" more than the "shrill cicada" (Call. *Aet.* fr. 1.18, 32–6 Pf.; Harder in this volume). Book 6, for instance, which tells of the war with Pyrrhus, opens with the programmatic line *quis potis ingentis oras evolvere belli?* ("who can unroll the huge boundaries of this war?" 164 Sk.). *Evolvere* is a metaphor for poetic composition that comes from unrolling a papyrus (*OLD* s.v. 7). Knowing that Ennius was fully conversant with Callimachus' poetry, might we find in his choice of words an inversion of the equally programmatic ἔπος δ' ἐπὶ τυτθὸν ἑλίϲϲω at the opening of the *Aetia* ("and I unroll a small poem," 1.5 Pf.) in order to signal his intention to write the seemingly paradoxical Callimachean epic? If so, the substitution of *ingentis* for τυτθόν is striking. We are perhaps on firmer ground in the line *deducunt habilies gladios filo gracilento* ("they make fine and nimble swords of delicate quality," 239 Sk.). The verb *deduco*, used literally of spinning and metaphorically of poetic composition, implies *tenuitas*, as Servius notes on Vergil's phrase *deductum dicere carmen* at *Eclogue* 6.5 (*translatio a lana quae deducitur in tenuitatem*). Ennius' *filo* introduces the metaphor of spinning and *gracilento* engages a stylistic nuance (cf. *tenui deducta poemata filo*, Hor. *Ep.* 2.1.225). The description of the making of swords (military) in terms that evoke elegant verse (Callimachean) offers up the sort of inverted imagery we find in Late Republican and Augustan authors and leads to the conclusion that Roman poets as early as Ennius not only employed programmatic language but possessed considerable freedom in manipulating it to suit their interests.

***

From what we have seen, Livius, Naevius, and Ennius engaged in a sophisticated and self-conscious literary practice that might have been as much at home in Alexandria as it was in Rome. The only true "fauns and soothsayers" who composed Latin literature were those who antedated the arrival of Livius Andronicus, the first *doctus poeta*, who came on the scene with an already impressive panoply of philological weapons. Thereafter, Roman poets continuously improved upon the literary *doctrina* of their antecedents. In time, the works of many Hellenistic artists would perish but their scholarly approach to writing would live on in the Roman *epigonoi* of the first and subsequent generations of writers and even beyond the fall of the Roman Empire, when Medieval and Renaissance thinkers discovered and rediscovered their Classical past that was deeply invested in Hellenistic aesthetics. What is more, as we have seen elsewhere in this collection, when Greek and non-Greek writers composed literature, in verse or prose, subsequent to the first generation of Hellenistic writers, they were primarily responding not to Archaic or Classical artists but to their successors, who set the literary agenda throughout the Mediterranean for centuries to come, an agenda that was fully and unmistakably Hellenistic.

FURTHER READING

A myriad of studies that describe and analyze the influence of Hellenistic literature on Roman writers of all eras, many excellent and not a few groundbreaking, have appeared over the past decades. In the interest of space, I cite only a small selection of recent works, especially those that relate to some of the ideas presented here: Thomas 1993 (an article-length update of Wimmel's authoritative 1960 study), Cameron 1995a: 454–83, Fantuzzi and Hunter 2004: 444–85, and Hunter 2006a. Since Hellenistic literature is primarily intertextual, studies on intertextuality in Rome, particularly as it was directly influenced by Hellenistic authors, form an important part of any discussion of Roman literature, especially poetry. Key works on the subject include Barchiesi 1984, Conte 1986, Hinds 1998, Thomas 1999, and Barchiesi 2001a. For current surveys of early Roman literature in general, see Conte 1994, Albrecht 1997, Suerbaum 2002, and the magisterial review of the latter by Feeney 2005. On the early epic tradition in Rome, I can think of no better place to start than Goldberg 1995. On the blending of cultures on the Italian peninsula, see Veyne 1979. Horsfall 1994 offers a useful survey of our evidence for Latin literature before Livius. Regarding the appropriation of the Trojan legend by Roman writers, see above all Gruen 1992: 6–51 and Erskine 2001.

Blänsdorf 1995 provides up-to-date Latin texts of the *Odusia* and *Bellum Poenicum*; for the *Annales*, see Skutsch 1985. Volumes 1 and 2 of Warmington 1932 remain the most readily available collection and translation of the fragments of early Latin poetry. As for studies on the individual poets examined here, for Livius Andronicus see, for instance, Mariotti 1986 and Livingston 2004; for Naevius, Barchiesi 1962, a truly extraordinary work of scholarship, and Mariotti 2001. Regarding the *Annales*, in addition to the monumental commentary of Skutsch 1985, a number of edited collections have appeared that touch upon many of the central issues pertaining to the first hexametric epic in Rome: Skutsch 1972, more recently Breed and Rossi 2006, and Fitzgerald and Gowers 2007. In short, our understanding of the influence of Hellenistic literature on Roman writers has come far, but more work remains to be done as we continue to discover the extent to which Romans, like other Mediterranean peoples, made Greek literature their own.

Bibliography

el-Abbadi, M. 2004. "The Island of Pharos in Myth and History." In Harris and Ruffini 2004: 259–67.

Abbenes, J. G. J., Slings, S. R. and Sluiter, I. 1995 (eds.). *Greek Literary Theory after Aristotle.* Amsterdam.

Accorinti, D. and Chuvin, P. 2003 (eds.). *Des Géants à Dionysos: Mélanges de mythologie et de poésie grecques offerts à Francis Vian.* Alessandria.

Acosta-Hughes, B. 2002. *Polyeideia: The Iambi of Callimachus and the Archaic Iambic Tradition.* Berkeley.

Acosta-Hughes, B. 2010. *Arion's Lyre: Archaic Lyric in Hellenistic Poetry.* Princeton.

Acosta-Hughes, B. and Stephens, S. A. 2002. "Rereading Callimachus' *Aetia* Fragment 1." *Classical Philology* 97: 238–55.

Acosta-Hughes, B. and Stephens, S. A. 2007. "The Cicala's Song: Plato in the *Aetia*" and "Literary Quarrels." *Princeton/Stanford Working Papers*, www.princeton.edu/~pswpc.

Acosta-Hughes, B., Kosmetatou, E. and Baumbach, M. 2004 (eds.). *Labored in Papyrus Leaves: Perspectives on an Epigram Collection Attributed to Posidippus (P.Mil.Vogl. VIII 309).* Washington, DC and Cambridge, MA.

Adamson, J. 1999 (ed.). *The Princely Courts of Europe, 1500–1750.* London.

Adler, A. 1928–38. *Suidae Lexicon.* 5 vols. Leipzig.

Adorno, F. et al. 1977 (eds.). *La cultura ellenistica: filosofia, scienza, letteratura.* Milan.

Albrecht, M. von 1997. *A History of Roman Literature.* 2 vols. Leiden.

Alcock, S. E., Cherry, J. and Elsner, J. 2001 (eds.). *Pausanias: Travel and Memory in Roman Greece.* Oxford.

Alexandria and Alexandrianism. 1996. *Papers Delivered at a Symposium Organized by the John Paul Getty Museum and Getty Center for the History of Art.* Malibu.

Algra, K., Barnes, J., Mansfeld, J. and Schofield, M. 1999 (eds.). *The Cambridge History of Hellenistic Philosophy.* Cambridge.

Allan, W. 2000. *The Andromache and Euripidean Tragedy.* Oxford.

Allen, A. 1993. *The Fragments of Mimnermus: Text and Commentary.* Stuttgart.

Allen, J. 2001. *Inference from Signs: Ancient Debates about the Nature of Evidence.* Oxford.

Allen, W. 1940. "The Epyllion: A Chapter in the History of Literary Criticism." *Transactions of the American Philological Association* 71: 1–26.

Aloni, A. 1981. *Le Muse di Archiloco: richerche sullo stile archilocheo.* Copenhagen.

Aloni, A. 1989. *L'aedo e i tiranni: ricerche sull'Inno omerico a Apollo.* Rome.

Aloni, A. 2001. "The Proem of Simonides' Plataea Elegy and the Circumstances of Its Performance." In Boedeker and Sider 2001: 86–105.

Alonso Nuñez, J.-M. 1989. "Un historien entre deux cultures: Apollodore d'Artemita." In Mactoux and Geny 1989: 1–6.

Alpers, P. 1996. *What is Pastoral?* Chicago.

Ambühl, A. 2004. "Entertaining Theseus and Heracles: The *Hecale* and the *Victoria Berenices* as a Diptych." In Harder, Regtuit, and Wakker 2004: 23–47.

Ambühl, A. 2005. *Kinder und junge Helden: Innovative Aspekte des Umgangs mit der literarischen Tradition bei Kallimachos.* Leuven.

Ameling, W. 2004. "Wohltäter im hellenistischen Gymnasion." In Kah and Scholz 2004: 129–61.

Anderson, G. 1984. *Ancient Fiction: The Novel in the Graeco-Roman World.* London.

Andreassi, M. 1997. "Osmosis and Contiguity between 'Low' and 'High' Literature." In Hofmann and Zimmermann 1997: 1–21.

Andreassi, M. 2001a. *Mimi greci in Egitto.* Bari.

Andreassi, M. 2001b. "Esopo sulla scena: il mimo della *Moicheutria* e la *Vita Aesopi.*" *Rheinisches Museum für Philologie* 144: 203–25.

Andreassi, M. 2002. "Il mimo tra 'consumo' e 'letteratura': *Charition* e *Moicheutria.*" *Ancient Narrative* 2: 30–46.

Aneziri, S. and Damaskos, D. 2004. "Städtische Kulte im hellenistischen Gymnasion." In Kah and Scholz 2004: 247–71.

Annas, J. and Barnes, J. 1994. *Sextus Empiricus: Outlines of Scepticism.* Cambridge.

Annas, J. and Woolf, R. 2001. *Cicero: On Moral Ends.* Cambridge.

Aperghis, M. 2004. *The Seleukid Royal Economy: The Finances and Financial Administration of the Seleukid Empire.* Cambridge.

Ardizzoni, A. 1958. *Apollonio Rodio, Le Argonautiche: libro III.* Bari.

Ardizzoni, A. 1967. *Apollonio Rodio, Le Argonautiche: libro I.* Rome.

Argentieri, L. 2007. "Meleager and Philip as Epigram Collectors." In Bing and Bruss 2007: 147–64.

Argoud, G. and Guillaumin, J.-Y. 1998 (eds.). *Sciences exactes et sciences appliquées à Alexandrie (IIIième siècle av. J.-C.–Ier siècle ap. J.-C.).* Saint-Étienne.

Arland, W. 1937. *Nachtheokritische Bukolik bis an die Schwelle der lateinischen Bukolik.* Leipzig.

Armstrong, D. 1995. "Appendix 1: Philodemus, *On Poems* Book 5." In Obbink 1995: 255–69.

Armstrong, D., Fish, J., Johnston, P. A. and Skinner, M. B. 2004 (eds.). *Vergil, Philodemus, and the Augustans.* Austin.

Arnott, W. G. 1971. "Herodas and the Kitchen Sink." *Greece and Rome* 18: 121–32.

Arnott, W. G. 1979, 1996a, 2000a. *Menander.* 3 vols. Cambridge, MA.

Arnott, W. G. 1996b. *Alexis, the Fragments: A Commentary.* Cambridge.

Arnott, W. G. 2000b. "Stage Business in Menander's *Samia.*" In Gödde and Heinze 2000: 113–24.

Arrighetti, G. and Montanari, F. 1993 (eds.). *La componente autobiografica nella poesia greca e latina fra realtà e artificio letterario.* Pisa.

Asch, R. G. and Birke, A. 1991 (eds.). *Princes, Patronage, and the Nobility: The Court at the Beginning of the Modern Age, c. 1450–1650.* London and Oxford.

Asche, U. 1983. *Roms Weltherrschaftsidee und Außenpolitik in der Spätantike im Spiegel der Panegyrici Latini.* Bonn.

Ashton, S.-A. 2004. "Ptolemaic Alexandria and the Egyptian Tradition." In Hirst and Silk 2004: 15–40.

Asmis, E. 1990. "The Poetic Theory of the Stoic 'Aristo'." *Apeiron* 23: 147–201.

Asmis, E. 1991. "Philodemus's Poetry Theory and *On the Good King According to Homer*." *Classical Antiquity* 10: 1–45.

Asmis, E. 1992a. "Crates on Poetic Criticism." *Phoenix* 46: 138–69.

Asmis, E. 1992b. "An Epicurean Survey of Poetic Theories (Philodemus *On Poems* 5, Cols. 26–36)." *Classical Quarterly* 42: 395–415.

Asmis, E. 1992c. "Neoptolemus and the Classification of Poetry." *Classical Philology* 87: 206–31.

Asmis, E. 1995. "Epicurean Poetics." In Obbink 1995: 15–34. Reprinted in Laird 2006: 238–66.

Asmis, E. 2001. "Basic Education in Epicureanism." In Too 2001: 209–39.

Asmis, E. 2002. Review of R. Janko, *Philodemus 'On Poems' Book One*. *Classical Philology* 97: 383–94.

Asmis, E. 2004. "Philodemus on Sound and Sense in Poetry." *Cronache Ercolanesi* 34: 5–27.

Asper, M. 1997. *"Onomata allotria": Zur Genese, Struktur und Funktion poetologischer Metaphern bei Kallimachos*. Stuttgart.

Asper, M. 2001. "Gruppen und Dichter." *Antike und Abendland* 47: 84–116.

Asper, M. 2004. *Kallimachos, Werke*. Darmstadt.

Asper, M. 2007. *Griechische Wissenschaftsgeschichte: Formen, Funktionen, Differenzierungsgeschichten*. Stuttgart.

Asquith, H. 2005. "From Genealogy to Catalogue: The Hellenistic Adaptation of the Hesiodic Catalogue Form." In Hunter 2005b: 266–86.

Assmann, J. 2003. *The Mind of Egypt: History and Meaning in the Time of the Pharaohs*. New York. Orig. *Ägypten: Eine Sinngeschichte*. Munich 1996.

Assmann, J. and Blumenthal, E. 1999 (eds.). *Literatur und Politik im pharaonischen und ptolemäischen Ägypten*. Cairo.

Astbury, R. 2002. *M. Terentius Varro, Saturarum Menippearum fragmenta*. 2nd edition. Munich and Leipzig.

Aujac, G. 2001. *Ératosthène de Cyrène, le pionnier de la géographie: Sa mesure de la circonférence terrestre*. Paris.

Austin, C. and Bastianini, G. 2002. *Posidippi Pellaei quae supersunt omnia*. Milan.

Austin, M. M. 1986. "Hellenistic Kings, War and the Economy." *Classical Quarterly* 36: 450–66.

Austin, M. M. 2003. "The Seleukids and Asia." In Erskine 2003: 121–33.

Austin, M. M. 2006. *The Hellenistic World from Alexander to the Roman Conquest: A Selection of Ancient Sources in Translation*. 2nd edition. Cambridge.

Ax, W. and Glei, R. F. 1993 (eds.). *Literaturparodie in Antike und Mittelalter*. Trier.

Ayres, L. 1995 (ed.). *The Passionate Intellect: Essays on the Transformation of Classical Traditions Presented to Professor I. G. Kidd*. New Brunswick.

Badian, E. 1972. "Ennius and his Friends." In Skutsch 1972: 149–208.

Badian, E. 1982. "Greeks and Macedonians." In Barr-Sharrar and Borza 1982: 33–51.

Bagnall, R. S. 2002. "Alexandria: Library of Dreams." *Proceedings of the American Philosophical Society* 146: 348–62.

Bagnall, R. S. and Derow, P. 2004. *The Hellenistic Period: Historical Sources in Translation*. Oxford.

Bagnall, R. S. and Rathbone, D. 2004. *Egypt from Alexander to the Early Christians: An Archaeological and Historical Guide*. Los Angeles.

Baines, J. 2004. "Egyptian Elite Self-Presentation in the Context of Ptolemaic Rule." In Harris and Ruffini 2004: 33–61.

Barbantani, S. 2001. *Φάτις νικηφόρος: frammenti di elegia encomiastica nell'età delle Guerre Galatiche*. Milan.

Barbantani, S. 2002/3. "Callimachus and the Contemporary Historical 'Epic'." *Hermathena* 173/4: 29–47.

Barber, E. A. 1928. "Alexandrian Literature." *The Cambridge Ancient History* (1st edition) 7: 249–83.

Barchiesi, A. 1984. *La traccia del modello: effetti omerici nella narrazione virgiliana*. Rome.

Barchiesi, A. 1995. "Genealogie: Callimaco, Ennio e l'autocoscienza dei poeti augustei." In Belloni, Milanese, and Porro 1995: 5–18.

Barchiesi, A. 2001a. *Speaking Volumes: Narrative and Intertext in Ovid and Other Latin Poets.* London.

Barchiesi, A. 2001b. "Simonides and Horace on the Death of Achilles." In Boedeker and Sider 2001: 255–60.

Barchiesi, M. 1962. *Nevio epico.* Padua.

Barclay, J. M. G. 1996. *Jews in the Mediterranean Diaspora from Alexander to Trajan (323 BCE–117 CE).* Edinburgh.

Barnes, J. and Griffin, M. 1997 (eds.). *Philosophia Togata II: Plato and Aristotle at Rome.* Oxford.

Barnouw, J. 2002. *Propositional Perception: Phantasia, Predication and Sign in Plato, Aristotle and the Stoics.* Lanham.

Barns, J. W. B. 1956. "Egypt and the Greek Romance." In Gerstinger 1956: 29–36.

Barrett, J. 2002. *Staged Narrative: Poetics and the Messenger in Greek Tragedy.* Berkeley.

Barr-Sharrar, B. and Borza, E. N. 1982 (eds.). *Macedonia and Greece in Late Classical and Early Hellenistic Times.* Washington, DC.

Bartalucci, A. 1963. "Gli aggettivi in -εις in Nicandro." *Studi classici e orientali* 12: 118–44.

Bartels, A. 2004. *Vergleichende Studien zur Erzählkunst des römischen Epyllion.* Göttingen.

Barthes, R. 1977. "Introduction to the Structural Analysis of Narratives." In *Image, Music, Text.* New York.

Barton, T. 1994. *Ancient Astrology.* London and New York.

Barwick, K. 1928. "Die Gliederung der *Narratio* in der rhetorischen Theorie und ihre Bedeutung für die Geschichte des antiken Romans." *Hermes* 68: 261–87.

Basile, C. and Di Natale, A. 1996 (eds.). *Atti del II Convegno Nazionale di Egittologia e Papirologia, Siracusa 1–3 dicembre 1995.* Syracuse.

Bassi, K. and Euben, P. 2003 (eds.). *Declassifying Hellenism: Cultural Studies and the Classics = Parallax* 9.3.

Bastianini, G. 1996a. "Un luogo di ritrovamento fantasma." In Basile and Di Natale 1996: 69–84.

Bastianini, G. 1996b. "Κατὰ λεπτόν in Callimaco (fr. 1.11 Pfeiffer)." In Funghi 1996: 69–80.

Bastianini, G. and Casanova, A. 2002 (eds.). *Il papiro di Posidippo un anno dopo.* Florence.

Bastianini, G. and Gallazzi, C. 2001. *Posidippo di Pella, Epigrammi (P.Mil.Vogl. VIII 309).* Milan.

Bates, D. 1995 (ed.). *Knowledge and the Scholarly Medical Traditions.* Cambridge.

Battezzato, L. 1995. *Il monologo nel teatro di Euripide.* Pisa.

Bearzot, C. 1992. "Πτολεμαῖος Μακεδών: sentimento nazionale macedone e contrapposizioni etniche all'inizio del regno tolemaico." In Sordi 1992: 39–53.

Beck, F. A. G. 1975. *Album of Greek Education.* Sydney.

Beck, R. 2006. *A Brief History of Ancient Astrology.* Malden.

Beckby, H. 1975. *Die griechischen Bukoliker: Theokrit–Moschos–Bion.* Meisenheim.

Bélis, A. 1988. "A proposito degli Inni Delfici ad Apollo." In Gentili and Pretagostini 1988: 205–18.

Bellandi, F., Berti, E. and Ciappi, M. 2001. *Iustissima Virgo: il mito della Vergine in Germanico e in Avieno.* Pisa.

Belloni, L. 2004. *Teocrito, I pescatori*. Como.

Belloni, L., Milanese, G. and Porro, A. 1995 (eds.). *Studia classica Iohanni Tarditi oblata*. 2 vols. Milan.

Benedetto, G. 1993. *Il sogno e l'invettiva: momenti di storia dell'esegesi callimachea*. Florence.

Benz, L., Stärk, E. and Vogt-Spira, G. 1995 (eds.). *Plautus und die Tradition des Stegreifspiels*. Tübingen.

Berggren, J. L. and Thomas, R. S. D. 1996. *Euclid's Phaenomena: A Translation and Study of a Hellenistic Treatise in Spherical Astronomy*. New York.

Bergmann, M. 1998. *Die Strahlen der Herrscher: Theomorphes Herrscherbild und politische Symbolik im Hellenismus und in der römischen Kaiserzeit*. Mainz.

Bernabò Brea, L. 1981. *Menandro e il teatro greco nelle terracotte liparesi*. Genova.

Bernand, É. 1969. *Inscriptions métriques de l'Égypte gréco-romaine: recherches sur la poésie épigrammatique des grecs en Égypte*. Paris.

Bernsdorff, H. 1994. "Polyphem und Daphnis: Zu Theokrits sechstem Idyll." *Philologus* 138: 38–51.

Bernsdorff, H. 2006. "The Idea of Bucolic in the Imitators of Theocritus, 3rd–1st cent. BC." In Fantuzzi and Papanghelis 2006: 167–207.

Bernsdorff, H. 2008. "Mythen, die unter die Haut gehen: Zur literarischen Form der Tätowierelegie (*P.Brux.* Inv. e8934 und *P.Sorb.* Inv. 2254)." *Mnemosyne* 61: 45–65.

Berry, D. H. and Heath, M. 1997. "Oratory and Declamation." In Porter 1997: 393–420.

Bertelli, S. 1986. "The Courtly Universe." In Bertelli, Cardini, and Garbero Zorzi 1986: 7–38.

Bertelli, S., Cardini, F. and Garbero Zorzi, E. 1986 (eds.). *The Courts of the Italian Renaissance*. Milan.

Berve, H. 1926. *Das Alexanderreich auf prosopographischer Grundlage*. Munich.

Bett, R. 1997. *Sextus Empiricus: Against the Ethicists*. Oxford.

Bett, R. 2005. *Sextus Empiricus: Against the Logicians*. Cambridge.

Bett, R. 2010 (ed.). *The Cambridge Companion to Ancient Scepticism*. Cambridge.

Bettenworth, A. 2002. "Asclepiades XXV GP (*AP* 5.181): Ein Beitrag zum sympotisch-erotischen Epigramm." In Harder, Regtuit, and Wakker 2002: 27–38.

Bettenworth, A. 2006. "Die Darstellung nonverbaler Handlungen bei Herodas." In Harder, Regtuit, and Wakker 2006: 1–20.

Bettenworth, A. 2007. "The Mutual Influence of Inscribed and Literary Epigram." In Bing and Bruss 2007: 69–93.

Beye, C. R. 1969. "Jason as Love-hero in Apollonius' *Argonautika*." *Greek, Roman and Byzantine Studies* 10: 31–55.

Beye, C. R. 1982. *Epic and Romance in the Argonautica of Apollonius*. Carbondale.

Biagioli, M. 1993. *Galileo, Courtier: The Practice of Science in the Culture of Absolutism*. Chicago.

Bianchetti, S. 1990. *Sulle tracce di una periegesi anonima*. Florence.

Bianchetti, S. 1998. *Pitea di Massalia, L'Oceano*. Pisa.

Bickerman, E. J. 1975. "The Jewish Historian Demetrius." In Neusner 1975: 72–84.

Billault, A. 2004. "Histoire et roman dans les fragments du *Roman de Ninos*." *Ktema* 29: 215–21.

Billows, R. 1990. *Antigonos the One-Eyed and the Creation of the Hellenistic State*. Berkeley.

Billows, R. 2003. "Cities." In Erskine 2003: 196–215.

Bing, P. 1985. "Kastorion of Soloi's *Hymn to Pan*." *American Journal of Philology* 106: 502–9.

Bing, P. 1988. *The Well-Read Muse: Present and Past in Callimachus and the Hellenistic Poets*. Göttingen.

Bing, P. 1989. "Impersonations of Voice in Callimachus' *Hymn to Apollo*." *Transactions of the American Philological Association* 123: 181–98.

Bing, P. 1990. "A Pun on Aratus' Name in Verse 2 of the *Phainomena*?" *Harvard Studies in Classical Philology* 93: 281–5.

Bing, P. 1993. "Aratus and his Audiences." In Schiesaro, Mitsis, and Clay 1993: 99–109.

Bing, P. 1995. "*Ergänzungsspiel* in the Epigrams of Callimachus." *Antike und Abendland* 41: 115–31.

Bing, P. 2005. "The Politics and Poetics of Geography in the Milan Posidippus, Section One: On Stones (AB 1–20)." In Gutzwiller 2005: 119–40.

Bing, P. and Bruss, J. S. 2007 (eds.). *Brill's Companion to Hellenistic Epigram: Down to Philip*. Leiden.

Bing, P. and Uhrmeister, V. 1994. "The Unity of Callimachus' *Hymn to Artemis*." *Journal of Hellenic Studies* 114: 19–34.

Blank, D. 1998. *Sextus Empiricus: Against the Grammarians*. Oxford.

Blänsdorf, J. 1982. "Die Komödienintrige als Spiel im Spiel." *Antike und Abendland* 28: 131–54.

Blänsdorf, J. 1995. *Fragmenta poetarum latinorum epicorum et lyricorum praeter Ennium et Lucilium*. Stuttgart and Leipzig.

Blasius, A. and Schipper, B. U. 2002 (eds.). *Apokalyptik und Ägypten: Eine kritische Analyse der relevanten Texte aus dem griechisch-römischen Ägypten*. Leuven.

Blass, F. 1887. *Eudoxi Ars astronomica qualis in charta Aegyptiaca superest*. Kiel. Reprinted in *Zeitschrift für Papyrologie und Epigraphik* 115 (1997): 79–101.

Blass, F. 1892. Review of F. Bücheler, *Herondae Mimiambi* (1892). *Göttingische Gelehrte Anzeigen*: 230–7.

Blum, R. 1991. *Kallimachos: The Alexandrian Library and the Origins of Bibliography*. London.

Blume, H.-D. 1974. *Menanders Samia: Eine Interpretation*. Darmstadt.

Bo, D. 1962. *La lingua di Eroda*. Turin.

Bodnár, I. and Fortenbaugh, W. W. 2002 (eds.). *Eudemus of Rhodes*. New Brunswick.

Boedeker, D. 1995. "Simonides on Plataea: Narrative Elegy, Mythodic History." *Zeitschrift für Papyrologie und Epigraphik* 107: 217–29.

Boedeker, D. and Sider, D. 2001 (eds.). *The New Simonides: Contexts of Praise and Desire*. Oxford.

Boiy, T. 2004. *Late Achaemenid and Hellenistic Babylon*. Leuven.

Bollansée, J. 1999. *Hermippos of Smyrna and His Biographical Writings = Fragmente der Griechischen Historiker* 4.3. Leiden.

Bollók, J. 1974. "Du problème de la datation des hymnes d'Isidore." *Studia Aegyptiaca* 1: 27–37.

Bonanno, M. G. 1990. *L'allusione necessaria: ricerche intertestuali sulla poesia greca e latina*. Rome.

Bonanno, M. G. 1995. "*Poetae ut Homeri interpretes* (Teocrito, Apollonio)." *Aevum antiquum* 8: 65–85.

Bonanno, M. G. 2004. "Il poeta scienziato di età ellenistica: appunti per una ridefinizione del *poeta doctus* alessandrino." In Pretagostini and Dettori 2004: 451–77.

Bonner, S. F. 1949. *Roman Declamation*. Liverpool.

Borger, R. 1996. *Beiträge zum Inschriftenwerk Assurbanipals: Die Prismenklassen A, B, C = K, D, E, F, G, H, J und T sowie andere Inschriften*. Wiesbaden.

Bornmann, F. 1968. *Callimachus, Hymnus in Dianam*. Florence.

Bosworth, A. B. 2000. "Ptolemy and the Will of Alexander." In Bosworth and Baynham 2000: 207–41.

Bosworth, A. B. 2002. *The Legacy of Alexander: Politics, Propaganda and Warfare under the Successors*. Oxford.

Bosworth, A. B. and Baynham, E. J. 2000 (eds.). *Alexander the Great in Fact and Fiction*. Oxford.

Bousquet, J. 1988. "La stèle des kyténiens au Letôon de Xanthos." *Revue des études grecques* 101: 12–53.

Bousquet, J. 1992. "Les inscriptions gréco-lydiennes." *Fouilles de Xanthos* 9: 147–96.

Bowen, A. C. and Todd, R. B. 2004. *Cleomedes' Lectures on Astronomy: A Translation of The Heavens with an Introduction and Commentary*. Berkeley.

Bowersock, G. W., Burkert, W. and Putnam, M. C. J. 1979 (eds.). *Arktouros: Hellenic Studies Presented to B. Knox*. Berlin.

Bowie, E. L. 1986. "Early Greek Elegy, Symposium and Public Festival." *Journal of Hellenic Studies* 106: 13–35.

Bowie, E. L. 1993. "Lies, Fiction and Slander in Early Greek Poetry." In Gill and Wiseman 1993: 1–37.

Bowie, E. L. 1994. "Greek Table-Talk before Plato." *Rhetorica* 11: 355–73.

Bowie, E. L. 1996. "Frame and Framed in Theocritus Poems 6 and 7." In Harder, Regtuit, and Wakker 1996: 91–100.

Bowie, E. L. 2002. "The Chronology of the Greek Novel since B. E. Perry: Revisions and Precisions." *Ancient Narrative* 2: 47–63.

Bowie, E. L. 2007. "From Archaic Elegy to Hellenistic Sympotic Epigram?" In Bing and Bruss 2007: 95–112.

Bowman, A. K. and Woolf, G. 1994 (ed.). *Literacy and Power in the Ancient World*. Cambridge.

Boys-Stones, G. R. 2001. *Post-Hellenistic Philosophy: A Study of its Developments from Stoics to Origen*. Oxford.

Boys-Stones, G. R. 2003a. "The Stoics' Two Types of Allegory." In Boys-Stones 2003b: 189–216.

Boys-Stones, G. R. 2003b (ed.). *Metaphor, Allegory, and the Classical Tradition: Ancient Thought and Modern Revisions*. Oxford.

Brands, G. and Hoepfner, W. 1996 (eds.). *Basileia: Die Paläste der hellenistischen Könige*. Mainz.

Brandt, P. 1888. *Parodorum epicorum Graecorum et Archestrati reliquiae*. Leipzig.

Branham, R. B. and Goulet-Cazé, M.-O. 1996 (eds.). *The Cynics: The Cynic Movement in Antiquity and its Legacy*. Berkeley.

Braun, M. 1934. *Griechischer Roman und hellenistische Geschichtschreibung*. Frankfurt am Main.

Bravo, B. 2007. "Antiquarianism and History." In Marincola 2007: 515–27.

Breed, B. W. and Rossi, A. 2006 (eds.). *Ennius and the Invention of Roman Epic = Arethusa* 39.

Breitenstein, T. 1966. *Recherches sur le poème Mégara*. Copenhagen.

Brelich, A. 1958. "Un mito prometeico." *Studi e Materiali di Storia delle Religioni* 29: 23–40.

Bridges, M. and Bürgel, J. C. 1996 (eds.). *The Problematics of Power: Eastern and Western Representations of Alexander the Great*. Bern.

Brink, C. O. 1946. "Callimachus and Aristotle: An Inquiry into Callimachus' Πρὸς Πραξιφάνην." *Classical Quarterly* 40: 11–26.

Brink, C. O. 1963. *Horace on Poetry: Prolegomena to the Literary Epistles*. Cambridge.

Brinker, C. 1884. *De Theocriti vita carminibusque subditiciis*. Rostock.

Brioso Sánchez, M. 1974. "Nicandro y los esquemas del hexámetro." *Habis* 5: 9–23.

Brioso Sánchez, M. 1994. "La épica didáctica helenístico-imperial." In López Férez 1994: 253–82.

Brittain, C. 2006. *Cicero: On Academic Scepticism.* Indianapolis.

Broggiato, M. 2001. *Cratete di Mallo, I frammenti.* La Spezia.

Brown, M. K. 2002. *The Narratives of Konon.* Munich and Leipzig.

Brown, P. G. McC. 1983. "Menander's Dramatic Technique and the Law of Athens." *Classical Quarterly* 33: 412–20.

Brown, T. S. 1967. "Alexander's Book Order." *Historia* 16: 359–68.

Brugnoli, G. 1963. *C. Suetoni Tranquilli praeter Caesarum libros reliquiae.* Vol. 1. Leipzig.

Brunner-Traut, E. 1968. *Altägyptische Tiergeschichte und Fabel: Gestalt und Strahlkraft.* Darmstadt.

Brunt, P. A. 1980. "On Historical Fragments and Epitomes." *Classical Quarterly* 30: 477–94.

Bruss, J. S. 2002. "An Emendation in Callimachus Ep. 9 GP (= 44 Pf. = *AP* 12.139)." *Mnemosyne* 55: 728–31.

Bruss, J. S. 2002/3. "A Program Poem of Alcaeus of Messene: Epigram 16 GP (= *AP* 7.429)." *Classical Journal* 98: 161–80.

Bruss, J. S. 2005. *Hidden Presences: Monuments, Gravesites and Corpses in Greek Funerary Epigram.* Leuven.

Bryce, T. 1986. *The Lycians.* Vol. 1: *The Lycians in Literary and Epigraphic Sources.* Copenhagen.

Bugh, G. R. 2006 (ed.). *The Cambridge Companion to the Hellenistic World.* Cambridge.

Bühler, W. 1960. *Die Europa des Moschos.* Wiesbaden.

Buitenwerf, R. 2003. *Book III of the Sibylline Oracles and its Social Setting.* Leiden.

Bulloch, A. W. 1985. *Callimachus, The Fifth Hymn.* Cambridge.

Bulloch, A. W. 1989. "Hellenistic Poetry." In Easterling and Knox 1989: 4.1–81.

Bulloch, A. W. 2006. "Jason's Cloak." *Hermes* 134: 44–68.

Bulloch, A. W., Gruen, E. S., Long, A. A. and Stewart, A. 1993 (eds.). *Images and Ideologies: Self-Definition in the Hellenistic World.* Berkeley.

Burckhardt, L. 2004. "Die attische Ephebie in hellenistischer Zeit." In Kah and Scholz 2004: 193–206.

Burkard, G. and Magen, B. 2004 (eds.). *Kon-Texte: Akten des Symposions "Spurensuche: Altägypten im Spiegel seiner Texte."* Wiesbaden.

Burke, P. 1992. *History and Social Theory.* Cambridge.

Burkert, W. 1979. "Kynaithos, Polykrates, and the *Homeric Hymn to Apollo*." In Bowersock, Burkert, and Putnam 1979: 53–62.

Burstein, S. M. 1985. *The Hellenistic Age from the Battle of Ipsos to the Death of Kleopatra VII.* Cambridge.

Burstein, S. M. 1989. *Agatharchides of Cnidus, On the Erythraean Sea.* London.

Burton, H. 1945. "Euclid, *Optics*." *Journal of the Optical Society of America* 35: 357–72.

Busch, S. 1993. "Orpheus bei Apollonios Rhodios." *Hermes* 121: 301–24.

Buxton, R. 1999 (ed.). *From Myth to Reason? Studies in the Development of Greek Thought.* Oxford.

Byre, C. S. 2002. *A Reading of Apollonius Rhodius' Argonautica: The Poetics of Uncertainty.* Lewiston.

Cairns, F. 1979. *Tibullus: A Hellenistic Poet at Rome.* Cambridge.

Cairns, F. and Heath, M. 1998 (eds.). *Papers of the International Leeds Latin Seminar*, 10: *Greek Poetry, Drama, Prose, Roman Poetry.* Leeds.

Cambiano G., Canfora L. and Lanza, D. 1993 (eds.). *Lo spazio letterario della Grecia antica.* Vol. I/2. Rome.

Cameron, A. 1992. "Genre and Style in Callimachus." *Transactions of the American Philological Association* 122: 305–12.

Cameron, A. 1993. *The Greek Anthology from Meleager to Planudes.* Oxford.

Cameron, A. 1995a. *Callimachus and His Critics*. Princeton.

Cameron, A. 1995b. "Avienus or Avienius?" *Zeitschrift für Papyrologie und Epigraphik* 108: 252–62.

Campbell, D. and Delf, B. 2003a. *Greek and Roman Artillery 399 BC–AD 363*. Oxford.

Campbell, D. and Delf, B. 2003b. *Greek and Roman Siege Machinery 399 BC–AD 363*. Oxford.

Campbell, M. 1991. *Moschus, Europa*. Hildesheim.

Campbell, M. 1994. *A Commentary on Apollonius Rhodius, Argonautica III 1–471*. Leiden.

Capasso, M. 1992. *Papiri letterari greci e latini*. Galatina.

Carey, C. 1995. "Pindar and the Victory Ode." In Ayres 1995: 83–103.

Carey, C. 2004. "Offence and Procedure in Athenian Law." In Harris and Rubinstein 2004: 111–36.

Carspecken, J. F. 1952. "Apollonius and the Homeric Epic." *Yale Classical Studies* 13: 33–143.

Cartledge, P., Garnsey, P. and Gruen, E. S. 1997 (eds.). *Hellenistic Constructs: Essays in Culture, History and Historiography*. Berkeley.

Cary, E. 1943. *Dionysius of Halicarnassus, The Roman Antiquities*. Cambridge, MA.

Caspers, C. L. 2006. "The Loves of the Poets: Allusions in Hermesianax fr. 7 Powell." In Harder, Regtuit, and Wakker 2006: 21–42.

Cazzaniga, I. 1960. "Colori nicandrei in Virgilio." *Studi italiani di filologia classica* 32: 18–37. Reprinted in Gioseffi 2000: 51–72.

Cazzaniga, I. 1972. "L'inno di Nicandro ad Attalo I (fr. 104): esegesi e problematica." *La Parola del Passato* 27: 369–96.

Cazzaniga, I. 1973. "Gli *Aetolika* di Nicandro: esegesi dei frammenti." *Annali della Scuola Normale Superiore di Pisa* 3: 357–80.

Cazzaniga, I. 1975. "Per Nicandro Colofonio la *Titanomachia* fu opera autentica di Esiodo." *Rendiconti del'Istituto Lombardo* 109: 173–80.

Cazzaniga, I. 1976. "Note nicandree." *Studi classici e orientali* 25: 317–24.

Celentano, M. S. 2003 (ed.). *Ars–Techne: il manuale tecnico nelle civiltà greca e romana*. Alessandria.

Champion, C. B. 1997. "The Nature of Authoritative Evidence in Polybius and Agelaus' Speech at Naupactus." *Transactions of the American Philological Association* 127: 111–28.

Champion, C. B. 2004. *Cultural Politics in Polybius' Histories*. Berkeley.

Chandler, C. 2006. *Philodemus "On Rhetoric" Books 1 and 2: Translation and Exegetical Essays*. New York.

Chaniotis, A. 2003. "The Divinity of Hellenistic Rulers." In Erskine 2003: 431–46.

Chaniotis, A. 2004. *War in the Hellenistic World: A Social and Cultural History*. Oxford.

Charlesworth, J. H. 1983, 1985. *The Old Testament Pseudepigrapha*. 2 vols. London.

Chavis, D. and Cazotte, M. 1792. *Arabian Tales, Being a Continuation of the Arabian Nights Entertainment*, trans. R. Heron. Edinburgh and London. Original French edition 1788–90. Cited after the 2nd edition of 1794.

Chesnutt, R. D. 1995. *From Death to Life: Conversion in Joseph and Aseneth*. Sheffield.

Chiron, P. 1993. *Demetrios, Du Style*. Paris.

Christ, M. 1998. *The Litigious Athenian*. Baltimore.

Christ, W. von, Schmid, W. and Stählin, O. 1911, 1920. *Geschichte der griechischen Literatur*, Teil 2: *Die nachklassische Periode*, 1. Hälfte: *Von 320 v.Chr. bis 100 n.Chr.* Vol. 2.1. 5th and 6th editions. Munich.

Cipolla, P. 2003. *Poeti minori del dramma satiresco*. Amsterdam.

Clare, R. J. 2002. *The Path of the Argo: Language, Imagery and Narrative in the Argonautica of Apollonius Rhodius.* Cambridge.

Clarke, K. 1999. *Between Geography and History: Hellenistic Constructions of the Roman World.* Oxford.

Clarke, K. 2008. *Making Time for the Past: Local History and the Polis.* Oxford.

Clarke, M. 1996. *Rhetoric at Rome.* London.

Clarysse, W. 1985. "Greeks and Egyptians in the Ptolemaic Army and Administration." *Aegyptus* 65: 57–66.

Clarysse, W. 1991. "Ptolemaeïsch Egypte: een maatschappij met twee gezichten." *Handelingen van de Koninklijke Zuidnederlandse Maatschappij voor Taal- en Letterkunde en Geschiedenis* 45: 21–38.

Clarysse, W. and Thompson, D. J. 2006. *Counting the People in Hellenistic Egypt.* 2 vols. Cambridge.

Clauss, J. J. 1986. "Lies and Allusions: The Addressee and Date of Callimachus' *Hymn to Zeus.*" *Classical Antiquity* 5: 155–70.

Clauss, J. J. 1989. "The Episode of the Lycian Farmers in Ovid's *Metamorphoses.*" *Harvard Studies in Classical Philology* 92: 297–314.

Clauss, J. J. 1993. *The Best of the Argonauts: The Redefinition of the Epic Hero in Book One of Apollonius' Argonautica.* Berkeley.

Clauss, J. J. 1995. "A Delicate Foot on the Well-worn Threshold: Paradoxical Imagery in Catullus 68b." *American Journal of Philology* 116: 237–53.

Clauss, J. J. 1997. "Conquest of the Mephistophelian Nausicaa: Medea's Role in Apollonius' Redefinition of the Epic Hero." In Clauss and Johnston 1997: 149–77.

Clauss, J. J. 2000. "Cosmos without Imperium: The Argonautic Journey through Time." In Harder, Regtuit, and Wakker 2000: 11–32.

Clauss, J. J. 2004. "Vergil's Sixth *Eclogue*: The *Aetia* in Rome." In Harder, Regtuit, and Wakker 2004: 71–93.

Clauss, J. J. 2006. "*Theriaca*: Nicander's Poem of the Earth." *Studi italiani di filologia classica* n.s. 4: 160–82.

Clauss, J. J. and Johnston, S. I. 1997 (eds.). *Medea: Essays on Medea in Myth, Literature, Philosophy, and Art.* Princeton.

Clay, D. 1998. *Paradosis and Survival: Three Chapters in the History of Epicurean Philosophy.* Ann Arbor.

Clay, D. 2004. *Archilochus Heros: The Cult of Poets in the Greek Polis.* Washington, DC.

Clayman, D. 2007. "Philosophers and Philosophy in Greek Epigram." In Bing and Bruss 2007: 497–517.

Clements, W. 2004. "At Arlington." *First Things* 145: 45.

Clère, J. J. 1951. "Une statuette du fils aîné du roi Nectanabô." *Revue d'Égyptologie* 6: 135–55.

Cohen, D. 1995. *Law, Violence, and Community in Classical Athens.* Cambridge.

Collins, D. 2004. *Master of the Game: Competition and Performance in Greek Poetry.* Cambridge, MA.

Collins, J. J. 2000. *Between Athens and Jerusalem.* 2nd edition. Grand Rapids.

Collombert, P. 2002. "Le conte de l'hirondelle et de la mer." In Ryholt 2002b: 59–76.

Condello, F. and Esposito, E. 2003. "Eronda, Saba e il monello Còttalo: storia e modi di una riscrittura." *Studi e Problemi di Critica Testuale* 67: 43–69.

Connolly, J. 2007. "The New World Order: Greek Rhetoric in Rome." In Worthington 2007: 139–65.

Connor, W. R. 1985. "Historical Writing in the Fourth Century BC and in the Hellenistic Period." In Easterling and Knox 1985: 458–71, 786–7.

Conrad, L., Neve, M., Nutton, V., Porter, R. and Wear, A. 1995. *The Western Medical Tradition*. Cambridge.
Conte, G. B. 1985. *Memoria dei poeti e sistema letterario*. Turin.
Conte, G. B. 1986. *The Rhetoric of Imitation: Genre and Poetic Memory in Virgil and Other Latin Poets*. Ithaca, NY.
Conte, G. B. 1994. *Latin Literature: A History*. Baltimore.
Couat, A. 1882. *La poésie alexandrine sous les trois premiers Ptolemées (324–222 av. J.C.)*. Paris.
Couat, A. 1931. *Alexandrian Poetry under the First Three Ptolemies, 324–222 BC*, with a supplementary chapter by E. Cahen. London.
Cozzoli, A.-T. 1994. "Dalla catarsi mimetica aristotelica all'auto-catarsi dei poeti ellenistici." *Quaderni urbinati di cultura classica* 48: 95–110.
Cozzoli, A.-T. 2003. "Sositeo e il nuovo dramma satiresco." In Martina 2003: 265–91.
Crevatin, F. and Tedeschi, G. 2005 (eds.). *Scrivere leggere interpretare: studi di antichità in onore di S. Daris*. At http://140.105.59.2/crevatin/Daris.htm.
Cribiore, R. 1994. "A Homeric Writing Exercise and Reading Homer in School." *Tyche* 9: 1–8.
Cribiore, R. 1996. *Writing, Teachers, and Students in Graeco-Roman Egypt*. Atlanta.
Cribiore, R. 1997. "Literary School Exercises." *Zeitschrift für Papyrologie und Epigraphik* 116: 53–60 and 117: 162.
Cribiore, R. 2001a. *Gymnastics of the Mind: Greek Education in Hellenistic and Roman Egypt*. Princeton.
Cribiore, R. 2001b. "The Grammarian's Choice: The Popularity of Euripides' *Phoenissae* in Hellenistic and Roman Education." In Too 2001: 243–59.
Cristante, L. 2006 (ed.). *Incontri triestini di filologia classica* 5. Trieste.
Crugnola, A. 1961. "La lingua poetica di Nicandro." *Acme* 14: 119–52.
Crugnola, A. 1971. *Scholia in Nicandri Theriaca cum glossis*. Milan.
Crump, M. M. 1931. *The Epyllion from Theocritus to Ovid*. Oxford.
Crusius, O. 1904. "Studien zu neueren Papyrusfunden." *Sitzungsberichte der Berliner Akademie der Wissenschaften*: 357–8.
Csapo, E. 2004. "The Politics of the New Music." In Murray and Wilson 2004: 207–48.
Cunningham, I. C. 1971. *Herodas, Mimiambi: Edited with Introduction, Commentary, and Appendices*. Oxford.
Cunningham, I. C. 1987. *Herodae Mimiambi, cum appendice fragmentorum mimorum papyraceorum*. Leipzig. Reprinted with *addenda et corrigenda* Munich and Leipzig 2004.
Cunningham, I. C. 2002. *Herodas, Mimes; Sophron and Other Mime Fragments*. In Rusten and Cunningham 2002.
Cuomo, S. 2001. *Ancient Mathematics*. London.
Cuomo, S. 2007. *Technology and Culture in Greek and Roman Antiquity*. Cambridge.
Currie, G. 1990. *The Nature of Fiction*. Cambridge.
Cusset, C. 1995. "Exercises rhétoriques d'Aratos autour du terme ΗΧΗ." *Revue de philologie* 69: 245–8.
Cusset, C. 1999. *La Muse dans la bibliothèque: réécriture et intertextualité dans la poésie alexandrine*. Paris.
Cusset, C. 2001. "Le bestiaire de Lycophron: entre chien et loup." *Anthropozoologica* 33/4: 61–72.
Cusset, C. 2003a. "Tragic Elements in Lycophron's *Alexandra*." *Hermathena* 173/4: 137–53.
Cusset, C. 2003b (ed.). *La météorologie dans l'Antiquité: entre science et croyance*. Saint-Étienne.

Cusset, C. 2006a. "Les images dans la poésie scientifique alexandrine: les *Phénomènes* d'Aratos et les *Thériaques* de Nicandre." In Cusset 2006b: 49–104.

Cusset, C. 2006b (ed.). *Musa docta: recherches sur la poésie scientifique dans l'Antiquité.* Saint-Étienne.

Cusset, C. 2006c. "Dit et non-dit dans l'*Alexandra* de Lycophron." In Harder, Regtuit, and Wakker 2006: 43–60.

Cusset, C. and Frangoulis, H. 2008 (eds.). *Eratosthène: un athlète du savoir.* Saint-Étienne.

Cuypers, M. 1997. "Apollonius Rhodius, *Argonautica* 2.1–310: A Commentary." Diss. Leiden.

Cuypers, M. 2004a. "Apollonius of Rhodes." In De Jong, Nünlist, and Bowie 2004: 43–62.

Cuypers, M. 2004b. "Prince and Principle: The Philosophy of Callimachus' *Hymn to Zeus.*" In Harder, Regtuit, and Wakker 2004: 95–115.

Cuypers, M. 2005. "Interactional Particles and Narrative Voice in Apollonius and Homer." In Harder and Cuypers 2005: 35–69.

D'Alessio, G. B. 1995. "Sull'epigramma dal Polyandrion di Ambracia." *Zeitschrift für Papyrologie und Epigraphik* 106: 22–6.

D'Alessio, G. B. 1997. "Pindar's *Prosodia* and the Classification of Pindaric Papyrus Fragments." *Zeitschrift für Papyrologie und Epigraphik* 118: 23–60.

D'Alessio, G. B. 2007. *Callimaco.* 4th edition. 2 vols. Milan.

D'Alessio, G. B. and Ferrari, F. 1988. "Pindaro, *Peana* 6, 175–183: una ricostruzione." *Studi classici e orientali* 38: 159–80.

Dalley, S. 2005. "Semiramis in History and Legend: A Case Study in Interpretation of an Assyrian Historical Tradition." In Gruen 2005: 11–22.

Daniel, R. W. 1996. "Epicharmus in Trier: A Note on the Monnus Mosaic." *Zeitschrift für Papyrologie und Epigraphik* 114: 30–6.

Davies, M. 1987. "The Ancient Greeks on Why Mankind Does Not Live Forever." *Museum Helveticum* 44: 65–75.

Dawson, D. 1992a. *Allegorical Readers and Cultural Revision in Ancient Alexandria.* Berkeley.

Dawson, D. 1992b. *Cities of the Gods: Communist Utopias in Ancient Thought.* New York and Oxford.

Day, J. W. 1989. "Rituals in Stone: Early Greek Grave Epigrams and Monuments." *Journal of Hellenic Studies* 111: 16–28.

Day, J. W. 2007. "Poems on Stone: The Inscribed Antecedents of Hellenistic Epigram." In Bing and Bruss 2007: 29–48.

De Bruijn, J. T. P., Idema, W. L. and Van Oostrom, F. P. 1986 (eds.). *Dichter en hof: verkenningen in veertien culturen.* Utrecht.

de Grummond, N. and Ridgway, B. 2000 (eds.). *From Pergamon to Sperlonga.* Berkeley.

De Jong, I. J. F. and Sullivan, J. P. 1994 (eds.). *Modern Critical Theory and Classical Literature.* Leiden.

De Jong, I. J. F., Nünlist, R. and Bowie, A. 2004 (eds.). *Narrators, Narratees, and Narratives in Ancient Greek Literature.* Leiden.

De Jonge, C. C. 2005. "Dionysius of Halicarnassus and the Method of Metathesis." *Classical Quarterly* 55: 463–80.

De Jonge, C. C. 2008. *Between Grammar and Rhetoric: Dionysius of Halicarnassus on Language, Linguistics and Literature.* Leiden.

De Lacy, P. 1978. *Galen, On the Doctrines of Hippocrates and Plato.* Berlin.

De Martino, F. 1982. "Nicandro e la 'questione omerica' dell'*Inno ad Apollo.*" *Atene e Roma* 27: 46–50.

De Stefani, C. 2002. "Fenice di Colofone fr. 2 Diehl: introduzione, testo critico, commento." *Studi classici e orientali* 47: 81–121.

De Stefani, C. 2006a. "I *Theriaca* nicandrei di Jean-Marie Jacques." *Rivista di filologia e di istruzione classica* 134: 100–25.

De Stefani, C. 2006b. "La poesia didascalica di Nicandro: un modello prosastico?" In Cristante 2006: 55–72.

Deacy, S. and Pierce, K. 1997 (eds.). *Rape in Antiquity.* London.

DeForest, M. M. 1994. *Apollonius' Argonautica: A Callimachean Epic.* Leiden.

Degani, E. 1982. *Poesia parodica greca.* Bologna.

Degani, E. 1984. *Studi su Ipponatte.* Bari.

Degani, E. 1991. *Hipponax, testimonia et fragmenta.* 2nd edition. Stuttgart and Leipzig.

Degani, E. 1995. "Ipponatte e i poeti filologi." *Aevum antiquum* 8: 105–36.

Deichgräber, K. 1965. *Die griechische Empirikerschule: Sammlung der Fragmente und Darstellung der Lehre.* 2nd edition. Berlin.

Del Corno, D. 1962. "Ricerche intorno alla *Lyde* di Antimaco." *Acme* 15: 57–95

Del Monte, G. F. 1997. *Testi dalla Babilonia ellenistica.* Vol. 1. Pisa and Rome.

Del Ponte, A. 1981. "Lycophronis *Alexandra*: la versificazione ed il mezzo espressivo." *Studi italiani di filologia classica* 53: 101–33.

Delattre, D. 2006. *La Villa des Papyrus et les rouleaux d'Herculanum.* Liège.

Delattre, D. 2007. *Philodème de Gadara, Sur la musique, Livre IV.* 2 vols. Paris.

Delev, P. 2000. "Lysimachus, the Getae and Archaeology." *Classical Quarterly* 50: 384–401.

Delia, D. 1996, "All Army Boots and Uniforms? Ethnicity in Ptolemaic Egypt." In *Alexandria and Alexandrianism* 1996: 41–52.

Delorme, J. 1960. *Gymnasion: étude sur les monuments consacrés à l'éducation en Grèce.* Paris.

Dench, E. 2007. "Ethnography and History." In Marincola 2007: 493–503.

Depauw M. 1997. *A Companion to Demotic Studies.* Brussels.

Depauw, M. and Smith, M. 2004. "Visions of Ecstasy: Cultic Revelry before the Goddess Ai/Nehemanit; Ostraca Faculteit Letteren (K.U. Leuven) dem. 1–2." In Hoffmann and Thissen 2004: 67–93.

Depew, M. 2000. "Enacted and Represented Dedications: Genre and Greek Hymn." In Depew and Obbink 2000: 59–79, 254–63.

Depew, M. 2004. "Gender, Power, and Poetics in Callimachus' Book of Hymns." In Harder, Regtuit, and Wakker 2004: 117–37.

Depew, M. and Obbink, D. 2000 (eds.). *Matrices of Genre: Authors, Canons, and Society.* Cambridge, MA.

Derchain, P. 2000. *Les impondérables de l'hellénisation: littérature d'hiérogrammates.* Brussels.

Deroux, C. 1992 (ed.). *Studies in Latin Literature and Roman History* 6. Brussels.

Derow, P. 1979. "Polybius, Rome and the East." *Journal of Roman Studies* 69: 1–15.

Derow, P. 1989. "Rome, the Fall of Macedon, and the Sack of Corinth." *The Cambridge Ancient History* (2nd edition) 8: 290–323.

Derow, P. 2003. "The Arrival of Rome." In Erskine 2003: 51–70.

Detienne, M. 1996. *The Masters of Truth in Archaic Greece.* New York.

Di Benedetto, V. 1956. "Omerismi e struttura metrica negli idilli dorici di Teocrito." *Annali della Scuola Normale Superiore di Pisa* 25: 48–60.

Di Gregorio, L. 1995. "La figura di Metriche nel primo mimiambo di Eronda." In Belloni, Milanese, and Porro 1995: 675–94.

Di Gregorio, L. 1997, 2004. *Eronda, Mimiambi.* 2 vols. Milan.

Di Marco, M. 1989. *Timone di Fliunte, Silli.* Rome.

Dickens, A. G. 1977 (ed.). *The Courts of the Italian Renaissance: Politics, Patronage, and Royalty, 1400–1800*. London.

Dicks, D. R. 1960. *The Geographical Fragments of Hipparchus*. London.

Dieleman, J. 1998. "Fear of Women? Representations of Women in Demotic Wisdom Texts." *Studien zur altägyptischen Kultur* 25: 7–46.

Dieleman, J. 2005. *Priests, Tongues, and Rites: The London–Leiden Magical Manuscripts and Translation in Egyptian Ritual (100–300 CE)*. Leiden.

Diels, H. 1879. *Doxographi Graeci*. Berlin.

Dieter, O. 1950. "*Stasis*." *Speech Monographs* 17: 345–69.

Dihle, A. 1961. "Zur hellenistischen Ethnographie." In Reverdin 1961: 205–39.

Dihle, A. 1968 (ed.). *L'Épigramme grecque*. Geneva.

Dihle, A. 1991. *Griechische Literaturgeschichte: von Homer bis zum Hellenismus*. Munich.

Dihle, A. 1994. *A History of Greek Literature: From Homer to the Hellenistic Period*, trans. C. Krojzl. London and New York.

Dijksterhuis, E. J. 1987. *Archimedes*. Princeton.

Dilke, O. A. W. 1985. *Greek and Roman Maps*. London.

Dillery, J. 1999. "The First Egyptian Narrative History: Manetho and Greek Historiography." *Zeitschrift für Papyrologie und Epigraphik* 127: 93–116.

Dillery, J. 2007. "Greek Historians of the Near East: Clio's 'Other' Sons." In Marincola 2007: 221–30.

Dillon, J. M. 1997. "Medea among the Philosophers." In Clauss and Johnston 1997: 211–18.

Doležel, L. 1998. *Heterocosmica*. Baltimore.

Dominik, W. J. 1997 (ed.). *Roman Eloquence*. London.

Dominik, W. J. and Hall, J. 2007 (eds.). *A Companion to Roman Rhetoric*. Malden.

Doran, R. 1987. "The Jewish Hellenistic Historians before Josephus." *ANRW* II.20.1: 246–97.

Dorandi, T. 1991. *Filodemo, Storia dei filosofi: Platone e l'Academia (PHerc. 1021 e 164)*. Naples.

Dorandi, T. 1994. *Filodemo, Storia dei filosofi: la Stoà da Zenone a Panezio (PHerc. 1018)*. Leiden.

Dorandi, T. 1999. *Antigone de Caryste*. Paris.

Dougherty, C. 1994. "Archaic Greek Foundation Poetry: Questions of Genre and Occasion." *Journal of Hellenic Studies* 114: 35–46.

Dousa, T. 2002. "Imagining Isis: On Some Continuities and Discontinuities in the Image of Isis in Greek Isis Hymns and Demotic Texts." In Ryholt 2002b: 149–84.

Dover, K. J. 1971. *Theocritus, Select Poems*. London.

Dover, K. J. 1974. *Greek Popular Morality in the Time of Plato and Aristotle*. Oxford.

Dover, K. J. 1993. *Aristophanes, Frogs*. Oxford.

Drachmann, A. B. 1903–27. *Scholia vetera in Pindari carmina*. 3 vols. Leipzig.

Drachmann, A. G. 1963. *The Mechanical Technology of Greek and Roman Antiquity*. Copenhagen.

Droysen, J. G. 1833–43. *Geschichte des Hellenismus*. 3 vols. Reprinted Darmstadt 1998.

duBois, P. 2006. "The History of the Impossible: Ancient Utopia." *Classical Philology* 101: 1–14.

Duchemin, J. 1968. *L'Agon dans la tragédie grecque*. Paris.

Duindam, J. 1995. *Myths of Power: Norbert Elias and the Early Modern European Court*. Amsterdam.

Duindam, J. 2003. *Vienna and Versailles: The Courts of Europe's Dynastic Rivals*. Cambridge.

Duindam, J., Kunt, M. and Artan, T. forthcoming (eds.). *Royal Courts in Dynastic States and Empires: A Global Perspective*. Leiden.

Durbec, Y. 2006. "Lycophron et la poétique de Callimaque: le prologue de l'*Alexandra*, 1–15." *Appunti romani di filologia* 8: 81–3.

Dyck, A. R. 1989. "On the Way from Colchis to Corinth: Medea in Book 4 of the *Argonautica*." *Hermes* 117: 455–70.

Eamon, W. 1991. "Court, Academy, and Printing House: Patronage and Scientific Careers in Late Renaissance Italy." In Moran 1991b: 125–50.

Earp, F. R. 1936 (ed.). *Essays in Honour of Gilbert Murray: Greek Poetry and Life*. Cambridge.

Easterling, P. E. and Hall, E. 2002 (eds.). *Greek and Roman Actors*. Cambridge.

Easterling, P. E. and Knox, B. M. W. 1985, 1989 (eds.). *The Cambridge History of Classical Literature*. Vol. 1: *Greek Literature*. Cambridge. Reprinted in 4 fascicles 1989. Vol. 1.4: *The Hellenistic Period and the Empire*.

Eckstein, A. 2008. *Rome Enters the Greek East*. Oxford.

Edelstein, L. and Kidd, I. G. 1972. *Posidonius I: The Fragments*. Cambridge. Cf. Kidd 1988.

Edmunds, L. 2001. *Intertextuality and the Reading of Roman Poetry.* Baltimore.

Effe, B. 1974a. "Zum Eingang von Nikanders *Theriaka*." *Hermes* 102: 119–21.

Effe, B. 1974b. "Der Aufbau von Nikanders *Theriaka* und *Alexipharmaka*." *Rheinisches Museum für Philologie* 117: 53–66.

Effe, B. 1977a. *Dichtung und Lehre: Untersuchungen zur Typologie des antiken Lehrgedichts*. Munich.

Effe, B. 1977b. *Die Genese einer literarischen Gattung: Die Bukolik*. Konstanz.

Effe, B. 1978. "Die Destruktion der Tradition: Theokrits mythologische Gedichte." *Rheinisches Museum für Philologie* 121: 48–77. Reprinted in Effe 1986: 56–88.

Effe, B. 1980. "Held und Literatur: Der Funktionswandel des Herakles-Mythos in der griechischen Literatur." *Poetica* 12: 145–66.

Effe, B. 1986 (ed.). *Theokrit und die griechische Bukolik*. Darmstadt.

Effe, B. 2001. "The Similes of Apollonius Rhodius: Intertextuality and Epic Convention." In Papanghelis and Rengakos 2001: 147–69.

Elias, N. 1969. *Die höfische Gesellschaft: Untersuchungen zur Soziologie des Königtums und der höfischen Aristokratie*. Neuwied and Berlin.

Elliott, J. M. 2003. "A New Mime Fragment (*P.Col.* inv. 546 A)." *Zeitschrift für Papyrologie und Epigraphik* 145: 60–6.

Enenkel, K. A. E. and Pfeijffer, I. L. 2005 (eds.). *The Manipulative Mode: Political Propaganda in Antiquity.* Leiden.

Engels, J. "Geography and History." In Marincola 2007: 541–52.

Erbse, H. 1953. "Homerscholien und hellenistische Glossare bei Apollonios Rhodios." *Hermes* 81: 163–96.

Erler, M. 1993. "*Philologia medicans*: Wie die Epikureer die Texte ihres Meisters lasen." In Kullmann and Althoff 1993: 281–303.

Erler, M. and Schorn, S. 2007 (eds.). *Die griechische Biographie in hellenistischer Zeit*. Berlin.

Erren, M. 1967. *Die Phainomena des Aratos von Soloi: Untersuchungen zum Sach- und Sinnverständnis*. Wiesbaden.

Errington, R. M. 1990. *A History of Macedonia*. Berkeley.

Erskine, A. 1990. *The Hellenistic Stoa: Political Thought and Action*. London.

Erskine, A. 1995. "Culture and Power in Ptolemaic Egypt: The Museum and Library of Alexandria." *Greece and Rome* 42: 38–48.

Erskine, A. 2001. *Troy between Greece and Rome: Local Tradition and Imperial Power.* Oxford.

Erskine, A. 2002. "Life after Death: Alexandria and the Body of Alexander." *Greece and Rome* 49: 163–79.

Erskine, A. 2003 (ed.). *A Companion to the Hellenistic World*. Malden.

Erskine, A. 2005. "Unity and Identity: Shaping the Past in the Greek Mediterranean." In Gruen 2005: 121–36.

Erskine, A. 2007. "Rhetoric and Persuasion in the Hellenistic World: Speaking up for the *Polis*." In Worthington 2007: 272–85.

Erskine, A. 2009 (ed.). *A Companion to Ancient History.* Malden.

Esposito, E. 2000. "A proposito di una nuova edizione di Eronda." *Eikasmós* 11: 219–34.

Esposito, E. 2001a. "Allusività epica e ispirazione giambica in Herond. 1 e 8." *Eikasmós* 12: 141–59.

Esposito, E. 2001b. Review of Andreassi 2001a. *Eikasmós* 12: 456–61.

Esposito, E. 2004. "Posidippo, Eronda e l'arte tolemaica." *Appunti romani di filologia* 6: 191–202.

Esposito, E. 2005. *Il Fragmentum Grenfellianum (P.Dryton 50)*. Bologna.

Evans, J. 1998. *The History and Practice of Ancient Astronomy.* Oxford.

Eyre, C. J., Leahy, M. A. and Leahy, L. M. 1994 (eds.). *The Unbroken Reed: Studies in the Culture and Heritage of Ancient Egypt in Honour of A. F. Shore.* London.

Fabian, K. 1992. *Callimaco, Aitia II.* Alessandria.

Fabiano, G. 1971. "Fluctuation in Theocritus' Style." *Greek, Roman and Byzantine Studies* 12: 517–37.

Fakas, C. 1999. "Ein unbeachtetes Telestichon bei Arat." *Philologus* 143: 356–9.

Fakas, C. 2001. *Der hellenistische Hesiod: Arats Phainomena und die Tradition der antiken Lehrepik.* Wiesbaden.

Fantuzzi, M. 1979. Review of Mastromarco 1979. *Lingua e Stile* 14: 721–4.

Fantuzzi, M. 1985. *Bionis Smyrnaei Adonidis Epitaphium.* Liverpool.

Fantuzzi, M. 1988. *Ricerche su Apollonio Rodio: diacronie della dizione epica.* Rome.

Fantuzzi, M. 1993. "Il sistema letterario della poesia alessandrina nel III sec. a.C." In Cambiano, Canfora, and Lanza 1993: 31–73.

Fantuzzi, M. 1995. "Mythological Paradigms in the Bucolic Poetry of Theocritus." *Proceedings of the Cambridge Philological Society* 41: 16–35.

Fantuzzi, M. 1998. "Textual Misadventures of Daphnis: The Pseudo-Theocritean *Id.* 8 and the Origins of the Bucolic 'Manner'." In Harder, Regtuit, and Wakker 1998: 61–79.

Fantuzzi, M. 2000. "Theocritus and the Demythologizing of Poetry." In Depew and Obbink 2000: 135–51.

Fantuzzi, M. 2001. "Heroes, Descendants of *hemitheoi*: The Proemium of Theocritus 17 and Simonides 11 W^2." In Boedeker and Sider 2001: 232–41.

Fantuzzi, M. 2005. "Posidippus at Court: The Contribution of the Ἱππικά of *P.Mil.Vogl.* VIII 309 to the Ideology of Ptolemaic Kingship." In Gutzwiller 2005: 249–68.

Fantuzzi, M. and Hunter, R. 2004. *Tradition and Innovation in Hellenistic Poetry.* Cambridge.

Fantuzzi, M. and Papanghelis, T. 2006 (eds.). *Brill's Companion to Greek and Latin Pastoral.* Leiden.

Faraone, C. A. 2005a. "Exhortation and Meditation: Alternating Stanzas as a Structural Device in Early Greek Elegy." *Classical Philology* 100: 317–36.

Faraone, C. A. 2005b. "Catalogues, Priamels, and Stanzaic Structure in Early Greek Elegy." *Transactions of the American Philological Association* 135: 249–65.

Faraone, C. A. 2008. *The Stanzaic Architecture of Early Greek Elegy.* Oxford.

Faubion, J. D. 2001a. "Introduction: Toward an Anthropology of the Ethics of Kinship." In Faubion 2001b: 1–28.

Faubion, J. D. 2001b (ed.). *The Ethics of Kinship: Ethnographic Inquiries.* Lanham.

Feeney, D. C. 1991. *The Gods in Epic: Poets and Critics of the Classical Tradition.* Oxford.

Feeney, D. C. 1993. "Towards an Account of the Ancient World's Concepts of Fictive Belief." In Gill and Wiseman 1993: 230–44.

Feeney, D. C. 2005. "The Beginnings of Literature in Latin." *Journal of Roman Studies* 95: 226–40.

Feeney, D. C. 2007. *Caesar's Calendar: Ancient Time and the Beginnings of History.* Berkeley.

Felber, H. 2002. "Die demotische Chronik." In Blasius and Schipper 2002: 65–111.

Ferguson, J. 1975. *Utopias of the Classical World.* Ithaca, NY.

Fernández, C. N. 2006. "Herondas por Herondas: autoficción en el mimo helenístico." *L'Antiquité classique* 75: 23–40.

Fernández Galiano, M. 1991. "Sobre la fecha de la *Alejandra* de Licofrón." In *Studi di filologia classica in onore di Giusto Monaco.* Palermo: 1.401–13.

Ferrary, J.-L. 1988. *Philhellénisme et impérialisme: aspects idéologiques de la conquête romaine du monde hellénistique.* Rome.

Finkel, I. and Van der Spek, R. J. forthcoming. *Babylonian Chronicles of the Hellenistic Period.* Prepublished at www.livius.org/babylonia.html.

Finkelberg, M. 1998. *The Birth of Literary Fiction in Ancient Greece.* Oxford.

Fitzgerald, J. T., Obbink, D. and Holland, G. 2004 (eds.). *Philodemus and the New Testament World.* Leiden.

Fitzgerald, W. and Gowers, E. 2007 (eds.). *Ennius Perennis: The Annals and Beyond.* Cambridge.

Flemming, R. 2003. "Empires of Knowledge: Medicine and Health in the Hellenistic World." In Erskine 2003: 449–63.

Foley, J. M. 2005 (ed.). *A Companion to Ancient Epic.* Malden.

Ford, A. 2002. *The Origins of Criticism.* Princeton.

Ford, A. 2006. "The Genre of Genres: Paeans and *Paian* in Early Greek Poetry." *Poetica* 38: 277–95.

Formisano, M. 2001. *Tecnica e scrittura: le letterature tecnico-scientifiche nello spazio letterario tardolatino.* Rome.

Fortenbaugh, W. W. 2005. *Theophrastus of Eresus, Sources for His Life, Writings, Thought and Influence: Commentary.* Vol. 8: *Sources on Rhetoric and Poetics (Texts 666–713).* Leiden.

Fortenbaugh, W. W. and Gutas, D. 1992 (eds.). *Theophrastus: His Psychological, Doxographical, and Scientific Writings.* London.

Fortenbaugh, W. W. and Mirhady, D. C. 1993 (eds.). *Peripatetic Rhetoric after Aristotle.* New Brunswick.

Fortenbaugh, W. W. and Pellegrin, P. forthcoming (eds.). *Strato of Lampsacus.* New Brunswick.

Fortenbaugh, W. W. and Schütrumpf, E. 2000 (eds.). *Demetrius of Phalerum.* New Brunswick.

Fortenbaugh, W. W. and White, S. 2004 (eds.). *Lyco of Troas and Hieronymus of Rhodes.* New Brunswick.

Fortenbaugh, W. W. and White, S. 2006 (eds.). *Aristo of Ceos.* New Brunswick.

Fortenbaugh, W. W., Huby, P. and Long, A. A. 1985 (eds.). *Theophrastus of Eresus: On His Life and Work.* New Brunswick.

Fortenbaugh, W. W., Huby, P., Sharples, R. and Gutas, D. 1992 (eds.). *Theophrastus of Eresus: Sources for his Life, Writings, Thought, and Influence.* 2 vols. Leiden.

Fountoulakis, A. 1998. "On the Literary Genre of Lycophron's *Alexandra.*" *Acta Antiqua Academiae Scientiarum Hungaricae* 38: 291–5.

Fountoulakis, A. 2000. "The Artists of Aphrodite." *L'Antiquité classique* 69: 133–47.

Fountoulakis, A. 2002. "Herodas 8.66–79: Generic Self-consciousness and Artistic Claims in Herodas' *Mimiambs.*" *Mnemosyne* 55: 301–19.

Fowden, G. 1986. *The Egyptian Hermes: A Historical Approach to the Late Pagan Mind.* Cambridge.

Fowler, B. H. 1989. *The Hellenistic Aesthetic.* Madison.

Fowler, B. H. 1990. *Hellenistic Poetry: An Anthology.* Madison.

Fox, M. and Livingstone, N. 2007. "Rhetoric and Historiography." In Worthington 2007: 544–61.

Foxhall, L. and Salmon, J. (eds.). *Thinking Men: Masculinity and its Self-Representation in the Classical Tradition*. London.

Fränkel, H. 1961. *Apollonii Rhodii Argonautica*. Oxford.

Fränkel, H. 1968. *Noten zu den Argonautika des Apollonios Rhodios*. Munich.

Fraser, P. M. 1972. *Ptolemaic Alexandria*. 3 vols. Oxford.

Fraser, P. M. 1979. "Lycophron on Cyprus." *Report of the Department of Antiquities, Cyprus*: 328–43.

Fraser, P. M. 1996. *Cities of Alexander the Great*. Oxford.

Frede, D. and Inwood, B. 2005 (eds.). *Language and Learning: Philosophy of Language in the Hellenistic Age*. Oxford.

Fredershausen, O. 1912. "Weitere Studien über das Recht bei Plautus und Terenz." *Hermes* 47: 199–249.

French, R. 1994. *Ancient Natural History*. London and New York.

Fried, M. N. 2002. *Apollonius of Perga, Conics, Book IV*. Santa Fe.

Friedländer, P. and Hoffleit, H. B. 1948. *Epigrammata: Greek Inscriptions in Verse from the Beginnings to the Persian Wars*. Berkeley.

Fromentin, V. 1998. *Denys d'Halicarnasse, Antiquités Romaines*. Vol. 1. Paris.

Fryer, E. F. 1993. "Greek Literary Mime." Diss. Indiana University.

Fuhrer, T. 1992. *Die Auseinandersetzung mit den Chorlyrikern in den Epinikien des Kallimachos*. Basel.

Funghi, M. S. 1996 (ed.). *Ὁδοὶ διζήcιοc, Le vie della ricerca: studi in onore di Francesco Adorno*. Florence.

Furley, W. D. 1993. "Types of Greek Hymns." *Eos* 81: 21–41.

Furley, W. D. 1994. "Apollo Humbled: Phoenix of Kolophon's *Koronisma* in its Hellenistic Literary Setting." *Materiali e discussioni* 33: 9–31.

Furley, W. D. and Bremer, J. M. 2001. *Greek Hymns: Selected Cult Songs from the Archaic to the Hellenistic Period*. 2 vols. Tübingen.

Fusillo, M. 1984. "L'*Alessandra* di Licofrone: racconto epico e discorso drammatico." *Annali della Scuola Normale Superiore di Pisa* 14: 495–525.

Fusillo, M. 1985. *Il tempo delle Argonautiche*. Rome.

Fusillo, M. 1989. *Il romanzo greco: polifonia ed eros*. Venice.

Fusillo, M. 2001. "Apollonius Rhodius as 'Inventor' of the Interior Monologue." In Papanghelis and Rengakos 2001: 127–46.

Fusillo, M., Hurst, A. and Paduano, G. 1991. *Licofrone, Alessandra*. Milan.

Gabathuler, M. 1937. *Hellenistische Epigramme auf Dichter*. St. Gallen.

Gabba, E. 1991. *Dionysius and the History of Archaic Rome*. Berkeley.

Gagarin, M. and Cohen, D. 2005 (eds.). *The Cambridge Companion to Ancient Greek Law*. Cambridge.

Gain, D. B. 1976. *The Aratus Ascribed to Germanicus Caesar*. London.

Galán Vioque, G. 2001. *Dioscórides, Epigramas*. Huelva.

Gale, M. R. 2004 (ed.). *Latin Epic and Didactic Poetry*. Swansea.

Galinsky, G. K. 1972. *The Herakles Theme: The Adaptations of the Hero in Literature from Homer to the Twentieth Century*. Oxford.

Galinsky, K. 1996. *Augustan Culture*. Princeton.

Gardini, F. 1986. "The Sacred Circle of Mantua." In Bertelli, Cardini, and Garbero Zorzi 1986: 77–126.

Garlan, Y. 1974. *Recherches de poliorcétique grecque*. Paris.

Garofalo, I. 1988. *Erasistrati fragmenta*. Pisa.

Garrison, D. 1978. *Mild Frenzy: A Reading of Hellenistic Love Epigram*. Wiesbaden.

Gärtner, H. 1984 (ed.). *Beiträge zum griechischen Liebesroman*. Hildesheim.

Gauger, J.-D. 2002. "Der 'Traum des Nektanebos' – Die griechische Fassung." In Blasius and Schipper 2002: 189–219.

Gauthier, P. 1985. *Les cités grecques et leurs bienfaiteurs (IVe–Ier siècle avant J.-C.): contribution à l'histoire des institutions*. Paris.

Gauthier, P. 1993. "Les cités hellénistiques." In Hansen 1993: 211–31.

Gauthier, P. 1995. "Notes sur le rôle du gymnase dans les cités hellénistiques." In Wörrle and Zanker 1995: 1–11.

Gee, E. 2000. *Ovid, Aratus and Augustus: Astronomy in Ovid's Fasti*. Cambridge.

Gee, E. 2001. "Cicero's Astronomy." *Classical Quarterly* 51: 520–36.

Gehrke, H.-J. 1982. "Der siegreiche König: Überlegungen zur hellenistischen Monarchie." *Archiv für Kulturgeschichte* 64: 247–77.

Geller, M. J. 1995. "The Influence of Ancient Mesopotamia on Hellenistic Judaism." In Sasson 1995: 43–54.

Geller, M. J. 1997. "The Last Wedge." *Zeitschrift für Assyriologie* 87: 43–95.

Geller, M. J., Greenfield, J. C. and Weitzman, M. P. 1995 (eds.). *Studia Aramaica*. Oxford.

Gelzer, T. 1982. "Kallimachos und das Zeremoniell des ptolemäischen Königshauses." In Stagl 1982: 13–30.

Gengler, O. 2003. "Héritage épique et lyrique dans la poésie alexandrine: les Dioscures et les Apharétides d'Homère à Lycophron." In Guglielmo and Bona 2003: 135–47.

Gentili, B. 1968. "Epigramma ed elegia." In Dihle 1968: 39–81.

Gentili, B. and Prato, C. 2002. *Poetae elegiaci, testimonia et fragmenta*. Part II. 2nd edition. Munich.

Gentili, B. and Pretagostini, R. 1988 (eds.). *La musica in Grecia*. Rome and Bari.

George, A. R. 2003. *The Babylonian Gilgamesh Epic*. Oxford.

Gerber, D. E. 1997 (ed.). *A Companion to the Greek Lyric Poets*. Leiden.

Gerber, D. E. 1999. *Greek Elegiac Poetry*. Cambridge, MA.

Gerhard, G. A. 1909. *Phoinix von Kolophon: Texte und Untersuchungen*. Leipzig and Berlin.

Gernet, L. 1921. "Sur l'epiclérat." *Revue des études grecques* 34: 337–79.

Gerstinger, H. 1956 (ed.). *Akten des VIII. internationalen Kongress für Papyrologie*. Vienna.

Geus, K. 2000. "'Hermes' und 'Hermeneia': Dichtung und Grammatik bei Philitas von Kos." *Würzburger Jahrbücher für die Altertumswissenschaft* 24: 65–78.

Geus, K. 2002. *Eratosthenes von Kyrene: Studien zur hellenistischen Kultur- und Wissenschaftsgeschichte*. Munich.

Geus, K. 2003. "Space and Geography." In Erskine 2003: 232–46.

Geymonat, M. 1974. *Scholia in Nicandri Alexipharmaca cum glossis*. Milan.

Geymonat, M. 1976. *Eutecnii paraphrasis in Nicandri Alexipharmaca*. Milan.

Ghiron-Bistagne, P. 1976. *Recherches sur les acteurs dans la Grèce antique*. Paris.

Giangrande, G. 1962. "On the Origins of the Greek Romance: The Birth of a Literary Form." *Eranos* 60: 132–59. Reprinted in Gärtner 1984: 125–52.

Giangrande, G. 1968. "Sympotic Literature and Epigram." In Dihle 1968: 93–174.

Giannantoni, G. and Vegetti, M. 1985 (eds.). *La scienza ellenistica: atti delle tre giornate di studio tenutesi a Pavia dal 14 al 16 aprile 1982*. Naples.

Gianotti, G. F. 1996. "Forme di consumo teatrale: mimo e spettacoli affini." In Pecere and Stramaglia 1996: 265–92.

Gianotti, G. F. 2005. "Odisseo mendico a Troia (*P.Köln VI 245*)." In Crevatin and Tedeschi 2005: 8 pp.

Gigante Lanzara, V. 1995. "I vaticini di Cassandra e l'interpretazione trasgressiva del mito." *Studi classici e orientali* 45: 85–98.

Gigante Lanzara, V. 1997. "Il νόcτοc di Odisseo e la prospezione della memoria." *Maia* 49: 43–68.

Gigante Lanzara, V. 1998. "Il tempo dell'*Alessandra* e i modelli ellenistici di Licofrone." *La parola del passato* 53: 401–18.

Gigante Lanzara, V. 2000. *Licofrone, Alessandra*. Milan.

Gill, C. 1983. "Did Chrysippus Understand Medea?" *Phronesis* 28: 136–49.

Gill, C. 1993. "Plato on Falsehood – Not Fiction." In Gill and Wiseman 1993: 38–87.

Gill, C. 1996. *Personality in Greek Epic, Tragedy, and Philosophy*. Oxford.

Gill, C. and Wiseman, T. P. 1993 (eds.). *Lies and Fiction in the Ancient World*. Exeter.

Gill, M. L. and Pellegrin, P. 2006 (eds.). *A Companion to Ancient Philosophy*. Oxford.

Gillies, M. M. 1928. *The Argonautica of Apollonius Rhodius, Book III*. Cambridge.

Gioseffi, M. 2000 (ed.). *"E io sarò tua guida": raccolta di saggi su Virgilio e gli studi virgiliani*. Milan.

Giovannini, A. 1993. "Greek Cities and Greek Commonwealth." In Bulloch, Gruen, Long, and Stewart 1993: 265–86.

Girard, R. 1978. *To Double Business Bound: Essays on Literature, Mimesis, and Anthropology*. Baltimore.

Glassner, J.-J. 2004. *Mesopotamian Chronicles*. Leiden.

Gödde, S. and Heinze, T. 2000 (eds.). *Skenika: Beiträge zum antiken Theater und seiner Rezeption*. Darmstadt.

Gold, B. K. 1987. *Literary Patronage in Greece and Rome*. Chapel Hill.

Goldberg, S. 1980. *The Making of Menander's Comedy*. London.

Goldberg, S. 1995. *Epic in Republican Rome*. Oxford.

Golden, M. 1990. *Children and Childhood in Classical Athens*. Baltimore.

Goldhill, S. 1991. *The Poet's Voice: Essays on Poetics and Greek Literature*. Cambridge.

Goldhill, S. 2002. *The Invention of Prose*. Oxford.

Goldhill, S. 2005. Review of Stephens 2003. *Gnomon* 77: 99–104.

Gomme, A. W. and Sandbach, F. H. 1973. *Menander, A Commentary*. Oxford.

Göransson, T. 1995. *Albinus, Alcinous, Arius Didymus*. Gothenburg.

Goulet, R. 1989– (ed.). *Dictionnaire des philosophes antiques*. Paris.

Goulet-Cazé, M. O. 1999 (ed.). *Diogène Laërce, Vies et doctrines des philosophes illustres*. Paris.

Gow, A. S. F. 1951. "Nicandrea, with Reference to Liddell and Scott, Edition 9." *Classical Quarterly* 1: 95–118.

Gow, A. S. F. 1952a. *Bucolici Graeci*. Oxford.

Gow, A. S. F. 1952b. *Theocritus*. 2 vols. 2nd edition. Cambridge.

Gow, A. S. F. 1965. *Machon*. Cambridge.

Gow, A. S. F. and Page, D. L. 1965. *The Greek Anthology: Hellenistic Epigrams*. 2 vols. Cambridge.

Gow, A. S. F. and Page, D. L. 1968. *The Greek Anthology: The Garland of Philip*. 2 vols. Cambridge.

Gow, A. S. F. and Scholfield, A. F. 1953. *Nicander, The Poems and Poetical Fragments*. Cambridge.

Grainger, J. D. 1990. *Seleukos Nikator: Constructing a Hellenistic Kingdom*. London.

Grandjean, Y. 1975. *Une nouvelle arétalogie d'Isis à Maronée*. Leiden.

Granger, F. 1931, 1934. *Vitruvius, On Architecture*. 2 vols. Cambridge, MA.

Gratwick, A. S. 1982. "Ennius *Annales*." In Kenney and Clausen 1982: 60–76.

Graver, M. 2002. *Cicero on the Emotions: Tusculan Disputations 3 and 4*. Chicago.

Grayson, A. K. 1975. *Assyrian and Babylonian Chronicles*. Locust Valley.

Green, P. 1990. *Alexander to Actium: The Historical Evolution of the Hellenistic Age*. Berkeley. Corrected edition 1993.

Green, P. 1993 (ed.). *Hellenistic History and Culture.* Berkeley.

Green, P. 1997. *The Argonautika by Apollonios Rhodios.* Berkeley.

Greenberg, N. A. 1955. "The Poetic Theory of Philodemus." Diss. Harvard. Reprinted New York and London 1990.

Griffin, A. H. F. 1991. "Philemon and Baucis in Ovid's *Metamorphoses.*" *Greece and Rome* 38: 62–74.

Griffin, D. 1996. *Literary Patronage in England, 1650–1800.* Cambridge.

Griffin, M. and Barnes, J. 1989 (eds.). *Philosophia Togata: Essays on Philosophy and Roman Society.* Oxford.

Griffiths, F. T. 1976. "Theocritus' Silent Dioscuri." *Greek, Roman and Byzantine Studies* 17: 353–67.

Griffiths, F. T. 1979. *Theocritus at Court.* Leiden.

Griffiths, J. G. 1965. "A Translation from the Egyptian by Eudoxus." *Classical Quarterly* 59: 75–8.

Grilli, A. 1973. "Σύγγραμμα e ποίηcιc in Dionigi Faselite (*Vita Nicandri*)." *Annali della Scuola Normale Superiore di Pisa* 3: 381–6.

Grimm, G. 1996. "City Planning?" In *Alexandria and Alexandrianism* 1996: 55–74.

Groeneboom, P. 1922. *Les Mimiambes d'Hérondas, I–VI.* Groningen.

Gruen, E. S. 1984. *The Hellenistic World and the Coming of Rome.* Berkeley.

Gruen, E. S. 1990. *Studies in Greek Culture and Roman Policy.* Leiden.

Gruen, E. S. 1992. *Culture and National Identity in Republican Rome.* Ithaca, NY.

Gruen, E. S. 1993. "The Polis in the Hellenistic World." In Rosen and Farrell 1993: 339–54.

Gruen, E. S. 1998. *Heritage and Hellenism: The Reinvention of Jewish Tradition.* Berkeley.

Gruen, E. S. 2000. "Culture as Policy: The Attalids of Pergamon." In de Grummond and Ridgway 2000: 17–31.

Gruen, E. S. 2005 (ed.). *Cultural Borrowings and Ethnic Appropriations in Antiquity.* Stuttgart.

Gualandri, I. 1968. *Eutecnii paraphrasis in Nicandri Theriaca.* Milan.

Guglielmo, M. and Bona, E. 2003 (eds.). *Forme di comunicazione nel mondo antico e metamorfosi del mito: dal teatro al romanzo.* Alessandria.

Guichard, L. A. 2004. *Asclepíades de Samos, Epigramas y fragmentos.* Bern.

Gummert, P. 1992. *Die Erzählstruktur in den Argonautika des Apollonios.* Frankfurt am Main.

Gurney, O. R. 1957. "The Sultantepe Tablets V: The Poor Man of Nippur." *Anatolian Studies* 6: 145–64.

Gurney, O. R. 1972. "The Tale of the Poor Man of Nippur and its Folktale Parallels." *Anatolian Studies* 22: 149–158.

Gutman, Y. 1958, 1963. *The Beginnings of Jewish-Hellenistic Literature.* 2 vols. Jerusalem.

Gutzwiller, K. J. 1981. *Studies in the Hellenistic Epyllion.* Königstein.

Gutzwiller, K. J. 1983. "Charites or Hiero: Theocritus' *Idyll* 16." *Rheinisches Museum für Philologie* 126: 212–38.

Gutzwiller, K. J. 1991. *Theocritus' Pastoral Analogies: The Formation of a Genre.* Madison.

Gutzwiller, K. J. 1992. "Callimachus' *Lock of Berenice*: Fantasy, Romance, and Propaganda." *American Journal of Philology* 113: 359–85.

Gutzwiller, K. J. 1998. *Poetic Garlands: Hellenistic Epigrams in Context.* Berkeley.

Gutzwiller, K. J. 2000. "The Tragic Mask of Comedy: Metatheatricality in Menander." *Classical Antiquity* 19: 102–37.

Gutzwiller, K. J. 2002. "Posidippus on Statuary." In Bastianini and Casanova 2003: 41–60.

Gutzwiller, K. J. 2005 (ed.). *The New Posidippus: A Hellenistic Poetry Book.* Oxford.

Gutzwiller, K. J. 2006. "The Bucolic Problem." *Classical Philology* 101: 380–404.

Gutzwiller, K. J. 2007a. *A Guide to Hellenistic Literature.* Malden.

Gutzwiller, K. J. 2007b. "The Paradox of Amatory Epigram." In Bing and Bruss 2007: 313–32.

Habicht, C. 1958. "Die herrschende Gesellschaft in den hellenistischen Monarchien." *Vierteljahrschrift für Sozial- und Wirtschaftsgeschichte* 45: 1–16.

Habicht, C. 1970. *Gottmenschentum und Griechische Städte.* 2nd edition. Munich.

Habicht, C. 1988. *Hellenistic Athens and Her Philosophers* (*David Magie Lecture*). Princeton. Reprinted in Habicht 1994.

Habicht, C. 1992. "Athens and the Ptolemies." *Classical Antiquity* 11: 68–90.

Habicht, C. 1994. *Athen in hellenistischer Zeit.* Munich.

Habicht, C. 1997. *Athens from Alexander to Antony.* Cambridge.

Habinek, T. 2005. *Ancient Rhetoric and Oratory.* London.

Hadas, M. 1951. *Aristeas to Philocrates (Letter of Aristeas).* New York.

Hägg, T. 1984. *The Novel in Antiquity.* Oxford.

Hägg, T. and Utas, B. 2003. *The Virgin and Her Lover: Fragments of an Ancient Greek Novel.* Leiden.

Halliwell, S. 2002. *The Aesthetics of Mimesis: Ancient Texts and Modern Problems.* Princeton.

Halperin, D. M. 1983. *Before Pastoral: Theocritus and the Ancient Tradition of Bucolic Poetry.* New Haven.

Hammond, N. G. L. and Walbank, F. W. 1988. *A History of Macedonia III: 336–167 BC.* Oxford.

Hankinson, R. J. 1988a. "Stoicism, Science and Divination." In Hankinson 1988b: 123–60.

Hankinson, R. J. 1988b (ed.). *Method, Medicine and Metaphysics: Studies in the Philosophy of Ancient Science* = *Apeiron* 21.2.

Hankinson, R. J. 1995. "The Growth of Medical Empiricism." In Bates 1995: 60–83.

Hannah, R. 2008. *Time in Antiquity.* London and New York.

Hans, L.-M. 1985. "Theokrits XVI. *Idylle* und die Politik Hierons II. von Syrakus." *Historia* 34: 117–25.

Hansen, E. V. 1971. *The Attalids of Pergamon.* 2nd edition. Ithaca, NY.

Hansen, M. H. 1989. "Solonian Democracy in Fourth-Century Athens." *Classica et Mediaevalia* 40: 71–99.

Hansen, M. H. 1993 (ed.). *The Ancient Greek City-State.* Copenhagen.

Hansen, P. A. 1983, 1989. *Carmina epigraphica Graeca.* 2 vols. Berlin.

Hansen W. 1996. *Phlegon of Tralles' Book of Marvels.* Exeter.

Harder, M. A. 1992. "Insubstantial Voices: Some Observations on the *Hymns* of Callimachus." *Classical Quarterly* 42: 384–94.

Harder, M. A. 1993. "Aspects of the Structure of Callimachus' *Aetia.*" In Harder, Regtuit, and Wakker 1993: 99–110.

Harder, M. A. 1998. "Generic Games in Callimachus' *Aetia.*" In Harder, Regtuit, and Wakker 1998: 95–113.

Harder, M. A. 2002a. "Intertextuality in Callimachus' *Aetia.*" In Montanari and Lehnus 2002: 189–233.

Harder, M. A. 2002b. Review of Cameron 1995a. *Mnemosyne* 55: 599–611.

Harder, M. A. 2003a. "Allowed to Speak: The Use of Direct Speech in Callimachus' *Hymns* and *Aetia.*" *Hermathena* 173/4: 49–60.

Harder, M. A. 2003b. "The Invention of Past, Present and Future in Callimachus' *Aetia.*" *Hermes* 131: 290–306.

Harder, M. A. 2004. "Callimachus." In De Jong, Nünlist, and Bowie 2004: 63–81.

Harder, M. A. and Cuypers M. 2005 (eds.). *Beginning from Apollo: Studies in Apollonius Rhodius and the Argonautic Tradition.* Leuven.

Harder, M. A., Regtuit, R. F. and Wakker, G. C. 1993 (eds.). *Callimachus.* Groningen.

Harder, M. A., Regtuit, R. F. and Wakker, G. C. 1996 (eds.). *Theocritus.* Groningen.

Harder, M. A., Regtuit, R. F. and Wakker, G. C. 1998 (eds.). *Genre in Hellenistic Poetry.* Groningen.

Harder, M. A., Regtuit, R. F. and Wakker, G. C. 2000 (eds.). *Apollonius Rhodius.* Leuven.

Harder, M. A., Regtuit, R. F. and Wakker, G. C. 2002 (eds.). *Hellenistic Epigrams.* Leuven.

Harder, M. A., Regtuit, R. F. and Wakker, G. C. 2004 (eds.). *Callimachus II.* Leuven.

Harder, M. A., Regtuit, R. F. and Wakker, G. C. 2006 (eds.). *Beyond the Canon.* Leuven.

Harder, M. A., Regtuit, R. F. and Wakker, G. C. 2009 (eds.). *Nature and Science in Hellenistic Poetry.* Leuven.

Harder, M. A., Regtuit, R. F. and Wakker, G. C. forthcoming (eds.). *Hellenistic Poetry and Religion.* Leuven.

Harder, R. 1944. *Karpokrates von Chalkis und die memphitische Isispropaganda.* Berlin.

Hardie, A. 1983. *Statius and the Silvae: Poets, Patrons and Epideixis in the Graeco-Roman World.* Liverpool.

Hardie, P. 2002. *Ovid's Poetics of Illusion.* Cambridge.

Harris, E. M. 1990. "Did the Athenians Regard Seduction as a Worse Crime than Rape?" *Classical Quarterly* 40: 370–7.

Harris, E. M. and Rubinstein, L. 2004 (eds.). *The Law and the Courts in Ancient Greece.* London.

Harris, W. V. and Ruffini, G. 2004 (eds.). *Ancient Alexandria between Egypt and Greece.* Leiden.

Harrison, A. R. W. 1968. *The Law of Athens.* Vol. 1. Oxford.

Harrison, S. 2004. "Virgil's *Corycius senex* and Nicander's *Georgica*: *Georgics* 4.116–48." In Gale 2004: 109–23.

Haslam, M. 1992. "Hidden Signs: Aratus *Diosemeiai* 46ff., Vergil *Georgics* 1.424ff." *Harvard Studies in Classical Philology* 94: 199–204.

Haslam, M. 1993. "Callimachus' *Hymns.*" In Harder, Regtuit, and Wakker 1993: 111–25.

Häusle, H. 1979. *Einfache und frühe Formen des griechischen Epigramms.* Innsbruck.

Hausrath, A. and Hunger, H. 1957–70. *Corpus fabularum Aesopicarum.* 2nd edition revised by H. Hunger. Leipzig.

Hautcourt, A. d' 2001. "Héraclée du Pont dans les *Alexipharmaca* de Nicandre de Colophon: un nouvel indice de chronologie?" In Virgilio 2001: 191–8.

Hazzard, R. A. 2000. *Imagination of a Monarchy: Studies in Ptolemaic Propaganda.* Toronto.

Headlam, W. and Knox, A. D. 1922. *Herodas, The Mimes and Fragments.* Cambridge.

Heath, M. 1994. "The Sub-structure of *Stasis*-theory from Hermagoras to Hermogenes." *Classical Quarterly* 44: 114–29.

Heath, M. 1995. *Hermogenes, On Issues.* Oxford.

Heath, T. B. L. 1896. *Apollonius of Perga, Treatise on Conic Sections.* Cambridge.

Heath, T. B. L. 1912. *The Works of Archimedes.* 2nd edition. Cambridge.

Heath, T. B. L. 1913. *Aristarchus of Samos: The Ancient Copernicus.* Oxford.

Heath, T. B. L. 1921. *A History of Greek Mathematics.* 2 vols. Oxford.

Heath, T. B. L. 1926. *Euclid's Elements.* 2nd edition. Cambridge.

Heath, T. B. L. 1932. *Greek Astronomy.* London and Toronto.

Heckel, W. 1992. *The Marshals of Alexander's Empire.* London and New York.

Heinze, R. 1919. *Ovids elegische Erzählung.* Leipzig.

Heiserman, A. 1977. *The Novel before the Novel: Essays and Discussions about the Beginnings of Prose Fiction in the West.* Chicago.

Henderson, J. 1991. *The Maculate Muse: Obscene Language in Attic Comedy.* 2nd edition. Oxford.

Hendry, M. 1994. "A Martial Acronym in Ennius?" *Liverpool Classical Monthly* 19: 108–9.
Hengel, M. 1974. *Judaism and Hellenism.* 2 vols. London.
Henrichs, A. 1975. "Two Doxographical Notes: Democritus and Prodicus on Religion." *Harvard Studies in Classical Philology* 79: 93–123.
Henrichs, A. 1993a. "Gods in Action: The Poetics of Divine Performance in the *Hymns* of Callimachus." In Harder, Regtuit, and Wakker 1993: 127–47.
Henrichs, A. 1993b. "Response (to Bulloch, Gelzer, Parsons)." In Bulloch, Gruen, Long, and Stewart 1993: 171–95.
Henrichs, A. 1999. "Demythologizing the Past, Mythicizing the Present: Myth, History, and the Supernatural at the Dawn of the Hellenistic Period." In Buxton 1999: 223–48.
Hense, O. 1909. *Teletis reliquiae.* 2nd edition. Tübingen.
Herda, A. 2006. *Der Apollon-Delphinion-Kult in Milet und die Neujahrsprozession nach Didyma: Eine neuer Kommentar der sog. Molpoi-Satzung.* Mainz.
Herington, J. 1985. *Poetry into Drama: Early Tragedy and the Greek Poetic Tradition.* Berkeley.
Herman, G. 1981. "The 'Friends' of the Early Hellenistic Rulers: Servants or Officials?" *Talanta* 12/13: 103–49.
Herman, G. 1987. *Ritualised Friendship and the Greek City.* Cambridge.
Herman, G. 1997. "The Court Society of the Hellenistic Age." In Cartledge, Garnsey, and Gruen 1997: 199–224.
Herter, H. 1941. "Ovids Persephone-Erzählungen und ihre hellenistischen Quellen." *Rheinisches Museum für Philologie* 90: 236–68.
Herter, H. 1955. "Bericht über die Literatur zur hellenistischen Dichtung seit dem Jahre 1921. 2. Teil: Apollonios von Rhodos." *Bursian's Jahresbericht* 285: 213–410.
Herzog, R. 1924. "Der Traum des Herodas." *Philologus* 79: 387–433.
Hesberg, H. von. 1995. "Das griechische Gymnasion im 2. Jh. v.Chr." In Wörrle and Zanker 1995: 13–27.
Hidber, T. 1996. *Das klassizistische Manifest des Dionys von Halikarnas.* Stuttgart and Leipzig.
Hilgard, A. 1901. *Scholia in Dionysii Thracis Artem Grammaticam.* Part 1, Vol. 3. Leipzig.
Hinds, S. 1987. *The Metamorphosis of Persephone: Ovid and the Self-Conscious Muse.* Cambridge.
Hinds, S. 1998. *Allusion and Intertext: Dynamics of Appropriation in Roman Poetry.* Cambridge.
Hinneberg, P. 1912 (ed.). *Die Kultur der Gegenwart, ihre Entwicklung und ihre Ziele.* 3rd edition (1st edition 1905). Berlin and Leipzig.
Hinske, N. 1981 (ed.). *Alexandrien: Kulturbegegnungen dreier Jahrtausende im Schmelztiegel einer mediterranen Großstadt.* Mainz.
Hirst, A. and Silk, M. S. 2004 (eds.). *Alexandria, Real and Imagined.* Aldershot.
Hoff, M. 1997. "*Laceratae Athenae*: Sulla's Siege of Athens in 87/6 BC and its Aftermath." In Hoff and Rotroff 1997: 33–51.
Hoff, M. and Rotroff, S. 1997 (eds.). *The Romanization of Athens.* Oxford.
Hoffmann, F. 1996. *Der Kampf um den Panzer des Inaros: Studien zum P.Krall und seiner Stellung innerhalb des Inaros-Petubastis-Zyklus.* Vienna.
Hoffmann, F. 2000. *Ägypten: Kultur und Lebenswelt in griechisch-römischer Zeit; Eine Darstellung nach den demotischen Quellen.* Berlin.
Hoffmann, F. and Quack, J. F. 2007. *Anthologie der demotischen Literatur.* Münster.
Hoffmann, F. and Thissen, H. J. 2004 (eds.). *Res severa verum gaudium: Festschrift K.-Th. Zauzich.* Leuven.
Hofmann, H. and Zimmermann, M. 1997 (eds.). *Groningen Colloquia on the Novel* 8. Groningen.
Hölbl, G. 2001. *A History of the Ptolemaic Empire.* London.

Holder, A. 1894. *Pomponi Porfyrionis commentum in Horatium Flaccum*. Innsbruck.

Holladay, C. R. 1983, 1989, 1995, 1996. *Fragments from Hellenistic Jewish Authors*. Vol. 1: *Historians*. Chico. Vol. 2: *Poets*. Vol. 3: *Aristobulus*. Vol. 4: *Orphica*. Atlanta.

Holleaux, M. 1921. *Rome, la Grèce et les monarchies hellénistiques au IIème siècle avant J.-C.* Paris.

Hollis, A. S. 1994. "*Supplementum Hellenisticum* 948–9: Callimachus, *Hecale*?" *Zeitschrift für Papyrologie und Epigraphik* 100: 17–21.

Hollis, A. S. 1998. "Nicander and Lucretius." In Cairns and Heath 1998: 169–84.

Hollis, A. S. 2009. *Callimachus, Hecale*. 2nd edition. Oxford.

Holt, F. 1999. *Thundering Zeus: The Making of Hellenistic Bactria*. Berkeley.

Holtsmark, E. B. 1966. "Poetry as Self-enlightenment: Theocritus 11." *Transactions of the American Philological Association* 97: 253–9.

Holzberg, N. 1993. "Ktesias von Knidos und der griechische Roman." *Würzburger Jahrbücher für die Altertumswissenschaft* 19: 79–84.

Holzberg, N. 2003. "Utopias and Fantastic Travel." In Schmeling 2003: 621–32.

Honigman, S. 2003. *The Septuagint and Homeric Scholarship in Alexandria: A Study in the Narrative of the Letter of Aristeas*. London.

Hopkinson, N. 1984a. *Callimachus, Hymn to Demeter*. Cambridge.

Hopkinson, N. 1984b. "Callimachus' *Hymn to Zeus*." *Classical Quarterly* 34: 139–48.

Hopkinson, N. 1988. *A Hellenistic Anthology*. Cambridge.

Hordern, J. H. 2002a. *Timotheus of Miletus, The Fragments*. Oxford.

Hordern, J. H. 2002b. "Word-Order and ἐκλογή in Sophron and Demetrius, *On Poems* 2, Cols. 55–60." *Zeitschrift für Papyrologie und Epigraphik* 141: 75–82.

Hordern, J. H. 2004. *Sophron's Mimes*. Oxford.

Horsfall, N. 1994. "The Prehistory of Latin Poetry: Some Problems of Method." *Rivista di filologia e di istruzione classica* 122: 50–75.

Horster, M. and Reitz, C. 2003 (eds.). *Antike Fachschriftsteller: Literarischer Diskurs und sozialer Kontext*. Stuttgart.

Horster, M. and Reitz, C. 2005 (eds.). *Wissensvermittlung in dichterischer Gestalt*. Stuttgart.

Hose, M. 1997. "Der alexandrinische Zeus: Zur Stellung der Dichtkunst im Reich der ersten Ptolemäer." *Philologus* 141: 3–20.

Hubbard, T. K. 1998. *The Pipes of Pan*. Ann Arbor.

Hübner, W. 2000 (ed.). *Geschichte der Mathematik und der Naturwissenschaften in der Antike 2: Geographie und verwandte Wissenschaften*. Stuttgart.

Hübner, W. 2005. "Die Rezeption der *Phainomena* Arats in der lateinischen Literatur." In Horster and Reitz 2005: 133–54.

Hughes, B. 1996. "Callimachus, Hipponax and the Persona of the Iambographer." *Materiali e discussioni* 37: 205–16.

Humphrey, E. 2000. *Joseph and Aseneth*. Sheffield.

Humphrey, J. W., Oleson, J. and Sherwood, A. 1998. *Greek and Roman Technology: A Sourcebook*. London.

Humphreys, S. C. 1974. "The Nothoi of Kynosarges." *Journal of Hellenic Studies* 94: 88–95.

Humphreys, S. C. 1983. *The Family, Women and Death: Comparative Studies*. London.

Hunger, H. and Sachs, A. 1988–96. *Astronomical Diaries and Related Texts from Babylonia*. Vienna.

Hunter, R. 1985. *The New Comedy of Greece and Rome*. Cambridge.

Hunter, R. 1987. "Medea's Flight: The Fourth Book of the *Argonautica*." *Classical Quarterly* 37: 129–39.

Hunter, R. 1988. "'Short on Heroics': Jason in the *Argonautica*." *Classical Quarterly* 38: 436–53.

Hunter, R. 1989. *Apollonius of Rhodes, Argonautica Book III*. Cambridge.

Hunter, R. 1992. "Writing the God: Form and Meaning in Callimachus, *Hymn to Athena*." *Materiali e discussioni* 29: 9–34.

Hunter, R. 1993a. *The Argonautica of Apollonius: Literary Studies*. Cambridge.

Hunter, R. 1993b. *Apollonius of Rhodes, Jason and the Golden Fleece (Argonautica)*. Oxford.

Hunter, R. 1993c. "The Presentation of Herodas' *Mimiamboi*." *Antichthon* 27: 31–44.

Hunter, R. 1995. "Plautus and Herodas." In Benz, Stärk, and Vogt-Spira 1995: 155–69.

Hunter, R. 1996. *Theocritus and the Archaeology of Greek Poetry.* Cambridge.

Hunter, R. 1998. "Before and After Epic: Theocritus(?), *Idyll* 25." In Harder, Regtuit, and Wakker 1998: 115–32.

Hunter, R. 1999. *Theocritus, A Selection (Idylls 1, 3, 4, 6, 7, 10, 11 and 13)*. Cambridge.

Hunter, R. 2001. "The Poetics of Narrative in the *Argonautica*." In Papanghelis and Rengakos 2001: 93–125.

Hunter, R. 2003a. *Theocritus, Encomium of Ptolemy Philadelphus*. Berkeley.

Hunter, R. 2003b. "Literature and its Contexts." In Erskine 2003: 477–93.

Hunter, R. 2004a. "Theocritus and Moschus." In De Jong, Nünlist, and Bowie 2004: 83–97.

Hunter, R. 2004b. "The *Periegesis* of Dionysius and the Traditions of Hellenistic Poetry." *Revue des études anciennes* 106: 217–31.

Hunter, R. 2005a. "The Hesiodic Catalogue and Hellenistic poetry." In Hunter 2005b: 239–65.

Hunter, R. 2005b (ed.). *The Hesiodic Catalogue of Women: Constructions and Reconstructions.* Cambridge.

Hunter, R. 2006a. *The Shadow of Callimachus: Studies in the Reception of Hellenistic Poetry at Rome*. Cambridge.

Hunter, R. 2006b. "The Prologue of the *Periodos to Nicomedes* ('Pseudo-Scymnus')." In Harder, Regtuit, and Wakker 2006: 123–40.

Hunter, R. 2008a. "Written in the Stars: Poetry and Philosophy in the *Phaenomena* of Aratus." In Hunter 2008b: 1.153–88. Originally published in *Arachnion* 1.2 (1995).

Hunter, R. 2008b. *On Coming After: Studies in Post-Classical Greek Literature and its Reception*. 2 vols. Berlin.

Hunter, R. and Fuhrer, T. 2002. "Imaginary Gods? Poetic Theology in the *Hymns* of Callimachus." In Montanari and Lehnus 2002: 143–87.

Hunter, R. and Rutherford, I. C. 2009 (eds.). *Wandering Poets in Ancient Greek Culture: Travel, Locality and Panhellenism*. Cambridge.

Hurst, A. 1967. *Apollonios de Rhodes: manière et cohérence*. Rome.

Hurst, A. 1976. "Sur le date de Lycophron." In *Mélanges d'histoire ancienne et d'archéologie offerts à Paul Collart*. Lausanne: 231–5.

Hurst, A. 1996. "Alexandre médiateur dans l'*Alexandra* de Lycophron." In Bridges and Bürgel 1996: 61–8.

Hurst, A. 1999. "L''Odyssée' de Lycophron." In Hurst and Létoublon 1999: 115–27.

Hurst, A. and Kolde, A. 2008. *Lycophron, Alexandra*. Paris.

Hurst, A. and Létoublon, F. 1999 (eds.). *La mythologie et l'Odyssée: Hommage à Gabriel Germain*. Geneva.

Huss, W. 1994. "Das Haus des Nektanebis und das Haus des Ptolemaios." *Ancient Society* 25: 111–17.

Huss, W. 2001. *Ägypten in hellenistischer Zeit, 332–30 BC*. Munich.

Hutchinson, G. O. 1988. *Hellenistic Poetry.* Oxford.

Hutchinson, G. O. 2001. *Greek Lyric Poetry: A Commentary on Selected Larger Pieces.* Oxford.

Hutchinson, G. O. 2003. "The *Aetia*: Callimachus' Poem of Knowledge." *Zeitschrift für Papyrologie und Epigraphik* 145: 47–59.

Huttner, U. 1997. *Die politische Rolle der Heraklesgestalt im griechischen Herrschertum*. Stuttgart.

Huys, M. 1991. *Le poème élégiaque hellénistique P.Brux. inv. E 8934 et P.Sorb. inv. 2254*. Brussels.

Ieranò, G. 1992. "Dioniso Ikarios e Apollo Pizio." *Quaderni di storia* 36: 171–80.

Ierodiakonou, K. 1999 (ed.). *Topics in Stoic Philosophy*. Oxford.

Ildefonse, F. 1997. *La naissance de la grammaire dans l'antiquité grecque*. Paris.

Immerwahr, R. 1964. *Some Inscriptions on Attic Pottery*. Chapel Hill.

Innes, D. 1995. *Demetrius, On Style*. Cambridge, MA.

Innes, D. 2003. "Metaphor, Simile, and Allegory as Ornaments of Style." In Boys-Stones 2003b: 7–27.

Inwood, B. 2003 (ed.). *The Cambridge Companion to the Stoics*. Cambridge.

Inwood, B. and Donini, P. 1999. "Stoic Ethics." In Algra, Barnes, Mansfeld, and Schofield 1999: 675–738.

Inwood, B. and Gerson, L. P. 1997. *Hellenistic Philosophy: Introductory Readings*. 2nd edition. Indianapolis.

Ioppolo, A.-M. 1980. *Aristone di Chio e lo Stoicismo antico*. Naples.

Ioppolo, A.-M. and Sedley, D. N. 2007 (eds.). *Pyrrhonists, Patricians, Platonizers: Hellenistic Philosophy in the Period 155–86 BC*. Naples.

Irby-Massie, G. L. and Keyser, P. T. 2002. *Greek Science of the Hellenistic Era: A Sourcebook*. London.

Isaacs, H. R. 1975. *Idols of the Tribe: Group Identity and Political Change*. New York.

Isager, S. 1980/1. "The Marriage Pattern in Classical Athens: Men and Women in Isaios." *Classica et Mediaevalia* 33: 81–96.

Isager, S. 1998. "The Pride of Halikarnassos: Editio Princeps of an Inscription from Salmakis." *Zeitschrift für Papyrologie und Epigraphik* 123: 1–23.

Iser, W. 1989. *Prospecting: From Reader Response to Literary Anthropology*. Baltimore.

Iser, W. 1993. *The Fictive and the Imaginary*. Baltimore.

Jackson, S. 1987. "Apollonius' *Argonautica*: Euphemus, a Clod and a Tripod." *Illinois Classical Studies* 12: 23–30.

Jacob, C. 1991. *Géographie et ethnographie en Grèce ancienne*. Paris.

Jacobson, H. 1983. *The Exagoge of Ezekiel*. Cambridge.

Jacoby, F. 1905. "Zur Entstehung der römischen Elegie." *Rheinisches Museum für Philologie* 60: 38–105. Reprinted in *Kleine philologische Schriften*. Berlin 1961: 2.65–121.

Jacoby, F. 1909. "Über die Entwicklung der griechischen Historiographie und den Plan einer neuen Sammlung der Historikerfragmente." *Klio* 9: 80–123. Reprinted in Jacoby 1956: 16–64.

Jacoby, F. 1923–58. *Die Fragmente der griechischen Historiker*. Berlin and Leiden.

Jacoby, F. 1956. *Abhandlungen zur griechischen Geschichtsschreibung*. Leiden.

Jacques, J.-M. 1955. "Les *Alexipharmaques* de Nicandre." *Revue des études anciennes* 57: 5–35.

Jacques, J.-M. 1960. "Sur un acrostiche d'Aratos (*Phén*. 783–787)." *Revue des études anciennes* 62: 48–61.

Jacques, J.-M. 1979. "Nicandre de Colophon poète et médecin." *Ktema* 4: 133–49.

Jacques, J.-M. 2002. *Nicandre, Œuvres*. Vol. 2: *Les Thériaques*. Paris.

Jacques, J.-M. 2004. "Médecine et poésie: Nicandre de Colophon et ses poèmes iologiques." In Jouanna and Leclant 2004: 109–24.

Jacques, J.-M. 2006. "Nicandre de Colophon, poète et médecin." In Cusset 2006b: 19–48.

Jacques, J.-M. 2007a. *Nicandre, Œuvres*. Vol. 3: *Les Alexipharmaques*. Paris.

Jacques, J.-M. 2007b. "Situation de Nicandre de Colophon." *Revue des études anciennes* 109: 99–121.

Jaeger, M. 2008. *Archimedes and the Roman Imagination.* Ann Arbor.

James, A. W. 1972. "The Zeus Hymns of Cleanthes and Aratus." *Antichthon* 6: 28–38.

Janko, R. 2011 *Philodemus, 'On Poems' Books 3–4, with the Fragments of Aristotle, 'On Poets.'* Oxford.

Janko, R. 2000. *Philodemus 'On Poems' Book One.* Oxford.

Jansen-Winkeln, K. 2001. *Biografische und religiöse Inschriften der Spätzeit aus dem Ägyptischen Museum Kairo.* Wiesbaden.

Jasnow, R. 1992. *A Late Period Hieratic Wisdom Text (P.Brooklyn 47.218.135).* Chicago.

Jasnow, R. 1997. "The Greek *Alexander Romance* and Demotic Egyptian Literature." *Journal of Near-Eastern Studies* 56: 95–103.

Jasnow, R. 1999. "Remarks on Continuity in Egyptian Literary Tradition." In Teeter and Larson 1999: 193–210.

Jasnow, R. and Zauzich, K.-Th. 2005. *The Ancient Egyptian Book of Thoth: A Demotic Discourse on Knowledge and Pendant to the Classical Hermetica.* Wiesbaden.

Jensen, C. 1923. *Philodemos über die Gedichte, Fünftes Buch.* Berlin.

Jensen, C. 1936. "Herakleides vom Pontos bei Philodem und Horaz." *Sitzungsberichte der Preussischen Akademie der Wissenschaften*, phil.-hist. Klasse: 292–320.

Johnson, J. H. 1983. "The Demotic Chronicle as a Statement of a Theory of Kingship." *Journal of the Society for the Study of Egyptian Antiquities* 13: 61–76.

Johnson, J. H. 1992 (ed.). *Life in a Multi-Cultural Society: Egypt from Cambyses to Constantine and Beyond.* Chicago.

Johnson, S. R. 2004. *Historical Fictions and Hellenistic Jewish Identity.* Berkeley.

Jones, A. 1999. *Astronomical Papyri from Oxyrhynchus (P.Oxy. 4133–4300a).* Philadelphia.

Jones, C. P. 1978. *The Roman World of Dio Chrysostom.* Cambridge, MA.

Jones, C. P. 1996. "*Ethnos* and *genos* in Herodotus." *Classical Quarterly* 46: 315–20.

Jones, C. P. 2001. "Pausanias and His Guides." In Alcock, Cherry, and Elsner 2001: 33–9.

Jonnes, L. and Ricl, M. 1997. "A New Royal Inscription from Phrygia Paroreios: Eumenes II Grants Tyriaion the Status of a *polis*." *Epigraphica Anatolica* 29: 1–30.

Jouanna, J. and Leclant, J. 2004 (eds.). *Colloque La médecine grecque antique: Actes.* Paris.

Jouanno, C. 2002. *Naissance et métamorphoses du Roman d'Alexandre: domaine grec.* Paris.

Kah, D. and Scholz, P. 2004 (eds.). *Das hellenistische Gymnasion.* Berlin.

Kaibel, G. 1894. "Aratea." *Hermes* 29: 82–123.

Kamtekar, R. 2002. "Distinction without a Difference? Race and *genos* in Plato." In Ward and Lott 2002: 1–13.

Käppel, L. 1992. *Paian: Studien zur Geschichte einer Gattung.* Berlin.

Karabelias, E. 1970. "Une nouvelle source pour l'étude du droit attique: le *Bouclier* de Ménandre." *Revue de droit* 48: 357–89.

Karnezis, J. E. 1977. "Law in the *Aspis*." *Platon* 29: 152–5.

Kassel, R. 1987. *Die Abgrenzung des Hellenismus in der griechischen Literaturgeschichte.* Berlin.

Kassel, R. and Austin, C. 1983–. *Poetae Comici Graeci.* Berlin.

Kaster, R. A. 1995. *Suetonius, De grammaticis et rhetoribus.* Oxford.

Katsouris, A. G. 1995. *Menander Bibliography.* Thessaloniki.

Kattein, C. 1901. *Theocriti Idylliis octavo et nono cur abroganda sit fides theocritea.* Paris.

Kazazis, J. N. and Rengakos, A. 1999 (eds.). *Euphrosyne: Studies in Ancient Epic and Its Legacy in Honor of Dimitris N. Maronitis.* Stuttgart.

Keller, O. 1877. *Rerum naturalium scriptores.* Vol. 1. Leipzig.

Kennedy, G. A. 1968. *The Art of Persuasion in Greece.* Princeton.

Kennedy, G. A. 1969. *Quintilian*. New York.

Kennedy, G. A. 1989 (ed.). *The Cambridge History of Literary Criticism* Vol. 1: *Classical Criticism*. Cambridge.

Kennedy, G. A. 1994. *A New History of Classical Rhetoric*. Princeton.

Kennedy, G. A. 2003. *Progymnasmata: Greek Textbooks of Prose Composition and Rhetoric*. Leiden.

Kenney, E. J. and Clausen, W. V. 1982 (eds.). *The Cambridge History of Classical Literature*. Vol. 2: *Latin Literature*. Cambridge.

Kent, W. F., Simons, P. and Eade, J. C. 1987 (eds.). *Patronage, Art, and Society in Renaissance Italy.* Oxford.

Kenyon, F. G. 1891. *Classical Texts from Papyri in the British Museum, Including the Newly Discovered Poems of Herodas*. London.

Kerkhecker, A. 1997. "Μουcέων ἐν ταλάρῳ: Dichter und Dichtung am Ptolemäerhof." *Antike und Abendland* 43: 124–44.

Kerkhecker, A. 1999. *Callimachus' Book of Iambi*. Oxford.

Keuls, E. 1973. "The *Samia* of Menander: An Interpretation of its Plot and Theme." *Zeitschrift für Papyrologie und Epigraphik* 10: 1–12.

Keyser, P. T. and Irby-Massie, G. L. 2006. "Science, Medicine, and Technology." In Bugh 2006: 241–64.

Keyser, P. T. and Irby-Massie, G. L. 2008 (eds.). *The Encyclopedia of Ancient Natural Scientists: The Greek Tradition and its Many Heirs*. London and New York.

Kidd, D. A. 1981. "Notes on Aratus, *Phaenomena*." *Classical Quarterly* 31: 355–62.

Kidd, D. A. 1997. *Aratus, Phaenomena*. Cambridge.

Kidd, I. G. 1988. *Posidonius II: The Commentary.* 2 vols. Cambridge. Cf. Edelstein and Kidd 1972.

Kingsley, P. 1996. "Empedocles' Two Poems." *Hermes* 124: 108–11.

Kirk, G. S. 1966. "Formular Language and Oral Quality." *Yale Classical Studies* 20: 155–74. Reprinted in Kirk 1976: 183–201.

Kirk, G. S. 1976 (ed.). *Homer and Oral Tradition*. Cambridge.

Kish, G. 1978. *A Source Book in Geography.* Cambridge.

Kirstein, R. 2007. *Junge Hirten und alte Fischer: Die Gedichte 27, 20 und 21 des Corpus Theocriteum*. Berlin.

Klauser, H. 1898. "De dicendi genere in Nicandri *Theriacis* et *Alexipharmacis* quaestiones selectae." *Dissertationes Philologae Vindobonenses* 6: 1–92.

Klein, L. 1931. "Die Göttertechnik in den *Argonautika* des Apollonios Rhodios." *Philologus* 40: 18–51, 215–57.

Knight, V. H. 1995. *The Renewal of Epic: Responses to Homer in the Argonautica of Apollonius*. Leiden.

Knox, A. D. 1925. "The Dream of Herodas." *Classical Review* 39: 13–15.

Knox, A. D. 1929. *Herodas, Cercidas and the Greek Choliambic Poets*. London. Partially reprinted in Rusten, Cunningham, and Knox 1993.

Kock, T. 1880–8. *Comicorum Atticorum fragmenta*. 3 vols. Leipzig.

Koenen, L. 1977. *Eine agonistische Inschrift aus Ägypten und frühptolemäische Königsfeste*. Meisenheim.

Koenen, L. 1983. "Die Adaptation ägyptischer Königsideologie am Ptolemäerhof." In Van't Dack, Van Dessel, and Van Gucht 1983: 143–90.

Koenen, L. 1985. "The Dream of Nektanebos." *Bulletin of the American Society of Papyrologists* 22: 161–94.

Koenen, L. 1993. "The Ptolemaic King as a Religious Figure." In Bulloch, Gruen, Long, and Stewart 1993: 25–115.

Koester, H. (ed.). 1998. *Pergamon, Citadel of the Gods: Archaeological Record, Literary Description, and Religious Development.* Harrisburg.

Köhnken, A. 1965. *Apollonios und Theokrit: Die Hylas- und die Amykos-Geschichten beider Dichter und die Frage der Priorität.* Göttingen.

Köhnken, A. 1996. "Theokrits Polyphemgedichte." In Harder, Regtuit, and Wakker 1996: 171–86.

Köhnken, A. 2000. "Der Status Jasons: Besonderheiten der Darstellungstechnik in den *Argonautika* des Apollonios Rhodios." In Harder, Regtuit, and Wakker 2000: 55–68.

Köhnken, A. 2001. "Hellenistic Chronology: Theocritus, Callimachus, and Apollonius Rhodius." In Papanghelis and Rengakos 2001: 73–92.

Köhnken, A. 2003. "Apoll-Aitien bei Kallimachos und Apollonios." In Accorinti and Chuvin 2003: 207–13.

Köhnken, A. 2004. "Artemis im *Artemishymnos* des Kallimachos." In Harder, Regtuit, and Wakker 2004: 161–71.

Köhnken, A. 2005. "Der Argonaut Euphemos." In Harder and Cuypers 2005: 70–5.

Köhnken, A. 2007. "Epinician Epigram." In Bing and Bruss 2007: 295–312.

Kolde, A. 2002/3. "Is Isyllos of Epidauros' Poetry Typically Hellenistic?" *Hermathena* 173/4: 155–64.

Kolde, A. 2003. *Politique et religion chez Isyllos d'Épidaure.* Basel.

Kollesch, J., Kudlien, F. and Nickel, D. 1965. *Apollonii Citiensis in Hippocratis de articulis commentarius.* Berlin.

König, F. W. 1972. *Die Persika des Ktesias von Knidos.* Graz.

König, J. and Whitmarsh, T. 2007 (eds.). *Ordering Knowledge in the Roman Empire.* Cambridge.

Konstan, D. 1995. *Greek Comedy and Ideology.* Oxford.

Konstan, D. 1997. *Friendship in the Classical World.* Cambridge.

Konstan, D. and Saïd, S. 2006 (eds.). *Greeks on Greekness: Viewing the Greek Past under the Roman Empire.* Cambridge.

Korenjak, M. 2003. *Die Weltrundreise eines anonymen Autors ('Pseudo-Skymnos').* Hildesheim.

Körte, A. 1925. *Die hellenistische Dichtung.* Leipzig.

Körte, A. 1929. *Hellenistic Poetry,* trans. J. Hammer and M. Hadas. New York.

Körte, A. 1938. *Menandri quae supersunt.* Vol. 1. 3rd edition. Leipzig.

Körte, A. and Händel, P. 1960. *Die hellenistische Dichtung.* Stuttgart.

Kosmetatou, E. 2000. "Lycophron's *Alexandra* Reconsidered: The Attalid Connection." *Hermes* 128: 32–53.

Kosmetatou, E. 2003. "The Attalids." In Erskine 2003: 159–74.

Kosmetatou, E. 2004. "Vision and Visibility: Art Historical Theory Paints a Portrait of New Leadership in Posidippus' *Andriantopoiika.*" In Acosta-Hughes, Kosmetatou, and Baumbach 2004: 187–211.

Kossaifi, C. 2002. "L'onomastique bucolique dans les *Idylles* de Théocrite: un poète face aux noms." *Revue des études anciennes* 104: 349–61.

Kottsieper, I. 1991. "Die Geschichte und die Sprüche des weisen Achiqar." In *Texte aus der Umwelt des Alten Testaments* III.2. Gütersloh: 320–47.

Kraemer, R. S. 1998. *When Aseneth Met Joseph: A Late Antique Tale of the Biblical Patriarch and his Egyptian Wife, Reconsidered.* Oxford.

Krevans, N. 1993. "Fighting against Antimachus: The *Lyde* and the *Aetia* Reconsidered." In Harder, Regtuit, and Wakker 1993: 149–60.

Krevans, N. 2000. "The Foundation Poems of Apollonius." In Harder, Regtuit, and Wakker 2000: 69–84.

Krevans, N. 2007. "The Arrangement of Epigrams in Collections." In Bing and Bruss 2007: 131–46.

Krevans, N. and Sens, A. 2006. "Language and Literature." In Bugh 2006: 186–207.

Kroll, W. 1924. *Studien zum Verständnis der römischen Literatur.* Stuttgart.

Kroll, W. 1925. "Lehrgedicht." *RE* 12.2: 1842–57.

Kroll, W. 1926. *Historia Alexandri Magni (Pseudo-Callisthenes).* Berlin.

Kroll, W. 1930. "Cn. Matius." *RE* 14.2: 2211–2.

Kroll, W. 1936. "Nikandros (11)." *RE* 17.1: 250–65.

Kruedener, J. von 1973. *Die Rolle des Hofes im Absolutismus.* Stuttgart.

Kühn, C. G. 1821–33. *Claudii Galeni Opera Omnia.* 22 vols. Leipzig.

Kühn, J.-H. 1958. "Die *Thalysien* Theokrits (*id.* 7)." *Hermes* 86: 40–79.

Kühnert, F. 1993. "Rhetorik." In Schmitt and Vogt 1993: 665–78.

Kuhrt, A. 1987. "Berossus' *Babyloniaka* and Seleucid Rule in Babylonia." In Kuhrt and Sherwin-White 1987: 32–56.

Kuhrt, A. 1995. "Ancient Mesopotamia in Classical Greek and Hellenistic Thought." In Sasson 1995: 55–65.

Kuhrt, A. and Sherwin-White, S. 1987 (eds.). *Hellenism in the East: The Interaction of Greek and Non-Greek Civilizations from Syria to Central Asia after Alexander.* Berkeley.

Kuhrt, A. and Sherwin-White, S. 1991. "Aspects of Seleucid Royal Ideology: The Cylinder of Antiochus I from Borsippa." *Journal of Hellenic Studies* 111: 71–86.

Kullmann, W. and Althoff, J. 1993 (eds.). *Vermittlung und Tradierung von Wissen in der griechischen Kultur.* Tübingen.

Kurke, L. 2002. "Gender, Politics and Subversion in the *Chreiai* of Machon." *Proceedings of the Cambridge Philological Society* 48: 20–65.

Kuttner, A. 2005. " 'Do You Look Like You Belong Here?' Asianism at Pergamon and the Makedonian Diaspora." In Gruen 2005: 137–206.

Kutzko, D. 2003. "Cafavy and the Discovery of Herodas." *Classical and Modern Literature* 23.2: 89–109.

Kutzko, D. 2006. "The Major Importance of a Minor Poet: Herodas 6 and 7 as a Quasi-dramatic Diptych." In Harder, Regtuit, and Wakker 2006: 167–84.

La'da, C. A. 2003. "Encounters with Ancient Egypt: The Hellenistic Greek Experience." In Matthews and Roemer 2003: 157–69.

Laird, A. 2006 (ed.). *Oxford Readings in Ancient Literary Criticism.* Oxford.

Lallot, J. 1998. *La grammaire de Denys le Thrace.* Paris.

Lamberton, R. and Keaney, J. J. 1992 (eds.). *Homer's Ancient Readers: The Hermeneutics of Greek Epic's Earliest Exegetes.* Princeton.

Lambin, G. 2003. "Une poétique de la parole: à propos de l'*Alexandra* de Lycophron." *Les études classiques* 71: 129–50.

Lambin, G. 2005. *La Alexandra de Lycophron: études et traduction.* Rennes.

Landels, J. G. 1978. *Engineering in the Ancient World.* Berkeley.

Lang, P. 2005 (ed.). *Re-Inventions: Essays on Hellenistic and Early Roman Science* = *Apeiron* 37.4.

Lang, P. 2009. "Goats and the Sacred Disease in Callimachus' Acontius and Cydippe." *Classical Philology* 104: 85–90.

Lape, S. 2001. "Democratic Ideology and the Poetics of Rape in Menandrian Comedy." *Classical Antiquity* 20: 79–120.

Lape, S. 2002/3. "Solon and the Institution of the Democratic Family Form." *Classical Journal* 98: 117–39.

Lape, S. 2003. "Racializing Democracy: The Politics of Sexual Reproduction in Classical Athens." In Bassi and Euben 2003: 52–62.

Lape, S. 2004a. *Reproducing Athens: Menander's Comedy, Democratic Culture, and the Hellenistic City.* Princeton.

Lape, S. 2004b. "The Terentian Marriage Plot: Reproducing Fathers and Sons." *Ramus* 33: 35–52.

Lasserre, F. 1966. *Die Fragmente des Eudoxos von Knidos.* Berlin.

Latacz, J. 1999. "Philitas und Homer: Bemerkungen zu Philitas' *Hermes.*" In Kazazis and Rengakos 1999: 202–10.

Lausberg, H. 1973. *Handbuch der literarischen Rhetorik: Eine Grundlegung der Literaturwissenschaft.* Second edition. Munich.

Lausberg, H. 1998. *Handbook of Literary Rhetorik: A Foundation for Literary Study.* Leiden.

Lavagnini, B. 1921. "Le origini del romanzo greco." *Annali della Scuola Normale Superiore di Pisa* 28: 9–104. Reprinted in Gärtner 1984: 41–101.

Lawall, G. 1966. "Apollonius' *Argonautica*: Jason as Anti-Hero." *Yale Classical Studies* 19: 119–69.

Lawrence, A. W. 1979. *Greek Aims in Fortification.* Oxford.

Lazaridis, N. 2007. *Wisdom in Loose Form: The Language of Egyptian and Greek Proverbs in Collections of the Hellenistic and Roman Periods.* Leiden.

Le Boeuffle, A. 1975. *Germanicus, Les Phénomènes d'Aratos.* Paris.

Legrand, P.-E. 1924. *La poésie alexandrine.* Paris.

Lehnus, L. 2002. "Posidippean and Callimachean Queries." *Zeitschrift für Papyrologie und Epigraphik* 138: 11–13.

Lehoux, D. 2006. "Logic, Physics, and Prediction in Hellenistic Philosophy: *x* happens, but *y*?" In Löwe, Peckhaus, and Räsch 2006: 125–42.

Lehoux, D. 2007. *Astronomy, Weather, and Calendars in the Ancient World.* Cambridge.

Lejeune, P. 1989. *On Autobiography.* Minneapolis.

Lelli, E. 2004. *Critica e polemiche letterarie nei Giambi di Callimaco.* Alessandria.

Lendering, J. 2008. "Astronomical Diaries." At www.livius.org, accessed on April 30, 2008.

Lenfant, D. 2004. *Ctésias de Cnide: La Perse, L'Inde, autres fragments.* Paris.

Lenfant, D. 2007. "Greek Historians of Persia." In Marincola 2007: 200–9.

Leone, P. L. 2002. *Scholia vetera et paraphrases in Lycophronis Alexandram.* Galatina.

Leontis, A. 1995. *Topographies of Hellenism: Mapping the Homeland.* Ithaca, NY.

Leppin, H. 1992. *Histrionen: Untersuchungen zur sozialen Stellung von Bühnenkünstlern im Westen des Römischen Reiches zur Zeit der Republik und des Principats.* Bonn.

Lesky, A. 1966. *A History of Greek Literature.* Translated from the 2nd German edition. London.

Lesky, A. 1971. *Geschichte der griechischen Literatur.* 3rd edition. Berlin.

LeVen, P. 2008. "The Many-Headed Muse: Tradition and Innovation in Fourth-Century BC Greek Lyric Poetry." Diss. Sorbonne/École Normale Supérieure, Paris.

Levitan, W. 1979. "Plexed Artistry: Aratean Acrostics." *Glyph* 5: 55–68.

Lewis, A.-M. 1992. "The Popularity of the *Phaenomena* of Aratus: A Reevaluation." In Deroux 1992: 94–118.

Liampi, K. 1998. *Der Makedonische Schild.* Berlin.

Lichtheim, M. 1980. *Ancient Egyptian Literature: A Book of Readings.* Vol. 3: *The Late Period.* Berkeley.

Lichtheim, M. 1983. *Late-Egyptian Wisdom Literature in its International Context: A Study of Demotic Instructions.* Freiburg and Göttingen.

Lightfoot, J. L. 1999. *Parthenius of Nicaea, The Poetical Fragments and the* Ἐρωτικὰ παθήματα. Oxford.

Lightfoot, J. L. 2002. "Nothing to do with the *technitai* of Dionysus?" In Easterling and Hall 2002: 209–224.

Lightfoot, J. L. 2003. *Lucian, On the Syrian Goddess.* Oxford.

Lightfoot, J. L. 2007. *The Sibylline Oracles, with Introduction, Translation, and Commentary on the First and Second Books.* Oxford.

Lindberg, D. C. 2007. *The Beginnings of Western Science: The European Scientific Tradition in Philosophical, Religious, and Institutional Context, Prehistory to A.D. 1450.* 2nd edition. Chicago.

Linssen, M. J. H. 2003. *The Cults of Uruk and Babylon: The Temple Ritual Texts as Evidence for Hellenistic Cult Practice.* Leiden.

Lippert, S. and Schentuleit, M. 2005 (eds.). *Tebtynis und Soknopaiu Nesos: Leben im römerzeitlichen Fajum.* Wiesbaden.

Liverani, M. 1990. *Prestige and Interest: International Relations in the Near East ca. 1600–1100.* Padua.

Livingston, I. 2004. *A Linguistic Commentary on Livius Andronicus.* New York.

Livrea, E. 1973. *Apollonii Rhodii Argonauticon liber IV.* Florence.

Livrea, E. 1986. *Studi Cercidei.* Bonn.

Livrea, E. and Privitera, G. 1978 (eds.). *Studi in onore di Anthos Ardizzoni.* 2 vols. Rome.

Lloyd, A. B. 1975–88. *Herodotus Book II.* 3 vols. Leiden.

Lloyd, A. B. 1988. "Herodotus' Account of Pharaonic History." *Historia* 37: 22–53.

Lloyd, A. B. 2002. "The Egyptian Elite in the Early Ptolemaic Period: Some Hieroglyphic Evidence." In Ogden 2002: 117–36.

Lloyd, G. E. R. 1973. *Greek Science after Aristotle.* London and New York.

Lloyd, G. E. R. 1983. *Science, Folklore, and Ideology.* Cambridge.

Lloyd, G. E. R. 1987. *The Revolutions of Wisdom: Studies in the Claims and Practice of Ancient Greek Science.* Berkeley.

Lloyd, G. E. R. 1991. *Methods and Problems in Greek Science.* Cambridge.

Lloyd, G. E. R. 1995. "Epistemological Arguments in Early Greek Medicine in Comparativist Perspective." In Bates 1995: 25–40.

Lloyd, G. E. R. 1996. *Adversaries and Authorities.* Cambridge.

Lloyd-Jones, H. 1963. "The Seal of Posidippus." *Journal of Hellenic Studies* 83: 75–99.

Lloyd-Jones, H. 1990. "A Hellenistic Miscellany." In *Greek Comedy, Hellenistic Literature, Greek Religion, and Miscellanea: The Academic Papers of Sir Hugh Lloyd-Jones.* Oxford: 231–49. Originally published *Studi italiani di filologia classica* 3rd ser. 2 (1984): 52–71.

Lloyd-Jones, H. 1994. "Again the Tattoo Elegy." *Zeitschrift für Papyrologie und Epigraphik* 101: 4–7.

Lloyd-Jones, H. 1999. "The Pride of Halicarnassus." *Zeitschrift für Papyrologie und Epigraphik* 124: 1–14 and 127: 63–5.

Lloyd-Jones, H. 2005. *Supplementum Supplementi Hellenistici.* Berlin.

Lloyd-Jones, H. and Parsons, P. 1983. *Supplementum Hellenisticum.* Berlin.

Lobel, E. 1928. "Nicander's Signature." *Classical Quarterly* 22: 114.

Lobel, E. and Page, D. L. 1963. *Poetarum Lesbiorum fragmenta.* 2nd edition. Oxford.

Lombardo, S and Rayor, D. 1988. *Callimachus: Hymns, Epigrams, Select Fragments.* Baltimore.

Lomiento, L. 1993. *Cercidas, testimonia et fragmenta.* Rome.

Long, A. A. 1978. "Timon of Phlius: Pyrrhonist and Satirist." *Proceedings of the Cambridge Philological Society* 24: 68–91.

Long, A. A. 1986. "Diogenes Laertius, *Life of Arcesilaus.*" *Elenchos* 7: 429–49.

Long, A. A. 1992. "Stoic Readings of Homer." In Lamberton and Keaney 1992: 41–66. Reprinted in Long 1996b: 58–84 and Laird 2006: 211–37.

Long, A. A. 1996a. "The Socratic Tradition: Diogenes, Crates, and Hellenistic Ethics." In Branham and Goulet-Cazé 1996: 28–46.

Long, A. A. 1996b. *Stoic Studies*. Berkeley.

Long, A. A. and Sedley, D. N. 1987. *The Hellenistic Philosophers*. Cambridge.

Long, L. 2001. *Openness, Secrecy, Authorship: Technical Arts and the Culture of Knowledge from Antiquity to the Renaissance*. Baltimore.

Longo Auricchio, F. 1977. *Φιλοδήμου Περὶ Ῥητορικῆς, libri primus et secundus* = Sbordone 1977.

Longrigg, J. 1998. *Greek Medicine: A Sourcebook*. London.

Lonis, R. 1992 (ed.). *L'étranger dans le monde grec II*. Nancy.

Lonsdale, S. H. 1993. *Dance and Ritual in Greek Religion*. Baltimore.

López Cruces, J. L. 1995. *Les Méliambes de Cercidas de Mégalopolis: politique et tradition littéraire*. Amsterdam.

López Férez, J. A. 1994 (ed.). *La épica griega y su influencia en la literatura española*. Madrid.

López Férez, J. A. 2003 (ed.). *Mitos en la literatura griega helenística e imperial*. Madrid.

Loprieno, A. 1996 (ed.). *Ancient Egyptian Literature: History and Forms*. Leiden.

L'Orange, H. P. 1953. *Studies in the Iconography of Cosmic Kingship in the Ancient World*. Oslo.

Loraux, N. 1986. *The Invention of Athens: The Funeral Oration in the Classical City*. Cambridge.

Loraux, N. 1993. *The Children of Athena*. Princeton.

Löwe, B., Peckhaus, V. and Räsch, T. 2006 (eds.). *Foundations of the Formal Sciences IV: The History of the Concept of the Formal Sciences*. London.

Lowe, N. 2004. "Lycophron." in De Jong, Nünlist, and Bowie 2004: 307–14.

Ludwig, W. 1963. "Die *Phainomena* Arats als hellenistische Dichtung." *Hermes* 91: 425–48.

Ludwig, W. 1968. "Die Kunst der Variation im hellenistischen Liebesepigramm." In Dihle 1968: 299–334.

Lund, H. S. 1992. *Lysimachus: A Study in Hellenistic Kingship*. London.

Luppe, W. 1997. "Kallimachos, *Aitien*-Prolog, V. 7–12." *Zeitschrift für Papyrologie und Epigraphik* 115: 50–4.

Lupu, E. 2005. *Greek Sacred Law: A Collection of New Documents*. Leiden.

Luria, S. 1963. "Herodas' Kampf für die veristische Kunst." In *Miscellanea di studi alessandrini in memoria di Augusto Rostagni*. Turin: 394–415.

Lushkov, A. H. 2003. "Watching Daphnis: Frustration of Viewing in *Idylls* 1 and 6." At www.chs.harvard.edu.

Lytle, G. F. and Orgel, S. 1981 (eds.). *Patronage in the Renaissance*. Princeton.

Ma, J. 1999. *Antiochos III and the Cities of Western Asia Minor*. Oxford.

Ma, J. 2003. "Kings." In Erskine 2003: 177–95.

Maass, E. 1898. *Commentariorum in Aratum reliquiae*. Berlin.

MacCormack, S. G. 1981. *Art and Ceremonial in Late Antiquity*. Berkeley.

MacDowell, D. M. 1978. *The Law in Classical Athens*. Ithaca, NY.

MacDowell, D. M. 1982. "Love versus the Law: An Essay on Menander's *Aspis*." *Greece and Rome* 29: 42–52.

Mace, S. 2001. "Utopian and Erotic Fusion in a New Elegy by Simonides." In Boedeker and Sider 2001: 185–207.

MacFarlane, K. 2002. "To Lay the Shining Foundation: The Theme of the Persian Wars in Classical Greek Poetry." Diss. University of Alberta.

MacFarlane, K. 2006. "Choerilus of Samos and Darius' Bridge: The Scope and Content of the *Persica* (*SH* 316–323)." *Mouseion* 6: 15–26.

MacFarlane, K. 2009. "Choerilus of Samos' Lament (*SH* 317) and the Revitalization of Epic." *American Journal of Philology* 130: 219–34.

MacGinnis, J. D. A. 1988. "Ctesias and the Fall of Nineveh." *Illinois Classical Studies* 13: 37–42.

Mactoux, M. M. and Geny, E. 1989 (eds.). *Mélanges Pierre Lévêque*. Paris.

Magnelli, E. 1999. *Alexandri Aetoli testimonia et fragmenta*. Florence.

Magnelli, E. 2002. *Studi su Euforione*. Rome.

Magnelli, E. 2006a. "Nicander's Chronology: A Literary Approach." In Harder, Regtuit, and Wakker 2006: 185–204.

Magnelli, E. 2006b. "La chiusa degli *Alexipharmaca* e la struttura dei due poemi iologici di Nicandro." In Cusset 2006b: 105–18.

Mair, A. W. 1921. *Callimachus, Hymns and Epigrams; Aratus, Phaenomena*. Cambridge, MA.

Malaise, M. 1966. "Sésostris, Pharaon de légende et d'histoire." *Chronique d'Égypte* 41: 244–272.

Manakidou, F. 1995. "Die Seher in den *Argonautika* des Apollonios Rhodios." *Studi italiani di filologia classica* 13: 190–208.

Manakidou, F. P. and Spanoudakis, K. 2008 (eds.). *Αλεξανδρινή Μούσα: συνέχεια και νεωτερισμός στην Ελληνιστική ποίηση*. Athens.

Manetti, G. 1993. *Theories of the Sign in Classical Antiquity*. Bloomington.

Mangoni, C. 1993. *Filodemo, Il quinto libro della poetica (P.Herc. 1425 e 1538)*. Naples.

Manitius, K. 1894. *Hipparchi in Arati et Eudoxi Phaenomena commentariorum libri tres*. Leipzig.

Männlein-Robert, I. 2006. "Hinkende Nachahmung: Desillusionierung und Grenzüberspielungen in Herodas' viertem *Mimiambos*." In Harder, Regtuit, and Wakker 2006: 205–28.

Männlein-Robert, I. 2007. *Stimme, Schrift und Bild: Zum Verhälnis der Künste in der hellenistischen Dichtung*. Heidelberg.

Marcovich, M. 1980. "Over Troubled Waters: *Megara* 62–71." *Illinois Classical Studies* 5: 49–56.

Marincola, J. 1997. *Authority and Tradition in Ancient Historiography*. Cambridge.

Marincola, J. 2001. *Greek Historians*. Oxford.

Marincola, J. 2007 (ed.). *A Companion to Greek and Roman Historiography*. 2 vols. Malden.

Marinone, N. 1997. *Berenice da Callimaco a Catullo*. 2nd edition. Bologna.

Mariotti, S. 1986. *Livio Andronico e la traduzione artistica*. Urbino.

Mariotti, S. 2001. *Il Bellum Poenicum e l'arte di Nevio*. 3rd edition. Bologna.

Marrou, H. I. 1948. *Histoire de l'éducation dans l'antiquité*. Paris.

Marrou, H. I. 1982. *A History of Education in Antiquity*. Madison.

Marsden, E. W. 1969, 1971. *Greek and Roman Artillery*. 2 vols. Oxford.

Martin, A. 2002. "Heurs and malheurs d'un manuscrit: deux notes à propos du papyrus d'Hérondas." *Zeitschrift für Papyrologie und Epigraphik* 139: 22–6.

Martin, Jean. 1974. *Scholia in Aratum Vetera*. Stuttgart.

Martin, Jean. 1998. *Aratos, Phénomènes*. 2 vols. Paris.

Martin, Joseph. 1974. *Antike Rhetorik: Technik und Methode*. Munich.

Martin, R. P. 1989. *The Language of Heroes: Speech and Performance in the Iliad*. Ithaca, NY.

Martina, A. 2003 (ed.). *Teatro greco postclassico e teatro latino: teorie e prassi drammatica*. Rome.

Martindale, C. 1997a. "Green Politics: The *Eclogues*." In Martindale 1997b: 107–24.

Martindale, C. 1997b (ed.). *The Cambridge Companion to Virgil*. Cambridge.

Martínez, S. 2000. "Los *Cynegetica* fragmentarios y el fracaso del cazador." *Myrtia* 15: 177–85.

Marx, F. 1904. *C. Lucilii carminum reliquiae*. 2 vols. Leipzig.

Marzolph, U., Van Leeuwen, R. and Wassouf, H. 2004. *The Arabian Nights Encyclopedia*. Santa Barbara and Oxford.

Mascialino, L. 1964. *Lycophronis Alexandra*. Leipzig.
Massimilla, G. 1996. *Callimaco, Aitia: libri primo e secondo*. Pisa.
Massimilla, G. 2000. "Nuovi elementi per la cronologia di Nicandro." In Pretagostini 2000: 127–37.
Mastromarco, G. 1979. *Il pubblico di Eronda*. Padua.
Mastromarco, G. 1984. *The Public of Herondas*. Amsterdam.
Mastromarco, G. 1991. "Il mimo greco letterario." *Dioniso* 61: 169–92.
Matteo, R. 2007. *Apollonio Rodio, Argonautiche: libro II*. Lecce.
Matthes, D. 1958. "Hermagoras von Temnos 1904–1955." *Lustrum* 3: 58–214.
Matthes, D. 1962. *Hermagorae Temnitae testimonia et fragmenta*. Leipzig.
Matthews, R. and Roemer, C. 2003 (eds.). *Ancient Perspectives on Egypt*. London.
Matthews, V. J. 1974. *Panyassis of Halikarnassos: Text and Commentary*. Leiden.
Matthews, V. J. 1996. *Antimachus of Colophon: Text and Commentary*. Leiden.
Maul, S. M. 1991. "Neues zu den Graeco-Babyloniaca." *Zeitschrift für Assyriologie* 81: 87–107.
Maxwell, R. L. 1992. "The Documentary Evidence for Ancient Mime." Diss. Toronto.
May, J. 2003 (ed.). *Brill's Companion to Cicero*. Leiden.
McCarthy, K. 2000. *Slaves, Masters, and the Art of Authority in Plautine Comedy*. Princeton.
McGing, B. C. 1997. "Revolt Egyptian Style: Internal Opposition to Ptolemaic Rule." *Archiv für Papyrusforschung* 43: 273–314.
McGing, B. C. 2006. Review of Veïsse 2004. *Archiv für Papyrusforschung* 52: 58–63.
McHale, B. 1987. *Postmodernist Fiction*. London.
McKenzie, J. 2003. "Glimpsing Alexandria from Archaeological Evidence." *Journal of Roman Archaeology* 16: 35–61.
McKenzie, J. 2007. *The Architecture of Alexandria and Egypt: 300 BC–AD 700*. New Haven and London.
McLennan, G. R. 1977. *Callimachus, Hymn to Zeus*. Rome.
Mehl, A. 1986. *Seleukos Nikator und sein Reich*. Vol. 1: *Seleukos' Leben und die Entwicklung seiner Machtposition*. Leuven.
Meijering, R. 1987. *Literary and Rhetorical Theories in Greek Scholia*. Groningen.
Meillier, C. 1993. "Théocrite, *Idylle* VII et autour de l'*Idylle* VII: ambiguïtés et contradictions de l'autobiographique." In Arrighetti and Montanari 1993: 101–28.
Meissner, B. 1992. *Historiker zwischen Polis und Königshof: Studien zur Stellung der Geschichtsschreiber in der griechischen Gesellschaft in spätklassischer und hellenistischer Zeit*. Göttingen.
Meissner, B. 1999. *Die technologische Fachliteratur der Antike: Struktur, Überlieferung und Wirkung technischen Wissens in der Antike (ca. 400 v.Chr. – ca. 500 n.Chr.)*. Berlin.
Merkelbach, R. 1956. "Βουκολιασταί (Der Wettgesang der Hirten)." *Rheinisches Museum für Philologie* 99: 97–133.
Merkelbach, R. 1981. "Das Königtum der Ptolemäer und die hellenistischen Dichter." In Hinske 1981: 27–35.
Merkelbach, R. and Stauber, J. 1998–2004. *Steinepigramme aus dem griechischen Osten*. 5 vols. Stuttgart, Munich, and Leipzig.
Merkelbach, R. and West, M. L. 1969. *Fragmenta Hesiodea*. Oxford.
Merriam, C. U. 2001. *The Development of the Epyllion Genre through the Hellenistic and Roman Periods*. Lewiston.
Mette, H. J. 1936. *Sphairopoiia: Untersuchungen zur Kosmologie des Krates von Pergamon*. Munich.
Mette, H. J. 1980. "Neoptolemos von Parion." *Rheinisches Museum für Philologie* 123: 1–24.
Meyer, D. 2007. "The Act of Reading and the Act of Writing in Hellenistic Epigram." In Bing and Bruss 2007: 187–210.

Meyer, E. 1912. *Der Papyrusfund von Elephantine: Dokumente einer jüdischen Gemeinde aus der Perserzeit und das älteste erhaltene Buch der Welt.* Leipzig.

Meyer, S. 2003 (ed.). *Egypt, Temple of the Whole World: Studies in Honour of Jan Assmann.* Leiden.

Miles, G. B. 1977. "Characterization and the Ideal of Innocence in Theocritus' *Idylls.*" *Ramus* 6: 139–64.

Miller, S. G. 2004. *Arete: Greek Sports from Ancient Sources.* 3rd edition. Berkeley.

Mineur, W. H. 1984. *Callimachus, Hymn to Delos.* Leiden.

Miralles, C. 1992. "La poetica di Eroda." *Aevum antiquum* 5: 89–113.

Miralles, C. and Pòrtulas, J. 1988. *The Poetry of Hipponax.* Rome.

Mitchell, S. 2003. "The Galatians: Representation and Reality." In Erskine 2003: 280–93.

Modrzejewski, J. M. 2005. "Greek Law in the Hellenistic Period: Family and Marriage." In Gagarin and Cohen 2005: 343–56.

Molyneux, J. H. 1992. *Simonides: A Historical Study.* Wauconda.

Momigliano, A. 1942. "*Terra marique.*" *Journal of Roman Studies* 32: 53–64.

Momigliano, A. 1945. "The Locrian Maidens and the Date of Lycophron's *Alexandra.*" *Classical Quarterly* 39: 49–53.

Montanari Caldini, R. 1973. "L'astrologia nei *Prognostica* di Germanico." *Studi italiani di filologia classica* 45: 137–204.

Montanari, F. 1974. "L'episodio eleusino delle peregrinazioni di Demetra: a proposito delle fonti di Ovidio, *Fast.* 4.502–562 e *Metam.* 5.446–461." *Annali della Scuola Normale Superiore di Pisa* 4: 109–37.

Montanari, F. and Lehnus, L. 2002 (eds.). *Callimaque: sept exposés suivis de discussions.* Geneva.

Mooney, G. W. 1912. *The Argonautica of Apollonius Rhodius.* London and Dublin.

Mooney, G. W. 1921. *The Alexandra of Lycophron.* London.

Mooren, L. 1975. *The Aulic Titulature in Ptolemaic Egypt: Introduction and Prosopography.* Brussels.

Mooren, L. 1977. *La hierarchie de cour ptolémaïque: contribution à l'étude des institutions et des classes dirigeantes à l'époque hellénistique.* Leuven.

Moran, B. T. 1991a. "Patronage and Institutions: Courts, Universities, and Academies in Germany: An Overview, 1550–1750." In Moran 1991b: 169–83.

Moran, B. T. 1991b (ed.). *Patronage and Institutions: Science, Technology, and Medicine at the European Court, 1500–1750.* Rochester, NY.

Morgan, J. R. 1993. "Make-believe and Make Believe: The Fictionality of the Greek Novels." In Gill and Wiseman 1993: 175–229.

Morgan, J. R. 2007. "Fiction and History." In Marincola 2007: 553–64.

Morgan, J. R. and Stoneman, R. 1994 (eds.). *Greek Fiction: The Greek Novel in Context.* New York and London.

Morgan, T. 1998a. *Literate Education in the Hellenistic and Roman Worlds.* Cambridge.

Morgan, T. 1998b. "A Good Man Skilled in Politics: Quintilian's Political Theory." In Too 1998: 245–62.

Morgan, T. 2007. "Rhetoric and Education." In Worthington 2007: 303–19.

Mori, A. 2007. "Acts of Persuasion in Hellenistic Epic: Honey-Sweet Words in Apollonius." In Worthington 2007: 558–72.

Mori, A. 2008. *The Politics of Apollonius Rhodius' Argonautica.* Cambridge.

Morrison, A. D. 2005. "Sexual Ambiguity and the Identity of the Narrator in Callimachus' *Hymn to Athena.*" *Bulletin of the Institute of Classical Studies* 48: 27–46.

Morrison, A. D. 2007. *The Narrator in Archaic Greek and Hellenistic Poetry.* Cambridge.

Mossé, C. 1992. "L'étranger dans le théâtre de Ménandre." In Lonis 1992: 271–7.

Most, G. W. 1982. "Neues zur Geschichte des Terminus 'Epyllion'." *Philologus* 126: 153–6.

Most, G. W. 1989. "Cornutus and Stoic Allegoresis: A Preliminary Report." *ANRW* II.36.3: 2014–65.

Most, G. W. 1993. "Die *Batrachomyomachia* als ernste Parodie." In Ax and Glei 1993: 27–40.

Most, G. W. 1997 (ed.). *Collecting Fragments / Fragmente sammeln*. Göttingen.

Moxon, I. S., Smart, J. D. and Woodman, A. J. 1986 (eds.). *Past Perspectives: Studies in Greek and Roman Historical Writing*. Cambridge.

Moyer, I. S. 2002. "Herodotus and an Egyptian Mirage: The Genealogies of the Theban Priests." *Journal of Hellenic Studies* 122: 70–90.

Mueller, K. 2005. "Geographical Information Systems (GIS) in Papyrology: Mapping Fragmentation and Migration Flow to Hellenistic Egypt." *Bulletin of the American Society of Papyrologists* 42: 63–92.

Müller, C. W. 1987. *Erysichthon: Der Mythos als narrative Metapher im Demeterhymnos des Kallimachos*. Stuttgart.

Müller, C. W. 1998. "Wanted! Die Kallimachosforschung auf der Suche nach einem einsilbigen Substantiv." *Zeitschrift für Papyrologie und Epigraphik* 122: 36–40.

Murphy, S. 1995. "Heron's *Automatopoiikēs*." *History of Technology* 17: 1–44.

Murray, J. 2004. "The Metamorphoses of Erysichthon: Callimachus, Apollonius, and Ovid." In Harder, Regtuit, and Wakker 2004: 207–41.

Murray, O. 1972. "Herodotus and Hellenistic Culture." *Classical Quarterly* 22: 200–13.

Murray, O. 1990 (ed.). *Sympotica: A Symposium on the Symposion*. Oxford.

Murray, P. and Wilson, P. 2004 (eds.). *Music and the Muses: The Culture of Mousikē in the Classical Athenian City*. Oxford.

Musti, D. 2001. "Punti fermi e prospettive di ricerca sulla cronologia dell'*Alessandra* di Licofrone." *Hespería* 14: 201–26.

Nagy, G. 1987. "Herodotus the *logios*." *Arethusa* 20: 175–84.

Nagy, G. 1998. "The Library of Pergamon as a Classical Model." In Koester 1998: 185–232.

Nairn, J. A. 1904. *The Mimes of Herodas*. Oxford.

Nauta, R. R. 1990. "Gattungsgeschichte als Rezeptionsgeschichte am Beispiel der Entstehung der Bukolik." *Antike und Abendland* 36: 116–37.

Negri, M. 2000. "L'ultima(?) parola sul presunto incontro tra Arato e Callimaco." *Studi classici e orientali* 47: 495–8.

Nelis, D. 2001. *Vergil's Aeneid and the Argonautica of Apollonius Rhodius*. Leeds.

Nelis, D. 2005. "Apollonius of Rhodes." In Foley 2005: 353–63.

Nesselrath, H.-G. 1990. *Die attische Mittlere Komödie: Ihre Stellung in der antiken Literaturkritik und Literaturgeschichte*. Berlin.

Netz, R. 1999. *The Shaping of Deduction in Greek Mathematics: A Study of Cognitive History*. Cambridge.

Netz, R. 2004a. *The Transformation of Mathematics in the Early Mediterranean World: From Problems to Equations*. Cambridge.

Netz, R. 2004b. *The Works of Archimedes*. Vol. 1: *The Two Books On the Sphere and the Cylinder*. Cambridge.

Netz, R. 2009. *Ludic Proof: Greek Mathematics and the Alexandrian Aesthetic*. Cambridge.

Netz, R. and Noel, W. 2007. *The Archimedes Codex*. Cambridge, MA and New York.

Neugebauer, O. 1975. *A History of Ancient Mathematical Astronomy*. 3 vols. Berlin.

Neugebauer, O. and Van Hoesen, H. B. 1959. *Greek Horoscopes*. Philadelphia.

Neusner, J. 1975 (ed.). *Christianity, Judaism, and Other Greco-Roman Cults*. Vol. 3. Leiden.

Newsom, R. 1988. *A Likely Story: Probability and Play in Fiction*. New Brunswick.

Nicastro, N. 2008. *Circumference: Eratosthenes and the Ancient Quest to Measure the Globe.* New York.

Nicolet, C. 1970 (ed.). *Recherches sur les structures sociales dans l'antiquité classique.* Paris.

Nielsen, I. 1994. *Hellenistic Palaces: Tradition and Renewal.* Aarhus.

Nikonov, V. P. 1998. "Apollodorus of Artemita and the Date of his *Parthika* Revisited." *Electrum* 2: 107–22.

Nilsson, M. 1955. *Die hellenistische Schule.* Munich.

Nisbet, G. 2003. *Greek Epigram in the Roman Empire: Martial's Forgotten Rivals.* Oxford.

Nisbet, G. 2007. "Satiric Epigram." In Bing and Bruss 2007: 353–69.

Nisetich, F. 2001. *The Poems of Callimachus.* Oxford.

Noegel, S. 2004. "Apollonius' *Argonautika* and Egyptian Solar Mythology." *Classical World* 97: 123–36.

Noussia, M. forthcoming. *Solon of Athens: The Poetic Fragments.* Leiden.

Nünlist, R. 2004. "The Homeric Hymns." In De Jong, Nünlist, and Bowie 2004: 35–42.

Nussbaum, M. 1997. "Serpents in the Soul: A Reading of Seneca's *Medea.*" In Clauss and Johnston 1997: 219–49.

Nutton, V. 2004. *Ancient Medicine.* London and New York.

Obbink, D. 1995 (ed.). *Philodemus and Poetry: Poetic Theory and Practice in Lucretius, Philodemus, and Horace.* New York and Oxford.

Obbink, D. 2001. "The Genre of *Plataea*: Generic Unity in the New Simonides." In Boedeker and Sider 2001: 65–85.

Obbink, D. 2003. "Allegory and Exegesis in the Derveni Papyrus." In Boys-Stones 2003b: 177–88.

Ober, J. 1989. *Mass and Elite in Democratic Athens: Rhetoric, Ideology, and the Power of the People.* Princeton.

Oelsner, J. 1986. *Materialien zur babylonischen Gesellschaft und Kultur in hellenistischer Zeit.* Budapest.

Ogden, D. 1996. *Greek Bastardy in the Classical and Hellenistic Periods.* Oxford.

Ogden, D. 1999. *Polygamy, Prostitutes and Death: The Hellenistic Dynasties.* London.

Ogden, D. 2002 (ed.). *The Hellenistic World: New Perspectives.* London.

Ogilvie, R. M. 1962. "The Song of Thyrsis." *Journal of Hellenic Studies* 82: 106–10.

Oikonomakos, K. 1999. "Les *Alexipharmaques* et le *Corpus Hippocraticum*: Nicandre lecteur d'Hippocrate(?)." *Revue des études grecques* 112: 238–52.

Oikonomakos, K. 2002a. *Νικάνδρου Ἀλεξιφάρμακα.* Athens.

Oikonomakos, K. 2002b. *Προλεγόμενα στὴν κριτικὴ ἔκδοση τῶν Ἀλεξιφαρμάκων τοῦ Νικάνδρου.* Athens.

Oikonomides, A. N. 1980. "The Lost Delphic Inscription with the Commandments of the Seven and *P.Univ.Athen.* 2782." *Zeitschrift für Papyrologie und Epigraphik* 37: 179–83.

Oleson, J. P. 2008 (ed.). *The Oxford Handbook of Engineering and Technology in the Classical World.* Oxford.

Oliver, G. J. 2006. "History and Rhetoric." In Bugh 2006: 113–35.

Olney, J. 1980 (ed.). *Autobiography: Essays Theoretical and Critical.* Princeton.

Olson, S. D. 2007–. *Athenaeus, The Learned Banqueters.* Cambridge, MA.

Olson, S. D. and Sens, A. 1999. *Matro of Pitane and the Tradition of Epic Parody in the Fourth Centuy BCE.* Atlanta.

Olson, S. D. and Sens, A. 2000. *Archestratos of Gela: Greek Culture and Cuisine in the Fourth Century BCE.* Oxford.

Omitowoju, R. 2002. *Rape and the Politics of Consent in Classical Athens.* Cambridge.

Osborne, R. G. 1985. "Law in Action in Classical Athens." *Journal of Hellenic Studies* 105: 40–58.

O'Sullivan, N. 1992. *Alcidamas, Aristophanes and the Beginnings of Greek Stylistic Theory.* Stuttgart.

Ott, U. 1969. *Die Kunst des Gegensatzes in Theokrits Hirtengedichten.* Hildesheim.

Otto, E. 1954. *Die biographischen Inschriften der ägyptischen Spätzeit: Ihre geistesgeschichtliche und literarische Bedeutung.* Leiden.

Pace, B. 1932. "Mimo e attor mimico." *Dioniso* 3: 162–72.

Packman, Z. 1991. "The Incredible and the Incredulous: The Vocabulary of Disbelief in Herodotus, Thucydides and Xenophon." *Hermes* 199: 399–414.

Paduano Faedo, L. 1970. "L'inversione del rapporto *poeta–musa* nella cultura ellenistica." *Annali della Scuola Normale Superiore di Pisa* 39: 377–86.

Pagani, L. 2004. "Asclepiade di Mirlea e la coppa di Nestore." In Pretagostini and Dettori 2004: 353–69.

Page, D. L. 1936. "The Elegiacs in Euripides' *Andromache.*" In Earp 1936.

Page, D. L. 1975. *Epigrammata Graeca.* Oxford.

Page, D. L. 1981. *Further Greek Epigrams.* Cambridge.

Palumbo Stracca, B. M. 2006. "Eronda 'ipponatteo' (mim. IV, vv. 72–78)." *Rivista di cultura classica e medioevale* 48: 49–54.

Pàmias, J. and Geus, K. 2007. *Eratosthenes, Sternsagen (Catasterismi).* Oberhaid.

Papanghelis, T. D. and Rengakos, A. 2001 (eds.). *A Companion to Apollonius Rhodius.* Leiden. 2nd edition 2008.

Papathomopoulos, M. 1976. *Εὐτεκνίου παραφράcειc εἰc τὰ Νικάνδρου Θηριακὰ καὶ Ἀλεξιφάρμακα.* Ioannina.

Parca, M. G. 1991. *Ptocheia or Odysseus in Disguise at Troy (P.Köln VI 245).* Atlanta.

Parke, H. W. 1988. *Sibyls and Sibylline Prophecy in Classical Antiquity.* London.

Parker, L. P. E. 2001. "*Consilium et ratio*? Papyrus A of Bacchylides and Alexandrian Metrical Scholarship." *Classical Quarterly* 51: 23–52.

Parkinson, R. 2002. *Poetry and Culture in Middle Kingdom Egypt: A Dark Side to Perfection.* London.

Parlasca, K. 1959. *Die römischen Mosaiken in Deutschland.* Berlin.

Parpola, S. and Watanabe, K. 1988. *Neo-Assyrian Treaties and Loyalty Oaths.* Helsinki.

Parsons, P. J. 1977. "Callimachus, *Victoria Berenices.*" *Zeitschrift für Papyrologie und Epigraphik* 25: 1–50.

Parsons, P. J. 1981. Review of Mastromarco 1979. *Classical Review* 31: 110.

Paskiewicz, T. M. 1988. "Aitia in the Second Book of Apollonius' *Argonautica.*" *Illinois Classical Studies* 13: 57–61.

Pasquali, G. 1913. "I due Nicandri." *Studi italiani di filologia classica* 20: 55–111. Reprinted in *Scritti filologici.* Florence 1986: 1.340–87.

Paton, W. R. 1916–19. *The Greek Anthology.* 5 vols. Cambridge, MA.

Patterson, A. 1987. *Pastoral and Ideology.* Berkeley.

Patterson, C. 1998. *The Family in Greek History.* Cambridge.

Pavel, T. G. 1986. *Fictional Worlds.* Cambridge, MA.

Payne, M. 2007. *Theocritus and the Invention of Fiction.* Cambridge.

Pecere, O. and Stramaglia, A. 1996 (eds.). *La letteratura di consumo nel mondo greco-latino.* Cassino.

Peek, W. 1955. *Griechische Vers-Inschriften I: Grabinschriften.* Berlin.

Pelling, C. 2007. "The Greek Historians of Rome." In Marincola 2007: 244–58.

Pendergraft, M. L. B. 1990. "On the Nature of the Constellations: Aratus, *Ph.* 367–85." *Eranos* 88: 99–106.

Peremans, W. 1970. "Ethnies et classes dans l'Égypte ptolémaïque." In Nicolet 1970: 213–23.

Peremans, W., Van't Dack, E. and Mooren, L. 1968. *Prosopographia Ptolemaica VI: la cour, les relations internationales et les possessions extérieures, la vie culturelle*. Leuven.

Peretti, A. 1979. *Il Periplo di Scilace: studio sul primo portolano del Mediterraneo*. Pisa.

Pernot, L. 2000. *La rhétorique dans l'antiquité*. Paris.

Pernot, L. 2005. *Rethoric in Antiquity*. Washington, DC.

Perpillou-Thomas, F. 1993. *Fêtes d'Égypte ptolémaïque et romaine d'après la documentation papyrologique grecque*. Leuven.

Perry, B. E. 1967. *The Ancient Romances: A Literary-Historical Account of their Origins*. Berkeley.

Perutelli, A. 1979. *La narrazione commentata: studi sull'epillio latino*. Pisa.

Pessoa, F. 1998. *Fernando Pessoa & Co*. New York.

Pessoa, F. 2001. *The Selected Prose of Fernando Pessoa*. New York.

Petrain, D. 2005. "Gems, Metapoetics, and Value: Greek and Roman Responses to a Third-Century Discourse on Precious Stones." *Transactions of the American Philological Association* 135: 329–57.

Petrovic, A. 2007. "Inscribed Epigram in Pre-Hellenistic Literary Sources." In Bing and Bruss 2007: 49–68.

Petrovic, A. and Petrovic, I. 2006. "'Look Who Is Talking Now!': Speaker and Communication in Greek Metrical Sacred Regulations." In Stavrianopoulou 2006: 151–79.

Petrovic, I. 2007. *Von den Toren des Hades zu den Hallen des Olymp: Artemiskult bei Theokrit und Kallimachos*. Leiden.

Petrovic, I. forthcoming. "Callimachus' *Hymn to Apollo* and Greek Metrical Sacred Regulations." In Harder, Regtuit, and Wakker forthcoming.

Pfeiffer, R. 1949, 1953. *Callimachus*. 2 vols. Oxford.

Pfeiffer, R. 1968. *History of Classical Scholarship: From the Beginnings to the End of the Hellenistic Age*. Oxford.

Pfeijffer, I. L. 1999. *First Person Futures in Pindar*. Stuttgart.

Philonenko, M. 1968. *Joseph et Aséneth*. Leiden.

Pickard-Cambridge, A. 1968. *The Dramatic Festivals of Athens*. 2nd edition, revised by J. Gould and D. M. Lewis. Oxford.

Picone, M. and Zimmermann, B. (eds.). *Der antike Roman und seine mittelalterliche Rezeption*. Basel.

Pierce, K. 1997. "The Portrayal of Rape in New Comedy." In Deacy and Pierce 1997: 163–84.

Plantinga, M. 2004. "A Parade of Learning: Callimachus' *Hymn to Artemis* (lines 170–268)." In Harder, Regtuit, and Wakker 2004: 257–77.

Pöhlmann, E. and West, M. L. 2001. *Documents of Ancient Greek Music*. Oxford.

Pomeroy, S. B. 1984. *Women in Hellenistic Egypt: From Alexander to Cleopatra*. New York.

Porten, B. 2004. "The Prophecy of Hor bar Punesh and the Demise of Righteousness: An Aramaic Papyrus in the British Library." In Hoffmann and Thissen 2004: 427–66.

Porten, B. and Yardeni, A. 1993. *Textbook of Aramaic Documents from Ancient Egypt*. Vol. 3: *Literature, Accounts, Lists*. Jerusalem and Winona Lake.

Porter, H. N. 1946. "Hesiod and Aratus." *Transactions of the American Philological Association* 77: 158–70.

Porter, J. 1992. "Hermeneutic Lines and Circles: Aristarchus and Crates on the Exegesis of Homer." In Lamberton and Keaney 1992: 67–114.

Porter, J. 1994. "Stoic Morals and Poetics in Philodemus." *Cronache ercolanesi* 24: 63–88.

Porter, J. 1995. "Content and Form in Philodemus: The History of an Evasion." In Obbink 1995: 97–147.

Porter, J. 2004. "Aristotle and the Origins of Euphonism." In *Mathesis e mneme: studi in memoria di Marcello Gigante*. Naples: 131–48.

Porter, S. E. 1997 (ed.). *Handbook of Classical Rhetoric in the Hellenistic Period, 330 BC–AD 400*. Leiden.

Posener, G. 1985. *Le Papyrus Vandier*. Cairo.

Possanza, D. M. 2004. *Translating the Heavens: Aratus, Germanicus, and the Poetics of Latin Translation*. New York.

Potter, D. 1994. *Prophets and Emperors*. Cambridge, MA.

Powell, B. 1991. *Homer and the Origin of the Greek Alphabet*. Cambridge.

Powell, J. U. 1925. *Collectanea Alexandrina: reliquiae minores poetarum Graecorum aetatis Ptolemaicae, 323–146 A.C.* Oxford.

Pratt, L. 1983. *Lying and Poetry from Homer to Pindar: Falsehood and Deception in Archaic Greek Poetics*. Ann Arbor.

Prauscello, L. 2006. *Singing Alexandria: Music between Practice and Textual Transmission*. Leiden.

Prauscello, L. 2009. "Wandering Poetry, 'Travelling' Music: Timotheus' Muse and Some Case-studies of Shifting Cultural Identities." In Hunter and Rutherford 2009: 168–94.

Préaux, C. 1960. "Les fonctions du droit dans la comédie nouvelle." *Chronique d'Égypte* 25: 222–39.

Préaux, C. 1978. *Le Monde hellénistique: la Grèce et l'Orient de la mort d'Alexandre à la conquête romaine de la Grèce (323–146 av. J.-C.)*. 2 vols. Paris.

Pretagostini, R. 1992. "Tracce di poesia orale nei carmi di Teocrito." *Aevum antiquum* 5: 67–87.

Pretagostini, R. 2000 (ed.). *La letteratura ellenistica: problemi e prospettive di ricerca*. Rome.

Pretagostini, R. and Dettori, E. 2004 (eds.). *La cultura ellenistica: l'opera letteraria e l'esegesi antica*. Rome.

Price, S. R. F. 1984. *Rituals and Power: The Roman Imperial Cult in Asia Minor*. Cambridge.

Puccioni, G. 1950. "Due note a Eroda." *Annali della Scuola Normale Superiore di Pisa* 19: 51–2.

Puchner, W. 1993. "Zur Raumkonzeption der *Mimiamben* des Herodas." *Wiener Studien* 106: 9–34.

Puelma, M. 1960. "Die Dichterbegegnung in Theokrits *Thalysien*." *Museum Helveticum* 17: 144–64.

Puelma, M. 1996. "Ἐπίγραμμα–*epigramma*: Aspekte einer Wortgeschichte." *Museum Helveticum* 53: 123–39.

Pummer, R. 1982. "*Genesis* 34 in Jewish Writings of the Hellenistic and Roman Periods." *Harvard Theological Review* 75: 177–88.

Quack, J. F. 2002. "Die Spur des Magiers Petese." *Chronique d'Égypte* 77: 76–92.

Quack, J. F. 2003. "'Ich bin Isis, die Herrin der beiden Länder': Versuch zum demotischen Hintergrund der memphitischen Isisaretalogie." In Meyer 2003: 319–65.

Quack, J. F. 2005. *Einführung in die altägyptische Literaturgeschichte*. Vol. 3: *Die demotische und gräko-ägyptische Literatur*. Münster.

Quack, J. F. 2007. "Die Initiation zum Schreiberberuf." *Studien zur altägyptischen Kultur* 36: 249–95.

Race, W. H. 2008. *Apollonius Rhodius, Argonautica*. Cambridge, MA.

Radici Colace, P. and Zumbo, A. 2004 (eds.). *La riscrittura e il teatro dall'antico al moderno e dai testi alla scena*. Messina.

Radke, G. 2007. *Die Kindheit des Mythos: Die Erfindung der Literaturgeschichte in der Antike*. Munich.

Rajak, T. 2009. *Translation and Survival: The Greek Bible of the Ancient Jewish Diaspora*. Oxford.
Ramelli, I. and Lucchetta, G. 2004. *Allegoria*. Vol. 1: *L'età classica*. Milan.
Rapp, C. forthcoming (ed.). *City–Empire–Christendom: Changing Contexts of Power and Identity in Antiquity.* Cambridge.
Rashed, R., Decorps-Foulquier, M., and Federspiel, M. 2008–. *Apollonius de Perge, Coniques*. Vols. 1, 2.1, 2.2, 2.3, 3, 4. Berlin.
Raubitschek, A. E. 1968. "Das Denkmal-Epigramm." In Dihle 1968: 3–36.
Rawles, R. 2006. "Homeric Beginnings in the 'Tattoo Elegy'." *Classical Quarterly* 56: 486–95.
Rawson, E. 1985. *Intellectual Life in the Late Roman Republic*. London.
Ray, J. D. 1976. *The Archive of Hor.*. London.
Reardon, B. P. 1989. *Collected Ancient Greek Novels*. Berkeley.
Redford, D. B. 1986. *Pharaonic King-Lists, Annals, and Day-Books*. Mississauga.
Redondo Moyano, E. 1995. *Estudio sintáctico de las partículas en el período helenístico: Herodas*. Amsterdam.
Reed, J. D. 1997. *Bion of Smyrna, The Fragments and the Adonis*. Cambridge.
Reed, J. D. 2000. "Arsinoe's Adonis and the Poetics of Ptolemaic Imperialism." *Transactions of the American Philological Association* 130: 319–51.
Reed, J. D. 2006. "Continuity and Change in Greek Bucolic between Theocritus and Virgil." In Fantuzzi and Papanghelis 2006: 209–34.
Rees, R. 2002. *Layers of Loyalty: Latin Panegyric, AD 289–307*. Oxford.
Reeve, M. D. 1996/7. "A Rejuvenated Snake." *Acta Antiqua Academiae Scientiarum Hungaricae* 37: 245–58.
Reiner, L. 1975. "Philodamus' *Paean to Dionysus*: A Literary Expression of Delphic Propaganda." Diss. University of Illinois, Urbana-Champaign.
Reinsch-Werner, H. 1976. *Callimachus Hesiodicus: Die Rezeption der hesiodischen Dichtung durch Kallimachos von Kyrene*. Berlin.
Reitz, C. 1996. *Zur Gleichnistechnik des Apollonios Rhodios*. Frankfurt am Main.
Reitzenstein, E. 1931. "Zur Stiltheorie des Kallimachos." In *Festschrift Richard Reitzenstein*. Leipzig: 23–69.
Reitzenstein, R. 1893. *Epigramm und Skolion: Ein Beitrag zur Geschichte der alexandrinischen Dichtung*. Giessen.
Rengakos, A. 1992. "Homerische Wörter bei Kallimachos." *Zeitschrift für Papyrologie und Epigraphik* 94: 21–47.
Rengakos, A. 1993. *Der Homertext und die hellenistischen Dichter*. Stuttgart.
Rengakos, A. 1994a. *Apollonios Rhodios und die antike Homererklärung*. Munich.
Rengakos, A. 1994b. "Lykophron als Homererklärer." *Zeitschrift für Papyrologie und Epigraphik* 102: 111–30.
Rengakos, A. 2001. "Apollonius Rhodius as a Homeric Scholar." In Papanghelis and Rengakos 2001: 193–216.
Reverdin, M. 1961 (ed.). *Grecs et barbares*. Geneva.
Rhodes, P. J. 1981. *A Commentary on the Aristotelian Athenaion Politeia*. Oxford.
Rhys Davids, T. W. 1975. *The Questions of King Milinda*. Delhi.
Rice, E. E. 1983. *The Grand Procession of Ptolemy Philadelphus*. New York.
Riess, E. 1892. "Nechepsonis et Petosiridis fragmenta magica." *Philologus Supplement* 6: 325–94.
Rigsby, K. 1996. *Asylia: Territorial Inviolability in the Hellenistic World*. Berkeley.
Rihll, T. E. 1999. *Greek Science*. Oxford.
Rihll, T. E. 2009. "Ancient Technology." In Erskine 2009.

Rihll, T. E. and Tuplin, C. J. 2002 (eds.). *Science and Mathematics in Ancient Greek Culture*. Oxford.

Robert, L. 1966. "Sur un décret d'Ilion et sur un papyrus concernant des cultes royaux." In Samuel 1966: 175–211.

Robert, L. 1969. "Théophane de Mytilène à Constantinople." *Comptes rendues de l'Académie des Inscriptions et Belles-Lettres* 1969: 42–64.

Rohde, E. 1914 [1876]. *Der griechische Roman und seine Vorläufer*. 3rd edition. Berlin.

Romeo, C. 1988. *Demetrio Lacone, La Poesia (PHerc. 188 e 1014)*. Naples.

Romeo, C. 1992. "Un contributo inedito di Filodemo alla critica omerica (*PHerc*. 1677 coll. V–VII)." In Capasso 1992: 193–202.

Romm, J. S. 1992. *The Edges of the Earth in Ancient Thought: Geography, Exploration, and Fiction*. Princeton.

Ronen, R. 1994. *Possible Worlds in Literary Theory*. Cambridge.

Rose, V. 1886. *Aristotelis qui ferebantur librorum fragmenta*. Leipzig.

Rose, V. 1894. *Theodori Prisciani Euporiston libri tres*. Leipzig.

Roseman, C. 1994. *Pytheas, On the Ocean*. Chicago.

Rosen, R. 1990. "Hipponax and the Homeric Odysseus." *Eikasmós* 1: 11–25.

Rosen, R. and Farrell, J. 1993 (eds.). *Nomodeiktes: Greek Studies in Honor of Martin Ostwald*. Ann Arbor.

Rosenmeyer, P. A. 1996. "Love Letters in Callimachus, Ovid and Aristaenetus, or the Sad Fate of a Mailorder Bride." *Materiali e discussioni* 36: 9–31.

Rosivach, V. 1998. *When a Young Man Falls in Love: The Sexual Exploitation of Women in New Comedy*. London.

Rösler, W. 1980. "Die Entdeckung der Fiktionalität." *Poetica* 12: 283–319.

Rosokoki, A. 1995. *Die Erigone des Eratosthenes*. Heidelberg.

Rossi, L. 2001. *The Epigrams Ascribed to Theocritus: A Method of Approach*. Leuven.

Rossi, L. E. 1971a. "I generi letterari e le loro leggi scritte e non scritte nelle letterature classiche." *Bulletin of the Institute of Classical Studies* 18: 69–94.

Rossi, L. E. 1971b. "Mondo pastorale e poesia bucolica di maniera: l'idillio ottavo del *corpus* teocriteo." *Studi italiani di filologia classica* 43: 5–25.

Rossi, L. E. 1995. "Letteratura di filologi e filologia di letterati." *Aevum antiquum* 8: 9–32.

Rossi, L. E. 2000. "La letteratura alessandrina e il rinnovamento dei generi letterari della tradizione." In Pretagostini 2000: 149–61.

Rostovtzeff, M. 1941. *Social and Economic History of the Hellenistic World*. 3 vols. Oxford.

Roueché, C. 1993. *Performers and Partisans at Aphrodisias in the Roman and Late Roman Periods*. London.

Rowland, I. D. and Howe, T. N. 1999. *Vitruvius, Ten Books on Architecture*. Cambridge.

Rubinstein, L. 1993. *Adoption in Fourth-century Athens*. Copenhagen.

Ruschenbusch, E. 1958. "Πάτριος πολιτεία." *Historia* 7: 398–424.

Ruschenbusch, E. 2004. *Die frühen römischen Annalisten: Untersuchungen zur Geschichtsschreibung des 2. Jahrhunderts v.Chr.* Wiesbaden.

Russell, D. A. 1983. *Greek Declamation*. Cambridge.

Russell, D. A. and Konstan, D. 2005. *Heraclitus, Homeric Problems*. Leiden.

Rusten, J. S. 1982. *Dionysius Scytobrachion*. Opladen.

Rusten, J. S. 1985. "Maron in School (on *P.Köln* 3.125)." *Zeitschrift für Papyrologie und Epigraphik* 60: 21–2.

Rusten, J. S. and Cunningham, I. C. 2002. *Theophrastus, Characters; Herodas, Mimes; Sophron and Other Mime Fragments*. Cambridge, MA.

Rusten, J. S., Cunningham, I. C. and Knox, A. D. 1993. *Theophrastus, Characters; Herodas, Mimes; Cercidas and the Choliambic Poets.* Cambridge, MA.

Rutherford, I. 1997. "Kalasiris and Setne Khamwas: A Greek Novel and Some Egyptian Models." *Zeitschrift für Papyrologie und Epigraphik* 117: 203–9.

Rutherford, I. 2000. "The Genealogy of the *boukoloi*: How Greek Literature Appropriated an Egyptian Narrative Motif." *Journal of Hellenic Studies* 120: 106–21.

Rutherford, I. 2001a. *Pindar's Paeans: A Reading of the Fragments with a Survey of the Genre.* Oxford.

Rutherford, I. 2001b. "The New Simonides: Toward a Commentary." In Boedeker and Sider 2001: 33–54.

Ryholt, K. 1999. *The Carlsberg Papyri 4: The Story of Petese Son of Petetum and Seventy Other Good and Bad Stories.* Copenhagen.

Ryholt, K. 2002a. "Nectanebo's Dream, or the Prophecy of Petesis." In Blasius and Schipper 2002: 221–41.

Ryholt, K. 2002b (ed.). *Acts of the Seventh International Conference of Demotic Studies, Copenhagen, 23–27 August 1999.* Copenhagen.

Ryholt, K. 2005. "On the Contents and Nature of the Tebtunis Temple Library." In Lippert and Schentuleit 2005: 141–70.

Ryholt, K. 2006. *The Carlsberg Papyri 6: The Petese Stories II (P.Petese II).* Copenhagen.

Ryholt, K. 2008. Unpublished paper, "New Light on the Legendary King Nechepsos of Egypt," delivered at the 10th International Congress of Demotic Studies, Leuven.

Saïd, S. 1997. "L'Époque hellénistique: des conquêtes d'Alexandre à Actium." In Saïd, Trédé, and Le Boulluec 1997: 277–402.

Saïd, S. and Trédé, M. 1999. *A Short History of Greek Literature.* London and New York.

Saïd, S., Trédé, M. and Le Boulluec, A. 1997. *Histoire de la littérature grecque.* Paris.

Samuel, A. E. 1966 (ed.). *Essays in Honor of C. Bradford Welles.* New Haven.

Samuel, A. E. 1983. *From Athens to Alexandria: Hellenism and Social Goals in Ptolemaic Egypt.* Leuven.

Sandbach, F. H. 1990 (ed.). *Menandri reliquiae selectae.* 2nd edition. Oxford.

Santelia, S. 1991. *Charition liberata (P.Oxy. 413).* Bari.

Santini, C. 2002 (ed.). *Letteratura scientifica e tecnica di Grecia e Roma.* Rome.

Sargent, T. 1982. *The Idylls of Theocritus: A Verse Translation.* New York and London.

Sasson, J. 1995 (ed.). *Civilizations of the Ancient Near East.* New York.

Savalli-Lestrade, I. 1998. *Les philoi royaux dans l'Asie hellénistique.* Geneva.

Sbordone, F. 1976 (ed.). *Ricerche sui papiri ercolanesi* 2. Naples.

Sbordone, F. 1977 (ed.). *Ricerche sui papiri ercolanesi* 3. Naples.

Scafuro, A. 1997. *The Forensic Stage.* Cambridge.

Schaaf, H. 1992. *Untersuchungen zu Gebäudestiftungen in hellenistischer Zeit.* Cologne.

Schade, G. 1999. *Lycophrons "Odyssee": Alexandra 648–819.* Berlin.

Schaps, D. 1977. "The Woman Least Mentioned: Etiquette and Women's Names." *Classical Quarterly* 27: 323–31.

Schaps, D. 1979. *Economic Rights of Women in Ancient Greece.* Edinburgh.

Scheer, E. 1881–1908. *Lycophronis Alexandra.* 2 vols. Berlin.

Scheer, T. 2003. "The Past in a Hellenistic Present: Myth and Local Tradition." In Erskine 2003: 216–31.

Scheidel, W. 2004. "Creating a Metropolis." In Harris and Ruffini 2004: 1–31.

Schepens, G. 1997. "Jacoby's *FGrHist*: Problems, Methods, Prospects." In Most 1997: 144–72.

Schepens, G. and Bollansée, J. 2005 (eds.). *The Shadow of Polybius: Intertextuality as a Research Tool in Greek Historiography.* Leuven.

Schepens, G. and Delcroix, K. 1996. "Ancient Paradoxography: Origin, Evolution, Production and Reception." In Pecere and Stramaglia 1996: 373–460.

Schibli, H. 1983. "Fragments of a *Weasel and Mouse War*." *Zeitschrift für Papyrologie und Epigraphik* 53: 1–26.

Schiesaro, A. 1996. "Aratus' Myth of Dike." *Materiali e discussioni* 37: 9–26.

Schiesaro, A., Mitsis, P. and Clay, J. S. 1993 (eds.). *"Mega nepios": il destinatario nell'epos didascalico / The Addressee in Didactic Epic = Materiali e discussioni* 31. Pisa.

Schirren, T. 2005. *Philosophos bios: Die antike Philosophenbiographie als symbolische Form*. Heidelberg.

Schmakeit-Bean, I. 2006. "Ein Beitrag zur Entschlüsselung eines Rätsels: Die Argonauten in Lykophrons *Alexandra*." In Harder, Regtuit, and Wakker 2006: 271–86.

Schmeling, G. 2003 (ed.). *The Novel in the Ancient World*. 2nd edition. Leiden.

Schmidt, V. 1968. *Sprachliche Untersuchungen zu Herodas*. Berlin.

Schmidt, W., Nix, L., Schöne, H. and Heiberg, J. L. 1899–1914. *Heronis Alexandrini opera quae supersunt omnia*. 6 vols. Leipzig.

Schmitt, H. H. and Vogt, E. 1993 (eds.). *Kleines Lexikon des Hellenismus*. Wiesbaden.

Schmitt, H. H. and Vogt, E. 2005 (eds.). *Lexikon des Hellenismus*. Wiesbaden.

Schmitz, T. A. 1999. "'I Hate All Common Things': The Reader's Role in Callimachus' *Aetia* Prologue." *Harvard Studies in Classical Philology* 99: 151–78.

Schneider, D. 1984. *A Critique of the Study of Kinship*. Ann Arbor.

Schneider, H. 1962. *Vergleichende Untersuchungen zur sprachlichen Struktur der beiden erhaltenen Lehrgedichte des Nikander von Kolophon*. Wiesbaden.

Schneider, H. 1992. *Einführung in die antike Technikgeschichte*. Darmstadt.

Schneider, H. 2007. *Geschichte der antiken Technik*. Munich.

Schneider, O. 1856. *Nicandrea*. Leipzig.

Schofield, M. 1983. "The Syllogisms of Zeno of Citium." *Phronesis* 28: 31–58.

Schofield, M. 1991. *The Stoic Idea of the City*. Cambridge.

Scholz, P. 2004a. "Elementarunterricht und intellektuelle Bildung im hellenistischen Gymnasion." In Kah and Scholz 2004: 103–28.

Scholz, P. 2004b. "Peripatetic Philosophers as Wandering Scholars: Some Historical Remarks on the Socio-Political Conditions of Philosophizing in the Third Century BCE." In Fortenbaugh and White 2004: 315–53.

Schröder, S. 1999. *Geschichte und Theorie der Gattung Paian*. Stuttgart and Leipzig.

Schuler, C. 2004. "Die Gymnasiarchie in hellenistischer Zeit." In Kah and Scholz 2004: 163–91.

Schultze, C. 1986. "Dionysius of Halicarnassus and his Audience." In Moxon, Smart, and Woodman 1986: 121–41.

Schürer, E. 1986. *The History of the Jewish People in the Age of Jesus Christ*. Vol. 3.1, revised by G. Vermes, F. Millar and M. Goodman. Edinburgh.

Schürmann, A. 1991. *Griechische Mechanik und antike Gesellschaft: Studien zur staatlichen Förderungen einer technischen Wissenschaft*. Stuttgart.

Schürmann, A. 2005 (ed.). *Geschichte der Mathematik und der Naturwissenschaften in der Antike* 3: *Physik / Mechanik*. Stuttgart.

Schwinge, E.-R. 1986. *Künstlichkeit von Kunst: Zur Geschichtlichkeit der alexandrinischen Poesie*. Munich.

Scodel, R. 2003. "Preface." *Classical and Modern Literature* 23.2: 1–3.

Sealey, R. 1990. *Women and Law in Classical Greece*. Chapel Hill.

Seaton, R. C. 1912. *Apollonius Rhodius, The Argonautica*. Cambridge, MA.

Sedley, D. N. 1977. "Diodorus Cronus and Hellenistic Philosophy." *Proceedings of the Cambridge Philological Society* 23: 74–120.

Sedley, D. N. 1989. "Philosophical Allegiance in the Greco-Roman World." In Griffin and Barnes 1989: 97–119.

Sedley, D. N. 1997. "Plato's *auctoritas* and the Rebirth of the Commentary Tradition." In Barnes and Griffin 1997: 110–29.

Sedley, D. N. 1998. *Lucretius and the Transformation of Greek Wisdom*. Cambridge.

Sedley, D. N. 1999. "The Stoic-Platonist Debate on *kathēkonta*." In Ierodiakonou 1999: 128–52.

Seiler, M. A. 1997. *Ποίησις ποιήσεως: Alexandrinische Dichtung κατὰ λεπτόν in strukturaler und humanethologischer Deutung*. Stuttgart and Leipzig.

Selden, D. L. 1994. "The Genre of Genre." In Tatum 1994: 39–64.

Selden, D. L. 1998. "Alibis." *Classical Antiquity* 17: 299–412.

Semanoff, M. 2006. "Undermining Authority: Pedagogy in Aratus' *Phaenomena*." In Harder, Regtuit, and Wakker 2006: 303–18.

Sens, A. 1992. "Theocritus, Homer, and the Dioscuri: *Idyll* 22.137–223." *Transactions of the American Philological Association* 122: 335–50.

Sens, A. 1997. *Theocritus, Dioscuri (Idyll 22)*. Göttingen.

Sens, A. 2004. "Doricisms in the New and Old Posidippus." In Acosta-Hughes, Kosmetatou, and Baumbach 2004: 63–83.

Sens, A. 2005. "The Art of Poetry and the Poetry of Art: The Unity and Poetics of Posidippus' Statue-poems." In Gutzwiller 2005: 206–25.

Sens, A. forthcoming. *Hellenistic Epigram: A Selection*. Cambridge.

Serrao, G. 1977. "La poesia bucolica: realtà campestre e stilizzazione letteraria." In Adorno et al. 1977: 180–99.

Shackleton Bailey, D. R. 1965. *Cicero's Letters to Atticus*. Vol. 1. Cambridge.

Sharples, R. W. forthcoming. "Strato of Lampsacus: The Sources, Text and Translation." In Fortenbaugh and Pellegrin, forthcoming.

Sheets, G. A. 1981. "The Dialect Gloss, Hellenistic Poetry, and Livius Andronicus." *American Journal of Philology* 102: 58–78.

Sherk, R. K. 1970. "Daos and Spinther in Menander's *Aspis*." *American Journal of Philology* 91: 341–3.

Sherk, R. K. 1984. *Rome and the Greek East to the Death of Augustus*. Cambridge.

Sherwin-White, S. 1978. *Ancient Cos: An Historical Study from Dorian Settlement to the Imperial Period*. Göttingen.

Sherwin-White, S. 1987. "Seleucid Babylonia: A Case Study for the Installation and Development of Greek Rule." In Kuhrt and Sherwin-White 1987: 1–31.

Sherwin-White, S. and Kuhrt, A. 1993. *From Samarkhand to Sardis: A New Approach to the Seleucid Empire*. London.

Shipley, G. 2000. *The Greek World after Alexander 323–30 BC*. London.

Shipley, G. 2002. *The Periplous of Pseudo-Scylax: An Interim Translation*. At www.le.ac.uk/ar/gjs/skylax_for_www_02214.pdf.

Shipley, G. and Hansen, M. H. 2006. "The *polis* and Federalism." In Bugh 2006: 52–72.

Sider, D. 1982. "Empedocles' *Persika*." *Ancient Philosophy* 2: 76–8.

Sider, D. 1997. *The Epigrams of Philodemos*. Oxford.

Sider, D. 2001. "Simonides, Fragments 1–22 W^2: Text, Apparatus Criticus, and Translation." In Boedeker and Sider 2001: 13–29.

Sider, D. 2004. "How to Commit Philosophy Obliquely: Philodemus' Epigrams in the Light of his *Peri Parrhesias*." In Fitzgerald, Obbink, and Holland 2004: 85–101.

Sider, D. 2005a. *The Library of the Villa dei Papiri at Herculaneum*. Los Angeles.

Sider, D. 2005b. "Posidippus on Weather signs and the Tradition of Didactic Poetry." In Gutzwiller 2005: 164–82.

Sider, D. 2007. "Sylloge Simonidea." In Bing and Bruss 2007: 113–30.

Sider, D. and Brunschön, C. W. 2007. *Theophrastus, On Weather Signs.* Leiden.

Sifakis, G. M. 1967. *Studies in the History of Hellenistic Drama.* London.

Simon, F.-J. 1991. *Τὰ κύλλ' ἀείδειν: Interpretationen zu den Mimiamben des Herodas.* Frankfurt am Main.

Simpson, W. K. 2003. *The Literature of Ancient Egypt: An Anthology of Stories, Instructions, Stelae, Autobiographies, and Poetry.* 3rd edition. New Haven.

Sineux, P. 1999. "Le péan d'Isyllos: forme et finalités d'un chant religieux dans le culte d'Asklepios à Épidaure." *Kernos* 12: 153–66.

Sistakou, E. 2008. *Reconstructing the Epic: Cross-Readings of the Trojan Myth in Hellenistic Poetry.* Leuven.

Skutsch, O. 1972 (ed.). *Ennius: Sept exposés suivis de discussions.* Geneva.

Skutsch, O. 1985. *The Annals of Quintus Ennius.* Oxford.

Slater, W. J. 1969. "Futures in Pindar." *Classical Quarterly* 19: 86–94.

Slater, W. J. 1986. *Aristophanis Byzantii fragmenta.* Berlin.

Slings, S. R. 1993. "Hermesianax and the Tattoo Elegy (*P.Brux.* Inv. E 8934 and *P.Sorb.* Inv. 2254)." *Zeitschrift für Papyrologie und Epigraphik* 98: 29–35.

Sluiter, I. 1990. *Ancient Grammar in Context: Contributions to the Study of Ancient Linguistic Thought.* Amsterdam.

Sluiter, I. 1997. "The Greek Tradition." In Van Bekkum, Houben, Sluiter, and Versteeg 1997: 147–224.

Smith, H. S. and Tait, W.J. 1983. *Saqqâra Demotic Papyri I.* London.

Smith, M. 1994. "Budge at Akhmim, January 1896." In Eyre, Leahy, and Leahy 1994: 293–303.

Smith, M. 2000. "Egyptian Invective." *Journal of Egyptian Archaeology* 86: 173–87.

Smith, R. W. 1974. *The Art of Rhetoric in Alexandria.* The Hague.

Smotrytsch, A. P. 1962. "Eronda e il vecchio." *Helikon* 2: 605–14.

Smotrytsch, A. P. 1966. "Izobraženie ljudei ellinističeskogo obščestva v mimiambach Geronda." Diss. Kiev. Summary: "Die Darstellung der Menschen der hellenistischen Gesellschaft in den *Mimiamben* des Herodas." *Bibliotheca Classica Orientalis* 11: 323–35.

Snell, B. and Maehler, H. 1964. *Pindari carmina cum fragmentis.* 2 vols. 3rd edition. Leipzig.

Sokolowski, F. 1962. *Lois sacrées des cités grecques.* Paris.

Solimano, G. 1976. *Asclepio: le aree del mito.* Genova.

Sommerstein, A. 1998. "Rape and Young Manhood in Athenian Comedy." In Foxhall and Salmon 1998: 100–14.

Sorabji, R. and Sharples, R. W. 2007 (eds.). *Greek and Roman Philosophy 100 BC–200 AD.* London.

Sordi, M. 1992 (ed.). *Autocoscienza e rappresentazione dei popoli nell'antichità.* Milan.

Soubiran, J. 1972. *Ciceron, Aratea, fragments poétiques.* Paris.

Soubiran, J. 1981. *Aviénus, Les Phénomènes d'Aratos.* Paris.

Spanoudakis, K. 2002. *Philitas of Cos.* Leiden.

Spanoudakis, K. 2005. Review of Jacques 2002. *Gnomon* 77: 402–10.

Spatafora, G. 2005. "Riflessioni sull'arte poetica di Nicandro." *Giornale italiano di filologia* 57: 231–62.

Spatafora, G. 2007. *Nicandro, Theriaka e Alexipharmaka.* Rome.

Spawforth, A. J. S. 2007 (ed). *The Court and Court Society in Ancient Monarchies.* Cambridge.

Spengel, L. 1856. *Rhetores Graeci.* Vol. 3. Leipzig.

Spofford, E. W. 1969. "Theocritus and Polyphemus." *American Journal of Philology* 90: 22–35.

Staden, H. von. 1989. *Herophilus: The Art of Medicine in Early Alexandria*. Cambridge.

Staden, H. von. 1996. "Body and Machine: Interactions between Medicine, Mechanics, and Philosophy." In *Alexandria and Alexandrianism* 1996: 85–106.

Stagl, J. 1982 (ed.). *Aspekte der Kultursoziologie: Aufsätze zur Soziologie, Philosophie, Anthropologie und Geschichte der Kultur zum 60. Geburtstag von Mohammed Rassem*. Berlin.

Stanwick, P. E. 2002. *Portraits of the Ptolemies: Greek Kings as Egyptian Pharaohs*. Austin.

Stanzel, K.-H. 1995. *Liebende Hirten: Theokrits Bukolik und die alexandrinische Poesie*. Stuttgart.

Stanzel, K.-H. 1998. "Mimen, Mimepen und Mimiamben: Theokrit, Herodas und die Kreuzung der Gattungen." In Harder, Regtuit, and Wakker 1998: 143–65.

Starobinski, J. 1980. "The Style of Autobiography." In Olney 1980: 73–83.

Stavrianopoulou, E. 2006 (ed.). *Ritual and Communication in the Graeco-Roman World*. Liège.

Stehle, E. 1997. *Performance and Gender in Ancient Greece: Nondramatic Poetry in its Setting*. Princeton.

Stehle, E. 2001. "A Bard of the Iron Age and His Auxiliary Muse." In Boedeker and Sider 2001: 106–19.

Steiner, R. C. 1995. "Papyrus Amherst 63: A New Source for the Language, Literature, Religion, and History of the Aramaeans." In Geller, Greenfield, and Weitzman 1995: 199–207.

Steiner, R. C. and Nims, C. F. 1985. "Ashurbanipal and Shamash-shum-ukin: A Tale of Two Brothers from the Aramaic text in Demotic Script." *Revue biblique* 92: 60–81.

Stephens, S. A. 1998. "Callimachus at Court." In Harder, Regtuit, and Wakker 1998: 167–85.

Stephens, S. A. 2000. "Writing Epic for the Ptolemaic Court." In Harder, Regtuit, and Wakker 2000: 195–215.

Stephens, S. A. 2002. "Egyptian Callimachus." In Montanari and Lehnus 2002: 235–69.

Stephens, S. A. 2003. *Seeing Double: Intercultural Poetics in Ptolemaic Alexandria*. Berkeley.

Stephens, S. A. 2004. "Posidippus' Poetry Book: Where Macedon Meets Egypt." In Harris and Ruffini 2004: 63–86.

Stephens, S. A. 2006. "Ptolemaic Pastoral." In Fantuzzi and Papanghelis 2006: 91–117.

Stephens, S. A. and Winkler, J. J. 1995. *Ancient Greek Novels: The Fragments*. Princeton.

Sterling, G. E. 1992. *Historiography and Self-Definition: Josephos, Luke-Acts, and Apologetic Historiography*. Leiden.

Stevens, J. 1999. *Reproducing the State*. Princeton.

Stewart, A. 1982. "Dionysus at Delphi: The Pediments of the Sixth Temple of Apollo and the Religious Reform in the Age of Alexander." In Barr-Sharrar and Borza 1982: 205–27.

Stewart, A. 1993. *Faces of Power: Alexander's Image and Hellenistic Politics*. Berkeley.

Stinton, T. C. W. 1976. "*Si credere dignum est*: Some Expressions of Disbelief in Euripides and Others." *Proceedings of the Cambridge Philological Society* 22: 60–89. Reprinted in *Collected Papers on Greek Tragedy*. Oxford 1990: 236–64.

Stirpe, P. 2002. "Perseo nell'*Alessandra* di Licofrone e sulle monete macedoni del II secolo a. C." *Rivista di filologia e di istruzione classica* 130: 5–20.

Stoneman, R. 1991. *The Greek Alexander Romance*. London.

Stoneman, R. 1994. "The *Alexander Romance*: From History to Fiction." In Morgan and Stoneman 1994: 117–29.

Stoneman, R. 2003. "The Metamorphoses of the *Alexander Romance*." In Schmeling 2003: 601–12.

Stoneman, R. 2007. *Il romanzo d'Alessandro*. Vol. 1. Milan.

Stoneman, R. 2008. *Alexander the Great: A Life in Legend*. New Haven.

Stork, P. 2006. "Aristo of Ceos: The Sources, Text and Translation." In Fortenbaugh and White 2006: 1–177.

Streck, M. P. 2005. "Oannes 2" In *Reallexikon der Assyriologie* 10. Winona Lake.

Strootman, R. 2005. "Kings against Celts: Deliverance from Barbarians as a Theme in Hellenistic Royal Propaganda." In Enenkel and Pfeijffer 2005: 101–41.

Strootman, R. 2007. "The Hellenistic Royal Court: Court Culture, Ceremonial and Ideology in Greece, Egypt and the Near East, 336–30 BCE." Diss. Utrecht.

Strootman, R. forthcoming a. "Hellenistic Imperialism and the Ideal of Universal Hegemony." In Rapp forthcoming.

Strootman, R. forthcoming b. "Hellenistic Court Society: The Seleukid Imperial Court under Antiochos the Great, 223–187 BCE." In Duindam, Kunt, and Artan forthcoming.

Strouhal, E. 1989. *Life of the Ancient Egyptians.* Norman.

Stroup, A. 1991. "The Political Theory and Practice of Technology under Louis XIV." In Moran 1991b: 211–34.

Struck, P. T. 2004. *Birth of the Symbol: Ancient Readers at the Limits of Their Texts.* Berkeley.

Sudhaus, S. 1892, 1896. *Philodemi volumina rhetorica.* 2 vols. Leipzig.

Sudhaus, S. 1895. *Philodemi volumina rhetorica, supplementum.* Leipzig.

Suerbaum, W. 2002 (ed.). *Handbuch der Lateinischen Literature der Antike.* Vol. 1: *Die archaische Literatur.* Munich.

Susemihl, F. 1891–1892. *Geschichte der griechischen Literatur in der Alexandrinerzeit.* 2 vols. Leipzig.

Sussman, L. 1978. *Seneca the Elder.* Leiden.

Svenbro, J. 1993. *Phrasikleia: An Anthropology of Reading in Ancient Greece.* Ithaca, NY.

Swerdlow, N. M. 2000. *Ancient Astronomy and Celestial Divination.* Cambridge, MA.

Swiderek, A. 1954. "Le mime grec en Égypte." *Eos* 47: 63–74.

Tait, W. J. 1992. "Demotic Literature and Egyptian Society." In Johnson 1992: 303–10.

Tait, W. J. 1994. "Egyptian Fiction in Demotic and Greek." In Morgan and Stoneman 1994: 203–22.

Tait, W. J. 1996. "Demotic Literature: Forms and Genres." In Loprieno 1996: 175–87.

Talbert, R. J. A. and Unger, R. W. 2008 (eds.). *Cartography in Antiquity and the Middle Ages: Fresh Perspectives, New Methods.* Leiden.

Tandy, D. W. 1979. "Callimachus, *Hymn to Zeus.*" Diss. Yale.

Tarán, S. L. 1979. *The Art of Variation in Hellenistic Epigram.* Leiden.

Tarn, W. W. 1913. *Antigonus Gonatas.* London.

Tarn, W. W. 1927. *Hellenistic Civilisation.* London.

Tarn, W. W. 1938. *The Greeks in Bactria and India.* Cambridge.

Tartari Chersoni, M. 2003. "I *Choliambi* di Persio: osservazioni metrico-stilistiche." *Philologus* 147: 270–88.

Tatum, J. 1994 (ed.). *The Search for the Ancient Novel.* Baltimore.

Tatum, J. 1997. "Herodotus the Fabulist." In Picone and Zimmermann 1997: 29–48.

Taub, L. 2003. *Ancient Meteorology.* London and New York.

Tcherikover, V. 1956. "Jewish Apologetic Literature Reconsidered." *Eos* 48: 169–93.

Tedeschi, G. 2011. *Intrattenimenti e spettacoli nell'Egitto ellenistico-romano.* Trieste.

Teeter, E. and Larson, J. A. 1999 (eds.). *Gold of Praise: Studies in Honor of Edward F. Wente.* Chicago.

Thissen, H. J. 1992. *Der verkommene Harfenspieler: Eine altägyptische Invektive (P.Wien KM 3877).* Sommerhausen.

Thissen, H. J. 1999. "Homerischer Einfluss im Inaros-Petubastis-Zyklus?" *Studien zur Altägyptischen Kultur* 27: 369–87.

Thissen, H. J. 2002. "Das Lamm des Bokchoris." In Blasius and Schipper 2002: 113–38.

Thissen, H. J. 2004. "Die demotische Literatur als Medium spätägyptischer Geisteshaltung." In Burkard and Magen 2004: 91–101.

Thom, J. C. 2005. *Cleanthes' Hymn to Zeus.* Tübingen.

Thomas, I. 1939, 1941. *Greek Mathematical Works.* 2 vols. Cambridge, MA.

Thomas, R. 1989. *Oral Tradition and Written Record in Classical Athens.* Cambridge.

Thomas, R. F. 1985. "From *recusatio* to Commitment: The Evolution of the Vergilian Programme." *Proceedings of the Liverpool Latin Seminar* 5: 61–73.

Thomas, R. F. 1988. *Virgil, Georgics.* 2 vols. Cambridge.

Thomas, R. F. 1993. "Callimachus Back in Rome." In Harder, Regtuit, and Wakker 1993: 197–215.

Thomas, R. F. 1996. "Genre through Intertextuality: Theocritus to Virgil and Propertius." In Harder, Regtuit, and Wakker 1996: 227–46. Reprinted in Thomas 1999: 246–66.

Thomas, R. F. 1999. *Reading Virgil and his Texts: Studies in Intertextuality.* Ann Arbor.

Thompson, D. 1988. *Memphis under the Ptolemies.* Princeton.

Thompson, D. 1994. "Literacy and Power in Ptolemaic Egypt." In Bowman and Woolf 1994: 67–83.

Thompson, D. 2005. "Posidippus, Poet of the Ptolemies." In Gutzwiller 2005: 269–83.

Thomson, J. 1948. *History of Ancient Geography.* Cambridge.

Todd, S. 1993. *The Shape of Athenian Law.* Oxford.

Too, Y. L. 1998 (ed.). *Pedagogy and Power: Rhetorics of Classical Learning.* Cambridge.

Too, Y. L. 2001 (ed.). *Education in Greek and Roman Antiquity.* Leiden.

Toohey, P. 1992. *Reading Epic: An Introduction to the Ancient Narratives.* London and New York.

Toohey, P. 1996. *Epic Lessons: An Introduction to Ancient Didactic Poetry.* London.

Toomer, G. J. 1976. *Diocles, On Burning Mirrors: The Arabic Translation of the Lost Greek Original.* Berlin.

Torraca, L. 1973. *Il prologo dei Telchini e l'inizio degli Aitia di Callimaco.* 2nd edition. Naples.

Tosi, R. 1997. "Callimaco e i Glossografi omerici." *Eikasmós* 8: 223–40.

Totti, M. 1985. *Ausgewählte Texte der Isis- und Sarapis-Religion.* Hildesheim.

Touwaide, A. 1991. "Nicandre, de la science à la poésie: contribution à l'exégèse de la poésie médicale grecque." *Aevum* 65: 65–101.

Tozer, H. F. 1964. *A History of Ancient Geography,* revised by M. Cary. New York.

Trachsel, A. 2009. "Astronomy in Mythology and Mythology in Astronomy: The Case of Eratosthenes." In Harder, Regtuit, and Wakker 2009: 201–25.

Traill, A. 2008. *Women and the Comic Plot in Menander.* Cambridge.

Trapp, M. 2007. "Cynics." In Sorabji and Sharples 2007: 189–203.

Trevor-Roper, H. 1976. *Princes and Patronage: Patronage and Ideology at Four Habsburg Courts, 1517–1633.* London.

Trovati, G. 2001. "Gli ultimi sviluppi della poesia bucolica greca." *Acme* 54: 35–72.

Tybjerg, K. 2005. "Hero of Alexandria's Mechanical Geometry." *Apeiron* 37: 29–56.

Tzamali, E. 2000. "Zum Gebrauch der präpositionalen Umschreibungen bei Herodas." *Classica et Mediaevalia* 51: 118–28.

Ukleja, K. 2005. *Der Delos-Hymnus des Kallimachos innerhalb seines Hymnensextetts.* Münster.

Usher, S. 1974–85. *Dionysius of Halicarnassus, Critical Essays.* 2 vols. Cambridge, MA.

Usher, S. 1999. *Greek Oratory: Tradition and Originality.* Oxford.

Valckenaer, L. C. 1779. *Theocriti, Bionis, et Moschi carmina bucolica.* Leiden.

Vallance, J. T. 1990. *The Lost Theory of Asclepiades of Bithynia.* Oxford.

Valverde Sánchez, M. 1989. *El aition en las Argonáuticas de Apolonio de Rodas.* Murcia.

Vamvouri, M. 1998. "Fiction poétique et réalité historique à propos du *Péan* de Liménios." *Gaia* 3: 37–57.

Vamvouri, M. 2004. *La fabrique du divin: les Hymnes de Callimaque à la lumière des Hymnes homériques et des Hymnes épigraphiques.* Liège.

Van Bekkum, W., Houben, J., Sluiter, I. and Versteeg, K. 1997 (eds.). *The Emergence of Semantics in Four Linguistic Traditions.* Amsterdam.

Van de Mieroop, M. 2004. "A Tale of Two Cities: Nineveh and Babylon." *Iraq* 66: 1–5.

Van Dijk, J. 1963. "Ausgrabungen in Warka." *Archiv für Orientforschung* 20: 215–18.

Van Erp Taalman Kip, A. M. 1994. "Intertextuality and Theocritus 13." In De Jong and Sullivan 1994: 153–69.

Van Groningen, B. A. 1977. *Euphorion.* Amsterdam.

Van Minnen, P. 1998. "Boorish or Bookish? Literature in Egyptian Villages in the Fayum in the Graeco-Roman Period." *Journal of Juristic Papyrology* 28: 99–184.

Van Sickle, J. 1976. "Theocritus and the Development of the Conception of the Bucolic Genre." *Ramus* 5: 18–44.

Van Sickle, J. 1981. "Poetics of Opening and Closure in Meleager, Catullus, and Gallus." *Classical World* 75: 65–75.

Van Sickle, J. 1987. "The *Elogia* of the Cornelii Scipiones and the Origin of Epigram at Rome." *American Journal of Philology* 108: 41–55.

Van Thiel, H. 1974. *Leben und Taten Alexanders von Makedonien: Der griechische Alexanderroman nach der Handschrift L.* Darmstadt.

Van't Dack, E., Van Dessel, P. and Van Gucht, W. 1983 (eds.). *Egypt and the Hellenistic World: Proceedings of the International Colloquium, Leuven, 24–26 May 1982.* Leuven.

Vanderlip, V. F. 1972. *The Four Greek Hymns of Isidorus and the Cult of Isis.* Toronto.

Vanderspoel, J. 2007. "Hellenistic Rhetoric in Theory and Practice." In Worthington 2007: 124–38.

Vasilaros, G. 2004. *Apollōniou Rhodiou Argonautikōn A.* Athens.

Vatin, C. 1970. *Recherches sur le mariage et la condition de la femme mariée à l'époque hellénistique.* Paris.

Vaughn, J. W. 1976. *The Megara (Moschus IV).* Bern and Stuttgart.

Veïsse, A.-E. 2004. *Les "révoltes égyptiennes": recherches sur les troubles intérieurs en Égypte du règne de Ptolémée III à la conquête romaine.* Leuven.

Verbrugge, G. P. and Wickersham, J. M. 1996. *Berossus and Manetho: Native Traditions in Ancient Mesopotamia and Egypt.* Ann Arbor.

Verhoeven, U. 1999. "Von hieratischen Literaturwerken in der Spätzeit." In Assmann and Blumenthal 1999: 255–66.

Verity, A. 2002. *Theocritus, Idylls.* Oxford.

Versnel, H. S. 1998. *Ter Unus – Isis, Dionysos, Hermes: Three Studies in Henotheism.* Vol. 1. 2nd edition. Leiden.

Veyne, P. 1979. "The Hellenization of Rome and the Question of Acculturations." *Diogenes* 106: 1–27.

Vian, F. 1961. *Apollonios de Rhodes, Argonautiques, Chant III.* Paris.

Vian, F. 1978. "Ἰήσων ἀμηχανέων." In Livrea and Privitera 1978: 1025–41. Reprinted in Vian 2005: 49–62.

Vian, F. 1991. "Nonno ed Omero." *Κοινωνία* 15: 5–18. Reprinted in Vian 2005: 469–82.

Vian, F. 2005. *L'épopée posthomérique: recueil d'études.* Alessandria.

Vian, F. and Delage, E. 1974, ^{2}1995 (1980), ^{2}1996 (1981). *Apollonios de Rhodes, Argonautiques.* 3 vols. Paris.

Viereck, P. 1925. "Drei Ostraka des Berliner Museums." In *Raccolta di scritti in onore di Giacomo Lumbroso.* Milan: 253–9.

Vinagre, M. A. 2001. "Tragedia griega del siglo IV a.C. y tragedia helenística." *Habis* 32: 81–95.

Virgilio, B. 2001 (ed.). *Studi ellenistici* 13. Pisa.

Vittmann, G. 1998. "Tradition und Neuerung in der demotischen Literatur." *Zeitschrift für ägyptische Sprache* 125: 62–77.

Vittmann, G. 2006. "Zur Rolle des 'Auslands' im demotischen Inaros-Petubastis-Zyklus." *Wiener Zeitschrift für die Kunde des Morgenlandes* 96: 305–37.

Vogt-Spira, G. 1992. *Dramaturgie des Zufalls.* Munich.

Voigt, E. M. 1971. *Sappho et Alcaeus.* Amsterdam.

Vollgraff, W. 1919. *Nikander und Ovid.* Groningen.

Vollgraff, W. 1924–27. "Le péan delphique à Dionysus." *Bulletin de correspondence hellénique* 48: 97–208; 49: 104–42; 50: 263–304; 51: 423–68.

Volten, A. 1956. "Der demotische Petubastisroman und seine Beziehung zur griechischen Literatur." In Gerstinger 1956: 147–152.

Wacholder, B. Z. 1974. *Eupolemus: A Study of Judaeo-Greek Literature.* Cincinnati.

Waddell, W. G. 1940. *Manetho.* Cambridge, MA.

Walbank, F. W, 1957–79. *A Historical Commentary on Polybius.* 3 vols. Oxford.

Walbank, F. W. 1960. "History and Tragedy." *Historia* 9: 216–34.

Walbank, F. W. 1972. *Polybius.* Berkeley.

Walbank, F. W. 1984. "Monarchies and Monarchic Ideas." *The Cambridge Ancient History* (2nd edition) 7.1: 62–100.

Walbank, F. W. 1985a. "Speeches in Greek Historians." In Walbank 1985b: 242–61.

Walbank, F. W. 1985b. *Selected Papers.* Cambridge.

Walbank, F. W. 1992. *The Hellenistic World.* 2nd edition. London.

Walker, C. B. F. 1972. *Cuneiform Texts from Babylonian Tablets in the British Museum* 51. London.

Walker, S. and Higgs, P. 2001 (eds.). *Cleopatra of Egypt: From History to Myth.* London.

Walker, S. F. 1980. *Theocritus.* Boston.

Walsh, G. B. 1985. "Seeing and Feeling: Representation in Two Poems of Theocritus." *Classical Philology* 80: 1–19.

Walsh, G. B. 1990. "Surprised by Self: Audible Thought in Hellenistic Poetry." *Classical Philology* 85: 1–21.

Walsh, P. G. 1997. *Cicero, The Nature of the Gods.* Oxford.

Walsh, P. G. 2000. *Cicero, On Obligations.* Oxford.

Walter, N. 1964. *Der Thoraausleger Aristobulos.* Berlin.

Ward, J. K. and Lott, T. L. 2002 (eds.), *Philosophers on Race: Critical Essays.* Malden.

Warmington, E. H. 1932. *Remains of Old Latin.* 4 vols. Cambridge, MA.

Warren, J. 2007. "Diogenes Laertius, Biographer of Philosophy." In König and Whitmarsh 2007: 133–49.

Warren, J. 2009 (ed.). *The Cambridge Companion to Epicureanism.* Cambridge.

Waszink, J. H. 1972. "Problems Concerning the *Satura* of Ennius." In Skutsch 1972: 97–147.

Waszink, J. H. 1979. *Opuscula selecta.* Leiden.

Watson, L. 1991. *Arae: The Curse Poetry of Antiquity.* Leeds.

Webb, R. 2006. "Fiction, *mimesis* and the Performance of the Greek Past in the Second Sophistic." In Konstan and Saïd 2006: 27–46.

Weber, G. 1992. "Poesie und Poeten an den Höfen vorhellenistischer Monarchen." *Klio* 74: 25–77.

Weber, G. 1993. *Dichtung und höfische Gesellschaft: Die Rezeption von Zeitgeschichte am Hof der ersten drei Ptolemäer.* Stuttgart.

Weber, G. 1995. "Herrscher, Hof und Dichter: Aspekte der Legitimierung und Repräsentation hellenistischer Könige am Beispiel der ersten drei Antigoniden." *Historia* 44: 283–316.

Weber, G. 1997. "Interaktion, Repräsentation und Herrschaft: Der Königshof im Hellenismus." In Winterling 1997: 27–71.

Webster, T. B. L. 1964. *Hellenistic Poetry and Art.* London.

Webster, T. B. L. 1970. *Studies in Later Greek Comedy.* 2nd edition. Manchester.

Webster, T. B. L. 1974. *An Introduction to Menander.* Oxford.

Webster, T. B. L. 1995. *Monuments Illustrating New Comedy.* 3rd edition, revised and enlarged by J. R. Green and A. Seeberg. London.

Wehrli, C. 1968. *Antigone et Démétrios.* Geneva.

Weineck, S.-M. 1992. *The Abyss Above: Philosophy and Poetic Madness in Plato, Hölderlin, and Nietzsche.* New York.

Weinhold, H. 1912. "Die Astronomie in der antiken Schule." Diss. Munich.

Weinstock, S. 1971. *Divus Iulius.* Oxford.

Wendel, C. 1914. *Scholia in Theocritum vetera.* Leipzig.

Wendel, C. 1935. *Scholia in Apollonium Rhodium vetera.* Berlin.

West, M. L. 1965. "Tryphon *De Tropis.*" *Classical Quarterly* 15: 230–48.

West, M. L. 1970. "Melica." *Classical Quarterly* 20: 205–15.

West, M. L. 1974. *Studies in Greek Elegy and Iambus.* Berlin.

West, M. L. 1982. *Greek Metre.* Oxford.

West, M. L. 1989, 1992. *Iambi et Elegi Graeci ante Alexandrum cantati.* 2 vols. 2nd edition. Oxford.

West, S. 1974. "*Joseph and Aseneth*: A Neglected Greek Romance." *Classical Quarterly* 68: 70–81.

West, S. 1983. "Notes on the Text of Lycophron." *Classical Quarterly* 33: 114–35.

West, S. 1984. "Lycophron Italicised." *Journal of Hellenic Studies* 104: 127–51.

West, S. 2000. "Lycophron's *Alexandra*: 'Hindsight as Foresight Makes No Sense?'" In Depew and Obbink 2000: 153–66 and 284–9.

West, S. 2003a. "Lycophron's *Alexandra*: Something Old and Something New." In López Férez 2003: 79–95.

West, S. 2003b. "Croesus' Second Reprieve and Other Tales of the Persian Court." *Classical Quarterly* 53: 416–37.

Westenholz, A. 2007. "The Graeco-Babyloniaca Once Again." *Zeitschrift für Assyriologie* 97: 262–313.

White, H. 1899. *Appian's Roman History.* 2 vols. New York.

White, K. D. 1984. *Greek and Roman Technology.* London.

White, K. D. 1993. "'The Base Mechanic Arts'? Some Thoughts on the Contribution of Science (Pure and Applied) to the Culture of the Hellenistic Age." In Green 1993: 220–32.

White, S. 1994. "Callimachus on Plato and Cleombrotus." *Transactions of the American Philological Association* 124: 135–61.

White, S. forthcoming. *Diogenes Laertius: Lives and Doctrines of the Ancient Philosophers.* Cambridge.

Whitman, J. 1987. *Allegory: The Dynamics of an Ancient and Medieval Technique.* Cambridge, MA.

Whitmarsh, T. 2005a. *The Second Sophistic.* Oxford.

Whitmarsh, T. 2005b. "The Greek Novel: Titles and Genre." *American Journal of Philology* 126: 587–611.

Widmer, G. 2002. "Pharaoh Mââ-Rê, Pharaoh Amenemhat and Sesostris: Three Figures from Egypt's Past as Seen in Sources of the Graeco-Roman Period." In Ryholt 2002b: 377–93.

Wilamowitz-Moellendorff, U. von. 1886. *Isyllos von Epidauros.* Berlin.

Wilamowitz-Moellendorff, U. von. 1896. "Des Mädchens Klage: Eine alexandrinische Arie." *Nachrichten von der Gesellschaft der Wissenschaften zu Göttingen*, phil.–hist. Klasse: 209–32. Reprinted in *Kleine Schriften* 2 (Berlin 1941): 95–120.

Wilamowitz-Moellendorff, U. von. 1906. *Die Textgeschichte der griechischen Bukoliker.* Berlin.

Wilamowitz-Moellendorff, U. von. 1912. "Die griechische Literatur des Altertums." In Hinneberg 1912: I.8.

Wilamowitz-Moellendorff, U. von. 1924. *Hellenistische Dichtung in der Zeit des Kallimachos.* 2 vols. Berlin.

Wiles, D. 1984. "Menander's *Dyskolos* and Demetrius of Phaleron's Dilemma: A Study of the Play in its Historical Context – the Trial of Phokion, the Ideals of a Moderate Oligarch, and the Rancor of the Disfranchised." *Greece and Rome* 31: 170–80.

Wiles, D. 1991. *The Masks of Menander: Sign and Meaning in Greek and Roman Performance.* Cambridge.

Will, E. 1979–82. *Histoire politique du monde hellénistique.* 2 vols. 2nd edition. Nancy.

Will, F. 1973. *Herodas.* New York.

Williams, F. 1971. "A Theophany in Theocritus." *Classical Quarterly* 21: 137–45.

Williams, F. 1978. *Callimachus, Hymn to Apollo.* Oxford.

Williams, F. 2002. "Cercidas fr. 3 Liv.: Canine Language in a Cynic Poet?" *Zeitschrift für Papyrologie und Epigraphik* 139: 40–2.

Williams, G. 1982. "The Genesis of Poetry in Rome." In Kenney and Clausen 1982: 53–9.

Williams, M. F. 1991. *Landscape in the Argonautica of Apollonius Rhodius.* Frankfurt am Main.

Wills, G. 1970. "Phoenix of Colophon's *Κορώνισμα*." *Classical Quarterly* 20: 112–18.

Wills, L. M. 1995. *The Jewish Novel in the Ancient World.* Ithaca, NY.

Wills, L. M. 2002. *Ancient Jewish Novels: An Anthology.* New York and Oxford.

Wimmel, W. 1960. *Kallimachos in Rom.* Wiesbaden.

Winder, S. J. 1997. "The Ancient Quarrel between Poetry and Philosophy in Callimachus' *Hymn to Zeus.*" Diss. Ohio State University, Columbus.

Winiarczyk, M. 2002. *Euhemeros von Messene: Leben, Werk und Nachwirkung.* Munich.

Winston, D. 1976. "Iambulus' Island of the Sun and Hellenistic Literary Utopias." *Science Fiction Studies* 3: 219–27.

Winterling, A. 1997 (ed.). *Zwischen Haus und Staat: Antike Höfe im Vergleich.* Munich.

Wirth, G. 1993. *Diodor und das Ende des Hellenismus.* Vienna.

Wiseman, T. P. 1979. *Clio's Cosmetics.* Lanham.

Wisse, J. 1995. "Greeks, Romans, and the Rise of Atticism." In Abbenes, Slings, and Sluiter 1995: 65–82.

Wissmann, J. 2002. "Hellenistic Epigrams as School-texts." In Harder, Regtuit, and Wakker 2002: 215–30.

Wöhrle, G. 1999 (ed.). *Geschichte der Mathematik und der Naturwissenschaften in der Antike 1: Biologie.* Stuttgart.

Wolff, H. J. 1944. "Marriage Law and Family Organization in Ancient Athens: A Study of the Interrelation of Public and Private Law in the Greek City." *Traditio* 2: 43–95.

Wölke, H. 1978. *Untersuchungen zur Batrachomyomachie.* Meisenheim.

Woodcroft, B. 1971. *Hero's Pneumatics.* Reprinted with an introduction by M. B. Hall. London. Originally published 1851.

Wooten, C. 1973. "The Ambassador's Speech: A Particularly Hellenistic Genre of Oratory." *Quarterly Journal of Speech* 59: 209–12.

Wooten, C. 1974. "The Speeches in Polybius: An Insight into the Nature of Hellenistic Oratory." *American Journal of Philology* 95: 235–51.

Wooten, C. 1975. "Le développement du style asiatique pendant l'époque hellénistique." *Revue des études grecques* 83: 94–104.

Wörrle, M. and Zanker, P. (eds.). 1995. *Stadtbild und Bürgerbild im Hellenismus.* Munich.

Worthington, I. 2006– (ed.). *Brill's New Jacoby: The Fragments of the Greek Historians.* At www.brillonline.nl.
Worthington, I. 2007 (ed.). *A Companion to Greek Rhetoric.* Malden.
Xanthakis-Karamanos, G. 1994. "The *Daphnis or Lityerses* of Sositheus." *L'Antiquité classique* 63: 237–50.
Xanthakis-Karamanos, G. 1996. "The *Menedemus* of Lycophron." *Athena* 81: 339–65.
Xanthakis-Karamanos, G. 1997. "Echoes of Earlier Drama in Sositheus and Lycophron." *L'Antiquité classique* 66: 121–43.
Yarrow, L. M. 2006. *Historiography at the End of the Roman Republic: Provincial Perspectives on Roman Rule.* Oxford.
Yatromanolakis, D. 2001. "To Sing or to Mourn." In Boedeker and Sider 2001: 208–25.
Yoyotte, J. 1969. "Bakhtis: religion égyptien et culture grecque à Edfou." In *Religions en Égypte hellénistique et romaine.* Paris: 127–41.
Ypsilanti, M. 2006. "Mime in Verse: Strategic Affinities in Theocritus and Herodas." *Maia* 58: 411–32.
Yunis, H. 2005. "The Rhetoric of Law in Fourth-century Athens." In Gagarin and Cohen 2005: 191–210.
Žabkar, L. V. 1988. *Hymns to Isis in her Temple at Philae.* Hanover and London.
Zagagi, N. 1994. *The Comedy of Menander: Convention, Variation and Originality.* London.
Zanker, G. 1983. "The Nature and Origin of Realism in Alexandrian Poetry." *Antike und Abendland* 29: 125–45.
Zanker, G. 1987. *Realism in Alexandrian Poetry: A Literature and its Audience.* London.
Zanker, G. 1989. "Current Trends in the Study of Hellenic Myth in Early Third-Century Alexandrian Poetry: The Case of Theocritus." *Antike und Abendland* 35: 83–103.
Zanker, G. 1996. "Pictorial Description as a Supplement for Narrative: The Labour of Augeas' Stables in *Herakles Leontophonos.*" *American Journal of Philology* 117: 411–23.
Zanker, G. 1998. "The Concept and the Use of Genre-Marking in Hellenistic Epic and Fine Art." In Harder, Regtuit, and Wakker 1998: 225–38.
Zanker, G. 2004. *Modes of Viewing in Hellenistic Poetry and Art.* Madison.
Zanker, G. 2006. "Poetry and Art in Herodas, *Mimiamb* 4." In Harder, Regtuit, and Wakker 2006: 357–78.
Zanker, G. 2009. *Herodas: Mimiambs.* Oxford.
Zetzel, J. E. G. 1974. "Ennian Experiments." *American Journal of Philology* 95: 137–40.
Zetzel, J. E. G. 1981. "On the Opening of Callimachus, *Aetia* II." *Zeitschrift für Papyrologie und Epigraphik* 42: 31–3.
Zhmud, L. 2006. *The Origin of the History of Science in Classical Antiquity.* Berlin.
Ziegler, K. 1949. "*Paradoxographoi.*" *RE* 18.3: 1137–66.
Ziegler, K. 1966. *Das hellenistische Epos: Ein vergessenes Kapitel griechischer Dichtung.* 2nd edition. Leipzig. Originally published 1934.
Zivie-Coche, C. 2004. *Tanis: statues et autobiographies de dignitaires; Tanis à l'époque ptolémaïque.* Paris.
Zumbo, A. 2004. "La *Lunga notte di Medea* di Corrado Alvaro." In Radici Colace and Zumbo 2004: 135–47.

Index

Printed and bound by CPI Group (UK) Ltd, Croydon, CR0 4YY